Custom Version for the University of Houston - Third Edition

AMERICA AND ITS PEOPLES

A Mosaic in the Making

Volume I - to 1877

James Kirby Martin   *Randy Roberts*   *Steven Mintz*
Linda O. McMurry   *James H. Jones*

Containing Material From

America and Its Peoples: A Mosaic in the Making, Volume 1-to 1877, Fifth Edition
by James Kirby Martin, Randy Roberts, Steven Mintz,
Linda O. McMurry, James H. Jones

PEARSON
Custom
Publishing

PEARSON
Longman

Cover art: *Minute Man*, by Angela Sciaraffa.

Taken from:

America and Its Peoples, Fifth Edition, Volume 1—to 1877
by James Kirby Martin, Randy Roberts, Steven Mintz, Linda O. McMurry, and James H. Jones
Copyright © 2003 by James Kirby Martin, Randy Roberts, Steven Mintz, Linda O. McMurry, and James H. Jones
Published by Longman, Inc.
A Pearson Education Company
New York, New York 10036

This special edition published in cooperation with Pearson Custom Publishing.

Printed in the United States of America

10 9 8 7 6 5 4 3 2

ISBN 0-536-86087-4

2004300081

LW

Please visit our web site at *www.pearsoncustom.com*

PEARSON CUSTOM PUBLISHING
75 Arlington Street, Suite 300, Boston, MA 02116
A Pearson Education Company

BRIEF CONTENTS

DETAILED CONTENTS

4 BREAKING THE BONDS OF EMPIRE, 1760–1775 92

5 THE TIMES THAT TRIED MANY SOULS, 1775–1783 120

MAPS

TABLES AND FIGURES

FEATURES

PREFACE

Americans are of two minds about history. Popular history fascinates us. Many of Hollywood's most popular films—from *Birth of a Nation* to *Gangs of New York*—draw on history for their themes, characters, and drama. Nothing better underscores this fascination with history than the fact that more Americans visit historical sites and museums like Colonial Williamsburg or the National Museum of American History each year than attend major league baseball games.

Academic history is far less popular, however. "Boring" and "irrelevant" are adjectives often appended to the word *history*. At the high school level, history requirements have increasingly been replaced by courses in social studies. At colleges and universities, the number of history majors and enrollment in history courses has fallen at an alarming rate.

A disturbingly large number of students are ignorant about the most basic facts of our country's past. A recent survey of high school seniors showed that just two thirds of them knew that the Great Depression occurred during the twentieth century or that Germany and Japan were America's adversaries in World War II. A history report card issued by the U.S. Department of Education reported that 57 percent of high school seniors could not perform even "at the bottom of the achievement ladder" and that only 1 percent were advanced or superior.

Historical illiteracy is not a victimless crime. Time travel broadens our perspective just as physical travel does. Historical perspective is essential if we are to learn from the mistakes of the past and not repeat them. History reveals the debt we owe to past generations and reminds us that progress is not inevitable, but is the product of past decisions, choices, and struggles.

We have designed *America and Its Peoples* to convey American history's excitement and drama. The story that we tell is fraught with conflict, suspense, and controversy, and we have sought to recapture this excitement by writing a book built around vivid character sketches, colorful anecdotes, a strong narrative pulse, and a wide-angle view that allows us to examine such subjects as crime, disease, private life, and sports.

A history textbook, in our view, need not be dull, humorless, or lifeless. Rather, it should bring the past back to life in all of its complexity, underscoring history's relevance to our daily lives. The issues addressed in this book—colonialism, revolution, the origins of racial prejudice, the costs and benefits of industrialization and urbanization—are anything but trivial. They remain very much a part of the human story today.

Nor do we think that a textbook should insulate readers from controversy. One of history's greatest benefits is that it allows us to second guess the decisions and choices made in the past, to reassess the meaning of past events, and to reevaluate real-life heroes and villains. History, we believe, is the ideal laboratory for critical thinking. By engaging the past, we can assess the roles of individuals and of social forces in producing historical transformations and learn to evaluate conflicting interpretations of people and events. This textbook demonstrates that history is an arena of debate and contention as exciting as any other.

Each generation must produce a history that addresses the concerns of its own time. In writing *America and Its Peoples,* we have sought to fashion a history of the United States that speaks to the realities of a changing America. Today, the United States is the most ethnically diverse nation in the world. Over the past four centuries, 45 million people arrived in the United States from Africa, Asia, Latin America, and Europe. In *America and Its Peoples*, we recount the histories of the diverse ethnic, religious, and racial groups that have come to make up our society and underscore the pivotal role that ethnicity, race, and religion have played in our nation's social, cultural, and political development. From its earliest settlement, America has been a multicultural society, and by placing ethnicity, race, gender, and class at the very heart of our narrative, we have sought to present a new perspective on how our multifaceted culture and politics functioned through time.

Contemporary American society perceives itself as beset by unprecedented problems—of ethnic and racial tension, economic stagnation and inequality, crime, family upheaval, and environmental degradation. In *America and Its Peoples,* we have made a special point of uncovering the historical roots of the problems confronting American society today. One of history's values is that it can show how previous generations confronted the controversial issues of their times, allowing us to assess their achievements as well as their failures.

Americans are an optimistic, forward-looking people who, in the course of everyday life, care little about the past. More than two centuries ago, Thomas Jefferson gave pointed expression to this attitude when he declared "the earth belongs to the living and not the dead." But as the novelist William Faulkner once observed, "the past is never dead. It's not even past." We are convinced that the very worst forms of bigotry, fanaticism, and racism are ultimately grounded in historical ignorance and mythology. History reminds us that our values, our identities, and our most pressing social problems are rooted in our historical experience. Thus, in writing this book, we have not sought simply to create an encyclopedic compendium of names, dates, events, and concepts; we have conceived of U.S. history as a dramatic story: a story involving contention, struggle, compromise, and, above all, conflicting visions of the nation's dominant values.

Today, many Americans are wary about the future and uneasy about the state of their society. In *American and Its Peoples,* we have written a textbook that emphasizes historical contingency—the idea that different decisions and choices in the past would have created a very different world today. Ours is a history that emphasizes the importance of personal choice and collective action; a history that stresses peoples' capacity to shape their own destiny. We believe that this is an inspiring historical lesson with profound implications for the nation's future.

APPROACH AND THEMES

Written by scholars who regularly teach the introductory U.S. history survey, *America and Its Peoples* brings history to life through the stories of the women and men who have shaped our history as a people. Highly sensitive to students' needs and interests, the authors place ethnicity, race, and gender at the core of the historical narrative. Carefully balancing cultural, diplomatic, economic, military, political, religious, and social history, the authors pay special attention to the clash of ideas and peoples that has shaped American history. This fifth edition contains up-to-date coverage of the controversial presidential election of 2000, the terrorist attacks of September 11, 2001, and the presidency of George W. Bush.

America and Its Peoples thoroughly treats the history of *all* Americans, providing extensive coverage of women, African Americans, Asian Americans, Hispanic Americans, and Native Americans. It offers exceptionally complete coverage of the areas that were originally colonized by Spain, to meet the special needs of students who live in the Sunbelt. Concisely and vividly written, the textbook contains a wealth of special features designed to stimulate student interest in history and reinforce student learning.

FEATURES

America and Its Peoples, Fifth Edition, includes a wealth of features and pedagogical aids designed to engage students' interest and enhance their learning:

- *Chapter-opening outlines* help students prepare for their study of the chapter by listing the main topics and subtopics to be discussed.
- *Chapter-opening vignettes* capture students' interest through the story of an individual or a specific event. Set-off paragraphs at the end of the vignette succinctly introduce chapter themes and explain how the vignette relates to or exemplifies the chapter's themes and topics.
- *"The American Mosaic" essays* offer an in-depth examination of some aspect of such high-interest topics as crime, medicine, sports and other leisure-time activities, the experience of combat, and the reshaping of private life.
- *"The People Speak"* These excerpts from primary sources introduce students to critical documents in American history and allow them to hear the people of the past speak in their own voices. Brief introductions provide the historical context for each document.
- *Key Terms* In each chapter, key terms are highlighted in boldface type to alert students to the principal concepts and events discussed in the chapter. A page-referenced list of the key terms at the end of each chapter helps students review the main ideas and events covered in the chapter.
- *Battlefield Maps* Five watercolor maps offer close examination of some of the key battles in America's wars. An essay accompanying each battlefield map describes the battle in detail and explores its historical significance.
- *"Road to War" Tables* These specialized chronologies summarize the key events that led up to the declaration of each of America's wars, summarizing for students the background for these pivotal events in U.S. history.

- *Review Questions* End-of-the-chapter review questions allow students to examine how well they have absorbed the chapter content and invite them to think critically about the issues discussed in the chapter. The review questions can be used to spark class discussions or for written assignments.
- *Comprehensive Reference Resources* Reference material at the end of each chapter includes both print and media resources. Print resources are a selective list of scholarly works that provide additional depth and insight on the chapter content and novels that illuminate the era covered in the chapter; media resources include films, videos, and documentaries related to the chapter content and an annotated list of Web sites identifying for students sources of additional information that can be easily accessed online.
- *Glossary* An expanded glossary at the end of the book provides definitions for the key terms in each chapter. Each glossary term is page referenced so that students can easily locate discussion of the term in its historical context.

NEW TO THIS EDITION

- *Chapter 32* This new chapter offers a full account of the presidency of Bill Clinton, the disputed presidential election of 2000, the terrorist attacks of September 11, 2001, the presidency of George W. Bush, the globalization of the American economy, and the increasing diversity of the U.S. population.
- *New chapter-opening vignettes* New vignettes on Prudence Crandall (Chapter 11), the 1893 World's Columbian Exposition in Chicago (Chapter 17), and Muhammad Ali (Chapter 29) use the stories of these individuals and events to bring to life the era covered in the chapter—the age of reform, the age of industrialization and the rise of big business, and the struggle for civil rights and the liberation movements of the 1960s, respectively.
- *New "The People Speak" document excerpts.* This edition of *America and Its Peoples* contains several new primary source excerpts, among them John Winthrop, "A Model of Christian Charity" (Chapter 2); documents on the Trail of Tears (Chapter 11) and the Irish potato famine (Chapter 13); Senator William Alfred Peffer, "The Mission of the Populist Party" (Chapter 19); the Watergate tapes (Chapter 31); and international

reactions to the terrorist attacks of September 11, 2001 (Chapter 32).
- *New "The American Mosaic" essays* Two new American Mosaic essays—New Powers in the South and West (Chapter 30) and Terrorism in Historical Perspective (Chapter 32)—discuss the new immigration of the late twentieth century and the language, history, and acts of terrorism from ancient Rome to the present day.
- *Chapter Summary and Key Points* This new pedagogical device aids student understanding of the chapter by recalling chapter themes and recapping major events, topics, and concepts covered in the chapter.
- *People You Should Know* At the end of each chapter is a list of the prominent individuals discussed in the chapter, reminding students of the major players involved in the events covered in the chapter.
- *New maps* Fourteen new maps have been added in the fifth edition to provide geographical context for text discussions. Among these new maps are Ratification of the Constitution (Chapter 6), Territorial Growth to 1853 (Chapter 13), African American Population Distribution in 1890 (Chapter 19), World War I Casualties (Chapter 22), Events of the Civil Rights Movement (Chapter 29), and McDonald's Around the World (Chapter 32).

SUPPLEMENTS

A comprehensive and up-to-date supplements package accompanies *America and Its Peoples*.

For Qualified College Adopters

Companion Website (*www.ablongman.com/martin*) The instructor section of the Website includes the instructor's manual, teaching links, and PowerPoint presentations with the maps, graphs, and charts from the text.

Course Management   Longman offers an American history course in CourseCompass™, Blackboard, and WebCT. These courses include primary sources, atlas maps, and map exercises. Ask your Longman representative for more details.

Digital Media Archive CD-ROM   Free to qualified college adopters, this CD-ROM contains hundreds of images and maps and dozens of interactive maps and video clips.

Instructor's Manual This resource, prepared by Austin Allen of the University of Houston–Downtown, contains a synopsis, sample discussion questions, lecture supplements, and instructional flowcharts for each chapter.

Test Bank Written by Marc Maltby of Owensboro Community College, the test bank contains multiple choice, true/false, and essay test items. The questions are keyed to topic, cognitive type, and relevant text page.

TestGen-EQ Computerized Testing System This flexible, easy-to-master computerized test bank on a dual-platform CD includes all the test items in the printed test bank. The software allows instructors to select specific questions, edit existing questions, and add their own items to create exams. Tests can be printed in several different fonts and formats and can include figures, such as graphs and tables.

Text Map Transparencies A set of 40 four-color transparencies from the maps and figures in *America and Its Peoples*.

Comprehensive American History Transparency Set This vast collection of American history transparencies is a necessary teaching aid. It includes over 200 maps covering social trends, wars, elections, immigrations, and demographics. Included is a set of reproducible map exercises.

Discovering American History Through Maps and Views Transparency Set Created by Gerald Danzer of the University of Illinois at Chicago, the recipient of the AHA's 1990 James Harvey Robinson Prize for his work in the development of map transparencies, this set of 140 four-color acetates is a unique instructional tool. It contains an introduction on teaching history through maps and a detailed commentary on each transparency. The collection includes cartographic and pictorial maps, views and photos, urban plans, building diagrams, and works of art.

Video Lecture Launchers Prepared by Mark Newman of the University of Illinois at Chicago, these video lecture launchers (each two to five minutes in duration) cover key issues in American history from 1877 to the present. The launchers are accompanied by an instructor's manual.

"This Is America" Immigration Video Produced by the American Museum of Immigration, this video tells the story of American immigrants. By showing how the richness of our culture is due to the contributions of millions of immigrant Americans, the videos make the point that America's strength lies in the ethnically and culturally diverse backgrounds of its citizens.

For Students

Companion Website (*www.ablongman.com/martin*) Students will find summaries, practice test questions, Web links, and flashcards for every chapter.

Study Guide This two-volume study guide, prepared by Karen Guenther of Mansfield University, is designed to provide students with a comprehensive review of the text material and to encourage application and critical analysis of the material. Each chapter contains an overview, learning objectives, important glossary terms, and multiple choice and essay questions.

Longman American History Atlas This four-color reference tool and visual guide to American history includes almost 100 maps and covers the full scope of history. Atlas overhead transparencies are available to adopters.

Mapping American History: Student Activities Created by Gerald Danzer of the University of Illinois at Chicago, this workbook may be used in conjunction with *Discovering American History Through Maps and Views* and is designed to teach students to interpret and analyze cartographic materials as historical documents.

Mapping America: A Guide to Historical Geography, Second Edition This two-volume workbook by Ken Weatherbie of Del Mar College presents the basic geography of the United States and helps students place the history of the United States into spatial perspective. *Available free to college adopters when bundled with the book.*

Research Navigator Guide This guidebook includes exercises and tips on how to use the Internet. It also includes an access code for Research Navigator™—the easiest way for students to start a research assignment or research paper. Research Navigator™ is composed of three exclusive databases of credible and reliable source material, including EBSCO's ContentSelect™ Academic Journal Database, New York Times Search by Subject Archive, and "Best of the Web" Link Library. This comprehensive site also includes a detailed help section.

America Through the Eyes of Its People, Second Edition This comprehensive anthology makes primary sources widely available in an inexpensive format, balancing social and political history and providing up-to-date narrative material. The documents reflect the rich and varied tapestry of American life. *Free to qualified college adopters when bundled with the book.*

Sources of the African-American Past, Second Edition Edited by Roy Finkenbine of the University of Detroit at Mercy, this collection of primary sources covers themes in the African American experience from the West African background to the present. Balanced between political and social history, the documents offer a vivid snapshot of the lives of African Americans in different historical periods. The collection includes documents representing women and different regions of the United States. *Available to qualified college adopters at a reduced price when bundled with the text.*

Women and the National Experience, Second Edition Edited by Ellen Skinner of Pace University, this primary source reader contains both classic and unusual documents describing the history of women in the United States. The documents provide dramatic evidence that outspoken women attained a public voice and participated in the development of national events and policies long before they could vote. Chronologically organized and balanced between social and political history, this reader offers a striking picture of the lives of women across American history. *Available to qualified college adopters at a reduced price when bundled with the text.*

Reading the American West Edited by Mitchel Roth of Sam Houston State University, this primary source reader uses letters, diary excerpts, speeches, interviews, and newspaper articles to let students experience how historians research and how history is written. Every document is accompanied by a contextual headnote and study questions. The book is divided into chapters with extensive introductions. *Available to qualified college adopters at a reduced price when bundled with the text.*

Library of American Biography Series Each of these interpretive biographies focuses on a figure whose actions and ideas significantly influenced the course of American history and national life. At the same time, each biography relates the life of its subject to the broader themes and developments of the era. Brief and inexpensive, they are ideal for any U.S.

history course. *Available to qualified college adopters at a discounted price when bundled with the book.*

A Short Guide to Writing About History, Fourth Edition Written by Richard Marius of Harvard University and Melvin E. Page of Eastern Tennessee University, this engaging and practical text helps students get beyond merely compiling dates and facts. This guide teaches them how to incorporate their own ideas into their papers and to tell a story about history that interests them and their peers. Covering both brief essays and the documented resource paper, the text explores the writing and research processes, as well as different modes of historical writing including argument, and concludes with guidelines for improving style.

Constructing the American Past, Fourth Edition Compiled and edited by Elliot Gorn and Randy Roberts of Purdue University along with Terry Bilhartz of Sam Houston State University, this two-volume popular reader consists of a wide variety of primary sources grouped around central themes in American history. Each chapter focuses on a particular problem in American history, providing students with several points of view from which to examine the historical evidence. Introductions and study questions prompt students to participate in interpreting the past and challenge them to understand the problems in relation to the big picture of American history.

American Experiences: Readings in American History. Fifth Edition This two-volume collection of secondary source readings, compiled and edited by Randy Roberts of Purdue University and James Olson of Sam Houston State University, contains articles that emphasize social history in order to illuminate important aspects of America's past. *American Experiences* addresses the complexity and richness of the nation's past by focusing on the people themselves—how they coped with, adjusted to, or rebelled against America. The readings examine people as they worked and played, fought and loved, lived and died.

Penguin Books
The partnership between Penguin-Putnam USA and Longman Publishers offers qualified college adopters a discount on many titles when bundled with any Longman survey. Penguin titles include *Narrative of the Life of Frederick Douglass* by Frederick Douglass; *Benjamin Franklin: The Autobiography & Other Writings,* L. Jesse Lemisch (Editor); *The Jungle* by Upton Sinclair; and *Uncle Tom's Cabin* by Harriet Beecher Stowe.

ACKNOWLEDGMENTS

Any textbook project is very much a team effort. Here we acknowledge with gratitude the assistance of the many talented historians who have served as reviewers and whose valuable critiques have greatly strengthened the fifth edition of *America and Its Peoples.*

Robert Carriker, *University of Louisiana at Lafayette*
Karen Guenther, *Mansfield University*
David M. Head, *John Tyler Community College*
James R. Hedtke, *Cabrini College*
Douglas E. Kupel, *Gateway Community College*
James M. McCaffrey, *University of Houston– Downtown*
Robert E. McCarthy, *Providence College*
Kenneth T. Osborne, *Metropolitan College, Roger Williams University*
Susan A. Strauss, *Santa Fe Community College*
Jerry K. Sweeney, *South Dakota State University*
Lynn Yerby, *Cypress College*

This book also owes much to the many conscientious historians who reviewed previous editions and offered valuable suggestions that led to many improvements in the text. We acknowledge with gratitude the contributions of the following:

Joe S. Anderson, *Azusa Pacific University*
Elizabeth Reilly Ansnes, *San Jose State University*
Larry Balsamo, *Western Illinois University*
James Banks, *Cuyahoga Community College*
Lois W. Banner, *University of Southern California*
Robert A. Becker, *Louisiana State University*
Delmar L. Beene, *Glendale Community College*
Surendra Bhana, *University of Kansas*
Nancy Bowen, *Del Mar College*
Blanche Brick, *Blinn College*
Larry Burke, *Dodge City Community Junior College*
Frank L. Byrne, *Kent State University*
Colin G. Calloway, *University of Wyoming*
Albert Camarillo, *Stanford University*
Ballard Campbell, *Northeastern University*
Clayborne Carson, *Stanford University*
Jay Caughtry, *University of Nevada at Las Vegas*
Raymond W. Champagne, Jr., *University of Scranton*
Paul G. E. Clemens, *Rutgers University*
Kenton Clymer, *University of Texas at El Paso*
Berry Craig, *Paducah Community College*
John P. Crevelli, *Santa Rosa Junior College*
Shannon J. Doyle, *University of Houston*
Thelma Epstein, *DeAnza College*
John Findlay, *University of Washington*
Roy E. Finkenbine, *University of Detroit*
Mark S. Foster, *University of Colorado at Denver*
Ronald H. Fritze, *Lamar University*

David Glassberg, *University of Massachusetts*
James P. Gormly, *Washington and Jefferson College*
Elliott Gorn, *Purdue University*
Neil Hamilton, *Brevard Community College*
Sam W. Haynes, *University of Texas at Arlington*
Nancy Hewitt, *Rutgers University*
J. David Hoeveler, *University of Wisconsin at Milwaukee*
Steven R. Hoffbeck, *Minot State University*
Melissa M. Hovsepian, *University of St. Thomas, Texas*
Alphine W. Jefferson, *Southern Methodist University*
David R. Johnson, *University of Texas at San Antonio*
Ellen K. Johnson, *Northern Virginia Community College*
Deborah M. Jones, *Bristol Community College*
Kathleen Kennedy, *Western Washington University*
Sterling J. Kernek, *Western Illinois University*
Stuart E. Knee, *College of Charleston*
George W. Knepper, *University of Akron*
Tim Koerner, *Oakland Community College*
Lee Bruce Kress, *Rowan University*
Barbara E. Lacey, *Saint Joseph College*
Steven F. Lawson, *Rutgers University*
Irene Ledesma, *University of Texas–Pan American*
Barbara LeUnes, *Blinn College*
Thomas Lewis, *Mount Senario College*
Terrence Lindell, *Wartburg College*
Ann E. Liston, *Fort Hays State University*
James McMillan, *Arizona State University*
Myron Marty, *Drake University*
M. Catherine Miller, *Texas Tech University*
Otis Miller, *Belleville Area College*
William Howard Moore, *University of Wyoming*
Peter Myers, *Palo Alto College*
Daniel Nelson, *University of Akron*
Mark Newell, *Ramapo College*
Roger L. Nichols, *University of Arizona*
Barbara J. Oberlander, *Santa Fe Community College*
Michael Perman, *University of Illinois at Chicago*
Peter L. Petersen, *West Texas A&M University*
Paula Petrik, *University of Maine*
Robert Pierce, *Foothill College*
George Rable, *Anderson College*
Max Reichard, *Delgado Junior College*
Leonard R. Riforgiato, *Pennsylvania State University, Shenango Valley Campus*
Marilyn Rinehart, *North Harris County College*
Jon H. Roberts, *University of Wisconsin at Stevens Point*
Randall Rosenberg, *University of Northern Alabama*
James G. Ryan, *Texas A&M University at Galveston*
David P. Shriver, *Cuyahoga Community College*
Jason H. Silverman, *Winthrop University*
John Ray Skates, *University of Southern Mississippi*
Sheila Skemp, *University of Mississippi*

Kathryn Kish Sklar, *State University of New York at Binghamton*
Larry Steck, *Lake Michigan College*
Robert Striplin, *American River College*
Alan Taylor, *Boston University*
Jason Tetzloff, *Defiance College*
Gary E. Thompson, *Tulsa Junior College*
Jose Torres, *Mesa Community College*
Philip Vaughn, *Rose State College*
Peter H. Wang, *Cabrillo Community College*
Eddie Weller, *San Jacinto College South*
Larry Wilson, *San Jacinto College Central*
Valdenia Winn, *Kansas City Kansas Community College*
Bill Worley, *Sterling College*
Eli Zaretsky, *University of Missouri*

Each author has received invaluable assistance from friends, colleagues, and family. James Kirby Martin thanks Don R. Gerlach, Joseph T. Glatthaar, Irene Guenther, Karen Guenther, Katie Harrison, J. Kent McGaughy, David M. Oshinsky, Cathy Patterson, Jeffrey T. Sammons, Halt T. Shelton, and Karen Martin, whose talents as an editor and critic are too often overlooked. Randy Roberts thanks Terry Bilhartz, Aram Goudsouzian, James S. Olson, and Joan Randall. Steven Mintz thanks Susan Kellogg for her encouragement, support, and counsel. Linda O. McMurry thanks Joseph P. Hobbs, John David Smith, Richard McMurry, and William C. Harris. James H. Jones thanks Kimberley Weathers for her assistance in revising the fifth edition. All of the authors thank Gerard F. McCauley, whose infectious enthusiasm for this project has never wavered. And above all else, we wish to thank our students to whom we have dedicated this book.

The Authors

James Kirby Martin holds the rank of Distinguished University Professor of History at the University of Houston. He received his Ph.D. in history from the University of Wisconsin, Madison. His areas of special interest include early American history, including the era of the American Revolution, American military history through the years of the Civil War, and the history of such social-behavioral issues as drinking and smoking in America. He is the author, co-author, or editor of eleven books, including *Men in Rebellion* (1973), *In the Course of Human Events* (1979), *A Respectable Army: The Military Origins of the Republic* (1982), and *Drinking in America* (1982, revised edition 1987). His most recent book, *Benedict Arnold, Revolutionary Hero: An American Warrior Reconsidered* (1997), was the recipient of the Homer D. Babbidge, Jr. Award and was named by the *Los Angeles Times* to its list of the best 100 books published that year. Martin has served as general editor of the *American Social Experience* series, New York University Press. His many interests also include the study of ordinary persons and the ways in which their lives have shaped the course of American historical development. His capacity to present these lives in meaningful historical contexts helps explain why his students consistently rank him among the very best teachers in the department.

Randy Roberts earned his Ph.D. degree from Louisiana State University. His areas of special interest include modern U.S. history and popular culture in America. He is a faculty member at Purdue University, where he has won the Murphy Award for outstanding undergraduate teaching, the School of Liberal Arts Teacher of the Year award, and the Society of Professional Journalists Teacher of the Year award. The books on which he is author or co-author include *Jack Dempsey: The Manassa Mauler* (1979, expanded edition, 1984), *Papa Jack: Jack Johnson and the Era of White Hopes* (1983), *Heavy Justice:* The State of Indiana *v.* Michael G. Tyson (1994), *My Lai: A Brief History with Documents* (1998), *John Wayne: American* (1995), *Where the Domino Fell: America in Vietnam, 1945–1990* (1990, revised edition 1996), *Winning Is the Only Thing: Sports in America Since 1945* (1989), *A Line in the Sand: The Alamo in Blood and Memory* (2001), and *Pittsburgh Sports: Stories from the Steel City* (2000), among others. Roberts serves as the co-editor of the Sports and Society series, University of Illinois Press, and is on the editorial board of the *Journal of Sports History.* In addition, he has made frequent appearances on television and been involved in numerous documentaries.

Steven Mintz is the John and Rebecca Moores Professor of History and director of the American Cultures Program at the University of Houston. A leading authority on the history of the family as well as a noted expert on slavery, social reform, and the history of film, his books include *The Boisterous Sea of Liberty* (with David Brion Davis, 1998), *Moralists & Modernizers: America's Pre–Civil War Reformers* (1995), *Domestic Revolutions: A Social History of American Family Life* (with Susan Kellogg, 1989), and *A Prison of Expectations: The Family in Victorian Culture* (1983). A pioneer in the application of new computer technologies in history, he moderates a scholarly discussion list on the history of slavery and has served as Vice President for Teaching of H-Net: Humanities and Social Sciences Online. He is also the recipient of two "Teaching American History" grants from the U.S. Department of Education.

Linda O. McMurry is an emeritus professor of history at North Carolina State University, specializing in African American history. Her interest in personal perspectives and experiences of history has led her to write three biographies: *To Keep the Waters Troubled: The Life of Ida B. Wells* (1998), *Recorder of the Black Experience: A Biography of Monroe Nathan Work* (1985), and *George Washington Carver: Scientist and Symbol* (1981). Both the Wells and Carver biographies are listed in the *New York Review of Books Readers' Catalog* of the best books in print. A recipient of a Rockefeller Foundation Humanities fellowship, McMurry has been active as a consultant and lecturer on topics relating to the black experience in America, appearing on such programs as NPR's "Morning Edition" and C-SPAN's "Booknotes." In 1999, she won both the top teaching and research awards from her college. Although she is retired from full-time teaching, she continues to work with graduate students and plans to return to the classroom on a part-time basis.

James H. Jones earned his Ph.D. degree at Indiana University. His areas of specialization include modern U.S. history, the history of medical ethics and medicine, and the history of sexual behavior. Jones has been a member of the advisory board of the Arkansas Center for Oral and Visual History, a senior fellow of the National Endowment for the Humanities, a Kennedy fellow at Harvard University, a senior research fellow at the Kennedy Institute of Ethics, Georgetown University, and a Rockefeller fellow at the University of Texas Medical Branch, Galveston. His published works include *Bad Blood: The Tuskegee Syphilis Experiment, A Tragedy of Race and Medicine* (1981), revised edition (1993), which was named to the *New York Times Book Review* list of best books of 1981 and received the Arthur Viseltear prize for the Best Book in Public Health History. His most recent publication, *Alfred C. Kinsey: A Public/Private Life* (1997), was a finalist for both the Pulitzer Prize in biography and the Penn Center Award. Recently retired from teaching, Jones is now living in Santa Fe, New Mexico, where he devotes all his time to research and writing.

AMERICA
AND ITS
PEOPLES
A MOSAIC IN THE MAKING

1 The Peopling and Unpeopling of America

SQUANTO SAVES THE PILGRIMS

The Pilgrims called him **Squanto,** a corruption of his given name, **Tisquantum.** Each Thanksgiving Americans remember him as the valued native friend who saved the suffering Pilgrims from starvation. Few know the other ways in which Tisquantum's life reflected the disastrous collision of human beings that occurred in the wake of Christopher Columbus's first voyage of discovery to America in 1492. European explorers believed they had stumbled upon two empty continents, which they referred to as the "new world." In actuality, the new world was both very old and the home of millions of people. These Native Americans experienced chaos and death when they came into contact with the Europeans. A little more than 100 years after Columbus, at the time of the Pilgrims, the American Indian population had declined by as much as 90 percent. The tragic story of Tisquantum and his tribe, the Patuxets of eastern Massachusetts, vividly portrays what happened.

Born about 1590, Tisquantum acquired the values of his Algonquian-speaking elders before experiencing much contact with adventurers from overseas. Tribal fathers taught him that personal dignity came from respecting the bounties of nature and serving one's clan and village, not from acquiring material possessions. He also learned the importance of physical and mental endurance. To be accepted as an adult, he spent a harrowing winter surviving alone in the wilderness. When he returned the next spring, his Patuxet fathers fed him poisonous herbs for days on end, which he unflinchingly ate—and survived by forced vomiting. Having demonstrated his fortitude, tribal members declared him a man.

Living among 2000 souls in the Patuxet's principal village, located on the very spot where the Pilgrims settled in 1620, Tisquantum may well have foreseen trouble ahead when fair-skinned Europeans started visiting the region. First there were fishermen; then in 1605 the French explorer, Samuel de Champlain, stopped at Plymouth Bay. More fatefully, Captain John Smith, late of the Virginia colony, passed through in 1614. Smith's party treated the Patuxets with respect, but they viewed the natives as little more than wild beasts, to be exploited if necessary. Before sailing away, Smith ordered one of his lieutenants, Captain Thomas Hunt, to stay behind with a crew of mariners and gather up a rich harvest of fish. After completing his assignment, Hunt lured 20 Indians, among them Tisquantum, on board his vessel and, without warning, set his course for the slave market in Malaga, Spain.

Somehow Tisquantum avoided a lifetime of slavery. By 1617 he was in England, where he devoted himself to mastering the English tongue. One of his sponsors, Captain Thomas Dermer, who had been with Smith in 1614, asked Tisquantum to serve as an interpreter and guide for yet another New England expedition. Eager to return home, the native readily agreed and sailed back to America in 1619.

When Dermer's party put in at Plymouth Bay, a shocked Tisquantum discovered that nothing remained of his once-thriving village, except overgrown fields and rotting human bones. As if swept away by some unnamed force, the Patuxets had disappeared from the face of the earth. Trained to hide his emotions, Tisquantum grieved privately. Soon he learned about a disastrous epidemic. Thousands of

Tisquantum is best remembered for the assistance he gave the Pilgrims in providing for the necessities of life, but his own life—and death—illustrate the tensions and problems created by contact between Native American and European cultures.

natives had died in the Cape Cod vicinity of diseases heretofore unknown in New England—in this case probably chicken pox carried there from Europe by fishermen and explorers. When these microparasites struck, the native populace, lacking antibodies, had no way of fending them off.

Tisquantum soon left Dermer's party and went in search of possible survivors. He was living with the Pokanoket Indians when the Pilgrims stepped ashore in December 1620 at the site of his old village. The Pilgrims endured a terrible winter in which half their numbers died. Then in the early spring of 1621 a lone Indian, Samoset, appeared in Plymouth Colony. He spoke halting English and told of another who had actually lived in England. Within a week Tisquantum arrived and agreed to stay and help the Pilgrims produce the necessities of life.

Tisquantum taught them how to grow Indian corn (maize), a crop unknown in Europe, and how to catch great quantities of fish. His efforts resulted in an abundance of food, celebrated in the first Thanksgiving feast during the fall of 1621. To future Pilgrim Governor William Bradford, Squanto "was a special instrument sent of God for their good beyond their expectation."

The story does not have a pleasant ending. Contact with the English had changed Tisquantum, and he adopted some of their practices. In violation of his childhood training, he started to serve himself. As Bradford recorded, Squanto told neighboring Indian tribes that the Pilgrims would make war on them unless they gave him gifts. Further, he would unleash the plague, which the English "kept . . . buried in the ground, and could send it among whom they would." By the summer of 1622 Squanto had become a problem for the Pilgrims, who were eager for peace. Then he fell sick, "bleeding much at the nose," and died within a few days as yet another victim of some European disease.

As demonstrated by Tisquantum's life, white-Indian contacts did not point toward a fusing of Native American and European customs, values, and ideals. Rather, the westward movement of peoples destroyed Indian societies and replaced them with European-based communities. The history of the Americas (and of the United States) cannot be fully appreciated without considering the reasons that thousands of Europeans crossed the Atlantic Ocean and sought dominance over the American continents and their native peoples. Three groups in particular, the Spanish, French, and English, succeeded in this life-and-death struggle that changed forever the course of human history.

The First Discovery of America

The world was a much colder place 75,000 years ago. A great ice age, known as the Wisconsin glaciation, had begun. Year after year, water being drawn from the oceans formed into mighty ice caps, which in turn spread over vast reaches of land. This process dramatically lowered ocean levels. In the area of the Bering Straits, where today 56 miles of ocean separate Siberia from Alaska, a land bridge emerged. At times this link between Asia and America, *Beringia,* may have been 1000 miles wide. Most experts believe it provided the pathway used by early humans to enter a new world.

These people, known as **Paleo-Indians,** were nomads and predators. With stone-tipped spears, they hunted mastodons, woolly mammoths, giant beavers, giant sloths, and bighorn bison, as well as many smaller animals. The mammals led prehistoric men and women to America up to 30,000 or more years ago. For generations, these humans roamed Alaska in small bands, gathering seeds and berries when not hunting the big game or attacking and killing one another.

Eventually, corridors opened through the Rocky Mountains as the ice started to recede. The migratory cycle began anew. Animals and humans trekked southward and eastward, reaching the bottom of South America and the east coast of North America by about 8000 B.C. This long journey covered thousands of miles and took several centuries to complete. In the process Paleo-Indians had become Native Americans.

A Diversity of Cultures

As these first Americans fanned out over two continents, they improved their weapons. They flaked and crafted such hard quartz stones as flint into sharper spear points, which allowed them to slaughter the big game more easily. Also, with the passing of time, the atmosphere began to warm as the ice age came to an end. Mammoths, mastodons, and other giant mammals did not survive the warming climate and needless overkilling.

The first Americans now faced a serious food crisis. Their solution was ingenious. Beginning in Central America between roughly 8000 and 5000 B.C., groups of humans started cultivating plant life as an alternative food source. They soon mastered the basic techniques of agriculture. They raked the earth with stone hoes and planted seeds that produced

Routes of the First Americans

The Paleo-Indians migrated across the land bridge that once linked Asia and America. They then journeyed southward and eastward in populating North and South America.

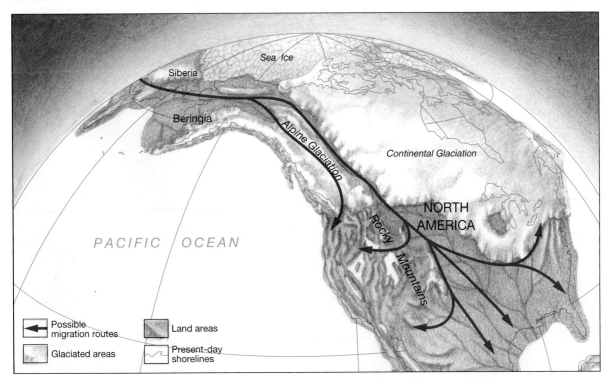

The mural above depicts the many facets of Maya civilization, which involved extensive agricultural production, far-reaching trading networks, complex architectural designs in urban centers, and the crafting of jewelry from rare metals.

crops as varied as maize, potatoes, squashes, pumpkins, and tomatoes.

This agricultural revolution profoundly affected Native American life. Those who engaged in farming were no longer as nomadic. They constructed villages and ordered their religious beliefs around such elements of nature as the sun and rain. With dependable food supplies, they had more children, resulting in a population explosion. Work roles became differentiated by gender. Men still hunted and fished for game, but they also prepared the fields for crops. When not caring for children, women did the planting, weeding, and harvesting.

Ultimately, out of these agriculturally oriented cultures evolved complex Native American societies, the most sophisticated of which appeared in Central America and the Ohio and Mississippi river valleys. Emerging before A.D. 300, the Mayas of Mexico and Guatemala based their civilization on abundant agricultural production. They also built elaborate cities and temples. Their craft workers produced jewelry of gold, silver, and other precious metals, and their merchants developed extensive trading networks. Their intellectuals devised forms of hieroglyphic writing, mathematical systems, and several calendars, one of which was the most accurate in the world at that time.

Powerful nobles and priests ruled over ordinary inhabitants in the highly stratified Maya social order. However, no strong central government existed, and warfare eventually broke out among the principal population centers. This internal strife so weakened the Mayas that after A.D. 1000 warlike peoples from the north began to overrun and conquer them. First came the Toltecs, then the Aztecs. The Aztecs called their principal city Tenochtitlán (the site of present-day Mexico City). At its zenith just before the Spanish con-

quistadores appeared in 1519, Tenochtitlán had a population of 300,000, making it one of the largest cities in the world at that time. The Aztecs imitated many aspects of Maya culture, and they brutally extracted trib-

The Aztecs, Mayas, and Incas

The Aztecs, Mayas, and Incas evolved from simple agriculturally based groups to become politically and socially complex civilizations.

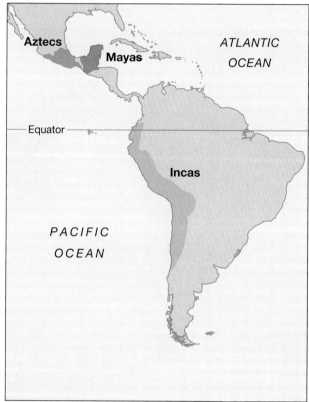

ute, both in wealth and lives, from subject tribes. Their priests reveled in human sacrifice, since Huitzilopochtli, the Aztec war god, voraciously craved human hearts. At one temple dedication, Aztec priests sacrificed some 20,000 subject peoples. Not surprisingly, these tribes hated their oppressors. Many later cooperated with the Spanish in destroying the Aztecs.

Other mighty civilizations also emerged, such as the Incas of Peru, who came into prominence after A.D. 1100. Settling in the Andes Mountains, the Incas developed a sophisticated food supply network. They trained all young males as warriors to protect the empire and their kings, whom they thought of as gods and to whom all riches belonged. The Incas were even wealthier than the Aztecs, and they particularly prized gold and silver, which they mined in huge quantities—and which made them a special target for Spanish conquerors.

In North America the Mound Builders (Adena and Hopewell peoples) appeared in the Ohio River valley around 1000 B.C. and lasted until A.D. 700. These natives hunted and gathered food, but they obtained most of their diet from agriculture. They also raised such crops as tobacco for ceremonial functions. Their merchants traded far and wide. Fascinated with death, they built elaborate burial sites, such as the Great Serpent Mound in Ohio. In time they gave way to the Temple Mound Builders (Mississippian peoples), who were even more sedentary and agriculturally minded. They too were great traders, and they constructed large cities, including a huge site near Cahokia, Illinois, where as many as 75,000 people lived amid 85 large temple mounds.

For unknown reasons the Mississippian culture broke apart before European contact. Remnant groups may have included the Choctaws and Creeks of Mississippi and Alabama, as well as the Natchez Indians. In the rigidly stratified Natchez society the Great Sun was the all-powerful chief, and he ruled over nobles and commoners, the latter bearing the unpleasant name of "stinkards." As with their Mississippian forebears, when eminent individuals died, others gave up their lives so that central figures would have company as they passed into eternity. All but exterminated by the French in the 1730s, the Natchez were the last of the Mound Builders in North America.

The Myth of the "Virgin" Land

Beginning with the agricultural revolution, population in the Americas increased rapidly. Estimates vary widely. One authority has claimed a native populace of up to 120 million persons by the 1490s, whereas other experts suggest a figure of 50 to 80 million, with 5 to 8 million of these people inhabiting North America. Europe's population, by comparison, was roughly 75 million at the time of Columbus, which underscores the mistaken impression of European explorers that America was a "virgin" or "vacant" land.

Over several centuries the Native American populace developed as many as 2200 different languages, some 550 to 650 of which were in use in Central and North America at the time of Columbian contact. So many languages implied immense cultural diversity. Although sophisticated civilizations of enormous wealth did exist, most natives belonged to small, less complex groups in which families formed into clans—and clans into tribes.

Developing lifestyles to fit their environments, native groups varied greatly. Tribes in Oregon and

The snake-shaped Great Serpent Mound, located in southern Ohio, is one of the lasting legacies of the Adena and Hopewell cultures. The mound is about 20 feet wide; uncoiled, its length would be more than 1300 feet.

Washington, such as the Chinooks, did some farming, but fishing for salmon was their primary means of subsistence. In the Great Plains region, Indians such as the Arapahos and Pawnees did not wander to the extent of their ancestors but pursued wild game within more or less fixed hunting zones. In the Southwest, the Hopi and Zuni tribes relied on agriculture, since edible plant and animal life was scarce in their desert environment. These natives even practiced irrigation. Perhaps they are best known for their flat-roofed, multitiered villages, which the Spanish called *pueblos.*

Eastern Indians on the Eve of Contact

In the East, where English explorers and settlers first made contact with Native Americans, dozens of small tribal groupings dotted the landscape. Southeastern Indians, including the Cherokees, Chickasaws, Creeks, Choctaws, and Seminoles, were more attuned to agriculture than to hunting because of lengthy growing seasons. Northeastern tribes, such as the Mahicans and Micmacs, placed more emphasis on hunting and gathering.

Eastern Woodland natives spoke several different languages but held many cultural traits in common. Perhaps linked to memories of the period of overkilling, they treated plant and animal life with respect. Essential to their religious values was the notion of an animate universe. They considered trees, plants, and animals to be spiritually alive (filled with **manitou**). As such, animals were not inferior to humans. They too organized themselves into nations, and through their "boss spirits" permitted some thinning of their numbers for humans to have food and survive. Boss spirits, however, would not tolerate overkilling. If tribes became gluttonous, animal nations could either leave the region or declare war, causing starvation and death.

Tribal **shamans,** or medicine men, communicated with the boss spirits and prescribed elaborate rules, or taboos, regarding the treatment of plants and animals. Indian parents, having mastered such customs, taught children like Tisquantum that nature contained the resources of life. Although intertribal trading was common, as was gift-giving in pottery, baskets, jewelry, furs, and wampum (conch and clam shells), religious values precluded tribal members from exploiting the landscape for the sake of acquiring great personal wealth.

Eastern Woodland parents introduced their children to many other concepts. Individual ownership of land was not known. Tribal boundaries consisted of geographic locales large enough to provide basic food supplies. Although individual dignity did matter, cooperation with tribal members rather than individual competitiveness was the essential ideal, even in sports. Eastern Woodland tribes enjoyed squaring off with one another in lacrosse matches, archery contests, and foot races. Betting and bragging occurred regularly, as did serious injuries in the heat of competition, but the matches had a decided group orientation. Individuals did not participate to gain personal glory but to bring accolades to their tribes.

The refinement of athletic skills also represented useful training for war. Intertribal warfare was sporadic and resulted from any number of factors, such as competition over valued hunting grounds. Skirmishes and the taking of a few lives by roving bands of warriors usually ended the conflict, but not necessarily the ill will, especially among different language groups. Festering tensions and language barriers worked against intertribal cooperation in repelling the Europeans.

Even though males served as warriors, they did not always control tribal decision making. Among the powerful Five Nations of Iroquois (Mohawks, Oneidas, Onondagas, Cayugas, and Senecas) in central New York, tribal organization was **matrilineal.** Women headed individual family units that in turn formed into clans. Clan leaders were also women, and they decided which males would sit on tribal councils charged with determining policies on diplomacy and war. Women held the power of removal as well, so males had no choice but to respect the authority of female clan heads. Among other Eastern Woodland Indians, women occasionally served as tribal *sachems* (chiefs), much to the shock of Europeans.

When European fishermen and explorers started making contact, an estimated 500,000 to 800,000 Indians inhabited the land between the North Atlantic coastline and the Appalachian Mountains. The Europeans, in a pattern that was essentially the same throughout the Americas, were initially curious as well as fearful in approaching the natives, but these feelings soon gave way to expressions of contempt. Judging all persons by their own cultural standards, Europeans came to regard the Indians as inferior. Native Americans looked and dressed differently. Their religious beliefs did not conform to European forms of Christianity. The men seemed lazy since women did the bulk of the farming, and they lacked a consuming drive to acquire personal wealth, leaving the mistaken impression of much "want in a land of plenty," as one historian has summarized European perceptions.

To make matters worse, the native populace, as was the case with Tisquantum's Patuxet tribe, quickly began to die in huge numbers, further confirming European perceptions that Indian peoples were inferior rather than merely different. These native "savages," or so Europeans stated, were blocking the path of a more advanced civilization desirous of expansion. Thus commenced what historians have come to call the "invasion" of America.

PREPARING EUROPE FOR WESTWARD EXPANSION

Nearly 500 years before Columbus's initial westward voyage, Europeans made their first known contacts with North America. Around A.D. 1000, the Vikings (Scandinavians) explored barren regions of the North Atlantic. Eric the Red led an expedition of Vikings to Greenland, and one of his sons, Leif Ericson, continued exploring south and westward, stopping at Baffin Island, Labrador, and Newfoundland (described as *Vinland*). There were some attempts at settlement, but none survived. The Viking voyages had no long-term impact because Europe was not yet ripe for westward expansion.

Changing Population Pressures

Most Europeans of the Middle Ages (approximately A.D. 500–1400) lived short, demanding lives. Many tilled the soil as peasants, owing allegiance to manor lords and eking out a meager subsistence. Their crops, grown on overworked soil, were not nutritious. Because they rarely ate fruits, they suffered from constipation and rickets among other diseases. These peasants worshipped as Roman Catholics, regularly attending church services that emphasized the importance of preparing for a better life after death. Meanwhile, the dominant concern was to survive long enough to help the next generation begin the cycle anew.

A variety of factors, including rapid population growth, gradually altered the established rhythms of life in the Middle Ages. Between A.D. 1000 and 1340, Europe's population doubled, reaching over 70 million people. Even with improved methods of agricultural production, a new problem—overcrowding on the land—emerged. Overcrowding represents a condition in which too many individuals try to provide for themselves and their families on fixed parcels of farmland. To ease the pressure, manor lords forced some peasants off the land. These dispossessed persons struggled to avoid starvation. Some joined the growing class of beggars, or they became highway bandits. Others moved into the developing towns where they offered their labor for wages of any kind while seeking to acquire craft skills. Only a handful advanced beyond a marginal existence.

By 1340 Europe was bulging at the seams, but the knowledge and technology were not yet in place to

The Atlantic Community, Late 1400s

Native Americans, Europeans, and Africans made up a triad of peoples around the Atlantic Ocean.

facilitate the movement of people to distant regions. Then, suddenly, a frightening disaster relieved the population pressure. Italian merchant ships trading in Muslim ports in the eastern Mediterranean hauled rats as well as cargoes back to their home ports. These rats carried fleas infested with microbes that caused bubonic plague. The plague, or "Black Death," spread mercilessly through a populace already suffering less virulent maladies related to inadequate diet and poor personal hygiene. When the plague struck the Italian city of Florence in 1348, for example, between half and two-thirds of the population of 85,000 died. More generally, between 1347 and 1353 about one-third of all Europeans died in a medical calamity not to be outdone until the plague and other killer diseases started wiping out Native Americans.

The unpeopling of Europe resulting from the Black Death temporarily checked any desire to find and inhabit new lands. In another two centuries rapid population growth, overcrowding, and consequent problems of destitution and starvation would again come to characterize life in Europe. By this time other factors were in place to facilitate the westward migration of peoples in search of new beginnings.

Crusades, Commerce, and the New Learning

Long before the Black Death, Europeans were gathering knowledge about previously unknown peoples and places. The Crusades, designed to oust the Muslim "infidels" from such Christian holy sites as Jerusalem, broadened their horizons. Sanctioned by the Roman Catholic church and begun in 1095, the Crusades lasted for two centuries. Although European warriors failed to break Muslim hegemony, they did discover that they could carry on trade with the Orient. They learned of spices that would preserve meats over long winters, fruits that would bring greater balance to diets, silk and velvet clothing, hand-crafted rugs, delicate glassware, and dozens of other commodities that would make European lives more comfortable.

Italian merchants, living in independent city-states such as Venice and Genoa, took the lead in developing the Mediterranean trade. Other European cities mushroomed in size at key trading points when Oriental goods started making their way from Italy into Switzerland, France, and Germany. One benefit of this striking increase in commercial activity was to create work for dislocated peasants. Also of major consequence was the rise of great merchants who devoted themselves to securing scarce commodities—and selling them for handsome profits.

The new wealth displayed by the great merchants promoted a pervasive spirit of material acquisition. The merchants, however, did more than merely reinvest profits in additional trading ventures. They also underwrote a resurgence in learning, known as the **Renaissance.** Beginning in Italy, the Renaissance soon captivated much of Continental Europe. New probings took place in all subjects. Learned individuals rediscovered the writings of

This engraving depicts the horrible destruction of the "Black Death" in Florence, a city visited by the plague sixteen times in the thirteenth and fourteenth centuries. Between 1347 and 1353, the plague claimed the lives of nearly 20 million Europeans.

such ancient scholars as Ptolemy, who had mapped the Earth, and Eratosthenes, who had estimated the circumference of the planet. By the mid-fifteenth century educated Europeans knew the world was not flat. Indeed, early in 1492, just a few months before Columbus sailed, a German geographer, Martin Behaim, constructed a round globe for all to see.

Enhanced geographical knowledge went hand in hand with developments in naval science. Before the fifteenth century, Europeans risked their lives when they did not sail within sight of land. The Muslims provided knowledge about the astrolabe and sextant and their uses as basic navigational instruments. Contact with the Arabs also introduced Europeans to more advanced ship and sail designs. Europeans soon abandoned their outmoded square-rigged galleys, which required oarsmen to maneuver these craft against the wind, in favor of lateen-rigged caravels. These vessels were sleeker in design, making them faster. Since their triangular sails could also swivel, the caravels were more mobile. Tacking, or sailing at angles into the wind, was now possible. Such nautical breakthroughs heightened prospects for worldwide exploration in the ongoing search for valuable trading commodities.

Developed by the Portuguese in the late 1400s for exploration of the African coast, the caravel was a light sailing ship about 165 feet long and able to carry 130 tons of cargo. Christopher Columbus's ships, the *Niña* and the *Pinta*, were caravels.

The adventures of **Marco Polo** (1254?–1324?) underscored the new learning and exemplified its relationship to commerce and exploration. Late in the thirteenth century, this young Venetian trader traveled throughout the Orient. He recorded his findings and told of unbelievable wealth in Asian kingdoms such as Cathay (China). Around 1450, Johannes Gutenberg, a German printer, perfected movable type, making it possible to reprint limitless copies of manuscripts, heretofore laboriously copied by hand. The first printed edition of Marco Polo's *Journals* appeared in 1477. Merchants and explorers alike, among them Christopher Columbus, read Polo's *Journals,* which spurred them forward in their quest to gain complete access to Oriental riches.

Nation-States Support the First Explorations

Not all elements of European society embraced the new vitality. Powerful manor lords still controlled the countryside, and they made it difficult for merchants to move goods across their lands, unless traders paid heavy tolls. These nobles also sneered at monarchs wanting to collect taxes. Tapping into peasant manpower, manor lords quite often had stronger armies, leaving royal figures unable to enforce their will. Over time, merchants and monarchs started working together. Using mercantile capital, they formed armies that challenged the nobility.

The process of forming modern nation-states commenced during the fifteenth century. The marriage of Ferdinand of Aragon to Isabella of Castile in 1469 represented the beginnings of national unity in Spain. These joint monarchs hired mercenary soldiers to break the power of defiant nobles. In 1492 they also crushed the Muslims (Moors) inhabiting southern Spain, driving them as well as Jewish inhabitants out of the country. Working closely with the Roman Catholic church, Ferdinand and Isabella used inquisition torture chambers to break the will of those whose loyalty they doubted. By 1500 their subjects had become full-fledged Spaniards who expected to serve their nation with loyalty.

Portugal, France, and England also reckoned with the turbulent process of nation-making. John I led the way by consolidating Portugal in the 1380s. Louis XI, known as the "Spider King," was responsible for unifying France in the 1460s at the end of more than 100 years of intermittent but debilitating warfare with England. Two powerful English noble lines, the houses of York and Lancaster, fought endlessly and devastated themselves in the Wars of the

Indian Scalping and European War Dogs

When Native Americans and Europeans first came into contact, each seemed genuinely curious about the other. Curiosity, however, soon turned to mistrust, and mistrust to a state of unending warfare. Both sides employed "the tactics of remorseless terrorism" in their combat, as one student of early Indian-white relations has written, because both were fighting for control of the landscape—the natives to retain their ancient tribal homes and the Europeans to inhabit the same.

In their life-and-death struggle, Europeans and Indians drew upon long-accepted styles of waging combat. Neither showed much mercy toward the other. Europeans rationalized their acts of butchery by claiming they were dealing with "savages" who were at best "inhumanely cruel" and at worst "carnivorous beasts of the forest." Because of language barriers, the thoughts of Native Americans are not known, but they learned to fear and hate the invaders from across the ocean, and they too fought with a vengeance, although at times with more mercy than Europeans.

Long before the English first made contact, Eastern Woodland Indians regularly engaged in small-scale, intertribal wars. Their weapons included bows and arrows, knives, tomahawks, spears, and clubs. War parties did not attack in battle formations but used the forest as their cover as they ambushed enemies in surprise guerrilla-like raids. Employing hit-and-run tactics, intertribal combat rarely resulted in much bloodshed, since battles seldom lasted for more than a few minutes before attacking warriors melted back into the forest.

When possible, Indian war parties celebrated their victories by the taking of enemy scalps, which for them were war trophies filled with religious meaning. Native Americans believed the piece of scalp and hair sliced from an enemy's head contained the victim's living spirit, which now belonged to the holder of the scalp. To take a scalp, then, was to gain control over that person's spirit (*manitou*). Even if victims survived scalping, which happened on occasion, they were spiritually dead, since they no longer possessed the essence of human life.

Because of their spiritual meaning and power, scalps were treated with great respect. Indians decorated them with jewelry and paint, and warriors kept them on display, even strapping them on their belts as symbols of individual prowess. In other instances warriors gave scalps to families who had lost relatives in battle. Since they contained life, scalps took the place of deceased tribal members.

When Europeans first saw scalps, they were not sure what to think. They certainly attached no spiritual significance to them. Frenchman Jacques Cartier, exploring along the St. Lawrence River in 1535, wrote about local Indians who showed him "the skins of five men's heads, stretched on hoops, like parchment." The local chief explained that the scalps were from Micmacs living to "the south, who waged war continually against his people." Just five years later in west Florida, natives killed two Spanish conquistadores exploring with Hernando de Soto. The Indians then "removed" the "head" of one victim, "or rather all around his skull—it is unknown with what skill they removed it with great ease—and carried it off as evidence of their deed."

Europeans quickly concluded that scalping was another barbarous practice of "savage" Native Americans. Also frightening was the way in which Indians conducted combat. They would not stand and fight in "civilized" fashion, holding to complex linear formations as Europeans did. Rather "they are always running and traversing from one place to another," complained de Soto, making it impossible for musket-wielding Europeans to shoot them down. Worse yet, an expert Indian bowman could easily "discharge three or four arrows" with great accuracy by the time musketeers went through the elaborate steps of preparing their cumbersome weapons for firing. This made combat with Native Americans particularly dangerous because, as de Soto concluded, an Indian bowman "seldom misses what he shoots at."

The Indian style of fighting caused a stream of negative commentary from various European New World adventurers. Natives did not fight fairly, they wrote, but used "cunning tricks" and "slippery designs" to defeat their adversaries. Rather than engaging in manly combat, they were "as greedy after their prey as a wolf," wanting above all else to mutilate their opponents by taking their scalps. The only effective way to deal with native tactics, reasoned these early adventurers, was

to counter them with the most brutal forms of corporal punishment then known—and commonly used—in Europe.

In times of combat the Europeans treated Indians as if they were criminals. As such, natives, in various combinations, would be hanged, drawn and quartered, disemboweled, and like the "savage" and "wild" Irish, beheaded. Captain Miles Standish, charged with protecting the Pilgrims, killed one troublesome Indian and then carried his head back to Plymouth where he had it publicly displayed. When the Dutch in New Netherland went to war with local natives in the 1640s, they regularly beheaded their opponents and had their "gory heads . . . laid in the streets of New Amsterdam, where the governor's mother kicked them like footballs."

Such wanton cruelty, when measured by modern standards, recently resulted in claims from some students of Native American history that Indians, before making contact with Europeans, did not scalp their enemies. Scalping, they claimed, was modeled on beheading but was a more efficient means of gaining war trophies for highly mobile Indian warriors not wanting to carry the extra weight of human heads.

Seeking to demonstrate the "barbarous" influence of "civilized" Europeans expanding westward, this line of reasoning has been thoroughly refuted. Among other forms of evidence, Indian cultural traditions and the astonishment of explorers who first saw scalps support the conclusion that Europeans learned about scalping from Indians and soon incorporated the practice into their arsenal of punishments.

In at least one area, however, European adventurers reached beyond ac-

cepted methods for exacting terror, pain, and death. The Spanish conquistadores used war dogs to maim and kill their victims. The English, who during the sixteenth century reveled in horror stories about Spanish New World barbarities (the so-called Black Legend), thought of war dogs as a new low point in human warfare. Yet within a few years of founding their first settlements, the English likewise were training and unleashing war dogs on Native Americans.

Apparently the favored breed was the English mastiff. These were huge, ugly dogs, weighing up to 150 pounds and naturally protective of their masters. In sixteenth-century England their owners trained them to "bait the bear, to bait the bull and other such like cruel and bloody beasts." The next logical step was to turn these dogs loose on the "heavy beast" in America. In retaliation for Opechancanough's 1622 massacre of Virginians, surviving settlers used dogs, presumably mastiffs, to track down and kill local Indians. War dogs participated in the slaughter of Pequot Indians in Connecticut during 1637 and would perform similar duty throughout the colonial period.

If prospects of facing the scalping knife filled European New World settlers with horror, war dogs, whether on guard duty or on the attack, represented an "extreme terror to the Indians," as a New England minister wrote in the early eighteenth century. This clergyman wanted yet more dogs "trained up to hunt Indians as they do the bear." He understood the nature of "total war" between Indians and whites in the bloody contest for the Americas, and he wanted to survive.

Roses (1455–1485). Henry Tudor, who became Henry VII (reigned 1485–1509), arose from the chaos, worked to crush forever the power of the nobility, and initiated a lengthy internal unification process that set the stage for England's westward expansion.

Unification was critical to focusing national efforts on exploration, as demonstrated by Portugal. Secure in his throne, King John I was able to support his son, Prince Henry (1394–1460), called "the Navigator," in the latter's efforts to learn more about the world. Henry set up a school of navigation at Sagres on the rocky southwestern coast of Portugal. With official state support, he sent out ships on exploratory missions. When the crews returned, they worked to improve maps, sailing techniques, navigational procedures, and ship designs.

Initially, the emphasis was on learning, but then it shifted to a quest for valuable trade goods. Henry's mariners conquered such islands as the Azores and brought back raw wealth (gold, silver, and ivory) from the west coast of Africa. During the 1420s trading ties developed with Africans, including the first dealings in black slaves by early modern Europeans. The lure of wealth drove Portuguese ships farther south along the African coast. Bartholomeu Dias made it to the Cape of Good Hope in 1487. Ten years later, Vasco da Gama took a small flotilla around the lower tip of Africa and on to the riches of India.

Besides returning a 400 percent profit, da Gama's expedition led to the development of Portugal's Far Eastern empire. It also proved that the Muslim world, with its heavy trade tolls, could be circumvented in getting European hands on Oriental riches. None of this would have been possible without a unified Portuguese government able to tax the populace and thus sponsor Prince Henry's attempts to probe the boundaries of the unknown.

Ferdinand and Isabella were intensely aware of Portugal's triumphs when a young Genoese mariner, **Christopher Columbus** (1451–1506), asked them to underwrite his dream of sailing west to reach the Orient. Consumed by their struggle for internal unification, they refused him, but Columbus persisted. He had already contacted King John II of Portugal, who rebuffed him as "a big talker and boastful." Columbus also turned to France and England but gained no sponsorship. Ultimately, Queen Isabella reconsidered. She met Columbus's terms, which included 10 percent of all profits from his discoveries, and proclaimed him "Admiral of the Ocean Sea." Her decision, made possible by Spain's unification, had monumental consequences.

On August 3, 1492, Columbus and some 90 mariners set sail from Palos, Spain, in the *Niña, Pinta,* and *Santa María.* Using faulty calculations, the admi-

Columbus first landed on the Bahamian island that he named San Salvador. He described the local natives as peaceful and generous, an image that changed rapidly as conquistadores swept over the native populace in their rush to tap into the riches of the Americas.

ral estimated Asia to be no more than 4500 miles to the west (the actual distance is closer to 12,000 miles). Some 3000 miles out, his crew became fearful and almost rebelled. They wanted to return home, but he persuaded them to keep sailing west. Just two days later, on October 12, they landed on a small island in the Bahamas, which Columbus named San Salvador (holy savior). There they found hospitable natives, the Arawaks, whom Columbus described as "a loving people without covetousness." He called them Indians, a misnomer that stuck, because he believed he was near Asia (the Indies). Proceeding on, Columbus landed on Cuba, which he thought was Japan, and then on Hispaniola, where he traded for gold-laden native jewelry. In 1493 Columbus and his crew returned home to a hero's welcome and to funding for three more expeditions to America.

EXPLORERS, CONQUERORS, AND THE MAKING OF NEW SPAIN

A fearless explorer, Columbus proved to be an ineffective administrator and a poor geographer. He ended up in debtors' prison, and to his dying day in 1506 he never admitted to locating a world unknown to Europeans. Geographers named the western continents after another mariner, Amerigo Vespucci, a merchant from Florence who participated in a Portuguese expedition to South America in 1501. In a widely reprinted letter, Vespucci insisted that a new world had been found. His first name soon became associated with the two continents.

Columbus's significance lay elsewhere. His 1492 venture garnered enough extractable wealth to exhilarate the Spanish monarchs. They did not care whether Columbus had reached Asia, only that further exploratory voyages might produce unimaginable riches. Because they feared Portuguese interference, Ferdinand and Isabella moved quickly to validate their interests. They went to Pope Alexander VI, who issued a papal bull, *Inter Caetera,* that divided the unknown world between Portugal and Spain.

In 1494 the Spanish monarchs worked out a formal agreement with Portugal in the Treaty of Tordesillas, drawing a line some 1100 miles west of the Cape Verde Islands. All undiscovered lands to the west of the demarcation line belonged to Spain. Those to the east were Portugal's. Inadvertently, Ferdinand and Isabella had given away the easternmost portion of South America. In 1500 a Portuguese mariner, Pedro Alvares Cabral, laid claim to this territory, which came to be known as Brazil. Spain claimed title to everything else, which of course left nothing for emerging nation-states such as France and England.

The Spanish monarchs used their strong army, seasoned by the struggle for unification, as a weapon to conquer the Americas. These *conquistadores* did so with relish. Befitting their crusader's ideology, they agreed to subdue the natives and, with the support of church leaders, to convert them to Roman Catholicism. Bravery and courage, these warriors believed, would bring distinction to themselves and to Spain. Further, they could gain much personal wealth, even if shared with the Crown. Gold, glory, and the gospel formed a triad of factors motivating the Spanish conquistadores, and their efforts resulted in a far-flung American empire known as New Spain.

Conquistadores Overrun Native Americans

Before 1510 the Spanish confined their explorations and settlements to the Caribbean islands. The conquistadores parleyed with Indians, searched diligently for rare metals and spices, and listened to tales of fabulous cities of gold somewhere over the horizon. Most natives remained friendly, but they were hostile in some locales, such as the Lesser Antilles where the cannibalistic Caribs dined on more than one Spanish warrior.

Unwittingly, the conquistadores with their microbial weapons retaliated against all Indians—friend and foe alike. Natives on all the islands lacked the antibodies to fend off European diseases. Smallpox, typhoid, diphtheria, the measles, and various plagues and fevers took a rapid toll. In 1492, for example, more than 200,000 Indians inhabited Hispaniola. Just 20 years later, fewer than 30,000 were alive.

After 1510 the conquistadores moved onto the mainland. Vasco Núñez de Balboa reached Panama in 1513. He organized an exploratory expedition, cut across the isthmus, and became the first European to see the Pacific Ocean, which he dutifully claimed for Spain. The same year Juan Ponce de León, governor of Puerto Rico, led a party to Florida in search of gold and a rumored fountain of youth. Although disappointed on both counts, he claimed Florida for Spain.

Then in 1519 **Hernán Cortés** (1485–1547), a leader of great bravado, mounted his dramatic expedition against the Aztecs. Landing on the Mexican coast with 600 soldiers, his party began a difficult overland march toward Tenochtitlán. Along the way Cortés won to his side various tribes subservient to the Aztecs. These natives may have thought Cortés a god. They certainly admired his horses—unknown in America—as well as the armor and weapons of his soldiers. Still, so small an invading force, even if well armed, could never have prevailed over thousands of Aztec warriors if other factors had not intervened.

Aztec emperor **Montezuma II,** who feared that Cortés was the old Toltec war god Quetzalcoatl coming back to destroy the Aztecs, tried to keep the Spaniards out of Tenochtitlán. He offered mounds of gold and silver, but this gesture only intensified the conquistadores' greed. They boldly marched into the city and took Montezuma prisoner. The Aztecs finally drove off Cortés's army in 1520, but not before smallpox had broken out. Less than a year later, the Spaniards retook Tenochtitlán and claimed all Aztec wealth and political authority as their prize.

Carried away with success, Cortés's soldiers razed the city and boasted of their great prowess as warriors and the superiority of their weapons and knowledge of warfare. They even claimed that God had willed their victory. However, the microbes they brought with them were the true victors. As a participant wrote, when they reentered Tenochtitlán, "the streets, squares, houses, and courts were filled with bodies, so that it was almost impossible to pass. Even Cortés was sick from the stench in his nostrils."

European diseases resulted in at least 17 major epidemics in the Americas during the sixteenth century; there were 14 in Europe. One of these 17 epidemics broke the Aztecs' ability to keep resisting the

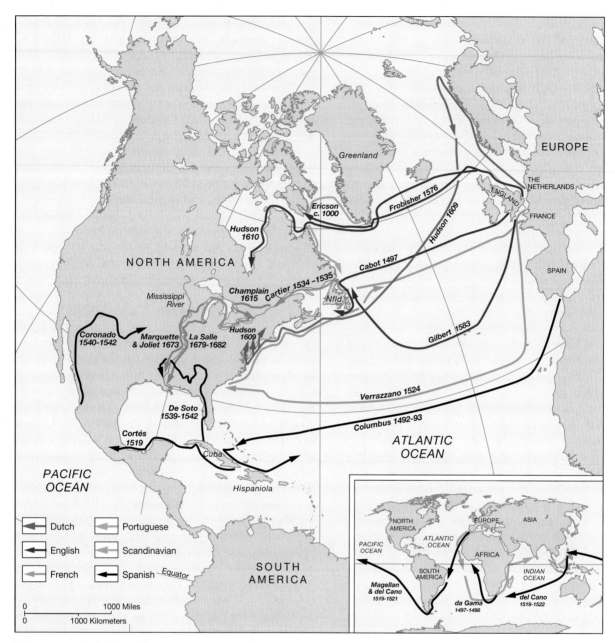

Voyages of Exploration

The European exploration of the Americas came in waves after Columbus's initial voyages in the late 1400s. In the 1500s Spain's American empire took shape, and in the early 1600s England, France, Holland, and Sweden located settlements north of New Spain along the Atlantic coast.

Spanish. As additional epidemics struck, the native populace of 20 to 25 million in Mexico declined dramatically—by about 90 percent during the 50 years following the invasion of Cortés's small army.

Cortés's stunning victory spurred on many other conquistadores, such as aggressive **Francisco Pizarro** (1470–1541). With about 180 soldiers, he overwhelmed thousands of Incas in Peru, seizing the capital city of Cuzco in 1533 after hardly any fighting.

Inca rulers, paralyzed by fear, provided little leadership in resisting the Spanish and their powerful microbial allies. Pizarro showed no mercy; he executed the great chief Atahualpa and proclaimed Spain's sovereignty. By the 1550s the Spanish had conquered much of the rest of South America.

To the north, various expeditions found nothing comparable to the wealth of the Aztecs and Incas. Four hundred men under Pánfilo de Narváez began

This Aztec drawing presumably represents Cortés's conquest of Tenochtitlán in 1519–1522.

a disastrous adventure in 1528. They landed in Florida and searched the Gulf Coast region before being shipwrecked in Texas. Only four men survived, one of whom, Cabeza de Vaca, wrote a tract telling of seven great cities laden with gold. Vaca's writings stimulated Hernando de Soto and 600 others, beginning in 1539, to investigate the lower Mississippi River valley. In 1540 another party under Francisco Vásquez de Coronado began exploring parts of New Mexico, Texas, Oklahoma, and Kansas. They were the first Europeans to see the Grand Canyon. During 1542–1543 mariners under Juan Rodríguez Cabrillo sailed along the California coast as far north as Oregon. None of these groups ever located the fabled cities, but they advanced geographic knowledge of North America while claiming everything they came in contact with for Spain.

Constructing the Spanish Empire

To keep out intruders and to maintain order in New Spain, the Spanish Crown set up two home-based administrative agencies in Madrid. The House of Trade formulated economic policies and provided for annual convoys of galleons, called plate fleets, to haul extractable forms of American wealth back to Spain. The Council for the Indies controlled all political matters in what became an autocratic, rigidly managed empire for the exclusive benefit of the parent state.

The Council for the Indies ruled through viceroys that headed four regional areas of administration. Viceroys, in turn, consulted with *audiencias*

(appointed councils) on matters of local concern, but there were no popularly based representative assemblies. Normally, only pure-blooded Spaniards could influence local decision making—and only if they had ties to councilors or viceroys. Those who questioned their political superiors soon learned there was little tolerance for divergent opinions.

During the sixteenth century the incentive to resettle in New Spain was lacking. Work was plentiful at home, and Spain's population was in decline, reflecting the government's constant warfare in Europe. Consequently, only about 200,000 Spaniards, a modest number, migrated to New Spain. Most migrants were young males looking for adventure and material riches. They did not find much of either, but a few became wealthy as manor holders, ranchers, miners, and government officials.

From the very outset, Spanish migrants complained about a shortage of laborers in America. One solution was the *encomienda* **system,** initially approved by the Crown to reward conquistadores for outstanding service. Favored warriors and settlers received land titles to Indian villages and the surrounding countryside. As *encomenderos,* or landlords, they agreed to educate the natives under their jurisdiction and to guarantee instruction in the Roman Catholic faith. In return, the landlords gained control of the labor of whole villages of people and received portions of annual crops and other forms of forced tribute in recognition of their efforts to "civilize" the native populace.

The *encomienda* system fostered serious problems. Landlords regularly abused the Indians, treating them like slave property. They maimed or put troublemakers to death and bought and sold many others as if they were commodities. The exploitation was so outrageous that one Dominican priest, Bartolomé de Las Casas (1474–1566), later a bishop in southern Mexico, repeatedly begged officials in Madrid to stop such barbarities.

In 1542 the Crown settled the issue by outlawing both the *encomienda* system and the enslavement of Indians. This ruling did not change matters that much. Governing officials continued to award pure-blooded Spaniards vast landed estates *(haciendas),* on which Indians lived in a state of peonage, cultivating the soil and sharing their crops with their landlords *(hacendados).*

Since the native populace also kept dying from European diseases, a second solution to the labor problem was to import Africans. In 1501 the Spanish Crown authorized the first shipment of slaves to the Caribbean islands, a small beginning to what became a vast, forced migration of some 10 million human beings to the Americas.

Slavery as it developed in New Spain was harsh. *Hacienda* owners and mine operators wanted only young adult males who could literally be worked to death, then replaced by new shiploads of Africans. On the other hand, Spanish law and Roman Catholic doctrine restrained some brutality. The Church believed that all souls should be saved, and it recognized marriage as a sacrament, meaning that slaves could wed and aspire to family life. Spanish law even permitted slaves to purchase their freedom. Such allowances were well beyond those made in future English-speaking colonies, and many blacks, particularly those who became artisans and house servants in the cities, did gain their independence.

Also easing slavery's harsh realities was the matter of skin color gradation: The lighter the skin, the greater the range of privileges. Pure-blooded natives of Spain *(peninsulares)* were at the apex of society. Next came the creoles *(criollos)*, or whites born in New Spain. Since so many of the first Spanish migrants were males, they often intermarried with Indians, their children forming the *mestizo* class; or they intermarried with Africans, their children making up the *mulatto* class. The mixture of skin colors in New Spain helped Africans escape some of the racial contempt experienced by blacks in English North America, where legal restrictions against racial intermarriage resulted in less skin color variation.

Success Breeds Envy and Contempt

Still, most slaves and Indians lived in privation at the bottom of New Spain's society. Many church officials, as suggested by the pleas of Las Casas, worked to ease their burdens. Las Casas even went so far as to denounce the enslavement of Africans; but the Crown ignored him, realizing that without slavery Spain would receive fewer shipments of gold, silver, and other valuable commodities.

As Spanish authority spread north into New Mexico, Arizona, California, and other areas, Franciscan, Dominican, and Jesuit friars opened missions and offered protection to natives who would accept Roman Catholic beliefs. Quite often local Indians simply incorporated Catholic doctrines into their own belief systems.

When in the late 1660s and early 1670s a prolonged drought followed by a devastating epidemic ravaged Pueblos living in the upper Rio Grande valley of New Mexico, these natives openly questioned their new Catholic faith—and conquering masters. Spanish friars and magistrates reacted harshly and imprisoned some of the leading dissidents. The Pueblos eventually rallied around a native spiritual leader named Popé. In 1680 they rose in rebellion and killed or drove some 2500 Spanish inhabitants out of New Mexico. By 1700 Spanish soldiers had reconquered the region, maiming and killing hundreds of Pueblos in the process. With their numbers already in rapid decline, the Pueblos never again seriously challenged what seemed like the everexpanding reach of Spanish authority.

As it took shape, then, the Spanish empire was more brutal than tolerant and contained many sharp contrasts. The construction of European-like cathedrals and the founding of great universities could not mask the terrible price in native lives lost, the endemic poverty of surviving Indian and *mestizo* villagers on *haciendas,* or the brutal treatment of slaves in gold and silver mines. These contrasts reflected the acquisitive beginnings of New Spain, which operated first and foremost as a treasure chest for the monarchs back in Madrid.

The flow of wealth made Spain the most powerful—and envied—nation in Europe during the sixteenth century. Such success also became a source of contempt. When Las Casas, for example, published *A Very Brief Relation of the Destruction of the Indies* (1552), he described the Indians as "patient, meek, and peaceful . . . lambs" whom bloodthirsty conquistadores had "cruelly and inhumanely butchered." Las Casas's listing of atrocities became the basis of the "Black Legend," a tale that other Europeans started to employ as a rationale for challenging Spain's New World supremacy. They promised to treat Native Americans more humanely, but in reality their primary motivation was to garner a share of America's riches for themselves.

CHALLENGERS FOR NORTH AMERICA: FRANCE AND ENGLAND

When Henry VII of England realized how successful Columbus had been, he chose to ignore the Treaty of Tordesillas. He underwrote another Italian explorer, **Giovanni Caboto (John Cabot)**, to seek Cathay on behalf of the Tudor monarchy. Cabot's was the first exploratory expedition to touch North America since the Viking voyages. He landed on Newfoundland and Cape Breton Island in 1497. A second expedition in 1498 ended in misfortune when Cabot was lost at sea. Still, his voyages served as the basis for English claims to North America.

Soon France joined the exploration race. In 1524 King Francis I authorized yet another Italian mariner, Giovanni da Verrazzano, to sail westward. Verrazzano tracked along the American coast from North

Carolina to Maine. Unfortunately, during another voyage in 1528 he died somewhere in the Lesser Antilles, where either Spaniards hanged him as an intruder or Caribs killed him. More important for later French claims, Jacques Cartier mounted three expeditions to the St. Lawrence River area, beginning in 1534. He scouted as far inland as modern-day Quebec and Montreal. Cartier even started a colony in 1541–1542, but too much political turmoil in France diverted the Crown from supporting trading stations or permanent settlements.

Verrazzano and Cartier were among the first to show interest in finding an all-water route—the **Northwest Passage**—through North America to the Orient. Seeking a northerly route was partially a response to the epic voyage of **Ferdinand Magellan** (1519–1522) under the Spanish flag. Magellan's party circumnavigated the globe by sailing around the southern tip of South America and proved, once and for all, that the world was round and that a vast ocean lay between America and Asia. The Northwest Passage, had it existed, would have allowed the English and French, among other Europeans, to avoid contact with New Spain while gaining access to Oriental wealth, since no one, as yet, had found readily extractable riches in North America. Searching for the passage was also a challenge to the worldwide ambitions of Portugal and Spain, especially after 1529 when these two powers extended their demarcation line down through the Pacific Ocean.

The Protestant Reformation Stirs Deep Tensions

Throughout the sixteenth century, the monarchs of England and France did not directly challenge Spain's supremacy in the Americas. They had too many problems at home, such as those related to religious strife. The **Protestant Reformation** shattered the unity of the Roman Catholic church, convulsed Europe, and provoked bloody wars. At the same time, the Reformation helped stimulate many Europeans, experiencing repression at home because of their newfound beliefs, to consider moving and resettling elsewhere. This was particularly the case in England.

The Roman Catholic church was the most powerful institution in medieval Europe. When dissenters spoke out, they were invariably punished, unless they publicly recanted their heretical views. Then in 1517, **Martin Luther** (1483–1546), an obscure friar of the Augustinian order and a professor of Scripture at the University of Wittenberg in Germany, tacked "Ninety-Five Theses" on a local church

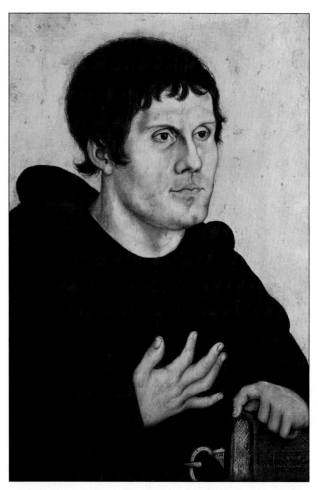

A portrait of young Martin Luther by Lucas Cranach the Elder. Luther's call for reform of church abuses helped spur the Protestant Reformation and sparked political and social upheaval in Europe, as well as in the new settlements across the Atlantic in the Americas.

door. Luther was upset with what he thought were a number of unscriptural practices, particularly the selling of **indulgences** in the form of cash payments to the church to make amends for sins. As a form of penance, individuals could purchase indulgences for themselves or for others, such as deceased loved ones, to assure quick journeys through purgatory to heaven.

Luther found no biblical basis for indulgences. He could not understand why the church, which he described as "wealthiest of the wealthy," wanted money from hard-pressed peasants to help complete such building projects as St. Peter's Basilica in Rome. He also despised agents who were selling indulgences with clever sayings like: "As soon as coin in the coffer rings, the soul from purgatory springs." Luther had agonized for years over the ways to earn God's grace. He concluded that faith was all that mattered, not ritual or good works. The papacy demanded that Luther recant his heretical notions, but he refused, knowing full well that his penalty would be excommunication from the church.

Among other ideas, Luther contended that people did not need priests to interpret scriptures. All persons should have the right to read the Bible for themselves in cultivating their own faith in God. Luther thus advocated a "priesthood of all believers" in comprehending the mysteries of Christianity. In effect, he was attacking the widespread illiteracy of his era. Luther envisioned an educated populace capable of improving its lot in life. By the 1550s the doctrines of Lutheranism had taken firm hold in parts of Germany and the Scandinavian countries, often in the wake of enormous social turmoil and bloodshed.

Once under way, the Reformation, as this religious reform movement came to be known, gained rapid momentum. It also took many forms. In England politics rather than theology dictated the split with Rome. Henry VIII (reigned 1509–1547) prided himself on his devotion to Roman Catholicism. In 1521 he published a *Defense of the Seven Sacraments,* which berated Luther for arguing in favor of only two sacraments—baptism and communion. The Pope responded by awarding Henry a new title, "Defender of the Faith." At the same time, Henry worried about producing a male heir. His queen, Catherine of Aragon, daughter of Ferdinand and Isabella, bore him six children; but only one, a daughter named Mary, survived early childhood. Henry still wanted a male heir to ensure perpetuation of the Tudor line. In 1527 he asked Pope Clement VII to annul his marriage. When the Pope refused, Henry severed all ties with Rome.

Henry's actions were also spurred by his infatuation with Anne Boleyn, who bore him Elizabeth before being beheaded as an alleged adulteress. Through a series of parliamentary acts, Henry closed monasteries and seized church property. In the 1534 Act of Supremacy he formally repudiated the Pope and declared himself God's regent over England. Henceforth, all subjects would belong to the Anglican (English) church. The Church of England, unlike the Lutheran church, was similar to Catholicism in doctrine and ritual.

After his death Henry's reformation became a source of internal political chaos. When his daughter Mary I (reigned 1553–1558) came to the throne, she tried to return England to the Roman Catholic faith.

Her government persecuted Protestants relentlessly, condemning nearly 300 to fiery deaths at the stake. Her opponents dubbed her "Bloody Mary," and many church leaders fled the land. Some of these "Marian exiles" went to Geneva, Switzerland, to study with John Calvin, whose Biblical ideas formed the basis of the Reformed Protestant tradition.

John Calvin (1509–1564) was a French lawyer who had fled to Switzerland because of his controversial theological ideas. Brilliant and persuasive, he soon controlled Geneva and reordered life there according to his understanding of Scripture. Calvin believed God to be both all-powerful and wrathful. To avoid eternal damnation, persons had to gain God's grace through a conversion experience denoted by accepting Jesus Christ as their savior. All had to seek, insisted Calvin, even though God had already predestined who would be saved and who would be damned. Since no one could be sure which persons were God's chosen "saints," Calvin taught that correct moral behavior and outward prosperity—physical and mental as well as material—represented possible signs of divine favor.

Individuals disenchanted with Catholicism studied Calvin's famous *Institutes of the Christian Religion* (1536). Many, such as the Marian exiles, traveled to Geneva to learn more about the concepts that came to be known as **Calvinism.** Then they returned to their homelands eager to set up godly communities. Their numbers included founders of the German and Dutch Reformed churches, as well as Huguenots who eventually suffered from organized state persecution back in France. John Knox, another disciple of Calvin, established the Presbyterian church in Scotland.

The Marian exiles began reappearing in England after the death of Queen Mary. In time, they developed a large following and came to be known as "Puritans." They wanted to continue Henry's reformation but now along theological lines. Fiercely dedicated to their beliefs, they had a startling impact on the course of English history, particularly after the time of Elizabeth I (reigned 1558–1603), when some of them moved to North America and others precipitated a civil war in England.

Defying the Supremacy of Spain

Spain's success in the Americas in combination with religious contention between Catholics and Protestants fostered unending turmoil among sixteenth-century nation-states. Some of the tension related to America, where French, Dutch, and English "sea dogs" attacked Spanish commerce or traded covertly within the empire. Some related to attempted

The defeat of the Spanish Armada on May 30, 1588, and the destruction of so many of Philip II's ships opened the way for overseas exploration and expansion by both England and the Dutch Republic.

Huguenot (French Protestant) settlements in South Carolina and Florida. Spain, cast as the primary defender of Roman Catholicism, fought back, using wealth extracted from America to pay for military forces capable of protecting its interests.

France remained overwhelmingly Roman Catholic but was at first tolerant of the Huguenots. The Crown, however, encouraged Huguenot emigration to America as a way to rid the realm of these zealous dissenters. Two attempts by Huguenots to settle in the Americas failed. Yet a third colonization undertaking occurred in 1564. These Huguenots located in northern Florida and called their settlement site Fort Caroline.

Spanish officials responded decisively. In 1565 they sent out a small army under Pedro Menéndez de Avilés, who first set up a garrison at San Augustín (the beginnings of St. Augustine, the oldest European-style city in North America), then turned on the Huguenots. Menéndez's troops massacred the Fort Caroline settlers, killing 132 of them but sparing about 50 women and children. To make sure other outsiders, especially Protestants, understood the danger of trying to colonize in Spanish territory, Menéndez ordered his soldiers to hack up the bodies before dumping the remains into a river. The butchery of Menéndez helped curtail sixteenth-century French settlement ventures.

Raids on Spanish treasure ships served as another source of tension. As early as the 1520s French freebooters started attacking Spanish vessels. The most daring of the sea dogs were Englishmen such as

John Hawkins and **Francis Drake.** During the 1560s and 1570s Hawkins traded illegally and raided for booty in New Spain. Drake's adventures were even more dramatic. With private financial backing, including funds from **Queen Elizabeth I,** he began a voyage in 1577 that took him around the world. Drake attacked wherever Spanish ports of call existed before returning home in 1580. Elizabeth gratefully dubbed him a knight, not only for being the first Englishman to circumnavigate the globe but also for securing a 4600 percent profit for his investors.

Elizabeth's professions of innocence to the contrary, King Philip II of Spain suspected her of actively supporting the sea dogs, whom he considered piratical scum. Further, he was furious with the English for giving military aid to the Protestant Dutch, who since 1567 had been fighting to free themselves from Spanish rule. Philip so despised Elizabeth that he conspired with her Catholic cousin Mary Stuart, Queen of Scots, to overthrow the English Protestant government. Wary of such plots, Elizabeth had Mary beheaded in 1587, at which point Philip decided to conquer the troublesome English heretics.

Philip and his military advisers pulled together an armada of Spanish vessels. They planned to sail 130 ships, including many hulking galleons, through the English Channel, pick up thousands of Spanish troops fighting the Dutch, and then invade England. The expedition ended in disaster for the Spanish when a flotilla of English ships, most of them smaller but far more maneuverable than the slow-moving galleons, appeared in the channel under Drake's command and offered battle. Then the famous "Protestant Wind" blew the Spanish Armada to bits. The war with Spain did not officially end until 1604; however, the destruction of the Armada in 1588 established England's reputation as a naval power. It also demonstrated that little England, heretofore a minor kingdom, could prevail over Europe's mightiest nation, which caused some English subjects to press forward with plans to secure territories in North America.

England Prepares for Westward Expansion

Besides the diminished Spanish threat, other factors helped pave the way for England's westward expansion. None was more important than rapid population growth. During the sixteenth century, England's population doubled, reaching 4 million by the 1590s. Yet opportunities for employment and decent wages lagged behind the population explosion. The phenomenal growth of the woolen industry, for instance, forced peasants off the land as manor lords fenced in their fields to make pastures for sheep. Because of this **enclosure movement,** England in 1600 had three times as many sheep as people. Meanwhile, London and other cities exploded in size as persons displaced from the countryside poured in and subsisted as best they could under miserable conditions.

In addition, all Europeans faced the major problem of rapid inflation, a reflection of what has been called the **price revolution.** Between 1500 and 1600 the cost of goods and services spiraled upward by as much as 500 percent. The principal inflationary culprit was an overabundance of precious metal, mostly Spanish silver mined in America (7 million pounds in weight by about 1650) and then pumped into the European economy in exchange for various commodities. The amount of money in circulation expanded more quickly than did the supply of goods or services. As a result, prices jumped dramatically.

In England, even farmers who owned their own land struggled to make ends meet. What they had to pay for necessities rose faster than what they received in the marketplace for their agricultural produce. A prolonged decline in real income on top of heavy taxes under the Tudors left many independent farmers destitute. In time, the abundant land of America attracted great numbers of England's failing yeoman farmers and permanently poor (sometimes called "sturdy beggars").

Apparent overpopulation and so much poverty and suffering became powerful arguments for west-

ward expansion. As the eminent Elizabethan expansionist **Richard Hakluyt** wrote in his influential *Discourse of Western Planting* (1584), "infinite numbers may be set to work" in America, "to the unburdening of the realm . . . at home." Hakluyt also viewed American settlements as the key to achieving national greatness, since colonies could serve as sources of valuable commodities. They would likewise stimulate England's shipbuilding industry. They would help "enlarge the glory of the gospel" by offering the Indians "sincere religion" in the form of the Protestant Anglican faith. Further, argued Hakluyt, no one, certainly not the native populace, could enjoy "humanity, courtesy, and freedom" in America unless England challenged Spain's tyrannical sway by planting true "liberty" in its overseas settlements.

As with other New World colonizers, the English viewed their motives as above reproach on all counts. Certainly Queen Elizabeth recognized the merits of Richard Hakluyt's arguments, especially as they related to increasing the power of her realm. Still, she was a tightfisted monarch who refused to plunge vast sums of royal funds into highly speculative American ventures. She preferred having her favored courtiers, such as those then subduing Ireland, expend their own capital and energies in the quest for riches across the Atlantic Ocean.

JOINING IN THE INVASION OF AMERICA

England's path to America lay through Ireland. Off and on over four centuries the English had conducted sporadic raids on the "wild" Irish, as they thought of their Gaelic-speaking neighbors. During Elizabeth's reign, these forays became routine. The goal was to gain political control of Ireland and to establish agricultural colonies, since ample food supplies had become a problem at home with the spread of the enclosure movement.

Elizabeth named as governor one of her court favorites, Sir Humphrey Gilbert (1539?–1583), and instructed him to subdue the Irish. Gilbert did so with a vengeance, operating as if the only good Irish subject was one who had been beheaded. The Irish, a million strong, fought back relentlessly, causing the English "plantations" there to exist precariously as military outposts in an alien environment.

For Elizabethan courtiers, Ireland became a laboratory for learning how to crush one's adversaries. Assumptions of cultural superiority abetted the English onslaught. The conquerors condemned the Irish,

A Festive Dance is one of John White's drawings depicting life among the Native Americans in the village of Secoton, near the Roanoke settlement.

who were Roman Catholics, as religious heathens. They faulted them for using the land improperly, since the Irish were not sedentary farmers but people of migratory habits who tilled the soil only when they needed food. England's expansionists held these same attitudes when they began their American settlements. This time, however, the Indians would be the wild, unkempt, "savage" peoples in need of subjugation or eradication.

The Roanoke Disaster

Sir Humphrey Gilbert was as intolerant and contemptuous of the Spanish as he was of the Irish. He resented their pretensions to everything in America. He dreamed of finding the Northwest Passage to facilitate a flow of Oriental riches back to England, and he was willing to risk his personal fortune in that quest. Gilbert had other visions as well, including the effective occupation of North America and the founding of American colonies. He appealed to Elizabeth for exclusive rights to carry out his plans, and she acceded in 1578.

Gilbert's patent represented an important statement with respect to future guidelines for England's westward expansion. On the monarch's authority, he could occupy "heathen and barbarous lands . . . not actually possessed of any Christian prince or people." He would share in profits from extractable wealth, as would the Crown. Even more significant, prospective settlers would be assured the same

rights of Englishmen "as if they were born and personally resident" at home. Not guaranteeing fundamental liberties would have inhibited the development of American colonies.

Gilbert did not live to see his dreams fulfilled. He disappeared in a North Atlantic storm after searching for the Northwest Passage. In 1584 his half-brother, **Sir Walter Raleigh** (1552?–1618), requested permission to carry on Gilbert's work. Elizabeth agreed, and Raleigh took quick action. He sent out a reconnoitering party, which explored the North Carolina coast and surveyed Roanoke Island. Then in 1585 Raleigh sponsored an expedition of 600 men, many of them veterans of the Irish wars. After some raiding for booty in New Spain, Raleigh's adventurers sailed north and dropped off 107 men under Governor Ralph Lane at the chosen site.

Lane's party found the local Croatoan and Roanoak Indians to be friendly. Then diseases struck. "That people," an eyewitness exclaimed, "began to die very fast, and many in short space." In the spring of 1586 a local chief, Wingina, probably trying to protect his tribe from an illness "so strange that they neither knew what it was, nor how to cure it," moved inland. Ralph Lane went after the natives and ordered an attack, during which one of his men beheaded Wingina in the tradition of dealing with the "wild" Irish. Fortunately for Lane, Sir Francis Drake appeared and carried the English party away before the Indians counterattacked.

Raleigh persisted. He decided to send out families in 1587, with John White, a capable, gentle person, as their governor. White had been on the 1585 expedition. Besides preparing many famous drawings of native life in the Roanoke area, he had spoken out against butchering the Indians. White and the other 114 settlers arrived at Roanoke Island in late July. In mid-August his daughter Elinor gave birth to Virginia Dare, the first English subject born in America. A few days later, White sailed back to England to obtain additional supplies. The outbreak of warfare between Spain and England delayed his return, and he did not get back to Roanoke until 1590. Nothing was left, except the word CROATOAN carved on a tree.

What happened to the lost colony may never be known. No European saw the settlers again. Local Indians either killed or absorbed them into their tribes. As for Raleigh, he had ruined himself financially, proving that funding overseas ventures lay beyond the means of any one person. All that he had left was a patent that he gave up in the 1590s, a sense that colonizing in America was a hazardous undertaking at best, and a name, Virginia, which Raleigh had offered in thanks to his patron, Elizabeth, the Virgin Queen.

Merchant Capitalists Sponsor the Founding of Virginia

A few sixteenth-century English subjects did prosper in the wake of economic dislocation and spiraling inflation. Among these fortunate few were manufacturers of woolen goods and merchants who made Europe a major marketplace for English cloth. With their profits, these gentlemen of capital gained social respectability. Many purchased landed estates, and some even married into England's titled nobility. As members of the gentry class, they started pooling their capital and sponsoring risky overseas business ventures by investing in **joint-stock trading companies.**

In 1555 the Crown chartered the Muscovy Company, giving that business venture the exclusive right to develop England's trade with Russia. Having a monopoly made the enterprise more attractive to potential stockholders. Although they hoped to make handsome profits, they would lose no more than the money they had subscribed. Meanwhile, the company could draw on a large pool of working capital to underwrite its activities. Queen Elizabeth liked this model of business organization, which depended on private capital rather than royal funds to finance England's economic—and eventually political—expansion abroad. The Crown, of course, was to share in any profits.

The Muscovy Company was a success, and other joint-stock undertakings followed, such as the East India Company, chartered in 1600 to develop England's Far Eastern interests. Then in 1606 a charter for the Virginia Company received royal approval. Ironically, even though this business enterprise failed its stockholders, company activities produced England's first enduring settlement in North America.

During the 1590s, English courtiers and merchant capitalists did not pick up on Raleigh's failed efforts. The ongoing war with Spain took precedence, and profits came easily from capturing Spanish vessels on the high seas. When peace returned, influential merchants stood ready to pool their capital, spread the financial risk, and pursue Raleigh's patent. They took their case to the new king, the Stuart monarch **James I** (reigned 1603–1625), who willingly granted them a generous trading company charter.

Initially, the Virginia Company had two sets of investors. The first, a group of London merchants,

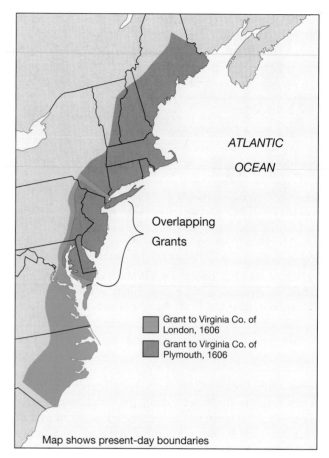

Grant to Virginia Co. of London, 1606

Grant to Virginia Co. of Plymouth, 1606

Map shows present-day boundaries

Conflicting Land Claims

held Raleigh's patent. They had earned bountiful profits from other joint-stock ventures and were ready to take further risks. Foolishly, they dreamed of heaping piles of gold and silver. More realistically, they hoped to trade for valuable commodities with the native populace and to plant vineyards and silk-producing mulberry trees. The London merchants had first claim to all land between the Cape Fear River in southern North Carolina and present-day New York City.

In December 1606, they sent out 144 adventurers under Captain Christopher Newport aboard the *Susan Constant, Godspeed,* and *Discovery.* The crossing was difficult, and 39 men died. In May 1607 the survivors located on an island some 30 miles up the James River off Chesapeake Bay. They called their settlement, really meant as a trading post, Jamestown.

The second set of investors were from such West Country port towns as Plymouth. In response to bitter complaints over the years about London's dominance of joint-stock ventures, the Virginia Company granted the West Country merchants lands lying between the mouth of the Potomac River and northern Maine. Thus the charter allowed for an overlapping middle zone that both investor groups could develop, so long as their settlements were at least 100 miles apart.

The West Country merchants hoped to reap profits by harvesting great stands of American timber and from fur trading with the Indians and fishing off the New England coast. They dispatched a party in 1607 that located at Sagadahoc, Maine, near the mouth of the Kennebec River. These 44 adventurers squabbled incessantly among themselves and failed to maintain harmonious relations with local natives. Those who survived the first winter gave up and returned home in 1608. The Plymouth investors refused to expend more funds, and their patent fell dormant.

As with the Irish invasion, both groups of adventurers came forth in military fashion. They built forts to protect themselves from unfriendly Indians and Spanish raiding parties. In its early days, Jamestown functioned as an outpost in another alien environment. The early participants were not settlers. They wanted to get in, gain access to easy forms of wealth, and get out before losing their lives.

Struggling Jamestown Survives

That Jamestown survived is amazing. Newport's adventurers were miscast for the American wilderness. Many were second and third sons of English noblemen. Because of primogeniture and entail (laws that specified that only firstborn male heirs could inherit landed estates and family titles), these younger sons had to choose alternate careers. Many became lawyers, clergymen, or high-ranking military officers, but none toiled in the fields, as farming was hardly a gentleman's calling. When Jamestown ran short of food, these company adventurers still avoided agricultural work, preferring to search for gold, silver, or the Northwest Passage. Some starved to death as a result.

Besides gentleman-adventurers, other equally ill-prepared individuals, such as valets and footmen, joined the expedition. Their duties extended only to waiting on their aristocratic masters. Also present were goldsmiths and jewelers, plus a collection of ne'er-do-wells who knew no occupation but apparently functioned as soldiers under gentleman-officers in dealings with the natives.

The social and economic characteristics of these first adventurers suggest that the London investors may have modeled the expedition after the early Spanish conquests—with the idea of forcing local Indians to become agricultural workers as peons or slaves. As matters turned out, the natives supplied food, but even with their assistance, only 38 Englishmen were still alive by the early spring of 1608.

Another problem was the settlement site. Company directors had ordered the adventurers to locate on high ground far enough inland so as to go undetected by the Spanish. Jamestown Island met the second requirement, but it was a low, swampy place lying at a point on the James River where salt and fresh water mingled. The brackish water was

A fortified palisade surrounded the simple one- and two-room dwellings at Jamestown, but could not protect the settlers from the disease and starvation that claimed the lives of nearly two-thirds of them.

"full of slime and filth," as one observer noted. The water could cause salt poisoning and was also a breeding ground for malaria, typhoid fever, and dysentery.

Several factors saved the Jamestown settlement. The local Indians under **Powhatan,** an Algonquian-speaking Pamunkey, initially offered sustenance. Powhatan had organized a confederacy of some 30 coastal tribes, numbering about 20,000 people, to defend themselves against aggressive interior neighbors. Powhatan tried to stay clear of the Jamestown adventurers, but when he was around them, he could not help but notice their large ships, gaudy body armor, and noisy firearms. He viewed the English as potential allies in warfare with interior tribes, a faulty assessment but one that kept him from wiping out the weakened adventurers.

At the same time, Company investors in London refused to quit. They kept sending out supplies and adventurers, as many as 800 more young men plus a few women in 1608 and 1609. Upon their arrival, however, many quickly died of malaria and other diseases. Others, debilitated from illnesses, were unable to work. They became a drain on Jamestown's precarious food supply.

In these early days the dynamic and ruthless local leadership of **Captain John Smith** (1580?–1631) kept the Jamestown outpost from totally collapsing. Smith had crossed the Atlantic with the original adventurers. Once in Jamestown, he emerged as a virtual dictator. Smith helped save many lives by imposing discipline and forcing everyone—gentleman or servant, sick or well—to adhere to one rule: "He who works not, eats not."

In October 1609 Smith returned to England after suffering severe burns from an accidental explosion of gunpowder. Lacking authoritarian leadership, the adventurers experienced a tragic "starving time" during the winter of 1609–1610. Hundreds died as food supplies, described as "moldy, rotten, full of cobwebs and maggots," gave out. Only about 60 persons survived by eating everything from rats to snakes, and there was even an alleged instance of cannibalism. One man completely lost his mind; he murdered his wife, then "powdered [salted] her up to eat her, for which he was burned" at the stake.

Smith's presence might not have averted the disaster. Too often, he, like the other early adventurers, had treated the Indians with contempt. Bad relations caused Powhatan to cut off food supplies. For some reason, however, the native leader did not seize the opportunity to wipe out Jamestown. Perhaps still hoping for an alliance, he simply allowed the feeble English to die on their own.

Back in England, Virginia Company stockholders refused to concede defeat. By 1610 they realized that mineral wealth was an illusion, but still they sent out more people. One of them, **John Rolfe,** experimented with local tobacco plants, which produced a harsh-tasting crop. Rolfe, like the company, persisted. He procured some plants from Trinidad in the West Indies and grew a milder, more flavorful leaf. Tobacco soon became Virginia's gold and silver. The colony now had a valuable trading commodity, and settlements quickly spread along the banks of the James River. Englishmen had found an economic reason to stay in the Americas.

Dutch and French Adventurers

In the early 1600s the Spanish contented themselves with drawing wealth from their Caribbean basin empire. They did not challenge various European interlopers seeking to stake North American claims. Ultimately, Dutch settlements in New York were seized by the English, but France's efforts resulted in a Canadian empire capable of rivaling those of Spain and England.

Once fully liberated from Spanish domination at home, the Dutch grabbed at a portion of North America. In 1609 they sent out an English sea captain, Henry Hudson, to search for the Northwest Passage. He explored Delaware Bay, then the New York waterway that bears his name. Hudson made contact with the Iroquois Indians, probably the Mohawks, and talked of trade in furs. Broad-brimmed beaver hats were then the fashion rage in Europe, but fur supplies were dwindling. North America could become a new source of pelts, if the natives would cooperate. The Dutch established trading stations on Manhattan Island (later called New Amsterdam) and Albany (Fort Orange) in 1624. The Iroquois did their part in delivering furs, and the colony of New Netherland took hold under the auspices of the Dutch West India Company.

Profits from furs also helped motivate the French. In 1608 Samuel de Champlain set up an outpost at Quebec on the St. Lawrence River, and he found local Indians ready to trade. Quebec was the base from which New France spread. Yet only after 1663, when the Crown took control of managing the colony, did the French population in Canada grow significantly, reaching 10,000 people by the 1680s.

The French Canadians were energetic. Following Champlain's lead, they explored everywhere and claimed everything in sight. They established harmo-

THE PEOPLE SPEAK

Powhatan Pleads for Peace and Harmony (1609)

The aging Chief Powhatan hoped to befriend the English adventurers who began appearing in the midst of his Confederacy in 1607. However, he quickly learned that they were just as likely to maim and kill his followers as to respond gratefully for the food that he was supplying them. Skeptics among the native populace started warning Powhatan that the English had but one goal—to kill them all and take their lands. In 1609, Powhatan, still hoping for peace, met with Captain John Smith and warned him of grave consequences should the English persist in their belligerent ways. The Jamestown adventurers did not listen. Powhatan cut off their food supplies, which resulted in the "starving time" of 1609–1610 and protracted warfare in the years ahead. Smith recorded the text of Powhatan's speech as follows:

> Captaine Smith, . . . I knowe the difference of peace and warre better than any in my Countrie. But now I am old, and ere long must die. My brethren, namely Opichapam, Opechankanough, and Kekataugh, my two sisters, and their two daughters, are distinctly each others successours. I wish their experience no lesse then mine, and your love to them, no less then mine to you: but this brute [rumor] from Nansamund, that you are come to destroy my Countrie, so much affrighteth all my people, as they dare not visit you. What will it availe you to take that perforce you may quietly have with love, or to destroy them that provide you food? What can you get by war, when we can hide our provision and flie to the woodes, whereby you must famish, by wronging us your friends? And whie are you thus jealous of our loves, seeing us unarmed, and both doe, and are willing still to feed you with that you cannot get but by our labours? Think you I am so simple not to knowe it is better to eate good meate, lie well, and sleepe quietly with my women and children, laugh, and be merrie with you, have copper, hatchets, or what I want being your friend; then bee forced to flie from all, to lie cold in the woods, feed upon acorns roots and such trash, and be so hunted by you that I can neither rest eat nor sleepe, but my tired men must watch, and if a twig but breake, everie one crie, there comes Captaine Smith: then must I flie I knowe not whether and thus with miserable feare end my miserable life, leaving my pleasures to such youths as you, which, through your rash unadvisednesse, may quickly as miserably ende, for want of that you never knowe how to find? Let this therefore assure you of our loves, and everie yeare our friendly trade shall furnish you with corn; and now also if you would come in friendly manner to us, and not thus with your gunnes and swords, as to invade your foes.

Source: Samuel G. Drake, *Biography and History of the Indians of North America* (Boston, 1841), 353.

nious relations with dozens of different Indian nations, and they even joined in native wars as a way of solidifying trading ties. The French, with their small numbers, could not completely impose their cultural values. They did use the natives for their own purposes, especially in relation to the fur trade. At the same time, they also showed respect, which paid off handsomely when their many Indian allies willingly fought beside them in a series of imperial wars that beset America beginning in 1689.

CONCLUSION

Except in Canada, the Europeans who explored the Americas and began colonies after 1492 acted as foreign invaders. Although a few were at first curious, they generally viewed the natives as their adversaries, describing them as "worse than those beasts which are of the most wild and savage nature." Judgments of cultural superiority seemed to justify the destruction of Native Americans.

Still, there was a **Columbian exchange** of sorts. The Indians taught the Europeans about tobacco, corn, potatoes, varieties of beans, peanuts, tomatoes, and many other crops then unknown in Europe. In return, Europeans introduced the native populace to wheat, oats, barley, and rice, as well as to grapes for wine and various melons. The Europeans also brought with them domesticated animals, including horses, pigs, sheep, goats, and cattle. Horses proved to be important, particularly for Great Plains Indians, who used them in fighting against future generations of white settlers, just as tobacco production in the Chesapeake

CHRONOLOGY OF KEY EVENTS

30,000–20,000 B.C.	First humans arrive in North America from Asia across what is now the Bering Strait
8000–5000 B.C.	Central American Indians begin to practice agriculture
A.D. 300–900	Maya civilization flourishes in present-day Mexico and Guatemala
c. 900	Toltecs rise to power in the Valley of Mexico and later conquer the Mayas
c. 1000	Vikings led by Leif Ericson reach Labrador and Newfoundland (*Vinland*)
1095	European Christians launch the Crusades to capture the Holy Lands from Muslims
c. 1100	Inca civilization emerges in what is now Peru
1271	Marco Polo begins a 20-year journey to China
1347–1353	"Black Death" kills about one-third of Europe's population
1420s	Prince Henry the Navigator of Portugal sends mariners to explore Africa's western coast
c. 1450	Johannes Gutenberg, a German printer, develops movable type, the basis of modern printing
1469	Ferdinand and Isabella marry and begin to unify Spain
1492	Columbus makes the first of his voyages of discovery to the Americas
1494	Treaty of Tordesillas divides the known world between Portugal and Spain
1497–1498	John Cabot's two voyages to Newfoundland and Cape Breton Island lay the basis for English claims to North America
1501	Spain authorizes the first shipment of African slaves to the Caribbean islands
1517	Martin Luther's public protests against the sale of indulgences (pardons of punishment in Purgatory) mark the beginning of the Protestant Reformation
1519	Hernán Cortés and 600 Spanish conquistadores begin the conquest of the Aztec empire
1527	Henry VIII of England begins to sever ties with the Roman Catholic church
1531	Francisco Pizarro and 180 Spanish soldiers start the conquest of the Inca empire
1534	Jacques Cartier explores the St. Lawrence River and claims the region for France
1542	Spain outlaws the *encomienda* system and the enslavement of Indians
1585–1587	Sir Walter Raleigh sponsors England's first North American settlement at Roanoke Island in present-day North Carolina
1607	English adventurers establish the first permanent English settlement at Jamestown in present-day Virginia

area had the unintended effect of attracting enough Europeans to end native control of that area.

Perhaps more than anything else, killer diseases served to unbalance the exchange. From the first moments of contact, great civilizations like the Aztecs and more humble groups like Tisquantum's Patuxets faced devastation. In some cases the Indians who survived, as in New Spain, had to accept the status of peons. Along the Atlantic coastline, survivors were drawn into the European trading network. In exchange for furs, the Indians wanted firearms to kill yet more animals whose pelts could be traded for still more guns and for alcohol to help them forget, even for a moment, what was happening to their way of life in the wake of European westward expansion.

The English would eventually send the most settlers. They left home for various reasons. Some, like the Pilgrims, crossed the Atlantic to avoid further religious persecution. Others, such as the Puritans, sought to build a holy community that would shine as a light upon Europe. Still others, including colonists in the Chesapeake Bay area, desired land for growing tobacco. The latter group wanted laborers to help them raise their crops. Unable to enslave the Indians, they ultimately borrowed from the Spanish model and enslaved Africans. In so doing, they forced blacks to enter their settlements in chains and to become a part of a peopling and unpeopling process that helped shape the contours of life in colonial America.

- The exchange was not evenly balanced. Killer diseases wiped out millions of Native Americans. The survivors were drawn into European trading networks that disrupted earlier patterns of life.

- The Spanish constructed the first large European empire in the Americas, but the English and French would eventually find space for colonization in North America. The first English settlement attempt failed at Roanoke but later succeeded at Jamestown in the colony of Virginia. The first permanent French settlement was on the St. Lawrence River and would be called Quebec.

CHAPTER SUMMARY AND KEY POINTS

A diverse variety of cultures and peoples were present in North and South America at the time of initial Columbian contact. Regardless of cultural levels, these groups had a hard time resisting encroaching Europeans. Critical among the factors that made resistance so difficult was exposure to varieties of diseases unwittingly carried westward by the invading Europeans. The Europeans conquered vast territories as Native Americans succumbed to heretofore unknown diseases by the hundreds of thousands. The Spanish were the initial conquerors, and they built the first European empire in the Americas. In time, the French and the English, who would also succeed in establishing long enduring settlements, would follow them. Many factors influenced the expansion of Europeans into what they viewed as the "new world." These included rapid population growth after the great plague of the mid-fourteenth century, the rise of dynastic states such as Portugal and Spain, the search for commercial opportunities and expanded trade in prized goods, and religious factors related to the Roman Catholic church and the Protestant Reformation.

- Millions of native peoples had inhabited the Americas for centuries and had formed themselves into sophisticated tribes and nations long before Europeans "discovered" what for them was the "new world."

- The European voyages of exploration brought two worlds into direct contact, producing what scholars call the Columbian Exchange.

SUGGESTIONS FOR FURTHER READING

Alfred W. Crosby, *Ecological Imperialism: The Biological Expansion of Europe, 900–1900* (1986). Revealing examination of biological encounters that devastated Native Americans in the process of European westward expansion.

John Guy, *Tudor England* (1990). Admirable summary of the rise of a powerful monarchy, with implications for westward expansion, in the emerging nation-state of England.

Francis Jennings, *The Invasion of America: Indians, Colonialism, and the Cant of Conquest* (1976). Controversial introduction to discordant relations between Native Americans and Europeans with particular reference to white aggression in New England.

Steven Ozment, *The Age of Reform (1250–1550): An Intellectual and Religious History of Late Medieval and Reformation Europe* (1980). Balanced, readable investigation of growing religious tensions and the rise of Protestantism in Europe.

Daniel K. Richter, *Facing East from Indian Country: A Native History of Early America* (2002). Imaginative and informative reconstruction of contact and conflict among peoples in early America from a Native American perspective.

Ian K. Steele, *Warpaths: Invasions of North America* (1994). Broad-ranging assessment of European encounters with Native Americans and patterns of Indian resistance up to the 1760s.

John Thornton, *Africa and Africans in the Making of the Atlantic World, 1400–1800*, 2d ed. (1998). Invaluable examination of the slave trade and its impact on African and American societies.

Tzvetan Todorov, *The Conquest of America: The Question of the Other* (1992). Engrossing analysis of early Spanish conquests and the human dilemmas posed by cultural intolerance and conflict.

David J. Weber, *The Spanish Frontier in North America* (1992). Revisionist overview that treats the Spanish as much more than plunderers in their American explorations and settlements.

Media Resources
Web Sites
Sir Francis Drake
http://www.mcn.org/2/oseeler/drake.htm
This comprehensive site covers much of Drake's life and voyages.

1492: An Ongoing Voyage
http://metalab.unc.edu/expo/1492.exhibit/Intro.html
An exhibit of the Library of Congress, Washington, D.C., with brief essays and images about early civilizations and contact in the Americas.

The Computerized Information Retrieval System on Columbus and the Age of Discovery
http://muweb.millersville.edu
The History Department and Academic Computing Services of Millersville University of Pennsylvania provide this text retrieval system containing over 1000 text articles from various magazines, journals, newspapers, speeches, official calendars, and other sources relating to various encounter themes.

Cahokia Mounds
http://medicine.wustl.edu/~mckinney/cahokia/cahokia.html
The Cahokia Mounds State Historical Site gives information about a fascinating pre-Columbian culture in North America.

Mexico Pre-Columbian History
http://www.mexonline.com/precolum.htm
This site provides information on the Aztecs, Maya, Mexica, Olmecs, Toltec, Zapotecs, and other pre-European cultures, as well as information on museums, archeology, language, and education.

The Discoverers' Web
http://www.win.tue.nl/cs/fm/engels/discovery/
Andre Engels maintains this most complete collection of information on the various efforts at exploration.

Key Terms
Paleo-Indians   (p. 5)

Shamans   (p. 8)

Matrilineal   (p. 8)

Renaissance   (p. 10)

Manitou   (p. 12)

Encomienda system   (p. 17)

Haciendas   (p. 17)

Northwest Passage   (p. 19)

Protestant Reformation   (p. 19)

Indulgences   (p. 19)

Calvinism   (p. 20)

Enclosure movement   (p. 22)

Price revolution   (p. 22)

Joint-stock trading companies   (p. 24)

Columbian exchange   (p. 27)

People You Should Know
Tisquantum (Squanto)   (p. 3)

Marco Polo   (p. 11)

Christopher Columbus   (p. 14)

Hernán Cortés   (p. 15)

Montezuma II   (p. 15)

Francisco Pizarro   (p. 16)

Giovanni Caboto (John Cabot)   (p. 18)

Ferdinand Magellan   (p. 19)

Martin Luther   (p. 19)

John Calvin   (p. 20)

Francis Drake   (p. 21)

Queen Elizabeth I   (p. 21)

Richard Hakluyt   (p. 22)

Sir Walter Raleigh   (p. 23)

King James I   (p. 24)

Powhatan   (p. 26)

Captain John Smith   (p. 26)

John Rolfe   (p. 26)

Review Questions
1. Describe the principal regions of the Americas, and discuss how factors such as climate and the environment affected the economic and social development of various Native American peoples before the time of Columbus. Why did Native Americans not offer more resistance to the first European explorers and settlers?

2. What factors were in place by the late fifteenth century that facilitated European exploration and, ultimately, expansion into the Americas? Why were Portugal and Spain the first to become involved in these exploratory ventures?

3. How did the European Renaissance and Protestant Reformation affect the process of European westward

expansion? Was one more important than the other? If so, why?

4. Compare and contrast the Spanish colonial system and its organization and objectives to those of the English, French, and Dutch. What elements did they have in common? What were the most significant differences, if any?

5. Why did Native Americans fail in their attempts to live in harmony with or drive off the Europeans? What else could they have done to maintain rather than lose control of their ancient tribal lands? Was the Columbian exchange, then, a failure for the original inhabitants of the Americas?

2 Plantations and Cities upon a Hill, 1620–1700

JOHN PUNCH: FROM SERVANT TO SLAVE

John Punch wanted his freedom. He was a black indentured servant who joined two white servants and tried to flee Virginia in 1640, only to be caught by local residents and brought before the governor's council, the colony's highest court. The judges ordered the flogging of each runaway—30 lashes well laid on. Then in a telling ruling, these officials revealed their thinking about the future status of blacks in England's North American colonies. The two whites had their terms of service extended by four years, but they ordered John Punch to "serve his said master . . . for the time of his natural life here or elsewhere."

Persons of African heritage were first transported to Virginia in 1619. In August of that year a Dutch vessel sailed north from the West Indies, where it had been trading or, more likely, stealing slaves from the Spanish. The Dutch ship entered Chesapeake Bay and sold some 20 "Negars," as John Rolfe described the human cargo, to settlers caught up in the early tobacco boom.

Virginia's first white settlers did not automatically assume that transplanted Africans were permanently unfree. They treated some blacks as indentured servants, a status that conveyed the prospect of personal freedom after four to seven years of laboring for someone else. English law did not recognize human slavery. The key phrase was *in favorem libertatis* (in favor of liberty), and the central tenet, wrote a contemporary legal authority, held that no person should ever "make or keep his brother in Christ, servile, bond, and underling forever unto him, as a beast rather than as a man."

Into the 1630s some black Virginians did gain their personal freedom. Others not only owned land but held servants of African origin as well, proof that permanent, inheritable slavery for blacks was a concept not yet fully developed in the Chesapeake Bay region.

By the 1640s, however, blacks faced a deteriorating legal status, ultimately leaving them outside the bounds of English liberty. In 1639 the new colony of Maryland guaranteed "all . . . Christians (slaves excepted)" the same "rights, liberties, . . . and free customs" as enjoyed by "any natural born subject of England." Worried about sporadic Indian raids, the Virginia assembly in 1640 ordered planters to arm

An African slave trader marches a group of yoked and chained captives—including women and children—from the interior of Africa to a trading post on the coast. There the captives awaited transport to the Americas.

themselves and "all those of their families which be capable of [bearing] arms . . . (excepting Negroes)." In 1643 the same assembly decreed that black women, like all adult males, would henceforth be "tithables"— those counted for local taxes because they worked in the fields. Black female servants planted, tended, and harvested tobacco crops while white female servants mainly performed household work—further evidence of discrimination based on skin color.

Local laws were catching up with the growing reality of lifetime slavery for blacks, as compared to temporary servitude for whites. In 1640 the Virginia council considered other runaway cases, besides that of John Punch. One of these involved a black named Emmanuel, who ran away with several whites. The judges handed out severe penalties, including whippings and extended terms of service for the whites. The leader of the group endured branding with an "R" on his face and had one of his legs shackled in irons for a year. Emmanuel received the same penalty, but the court made no mention of an extension of service. Apparently Emmanuel was already a slave for life.

Between 1640 and 1670 the distinction between short-term servitude for whites and permanent, inheritable slavery for blacks became firmly fixed. In appearance and by cultural and religious tradition, Africans were not like the English. As with the "wild" Irish and Indian "savages," noticeable differences translated into assumptions of inferiority, and blacks became "beastly heathens," not quite human.

Such thinking helped justify the mixing of words like "black" and "slave," so that by the 1690s slavery in the English colonies had emerged as a caste status for blacks only. Now fully excluded from the tradition of English liberty, local law defined Africans as chattels (movable property), and their masters held absolute control over their lives.

J ohn Punch and Emmanuel were among those first African Americans in the Chesapeake Bay area who felt the stinging transition from servitude to slavery. They were also among the thousands of Europeans and Africans who helped settle England's North American colonies between 1620 and 1700. The societies and lifestyles of these migrants had many differences, as comparisons between the founding of the northern and southern colonies demonstrate. A common point for all migrants, regardless of status or condition, however, was their titanic struggle to survive in an alien land. Although thousands died, some 250,000 settlers inhabited England's mainland colonies by 1700, which resulted in the formation of another powerful European empire in the Americas.

FROM SETTLEMENTS TO SOCIETIES IN THE SOUTH

Smoking tobacco, wrote King James I, was "loathsome to the eye, hateful to the nose, harmful to the brain, [and] dangerous to the lungs." Despite the king's admonition, John Rolfe's experiments saved the Virginia Company—at least temporarily—by providing the struggling colony with an economic base. Early migrants grew tobacco with enthusiasm. The first exports occurred in 1617. By the mid-1630s Virginians were selling a million pounds a year, and

The rise of the tobacco industry in the colonies spurred tobacco consumption in England.

by the mid-1660s annual tobacco crops for export reached 15 million pounds.

Company directors did not initially encourage the tobacco boom. Wanting a diversified economy, they sent out workers knowledgeable in the production of such commodities as silk, wine, glass, and iron, but all these efforts failed. Virginia's climate and soil were ideal for raising tobacco. Also, new land for cultivation was plentiful, since the "stinking weed" quickly depleted the soil of its minerals. Accepting reality, the London investors soon hailed tobacco as the savior of their venture. Other difficulties, however, cost the directors their charter, but not before company activities laid the basis for England's first enduring colony in North America.

Searching for Laborers

Life in early Virginia presented constant hardships. Migrants quickly succumbed to diseases such as malaria, typhoid fever, and dysentery. Survival, it seemed, depended upon "seasoning," or getting used to an inhospitable climate. Bad relations with Powhatan's Indians also was a source of mayhem and death, since the English and Native Americans fought in many isolated clashes. All told, the company convinced nearly 14,000 persons to attempt new lives in America. Only about 1150 were still alive and residing in the James River area in 1624, the year the company lost its charter.

Trying to overcome "a slaughter house" reputation, company leaders pursued various policies. Sir Thomas Smythe, a wealthy London merchant, used his boundless energy to keep the venture going. He tied company fortunes to England's potential for national greatness. His influence at court resulted in more generous charter rights in 1609 and 1612, the latter of which expanded company boundaries to include the island of Bermuda—soon a source of profitable cash crops. Also under Smythe's guidance, the company secured a steady supply of laborers. It also managed affairs in Virginia with an iron hand while attempting to improve Indian relations. Each activity was crucial to long-term development.

To encourage prospective laborers, company directors mounted publicity campaigns. These efforts helped neutralize Virginia's reputation as a death trap. More successful in securing workers was the development of the system of **indentured servitude,** modeled along the lines of contractual farm service. During early Stuart times, between one-fourth and one-third of England's families had servants. Many young men and women, having no access to land, made agreements to work for a year or more as farm laborers in return for food, lodging, and modest wages. They had few other prospects for employment and virtually no chance of gaining title to their own freehold farms.

In theory, Virginia held out the opportunity of potential economic independence for rapidly growing numbers of landless farm servants and the urban poor. As early as 1609, the mayor of London asked the company "to ease the city and suburbs of a swarm of unnecessary inmates." The challenge was to get these struggling poor to America. Persons without money needed only to sign bonded contracts, or indentures, in which they legally exchanged up to seven years of labor in return for passage costs. After completing their terms of service, their masters owed them "freedom dues," including clothing, farm tools, and in some cases land on which to begin anew as free persons.

The system of indentured servitude slowly took shape after 1609. At first, the company offered free passage along with shares of stock to those who signed up for seven years of labor. When terms were up, workers were to gain title to 100 acres of land as well as any stock dividends. The bait was eventual economic freedom, but even with so many unemployed persons in England, few applied. Getting by marginally or facing a hangman's noose remained more attractive than an early—and often brutal—death in America.

Some venturesome souls, mostly young, unattached males, signed on as company-managed laborers. To make sure these servants would take orders and work, Sir Thomas Smythe and his advisers gave dictatorial powers to their governors in Virginia. Lord De La Warr, a veteran of the Irish wars who arrived in 1610, organized the colony along military lines. He ruled by martial law, as did his surrogates, Sir Thomas Gates and Sir Thomas Dale, once he returned to England. Their *Lawes Divine, Moral, and Martiall* (1612) provided harsh penalties for even the smallest offenses.

Company servants were an undisciplined lot, less interested in work than in "bowling in the streets" of Jamestown, as an observer described their attitudes. When caught loafing, they paid with bloodied backs from public floggings, and when some laborers stole boats and tried to escape in 1612, Deputy Governor Gates showed no mercy. Their sentences included death by firing squad, hanging, or breaking upon the wheel, all as a warning to others with ideas of violating company contracts.

To Be Like English Subjects at Home

Stories of brutal treatment and high mortality rates undercut company efforts to secure a steady supply of laborers. Changes had to be made, and that process culminated when a reform-minded faction led by Sir Edwin Sandys prepared new instructions, since known as the "great charter" of 1618. The overriding goal was to frame incentives that would make risking settlement more attractive. Key provisions included an end to martial rule and a declaration assuring Virginians government "by those free laws which his Majesty's subjects live under in England." The charter promised a local representative assembly, which came to be known as the House of Burgesses. Its first deliberations took place in July 1619, a small cornerstone gathering pointing toward governments with a popular voice in England's North American colonies.

Besides guaranteeing political rights, the charter addressed economic incentives, including the notion of "private plantations" and **headrights.** Heretofore, the company controlled all acreage, but now potential settlers could purchase land without first serving as company laborers. Fifty acres per person would be given to those who migrated or those who paid for the passage of others to Virginia. Headrights would permit English families with funds to relocate and

get title to enough property to grow tobacco and, perhaps, prosper. After all, Virginia had land in abundance but very few laborers, whereas England had a shortage of land and an oversupply of workers.

Even with these reforms, Virginia's unhealthful reputation kept families from migrating. English merchants and sea captains, however, developed a booming trade in indentured servants. They made substantial profits from delivering servants to labor-hungry planters and from headright patents, which they accumulated and sold to others with enough capital to purchase large tracts of land before migrating. In a few cases, buying up headrights resulted in the establishment of large plantations; still, three-fourths of all English settlers entering seventeenth-century Virginia were indentured servants.

The vast bulk of these migrants were single males under the age of 25 with no employment prospects in England. The unbalanced sex ratio concerned company officials. Wanting to give Virginia a "more settled" feeling, they contracted with 90 "uncorrupt" young women in 1619 to go to Jamestown and be sold as wives. The plan worked well, but because of other problems the company sent over only one more shipment of women. Stable family life was not a characteristic of the rough-and-tumble society of early Virginia.

Crushing Powhatan's Confederacy

Bickering, bloodshed, and death denoted relations with Powhatan's Indians as the English planted tobacco farms along the James River. John Rolfe's marriage to Powhatan's daughter, **Pocahontas,** in 1614, which implied a political alliance of sorts, eased tensions—but only briefly. Rolfe soon took Pocahontas to England, where she became an instant celebrity, and both of them encouraged settlement in Virginia. Unfortunately, while preparing to return home in 1616, Pocahontas contracted smallpox and died.

Two years later, Powhatan also died, leaving his more militant half-brother **Opechancanough** in charge of the Confederacy. Watching the growing English presence with misgivings, Opechancanough decided that slaughtering the intruders was the only means left to save his people. On Good Friday, March 22, 1622, his warriors struck everywhere. Before the massacre was over, the Indians killed 347 settlers, or about 30 percent of the English colonists, including John Rolfe. Opechancanough, however, had failed to exterminate the enemy, and in many ways the massacre of 1622 was the beginning of the end for Virginia's coastal natives. White settlers, now more convinced than ever that Indians were savages, took vengeance whenever they could.

This sketch of a Virginia native appeared in about 1645, shortly after Virginia's coastal Indians failed in their second attempt to drive out the white settlers.

Retreating inland, Opechancanough waited 22 years before striking again. The attack came in April 1644, and another 400 or more colonists died (about 5 percent of the white population). The 1644 massacre was a last desperate gasp by Virginia's coastal natives. The numbers of whites were now too overwhelming for total destruction. As for Opechancanough, the settlers took him prisoner. A white guard, seeking personal vengeance, shot the old, enfeebled native leader to death in 1646. That same year, Confederacy chiefs signed a treaty agreeing to submit to English rule. The survivors of Powhatan's once-mighty league eventually accepted life on a reservation, as many other remnant Indian peoples would be forced to do as Europeans pushed westward across the North American continent.

A Model for Other Royal Colonies

The massacre of 1622 was one of two fatal blows to the Virginia Company. James I had started to dream about huge sums of money flowing into the royal treasury from taxes on tobacco. Company leaders, trying to stabilize their debt-ridden interests after the massacre, negotiated an exclusive contract with the Crown to deliver tobacco to England with the king receiving tax revenues on every pound shipped. However, a rumor spread that company leaders intended to charge exorbitant fees for handling the tobacco. The Crown, as a second fatal blow, quickly voided the tobacco contract. Then the king's advisers used court proceedings to revoke the company charter, thereby dissolving the enterprise in 1624.

King James next declared Virginia a royal colony and sent out his own governor. He did not promise basic political rights to the settlers and canceled the privilege of a local assembly. In a virtual throwback to the days of martial law, the king authorized his officials to rule absolutely.

Neither James nor his son, **King Charles I** (reigned 1625–1649), were advocates of popular rights or representative forms of government. Rather, they adhered to **divine right** theories of kingship, which meant that monarchs were literally God's political stewards on earth.

Virginia's planters, however, would not be denied a voice in government, and the royal governors shrewdly called upon locally prominent men to serve as advisory councilors. The governors also began authorizing assemblies, conveniently referred to as conventions, to deal with local problems. Still, relations between royal governors and colonists could become turbulent. In 1634 one governor, Sir John Harvey, known as a "choleric and impatient" man, got into a fist fight with one of his councilors. He punched out his opponent's teeth and threatened to hang the other councilors. In response, the councilors had Harvey arrested and sent him back to England in chains.

In 1639 King Charles, facing popular dissent at home because of his high-handed rule, finally relieved some of the pressure by granting Virginians a representative assembly, thereby assuring some local participation in colony-related decision making. Unlike the Spanish and French, English subjects had refused to accede to political domination by a far-off parent nation. They would share in the decision making affecting their lives as colonists in America.

Proprietary Maryland and the Carolinas

Charles's concession suggests the expediency with which the Stuart kings viewed colonization. Assuring basic rights did attract more settlers, which in turn meant larger tobacco crops and more tax revenues for the Crown. Founding additional colonies, moreover, would enhance England's stature among the nations of Europe. These same settlements could be used as dumping grounds for troublesome groups in England, such as the Puritans. Vast stretches of territory could also be granted to court favorites. The Stuarts had the power to make wealthy men even wealthier by awarding them huge "proprietary" estates in America, which would foster loyalty among powerful gentlemen at court who might otherwise choose, at some point, to challenge the authority of the Crown.

Sir George Calvert, described as a "forward and knowing person," was one such favored courtier. Serving as James I's secretary of state, he took charge of dissolving the Virginia Company. A year later he converted to Roman Catholicism and had to leave the government. To reward his loyal service, however, the king named Calvert the first Lord Baltimore and granted him permission to colonize Newfoundland, an effort that failed. Then in 1632 Charles I awarded Calvert title to 10 million acres surrounding the northern end of Chesapeake Bay. The king named the territory "Maryland" after his own Catholic wife, Queen Henrietta Maria, and he named Calvert lord proprietor over these lands.

Chesapeake Settlements, 1650

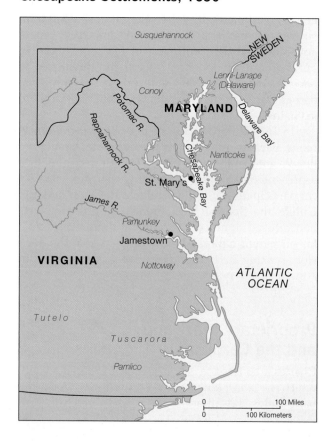

When Calvert died, his son Cecilius, the second Lord Baltimore, took charge and sent out the first settlement parties. The idea was for Maryland to function as a haven for persecuted Roman Catholics. Those Catholics who migrated received substantial personal estates in return for annual quitrents, or land taxes, paid to Lord Baltimore. Many more Protestants than Catholics secured land patents, also with quitrents. The colony soon bore a striking similarity to its Chesapeake neighbor Virginia, since Marylanders also devoted themselves to cultivating tobacco.

The Maryland charter granted the Baltimore proprietors absolute political authority, but in 1635 Cecilius Calvert, hoping to induce further settlements, granted a representative assembly. As the colony grew, Catholics and Protestants dueled bitterly over control of local politics. In an attempt to protect the minority Catholics, Calvert proposed an Act of Religious Toleration in 1649, which guaranteed all adult males voting or officeholding rights, so long as they subscribed to the doctrine of the Trinity. Although not full toleration, this act, which the assembly approved, was a key step toward liberty of conscience. Still, bickering between Maryland's Catholic and Protestant settlers continued for several decades.

Religious warfare, meanwhile, convulsed England. During the 1640s civil war turned English subjects against one another. Puritan "Roundheads" rose up against the "Cavalier" supporters of Charles I, who had refused to let Parliament meet for several years. In 1649 the victorious Puritans showed willful contempt for divine right theories of kingship by beheading Charles. Oliver Cromwell, the leader of Puritan military forces, then took political control of England as Lord Protector. After Cromwell's death and a brief, disastrous period of rule by his son, Parliament invited Charles I's exiled son to reestablish the Stuart monarchy—in exchange for promises to assemble Parliament regularly and to support the Anglican church.

The restoration of **Charles II** (reigned 1660–1685) left the new king with many political debts. In 1663 he paid off eight powerful gentlemen by awarding them title to all lands lying south of Virginia and north of Spanish Florida. The region was already known as Carolus, the Latin equivalent of Charles. The new proprietors quickly set about the task of finding settlers for the Carolinas, which proved difficult because of a dramatic new boom in England's economy—and a consequent decrease in the numbers of unemployed subjects.

Trying to spark the settlement process, one of the proprietors, Sir Anthony Ashley Cooper, assisted by his brilliant secretary, political philosopher **John Locke,** produced the "Fundamental Constitutions for Carolina" (1669). This document spelled out unworkable plans for a complex social order in which "landgraves" and "caciques" held vast estates and functioned as an American nobility but shared the responsibilities of local government with smaller landholders. More important, the proprietors offered attractive headright provisions of up to 150 acres per person, guarantees of a representative assembly and religious toleration, and a fateful promise that free persons "shall have absolute power and authority over . . . negro slaves."

Even with such generous terms, the Carolinas grew slowly. The Albemarle region of northeastern North Carolina developed as settlers spilled over from Virginia. William Byrd II, a prominent Virginia planter of the early eighteenth century, described the Albemarle inhabitants as having a "disposition to laziness for their whole lives." Most inhabitants subsisted marginally by exporting tobacco and various timber-derived products, including pitch, tar, and potash.

The proprietors focused on settling South Carolina. They contacted small-scale English farmers on the island of Barbados who were selling out to well-capitalized gentlemen building large sugar plantations. In 1670 a group of these Barbadians founded Charleston (then known as Charles Town), and a steady trade in deerskins and horsehides soon developed with interior natives. A few greedy migrants even dealt in humans by getting local Indians to capture tribal enemies, who were then sold off as slaves to the West Indies.

Picking up on the proprietors' promise, Barbadian migrants who owned slaves brought their chattels with them. Unlike in the Chesapeake area, slavery existed from the outset in South Carolina and took even firmer hold when rice production became the mainstay of economic activity after 1690. By the end of the seventeenth century, English colonists in the southern colonies had constructed their lives around the exportation of cash crops, particularly tobacco and rice, supported increasingly by black slave labor. Over time the institution of slavery gave white southerners a common identity—with serious long-term consequences.

RELIGIOUS DISSENTERS COLONIZE NEW ENGLAND

English men and women migrated to America for many reasons. Certainly the hope of economic betterment was a prime motivating factor, but in New England the initial emphasis reflected more directly on a communal desire to provide a hospitable environment for Calvinist religious values. Beginning in the 1620s New England emerged as a haven for religious dissenters of two types: **separatists,** such as the Pilgrims, and **nonseparatists,** such as the Puritans.

Separatists believed the Church of England to be so corrupt that it could not be salvaged. So as not to compromise their beliefs, their only course was to sever all ties with the Anglican church and establish their own religious communities of like-minded believers.

The dauntless band known as the Pilgrims were separatists from Scrooby Manor, a village in northeastern England. Facing official harassment, they fled to the Netherlands in 1608 but found it difficult to make a decent living there. Furthermore, they worried about their children, who not only were losing their sense of identity as English persons but also appeared "to degenerate and be corrupted" by frequent exposure to various worldly pleasures. As a result, Pilgrim leaders sought a land grant to settle in America, where they could set up their own religious community and worship as they pleased.

In September 1620 the first party of Pilgrims sailed west on the *Mayflower* under a land patent of the Virginia Company. Only one-third of the 102 migrants aboard were Pilgrims. The rest were employees of the London merchant Thomas Weston, who financed the venture in return for an exclusive seven-year monopoly over all trading commodities

English Barbadians settled Charleston, South Carolina. The local economy would develop around crops, such as rice, produced by slave labor.

sent back to England. After surviving nine harrowing, storm-tossed weeks at sea, the *Mayflower* made first landfall on the northern tip of Cape Cod.

Knowing they were well to the north of Virginia territory and outnumbered by "strangers," the Pilgrims drafted a plan of government, called the Mayflower Compact, before proceeding to the mainland in December 1620 and selecting the site of Tisquantum's old Patuxet village for their permanent settlement. The Compact guaranteed settlers the right to elect governing officials to a representative assembly, but only Pilgrim "saints"—those who were church members—could vote. The Pilgrims would tolerate "strangers" in their midst and encourage them to seek God's grace—the basis of church membership—as long as they showed "due submission and obedience" to the authority of the congregation of church members. In this sense the Compact was not an advanced statement of popular government; its purpose was to assure the Pilgrims full political control of Plymouth Colony.

Plymouth Plantation struggled to survive. Under the effective, persistent leadership of Governor **William Bradford** (1590–1657), the settlers overcame all obstacles. Besides a deadly first winter, the Pilgrims had to reckon with no clear title to their land. In 1621 they obtained a proper patent, but several years passed before they fulfilled their financial obligations to Weston and a variety of other sponsors. They did so mostly by shipping fish and furs back to England.

At the outset the Pilgrims worked hard to maintain peace with local Indians. Under Miles Standish, the one professional soldier in their midst, they also trained for war, should serious discord with the natives develop. They certainly did not hesitate to discipline other whites in the region, such as the rowdy band of men at Thomas Morton's "Merry Mount" trading post not far from Plymouth. Not only was Morton selling alcohol and firearms, but his traders were regularly "dancing and frisking together" with native women around a maypole, in addition to "worse practices," according to Bradford. Morton's arming of the natives, as well as the lustful scenes at Merry Mount, incensed the Pilgrims. Above all else, they did not want to face the kind of massacre that had occurred in Virginia during 1622. With Standish in the lead, they closed down the Merry Mount post in 1628 and sent Morton packing off to England.

Slowly but surely the Pilgrim colony began to prosper, as recorded in Bradford's valuable account, *History Of Plymouth Plantation,* which covers the first 26 years of the colony's history. Through all of their adventures and travails, the Pilgrims never lost sight of their original purpose—freedom to worship God according to their own understanding of scripture.

Their numbers increased to 7000 persons by 1691, the year they accepted annexation to the much more populous Puritan colony of Massachusetts Bay.

The Rise of Puritan Dissenters at Home

Far more numerous in England were nonseparatists, who wanted to "purify" rather than separate from the Church of England. The Puritans, as these dissenters were known, have often been characterized as prudish, ignorant bigots who hated the thought of having a good time. Modern historical research, however, has shattered this stereotype. The Puritans were reformers who, as recipients of John Calvin's legacy, took Biblical matters seriously. They believed that God's word should order the steps of every person's life. What troubled them most was their conviction that the Protestant Reformation in England had not gone far enough. They viewed the Church of England as "corrupt" in organization and guided by unscriptural doctrine; they longed for far-reaching institutional change that would rid the Anglican church of its imperfections. When church and state leaders harassed them, they responded in various ways, including the planting of a model utopian society—Massachusetts Bay Colony—in New England.

In the early 1600s the Puritans numbered in the hundreds of thousands. Their emphasis upon reading Scripture particularly appealed to literate members of the middle classes and lesser gentry—merchants, skilled craft workers, professionals, and freehold farmers. The Puritans prided themselves on hard work and the pursuit of one's "calling" as a way to glorify the Almighty. They also searched for signs of having earned God's saving grace through a personal conversion experience. The goal was to become one of God's "visible saints" on earth. To be a visible saint meant that a person was fit for church membership.

By comparison, the Church of England, as a state-supported institution, claimed all citizens, regardless of their spiritual nature, as church members. Besides this problem, the Anglican church, from the Puritan perspective, put too much emphasis on ritual. Its elaborate hierarchy of church officials did not include enough educated ministers who understood the Bible, let alone the need to teach parishioners to seek God's grace; rather, Anglican clergymen were the friends and relatives of the well connected. They were like "Mr. Atkins, curate of Romford, thrice presented for a drunkard," "Mr. Goldringe, parson of Laingdon Hills, . . . convicted of fornication," and "Mr. Cuckson, vicar of Linsell, . . . a pilferer, of scandalous life."

In his youth in Scotland, James Stuart, who became King James I, had regular dealings with John Knox and his Presbyterian (Scottish Puritan) followers. He developed a decided distaste for religious dissenters. "I will harry them out of the land," James boldly proclaimed after becoming king of England, "or else do worse." Like Queen Elizabeth before him, however, he endured the Puritans. He never felt secure enough in his own authority to test his will against their rapidly expanding influence.

During King James's reign, the Puritans moved aggressively to realize their goals. They built a political base from which to demand church reform by winning elections for seats in Parliament. James put up with their protests, but his son, Charles I, was more confrontational. He named William Laud, whom the Puritans considered a Roman Catholic in Anglican garb, as archbishop of the Church of England. Laud was particularly adept at persecuting his opponents. In response, the Puritans pushed a bill through Parliament denouncing "popish" practices in church and state. Finally, Charles used his royal prerogatives to disband Parliament and tried to rule by himself between 1629 and 1640, thus contributing to the advent of the bloody English Civil War.

In the late 1620s the Puritans were not ready for rebellion, but some in their numbers had decided upon an "errand into the wilderness." In 1629 they secured a joint-stock charter for the Massachusetts Bay Company. Investors knew they were underwriting the peopling of a utopian religious experiment in America. As for King Charles, the prospect of ridding the realm of thousands of Puritans was incentive enough to give royal approval to the Bay Company charter.

Godly Mission to New England

The Puritans organized their venture carefully. They placed their settlement effort under **John Winthrop** (1588–1649), a prominent lawyer and landholder. In 1630 some 700 Puritans crowded onto 11 ships and joined Winthrop in sailing to Massachusetts. They were the vanguard of what became the *Great Migration*, or the movement of an estimated 20,000 persons to New England by 1642. These men and women left not as indentured servants but as families fleeing the religious repression and worsening economic conditions of Charles I's England.

More than any other person, John Winthrop worked tirelessly to promote the Puritan mission. Before landing in Massachusetts Bay, he delivered a sermon entitled "A Model of Christian Charity," in which he asserted: "We must consider that we shall be as a **city upon a hill;** the eyes of all people are

John Winthrop led the Puritans to New England, where he served several terms as governor of the Massachusetts Bay Colony.

upon us." The Puritans' mission was to order human existence in the Bay Colony according to God's word. Their example, Winthrop and other company leaders hoped, would inspire England and the rest of Europe to change, thereby causing the full realization of the Protestant Reformation.

Curious events back in England facilitated attempts to build a model society in the wilderness. For some reason, perhaps because of a well-placed bribe, the Bay Company charter did not specify a location for stockholder (General Court) meetings. Seizing the opportunity, Winthrop and others drafted the Cambridge Agreement in August 1629; they decided to carry the charter with them and hold all stockholder meetings in New England—3000 miles from meddlesome king's officials. Of the stockholders who migrated, all were fervent Puritans, which meant that decision making for the colony would be controlled in General Court sessions by a handful of men fully committed to the Puritan mission.

THE PEOPLE SPEAK

John Winthrop, "A Model of Christian Charity"

John Winthrop (1588–1649) was a well-educated lawyer and landholder who was also prominent in the Puritan movement in England. In 1629 he assumed the responsibility of leading some 700 Puritans to America. He went on to serve several terms as governor of the Massachusetts Bay Colony. When sailing for America in 1630, he prepared a speech, which he entitled "A Model of Christian Charity." Speaking aboard the flagship *Arbella* while still at sea, he called upon his fellow Puritans to devote themselves to building a model Christian society in New England. Winthrop envisioned "a city upon a hill" to shine as a beacon of light back on England where the "corrupt" King Charles I refused to halt the oppressive, impure practices of the Church of England. By comparison, the Puritans who intended to reside in New England, stated Winthrop, had made a covenant with God to establish an ideal representation of a biblical community on earth. Should they succeed in their mission, God would greatly bless their lives. Should they fail, they would surely "perish" in the wake of afflictions that God would visit upon them. Winthrop thus conveyed a sense of high purpose regarding the founding of New England. The theme of a special calling has persisted in many different forms throughout the American experience.

> Thus stands the cause between God and us. We are entered into covenant with Him for this work; we have taken out a commission. . . . We have hereupon besought Him of favor and blessing. Now if the Lord shall please to hear us, and bring us in peace to the place we desire, then hath He ratified this covenant and sealed our commission, and will expect a strict performance of the articles contained in it. But if we shall neglect the observation of these articles, . . . the Lord will surely break out in wrath against us, be revenged of such a perjured people, and make us know the price of the breach of such a covenant.

Now the only way to avoid this shipwreck and to provide for our posterity is to follow the counsel of Micah: to do justly, to love mercy, to walk humbly with our God. For this end we must be knit together in this work as one man; we must entertain each other in brotherly affection; we must be willing to abridge ourselves of our superfluities for the supply of others' necessities; we must uphold a familiar commerce together in all meekness, gentleness, patience, and liberality; we must delight in each other, make others' conditions our own, rejoice together, mourn together, labor and suffer together always having before our eyes our commission and community in the work, our community as members of the same body, so shall we keep the unity of the spirit in the bond of peace. The Lord will be our God and delight to dwell among us as His own people and will command a blessing upon us in all our ways, so that we shall see much more of His wisdom, power, goodness, and truth than formerly we have been acquainted with. We shall find that the God of Israel is among us when ten of us shall be able to resist a thousand of our enemies; when He shall make us a praise and glory, that men shall say of succeeding plantations: the Lord make it like that of New England. For we must consider that we shall be as a city upon a hill, the eyes of all people are upon us; so that if we shall deal falsely with our God in this work we have undertaken and so cause Him to withdraw His present help from us, we shall be made a story and a byword through the world. . . . Beloved, there is now set before us life, and good, death and evil, in that we are commanded this day to love the Lord our God and to love one another, to walk in His ways and to keep His commandments and His ordinances and His laws, and the articles of our covenant with Him, that we may live and be multiplied, and that the Lord our God may bless us in the land whither we go to possess it. But if our hearts shall turn away so that we will not obey, but shall be seduced and worship other gods, our pleasures and profits, and serve them, it is propounded unto us this day, we shall surely perish out of the good land whither we pass over this vast sea to possess it.

> Therefore let us choose life,
> that we, and our seed,
> may live by obeying His
> voice, and cleaving to Him,
> for He is our life, and
> our prosperity.

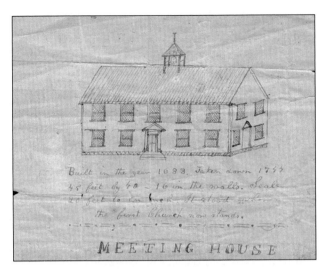

MEETING HOUSE

The Puritan meetinghouse was the gathering place not only for religious services but for the town meeting as well. The meetinghouse's location, usually in the center of town, reinforced the centrality of religion in the community. Meetings, whether for religious or political purposes, also helped strengthen the communal bonds among the townspeople.

Court started to issue town charters, and settlements fanned out in semicircular fashion from Boston into the interior.

Designated proprietors guided the establishment of Puritan towns, emphasizing community control over individual lives. A 1635 law—later repealed—stated that inhabitants had to live within a half mile of the town church. Each family received a house lot near the village green, farmland away from the center of town, and access to pasture land and woodlots. Some towns perpetuated the European open-field system. Families gained title to strips of land in several fields and worked in common with other townspeople to bring in yearly crops. In other towns, families had all their farmland concentrated in one area.

These property arrangements reflected English patterns of land distribution as well as the desire to promote godly behavior, especially since some first-generation settlers were not Puritans. Village life was not wholly restrictive, however, so long as families viewed the Bay Colony, in the words of the Reverend **John Cotton**, as "the setting forth of God's house, which is His church."

Once in Massachusetts, the stockholders soon faced challenges to their all-inclusive authority. Typical was a protest in 1632 by settlers who refused to pay taxes under the "bondage" of no voice in government. The solution was to create a category of citizenship known as "freeman." Freemen would be like stockholders; they could participate in government. As with the Pilgrims, however, only male church members gained full citizenship status as voters. The leaders assumed that these visible saints would not subvert the colony's mission.

The government of Massachusetts developed out of this arrangement. As the colony grew, the General Court became an elective assembly with freemen (full church members) from each town sending delegates to Boston to represent local concerns. The governorship, too, was elective on an annual basis, and John Winthrop dominated the office until his death in 1649. Ministers were not eligible for political offices, so the government was not technically a theocracy. Clergymen, however, met occasionally in synods and offered written advice to colony leaders regarding religious issues, which did affect political decision making.

Initially, Winthrop wanted all settlers to live in towns close to Boston, but with migrants pouring into the colony, that proved impossible. The General

New England Colonies, 1650

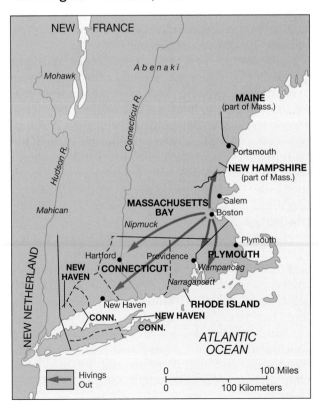

Town leaders promoted harmonious living conditions. They set off lots for taverns, schools, and meeting houses. Taverns served as community centers in which people socialized and cheerfully drank alcohol, which they believed was essential to good health. School lots satisfied concerns about education. The Puritans advocated literacy so that everyone could read Scripture and "understand the principles of religion and . . . laws of the country." (The desire to have a learned clergy led to the founding of Harvard College in 1636.) Beginning in the 1640s, the General Court ordered each town to tax inhabitants to pay for formal schooling in reading and writing for all children. The meeting house was the gathering place for town meetings and church services. Church members had the duty to encourage non-Puritans in their midst to study the Bible, pray fervently, and seek God's grace so that they might also enjoy political and religious rights—as well as eternal salvation.

Testing the Limits of Toleration

The first generation of Puritans worked hard and prospered. Farming was the primary means of gaining a livelihood, although some coastal inhabitants took to shipbuilding, fishing, and mercantile activity. Prosperity did not stand in the way of serious internal controversies. These disagreements suggested how the Puritan system functioned on behalf of orthodoxy—and against diverse opinions—to assure adherence to the wilderness mission.

No Puritan was purer than **Roger Williams** (1603?–1683). When this well-educated clergyman arrived in Boston in 1631 and announced that "Bishop Laud pursued me out of the land," John Winthrop graciously welcomed him. Soon Williams received an offer to teach in the Boston church, but he refused because of rules about mandatory worship. To hold services with the unconverted in attendance was to be no purer than the Church of England. It "stinks in God's nostrils," Williams proclaimed.

So off Williams went, first to Salem and then to Plymouth Colony, where Governor William Bradford and the Pilgrims embraced him. Only the visible saints attended church services in Plymouth. The Pilgrims soon dismissed Williams for "strange opinions" having to do with questions of land ownership. He had become friendly with local Indians and had concluded that any Crown-based land patent was fraudulent—and that Puritans and Pilgrims alike were thieves because they had not purchased their land from the natives. Moving back to Salem,

Williams next denounced Bay Colony leaders who meddled in church affairs. So long as churches were subject in any way to political influences, they would be as corrupt as the Church of England.

John Winthrop remained Williams's friend and kept advising him to keep his opinions to himself, but other Puritan leaders had endured enough. Orthodox adherence to the Puritan mission meant that this contentious young minister, no matter how logical in his criticisms, could not be tolerated. With Winthrop's reluctant approval, the General Court banished Williams in October 1635. To avoid being sent back to England, Williams fled to the Narragansett Indians, with whom he spent the winter and from whom he eventually purchased land for a new community—Providence, Rhode Island.

Partly because of Roger Williams's influence, the colony of Rhode Island took form as a center of religious toleration. Settlers there welcomed all faiths, including Judaism, and the government stayed out of matters of personal conscience. Personal conscience was truly sacred, Williams thought, which made him an advance agent for such concepts as religious freedom and separation of church and state.

Meanwhile, others such as **Anne Hutchinson** (1591–1643), also tested the limits of orthodoxy. Hutchinson was a woman of powerful mind and commanding presence who frightened leaders like John Winthrop. Hutchinson, the mother of 13 children, moved with her family to Boston in 1634,

Charged and convicted of spreading "dangerous opinions," Roger Williams was banished from Massachusetts Bay Colony in October 1635.

Tried for her controversial religious ideas before the General Court, Anne Hutchinson refused to recant. The court banished her from the Bay Colony.

1637 Bay Colony clergymen assembled in a synod and denounced Antinomianism as "blasphemous." They also insisted that Hutchinson's brother-in-law, the Reverend John Wheelwright, recant his Antinomian views. Wheelwright held his ground, and he was banished. He and his followers went off to found Exeter, New Hampshire.

Now the target was Hutchinson. Ordered to appear before the General Court, she masterfully defended herself for two days, only to be declared guilty of sedition for dishonoring her spiritual parents, Winthrop and the other magistrates. As "a woman not fit for our society," she too was banished. In the spring of 1638 she migrated to Rhode Island where she helped establish the community of Portsmouth.

"Hivings Out" Provoke Bloody Indian Relations

For those who accepted mainstream Puritan orthodoxy, Massachusetts was paradise compared to England. But for dissidents like the Antinomians, Bay Colony leaders seemed just as intolerant as Charles I or Archbishop Laud. As a result, they felt compelled to locate elsewhere, and that is how Rhode Island began. Eventually settlers there pulled themselves together into a confederation and, thanks to Roger Williams, gained a separate patent from Parliament in 1644. Then in 1663 King Charles II granted a more generous charter. Local political offices, even including the governorship, were to be elective, and the Crown also declared that no person should ever be "molested, . . . [or] punished for any differences of opinion in matters of religion." This clause made Rhode Island a unique haven for religious freedom in Puritan New England.

Even before John Wheelwright's exodus to New Hampshire, a few hardy settlers had located in that region. Others established themselves along the coast of Maine. Massachusetts tried to maintain control of both areas, but in 1681 New Hampshire became a separate royal colony. The Bay Colony did sustain its authority over Maine by purchasing the land patents of rival claimants. This territory remained a thinly settled appendage of Massachusetts until it gained statehood in 1820.

Connecticut also started to emerge as a Puritan colony during the 1630s. The Reverend Thomas Hooker, who viewed John Winthrop as too dictatorial, led 100 settlers into the Connecticut River Valley in May 1636. By year's end, another 700 Puritans had followed Hooker's path, resulting in the founding of

where she served as a midwife. She also spoke openly about her religious views, which had a strong mystical element. Once humans experienced saving grace, she believed, the "Holy Spirit illumines the heart," and God would offer direct revelation. This meant that his true saints no longer needed the church or the state to help order their daily existence.

Such ideas gained the label **Antinomian,** which Puritans defined as against the laws of human governance. To Winthrop, Hutchinson appeared as an advocate of social anarchy. She was threatening to ruin the Puritan mission, since human institutions of any kind would have no purpose, except to control the unregenerate. Winthrop viewed the Antinomian crisis as very serious, especially since the movement came to involve large numbers of people.

With Antinomian thinking spreading so rapidly, orthodox Puritans girded themselves for battle. In such towns as Hartford, Wethersfield, and Windsor. John Davenport guided a party of London Puritans to Boston in 1637 but after a few months decided that Winthrop was not dictatorial enough. He led his flock to the mouth of the Quinnipiac River, where they established New Haven.

In 1639 the three Connecticut river towns founded by Hooker adopted a plan of general government, known as the Fundamental Orders of Connecticut. Although based on the Bay Colony's political organization, this plan did permit all adult male property holders, not just church members, to vote, a step toward more inclusive franchise rights. Eventually, all the Connecticut settlements came together to form one political unit and gained a Crown charter (1662) as generous as Rhode Island's. Connecticut Puritans, however, had little interest in encouraging religious diversity; as in Massachusetts, the Congregational church dominated spiritual life.

These "hivings out" from Massachusetts, as Winthrop called them, adversely affected relations with the native populace. A devastating smallpox epidemic in 1633 temporarily delayed Indian resistance. When Hooker's followers moved into the Connecticut River Valley, they settled on land claimed by the Pequots, who decided to resist and struck at Wethersfield in April 1637, killing several people. A force of Puritans and Narragansett Indians, who hated the Pequots, retaliated a month later by surrounding and setting fire to the main Pequot village on the Mystic River. Some 400 men, women, and children died in the flames. "Horrible was the stink and scent thereof," wrote one Puritan, but destroying the Pequots "seemed a sweet sacrifice" to assure the

peace and safety of those seeking to plant themselves on fertile Connecticut lands.

The Puritans were no worse than Virginians or Carolinians in their treatment of Native Americans. In some ways they tried to be better. The Bay Colony charter mandated that Indians be brought "to the knowledge . . . of the only true God and . . . the Christian faith." Most Puritans ignored this mandate, but the Reverend John Eliot devoted his ministry to converting the natives. Besides translating the Bible into an Algonquian tongue, he established four towns for "praying Indians," which by 1650 held a population of over 1000. Most of these natives did not actually seek conversion. They were remnant members of once vital tribes, and they were trying to survive while retaining as much of their cultural heritage as possible in the face of what had become an irreversible European tide of westward migration.

FAMILIES, INDIVIDUALS, AND COMMUNITIES: SURVIVING IN EARLY AMERICA

Just as Opechancanough tried to wipe out the Virginians, **Metacomet**, better known to the Puritans as King Philip, attempted the same in New England. The son of Massasoit, a Wampanoag chieftain who, like Tisquantum, had aided the early Pilgrims, Metacomet felt threatened by the spread of white settlements. In 1671 the Pilgrims hauled him into court on the grounds of plotting against their colony and extracted a statement of submission to English authority. Thoroughly humiliated, Metacomet swore revenge.

The life-and-death struggle known as King Philip's War began during the summer of 1675 when various Indian tribes joined Metacomet's warriors in raiding towns along the Massachusetts–Connecticut frontier. Taking advantage of the settlers' habits, the natives often struck during Sunday church meetings. By early 1676 much of New England was in chaos. Metacomet's forces even attacked towns within 20 miles of Boston, but there were too many Puritans (around 50,000) and not enough Indians (fewer than 12,000) to annihilate the whites. When a "praying" Indian shot and killed Metacomet, King Philip's War rapidly lost its momentum.

Metacomet's warriors had leveled or done substantial damage to several towns, and around 2000 Puritan settlers died in the war. Roughly twice as many Indians lost their lives in what proved to be a futile effort to drive away the ever-expansive English. Still, King Philip's War was not the Indians' last

John Eliot was known as the Puritan Apostle to the Indians. Also shown below is the title page from the Bible as translated by Eliot into an Algonquian tongue.

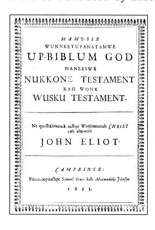

gasp. In a few years remnant native groups started receiving support from the French in Canada and once again began attacking New England's frontier towns.

King Philip's War was very bloody. However, surviving in New England was less difficult than surviving in the Chesapeake region, as comparative experiences graphically reveal.

Life and Death, North and South

During the seventeenth century New England's population grew steadily by natural increase. Most of the 25,000 migrants crossed the ocean before the outbreak of England's civil war in the 1640s; yet by the end of the century some 93,000 colonists inhabited New England. In the Chesapeake, by comparison, as many as 100,000 persons had attempted settlement, but only about 85,000 were living in Virginia and Maryland in 1700. Had these two colonies not had a

Population Comparison of New England and Chesapeake, Mid-1600s

Virulent disease and brackish water in the Chesapeake Bay region resulted in shorter life spans than in New England.

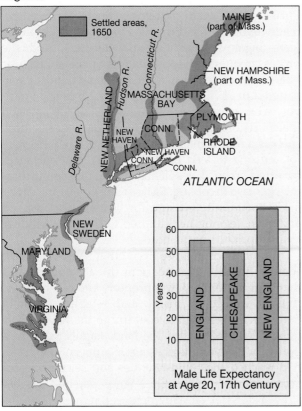

Male Life Expectancy at Age 20, 17th Century

steady influx of new migrants, they might have ceased to exist altogether.

The Chesapeake colonists experienced shorter, less fertile lives than their New England counterparts. In 1640, for example, Chesapeake migrants had no more than a 50 percent chance of surviving their first year in America. Hot, steamy summers fostered repeated outbreaks of malaria and typhoid fever, which, along with dysentery and poisoning from brackish drinking water, killed thousands. New England's drinking water was safer, although Puritans generally preferred home-brewed beer, and the harsher winter climate helped kill off deadly germs. As a result, the Puritans enjoyed longer, healthier lives.

In New England 20 percent of all Puritan males who survived infancy lived into their seventies. Even with the hazards of childbirth, Puritan women lived almost as long. In Virginia and Maryland, men who survived into their early twenties had reached middle age; on the average, they would not live beyond their mid-forties. Women in their early twenties could not expect to survive too far beyond their late thirties. Given an average life expectancy of 50 to 55 years back in England, the Chesapeake region deserved its reputation as a human graveyard. In comparison early New England represented a utopian health environment.

Good health sustained life and meant longer marriages and more children. Men in New England were usually in their mid-twenties when they married, and their wives were only two to three years younger. Marriages lasted an average of 25 years before one or the other spouse died. Longevity also resulted in large families, averaging seven to eight children per household. In some locales, nine out of ten children survived infant diseases and grew to adulthood knowing not only their parents but their grandparents as well. Families with living grandparents were a unique characteristic of Puritan New England, reflecting life spans more typical of modern America than early modern Europe.

From a demographic perspective, then, New England families were far more stable and secure than those of the Chesapeake. Because Puritans crossed the Atlantic in family units, the ratio of women to men was more evenly balanced than in Virginia or Maryland, where most migrants were not married. Planters seeking laborers for their tobacco fields preferred young males, which skewed the gender ratio against women and retarded the development of family life. Before 1640 only one woman migrated to the Chesapeake for every six men; and as late as 1700, males still outnumbered females by a ratio of more than three to two.

The system of indentured servitude also affected population patterns. Servants could not marry until

Living grandparents were a unique characteristic of New England families, as illustrated by this portrait of Abigail Gerrish and her grandmother.

they had completed their terms. Typically, women were in their mid-twenties before they first wed, which in combination with short adult life expectancies curbed the numbers of children they could bear. Seventeenth-century Chesapeake families averaged only two to three children, and a quarter of them did not survive their first year of life. Marriages lasted an average of seven years before one or the other spouse died. Two-thirds of all surviving children lost one parent by the age of 18, and one-third lost both. Rarely did children know grandparents. Death was as much a daily reality as life for Chesapeake families, at least until the early eighteenth century when killer diseases stopped wreaking such havoc.

Roles for Men, Women, and Children

The early Puritans looked at their mission as a family undertaking, and they referred to families as "little commonwealths." Not only were families to "be fruitful and multiply," but they also served as agencies of education and religious instruction as well as

centers of vocational training and social welfare. Families cared for the destitute and elderly; they took in orphans; and they housed servants and apprentices—all under one roof and subject to the authority of the father.

The Puritans carried **patriarchal** values across the Atlantic and planted them in America. New England law, reflecting its English base, subscribed to the doctrine of **coverture,** or subordinating the legal identity of women to their husbands, who were the undisputed heads of households. Unless there were prenuptial agreements, all property brought by women to marriages belonged to their mates. Husbands were responsible for assuring decency and good order in family life. They also represented their families in all community political, economic, and religious activities.

Wives also had major family responsibilities. "For though the husband be the head of the wife," the Reverend Samuel Willard explained, "yet she is the head of the family." The particular calling of mothers was to nurture their children in godly living, as well as to perform many other tasks—tending gardens, brewing beer, raising chickens, cooking, spinning, and sewing—when not helping in the planting and harvesting of crops.

Most Puritan marriages functioned in at least outward harmony. If serious problems arose, local churches and courts intervened to end the turmoil. Puritan law, again reflecting English precedent, made divorce quite difficult. The only legal grounds were bigamy, desertion, and adultery, and the process required the petitioning of assemblies for bills of separation. A handful of women, most likely battered or abandoned wives, effected their own divorces by setting up separate residences. On occasion the courts brought abusive husbands under control, such as a Maine man who brutally clubbed his wife for refusing to feed the family pig. Some instances occurred when wives defied patriarchalism, including one case involving a Massachusetts woman who faced community censure for beating her husband and even "egging her children to help her, bidding them knock him in the head."

Family friction arose from other sources as well, some of which stemmed from the absolute control that fathers exercised over property and inheritances. If sons wanted to marry and establish separate households, they had to conform to the will of their fathers, who controlled the land. Family patriarchs normally delayed the passing of property until sons had reached their mid-twenties and selected mates acceptable to their parents. Since parents also bestowed dowries on daughters as their contributions to new family units, romantic love had less to do with mate selection than parental desires to unite particular family names and estates.

Puritans expected brides and grooms to learn to love one another as they went about their duty of conceiving and raising the next generation of children. In most cases spouses did develop lasting affection for one another, as captured by the gifted Puritan poet Anne Bradstreet in 1666 when she wrote to her "Dear and loving Husband":

If ever two were one, then surely we.
If ever man were lov'd by wife, then thee;
If ever wife was happy in a man,
Compare with me the women if you can.

Young adults who openly defied patriarchal authority were rare. Also unusual were instances of illegitimate children, despite the lengthy gap between puberty and marriage. As measured by illegitimate births, premarital sex could not have been that common in early New England. This is not a surprising finding among people living in closely controlled communities and seeking to honor the Almighty by reforming human society.

The experiences of seventeenth-century Chesapeake colonists were very different. The system of indentured servitude was open to abuse. Free planters ruled as patriarchs but with no sense of nurturing the next generation; rather, they presumed they were dealing with "simple people" who "professed idleness and will rather beg than work," as a contemporary claimed. The goal was to get as much labor as possible out of servants, since 40 percent died before completing their contracts. Disease was the major killer, but hard-driving planters also contributed to many early deaths.

Servants responded to cruel treatment in various ways. A few committed suicide. Others, like John Punch, ran away. Some killed farm animals, set buildings on fire, or broke tools. Local laws, as drafted by freeholding planters, specified harsh penalties. Besides floggings and brandings, resisting servants faced long extensions of service, as one unfortunate man learned after he killed three pigs belonging to his master. The court added six years to his term of service.

Indentured servitude also inhibited family life. Since servants could not marry, the likelihood of illicit sexual activity increased. Quite frequently, women became the unwilling sexual partners of lustful masters or male servants. Margerie Goold, for example, warded off attempted rape by her master in 1663, but another servant, Elizabeth Wild, was less successful. The planter, however, helped her induce an abortion. One-fifth of Maryland's indentured females faced charges of "bastardy," reflecting both a shortage of women and a labor system controlled by all-powerful masters. Finally in 1692, Virginia officials tried to improve the situation by adopting a statute that mandated harsh penalties for "dissolute masters" getting "their maids with child."

Still, the fate of female and male servants was not always abuse or death. Some survived, gained title to land, and enjoyed, however briefly, personal freedom in America. A few women, usually widows, acquired influence. **Margaret Brent**, for example, controlled over 1000 acres in Maryland and served as the executor of Governor Leonard Calvert's estate in 1647. She even dared to demand the right to vote, a plea dismissed by male legislators.

Brent's case suggests that high death rates in combination with an unbalanced sex ratio may have, at least temporarily, enhanced the status of some Chesapeake women. English and colonial law recognized the category of *femes sole*, which permitted single, adult women and widows to own and manage property and households for themselves. Chesapeake women who outlived two or three husbands could acquire significant holdings through inheritances and then maintain control by requiring prenuptial contracts from future spouses. Once married, however, any property not so protected fell to new husbands because of *coverture.*

Since widowed mothers could presume they would outlive new husbands, most prenuptial contracts protected property for children by previous marriages. Indeed, few children grew to adulthood without burying one or both parents, and there were extreme cases like that of Agatha Vause, a Virginia child whose father, two stepfathers, mother, and guardian uncle all died before she was 11 years old.

The fragility of Chesapeake life resulted in complex family genealogies with some households containing children from three or four marriages. In some instances local Orphans' Courts had to take charge because all adult relatives had died. Because parents did not live that long, children quite often received their inheritances by their late teens, much earlier than in New England. This advantage meant only that economic independence, like death, came earlier in life.

COMMERCIAL VALUES AND THE RISE OF CHATTEL SLAVERY

By 1650 signs were abundant that the Puritan mission was in trouble. From the outset many non-Puritan settlers, including merchants in Boston, had shunned

Childbirth in Early America

When the *Mayflower* left Plymouth, England, September 16, 1620, on its historic voyage to the New World, 3 of its 102 passengers were pregnant. Elizabeth Hopkins and Susanna White were each in their seventh month of pregnancy. Mary Norris Allerton was in her second or third month.

Their pregnancies must have been excruciatingly difficult. After a few days of clear weather, the *Mayflower* ran into "fierce storms" that lasted for six of the voyage's nine and a half weeks. For days on end, passengers were confined to the low spaces between decks, while high winds blew away clothing and supplies and the ship tossed and rolled on the heavy seas.

While the ship was still at sea, Elizabeth Hopkins gave birth to a baby boy named Oceanus after his birthplace. Two weeks later, while the Mayflower was anchored off Cape Cod, Susanna White also had a baby boy. He was christened Peregrine, a name that means "pilgrim." Peregrine White would live into his eighties, but Oceanus Hopkins died during the Pilgrims' first winter in Plymouth. In the spring of 1621, Mary Norris Allerton died in childbirth; her baby was stillborn.

Childbirth in colonial America was a difficult and sometimes dangerous experience for women. During the seventeenth and eighteenth centuries, between 1 and 1.5 percent of all births ended in the mother's death—as a result of exhaustion, dehydration, infection, hemorrhage, or convulsions.

Since the typical mother gave birth to between five and eight children, her lifetime chances of dying in childbirth ran as high as one in eight. This meant that if a woman had eight female friends, it was likely that one would die in childbirth.

Understandably, many colonial women regarded pregnancy with dread. In their letters, women often referred to childbirth as "the Dreaded apparition," "the greatest of earthly miserys," or "that evel hour I loock forward to with dread." Many, like New England poet Anne Bradstreet, approached childbirth with a fear of impending death. In a poem entitled "Before the Birth of One of Her Children," Bradstreet wrote,

> How soon, my Dear, death may
> my steps attend,
> How soon't may be thy lot to
> lose thy friend.

In addition to her anxieties about pregnancy, an expectant mother was filled with apprehensions about the survival of her newborn child. The death of a child in infancy was far more common than it is today. In the healthiest seventeenth-century communities, 1 infant in 10 died before the age of 5. In less healthy environments, 3 children in 10 died before their fifth birthday. Puritan minister Cotton Mather saw 8 of his 15 children die before reaching the age of 2. "We have our children taken from us," Mather cried out, "the Desire of our Eyes taken away with a stroke."

Given the high risk of birth complications and infant death, it is not surprising to learn that pregnancy was surrounded by superstitions. It was widely believed that if a mother-to-be looked upon a "horrible spectre" or was startled by a loud noise

her child would be disfigured. If a hare jumped in front of her, her child was in danger of suffering a harelip. There was also fear that if the mother looked at the moon, her child might become a lunatic or sleepwalker. A mother's ungratified longings, it was thought, could cause a miscarriage or leave a mark imprinted on her child's body. At the same time, however, women were expected to continue to perform work until the onset of labor, since hard work supposedly made for an easier labor. Pregnant women regularly spun thread, wove fabric on looms, performed heavy lifting and carrying, milked cows, and slaughtered and salted down meat.

Today, most women give birth in hospitals under close medical supervision. If they wish, women can take anesthetics to relieve labor pangs. During the seventeenth and eighteenth centuries, the process of childbirth was almost wholly different. In colonial America, the typical woman gave birth to her children at home, while female kin and neighbors clustered at her bedside to offer support and encouragement. When the daughter of Samuel Sewall, a Puritan magistrate, gave birth to her first child on the last day of January 1701, at least eight other women were present at her bedside, including her mother, her mother-in-law, a midwife, a nurse, and at least four other neighbors.

Most women were assisted in childbirth not by a doctor but by a midwife. Most midwives were older women who relied on practical experience in delivering children. One midwife, Martha Ballard, who practiced in Augusta, Maine, delivered 996 babies with only 4 recorded fatalities. Skilled midwives were highly

valued. Communities tried to attract experienced midwives by offering a salary or a rent-free house. In addition to assisting in childbirth, midwives helped deliver the offspring of animals, attended the baptisms and burials of infants, and testified in court in cases of bastardy.

During labor, midwives administered no painkillers, except for alcohol. Pain in childbirth was considered God's punishment for Eve's sin of eating the forbidden fruit in the Garden of Eden. Women were merely advised to "arm themselves with patience" and prayer and to try, during labor, to restrain "those dreadful groans and cries which do so much discourage their friends and relations that are near them."

After delivery, new mothers were often treated to a banquet. At one such event, visitors feasted on "boil'd pork, beef, fowls, very good roast beef, turkey-pye, [and] tarts." Women

from well-to-do families were then expected to spend three to four weeks in bed convalescing. Their attendants kept the fireplace burning and wrapped them in a heavy blanket in order to help them sweat out "poisons." Women from poorer families were generally back at work in one or two days.

During the second half of the eighteenth century, customs of childbirth began to change. One early sign of change was the growing insistence among women from well-to-do urban families that their children be delivered by male midwives and doctors. Many upper-class families assumed that in a difficult birth trained physicians would make childbirth safer and less painful. In order to justify their presence, physicians tended to take an active role in the birth process. They were much more likely than midwives to intervene in labor with forceps and drugs.

Another important change was the introduction in 1847 of two drugs— ether and chloroform—to relieve pain in childbirth. By the 1920s, the use of anesthesia in childbirth was almost universal. The practice of putting women to sleep during labor contributed to a shift from having children at home to having children in hospitals. In 1900, over 90 percent of all births occurred in the mother's home. But by 1940, over half took place in hospitals and by 1950, the figure had reached 90 percent.

The substitution of doctors for midwives and of hospital delivery for home delivery did little in itself to reduce mortality rates for mothers. It was not until around 1935, when antibiotics and transfusions were introduced, that a sharp reduction in the maternal mortality rate occurred. In 1900 maternal mortality was about 65 times higher than it is today, and not much lower than it had been in the mid-nineteenth century. By World War II, however, death in childbirth had been cut to its present low level.

In recent years, a reaction has occurred against the sterile impersonality of modern hospital delivery. Women today are much more likely than their mothers or grandmothers to want a "natural childbirth." Beginning in the 1960s, a growing number of women elected to bear their children without anesthesia, so that they could be fully conscious during childbirth. Many women also chose to have their husbands or a relative or a friend present during labor and delivery and to bear their children in special "birthing rooms" that provide a homelike environment. In these ways, many contemporary women have sought to recapture the broader support network that characterized childbearing in the colonial past, without sacrificing the tremendous advances that have been made in maternal and infant health.

the religious values of the Bay Colony's founders. By the 1660s children and grandchildren of the migrating generation displayed less zeal about earning God's grace; they were becoming more like southern settlers in their eagerness to get ahead economically. By 1700 their search for worldly prosperity even brought some New Englanders into the international slave trade.

Declension in New England

Declension, or movement away from the ideals of the Bay Colony's founding fathers, resulted in tensions between settlers adhering to the original mission and those attracted to rising commercial values. Clergymen proposed a major compromise known as the **Half-Way Covenant** in 1662. The Covenant recognized that many children were not preparing for salvation, a necessary condition for full church membership, as their parents had done. The question was how to keep them—and their offspring—aspiring toward a spiritual life. The solution was half-way membership, which permitted the baptism of the children and grandchildren of professing saints. If still in the church, ministers and full members could continue to urge them to focus their lives on seeking God's eternal rewards.

Many communities disdained the Half-Way Covenant because of what it implied about changing values. As one minister wrote, too many individuals were acting "as if the Lord had no further work for his people to do but every bird to feather his own nest." With the passage of time, however, most accepted the covenant to help preserve some semblance of a godly society in New England.

Spreading commercial values took hold for many reasons, including the natural abundance of the New England environment and an inability to sustain fervency of purpose among American-born offspring who had not personally felt the religious repression of early Stuart England. Also, Puritans back in England, after overthrowing Charles I, generally ignored the model society in America, which left the impression that the mission had been futile, that no one back in Europe really cared.

The transition in values occurred gradually, as shown in various towns where families bought and sold common field strips so that all of their landholdings were in one place. The next step was to build homes on these sites and become "outlivers," certainly a more efficient way to practice agriculture, yet also a statement that making one's living was more important than daily participation in village life—with its emphasis on laboring together in God's love.

In Boston and other port towns, such as Salem, merchants gained increasing community stature because of their wealth. By the early eighteenth century some of them were earning profits by participating in the African slave trade. Retinues of household servants or, more properly, slaves taken from Africa, symbolized their newfound status.

Clergymen disapproved of these trends. Their sermons took on the tone of "jeremiads," modeled on the prophet Jeremiah who kept urging Israel to return to the path of godliness. In Calvinist fashion, they warned of divine retribution or "afflictions" from the Almighty, and they pointed to events like King Philip's War as proof that Jehovah was punishing New England. In 1679 the ministers met in another synod and listed several problems, everything from working on the Sabbath to swearing in public and sleeping during sermons. Human competitiveness and contention, they sadly concluded, were in ascendance. Worse yet, the populace, in its rush to garner worldly riches, showed little concern that Winthrop's "city upon a hill" was becoming the home of the acquisitive Yankee trader.

Stabilizing Life in the Chesapeake Region

By 1675 certain trends indicated that life in Maryland and Virginia could be something more than brief and unkind. The death rate was dropping; more children were surviving; the gender ratio was starting to balance out; and life expectancy was rising. By the early 1700s Chesapeake residents were living well into their fifties. This figure was comparable to longevity estimates for England but still 10 to 15 years shorter than that of New England. The patterns also indicate greater family stability, as shown by longer marriages and more children.

Not only did life become more stable, but also an elite group of families, controlling significant property and wealth, had begun to emerge. By 1700 the great tidewater families—the Byrds, Carters, Fitzhughs, Lees, and Randolphs, among others—were making their presence felt and had started to dominate social and political affairs in the Chesapeake area. These gentleman-planters aped the lifestyle of England's rural gentry class. They constructed lavish manor houses from which they ruled over their plantation estates, dispensing hospitality and wisdom as the most illustrious and powerful residents of their tobacco-producing region.

Such a person was **William Byrd II** (1674–1744), who inherited 26,000 fertile acres along the James River in 1705. He built the magnificent Westover plan-

Lavish estates like Westover plantation, built by William Byrd II on the James River, illustrate the wealth and social dominance of rising gentleman-planters in Virginia.

tation, raised a large family, served on the governor's council, and assumed, as he wrote to an English correspondent, that he was "one of the patriarchs" of Virginia society. By the time of his death, Byrd had holdings of 180,000 acres, and he owned at least 200 slaves.

Byrd read widely, put together an impressive personal library, and wrote extensively on any subject that interested him. His "secret" diaries describe how he treated others, including his wife, Lucy Parke Byrd. When they argued, Byrd on occasion demonstrated his presumed masculine superiority with sexual bravado. In 1710 "a little quarrel" was "reconciled with a flourish . . . performed on the billiard table." Byrd's behavior was part of his assertive, self-confident manner. He was the master of everything on his magnificent plantation, making him a patriarch of the realm of Virginia.

For every great planter, there were dozens of small farmers who lacked the wealth to obtain land, slaves, and high status in society. Most eked out bare livings, yet they dreamed of the day when they, or their children, might live in the style of a William Byrd. Meanwhile, they deferred to their "betters" among the planter elite, who in turn "treated" them to large quantities of alcohol on election days and expressed gentlemanly concern about the welfare of their families. Such behavior was part of an ongoing bonding ritual among white inhabitants who, no matter how high or low in status, considered themselves superior to black slaves—whose numbers were now growing rapidly on the bottom rung of Maryland and Virginia society.

The Beginnings of American Slavery

The system of **perpetual servitude** that shaped the lives of persons of African heritage like John Punch and Emmanuel had ancient roots. However, slavery was dying out in much of Europe by the fifteenth century. Then the Portuguese mariners of Prince Henry started coasting along sub-Saharan Africa, making contact with various peoples and cultures, some of whom were willing to barter in human flesh as well as in gold and ivory. The first Portuguese expeditions represented the small beginnings of a trade that forcibly relocated an estimated 10 million Africans to the Americas during the next 350 years.

Africa, a continent of immense geographical diversity with vast deserts, grassy plains, and tropical rain forests, had a population of about 50 million people at the time of Columbus. Mighty kingdoms like Ghana had flourished in West Africa but had been overrun by Muslims from the north during the eleventh century, resulting in the empire of Mali and its magnificent trading and learning center, Timbuktu. Farther to the south in Guinea were smaller kingdoms such as Benin in which the populace farmed or worked at such crafts as pottery making, weaving, and metalworking. These cultures valued family life and were mostly matrilineal in the organization of kinship networks. They also had well-developed political systems and legal codes.

In addition, these kingdoms thrived on elaborate regional trading networks, which the Portuguese and other Europeans, offering guns and various iron products, tapped into easily. As time passed Europeans came to identify certain coastal areas with particular commodities. Upper Guinea contained the rice and grain coasts, and Lower Guinea the ivory, gold, and slave coasts.

Early modern European traders learned that some Africans held slaves—mainly individuals captured in tribal wars—who had the status of family members. The Portuguese found that coastal chiefs were willing to trade humans for European firearms, which they could use when attacking interior kingdoms. A new objective of this tribal warfare became the capturing of peoples who would then be transported back to the coast and sold into slavery in exchange for yet more European goods.

Once this vicious slave trading cycle began, it expanded rapidly. Decade after decade, thousands of Africans experienced the agony of being shackled in collars and ankle chains; marched in gangs, or *coffles*, to the coast; thrown into *barracoons*, or slave pens; and then packed aboard waiting European ships destined for ports of call in the Americas. One slave, **Olaudah Equiano,** who made the voyage during the eighteenth century, recalled the "loathsomeness of the stench" from overcrowded conditions, which made him "so sick and low" that he neither was "able to eat, nor had . . . the desire to taste anything."

Some Africans resisted by refusing to eat and starved to death. In response the Europeans made tools to break jaws and pry open mouths so that food could be jammed down unwilling throats. Other resisters jumped overboard and drowned, but the Europeans soon placed large nets on the sides of their vessels. About 15 percent of those Africans forced onto slave ships did not survive. Those who did had to reckon with the frightening realization of having lost everything familiar in their lives—with no knowledge of what might happen next.

During the sixteenth century the Spanish and Portuguese started pouring Africans into their colonies. These slaves were not thought of as family members, but as disposable beings whose energy was to be used up in mining or agricultural operations. High mortality rates among the migrants did not seem to bother their European masters because more slave ships kept appearing on the horizon. As a result, areas such as Brazil and the West Indian sugar islands earned deserved reputations as centers of human exploitation and death.

Cramped and crowded conditions were common on the decks of slave vessels. As shown here, slaves invariably became emaciated from deficient food during their passage across the Atlantic.

Shifting to Slavery in Maryland and Virginia

The English North American colonies existed at the outer edge of the African slave trade until the very end of the seventeenth century. In 1650 the population of Virginia approached 15,000 settlers, including only 500 persons of African descent. By comparison, the English sugar colony of Barbados already held 10,000 slaves, a majority of the population. English Barbadians had started to model their economy on that of other Caribbean sugar islands, whereas Virginians, with a steady supply of indentured servants, had not yet made the transition to slave labor.

Factors supporting a shift, however, were present by the 1640s, as evidenced in laws discriminating against Africans and court cases involving blacks like John Punch and Emmanuel. During the same decade, a few Chesapeake planters started to invest in Africans. Governor Leonard Calvert of Maryland, for example, asked "John Skinner mariner" to ship him "fourteen negro-men-slaves and three women-slaves." Planters like Calvert were ahead of their time because slaves cost significantly more to purchase than indentured servants. Yet for those who invested, they owned their laborers for their lifetimes and did

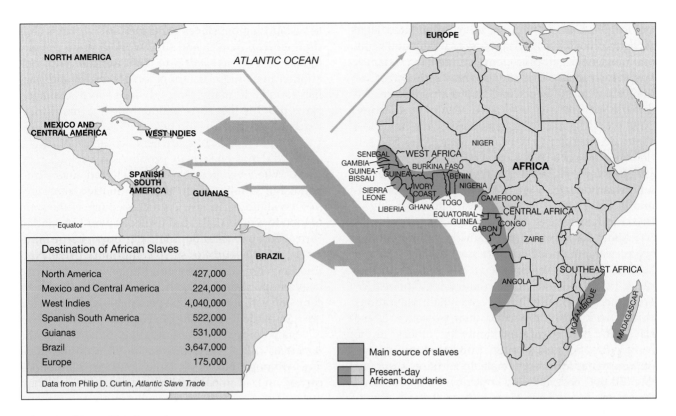

Destination of African Slaves	
North America	427,000
Mexico and Central America	224,000
West Indies	4,040,000
Spanish South America	522,000
Guianas	531,000
Brazil	3,647,000
Europe	175,000
Data from Philip D. Curtin, *Atlantic Slave Trade*	

African Slave Trade

Central and South America represented the most common destination for slaves traded to the Americas between 1520 and 1810.

not have to pay "freedom dues." Moreover, they soon discovered that Africans, having built up immunities to tropical diseases like malaria and typhoid fever, generally lived longer than white servants. Resistance to such diseases made Africans a better long-term investment, at least for well-capitalized planters.

Then in the 1660s two additional factors spurred on the shift toward slave labor. First, Virginia legislators in 1662 decreed that slavery was an inheritable status, "according to the condition of the mother." The law made yet unborn generations subject to slavery, a powerful incentive for risking an initial investment in human chattels. If slaves kept reproducing, planters would control a never-ending supply of laborers. Second, the numbers of new indentured servants began to shrink as economic conditions improved in England. With expanded opportunities for work, poorer citizens were less willing to risk life and limb for a chance at economic independence in America.

Also assisting the shift was the chartering of the Royal African Company in 1672 to develop England's role in the slave trade. Royal African vessels soon made regular visits to Chesapeake Bay. As the supply of slaves increased, asking prices started to drop—at the very time that the cost of buying inden-

tured servants began to climb. In 1698 the company lost its monopoly, which spurred some New England traders to engage actively in the slave trade. Yankee merchants now had something in common with Chesapeake planters besides English roots and language. Both were profiting from the international traffic in human beings.

Population figures explain the rest. In 1670 Virginia contained about 40,000 settlers, which included an estimated 6000 white servants and 2000 black slaves. By 1700 the number of slaves had grown to 16,000, and by 1750 white Virginians owned 120,000 slaves—about 40 percent of the total population. The same general pattern characterized Maryland, where by 1750 there were 40,000 slaves—some 30 percent of the populace. In the Chesapeake area, indentured servitude was by then a moribund institution. White planters, great and small, now measured their wealth and status in terms of plantations and slaves owned and managed.

The World the Slaves Made

Historians once argued that slavery in English North America was harsher than the Spanish-American version. They pointed to the moderating influence of the Roman Catholic church, which mandated legal recognition of slave marriages as a sacramental right, and ancient legal precedents influencing Spanish law, which meant that slaves could earn wages for their labor in off hours and buy their freedom. Although Spanish laws may have been more humane, daily working and living conditions were not. Most slaves destined for Caribbean or South American settlements did not survive long enough to marry or enjoy other legal rights. By contrast, in North America, where early deaths were not as pervasive among migrants, slaves more easily reconstructed meaningful lives for themselves.

About 10 percent of those Africans coming to the colonies entered northern port towns like Boston and became domestic servants, craft workers, or in rare cases, farmhands out in the countryside. The rest labored in the South, mostly on small plantations where field work dominated their existence. These slaves had little chance for family life, at least in the early years, because planters purchased an average of three males for every female. In addition, southern law did not recognize slave marriages—in case masters wanted to sell off some of their chattels. Anglican church leaders accepted the situation. In New England, by comparison, the Congregational church insisted that slave marriages be recognized and respected by masters.

Facing a loss of personal freedom and pervasive racism, southern slaves made separate lives for themselves, particularly on large plantations where their substantial numbers allowed them to form their own communities in the slave quarters. Here they maintained African cultural traditions and developed distinctive forms of music. In South Carolina's

sea island region, slaves continued to give their children African names, and they worked out a distinct dialect, known as *Gullah,* to communicate with one another in a unique combination of African and English sounds. In many places, female slaves managed slave quarter life, thus maintaining the matrilineal nature of African kinship ties.

Contrary to white owners' contentions, most slaves did not engage in promiscuous sexual relations. Whenever possible, they selected mates and had large families, even if slave quarter marriages had no standing in law. As a consequence, the ratio of men to women balanced itself out over time and in turn sped up natural population growth. Large families became a source of slave community pride. Natural increase also undercut the need to continue heavy importation of chattels. As a result, only 5 percent—an estimated 399,000 persons—of all imported Africans ended up in English North America.

Such comparisons are relative. Nowhere in the Americas did slavery function in an uplifting fashion. Although blacks on large southern plantations carried on traditional cultural practices, they still had to face masters or overseers who might whip them, sell off their children, or maim or kill them if they tried to run away. Always present was the realization that whites considered them to be a subhuman species of property, which left scant room for human dignity in life beyond the slave quarters.

Despite the oppression, Africans made substantial contributions to colonial life. In South Carolina, for example, many early slave migrants were expert at raising and herding animals, and they helped develop and support a thriving trade in cattle. Others who came from the rice coast region of Africa used their agricultural skills in fostering South Carolina's emergence as a major center of rice production. These and many other contributions went unrecognized in the rush for profits in the maturing commercial world of the American colonies, except in the ironic sense of creating further demand among white settlers for additional black laborers.

The drawing *Old Plantation* shows that slaves, even though defined as property and without legal rights, succeeded in making meaningful lives for themselves in their own quarters.

CONCLUSION

Although most Africans adapted to slavery, some remained defiant. They stole food, broke farm tools, or in a few cases poisoned their masters. In rare instances they resorted to rebellion. In September 1739 twenty slaves in the Stono River area of South Carolina rose up, seized some weapons, killed a few whites, and started marching toward Spanish Florida. Within a few days frightened planters rallied together and crushed the Stono uprising by shooting or hanging the rebels.

The South Carolina legislature soon approved a more repressive slave code, which all but restricted the movement of blacks from their home plantations. No legislator gave thought to the other possibility, which was to abandon the institution of slavery. Even though long in development, slavery now supported southern plantation agriculture and the production of such cash crops as tobacco and rice.

Just as the southern colonies had made a fateful shift from servitude to slavery, New Englanders experienced another kind of transition. Slowly but surely, they had forsaken their utopian, religiously oriented mission into the wilderness. Service to mammon had started to replace loyalty to God and community. The religious side would remain, but the fervor of a nobler spiritual mission was in rapid decline by 1700. Material gain was now a quality shared by white English colonists in America—North and South.

Prosperity, which had come after so much travail and death, promoted a sense of unlimited opportunity in profiting from the abundance of the American environment. Other realities, however, were also taking shape. The colonists had learned that Crown officials now expected them to conform to new laws governing the emerging English empire. Because of these imperial rules, much turmoil lay ahead for the diversity of peoples now inhabiting English North America.

CHAPTER SUMMARY AND KEY POINTS

Europeans came to North America in the 1600s for reasons that ranged from making quick profits to seeking religious freedom. Initially they faced problems of survival as they made contact with Native American peoples and adjusted to diverse geographic settings and climates. In time thriving colonies developed, and settlers focused as much as possible on achieving economic success. This trend toward expanded economic opportunities for some colonists caused discontent among others and played a part in the enslavement of Africans as chattel slavery took root in English North America, especially in the southernmost colonies.

- The quest of economic success led to a stabilization of the early Chesapeake settlements as the production of tobacco took hold in the area.

- Religious controversy and dissent in England led to the establishment of the Massachusetts Bay Colony in New England, which tried to function as an ideal version of how societies should be organized along biblical lines.

- Initially, settlers in the Chesapeake Bay area relied on white indentured servants as their labor force. A few blacks who arrived in the region were able to acquire property and maintain their freedom.

- Permanent, hereditary slavery took root slowly in the English North American colonies.

- Between 1640 and 1670, a sharp distinction emerged between short-term servitude for whites and permanent slavery for blacks amid valiant attempts by African Americans to make meaningful lives for themselves throughout the Americas.

SUGGESTIONS FOR FURTHER READING

Ira Berlin, *Many Thousands Gone: The First Two Centuries of Slavery in North America* (1998). Detailed, highly readable account of the diverse and complex experiences of slaves during the colonial period and beyond.

David Hackett Fischer, *Albion's Seed: Four British Folkways in America* (1989). Broad-ranging investigation of the implantation of traditional cultural values and practices in North America by distinct groups of English-speaking colonists.

David D. Hall, *Worlds of Wonder, Days of Judgment: Popular Religious Belief in Early New England* (1990). Probing analysis of the mentality of ordinary Puritan settlers in relation to the publicly enunciated ideals of their leaders.

James Horn, *Adapting to a New World: English Society in the Seventeenth-Century Chesapeake* (1994). Comprehensive examination of migratory patterns and the construction of English society in the Chesapeake Bay region.

Jill Lepore, *The Name of War: King Philip's War and the Origins of American Identity* (1998). An evocative study of recollections and understanding of one of the bloodiest wars to take place on American soil.

Gloria L. Main, *Peoples of a Spacious Land: Families and Cultures in Colonial New England* (2001). Fascinating study of life patterns among Puritan settlers in comparison to Native American customs and habits.

Edmund S. Morgan, *American Slavery, American Freedom: The Ordeal of Colonial Virginia* (1975). Valuable discussion of the emergence of slavery in Virginia and the paradoxical evolution of freedom and slavery in British North America.

———, *The Puritan Dilemma: The Story of John Winthrop*, 2d ed. (1999). Classic introduction to Puritan religious beliefs and their implementation in the structure of life in Massachusetts Bay Colony.

Mary Beth Norton, *Founding Mothers and Fathers: Gendered Power and the Forming of American Society* (1996). A probing analysis of the evolution of gender relations in New England and the Chesapeake Bay region during the seventeenth century.

Peter H. Wood, *Black Majority: Negroes in Colonial South Carolina from 1670 Through the Stono Rebellion* (1974). Influential exploration of the lives and contributions of African-American slaves in the development of this Deep South colony.

Novels

John Barth, *The Sot-Weed Factor* (1960).

Virginia Bernhard, *A Durable Fire* (1990).

Nathaniel Hawthorne, *The Scarlet Letter* (1850).

Brian Moore, *Black Robe: A Novel* (1985).

MEDIA RESOURCES

Web Sites

The Plymouth Colony Archive Project at the University of Virginia

http://www.people.virginia.edu/~jfd3a/

This site contains fairly extensive information about late seventeenth century Plymouth Colony.

DPLS Archive: Slave Movement During the 18th and 19th Centuries (Wisconsin)

http://dpls.dacc.wisc.edu/slavedata/index.html

This site explores the slave ships and the slave trade that carried thousands of Africans to the Americas.

CHRONOLOGY OF KEY EVENTS

1608	Pilgrims flee to Holland to avoid religious persecution in England
1617	Virginia begins to export tobacco
1619	The first persons of African descent arrive in Virginia; first representative assembly in English North America meets in Jamestown
1620	Pilgrims arrive at Cape Cod on the *Mayflower* and establish Plymouth Colony
1622	Opechancanough's Indians fail in an attempt to massacre all English settlers in Virginia
1624	English Crown takes control of Virginia; the Dutch begin to settle New York and name their colony New Netherland
1630	Puritans establish the Massachusetts Bay Colony
1632	Maryland becomes the first proprietary colony
1635	Leaders in Massachusetts Bay Colony banish Roger Williams
1636	Harvard College is founded; first permanent English settlements established in Connecticut and Rhode Island
1637– 1638	Anne Hutchinson is convicted of heresy in Massachusetts and flees to Rhode Island
1640s	Legal status of African Americans in the Chesapeake Bay region deteriorates
1644	Second attempted Native American massacre of Virginia colonists fails
1646	Powhatan's Confederacy accepts English rule
1647	Massachusetts Bay Colony adopts the first public school law in the colonies
1649	Maryland's Act of Toleration affirms religious freedom for Christians in the colony; Charles I of England is beheaded
1660	Charles II is restored to the English throne
1664	English conquer New Netherland and rename the colony New York
1675– 1676	King Philip's (Metacomet's) War inflicts heavy casualties on New Englanders
1681– 1682	William Penn founds Pennsylvania as a "holy experiment" in which diverse groups of people can live together harmoniously
1688	Glorious Revolution drives James II from England
1732	Georgia is founded as a haven for debtors and a buffer colony against Spanish Florida
1739	Stono slave uprising occurs in South Carolina

Excerpts from Slave Narratives
http://vi.uh.edu/pages/mintz/primary.htm
The seventeenth- through nineteenth-century accounts of slavery housed in this site speak volumes about the many impacts of slavery.

KEY TERMS

Indentured servitude   (p. 35)

Headrights   (p. 36)

Divine right   (p. 37)

Separatists   (p. 39)

Nonseparatists   (p. 39)

"City upon a hill"   (p. 41)

Antinomian   (p. 45)

Patriarchal   (p. 48)

Coverture   (p. 48)

femes sole   (p. 49)

Declension   (p. 52)

Half-Way Covenant   (p. 52)

Perpetual servitude   (p. 53)

PEOPLE YOU SHOULD KNOW

John Punch   (p. 33)

Pocahontas   (p. 36)

Opechancanough   (p. 36)

King Charles I   (p. 37)

Sir George Calvert (Lord Baltimore)   (p. 38)

Charles II   (p. 38)

John Locke   (p. 38)

William Bradford   (p. 40)

John Winthrop   (p. 41)

John Cotton   (p. 43)

Roger Williams   (p. 44)

Anne Hutchinson   (p. 44)

Metacomet (King Philip)   (p. 46)

Margaret Brent   (p. 49)

William Byrd II   (p. 52)

Olaudah Equiano   (p. 54)

REVIEW QUESTIONS

1. What were the major difficulties that early English settlers in the area of Jamestown had to overcome? What developments allowed the Virginia colony to survive and endure?

2. Compare and contrast Indian-white relations in the Chesapeake and New England colonies. What were the differences and similarities? Did they matter in the end?

3. Describe the original mission of the Puritans who settled in New England. How did the Puritans attempt to implement their mission in the organization of their society? How successful were they in fulfilling their mission?

4. Compare and contrast the characteristics of living in New England and the Chesapeake colonies during the seventeenth century. Why did life seem so much harsher in the Chesapeake region than in New England?

5. What were the differences between indentured servitude and chattel slavery? What factors supported the shift from indentured servitude to slavery and the enslavement of Africans in the southern colonies?

3 Provincial America in Upheaval, 1660–1760

HANNAH DUSTAN AND ELIZA LUCAS: COLONIAL WOMEN IN TIME OF WAR

Hannah Dustan (1657–1736) and **Eliza Lucas** (1722–1793) never knew one another. Dustan lived in the town of Haverhill on the Massachusetts frontier, and Lucas spent her adult years in the vicinity of Charleston, South Carolina. Even though of different generations, both were inhabitants of England's developing North American empire. Along with so many other colonists, perpetual imperial warfare profoundly affected their lives as England, France, and Spain repeatedly battled for supremacy in Europe and America between 1689 and 1763.

During the 1690s, as part of a war involving England and France, frontier New Englanders experienced devastating raids by Indian parties from French Canada. On the morning of March 15, 1697, a band of Abenakis struck Haverhill. Hannah Dustan's husband and seven of her children saved themselves by racing for the community's blockhouse. Hannah, who had just given birth a few days before, was not so fortunate. The Abenakis captured her, as well as her baby and midwife Mary Neff.

After some discussion, the natives "dashed out the brains of the infant against a tree," the well-known Puritan minister, the Reverend Cotton Mather, later wrote; but they decided to spare Hannah and Mary along with a few other captives. Their plan was to march these residents to the principal Abenaki village in Canada where they would "be stripped and scourged and [made to] run the gauntlet through the whole army of Indians." If they survived, they would be adopted into the tribe, literally to become white Indians.

The Abenakis split up their captives. Two male warriors, three women, and seven children escorted Hannah, Mary, and a young boy named Samuel Lenorson. Hannah, although still in a state of shock, maintained her composure as the party walked northward day after day. She prayed fervently for some means of escape.

Just before dawn one morning, she awoke to find all her captors sound asleep. Seizing the moment, she roused Mary and Samuel, handed them hatchets, and told them to crush as many skulls as possible. Suddenly the Indians were dying, and only two, a badly wounded woman and a child, escaped.

Hannah then took a scalping knife and finished the bloody work. When she and the other captives got back to Haverhill, they had ten scalps, for which the Massachusetts General Court awarded them a bounty of £50 in local currency. New Englanders hailed Hannah Dustan as a true heroine—a woman whose courage overcame the French and Indian enemies of England's empire in America.

Cotton Mather spread Dustan's story far and wide, hoping to rekindle the faith of New England's founders. If citizens would just "humble" themselves before God, he argued, the Almighty would stop afflicting society with the horrors of war and provide for the "quick extirpation" of all "bloody and crafty" enemies. Mather's jeremiad had little effect. The war

This heroic statue of Hannah Dustan in Haverhill, Massachusetts, shows her with the hatchet she used to escape from her captors. Dustan brought the scalps back with her to Haverhill to prove her story and collect a bounty.

soon ended, and New Englanders devoted themselves more than ever before to acquiring personal wealth.

After a long and full life, Hannah Dustan died in 1736. Two years later, George Lucas, a prosperous Antigua planter who was also an officer in the British army, moved to South Carolina, where he owned three rice plantations. He wanted to get his family away from the Caribbean region, since hostilities were brewing with Spain.

When war did come a year later, Lucas returned to Antigua to resume his military duties. Leaving an ailing wife, he placed his 17-year-old daughter Eliza in charge of his Carolina properties. The responsibility did not faze her; she wrote regularly to her "Dear Papa" for advice, and the plantations prospered. The war, however, disrupted rice trading routes into the West Indies, and planters needed other cash crops to be sold elsewhere. George Lucas was aware of the problem and sent Eliza seeds for indigo plants, the source of a valued deep-blue dye, to see whether indigo could be grown profitably in South Carolina.

With the help of knowledgeable slaves, Eliza conducted successful experiments. In 1744 a major dye broker in England tested her product "against some of the best French" indigo and rated it "in his opinion . . . as good." Just 22 years old, Eliza had pioneered a cash crop that brought additional wealth to Carolina's planters and became a major trading staple of the British empire.

Had Eliza chosen to marry before this time, she could have lost the legal independence to conduct her experiments; but she favored no suitor until she met and wed Charles Pinckney, a widower of great wealth and high social standing. In later life she took pride in the success of her children. Charles Cotesworth Pinckney (b. 1746) was a powerful voice in the Constitutional Convention of 1787, and Thomas Pinckney (b. 1750) represented President Washington during 1795 in negotiating an agreement called Pinckney's Treaty (see p. 192), which resolved western boundary questions with Spain.

A heralded woman of her generation, Eliza Lucas Pinckney died at the end of the revolutionary era, nearly 140 years after the birth of Hannah Dustan. Dustan's life paralleled the years in which England laid the foundations for a mighty empire in America. Between 1660 and 1700, the colonists offered resistance but had to adjust to new imperial laws governing their lives. Then a series of wars with France and Spain that affected both Dustan and Pinckney caused yet more turbulence. Even with so much upheaval, the colonies grew and prospered. After 1760 provincial Americans were in a position to question their subordinate relationship with England. The coming of the American Revolution cannot be appreciated without looking at the development of the English empire in America—and how that experience related to the lives of passing generations of colonists like Hannah Dustan and Eliza Lucas Pinckney.

DESIGNING ENGLAND'S NORTH AMERICAN EMPIRE

During the 1760s Benjamin Franklin tried to explain why relations between England and the colonies had turned sour. He blamed British trade policies designed to control American commerce. "Most of the statutes, or acts, . . . of parliaments . . . for regulating, directing, or restraining of trade," Franklin declared, "have been . . . political blunders . . . for private advantage, under pretense of public good." The trade system, he believed, had become both oppressive and corrupt.

Little more than a hundred years before, the colonists had traded as they pleased. After 1650, however, Oliver Cromwell and then the restored Stuart monarch Charles II (reigned 1660–1685) worked closely with Parliament to design trade policies that exerted greater control over the activities of the American colonists.

To Benefit the Parent Nation

Certain key ideas underlay the new, more restrictive policies. Most important was the concept of **mercantilism,** a term not invented until the late eighteenth century but one that describes what England's leaders set out to accomplish. Their goal was national greatness and, as one courtier told Charles II, the challenge was to develop "trade and commerce" so that it "draws [a] store of wealth" into England.

Mercantilist thinkers believed the world's supply of wealth was not infinite but fixed in quantity. Any nation that gained wealth automatically did so at the expense of another. In economic dealings, then, the most powerful nations always maintained a favorable balance of trade by exporting a greater value of goods than they imported. To square accounts, hard money in the form of gold and silver would flow into creditor nations. Governments controlling the most precious metals would be the most self-sufficient. They could use such wealth to stimulate internal economic development as well as to strengthen military forces, both of which were critical to economic survival and ascendancy over other nations.

Mercantilist theory also demonstrated how colonies could best serve their parent nations. Gold and silver extracted from Central and South America had underwritten Spain's rise to great power and glory in the sixteenth century. Although such easy wealth did not exist in eastern North America, the colonies could contribute to a favorable trade balance for England by producing such staple crops as tobacco, rice, and sugar, thus ending any need to import these goods from other countries.

The American provinces, in addition, could supply valuable raw materials—for example, timber products. England had plundered its own forests to have winter fuel and construct a strong naval fleet, making it necessary to import wood from the Baltic region. Now the colonies could help fill timber demands, again reducing foreign imports while supplying a commodity vital to national security. Great stands of American timber could also be fashioned into fine furniture and sold back to the colonists. Ideally, England's overseas colonies would serve as a source of raw materials and staple crops as well as a marketplace for manufactured goods.

Mercantilist thinking affirmed the principle that the colonies existed to benefit and strengthen the parent nation. As such, provincial economic and political activities required close management. To effect these goals, Parliament passed a series of Navigation Acts (1651, 1660, 1663, and 1673), which formed the cornerstone of England's commercial relations with the colonies and the rest of the world. The acts banned foreign merchants and vessels from participating in the colonial trade; proclaimed that certain **enumerated goods** could be shipped only to England or other colonies (the first list included dyewoods, indigo, sugar, and tobacco, and furs, molasses, rice, and wood products such as masts, pitch, and tar were added later); and specified that European goods destined for America had to pass through England.

Through the **Navigation System,** England became the central trading hub of its empire, which resulted in a great economic boom at home. Before 1660, for example, the Dutch operated the largest merchant fleet in Europe and dominated the colonial tobacco trade. With stimulus from the Navigation Acts, the shipbuilding industry began to boom in England as never before. By the late 1690s the English merchant fleet had outdistanced all competitors, including the Dutch, which seemed to bear out mercantilist ideas regarding one nation's strength coming at another's expense.

In the colonies the Navigation Acts had mixed effects. New Englanders, taking advantage of local

The ship's carpenter was typical of colonists who benefited from a thriving imperial economy. The colonies produced one-fourth or more of all English-registered vessels.

timber supplies, bolstered their economy by heavy involvement in shipbuilding. By the early 1700s Americans were constructing one-fourth or more of all English merchant vessels. In the Chesapeake Bay region, however, the enumeration of tobacco resulted in economic problems. By the 1660s planters were producing too much tobacco for consumption in the British Isles alone. Because of the costs of merchandising the crop through England, the final market price was too high to support large sales in Europe. Consequently, the tobacco glut in England caused wholesale prices to decline, resulting in hard times in the Chesapeake region and much furor among planters.

Seizing Dutch New Netherland

Charles II learned from his father's mistakes. He never claimed divine authority in decision making; and so as not to appear too power hungry, he passed himself off at court as a sensuous, lazy, vulgar man whose major objectives were to attend horse races, tell bawdy jokes, and seduce women. His mistresses, like Nell Gwynn, became national celebrities and bore him at least 14 illegitimate children. When asked about his lustful ways, he replied, as if mocking the Puritans who had beheaded his father, "God will not damn a man for taking a little unregular pleasure by the way."

Charles often played the foppish fool, but he was an intelligent person with a vision for England's greatness. Besides urging Parliament to legislate the Navigation System, Charles pursued other plans for enhancing England's imperial power. None was more important than challenging Dutch supremacy over the Hudson and Delaware river valleys.

The precedent for attacking territory claimed by England's imperial rivals came in 1654 when Cromwell launched a fleet with 8000 troops to strike at the heart of New Spain. Cromwell's "Western Design" expedition failed to conquer the primary targets of Puerto Rico, Hispaniola, or the port city of Cartagena (located in modern-day Colombia). The fleet, however, seized the island of Jamaica, which in time became a center for illegal commerce with New Spain as well as a major slave trade marketing center.

Charles hated everything about Cromwell, which he proved by having the Lord Protector's corpse exhumed and hanged in public before a cheering crowd. Yet Charles borrowed freely from Cromwell's precedents. New Netherland, a colony having the geographic misfortune of lying between New England and the southern colonies, was an obvious target, especially since Dutch sea captains used New Amsterdam as a base for illegal trade with English settlers. To enforce the Navigation Acts, reasoned Charles and his advisers, the Dutch colony had to be conquered.

New Netherland was the handiwork of the Dutch West India Company, a joint-stock venture chartered in 1621. The company soon sent out a governor and employees to the Hudson River area to develop the fur trade with local Indians, particularly the Five Nations of Iroquois inhabiting upper New York west of Fort Orange (Albany).

Initially the company showed little interest in settlement, but its leaders had to reckon with food shortages. To encourage local agricultural production, the company announced in 1629 that vast landed estates, known as *patroonships,* would be made available to wealthy individuals who transported at least 50 families to New Netherland. The migrants would become tenant farmers for their masters, or *patroons,* who hoped to live like medieval lords on manorial estates. With the Dutch home economy booming, few subjects accepted these less-than-generous terms.

The New Netherland colony was also internally weak and unstable. The governors were a sorry lot, typified by Wouter van Twiller (served 1633–1638), who was pleasant, claimed a contemporary, only "as long as there is any wine." In 1643 his successor, William Kieft, started a war with natives around New Amsterdam (New York City) that devastated the colony's settlers. Facing bankruptcy in 1647, company directors called on Peter Stuyvesant to save the venture. Stuyvesant, however, became embroiled in many disputes with the settlers, whom he repeatedly infuriated with his highhanded policies.

Despite everything, New Netherland's population pushed toward 8000 by 1660, counting Puritans who had settled on Long Island. New Amsterdam was home to people from all over Europe, as well as many African slaves. The unpopularity of Stuyvesant, the absence of any voice in government, and the denial of freedom of worship separate from the Dutch Reformed church all combined to favor a possible English takeover.

In the early days of his monarchy, Charles II strengthened his political base at home by making generous land grants in America, such as rewarding eight loyal court favorites with the Carolinas patent. In 1664 the king gave his brother, **James, the Duke of York,** title to all Dutch lands in North America, on the obvious condition that they be conquered. James quickly hired Colonel Richard Nicolls to organize a small invasion fleet. When the flotilla appeared before New Amsterdam in August 1664, Stuyvesant could not rally the populace. With hardly an exchange of shots, New Netherland became the Duke of York's English province of New York.

Proprietary Difficulties in New York and New Jersey

Unlike his older brother, James was an inflexible person. Although hard-working, he was a humorless autocrat. He even treated his mistresses coldly, as if they were "given him by priests for penance," wrote one court wag. Nor was James sensitive to the political trends of his time. He hated Parliament for having executed his father and was intolerant of representative government.

James's proprietary charter had no clause mandating a popular assembly for his colony, and he instructed Nicolls to make no concessions. As an adept administrator, Nicolls maneuvered around the issue by granting other rights. In his Articles of Capitulation, he confirmed the land titles of all inhabitants, including the Dutch. Next Nicolls announced the

Duke's Laws, which provided for local government and guaranteed such basic liberties as trial by jury and religious toleration, so long as settlers belonged to and supported some church.

The Long Island Puritans kept pressing for a popularly elected assembly. They refused to pay local taxes, arguing that they were "enslaved under an arbitrary power." The absence of an assembly for New York's colonists remained a source of friction for several years. Finally, James conceded the point, and an assembly met for the first time in 1683. Once he became king in 1685, however, James disavowed further assembly meetings.

Making matters more confusing, in 1664 James turned over all his proprietary lands between the Hudson and Delaware rivers to John, Lord Berkeley, and Sir George Carteret, two court favorites who were also Carolina proprietors. Nicolls, however, did not learn of this grant until after he had offered some Puritans land patents in the eastern portion of what became the colony of New Jersey.

Until the end of the century, questions regarding proprietary ownership of New Jersey plagued the colony's development. Settlement proceeded slowly, with the population moving toward 15,000 by 1700.

Middle Colonies, 1685

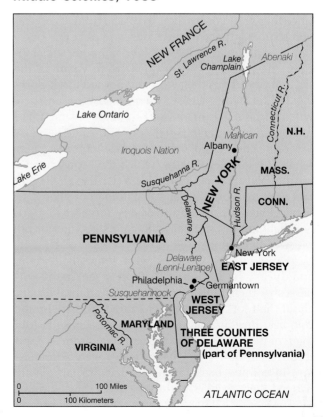

Most New Jersey colonists engaged in commercial farming and raised grain crops, which they marketed through New York City and Philadelphia, the two port towns that would dominate the region. Because of endless bickering over land titles and proprietary political authority, the Crown declared in 1702 that New Jersey would henceforth be a royal province.

Planting William Penn's "Holy Experiment"

During the English Civil War of the 1640s a number of radical religious sects—Ranters, Seekers, and Quakers among them—began to appear in England. Each represented a small band of fervent believers determined to recast human society in the mold of a particular religious vision. George Fox founded the Society of Friends. His followers came to be called "Quakers," because Fox, who went to jail many times, warned one judge to "tremble at the word of the Lord."

The Quakers adhered to many controversial ideas. They believed that all persons had a divine spark, or "inner light," which, when fully nurtured, allowed them to commune directly with God. Like Anne Hutchinson before them, they saw little need for human institutions. They had no ordained ministers and downplayed the importance of the Bible, since they could order their lives according to revelation received directly from God.

In addition, the Quakers held a unique social vision. All humans, they argued, were equal in the sight of God. Thus they wore unadorned black clothing and refused to remove their broad-brimmed hats when social superiors passed by them. Women had full access to leadership positions and could serve as preachers and missionaries. Members of the sect also refused to take legal oaths, which they considered a form of swearing, and they were pacifists, believing that warfare would never solve human problems. In time, Quakers became antislavery advocates, arguing that God did not hold some persons inferior because of skin color.

Early English Quakers were intensely fervent, and during the 1650s and 1660s they sent many witnesses of their faith to America. These individuals, about half of them women, fared poorly in the colonies. Puritan magistrates in Massachusetts told them of their "free liberty to keep away from us" and threw them out. Two Quaker males were so persistent in coming back to Boston that officials finally hanged them in 1659, and they gave a third witness, Mary Dyer, a gallows reprieve. Dyer, however, re-turned the next year, was hanged, and became a martyr to her vision of a more harmonious world.

William Penn (1644–1718) first became a Quaker in the early 1660s while a college student at Oxford. Hoping to cure his son's zealousness, Penn's father sent William on a tour of the Continent. Penn returned in a more worldly frame of mind, but he soon readopted Quaker beliefs. He was so outspoken that he even spent time in jail, but his father's high standing at court—he had supported the Stuart restoration—assured the family access to Charles II.

During the 1670s George Fox traveled to America, hoping to find a haven for his followers. He also encouraged William Penn to use his family connections to obtain a land grant. King Charles acceded to Penn's request for a proprietary charter in 1681, stating that the purpose was to "enlarge our British empire" and pay off a £16,000 debt long since due the estate of Penn's father. Years later, Penn claimed that Charles's real motivation was "to be rid of" the Quakers "at so cheap a rate" by conveying to him title to "a desert [wilderness] three thousand miles off."

Pennsylvania, which means Penn's woods, was hardly a desert. The tract was bountiful, and Penn tried to make the most of it, both as a sanctuary for oppressed religious groups and as a source of personal income from quitrents. He laid his plans carefully, making large grants to English Quakers, and he drew up a blueprint for a commercial center—Philadelphia, or the City of Brotherly Love. Penn sent agents to Europe in search of settlers, offering generous land packages with low annual quitrents. He also wrote his First Frame of Government (1682), which guaranteed a legislative assembly and full freedom of religion.

Like the Puritans before him, Penn had a utopian vision, in this case captured by the phrase **holy experiment.** Unlike the Puritans, Penn wanted to mold a society in which peoples of diverse backgrounds and religious beliefs lived together harmoniously—a bold idea in an era not known for its toleration.

Determined to succeed, Penn sailed to America in 1682, landing first in the area known as the Three Lower Counties, later to become the colony of Delaware. He had purchased this strip of land from the Duke of York to assure an easy exit for commerce flowing out of Philadelphia to Atlantic trade routes. Until 1701, Delaware existed as an appendage of Pennsylvania, but then Penn granted the colonists there a separate assembly. Until the Revolution, however, the proprietary governors of Pennsylvania also headed Delaware's government.

Penn next journeyed upriver to lay out Philadelphia. Some settlers were already present, and during

In his dealings with Native Americans, William Penn sought to negotiate land rights fairly. However, Pennsylvania's settlers and Penn's own officials were not so scrupulous. They used many underhanded means to push the native populace off ancient tribal lands as rapidly as possible.

the next few years others migrated from England as well as from Wales, Scotland, Ireland, Holland, Germany, and Switzerland. Typical were Germans from the Rhineland who followed their religious leader, Francis Daniel Pastorius, and founded Germantown to the north of Philadelphia. From the very outset, Pennsylvania developed along pluralist lines, an early sign of what later characterized the cultural ideal of the United States as a whole.

Penn envisioned a "peaceable kingdom" and sought cordial relations with local Indians. Before traveling to America, he wrote to the Delawares, the dominant tribe in the region, explaining that the king of England "hath given me a great province." He asked that "we may always live together as neighbors and friends." True to his word, Penn met with the Delawares and told them that he would not take land from them unless sanctioned by tribal chieftains. What emerged was the "walking purchase" system in which the natives sold land based on the distance that a person could travel on foot in a day. Even though the system was open to abuse, Penn's goal was honest dealing, which had rarely been the case in other colonies.

Completing these and other tasks, Penn returned to England in 1684 to encourage further settlement. That was no problem. Pennsylvania was very attractive, particularly for dissenter religious groups. By the early 1700s the population exceeded 20,000. Colonists poured through the booming port of Philadelphia and then fanned out into the fertile countryside. There they established family farms, raising livestock and growing abundant grain crops, which they marketed to the West Indies and Europe. The settlers prospered, and Pennsylvania gained a reputation as "one of the best poor man's countries in the world."

Still, not all was perfect in the peaceable kingdom. Religious sects segregated themselves, wanting little to do with one another. To Penn's dismay, life in Philadelphia was more raucous than pious. Drinking establishments and brothels sprang up in large numbers, and endless bickering characterized local politics. Quakers dominated the government but fought endlessly over the prerogatives of power. Penn thought these "brutish, . . . scurvy quarrels" were a "disgrace" to the colony, but his pleas for harmony went unheeded. Equally disturbing from his point of view, settlers refused to pay quitrents "to supply me with bread," yet he kept funding the colony's development.

Hoping to solve such problems, Penn returned in 1699. His presence had a moderating influence—but only so long as he stayed. Before leaving for the last time, he announced a new Charter of Liberties (1701), which placed all legislative authority in an elective assembly, to be checked only by a proprietary governor with the advice of a council of well-to-do local gentlemen. The charter served as the basis of Pennsylvania's unicameral government until the Revolution.

Peace, prosperity, pluralism, and religious toleration were the hallmarks of Penn's utopian vision. In his old age, however, he considered the "holy experiment" a failure. He concluded that peaceable kingdoms on earth lay beyond human reach. Having even spent time in prison for debts contracted on behalf of his colony, Penn died an embittered man in 1718. Still, by seeking a better life for all peoples, he helped infuse the American experience with a profound sense of social purpose.

DEFYING THE IMPERIAL WILL: PROVINCIAL CONVULSIONS AND REBELLIONS

Establishing the Middle Colonies was an integral part of England's imperial expansion within the framework of mercantilist thinking. Certainly the Dutch understood this, and they fought two wars with England (1664–1667 and 1672–1674), hoping to recoup their losses. In the second war they recaptured New York, only to renounce all claims in the peace settlement. After that time, the Dutch focused their activities on other parts of the world, even though some of their mariners continued to trade illegally with the English North American colonists.

Besides reckoning with the Dutch, Charles II and his advisers endeavored to shape the emerging empire in other ways. Crown representatives crossed the Atlantic to determine whether the colonists were cooperating with the Navigation System. Also traveling to America were the first customs officers, who were to collect duties on enumerated goods being traded between colonies—and then to foreign ports. Increasingly the Americans felt England's constraining hand, which in some locales resulted in violent confrontations.

Bacon's Bloody Rebellion in Virginia

With tobacco glutting the market in England, Virginia's economy went into a tailspin during the 1660s. The planters blamed the Navigation Acts, which stopped them from dealing directly with such foreign merchants as the Dutch. The planters' mood did not improve when, in 1667, Dutch war vessels captured nearly the whole English merchant fleet hauling the annual tobacco crop out of Chesapeake Bay, resulting in the virtual loss of a year's worth of labor, harvest, and income.

Besides economic woes, other problems existed. Some Virginians thought their long-time royal governor, **Sir William Berkeley** (1606–1677), had become a tyrant. Berkeley handed out patronage jobs to a few favored planters, known as the "Green Spring" faction (named after Berkeley's plantation). Such favors allowed the governor to dominate the assembly and levy heavy taxes at a time when settlers were suffering economically. As a consequence, some planters lost their property, and young males just completing terms of indentured service saw few prospects for ever gaining title to land and achieving economic independence. In 1670 Berkeley and the assembly approved a 50-acre property holding requirement for voting privileges. This action fed suspicions that the governor and his cronies were out to amass all power for themselves.

In 1674 young **Nathaniel Bacon** (1647–1676) jumped into the simmering pot. From a wealthy English family and educated at Cambridge, he had squandered his inheritance before reaching his mid-twenties. Bacon's despairing father sent him to Virginia with a stipend to start a plantation, hoping the experience would force his son to grow up. When Bacon arrived, Berkeley greeted him warmly, stating that "gentlemen of your quality come very rarely into this country."

Bacon was ambitious, and he sought acceptance among Berkeley's favored friends, who controlled the lucrative Indian trade. He asked the governor for a trading license, but Berkeley denied the request, feeling that the young man had not yet proven his worth. Incensed by his rejection, Bacon started opposing Berkeley at every turn. He organized other substantial planters—also not favored by Berkeley—into his own "Castle" faction (the name of his plantation), and he appealed to Virginia's growing numbers of propertyless poor for support.

Stirrings among native peoples made matters worse. Far to the north in New York, the Five Nations of Iroquois had become more aggressive in their quest for furs. They started pushing other tribes southward toward Virginia, and some groups spilled onto frontier plantations, resulting in a few killings.

Bacon demanded reprisals, but Berkeley urged caution. A war, he stressed, would only add to Virginia's tax burdens. Bacon asked for a military commission, stating that he would organize an army of volunteers. The governor refused, at which point Bacon charged his adversary with being more interested in protecting profits from his Indian trading monopoly than in saving settlers' lives. Bacon pulled together a force of over 1000 men, described as "the scum of the country" by Berkeley's supporters, and indiscriminately started killing local natives.

In response, Berkeley declared Bacon "the greatest rebel that ever was in Virginia" and sent out militiamen to corral the volunteers, but Bacon's force eluded them. The governor also called a new assembly, which met at Jamestown in June 1676. Among reforms designed to pacify the "mutineers," the burgesses restored voting rights to all adult freemen, even if they did not own property. Events had gone too far, however, and a shooting war broke out. Before the fighting ceased, Bacon's force burned Jamestown to the ground, and Berkeley fled across Chesapeake Bay. What finally precipitated an end to the struggle was Bacon's death from dysentery in October 1676.

When Charles II learned of the uprising, he considered it an affront to royal authority and a threat to his tax revenues on tobacco. The colonists had to be disciplined, so he authorized a flotilla of 11 ships and 1000 troops to cross the Atlantic and restore order. By the time the troops arrived, Berkeley was back in control. Royal advisers with the king's army, however, removed the aging governor from office on the grounds that his policies had helped stir up trouble. Governors who placed self-interest above the need for stability and order in the empire would no longer be tolerated.

After 1676 the Crown started sending royal governors to Virginia with detailed instructions about managing the colony as an imperial enterprise—at times at the expense of local interests. In response, Virginia's leading gentleman-planters, previously divided into pro- and anti-Berkeley factions, settled their differences in the face of what they viewed as threats to local autonomy. They rallied the people to their side, got themselves elected regularly to the House of Burgesses, and worked together to protect the colony's interests.

This fundamental recasting of political lines was an important development. No longer would rising planter elite leaders fight to the death among themselves. They would stand united in defense of local rights and privileges, making sure Crown officials understood that harmony and stability depended on their showing basic respect for the welfare of the colonists.

The Glorious Revolution Spills into America

The king's reaction to Bacon's Rebellion fit a larger pattern of asserting more authority over America. New England, with its independent ways, was an obvious target. Back in the mid-1660s royal commissioners had visited Massachusetts and seen Dutch merchant vessels trading in Boston harbor in violation of the Navigation Acts. Puritan leaders were surly about the matter. "The laws of England . . . do not reach [to] America," they declared. Once back in England, the angry commissioners urged the Crown to take over the colony, but nothing happened—at least not for a few years.

Then in 1675 King Charles, seeking more effective control over the colonies, designated certain Privy Council members to serve as the Lords of Trade and Plantations. The lords, in turn, sent agents and customs officials to America. The most notorious was Edward Randolph, a grim, dedicated bureaucrat who never met a Puritan he liked. Soon he was bombarding the lords with negative reports. In response to Randolph's accusations the lords began legal proceedings and got the Bay Colony charter revoked in 1684.

Randolph was not solely responsible for voiding the charter. The Lords of Trade had developed plans for setting up two or three large administrative territories in North America. New England made a natural unit, based on geographic cohesion and forms of economic production. Charles thought the scheme too radical, but when James became king in 1685, the lords gained permission to set up the Dominion of New England, which stretched from Nova Scotia to the Delaware River.

James II liked the Dominion concept not only because it favored the Church of England but also because it centralized political power in the hands of a governor and a large advisory council made up of Crown appointees. Local representative assemblies would likewise cease to exist. James gladly wrote New York's local leaders and informed them that they would now exist under the authority of the Dominion. As for Connecticut and Rhode Island, the lords were working to void their charters in court.

From the outset the Dominion was a bad idea, perhaps made worse by naming as governor **Sir Edmund Andros** (1637–1714), a man of aristocratic bearing with impressive military credentials. Among his councilors was the despised Edward Randolph. Images of political tyranny wafted through Puritan minds when Andros debarked in Boston in late 1686 and demanded that a building be found for holding Anglican church services. It all smacked of garrison government in which the highest ranking military officer had complete authority, with no popular checks whatsoever.

Andros expected the Puritans to conform to the imperial will. He announced plans to rewrite all land deeds, none of which the General Court had awarded in the king's name and, then, to impose quitrents, which New Englanders had never paid. He announced import taxes to underwrite the expenses of his government, and he started prosecuting violators of the Navigation Acts.

Meanwhile, back in England, James II had created an uproar by pushing royal authority too far. In defiance of England's Protestant tradition, he flaunted his Roman Catholic beliefs and announced that his newborn son, now next in line for the throne, would be raised a Catholic. The thought of yet more turbulence over religious beliefs was too much for influential English leaders to bear. In December 1688 they drove James from the realm and offered the throne to his Protestant daughter, Mary, and her husband, the Dutch prince, William of Orange, as joint monarchs. As part of the Glorious Revolution, Parliament also placed strict limitations on royal prerogatives by adopting the Declaration of Rights (1689), which at long last assured Parliament an equal, if not dominant, voice in Britain's political affairs.

When news of the Glorious Revolution reached Boston, local Puritan leaders went into action. They believed wild rumors about James, who had fled to France, conspiring with Andros, French Canadians, and Indians to seize New England and turn it into a new bastion of Roman Catholicism. They seized the governor on April 18, 1689, threw him in jail, and then shipped him back to England. They did so, they insisted, to end Andros's arbitrary rule, and they asked William and Mary to restore their original corporate charter.

The coup in Massachusetts helped spark a rebellion in New York, where a volatile mix of ethnic and class tensions resulted in a violent upheaval. Francis Nicholson served in New York City as the Dominion's lieutenant governor. Wealthy Dutch and English landholders and merchants cooperated with his rule, which bred resentment among poorer Dutch and English settlers, such as the Puritans on Long Island. Jacob Leisler, a combative local merchant of German origin, also hated the favored families. They had snubbed him socially, despite his marriage to a wealthy Dutch widow. Even worse, from his point of view, they cared little about securing popular political rights.

When reports of the rumored "popish" plot and the Massachusetts coup reached New York, Leisler exhorted the anti-Nicholson settlers to rise up and defend themselves. He organized 500 of them into a military force, and on May 31 they captured Fort James which guarded New York harbor. Within a few days, Nicholson fled to England. Leisler set up an interim government and waited for advice from England, hoping that the new monarchs would make a permanent grant of a popularly based assembly. In addition, Leisler made no attempt to stop mobs from harassing and robbing wealthy families.

The third colony jolted by a revolt in 1689 was Maryland, where quarrels between Roman Catholics and Protestants remained a perpetual source of tension. The proprietary governor, William Joseph, tried to contain the popish conspiracy rumors, but John Coode, an anxious local planter, organized the Protestant Association to defend Marylanders from the impending slaughter. Rumormongers soon were whispering that the Catholic proprietor and his local governor were in on the plot. That was all Coode needed. He led 250 followers to St. Mary's, where in July 1689 they removed Joseph from office, called their own assembly, and then sent representatives to England to plead for royal government.

In a chain reaction, three political uprisings had occurred in the American colonies in just four months. Although each had its own individual character, the common issue, besides the rumored Catholic conspiracy, was the question of how extensive colonial rights would be in the face of tightening imperial administration. All the colonists could do now was wait to hear from the new monarchs—and hope for the best.

New England's Witchcraft Hysteria

William and Mary, at first, had little time to deal with the provincial rebellions. Warfare had broken out in Europe (the War of the League of Augsburg, 1689–1697). Spilling over into America, this contest caused havoc in the lives of frontier settlers like Hannah Dustan. French and Indian raiding parties made orphans of many children, including a few who ended up in Salem Village (now Danvers), Massachusetts, the center of the 1692 witchcraft episode.

Puritans, like most Europeans and colonists elsewhere, believed in witchcraft. They thought the devil could materialize in various shapes and forms, damaging lives at will. Satan's agents included witches and wizards, women and men possessed by his evil spirits. Eighty-one New Englanders had faced accusations of practicing witchcraft before 1692, 16 of whom were put to death. These numbers were insignificant in comparison to accused witches hunted down and executed in Europe.

Reasons abound for the outbreak of the witchcraft hysteria. By the early 1690s New Englanders had lost their charter, lived under the Dominion, rebelled against Edmund Andros, and engaged in war with the hated French. These unsettled conditions may have made the populace overly suspicious and anxious about evil influences in their midst.

In addition, specific tensions affected the Salem area. Salem Town, the port, was caught up in New England's commercial life while outlying settlers around Salem Village remained traditional in seeking God's grace before material wealth. Resentment by the villagers was growing, described even before 1690 as "uncharitable expressions and uncomely reflections tossed to and fro."

These tensions came out in the pattern of accusations when in early 1692 a few adolescent girls, among them some of the war orphans from Maine, started having their "fits." Anxious about their own

As the Salem witchcraft trials unfolded, the young "afflicted" girls became more bold in their accusations. They often fell into fits and shouted that the accused had cast evil satanic spells over them.

lives, the girls had asked Tituba, a local slave woman from the West Indies, to tell them their fortunes. She did so. Soon thereafter the girls started acting hysterically, observers claimed, as if possessed by Satan's demons. When asked to name possible witches, the girls did not stop with Tituba.

Before the hysteria ended, the "afflicted" girls made hundreds of accusations before a special court appointed to root the devil out of Massachusetts. With increasing frequency they pointed to more urbane, prospering citizens like those of Salem Town. The penalty for practicing witchcraft was death. Some 50 defendants, among them Tituba, saved themselves by admitting their guilt; but 20 men and women were executed (19 by hanging and 1 by the crushing weight of stones) after steadfastly refusing to admit that they had practiced witchcraft.

By the end of 1692 the craze was over, probably because too many citizens of rank and influence, including the wife of the new royal governor, Sir William Phips, had been accused of doing the devil's work. In time, most participants in the Salem witchcraft trials admitted to being deluded. While victims could not be brought back to life, the episode stood as a warning in the colonies about the dangers of mass hysteria at a time when Europeans were still actively ferreting out and prosecuting alleged witches. The playing out of events also helped sustain New England's transition to a commercial society by making traditional folk beliefs—and those who espoused them—appear foolish.

Settling Anglo-American Differences

In 1691 William and Mary began to address colonial issues. As constitutional monarchs, they were not afraid of popularly elected assemblies. In the case of Massachusetts they approved a royal charter that gave the Crown the authority to name royal governors and stated that all male property holders, not just church members, had the right to vote. On the other hand, the monarchs did not tamper with the established Congregational church, thereby reassuring old-line Puritans that conforming to the Church of England was not necessary so long as Bay Colony residents supported England's imperial aspirations.

New York also became a royal colony in 1691, complete with a local representative assembly. Henry Sloughter, the governor, delivered the news; but Jacob Leisler hesitated to step aside, fearing that Sloughter might be an agent of King James. Leisler's obstinacy led to his arrest and hasty trial for treason. His enemies gave all the testimony that the court needed to sentence him to a ghastly death by hanging, disemboweling, drawing and quartering and, if that were not enough, decapitation. It was little solace to Leisler's followers that Parliament, in later reviewing the evidence, declared him innocent of treason.

In Maryland's case the Calverts lost political control in 1692 in favor of royal government, although they still held title to the land and could collect quitrents. Shortly thereafter, a Protestant assembly banned Roman Catholics from political office. Not until 1715 did the Calverts regain political control. By then the proprietary family had converted to

Anglicanism and was no longer a threat to Protestant sensibilities.

The transformation revealed a movement toward the royal model of government in which the colonies established legislative assemblies to express and defend their local concerns. Crown-appointed governors, in turn, pledged themselves to enforce the Navigation Acts and other imperial laws. So long as the colonists cooperated, they would not face autocratic forms of government. Nor would the Crown permit the kind of loose freedom of earlier times, because in gaining basic rights, the colonists also accepted responsibility for conducting their daily affairs within the imperial framework. The Glorious Revolution and its reverberations in America had made this compromise possible.

Maintaining the delicate balance between imperial authority and local autonomy was the major challenge of the eighteenth century. Until the 1760s both sides succeeded in doing so. The Crown, for example, adopted the Navigation Act of 1696, which set up the Board of Trade and Plantations as an administrative agency to advise England's leaders on colonial issues. This act also mandated the establishment of vice-admiralty courts in America to punish with stiff penalties smugglers and others who violated the rules of trade.

The Board of Trade generally acted with discretion, even in recommending a few acts to restrain colonial manufacturers competing with home industries. Parliament in 1699 adopted legislation (the Woolen Act) that outlawed any exportation of woolen products from America or from one colony to another. The intent was to get the colonists to buy finished woolens from English manufacturers rather than develop their own industry. In 1732 the Hat Act barred the colonial production of beaver and felt hats. Then in 1750 Parliament passed the Iron Act, which forbade the colonists from building new facilities or expanding old ones for the manufacture of finished iron or steel products. On the other hand, the act encouraged them to keep preparing raw iron for final processing in England. As a whole, these acts had little adverse effect on the provincial economy. They simply reinforced fundamental mercantile notions regarding colonies as sources of raw materials and as markets for finished goods.

Occasionally, imperial leaders went too far, such as with the Molasses Act of 1733. In support of a thriving rum industry based mostly in New England, colonial merchants roamed the Caribbean for molasses, which cost less on French and Dutch West Indian islands. To placate British West Indian planters,

Colonial Trade Routes, 1750

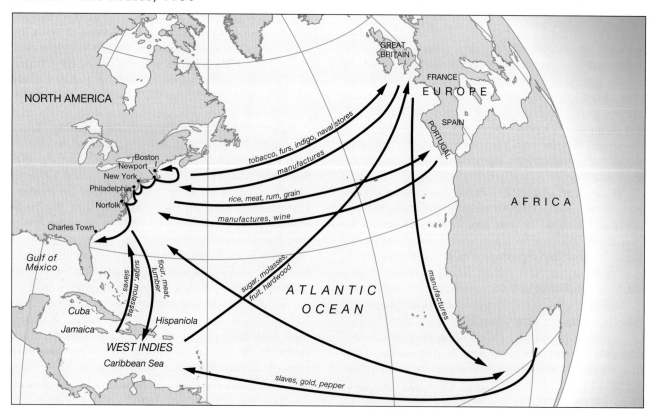

Parliament tried to redirect the trade with a heavy duty (6 pence per gallon) on foreign molasses transported into the colonies. Enforcing the trade duty could have ruined the booming North American rum industry, but customs officers wisely ignored collecting the duty, a sensible solution to a potentially inflammatory issue.

As the eighteenth century progressed, imperial officials tried hard not to be overbearing. In certain instances they even stimulated provincial economic development by offering large cash bounties for raising indigo plants. (Thus, Eliza Lucas's efforts held the long-term potential to challenge France's dominant position in the production of that valued dye.) Caught up as the empire was in warfare with France and Spain, home leaders did not want to tamper with a system that, by and large, worked. The colonists, in turn, gladly accepted the relative autonomy that characterized their lives during the so-called era of **salutary neglect.**

MATURING COLONIAL SOCIETIES IN UNSETTLED TIMES

Stable relations with the parent nation and other factors nourished the maturing of the American provinces after 1700. Certainly a rapidly expanding population that nearly doubled every 20 years strengthened the colonies, as did widespread economic prosperity, even though it was not shared evenly among the populace. In times of internal social turmoil, such as during the religious upheaval known as the Great Awakening, the colonists disagreed heatedly among themselves but did not lose sight of the need for mutual respect and cooperation in further building their communities. Finally, participation in a series of imperial wars, in which the colonists contributed greatly to Britain's military success while also wresting yet more land for themselves from the native populace, underpinned a growing sense of self-confidence. By the 1760s, however, many colonists had come to doubt whether the home government truly appreciated what they had accomplished for the expanding British empire—portending an end to the long period of stable relations.

An Exploding Population Base

Between 1700 and 1760 the colonial population mushroomed from 250,000 to 1.6 million persons—and to 2.5 million by 1775. Natural population increase—predicated upon abundant land, early marriages, and high fertility rates—was only one source of the population explosion. Equally significant was the introduction of non-English peoples. Between 1700 and 1775 the British North American slave trade reached its peak, resulting in the involuntary entry of an estimated 250,000 Africans into the colonies. The black population grew from 28,000 in 1700 to over 500,000 in 1775, with most living as chattel slaves in the South. At least 40 to 50 percent of the African population increase in the colonies was attributable to the booming slave trade.

Among European groups, Scots-Irish and Germans predominated, although a smattering of French Huguenot, Swiss, Scottish, Irish, and Jewish migrants joined the westward stream. The Scots-Irish had endured many privations. Originally Presbyterian lowlanders from Scotland, they had migrated to Ulster (northern Ireland) in the seventeenth century at the invitation of the Crown. Once there, they harassed the Catholic Irish with a vengeance, only to face discrimination themselves when a new Parliamentary law, the Test Act of 1704, stripped non-Anglicans of political rights. During the next several years they also endured crop failures and huge rent increases from their English landlords.

In a series of waves between 1725 and 1775 over 100,000 Scots-Irish descended on North America, lured by reports of "a rich, fine soil before them, laying as loose . . . as the best bed in the garden." Philadelphia was their main port of entry. They then moved out into the backcountry where they squatted on open land and earned reputations as bloodthirsty Indian fighters. In time, the Scots-Irish took the Great Wagon Road through the Shenandoah Valley and started filling in the southern backcountry.

TABLE 3.1
Colonial Population Growth, 1660–1780

Year	White	Black	Total
1660	70,200	2900	73,100*
1680	138,100	7000	145,100
1700	223,100	27,800	250,900
1720	397,300	68,900	466,200
1740	755,500	150,000	905,500
1760	1,267,800	325,800	1,593,600
1780	2,111,100	566,700	2,677,800

Note: All estimates rounded to the nearest hundred.

*Includes the population of New Netherland.

Source: The American Colonies: From Settlement to Independence by R. C. Simmons. Copyright © 1976 by R. C. Simmons. Reprinted by permission of Harold Matson, Inc.

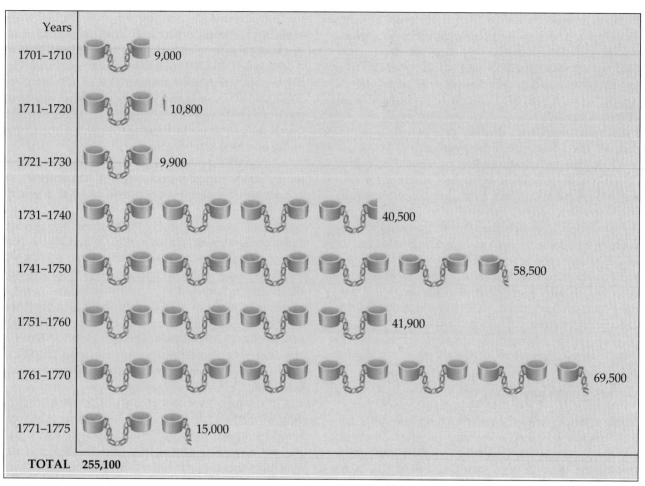

Years	
1701–1710	9,000
1711–1720	10,800
1721–1730	9,900
1731–1740	40,500
1741–1750	58,500
1751–1760	41,900
1761–1770	69,500
1771–1775	15,000
TOTAL	**255,100**

FIGURE 3.1
Slave Importation Estimates, 1701–1775

Even before the first Scots-Irish wave, Germans from the area of the upper Rhine River began streaming into the Middle Colonies. Some, like Amish, Moravian, and Mennonite sectarians, fled religious persecution; others escaped from crushing economic circumstances caused by overpopulation, crop failures, and heavy local taxes. So many Germans came through Philadelphia that Benjamin Franklin questioned whether "Pennsylvania . . . [will] become a colony of aliens, who will shortly be so numerous as to Germanize us, instead of our Anglifying them." Franklin's worries could not stop the German migrants, whose numbers exceeded 100,000 by 1775.

Many destitute Germans crossed the Atlantic as **redemptioners.** This system was similar to indentured servitude, except that families migrated together and shippers promised heads of households a few days' time, upon arrival in America, to locate some person or group to pay for the family's passage in return for a set number of years of labor (usually three to six years per family member). If they failed, then ship captains held auctions at market with the expectation of making tidy profits. The redemptioner system was full of abuses, such as packing passengers on vessels like cattle and serving them worm-infested food. Hundreds died before seeing America. For those who survived, the dream of prospering someday as free colonists remained viable.

One reason for such optimism was that more settlers were enjoying longer life spans, as reflected in higher birth and lower death rates. Estimates indicate that post-1700 Americans were dying at an average of 20 to 25 per 1000 annually, but births numbered 45 to 50 per 1000 settlers.

Longer lives reflected improved health and agricultural abundance. Colonists had plentiful supplies

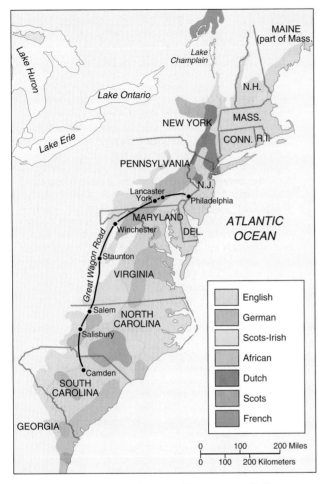

Distribution of Immigrant Groups and the Great Wagon Road, Mid-1700s

Many settlers carried their possessions in Conestoga wagons as they migrated south from Pennsylvania along the Great Wagon Road in search of new homesteads.

of food. Nutritious diets led to better overall health, making it easier for Americans to fight virulent diseases. Even the poorest people, claimed a New England doctor, had regular meals of "salt pork and beans, with bread of Indian corn meal," as well as ample quantities of home-brewed beer and distilled spirits. In the same period, food supplies in Europe were dangerously sparse. Thousands of western Europeans starved to death between 1740 and 1743 because of widespread crop failures.

The "Europeanizing" of America

Compared to Europe, America was a land of boundless prosperity. To be sure, however, the colonists accepted wide disparities in wealth, rank, and privilege as part of the natural order of life. They did so

because of the pervasive influence of European values, such as the need for hierarchy and deference in social and political relations. The eighteenth century was still an era in which individuals believed in three distinct social orders—the monarchy, the aristocracy, and the "democracy" of common citizens. All persons had an identifiable place in society, fixed at birth; and to try to improve one's lot was to risk instability in the established rhythms of the universe.

These notions, dating back to Aristotle and other ancient thinkers, helped justify the highly stratified world of early modern Europe, featuring monarchical families such as the Tudors and Stuarts and bloodline aristocrats who passed hereditary titles from one generation to the next. Among those threatening Europe's established social order were ambitious commoners who had acquired great wealth through commerce. They too craved public recognition and high status, and they tried to earn a place for themselves at the top of the social pyramid by aping the manners and customs of those born into privileged social stations.

Western European Migration

Western Europeans, escaping religious persecution and dwindling food supplies, migrated in great numbers to North America.

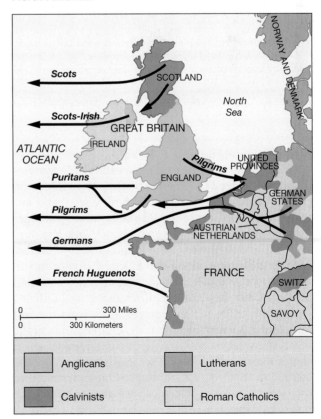

THE PEOPLE SPEAK

Olaudah Equiano on His Ship Passage to America as a Slave

For free persons of great wealth, migrating to America in the eighteenth century was invariably an unpleasant undertaking. For unfree persons such as Olaudah Equiano (c. 1745–1797), the experience was truly mortifying. Stolen from his village in Nigeria by Africans involved in the slave trade, 11-year-old Equiano had to face the unknown with no sense of what his prospects were for the future. He had become one of about 250,000 Africans forced into migrating to the British North American colonies between 1700 and 1775. As events for young Equiano turned out, he was among the luckier slaves. A British naval officer purchased him in Virginia and later sold him to a Quaker merchant in the West Indies. This gentleman allowed Equiano the opportunity to trade on his own, enough so that he was able to purchase his freedom in 1766. For much of the rest of his life, Equiano lived in England and worked to halt the slave trade. His *Narrative* was part of his effort to bring an end to such human exploitation, as these passages about what he experienced on a slave ship attest.

> The first object which saluted my eyes when I arrived on the coast was the sea, and a slave ship, which was then riding at anchor, and waiting for its cargo. These filled me with astonishment, which was soon converted into terror, which I am yet at a loss to describe, nor the then feelings of my mind. When I was carried on board I was immediately handled, and tossed up, to see if I were sound, by some of the crew; and I was now persuaded that I had got into a world of bad spirits, and that they were going to kill me. Their complexions too differing so much from ours, their long hair, and the language they spoke, which was very different from any I had ever heard, united to confirm me in this belief. . . . When I looked round the ship too, and saw a large furnace or copper boiling, and a multitude of black people of every description chained together, every one of our countenances expressing dejection and sorrow, I no longer doubted of my fate; and, quite overpowered with horror and anguish, I fell motionless on the deck and fainted.
>
> When I recovered a little, I found some black people about me, who I believed were some of those who brought me on board, and had been receiving their pay; they talked to me in order to cheer me, but all in vain. I asked them if we were not to be eaten by those white men with horrible looks, red faces, and long hair. They told me I was not. . . .
>
> I was not long suffered to indulge my grief; I was soon put down under the decks, and there I received such a salutation in my nostrils as I had never experienced in my life; so that, with the loathsomeness of the stench, and crying together, I became so sick and low that I was not able to eat, nor had I the least desire to taste any thing. I now wished for the last friend, death, to relieve me; but soon, to my grief, two of the white men offered me eatables; and, on my refusing to eat, one of them held me fast by the hands, and laid me across, I think, the windlass, and tied my feet while the other flogged me severely. I had never experienced any thing of this kind before. . . .
>
> In a little time after, amongst the poor chained men, I found some of my own nation, which in a small

The same could be said for wealthy elite families that had emerged in America by the early eighteenth century. In Virginia names like Byrd, Carter, and Lee were of the first rank; the Pinckneys and Rutledges dominated South Carolina; in New York the Livingstons and Schuylers were among the favored few with great estates along the Hudson River; and in Massachusetts those of major consequence included merchant families like the Hutchinsons and Olivers.

Elite families set themselves apart from the rest of colonial society by imitating English aristocratic lifestyles. Wealthy southern gentlemen used gangs of slaves to produce the staple crops that generated the income to construct lavish manor houses with elaborate formal gardens. Northern merchants built large residences of Georgian design and filled them with fashionable Hepplewhite or Chippendale furniture. Together, they thought of themselves as the "better sort," and they expected the "lower sort" (also described as the "common herd" or "rabble") to defer to their judgment in social and political decision making.

One characteristic, then, of the **Europeanizing** of colonial society was growing economic stratification, with extremes of wealth and poverty becoming more visible. In Chester County, Pennsylvania, where commercial farming was predominant, the wealthiest 10 percent of the people owned 24 percent of the taxable property in the 1690s, which jumped to 34 percent by 1760. Their gain came at the expense of the bottom 30 percent, who held 17 percent in the 1690s but only 6 percent in 1760. The pattern was

degree gave ease to my mind. I inquired of them what was to be done with us? They gave me to understand we were to be carried to these white people's country to work for them. I then was a little revived, and thought, if it were no worse than working, my situation was not so desperate; but still I feared I should be put to death, the white people looked and acted, as I thought, in so savage a manner; for I had never seen among any people such instances of brutal cruelty; and this not only shown toward us blacks, but also to some of the whites themselves. . . .

At last, when the ship we were in had got in all her cargo, they made ready with many fearful noises, and we were all put under deck. . . . The stench of the hold . . . became absolutely pestilential. The closeness of the place, and the heat of the climate, added to the number in the ship, which was so crowded that each had scarcely room to turn himself, almost suffocated us. This produced copious perspirations, so that the air soon became unfit for respiration, from a variety of loathsome smells, and brought on a sickness amongst the slaves, of which many died, thus falling victims to the improvident avarice, as I may call it, of their purchasers. This wretched situation was again aggravated by the galling of the chains, now become insupportable; and the filth of the necessary tubs, into which the children often fell, and were almost suffocated. The shrieks of the women, and the groans of the dying, rendered the whole scene of horror almost inconceivable. Happily perhaps for myself I was soon reduced so low here that it was thought necessary to keep me almost always on deck; and from my extreme youth I was not put in fetters.

In this situation I expected every hour to share the fate of my companions, some of whom were almost daily brought upon deck at the point of death, which I began to hope would soon put an end to my miseries. Often did I think many of the inhabitants of the deep much more happy than myself; I envied them the freedom they enjoyed, and as often wished I could change my condition for theirs. . . .

One day, when we had a smooth sea, and moderate wind, two of my wearied countrymen, who were chained together (I was near them at the time), preferring death to such a life of misery, somehow made through the nettings, and jumped into the sea; immediately another quite dejected fellow, who, on account of his illness, was suffered to be out of irons, also followed their example; and I believe many more would very soon have done the same, if they had not been prevented by the ship's crew, who were instantly alarmed. Those of us that were the most active were in a moment put down under the deck; and there was such a noise and confusion amongst the people of the ship as I never heard before, to stop her, and get the boat out to go after the slaves. However, two of the wretches were drowned, but they got the other, and afterwards flogged him unmercifully, for thus attempting to prefer death to slavery. In this manner we continued to undergo more hardships than I can now relate; hardships which are inseparable from this accursed trade. Many a time we were near suffocation, from the want of fresh air, which we were often without for whole days together. This, and the stench of the necessary tubs, carried off many. . . .

Source: Olaudah Equiano, *The Interesting Narrative of the Life of Olaudah Equiano or Gustavus Vassa, the African* (New York, 1791).

even more striking in urban areas like Boston and Philadelphia. By 1760 the top 10 percent controlled over 60 percent of the available wealth; the bottom 30 percent owned less than 2 percent.

Nevertheless, the colonies featured a large middle class, and it was still possible to get ahead in provincial America. Over 90 percent of the people lived in the countryside and engaged in some form of agricultural production. By European standards, property ownership was widespread, yet poverty was also common. Some of the worst instances were among urban dwellers, many of whom eked out the barest of livelihoods as unskilled day laborers or merchant seamen. These individuals at least enjoyed some personal freedom, which placed them above those persons trapped in slavery, who formed 20 percent of the populace but enjoyed none of its prosperity or political rights.

With colonial wealth concentrated in fewer and fewer hands, a second "Europeanizing" trend was toward the hardening of class lines. Elite families increasingly intermarried, and they spoke openly of an assumed right to serve as political stewards for the people. As one Virginia gentleman proclaimed in the 1760s, "men of *birth and fortune,* in every government that is free, should be invested with power, and enjoy higher honors than the people. If it were otherwise, their privileges would be less, and they would not enjoy an equal degree of liberty with the people."

Here was a classic statement of "deferential" thinking. Although widespread property holding allowed substantial numbers of free white males to vote, they most often chose among members of the elite to represent them in elective offices, particularly in colonial assemblies. Once elected, these stewards regularly contested with Crown-appointed governors and councilors in upper houses over the prerogatives of decision making. In colony after colony during the eighteenth century, elite leaders chipped away at royal authority, arguing that the assemblies were "little parliaments" with the same legislative rights in their respective territorial spheres as Parliament had over all British subjects.

More often than not, governors had only feeble backing from the home government and lost these disputes. Consequently, the assemblies gained many prerogatives, including the right to initiate all provincial money and taxation bills. Because governors depended on the assemblies for their salaries, they often approved local legislation not in the best interests of the Crown in exchange for bills appropriating their annual salaries. By the 1760s the colonial assemblies had thus emerged as powerful agencies of government.

As self-conscious, assertive elite leaders, colonial gentlemen also read widely and kept themselves informed about European political activities. They were particularly attracted to the writings of a band of "radical" whig pamphleteers in England who repeatedly warned of ministerial officials who would use every corrupting device to grab all power and authority as potential tyrants at home. The radical whigs spoke of the delicate fabric of liberty; and provincial leaders, viewing themselves as the protectors of American rights, were increasingly on guard, in case the Crown became too oppressive, as it had been during the 1680s in demanding conformity to the imperial will.

These colonial leaders took challenges to their local autonomy seriously. At least some in their number were ready to mobilize and lead the populace in resisting any new wave of perceived imperial tyranny, should a time ever come when the parent nation attempted to return to arbitrary government.

Intellectual and Religious Awakening

Besides politics, colonial leaders paid close attention to Europe's dawning Age of Reason, also called the **Enlightenment.** The new approach to learning was secular, based on scientific inquiry and the systematic collection of information. A major goal was to unlock the physical laws of nature, as the great English physicist **Sir Isaac Newton** (1642–1727), often considered the father of the Enlightenment, had done in explaining how the force

of gravity held the universe together (*Principia Mathematica*, 1687).

Europe's intellectuals, heavily influenced by the English political thinker John Locke (1632–1704), tried to identify laws governing human behavior. In his *Essay Concerning Human Understanding* (1690), Locke described the human mind as a blank sheet (*tabula rasa*) at birth waiting to be influenced by the experiences of life. If people followed the insights of reason, social and political ills could be reduced or eliminated from society, and each person, as well as humanity as a whole, could advance toward greater harmony and perfection. As such, the key watchword of the Enlightenment was **rationalism,** meaning a firm trust in the ability of the human mind to solve earthly problems—with much less faith in the centrality of God as an active, judgmental force in the universe.

Like their counterparts in Europe, educated colonists pursued all forms of knowledge. Naturalists John Bartram of Pennsylvania and Dr. Alexander Garden of Charleston, South Carolina, were among those who systematically collected and classified American plants. The wealthy merchant James Logan of Philadelphia was a skilled mathematician who also conducted experiments in botany that revealed how pollen functioned as a fertilizing agent in corn.

Benjamin Franklin (1706–1790) became the best-known colonial student of science. In the early 1720s he organized the Junto, a club in Philadelphia devoted to exploring useful knowledge. In 1743 he helped found the American Philosophical Society, which focused on compiling scientific knowledge that would help "multiply the conveniences and pleasures of life." Flying his famous kite, Franklin himself performed experiments with lightning, seeking to reveal the mysteries of electrical energy. After publishing his *Experiments and Observations on Electricity* (1751), Franklin's fame spread throughout the Western world. The next year he invented the lightning rod (1752), which he first developed to protect his own home from the destructive energy contained in flashes of lightning.

Franklin was very much a man of secular learning. So were some clergymen, such as Boston's **Cotton Mather,** who dabbled in science without forsaking strongly held religious beliefs. During a deadly New England smallpox epidemic in 1720 and 1721, Mather was outspokenly in favor of inoculation, which involved purposely inducing slight infections. Many thought inoculations would only spread the disease, but Mather collected statistics that proved the procedure's preventive effects. Whereas 15 percent of uninoculated smallpox victims did not survive, just 3 percent died as a result of inoculation.

Benjamin Franklin epitomized Enlightenment thinking in the colonies. As a student of science he wanted to unlock the mysterious laws of nature, such as in his lightning experiments. Franklin was also a printer, inventor, philosopher, and statesman.

Mather conducted his experiment in the face of strong public opposition. Even local physicians railed against him, and one irate citizen threw a rock through the window of his home with the message: "Mather, you dog; damn you: I'll enoculate you with this, with a pox to you." Years would pass before most provincial Americans accepted inoculation as a sensible medical procedure for controlling deadly smallpox epidemics.

Unlike Mather, many ministers viewed the Enlightenment with great suspicion. Rationalism seemed to undermine orthodox religious values by reducing God to a prime mover who had set the universe in motion only to leave humans to chart their own destiny. (This system of thought was known as Deism.) Others perceived a decline in religious faith, as the populace rushed to achieve material rather than spiritual abundance. For some clergymen, the time was at hand for a renewed emphasis on vital religion.

During the 1720s and 1730s in Europe and America, some ministers started holding revivals. They did so in the face of dwindling church attendance in many locales. The first colonial outpouring of rejuvenated faith occurred during the mid-1720s in New Jersey and eastern Pennsylvania, where the determined Dutch Reformed minister, Theodorus Frelinghuysen, and his Presbyterian counterpart, Gilbert Tennent, attacked what the latter called the "presumptuous security" of his parishioners. Delivering impassioned sermons, these two ministers exhorted great numbers of people to seek after God's saving grace. Theirs was the first in a succession of revival "harvests" known collectively as the **Great Awakening.**

The next harvest came in New England. With each passing year fewer descendants of the Puritans showed interest in seeking God's grace and gaining full church membership. Attempting to reverse matters in the early eighteenth century, the longtime Congregational minister, Solomon Stoddard (c. 1643–1729) of Northampton, Massachusetts, threw open the doors of his church and encouraged everyone to join in communion services—the hallmark of full church membership. Stoddard's method worked, and he temporarily reversed the slide.

Then in 1734 **Jonathan Edwards** (1703–1758), who had succeeded Stoddard, his grandfather, in the Northampton pulpit, initiated a series of revival meetings aimed at young persons. Edwards was a learned student of the Enlightenment who argued that experiencing God's grace was essential to the full appreciation of the universe and its laws. Like his grandfather before him, he joyously preached about seeking redemption and salvation, soon noting that Northampton's inhabitants, both young and old, were now "full of love."

In 1741 Edwards delivered his best known sermon, "Sinners in the Hands of an Angry God." Preaching fervently, he reminded his listeners of the "manifold . . . abominations of your life," vividly picturing how each of them was "wallowing in sensual filthiness, as swine in mire." He also dangled his audience over "the abyss of *hell*" as a jarring reminder to place God at the center of human existence. Appealing to the senses more than to rational inquiry, Edwards felt, was the surest way to uplift individual lives, win souls for God, and improve society as a whole.

Such local revivals did not become broad and general until after the dynamic English preacher, **George Whitefield** (1714–1770), arrived in America. Whitefield was a disciple of John Wesley, the founder of the revival-oriented Methodist movement in England. Possessing a booming voice and charismatic

Colonial Pastimes

For much of the past 300 years, Puritans have been the subject of considerable bad press. Novelists and historians have pictured them as dour, sour individuals, dressed in black with faces cast in a permanently disapproving expression. H. L. Mencken, the twentieth-century opponent of what he saw as the Puritan legacy in America, defined Puritanism as "the haunting fear that some one, some where, may be happy." Thomas Babington Macaulay, the nineteenth-century English writer, perhaps best set the tone for Mencken. "The Puritan," Macaulay noted, "hated bearbaiting, not because it gave pain to the bear, but because it gave pleasure to the spectators."

Is there any truth to such broad-brushed stereotyping? What was the Puritans' attitude toward games, sports, and amusements? And how did their attitudes differ from southern Americans? The answers to such questions indicate the differences between Americans North and South.

Commenting on Puritan religious leaders Increase and Cotton Mather, one historian observed, "Though father and son walked the streets of Boston at noonday, they were only twilight figures, communing with ghosts, building with shadows." Certainly, as the quote suggests, the Puritan clergy were sober figures. They looked askance at frivolous behavior. Into this category they lumped sports, games, and amusements played for the pure joy of play. In 1647 the Massachusetts Bay Colony outlawed shuffleboard. A ban against bowling followed in 1650. Football and other sports were similarly treated.

Puritan leaders were opposed to any Sabbath amusements. Sunday was a day for worship—not work, and certainly not play. Remaining true to the teachings of the Prophet Isaiah, Cotton Mather condemned those who tried to justify Sabbath sports: "Never did anything sound more sorrowfully or odious since the day the World was first bless'd with such a day." Those who broke the Sabbath were punished. They were denied food, publicly whipped, or placed in stocks.

Nor did Puritans condone pit sports, which matched animal against animal. Before the eighteenth century, pit sports (or blood sports) were popular and commonplace in Europe and the American South. People would travel long distances to watch dogs fight bulls, bears, badgers, or other dogs. Cockfighting was equally popular. Were these spectators cruel? Perhaps not. The "bloodied animals," noted a historian of humanitarianism, "were probably not victims of cruelty. Cruelty implies a desire to inflict pain and thus presupposes an empathic appreciation of the suffering of the object of cruelty. Empathy, however, seems not to have been a highly developed trait in premodern Europe."

Unlike Europeans and southerners, Puritans condemned such activity. They did empathize with the animals. "What Christen [sic] heart," wrote Puritan Philip Stubbes, "can take pleasure to see one poor beast to rent, teare, and kill another, and all for his foolish pleasure?"

Although Puritans outlawed pit sports and insisted on the strict observance of the Sabbath, they did not oppose all sports and games. They supported such activities as walking, archery, running, wrestling, fencing, hunting, fishing, and hawking—as long as they were engaged in at a proper time and in a proper manner. Moderate recreation devoid of gambling, drunkenness, idleness, and frivolousness could refresh the body and spirit and, thus, serve the greater glory of God. This last point was the most important for the Puritans. Recreations had to help men and women better serve God; they were never to be ends in themselves.

Different attitudes toward sports and games emerged in the southern colonies. Almost from the time of settlement, southerners exhibited an interest—oftentimes bordering on a passion—for various sports. They were particularly attracted to sports that involved opportunities for betting and demonstrations of physical prowess.

Cockfights attracted southerners from every class. The matches were advertised in newspapers and eagerly anticipated; at important events thousands of dollars in bets would change hands. For northern observers the entire affair attracted only scorn and disgust. Elkanah Watson, who traveled to the South in the mid-1800s, was upset to see "men of character and intelligence giving their countenance to an amusement so frivolous and scandalous, so abhorrent to every feeling of humanity, and so injurious in its moral influence."

Horse racing surpassed even cockfighting as a favorite southern pastime. Wealthy southerners liked to trace their ancestry to the English aristocracy, and they viewed horse racing and horse breeding as aristocratic occupations. In fact, by the eighteenth

century the ownership of horses had taken on a cultural significance. As one student of the subject explained, "By the turn of the century possession of . . . these animals had become a social necessity. Without a horse, a planter felt despised, an object of ridicule. Owning even a slow footed saddle horse made the common planter more of a man in his own eyes as well as those of his neighbors."

Horse races matched owner against owner, planter against planter, in contests where large sums of money and sense of personal worth often rode on the outcome. In most races planters rode their own horses,

making the outcome even more important. Intensely competitive men, planters sometimes cheated to win, and many races ended in legal courts rather than on the racetrack.

If planters willingly battled each other on the racetrack, they did not ride against their social inferiors. When James Bullocke, a tailor, challenged Mr. Mathew Slader to a race in 1674, the county court informed the tailor that it was "contrary to Law for a Labourer to make a race being a Sport for Gentlemen." For his efforts, the court fined Bullocke 200 pounds of tobacco and cask. Although laborers and slaves watched the contests,

and even bet among each other, they did not mix socially with the gentry.

Unlike the Puritans who believed sports should serve God, southerners participated in sports as an outlet for their very secular materialistic, individualistic, and competitive urges. But neither North nor South had a modern concept of sports. Colonial Americans seldom kept records, respected equality of competition, established sports bureaucracies, standardized rules, or quantified results—all hallmarks of modern sports. Yet each section engaged in leisure activities that reflected their social and religious outlooks.

presence, he preached with great simplicity, always stressing the essentials of God's "free gift" of grace for those seeking conversion. Even Benjamin Franklin, a confirmed skeptic, felt moved when Whitefield appeared in Philadelphia. He went to the meeting determined to give no money but relented in the end: Franklin confessed, "I emptied my pocket wholly into the collector's dish, gold and all."

Whitefield, known as the "grand itinerant," made seven preaching tours to the colonies, traveled thousands of miles, and delivered hundreds of sermons. Perhaps his most dramatic tour was to New England in the autumn of 1740. In Boston alone over 20,000 persons heard him preach in a three-day period. Concluding his tour in less than a month, Whitefield left behind churches full of congregants anxious to experience conversion and bask in the glow of their newfound fellowship with God.

The Awakening soon became a source of much contention, splitting America's religious community into new and old light camps. When in 1740 Gilbert Tennent preached his widely read sermon,

Although George Whitefield failed to convert Benjamin Franklin, the evangelist's eloquence moved Franklin to make a generous contribution to the preacher's collection.

"The Danger of an Unconverted Ministry," he expressed the feeling of many revivalists in advising their flocks of believers to shun clergymen who, although formally educated in theology, showed no visible signs of having gained God's saving grace. Thousands paid attention, and they started breaking away from congregations where ministers were suspect.

In response, Old Light clergymen, who at first rejoiced about having so many people return to the fold, began denouncing the Awakening as a fraudulent hoax being perpetrated by unlettered fools with no theological training. In New England ministers of the established Congregational church got their legislative assemblies to adopt anti-itinerancy laws, which barred traveling evangelists such as Whitefield and Tennent from preaching in their communities. The contention between **Old Lights** and **New Lights** became so heated in many New England towns that friends and neighbors, when not arguing, stopped speaking.

So much turmoil had significant long-term repercussions. Those feeling a new relationship with God were less willing to submit to established authority and more determined to speak out on behalf of basic liberties. Typical were colonists in New England who had started calling themselves Baptists. Under the resolute leadership of Isaac Backus, they demanded the right to separate completely from the established Congregational church, to which all citizens owed taxes, and the right to support their own ministers and churches. Theirs would be a long and hard-fought campaign to end state-supported religion.

The liberty to worship and support whatever church one pleased was a central outcome of the Awakening movement, as was a concern with the proper training of clergymen. Before the 1740s, the colonies had only three colleges: Harvard (1636), William and Mary (1693), and Yale (1701). In demanding toleration for diverse ideas, Presbyterian revivalists set up the College of New Jersey (1747, later Princeton), to train New Light clergymen; Baptists founded the College of Rhode Island (1764, later Brown); and the Dutch Reformed established Queen's College (1766, later Rutgers). In 1769 a New Light Congregational minister, Eleazar Wheelock, received a charter for Dartmouth College to carry the new-birth message to Native Americans. Only King's College (1757, later Columbia), founded by Anglicans, and the College of Philadelphia (1755, later the University of Pennsylvania) had no special interest in training New Light clergymen; but in recognizing growing religious pluralism, these two colleges regularly admitted students on a nonsectarian basis.

The Great Awakening, the religious revival that swept through the colonies in the mid-eighteenth century, swelled the ranks of many "New Light" denominations including the Baptists who founded the College of Rhode Island (later Brown University) in 1764.

As the Great Awakening spread into the South, it had a variety of lasting effects. During the late 1740s and 1750s the Reverend Samuel Davies inspired the emergence of Presbyterian congregations in Virginia, thereby calling into question the authority of the established Anglican church. By the mid-1750s swelling numbers of Baptists were openly criticizing the mores of Virginia's planter elite. They started to demand, for example, the "entire banishment of *dancing, gaming,* and sabbath-day diversions."

Sometimes those in authority reacted viciously. A Virginia sheriff "violently jerked" a Baptist speaker off a platform and "beat his head against the ground" before administering "twenty lashes with his horse whip." The victim responded by returning to the stage and preaching even more vigorously "with a great deal of liberty." Persistence in the face of official hostility even led Awakening preachers to spread the gospel among the expanding slave population of the Chesapeake Bay region. This activity stimulated Protestant forms of worship among blacks, who did not forsake their African religious traditions but blended them with Christian faith in a savior who offered eternal life as well as hope for triumphing over oppression in their search for human freedom.

Throughout the British North American provinces, the Great Awakening caused its proponents to question established authority. It also provoked movement toward a clearer definition of fundamental human rights as well as a greater toleration of divergent ideas and the eventual acceptance of religious pluralism. These were hallmark legacies of the Awakening.

None of this came easily, and some of it—especially the emphasis on the search for personal liberty and freedom of conscience, along with the questioning of established authority—may have unwittingly helped prepare many colonists for the political rebellion against Great Britain that lay ahead. Historians have divided opinions on this subject, but most would agree that the Awakening demonstrated that American communities showed considerable strength and resiliency in weathering so much internal divisiveness—a sure sign that Britain's colonists had grown up and matured during the previous 100-year period.

International Wars Beset America

As the seventeenth century unfolded on the North American continent, Spain maintained its grip on Florida as well as on the Gulf coast. French Canadians, operating from bases in Montreal and Quebec, explored throughout the Great Lakes region and then down into the Mississippi Valley. In 1682 an expedition headed by René-Robert Cavelier, Sieur de La Salle, reached the mouth of the Mississippi River. La Salle, who dreamed of a mighty French empire west of the Appalachian Mountains, claimed the whole region for his monarch, Louis XIV.

René-Robert Cavelier, Sieur de La Salle, claimed the whole of the Mississippi Valley for France. He inspired other French leaders with his dream of an empire encircling the British North American colonies.

La Salle's grand vision was ahead of its time. In 1699 the French located their first Louisiana country settlement at Biloxi, Mississippi. A second community soon sprang up on Mobile Bay (present-day Mobile, Alabama). Then in 1718 Jean Baptiste le Moyne, Sieur de Bienville, founded New Orleans, which became the French capital in the region. None of these posts contained a significant population, and they survived by developing close trading ties with various Indian nations.

The French monarchy, consumed by European affairs, did not actively encourage settlement in New France. As late as 1760, no more than 75,000 French subjects lived in all of Canada and the Mississippi Valley. Some farmed or fished, and others traded in furs. Because French numbers were so small, Native Americans did not fear losing ancient tribal lands to them. Solid relations with the Indians was an important advantage for the French, especially after European warfare spilled over into America. Having thousands of potential native allies willing to join in combat against the British colonists made the French a very dangerous foe in North America, as events proved during the imperial wars between 1689 and 1763.

Each of the four wars had a European as well as an American name. The first, the War of the League of Augsburg (1689–1697), known in the colonies as King William's War, was a limited conflict with no major battles in America. What made this war so frightening were bloody border raids—typical was the French and Indian attack on Hannah Dustan's Haverhill—that resulted in a total of about 650 deaths among the English colonists. The Treaty of Ryswick ended the contest without upsetting the balance of international power, since no major exchanges of territory occurred.

Five years later warfare erupted again when Louis XIV of France succeeded in placing his grandson, Philip of Anjou, on the Spanish throne. Other nations believed Louis intended to govern Spain himself, which they viewed as a serious threat to the European balance of power. What ensued was the War of the Spanish Succession (1702–1713), which the colonists called Queen Anne's War—named after the new English monarch Anne (reigned 1702–1714), another Protestant daughter of James II. This time, the British colonists found themselves dueling with Spain as well as France. The French and their native allies launched forays against frontier communities in New England. In 1702 South Carolinians assaulted the Spanish stronghold of St. Augustine, Florida, only to have to stave off a strong counterassault against Charleston four years later. In terms of casualties the war was not particularly bloody. The English colonists lost fewer than 500 persons over an 11-year period.

The peace settlement embodied in the Treaty of Utrecht was a virtual declaration of Britain's growing imperial might. The British realized major territorial gains, including Hudson Bay, Newfoundland, and Nova Scotia in Canada. In addition, they secured from Spain the strategically vital Rock of Gibraltar, guarding the entrance to the Mediterranean Sea, as well as the *Asiento*—a trading pact allowing the English to sell 4800 slaves annually in New Spain.

The scope of Britain's triumph, coming at the expense of its two major European rivals, deterred additional warfare for a quarter century, but further conflict seemed inevitable. In 1721 the Board of Trade urged the "enlarging and extending of the British settlements" in North America as "the most effectual means to prevent the growing power . . . of the French in those parts." Ten years later, board members called for the creation of a military colony in the buffer zone between South Carolina and Florida, and they talked of sending over convicted felons and other desperate persons to act as soldier-settlers.

General **James Oglethorpe** (1696–1785), a wealthy member of Parliament known for his "strong benevolence of soul," heard of these discussions and pursued the idea. A true philanthropist as well as imperialist, Oglethorpe hoped to roll back Spanish influence in America while improving the lot of England's downcast poor, especially imprisoned debtors. In 1732 King George II (reigned 1727–1760) issued a charter for Georgia, granting 21 trustees all the land between the Savannah and Altamaha rivers for 21 years to develop the region, after which the colony

TABLE 3.2

The Imperial Wars, 1689–1763

European Name	American Name	Dates	Peace Treaty
War of the League of Augsburg	King William's War	1689–1697	Ryswick
War of the Spanish Succession	Queen Anne's War	1702–1713	Utrecht
War of Jenkins's Ear		1739–1748	
War of the Austrian Succession	King George's War	1744–1748	Aix-la-Chapelle
Seven Years' War	French and Indian War*	1756–1763	Paris

*This term came into vogue when nineteenth-century historians first employed it. The colonists most often referred to this contest as "the war."

would revert to the Crown and function under royal authority.

Oglethorpe played on anti-Spanish sentiment, and large monetary donations poured in to underwrite the first settlements. Colonists, however, were hard to find, largely because of laws devised by Oglethorpe and the other trustees. To assure good order, they outlawed liquor. To promote personal industry and hard work as well as to spread out settlements in an effective defensive line, they limited individual grants to 500 acres, and they banned slavery. To guard against breaches in the settlement line, parcels of land could be passed only from father to son. Should no male heirs exist, grants would then revert to the trustees.

Those who did migrate to Georgia complained endlessly. Some wanted slaves; others, referring to Oglethorpe as "our perpetual dictator," called for a popular assembly; and they all demanded alcohol. The colony floundered as a social experiment to uplift the poor. The trustees admitted failure by turning Georgia back over to the Crown in 1752, a year ahead of schedule. By that time, they had already conceded on the issues of slavery and strong drink. Thereafter, Georgia looked more and more like South Carolina, with large rice and indigo plantations sustaining the local economy. By 1770, the colony's populace was pushing toward 25,000, nearly half of whom were slaves.

The founding of Georgia angered the Spanish, as did England's cheating on the *Asiento* agreement, especially in relation to a clause that permitted only one English vessel a year to sell goods off the coast of Panama. The *one* turned into shiploads, involving reputed smugglers like Captain Robert Jenkins, whom the Spanish caught in 1731. As a warning to others, his captors cut off his ear. Seven years later Jenkins appeared before Parliament and held high the severed remains of his ear to affirm Spanish brutality. When asked to describe his feelings while facing mu-

tilation, he boldly stated: "I commended my soul to God, and my cause to my country!"

Jenkins's testimony was part of an orchestrated campaign by powerful merchants in England to provoke anti-Spanish sentiment, with the hope of using cries for war to gain more trading rights in New Spain. In 1739 the War of Jenkins's Ear resulted. Then a dispute among rival European claimants over who belonged on the Austrian throne—male aspirants were upset by the rightful accession of Queen Maria Theresa—brought England and France to formal blows in the War of the Austrian Succession, which the colonists called King George's War (1744–1748).

In 1740, before the French became involved, James Oglethorpe mounted an unsuccessful expedition against Florida. In 1741 a combined British-colonial force attempted to capture the major Spanish port of Cartagena. The effort was a disaster, with three-fourths of the 3000 American troops dying from disease. Then in June 1745 a New England army achieved a brilliant victory against the French: After a lengthy siege some 4000 colonists under the command of William Pepperrell, a prominent merchant from Maine, captured the mighty fortress of Louisbourg, the so-called Gibraltar of the New World guarding the entrance to the St. Lawrence River. Here was a remarkable American victory, since the British offered only limited naval assistance.

The war cost the British colonists as many as 5000 lives, but the victory at Louisbourg represented the valued harvest of that sacrifice. In 1748 Britain approved the Treaty of Aix-la-Chapelle, a peace settlement that returned Louisbourg to the French in exchange for Madras, India, which the French had captured. The king's negotiators reasoned that Madras was of much greater value as a center for imperial trade—and expansion into other eastern markets—than a huge, non-income-producing fortress in the American wilderness. The colonists were furious

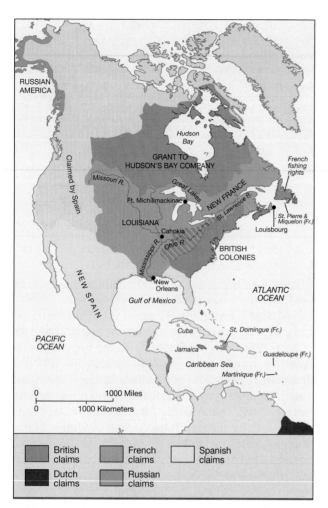

European Claims in North America, 1750

Virginia were among those casting a covetous eye on the development of the Ohio valley. With the backing of London merchants one group formed the Ohio Company in 1747 and two years later secured a grant of 200,000 acres from the Crown. Should the company settle 200 families in the valley within seven years, its investors would receive a patent to an additional 300,000 acres.

Determined to secure the region against encroaching Anglo-American traders and land speculators, the French in the early 1750s started constructing a chain of forts in a line running southward from Lake Erie in western Pennsylvania. They decided to locate their principal fortress—and trading station—at the strategic point where the Monongahela and Allegheny rivers join to form the Ohio River (the site of modern-day Pittsburgh).

By 1753 the British ministry knew of these plans and ordered colonial governors to challenge the French advance and "repel force by force" if necessary. Virginia's Governor Robert Dinwiddie, an investor in the Ohio Company, acted quickly. He sent a young major of militia, 21-year-old **George Washington,** whose older half-brother Lawrence was also an Ohio Company investor, to northwestern Pennsylvania with a message to get out. Politely, the French declined.

In the spring of 1754 Washington led 200 Virginia soldiers toward the forks of the Ohio River and learned that the French were already there constructing Fort Duquesne. Foolishly, he skirmished with a French party, killing 10 and capturing 21. Washington then hastily retreated and constructed Fort Necessity, but a superior French and Indian force attacked on July 3. Facing extermination, Washington surrendered and signed articles of capitulation on July 4, 1754, which permitted him to lead his troops back to Virginia as prisoners of war. Out of these circumstances erupted a world war that cost France the whole of its North American empire.

At the very time (June 1754) that Washington was preparing to defend Fort Necessity, delegates from seven colonies had gathered in Albany, New York, to plan for their defense in case of war and to secure active support from the powerful Iroquois Confederacy. The Indian chiefs readily accepted 30 wagons loaded with gifts but did not promise to turn their warriors loose on the French. So as not to get caught on the losing side and face eviction from their ancient tribal lands in New York, the Iroquois assumed a posture of neutrality, waiting to see which side was winning the war. Some Senecas did fight for the French; but when the tide shifted in favor of the English after 1758, the Iroquois helped crush the French.

In other major business at the conference, delegates Benjamin Franklin and Thomas Hutchinson

about this decision, but they were powerless to do anything except complain among themselves about their subordinate—and unappreciated—status in the empire.

Showdown: The Great War for the Empire

The treaty of Aix-la-Chapelle really settled nothing. The three combatants were on a showdown course, and this time warfare would result from conflicting interests in America. In 1748 fur traders from Pennsylvania and Virginia began establishing contacts with natives in the Ohio River valley. The French, who had controlled the fur trade in that region, responded by warning all tribes to stop dealing with the land-hungry English who, as one French envoy stated, "are much less anxious to take away your peltries than to become masters of your lands."

This observation was essentially correct. With the boom in colonial population, leading planters in

This woodcut, displayed in the *Pennsylvania Gazette*, failed to overcome long-standing jealousies that thwarted attempts at intercolonial cooperation.

proposed an intercolonial plan of government, known as the Albany Plan of Union. The idea was to have a "grand council" made up of representatives from each colony who would meet with a "president general" appointed by the Crown to plan for defense, and even to tax the provinces on an equitable basis, in keeping the North American colonies secure from external enemies. The Plan of Union stirred little interest at the time, since the provincial assemblies were not anxious to share their prerogatives, especially that of taxation, with anyone. The plan's significance lay in its attempt to effect intercolonial cooperation against a common enemy—an important precedent for later years.

Leaders in England ignored the Albany Plan of Union, but the Fort Necessity debacle resulted in a fateful decision to send Major General **Edward Braddock,** an unimaginative 60-year-old officer who had never commanded troops in battle, to Virginia. Braddock arrived in February 1755 with two regiments of redcoats and orders to raise additional troops among the Americans. He eventually got his army of 3000 moving—Washington came along as a volunteer officer—toward Fort Duquesne. On July 9, about eight miles from the French fort, a much smaller French and Indian force nearly destroyed the British column, leaving two-thirds of Braddock's soldiers dead or wounded.

Washington, appalled by one of the worst defeats in British military history, spoke of being "most scandalously beaten by a trifling body of men." Braddock himself sustained mortal wounds; but before he died, he stated wryly: "We shall better know how to deal with them another time."

Braddock's defeat was an international embarrassment, yet King George II and his advisers hesi-

tated to plunge into full-scale war. They knew the financial burden would be immense. Finally, a formal declaration of war came in May 1756. The Seven Years' War (1756–1763), later referred to in America as the French and Indian War, more accurately should be called "the great war for the empire." Certainly **William Pitt** (1708–1778), the king's new chief minister, viewed North America as the place "where England and Europe are to be fought for." Not a modest man, Pitt stated categorically that he alone could "save England and no one else can."

Pitt's strategic plan was straightforward. Letting King Frederick the Great of Prussia, Britain's ally, bear the brunt of warfare in Europe, Pitt placed the bulk of England's military resources in America with the intent of eradicating New France. He also advanced a group of talented young officers, such as General **James Wolfe,** over the heads of less capable men. His plans paid off in a series of carefully orchestrated military advances that saw Quebec fall in

Significant Battles of the French and Indian War, 1756–1763

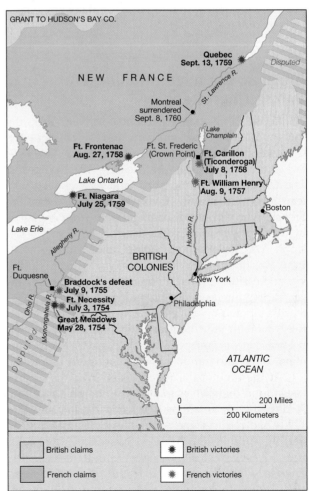

General Edward Braddock's failure to understand the nature of forest warfare and his underestimation of his opponents' abilities led to his disastrous defeat at Fort Duquesne. Braddock and his troops were ambushed by a force of French and Indian warriors numbering less than half the size of the English group. The General was wounded in the attack and died three days later.

September 1759 to the forces of General Wolfe. Then in September 1760 with hardly an exchange of musket fire, Montreal surrendered to the army of General Jeffrey Amherst.

Allies as Enemies: Making War on the Cherokees

Unlike the Six Nations of Iroquois in New York, the four most powerful southern Indian nations—the Cherokees, Chickasaws, Choctaws, and Creeks—lacked unity of purpose when dealing with Europeans. The Choctaws, residing north and east of New Orleans, became heavily involved in trade with the French, who did not discourage them from engaging in warfare with the Chickasaws of northern Mississippi. The Creeks, who inhabited lands running north from Florida into central Alabama and western Georgia, successfully played off English, French, and Spanish trading interests in maintaining their territorial integrity. Sporadic warfare, however, denoted Creek relations with the Cherokees, whose territory encompassed the western portions of Virginia, North Carolina, and South Carolina as well as eastern Tennessee.

At the time of the Seven Years' War, the Cherokees found themselves in a very vulnerable position. A devastating smallpox epidemic during the late 1730s had reduced their numbers by as much as 50 percent to about 10,000 persons. In seeking to restabilize themselves, the Cherokees drew closer to the English. They strengthened trading ties and generally ignored the ominous appearance of frontier set-

tlers, among them many Scots-Irish, who were beginning to squat and farm in the easternmost portions of their tribal lands. After Braddock's defeat, the Cherokees even agreed to help fight the French, hoping in return to get lower prices for British trade goods along with increased supplies of gunpowder.

Then in 1758 a handful of Cherokee warriors coming home from service in the British ranks fell to fighting with western Virginia militiamen and settlers. Both sides lifted scalps, and two years of bloody combat ensued. The Cherokee War of 1759–1761 cost many lives and did not end until an expeditionary force of 2800 British regulars and frontier militiamen, accompanied by Indian support units, among them some Chickasaws, marched into the heart of Cherokee territory and destroyed at least 15 principal villages and hundreds of acres of crops. In the peace settlement that followed in December 1761, the Cherokees made land concessions along the eastern edge of their territory, based on the soon-to-be-broken promise that white settlers would not push beyond this boundary.

A determined people, the Cherokees eventually recovered from the devastation rained upon them in the midst of the Seven Years' War by their English allies. They would keep resisting, but in another seventy years they would have to accept, as would other Native Americans of the Southeast, resettlement in designated enclaves across the Mississippi River (see Chapter 10). Whether this long-term outcome would have been different had the southern nations found the means to rally together in some form of pan-Indian resistance movement will never be known.

CHRONOLOGY OF KEY EVENTS

1651–
1673   Parliament passes Navigation Acts to ensure that the colonies trade within the emerging English empire

1664   Dutch settlers in New Netherland surrender to the English, who rename the colony New York

1676   Bacon's Rebellion occurs in Virginia

1681–
1682   William Penn founds Pennsylvania as a "holy experiment" in which diverse groups of people all live together homogeneously

1682   La Salle claims the Louisiana country for France

1684–
1688   England revokes the Massachusetts Bay Colony charter and eliminates representative assemblies in all colonies east of New Jersey

1686   The Crown establishes the Dominion of New England

1688–
1689   The English drive James II from the throne in the Glorious Revolution and replace him with William and Mary

1689   Massachusetts successfully rebels against the Dominion of New England; Leisler's Rebellion occurs in New York; Coode's uprising disrupts Maryland's government

1692   Witchcraft scare in Salem, Massachusetts, results in the execution of 20 women and men

1699   Parliament prohibits the export of woolen products from America

1733   Parliament passes the Molasses Act, which requires colonies to pay a high duty on molasses or rum imported from the foreign West Indies

1739–
1740   George Whitefield begins preaching tours that turn local revivals into the Great Awakening

1749   Ohio Company obtains from the British government a 200,000-acre grant to western territory

1750   Parliament passes the Iron Act, which prohibits colonists from expanding the production of finished iron or steel products

1754   Albany Congress draws up a plan to unite the 13 colonies under a single government; George Washington defends Fort Necessity and helps to bring on the Seven Years' War

1759   British forces under General James Wolfe conquer Quebec; warfare erupts along the southern frontier between the Cherokee Nation and English settlers

1763   Treaty of Paris ends the Seven Years' War

CONCLUSION

The fall of the French empire in North America took place in the face of mounting antagonism between British military leaders and the colonists. Americans enlisted in provincial regiments and fought beside British redcoats, but most did not care for the experience. They found the king's regulars to be rough, crude, and morally delinquent. They viewed the king's officers as needlessly overbearing and aristocratic. They resented being treated as inferiors by the British.

Young George Washington explained how Virginia's recruits "behaved like men, and died like soldiers" during Braddock's defeat, as compared to the British regulars, who "behaved with more cowardice than it is possible to conceive." On the other hand,

General James Wolfe later described provincial troops as "the dirtiest most contemptible cowardly dogs that you can conceive." The provincials, concluded another British officer, were a "naturally obstinate and ungovernable people, . . . utterly unacquainted with the nature of subordination in general."

The Americans were proud of their contributions to the triumphant British empire. They hoped the Crown would begin treating them with greater respect. Home government leaders, however, thought more like the British military officers in America. They believed that the colonists had done more to serve themselves than the British empire during the Seven Years' War. Because of so many problems related to the war, the Crown would soon prove to be less indulgent toward the "obstinate and ungovernable" American colonists.

Apparently the king's ministers had learned little from the previous 100 years of British-American history. Before 1690, when the laws by which the empire operated became too restrictive, colonial resistance ensued. After 1690, during the so-called era of salutary neglect, an accommodation of differences assured the Americans of basic rights and some local autonomy, so long as they supported the empire's economic and political objectives. Now more self-assertive than ever before, provincial Americans would once again resist imperial plans to make them more fully subordinate to the will of the parent nation. This time they would even challenge the bonds of empire.

CHAPTER SUMMARY AND KEY POINTS

Toward the middle of the seventeenth century, England began to construct a transatlantic empire based on mercantilist principles. In trying to assert its authority over the flow of commerce and trade, the English home government helped provoke a series of provincial convulsions and rebellions. In the long run an attitude of accommodation prevailed and resulted in the so-called era of salutary neglect toward the colonies, which promoted long-term prosperity in the emerging British Empire. At the same time, various elements worked to transform colonial life, including an expanding population base, Enlightenment thinking, the Great Awakening, and imperial warfare, all of which set the stage for renewed conflict after 1760 between thirteen of England's North American colonies and the home government.

- Between 1660 and 1760, England laid the foundations for a great empire. The home government did so by adopting navigation laws, or rules of trade, designed to promote dynamic economic activity and by developing or acquiring more colonies in the Americas and other parts of the globe.

- In some instances, the colonists openly defied and resisted imperial laws that threatened to undercut their economic prosperity or their claims to basic political rights as freeborn English subjects.

- As Great Britain became embroiled in a series of military contests with France and Spain, leaders in England relied on appointed royal governors and other officials not only to enforce imperial laws in America but also to allow the colonies greater latitude in managing their own local affairs, a key characteristic of the so-called era of salutary neglect.

- The colonists also made substantial contributions when the fighting with France and Spain spilled over into North America. By the early 1760s—after the French had been decisively defeated—the colonists were in a position to challenge their subordinate status with the British Empire.

SUGGESTIONS FOR FURTHER READING

Fred Anderson, *The Crucible of War: The Seven Years' War and the Fate of Empire in British North America, 1754–1766* (2000). Masterful analysis of the war that shaped so many of the issues and events leading to the American Revolution.

Patricia U. Bonomi, *Under the Cope of Heaven: Religion, Society, and Politics in Colonial America* (1986). Balanced account of the Great Awakening in the framework of the firm commitment to religious beliefs among passing generations of English settlers.

John Demos, *The Unredeemed Captive: A Family Story from Early America* (1994). Fascinating study of a Puritan family captured by Indians during Queen Anne's War and one daughter's crossing of cultural boundaries by embracing the Mohawk way of life.

Carol F. Karlsen, *The Devil in the Shape of a Woman: Witchcraft in New England* (1987). Informative investigation that probes the meaning of witchcraft cases in assessing the constrained status of women in colonial society.

Douglas E. Leach, *Roots of Conflict: British Armed Forces and Colonial Americans, 1677–1763* (1986). Suggestive appraisal of the mounting mistrust between British regulars and American colonists that provoked imperial disunity pointing toward rebellion.

Philip D. Morgan, *Slave Counterpoint: Black Life and Culture in the Eighteenth-Century Chesapeake and Lowcountry* (1998). Thoroughly researched comparative study of the social, economic, and cultural interactions between black and white populations in Virginia and South Carolina.

Mary Beth Norton, *In the Devil's Snare: The Salem Witchcraft Crisis of 1692* (2002). Comprehensive effort to place the much-studied witchcraft crisis in its most appropriate contemporary context.

Stephen S. Webb, *1676: The End of American Independence* (1984). Engaging analysis of Bacon's Rebellion, King Philip's War, and the long-term evolution of white-Indian and colonial-imperial relations.

Novels

James Fenimore Cooper, *The Last of the Mohicans* (1826).

_____, *The Pathfinder; or, The Inland Sea* (1840).

Allan W. Eckert, *Wilderness Empire: A Narrative* (1968).

Charles McCarry, *The Bride of the Wilderness* (1988).

Arthur Miller, *The Crucible: A Play in Four Acts* (1953).

Kenneth Roberts, *Northwest Passage* (1937).

MEDIA RESOURCES

Web Sites

Witchcraft in Salem Village
http://etext.virginia.edu/salem/witchcraft/
Extensive archive of the 1692 trials and life in late seventeenth-century Massachusetts.

Salem WitchcraftTrials (1692)
http://www.law.umkc.edu/faculty/projects/ftrials/salem/salem.htm
Images, chronology, court, and official documents from the University of Missouri—Kansas City Law School.

Colonial Documents
http://www.yale.edu/lawweb/avalon/18th.htm
The key documents of the Colonial Era are reproduced here, as are some of the important documents from earlier and later time periods in American History.

History Buff's Reference Library
http://www.historybuff.com/library/refseventeen.html
Brief journalistic essays on newspaper coverage of sixteenth- to eighteenth-century American history.

Benjamin Franklin Documentary History Web Site
http://www.english.udel.edu/lemay/franklin/
University of Delaware professor J. A. Leo LeMay tells the story of Franklin's varied life in seven parts on this intriguing site.

Jonathan Edwards
http://www.jonathanedwards.com/
Speeches by this famous minister of the Great Awakening are on this site.

The French and Indian War
http://web.syr.edu/~laroux/
This site is about French soldiers who came to New France between 1755 and 1760 to fight in the French and Indian War.

KEY TERMS

Mercantilism   (p. 63)

Enumerated goods   (p. 63)

Navigation System   (p. 63)

Holy experiment   (p. 66)

Salutary neglect   (p. 73)

Redemptioners   (p. 74)

Europeanizing   (p. 76)

Enlightenment   (p. 78)

Rationalism   (p. 78)

Great Awakening   (p. 79)

New Lights   (p. 82)

Old Lights   (p. 82)

Asiento   (p. 84)

PEOPLE YOU SHOULD KNOW

Hannah Dustan   (p. 61)

Eliza Lucas Pinckney   (p. 61)

James, Duke of York (King James II)   (p. 65)

William Penn   (p. 66)

Sir William Berkeley   (p. 68)

Nathaniel Bacon   (p. 68)

Sir Edmund Andros   (p. 69)

Sir Isaac Newton   (p. 78)

Benjamin Franklin   (p. 78)

Cotton Mather   (p. 78)

Jonathan Edwards   (p. 79)

George Whitefield   (p. 79)

James Oglethorpe   (p. 84)

George Washington   (p. 86)

Edward Braddock   (p. 87)

William Pitt   (p. 87)

James Wolfe   (p. 87)

REVIEW QUESTIONS

1. Define *mercantilism* and trace its implementation in relation to England's North American colonies after 1650. Were the Navigation Acts a burden or a benefit to these colonies?

2. Compare and contrast the factors that led to the establishment of the Middle Colonies (New York, New Jersey, Pennsylvania, and Delaware) in relation to those that resulted in the founding of the New England and southern colonies. What were the most important differences and similarities?

3. What were the major reasons for the political and social upheavals in Virginia, Massachusetts, New York, and Maryland during the 1670s and 1680s? What impact did all of this turmoil have on the long-term development of the colonies?

4. What were the Enlightenment and the Great Awakening, and how did they affect colonial society, culture, and politics? How did these movements relate to the "Europeanizing" of the colonies?

5. Describe the ongoing military conflict among the British, French, and Spanish in the Americas from the 1690s through the 1750s. What competing interests were at stake, and why did the British ultimately emerge triumphant in 1763?

4 Breaking the Bonds of Empire, 1760–1775

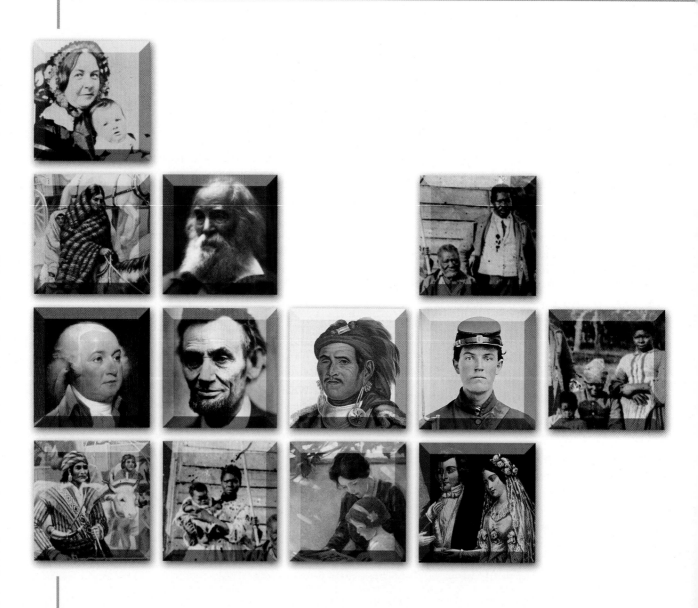

SAMUEL ADAMS: THE MAN OF THE REVOLUTION

Samuel Adams (1722–1803) was "truly the *man of the Revolution*," wrote Thomas Jefferson. In the port city of Boston, Massachusetts, Adams was the prime instigator of protest against the new wave of imperial policies adopted by King and Parliament after the Seven Years' War. He was an authentic popular leader, but he preferred to operate as anonymously as possible in guiding the resistance movement. Adams was by nature a secretive person who late in life destroyed many personal records relating to his revolutionary political activities. Perhaps he had something to hide.

"The great Mr. Adams," as one contemporary referred to him during the 1760s, had grown up with many advantages in life. His father, "Deacon" Samuel, was a prospering maltster (manufacturer of malt, a basic ingredient in beer and distilled spirits). The deacon wanted his son to become a Congregational minister, so he sent him off to Harvard College. In 1740 Samuel emerged with a bachelor's degree, a reputation for free spending and excessive drinking, for which he once paid a heavy fine, and little desire to become a clergyman. Always proud of his Puritan heritage, Adams remained a lifelong student of Scripture, but his primary career interest was politics.

The year 1740 turned out to be disastrous for Adams's father. As a community leader the deacon had become deeply involved in a plan to provide individuals with paper currency for local business transactions. The deacon and others established a "land bank" that would lend out money to persons who put up collateral in the form of real estate. The bank's paper money could then be used to purchase goods and services—and even pay debts as legal tender.

The directors of the Massachusetts Land Bank believed they were performing a public service. Wealthy merchants, however, thought otherwise. They viewed such paper currencies with great skepticism. Only money properly backed by **specie,** such as gold or silver, they argued, could hold its value in the marketplace. Under the leadership of a powerful local merchant, **Thomas Hutchinson** (1711–1780), they appealed to the royal governor, who declared the land bank illegal, a position sustained in 1741 by Parliament.

The crushing of the land bank cost Deacon Adams large sums of money that he had invested to help underwrite the venture. As a bank director, he became a

Samuel Adams believed that royalist leaders in Massachusetts wanted to destroy American liberties. He was an organizer of Boston's Sons of Liberty, a vigorous opponent of the Stamp Act, and eventually a leader in the movement for independence. Later he served as governor of Massachusetts.

defendant in lawsuits from others trying to regain funds. He never recovered financially. When the deacon died in 1748, he left his son a legacy of bitterness toward arbitrary royal authority and Crown favorites, such as Thomas Hutchinson, whose actions had ravaged his family's prosperity. In addition, the deacon left Samuel a bequest of lawsuits rather than a handsome patrimony.

Samuel Adams considered his father's ruin an instructive lesson in high-handed, oppressive government, a matter very much on his mind when he accepted an M.A. degree at Harvard's commencement in 1743. Although Samuel did not address those in attendance, his printed topic was "whether it be lawful to resist the supreme magistrate, if the commonwealth cannot be otherwise preserved?" Five years later he helped found a short-lived newspaper, the *Independent Advertiser*, in which he repeatedly warned his readers to be on guard against power-hungry royal officials, men under whose authority "our liberties must needs degenerate."

Having no desire to continue his father's business, Samuel barely kept his own family in food and clothing. What little income he earned came from a number of minor political offices. In 1746 he won election as a clerk of the Boston market; in 1753 he became town scavenger; and in 1756 he assumed duties as a collector of local taxes for the town government. He held the latter post until declining reelection in 1765. Samuel had no other choice, since he was £8000 behind in his tax collections and facing legal prosecution to produce the delinquent sum.

Samuel Adams had not taken the money for himself. He simply had not collected taxes from hard-pressed Bostonians who, like himself, were struggling to make ends meet. Adams regularly accepted any good explanation—the outbreak of illness in some families and the loss of jobs in others. Boston's economy was stagnant, and unskilled workers were especially hard pressed. As Adams was also aware, each time he did not enforce a collection he made a friend. By the early 1760s he had built up a loyal following of admirers who considered him a good and decent man committed to protecting their interests.

Even as he earned the gratitude of Boston's ordinary citizens, Adams did not lose sight of his adversaries. He particularly loathed Thomas Hutchinson, whose stature as a wealthy merchant with wide-ranging imperial connections had helped him gain a number of prominent offices. In 1758 Hutchinson secured a Crown appointment as the Bay Colony's lieutenant governor. He was already holding a local probate judgeship, was the ranking local militia officer, and was serving as an elected member of the governor's council (the upper house of the General Court). Then in 1760 Hutchinson received appointment to the post of chief judge of the superior court. His combined annual salary from these offices was around £400 sterling, ten times the amount of an average family's yearly income.

Samuel Adams worried about having so much power placed in the hands of one favored plural officeholder, especially Hutchinson, the very person he held most responsible for wrecking the land bank and his father's finances. In the days ahead when Hutchinson and other royal officials in Massachusetts tried to implement the new imperial policies, Adams was ready to protest and resist. His allies in the streets would be the ordinary people, and they set a particularly defiant example for the broader resistance movement throughout the 13 provinces. Whether Adams acted out of personal rancor toward Hutchinson or purely to defend American liberties was one of the secrets he carried to his grave, even as contemporaries remembered him both in Europe and America as "one of the prime movers of the late Revolution."

The outbreak of the American Revolution can be traced directly to the year 1763 when British leaders began to tighten the imperial reins. The colonists protested vigorously, and communications started to break down, so much so that a permanent rupture of political affections began to take place. No one in 1763 had any idea the developing crisis would shatter the bonds of empire. That, however, is exactly what took place when the American colonists, after a dozen years of bitter contention with their parent nation, finally proceeded to open rebellion in 1775.

PROVOKING AN IMPERIAL CRISIS

In 1763 British subjects everywhere toasted the Treaty of Paris which ended the Seven Years' War. The empire had gained territorial jurisdiction over

North America, 1763

With the signing of the Treaty of Paris, Great Britain received almost all of France's holdings in North America.

British

Dutch

French

Russian

Spanish

French Canada and all territory east of the Mississippi River, except for a tiny strip of land around New Orleans that France deeded to Spain. The Spanish, in turn, who also took over French territory west of the Mississippi River, had to cede the Floridas to Britain to regain the Philippines and Cuba, the latter having fallen to a combined Anglo-American force in 1762. The British likewise made substantial gains in India. From the colonists' perspective, eradicating the French "menace" from North America was a cause for jubilation that should have signaled a new era of imperial harmony. Such was not to be the case.

A Legacy of War-Related Problems

For the chief ministers in Great Britain under the vigorous new monarch **George III** (reigned 1760–1820), who was 25 years old in 1763, the most pressing issue was Britain's national debt. During the Seven Years' War it had skyrocketed from £75 million to £137 million sterling. Annual interest payments on the debt amounted to £5 million alone. Advisers to the Crown worried about ways to get the debt under control, a most difficult problem considering the newly won territories that the home government now had to govern.

King George III, shown here in his coronation robes, was 22 when he acceded to the English throne in 1760.

Closely linked to the debt issue was the question of American smuggling activity. Many colonial merchants, eager for profits of any kind, had traded illegally with the enemy during the war. Even though the Royal Navy had blockaded French and Spanish ports in the Caribbean, traders from New England and elsewhere used various pretexts to effect business deals. Some claimed to sail on missions of benevolence and exchanged prisoners of war to cover up illegal trading operations. These wily merchants and seamen carried more goods than prisoners, and the products they traded helped sustain the French and Spanish war efforts.

When chief war minister William Pitt, normally an advocate of American interests, learned in 1760 that 100 or more colonial vessels flying British flags were in the Spanish port of Montecristi, he sputtered with rage and ordered customs officers in North America to search inbound vessels with greater rigor. The minister was furious about such quasi-treasonous activity and was ready in 1763 to tighten controls on colonial commerce.

A host of issues relating to newly won territories to the north and west of the Anglo-American settlements also concerned the king's ministers. They especially worried about the financial burden of prolonged warfare on the frontier, should land-hungry white settlers keep pushing into Indian hunting grounds. The vacuum created by the end of French authority greatly concerned Native Americans. They had little reason to trust British traders and settlers. Trade goods, they soon found out, were suddenly more expensive in the absence of French competition. Furthermore, British officials hesitated to deal in firearms and gunpowder. Also aggravating relations were tribal suspicions that royal military officers had given them diseased blankets—taken from soldiers who had died of smallpox—during recent wartime parleys.

Native American prophets, among them Neolin, a Delaware Indian, started traveling among western tribes and arguing for resistance. Neolin urged a return to earlier tribal cultural practices and called for an alliance to drive the English from western forts. **Pontiac,** an Ottawa war chief who feared the loss of yet more land in the absence of French support, believed Neolin's words. He built a pan-Indian alliance that included Chippewas, Delawares, Hurons, Mingoes, Potawatomis, and Shawnees. Pontiac's initial targets were former French forts that the British now occupied and for which they refused to pay rents—as the French had regularly done in recognition of tribal ownership of the land.

Beginning in May 1763, Pontiac's warriors struck with a vengeance at these posts, putting the major fortress at Detroit under heavy siege and attacking

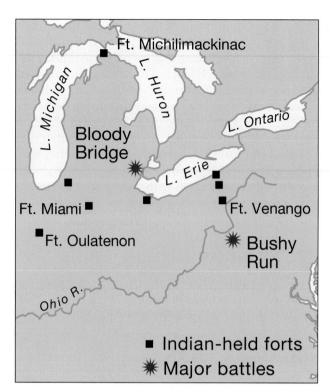

Pontiac's Rebellion

Pontiac, an Ottawa war chief, rebelled against white settlers who were moving onto tribal lands.

white settlements running in a southwesterly arc from New York through western Pennsylvania to Virginia. Only a severe drubbing at Bushy Run, Pennsylvania, in August 1763 turned the tide of bloody frontier warfare against the Indians. By autumn Pontiac's allies began drifting back to their villages, and they also lifted their siege of Detroit. When the final toll was taken, Pontiac's uprising had cost frontier white settlers some 2000 lives; a similar number of Native Americans died as well.

It fell to **George Grenville** (1712–1770), brother-in-law of William Pitt and a powerful leader in England, to solve these imperial problems. George III personally despised the humorless Grenville, but he needed the votes of Grenville's sizable following in Parliament, which was large enough to secure majorities for pressing legislative issues.

Grenville, who held strong anti-American feelings, became the king's chief minister in April 1763. In the common metaphor of the times, he viewed the provincials as spoiled children in need of a good spanking. As Grenville proclaimed before Parliament, "Great Britain protects America; America is bound to yield obedience." An ominous moment in British-American relations was at hand.

Getting Tough with the Americans

Grenville was not a rash man. A mercantilist in his thinking, he believed the colonists had forgotten their subordinate status in the empire. They needed to be reminded of their essential purpose, that of serving the parent nation. Having studied the issues carefully, Grenville struck hard on various fronts, leaving no doubt that a new era had dawned in Britain's administration of the American provinces.

Grenville made his first moves in early October 1763 through two administrative orders, each approved by the king's cabinet. The first, known as the Orders in Council of 1763, stationed British naval vessels in American waters with the intent of running down and seizing all colonial merchant ships suspected of illegal trading activity. Should juryless **vice-admiralty courts** condemn these vessels on charges of smuggling, British naval captains and crews would share in profits from the public sales of both the erring colonial ships and their cargoes. The goal was to put an end to American smuggling while compelling the colonists to start paying more trade duties into royal coffers.

The second order, known as the Proclamation of 1763, dealt with the West. It addressed matters of government for the new British territories, including the temporary organization of such provinces as Quebec. It also mandated that a line be drawn from north to south along "the heads or sources of any of the rivers which fell into the Atlantic Ocean from the west and northwest." Deeply concerned by the news of Pontiac's uprising, the ministry's objective was to stop white incursions onto native lands. As such, territory west of the Proclamation line was forever to be "reserved to the Indians."

The Proclamation policy may have reflected some desire for humane treatment of Native Americans; however, the cabinet's primary concern was to avoid costly Indian wars. Some cabinet leaders, furthermore, did not relish the prospect of American settlements spreading too far inland from the Atlantic coastline. If the colonists built communities across the mountains and out of the reach of the imperial trading network, they would of necessity begin manufacturing all sorts of products—and might, in time, compete with the British Isles for control of seaboard markets. From the imperial perspective, the parent nation's best interest lay in keeping the colonists on the eastern side of the Appalachian Mountains.

The Proclamation of 1763 also related to another policy decision of pivotal consequence. To keep control over both white settlers and Indians, the cabinet had already decided to garrison up to 10,000 British regulars in North America. Pontiac's uprising and the Proclamation policy determined that, at least initially, some of these redcoats would be ordered out onto the frontier.

The most critical matter was who would pay for these redcoats, an issue with the potential to provoke a serious imperial crisis if King and Parliament decided the colonists should assume that responsibility. Grenville had received estimates that the military force would cost at least £250,000 a year. Given the imposing home government debt, the chief minister soon went before Parliament with plans to tax His Majesty's subjects in America.

Grenville warmed to his task during 1764. He contacted the colonial agents who represented provincial interests in England and asked them for ideas

Colonial Products in the Mid-1700s

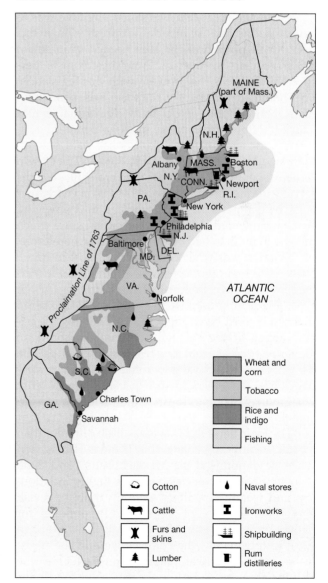

about taxing the colonists. Not surprisingly, they had few thoughts. Nevertheless, fully intent on taxing the colonists, Grenville proceeded with Parliamentary legislation to do just that.

The Revenue Act of April 1764, usually called the Sugar Act, embodied a series of complex regulations relating to the loading and unloading of trading vessels. The purpose was to aid customs collectors in ferreting out smugglers. Even more important, the Sugar Act placed trade duties on a number of foreign goods—coffee, indigo, sugar, and wine—regularly purchased by the colonists. The bill also lowered the trade duty on foreign molasses from 6 to 3 pence per gallon (Parliament further reduced this duty to 1 penny in 1766). The aim of revising downward the Molasses Act duty of 1733 (see p. 72) was to make the fee more collectible and to collect it—in contrast to the earlier period of lax enforcement.

Grenville projected initial annual revenue from the Sugar Act at £40,000. His stated objective was to help offset the costs of imperial administration, in this case only a portion of the sum needed to maintain British regulars in America. From the colonists' perspective, that was the problem with this legislation. The home government's purpose was something more than adopting slight trade duties that would adjust the flow of commerce in the imperial interest. In 1763, for instance, the colonists had paid only an estimated £1800 in imperial trade duties. (The Crown actually spent £8000 that year to operate the customs service in America.) A projected £40,000 in yearly revenue, by comparison, was a sure sign the home government intended to tax the Americans—and much more heavily than had ever been the case heretofore.

Taxation was what Grenville had most in mind; but he also had other concerns, as embodied in Parliament's passage in April of the Currency Act of 1764. This act represented an expansion of legislation directed against New England in 1751. Now the paper money of the colonial governments could no longer be used as legal tender in payment of private debts. Nor could these governments issue any new paper bills, and the Crown expected them to retire what money they had in circulation within a reasonable time frame.

The logic behind this act was little different than that of wealthy merchants like Thomas Hutchinson when he denounced the Massachusetts Land Bank of 1740. Paper currencies could be highly inflationary, and wealthy creditors were invariably peevish about having to accept depreciated local money for debts. They only wanted to deal in hard coin. In 1764, unfortunately, the colonies were in the midst of a severe postwar depression. Reducing the provincial money supply only worsened conditions by forcing colonists to scramble in obtaining money to conduct business—let alone pay increased taxes. If nothing else, the timing of the Currency Act was terrible; it made the Crown appear incredibly insensitive about promoting the economic welfare of the colonies.

Parliament Endorses Direct Taxes

George Grenville was indifferent about the opinions of the colonists. His major goal was to raise a substantial tax revenue in the colonies. He finally got what he wanted with the Stamp Act of March 1765, the capstone of his imperial program. Through the Stamp Act, Parliament asserted for the first time ever its full authority to lay direct taxes, as opposed to indirect (or hidden taxes, such as trade duties) on the colonists.

The Stamp Act was not very subtle. To take effect on November 1, 1765, this legislation required Americans to pay for stamps attached to some 50 items, everything from newspapers, pamphlets, almanacs, and playing cards to port clearance papers for ships, land deeds, wills, and college diplomas. The price of the stamps varied according to the value of the particular items. Grenville estimated the tax would yield about £100,000 per year. All stamps would have to be paid for in hard currency, a virtual impossibility since specie (hard money) continually flowed to Britain to pay for imported goods. Also, violators could be prosecuted in juryless vice-admiralty courts, as well as in regular criminal courts.

George Grenville knew the colonists would not like the Stamp Act, but he justified the plan by declaring that "the [parent] nation has run itself into an immense debt to give them protection." The time had come for Americans to pay for the benefits of being part of the mightiest empire in the western world. Grenville was not asking the colonists to help reduce the home debt, only to assist in meeting the actual costs of imperial administration. For that reason, Parliament earmarked Stamp Act revenues for maintaining the redcoats in America.

Grenville used three lines of reasoning in arguing for the Stamp Act. First, citizens in England had been paying stamp taxes for years. Second, the colonial public debt amounted to only £2.6 million, as compared to £137 million in England. On a per capita basis, each person living in Britain owed approximately 20 times as much as each American (£18 as compared to 18 shillings). With such a light per capita public debt load, the colonists could afford a heavier tax burden. Third, to counter arguments about taxation without representation, Grenville employed the concept of **virtual representation.** He maintained that all English subjects, regardless of where they resided in the empire, enjoyed representation in Parliament. His assertion was that members of Parliament (M.P.s), when they made legislative decisions, did not just represent particular constituents at home but every imperial subject, including all colonial Americans.

Testaments to virtual representation found favor in Parliament, where little pro-American sentiment existed, but proved unconvincing to the colonists. Grenville's thinking, moreover, did not encompass the whole picture. From an economic point of view, if from no other, the colonies were invaluable to the British empire. The provinces so stimulated the home economy, particularly with regard to buying manufactured goods, that a serious trade deficit had developed for the colonists. They had gotten into the habit of importing much more from the British Isles than they exported in return. The trade deficit amounted to £1.6 million for the year 1760. By the early 1770s provincial Americans owed more than £4 million to English and Scottish creditors. This was a major reason that hard money was so difficult to come by in America. It was being drained off constantly to pay these debts.

By only looking at specific governmental costs, Grenville had missed an essential point. Provincial subjects were not just taking from the empire; they also provided a ready, indeed, captive market for British-manufactured commodities. In this sense the Americans were paying a significant price, as measured by the trade deficit, in support of the parent nation.

A few members of Parliament appreciated the inherent value of the provinces and did not think of the colonists as overindulged children. Colonel Isaac Barré, who had served under General James Wolfe at Quebec, was one such person. "They grew by your neglect of them," he stated sharply during the Stamp Act debates in Parliament. Now, the tightening imperial grip would cause "the blood of those *sons of liberty* to recoil within them. . . . And remember I this day told you so, that same spirit of freedom which actuated that people at first, will accompany them still." Barré's words were prophetic. The Stamp Act would truly arouse the Americans.

"LIBERTY, PROPERTY, AND NO STAMPS"

Certainly the colonists were not plotting independence in 1763. They were proud to be subjects of the far-flung British empire, stretching as it did from India in the East across the globe to some 30 American colonies in the West, including such Caribbean is-

lands as Barbados and Jamaica. With the elimination of the French threat in North America, mainland colonists were also experiencing a buoyant new sensation of freedom. Paradoxically, the toughened imperial program came at the very time when the colonists, now needing much less government protection from across the ocean, hoped for a continuation if not expansion of the local autonomy to which they had become accustomed. Psychologically, they were ready for anything but new imperial constraints on their lives.

Emerging Patterns of Resistance

As the Grenville program took shape, the colonists evidenced various emotions. Dismay gave way to disappointment and anger. Initial reactions involved petitioning King and Parliament for a redress of grievances. By the summer of 1765 colonial protest took an extralegal turn as Americans resorted to such tactics of resistance as crowd intimidation and violence, economic boycott, and outright defiance of imperial law. The colonists did not think of themselves as Britain's children. Through their tactics of resistance they were asking to be treated more like adults. Few British officials, however, comprehended this message.

The first statements of protest were quite mild, expressed in a flurry of petitions and pamphlets that laid out an American position with respect to essen-

The Stamp Act, which required Americans to purchase stamps for everything from playing cards to marriage licenses, provoked intense colonial protest. Some newspaper printers expressed their outrage by using a skull and crossbones to mark the spot where the stamp was to be embossed, as shown here in the October 31, 1765, issue of the *Pennsylvania Journal* and *Weekly Advertiser*.

tial political rights. In reaction to the Sugar Act of 1764, Stephen Hopkins of Rhode Island expressed the sentiments of many in his widely read pamphlet, *The Rights of Colonies Examined.* He stated that "British subjects are governed only agreeable to laws to which [they] themselves have [in] some way consented." Hopkins then warned his fellow colonists: "Those who are governed at the will . . . of others, and whose property may be taken from them by taxes, or otherwise, without their own consent, and against their will, are in the miserable condition of slaves." Hopkins's words may be summarized in the phrase "no taxation without representation"—the core argument against Parliamentary taxation.

In many ways protest by pamphlet and petition was so mild in tone during 1764 that George Grenville did not hesitate to argue for more comprehensive taxation plans. The intensity of American ill feeling in reaction to the Stamp Act thus shocked the home government.

First news of the Stamp Act arrived in the provinces during April 1765, which left ample time to organize resistance before its November 1 effective date. Colonial protest soon became very turbulent, with Samuel Adams's Boston taking the lead in the use of more confrontational forms of resistance.

In Massachusetts, as in many other provinces, a small number of royal officials enjoyed the parent nation's political patronage. This group held the most prominent offices in colonial government, and they were known as the "royalist" or "court" political faction. Besides Lieutenant Governor and Chief Justice Thomas Hutchinson, other leading members of the royalist faction were Governor Francis Bernard, Secretary and Councilor **Andrew Oliver,** and Associate Justice and Councilor Peter Oliver (Andrew's younger brother). Hutchinson and the Oliver brothers were natives of New England and had all graduated from Harvard College. They were interrelated by marriage, and they were among the wealthiest citizens in America.

Even though these gentlemen were at the apex of provincial society, their opponents in the "popular" or "country" faction did not defer to them. Besides Samuel Adams, another local leader, the brilliant lawyer **James Otis, Jr.,** viewed the likes of Hutchinson and the Oliver brothers with contempt. In 1760 when Bernard became governor and appointed Hutchinson to the chief judgeship, he ignored the claims of assembly speaker James Otis, Sr., who had been promised this post by an earlier governor. Enraged by Bernard's slight to his father, Otis stated that he would "kindle such a fire in the province as shall singe the governor, though I myself perish in the flames."

Otis was soon speaking out on behalf of American rights and against royal appointees charged with enforcing imperial laws in Massachusetts. Before the end of 1760, for instance, customs collectors in the Bay Colony had started to use blanket search warrants, known as **writs of assistance,** to catch suspected smugglers, particularly those rumored to be trading with the enemy. The writs did not require any form of prior evidence to justify searches; as such, many respected attorneys in England questioned their legality, since they violated the fundamentals of due process in cases of search and seizure.

In 1761 on behalf of merchants in Boston, some number of whom were certainly smugglers, Otis argued against the writs in a well-publicized case before the Massachusetts superior court. Chief Justice Hutchinson ruled in favor of the writs, politely explaining how they were also then in use in England. In turn, Otis declared that the power of King and Parliament had specified boundaries, implying that only tyrants would uphold the use of writs.

Otis and the merchants may have lost, but they had put Hutchinson in an embarrassing position. They portrayed him as a person blinded to the protection of fundamental legal rights because of his insatiable lust for offices and power. Unfortunately for Otis, he would in a few years lose his mental stability. As a consequence, after the mid-1760s Samuel Adams assumed overall leadership of the popular rights faction in Massachusetts politics.

Adams won his first term to the Assembly in 1765 as a representative from Boston. The emerging Stamp Act crisis gave him an opportunity to launch a simultaneous attack on both unacceptable imperial policies and his old political adversaries. The combined assault commenced in August 1765, shortly after citizens learned that none other than Andrew Oliver was the Bay Colony's proposed Stamp Act distributor.

Protest Takes a Violent Turn

Samuel Adams did not participate directly in crowd actions, nor did the informal popular rights governing body, known as the **Loyal Nine.** (Adams and Otis were not members of this group but were the principal guides in directing the politics of defiance.) The Loyal Nine communicated specific protest plans to men like **Ebenezer Mackintosh,** a shoemaker living in the South End of town, and Henry Swift, a cobbler from the North End. Before 1765 these two craft workers were leaders of "leather apron" gangs (workers' associations) from their respective districts. The North End and South End gangs, as the "better sort" of citizens called them, were in reality fraternal organizations providing fellowship for artisans, apprentices, and day laborers.

Each year these leather apron workers looked forward to November 5, known as Pope's Day—referring to an alleged plot in 1605 by Guy Fawkes, a Roman Catholic, to blow up Parliament. November 5 was a traditional anti-Catholic holiday during which leaders like Swift and Mackintosh, holding high crude effigies of the devil and the pope, led throngs of North and South End workers in a march through the streets. These working people vented their anti-Catholic emotions and their fears of satanic influences as they marched; they also readied themselves for the annual fistfight that invariably took place after the two groups converged on the center of Boston. The fighting was so vicious in 1764 that at least one person died.

During the summer of 1765 Samuel Adams and the Loyal Nine convinced the North and South End associators to stop fighting among themselves and to unite in defense of essential political liberties. This juncture proved a critical step in ending any attempted implementation of the Stamp Act in Massachusetts.

On the morning of August 14, 1765, the local populace awoke to find an effigy of Peter Oliver (and a boot, representing Lord Bute, Grenville's predecessor) hanging in an elm tree—later called the Liberty Tree—in the South End of Boston. An appalled Governor Bernard demanded removal of the figures; but no one touched them, knowing they were under the protection of the associators—in time called the Sons of Liberty. That evening Ebenezer Mackintosh, who soon gained the title "Captain General of Liberty Tree," solemnly removed the effigies and exhorted the thousands of Bostonians present to join in a march through the streets. Holding the effigies high on a staff, Mackintosh and Swift led what was an orderly procession. As they marched, the people shouted: "Liberty, Property, and No Stamps."

The crowd worked its way to the dockyards, where the Sons of Liberty ripped apart a warehouse recently constructed by Andrew Oliver. Rumor had it that Oliver intended to store his quota of stamps there. Next, the crowd moved toward Oliver's stately home, which the family had fled. Some of the Sons of Liberty tore up the fence, ransacked the first floor, and imbibed from the well-stocked wine cellar. Others gathered on a hill behind the Oliver residence. Materials from Oliver's warehouse as well as his wooden fence provided kindling for a huge bonfire that ultimately consumed the effigies even as the working men and women of Boston cheered enthusiastically. This crucial crowd action was over by midnight.

Early the next morning, as Hutchinson later wrote, the thoroughly intimidated Oliver "despairing of protection, and finding his family in terror and distress, . . . came to the sudden resolution to resign his office before another night." Mackintosh's crowd, rather than Crown officials, now were in control of Boston. After this action of August 14, moreover, no one thought at all about assuming Oliver's stamp distributorship. Intimidating threats and selective property destruction had preserved the interests of the community over those of the Crown.

Crowds protesting imperial policies—in this case burning tax officials in effigy—were normally made up of ordinary citizens, particularly the working poor.

Had Boston's Sons of Liberty and their leaders been solely concerned with rendering the Stamp Act unenforceable, they would have ceased their rioting after Oliver's resignation; however, they had other accounts to settle. A misleading rumor began circulating through the streets, claiming that Thomas Hutchinson was very much in favor of the Stamp Act, indeed had even helped write the tax plan. As a result, the Sons of Liberty appeared again on the evening of August 26. After a few other intimidating stops, the crowd descended upon Hutchinson's opulent home, one of the most magnificent in the province. They ripped it apart. As the lieutenant governor later described the scene, "they continued their possession until daylight" and "demolished every part of it, except for walls, as lay in their power."

Who started the rumor remains a moot point, but Hutchinson's political enemies were well known. Further, some Bostonians may have vented their frustrations with the depressed local economy by ransacking the property of a well-placed person with key imperial connections who was prospering during difficult times. Whatever the explanation, royal authority in the Bay Colony had suffered another setback. The looming threat of crowd violence gave Samuel Adams and his popular rights faction a powerful presence that Hutchinson and other royalist officials never overcame.

Resistance Spreads Across the Landscape

By rendering the office of stamp distributor powerless, Boston had established a prototype for resistance. Colonists elsewhere were quick to act. Before the end of the month Augustus Johnston, Rhode Island's stamp distributor-designate, had been cowed into submission. In September Maryland's distributor, Zachariah Hood, not only resigned but fled the province after a crowd destroyed his home. Jared Ingersoll was the victim in Connecticut. The local Sons of Liberty met him on the road to Hartford, surrounded him, and demanded his resignation. They then rode with him to Hartford where the staid Ingersoll renounced the office in public, threw his periwig in the air, and cheered for liberty—to the delight of a menacing crowd. By November 1 virtually no one was foolish or bold enough to distribute stamps in America. Only Georgians experienced a short-lived implementation of the despised tax.

While the colonists employed intimidation and violence, they also petitioned King and Parliament. Assembly after assembly prepared remonstrances stating that taxation without representation was a fundamental violation of the rights of English subjects. **Patrick Henry,** a young and aggressive backcountry Virginia lawyer, had a profound influence on these official petitions. Henry first appeared in the Virginia House of Burgesses (lower house of the Assembly) in mid-May 1765. The session, meeting in Williamsburg, was coming to a close. Only a handful of burgesses were still present when Henry proposed seven resolutions. They endorsed the first four, which reiterated the no taxation without representation theme, but rejected the fifth as too categorical a denial of Parliament's authority. Henry did not bother to present his remaining two resolutions.

Some newspapers in other provinces reprinted all seven resolutions. The fifth stated that the Virginia Assembly held "the only exclusive right and power to lay taxes and impositions upon the inhabitants of this colony." The sixth asserted that Virginians were "not bound to yield obedience to any law" not approved by their own assembly. The seventh indicated that anyone thinking otherwise would "be deemed an enemy by His Majesty's colony."

These three resolutions read as if the Virginia burgesses had denied King and Parliament all legislative power over the American provinces. They seemed to advocate some form of dual sovereignty in which the American assemblies held final authority over legislative matters in America—comparable in scope to Parliament's authority over the British Isles. This was a radical concept, indeed too radical for the Virginia burgesses. Still, the reprinting of all seven of the Virginia Resolutions, as they came to be known, encouraged other assemblies to prepare strongly worded petitions during the summer and fall of 1765.

An important example of intercolonial unity, also bearing on the petitioning process, was the **Stamp Act Congress,** held in New York City during October 1765. At the urging of James Otis, Jr., the Massachusetts General Court called for an intercolonial congress to draft a joint statement of grievances. Nine colonies responded, and 27 delegates appeared in New York.

The delegates to the Stamp Act Congress were mostly cautious gentlemen from the upper ranks of society. Their "declarations" on behalf of American rights had a far more conciliatory tone than the Virginia Resolutions. They attested to "all due subordination to that august body, the Parliament of Great Britain." Since "from their local circumstances" Americans could not easily be represented in Parliament, the only way to protect "all the inherent rights and liberties" of the colonists was for Parliament to relinquish its right of taxation, more or less on a permanent basis, to the provincial assemblies. With these words the congress disbanded, having shown that leaders from different colonies could meet together and agree on common principles. The congress also suggested that unified resistance was possible, should events necessitate further intercolonial actions.

Another, more telling blow to the Stamp Act was a widespread economic boycott. Merchants in New York City were the first to act. On October 31 they pledged not to order "goods or merchandise of any nature, kind, or quality whatsoever, usually imported from Great Britain, . . . unless the Stamp Act be repealed." Within a month merchants in the other principal port cities, including Boston and Philadelphia, drafted similar agreements.

On November 1, 1765, commerce in the colonies came to a halt. Trading vessels remained in ports because no stamped clearance papers could be obtained. Courts ceased functioning, since so many legal documents required stamps. Newspapers stopped publication, at least temporarily. For all of their bravado the Americans really did not want to defy the law. As November gave way to December, however, popular leaders began to apply various forms of pressure on more timid citizens. By the beginning of 1766 colonial business and legal activity started returning to normal, and newspaper editors commenced printing again—all in open defiance of the Stamp Act.

George Grenville had grossly miscalculated. Not willing to be treated as errant children, the colonists, in defending their liberties, sent petitions to Parliament, intimidated and harassed royal officials, destroyed property, cut off the importation of British goods, and, finally, openly defied the law. Americans hoped for a return to the old days of salutary neglect, but they could not be sure whether the king's ministers would back down in the face of such determined resistance.

Parliament Retreats

Instability in the British cabinet, as much as American protest, helped bring about repeal of the Stamp Act. George III had never liked Grenville. In July 1765 the king asked him to step aside in favor of the Marquis of Rockingham, who was more sympathetic toward the Americans. Rockingham's political coalition was brittle, and his term as chief minister lasted just long enough to bring about repeal of the Stamp Act.

Looking for political allies, Rockingham took advantage of pressure from English traders and manufacturers who were extremely worried about the American boycott. He also linked arms with William Pitt, England's most influential politician. Pitt was eloquent in the repeal debates before Parliament. He exhorted his fellow M.P.s to recognize the colonists as "subjects of this kingdom equally entitled . . . to all the natural rights of mankind and peculiar privileges of Englishmen." The M.P.s listened and in March 1766 repealed the Stamp Act.

Home government leaders had by no means accepted colonial arguments. They insisted on a face-saving statement designed to make sure everyone understood that King and Parliament were the supreme legislative voices of the empire. In conjunction with rescinding the Stamp Act, the M.P.s approved the Declaratory Act, which denied the claims of American assemblies to "the sole and exclusive

In this political cartoon, mournful political leaders in England carry the dead Stamp Act to its grave after its repeal in 1766.

THE PEOPLE SPEAK

The Loyal Nine Plan a Stamp Act Protest

Henry Bass was a member of Boston's Loyal Nine, a group of artisans who worked closely with the likes of Samuel Adams and James Otis, Jr., in organizing resistance to unwanted British policies. Bass, a small-scale merchant, wrote the letter that follows to his future father-in-law after a crowd demonstration on December 17, 1765, directed against Andrew Oliver and the Stamp Act. A few months back on the evening of August 14, Oliver had been subjected to a boisterous crowd action that convinced him not to become the Stamp Act distributor for Massachusetts. In December 1765, Bostonians were hesitating to proceed to business as usual in open defiance of the act, which had become law on November 1. Samuel Adams was looking for a means to rally the local populace to more extreme resistance. Then he learned that Oliver's official commission as stamp distributor had just arrived on a vessel from England. Here was an issue the popular leader could draw upon to help bring about complete defiance.

The December 16 issue of the *Boston Gazette,* the popular rights paper edited by John Gill and Benjamin Edes, another Loyal Nine member, carried a warning about the commission's presence. With this news functioning as a signal, the Loyal Nine gathered secretly that very evening regarding "what further should be done" about Oliver, since they could not be sure "what had been done heretofore," referring to the crowd action back on August 14, was "Conclusive" enough in terms of his resignation.

Escorted from his home by street leader Ebenezer Mackintosh, the much-humiliated Oliver did appear before a boisterous crowd at the Liberty Tree near noontime on December 17. He again renounced his commission and even, with some prodding, cheered for liberty. Oliver's well-managed resignation helped galvanize the populace to defy the law and proceed with business without stamps.

Bass's letter tells the story of the December 17 crowd action and the role of the Loyal Nine in staging the event. Without this letter, their actions might have remained "a profound Secret" for all time with street leader Ebenezer Mackintosh getting all the credit as well as paying any consequences, had the Crown had the determination to enforce its will. These kinds of crowd actions, however, along with other forms of resistance, convinced King and Parliament to repeal the Stamp Act in March 1766.

> Boston 19 Dec. 1765
>
> Hon[d] Sir [Samuel Phillips Savage],
>
> On seeing Messrs. Edes & Gills last mondays Paper [December 16], the Loyall Nine repair'd the same Evg to Liberty Hall, in order to Consult what further should be done respecting Mr. Oliver's Resignation, as what had been done heretofore, we tho't not Conclusive & upon some little time debating we apprehended it would be most Satisfactory to the Publick to send a Letter to desire him to appear under Liberty tree at 12 o'Clock on Tuesday [December 17], to make a publick Resignation under Oath:—the copy of W[ch] the Advertisement, his Message, Resignation & Oath you have Inclos'd.
>
> the whole affair transacted by the Loyall Nine, in writing the Letter, getting the advertisements Printed, which were all done after 12 oClock monday Night, the advertisements Pasted up to the am[o] of a hun[4] was all done from 9 to 3 oClock.
>
> you also have a Copy, of w[t] he said to the publick as near as we can Recolect: he thank't the Gent[m] for the Polite Letter & treatment he Rec[d]. . . . The whole was Conducted to the General Satisfaction of the publick.
>
> & upon the Occasion we that Evg. Had a very Genteel Supper provided to which we invited your very good friends M[r] S.[amuel] A.[dams] and E.[des] & G.[ill] & three or four others & spent the Evening in a very agreeable manner Drinkg Healths &c.
>
> Dr. Sir, I must desire you'd keep this a profound Secret & not to Let any Person see these papers, & should be glad when you come to town youd bring them with you, as we have no other Copys, & choose to keep them as Archives. We do every thing in order to keep this & the first Affair Private: and are not a little pleas'd to hear that M[c]Intosh has the Credit of the whole Affair.
>
> we Endeavour to keep up the Spirit which I think is as great as ever.
>
> I give you joy in the Custom house being Opened, & I hope soon to advise you of the Courts of justice being the Same, I am w[t] my best wishes for you & Family, health & Happiness your affe. friend
>
> [Henry Bass]

Source: Letter printed in George P. Anderson, "A Note on Ebenezer Mackintosh," in *Proceedings of the Colonial Society of Massachusetts* (February 1926), pp. 355–356.

right of imposing duties and taxes . . . in the colonies." The Declaratory Act forcefully asserted that Parliament had "full power and authority to make laws and statutes . . . , *in all cases whatsoever.*" Repealing the Stamp Act had been only for the sake of imperial harmony; Parliament still had the right to tax all British subjects anytime it chose. The M.P.s had stated their position—and in terms at odds with the stance taken by the Americans.

A SECOND CRISIS: THE TOWNSHEND DUTIES

What everyone needed in 1766 was an extended cooling-off period, but that was not to happen. The Rockingham ministry, which might well have left the colonists alone, collapsed in the summer of 1766. George III called for a new cabinet. He wanted William Pitt to become his chief minister. In poor health, Pitt agreed to organize a ministry in return for peerage status as the Earl of Chatham. He retired to the House of Lords, letting others provide for legislation in the House of Commons. One man in particular, Chancellor of the Exchequer **Charles Townshend** (1725–1767), sometimes called "Champagne Charlie" because of his penchant for that bubbly drink, charged into the leadership void. To the amazement of many, Townshend proclaimed that he knew how to tax the colonists. The result was the ill-advised Townshend Duties of 1767.

Formulating a New Taxation Scheme

Benjamin Franklin, who was in England serving as an agent for various colonies, inadvertently helped formulate Townshend's plan. In a lengthy interview before Parliament during the repeal debates, Franklin, who was out of touch with American sentiment, stated emphatically that the colonists only objected to **direct** or "internal" **taxes,** such as those embodied in the Stamp Act. They did not object, he claimed, to **indirect** or "external" **taxes,** which may be defined as duties placed on trade goods for the purpose of obtaining imperial revenue. Pointing out that Franklin was the most respected of all American colonists, Townshend seized on this distinction as the basis for his taxation plan.

Townshend believed the Americans had to be taxed, if for no other reason than to establish once and for all the indivisible sovereignty of King and Parliament. In June 1767 Parliament agreed by authorizing the Townshend Duties, which were nothing more than import duties on a short list of trade items: British-manufactured glass, paper and lead

TABLE 4.1 Estimated Population of Colonial Port Towns Compared to London, England (1775)	
London	700,000
Philadelphia	28,000
New York City	23,000
Boston	16,000
Charleston	12,000
Newport	11,000
Baltimore	10,000

London, the capital of the British empire, had an enormous population by the standards of the largest cities in the colonies. The king's ministers were aware of this striking discrepancy, and they regarded American port towns like Boston as minor trading outposts in which a few well-trained redcoats could easily restore order among protesting colonists. Lord Hillsborough certainly believed so, but events proved him wrong.

products, painters' colors, and a three-pence-a-pound duty on tea. Townshend declared that his plan would net the Crown £35,000 to £40,000 per year. In time, once the colonists got used to paying the duties, the list of taxable products could be lengthened. Meanwhile, the revenue would help defray the costs of royal governments in America.

At first, it appeared that Townshend knew what he was doing. His scheme was subtle and generated very little colonial opposition. Except for tea, the duties were on luxury items, rarely used by the majority of colonists. The tea tax could be evaded by opening illicit trading connections with Dutch tea merchants—and Americans were still quite adept at the art of smuggling.

Mustering Further American Resistance

Late in the year **John Dickinson,** a landholder and lawyer residing in the area of Philadelphia, began publishing a series of newspaper essays, soon thereafter printed as a pamphlet entitled *Letters from a Farmer in Pennsylvania.* Dickinson assailed Townshend's logic. The colonists, he pointed out, had not distinguished between internal and external taxes. Certainly they had long accepted duties designed "to regulate trade" and facilitate the flow of imperial commerce. However, they now faced trade duties "for the single purpose" of raising revenue. Taxes disguised as trade duties, warned a suspicious Dickinson, were "a most dangerous innovation," having

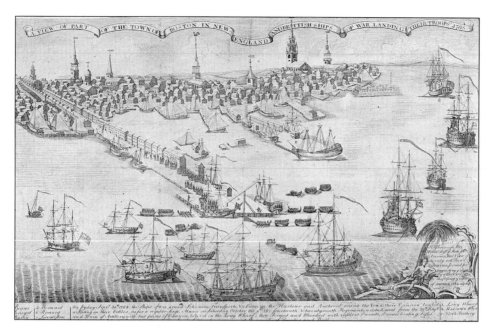

British redcoats landed at Boston's Long Wharf in 1768 with orders to put an end to ongoing political unrest in that port city.

the potential to turn the colonists into "abject slaves." Yet Dickinson, a man of considerable wealth who feared the destructive potential of violent crowds, urged moderation in resistance; he called for the colonial assemblies merely to petition Parliament, hoping the M.P.s would listen to reason.

In February 1768 the Massachusetts General Court, at the prompting of Samuel Adams, sent a Circular Letter to the other assemblies with arguments predicated on Dickinson's widely reprinted pamphlet and his call for petitions. If the British ministry had ignored the Massachusetts document, nothing of consequence might have happened. However, Wills Hill, Lord Hillsborough (1718–1793), who had recently taken the new cabinet post of Secretary for American Affairs, overreacted and provoked needless conflict.

Hillsborough considered the Circular Letter insubordinate. He quickly fired off orders to Governor Bernard to confront the General Court and demand an apology. If the delegates refused (they did overwhelmingly), Bernard was to dissolve the assembly and call for new elections. In addition, Hillsborough sent his own circular letter to the other colonial governors, insisting that they not allow their assemblies "to receive or give any countenance to this seditious paper" from Massachusetts. If they did, such assemblies were also to be dissolved. The result of Hillsborough's actions actually strengthened the colonists' resolve when new elections swelled the ranks of delegates firmly committed to resisting any form of Parliamentary taxation.

Just as the Massachusetts Circular Letter infuriated Hillsborough, so did the rough treatment experienced by royal customs officials, particularly in Boston where the Crown had recently located a new five-man Board of Customs Commissioners. When members of the board, which was to coordinate all customs collections in America, arrived at the end of 1767, jeering crowds greeted them at the docks. The commissioners found it virtually impossible to walk the streets or carry out their official duties without harassment.

More serious trouble erupted in June 1768 when a crowd attacked local customs collectors who had seized John Hancock's sloop *Liberty* on charges of smuggling in a cargo of Madeira wine. (Hancock was notorious for illegal trading.) For their personal safety, the new commissioners fled to Fort Castle William in Boston harbor. Even before the *Liberty* riots, they had sent reports to Hillsborough about the unruly behavior of Bostonians, and they had asked for military protection.

In the wake of the August 1765 Stamp Act riots, royalist political faction leaders had likewise talked in private about calling for military support. Governor Bernard demurred, thinking that the presence of redcoats might provoke even greater turmoil in the streets. Hillsborough, however, was not going to tolerate such abusive behavior from the Bostonians, even in the absence of a formal gubernatorial request for troops. Just before the *Liberty* riots took place, the American secretary issued orders for four regiments of redcoats to proceed to Boston. The troops were "to give every legal assistance to the civil magistrate in the preservation of the public peace; and to the officers of the revenue in the execution of the laws of trade and revenue."

When the first redcoats arrived in the fall of 1768 without serious incident, members of the royalist political faction went about their duties with newfound courage. Many inhabitants hoped that crowd rule, civil anarchy, and open harassment were tactics of the past.

Samuel Adams and the popular rights faction, however, kept demanding more resistance. On August 1, 1768, they convinced an enthusiastic town meeting to accept a nonimportation boycott of British goods. New Yorkers signed a similar agreement a few days later. Philadelphians refused at first to go along with their two northern neighbors, bowing to the pressure of influential merchants. Somewhat reluctantly, they finally joined the trade boycott in February 1769. Pressure from South Carolina's popular leader, Christopher Gadsden, backed by threats of crowd action, convinced Charleston merchants to come around in August 1769. A year had passed, but now all the major port cities had endorsed yet another trade boycott in defense of political liberties.

The colonists did more than boycott. In some communities talk was rife about producing manufactured goods, such as woolen cloth, in direct defiance of imperial restrictions. With the boycott in full force wealthier citizens could no longer get the most fashionable fabrics from London, and popular leaders encouraged them to join poorer colonists in wearing homespun cloth—a sign of personal sacrifice for the cause. Some leaders urged all "genteel ladies" to master the skills of spinning and weaving. The *Boston Gazette* asked "Daughters of Liberty" everywhere to:

First then throw aside your high top knots of
     pride
Wear none but your own country linen
Of economy boast. Let your pride be the most
To show clothes of your make and spinning.

Upper-class women, by and large, remained skeptical. They did not like the itchy feeling of homespun, and they considered spinning and weaving to be beneath their station in society. For poorer women, particularly those in the port cities, the trade boycott generated opportunities for piecemeal work in the production of homespun cloth. Such labor meant extra income, but there was virtually no long-term effect in improving the lot of the poor in Amer-

ica. Homespun was abundant, and the market price remained quite low. While wealthier women itched, complained, and worried about losing their status, poorer women were virtually donating their labor to the defense of American rights. For them the term "sacrifice" held a special meaning.

A "Bloody Massacre" in Boston

The citizens of Boston deeply resented the redcoats in their midst. When the king's troops had first debarked in October 1768, a concerned local minister proclaimed: "Good God! What can be worse to a people who have tasted the sweets of liberty! Things have come to an unhappy crisis, . . . and the moment there is any bloodshed all affection will cease."

Besides symbolizing political tyranny, the redcoats also competed for scarce jobs because, when not on duty, their officers allowed them to work for

This folk art painting depicts a well-to-do German farmer. The stock around his neck, his coat, and his walking stick all identify him with middle-class status.

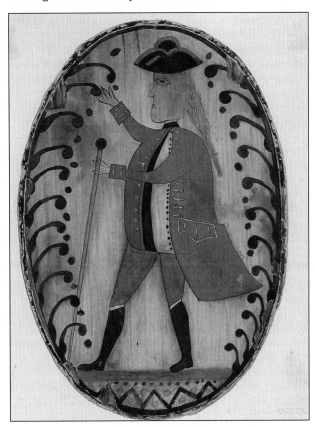

Those Hated Customs Informers

Benedict Arnold, who later became famous for turning against the American cause of liberty, was a prospering merchant in New Haven, Connecticut, before the Revolution. One of Arnold's trading vessels returned from the West Indies during January 1766 and managed to unload its cargo of rum and molasses without paying the required trade duties. Like hundreds of other colonial merchants, Arnold thought nothing of evading imperial customs collectors in American port towns. The economy was depressed, and many merchants were struggling to avoid bankruptcy. In addition, many argued that not paying duties at a time when the colonists were demanding repeal of the Stamp Act was a justifiable form of protest against the willfulness of the home government.

In attempting to stop colonial smuggling, British customs officers were in regular contact with informers, or local inhabitants who listened for rumors in the streets and secretly provided evidence about merchants evading the law. Informers expected cash payments for their services, and if vice-admiralty courts ruled against an offending merchant, informers sometimes shared in profits gained from the sale of confiscated cargoes. To be an informer could be lucrative, but it also assured the wrath of local citizens, should colonists caught smuggling find out who had broken the unwritten law of noncooperation with customs collectors.

Peter Boles was a seaman in the employ of Benedict Arnold who had helped to unload the smuggled cargo. Late in January he approached Arnold and asked for extra wages, implying that the money would help keep him quiet. Arnold responded tersely that he did not hand out bribes. Boles went straight to the New Haven customs office. The chief collector was not there, so the informer announced his intention to return later with important information.

When Arnold learned of Boles's action, he sought out the mariner, "gave him a little chastisement," and told him to get out of New Haven. Boles agreed to leave, but two days later he was still in town. Arnold, now backed by a number of seamen, confronted Boles at a local tavern and forced him to sign a prepared confession. "Being instigated by the devil," Boles acknowledged that "I justly deserve a halter for my malicious and cruel intentions." He also promised "never to enter the same [town] again."

Four hours later, at 11 P.M., Boles was still tippling at the tavern. This time Arnold returned with yet more followers. The party grabbed Boles and dragged the informer to the town's whipping post, where he "received forty lashes with a small cord, and was conducted out of town." Peter Boles was not heard from again.

Boles's punishment outraged more law-abiding community leaders. Arnold and a few members of his crowd were arrested for disturbing the peace, which ultimately cost each of them a small fine. In response, Arnold organized a demonstration and parade. Dozens of citizens participated in this evening spectacle, which saw effigies of the local magistrates who had issued the arrest warrants carried through the streets on pretended gallows and then consumed in a huge bonfire. As Arnold wrote later, these magistrates had acted as if they wanted to "vindicate, protect, and caress an informer," rather than stand up for American rights when colonial trade "is nearly ruined by the . . . detestable Stamp and other oppressive acts." Vigilante justice for "infamous informers" like Boles, Arnold maintained, was an effective way to loosen the stranglehold of imperial restrictions on provincial commerce and, at the same time, defend basic rights.

The whipping and banishment of Boles were relatively mild punishments. Angry crowds often covered informers with tar and feathers before strapping them onto wooden rails and "riding" them out of town. In some cases, such as that of Ebenezer Richardson of Boston, informers nearly lost their lives. A combative person and occasional employee of the customs office, Richardson provided damaging information about a prominent local merchant in 1766, for which this informer was "frequently abused by the people." Then in early 1770 Richardson gained the community's wrath by defying citizens enforcing Boston's nonimportation agreement protesting the Townshend Duties. Events got out of hand, and he became known as the greatest "monster of the times."

Since August 1768, when Bostonians accepted Samuel Adams's call for nonimportation, an informal group known as "the Body" directed the harassment of violators. Merchants who kept importing British goods endured much abuse as "importers." Roving bands of citizens struck at night, breaking windows and defacing importers' property; the damage in-

> O MURD'RER! RICHARDSON! *with their latest breath*
> *Millions will curse you when you sleep in death!*
> *Infernal horrors sure will shake your soul*
> *When o'er your head the awful thunders roll.*
> *Earth cannot hide you, always will the cry*
> *Of Murder! Murder! haunt you 'till you die!*
> *To yonder grave! with trembling joints repair,*
> *Remember* SEIDER'S *corps lies mould'ring there;*

cluded coating walls with a combination of mud and feces known as "Hillsborough treat." During the day, crowds moved from location to location, posting large wooden hands pointing toward the shops of offending merchants. As customers came and went, they received verbal abuse while dodging flying handfuls of Hillsborough treat.

On February 22, 1770, a crowd visited such a shop in Boston's North End, unfortunately across the street from Richardson's residence. The ever-belligerent informer suddenly appeared and, in the face of verbal taunts and flying debris, tried to remove the hand. Soon he retreated to his house with the crowd, including many boys, following close behind. "Come out, you damn son of a bitch," they shouted, and they started to break the windows. Inside, Richardson and another man loaded their muskets. When the crowd tried to enter the house, the informer first warned his assailants and then fired. He severely wounded an 11-year-old boy, Christopher Seider, who died several hours later. Only the intervention of well-known patriot gentlemen saved Richardson from being lynched.

Samuel Adams and other popular leaders in Boston took full advantage of this ugly incident. They planned an elaborate funeral during which some 2500 mourners solemnly marched in front and back of Seider's coffin from Liberty Tree to the burial ground. Hundreds more lined the streets as the procession passed by. Popular rights advocate John Adams considered young Seider a martyr to the cause of liberty. Lieutenant Governor Thomas Hutchinson was less charitable. Had his political adversaries had the power to restore Seider's life, he declared, they "would not have done it, but would have chosen the grand funeral."

Christopher Seider's death and emotional funeral were signs of the tension filling the streets of Boston over such imperial legislation as the Townshend Duties. That British redcoats were present to help enforce imperial law and keep the populace under control only made matters worse. In the week following Seider's funeral, there was a dramatic increase in incidents of troop baiting, including the fight at John Gray's ropemaking establishment, all of which culminated in the Boston Massacre.

As for Ebenezer Richardson, he soon stood trial on the charge of willfully murdering Seider. His argument was self-defense. His wife and two daughters were in the house and had been struck by eggs, stones, and flying Hillsborough treat. The Superior Court judges realized that manslaughter was the proper charge, not murder, as the enraged Bostonians urged with their cries of "damn him—hang him—murder not manslaughter" as the jurors left the courtroom to deliberate on a verdict.

The jury pronounced Richardson guilty of murder; however, the court, headed by Thomas Hutchinson, initiated a series of legal actions that in 1772 secured Richardson's freedom by king's pardon. Now an outcast, Boston's most notorious informer tried to find work, only to be reviled and sent on his way. Finally, he secured employment with the customs office in Philadelphia, but more than once he disappeared to avoid a coat of tar and feathers because everywhere colonists knew Richardson as the "execrable villain, . . . as yet unhanged" customs informer who had shot down young Christopher Seider.

extra wages on a piecemeal basis. As a result, the troops made hard economic times even harder for day laborers, semiskilled workers, and other poorer Bostonians already suffering from the prolonged economic depression besetting their community.

Throughout 1769 troop baiting by Boston's working men and women had resulted in fistfights and bloodied faces. Bad feelings continued to mount as winter snows covered the ground. Then on March 2, 1770, an ugly confrontation took place. A young off-duty soldier, Patrick Walker, entered John Gray's ropemaking establishment and asked for work. Seizing the opportunity to be insulting, one of Gray's workers snorted: "Well, then go and clean my shithouse." Taken aback, the soldier snapped in response: "Empty it yourself." Upset and angry, Walker fled amid taunts and threats from other laborers.

Walker told his story to comrades like Mathew Kilroy and William Warren of the 29th regiment. He convinced several of them to join him in teaching these workers a lesson. The soldiers soon appeared at Gray's, and a general brawl ensued before Gray's workers drove off the redcoats. This nasty fight

Effective propaganda, such as Paul Revere's engravings of the Boston Massacre, helped increase outrage over the event. Here, the British soldiers appear to be firing without provocation into an innocent-looking crowd.

would have been lost to history had it not been an important precursor to the so-called Boston Massacre three days later.

Monday, March 5, was bitterly cold, but heated emotions among workers and soldiers could have melted the deep piles of snow in the streets. A number of isolated fights had occurred over the weekend, but an eerie calm pervaded on Monday because Boston's working people had decided to challenge the redcoats' continued presence in their community. Toward evening small parties of day laborers, apprentices, and merchant seamen began milling about in the streets, eventually moving toward King Street, the site of the Customs House. Here a lone redcoat was on guard duty, and the growing crowd pressed in on him.

Then a small detachment from the 29th regiment, including privates Kilroy and Warren, appeared. After rescuing their isolated comrade, the redcoats retreated to the steps of the customs house with the Boston crowd harassing them with mud, snowballs, and rocks every step of the way. Captain Thomas Preston tried to steady his squad, but one of his soldiers, fearing for his life, panicked. He leveled his musket and shot into the crowd. Ignoring Preston's orders to stop, other soldiers also fired their weapons. Before the shooting was over, a number of civilians lay wounded and dying.

All told, five colonists lost their lives, including Samuel Gray, a relative of John Gray and a participant in the March 2 brawl; seventeen-year-old Samuel Maverick, brother-in-law of shoemaker Ebenezer Mackintosh; and **Crispus Attucks,** an unemployed mulatto merchant seaman. Bostonians would soon hail these men as martyred heroes in the struggle to defend American liberties.

Captain Preston and his troops faced trials for murder. The court found all but two of the redcoats innocent on the grounds of having been forced into a life-threatening situation by an enraged crowd of citizens. Private Kilroy and another soldier were declared guilty of manslaughter. By pleading benefit of clergy they had their thumbs seared with a hot branding iron before being sent back to their regiment.

Long before these verdicts, royal officials removed the hated redcoats from Boston. In this sense the working citizens of Boston had won—at the cost of five lives. They had freed their community of British regulars and unwanted economic competition. Just as important, the Boston Massacre caused colonists everywhere to ask just how far King and Parliament would go to sustain the imperial will. With lives now lost, Americans would be increasingly wary of British government actions that might result in some detestable form of political tyranny. In sum, the legacy of the Boston Massacre was even greater mistrust of the parent nation's intentions.

Parliament Backs Down Again

The colonists' trade boycott seriously hurt merchants and manufacturers in the British Isles. By the beginning of 1770 the Townshend program had netted only about £20,000 in revenue, a paltry sum when compared to the loss in American trade, estimated to be as high as £7 million. Once again, the colonists had found the means to get Parliament to reevaluate its position.

It may have been fortunate for Charles Townshend that he died unexpectedly in September 1767. He did not have to listen to the abuse that his infamous duties took before Parliament in early 1770. By that time the Pitt ministry had collapsed. In January 1770 George III asked amiable **Lord Frederick North** (1732–1792) to form a new cabinet and give some direction to drifting governmental affairs.

North, listening to the wrath of powerful merchants and manufacturers in the British Isles, moved quickly to settle differences with America. He went before Parliament on March 5, 1770 (ironically the same day as the Boston Massacre) and called for repeal of the Townshend Duties, except for the tax on tea, which was to stand as a face-saving, symbolic reminder of Parliament's right to tax and legislate for the Americans in all cases whatsoever. As with the Stamp Act confrontation, the colonial trade boycott of 1768–1770 most certainly had a telling effect. King and Parliament had backed down again—but for the last time.

The Rupturing of Imperial Relations

Lord North was a sensible leader who wanted to avoid taxation schemes and other forms of legislation that could provoke more trouble. He understood that imperial relations had been strained almost to a breaking point by too many controversial policies thrown at the colonists in too short a time after so many years of salutary neglect. North carefully avoided challenging the Americans between 1770 and 1773. In turn, the colonial resistance movement clearly waned. For a while, then, there were no new issues to stir further conflict—only old problems needing resolution.

When Parliament stepped back from the Townshend Duties, most colonists wanted to end the boycott and return to normal trade relations, despite the irritating tax on tea. That duty, they knew, could be avoided by the continued smuggling of Dutch tea. Slowly, economic relations with Great Britain improved, and His Majesty's subjects in England and America enjoyed a brief period of mutually beneficial economic prosperity.

The Necessity of Vigilance

Political relations were not so resilient. Many colonists had become very suspicious of the intentions of home government officials. Provincial leaders tried to explain what had happened since 1763 by drawing on the thoughts of England's "radical" **whig** opposition writers of the early eighteenth century. Men such as John Trenchard and Thomas Gordon, who had penned an extended series of essays known as *Cato's Letters* (1720–1723), had repeatedly warned about corruption in government caused by high ministerial officials lusting after power. If such officials were not stopped, citizens like the colonists would find themselves stripped of all liberties and living in a state of tyranny (often described as **political slavery**).

What took firm hold during the 1760s was an American worldview, or ideology, that saw liberties under attack by such grasping, power-hungry leaders as George Grenville and Charles Townshend in England and their royalist puppets in America, personified by such officials as Thomas Hutchinson and Andrew Oliver. Evidence of a conspiracy seemed overwhelming to those attempting to explain what had happened. Obvious signs included the hovering presence of British redcoats in such places as Boston and ships of the Royal Navy patrolling American waters, all during peacetime. The colonists had been cut off from frontier lands, and—perhaps worst of all from their perspective—they had experienced three willful attempts to tax them, literally to deprive them of property without any voice in the matter.

As never before, great numbers of colonists doubted the goodwill of the home government. Even if Lord North was behaving himself and keeping Parliament in check, many were sure that ministerial inaction was nothing more than a trick designed to lull Americans into a false sense of security while conspiring royal officials devised new and even more insidious plans to strip them of basic political rights.

Popular leaders exhorted the citizenry to be vigilant at all times. They employed various devices to ensure that the defense of liberties was not forgotten. In Boston Samuel Adams and his political lieutenants declared March 5 to be an annual commemorative holiday to honor the five fallen martyrs of the

Massacre. Each year there was a large public meeting and grand oration to stir memories and to remind the populace of the possible dangers of a new ministerial assault.

At the 1772 observance, Dr. Joseph Warren, a committed radical and close associate of Samuel Adams, delivered an impassioned speech. He vividly recalled *that dreadful night . . . when our streets were stained with the blood of our brethren; . . . and our eyes were tormented with the sight of the mangled bodies of the dead.* Then Warren turned to future prospects, reminding the hundreds in attendance that such an assault could happen again—and in much more destructive terms. Warren's "imagination" conjured up "our houses wrapped in flames, our children subjected to the barbarous caprice of a raging soldiery; our beauteous virgins exposed to all the insolence of unbridled passion." The message of constant vigilance to preserve liberties could not be missed.

Local confrontations also kept emotions stirred up. One such incident occurred in June 1772 and involved a Royal Naval vessel, the *Gaspée*, that regularly patrolled for smugglers in the waters off Rhode Island. The ship's crew and its captain, William Dudingston, were very efficient. Finally, Rhode Islanders had endured enough. One day they sent out a sloop that purposely flaunted itself before the *Gaspée*. Suspecting illicit trading activity, Dudingston gave chase but ran aground as the smaller vessel swept close to shore. That evening, a crowd, disguised as Indians, descended upon the stranded ship and burned it. One of the crowd delivered the supreme insult by firing a load of buckshot into Dudingston's buttocks.

Tension increased between British leaders and the American colonists when in June 1772 Rhode Islanders burned the *Gaspée*, a Royal Naval vessel charged with patrolling the area for smugglers.

Crown officials were furious about the *Gaspée's* destruction. They set up a royal commission of inquiry but never obtained any conclusive evidence regarding the perpetrators of this crowd action. Curiously, popular leaders, ignoring the reasons that the *Gaspée* was in American waters in the first place, set up a hue and cry about the royal commission. They feared that the intention was to send suspects to England for trial. Consequently, several provincial assemblies established **committees of correspondence** to communicate with one another, should home government leaders appear to jeopardize liberties of any kind—in this case holding trials of persons outside districts where they had allegedly committed crimes. These correspondence committees were soon writing back and forth regarding problems over tea.

The Tea Crisis of 1773

The final assault on American rights, as the colonists perceived reality, grew out of a rather inconspicuous piece of legislation known as the Tea Act of 1773. When Lord North proposed this bill, he had no idea that it would precipitate a disastrous sequence of events; indeed, he was hardly thinking about the American provinces. His primary concern was the East India Company, a joint-stock trading enterprise that dated back to the early seventeenth century whose officials ruled over British interests in India.

Once enormously prosperous, the company had descended into desperate economic straits by the early 1770s. One reason was that the recent colonial boycott had cost the company its place in the American tea market. With tea warehouses bulging, company directors sought marketing concessions from Parliament. They asked to have the authority to ship tea directly from India to America rather than through England, which would lower the final market price. In May 1773 King and Parliament acceded to this request and, in turn, forced the company to give up some of its political authority in India.

To reduce costs further, the company proceeded to name its own tea agents in the major American ports. The agents were to function as local distributors for 6 percent commissions. The net effect of these changes was to make company tea much more competitive with, if not cheaper than, smuggled Dutch blends—a fact that pleased Lord North very much.

North was even more pleased to have found a way, he thought, to get the Americans to accept the tea tax—and, symbolically at least, recognize Parliament's sovereignty. How could they refuse cheaper tea, even with the Townshend duty added to the

On the night of December 16, 1773, patriots—some of them disguised as Mohawk Indians—boarded ships of the British East India Company docked at Boston's harbor. Protesting the Tea Act of 1773, the patriots dumped the ships' cargo of tea into the harbor.

price? The chief minister should have listened to the M.P. who warned him during the debates on the Tea Act that "if we don't take off the duty they won't take the tea."

In September 1773 the company dipped into its warehouses and readied its first American consignment of 600,000 pounds of tea worth £60,000. Vigilant Americans were waiting. Conditioned by years of warding off undesirable imperial legislation, they were looking for signs of further conspiratorial acts. A small economic saving meant nothing in the face of what they believed to be another, more insidious plot to reduce them to a state of political slavery. East India Company tea had to be resisted.

Once again, the port city of Boston became the focal point of significant protest. In early November a crowd took to the streets and tried to intimidate the tea agents (among them Thomas and Elisha Hutchinson, sons of Thomas who was now the royal governor) into resigning. The merchant agents, who had not received official commissions as yet, refused to submit; the crowd did not press the matter, waiting for a more timely moment to force resignations.

On November 28 the first tea ship, the *Dartmouth*, docked in Boston. The local customs collectors fled to Fort Castle William, and the local committee of correspondence, headed by Samuel Adams and his associates, put guards on the *Dartmouth* and two other tea ships entering the port within the next few days. Repeatedly the popular rights faction insisted that the three tea ships be sent back to England. But Governor Hutchinson refused. This

native-son royal governor could be fair-minded but also stubborn, and this time Hutchinson decided that a showdown was necessary. He called on Royal Naval vessels in the vicinity to block off the port's entrance.

According to imperial law, unclaimed cargo had to be unloaded after 20 days in port and then sold at public auction. Since the tea ships could not escape the harbor, Hutchinson fully expected to have the vessels unloaded after the 20-day waiting period. Once the tea had been sold at auction, the Townshend duty would be paid from the revenues obtained, and the governor would have upheld the law of King and Parliament. Hutchinson's determination to stand firm on behalf of imperial authority—and against his troublesome, long-time local enemies—proved to be a bad idea.

The waiting period for the *Dartmouth* was over on December 16. That day a mass meeting of local citizens took place at Old South Church. The Samuel Adams faction made one last attempt to communicate the gravity of the situation to Hutchinson. They sent a messenger to him with a very clear message—remove the tea ships or else. Hutchinson refused again. Late in the day, Adams appeared before the huge gathering and reportedly shouted: "This meeting can do no more to save the country." The moment for crowd action had come. Several dozen artisans, apprentices, and day laborers, led by Ebenezer Mackintosh, went to the docks disguised as Indians. They clambered onto the tea ships and dumped 342 chests of tea valued at £10,000 into the harbor. It took them nearly three hours to complete the work of the Boston Tea Party.

Tea confrontations occurred later in other ports, but none were as destructive as that in Boston. Philadelphians used the threat of tar and feathers to convince local officials to send back the first tea ships to arrive there. The governor of South Carolina out-maneuvered the local populace and managed to get the tea landed, but the company product lay rotting in a warehouse and was never sold. New Yorkers had to wait until the spring of 1774 for tea ships to appear in their port. They jeered loudly at the docks, and an intelligent sea captain raised anchor and fled for the high seas. Once again, then, the Bostonians stood out for their bold defiance of imperial law.

Parliament Adopts the Coercive Acts

The Boston Tea Party shocked Lord North and other British leaders. North decided that the "rebellious" Bostonians had to be taught a lesson, and Parliament adopted a series of legislative bills, collectively known as the **Coercive Acts.** Although King and Parliament aimed these laws at Massachusetts, the Coercive Acts held implications for colonists elsewhere who believed that the tyrannical parent nation was using the Tea Party as a pretext for the final destruction of American liberties.

King George III signed the first act, known as the Boston Port Bill, into law at the end of March 1774. This act closed the port of Boston, making trade illegal until such time as local citizens paid for the tea. In May Parliament passed the Massachusetts Government Act and the Administration of Justice Act. The first suspended the colony's royal charter (which dated to 1691), vastly expanded the powers of the royal governor, abolished the elective council (upper house of the General Court), and replaced that body with appointed councilors of the Crown's choosing. Town meetings could be held only with the governor's permission, except for annual spring election gatherings.

Governor Hutchinson never exercised this vastly expanded range of authority. Distraught by the Tea Party, he asked for a leave of absence and traveled to England. The Crown replaced him with General **Thomas Gage,** Britain's North American military commander, who held the governorship until the final disruption of royal government in the Bay Colony.

The Administration of Justice Act provided greater protection for customs collectors and other imperial officials in Massachusetts. If they injured or killed anyone while carrying out their official duties, the governor would have the right to move trials to some other

Quebec Act of 1774

By making the Ohio River the new southwest boundary of Quebec, the Quebec Act cut into land the colonists wanted for expansion.

colony or to England. The assumption was that local juries were too biased to render fair judgments.

Finally, in early June 1774 Parliament sanctioned the fourth coercive bill, which was an amendment to the Quartering Act of 1765. The earlier law had outlined procedures relating to housing for the king's regulars and had specifically excluded the use of private dwellings of any kind. The 1774 amendment gave General Gage the power to billet his troops anywhere, including unoccupied private homes, so long as the army paid fair rental rates. Parliament passed this law because Gage was bringing several hundred troops to Boston with him.

The colonists also viewed the Quebec Act, approved in June 1774, as another piece of coercive legislation. Actually, this bill mainly concerned itself with the territorial administration of Canada by providing for a royal governor and a large appointed advisory council, but no popularly elected assembly. Roman Catholicism was to remain the established religion for the French-speaking populace. In addition, the Ohio River was to become the new southwestern boundary of Quebec.

Ever-vigilant colonial leaders viewed the Quebec Act as confirming all the worst tendencies of imperial rule over the past decade. Parliament had denied local representative government; it had ratified the establishment of a branch of the Christian faith that was repugnant to militantly Protestant Americans, especially New Englanders; and it had wiped out the claims of various colonial governments to millions of acres of western land, in this case all of the Ohio country. The latter decision particularly infuriated well-placed provincial land speculators, among them Benjamin Franklin and George Washington, who had fixed on this region for future development and population expansion. The Quebec Act, concluded thousands of Americans, smacked of abject political slavery.

Even without the Quebec Act, Lord North had made a tactical error by encouraging Parliament to pass so much legislation. The port bill punishing Boston was one thing; some Americans believed the Bostonians had gone too far and deserved some chastisement. The sum total of the Coercive Acts, however, caused widespread concern because they seemed to violate the sanctity of local political institutions, to distort normal judicial procedures, and to favor military over civil authority. For most colonists the acts resulted in feelings of solidarity with (rather than separateness from) the Bostonians, a critical factor in generating a unified resistance movement.

Hurling Back the Challenge: The First Continental Congress

News of the full array of Coercive Acts provoked an outburst of intercolonial activity, the most important expression of which was the calling of the **First Continental Congress.** This body began its deliberations in Philadelphia on September 5, 1774. Gentlemen of all political persuasions were in attendance (Georgia was the only colony not represented). Among the more radical delegates were Samuel Adams and his younger cousin John, as well as Patrick Henry. George Washington was present, mostly silent in debates but firmly committed to defending fundamental rights. Conservative delegates included **Joseph Galloway** of Pennsylvania and John Jay of New York. The core question was how confrontational the Congress should be. The more cautious delegates wanted to find some nonhostile means to settle differences with Britain, but the radicals believed that only a well-organized resistance effort would induce home government leaders to back down yet a third time.

Political maneuvering for control of the Congress began even before the sessions got under way. Con-

servative delegates favored meeting in the Pennsylvania State House, a building symbolizing ties with British rule. The radicals argued in favor of Carpenter's Hall, a gathering place for Philadelphia's laborers. The delegates chose the latter building, thus seeming to identify with the people and their desire to preserve political liberties. Then the radicals insisted on naming Charles Thomson, a popular leader in Philadelphia, secretary for the Congress. Thomson gained the post and was able to design the minutes so that more confrontational actions stood out in the official record.

These signs foreshadowed what was to come. Accounts of the work of the First Continental Congress make clear that Samuel Adams, Patrick Henry, and others of their radical persuasion dominated the proceedings. Although they went along with the preparation of an elaborate petition to Parliament, known as the "The Declaration of Colonial Rights and Grievances," these experienced molders of the colonial protest movement demanded much more. They drew upon the old weapons of resistance that had caused King and Parliament to retreat before, and they added a new cudgel. Just in case they could not convince home government leaders to repeal the Coercive Acts, they argued that Americans should begin to prepare for war.

To ensure that Congress moved in the right direction, Samuel Adams and his political allies back in

As the largest American city and a central geographic point, Philadelphia was a logical location for delegates of the First Continental Congress to gather in 1774.

Massachusetts had done some careful planning. Their efforts came to light on September 9, 1774, when a convention of citizens in Suffolk County (Boston and environs) adopted a series of resolutions written by Dr. Joseph Warren. Once approved, Paul Revere, talented silversmith and active member of Adams's popular rights faction, rode hard for Philadelphia. Revere arrived in mid-September and laid the Suffolk Resolves before Congress. Not only did these statements strongly profess American rights, but they also called for a complete economic boycott and the rigorous training of local militia companies, just in case military action became necessary to defend lives, liberty, and property against the redcoats of Thomas Gage.

Congress approved the Suffolk Resolves—and with them the initial step in organization for a possible military showdown. The delegates also committed themselves to a plan of economic boycott, which became known as the Continental Association. The association represented a comprehensive plan mandating the nonimportation and nonconsumption of British goods, to be phased in over the next few months, as well as the nonexportation of colonial products should Parliament not retreat within a year.

The association also called on every American community to establish a local committee of observation and inspection charged with having all citizens subscribe to the boycott. In reality, the association was a loyalty test. Citizens who refused to sign were about to become outcasts from the cause of liberty. The term of derision applied to them was *tory*; however, they thought of themselves as *loyalists*—maintaining their allegiance to the Crown.

The only conciliatory countercharge of any consequence during the first Congress came from Joseph Galloway, a wealthy Philadelphia lawyer who had long served as Pennsylvania's speaker of the house. Galloway desperately wanted to maintain imperial ties because he feared what the "common sort" of citizens might do if that attachment should be irrevocably severed. He could imagine nothing but rioting, dissipation, and the confiscation of the property of economically successful colonists. For Galloway, the continuation of any kind of political and social order in America depended on the stabilizing influence of British rule.

Galloway drew from the Albany Plan of Union of 1754 (see p. 86) in proposing a central government based in America that would be superior to the provincial assemblies. This government would consist of a "grand council" elected by colonial assemblymen and a "president general" appointed by the Crown. Grand council legislation would have to gain Parliament's approval; at the same time imperial acts

from King and Parliament would have to secure the assent of the grand council and president before becoming law.

Galloway's Plan of Union, as his blueprint came to be known, represented a structural alternative that would allow Americans a greater voice in imperial decisions affecting the colonies—and also foreshadowed the future commonwealth organization of the British empire. The more radical delegates, however, belittled it as an idea that would divert everyone from the task of the moment, which was to get King and Parliament to rescind the Coercive Acts. In a close vote the delegates remanded Galloway's plan to a committee, where it lay dormant for lack of majority support.

Later, at the urging of the radicals, Secretary Thomson expunged all references to Galloway's plan from the official minutes of Congress. He did so on the grounds of displaying full unity of purpose in resisting the home government. As for Galloway, he faced growing harassment as a loyalist in the months ahead and eventually fled to the British army for protection.

When the First Continental Congress ended its deliberations in late October 1774, its program was one of continued defiance. The delegates understood the course they had chosen. One of their last acts was to call for the Second Continental Congress, to convene in Philadelphia on May 10, 1775, "unless the redress of grievances, which we have desired, be obtained before that time."

As the fall of 1774 gave way to another cold winter, Americans awaited the verdict of King and Parliament. Would the Coercive Acts be repealed, or would the course of events lead to war? Local committees of observation and inspection were busily at work encouraging—and in some cases coercing—the populace to boycott British goods. Local militia companies were vigorously training. Even as they prepared for war, the colonists hoped that George III, Lord North, and Parliament would choose a less strident course. They would soon learn that imperial leaders had dismissed the work of the First Continental Congress, having decided the parent nation could not retreat a third time.

CONCLUSION

In September 1774 Lord North remarked: "The die is now cast, the colonies must either submit or triumph." Once-harmonious relations between Britain and America had become increasingly discordant between 1763 and the end of 1774. The colonists refused to accept undesirable imperial acts, and they successfully resisted such taxation plans as the

CHRONOLOGY OF KEY EVENTS

1760 George III becomes King of England

1763 Treaty of Paris ends the Seven Years' War (February); Pontiac begins an unsuccessful Indian rebellion on the western frontier (May); Orders in Council station Royal Naval vessels in American waters to run down smugglers (October); Proclamation of 1763 forbids white settlement west of the Appalachian Mountains (October)

1764 Sugar Act levies new trade duties on coffee, indigo, sugar, and wine (April); Currency Act prohibits colonial governments from issuing paper money and requires all debts to be paid in hard money (April)

1765 Stamp Act—which requires stamps to be affixed to all legal documents, almanacs, newspapers, pamphlets, and playing cards, among other items—provokes popular protests (March–December); Quartering Act directs colonists to provide barracks, candles, bedding, and beverages to soldiers stationed in their area (May); representatives from nine colonies at the Stamp Act Congress in New York City deny that Parliament has the right to tax the colonists (October)

1766 Parliament repeals the Stamp Act, but asserts its authority to tax the colonies in the Declaratory Act (March)

1767 Townshend Duties Act imposes taxes on imported glass, lead, paint, paper, and tea to defray the cost of colonial administration (June)

1768 British troops ordered to Boston (June); colonists begin to mount a trade boycott of British goods to protest the Townshend Duties (August)

1770 Boston Massacre leaves five colonists dead and others wounded (March)

1772 Rhode Island colonists attack and burn British naval vessel *Gaspée* (June)

1773 Tea Act allows the East India Company to sell tea directly to American retailers (May); Boston Tea Party occurs when a band of "Indians" boards three British vessels and dumps 342 chests of tea into Boston Harbor (December)

1774 Coercive Acts close the port of Boston (March), modify the Massachusetts charter (May), provide for trials outside colonies when royal officials are accused of serious crimes (May), and call for billeting of troops in unoccupied private homes (June); Quebec Act expands the boundaries of Quebec to the Mississippi and Ohio rivers (June); First Continental Congress, meeting in Philadelphia, protests oppressive Parliamentary legislation, votes to boycott trade with Britain, and defeats the Galloway Plan of Union (September–October)

Stamp Act and the Townshend Duties. In the process they came to believe that ministerial leaders in England were engaging in a deep-seated plot to deprive them of their fundamental liberties. When something as inconsequential as the Townshend duty on tea precipitated yet another crisis in 1773, neither side was willing to disengage. By early 1775 both had decided to show their resolve.

A small incident that well illustrates the deteriorating situation occurred in Boston during March 1774. At the state funeral of Andrew Oliver, the Bay Colony's most recent lieutenant governor and former stamp distributor-designate, a large gathering of ordinary citizens came out to watch the solemn procession. As Oliver's coffin was slowly lowered into the ground, these Bostonians, many of them veterans of the American resistance movement, suddenly burst into loud cheers.

This open expression of disaffection for the memory of so locally prominent a royalist leader epitomized the acute strain in British-American relations. Symbolically, the cheers almost seemed like a testament on behalf of the burial of imperial authority in America. Such striking changes in attitudes, over just a few years, pointed toward the fateful clash of arms known as the War for American Independence.

Chapter Summary and Key Points

"Breaking the Bonds of Empire" traces the events leading to the War for American Independence. The Seven Years' War (1756–1763) resulted in various problems for the British government, such as how to put an end to colonial smuggling and prevent frontier warfare between white settlers and Native Americans. Also pressing was the matter of paying the basic costs of imperial administration, which produced legislation by King and Parliament to tax the colonists. American responses included the writing of petitions and pamphlets as well as organized crowd actions and economic boycotts. The final rupturing of relations commenced in the wake of the Boston Tea Party and the response from England in the form of the Coercive Acts.

- The immediate causes of the Revolution can be traced to 1763 when British leaders began tightening the reins of imperial authority. Once the colonists began resisting the new imperial policies, relations became increasingly conflict-ridden.

- Britain's land policy prohibiting settlement in the West irritated the colonists, as did the presence of British troops during peacetime. A serious problem was the Crown's desire to tax the colonists to pay for the troops and other costs of imperial administration.

- King and Parliament approved various indirect and direct taxes in such legislation as the Sugar Act (1764), the Stamp Act (1765), and the Townshend Duties (1767). The colonists met each of these attempts with shouts of "no taxation without representation" and various forms of resistance.

- Tensions culminated in 1770 with a nasty altercation between British troops and American colonists in Boston—an event that came to be known as the Boston Massacre. A period of calm ensured, but tensions flared again during 1773 when angry Bostonians, in defiance of the imperial tax on tea, dumped 342 chests of tea into Boston Harbor.

- King and Parliament responded in punitive fashion with the Coercive Acts. American leaders in turn convened the First Continental Congress, which refused to submit but endorsed a complete economic boycott of British goods and military preparedness in responding to the Coercive Acts.

Suggestions for Further Reading

Bernard Bailyn, *The Ideological Origins of the American Revolution* (1967). Broadly influential, Pulitzer Prize-winning examination of the role of "radical" whig ideas in provoking the Revolution.

Ian R. Christie and Benjamin W. Labaree, *Empire or Independence, 1760–1776* (1976). Engaging appraisal of the reasons for revolution from the perspectives of British policymakers and ordinary American colonists.

John Ferling, *Setting the World Ablaze: Washington, Adams, Jefferson, and the American Revolution* (2000). Highly readable account of three principal leaders in the making of the Revolution.

Edmund S. Morgan, *Benjamin Franklin* (2002). Incisive biography of the masterful Franklin, including his role in key events leading to the Revolution.

Edmund S. and Helen M. Morgan, *The Stamp Act Crisis*, 3d ed. (1995). Classic account of the political, social, and constitutional aspects of the first major political confrontation pointing toward revolution.

Gary B. Nash, *The Urban Crucible: Social Change, Political Consciousness, and the Origins of the Revolution* (1979). Challenging analysis of the lives of ordinary persons in Boston, New York City, and Philadelphia, and the factors that propelled them toward revolution.

Ray Raphael, *A People's History of the American Revolution* (2001). Engaging narrative of various groups of people, including African-Americans, Native Americans, and women, reckoning with the events and realities of the Revolution.

Gordon S. Wood, *The Radicalism of the American Revolution* (1992). Winner of a Pulitzer Prize focusing on pre-Revolutionary social and political values and the transformations wrought by the Revolution.

Alfred F. Young, *The Shoemaker and the Tea Party: Memory and the American Revolution* (1999). Fascinating account of an ordinary Bostonian who participated in key events pointing toward rebellion against the British.

Novels

Kenneth Roberts, *Oliver Wiswell* (1940).

Jeffrey M. Shaara, *Rise to Rebellion: A Novel of the American Revolution* (2001).

Media Resources

American Revolution Maps and Charts, 1750–1790
http://memory.loc.gov/ammem/gmdhtml/armhtml/armhome.html
Valuable collection made available through the American Memory Project of the Library of Congress.

Benjamin Franklin: A Documentary History
http://www.english.udel.edu/lemay/franklin

A collection of documents and a year-by-year chronicle of Franklin's life with summations prepared by J. A. Leo Lemay.

The Maryland State Archives
http://www.mdarchives.state.md.us/msa/homepage/html/homepage.html
A variety of documents, including newspaper articles from the *Maryland Gazette* during the 1760s and 1770s, have been digitized for online study and use.

Stratford Hall Plantation
http://www.stratfordhall.org/
Stratford Hall was the home of various prominent generations of the Lee family, some of whom played noteworthy parts in the American Revolution. This site also includes information about eighteenth-century plantation slave life.

KEY TERMS

Specie   (p. 93)

Vice-admiralty courts   (p. 97)

Virtual representation   (p. 98)

Writs of assistance   (p. 100)

Loyal Nine   (p. 100)

Stamp Act Congress   (p. 102)

Direct taxes   (p. 105)

Indirect taxes   (p. 105)

Whig   (p. 111)

Political slavery   (p. 111)

Committees of correspondence   (p. 112)

Coercive Acts   (p. 114)

First Continental Congress   (p. 115)

PEOPLE YOU SHOULD KNOW

Samuel Adams   (p. 93)

Thomas Hutchinson   (p. 93)

George III   (p. 95)

Pontiac   (p. 96)

George Grenville   (p. 96)

Andrew Oliver   (p. 100)

James Otis, Jr.   (p. 100)

Ebenezer Mackintosh   (p. 100)

Patrick Henry   (p. 102)

Charles Townshend   (p. 105)

John Dickinson   (p. 105)

Crispus Attucks   (p. 110)

Lord Frederick North   (p. 111)

Thomas Gage   (p. 114)

Joseph Galloway   (p. 115)

REVIEW QUESTIONS

1. How did Great Britain's overwhelming success in the Seven Years' War (the French and Indian War in America) help produce an imperial crisis with the English colonies in North America after 1763?

2. Why did the Stamp Act cause such immense fury among the colonists? What various nonviolent and violent tactics were employed by the colonists in resisting British policy actions? Which proved to be most effective, and why?

3. What motivated George Grenville, Charles Townshend, and Lord Frederick North to attempt to tax the Americans? Prepare a brief defense of British colonial policies between 1763 and 1774.

4. The Boston Massacre and the Boston Tea Party were pivotal events in the colonial resistance movement. Examine both events by considering their short-term and long-term causes as well as their wide-reaching consequences.

5. Why did the combination of the Coercive Acts and the Quebec Act prove to be a legislative tactical blunder for Lord North's administration? How did the colonists respond to these measures, and why did their response seem to imply rebellion?

5 The Times That Tried Many Souls, 1775–1783

JOSEPH PLUMB MARTIN: PATRIOT SOLDIER

Joseph Plumb Martin was a dedicated patriot soldier, one of 11,000 men and women who formed the backbone of General George Washington's Continental army. When that force entered its Valley Forge winter campsite in December 1777, the soldiers' trail could "be tracked by their blood upon the rough frozen ground," Martin recorded despondently. The Continentals were "now in a truly forlorn condition,—no clothing, no provisions, and as disheartened as need be." They had fought hard against British regulars and Hessians that summer and autumn but had not prevented the army of General Sir William Howe from taking Philadelphia, the rebel capital. Washington had chosen Valley Forge as a winter encampment because, as a hilly area, it represented an easily defensible position some 20 miles northwest of Philadelphia, should Howe's soldiers venture forth from their far more comfortable quarters.

Washington was very worried about the conditions facing his troops. If something was not done, and soon, he stated, "this army must inevitably . . . starve, dissolve, or disperse." Private Martin thought the same. The weather was bitterly cold, but the Continentals, using what energy they had left, constructed "little shanties" described as "scarcely gayer than dungeon cells."

Making matters even more grim was the lack of food and clothing. Martin claimed that, upon first entering Valley Forge, he went a full day and two nights without anything to eat, "save half a small pumpkin, which I cooked by placing it upon a rock, the skin side uppermost, and making fire upon it." His comrades fared no better. Within two days of moving into Valley Forge, a common grumble could be heard everywhere: "No Meat! No Meat!" By the first of January the words had become more ominous: "No bread, no soldier!"

Thus began a tragic winter of desperation for Washington's Continentals. Some 2500 soldiers, or nearly one fourth of the troops, perished before the army broke camp in June 1778. They died from exposure to the elements, malnutrition, and such virulent diseases as typhus and smallpox. Not uncommonly, soldiers languished for days in their rudely constructed huts because they were too weak to drill or to participate in food-hunting expeditions. Sometimes for lack of straw and blankets, they simply froze to death in their beds. To add to the woes of the

George Washington led a bedraggled, half-starved army of 11,000 men and women into Valley Forge in December 1777.

camp, more than 500 of the army's horses starved to death that winter. Their carcasses could not be buried in the frozen ground, which only magnified the deplorable sanitation conditions and the consequent spread of disease.

Under such forsaken circumstances, hundreds of soldiers deserted. If Washington had not let his troops leave camp to requisition food in the countryside or if there had not been an unusually early shad run in the Schuylkill River, which flowed behind the encampment, the army might well have perished.

Commentators have usually attributed the extreme suffering at Valley Forge to the severe weather and a complete breakdown of the army's supply system. Actually, weather conditions were no worse than in other years. Certainly a major reason for the deprivation at Valley Forge was widespread civilian indifference toward an army made up of the poor, the expendable, and the unfree in American society.

Joseph Plumb Martin clearly thought this was the case. He was a young man from Connecticut, without material resources, who had first enlisted during 1776 at the very peak of patriot enthusiasm for the war—sometimes called the **rage militaire.** He soon learned that soldiering had few glorious moments. Camp life was both dull and dangerous,

given the many killer diseases that ravaged armies of the era, and battle was a frightening experience. Before 1776 was over, Martin had faced the hurtling musket balls and bloodied bayonets of British soldiers in the Continental army's futile attempt to defend New York City and vicinity. He did not renew his enlistment and returned to Connecticut.

For a poor, landless person, economic prospects at home were not much better than serving for promises of regular pay in the Continental army. So in 1777 Martin stepped forth again and agreed to enlist as a substitute for some local gentlemen being threatened by an attempted draft. For a specified sum of money (Martin "forgot the sum"), he became their substitute. As Martin later wrote, "they were now freed from further trouble, at least for the present, and I had become the scapegoat for them."

The experiences of Martin typified those of many others who performed long-term Continental service on behalf of the cause of liberty. After an initial rush to arms in defiance of British authority in 1775, the harsh realities of military life and pitched battles dampened patriot enthusiasm to the point that by December 1776 the

Continental army all but ceased to exist. Washington's major task became that of securing enough troop strength and material support to shape an army capable of standing up time after time to British forces.

The commander in chief found his long-term soldiers among the poor and deprived persons of revolutionary America. In addition, major European nations such as France, Spain, and Holland also came to the rescue with additional troops, supplies, and vital financial support. Working together, even in the face of so much popular indifference, these allies-in-arms outlasted the mighty land and sea forces of Great Britain, making possible a generous peace settlement in 1783 that guaranteed independence for the group of former British colonies that now called themselves the 13 United States.

RECONCILIATION OR INDEPENDENCE

Crown officials in England gave scant attention to the acts of the First Continental Congress. They believed the time had come to teach the American provincials a military lesson. George III explained why: The colonists, he asserted, "have boldly thrown off the mask and avowed nothing less than a total independence of the British legislature will satisfy them." The king's impression was inaccurate, but it lay behind the decision to turn the most powerful military machine in the western world, based on its record in recent wars, against the troublemakers in America and to crush resistance to British authority once and for all.

The Shooting War Starts

During the winter of 1774–1775 the king's ministers prepared for what they expected to be a brief but decisive demonstration of military force. General Gage received "secret" orders to employ the redcoats under his command "to arrest and imprison the principal actors and abettors" of rebellion; however, if the likes of Samuel Adams, John Hancock, and Joseph Warren could not be captured, then Gage was to challenge in any way he deemed appropriate "this rude [American] *rabble* without plan, without concert, and without conduct . . . unprepared to encounter with a regular force." Above all else, Gage was to strike hard with a crushing blow.

In a series of related showdown decisions, King and Parliament authorized funds for a larger force of regular troops in America and named three high-ranking generals—William Howe, Henry Clinton, and "Gentleman Johnny" Burgoyne—to sail to

Boston and join Gage. George III also declared Massachusetts to be in a state of rebellion, which permitted redcoats to shoot down suspected rebels on sight should that be necessary to quell opposition. Eventually this decree would be applied to all 13 provinces.

General Gage received the ministry's secret orders in mid-April 1775. Being on the scene, he was not quite as convinced as his superiors about American martial weakness. Gage had repeatedly urged caution in his reports to home officials, but now he had no choice; he had to act. Because the rebel leaders had already gotten word of the orders and fled to the countryside, Gage decided upon a reconnaissance in force mission. He would send a column of regulars to Concord, a town some 20 miles northwest of Boston that served as a storage point for patriot gunpowder and related military supplies. Once there, the troops were to seize or destroy as much weaponry and ammunition as possible. Gage hoped this maneuver could be effected without bloodshed; he feared the onset of full-scale warfare if patriot lives were lost.

After dark on April 18 some 700 British troops under Lieutenant Colonel Francis Smith moved out across Boston's back bay. Popular leaders monitored this deployment, and soon Paul Revere and William Dawes were riding through the countryside alerting the populace to what was happening. In Lexington, 5 miles east of Concord and on the road that the king's troops had taken, 70 militiamen, trained to respond at a moment's notice, gathered at the local tavern with their captain, John Parker. Samuel Adams and John Hancock were also present. Obviously outnumbered, the Minutemen debated possible actions. They decided to respond to the redcoats' provocative incursion into the countryside by acting as an army of observation.

Parker and his men lined up across the village green as the British column bore down on them at dawn (Adams and Hancock, as known enemies, fled into the woods). The Minutemen were not there to exchange shots, but to warn the regulars against trespassing on the property of free-born British subjects. As the redcoats came closer, Parker tried to shout out words to this effect. He could not be heard. A mysterious shot rang out just as the Minutemen, having made their protest, turned to leave the green. The shot caused troops at the front of the British column to level their arms and fire. Before order was restored, several of Parker's men lay wounded, mostly shot in their backs. Eight of them died in what was the opening volley of the War for American Independence.

The redcoats regrouped and continued their march to Concord. Once there, a detachment moved out to cross the Old North Bridge in search of weapons and gunpowder. Rallying militiamen repulsed them. Falling back to the center of town, the

TABLE 5.1

Road to War: The American Revolution

1763	Orders in Council	Places British naval vessels in American waters during peacetime to run down smugglers, thereby threatening highly profitable illegal trading activities.
	Proclamation of 1763	Denies colonists access to western lands with the purpose of avoiding frontier warfare with Native Americans; infuriates land-hungry settlers searching for tillable farmland.
1764	Sugar Act	Designed to collect trade duty on foreign molasses and toughen other trading regulations.
	Currency Act	Requires colonial governments to stop issuing paper currencies heretofore used to conduct local business transactions and pay private debts.
1765	Stamp Act	Unprecedented legislation to tax colonists directly; heavily resisted through crowd actions and the boycotting of British trade goods.
	Quartering Act	Shifts onto the colonists the financial burden of paying for the housing of imperial troops stationed in America.
1767	Townshend Duties	Another plan to tax the colonists, this time indirectly through a series of trade duties; provokes further resistance.
1770	Boston Massacre	Local crowd action against hated redcoats results in the death of five persons who are transformed into martyrs in the defense of American liberties.
1772	*Gaspée* Affair	Rhode Islanders destroy British naval vessel charged with seizing smugglers, thereby incensing the Crown.
	Committee organization	Colonial assemblies organize committees of correspondence to communicate about imperial policies; Massachusetts establishes local committees to be vigilant in relation to possible acts of tyranny.
1773	Tea Act	Colonists defy this plan to market cheaper tea with the Townshend duty attached; Boston Tea Party sets the tone of resistance.
1774	Coercive Acts	Crown closes port of Boston and makes various modifications in the Massachusetts government, actions that many colonists consider tyrannical.
	First Continental Congress	Offers something less than an olive branch in calling for a complete economic boycott of British trade goods and advising colonists to prepare for possible war.
1775	Lexington and Concord	Warfare breaks out when British regulars attempt to seize powder and arms at Concord.
	Lord Dunmore's Proclamation	Offers freedom to slaves and indentured servants in Virginia who will fight for the Crown.
	Invasion of Canada	Patriot attempt to conquer Quebec Province as the fourteenth colony in rebellion does not succeed.
1776	*Common Sense*	Thomas Paine demands independence and denounces colonists too faint-hearted to break free of perceived British tyranny.
	Massive British buildup	Crown musters huge martial force, including Hessians, to put down the American rebellion.
	Declaration of Independence	Second Continental Congress proclaims American desire to become a separate nation.

This painting, based on an eyewitness sketch, shows British troops under Lieutenant Colonel Francis Smith marching into Concord to destroy patriot stores of gunpowder and military supplies.

redcoats left behind three dead comrades. Now blood had been spilled on both sides.

Lieutenant Colonel Smith began to worry that his column might be cut to pieces by harassing citizen-soldiers, so he ordered a retreat. The rest of the day turned into a rout as an aroused citizenry fired away at the British from behind trees and stone fences. Only a relief column of some 1100 troops, which Gage had the foresight to send out, saved Smith's column. Final casualty figures showed 273 redcoats dead or wounded, as compared to 95 colonists. Lexington and Concord were clear blows to the notion of the invincibility of British arms and suggested that American citizens, when defending their own property, could and would hold their own against better-trained British soldiers.

As word of the bloodshed spread, New Englanders rallied to the patriot banner. Within days thousands of colonists poured into hastily assembled military camps surrounding Boston. Thomas Gage and his soldiers were now trapped, and they could only hope that promised reinforcements would soon reach them. The *rage militaire* was on. Everyone, it seemed, wanted to be a temporary soldier—and fire a few shots at a redcoat or two before returning home again.

Most colonists believed the ministry would soon regain its senses and quickly restore all American rights rather than engage in warfare. They did not realize that imperial leaders were irrevocably commit-ted to eradicating all American resistance, or that the conflict would become a long and grueling war in which the fortitude to endure would determine the eventual winner.

Moderates Versus Radicals in Congress

The shadow of Lexington and Concord loomed heavily as the **Second Continental Congress** convened in Philadelphia in May 1775. Despite the recent bloodshed, very few delegates had become advocates of independence. New Englanders like Samuel and John Adams were leaning that way, but the vast majority held out hope for a resolution of differences. By the summer of 1775 two factions had emerged in Congress: the one led by New Englanders, favoring a formal declaration of independence, and the opposing reconciliationist or moderate faction, whose strength lay in the Middle Colonies and whose most influential leader was John Dickinson of Pennsylvania. The two factions debated every issue with regard to possible effects on the subject of independence. The moderates remained the dominant faction into the spring of 1776, but then the weight of the spreading rebellion swung the pendulum decisively toward those favoring independence.

Early congressional wrangling centered on the organization of the Continental army. In mid-June 1775 the delegates, at the urging of the New Englanders, voted to adopt the patriot forces around Boston as a Continental military establishment. They asked the other colonies to supply additional troops and unanimously named wealthy Virginia planter George Washington, who had been appearing in Congress in his military uniform, to serve as commander in chief. Washington had qualifications for the job, including his combat experiences during the Seven Years' War. Also, he was a southerner. His presence at the head of the army was a way to involve the other colonies, at least symbolically, in what was still a localized conflict being fought by New Englanders.

Although the delegates agreed about the need for central military planning and coordination, the moderates worried about how British officials would view the formation of an independent American army. At the urging of John Dickinson, they wanted Congress to prepare a formal statement explaining this bold action. In early July the delegates approved the "Declaration of the Causes and Necessity for Taking up Arms," which they sent to England. The purpose of a Continental force, the "Declaration" stressed, was not "to dissolve that union which has so long and so happily subsisted between us." Rather, Congress had formed the army to assure the defense of American lives, liberty, and property until "hostilities shall cease on the part of the aggressors, and all danger of their being renewed shall be removed, and not before." Given home government attitudes about American intentions, this document received scant ministerial attention.

The moderates were persons caught in a bind. Even though deeply concerned about American rights, they feared independence. Like many other colonists of substantial wealth, they envisioned internal chaos in the colonies without the stabilizing influence of British rule. They also doubted whether a weak, independent American nation could long survive among aggressive European powers.

The moderates thus tried to keep open the channels of communication with the British government. Characteristic of such attempts was John Dickinson's "Olive Branch" petition, approved by Congress in July 1775. This document stated that "our breasts retain too tender a regard for the kingdom from which we derive our origin" to want independence. It implored George III to intercede with Parliament and find some means to preserve English liberties in America. Like so many other petitions, the Olive Branch had little impact in Britain. By the autumn of 1775 the home government was already mobilizing for full-scale war. This was one form of a response to the Olive Branch. The other was a public declaration that all the colonies were now in open rebellion.

LEXINGTON AND CONCORD

The Shot Heard 'Round the World

After the bloody skirmish at Lexington, Lieutenant Colonel Francis Smith's redcoats marched toward their intended target, the village of Concord, which served as a central storage point for patriot powder and arms. Smith's troops were to "seize and destroy" these military goods.

Just east of Concord, Smith's column found the road blocked by 250 Minutemen under Major John Buttrick. Choosing not to fight, Buttrick ordered his citizen-soldiers to retreat. They did so in disciplined fashion, marching into Concord just ahead of the redcoats and then to higher ground a mile north of the village across Old North Bridge.

Colonel Smith soon had his troops out hunting for supplies. He sent six companies up to North Bridge to seize any powder and weapons stored at farms in that area. Once there, Captain Lawrence Parsons led three companies across the bridge, right past the patriot militia. Captain Walter Laurie secured the bridge with the remaining companies.

At this juncture, just a little before 10 A.M., Buttrick's Minutemen saw a cloud of smoke rising from the village. The British were burning Concord's liberty tree, along with some gun carriages. An alarmed patriot officer shouted, "Would you let them burn down our town?" Angered by this prospect, Buttrick's troops advanced and engaged Laurie's redcoats; both contingents fired at each other across the bridge. The British, sustaining several casualties, fell back to Concord in reacting to these shots "heard 'round the world."

By late morning, Smith realized that the local patriots, fearing an incursion, had earlier that week moved most of the military supplies to other locales. The redcoat mission was a failure. Worse yet, hundreds of militiamen, enraged by news of events at Lexington, were gathering behind trees and stone fences, just waiting for Smith's retreat.

Had General Gage not sent out a relief force under Hugh, Lord Percy, Smith's redcoats might have been exterminated. The two British columns linked up just east of Lexington. By sundown, they had reached Charlestown peninsula, just north of Boston, having barely survived the opening encounter of the War for American Independence.

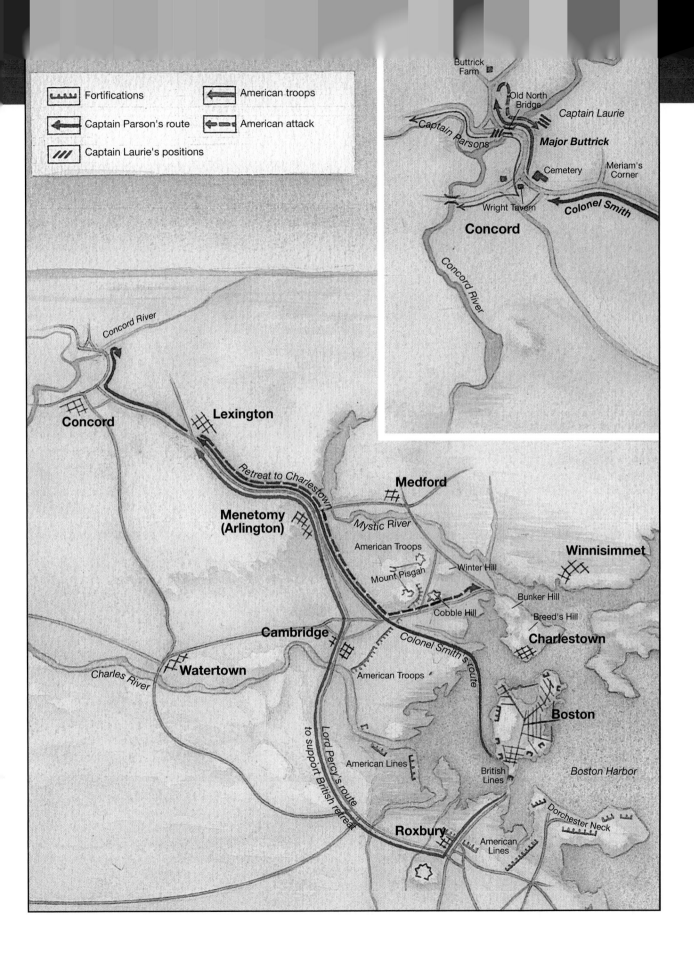

Legend:
- Fortifications
- Captain Parson's route
- Captain Laurie's positions
- American troops
- American attack

Inset map (Concord):
Buttrick Farm
Old North Bridge
Captain Laurie
Captain Parsons
Major Buttrick
Cemetery
Meriam's Corner
Wright Tavern
Colonel Smith
Concord
Concord River

Main map:
Concord River
Concord
Lexington
Retreat to Charlestown
Medford
Menetomy (Arlington)
Mystic River
American Troops
Mount Pisgah
Winter Hill
Winnisimmet
Bunker Hill
Cobble Hill
Breed's Hill
Charlestown
Cambridge
Colonel Smith's route
Watertown
Charles River
American Troops
Boston
British Lines
Boston Harbor
Lord Percy's route to support British retreat
American Lines
Roxbury
Dorchester Neck
American Lines

The Battle of Bunker Hill

Early on Friday evening, June 16, 1775, rebel military leaders held an urgent meeting in Cambridge, Massachusetts. Intelligence had just reached them that redcoats under Lieutenant General Thomas Gage would soon attempt to break out of Boston. The British plan was to cross the body of water south of Boston, take Dorchester Heights, then sweep north through Cambridge, the patriot army command base, and send the rebels, now numbering well over 10,000 volunteers, reeling back into the countryside. The target date for this operation was Sunday, June 18.

The assembled rebel officers decided to divert the British from their plans by moving patriot lines yet closer to Boston. They gave orders to Colonel William Prescott to fortify Bunker Hill on Charlestown peninsula, just to the north of Boston. The rebels would now control terrain from which they could cannonade British vessels in the harbor and even the city, if necessary. Should the British attempt to dislodge the rebels, they would have to storm up a hill rising 130 feet above sea level into withering patriot fire.

Before midnight on June 16, Prescott, leading more than 1000 troops, reached Bunker Hill. At this point he called together the other officers, including Colonel Richard Gridley, an experienced military engineer, to discuss the placement of earthworks. As they studied the terrain around them, they could see another hill some 600 yards closer to Boston,

which rose sharply to 75 feet above sea level. Gridley recommended a line of trenches and a redoubt on that site. Bunker Hill, the group concluded, should serve as a secondary line of defense.

Moving forward as quietly as possible, the Americans dug in rapidly on Breed's Hill, knowing that daylight would expose their activity. At dawn on Saturday, June 17, sailors on board a British war vessel in the harbor spied the new rebel position and opened up with artillery fire. The cannonade awoke everyone in the vicinity, including Gage, who soon met in a council of war with three other generals—William Howe, Henry Clinton, and John Burgoyne—all of whom had recently arrived in Boston.

Gage, despite his superior rank as commander of British military forces in North America, deferred to the three major generals in his presence. Since Gage had repeatedly urged caution in handling the rebels, many home leaders had started asking whether he was too timid for the task at hand. The appearance of Howe, Clinton, and Burgoyne, he knew, was hardly a vote of confidence.

During the imperial wars, British military officers had repeatedly characterized the colonists as fainthearted fighters. Reflecting this attitude, the three generals could not fathom how Gage had gotten his troops trapped in Boston by untrained, disorganized, and ill-disciplined rebels. The generals, not surprisingly, demanded an immediate offensive against Prescott's troops. They hoped for a victory so crushing that rebel resistance would disintegrate completely.

Then they debated tactics. Henry Clinton wanted to seize control of the narrow neck of land behind Bunker

Hill connecting Charlestown peninsula to the mainland. That maneuver would trap Prescott's force, which then could be defeated and captured in detail. Howe and Burgoyne favored a direct frontal assault. The rebels would wither and run, they argued, in the face of concentrated, disciplined British arms. Gage reluctantly agreed to a frontal assault. He hoped the other generals were correct, that the Americans would flee rather than fight, but deep inside he expected heavy casualties.

British regulars were very well trained soldiers. They would rather stand up to furious enemy fire than to the wrath of their officers and the brutal military penalties for insubordination of any kind. Insolence toward an officer or attempted desertion resulted in punishments of up to 1000 lashes well laid on, which few persons could survive.

New soldiers received rigorous training in the basics of combat. When deployed in front of the enemy, they moved easily from column formations into three battle lines. After troops in the first line fired their smoothbore muskets, affectionately known as the "Brown Bess," they reloaded as their comrades in the next two lines stepped in front of them and fired their muskets in turn.

Smoothbore muskets were inaccurate weapons with an effective range of less than 80 yards. Experienced soldiers going through the steps of ramming powder and ball down the barrel could rarely get off more than two shots a minute. Thus most battle casualties came from bayonet wounds when competing armies, once having fired three or four rounds at very close range, charged forward and engaged in hand-to-hand combat. The

bayonet, fastened to the end of the musket, was the major killing weapon of eighteenth-century European-style warfare, and the proficient soldier more often stabbed than shot his opponent to death.

Knowing all of this, General Howe, whom Gage placed in charge of the assault, envisioned an overwhelming victory over a motley band of rebels. By 3 P.M., more than 2000 redcoats had been ferried across the bay and were ready to advance. Howe sent forward troops on his left under General Robert Pigot directly at Breed's Hill to divert the Americans. In turn, he led his column along the shore to break through a patriot line behind a rail fence. He expected to sweep these defenders aside in a classic flanking maneuver, then swing sharply to the left and cut Prescott's soldiers off from retreat as they dueled with Pigot's redcoats on their front. Bayonets would finish the expected rout.

Galling rebel fire frustrated the first British assault. The patriots held off shooting until the last possible moment, then unleashed a furious series of blasts. The redcoats staggered and fell back. Wrote one British officer with Howe, we "were served up in companies against the grass fence, without being able to penetrate. . . . Most of our grenadiers and light infantry, in presenting themselves, lost three-fourths, and many nine-tenths, of their men." Far to the left Pigot's soldiers also ran back from the blistering volleys of musket fire being laid down by Prescott's defenders.

Retreating on all fronts, the British regrouped and then tried to execute Howe's plan a second time. "It was surprising," wrote an observer, to watch the redcoats "step over . . . dead bodies, as though they had been logs of wood." Once again, exclaimed one British officer, "an incessant stream of fire" forced them back. From his vantage point in Boston, General Burgoyne described what was happening as "a complication of horror . . . more dreadfully terrible" than anything he had ever seen. He wondered whether "defeat" would bring on "a final loss to the British empire in America."

At this critical juncture, Howe, reinforced by 400 fresh troops, decided to throw everything against the redoubt, where, unknown to him, Prescott's troops were running out of ammunition. Now the British, with regimental pride at stake, shouted "push on, push on." Within minutes they overran the Americans, most of whom lacked bayonets to defend themselves. Prescott's coolness under heavy fire resulted in an orderly retreat, but most of the rebel casualties occurred among defenders who did not evacuate in time. Included among them was Samuel Adams's valued political associate, Dr. Joseph Warren, already wounded but who died from bayonet wounds inflicted by an enraged redcoat who apparently recognized him and cried out that agitators like Warren were responsible for such horrible carnage.

The misnamed Battle of Bunker Hill was over within little more than an hour. Most of the patriots did escape, having no way of knowing that they had participated in the bloodiest fight of the Revolutionary War. The figure of 1465 combined casualties shocked everyone in what General Clinton called "a dear bought victory." The British had really gained nothing of consequence, since the American patriots still controlled the countryside surrounding Boston and Charlestown peninsula.

The Expanding Martial Conflict

Congressional moderates accomplished little, except to delay a declaration of independence. The war kept spreading, making a formal renunciation of British allegiance seem almost anticlimactic. On May 10, 1775, citizen-soldiers under Vermont's Ethan Allen and Connecticut's **Benedict Arnold** seized the once-mighty fortress of Ticonderoga at the southern end of Lake Champlain. This action netted the Americans more than 100 serviceable artillery pieces that would eventually be deployed to help drive British forces from Boston.

Taking Ticonderoga raised the question of luring Canada into the rebellion. Many hoped that Quebec Province would become the fourteenth colony, so much so that Congress approved a two-pronged invasion in the late summer of 1775. One column under General Richard Montgomery, a former British officer who had resettled in America, traveled down Lake Champlain and seized Montreal. The second column under Colonel Benedict Arnold proceeded on a harrowing march through the woods of Maine and finally emerged before the walls of Quebec City. Early on the morning of December 31, 1775, combined forces under these two commanders boldly tried to take the city but were repulsed. Montgomery lost his life, Arnold was seriously wounded, and great numbers of patriot troops were killed or captured. The rebel attempt to seize Canada had failed. This effort, however, made it increasingly difficult to argue that the colonists were only interested in defending their homes and families until political differences with Britain could be resolved.

Back in Boston, meanwhile, Generals Howe, Clinton, and Burgoyne arrived in May 1775 and urged General Gage to resume the offensive against the New Englanders. That opportunity came on June 17 just after patriot forces moved onto Charlestown peninsula north of Boston's back bay. The rebels planned to dig in on Bunker Hill but constructed the most extended portions of their line on Breed's Hill closer to Boston. After lengthy debate the British generals decided upon a frontal assault by some 2500 troops under William Howe's command to show the rebels the awesome power of concentrated British arms.

That afternoon, as citizens in Boston watched the misnamed Battle of Bunker Hill from rooftops, Howe's detachment made three separate charges, finally dislodging the patriots, who were running out of ammunition. This engagement was the bloodiest of the whole war. The British suffered 1054 casualties—40 percent of the redcoats engaged. American casualties amounted to 411, or 30 percent. Among those slain was Samuel Adams's close political associate, Dr. Joseph Warren, mourned by patriots everywhere.

The realization that patriot soldiers had been driven from the field undermined the euphoria that followed the rout of the redcoats at Lexington and Concord. Still, the British gained little advantage because they had failed to pursue the fleeing rebels. They remained trapped in Boston, surrounded by thousands of armed and angry colonists. Henry Clinton summarized matters best when he called Bunker Hill "a dear bought victory," adding dryly that "another such would have ruined us."

Lord Dunmore's Proclamation of Emancipation

New England and Canada did not long remain the only theaters of war. Before the end of 1775 fighting erupted in the South. In Virginia the protagonist was **John Murray, Lord Dunmore**, who was the last royal governor of the Old Dominion. In May 1774 Dunmore had dissolved the Assembly because the burgesses called for a day of fasting and prayer in support of the Bostonians. Incensed at Dunmore's arbitrary action, Virginia's gentleman-planters started meeting in provincial conventions, acting as if royal authority no longer existed.

Dunmore resented such impudence. In June 1775 he fled Williamsburg and announced that British subjects still loyal to the Crown should join him in bringing the planter elite to its senses. Very few citizens came forward. By autumn Dunmore, who used a naval vessel in Chesapeake Bay as his headquarters, had concluded that planter resistance could only be broken by turning Virginia's slaves against their masters. On November 7, 1775, he issued an emancipation proclamation. It read in part: "And I do hereby further declare all indentured servants, Negroes, or others . . . free, that are able and willing to bear arms."

Dunmore hoped that Virginia's slaves would break their chains and join with him in teaching their former masters that talk of liberty was a two-edged sword. The plan backfired. Irate planters suppressed copies of the proclamation and spread the rumor of a royal hoax designed to lure blacks into Dunmore's camp so that he could sell them to the owners of West Indian sugar plantations, where inhuman working conditions and very high mortality rates prevailed. Still, as many as 2000 slaves took their chances and escaped to the royal standard.

Those blacks who first fled became a part of **Dunmore's Ethiopian regiment**, which made the mistake of engaging Virginia militiamen in a battle at Great Bridge in December 1775. Having had no time for even the fundamentals of military training, the regiment took a drubbing. This battle ended any semblance of royal authority in Virginia. Dunmore and his following soon retreated to a flotilla of vessels in Chesapeake Bay. During the next few months the numbers of royalist adherents kept growing, but then smallpox struck, killing hundreds of people. In the summer of 1776 Dunmore sailed away, leaving behind planters who more closely guarded their human property while demanding independence from those in Britain whom they denounced as tyrants.

Resolving the Independence Question

Lord Dunmore's experiences highlighted the collapse of British political authority. Beginning in the summer of 1775, colony after colony witnessed an end to royal government. To fill the void, the patriots elected ad hoc provincial congresses. These bodies functioned as substitute legislatures and dealt with pressing local issues. They also took particular interest in suppressing suspected loyalists.

During that same summer Massachusetts asked the Continental Congress for permission to establish a more enduring government based on a written constitution. After ousting its royal governor, New Hampshire followed suit. These requests forced Congress to act. The delegates did so in early November, stating that Massachusetts, New Hampshire, and any others might adopt "such a form of government, as . . . will best produce the happiness of the people," yet only if written constitutions specified that these governments would exist until "the present dispute between Great Britain and the colonies" came to an end. The moderates realized that new state governments, as much if not more than a separate army, had the appearance of de facto independence. They did everything they could to prevent a total rejection of British political authority in America.

John Dickinson led the campaign in Congress to suppress discussion of a declaration of independence. In early November 1775 he got the Pennsylvania Assembly to instruct its congressional delegates to "dissent from, and utterly reject, any propositions . . . that may cause or lead to a separation from our mother country." New York, Delaware, Maryland, and South Carolina soon adopted similar instructions. Thus there was to be no resolution of the independence question before 1776.

Events outside of Congress were about to overwhelm the moderates. In January 1776 **Thomas Paine,** a recent migrant from England who had once been a corsetmaker's apprentice, published a pamphlet entitled *Common Sense.* It became an instant best-seller, running through 25 editions and 120,000 copies over the next three months.

Thomas Paine's *Common Sense,* first published in January 1776, urged the colonists to embrace independence and a bold new world of political freedom.

Common Sense electrified the populace with its dynamic, forceful language. Paine communicated a sense of urgency about moving toward independence. He attacked congressional moderates for not being bold enough to break with the past, and he likewise denounced the British monarchy, writing: "The folly of hereditary right in Kings, is that nature disapproves it . . . by giving mankind *an ass for a lion.*" He encouraged Americans to adopt republican forms of government, since "every spot of the old world is overrun with oppression." The fate of all humans everywhere, he concluded, hung in the balance. *Common Sense* put severe pressure on the moderates, but they held on doggedly, hoping against hope that Great Britain would turn from its belligerent course and begin serious negotiations with Congress.

At the end of February 1776 another significant incident took place in the form of a short, bloody battle between loyalists and patriot militia at Moore's Creek Bridge in North Carolina. This engagement resulted in more than a rout of local **tories.** Now facing a shooting war, North Carolina's provincial congress reversed instructions to its congressional delegates and allowed them to discuss independence and vote on a plan of national government. Soon thereafter the Virginians, furious about Lord Dunmore's activities, issued similar instructions. Then leaders in Rhode Island, impatient with everyone else, boldly declared their own independence in early May.

On June 7, 1776, **Richard Henry Lee,** speaking on behalf of the Virginia provincial convention, presented formal resolutions to Congress. Lee urged "that these United Colonies are, and of right ought to be, free and independent states, . . . and that all political connection between them and the State of Great Britain is, and ought to be, totally dissolved." The resolutions also called for the creation of a national government and the formation of alliances with foreign nations in support of the war effort.

Within a few days Congress established two committees, one headed by John Dickinson to produce a plan of central government and another to prepare a statement on independence. **Thomas Jefferson** (1743–1826), a tall, young Virginian, agreed to write a draft text on independence, which the committee laid before Congress on Friday, June 28. John Adams was expecting "the greatest debate of all" on Monday, July 1. In the session that day Dickinson spoke forcefully against a formal severance of ties with Great Britain. Americans, he argued, could not endure against superior British arms, especially "when we are in so wretched a state of preparation" for war. Nor did he think that significant foreign aid from France and other nations would be readily forthcoming. Moving forward with independence, he concluded, would be like reading "a little more in the Doomsday Book of America."

The delegates listened politely, but Dickinson was no longer in step with the mood of Congress. At the end of the day they voted on Lee's resolutions, and nine state delegations gave their assent. Political maneuvering produced what could be described as a unanimous vote the next day when 12 states voted affirmatively. New York's delegates had not yet received instructions from leaders back home, so they abstained, even though they were now personally in favor of independence. By so overwhelming a ratification of Lee's resolutions, Congress technically declared independence on Tuesday, July 2.

Congress next turned to the consideration of Jefferson's draft, which one delegate in a classic understatement called "a pretty good one." The delegates made only a few changes. They deleted a controversial statement blaming the slave trade on the king as well as a phrase repudiating friendship with the British people. By Thursday evening, July 4, 1776, everything was in place, and Congress unanimously adopted Jefferson's document, a masterful explanation of the reasons why the colonists were seeking independence.

The Declaration of Independence proclaimed to the world that Americans had been terribly mistreated by their parent nation. Much of the text represents a summary list of grievances, ranging from misuse of a standing army of redcoats in the colonies and the abuse of the rightful powers of popularly elected colonial assemblies to the ultimate crime, starting an unjustified war against loyal subjects. The Declaration blamed George III for the pattern of tyranny. He had failed to control his ministers, thereby abandoning his role as a true servant of the people.

Besides grievances, the Declaration also offered a long-range vision. Jefferson believed the Revolution would succeed only if Americans acted with a clear and noble purpose. Since "all men are created equal" and have "certain unalienable rights," which Jefferson defined as "life, liberty, and the pursuit of happiness," Americans needed to dedicate themselves to the establishment of a whole new set of political relationships guaranteeing all citizens fundamental lib-

Delegates to the Second Continental Congress formally debated whether to declare independence on July 1, 1776. After making minor modifications in Jefferson's draft, they unanimously approved the Declaration of Independence on July 4.

erties. The great task facing the revolutionary generation would be to institute republican forms of government, based on the rule of law and human reason. Governments had "to effect" the "safety and happiness" of all persons in the name of human decency, and all persons would be obligated to work for the greater good of the whole community.

Through Jefferson's words, the patriots of 1776 committed themselves to uplifting humanity in what they viewed as a world overrun by greed, petty ambition, and political tyranny. They would not realize their lofty purpose, however, unless they found the means to defeat the huge British military force arriving in America at the very time that Congress was debating and approving the Declaration of Independence.

WITHOUT VISIBLE ALLIES: THE WAR IN THE NORTH

British officials had made a great blunder in 1775. Disdaining the colonists as "a set of upstart vagabonds, the dregs and scorn of the human species," they had woefully underestimated their opponent. Lexington and Concord drove home this reality. Although the king's civil and military leaders continued to presume their superiority, they became far more serious about waging war. They had come to realize that snuffing out the rebellion was a complex military assignment, given the sheer geographic size of the colonies and the absence of a strategically vital center, such as a national capital, that, if captured, would end the contest. They also understood that the use of an invading army was not the easiest way to regain the political allegiance of a people no longer placing such great value on being British subjects.

Britain's Massive Military Buildup

Directing the imperial war effort were King George, Lord North, and **Lord George Germain** (1716–1785), who became the American secretary in 1775. Germain, who during the Seven Years' War had been court-martialed on charges of cowardice in battle and thrown out of the British army, was a surprisingly effective administrator. He proved adept at dealing with the bureaucratic and inefficient imperial military machine. His skills became evident in planning for the campaign of 1776—the largest land and sea offensive executed by any western nation until the Allied invasion of North Africa in 1942.

Step by step, Germain pulled the elements together. Of utmost importance was overall campaign strategy. It involved concentrating as many troops as possible on the port of New York City, where great numbers of loyalists lived, then subduing the surrounding countryside as a food and supply base. Loyalists would be used to reinstitute royal government, and the king's forces would engage and crush the rebel army. The American will to resist had to be shattered, and Germain hoped the king's forces could do so in only one campaign season. The longer the rebels lasted, he thought, the greater would be their prospects for success.

Next was the matter of assembling the military forces. It was not the practice in Britain, or elsewhere in Europe, to draw upon all able-bodied, adult males. By and large the middle classes were exempt from service because they were considered productive members of society. The rank and file would come from two sources. First would be the poorer, less productive subjects in the British Isles either recruited or dragooned into service. Since life in European armies was often brutal, it was not always possible to convince or coerce even the most destitute of subjects to sign enlistment papers.

A second source would be the principalities of Germany. Before the end of the war, six German states procured 30,000 soldiers. Some 17,000 came from Hesse-Cassel, where the local head of state coerced many unwilling subjects into service. In return, he received cash payments from the British Crown for each soldier supplied. **Hessians** and downtrodden Britons, including many Irish subjects, thus became the backbone of His Majesty's army.

Certainly as significant a matter as troop recruitment was military leadership. Home government leaders viewed General Gage as too timid and too respectful of Americans. The king recalled Gage in October 1775, naming **William Howe** (1729–1814) to replace him as commander in chief. William's brother Richard, Admiral Lord Howe (1726–1799), took charge of the naval flotilla that transported thousands of troops to America in 1776.

Lord Germain expected the Howe brothers to use their combined land and naval forces to smash and bayonet the rebels into submission. However, they did not turn out to be fearsome commanders. Politically, they identified with whig leaders in England who believed the colonists had some legitimate grievances. They intended to move in careful steps, using the presence of so many well-trained regulars to persuade Americans to sign loyalty oaths and renounce the rebellion. In failing to achieve the strategic objective of wiping out patriot resistance in only one campaign season, the less than daring Howe brothers actually helped save the patriot cause from early extinction.

The Campaign for New York

Not yet aware of the scale of British mobilization, New Englanders cheered loudly in mid-March 1776 when William Howe took redcoats and loyalists in tow and fled by sea to Halifax, Nova Scotia. British control of Boston had become untenable because Washington placed the cannons captured at Ticonderoga on Dorchester Heights overlooking the city. Howe's choice was to retreat or be bombarded into submission. Washington, however, did not relax. For months he had predicted the British would strike at New York City. He was absolutely right.

The king's army soon converged on Staten Island, across the bay from Manhattan. William Howe, sailing south from Halifax, arrived with 10,000 soldiers at the end of June. During July, even as Americans learned about the Declaration of Independence, more and more British troops appeared, another 20,000 by mid-August. They came in some 400 transports escorted by 70 naval vessels and 13,000 sailors under Admiral Lord Howe's supervision. All told, the Howe brothers had some 43,000 well-supplied, well-trained, and well-armed combatants. By comparison, George Washington had 28,000 troops on his muster rolls, but only 19,000 were present and fit for duty in August. Even worse, the bulk of the rebel army lacked good weapons or supplies and was deficient in training and discipline.

The decision to defend New York, which the Continental Congress insisted upon and to which Washington acceded, was one of the great rebel blunders of the war. Completely outnumbered, the American commander unwisely divided his soldiers between Manhattan and Brooklyn Heights, separated by the East River. The Howe brothers responded on August 22 by landing troops at Gravesend, Long Island, thereby putting them in an excellent position to trap Washington's force in Brooklyn. For some inexplicable reason, however, Lord Howe chose not to move his naval vessels into the East River, which would have sealed off Washington's escape route. The rebels took a severe beating from the redcoats and Hessians, but they escaped back across the East River. Washington had been lucky, and he clearly learned from his error. Never again did he place his troops in so potentially disastrous a position.

The Howe brothers moved along indecisively through the rest of the campaign season. Every time they had the advantage, they failed to destroy the rebel army. They drove Washington's forces northward out of Manhattan, then wheeled about and captured some 2000 rebels defending Fort Washington (November 16, 1776), located high on a bluff overlooking the Hudson River. Two days later a British column under **Charles, Lord Cornwallis** (1738–1805), nearly bagged another sizable patriot contingent at Fort Lee in New Jersey, across from Fort Washington. One of Washington's most talented field commanders, Nathanael Greene of Rhode Island, managed to extricate his force just in time.

Washington had already moved into New Jersey. He ordered a retreat, hoping to get his soldiers across the Delaware River and into Pennsylvania before the aggressive Cornwallis caught up with the dispirited rebel band. By early December 1776 what remained of Washington's army had reached Pennsylvania.

Although Washington's officers wanted to burn New York City to keep the British from using this port city as a base for military operations, Congress vetoed the proposal. When a fire broke out on September 20, 1776, the British and the Americans accused one another of starting the conflagration.

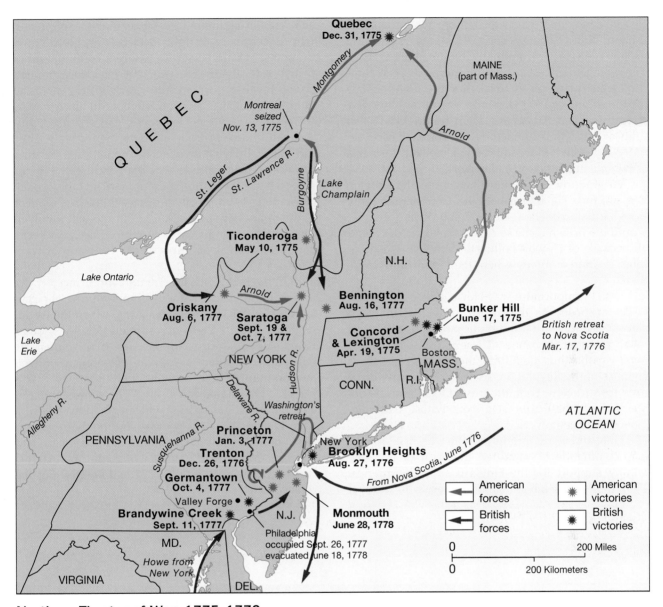

Northern Theater of War, 1775–1778

Saving the Cause at Trenton

As the half-starving, battle-wearied patriot troops fled, hundreds of them also deserted. They had learned that British muskets and bayonets could maim and kill. Others, ravaged by disease or wounded in battle, were left behind along the way with the hope of their receiving decent treatment from the enemy. The American army was on the verge of extinction. Washington wrote in mid-December, "I think the game is pretty near up. . . . No man, I believe, ever had a greater choice of difficulties and less means to extricate himself from them." Knowing he had virtually destroyed his prey, William Howe ordered his troops into winter camps

and returned to New York City. He was sure mopping up operations could be easily completed in the spring of 1777.

At this juncture George Washington earned his credentials as an innovative commander. He assessed his desperate position and decided upon a bold counterstroke. The success of this maneuver might save his army; defeat would surely ruin it. With muster rolls showing only 6000 troops, Washington divided his soldiers into three groups and tried to recross the icy Delaware River on Christmas evening. Their targets were British outposts in New Jersey. Of the three contingents, only Washington's near-frozen band of 2400 troops accomplished this daring maneuver.

At dawn they reached Trenton, where Colonel Johann Rall's unsuspecting Hessians were still groggy with liquor from their Christmas celebration. The engagement was over in a moment. Four hundred enemy troops escaped, but the Continentals captured almost 1000 Hessians. Within another few days the elated Americans again outdueled British units at Princeton. Stunned by this flurry of rebel activity, Howe redeployed his New Jersey outposts in a semicircle much closer to New York.

Washington had done much more than regain lost ground. He had saved the Continental army from virtual extinction. Never again during the war would the British come so close to total victory—and all because of Howe's failure to demolish Washington's shattered forces when the opportunity was there.

Also of importance was Howe's decision to pull in his outposts. As the British army had marched across New Jersey, it lured thousands of neutrals and loyalists under its banner. These individuals signed loyalty oaths, thus identifying themselves publicly as enemies of the Revolution. As the British army drew back toward New York, the fury of local patriots descended on these tory neighbors whose true allegiance had been revealed.

Time and again throughout the war, British military commanders committed the error of not sustaining support for the king's friends in America. They rarely took advantage of the reservoir of loyal subjects, an estimated 20 percent of the populace, who stood ready to fight the rebels and to do anything else within reason to assure a continuation of British rule. Before the war was over an estimated 50,000 loyalists formed into nearly 70 regiments to help the British army regain control in America. British commanders, however, largely used this valuable source of troop strength ineffectively. They did not really trust loyalists or respect their fighting prowess. Their attitude was that loyalists were just colonists, a part of the "rude" American rabble. Such presumed superiority represented a major blindspot, when an essential military task involved regaining the allegiance of enough citizens to effect a complete revival of imperial political authority in America.

On the rebel side, the Trenton and Princeton victories did not result in a revived outpouring of popular support for Washington's army. When the Continentals were in flight across New Jersey, Thomas Paine stepped forth with his first *Crisis* paper. He begged the populace to rally at this moment of deep desperation. "These are the times that try men's souls," Paine stated forcefully. "The summer soldier and the sunshine patriot will, in this crisis, shrink from the service of his country; but he that stands it now, deserves the love and thanks of man and woman." Many read Paine's words, but the massive British campaign effort of 1776 had snuffed out the *rage militaire*.

Emanuel Gottlieb Leutze, *George Washington Crossing the Delaware* (1851). The artist exercised considerable artistic license in recording the event. For example, he used the Rhine River of his native Germany to represent the Delaware, and the flag shown in the painting did not come into use until six months after the incident. Despite historical discrepancies, the painting captures the noble spirit of the American patriots.

The Real Continentals

One of the greatest problems facing Washington and the Continental Congress after 1776 was sustaining the rebel army's troop strength. In May 1777 the commander in chief had only 10,000 soldiers, of whom 7363 were present and fit for duty. This number increased substantially during the summer and fall, although only an estimated 11,000 Continentals entered Valley Forge. For the remainder of the war Washington's core of regulars rarely was more sizable. At times, as few as 5000 soldiers stood with him.

Certainly after his experiences in 1776, Washington understood that he must maintain "a respectable army" in the field, hoping ultimately to break Britain's will to continue the fight. He needed troops who would commit themselves to long-term service (three years or the duration), would submit to rigorous training and discipline, and would accept privation in the field. These were hardly glamorous prospects, especially when service often entailed death or dismemberment. Still, Washington, Congress, and the states could promise cash bounties for enlisting, as well as regular pay, decent clothing, adequate food, and even land at war's end. For people who had nothing to lose, long-term service in the Continental army was at least worth considering.

After 1776 the rank and file of the Continental army came to be made up of economically hard pressed and unfree citizens. Private Joseph Plumb Martin was probably better off than most who enlisted—or were forced into service. The bulk were young (ranging in age from their early teens to mid-twenties), landless, unskilled, poverty-stricken males whose families were likewise quite poor. Also well represented were indentured servants and slaves who stood as substitutes for their masters in return for guarantees of personal freedom at the war's end.

In 1777 Massachusetts became the first state to authorize the enlistment of African Americans—both slaves and freemen. Rhode Island soon followed suit by raising two black regiments. Southern states were far more reluctant to allow slaves to substitute for their masters. Maryland and Virginia ultimately did so, which caused one patriot general to query why so many "sons of freedom" seemed so anxious "to trust their all to be defended by slaves." Add to these groups captured British soldiers and deserters, particularly Hessians and Irishmen, as well as tories and criminals who were often given a choice between military service or the gallows, and a composite portrait of the real Continental army begins to emerge.

Eighteenth-century armies also accepted women in the ranks. Like their male counterparts, they were invariably living on the margins of society. These women "on the ration" (more literally half rations)

Dressed as a man, Deborah Sampson of Massachusetts served for more than a year in the Continental Army and was wounded in the fighting at Tarrytown, New York.

must be differentiated from so-called camp followers—those who marched along with their husbands or lovers or were prostitutes. Women in service performed various functions, ranging from caring for the sick and wounded, cooking, and mending clothes to scavenging battlefields for clothing and equipment and burying the dead. On occasion they became directly involved in combat. Such a person was hard-drinking **Margaret "Dirty Kate" Corbin**. Her husband, a cannoneer, was shot dead when British forces attacked and captured Fort Washington in November 1776. Kate Corbin stepped forth, took his place, and helped fire the artillery piece until she also sustained a serious wound, from which she eventually recovered. The British army allowed 1 woman in the ranks for every 10 men; the Continental ratio was closer to 1 in 15.

Whether male or female, a unifying characteristic of Washington's post-1776 Continentals was poverty and, in many cases, lack of personal freedom—much like their counterparts in the British army. As a group, they repeatedly risked their lives in return for promises: food, clothing, pay, and even land on which to make a decent living after the war. Their dreams of future opportunity depended upon the success of the rebellion, and that is one reason why they willingly endured, even though the far more prosperous civilian populace ignored their privation at such encampments as Valley Forge.

THE PEOPLE SPEAK

Thomas Paine's *American Crisis I* (December 1776)

In 1774 Benjamin Franklin, then residing in England, urged Thomas Paine to resettle in America and make his living as a writer. Paine was 37 years old at the time and had failed at virtually everything. He had nothing to lose, so he sailed for Philadelphia, where he gained the opportunity to become one of the great pamphleteers of the Revolution. His *Common Sense* (January 1776) was a runaway bestseller and clearly helped push American patriots toward independence. "We have it in our power to begin the world over again," Paine wrote excitedly in *Common Sense,* but that possibility depended on beating the British militarily. By the end of 1776 the Continental army was struggling to survive, having been shoved by British forces all the way across New Jersey into Pennsylvania. Paine, traveling with the army, penned his first *Crisis* paper to assist in reviving patriot fervor for the cause of liberty. His words, though powerful, had little effect in getting more Americans to commit to long-term military service against the British, a chronic patriot problem after 1776.

These are the times that try men's souls. The summer soldier and the sunshine patriot will, in this crisis, shrink from the service of his country: but he that stands it *now,* deserves the thanks of man and woman. Tyranny, like hell, is not easily conquered: yet we have this consolation with us, that the harder the conflict, the more glorious the triumph. What we obtain too cheap, we esteem too lightly: 'tis dearness only that gives every thing its value. Heaven knows how to set a proper price upon its goods; and it would be strange, indeed, if so celestial an article as freedom should not be highly rated. Britain, with an army to enforce her tyranny, has declared that she has a right, not only to tax, but 'to bind us in all cases whatsoever:' and if being bound in that manner is not slavery, there is not such a thing as slavery upon earth. Even the expression is impious: for so unlimited a power can belong only to God. . . .

I turn, with the warm ardour of a friend, to those who have nobly stood, and are yet determined to stand the matter out. I call not upon a few, but upon all; not on this state, or that state, but on every state. Up and help us. Lay your shoulders to the wheel. Better have too much force than too little, when so great an object is at stake. Let it be told to the future world, that in the depth of winter, when nothing but hope and virtue could survive, that the city and the country, alarmed at one common danger, came forth to meet and to repulse it. Say not that thousands are gone: turn out your tens of thousands: throw not the burden of the day upon providence, but show your faith by your good works, that God may bless you. It matters not where you live, or what rank of life you hold; the evil or the blessing will reach you all. The far and the near, the home counties and the back, the rich and the poor, shall suffer or rejoice alike. The heart that feels not now, is dead. The blood of his children shall curse his cowardice, who shrinks back at a time when a little might have saved the whole and made them happy. I love the man that can smile in trouble—that can gather strength from distress, and grow brave by reflection. It is the business of little minds to shrink; but he, whose heart is firm, and whose conscience approves his conduct, will pursue his principles unto death. My own line of reasoning is to myself, as strait and clear as a ray of light. Not all the treasures of the world, so far as I believe, could have induced me to support an offensive war; for I think it murder: but if a thief break into my house—burn and destroy my property, and kill, or threaten to kill me and those that are in it, and to 'bind me in all cases whatsoever,' to his absolute will, am I to suffer it? . . . Let them call me rebel, and welcome; I feel no concern from it; but I should suffer the misery of devils, were I to make a whore of my soul, by swearing allegiance to one whose character is that of a sottish, stupid, stubborn, worthless, brutish man. . . .

This is our situation—and who will, may know it. By perseverance and fortitude, we have the prospect of a glorious issue; by cowardice and submission, the sad choice of a variety of evils—a ravaged country—a depopulated city—habitations without safety—and slavery without hope—our homes turned into barracks and bawdy-houses for Hessians—and a future race to provide for, whose fathers we shall doubt of! Look on this picture, and weep over it! and if there yet remains one thoughtless wretch, who believes it not, let him suffer it unlamented.

December, 1776

Source: Thomas Paine, *American Crisis I* (December 1776).

RESCUING THE PATRIOTS: TOWARD GLOBAL CONFLICT

The struggles of the American rebels did not go unobserved in European diplomatic circles. France and Spain, in particular, hoped to see the rebellion succeed. Their concerns, however, were not wholly altruistic. Territorial losses sustained during the Seven Years' War had swung the European balance of power decisively toward Great Britain. From the perspective of the Duc de Choiseul, France's foreign minister, the growing rift between Britain and America after 1763 represented an opportunity to deflate the puffed-up British lion. Losing the colonies would weaken the British empire immeasurably. France, concluded Choiseul, could only benefit from the Americans gaining their independence.

Neither Choiseul nor his protégé, the **Comte de Vergennes,** who became France's foreign minister in 1774, were beacons of the Age of Enlightenment. They supported monarchism, not republicanism, and they had little interest in fostering political liberties. As hardened and cynical diplomatic veterans, they hoped to take advantage of the American rebellion. If they could shape events properly, they would enhance France's stature at the expense of an old and despised enemy. As Vergennes stated privately, "Providence had marked out this moment for the humiliation of England."

France Offers Covert Assistance

Before 1775, the French sent spies to America not only to report on events but, when possible, to help stir up ill-will toward Britain. Shortly after Congress established its Committee of Secret Correspondence in late November 1775 to open negotiations with other nations regarding war-related support, a young French aristocrat, Achard de Bonvouloir, appeared in Philadelphia. Although acting like a private citizen, Bonvouloir was actually an agent of Vergennes. His government, he told committee members, stood ready to support the rebel cause with arms and other war goods. Vergennes's role would be to provide secret assistance to the patriots while maintaining a public stance of disinterested neutrality. The French foreign minister did not want France to get caught between the colonies and England, should the Americans falter on the battlefield or suddenly reconcile differences. If the rebels demonstrated their long-term resolve and proved worthy in combat, then France would enter the war and help crush the British.

Vergennes was a master manipulator in the court of Louis XVI (reigned 1774–1793). In 1775 one of his diplomatic agents, the courtier **Pierre-Augustin Caron de Beaumarchais** (1732–1799), perhaps best known for writing librettos for the *Marriage of Figaro* and the *Barber of Seville,* made contacts with prominent Americans in London. Beaumarchais reported back to Vergennes, and the two of them pushed hard for the formation of a private trading company, **Roderigue Hortalez & Cie.,** the sole purpose of which was to funnel war *matériel* to the patriots. Vergennes had already convinced the Spanish government to join France in making possible the American purchases by loaning money to the rebel Congress.

Meanwhile, congressional delegates had selected one of their colleagues, Connecticut merchant Silas Deane, to travel to Europe in search of loans and war goods. In July 1776 Deane made his first contact with Beaumarchais, who informed him that the structure was already in place to provide covert aid to the rebels. A delighted Deane soon was working with Beaumarchais and others in obtaining supplies.

Although some of the merchandise was shoddy, much of it was invaluable to the patriot cause. Shipments made in 1777, for example, mostly went to the Continental army's Northern Department in upstate New York where weapons, gunpowder, tents, clothing, and shoes were in desperately short supply. French goods sustained the patriot army that defeated John Burgoyne's British army at Saratoga. Secret French aid, with a smaller portion from Spain, strengthened the rebel cause immeasurably, thereby helping the patriots to endure until the French government came out publicly against Great Britain.

In September 1776 Congress designated two additional commissioners to join Deane in France. They were Benjamin Franklin and Arthur Lee, Richard Henry's irascible younger brother who had lived for many years in England and had met Beaumarchais in 1775. Franklin, well known before his arrival in Paris (he had been admitted to the French Academy of Sciences during 1772 in recognition of his electrical experiments), dominated the American delegation, whose assignment was to seek full diplomatic recognition and a formal alliance. The aging Philadelphian became a popular celebrity. With his simple dress, witty personality, worldly charm, and shrewd mind, he embodied the ideals of republicanism. Painted likenesses of him appeared everywhere, even one place that Franklin did not find very flattering—inside chamber pots.

Despite Franklin's popularity, it was not simply the Philadelphian's charm and diplomatic skill that secured an alliance. Vergennes kept pronouncing France's neutrality to avoid serious problems with the British. Invariably at public gatherings, Vergennes all but snubbed the three commissioners. In private, however, he kept priming the government of Louis XVI to build up its land and naval forces in preparation for entering the war, should circumstances warrant such a

French artists and artisans celebrated the popular diplomat Benjamin Franklin by producing countless images of him in various forms—in paintings, both large and small, in medallions, on miniature enamels, and in this model of the Philadelphian at his writing table.

decisive move. Britain's military failures in 1777 triggered formal French intervention on behalf of the patriots.

The British Seize Philadelphia

Sir William Howe had ideas of his own regarding how to conduct the war in America. He may have been a good tactician in battle, but he had little appreciation of strategy. The home government's plan—called the **Hudson Highlands strategy**—for 1777 was to send an army under John Burgoyne south from Canada through the Lake Champlain corridor. In turn, Howe was to move troops up the Hudson River, eventually linking with Burgoyne at Albany. The overall objective was to cut off New England from the rest of the colonies before sweeping eastward in reconquering the very region that had been the seedbed of rebellion.

Sir William favored going after and destroying the main Continental army. During May and June 1777 he tried to lure Washington into a climactic battle, but the American commander refused the bait and held to a very defensible position in New Jersey's Watchung Mountains.

At this juncture Howe made a decision that may have cost Britain the war. All but abandoning the primary campaign goal of joining up with Burgoyne, he resolved to seize Philadelphia, the rebel capital, hoping at the same time to catch and crush Washington's Continentals as they moved into eastern Pennsylvania to protect the rebel capital. Howe loaded 15,000 soldiers onto vessels in New York harbor and sailed out to sea in the middle of the campaign season.

Howe's flotilla came up through Chesapeake Bay in August, landing at Head of Elk in Maryland. On September 11 the British mauled Washington's Continentals at Brandywine Creek, southwest of Philadelphia. The engagement, however, did not destroy the rebel army. Within another two weeks Sir William proudly led his troops into Philadelphia; yet, except for the establishment of comfortable winter quarters, the British commander had accomplished nothing of consequence. The Continental Congress had already moved westward to York, Pennsylvania. Howe's presence cheered local loyalists. All British proponents felt relief when Washington's attack on British troops at Germantown on October 4 failed. Then the realization began to sink in that chasing after the main rebel army and seizing the enemy's capital had represented a hollow quest that cost the British dearly.

Capturing Burgoyne's Army at Saratoga

The 1777 British descent from Canada had been planned carefully, at least on paper. One of its many aspects involved the use of Native-American allies as auxiliary troops. When the war broke out, both sides had asked the tribes of the North, particularly the powerful Six Nations of Iroquois, to remain neutral in what the Continental Congress called a "family quarrel." Soon, trying to gain every possible advantage, neither side could resist tapping into Indian manpower. Guy Johnson, Britain's Superintendent of Indian Affairs in the northern colonies, invited various tribes to fight under the king's banner. Similarly, American commissioners requested direct assistance. The British held the advantage in gifts and supplies, especially arms and gunpowder. In addition, they had the better argument, since colonial settlers were the obvious culprits in seizing tribal lands, whereas British officials had tried to stop these encroachments by insisting that territory west of the Appalachians was a permanent Indian reserve.

The army of General **John Burgoyne** (1722–1792), strengthened by hundreds of Indians now on the warpath, moved southward out of Canada in mid-June. The main column of nearly 8000 pushed into Lake Champlain and drove the rebels from Fort Ticonderoga in early July. A second column of 1700 under

Colonel Barry St. Leger proceeded up the St. Lawrence River and onto Lake Ontario, before sweeping south toward Fort Schuyler (formerly Fort Stanwix) at the western end of the Mohawk Valley. St. Leger's troops were to act as a diversionary force. Soon they had 750 desperate rebel defenders of Fort Schuyler under siege. Seemingly nothing could stop these two columns, which were to converge again in Albany.

After seizing Ticonderoga, Burgoyne became more tentative about his southward movement. Like William Howe in 1776, he did not take his opponent seriously enough. Under the leadership of General Philip Schuyler, the Continental army's Northern Department had started to rally. The rebels blocked Burgoyne's path by cutting down trees, ripping up bridges, and moving boulders into fording points on streams. Soon the British advance had been slowed to less than a mile a day. Then Congress confused matters by replacing Schuyler—New Englanders considered him too aristocratic in his behavior—with General **Horatio Gates**.

Burgoyne, meanwhile, was having problems controlling his Native-American allies. In late July a few of them murdered and scalped a young woman, **Jane McCrea**, who was betrothed to one of his loyalist officers. Burgoyne refused to punish the culprits, fearing he might drive off all his native allies. Despite his forbearance, the Indians found traveling with the slow moving British army tedious at best; most retreated back to Canada before the end of August. Moreover, not disciplining Jane McCrea's murderers conveyed a message of barbarism that helped convince at least some frontier New England militiamen, worried about shielding their own families from possible Indian depredations, to take up arms and come forward in support of the Continentals.

Just as bad for the British, St. Leger's diversionary force ran into trouble. Militiamen in the Mohawk Valley under General Nicholas Herkimer, in alliance with Oneidas and Tuscaroras of the Six Nations, tried to break through to Fort Schuyler. On August 6, 1777, they clashed with St. Leger's loyalists and Indians, among them Mohawks, Cayugas, and Senecas (also of the Six Nations) at the Battle of Oriskany. Herkimer and nearly half of his column were killed or wounded that day, one of the bloodiest of the war.

Oriskany represented the beginning of the end for the once mighty Iroquois nation, whose tribes were now hopelessly divided and consuming each other in combat. When war chieftain **Joseph Brant (Thayendanegea)** of the Mohawks led numerous bloody frontier raids for the British, a Continental army expedition under General John Sullivan marched into central New York in 1779 and destroyed every Iroquois village it came upon. After the Revolutionary War ended, the more aggressive Iroquois migrated north to Canada or west into the Ohio country, where they

fought to keep out white settlers; others, less militant, moved onto reservations in western New York.

St. Leger's victory was temporary. Continentals under Benedict Arnold rushed west from the Albany area and drove off St. Leger without a second major fight. Arnold sent a dim-witted local loyalist into St. Leger's camp with fabricated news of thousands of rebel soldiers moving rapidly toward Fort Schuyler. The Indians, already upset by the loss of so many warriors at Oriskany, quickly broke camp and fled, leaving the British colonel no alternative but to retreat back into Canada.

Burgoyne had now lost his diversionary force. He suffered another major setback on August 16 when New Hampshire militiamen under General John Stark overwhelmed some 900 Hessians who were out raiding for supplies near Bennington in the Vermont territory. Burgoyne's army was all but entrapped some 30 miles north of Albany along the Hudson River. In two desperate battles (September 19 and October 7) the British force tried to find a way around the well-entrenched rebels, but the brilliant field generalship of Benedict Arnold inspired the Americans to victory. Burgoyne finally surrendered what remained of his army—some 5000 soldiers and auxiliaries—to General Gates on October 17, 1777.

According to one British soldier on the Saratoga surrender field, "we marched out, . . . with drums beating and the honors of war, but the drums seemed to have lost their former inspiring sounds, . . . as if almost ashamed to be heard on such an occasion." Losing Burgoyne's army was an unnecessary disaster for Britain, caused primarily by William Howe's unwillingness to work in concert with Burgoyne and follow through on the Hudson Highlands strategy. The victory was a momentous triumph for the Americans and a key factor in convincing Vergennes that France could now commit itself publicly to the rebel cause.

On February 6, 1778, the French government signed two treaties with the American commissioners. The first, the Treaty of Amity and Commerce, recognized American independence and encouraged the development of close trading ties. For Vergennes the prospect of conducting—and perhaps even dominating—international trade with the Americans was another way to weaken the British. Still, trading concessions were really not enough to entice the French into an alliance. What Vergennes and Louis XVI really wanted was the opportunity to strike devastating military blows at the British. They knew the Treaty of Amity and Commerce would likely provoke Britain into an act of war with France, so they insisted upon a second agreement, the more entangling Treaty of Alliance, by which the young United States and France would stand as "good and faithful" allies in the event of such hostilities.

Joseph Brant (Thayendanegea), a Mohawk war chieftain, believed the Iroquois could not remain neutral and that their only chance was to side with the British.

On March 20 Louis XVI formally greeted the American commissioners at court and announced that the new nation had gained France's diplomatic recognition. In June 1778 a naval battle in the English Channel involving British and French warships resulted in formal warfare between these two powers. The drum beat for British rule over the 13 states had now taken on the cadence of a death march.

THE WORLD TURNED UPSIDE DOWN

When George Washington learned about the French alliance, he declared a holiday for "rejoicing throughout the whole army." On that spring day in early May 1778, the Continentals at Valley Forge thoroughly enjoyed themselves. They had much to celebrate. They had survived the winter, and they had also benefited from the rigorous field training of colorful Baron **Friedrich von Steuben,** a pretended Prussian nobleman who had volunteered to teach the soldiery how to fight in more disciplined fashion. Equally important was the announcement of open, direct aid from France, which would include not only land troops but critical naval support. Having gained the formal back-

ing of a powerful European nation certainly enhanced prospects for actually beating the British. Washington, so elated by this turn in events, even winked at the issuance of "more than the common quantity of liquor" to his soldiers, which he knew would result in "some little drunkenness among them."

Revamping British Strategy

The American alliance with France changed the fundamental character of the War for Independence. British officials realized that they were no longer just contending with upstart rebels in America. They were getting themselves ensnared in a world war. France, with its well-trained army and highly mobile navy, had the ability to strike British territories anytime and anywhere it chose. While renouncing any desire to retake Canada, the French did have designs on the valuable British sugar islands in the Caribbean. They built up troop strength in the French West Indies and soon had a four-to-one advantage in that region.

The British military problem became even more complex in 1779 when Spain joined the war but only after signing a secret agreement with France—the Convention of Aranjuez—stipulating that Louis XVI's military forces were not to stop fighting until the Spanish regained the Rock of Gibraltar (lost to the British at the end of the War of the Spanish Succession in 1713). Then in late 1780 the British declared war on the Netherlands, partly so they could capture the Dutch Caribbean island of St. Eustatius, which served as a key point of exchange for American patriots in obtaining war supplies from Dutch merchants.

The dawning reality of world war threatened the British empire with major territorial losses across the globe. One result was a redesigned imperial war plan—the **Southern strategy**—for reconquering the rebellious American provinces. The assumption was that his Majesty's troops could no longer be massed against the American rebels; instead, they would have to be dispersed to threatened points, such as islands in the West Indies.

The first step came in May 1778 when General **Sir Henry Clinton** (1738?–1795), who had taken over as North American commander from a discredited William Howe, received orders to evacuate Philadelphia. In June Clinton's troops retreated to New York City, narrowly averting a disastrous defeat by Washington's pursuing Continentals at Monmouth Court House (June 28) in central New Jersey. Clinton was to hang on as best he could at the main British base, but he would have to accept a reduction in forces for campaigns elsewhere. The process of dispersal began during the autumn of 1778. Sir Henry avoided major battles with Washington's army in the North while he implemented the Southern strategy.

Crown officials mistakenly assumed that, in the South, loyalists existed in far greater numbers than in the North. In a slight modification of the Hudson Highlands strategy, the idea was to employ the king's friends, primarily as substitutes for depleted British forces, in partisan (guerrilla) warfare. Bands of armed loyalists would operate in conjunction with a main redcoat army to break patriot resistance, beginning in Georgia and then moving in carefully planned steps northward. As soon as any rebel-dominated region had been fully resecured for the Crown, royal government would be reintroduced. Ultimately through attrition, the whole South would be brought back into the British fold, opening the way for eventual subjugation of the North.

The Southern strategy required patience as well as careful nurturing of loyalist sentiment. Both seemed very possible when a detachment of 3500 redcoats sailed south from New York City in November 1778 and quickly reconquered Georgia.

Until the French alliance the South was a secondary theater of war, marked mostly by sporadic partisan fighting between loyalists and rebel militia. Indian-white relations were bloodier. As in the North with Iroquois, both sides maneuvered to gain favor with the Cherokees, Chickasaws, Creeks, and Choctaws. These four nations had a total of about 10,000 warriors, compared to an estimated 2000 among the northern Iroquois.

John Stuart, Britain's Superintendent of Indian Affairs in the southern colonies, had a network of agents working among the native populace. Late in 1775 he focused on winning over the Cherokees and Creeks, who had the most warriors, urging them to fight in concert with loyalists. Stuart was particularly successful with the Cherokees, who had recovered somewhat from their losses during the Seven Years' War. Led by the Overhill chieftain Dragging Canoe (Chincohacina), Cherokee war parties in the summer of 1776 attacked frontier settlements from Virginia to South Carolina, massacring settlers who had unwisely moved onto traditional tribal hunting grounds.

Dragging Canoe's raids had two major effects. First, in September 1776 hundreds of Virginia and North Carolina frontiersmen came together as militia and wreaked mayhem on the most easterly Cherokee towns. During October the Virginians proceeded farther west to the Overhill Cherokee villages. Dragging Canoe and his warriors retreated, promising to foreswear further assistance to the British. This agreement took the Cherokees out of the war. Second, the other major nations, seeing what had happened, snubbed John Stuart's agents and backed off from the "family quarrel." By 1777 the southern Indians had been neutralized. Although a band of Creeks did support the British after their invasion of Georgia, Native Americans did not figure prominently in Britain's post-1778 strategy.

Sir Henry Clinton, who was probably less decisive than William Howe, was slow to expand on the redcoats' success in Georgia. Finally, in late 1779 he sailed with 7600 troops toward his target—Charleston, South Carolina. There General Benjamin Lincoln, with just 3000 Continental regulars and a smattering of militia, found himself completely outnumbered and trapped when part of Clinton's force moved inland and cut off escape routes. Facing prospects of extermination, Lincoln surrendered without much of a fight on May 12, 1780. This was the only occasion during the war that the British captured an American army.

Clinton's victory at Charleston was the second success in the Southern strategy. The British commander sailed back to New York in high spirits, leaving behind Lord Cornwallis to secure all of South Carolina. Clinton had ordered Cornwallis to advance with careful steps, making sure that loyalist partisans always had firm control of territory behind his army. Ironically, Cornwallis was one of the few aggressive British generals in America. His desire to rush forward and get on with the fight helped undermine the Southern strategy.

At first, Cornwallis's boldness reaped dividends. After learning about the fall of Charleston, the Continental Congress ordered Horatio Gates, now known as the "hero of Saratoga," to proceed south, pull together a new army, and check Cornwallis. Gates botched the job completely. He gathered troops, mostly raw militiamen, in Virginia and North Carolina, then hastily rushed his soldiers into the British lair.

Early on the morning of August 16, 1780, Cornwallis's force intercepted Gates's column near Camden, South Carolina. Not only did the American troops lack training, but tainted provisions had made them sick. The evening before the Battle of Camden they had supped on "a hasty meal of quick baked bread and fresh beef, with a dessert of molasses, mixed with mush or dumplings," which, according to one of Gates's officers, "operated so cathartically as to disorder many of the men" just before the engagement. Cornwallis's army overwhelmed the rebel force in yet another crushing American defeat in the South.

The Tide of War Turns at Last

During 1780 everything seemed to go wrong for the patriot cause. Besides major setbacks in the South, officers and soldiers directly under Washington's command were increasingly restive about long overdue wages and inadequate supplies. In July 1780 the officers threatened mass resignations unless Congress did something—and speedily. In September a frustrated Benedict Arnold switched his allegiance to the

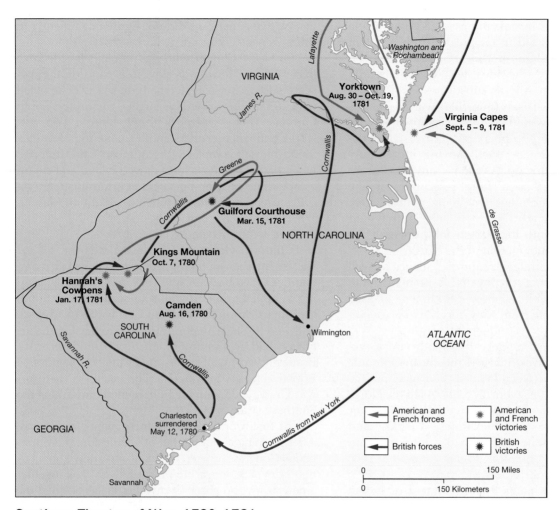

Southern Theater of War, 1780–1781

British. By the end of 1780 Continental army troop strength fell below 6000. Then, as the new year dawned, Washington faced successive mutinies among his hardened veterans in the Pennsylvania and New Jersey lines. The Continental army seemed to be disintegrating, so much so that the commander in chief put aside plans for a possible strike against New York City. Even though French troops under the Comte de Rochambeau were now in the vicinity, his own Continental numbers were too few to pursue such an elaborate venture.

Quite simply, the British seemed to be winning the endurance contest of wills: One despondent Continental officer wrote, "It really gives me great pain to think of our public affairs; where is the public spirit of the year 1775? Where are those flaming *patriots* who were ready to sacrifice their lives, their fortunes, their all, for the public?" At no time during the war, except for those dark days just before Washington's counterstrike at Trenton, had the rebel cause appeared more forlorn.

What could not yet be seen was that British successes in the South moved the redcoats toward far greater failure. Encouraged by its victories, the British southern army overreached itself. After Camden, Cornwallis started pushing toward North Carolina. His left wing under Major Patrick Ferguson, whose soldiers were mostly loyalists, was soon under the eye of growing numbers of "over-the-mountain" frontiersmen. Their goal was to protect their homesteads and families from Ferguson's loyalists, who repeatedly shot down or hanged patriots who fell into their path. Feeling their presence, Ferguson began retreating. When he spied Kings Mountain, Ferguson calculated that he and his 1100 followers could withstand any assault from atop that promontory. On October 7, 1780, the over-the-mountain force attacked from all sides. Ferguson fell mortally wounded; the rest of his column was killed, wounded, or captured; and the frontiersmen hanged nine of Ferguson's loyalists as a warning to others who might fight for the king.

The Battle of Kings Mountain destroyed the left wing of Cornwallis's army. Compounding the damage, the main British force had not completely secured South Carolina. Whenever Cornwallis moved his troops to a new locale, rebel guerrilla bands under such leaders as "Swamp Fox" Francis Marion emerged from their hiding places and wreaked vengeance on tories who had aided the British force or threatened rebels. Once again, the British had not effectively protected citizens favorably disposed toward them; this failing in combination with the debacle at Kings Mountain cut deeply into the reservoir of loyalist support available to Cornwallis.

Despite these reverses, Cornwallis seemed unconcerned. Like his fellow officers, he held Americans in contempt, believing it was only a matter of time until superior British arms would destroy the rebels. However, Cornwallis did not bargain on facing the likes of General **Nathanael Greene** (1742–1786), who replaced Gates as the Southern Department commander. Greene arrived in North Carolina during December 1780. Not surprisingly, very few troops were available for duty and, as Greene stated despondently, the "appearance" of those in camp "was wretched beyond description."

Greene was a military genius. Violating the military maxim of massing troop strength as much as possible, he decided to divide his soldiers into three small groups, one of which would work with partisan rebel bands. The idea was to let Cornwallis chase after the other two columns of just over 1000 each, until the redcoats were worn out. At that point Greene would stand and fight.

The aggressive Cornwallis took the bait. He went after Greene and sent a detached force after the other rebel column headed by shrewd, capable General Daniel Morgan of Virginia. Morgan's troops lured the onrushing British into a trap at Hannah's Cowpens in western South Carolina on January 17, 1781. Only 140 of the some 1100 British soldiers escaped being killed, captured, or wounded.

Meanwhile, Cornwallis relentlessly pursued Greene, who kept retreating northward before swinging back into central North Carolina. Then, on March 15, 1781, the rebels squared off for battle at Guilford Courthouse. The combatants fought throughout the afternoon, when the Americans abandoned the field. Greene's force had inflicted 506 casualties, as compared to taking 264 of their own. Cornwallis had gained a technical victory, but his troops were exhausted from Greene's game of "fox and hare," and the rebels were still very much in the field.

Franco-American Triumph at Yorktown

Cornwallis retreated to the seacoast to rest his army, then decided to take over British raiding operations in Virginia, which had begun in January 1781 under turncoat Benedict Arnold. In storming northward, Cornwallis totally abandoned the Southern strategy.

Nathanael Greene was now free to reassert full patriot authority in the states south of Virginia.

Back in New York, General Clinton fumed. He wanted to discipline his subordinate but was too timid to do so. Instead, he sent Cornwallis orders in July to establish a defensive base in Virginia and to refrain from conducting any offensive operations until such time as Clinton issued further orders. A most reluctant Cornwallis selected Yorktown, with easy access to Chesapeake Bay.

At this juncture everything fell into place for the Americans. Washington learned from General Rochambeau that a French naval fleet would be making its way north from the West Indies. If that fleet could seal off the entrance to Chesapeake Bay and combined Franco-American land forces could surround Cornwallis's army, a major victory would be in the making.

The rebel commander seized the opportunity. Washington and Rochambeau began marching soldiers south from New York, leaving only enough troops behind to keep Clinton tied down. In early September the French fleet, after dueling with British warships, took control of Chesapeake Bay. As the month came to a close, some 7800 French troops and 9000 Continentals and militiamen surrounded the British army of 8500 at Yorktown. Cornwallis wrote Clinton: "If you cannot relieve me very soon you must expect to hear the worst."

Using traditional siege tactics, Washington and Rochambeau slowly squeezed Cornwallis into submission. On October 17 a lone British drummer marched toward the Franco-American lines with a white flag showing. Two days later, on a bright, sunny autumn afternoon, the army of Charles, Lord Cornwallis, marched out from its lines in solemn procession and laid down its arms. As these troops did so, their musicians played an appropriate song, "The World Turned Upside Down." The surrender at Yorktown was an emotional scene. A second British army had been captured in America, and the linger-

Rebel guerrilla leaders like Francis Marion kept the patriot cause alive in South Carolina. In this scene, Marion is leading his troops across the Pee Dee River.

ing question was whether Great Britain still had the resolve to continue the war.

A Most Generous Peace Settlement

An accumulation of wounds, with the great Franco-American victory at Yorktown being the most damaging, brought the British to the peace table. As early as 1778 Britain had felt the effects of world war. Daring seaman John Paul Jones (1747–1792), known as the "father of the American navy," had conducted damaging raids along the English and Scottish coasts during that year. In 1779, while sailing in the North Sea, Jones lost his own warship, the *Bon Homme Richard,* but captured the British war frigate *Serapis* in a dramatic naval engagement, all within sight of England.

By 1781 French and Spanish warships were attacking British vessels at will in the English Channel, and French warships threatened British possessions in the West Indies. France and Spain were about to launch a major expedition against Gibraltar. In the spring of 1781 a Spanish force under Bernardo de Gálvez captured a sizable British garrison at Pensacola, Florida, and the British soon experienced defeats as far away as India. The allies had demonstrated they could carry the war anywhere, even to the shores of England, suggesting the possibility of much greater damage to the far-flung British empire than just the loss of 13 rebellious colonies in North America.

Keenly aware of these many setbacks, Lord North received the news about Yorktown "as he would have taken a [musket] ball in the breast." In March 1782 North's ministry collapsed, and a new cabinet opened negotiations with designated American peace commissioners—Benjamin Franklin, John Adams, and John Jay—in France. On November 30, 1782, the representatives agreed to preliminary peace terms, pending final ratification by both governments. The other belligerents also started coming to terms, largely because the naval war had turned against France and Spain and British troops had saved Gibraltar. All parties signed the final peace accords at Paris on September 3, 1783.

The major European powers now recognized the 13 rebellious colonies as a separate nation. Further, the peace accords established the Mississippi River as the western boundary line of the new nation and 31° north latitude as the southern boundary. Based on Gálvez's success, Britain returned the lands south of this line, constituting Florida, to Spain.

Although the American commissioners failed to obtain Canada, they had gained title to the vast reserve of Indian territory lying between the Appalachian Mountains and the Mississippi River. The treaty was silent about the rights of Indians, whose interests the British ignored, despite repeated promises during the war to protect the lands of Native Americans who joined the king's cause. All told, effective bargaining by the American peace commissioners gave the former colonists a huge geographic base on which to build their new republic.

The peace settlement also contained other important provisions. Britain recognized American fishing rights off the coast of eastern Canada, thus sustaining a major New England industry. The British promised not to carry away slaves when evacuating their troops (which they did anyway). At

This French print of the Battle of Yorktown celebrates the French contribution to the American victory in the Revolutionary War. French ships blocked the entrance to Chesapeake Bay, preventing British ships from landing there. French and American troops surrounded the British, "turning the world upside down" by forcing Cornwallis's surrender.

CHRONOLOGY OF KEY EVENTS

1775 The shot "heard 'round the world"—the first military clashes between British troops and colonists take place at Lexington and Concord (April); Second Continental Congress begins meeting in Philadelphia (May); fighting breaks out in New York, Massachusetts, and Canada (May–December); Continental army forms under the command of George Washington (June)

1776 Thomas Paine publishes *Common Sense* (January); Continental Congress adopts the Declaration of Independence (July); Virginia, North Carolina, and South Carolina frontiersmen neutralize southern Indians (July–November); British rout rebel soldiers in vicinity of New York City (August–November); American forces defeat British units at Trenton (December)

1777 Massachusetts begins enlisting free African Americans for Continental service (April); British forces seize Philadelphia after defeating Washington's troops at Brandywine Creek in Pennsylvania (September); American forces capture General Burgoyne's army at Saratoga (October)

1778 American patriots form an alliance with France (February–March); John Paul Jones raids along the British coastline (April–May); British troops invade the Deep South and conquer Savannah, Georgia (December)

1779 Spain joins the war against Britain

1780 British forces defeat American armies at Charleston (May) and Camden (August), South Carolina, but lose at Kings Mountain (October); Benedict Arnold, caught in his efforts to exchange West Point for a commission in the British army, flees to the British (September); British declare war on the Dutch (December)

1781 American forces defeat British soldiers at Hannah's Cowpens (January) in western South Carolina and fight to a draw at Guilford Courthouse (March) in central North Carolina; British surrender to combined Franco-American forces at Yorktown, Virginia (October)

1783 Treaty of Paris ends the War for American Independence

the same time, they demanded that prewar American debts be paid in full to British creditors (few actually would be paid) and insisted upon the complete restoration of the rights and property of loyalists. The American commissioners agreed to have Congress make such a recommendation to the states (which they generally ignored). The peace treaty, then, both established American independence and laid the groundwork for future conflict.

CONCLUSION

The rebellious Americans came out remarkably well in 1783. They emerged victorious not only in war but at the peace table as well. The young republic had endured over its parent nation, Great Britain, and with invaluable assistance from foreign allies, particularly France, had earned its freedom from European monarchism and imperialism. On the other hand, no one knew for sure whether the young United States could sustain its independence or have much of a future as a separate nation, given the many internal problems facing the 13 sovereign states.

Among those who did not cheer heartily at the prospect of peace were the officers and soldiers of the Continental army. They had made great personal sacrifices and had every reason to be proud of their accomplishments; however, they deeply resented the lack of civilian support that had plagued their efforts throughout the long conflict. Even in leaving the service, wrote Private Joseph Plumb Martin, the Continentals were "turned adrift like old worn-out horses" without just financial compensation for their services. Still, they had the personal satisfaction of knowing that their pain and suffering had sustained the grand vision of 1776, which would only prevail if revolutionary Americans resolved among themselves their many differences—especially those relating to the process of implanting republican ideals in the social and political fabric of the new nation.

CHAPTER SUMMARY AND KEY POINTS

Securing American independence depended on fighting and winning a long, bitter war with the British. Initially, many colonists hoped for a reconciliation of differences with the Crown, but once the initial combat occurred, no means could be found to contain the spread of warlike acts. The initial zone of warfare was in the northern colonies where General George Washington, amid many martial setbacks, sought to build an army capable of standing on an equal footing with British forces. The turning point came in 1777–1778 when patriot troops defeated and captured a British army at Saratoga in New York and the French came out formally for American independence. After Saratoga, the British shifted their operations southward. Another critical confrontation occurred in October 1781 when combined Franco-American forces entrapped another British army, this time at Yorktown in Virginia. In 1782 the British opened peace negotiations with American diplomatic representatives, which resulted in very favorable terms, including the full recognition of independence, as ratified by the Peace of Paris in September 1783.

- Fighting began between American patriots and British regulars at the battles of Lexington and Concord in Massachusetts on April 19, 1775.

- The British appeared to have the most advantages in going to war, including the capacity to maintain a large, well-trained army and navy, as well as an available pool of loyalists upon which they could draw to fight for the Crown. Still, British leaders had to find the means to regain through military means the allegiance of thousands of colonists who felt the home government had become wholly tyrannical in its administration of the American provinces.

- The British never found the way to destroy American martial resistance. Their clumsy execution of strategic plans and poor generalship worked to favor patriot forces, which struggled at times to overcome severe shortages in supplies and troop strength.

- Steady leadership by George Washington and a few of his generals as well as invaluable assistance from France in the form of supplies and land and naval forces were critical to the patriots winning the War for Independence and gaining very good peace terms in 1783.

SUGGESTIONS FOR FURTHER READING

Colin G. Calloway, *The American Revolution in Indian Country: Crisis and Diversity in Native American Villages* (1995). Thoughtful presentation of the ways in which eight Indian communities dealt with the American Revolution, viewed from the native as opposed to the British-American perspective.

Stephen Conway, *The War of American Independence, 1775–1783* (1995). Suggestive study that depicts the contest with Britain as the first modern war, a description usually reserved for the French Revolutionary and Napoleonic wars of a later period.

Jonathan R. Dull, *A Diplomatic History of the American Revolution* (1985). Succinct, incisive treatment of the competing national interests and rivalries that affected the outcome of the Revolutionary War.

Elizabeth A. Fenn, *Pox Americana: The Great Smallpox Epidemic of 1775–82* (2001). Valuable investigation of this killer disease as it affected not only those involved in the Revolutionary War but peoples across the whole of the North American continent.

David Hackett Fischer, *Paul Revere's Ride* (1994). Engaging narrative of Revere's life and the battles of Lexington and Concord in the context of New England's folkways.

Pauline Maier, *American Scripture: Making the Declaration of Independence* (1997). Fresh evaluation of the factors that helped shape Thomas Jefferson's landmark document.

James Kirby Martin, *Benedict Arnold, Revolutionary Hero: An American Warrior Reconsidered* (1997). Revisionist study of Arnold's life as a guide to the internal tensions that shaped the Revolution and made defeating the British so difficult a task.

James Kirby Martin and Mark Edward Lender, *A Respectable Army: The Military Origins of the Republic, 1763–1789* (1982). Overview analysis of Revolutionary ideals in contact with the realities of who served in the Continental army, their reasons for fighting, and their contributions to the nation-making process.

Charles Royster, *A Revolutionary People at War: The Continental Army and American Character, 1775–1783* (1979). Widely read study of the ways in which the Revolutionary populace perceived their involvement in the martial contest with Britain.

John Shy, *A People Numerous and Armed: Reflections on the Military Struggle for American Independence*, rev. ed. (1990). Classic essays illuminating the nature of eighteenth-century military values and practices and how the Revolutionary War helped foster a sense of national identity.

Novels

Allan W. Eckert, *The Frontiersmen: A Narrative* (1967).

Walter D. Edmonds, *Drums Along the Mohawk* (1936).

Howard Fast, *April Morning: A Novel* (1961).

_____, *The Crossing* (1971).

_____, *The Hessian: A Novel* (1972).

_____, *The Unvanquished: A Novel* (1942).

MacKinley Kantor, *Valley Forge* (1975).

Kenneth Roberts, *Arundel* (1930).

_____, *Rabble in Arms* (1933).

Jeffrey M. Shaara, *The Glorious Cause: A Novel of the American Revolution* (2002).

MEDIA RESOURCES

Web Sites

Exploring the West from Monticello: An Exhibition of Maps and Navigational Instruments

http://www.lib.virginia.edu/exhibits/lewis_clark/home.html

Maps and charts reveal knowledge and conceptions about the known and the unknown. This site includes a number of eighteenth century maps.

Georgia's Rare Map Collection

http://scarlett.libs.uga.edu/darchive/hargrett/maps/colamer.html

http://scarlett.libs.uga.edu/darchive/hargrett/maps/revamer.html

These two sites contain maps for Colonial and Revolutionary America.

LVA Colonial Records Project—Index of Digital Facsimiles of Documents on Early Virginia

http://eagle.vsla.edu/colonial/

This site contains numerous early documents, but it is unguided and a little difficult to use.

Thomas Paine National Historical Association

http://www.thomaspaine.org

This official site contains a large archive of Paine's works and information about the Association.

Maryland Loyalists and the American Revolution

http://www.erols.com/candidus/index.htm

This look at Maryland's loyalists promotes the author's book, but it has good information about an underappreciated phenomenon, including loyalist songs and poems.

Liberty!: **The American Revolution**

http://www.pbs.org/ktca/liberty/

Contains a variety of materials relating to the multi-part PBS television series about the Revolutionary era.

The American Revolution

http://revolution.h-net.msu.edu/

This site accompanies the PBS series *Liberty!* with essays and resource links.

Spy Letters of the American Revolution

http://www.si.umich.edu/spies/

Documents drawn from the collections of the William L. Clements Library at the University of Michigan, including the papers of British General Sir Henry Clinton.

KEY TERMS

Rage militaire   (p. 122)

Second Continental Congress   (p. 125)

Dunmore's Ethiopian regiment   (p. 130)

Common Sense   (p. 131)

Tory   (p. 131)

Hessians   (p. 133)

Roderigue Hortalez & Cie.   (p. 139)

Hudson Highlands strategy   (p. 140)

Southern strategy   (p. 142)

PEOPLE YOU SHOULD KNOW

Joseph Plumb Martin   (p. 121)

Benedict Arnold   (p. 130)

John Murray, Lord Dunmore   (p. 130)

Thomas Paine   (p. 131)

Richard Henry Lee   (p. 131)

Thomas Jefferson   (p. 132)

Lord George Germain   (p. 133)

Sir William Howe   (p. 133)

Charles, Lord Cornwallis   (p. 134)

Margaret "Dirty Kate" Corbin   (p. 137)

Comte de Vergennes   (p. 139)

Pierre-Augustin Caron de Beaumarchais   (p. 139)

John Burgoyne   (p. 140)

Horatio Gates   (p. 141)

Jane McCrea   (p. 141)

Joseph Brant (Thayendanegea)   (p. 141)

Friedrich von Steuben   (p. 142)

Sir Henry Clinton   (p. 142)

Nathanael Greene   (p. 145)

REVIEW QUESTIONS

1. What is meant by the concept *rage militaire*? What factors account for the widespread desire of the American colonists to challenge Great Britain militarily by the spring and summer of 1775?

2. Why were so many leaders in the Second Continental Congress so hesitant about moving toward formal independence? Discuss the text of the Declaration of Independence. How does the Declaration both summarize colonial grievances and provide a bold vision for the future of an independent American republic?

3. Examine the composition of British and American military forces. How did the Continental army change as the war progressed beyond 1775 and 1776? Who were the real Continentals, and what did they accomplish as the backbone of Washington's "respectable" army?

4. Assess the role of European powers such as the French, Spanish, and Dutch and the role of Native Americans in the colonists' fight for independence. Of these groups, did any seem to benefit from their support of the rebel cause? If so, how? If not, why not?

5. Why did the Americans emerge victorious in the Revolutionary War? Explain how all three of the following contributed to that final triumph—American strengths, British weaknesses, and the global diplomatic and strategic situation. How did these factors help secure a favorable peace settlement in 1783?

6 Securing the Republic and Its Ideals, 1776–1789

NANCY SHIPPEN AND PHILLIS WHEATLEY: SECOND-CLASS CITIZENS OF THE NEW REPUBLIC

Nancy Shippen was a product of Philadelphia's best lineage. Because she was born in 1763, the political turmoil leading to rebellion did not affect her early life. As a privileged daughter in an upper-class family, her duty was to blossom into a charming woman, admired for her beauty and social graces rather than her intellect. Nancy's education consisted of the refinement of skills that would please and entertain—dancing, cultivating her voice, playing musical instruments, painting on delicate china, and producing pieces of decorative needlework.

Had Nancy shown any interest in politics, an exclusively masculine preserve, she would have shocked everyone, including her father, William Shippen. Shippen was a noted local physician who espoused independence in 1776. That was his prerogative as paterfamilias; where he led, according to the customs of the time, his family followed. Indeed, he was a proud father in 1777 when, at his urging, Nancy displayed her patriotic virtue by sewing shirt ruffles for General Washington.

Three hundred miles away in Boston, another woman by the name of **Phillis Wheatley** was also reckoning with the American Revolution. Her life had been very different from Nancy's. Born on Africa's West Coast around 1753, she had been snatched from her parents by slave catchers. At the Boston slave market, Mrs. Susannah Wheatley, looking for a young female slave to train in domestic service, noticed her. In Phillis the Wheatley family got much more; their new slave yearned to express her thoughts and feelings through poetry.

Conventional wisdom dictated that slaves should not be educated. Exposure to reading and writing might make them resentful, perhaps even rebellious. Sensing Phillis's talents, the Wheatley family defied convention. She mastered English and Latin, even prepared translations of ancient writings. By 1770 some of her poems had been published, followed in 1773 by a collection entitled *Poems on Various Subjects, Religious and Moral.* In one verse addressed to Lord Dartmouth, Britain's secretary for American affairs, she queried:

Although from different social and racial backgrounds, Nancy Shippen and Phillis Wheatley shared one characteristic: As women, they were second-class citizens in Revolutionary America.

I young in life, by seeming cruel fate
Was snatch'd from Afric's fancy'd seat:
Such was my case. And can I then but pray
Others may never feel tyrannic sway?

Experiencing the tyranny of slavery influenced Phillis's feelings about the presence of redcoats in Boston. Late in 1775 she sent a flattering poem to George Washington. He responded gratefully and called her words "striking proof of your great poetical talents."

Little as Phillis Wheatley and Nancy Shippen had in common, they lived during an era in which men thought of all women, regardless of their rank in society, as second-class human beings. Phillis carried the additional burden of being black in an openly racist society. Like other women in revolutionary America, they could only hope that the ideals of human liberty might someday apply to them.

Nancy Shippen had two male tyrants in her life. The first was her father William, who in 1781 forced her into marriage with Henry Beekman Livingston, a son of one of New York's most powerful and wealthy families. The man she truly loved had only "honorable expectations" of a respectable income. So her father insisted that Nancy wed Livingston. The rejected suitor wanted to know "for what reason in this *free* country a lady . . . must be married in a hurry and given up to a man whom she dislikes." None of the Shippens responded. In truth, the answer was that Nancy legally belonged to her father until she became the property of the second tyrant in her life—her husband Henry.

The marriage was a disaster, most likely because Henry was a philanderer. Nancy eventually took her baby daughter and moved back to her family. She wanted full custody of the child, who by law was the property of her husband. Henry made it clear that he would never give up his legal rights to his daughter, should Nancy embarrass him in public by seeking a bill of divorcement. Even if she had defied him, divorce bills were very hard to get because they involved proving adultery or desertion.

To keep actual custody of her daughter, Nancy accepted her entrapment. Several years later Henry relented and arranged for a divorce, but by that time Nancy's spirit was broken. This former belle of Philadelphia society lived on unhappily in hermit-like fashion until her death in 1841. Having been so favored at birth, her adult years were a personal tragedy, primarily because of her legal dependence on the will of men.

Phillis Wheatley, by comparison, enjoyed some personal freedom before her untimely death in 1784. Mr. and Mrs. Wheatley died during the war period, and their will provided for Phillis's emancipation. She married John Peters, a free black man, and bore him three children. But John Peters was poor, and Phillis had scant time for poetry. Free blacks rarely got decent jobs, and Phillis struggled each day to help her family avoid destitution. She lived long enough to see slavery being challenged in the northern states; nevertheless, she died knowing that African Americans, even when free, invariably faced racial discrimination, which caused families like hers to exist on the margins of revolutionary society.

T he experiences of Phillis Wheatley and Nancy Shippen raise basic questions about the character of the Revolution. Did the cause of liberty really change the lives of Americans? If it was truly a movement to end tyranny, secure human rights, and ensure equality of opportunity, then why did individuals like Wheatley and Shippen benefit so little? A major reason was that white, adult males of property and community standing put much greater emphasis on establishing an independent nation between 1776 and 1789 than on securing human rights. Still, the ideology of liberty could not be denied. Primarily, the revolutionary era saw the creation of a new nation and the articulation of fundamental ideals regarding human freedom and dignity—ideals that have continued to shape the course of American historical development.

ESTABLISHING NEW REPUBLICAN GOVERNMENTS

Winning the war and working out a favorable peace settlement represented two of three crucial elements that made for a successful rebellion. The third centered on the formation of stable governments, certainly a challenging assignment because that process involved the careful definition of how governments should function to support life, liberty, and property (or happiness, as Jefferson framed the triad). A monarchical system, indeed any other capable of producing political tyranny, everyone agreed, was unacceptable. A second point of consensus was that governments should be republican in character. Sovereignty, or ultimate political authority, previously residing with King and Parliament, should be vested in the people. After all, political institutions presumably existed to serve them. As such, citizens should be governed by laws, not by power-hungry officials, and laws should be the product of the collective deliberations of representatives elected by the citizenry.

Defining the core ideals of **republicanism**—popular sovereignty, rule by law, and legislation by elected representatives—was not a source of disagreement. Revolutionary leaders, however, argued passionately about the organization and powers of new governments, both state and national, as well as the extent to which basic political rights should be put into practice. At the heart of the debate was the concept of **public virtue:** whether citizens were capable of subordinating their self-interest to the greater good of the whole community. Although some leaders answered in the affirmative, others did not. Their trust or distrust of the people directly affected how far they were willing to go in implementing republican ideals.

Leaders who believed that citizens could govern themselves and not abuse public privileges for private advantage were in the vanguard of political thinking in the western world. As such, they may be called radicals. They were willing to establish "the most democratic forms" of government, as Samuel Adams so aptly capsulized their thinking.

More cautious, elitist revolutionary leaders feared what the masses might do without the restraining hand of central political authority. As one of them wrote: "No one loves liberty more than I do, but of all tyranny I most dread that of the multitude." These leaders remained attached to traditional notions of hierarchy and deference in social and political relationships. They still thought that the "better sort" of citizens—men of education, wealth, and proven ability, whom they now defined as "natural aristocrats"—should be the stewards who guided the people. For such leaders the success of the Revolution depended on transferring power from the despoilers of liberty in Britain to "enlightened" gentlemen like themselves in America. As a precaution against a citizenry abusing liberties, they wanted a strong central government to replace King and Parliament, a government controlled by cautious revolutionaries in the interests of national political stability.

People Victorious: The New State Governments

In the wake of collapsing British authority during 1775 and 1776, **radical** and **cautious revolutionaries** squared off in constitutional conventions. Their heated debates produced ten new state constitutions by the end of 1777 and a plan of national government written by the Continental Congress. Connecticut and Rhode Island kept their liberal colonial charters, which had provided for the popular election of executive officials, and simply deleted all references to British sovereignty; Massachusetts ratified a new state constitution in 1780.

The first constitutional settlement of the Revolution shows that leaders who had firm faith in the people prevailed over those who did not, based on three essential characteristics. First, there was general agreement that governments derive their authority from the consent of the governed. This principle of popular sovereignty has prevailed to this day. Second, although state constitution-makers varied in their commitment, free, white, adult male citizens (about 20 percent of the total population) gained expanded voting and office holding rights. The movement clearly was toward greater popular participation in governmental decision making. Third, the central government would not have the power to inhibit the state governments and the people in the management of the republic's political affairs.

Pennsylvanians produced the most democratic of the first state constitutions. Decision-making authority resided in an annually elected unicameral, or one-chamber, assembly. All white male citizens, with or without property, could now vote for legislators. By comparison, Maryland's constitution-framers were much less trusting. They maintained a three-tiered structure of government, reminiscent of that of King and two houses of Parliament. Potential voters had to meet modest propertyholding requirements (at least a £30 valuation in local currency). At a minimum, those elected to the lower house had to own a 50-acre freehold farm while those chosen for the upper house needed to demonstrate a net worth of £1000 in local currency. For the governor the requirement was £5000. In Pennsylvania ordinary citizens could control their own political destiny, but in Maryland wealthier citizens were to act as stewards for the people, hence continuing the tradition of deferential politics. The other state constitutions varied between these two extremes.

Only New Jersey defined the electorate without regard to gender. Its 1776 constitution gave the vote to "all free inhabitants" meeting minimal property qualifications. This permitted some women to vote. Since all property in marriage belonged to husbands, New Jersey had technically extended franchise rights only to widows and spinsters (very few divorced women were to be found anywhere in America). Nonetheless, great numbers of married women went to the polls regularly. Not until 1807 did New Jersey

---

TABLE 6.1

Personal Wealth and Occupations of Approximately 900 Representatives Elected to Prewar and Postwar Assemblies (Expressed in Percentages)

	New Hampshire, New York, and New Jersey		Maryland, Virginia, and South Carolina	
	Prewar	Postwar	Prewar	Postwar
Property holdings				
Over £5000	36%	12%	52%	28%
£2000–£5000	47	26	36	42
Under £2000	17	62	12	30
Occupations				
Merchants and lawyers	43%	18%	23%	17%
Farmers*	23	55	12	26

Source: Derived from Jackson T. Main, "Government by the People: The American Revolution and the Democratization of the Legislatures," *William and Mary Quarterly*, 3d ser., 23 (1966), p. 45.

*Plantation owners with slaves are not included with farmers.

TABLE 6.2				
Family and Personal Wealth of Approximately 450 Executive Officials* in Late Colonial and Early Revolutionary Governments (Expressed in Percentages)				
	Family Wealth[†]		Personal Wealth	
	1774	1777	1774	1777
Over £5000	40%	26%	65%	37%
£2000–£5000	34	33	29	52
Under £2000	26	41	6	11

Source: Derived from James Kirby Martin, *Men in Rebellion: Higher Governmental Leaders and the Coming of the American Revolution* (New Brunswick, NJ: Rutgers University Press, 1973).

*Officeholders included are governors, lieutenant governors, secretaries, treasurers, members of upper houses of assemblies (councilors before the Revolution), attorneys general, chief judges, and associate judges of the highest provincial and state courts.

[†]Refers to the wealth of parents. A higher percentage of late colonial leaders (74 percent) than early revolutionary leaders (59 percent) came from upper-class and upper-middle-class families.

disenfranchise females, on the alleged grounds that they were more easily manipulated by self-serving political candidates. For a brief time, then, at least one state regarded women—not just free, white, adult males—as a legitimate voice in government. Even though the experiment worked, this concept proved too radical for the customary male-dominated political culture of revolutionary America.

Because of the first state constitutions, male citizens with more ordinary family backgrounds, less personal wealth, and a greater diversity of occupations began to hold higher political offices after the Revolution started. As an excited citizen noted in late 1776, elected delegates to the new Virginia assembly were more "plain and of consequence, less disguised, but I believe to be full[y] as honest, less intriguing, more sincere." Not "so politely educated, nor so highly born," these delegates were "the people's men (and the people in general are right)." Radical leaders throughout the states heartily endorsed these sentiments.

The Articles of Confederation

In June 1776 the Continental Congress called for a plan of national government. John Dickinson, the well-known reluctant revolutionary who refused to vote for independence, took the lead. Concerned about losing the stabilizing influence of British authority, Dickinson proposed a muscular central government in the draft constitution his committee presented to Congress. The Confederacy was to be called "THE UNITED STATES OF AMERICA" and was to exist "for their common defense, the security of their liberties, and their mutual and general welfare." Not surprisingly, the states would have little authority. Each would retain only "as much of its present laws, rights and customs, as it may think fit . . . in all matters that shall not interfere with the Articles of this Confederation."

The exigencies of war kept interrupting congressional debate on Dickinson's draft. Furthermore, the radical revolutionaries who dominated Congress in late 1776 and 1777 did not like this plan. They feared power too far removed from the people. After all, they had rebelled against a distant government that they had perceived as tyrannical. When Congress finally completed revisions in November 1777, the delegates had turned Dickinson's draft inside out. The Articles now stated: "Each state retains its sovereignty, freedom and independence, and every power, jurisdiction and right,

New Jersey extended the right to vote to all free inhabitants until 1807 when a new state law specifically limited the franchise to free white male citizens.

which is not . . . expressly delegated to the United States, in Congress assembled."

As a testament to the sovereignty of the 13 states, each had to ratify the Articles before this plan could go into full operation. At most the central government could coordinate activities among the states. It could manage the war, but it lacked taxation authority to support that effort. If Congress needed money (it obviously did), it could "requisition" the states. The states, however, would decide for themselves whether they would send funds to Congress.

Fundamentally penniless and powerless, the Confederation government represented the optimistic view that a virtuous citizenry did not require the constraining hand of central authority. This bold vision—fully in line with the rejection of King and Parliament as a remote, autocratic central government—pleased radicals like Samuel Adams, Thomas Paine, and Thomas Jefferson. Jefferson wrote glowingly of the "ease" with which the people "had deposited the monarchical and taken . . . republican government," as effortlessly as "throwing off an old and putting on a new suit of clothes." Cautious revolutionaries still harbored grave doubts, and events over the next few years convinced them that the first constitutional settlement had all but doomed the experiment in republicanism to failure.

CRISES OF THE CONFEDERATION

Internal difficulties soon beset the young American republic. Cautious revolutionaries viewed the years between 1776 and 1787 as a "critical period" because of problems encountered with the sovereign states and the people. These difficulties included ratifying the Articles of Confederation, establishing a national domain west of the Appalachian Mountains, finding some means to pay for the war, achieving stable diplomatic relations with foreign powers, and guarding against domestic upheavals.

Over time, those who advocated a strong central government formed an informal political alliance, and they have since come to be known as the **nationalists.** With each passing year the nationalists became more and more frustrated by the Confederation. In 1787 they finally overwhelmed their opposition by pressing for and getting a new plan of national government.

Struggle to Ratify the Articles

Given the wartime need for national unity in the face of a common enemy, Congress asked each state to approve the Articles of Confederation quickly.

Overcoming much indifference, 12 states had finally ratified by January 1779—but Maryland still held out.

The propertied gentlemen who controlled Maryland's revolutionary government objected to one specific provision in the Articles. Although Dickinson's draft had designated all lands west of the Appalachians as a **national domain,** belonging to all the people for future settlement, the final version left these lands in the hands of states having sea-to-sea clauses in their colonial charters—a logical extension of the principle of state sovereignty. Maryland, having a fixed western boundary, had no such western claim. Nor did Rhode Island, New Jersey, Pennsylvania, or Delaware.

Maryland's leaders refused to be cut off from western development. In public they talked in terms of high principle. Citizens from **landless states** should have as much right to resettle in the West as inhabitants of **landed states.** Equal access was not the only issue, however. Many Maryland leaders had invested in pre-Revolution land companies trying to gain title to large parcels of western territory. They had done so by appealing to the Crown and by making purchases from individual Native Americans, who without tribal approval often "sold" rights in return for alcohol and other "gifts." Wanting to avoid costly frontier warfare, the Crown had promulgated the Proclamation of 1763 (see p. 97) and thereafter refused to recognize any such titles. After independence there was new hope for these land speculators, but only if the Continental Congress rather than some of the states controlled the West.

The Maryland Assembly adamantly refused ratification unless the landed states agreed to turn over their charter titles to Congress. Virginia, which had the largest claim, including the vast region north of the Ohio River that came to be known as the "Old Northwest," faced the most pressure. Forsaking local land speculators for the national interest, the Virginia Assembly broke the deadlock in January 1781 by agreeing to cede its claims to Congress.

Had self-interest not been involved, ratification would have followed quickly; however, covetous Maryland leaders still held out. They pronounced Virginia's grant unacceptable because of a condition not permitting Congress to award lands on the basis of Indian deeds. Fortunately for the republic, the war intervened. In early 1781, with the British raiding in the Chesapeake Bay region, Marylanders became quite anxious about their defense. Congressional leaders urged ratification in exchange for promises of Continental military support. All but cornered, the Maryland Assembly reluctantly gave in and approved the Articles of Confederation.

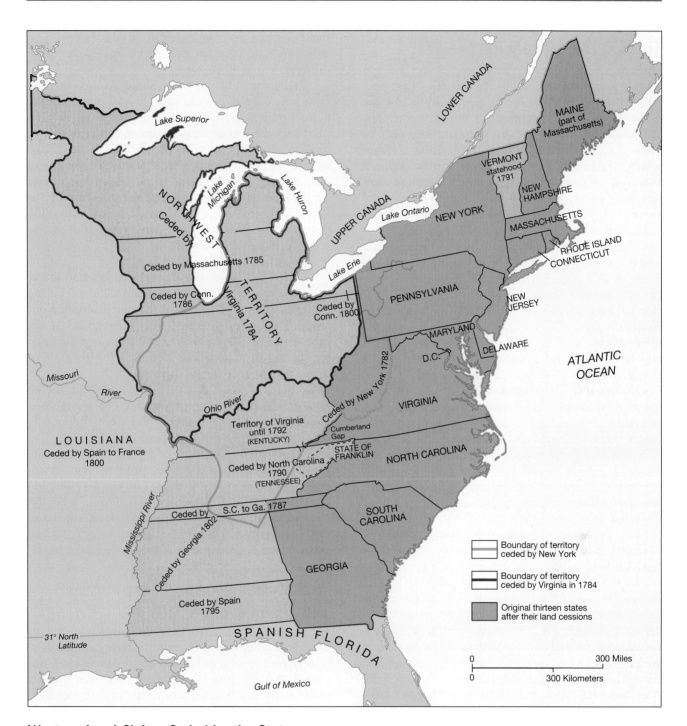

Western Land Claims Ceded by the States

The battle over conflicting state claims to western lands was a major issue facing the Continental Congress.

March 1, 1781, the day formal ratification ceremonies finally took place, elicited only muted celebrations. Some cheered "the union," at long last "indissolubly cemented," as an optimist wrote. Certainly, too, the prospect of a national domain for a rapidly expanding population pleased many citizens.

The nationalists, on the other hand, believed that Maryland's behavior showed how self-interest could be masked as public virtue. With so many problems needing solutions, they wondered how long the republic could endure when any sovereign state had the capacity to thwart the will of the other 12.

Turmoil over Financing the War

From the outset financial problems plagued the new central government. Under the Articles, Congress had no power of taxation; it repeatedly asked the states to pay a fair proportion of war costs. The states, also hard pressed for funds, rarely sent in more than 50 percent of their requisitions. Meanwhile, soldiers like Joseph Plumb Martin endured shortages of food, clothing, camp equipment, and pay. As a result, with each passing month the army grew increasingly angry about its role as a creditor to the republic.

The lack of tax revenues forced Congress to resort to various expedient measures to meet war costs. Between 1775 and 1780 it issued some $220 million in paper money, or Continental dollars. Lacking any financial backing, these "Continentals" became so worthless by 1779 that irate army officers complained how "four months' pay of a private [soldier] will not procure his wretched wife and children a single bushel of wheat." In addition, Congress, largely to get military supplies, issued interest-bearing certificates of indebtedness. Because Congress lacked the means to pay interest, these certificates, which also circulated as money, rapidly lost value. In 1780 Congress attempted to refinance Continental dollars at a 40 to 1 ratio, but the plan failed. Had it not been for grants and loans from allies like France and the Netherlands, the war effort might well have floundered.

Deeply disturbed by these conditions, many nationalists in the Continental Congress acted forcefully to institute financial reform. Their leader was the wealthy Philadelphia merchant, **Robert Morris** (1734–1806), sometimes called the "financier of the Revolution," who became Congress's Superintendent of Finance in 1781. His assistant superintendent, **Gouverneur Morris** (no relation), a wealthy New Yorker then practicing law in Philadelphia, was also critical to shaping the events that lay ahead, as were **Alexander Hamilton** of New York and **James Madison** of Virginia. Hamilton summarized their feelings this way: "The Confederation . . . gives the power of the purse too entirely to the state legislatures. . . . That power, which holds the purse strings absolutely, must rule."

At the urging of the nationalists, congressional delegates approved the Impost Plan of 1781. It called for import duties of 5 percent on all foreign trade goods entering the United States, the revenues to belong to Congress. These funds could be used to pay the army, to back a stable national currency, and, ultimately, to meet foreign loan obligations. Because the Plan would allow Congress some taxation authority,

the delegates recommended it in the form of an amendment to the Articles. Amendments required the approval of all 13 states.

Reluctant as they were to share taxation powers with the central government, many state leaders agreed with Robert Morris, who had warned: "The political existence of America depends on the accomplishment of this [Impost] plan." Twelve states had ratified by the autumn of 1782. Only Rhode Island hesitated. With so little land to tax, the easiest way to fund its own war debt was to collect state import duties. If a choice had to be made, state interests came first. The Assembly voted against ratification. Once again local interests had prevailed; a single state had blocked the will of the other 12.

In this crucial matter the nationalists had allies. Most prominent were disgruntled officers in the Continental army. Rarely had the soldiers been paid, and in 1780 the officers had exacted from Congress a promise of half-pay postwar pensions as their price for staying in the service. Without a fixed source of revenue, Congress lacked the ability to meet these obligations.

After a group of high-ranking officers learned about Rhode Island's decision, they sent a menacing petition to Congress in December 1782. It stated: "We have borne all that men can bear—our property is expended—our private resources are at an end." With no likelihood of pensions being funded, they insisted upon five years of full pay when mustering out of the service. Even with British troops still on American soil, the angry officers warned Congress: "Any further experiments on their patience may have fatal effects."

Threatened Military Coup: The Newburgh Conspiracy

For years Continental officers and soldiers alike had complained about the ungenerous treatment they received from revolutionary leaders and civilians. Convinced that the general populace had lived well at home while the army endured privation, sickness, and death in the field, they spoke out passionately about the absence of citizen virtue. As one officer bluntly wrote, "I hate my countrymen."

After the British force at Yorktown surrendered, Washington moved 11,000 troops north to the vicinity of Newburgh, New York. From this campsite on the Hudson River, the Continental army waited for peace terms and kept its eye on British forces in New York City. As peace negotiations dragged on during 1782, officers and soldiers worried about being demobilized without back pay and promised pensions. When Rhode Island refused to ratify the Impost Plan, their worst fears seemed to be realized.

Curiously, when the congressional nationalists received the officers' hotly worded petition, they were more pleased than alarmed. They soon devised a scheme to use these threats to extort taxation authority from the states. If need be, they would encourage the army to go back into the field and threaten the civilian populace with a military uprising. The danger, of course, was that the army might get out of control, seize the reins of government, and push the Revolution toward some form of military dictatorship.

When the states refused to be bullied, the nationalists turned to George Washington in February 1783. As his former military aide, Alexander Hamilton (1757?–1804), wrote to him, the critical issue was "the establishment of general funds. . . . In this the influence of the army, properly directed, may cooperate." Washington refused to help; perhaps better than anyone in revolutionary America, he understood that military power had to remain subordinate to civilian authority, or the republic would never be free.

At this juncture, Robert Morris and other congressional nationalists began "conspiring" with General Horatio Gates, second in command at Newburgh, who had often dreamed of replacing Washington at the head of the Continental army. Gates made his move in early March. He authorized two Newburgh Addresses, both prepared by members of his staff. The addresses warned the officers to "suspect the man [Washington] who would advise to more moderation and forbearance." If peace comes, let nothing separate you "from your arms but death," or at least not until the army had realized financial justice. The first address instructed the officers to attend a meeting to vent grievances—and take action. Dismayed, Washington called this proposal "disorderly"; he nevertheless approved a meeting for March 15. He would not attend, he stated, but would let Gates chair the gathering.

Despite his promise, Washington appeared at this showdown meeting. He pleaded with the officers to temper their rage and not go back into the field. That would destroy everything the army had accomplished during eight long years of war. The officers appeared unmoved. Then preparing to read a letter, Washington reached into his pocket, pulled out spectacles, and put them on. The officers, never having seen their commander wear eyeglasses before, started to murmur. Sensing a mood shift, Washington calmly stated, "Gentlemen, you must pardon me. I have grown gray in your service and now find myself growing blind." These heartfelt words caught the angry officers off guard. They recalled that they, as exemplars of truly virtuous citizenship, likewise

Gouverneur Morris (left) and Robert Morris (right) were key figures in the nationalist drive for financial reform. Robert Morris, who served as superintendent of finance under the Articles of Confederation, helped raise money in support of the American Revolution, including the funds needed to transport George Washington's army from New York to Yorktown to force Cornwallis's surrender. Morris was not so successful with his personal finances. Unwise investments in land speculation bankrupted him, and he was held for a time in debtor's prison. During the last years of his life, his former assistant, Gouverneur Morris, supported him.

had offered their lives for a cause larger than any of them. Many openly wept, even as the threat of a possible mutiny, or worse, a military coup directed against the states and the people, suddenly came to an end.

Washington promised to do everything in his power to secure "complete and ample justice" for the army. He did send a circular letter to the states imploring them to give more power to Congress. He warned them that "the Union could not be of a long duration" with a central government lacking in the capacity "to regulate and govern the general concerns of the Confederated republic." The states ignored Washington's plea for a strengthened national government.

Even though British troops were still in New York City, Washington also started "furloughing" soldiers, so that further troublesome incidents would not occur. After leaving the army one angry group of Pennsylvania Continentals marched on Philadelphia in

June 1783. They surrounded Independence Hall (the Pennsylvania State House), where Congress held its sessions. In threatening fashion these veterans refused to leave until they received back pay. The frightened delegates asked the Pennsylvania government to have local militia troops protect them, but state officials turned down their request. Amid the taunts and jeers of the angry soldiers, the delegates finally abandoned Independence Hall. They never came back.

Thoroughly humiliated by armed soldiers and a state government that would not defend them, the delegates first moved to Princeton, New Jersey, then to Annapolis, Maryland, and finally to New York City. One newspaper, in mocking the central government, spoke of "the itinerant genius of Congress," a body that would "float along from one end of the continent to the other" as would a hot-air balloon.

Many citizens did not seem to care much one way or the other, since Congress was so lacking in authority. Nationalist leaders, on the other hand, kept trying to redress the balance of power between the impotent central government and the sovereign states. They drafted the Impost Plan of 1783, but this proposal, too, failed to secure unanimous state ratification. The plan was still languishing in late 1786, but by that time the nationalists were pursuing other avenues of change.

Drifting Toward Disunion

Despite the Paris peace settlement and the final removal of British troops, most citizens were engaged in another battle beginning in late 1783—this one against a hard-hitting economic depression. It had many sources. Planters in the South had lost about 60,000 slaves, many of whom the British had carried off. In addition, crop yields for 1784 and 1785 were small, largely because of bad weather. Farmers in New England reeled from the effects of new British trade regulations—in essence turning the Navigation system against the independent Americans. The Orders in Council of 1783 prohibited the sale of many American agricultural products in the British West Indies, formerly a key market for New England goods, and required many commodities to be conveyed to and from the islands in British vessels. The orders represented a serious blow to New England's agricultural, shipping, and shipbuilding trades.

Making matters even worse, merchants in all the states rushed to reestablish old trading connections with their British counterparts. These overly optimistic traders quickly became oversupplied with British goods on easy credit terms. They soon discovered that they could not sell these commodities to citizens feeling the effects of the postwar depression. Many American merchants thus faced total economic ruin by 1785.

The central government could do little. Congress did send John Adams to Britain in 1785 as the first minister from the United States. Adams, however, made no headway in getting British officials to back off from the Orders in Council. He dejectedly reported to Congress: British leaders "rely upon our disunion" to avoid negotiations.

To add to these economic woes, significant postwar trading ties did not develop with France. In fact, American exports to France far exceeded the value of imports (by roughly $2 million a year during the 1780s). The same held true with the Dutch. Even though some venturesome merchants sent a trading vessel—the *Empress of China*—to the Far East in 1784, all the new activity was insignificant in comparison to the renewed American dependency on British manufactured goods. The former colonists stayed glued to the old imperial trading network; decades would pass before they would gain full economic independence.

Some merchants, primarily from the Middle Atlantic states, were anxious to break free of Britain's economic hold. An opportunity presented itself in 1784 after Congress named **John Jay** (1745–1829), one of the Paris peace commissioners, to be its secretary for foreign affairs. Jay soon started negotiations with **Don Diego de Gardoqui,** Spain's first minister to the United States. Gardoqui talked about his government's concern that Americans, now streaming into the trans-Appalachian west, would in time covet Spanish territory beyond the Mississippi River. To stem the tide, Gardoqui informed Congress that Spain would not allow the Mississippi to serve as an outlet for western agricultural goods. To ease possible bad feelings, Gardoqui offered an advantageous commercial treaty.

Jay and a number of powerful merchants from the Middle Atlantic states saw merit in the Spanish proposal. They viewed western development—settlements were sprouting in Kentucky and Tennessee—as a potential threat to eastern economic dominance. Meanwhile, Gardoqui had Spanish agents circulating through the west. They encouraged settlers to become Spanish subjects in return for trade access to the Mississippi River—a means to protect Spanish holdings beyond the Mississippi. Basically these agents did little more than stir up resentment, both toward Spain and eastern leaders like Jay, who appeared to be selling out western interests for a commercial treaty of undetermined value.

When Jay reported on his discussions to Congress in August 1786, tempers flared. The southern states voted as a bloc against any such treaty, which represented a mortal blow to the Jay-Gardoqui negotiations. Southerners and westerners remained suspicious that Jay and his eastern merchant allies would not hesitate to abandon them altogether for petty commercial gains. Some leaders in Congress, as one delegate explained, began to speak "lightly of a separation and dissolution of the Confederation." Such talk helped galvanize the nationalists for dramatic action, as did a rebellion that now convulsed Massachusetts.

Daniel Shays's Rebellion

Postwar economic conditions were so bad in several states that citizens began demanding tax relief from their governments. In western Massachusetts desperate farmers complained about huge property tax increases by the state government to pay off the state's war debt. Taxes on land rose by more than 60 percent in the period from 1783 to 1786, exactly when a depressed postwar economy meant that farmers were getting little income from the sale of excess agricultural goods.

Local courts, in the absence of tax payments, started to seize the property of persons like **Daniel Shays** (1747?–1825), a revolutionary war veteran. Some lost their freehold farms, and in certain cases the courts remanded delinquent taxpayers to debtors' prison. Viewing their plight in terms of tyranny, the farmers of western Massachusetts believed they had the right to break the chains of political oppression, just as they had done in resisting British rule a few years before. This time, however, the perceived enemy was their own state government.

The **Shaysites,** as they came to be known, tried to resist in orderly fashion. They first met in im-promptu conventions and sent petitions to the state assembly. Getting no relief, they turned to more confrontational means of resistance. In late August 1786 an estimated 1000 farmers poured into Northampton and shut down the county court. This crowd action represented the first of many such closures. By popular mandate citizens would no longer permit judges to seize property or condemn people to debtors' prison as the penalty for not paying taxes.

State leaders in Boston started to panic, fearing the "rebels" would soon descend upon them. Desperately, they conducted an emotional public appeal for funds. Frightened Bostonians opened their purses. They subscribed £5000 to pay for an eastern Massachusetts army headed by former Continental general Benjamin Lincoln. Lincoln's assignment was to march his army into western parts of the state and subdue the Shaysites.

The insurrection soon fizzled. Lacking weapons and suffering in bitterly cold weather, Daniel Shays and his followers lacked the essentials to sustain themselves. To get weapons, they attacked the federal arsenal at Springfield on January 25, 1787. A few well-placed cannon shots, which resulted in 24 Shaysite casualties (including 4 killed), drove them off. In early February the eastern Massachusetts army, after pursuing the western rebels through a driving snowstorm, fell upon Shays's followers at Petersham. Lincoln's force quickly routed the largely weaponless farmers. The Petersham engagement, along with tax relief from the assembly and amnesty for the leaders of the rebellion, ended the uprising.

Shays's Rebellion in Massachusetts convinced many citizens that the American republic needed a strong central government, if for no other reason than to control domestic insurrections.

Shays's Rebellion, however, held broader significance. The confrontation further coalesced the nationalists. Wrote George Washington: "Good God! . . . There are combustibles in every state, which a spark might set fire to." Only a national government of "energy" could save the republic from sinking "into the lowest state of humiliation and contempt." The nationalists thus intensified their campaign for a new constitutional settlement, one designed to bring the self-serving sovereign states and the people under control.

HUMAN RIGHTS AND SOCIAL CHANGE

The years between 1776 and 1787 represented much more than a time of mounting political confrontation between nationalists and localists. This period also witnessed the establishment of many fundamental human rights. When Thomas Jefferson penned his famous words, "all men are created equal," he informed George III that kings were not superior to the people by some assumed right of birth. Jefferson went on to say that all human beings had "certain unalienable rights," or rights literally beyond governmental control. Republican governments had the responsibility to guarantee and respect these rights, including "life, liberty, and the pursuit of happiness" for all citizens.

Americans had likewise rebelled against Britain to preserve property rights. Tyrannical governments, for example, threatened property through taxation without representation. In trying to protect property rights while expanding human rights, revolutionary leaders learned that the two could clash. They found it much easier to guarantee human rights when property rights, such as those relating to the ownership of slaves, were not also at stake. Thus the revolutionary era produced some striking contradictions in efforts to enshrine greater freedom for all persons living in the new American nation.

In Pursuit of Religious Freedom

Since the days of the Great Awakening, dissenter religious groups had expressed opposition to established churches in the colonies. The Baptists were particularly outspoken. They wanted official toleration and an end to taxes used exclusively for state-supported churches. A major breakthrough came in 1776, thanks to George Washington's close friend George Mason, who wrote the Virginia Declaration of Rights, a document appended to the new state constitution. It guaranteed all citizens equal entitle-

ment "to the free exercise of religion, according to the dictates of conscience." This statement provided for official toleration of dissenter sects but did not halt taxes going exclusively to the established Anglican church.

Three years later, Thomas Jefferson, with the support of Baptists from the backcountry, took up the cause. Jefferson presented legislation calling for the complete separation of church and state. On and off for seven years, the Virginia assembly debated this bill. In 1786 the will of those who argued for complete freedom of conscience, including the right to believe nothing and support no church, prevailed. In later years Jefferson would be labeled an atheist for his part in guaranteeing religious freedom. For him the Virginia Statute of Religious Freedom was just as significant as the Declaration of Independence, and he had these sentiments engraved on his tombstone.

Disestablishment quickly followed in other states, particularly in the South where the Anglican church (soon to become the Protestant Episcopal Church of America) had been dominant. In New England, only Rhode Islanders, following in the tradition of Roger Williams, had enjoyed full latitude in worship. With the Revolution the cause of religious freedom started to move forward in other New England states. Lawmakers began letting citizens decide which local church to support with their tax monies. This development represented a partial victory for individuals who preferred worshipping as Baptists or Presbyterians, but Congregationalism was still the established state church, continuing a pattern of official favoritism dating back to Puritan times. Complete separation of church and state, including the right not to support any church or to deny all religious creeds, did not occur in New England until the early nineteenth century.

Freedom of religion was one among a number of fundamental rights to make headway during the revolutionary era. Several of the states adopted bills of rights similar to Virginia's, guaranteeing freedom of speech, assembly, and the press, as well as trials by jury. Other states started revising their legal codes, making penalties for crimes less harsh. There was a sense that criminals could become useful citizens, which eventually resulted in prisons oriented more toward rehabilitation. Fewer crimes would now carry the death penalty.

In Virginia, Thomas Jefferson revised the state legal code. His work put an end to such feudal practices as primogeniture and entail (passing and committing property only to eldest sons through the generations). Running through all these acts was the republican assumption that citizens should have the opportunity to lead productive lives, uninhibited by laws violating personal conscience or denying the opportunity to acquire property.

The Propertyless Poor and the West

Gaining property remained only a dream for many revolutionary Americans. At least 20 percent of the population lived at the poverty level or below, eking out precarious existences as unskilled laborers. Indeed, wealth was more unevenly distributed in 1800 than in 1750. The striking increase in almshouses and other relief organizations was evidence in itself that poverty was spreading, especially in the large port cities.

One missed opportunity to help the poor related to the property of an estimated 500,000 loyalists, of whom one-fifth fled permanently to such places as England, Canada, the Bahamas, and various West Indian islands. State governments seized their land and other forms of property, worth millions, which could have been redistributed to poorer citizens. Instead, the states quickly sold off confiscated property to the highest bidders as a source of wartime revenues. This practice favored persons of wealth with investment capital and preempted any substantial redistribution of property.

Another opportunity lay with the enormous trans-Appalachian frontier. Washington's Continental soldiers, who ranked among the poorest members of revolutionary society, had been promised access to western lands for long-term service. When they mustered out in 1783, they received land warrant certificates. To survive, most veterans soon exchanged these paper certificates for the bare necessities of life. Consequently, very few were ever able to begin anew in the Ohio country, once military tracts had been set aside and surveyed.

Still, western lands remained a source of hope for economically downtrodden soldiers and civilians alike. In 1775 explorer Daniel Boone laid out the "Wilderness Road" to Kentucky. Others, like rugged Simon Kenton, scouted down the Ohio River from Pittsburgh. Where these frontiersmen went, thousands of land-hungry easterners soon followed. By 1790 Kentucky contained a population of 74,000, and Tennessee held 36,000. These settlers paid dearly for their invasion of Native-American lands. The Shawnees, Cherokees, and Chickasaws fought back in innumerable bloody clashes. The white death toll reached 1500. Besides losing ancient tribal lands, Native Americans also suffered considerable casualties.

White settlements in Kentucky and Tennessee generated pressure to open territory north of the Ohio River. After ceding the Old Northwest to the United States in 1783, however, the British did not abandon their military posts there. To maintain the lucrative fur trade, they bolstered the Miamis, Shawnees, Delawares, and remnant groups of the Iroquois nation with a steady supply of firearms. Americans foolish enough to venture north of the Ohio River rarely survived, and the region remained closed to large numbers of westward-moving settlers well into the 1790s.

Despite these circumstances, Congress was eager to open the Ohio country. With this goal in mind, the delegates approved three land ordinances. The 1784 Ordinance provided for territorial government and guaranteed settlers they would not remain in permanent colonial status. When enough people (later specified at 60,000) had moved in, a constitution could be written, state boundaries set, and admission to the union as a full partner would follow. The 1785 Ordinance called for orderly surveying of the region.

First Territorial Survey

Thomas Hutchins, a native of New Jersey, directed the first survey of territorial lands.

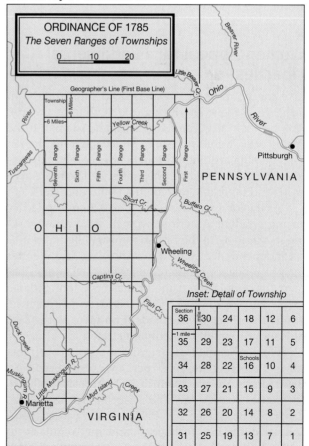

Townships of 6 miles square were to be laid out in gridlike fashion—each township to contain 36 sections of 640 acres each with proceeds from the sale of the sixteenth section to be used to finance public education. The Northwest Ordinance of 1787 refined governmental arrangements, gave a bill of rights to prospective settlers, and proclaimed slavery forever banned north of the Ohio River—a prohibition that Thomas Jefferson had sought but failed to get included in the 1784 Ordinance. In providing for orderly development and eventual statehood, the land ordinances may well have been the most significant legislation of the Confederation-period Congress.

The ordinances, however, were not fully enlightened. Congress, in its continuing search for revenue, viewed the Old Northwest as a source of long-term income. The smallest parcel individual settlers could buy was 640 acres, priced at $1.00 per acre, and there were to be no purchases on credit. Families of modest means, let alone poorer ones, could not meet such terms. As a result, Congress dealt mainly with well-to-do land speculators—and even extended them deeds to millions of acres on credit no less! These decisions cut off the poorest citizens from the West, unless they were willing to squat on uninhabited land until driven off, which thousands did to survive economically.

In her letters to her husband John, Abigail Adams spoke out in support of women's rights, but her message received little sympathetic attention.

Women Appeal for Fundamental Liberties

Like the poor, women experienced little success in improving their lot during the revolutionary era. Among their advocates was **Abigail Adams.** In the spring of 1776 she wrote to her husband John, then in Philadelphia arguing for independence, and admonished him to "remember the ladies, and be more generous and favorable to them than your ancestors."

As if joking with his wife, John Adams replied by asking whether American women were now working in league with the British ministry. Should political independence come, he wrote, "we know better than to repeal our masculine system," claiming that men "have only the name of masters." John Adams knew very well that by law and social practice, women were legally dependent on men, as the case of Nancy Shippen so vividly illustrates.

Women gained no significant political rights during the revolutionary period, except briefly in New Jersey. Yet they contributed enthusiastically to the cause. Some, like "The Association" headed by Esther DeBerdt Reed of Philadelphia, called themselves "daughters of liberty" and met regularly to make clothing for the Continental army. Others, such

as **Mary Ludwig Hays McCauly** of Carlisle, Pennsylvania, were not so well off economically. Living on a sparse income as a domestic servant, she accompanied her husband to war. A tough-talking, plucky woman, Mary helped fire a rebel artillery piece at the Battle of Monmouth Court House in June 1778 and was almost hit by a flying British cannon ball, which passed between her legs. To this she replied: "It was lucky it did not pass a little higher, for in that case it might have carried away something else." Later generations, worried lest America's youth be corrupted by Mary's earthy manner, redefined her role as a water bearer to troops and turned her into the far more feminine "Molly Pitcher," a change in persona that would have made Mary laugh. After the Revolution she lived in near poverty as a charwoman, although she did obtain a small war pension a few years before her death in 1832.

What held the greatest promise for women, at least for those of middling and affluent economic status, was the ideology of republicanism, which directly influenced family life by offering a broadened definition regarding the role of mothers. Patriot leaders repeatedly asserted that the republic would collapse without virtuous citizens. Hence a special task for mothers was to implant strong moral character

THE PEOPLE SPEAK

Abigail Adams Exhorts Her Husband to "Remember the Ladies" (1776)

In the spring of 1776 John Adams, who had become a staunch advocate of independence, was attending the Second Continental Congress in Philadelphia. His wife Abigail (1744–1818) was back in Massachusetts tending to the family homestead and their children. Abigail was a brilliant, insatiably curious person. She corresponded regularly with her husband, repeatedly asking him for news about the momentous events of the day. Moreover, she offered her own opinions, such as in late March 1776 when she wrote to John about the inferior status of women in American society. Should independence come about, Abigail wanted to see a real revolution as well that would include a vast expansion of social, political, and legal rights for women. In his reply, John was somewhat dismissive of Abigail's words. Her statement, however, did not go away but served as an important rallying cry for women as they struggled to obtain a full measure of equal rights for themselves over the next two centuries of United States history.

ABIGAIL TO JOHN ADAMS

Braintree March 31 1776

. . . I long to hear that you have declared an independancy—and by the way in the new Code of Laws which I suppose it will be necessary for you to make I desire you would Remember the Ladies, and be more generous and favourable to them than your ancestors. Do not put such unlimited power into the hands of the Husbands. Remember all Men would be tyrants if they could. If perticuliar care and attention is not paid to the Laidies we are determined to foment a Rebelion, and will not hold ourselves bound by any Laws in which we have no voice, or Representation.

That your Sex are Naturally Tyrannical is a Truth so thoroughly established as to admit of no dispute, but such of you as wish to be happy willingly give up the harsh title of Master for the more tender and endearing one of Friend. Why then, not put it out of the power of the vicious and the Lawless to use us with cruelty and indignity with impunity. Men of Sense in all Ages abhor those customs which treat us only as the vassals of your Sex. Regard us then as Beings placed by providence under your protection and in immitation of the Supreem Being make use of that power only for our happiness.

JOHN TO ABIGAIL ADAMS

Ap. 14. 1776

. . . As to your extraordinary Code of Laws, I cannot but laugh. We have been told that our Struggle has loosened the bands of Government every where. That Children and Apprentices were disobedient—that schools and Colledges were grown turbulent—that Indains slighted their Guardians and Negroes grew insolent to their Masters. But your Letter was the first Intimation that another Tribe more numerous and powerfull than all the rest were grown discontented.—This is rather too coarse a Compliment but you are so saucy, I wont blot it out.

Depend upon it, We know better than to repeal our Masculine systems. Altho they are in full Force, you know they are little more than Theory. We dare not exert our Power in its full Latitude. We are obliged to go fair, and softly, and in Practice you know We are the subjects. We have only the Name of Masters, and rather than give up this, which would compleatly subject Us to the Despotism of the Peticoat, I hope General Washington, and all our brave Heroes would fight. I am sure every good Politician would plot, as long as he would against Despotism, Empire, Monarchy, Aristocracy, Oligarchy, or Ochlocracy.—A fine Story indeed. I begin to think the Ministry as deep as they are wicked. After stirring up Tories, Landjobbers, Trimmers, Bigots, Canadians, Indians, Negroes, Hanoverians, Hessians, Russians, Irish Roman Catholicks, Scotch Renegadoes, at last they have stimulated the [text missing] to demand new Priviledges and threaten to rebell.

Source: L. H. Butterfield, et al., eds. *The Adams Papers,* Series II: *Adams Family Correspondence,* Vol 1: December 1761–May 1776 (New York, 1965), 369–371, 381–383.

and civic virtue in their children, especially their sons, so they would uphold the obligations of disinterested citizenship for the good of the nation.

The concept of **republican motherhood** had potentially liberating qualities. The calling of republican mothers was to manage the domestic sphere of family life, just as husbands were to take responsibility for the family's economic welfare. This duty reduced traditional male dominance in all family matters. Elevating the role of women in family life may also have affected the nature of courtship by putting more emphasis upon affection than on parental control in

Samplers stitched by young girls during the early days of the new republic combined the art of traditional crafts like needlework with messages extolling the value of education. This sampler is the work of Nabby Martin, a student at the Mary Balch School in Providence, Rhode Island. Students there studied reading, writing, geography, and music, but the school was renowned especially for the exquisite needlework produced by the students.

the making of marriages. However, the immediate effect of this emerging tendency should not be exaggerated, as Nancy Shippen's experiences indicate.

If women were to be responsible for instilling republican values in future generations, they needed more and better schooling. During the 1780s and 1790s some states started taxing the populace for the support of elementary education. Massachusetts broke new ground in 1789 by requiring its citizens to pay for female as well as male elementary education. In addition, these two decades saw the opening of many new private schools, such as the Young Ladies Academy of Philadelphia (founded in 1787). The academies offered more advanced education to

daughters of well-to-do families in subjects traditionally reserved for males, such as mathematics, science, and history. This was a major breakthrough because popular lore held that too much exposure to "masculine" subjects would addle the minds of young women. The female academies quickly demonstrated otherwise.

Still, the emphasis in expanding opportunities for middle- and upper-class women was upon service to the family and the republic, not on individual development and self-fulfillment. That is what bothered **Judith Sargent Murray** of Massachusetts, who wrote extensively about the need for comparable educational experiences for men and women. Murray insisted that women could exist independently of men and lead satisfying lives, but she was very much ahead of her times.

Most men in revolutionary America resisted further change for women. As a Marylander insisted in 1790, pursuit of the principle that "all mankind are born equal" was being "taken in too extensive a sense" in relation to females, and would undermine "those charms which it is the peculiar lot of the fair sex to excel in." Thus while republican motherhood offered potentially higher status, most men still thought of women as a form of property whose existence should be devoted to masculine welfare and happiness.

The Dilemma of Race and Racism

Revolutionary ideology placed a premium on such terms as liberty and equality. Almost everyone recognized that it was inconsistent to employ such terms, yet hold 500,000 African Americans (one-fifth of the population in 1776) in perpetual bondage. Phillis Wheatley addressed this incongruity in her poem to Lord Dartmouth. Lord Dunmore also pointed it out dramatically in November 1775 when he offered emancipation to Virginia's slaves (see p. 130) in return for bearing arms against their rebellious masters.

For generations colonial Americans had taken slavery for granted, as if the institution were part of the natural order of life. All of the talk about liberty and political slavery during the 1760s and 1770s began to undermine this unquestioning attitude, so much so that even slaveholding patriots like Patrick Henry asked whether holding persons in bondage was not "repugnant to humanity . . . and destructive to liberty?" Some revolutionary leaders decisively answered "yes."

These leaders did something else; they went into action. In 1774 Philadelphians, among them Benjamin Franklin, organized an abolition society. Pressure from this group and from antislavery Quakers

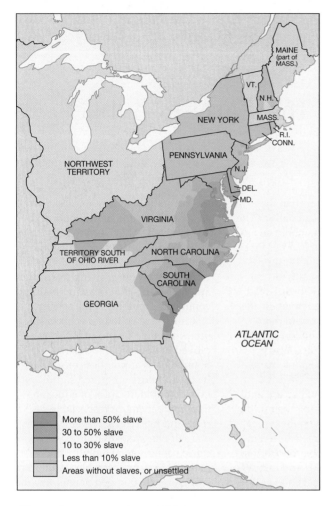

Slave Concentration, 1790

Many Americans considered slavery irreconcilable with the revolution's themes of liberty and equality.

Many revolutionary leaders hoped the campaign to abolish slavery would extend into the South. During the 1780s there were some positive signs. After 1783 only South Carolina and Georgia were still involved in the international slave trade. Maryland, Delaware, and Virginia passed laws making it easier for planters to manumit (free) individual slaves. George Washington was one among a few wealthy planters who took advantage of Virginia's **manumission** law. He referred to slavery as a "misfortune" that sullied revolutionary ideals, and in his will he made provision for the liberation of his slaves.

Washington was unusual. Far more typical was Thomas Jefferson. In his *Notes on the State of Virginia* (1785), he called slavery "a perpetual exercise" in "the most unremitting despotism." Fearing the worst should human bondage continue, he wrote: "I tremble for my country when I reflect that God is just." Such thinking led him to propose in Congress during 1784 that slavery never be allowed to spread north of the Ohio River. Jefferson, however, could not bring himself to free his own slaves. His chattels formed the economic base of his way of life. Their labor gave him the time that he needed for politics and, ironically, the time to work so persuasively on behalf of human liberty.

Support for his lifestyle was not the only reason Jefferson held back. He was representative of his times in believing blacks to be inherently inferior to whites. In his *Notes*, he made a number of comparisons of ability that were disparaging toward blacks, such as in the category of reasoning power. Trying to prove his point, Jefferson scoffed at the poems of Phillis Wheatley, which he described as "below the dignity of criticism." Jefferson thought, too, that the emancipation of African Americans would result in racial war and "the extermination of the one or the other race." Thus a man who labored so diligently for human rights in his own lifetime remained in bondage to the racist concepts of his era.

Negative racial attitudes were the norm in revolutionary America, as the growing number of freed African Americans learned again and again. Because of the general abolition and individual manumission movements, the free black population approached 60,000 by 1790 and 108,000 by 1800 (11 percent of the total African-American population). Like the some 5000 black Continental army veterans, Phillis Wheatley, and George Washington's former slaves, these individuals repeatedly had to struggle to survive in a hostile society.

Not only did they survive, but they led noteworthy lives. **Benjamin Banneker** (1731–1806) was such a person. He grew up in a free black family in Maryland, attended an interracial Quaker school, and

resulted in Pennsylvania's becoming the first state (1780) to declare human bondage illegal. Soon other Northern states followed, modeling their emancipation laws on Pennsylvania's, which specified that children born to slave mothers had to be set free by the age of 28. By 1800 slavery was a dying institution in the North.

Slaves themselves were also very active in challenging human bondage. **Quok Walker** of Massachusetts ran away from his master in April 1781 and sought refuge with a friendly neighbor. His master located Walker a few days later and accosted him with a whip. Although beaten severely, Walker stood his ground. He sued for his freedom, pointing out that the new state constitution had proclaimed that "all men are born free and equal." The State Superior Court upheld Walker in 1783, signaling the beginning of the end of slavery in Massachusetts.

Birth Control in the Early Republic

One of the most hotly debated questions in late eighteenth-century America and Europe was whether human beings were capable of improvement. Famous philosophers of the Enlightenment argued that people were naturally good and that all of society's problems could be solved by the application of reason. English philosopher William Godwin described the future in particularly glowing terms. He wrote that in the future "there would no longer be a handful of rich and a multitude of poor. . . . There will be no war, no crime, no administration of justice, as it is called, and no government. Beside this there will be no disease, anguish, melancholy, or resentment."

On the other side of the debate on human perfectibility was a young Anglican clergyman, Thomas Robert Malthus. Parson Malthus argued that human perfection was unattainable because human population growth would inevitably exceed the growth of the world's food supply. He asserted—on the basis of figures collected by Benjamin Franklin—that population tends to increase geometrically (1, 2, 4, 8) while subsistence only grows arithmetically (1, 2, 3, 4). Ultimately population would be held in check by famine, war, and disease.

Malthus's gloomy vision of the future failed to come true because large numbers of people began to limit the number of children through the use of birth control. Nowhere was the limitation of births more striking than in the United States. In 1800 the American birthrate was higher than the birthrate in any European nation. The typical American woman bore an average of 7 children. She had her first child around the age of 23 and proceeded to bear children at two-year intervals until her early forties. Had the American birthrate remained at this level, the nation's population would have reached 2 billion by 1990.

Late in the eighteenth century, however, Americans began to have fewer children. Between 1800 and 1900 the birthrate fell 40 percent and even more sharply among the middle and upper classes. Where the typical American mother bore 7 children in 1800, the average number of children had fallen to 3.5 in 1900. And instead of giving birth to her last child at the age of 40 or later, by 1900 the typical American woman bore her last child at the age of 33. The decline of the birthrate is such an important historical breakthrough that it has its own name: *the demographic transition.*

The sharp decline in birthrates is a phenomenon easier to describe than to explain. The drop in fertility was not the result of sudden improvements in contraceptive devices. The basic birth control techniques used before the Civil War—coitus interruptus (withdrawal), douching, and condoms—were known in ancient times. Ancient Egyptian papyri and the Old Testament describe cervical caps and spermicides, while ancient Greek physicians were aware of the contraceptive effects of douching. Contraception was not unknown in the past; it was simply used haphazardly and ineffectively. Nor was the imposition of limits on birthrates a result of urbanization. Although fertility fell earliest and most rapidly in the urban Northeast, the decline in fertility occurred in all parts of the country, in rural as well as urban areas and in the South and West as well as the Northeast.

What accounted for the declining birthrate? In part, the reduction in fertility reflected the growing realization among parents that in an increasingly commercial and industrial society children were no longer economic assets who could be productively employed in household industries or bound out as apprentices or servants. Instead, children required significant investment in the form of education to prepare them for respectable careers and marriages. The emergence of a self-conscious middle class concerned about social mobility and maintaining an acceptable standard of living also encouraged new limits on family size.

The shrinking size of families also reflected a growing desire among women to assert control over their lives. Much of the impetus behind birth control came from women who were weary of an unending cycle of pregnancy, birth, nursing, and new pregnancy. A letter written by a sister of Harriet Beecher Stowe suggests the desperation felt by many women who were single-handedly responsible for bearing and rearing a family's children. "Harriet," her sister observed, "has one baby put out for the winter, the other at home, and number three will be here the middle of January. Poor thing, she bears up wonderfully well. . . . She says she shall not have any more children, she knows for certain for one while."

How did Americans limit births? Periodic abstinence—or what is now known as the rhythm method—was the most widely advocated method of birth control. Unfortunately, knowledge about women's ovulation cycle,

menstruation, and conception was largely inaccurate and most advice writers suggested that the "safe period" was the ten days halfway between menstrual periods—which is in fact the time when a woman is most likely to conceive.

Other principal methods of contraception included coitus interruptus—withdrawal prior to ejaculation—and douches of the vagina after intercourse. Less common was the insertion of a sponge soaked in a spermicidal fluid into the vagina. None of these methods, however, were especially effective in preventing conception since each of these techniques can still allow small amounts of semen to reach the fallopian tubes. Other popular forms of contraception were heavily influenced by superstition. These included ingestion of teas concocted out of fruitless plants; having a woman engage in violent movements immediately after intercourse; and having intercourse on an inclined plane in order to prevent the sperm from reaching the egg or to prevent the egg from leaving the ovary.

Charles Goodyear's discovery in 1839 of the vulcanization of rubber permitted the mass production of an inexpensive and effective birth control device, the condom. But during the nineteenth century condoms were mainly used for protection against venereal disease, not for birth control.

Given the ineffectiveness of other methods of contraception, it is not surprising to learn that abortion was a major method of population control. By 1860, according to one estimate, 20 percent of pregnancies were terminated by abortion, compared to 30 percent today. Some of the popular practices for inducing abortion included taking hot baths, jumping off tables, performing heavy exercises, having someone jump on a pregnant woman's belly, drinking nauseating concoctions, and poking sharp instruments into the uterus.

Why were abortions so widespread during the nineteenth century? In part, it reflected the general ignorance of the reproductive process. It was not until 1827 that the existence of the human egg was established.

Before that time it was believed by many scientists that the human sperm constituted a miniature person that grew into a baby in the mother's womb. Thus there was no modern notion of a moment of conception when egg and sperm unite.

Furthermore, for most of the nineteenth century, it was difficult to determine whether a woman was pregnant or simply suffering menstrual irregularity. A woman only knew she was pregnant for sure when she could feel the child stir within her. This occurs around the fourth or fifth month of pregnancy and in most jurisdictions abortions prior to this time were not considered crimes. It was not until the late nineteenth century that most jurisdictions in the United States declared abortions to be criminal offenses.

The decline in the birthrate carried far-reaching consequences for family life. First of all, motherhood and the strain of pregnancy ended earlier for women. They had an increasing number of years when young children were no longer their primary responsibility. It also meant that parents were free to invest more time, energy, and financial resources in each individual child.

Benjamin Banneker taught himself calculus and spherical trigonometry, and in 1791 published an almanac in which he recorded the results of his mathematical and astronomical calculations and observations.

became a talented mathematician, astronomer, and surveyor. During the 1790s he published a series of almanacs and served on the commission that designed the new federal city of Washington, D.C. Throughout his life Banneker successfully disproved, as he wrote to Jefferson in 1791, the "train of absurd and false ideas and opinions" regarding the innate intelligence of African Americans.

Unlike Banneker, who spent his whole life in Maryland, many free blacks moved to the large northern port cities, where slavery was a fading threat. They built their own neighborhoods, and skilled workers opened shops to serve one another. Other urban free blacks, including both males and females, performed domestic service at low wages for well-to-do white families, but they did so as free persons with the opportunity to fashion independent lives for themselves.

Free African Americans also established their own schools and churches. With the assistance of the New York Society for the Promotion of Manumis-

sion, blacks helped found the African Free School in New York City during 1787. At first the school faced opposition from whites, who worried about educating blacks. This school survived, however, and would train hundreds of students in the fundamentals of reading and mathematics. In Delaware, **Richard Allen,** who purchased his own freedom in

In 1816 Richard Allen (top) became the first bishop of the African Methodist Episcopal Church (bottom), the first independent black denomination in the United States.

1777, became a powerful preacher within the Methodist ranks. After enduring incidents of intimidation from unfriendly whites, Allen moved to Philadelphia in 1786 where he became the founder of the African Methodist Episcopal Church. African Baptist and African Presbyterian denominations also developed in the northern port cities, and these churches provided opportunities for formal education, since African American children were rarely welcome in white schools.

Whether in the North or the South, the reality most often was overt discrimination. As a group, free African Americans responded by providing for one another and believing in a better day when revolutionary ideals regarding human freedom and liberty would have full meaning in their lives. In this sense they still had much in common with their brethren in slavery.

SECOND NEW BEGINNING, NEW NATIONAL GOVERNMENT

In 1787 many revolutionary leaders were more concerned about internal political stability than securing human rights. With all the talk of breaking up the Confederation, with Shays's Rebellion not yet completely quelled, and with the states arguing endlessly about almost everything, political leaders believed that matters of government should take primacy, or the republican experiment might be forever lost. Certainly the nationalists felt this way, and they were pushing hard for a revision of the first constitutional settlement.

In September 1786 representatives from five states met briefly in Annapolis, Maryland, to discuss pressing interstate commercial problems. Those present included such strong nationalists as Alexander Hamilton, John Dickinson, and James Madison. Since so few states were represented, the delegates abandoned their agenda in favor of an urgent plea asking all the states to send delegates to a special constitutional convention for remedying "such defects as exist" in the Articles of Confederation.

This time the states responded, largely because of the specter of civil turmoil associated with Shays's Rebellion. Twelve states—Rhode Island refused to participate—named 74 delegates, 55 of whom would attend the Constitutional Convention in Philadelphia. As the Continental Congress instructed the delegates in February 1787, their purpose was to revise the Articles of Confederation, making them "adequate to the exigencies . . . of the union." Some nationalists, however, had other ideas. They wanted a whole new plan of national government. Their ideas would dominate the proceedings from beginning to end, and their determination produced the Constitution of 1787.

The Framers of the Constitution

The men who gathered in Philadelphia were successful lawyers, planters, and merchants of education, wealth, and wide-ranging accomplishments, not ordinary citizens. They represented particular states, but most of them thought in national terms, based on experiences like serving in the Continental

George Washington (on the podium) presided at the Constitutional Convention in Philadelphia during the summer of 1787. Washington was a popular hero and a natural choice to serve as the first president of the United States.

Congress and the Continental army. They feared for the future of the republic, unless the weak central government was strengthened as a means of containing the selfishness of particular states. They seized this opportunity for change and made the most of it.

Among those present during the lengthy proceedings, which stretched from May 25 to September 17, was the revered George Washington, who served as the convention's president. Other notable leaders included James Madison, Alexander Hamilton, Gouverneur and Robert Morris, and John Dickinson. Benjamin Franklin, at 81, was the oldest delegate. He offered his finely tuned diplomatic tact in working out compromises that kept the proceedings moving forward.

Although the delegates disagreed vehemently over particular issues, they never let their differences deflect them from their main purpose—to find the constitutional means for an enduring republic. The Constitution was not perfect, as Benjamin Franklin stated on the last day of the convention, but it did bring stability and energy to national government—and it has endured.

James Madison, a strong nationalist, has been called the "father of the Constitution" for his plan of national government. He became the nation's fourth president.

A Document Constructed by Compromises

Had the nationalists been doctrinaire, their deliberations would have collapsed. They held fast to their objective—providing for a strong central government—but were flexible about ways to achieve their goal. Thus they were able to compromise on critical issues. The first great points of difference dealt with the structure of government and whether states should be represented equally or according to population distribution. The eventual compromise required the abandonment of the Articles of Confederation.

Slight of build and reserved, James Madison of Virginia (1751–1836) has been called the "father of the Constitution." A diligent student of history and politics, he drafted a proposed plan of national government, then made arrangements to have it presented by Edmund Randolph, Virginia's governor and a more adept public speaker, at the outset of the convention. This strategy worked, and the delegates gave the "Virginia Plan" their undivided attention. The plan outlined a three-tiered structure with an executive branch and two houses of Congress. Madison also envisioned a separate judicial branch.

Delegates from the less populous, smaller states objected. Under the Virginia Plan representatives to the two chambers of Congress would be apportioned to the states according to population, whereas under the Articles, each state, regardless of population, had an equal voice in national government. For such delegates as lawyer **William Paterson** of New Jersey, the latter practice ensured that the interests of the smaller states would not be sacrificed to those of the more populous, larger states. Paterson countered with his "New Jersey Plan" on June 15. It retained equal voting in a unicameral national legislature, and it also vested far greater authority, including the powers of taxation and regulation of interstate and foreign commerce, in the central government. Paterson's plan was far more consistent with the convention's original charge—an argument in its favor.

On June 19 the delegates voted to adopt a three-tiered structure of government, but they did not resolve the question of how the states should be represented in the two new legislative branches. The convention had reached an impasse, and some delegates now threatened to leave. At the end of June Benjamin Franklin made one of his well-timed speeches. He urged everyone present to put aside "our little partial local interests" so that future generations would not "despair of establishing governments by human wisdom and leave it to chance, war, and conquest."

The advice of Franklin and others calling for unity of purpose helped ease tensions. By July 12 the delegates had hammered out a settlement. Central to the "Great Compromise," which saved the convention from dissolving, was an agreement providing for proportional representation in the lower house (favoring the more populous states) and equality of representation in the upper house (favoring the less populous states). In the upper house each state would have two senators. Although the senators could vote independently of each other, they could also operate in tandem to protect state interests.

Having passed this crucial hurdle, the convention turned to other issues, not the least of which was slavery. Delegates from the Deep South wanted guarantees that would prevent any national tampering with their chattel property. Some Northerners, however, including those who had supported abolition in their states, preferred constitutional restrictions on slavery.

For a while, compromise did not seem possible. In the heat of debate South Carolinian Pierce Butler blurted out that the North and the South were "as different as . . . Russia and Turkey." Later on, Pennsylvania delegate Gouverneur Morris, a firm antislavery advocate, suggested that it was impossible "to blend incompatible things." Finally, both sides made concessions for the sake of union. What they produced was the first major national compromise on the continuation of slavery (to be followed by others, including the Compromises of 1820 and 1850).

In the North-South compromise of 1787, the delegates left matters purposely vague. By mutual agreement, the Constitution neither endorsed nor condemned slavery, nor can that word be found in the text. It did guarantee Southerners that slaves would count as "three-fifths" of white persons for purposes of determining representation in the lower house. While this meant more congressional seats for the South, direct taxes would also be based on population, including "three-fifths of all other persons." Thus the South would also pay more in taxes. The delegates also agreed to prohibit any national legislation against the importation of slaves from abroad until 1808.

Although these clauses gave implicit recognition to slavery, it should be noted that the Northwest Land Ordinance of 1787, adopted by the Continental Congress in New York at the same time, forever barred slavery north of the Ohio River. The timing has led some historians to conclude that inhibiting the spread of slavery was also part of the compromise, representing a major concession to northern interests.

The North-South compromise kept the convention and the republic together by temporarily mollifying most delegates on an extremely divisive issue. Still, slavery was so remarkably inconsistent with the ideals of human liberty that the problem could not be sidestepped for long.

A third set of issues provoking compromise had to do with the office of president. Nobody seemed sure what range of authority the national executive should have, how long the term of office should be, or how the president should be elected. By early September the delegates, fatigued by endless debates and extremely hot weather during three months of meetings, settled these questions quickly. The office of the president was potentially powerful. Besides serving as commander in chief of military forces, the incumbent could fashion treaties with foreign powers, subject to ratification by a two-thirds vote of the Senate. The president could veto congressional legislation, which both houses of Congress could only override with two-thirds majorities. Congress, in turn, had an important check on the president. It could impeach the executive if presidential powers were abused. Four years seemed like a reasonable term of office, and reelection would be permitted.

To help insulate the president from manipulation by public opinion, the delegates made the office indirectly elective. They did so by creating the electoral college. Each state would have the same number of electors as representatives and senators. In states that permitted popular voting for the presidency, citizens would cast ballots for electors who favored particular candidates. In turn the electors would meet and vote for the person they favored. The candidate with a majority of electoral college votes would become president. The person with the second highest total would become vice president. Should the electors fail to reach a majority decision (this happened in the elections of 1800 and 1824), the election would be turned over to the House of Representatives, where each state would have one vote in choosing a president.

The subject of the presidency might have been more contentious had no person of George Washington's universally acclaimed stature been on the scene. Washington was the one authentic popular hero and symbol of national unity to emerge from the Revolution, and the delegates were already thinking of him as the first president. Since he was so fully trusted as a firm apostle of republican principles who had disdained the mantle of a military dictator, defining the mode of election and powers of the national executive were not insurmountable tasks.

The Ratification Struggle

Thirty-nine delegates affixed their signatures to the proposed Constitution on September 17, 1787.

Benjamin Franklin hoped that more of the delegates would sign, and he echoed the thoughts of those who did so by indicating that "there are several parts of this Constitution which I do not at present approve. . . . It therefore astonishes me, Sir," he stated, "to find this system approaching so near to perfection as it does." Pointing toward a seal with a carving of the sun on the president's chair, Franklin concluded: "At length I have the happiness to know that it is a rising and not a setting sun."

The delegates who signed the Constitution of 1787 knew there would be significant opposition because their plan cut so heavily into state authority. So they made the shrewd move of agreeing that only nine states needed to ratify the Constitution—through special state conventions rather than through state legislatures—to allow the new central government to commence operations. The nationalists were not going to let one or two states destroy months of work—and what they viewed as the best last hope for a languishing republic.

In another astute move, the nationalists started referring to themselves as **Federalists,** and they disarmed their opponents by calling them **Antifederalists.** Actually, the Antifederalists were the real federalists; they wanted to continue the confederation of sovereign states, and they sought to keep power as close as possible to the people, mostly in the hands of state governments. This manipulation of terminology may have gotten some local Federalist candidates elected to state ratifying conventions, thus helping to secure victory for the Constitution.

The nationalists were also very effective in explaining the Convention's work. The essence of their argumentation appeared in **The Federalist Papers,** a series of 85 remarkably cogent newspaper essays written by James Madison, Alexander Hamilton, and John Jay on behalf of ratification in New York. Under the pseudonym "Publius," they discussed various aspects of the Constitution and tried to demonstrate how the document would ensure political stability and provide enlightened legislation.

The new government, they asserted, had been designed to protect the rights of all citizens. No one self-serving faction ("a landed interest, a manufacturing interest, a mercantile interest, a monied interest"), whether representing a minority or majority of citizens, could take power completely and deprive others of their liberties and property. The Constitution would check and balance these interest groups because basic powers (executive, legislative, judicial) would be divided among the various branches of government. Furthermore, the system was truly federal, they argued, because much decision-making authority remained with the states as a further protec-

tion against power-hungry, self-serving factional interest groups.

Beyond these advantages, the Constitution embodied the principle of representative republicanism, as Madison explained in *Federalist No. 10.* Large election districts for the House of Representatives would make it more difficult for particular interest groups to manipulate elections and send "unworthy candidates" to Congress. Citizens of true merit, hence, could rise up, emerge triumphant, and then meet in Congress to enact laws beneficial for all citizens of the republic.

The nationalists admitted they were overturning the first constitutional settlement of 1776. The emphasis would now be on a national government whose acts would be "the supreme law of the land." Federal leaders would be drawn from citizens of learning and wealth, many like those nationalists who had never fully trusted the people. From their perspective the people had failed the test of public virtue. They had shown more concern for their individual welfare than in making material or personal sacrifices to support the Continental war effort. They had formed into troublesome factions like the Maryland land speculators and the Massachusetts rebel followers of Daniel Shays, all to the detriment of the republic's political stability.

The nationalists, now expecting to function as the new nation's political stewards, did not repudiate the principle of popular sovereignty. Rather, they enshrined it in such concepts as representative republicanism. The people were to have a political voice, in the abstract at least, and they were to remain the constituent authority of American government. Their stewards, supposedly detached from selfish concerns, could now more easily check narrow interests inhibiting stable national development.

The Antifederalists understood, and they viewed this new settlement with grave alarm. One writer, "Centinel," stated that the Constitution would support "in practice a *permanent* ARISTOCRACY" of self-serving, wealthy citizens. Another, calling himself "Philadelphiensis," saw in the Constitution "a conspiracy against the liberties of his country, concerted by a few *tyrants,* whose views are to lord it over the rest of their fellow citizens."

These arguments, reminiscent of those that had stirred up revolutionary fervor in the 1760s and 1770s, lay at the heart of the Antifederalist critique of the proposed Constitution. Leading Antifederalists, among them Samuel Adams, Patrick Henry, and Richard Henry Lee, still had negative images of the distant British government, too far removed from the people to be checked in any effective way. Having rebelled against what they perceived as the

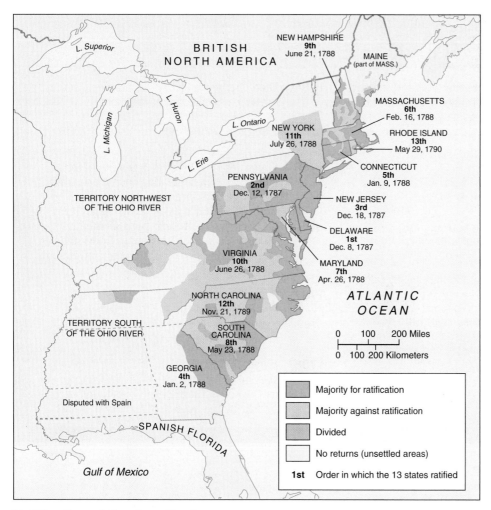

Ratification of the Constitution

The first ratifying convention in North Carolina (July 21, 1788) voted not to consider approval of the Constitution. A second convention (November 21, 1789) voted approval. Only after the United States Senate threatened to sever commercial ties with Rhode Island, which had refused to participate in the Constitutional Convention, did the state agree to hold a ratifying convention. On May 29, 1790, the convention reluctantly and by the narrowest of votes approved the Constitution.

tyranny of the British imperial government, they were not anxious to approve a plan for a new central government with enough power to threaten the states and the people with yet more political tyranny. They preferred life under the Articles of Confederation.

The Antifederalists failed to counter nationalist momentum. Close calls occurred in some ratifying conventions, such as in Massachusetts, New York, and Virginia. The well-organized nationalists were always ready to counter Antifederalist complaints. When some complained about the absence of a national bill of rights guaranteeing each citizen fundamental liberties, they promised that the first Con-

gress would prepare one. When some demanded a second convention that would not overturn but modify the Articles of Confederation, they argued that the new government should first be given a chance. If it did not work, the nationalists stated, they would support another convention.

Once the New Hampshire convention voted to ratify on June 21, 1788, the necessary nine states had given their approval. The two large states of Virginia and New York were still not in the fold, however, so everyone hesitated. Virginia was the most populous state, and New York was fourth behind Pennsylvania and Massachusetts. In addition, both Virginia and New York were so strategically located that it would

CHRONOLOGY OF KEY EVENTS

1775   Daniel Boone blazes the "Wilderness Road" to Kentucky; Lord Dunmore calls for the emancipation of Virginia's slaves (November)

1775–   Ten states adopt new state
1777   constitutions

1776–   Congress drafts the Articles of
1777   Confederation

1780   Pennsylvania becomes the first state to provide for the emancipation of slaves

1781   Articles of Confederation are finally ratified by all the states

1782   Rhode Island refuses to ratify the Impost Plan to provide Congress a tax revenue, thereby precipitating the threat of a military coup—the Newburgh Conspiracy

1783   Washington defuses the threat of a military coup

1784   Land Ordinance of 1784 guarantees western settlers territorial government

1785   Land Ordinance of 1785 provides for the survey and sale of western lands

1786   Virginia adopts Jefferson's Statute of Religious Freedom separating church and state (January); Jay-Gardoquí negotiations fail to produce a trading alliance with Spain (August); Shays's Rebellion gains momentum (August–December); Annapolis Convention calls for a national constitutional convention (September)

1787   Constitutional Convention convenes in Philadelphia (May); Congress passes the Northwest Ordinance, forever barring slavery north of the Ohio River (July)

1788   Hamilton, Madison, and Jay publish 85 essays on behalf of the Constitution, known as *The Federalist Papers;* Constitution is ratified by the necessary number of states

have been virtually impossible to operate the new national government without their involvement.

Promises of a bill of rights helped bring the Virginia convention around in a close vote (89 yeas to 79 nays) on June 25. A month later after much skillful Federalist maneuvering, including promises of a second constitutional convention should the 1787 plan fail to work, the dominant Antifederalists in New York's ratifying convention conceded enough votes for ratification to occur by the slim margin of 30 yeas to 27 nays. New York thus became the "eleventh pillar" of the union. Since the constitution did succeed, as demonstrated by George Washington's presidential administration, arguments for a second convention faded away.

CONCLUSION

In 1776 those radical revolutionaries who believed in a virtuous citizenry had sought to expand popular participation in government. By and large they succeeded. This first constitutional settlement proved to be unsatisfactory, however, largely because the weak central government under the Articles of Confedera-

tion lacked the authority to support even the minimal needs of the new nation. Blaming the states and the people, the nationalist leaders produced a second constitutional settlement in 1787 by drafting a plan for a more powerful central government. It was to be above the people and the states, strong enough to establish and preserve national unity and stability.

The new national government began functioning in April 1789. No sooner had these "diffusive and established" gentlemen started to govern, however, than they fell to fighting among themselves over a host of controversial issues. To gain allies, they turned back to the people. Against the wishes of many nationalists, some leaders started to organize political parties and urged the citizenry to support their candidates as a means of stopping the opposition. By the mid-1790s the people were emerging as much more than a token voice in national politics. Concepts of deference and stewardship were now in full retreat; common citizens were at last becoming the true foundation of what would one day be a system of political democracy.

The years between 1776 and 1789 thus secured the republic and republican ideals. On the other hand, notions regarding each American's right to enjoy life, liberty, happiness, and property in an equalitarian society fell far short of full implementation. Women remained second-class citizens, and the shackles of slavery and racist thinking still manacled African Americans. Even with the opening of the trans-Appalachian West, which came at the expense of thousands of Native Americans, poorer citizens found it difficult to gain access to farmland on which they could provide for themselves and secure their personal prosperity. Although future generations would argue and fight, even to the point of a bloody civil war, over how best to realize the full potential of republican ideals, there was no denying their rudimentary presence. In this sense the years before 1789 had witnessed a revolution in human expectations.

owners to manumit individual slaves. Despite the dominant language of liberty, however, slavery remained a firmly fixed institution in the southern states. Women gained more access to education but failed to obtain full citizenship rights.

- Concern for the new nation's political survival and stability caused nationalist-minded Revolutionary leaders to draft a new Constitution in 1787, which worked out compromises between large and small states over representation and between northern and southern states over maintaining the institution of slavery. In the end, the Revolutionary era, so full of triumphs, also left much undone in regard to extending the full range of political and social rights to all Americans.

CHAPTER SUMMARY AND KEY POINTS

Amid the War for Independence patriot leaders addressed the task of establishing new state governments and a national government. In each instance, the principles of republicanism, including popular sovereignty, rule by law, and legislation enacted by elected representatives, predominated. As leaders set up new governments, they were beset by a variety of vexing problems, including how to finance the war effort, the possible threat of a military coup, and popular demands for tax relief in the face of a hardhitting postwar depression. All the while, the rhetoric of liberty, which was at the core of the Revolutionary experience, raised questions about continuing the enslavement of African Americans and securing expanded rights for women as well as questions about such divisive issues as putting an end to state-supported religion and guaranteeing true religious freedom. Dealing with the political and economic problems facing the new nation took precedence, as did the matter of national unification, as shown in the drafting of the Constitution of 1787 and its ratification as a plan providing for a strong national government.

- Between 1776 and 1789 Revolutionary leaders made various efforts to implement the young nation's republican ideals. Most of the new state governments expanded voting and office holding rights, and some adopted statements guaranteeing such rights as freedom of speech, assembly, and the press as well as trial by jury.

- Some northern states began to abolish slavery or approved gradual emancipation plans, while some southern states made it easier for slave

SUGGESTIONS FOR FURTHER READING

Gregory Evans Dowd, *A Spirited Resistance: The North American Indian Struggle for Unity, 1745–1815* (1992). Incisive account of militant Native-American resistance in reaction to white expansion into the trans-Appalachian West.

Sylvia R. Frey, *Water from the Rock: Black Resistance in a Revolutionary Age* (1991). Revisionist investigation of southern slaves and how they sought to make better lives for themselves out of the turmoil of the Revolutionary era.

Robert A. Gross, ed., *In Debt to Shays: The Bicentennial of an Agrarian Rebellion* (1993). Illuminating essays focusing on Shays's Rebellion and the many problems besetting ordinary citizens in late eighteenth-century America.

Merrill Jensen, *The New Nation, 1781–1789* (1950). Classic examination of "critical period" politics and the nationalist mind-set of the Founding Fathers.

Jean B. Lee, *The Price of Nationhood: The American Revolution in Charles County* (1994). Suggestive appraisal of the impact of the Revolution on the inhabitants of this Maryland county.

Mary Beth Norton, *Liberty's Daughters: The Revolutionary Experience of American Women, 1750–1800* (1980). Valuable study of ways in which the Revolution affected the roles women defined for themselves.

Jack N. Rakove, *Original Meanings: Politics and Ideas in the Making of the Constitution* (1996). Prize-winning analysis of the ideas, concerns, and intentions that both shaped and gave meaning to the Constitution of 1787.

Leonard L. Richards, *Shays's Rebellion: The American Revolution's Final Battle* (2002). Well-written study that challenges the view of an uprising sparked by downtrodden, heavily indebted farmers.

Gordon S. Wood, *The Creation of the American Republic, 1776–1787* (1969). Influential analysis of changing conceptions of political thought and culture culminating in the Constitution of 1787 and a new national government.

Novels

Edward Bellamy, *The Duke of Stockbridge* (1879).

Howard Fast, *Citizen Tom Paine* (1943).

Irving Stone, *Those Who Love: A Biographical Novel of Abigail and John Adams* (1965).

MEDIA RESOURCES

Web Sites

Northwest Territory Alliance
http://www.nwta.com/main.html
This Revolutionary Era reenactment organization site contains several links and is an interesting look at historical reenactment.

Archiving Early America
http://earlyamerica.com/
Old newspapers are excellent windows into the issues of the past. This site includes the Keigwin and Matthews collection of historic newspapers.

Biographies of the Founding Fathers
http://www.colonialhall.com/
This site provides information about the men who signed the Declaration of Independence and includes a trivia section.

Religion and the Founding of the American Republic
http://lcweb.loc.gov/exhibits/religion/religion.html
This Library of Congress site is an online exhibit about religion and the creation of the United States.

The Federalist Papers
http://www.law.emory.edu/FEDERAL/federalist/
A collection of the most important *Federalist Papers*, a series of documents designed to convince people to support the new Constitution.

Anti-Federalist Papers
http://www.constitution.org/afp.htm
The Constitution Society has digitized several different works by leading Anti-Federalists who opposed the unconditional ratification of the Federal Constitution, including the *Letters from the Federal Farmer*.

The Constitution and the Amendments
http://www.law.emory.edu/FEDERAL/usconst.html
A searchable site to the Constitution, especially useful for its information about the Bill of Rights and other constitutional amendments.

Documents from the Continental Congress and the Constitutional Convention, 1774–1789
http://memory.loc.gov/ammem/bdsds/bdsdhome.html
This American Memory collection from the Library of Congress contains many valuable documents relating to the work of the Continental Congress and the drafting and ratification of the Constitution of 1787.

Debates on Ratifying the Constitution of 1787
http://www.constitution.org/elliot.htm
Jonathan Elliot's classic volumes, *The Debates in the Several State Conventions on the Adoption of the Federal Constitution*, are now readily available online.

KEY TERMS

Republicanism   (p. 153)

Public virtue   (p. 153)

Radical revolutionaries   (p. 154)

Cautious revolutionaries   (p. 154)

Nationalists   (p. 156)

National domain   (p. 156)

Landless states   (p. 156)

Landed states   (p. 156)

Shaysites   (p. 161)

Republican motherhood   (p. 165)

Manumission   (p. 167)

Federalists   (p. 174)

Antifederalists   (p. 174)

The Federalist Papers   (p. 174)

PEOPLE YOU SHOULD KNOW

Nancy Shippen   (p. 151)

Phillis Wheatley   (p. 151)

Robert Morris   (p. 158)

Gouverneur Morris   (p. 158)

Alexander Hamilton   (p. 158)

James Madison   (p. 158)

John Jay   (p. 160)

Don Diego de Gardoqui   (p. 160)

Daniel Shays   (p. 161)

Abigail Adams   (p. 164)

Mary Ludwig Hays McCauly   (p. 164)

Judith Sargent Murray   (p. 166)

Quok Walker   (p. 167)

Benjamin Banneker   (p. 167)

Richard Allen   (p. 170)

William Paterson   (p. 172)

REVIEW QUESTIONS

1. Examine the major points of disagreement between radical and reluctant revolutionaries. What characterized their viewpoints regarding the concept of public

virtue, and how did these differences affect constitution making during the Revolutionary era?

2. What were some of the numerous internal problems that plagued the early American republic? In what ways were these problems aggravated by having a weak national government under the Articles of Confederation and sovereign power granted to the states?

3. Compare and contrast the Newburgh Conspiracy of 1783 with Shays's Rebellion of 1786–1787. In what ways did these two events relate to the drive for a stronger national government, and what was their significance?

4. What were some of the contradictions between the Revolution's rhetoric of liberty and actual conditions faced by such groups as African Americans, women, and the propertyless poor? What effect, if any, did the rhetoric of liberty have on these groups during the Revolution and beyond?

5. Explain why the Constitution of 1787 might be described as a bundle of compromises? How did this plan of government address the major problems that had beset the struggling Confederation of states between 1776 and 1787? Why did the Constitution raise prospects for long-term political stability?

7 The Formative Decade, 1790–1800

JAMES CALLENDER AND THE POWER OF THE PRESS

A critic called **James Thomson Callender** "the most outrageous and wretched scandalmonger of a scurrilous age." During the 1790s, Callender, a pioneering muckraking journalist, published vicious attacks on George Washington, John Adams, Alexander Hamilton, and other leading political figures. Today, Callender is best known as the journalist who first published the story that Thomas Jefferson had a decades-long affair with one of his slaves.

Born in Scotland in 1758, Callender became an early proponent of Scottish independence from Britain. Indicted for sedition in 1793, he fled to Philadelphia, where he made a living as a congressional reporter and a political propagandist. Profoundly suspicious of Treasury Secretary Alexander Hamilton's pro-British views on foreign affairs, Callender used his pen to discredit Hamilton. In 1797 he published evidence—probably provided by supporters of Thomas Jefferson—that Hamilton had an adulterous extramarital affair with a woman named Maria Reynolds. Callender also accused Hamilton of involvement in illegal financial speculations with Reynolds's husband, an unsavory character who had been convicted of fraud and dealing in stolen goods. Hamilton acknowledged the affair, but denied the corruption charges, claiming that he was a victim of blackmail. Nevertheless, Hamilton's public reputation was hurt, and he never held public office again.

In 1798 Hamilton's political party, the Federalist party, pushed the Sedition Act through Congress, making it a crime to attack the government or the president with false, scandalous, or malicious statements. In 1800 Callender was one of several journalists indicted, tried, and convicted under the law. He was fined $200 and sentenced to nine months in prison, where he found himself "surrounded by thieves of every description."

By the time Callender was released, Thomas Jefferson had been elected president. Callender expected the new administration to refund his fine and appoint him to a government job. When repayment of the fine was delayed and Jefferson refused to appoint him as a postmaster, Callender struck back. In 1802, a year be-

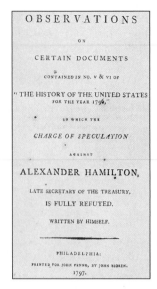

Alexander Hamilton responded to journalist James Thomson Callender's charges that he had engaged in illegal financial speculations by publishing a detailed denial.

fore his death, Callender publicly accused Jefferson of having a lifelong liaison with his slave Sally Hemings.

Sally Hemings was the half-sister of Jefferson's deceased wife Martha. Her mother had been impregnated by her master, John Wayles, the father of Martha Jefferson. Sally Hemings herself bore five mulatto children out of wedlock. Callender insisted that Jefferson fathered the children. Jefferson's defenders denied the assertion. In 1998 DNA testing indicated that Thomas Jefferson fathered at least one of Sally Hemings's children.

Despised by his critics as a "traitorous and truculent scoundrel," Callender defended himself on strikingly modern grounds: that the public had a right to know the moral character of people it elected to public office. Although he has often been dismissed as a "pen for hire," willing to defame anyone, Callender's work underscores one of the most radical consequences of the American Revolution. The revolution gave new meaning to the idea of popular sovereignty and ensured that ordinary Americans would be the ultimate arbiters of American politics. Passionately rejecting the notion that common people should express deference toward the educated and well to do, Callender aimed his political commentary at artisans and immigrants who flocked to seaport towns during the 1790s. Scandal, sensation, and suspicion of the powerful were the appeals he used to attract readers.

P olitically and economically, the 1790s was the nation's formative decade. During this time the United States implemented the new Constitution, adopted a bill of rights, created its first political parties, and built a new national capital city in Washington, D.C. The 1790s were also years of rapid economic and demographic growth, the time when the new United States established a strong and vigorous national government and a prosperous, growing economy.

THE ROOTS OF AMERICAN ECONOMIC GROWTH

Early in August 1790, David Howe, an assistant federal marshal, began the difficult task of counting all the people who lived in Hancock County, Maine. One of 650 federal census takers charged with making "a just and perfect enumeration and description of all persons" in the United States, he began by writing down his own name followed by his wife's and child's. He next listed the names of all the other people who lived in his hometown of Penobscot, then crisscrossed the Maine coast, recording the names of 9549 residents. In March 1791 he submitted his findings: 2436 free white males, 16 and older; 4544 free white females; 2631 white children; and 38 "other free persons," including Peter Williams, "a black," and his wife and child.

The United States was the first nation in history to institute a periodic national census. Since 1790, the country has tried to count each woman, man, and child every 10 years. The first census asked just six simple questions, yet when supplemented by other statistical information, it provides a treasure chest of information about the social and economic life of the American people.

Taking the nation's first census was an extraordinarily difficult challenge. The nation's sheer physical size—stretching across 867,980 square miles from Georgia to Maine—made it impossible to conduct an accurate count. Many people refused to speak to census takers; some because they feared that this was the first step toward enactment of new taxes, others because they believed that the Bible prohibited census taking. To make matters worse, census takers were abysmally paid; they received just $1 for every 150 rural residents and $1 for every 300 city dwellers counted. Indeed, the pay was so low that one judge found it difficult to find "any person whatever" to take the census.

What was the United States like in 1790? According to the first census, the United States contained just 3,929,214 people, about half living in the north-

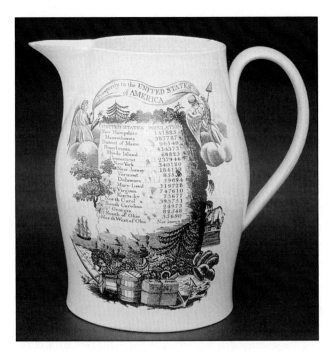

The Constitution provided for a census every 10 years. The first census, conducted in 1790, estimated the population of the United States at 3.9 million people. The jug, made in England after the 1790 census, shows the figures gathered in that census.

ern states, half in the South. At first glance, the population seems quite small (it was only about a quarter the size of England's and a sixth the size of France's), but it was growing extraordinarily rapidly. Just 1.17 million in 1750, the population would pass five million by 1800.

The 1790 census revealed a nation still overwhelmingly rural in character. In a population of nearly four million, only two cities had more than 25,000 people. Yet the urban population, while small, was growing extremely rapidly, especially in the West where frontier towns like Louisville started to sprout.

In 1790 most Americans still lived on the Atlantic coast. Nevertheless, the West was the most rapidly growing part of the nation. During the 1790s, the population of Kentucky and Tennessee increased nearly 300 percent, and by 1800, Kentucky had more people than five of the original 13 states.

The first census also revealed an extraordinarily youthful population, with half the people under the age of 16. Extraordinarily diverse, a fifth of the entire population was African American. Three-fifths of the white population was English in ancestry and another fifth was Scottish or Irish. The remainder was of German, Dutch, French, Swedish, or other background.

The American economy was still quite undeveloped. There were fewer than 100 newspapers in the entire country, three banks (with total capital of less than $5 million), and three insurance companies; yet, the United States was perched on the edge of an extraordinary decade of growth.

Over the next 10 years, American society made tremendous economic advances. During the 1790s, states chartered almost 10 times more corporations, banks, and transportation companies than during the 1780s. Exports climbed from $29 million to $107 million; cotton production rose from 3000 bales to 73,000. Altogether, 11 mechanized mills were built in the country during the 1790s, laying the foundations for future economic growth.

In 1800, as in 1790, the United States remained a nation of farms, plantations, and small towns, of yeomen farmers, slaves, and artisans. Nevertheless, the nation was undergoing far-reaching social and economic transformations. Improvements in education were particularly striking. Between 1783 and 1800 Americans founded 17 new colleges and a large number of female academies.

Why did the United States experience such rapid growth during the 1790s? In part, the answer lies in European wars, pitting France against Britain, which increased demand for U.S. products and stimulated American shipping and trade. The answer also lies in critical political developments, especially enactment of a financial program that secured the nation's credit.

IMPLEMENTING THE CONSTITUTION

The United States was one of the first modern nations to achieve independence through a successful revolution against colonial rule. Although many colonies in the nineteenth and twentieth centuries followed the example of the United States in winning independence through revolution, few were as successful in subsequent economic and political development. Even the United States, however, struggled to establish itself in its first decade under the Constitution.

The new nation faced severe economic and foreign policy problems. A huge debt remained from the Revolution, and paper money issued during and after the war was virtually worthless. Along with these pressing economic problems were foreign threats to the new nation's independence. In violation of the peace treaty of 1783 ending the Revolutionary War, Britain continued to occupy forts in the Old Northwest, and Spain refused to recognize the new nation's southern and western boundaries. In

1790 economic problems, domestic political conflict, and foreign policy issues challenged the new nation in its efforts to establish a stable republic.

Establishing the Machinery of Government

The first task facing American leaders was to establish the machinery of government. The new U.S. government consisted of 75 post offices, a large debt, a small number of unpaid clerks, and an army of just 46 officers and 672 soldiers. There was no federal court system, no navy, and no system for collecting taxes.

It fell to Congress to take the initial steps toward putting the new national government into operation: To raise revenue, it passed a tariff on imported goods and an excise tax on liquor; to encourage American shipping, it imposed duties on foreign vessels; and to provide a structure for the executive branch of the government, it created departments of State, Treasury, and War. By the **Judiciary Act of 1789** Congress organized a federal court system, which consisted of a Supreme Court with six justices, a district court in each state, and three appeals courts.

To strengthen popular support for the new government, Congress also approved a **Bill of Rights** in the form of 10 amendments to the Constitution. These first amendments guaranteed the rights of free press, free speech, and free exercise of religion; the right to peaceful assembly; and the right to petition government. The Bill of Rights also ensured that the national government could not infringe on the right to trial by jury. In an effort to reassure Antifederalists that the powers of the new government were limited, the tenth amendment "reserved to the States respectively, or to the people" all powers not specified in the Constitution.

Defining the Presidency

The Constitution provided only a broad outline of the office and powers of the president. It would be up to **George Washington,** as the first president, to define the office and establish many precedents regarding the president's relationship with the other branches of government. It was unclear, for example, whether the president was personally to run the executive branch or, instead, act like a constitutional monarch and delegate responsibility to the vice president and executive officers, called the **cabinet.** Washington favored a strong and active role for the president. Modeling the executive branch along the lines of a general's staff, Washington consulted his cabinet officers and listened to them carefully, but he made the final decisions, just as he had done as commander-in-chief.

The relationship between the executive and legislative branches was also uncertain. Should a president, like Britain's prime minister, personally appear before Congress to defend administration policies? Should the Senate have sole power to dismiss executive officers? The answers to such questions were not clear. Washington insisted that the president could dismiss presidential appointees without the Senate's permission. A bitterly divided Senate approved this principle by a single vote.

With regard to foreign policy, Washington tried to follow the literal words of the Constitution, which stated that the president should negotiate treaties with the advice and consent of the Senate. He appeared before the Senate to discuss a pending Indian treaty. The senators, however, refused to provide immediate answers and referred the matter to a committee. "This defeats every purpose of my coming here," Washington declared. In the future he negotiated treaties first and then sent them to the Senate for ratification.

The most difficult task that the president faced was deciding whom to nominate for public office.

This figurative drawing depicts President George Washington meeting with his first cabinet—Secretary of War Henry Knox, Secretary of State Thomas Jefferson, and Secretary of the Treasury Alexander Hamilton—at Washington's Mount Vernon home.

For secretary of war, Washington nominated Henry Knox, an old military comrade, who had held a similar position under the Articles of Confederation. As postmaster general, he named Samuel Osgood of Massachusetts, who carried out his tasks in a single room with the help of two clerks. For attorney general, he tapped fellow Virginian Edmund Randolph, and for chief justice of the Supreme Court, he selected New Yorker John Jay. Washington nominated another Virginian, Thomas Jefferson, for secretary of state. He named his former aide-de-camp, the 34-year-old Alexander Hamilton, to head the Treasury Department.

Alexander Hamilton's Financial Program

The most pressing problems facing the new government were economic. As a result of the revolution, the federal government had acquired a huge debt: $54 million including interest. The states owed another $25 million. Paper money issued under the Continental Congresses and Articles of Confederation was worthless. Foreign credit was unavailable.

Ten days after **Alexander Hamilton** became Treasury Secretary, Congress asked him to report on ways to solve the nation's financial problems. Hamilton, a man of strong political convictions, immediately realized that he had an opportunity to create a financial program that would embody his political principles.

Hamilton believed that the nation's stability depended on an alliance between the government and citizens of wealth and influence. No society could succeed, he maintained, "which did not unite the interest and credit of rich individuals with those of the state." Unlike Thomas Jefferson, Hamilton doubted the capacity of common people to govern themselves. "The people are turbulent and changing," he contended, "they seldom judge or determine right."

To keep the masses in check, Hamilton favored a strong national government. Born in the British West Indies, Hamilton never developed the intense loyalty to a state that was common among many Americans of the time. He intended to use government fiscal policies to strengthen federal power at the expense of the states and "make it in the immediate interest of the moneyed men to cooperate with government in its support."

The paramount problem facing Hamilton was the national debt. Hamilton argued that it was vital for the nation to repay the debts to establish the credit of the federal government. He proposed that the government assume the entire indebtedness—principal and interest—of the federal government and the states. His plan was to retire the old depreciated obligations by borrowing new money at a lower interest rate.

This proposal ignited a firestorm of controversy, because states like Maryland, Pennsylvania, North Carolina, and Virginia had already paid off their war debts. They saw no reason why they should be taxed by the federal government to pay off the debts of states like Massachusetts and South Carolina. Others opposed the scheme because it would provide enormous profits to speculators who had bought bonds from revolutionary war veterans for as little as 10 or 15 cents on the dollar. Many of these financial speculators were associates of Hamilton or members of Congress who knew that Hamilton's report would recommend full payment of the debt.

For six months, a bitter debate raged in Congress. The nation's future seemed in jeopardy until a compromise orchestrated by James Madison and Thomas Jefferson secured passage of Hamilton's plan. In exchange for southern votes in Congress, Hamilton promised his support for locating the future national capital on the banks of the Potomac River, the border between two southern states, Virginia and Maryland.

Hamilton's debt program was a remarkable success. By demonstrating Americans' willingness to repay their debts, he made America a good credit risk attractive to foreign investors. European investment capital poured into the new nation in large amounts.

Hamilton's next objective was to create a Bank of the United States, modeled after the Bank of England, to issue currency, collect taxes, hold government funds, and make loans to the government and borrowers. This proposal, like his debt scheme, unleashed a storm of protest.

One criticism was that a bank threatened to undermine the nation's republican values. Banks—and the paper money they issued—would simply encourage speculation and corruption. Some opposed the bank on constitutional grounds. Adopting a position known as **strict construction, Thomas Jefferson** and **James Madison** charged that a national bank was unconstitutional since the Constitution did not specifically give Congress the power to create a bank. Other grounds for criticism were that the bank would subject America to foreign influences (because foreigners would have to purchase a high percentage of the bank's stock) and give a propertied elite disproportionate influence over the nation's fiscal policies (since private investors would control the bank's board of directors).

Hamilton responded to the charge that a bank was unconstitutional by formulating the doctrine of **implied powers.** He argued that Congress did have

The National Bank of the United States, which opened in Philadelphia in 1791, was a key part of Alexander Hamilton's economic plan for a strong central government.

the power to create a bank since the Constitution granted the federal government authority to do anything "necessary and proper" to carry out its constitutional functions (in this case its fiscal duties). This represented the first attempt to defend a **loose interpretation** of the Constitution.

In 1791 Congress passed a bill creating a national bank for a term of 20 years, leaving the question of the bank's constitutionality up to President Washington. After listening to Madison, Jefferson, and Hamilton, the president reluctantly decided to sign the measure out of a conviction that a bank was necessary for the nation's financial well-being.

The first **Bank of the United States,** like Hamilton's debt plan, was a great success. It helped regulate the currency of private banks. It provided a reserve of capital on which the government and private investors drew. It helped attract foreign investment to the credit-short new nation. In 1811, however, the jealousy of private commercial banks convinced Congress to allow the bank to expire.

The final plank in Hamilton's economic program was a proposal to aid the nation's infant industries. Through high tariffs designed to protect American industry from foreign competition, government bounties and subsidies, and internal improvements of transportation, he hoped to break Britain's manufacturing hold on America.

Opposition to Hamilton's proposal came from many quarters. Many Americans feared that the proposal would excessively cut federal revenues by discouraging imports. Shippers worried that the plan would reduce foreign trade. Farmers feared the proposal would lead foreign countries to impose retaliatory tariffs on agricultural products. Many Southerners regarded the plan as a brazen attempt to promote Northern industry and commerce at the South's expense, since it provided no assistance to agriculture.

The most eloquent opposition to Hamilton's proposals came from Thomas Jefferson, who believed that the growth of manufacturing threatened the nation's agrarian way of life. Hamilton's vision of America's future directly challenged Jefferson's ideal of a nation of farmers, tilling the fields, communing with nature, and maintaining personal freedom by virtue of landownership. Manufacturing, Jefferson believed, should be left to European cities, which he considered to be cesspools of human corruption. Like slaves, factory workers would be manipulated by their masters, who not only would deny them satisfying lives but also would make it impossible for them to think and act as independent citizens.

Alexander Hamilton offered a remarkably modern economic vision based on investment, industry, and expanded commerce. Most strikingly, it was an economic vision that had no place for slavery. Before the 1790s the American economy—North and South—was intimately tied to a transatlantic system of slavery. States south of Pennsylvania depended on slave labor to produce tobacco, rice, indigo, and cotton. The northern states conducted their most profitable trade with the slave colonies of the West Indies. A member of New York's first antislavery society, Hamilton wanted to reorient the American economy away from slavery and trade with the slave colonies of the Caribbean.

Congress rejected most of Hamilton's proposals to aid industry. Nevertheless, the debate over Hamilton's plan carried with it fateful consequences. Fundamental disagreements had arisen between Hamiltonians and Jeffersonians over the federal government's role, constitutional interpretation, and distinct visions of how the republic should develop. To resolve these fundamental differences, Americans would create modern political parties—parties the writers of the Constitution never wanted nor anticipated.

THE BIRTH OF POLITICAL PARTIES

When George Washington assembled his first cabinet, there were no national political parties in the United States. In selecting cabinet members, he paid no attention to partisan labels and simply chose the individuals he believed were best qualified to run the new nation. Similarly, the new Congress had no party divisions. In the states, politics was waged not between parties but rather between impermanent factions built around leading families, ethnic groups, or interest groups such as debtors and creditors.

By the time Washington retired from the presidency in 1797, the nature of the American political system had changed radically. The first president devoted part of his "Farewell Address" to denouncing "the baneful effects of the Spirit of Party," which had come to dominate American politics. Local and state factions had given way to two competing national parties, known as the **Federalists** and the **Democratic-Republicans.** They nominated political candidates, managed electoral campaigns, and represented distinctive outlooks or ideologies. By 1796 the United States had produced its first modern party system.

The framers of the Constitution had not prepared their plan of government with political parties in mind. They associated parties with the political factions and interest groups that dominated the British government and hoped that in the United States the "better sort of citizens," rising above popular self-interest, would debate key issues and reach a harmonious consensus regarding how best to legislate for the nation's future. Thomas Jefferson reflected widespread sentiments when he declared in 1789, "If I could not go to heaven but with a party, I would not go there at all."

Yet despite a belief that parties were evil and posed a threat to enlightened government, political factions gradually coalesced into political parties during Washington's first administration. To build support for his financial program, Alexander Hamilton relied heavily on government patronage. Of 2000 federal officeholders appointed between 1789 and 1801, two-thirds were Federalist Party activists, who used positions as postmasters, tax collectors, judges, and customs house officials to favor the interests of the Federalists. By 1794 Hamilton's faction had evolved into the first national political party in history capable of nominating candidates, coordinating votes in Congress, staging public meetings, organizing petition campaigns, and disseminating propaganda.

Hamilton's opponents struck back. James Madison and his ally Thomas Jefferson saw in Hamilton's program an effort to establish the kind of corrupt patronage society that existed in Britain; that is, one with a huge public debt, a standing army, high taxes, and government-subsidized monopolies. Hamilton's aim, declared Jefferson, was to assimilate "the American government to the form and spirit of the British monarchy."

World Events and Political Polarization

World events intensified partisan divisions. On July 14, 1789 the Bastille, a hated royal fortress, was stormed by 20,000 French men and women, an event that marked the beginning of the **French Revolution.** For three years France experimented with a constitutional monarchy. Then, in 1792, the revolution took a violent turn after Austrian and Prussian troops invaded France to put an end to the revolution. French revolutionaries responded by officially deposing King Louis XVI and placing him on trial. He was found guilty and, in January 1793, beheaded. France declared itself a republic and launched a reign of terror against counterrevolutionary elements in the population. Three hundred thousand suspects were arrested; 17,000 were executed. A general war erupted in Europe pitting revolutionary France against a coalition of European monarchies, led by Britain. With two brief interruptions, this war would last 23 years.

Many Americans reacted enthusiastically to the overthrow of the French king and the creation of a French republic. The French people appeared to have joined America in a historic struggle against royal absolutism and aristocratic privilege. More cautious observers expressed horror at the cataclysm sweeping France. The French Revolution, they feared, was not merely a rebellion against royal authority, but a mass assault against property and Christianity. Conservatives urged President Washington to support England in its war against France.

Washington believed that involvement in the European war would weaken the new nation before it had firmly established its own independence. He proposed to keep the country "free from political connections with every other country, to see them independent of all, and under the influence of none." The president, however, faced a problem. During the War for American Independence, The United States had signed an alliance with France. Washington took the position that while the United States should continue to make payments on its war debts to France, it should refrain from directly supporting the new French republic. In April 1793 he issued a proclamation of neutrality, stating that the "conduct" of the United States would be "friendly and impartial toward the belligerent powers."

1793 and 1794: Years of Crisis

During 1793 and 1794 a series of explosive new controversies further divided the followers of Hamilton and Jefferson. Washington's administration confronted a French effort to entangle America in its war with England, an armed rebellion in western Pennsylvania, several Indian uprisings, and the threat of war with Britain. These controversies intensified party spirit and promoted an increase in voting along party lines in Congress.

Citizen Genêt Affair

In April 1793 "Citizen" Edmond Charles Genêt, minister of the French Republic, arrived in the United States. His mission was to persuade American citizens to join in France's "war of all peoples against all kings." Genêt proceeded to pass out military commissions as part of a plan to attack Spanish New Orleans, and letters authorizing Americans to attack British commercial vessels. Washington regarded these activities as clear violations of U.S. neutrality and demanded that France recall its hotheaded minister. Fearful that he would be executed if he returned to France, Genêt requested and was granted political asylum, bringing his ill-fated mission to an end. However, the Genêt affair did have an important effect—it intensified party feeling. From Vermont to South Carolina, citizens organized Democratic-Republican clubs to celebrate the triumphs of the French Revolution. Hamilton suspected that these societies really existed to stir up grass-roots opposition to the Washington administration. Jefferson hotly denied these accusations, but the practical consequence was to further divide followers of Hamilton and Jefferson.

Whiskey Rebellion

The outbreak of popular protests in western Pennsylvania against Hamilton's financial program further intensified political polarization. To help fund the nation's war debt, Congress in 1791 passed Hamilton's proposal for a whiskey excise tax. Frontier farmers objected to the tax on whiskey as unfair. On the frontier, because of high transportation costs, the only practical way to sell surplus corn was to distill it into whiskey. Thus, frontier farmers regarded a tax on whiskey in the same way as American colonists had regarded Britain's stamp tax.

By 1794 western Pennsylvanians had had enough. Like the Shaysites of 1786, they rose up in defense of their property and the fundamental right to earn a decent living. Some 7000 frontiersmen marched on Pittsburgh to stop collection of the tax. Determined to set a precedent for the federal government's authority, Washington gathered an army of 15,000 militiamen to disperse the rebels. In the face of this overwhelming force, the uprising collapsed. Two men were convicted of treason but later pardoned by the president. The new government

President Washington is reviewing the troops at Fort Cumberland, Maryland. These troops formed part of the force of 15,000 militiamen Washington assembled to disperse the Whiskey Rebellion in western Pennsylvania, a protest against the whiskey excise tax.

had proved that it would enforce laws enacted by Congress.

Thomas Jefferson viewed the Whiskey Rebellion from quite a different perspective. He saw the fiendish hand of Hamilton in putting down what he called a rebellion that "could never be found." Hamilton had "pronounced and proclaimed and armed against" the people for the sheer pleasure of suppressing liberties. And further, Jefferson claimed, Hamilton had done so because Westerners no longer supported Washington's administration. He had used the army to stifle legitimate opposition to unfair government policies.

Clearing the Ohio Country of Native Americans

The end of the American Revolution unleashed a mad rush of white settlers into frontier Georgia, Kentucky, Tennessee, Ohio, and western New York. In Kentucky and Tennessee, clashes between Cherokees, Chickasaws, Shawnees, and frontier settlers between 1784 and 1790 left some 1500 whites dead or captured, but ultimately warfare forced many Native Americans to migrate north of the Ohio River.

To clear the Ohio country, President Washington dispatched three armies. Twice, a confederacy of eight tribes led by Little Turtle, chief of the Miami, defeated American forces. But, in 1794, a third army defeated the Indian alliance. A 3000-man force under Anthony Wayne overwhelmed 1000 Native Americans at the **Battle of Fallen Timbers** in northwestern Ohio. Under the Treaty of Greenville (1795), Native Americans ceded much of the present state of Ohio in return for cash and a promise that the federal government would treat the Indian nations fairly in land dealings.

Native Americans responded to the loss of land and declining population in a variety of ways. One response was cultural renewal, the path taken by the Seneca, who lived in upstate New York. Displaced from their traditional lands and suffering from epidemic disease, the Seneca revitalized their culture under the leadership of a prophet named **Handsome Lake.** Handsome Lake preached a new religion that helped the Seneca adapt to a changing social environment while maintaining many traditional practices and religious tenets. Most strikingly, the prophet endorsed the demand of Quaker missionaries that the traditional Iroquois sexual division of labor emphasizing male hunting and female horticulture be replaced. Instead, men took up farming, even though this had been traditionally viewed as women's work.

Another response to cultural disruption was the formation of loosely knit Indian confederacies. In the

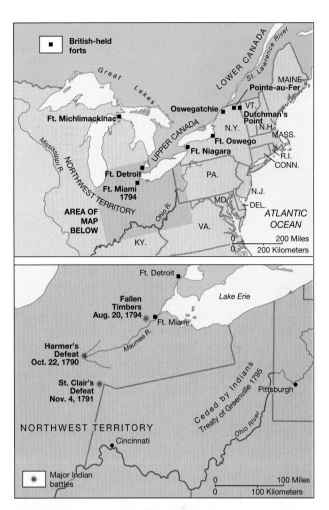

British Posts and Indian Battles

Because Americans still felt threatened by the continuing British refusal to evacuate forts and by Native American uprisings in the Northwest, John Jay, the first chief justice of the United States, was sent to negotiate a treaty with Great Britain.

Great Lakes region, the Shawnee, Delaware, and other Indian peoples banded together in an effort to resist white expansion, while across the Mississippi, the Chippewa, Fox, Kickapoo, Ottawa, Potawatomi, Sauk, and Sioux formed another confederation. But the ability of these confederacies to obstruct expansion depended on military support from Britain.

The Continuing Threat from Britain

The year 1794 brought a crisis in America's relations with Britain. For a decade, Britain had refused to evacuate forts in the Old Northwest as promised in the treaty ending the Revolution. Control of those forts impeded white settlement of the Great Lakes region and allowed the British to monopolize the fur trade.

Yellow Fever in Philadelphia: Pills and Politics

Death stalked the streets of Philadelphia in 1793 in the form of a yellow fever epidemic. The first case appeared in August, and by the time the epidemic disappeared in November, yellow fever had killed 10 percent of the city's population, while another 45 percent had fled in terror. At the height of the epidemic, Philadelphia was a city under siege, with city services interrupted; communications impaired; the port closed; the economy in shambles; and people locked in their homes, afraid to venture beyond their doorsteps. To make matters worse, the city's leaders—unable to reach agreement on what caused the disease or what should be done to combat it—attacked each other in endless debates. The result was that Philadelphia, America's premiere city, all but shut down.

Philadelphia's plight is not hard to explain, for yellow fever is a pulverizing, terrifying disease. Caused by a virus, the disease is spread by the female mosquito. Yellow fever's early symptoms are nearly identical to those of malaria; the victim feels flush and then develops chills, followed by a sizzling fever, accompanied by a severe headache or backache. The fever lasts for two or three days, and then the patient usually enjoys a remission.

Mild cases of yellow fever stop here. For the less fortunate, however, remission soon gives way to jaundice (hence "yellow" fever), and the victim starts to hallucinate. Massive internal hemorrhaging follows, and the suf-

ferer starts vomiting huge quantities of black blood. Next, the victim goes into a coma. A lucky few emerge from the coma to escape death, but the vast majority die from internal bleeding.

If any American city seemed well equipped to handle a medical crisis, it was Philadelphia. It was the nation's leading center of medicine, home to the prestigious College of Physicians, America's first medical school (1765), and to America's most famous physician, Dr. Benjamin Rush, a founder of the Pennsylvania Society for Promoting the Abolition of Slavery and a signer of the Declaration of Independence. The City of Brotherly Love could also point with pride to Franklin's Pennsylvania Hospital (1752), the first hospital in America and a model facility for the poor.

Yet for all of its luster, Philadelphia's medical community was no match for yellow fever. The basic problem was that doctors in 1793 could not agree on what caused the disease, how it spread, or how to treat it. Many physicians, including Dr. Rush, cited local factors. They blamed the disease on the decaying vegetation and rotting filth that littered Philadelphia's streets and docks, producing an atmospheric "miasma" that was carried by the wind, infecting anyone who breathed its noxious fumes. Rejecting local causes, other physicians argued that yellow fever was a contagious disease. It had been imported to Philadelphia, they insisted, by the 2000 French refugees who had fled the revolution (and a yellow fever epidemic!) in Haiti to seek political asylum in the United States.

Physicians in 1793 had no way of settling the dispute. Those who blamed the epidemic on dirty streets

sounded just as believable as those who pointed an accusing finger at sickly foreigners. What made the controversy truly remarkable, however, was the extent to which it became embroiled in politics, for what began as a purely medical debate quickly degenerated into a raging political battle.

With very few exceptions, the doctors who insisted that yellow fever was contagious were Federalists, while the anticontagionists were almost all Jeffersonian Republicans. Taught by the French Revolution to be wary of free-thinking political ideas, Federalist doctors regarded yellow fever as just another unwanted French import. Ablaze with pro-French sympathies, anticontagionist Republicans saw the French refugees as honored friends who brought virtue rather than death. The source of the epidemic, they insisted, lay with unvirtuous filth at their doorsteps.

Partisan leaders tried desperately to bend this medical debate to their political advantage. To Federalists, the doctrine of importation demanded that the United States protect itself from the French menace. Therefore, trade with French West Indian islands should be suspended; French refugees who had gained entry to the United States should be quarantined and future refugees excluded. Republicans, by contrast, denounced these demands as a federal plot to ruin profitable trade with the West Indies and to infect Americans with a new disease—hatred of all things French. Nor was their concern unfounded, for public hysteria was definitely building. At one point, amid persistent rumors that the French had poisoned the public drinking wells in preparation for a full-scale invasion, Philadel-

phians threatened violence against the innocent refugees.

At the height of the turmoil, politics even influenced how physicians treated the victims of yellow fever. At the beginning of the epidemic, doctors were pretty evenly divided, without regard to politics, into two schools. One prescribed stimulants—quinine bark, wine, and cold baths; while the other recommended bleeding—drawing off huge quantities of the patient's blood. (Dr. Rush had long been an advocate of the bleeding treatment. He recommended removing about four-fifths of the patient's blood supply, more than enough to kill all but the unkillable!)

Alexander Hamilton was personally responsible for converting this medical squabbling into a political issue. After managing to survive an attack of yellow fever, he published a ringing testimonial to the life-saving properties of the bark and wine cure. The treatment had been prescribed, he declared, by Dr. Edward Stevens of Philadelphia, a longtime friend of Hamilton. Dr. Stevens was the only physician in the City of Brotherly Love who was a publicly confessed Federalist.

A few days after his testimonial appeared, Hamilton published a second article in which he ridiculed Dr. Rush's "new treatment." Hamilton's attack was immediately echoed by

Federalist editors across the country, and in the wake of their articles, the public came to regard "bark" as the Federalist cure and "bleeding" as the Republican cure.

The controversy over yellow fever raged until the epidemic ended in the fall. Philadelphia's struggle against yellow fever was one of the many times that Americans would infuse their discussions of health problems with nonmedical concerns. In future epidemics, notions of class, race, individual virtue, and even gender would color public discussions of health, just as surely as politics enlivened the medical debate over yellow fever in Philadelphia in 1793 when the republic was young.

Frontiersmen believed that British officials at those posts sold firearms to Native Americans and incited uprisings against white settlers. War appeared imminent when British warships stopped 300 American ships carrying food supplies to France and to France's overseas possessions, seized their cargoes, and forced seamen suspected of deserting from British ships into the British navy.

Washington acted decisively to end the crisis. After Anthony Wayne's soldiers overwhelmed Indians at the Battle of Fallen Timbers, the president sent Chief Justice John Jay to London to seek a negotiated settlement with the British. The United States's strongest bargaining chip was a threat to join an alliance of European trading nations to resist British trade restrictions. Alexander Hamilton undercut Jay by secretly informing the British minister that the United States would not join the alliance.

Jay secured the best agreement he could under the circumstances. Britain agreed to evacuate its forts on American soil and promised to cease harassing American ships (provided the ships did not carry contraband to Britain's enemies). Britain agreed to pay damages for the ships it had seized, to permit trade with Indians, and to carry on restricted trade with the British West Indies; however, Jay failed to win concessions on a host of other American grievances, such as British incitement of the Indians and Britain's routine searching of American ships for escaping deserters.

As a result of the debate over **Jay's Treaty**, the first party system fully emerged. Publication of the terms of the treaty unleashed a storm of protest from the Jeffersonian Republicans. Republican newspapers and pamphlets denounced the treaty as craven submission to British imperial power and to wealthy commercial, shipping, and trading interests. In New York, a mob pelted Alexander Hamilton with stones. In Boston, graffiti appeared on a wall: "Damn John Jay! Damn everyone who won't damn John Jay!! Damn everyone that won't put lights in his windows and sit up all night damning John Jay!!!"

Washington never anticipated the wave of outrage that greeted his decision to sign the treaty. Republicans accused him of forming an Anglo-American alliance, and they made his last years in office miserable by attacking him for conducting himself like a "tyrant." James Thomson Callender denounced Washington in particularly negative terms: "If ever a nation was debauched by a man, the American Nation has been debauched by Washington. . . . If ever a nation has been deceived by a man, the American Nation has been deceived by Washington." It was even suggested that he should be impeached because he had overdrawn his $25,000 salary. Privately, Washington complained that he was

Angry Republicans denounced John Jay's treaty as submission to British power and hanged his effigy in Charleston, South Carolina.

being compared to the Roman emperor "Nero" and to a "common pickpocket."

Republicans sought to kill the treaty in the House of Representatives by refusing to appropriate the funds necessary to carry out the treaty's terms unless the president submitted all documents relating to the treaty negotiations. Washington refused to comply with the House's request for information, thereby establishing the principle of **executive privilege**. This precedent gives the chief executive authority to withhold information from Congress on grounds of national security. In the end, fear that rejection of the Jay Treaty would result in disunion or war convinced the House to approve the needed appropriations.

Washington's popularity returned within a few months when he was able to announce that a treaty had been negotiated with Spain opening up the Mississippi River to American trade. Spain, fearing joint British and American action against its American colonies, recognized the Mississippi River as the new nation's western boundary and the 31st parallel (the northern border of Florida) as America's southern boundary. In addition, Pinckney's Treaty (1795)—also known as the Treaty of San Lorenzo—granted Americans the right to navigate the Mississippi River as well as the right to export goods, duty free, through New Orleans, which was still a Spanish city.

Washington Retires

President Washington was now in a position to retire gracefully. He had avoided war, crushed the Native Americans, pushed the British out of western forts, established trade with selected parts of Asia, and opened the Northwest Territory to settlement. In his **Farewell Address,** published in a Philadelphia newspaper in September 1796, Washington warned his countrymen against the growth of partisan divisions. In foreign affairs, he warned against long-term alliances. Declaring the "primary interests" of America and Europe to be fundamentally different, he argued that "it is our true policy to steer clear of permanent alliance with any portion of the foreign world."

A NEW PRESIDENT AND NEW CHALLENGES

Washington's decision to retire set the stage for one of the most critical presidential elections in American history. The election of 1796 was the first in which voters could choose between competing political parties; it was also the first election in which candidates were nominated for the vice presidency. It was a critical test of whether the nation could transfer power through a contested election.

The Federalists chose **John Adams,** the first vice president, as their presidential candidate, and the Republicans selected Thomas Jefferson. In an effort to attract southern support, the Federalists named Thomas Pinckney of South Carolina as Adams's running mate. The Republicans, hoping to win votes in New York and New England, chose Aaron Burr of New York as their vice presidential nominee.

Both parties appealed directly to the people, rallying supporters through the use of posters, handbills, and mass rallies. Republicans portrayed their candidate as "a firm Republican" while they depicted his opponent as "the champion of rank, titles, and hereditary distinctions." Federalists countered by condemning Jefferson as the leader of a "French faction" intent on undermining religion and morality.

In the popular voting, Federalists drew support from New England; commercial, shipping, manufacturing, and banking interests; Congregational and Episcopalian clergy; professionals; and farmers who produced for markets. Republicans attracted votes from the South and from smaller planters; backcountry Baptists, Methodists, and Roman Catholics; small merchants, tradesmen, and craftsmen; and subsistence farmers.

John Adams won the election, despite backstage maneuvering by Alexander Hamilton against him. Hamilton developed a complicated scheme to elect Thomas Pinckney, the Federalist candidate for vice president. Under the electoral system originally set up by the Constitution, each presidential elector was allowed to vote twice, with the candidate who received the most votes becoming president, while the candidate who came in second was elected vice president. According to Hamilton's plan, southern electors would drop Adams's name from their ballots, while still voting for Pinckney. Thus Pinckney would receive more votes than Adams and be elected president. When New Englanders learned of this plan, they dropped Pinckney from their ballots, ensuring that Adams won the election. When the final votes were tallied, Adams received 71 votes, only 3 more than Jefferson. As a result, Jefferson became vice president.

The Presidency of John Adams

The new president was a 61-year-old Harvard-educated lawyer who had been an early leader in the struggle for independence. Short, bald, overweight, and vain (he was known, behind his back, as "His Rotundity"), John Adams had found the vice presi-

John Adams was elected the second president of the United States by only three electoral votes. During his presidency, he strengthened the military and averted war with France.

dency extremely frustrating. He complained to his wife Abigail: "My country has contrived for me the most insignificant office that ever the invention of man contrived or his imagination conceived."

His presidency also proved frustrating. He had failed to win a decisive electoral mandate and was saddled with the opposition leader as his vice president. He faced intense challenges within his own party and continuing problems from France throughout his four years in office. He avoided outright war with France, but he destroyed his political career in the process.

A New National Capital

John Adams was the first president to live in what would later be called the White House. In 1800 the national capital moved to Washington, D.C., from Philadelphia (in 1790 it had moved to Philadelphia from New York).

In planning the city of Washington, the architect Benjamin Latrobe hoped that "the days of Greece may be revived in the woods of America." Like many other late-eighteenth-century Americans, he hoped to build a country that would emulate the spirit of the ancient Greek and Roman republics.

The White House and the Capitol were designed along classical lines. Many new towns received classical names, such as Syracuse and Troy. Government institutions, like the Senate, also acquired classical names.

When John Adams moved into the unfinished executive mansion, only 6 of the structure's 30 rooms were plastered; the main staircases were not installed for another four years. The mansion's grounds were cluttered with workers' shanties, privies, and stagnant pools of water. The president's wife, Abigail, hung laundry to dry in the East Room.

The nation's Capitol was also uncompleted. Construction of the building's central portion had not even begun. All that stood were the House and Senate wings connected by a covered boardwalk.

The city of Washington consisted of a brewery, a half-finished hotel, an abandoned canal, an empty warehouse and wharf, and 372 "habitable" dwellings, "most of them small miserable huts." Cows and hogs ran freely in the capital's streets, and snakes frequented the city's many bogs and marshes. A bridge, supported by an arch of 13 stones—symbolizing the first 13 states—had collapsed. The entire population consisted of 500 families and some 300 members of government. A visitor saw "no fences, gardens, nor the least appearance of business."

The Quasi War with France

A decade after the Constitution was written, the United States faced its most serious international crisis: an undeclared naval war with France. In Jay's Treaty, France perceived an American tilt toward Britain, especially in the provision permitting the British to seize French goods from American ships in exchange for financial compensation. France retaliated by launching an aggressive campaign against American shipping, particularly in the West Indies, capturing hundreds of vessels flying the U.S. flag.

Adams attempted to negotiate with France, but the French government refused to receive the Ameri-

Abigail Adams supervises the work of a maidservant hanging laundry in the East Room of the White House.

can envoy and suspended commercial relations. Adams then called Congress into special session. Determined not to permit the United States to be "humiliated under a colonial spirit of fear and a sense of inferiority," he recommended that Congress arm American merchant ships, purchase new naval vessels, fortify harbors, and expand the artillery and cavalry. To pay for it all, Adams recommended a series of new taxes. By a single vote, a bitterly divided House of Representatives authorized the president to arm American merchant ships, but it postponed consideration of the other defense measures.

Adams then sent three commissioners to France to try to negotiate a settlement. Charles Maurice de Talleyrand, the French foreign minister, continually postponed official negotiations. In the meantime, three emissaries of the French minister (known later simply as X, Y, and Z) said that the only way the Americans could see the minister was to pay a bribe of $250,000 and provide a $10 million loan. The indignant American commissioners refused. When word of the "**XYZ affair**" became known in the United States, it aroused a popular demand for war. The popular slogan was "millions for defense, but not one cent for tribute." The Federalist-controlled Congress authorized a standing army of 20,000 troops, established a 30,000-man reserve army, and created the nation's first navy department. It also unilaterally abrogated America's 1778 treaty with France.

Adams named George Washington commanding general of the United States Army, and, at Washington's insistence, designated Alexander Hamilton second in command. During the winter of 1798, 14 American warships backed by some 200 armed merchant ships captured 80 French vessels and forced French warships out of American waters and back to bases in the West Indies. But the president refused to ask Congress for an official declaration of war. Thus, this conflict is known as the **quasi war with France.**

Despite intense pressure to declare war against France or to seize territory belonging to France's ally, Spain, President Adams managed to avert a full-scale war and achieve a peaceful settlement. Early in 1799, with the backing of moderate Federalists and Republicans, Adams proposed reestablishing diplomatic relations with France. When more extreme Federalists refused to go along with the plan, Adams threatened to resign and leave the presidency in the hands of Vice President Jefferson.

In 1800, after seven months of wearisome negotiations, negotiators worked out an agreement known as the Convention of 1800. The agreement freed the United States from its alliance with France; in exchange, America forgave $20 million in damages caused by the illegal seizure of American merchant ships during the 1790s.

Adams kept the peace, but at the cost of a second term as president. The more extreme Federalists reacted furiously to the negotiated settlement. Hamilton vowed to destroy Adams: "If we must have an enemy at the head of Government, let it be one whom we can oppose, and for whom we are not responsible."

The Alien and Sedition Acts

During the quasi war, the Federalist-controlled Congress attempted to suppress political opposition and stamp out sympathy for revolutionary France by enacting four laws in 1798 known as the **Alien and Sedition acts.** The Naturalization Act lengthened the period necessary before immigrants could receive citizenship from 5 to 14 years. The Alien Act gave the president the power to imprison or deport any foreigner believed to be dangerous to the United States. The Alien Enemies Act allowed the president to deport enemy aliens in time of war. Finally, the Sedition Act made it a crime to attack the government with "false, scandalous, or malicious" statements or writings. Adams, bitterly unhappy with the "spirit of falsehood and malignity" that threat-

In the early days of the republic, political dissent sometimes escalated into physical violence. This fight between Republican Matthew Lyon and Federalist Roger Griswold took place on the floor of Congress on February 15, 1798. Lyon was later arrested for violating the Sedition Act by publishing in his newspaper a letter attacking the government.

ened to undermine loyalty to the government, signed the measures.

The Alien acts were so broadly written that hundreds of foreign refugees—French intellectuals, Irish nationalists, and English radicals—fled to Europe fearing detention. But it was the Sedition Act that produced the greatest fear within the Republican opposition. Federalist prosecutors and judges used the Sedition Act to attack leading Republican newspapers, securing indictments against 25 people, mainly Republican editors and printers. Ten people were eventually convicted, one a Republican Representative from Vermont.

One of the most notorious uses of the law to suppress dissent took place in July 1798. Luther Baldwin, the pilot of a garbage scow, was arrested in a Newark, New Jersey, tavern on charges of criminal sedition. While cannons roared through Newark's streets to celebrate a presidential visit to the city, Baldwin was overheard saying "that he did not care if they fired through [the president's] arse." For his drunken remark, Baldwin was arrested, locked up for two months, and fined.

Republicans accused the Federalists of conspiring to subvert fundamental liberties. In Virginia, the state legislature adopted a resolution written by James Madison that advanced the idea that states have the right to determine the constitutionality of federal law and pronounced the Alien and Sedition acts unconstitutional. Kentucky's state legislature went even further, adopting a resolution written by Thomas Jefferson that declared the Alien and Sedition acts "void and of no force." The **Kentucky and Virginia resolutions** raised an issue that would grow increasingly important in American politics in the years before the Civil War: Did states have the power to declare acts of Congress null and void? In 1799, however, no other states were willing to go as far as Kentucky and Virginia.

With the Union in danger, violence erupted. In the spring of 1799 German settlers in eastern Pennsylvania rose up in defiance of federal tax collectors. President Adams called out federal troops to suppress the so-called Fries Rebellion. The leader of the rebellion, an auctioneer named John Fries, was captured, convicted of treason, and sentenced to be hanged. Adams followed Washington's example in the Whiskey Rebellion and pardoned Fries, but Republicans feared that the Federalists were prepared to use the nation's army to suppress dissent.

THE REVOLUTION OF 1800

In 1800 the young republic faced another critical test: Could national leadership pass peacefully from one political party to another? Once again, the na-

THE PEOPLE SPEAK

Gabriel's Revolt

In 1800 a group of slaves in Virginia plotted to seize the city of Richmond. Led by a man known as Gabriel, the insurrection was inspired in part by the slave revolt that began in the French colony of St. Domingue (Haiti) in 1791. It was also motivated by the ideals of liberty and natural rights that had led the American colonists to revolt against Britain. About 30 of the accused conspirators were executed, and many others were sold as slaves to Spanish and Portuguese colonies. Here, a visitor to Virginia describes why one of the slaves had decided to participate in Gabriel's revolt.

In the afternoon I passed by a field in which several poor slaves had lately been executed, on the charge of having an intention to rise against their masters. A lawyer who was present at their trials at Richmond, informed me that on one of them being asked, what he had to say to the court on his defence, he replied, in a manly tone of voice: "I have nothing more to offer than what General Washington would have had to offer, had he been taken by the British and put to trial by them. I have adventured my life in endeavouring to obtain the liberty of my countrymen, and am a willing sacrifice in their cause: and I beg, as a favour, that I may be immediately led to execution. I know that you have pre-determined to shed my blood, why then all this mockery of a trial?"

Source: Robert Sutcliff, *Travels in Some Parts of North America in the Years 1804, 1805, & 1806* (Philadelphia: B. & T. Kite, 1812).

tion had a choice between John Adams and Thomas Jefferson. But this election was more than a contest between two men; it was also a real party contest for control of the national government. Deep substantive and ideological issues divided the two parties, and partisan feelings ran deep. Federalists feared that Jefferson would reverse all the accomplishments of the preceding 12 years. A Republican president, they thought, would overthrow the Constitution by returning power to the states, dismantling the army and navy, and overturning Hamilton's financial system.

The Republicans charged that the Federalists, by creating a large standing army, imposing heavy taxes, and using federal troops and the federal courts to suppress dissent, had shown contempt for the liberties of the American people. They worried that the Federalists' ultimate goal was to centralize power in

TABLE 7.1 Election of 1800		
Candidate	**Party**	**Electoral Vote**
T. Jefferson	Republican	73
J. Adams	Federalist	65

the national government and involve the United States in the European war on the side of Britain.

The contest was one of the most vigorous in American history; emotions ran high. Federalist opponents called Jefferson an "atheist in religion, and a fanatic in politics." They claimed he was a drunkard, an enemy of religion, and the father of numerous mulatto children. Timothy Dwight, the president of Yale, predicted that a Jefferson administration would see "our wives and daughters the victims of legal prostitution; soberly dishonored; speciously polluted."

Jefferson's supporters responded by charging that President Adams was a warmonger, a spendthrift, and a monarchist who longed to reunite Britain with its former colonies. Republicans even claimed that the president had sent General Thomas Pinckney to England to procure four mistresses, two for himself and two for Adams. Adam's response: "I do declare if this be true, General Pinckney has kept them all for himself and cheated me out of my two."

The election was extremely close. The Federalists won all of New England's electoral votes, while the Republicans dominated the South and West. The final outcome hinged on the results in New York. Rural New York supported the Federalists, and Republican fortunes, therefore, depended on the voting in New York City. There, Jefferson's running mate, **Aaron Burr,** had created the most successful political organization the country had yet seen. Burr organized rallies, established ward committees, and promoted loyal supporters for public office. Burr's efforts paid off; Republicans won a majority in New York's legislature, thus giving the state's 12 electoral votes to Jefferson and Burr. Declared one Republican: The election "has been conducted . . . in so miraculous a manner that I cannot account for it but from the intervention of a Supreme Power and our friend Burr the agent."

Jefferson appeared to have won by a margin of eight electoral votes, but a complication soon arose. Because each Republican elector had cast one ballot

Thomas Jefferson described his election as president in 1800 as a "revolution." His goal was to reverse the centralizing policies of the Federalists.

for Jefferson and one for Burr, the two men received exactly the same number of electoral votes.

Under the Constitution, the election was now thrown into the Federalist-controlled House of Representatives. Instead of emphatically declaring that he would not accept the presidency, Burr failed to say anything. So the Federalists faced a choice. They could help elect the hated Jefferson—whom they had called "a brandy-soaked defamer of churches," "a contemptible hypocrite"—or they could throw their support to the opportunistic Burr—considered by Federalists to be "a profligate," "a voluptuary." Hamilton disliked Jefferson, but he believed he was a far more honorable man than Burr, whose "public principles have no other spring or aim than his own aggrandizement." Most other Federalists supported the New Yorker.

As the stalemate persisted, Virginia and Pennsylvania mobilized their state militias. Recognizing "the certainty that a legislative usurpation would be resisted by arms," as Jefferson noted, the Federalists finally backed down. On February 17, 1801, after six days of balloting and 36 ballots, the House of Representatives finally elected Thomas Jefferson the third president of the United States. As a result of the election, Congress adopted the Twelfth Amendment to the Constitution, by which electors in the Electoral College cast one ballot for president and a separate and distinct ballot for vice president.

Conclusion

Sometime between 2:00 A.M. and 3:00 A.M., on December 13, 1799, George Washington woke his wife, complaining of severe pains. Martha Washington called for an overseer, who inserted a lancet in the former president's arm and drew blood. Over the course of that day and the next, doctors arrived and attempted to ease General Washington's pain by applying blisters, administering purges, and additional bloodletting—eventually removing perhaps four pints of Washington's blood. Medical historians generally agree that Washington needed a tracheotomy (a surgical operation into the air passages), but this was too new a technique to be risked on the former president, who died on December 14.

During the early weeks of 1800 every city in the United States commemorated the death of the former leader. In Philadelphia, an empty coffin, a riderless horse, and a funeral cortege moved through the city streets. In Boston, business was suspended, cannons roared, bells pealed, and 6000 people—a fifth of the city's population—stood in the streets to express their last respects for the fallen general. In Washington, Richard Henry Lee delivered the most famous eulogy: "First in war, first in peace, and first in the hearts of his countrymen."

In 1789 the open question was whether the Constitution was a workable plan of government. Whether the new nation could establish a strong and vigorous national government or win the respect of foreign nations was still unclear. For a decade, the new nation battled threats to its existence. It faced bitter party conflict, threats of secession, and foreign interference with American shipping and commerce.

By any standard, the new nation's achievements were impressive. During the first decade under the Constitution, the country adopted a bill of rights, protecting the rights of the individual against the power of the central government; enacted a financial program that secured the government's credit and stimulated the economy; and created the first political parties that directly involved the enfranchised segment of the population in national politics. In the face of intense partisan conflict, the United States became the first nation to transfer peacefully political power from one party to another as a result of an election. A nation, strong and viable, had emerged from its baptism by fire.

Chapter Summary and Key Points

In this chapter you learned about the bill of rights that the United States adopted to protect the rights of the individual against the power of the central government. You also read about the financial program Congress enacted to secure the government's credit and stimulate the economy; about the creation of the first political parties to involve the voting population in national politics; and the construction of a new national capital in Washington, D.C.

- During the first 12 years under the new Constitution, the Federalists established a strong and vigorous national government.

- Alexander Hamilton's economic program attracted foreign investment and stimulated economic growth.

- The creation of political parties was an unexpected development that involved the voting population in politics.

- Presidents George Washington and John Adams succeeded in keeping the nation free from foreign entanglements during the nation's first crucial years.

CHRONOLOGY OF KEY EVENTS

1789 First session of Congress meets; Electoral College names George Washington the first president; Washington selects the first cabinet; Federal Judiciary Act establishes federal court system; French Revolution begins

1790 Congress adopts Hamilton's proposal to fund the national debt at full value and to assume all state debts from the Revolutionary War

1791 Bank of the United States is established; Congress adopts an excise tax on distilled liquors; the Bill of Rights becomes part of the Constitution

1793 King Louis XVI of France is beheaded and war breaks out in Europe; Washington issues the Proclamation of Neutrality; Citizen Genêt affair

1794 Jay's Treaty with Britain; Whiskey Rebellion in western Pennsylvania; General Anthony Wayne defeats an Indian alliance at the Battle of Fallen Timbers in Ohio

1795 Treaty of Greenville opens Ohio to white settlement; Pinckney's Treaty is negotiated with Spain

1796 Washington issues Farewell Address warning against political factionalism and foreign entanglements

1797 John Adams is inaugurated as second president

1798 Adams reports XYZ affair to Congress; undeclared naval war with France begins; Alien and Sedition acts give the president the power to imprison or deport dangerous foreigners and make it a crime to attack the government with "malicious" statements or writings; Virginia and Kentucky resolutions, drawn up by Jefferson and Madison, declare the Alien and Sedition acts unconstitutional

1800 Washington, D.C., replaces Philadelphia as the nation's capital; Convention of 1800 supplants treaties of 1778 with France

1801 House of Representatives elects Thomas Jefferson as third president

---

- Despite bitter party battles, threats of secession, and foreign interference with American shipping and commerce, the new nation had overcome every obstacle it had faced.

SUGGESTIONS FOR FURTHER READING

Richard Brookhiser, *Alexander Hamilton, American* (1999). This biography examines the professional, political, and personal life of the founder whose role in the emergence of a thriving American economy and a two-party political system is often underestimated.

Richard Brookhiser, *Founding Father: Rediscovering George Washington* (1997). Traces Washington's career as a general, a framer of the Constitution, and president and examines his character and sense of duty.

Stanley Elkins and Eric McKitrick, *The Age of Federalism: The Early American Republic, 1788–1800* (1993). Examines the major political and diplomatic controversies of the period from the beginning of the U.S. government under the Constitution to Thomas Jefferson's election as president.

Joseph J. Ellis, *Founding Brothers: The Revolutionary Generation* (2000). The story of the new republic's formative years is told through the lives of seven of the country's founders, John Adams, Aaron Burr, Benjamin Franklin, Alexander Hamilton, Thomas Jefferson, James Madison, and George Washington.

Joseph J. Ellis, *Passionate Sage: The Character and Legacy of John Adams* (1998). The life, character, and political career of the second president.

David McCullough, *John Adams* (2002). The Pulitzer Prize–winning life of the second president brings John Adams out of the shadows cast by George Washington and Thomas Jefferson.

James Roger Sharp, *American Politics in the Early Republic: The New Nation in Crisis* (1993). Vividly recaptures the atmosphere of passion, suspicion, and fear that marked the country's first 12 years under the new Constitution.

Novels

Charles Brockden Brown, *Wieland* (1798).

Herman Melville, *Billy Budd* (1924).

Susanna Rowson, *Charlotte Temple* (1794).

MEDIA RESOURCES

Web Sites

Alexander Hamilton
http://xroads.virginia.edu/~CAP/ham/hamilton.html
This site examines Hamilton's background, his experience during the revolutionary war, his political battles, and changes in his image over time.

Mount Vernon
http://www.mountvernon.org/education/
This site contains an online tour of Mount Vernon, a lesson plan about George Washington's life, and an online exhibit about George Washington and slavery.

Rediscovering George Washington
http://www.pbs.org/georgewashington/
The companion site to the PBS documentary contains transcripts of Washington letters.

Religion and Founding of Republic
http://lcweb.loc.gov/exhibits/religion/overview.html
This Library of Congress exhibit includes: Religion and the Congress of the Confederation, which examines the policies of America's first national government toward religion; Religion and the State Governments, which illuminates the policies of the revolutionary state governments toward religion, ranging from disestablishment in Virginia to multiple establishments in New England states; Religion and the Federal Government, which focuses on the status of religion in the new federal government; and Republican Religion, which traces the fortunes of religion.

Washington and Slavery
http://www.virginia.edu/gwpapers/articles/slavery/index.html
A leading authority on George Washington examines his place in the controversy over slavery.

Washington Papers
http://memory.loc.gov/ammem/gmdhtml/gwmaps.html
This site, created by the Library of Congress, includes a time line, essays drawing on George Washington's papers, and an on-line presentation about George Washington: Surveyor and Mapmaker.

Films and Videos

Alexander Hamilton (1931). Released early in the Depression, this film biography focuses on the Maria Reynolds affair and treats Hamilton as a man who placed his country above his personal interests.

Danton (1983). Focusing on Paris during the spring of 1794 and the Reign of Terror, the film raises probing questions about various forms of leadership and the horrors that they can create, including the idealist Robespierre and the more pragmatic Danton.

Jefferson in Paris (1995). Focusing on the mid-1780s, when widower and future president Jefferson replaced Benjamin Franklin as the U.S. representative in France, this film concentrates on his relationships with Maria Cosway and Sally Hemings.

Rediscovering George Washington (2002). A PBS documentary that discusses the character traits that allowed Washington to gain and wield power as well as those which taught him to use it justly and to give it up.

A Tale of Two Cities (1935, 1958, 1980). Charles Dickens's account of the era of the French Revolution has been filmed many times. The 1935 version starring Ronald Colman won several Academy Award nominations.

KEY TERMS

Judiciary Act of 1789   (p. 184)

Bill of Rights   (p. 184)

Cabinet   (p. 184)

Strict construction   (p.185)

Implied powers   (p. 185)

Loose interpretation   (p. 186)

Bank of the United States   (p. 186)

Federalist Party   (p. 187)

Democratic-Republican Party   (p. 187)

French Revolution   (p. 187)

Citizen Genêt Affair   (p. 188)

Whiskey Rebellion   (p. 188)

Battle of Fallen Timbers   (p. 189)

Jay's Treaty   (p. 192)

Executive privilege   (p. 192)

Farewell Address   (p. 193)

Quasi war with France   (p. 195)

XYZ affair   (p. 195)

Alien and Sedition acts   (p. 195)

Kentucky and Virginia resolutions   (p. 196)

PEOPLE YOU SHOULD KNOW

James Thomson Callender   (p. 181)

George Washington   (p. 184)

Alexander Hamilton   (p. 185)

Thomas Jefferson   (p. 185)

REVIEW QUESTIONS

1. What were the most serious problems facing the new nation when George Washington became president?

2. What strengths and skills did George Washington bring to the presidency?

3. What measures did Alexander Hamilton propose to create a strong central government and a prospering economy? Why did his opponents oppose these measures?

4. Which set of ideas and programs—Alexander Hamilton's or Thomas Jefferson's—best addressed the new country's needs?

5. Why did George Washington warn against permanent alliances and party divisions in his Farewell Address?

6. Why did Congress enact the Alien and Sedition Acts? Why did the Jeffersonians oppose these measures?

8 The Jeffersonians in Power, 1800–1815

THE BURR-HAMILTON DUEL

On the morning of June 18, 1804, a visitor handed a package to former treasury secretary **Alexander Hamilton.** Inside were a newspaper clipping and a terse three-sentence letter. The clipping said that Hamilton had called Vice President **Aaron Burr** "a dangerous man, and one who ought not to be trusted with the reins of government." It went on to say that Hamilton had "expressed" a "still more despicable opinion" of Burr—apparently a bitter personal attack on Burr's public and private morality, not merely a political criticism. The letter, signed by Burr, demanded a "prompt and unqualified" denial or an immediate apology.

Hamilton and Burr had sparred verbally for decades. Hamilton regarded Burr as an unscrupulous man and considered him partly responsible for a duel in 1801 that had left his son Philip dead. Burr, in turn, blamed Hamilton for his defeat in the race for governor of New York earlier in the year. When, after three weeks, Hamilton had failed to respond to his letter satisfactorily, Burr insisted that they settle the dispute according to the code of honor.

Shortly after 7 A.M., on July 11, 1804, Burr and Hamilton met on the wooded heights of Weehawken, New Jersey, a customary dueling ground directly across the Hudson River from New York. Hamilton's son died there in a duel in 1801.

Hamilton's second handed Burr one of two pistols equipped with hairspring triggers. After he and Burr took their positions 10 paces apart, Hamilton raised his pistol on the command to "Present!" and fired. His shot struck a tree a few feet to Burr's side. Then Burr fired. His shot struck Hamilton in the right side and passed through his liver. Hamilton died the following day.

The popular view was that Hamilton had intentionally fired to one side, while Burr had slain the Federalist leader in an act of cold-blooded murder. In fact, historians do not know whether Burr was guilty of willful murder. Burr had no way of knowing whether Hamilton had purposely missed. Hamilton, after all, had accepted the challenge, raised his pistol, and fired. According to the code of honor, if Burr missed on his first try, Hamilton would have a second chance to shoot.

On July 11, 1804, Vice President Aaron Burr critically wounded Alexander Hamilton in a duel.

The states of New York and New Jersey wanted to try Burr for murder; New Jersey actually indicted him. The vice president fled through New Jersey by foot and wagon to Philadelphia, then took refuge in Georgia and South Carolina, until the indictments were quashed and he could finish his term in office.

The Jeffersonian era—the period stretching from 1800 to 1815—was rife with conflict, partisan passion, and larger-than-life personalities. On the domestic front, a new political party, the **Democratic-Republicans,** came to office for the first time and a former vice president was charged with treason against his country. The era was also marked by foreign policy challenges. Pirates, operating from bases on the coast of North Africa, harassed American shipping and enslaved American sailors. Britain and France also interfered with American shipping. Finally, the United States once again waged war with Britain, the world's strongest power. These developments raised profound questions: Could the country peacefully transfer political power from one party to another? Could the country preserve political stability? And most important of all, could the nation preserve its neutral rights and national honor in the face of grave threats from Britain and France?

JEFFERSON TAKES COMMAND

Thomas Jefferson's goal as president was to restore the principles of the American Revolution. In his view, a decade of **Federalist Party** rule had threatened republican government. Not only had the Federalists levied oppressive taxes, stretched the provisions of the Constitution, and established a bastion of wealth and special privilege in the creation of a national bank, they also had subverted civil liberties and expanded the powers of the central government at the expense of the states. A new revolution was necessary, "as real a revolution in the principles of our government as that of 1776 was in its form."

Republicans celebrated Thomas Jefferson's victory in the election of 1800 with a flag inscribed: "T. Jefferson President . . . John Adams no more."

What was needed was a return to basic republican principles.

Beginning with his very first day in office, Jefferson sought to demonstrate his administration's commitment to republican principles. At noon, March 4, 1801, Jefferson, clad in clothes of plain cloth, walked from a nearby boardinghouse to the new United States Capitol in Washington. Without ceremony, he entered the Senate chamber and took the presidential oath of office. In his inaugural address Jefferson sought to allay fear that he planned a Republican reign of terror. "We are all Republicans," he said, "we are all Federalists." Echoing George Washington's Farewell Address, he asked his listeners to set aside partisan and sectional differences and remember that "every difference of opinion is not a difference of principle." He also laid out the principles that would guide his presidency: a frugal, limited government; reduction of the public debt; respect for states' rights; encouragement of agriculture; and a limited role for government in peoples' lives. He committed his administration to repealing oppressive taxes, slashing government expenses, cutting military expenditures, and paying off the public debt.

Who Was Thomas Jefferson?

In 1962 President John F. Kennedy hosted a White House dinner for America's Nobel Laureates. He told the assemblage that this was "probably the greatest concentration of talent and genius in this house except perhaps for those times when Thomas Jefferson ate alone."

Thomas Jefferson, the nation's third president, was a man of many talents. Though best known for his political accomplishments, he was also an architect, inventor, philosopher, planter, scientist, and talented violinist. Jefferson was an extremely complex man, and his life was filled with apparent inconsistencies. An idealist who repeatedly denounced slavery, the "Apostle of Liberty" owned 200 slaves when he wrote the Declaration of Independence and freed only five slaves at the time of his death. A vigorous opponent of all forms of human tyranny and staunch defender of human equality, he adopted a patronizing attitude toward women, declaring that their proper role was to "soothe and calm the minds of their husbands." Yet Jefferson remains this country's most eloquent exponent of democratic principles. A product of the Enlightenment, Jefferson was a stalwart defender of political freedom, equality, and religious and intellectual freedom. He was convinced that the yeoman farmer, who worked the land, provided the backbone of democracy. He popularized the idea that a democratic republic required an enlightened and educated citizenry and that government has a duty to assist in the education of a meritocracy based on talent and ability.

Jefferson's Goal: To Restore Republican Government

As president, Jefferson strove to return the nation to **republican values.** Through his personal conduct and public policies he sought to return the country to the principles of democratic simplicity, economy, and limited government. He took a number of steps to rid the White House of aristocratic customs that had prevailed during the administrations of Washington and Adams. He introduced the custom of having guests shake hands instead of bowing stiffly; he also placed dinner guests at a round table, so that no individual would sit in a more important place than any other. In an effort to discourage a "cult of personality," he refused to sanction public celebrations of his birthday declaring, "The only birthday I ever commemorate is that of our Independence, the Fourth of July." Jefferson also repudiated certain "monarchical practices" that had marked the Washington and Adams presidencies. Jefferson refused to ride in an elegant coach or host elegant dinner parties and balls and wore clothes made of homespun cloth. To dramatize his disdain for pomp and pageantry, he received the British minister in his dressing gown and slippers.

One of Thomas Jefferson's inventions was this polygraph machine, which made copies of Jefferson's letters as he wrote them.

THE PEOPLE SPEAK

Religion in the Early Republic

During the late eighteenth and early nineteenth centuries, America's churches were deprived of state tax support. Nevertheless, church membership soared, largely due to the success of religious revivals in converting thousands of Americans. Peter Cartwright (1785–1872), a Methodist minister in frontier Kentucky, Tennessee, and Illinois, describes the revival at Cane Ridge, Kentucky, which touched off a wave of revivals that continued until the Civil War. In 1846, Cartwright ran for Congress in Illinois but was defeated by a young Springfield attorney named Abraham Lincoln.

> Somewhere between 1800 and 1801, in the upper part of Kentucky, at a memorable place called "Cane Ridge," there was appointed a sacramental meeting by some of the Presbyterian ministers, at which meeting, seemingly unexpected by ministers or people, the mighty power of God was displayed in a very extraordinary manner; many were moved to tears, and bitter and loud crying for mercy. The meeting was protracted for weeks. Ministers of almost all denominations flocked in from far and near. The meeting was kept up by night and day. Thousands heard of the mighty work, and came on foot, on horseback, in carriages and wagons. It was supposed that there were in attendance at times

during the meeting from twelve to twenty-five thousand people. Hundreds fell prostrate under the mighty power of God, as men slain in battle. Stands were erected in the woods from which preachers of different Churches proclaimed repentance toward God and faith in our Lord Jesus Christ, and it was supposed, by eye and ear witnesses, that between one and two thousand souls were happily and powerfully converted to God during the meeting. It was not unusual for one, two, three, and four to seven preachers to be addressing the listening thousands at the same time from the different stands erected for the purpose. The heavenly fire spread in almost every direction. It was said, by truthful witnesses, that at times more than one thousand persons broke into loud shouting all at once, and that the shouts could be heard for miles around.

> From this camp-meeting, for so it ought to be called, the news spread through all the Churches, and through all the land, and it excited great wonder and surprise; but it kindled a religious flame that spread all over Kentucky and through many other states. And I may here be permitted to say, that this was the first camp-meeting ever held in the United States, and here our camp-meetings took their rise.

Source: W. P. Strickland, ed., *Autobiography of Peter Cartwright, The Backwoods Preacher* (New York: Carlton & Porter, 1856), 30–33.

Jefferson believed that presidents should not try to impose their will on Congress, and consequently he refused on policy grounds to initiate legislation openly or to veto congressional bills. Convinced that presidents Washington and Adams had acted like British monarchs by personally appearing before Congress and requesting legislation, Jefferson simply sent Congress written messages. Not until the presidency of Woodrow Wilson would another president publicly address Congress and call for legislation.

Jefferson matched his commitment to republican simplicity with an emphasis on economy in government. His ideal was "a wise and frugal Government, which shall . . . leave [Americans] free to regulate their own pursuits of industry and improvement." He slashed army and navy expenditures, cut the budget, eliminated taxes on whiskey, houses, and

slaves, and fired all federal tax collectors. He reduced the army to 3000 soldiers and 172 officers, the navy to 6 frigates, and foreign legations to 3—in Britain, France, and Spain. His budget cuts allowed him to cut the federal debt by a third, despite the elimination of all internal taxes.

Jefferson did not conceive of government in entirely negative terms. Convinced that ownership of land and honest labor in the earth were the firmest bases of political stability, Jefferson persuaded Congress to cut the price of public lands and extend credit to purchasers to encourage landownership and rapid western settlement. A firm believer in the idea that America should be the "asylum" for "oppressed humanity," he moved Congress to reduce the residence requirement for citizenship from 14 to 5 years. In the interest of protecting civil liberties, he allowed the Sedition Act to expire in 1801, freed all people imprisoned under the act, and refunded their fines. And finally, to ensure that the public knew the names and number of all government officials, Jefferson ordered publication of a register of all federal employees.

In one area Jefferson felt his hands were tied. He considered the **Bank of the United States** "the most deadly" institution to republican government. But Hamilton's bank had been legally chartered for 20 years and Jefferson's secretary of the treasury, Albert Gallatin, said that the bank was needed to provide credit for the nation's growing economy. So Jefferson allowed the bank to continue to operate, but he weakened its influence by distributing the federal government's deposits among 21 state banks. "What is practicable," Jefferson commented, "must often control pure theory."

Contemporaries were astonished by the sight of a president who had renounced all the practical tools of government: an army, a navy, and taxes. Jefferson's actions promised, said a British observer, "a sort of Millennium in government." Jefferson's goal was, indeed, to create a new kind of government, a republican government wholly unlike the centralized, corrupt, patronage-ridden one against which Americans had rebelled in 1776.

Reforming the Federal Government

Jefferson thought that the 3000 Federalist officeholders stood as the major obstacles to the restoration of republican government. Of the first 600 political appointees named to federal office by presidents Washington and Adams, all but six were Federalists. Even after learning of his defeat, Adams appointed Federalists to every vacant government position. His most dramatic postelection appointment was naming **John Marshall,** a Federalist, as chief justice of the Supreme Court.

Jefferson was committed to the idea that government office should be filled on the basis of merit, not political connections. Only government officeholders guilty of malfeasance or incompetence should be fired. Nothing more should be asked of government officials, he felt, than that they be honest, able, and loyal to the Constitution. Jefferson wholly rejected the idea that a victorious political party had a right to fill public offices with loyal party supporters.

Although many Republicans felt that Federalists should be replaced by loyal Republicans, Jefferson declared that he would remove only "midnight" appointees who had been named to office by

President Adams after he learned of his electoral defeat.

War on the Judiciary

When Thomas Jefferson took office, not a single Republican was serving as a federal judge. In Jefferson's view, the Federalists had prostituted the federal judiciary into a branch of their political party and intended to use the courts to frustrate Republican plans. "From that battery," said Jefferson, "all the works of republicanism are to be beaten down and erased."

The first major political battle of Jefferson's presidency involved his effort to weaken Federalist control of the federal judiciary. The specific issue that provoked Republican anger was the **Judiciary Act of 1801,** which was passed by Congress five days before Adams's term expired. The law created 16 new federal judgeships, positions that Adams promptly filled with Federalists. Even more damaging from a Republican perspective, the act strengthened the power of the central government by extending the jurisdiction of the federal courts over bankruptcy and land disputes, which were previously the exclusive domain of state courts. Finally, the act reduced the number of Supreme Court justices effective with the next vacancy, delaying Jefferson's opportunity to name a new Supreme Court justice.

Jefferson's supporters in Congress repealed the Judiciary Act, but the war over control of the federal courts continued. One of Adams's "midnight appointments" to a judgeship was William Marbury, a loyal Federalist. Although approved by the Senate, Marbury never received his letter of appointment from Adams. When Jefferson became president, Marbury demanded that the new secretary of state, James Madison, issue the commission. Madison refused and Marbury sued, claiming that under section 13 of the Judiciary Act of 1789, the Supreme Court had the power to issue a court order that would compel Madison to give him his judgeship.

The case threatened to provoke a direct confrontation between the judiciary on the one hand and the executive and legislative branches of the federal government on the other. If the Supreme Court ordered Madison to give Marbury his judgeship, the secretary of state was likely to ignore the Court, and Jeffersonians in Congress might try to limit the high court's power. This is precisely what had happened in 1793 when the Supreme Court had ruled that a state might be sued in federal court by nonresidents. Congress had retaliated by initiating the Eleventh Amendment, which restricted such suits.

In his opinion in *Marbury v. Madison,* John Marshall, the new chief justice of the Supreme Court, ingeniously expanded the court's power without directly provoking the Jeffersonians. Marshall conceded that Marbury had a right to his appointment but ruled the Court had no authority to order the secretary of state to act, since the section of the Judiciary Act that gave the Court the power to issue an order was unconstitutional. "A law repugnant to the constitution is void," Marshall declared. "It is emphatically the province and duty of the judicial department to say what the law is." For the first time, the Supreme Court had declared an act of Congress unconstitutional.

Marbury v. Madison was a landmark in American constitutional history. The decision firmly established the power of the federal courts to review the constitutionality of federal laws and to invalidate acts of Congress when they are determined to conflict with the Constitution. This power, known as **judicial review,** provides the basis for the important place that the Supreme Court occupies in American life today.

Marshall's decision in *Marbury v. Madison* intensified the Republican Party's distrust of the courts. Impeachment, Jefferson and his followers believed, was the only way to be rid of judges they considered unfit or overly partisan and make the courts responsive to the public will. "We shall see who is master of the ship," declared one Jeffersonian. "Whether men appointed for life or the immediate representatives of the people . . . are to give laws to the community." Federalists responded by accusing the administration of endangering the independence of the federal judiciary.

Three weeks before the Court handed down its decision in *Marbury v. Madison,* congressional Republicans launched impeachment proceedings against Federal District Judge John Pickering of New Hampshire. An alcoholic, who may have been insane, Pickering was convicted and removed from office.

On the day of Pickering's conviction, the House voted to impeach Supreme Court Justice **Samuel Chase,** a staunch Federalist and a signer of the Declaration of Independence. From the bench, he had openly denounced equal rights and universal suffrage and accused the Jeffersonians of atheism and being power hungry. Undoubtedly, Chase was guilty of unrestrained partisanship and injudicious statements. An irate President Jefferson called for Chase's impeachment.

Chase was put on trial for holding opinions "hurtful to the welfare of the country." The real issue, however, was whether Chase had committed an impeachable offense, since the Constitution specified that a judge could be removed from office only for "treason, bribery, or other high crimes" and not for partisanship or judicial misconduct. In a historic decision that helped to guarantee the independence of the judiciary, the Senate voted to acquit Chase. Although a majority of the Senate found Chase guilty, seven Republicans broke ranks and denied Jefferson the two-thirds majority needed for a conviction. "Impeachment is a farce which will not be tried again," Jefferson commented.

Chase's acquittal had momentous consequences for the future. If the Jeffersonians had succeeded in removing Chase, they would probably have removed other Federalist judges from the federal bench. Since Chase's acquittal, however, no further attempts have ever been made to remove federal judges solely on the grounds of partisanship or to reshape the federal courts through impeachment. Despite the Republicans' active hostility toward an independent judiciary, the Supreme Court had emerged as a vigorous third branch of government.

International Conflict

In his inaugural address, Thomas Jefferson declared that his fondest wish was for peace. "Peace is my passion," he repeatedly insisted. As president, however, Jefferson was unable to realize his wish. Like Washington and Adams before him, Jefferson faced the difficult task of preserving American independence and neutrality in a world torn by war and revolution.

The Barbary Pirates Jefferson's first major foreign policy crisis came from the "**Barbary pirates**" who preyed on American shipping off the coast of North Africa. In 1785, Algerian pirates boarded an American merchant schooner sailing off the coast of Portugal, took its 21-member crew to Algeria, and enslaved them for 12 years. During the next eight years, 100 more American hostages were seized from American ships. In 1795 Congress approved a $1 million ransom for their release, and by 1800, one-fifth of all federal revenues went to the North African states as tribute.

Early in Jefferson's first term, he refused to pay additional tribute. Determined to end the humiliating demands, he sent warships to the Mediterranean to enforce a blockade of Tripoli. The result was a protracted conflict with Tripoli, which lasted until 1805. Tripoli eventually agreed to make peace, though the United States continued to pay other Barbary States until 1816.

The Louisiana Purchase At the same time that conflict raged with the Barbary pirates, a more serious crisis loomed on the Mississippi River. In

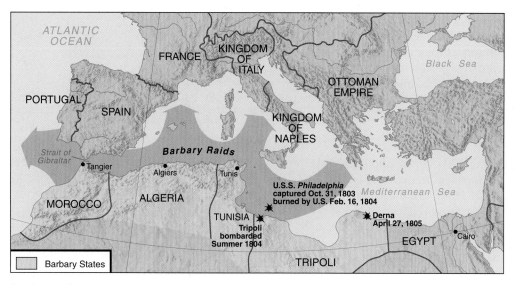

Barbary States

Thomas Jefferson's first foreign policy crisis occurred when he refused to pay tribute to the Barbary States for the release of hostages captured by Algerian pirates. Instead, he sent eight ships to enforce a blockade of Tripoli.

1795 Spain granted western farmers the right to ship their produce down the Mississippi River to New Orleans, where their cargoes of corn, whiskey, and pork were loaded aboard ships bound for the east coast and foreign ports. In 1800 Spain secretly ceded the Louisiana territory to France and closed the port of New Orleans to American farmers. West-

erners, left without a port from which to export their goods, exploded with anger. Many demanded war.

The prospect of French control of the Mississippi alarmed Jefferson. Spain had held only a weak and tenuous grip on the Mississippi, but France was a much stronger power. Jefferson feared the establish-

To avenge the capture of 307 crew members of the U.S. frigate *Philadelphia*, Lt. Stephen Decatur, Jr., and a small band of sailors boarded the ship and set it afire in 1804.

ment of a French colonial empire in North America blocking American expansion. The United States appeared to have only two options: diplomacy or war.

The president instructed his representatives in France to purchase New Orleans and as much of the Gulf Coast as they could for $2 million. Circumstances played into American hands when France failed to suppress a slave rebellion in Haiti. One hundred thousand slaves, inspired by the French Revolution, had revolted, destroying 1200 coffee and 200 sugar plantations. In 1800 France sent troops to crush the insurrection and reconquer Haiti, but they met a determined resistance led by a former slave named **Toussaint Louverture.** Then, mosquitoes carrying yellow fever wiped them out. "Damn sugar, damn coffee, damn colonies," **Napoleon Bonaparte,** the French leader, exclaimed. Without Haiti, which he regarded as the centerpiece of an American empire, Napoleon had little interest in keeping Louisiana.

Two days after Monroe's arrival, the French finance minister unexpectedly announced that France was willing to sell not just New Orleans but all of Louisiana Province, a territory extending from Canada

On his expedition with Meriwether Lewis to explore the Louisiana Territory, William Clark kept a detailed journal of field notes and drawings. This drawing shows how the Chinook Indians flattened their infants' heads by binding them between two boards.

The American flag was raised over New Orleans in 1803 after the Louisiana Purchase.

to the Gulf of Mexico and westward as far as the Rocky Mountains. The American negotiators agreed on a price of $15 million, or about 4 cents an acre.

Since the Constitution did not give the president specific authorization to purchase land, Jefferson considered asking for a constitutional amendment empowering the government to acquire territory. In Congress, Federalists bitterly denounced the **Louisiana Purchase,** fearing that the creation of new western states would weaken the influence of their party. In the end Jefferson, afraid that Napoleon might change his mind, simply sent the agreement to the Senate, which ratified it. "The less said about any constitutional difficulty, the better," he stated. In a single stroke, Jefferson had doubled the size of the country.

To gather information about the geography, natural resources, wildlife, and peoples of Louisiana, President Jefferson dispatched his private secretary Meriwether Lewis and William Clark, a Virginia-born military officer, to explore the area. For 2 years the **Lewis and Clark Expedition** of some 30 soldiers and 10 civilians traveled up the Missouri River as far as present-day central North Dakota and then west to the Pacific.

Disunionist Conspiracies

Anger over the acquisition of Louisiana led some Federalists to consider secession as a last resort to restore their party's former dominance. One group of Feder-

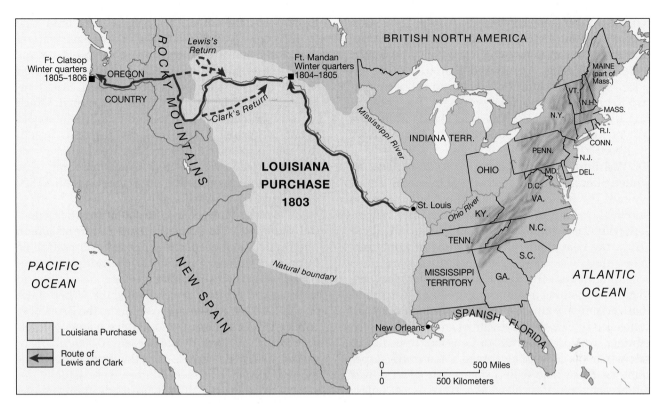

The Louisiana Purchase and Route of Lewis and Clark

No one realized how much territory Jefferson had acquired through the Louisiana Purchase until Lewis and Clark explored the far West.

alist congressmen plotted to establish a "**Northern Confederacy,**" which would consist of New Jersey, New York, the New England states, and Canada.

Alexander Hamilton repudiated this scheme, and the conspirators turned to Vice President Aaron Burr. In return for Federalist support in his campaign for the governorship of New York, Burr was to swing New York into the Northern Confederacy. Burr was badly beaten, in part because of Hamilton's opposition. Incensed and irate, Burr challenged Hamilton to the duel described at the beginning of this chapter.

The duel ruined Burr's career as a politician and made him a fugitive from the law. The Republican Party stripped away his control over political patronage in New York. In debt, disgraced, on the edge of bankruptcy, the desperate Burr became involved in a conspiracy for which he would be put on trial for treason.

During the spring of 1805 Burr traveled to the West, where he and an old friend, James Wilkinson, commander of United States forces in the Southwest and military governor of Louisiana, hatched an adventurous scheme. It is still uncertain what the conspirators' goal was, since Burr, in his efforts to attract support, told different stories to different people.

Spain's minister believed that Burr planned to set up an independent nation in the Mississippi Valley. Others reported that he planned to seize Spanish territory in what is now Texas, California, and New Mexico. The British minister was told that for $500,000 and British naval support, Burr would separate the states and territories west of the Appalachians from the rest of the Union and create an empire with himself as its head.

In the fall of 1806 Burr and some 60 schemers traveled down the Ohio River toward New Orleans to assess possibilities and perhaps to incite disgruntled French settlers to revolt. Wilkinson, recognizing that the scheme was doomed to failure, decided to betray Burr. He wrote a letter to Jefferson describing a "deep, dark, wicked, and widespread conspiracy, . . . to seize on New Orleans, revolutionize the territory, and carry an expedition against Mexico."

Burr fled, but was finally apprehended in the Mississippi Territory. He was then taken to the circuit court in Richmond, Virginia, where, in 1807, he was tried for treason. Jefferson, convinced that Burr was a dangerous man, wanted a conviction regardless of the evidence. Chief Justice John Marshall, who presided over the trial, was equally eager to discredit

Jefferson. Ultimately, Burr was acquitted. The reason for the acquittal was the Constitution's very strict definition of treason as "levying war against the United States" or "giving . . . aid and comfort" to the nation's enemies. In addition, each overt act of treason had to be attested to by two witnesses. The prosecution was unable to meet this strict standard; as a result of Burr's acquittal, few cases of treason have ever been tried in the United States.

Was Burr guilty of conspiring to destabilize the United States and separate the West by force? Probably not. The prosecution's case rested largely on the unreliable testimony of coconspirator James Wilkinson, who was a spy in the pay of Spain while also a U.S. army commander and governor of Louisiana. What, then, was the purpose of Burr's mysterious scheming? It appears likely that the former vice president was planning a filibuster expedition—an unauthorized military attack—on Mexico, which was then controlled by Spain. The dream of creating a western republic in Mexico, Florida, or Louisiana appealed to many early nineteenth-century Americans—especially to those who feared that a European power might seize Spain's New World colonies unless America launched a preemptive strike. Alexander Hamilton himself, back in 1798, had proposed a plan to conquer Louisiana and the Floridas.

To the end of his life, Burr denied that he had plotted treason against the United States. Asked by one of his closest friends whether he had sought to separate the West from the rest of the nation, Burr responded with an emphatic "No!" "I would as soon have thought of taking possession of the moon and informing my friends that I intended to divide it among them."

THE AMERICAN EAGLE CHALLENGES THE FRENCH TIGER AND THE BRITISH SHARK

In 1804, Jefferson was easily reelected, carrying every state except Connecticut and Delaware. He received 162 electoral votes to only 14 for his Federalist opponent, Charles C. Pinckney. Although his second term began, he later wrote, "without a cloud on the horizon," storm clouds soon gathered as a result of renewed war in Europe. Jefferson faced the difficult challenge of keeping the United States out of the European war, while defending the nation's rights as a neutral country.

In May 1803, only two weeks after Napoleon sold Louisiana to the United States, France declared war on Britain. As part of his overall strategy to bring

Britain to its knees, Napoleon instituted the "**Continental System,**" a policy of economic warfare that closed European ports to British goods and ordered the seizure of any neutral vessel that carried British goods or stopped in a British port. Britain retaliated in 1807 by issuing **Orders in Council,** which required all neutral ships to land at a British port to obtain a trading license and pay a tariff. Britain threatened to seize any ship that failed to obey the Orders in Council. United States shipping was caught in the crossfire. By 1807 France had seized 500 ships and Britain nearly 1000.

The most outrageous violation of America's neutral rights was the British practice of **impressment.** The British navy desperately needed sailors. Unable to procure sufficient volunteers, the British navy resorted to seizing—impressing—men on streets, in taverns, and on British merchant ships. When these efforts failed to muster sufficient men, the British began to stop foreign ships and remove seamen alleged to be British subjects. By 1811 nearly 10,000 American sailors had been forced into the British navy, although an undetermined number were actually deserters from British ships who made more money sailing on U.S. ships.

Outrage over impressment reached a fever pitch in 1807 when the British man-of-war *Leopard* fired three broadsides at the American naval frigate *Chesapeake* as the American crew had refused to allow British officers to search the American ship for Royal Navy deserters. The blasts killed three American sailors and wounded 18 more. British authorities then boarded the American ship and removed four sailors, only one of whom was really a British subject.

"Dambargo"

In a desperate attempt to stave off war, for which it was ill prepared, and to win respect for America's neutral rights, the United States imposed the **embargo of 1807** on foreign trade. Convinced that American trade was vital to European industry, Jefferson persuaded Congress in late 1807 to adopt a policy of "peaceable coercion": a ban on all foreign shipping and exports.

Jefferson regarded the embargo as an idealistic experiment—a moral alternative to war. Jefferson was not a doctrinaire pacifist, but he had long advocated economic coercion as an instrument of diplomacy. Now he had a chance to put his ideas into practice.

The embargo was an unpopular and costly failure. It hurt the American economy far more than it did the British or French and resulted in widespread smuggling. Without the European export market, harbors filled with idle ships, and nearly 30,000 sailors

TABLE 8.1		
Road to War: War of 1812		
1807	*Leopard-Chesapeake* **Affair**	British man-of-war H.M.S. *Leopard* fires upon the American warship U.S.S. *Chesapeake*, killing three; then the British forcibly remove four alleged deserters, bringing the United States and Great Britain to the brink of war.
	Embargo Act	Prohibits all American trade with foreign nations.
1809	**The Non-Intercourse Act**	Reopens overseas commerce except to Britain and France; trade with these countries is to be reinstituted if they halt interference with American shipping.
1810	**Macon's Bill No. 2**	Restores trade with Britain and France but stipulates that if either country lifts its restrictions on neutral trade, the United States would terminate trade with the other.
	Trade Disputes	France informs the United States that it will repeal its trade restrictions if the United States halts trade with Britain; United States forbids trade with Britain.
	Congressional Elections	Voters sweep the "War Hawks" into Congress.
1811	**The Battle of Tippecanoe**	Battle in Indiana Territory shatters the influence of the Shawnee Prophet, Tenskwatawa.
1812	**Declaration of War**	Congress declares war against Britain on grounds of British impressment of American seamen, interference with trade, and blockading of American ports.

found themselves jobless. The embargo resuscitated the Federalist Party, which regained power in several New England states and made substantial gains in the Congressional elections of 1808. "Would to God," said one American, "that the embargo had done as little evil to ourselves as it has done to foreign nations!"

Jefferson believed that Americans would cooperate with the embargo out of a sense of patriotism. Instead, evasions of the embargo were widespread, and smuggling flourished, particularly through Canada, and early in 1809, just three days before Jefferson left office, Congress repealed the embargo. In effect for 15 months, the embargo exacted no political concessions from either France or Britain. But it had produced economic hardship, evasion of the law, and political dissension at home. Upset by the failure of his policies, the 65-year-old Jefferson looked forward to his retirement: "Never did a prisoner, released from his chains, feel such relief as I shall on shaking off the shackles of power."

The problem of American neutrality now fell to Jefferson's handpicked successor, **James Madison.** "The Father of the Constitution" was small in stature and frail in health. A quiet and scholarly man, who secretly suffered from epilepsy, Madison brought a keen intellect and a wealth of experience to the presidency. At the Constitutional Convention, he had played a leading role in formulating the principles of federalism and separation of powers that underlie the American system of government. As a member of Congress, he had sponsored the Bill of Rights and founded the Republican Party. As Jefferson's secretary of state, he had kept the United States out of the Napoleonic wars and was committed to using economic coercion to force Britain and France to respect America's neutral rights.

In 1809 Congress replaced the failed embargo with the **Non-Intercourse Act,** which reopened trade with all nations except Britain and France.

Violations of American neutrality continued, and a year later Congress replaced the Non-Intercourse Act with a new measure, **Macon's Bill No. 2.** This policy reopened trade with France and Britain. It stated, however, that if either Britain or France agreed to respect America's neutral rights, the United States would immediately stop trade with the other nation. Napoleon seized on this new policy in an effort to entangle the United States in his war with Britain. In the summer of 1810, he announced repeal of all French restrictions on American trade. Even though France continued to seize American ships and cargoes, President Madison snapped at the bait. In early 1811 he cut off trade with Britain and recalled the American minister.

For 19 months the British went without American trade, but gradually economic coercion worked. Food shortages, mounting unemployment, and increasing inventories of unsold manufactured goods led Britain to end its trade restrictions (though not the British navy's policy of impressment). Unfortunately, Prime Minister Spencer Perceval was assassinated before he actually revoked the restrictions. When the restrictions were finally suspended on June 16, it was too late. President Madison had asked Congress for a declaration of war on June 1. A divided House and Senate concurred. The House voted to declare war on Britain by a vote of 79 to 49; the Senate by a vote of 19 to 13.

A Second War of Independence

Why did the United States declare war on Britain in 1812? Resentment at British interference with American rights on the high seas was certainly the most loudly voiced grievance. British trade restrictions, impressment of thousands of American seamen, and British blockades humiliated the country and undercut America's national honor and neutral rights.

But if British harassment of American shipping was the primary motivation for war, why then did the prowar majority in Congress come largely from the South, the West, and the frontier, and not from northeastern ship owners and sailors? The vote to declare war on Britain was divided along sharply regional lines. Representatives from western, southern, and frontier states voted 65 to 15 for war, while representatives from New England, New York, and New Jersey, states with strong shipping interests, voted 34 to 14 against war.

Northeastern Federalists and a handful of Republicans from coastal regions of the South regarded war with Britain as a grave mistake. The United States, they insisted, could not hope to challenge successfully British supremacy on the seas,

and the government could not finance a war without bankrupting the country. Southerners and Westerners, in contrast, were eager to avenge British insults against American honor and British actions that mocked American sovereignty on land and sea. Many Southerners and Westerners blamed British trade policies for depressing agricultural prices and producing an economic depression. War with Britain also offered another incentive: the possibility of clearing western lands of Indians by removing the Indians' strongest ally—the British. And finally, many Westerners and Southerners had their eye on expansion, viewing war as an opportunity to add Canada and Spanish-held Florida to the United States.

Weary of Jefferson and Madison's patient and pacifist policy of economic coercion, voters swept 63 of the 142 representatives out of Congress in 1810 and replaced them with young Republicans that Federalists dubbed "**War Hawks.**" These second-generation Republicans avidly supported national expansion and national honor. They elected **Henry Clay,** a representative from frontier Kentucky, Speaker of the House on his very first day in Congress. Clay then assigned other young Republicans, such as **John C. Calhoun,** a freshman representative from South Carolina, to key House committees.

Staunchly nationalist and rabidly anti-British, eager for territorial expansion and economic growth, the young Republicans regarded the Napoleonic Wars in Europe as an unparalleled opportunity to defend national honor, assert American interests, and conquer Canada and Florida.

Further contributing to their prowar fervor was the belief that the British incited Native Americans on the frontier to attack. Anti-British feeling soared in November 1811, when General **William Henry Harrison** precipitated a fight with a Native-American alliance led by the Shawnee Prophet, **Tenskwatawa,** at Tippecanoe Creek in Indiana. More than 60 American soldiers were killed and 100 were wounded at the **Battle of Tippecanoe,** but the Indian alliance was shattered, allowing the Americans to claim victory. Since British guns were found on the battlefield, young Republicans concluded that the British were responsible for the incident.

Early Defeats

Although Congress voted strongly in favor of war, the country entered the conflict deeply divided. Not only would many New Englanders refuse to subscribe to war loans, some merchants would actually ship provisions that Britain needed to support its

At the Battle of Tippecanoe, U.S. troops led by General William Henry Harrison routed the small force of Native Americans under the Shawnee Prophet Tenskwatawa.

army, which was fighting Napoleon in Europe. Moreover, the United States was woefully unprepared for war. The army consisted of fewer than 7000 soldiers and the navy was grotesquely overmatched.

The American strategy called for a three-pronged invasion of Canada and heavy harassment of British shipping. The attack on Canada, however, was a disastrous failure. At Detroit, 2000 American troops surrendered to a much smaller British and Native American force. An attack across the Niagara River, near Buffalo, resulted in 900 American prisoners of war when the New York state militia refused to provide support. Along Lake Champlain, a third army retreated into American territory after failing to cut undefended British supply lines. By the end of 1812, British forces controlled key forts in the Old Northwest, including Detroit and Fort Dearborn, the future site of Chicago. The only consolation for the Americans was a string of naval victories in single-ship encounters.

In 1813 America suffered new failures. In January, an American army advancing toward Detroit was defeated and captured in the swamps west of Lake Erie. Then, in April, Americans staged a raid across Lake Ontario to York (now Toronto). American soldiers set fire to the two houses of the provincial parliament, an act that brought retaliation in the burning of Washington, D.C., by the British. A plan to capture Montreal in the fall of 1813 also ended without an attack.

Only a series of unexpected victories at the end of the year raised American spirits. On September 10, 1813, America won a major naval victory at the Battle of Lake Erie near Put-in-Bay at the western end of Lake Erie. There, Master-Commandant Oliver Hazard Perry successfully engaged six British ships. Though Perry's flagship, the *Lawrence*, was disabled in the fighting, he went on to capture the British fleet. He reported his victory with the stirring words, "We have met the enemy and they are ours."

The Battle of Lake Erie was America's first major victory of the war. It forced the British to abandon Detroit and retreat toward Niagara. On October 5, 1813, Major General William Henry Harrison overtook the retreating British army and their Native American allies at the Thames River. He won a decisive victory in which the Indian leader **Tecumseh** was killed, thereby ending the fighting strength of the northwestern Indians.

The Tide Turns

In early 1814, prospects for an American victory dimmed. In the spring, Britain defeated Napoleon in Europe, freeing 18,000 veteran British troops to partic-

ipate in an invasion of the United States. The British planned to invade the United States at three points: upstate New York across the Niagara River and Lake Champlain, the Chesapeake Bay, and New Orleans. The London *Times* accurately reflected the confident English mood: "Oh, may no false liberality, no mistaken lenity, no weak and cowardly policy interpose to save the United States from the blow! Strike! Chastise the savages, for such they are. . . . Our demands may be couched in a single word—Submission!"

At Niagara, however, a small American army stopped the British advance, and on Lake Champlain, American naval forces commanded by Thomas Macdonough placed British supply lines in jeopardy, forcing 11,000 British troops to retreat into Canada. Outnumbered more than three to one, American forces had halted Britain's invasion from the north.

In a second attempt to invade the United States, Britain landed 4000 soldiers on the Chesapeake Bay coast and marched on Washington, D.C., where untrained soldiers lacking uniforms and standard equipment were protecting the capital.

The result was utter chaos. While President Madison was inspecting the troops and offering encouragement, he narrowly escaped capture by British forces. On August 24, 1814, the British humiliated the nation by capturing and burning Washington, D.C. President Madison and his wife Dolley were forced to flee the capital, carrying with them many of the nation's treasures, including the Declaration of Independence and Gilbert Stuart's portrait of George Washington. For 72 hours, the president was forced to hide in the Virginia and Maryland countryside. The British arrived so soon after the president fled that the officers dined on a White House meal that had been prepared for the Madisons and 40 invited guests.

Britain's next objective was Baltimore. To reach the city, British warships had to pass the guns of Fort McHenry, which was manned by 1000 American soldiers. Waving atop the fort was the largest garrison flag ever designed—30 feet by 42 feet. On September 13, 1814, British warships began a 25-hour bombardment of Fort McHenry. British vessels anchored two miles off shore—close enough so that their guns could hit the fort, but too far for American shells to reach them.

All through the night British cannons bombarded Fort McHenry. At dawn on September 14, Francis Scott Key, a young lawyer detained on a British ship, saw the flag still waving over the fort's ramparts. The Americans had repulsed the British attack, with only 4 soldiers killed and 24 wounded. Key was so moved by the American victory that he

The Shawnee Prophet Tenskwatawa and His Warrior Brother Tecumseh

During the last years of the eighteenth century, defeat, disease, and death were the bitter lot of Native Americans living in the Northwest Territory. In 1794 an American expeditionary force led by Major General "Mad" Anthony Wayne crushed an opposing Indian army at the Battle of Fallen Timbers near present-day Toledo, Ohio. This decisive victory eventually forced Native Americans to give up 25,000 square miles of land north of the Ohio River.

Forty-five thousand land-hungry white settlers poured into the Ohio Country during the next six years. They spread a variety of killer diseases, including smallpox, influenza, and measles, in their wake. Whole villages succumbed, and hundreds of natives died. High Indian mortality rates did not bother the intruding whites, who also considered the arbitrary "murdering of the Indians in the highest degree meritorious," according to William Henry Harrison, the territorial governor. Aggressive frontier settlers likewise infringed on Indian hunting grounds and rapidly killed off wild game that provided the natives with basic sustenance. Deprived of their ancestral homelands, faced with severe food shortages, and enduring a drastic loss of population, Native Americans in the Old Northwest saw the fabric of their society coming apart. Tribal unity eroded, villages broke apart, and violent disputes became widespread. To escape from their problems, some natives turned to alcohol for the mind-numbing relief it provided them.

One of the Native Americans who suffered from the breakdown of Indian society was a Shawnee youth named Laulewasika. A few months before he was born in 1774, white frontiersmen—they had crossed into the Ohio Country in violation of a recent treaty—killed his father, a respected Shawnee warrior chief. Shortly thereafter, his despondent mother, a Creek, fled westward, leaving behind her children to be raised by relatives.

As a young man Laulewasika lacked direction. He became a dissolute, drunken idler, known only for the handkerchief he wore to cover up the facial disfigurement he suffered when he lost an eye during an accident. Then in 1805 in the midst of a frightening epidemic, Laulewasika underwent a powerful transformation. Overcome by images of his own wickedness, he fell into a deep trance during which he met the Indian Master of Life. On the basis of this mystical experience, Laulewasika embarked on a crusade "to reclaim the Indians from bad habits." Adopting the name Tenskwatawa, meaning "the open door," he first called upon Indians everywhere to stop drinking the white traders' alcohol. He soon broadened his appeals. Like other Native-American revitalization prophets before and after him, Tenskwatawa vigorously demanded an end to intertribal fighting, a return to ancestral ways, and a complete rejection of all aspects of white civilization. His central message was native unity as the key to blocking further white encroachments on ancient tribal lands.

Tenskwatawa's reputation reached a high point in 1806 after Governor William Henry Harrison demanded the performance of a miracle. "If he is a prophet," an almost mocking Harrison said to some Indians, "ask him to cause the sun to stand still, the moon to alter its course, . . . or the dead to rise from their graves. If he does these things, you may then believe he has been sent from God." Tenskwatawa obliged. Most likely learning from the British about an upcoming solar eclipse, he pronounced that he would make the sun disappear on the morning of June 16. When the shadow of the moon darkened the rays of the sun that day, the prophet's fame and message of unity spread far and wide among Native Americans.

The doctrines of Tenskwatawa were not solely his own. His older brother, the famed Shawnee war chief Tecumseh (1768–1813), had come to recognize the futility of fighting piecemeal against the whites. He also emerged as a firm advocate of a broad-based Indian alliance. In conjunction with the Shawnee Prophet, he struggled to convince Native Americans as far north as Wisconsin, as far west as Arkansas, and as far south as Florida to join together in blocking white expansion.

Besides working to build an alliance, Tecumseh's immediate goal was to save Indiana territory, or "the country of Indians," for the native populace. In 1808 he and Tenskwatawa relocated their tribal village in northwestern Indiana along the shoreline of the Tippecanoe River where it flowed into the Wabash River. The presence of the so-called Prophet's Town greatly worried Governor Harrison, since it

Tenskwatawa

Tecumseh

served as a mecca for Indian unification. In reaction Harrison directly challenged the growing influence of the Shawnee brothers. He conducted negotiations with friendly local chiefs and plied them with alcohol until they turned over title to 3 million acres in Indiana for the paltry sum of $7000 and an annuity of $1750. This precipitous act put Harrison on a collision course with Tecumseh and Tenskwatawa.

Harrison eventually held a meeting with the outraged Shawnee brothers. The governor told them they could surely place their faith in treaties with the United States, but not before Tecumseh, a spellbinding orator, had queried: "How can we have confidence in the white people? When Jesus Christ came upon the earth, you killed Him and nailed Him to a cross. You thought He was dead, but you were mistaken." Harrison did not miss the point. Tecumseh and Tenskwatawa intended to revitalize Native Americans so that they too would regain life as a united nation of

peoples and put an end to legalized land grabbing as provided for in such treaties as the one recently negotiated by Harrison.

Tecumseh needed time to build his alliance, and he soon set off on another of his journeys to convince his native brethren to put aside their petty tribal squabbles and prepare to rise up as one to resist the whites. He warned Tenskwatawa to avoid any conflict with Harrison, but the prophet did not listen. In November 1811, while Tecumseh was away in the south attempting to rally support, Harrison approached the Prophet's Town with an army of nearly 1000 men. Tenskwatawa rose to the bait and allowed some 450 warriors to attack the Americans. What followed was a rout. As the battle raged, the prophet called upon the Master of Life to protect his native fighters. His prayer failed. Harrison's troops drove off the warriors and then sacked and burned the village. In so doing, they destroyed the prophet's credibility and prestige. They also inadvertently

gave Harrison the kind of impressive military victory that helped him successfully secure the presidency of the United States in 1840. "Tippecanoe and Tyler Too" was Harrison's catchy electioneering slogan.

Tecumseh returned home from his trip a few months later. He was in an optimistic frame of mind, believing the grand native alliance could yet become reality. Then he saw the devastated village. Shocked and enraged that his brother had challenged Harrison's force, he angrily denounced Tenskwatawa and sent him packing westward into obscurity. In frustration Tecumseh likewise abandoned his dream of a pan-Indian alliance, since he now doubted whether his native brethren had the patience to plan and work together. Then, in his own words, he "swore . . . eternal hatred—the hatred of an avenger" against white settlers everywhere. He would rally what warriors he could and fight with all his strength in the name of his way of life until death relieved him of the anguish he felt for the collapsing world of his native brethren.

When the War of 1812 broke out, Tecumseh allied himself with the British in his final effort to halt American expansion. In October 1813, after U.S. forces compelled the British to retreat from the area around Detroit, the Shawnee warrior and an army consisting of Indian and British troops tried to halt the American advance at the Thames River in the eastern part of Canada's Ontario Province. The day before the climactic encounter, Tecumseh told his native followers: "Brother warriors, we are about to enter an engagement from which I shall not return. My body will remain on the field of battle." Tecumseh's premonition was correct. The next afternoon he died from multiple wounds in combat. With his demise the vision of pan-Indian resistance to white encroachment on native lands in the Middle West also perished.

217

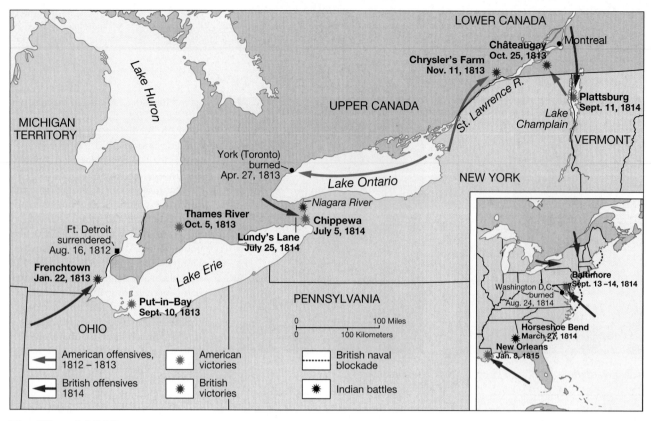

The War of 1812

wrote a poem entitled "The Star-Spangled Banner" on the back of an old envelope. The words were destined to become the young nation's national anthem.

The country still faced grave threats in the South. In 1813 the Creek Indians, encouraged by the British, attacked American settlements in what are now Alabama and Mississippi. Frontiersmen from Georgia, Mississippi, and Tennessee, led by Major General **Andrew Jackson,** retaliated and succeeded in defeating the Creeks in March 1814, at the **Battle of Horseshoe Bend** in Alabama. When the Creek War ended, Jackson proceeded to cut British supply lines in the South. He knew that Spain, supposedly neutral, allowed Britain to use the Florida port of Pensacola as a base of operations for a planned invasion of New Orleans. In a week, Jackson marched from Mobile, Alabama, to Pensacola and seized the city, forcing the British to delay their invasion.

On January 8, 1815, the British fleet and a battle-tested 10,000-man army finally attacked New Orleans in an attempt to seize control of the mouth of the Mississippi River. To defend the city, Jackson assembled a ragtag army, including French pirates, Choctaw Indians, western militia, and freed slaves.

Although British forces outnumbered Americans by more than two to one, American artillery and sharpshooters stopped the invasion. American losses totaled only 8 dead and 13 wounded, while British casualties were 2036, including their commanding officer. Almost 400 British soldiers were killed. Ironically, American and British negotiators in Ghent, Belgium, had signed the peace treaty ending the War of 1812 two weeks earlier. Britain, convinced that the American war was so difficult and costly that nothing would be gained from further fighting, agreed to return to the conditions that existed before the war. Left unmentioned in the peace treaty were the issues over which the Americans had fought the war—impressment, naval blockades, and the British Orders in Council.

The War's Significance

Although often treated as unimportant, a minor footnote to the bloody European war between France and Britain, the **War of 1812** was crucial for the United States. First, it effectively destroyed the Indi-

On August 24, 1814, British troops avenged an American attack on York, Ontario, by marching into Washington, D.C., and setting fire to the Capitol and the White House.

ans' ability to resist American expansion east of the Mississippi. Native Americans were crushed in the North by General William Henry Harrison and in the South by General Andrew Jackson. Abandoned by their British allies, the Indians made the best treaties they could. Reluctantly, they ceded most of their lands north of the Ohio River and in southern and western Alabama to the U.S. government.

Second, the war strengthened America's position relative to Spain in the South and Southwest. It allowed the United States to rewrite its boundaries with Spain and solidify control over the lower Mississippi River and the Gulf of Mexico. Although the United States failed to conquer Canada or defeat the British Empire, it had fought the world's strongest power to a stalemate. Spain recognized the significance of this fact, and in 1819 Spanish leaders abandoned Florida and agreed to an American boundary running clear to the Pacific Ocean.

Third, the Federalist Party never recovered from its opposition to the war. Many Federalists believed that the War of 1812 was really fought to help Napoleon in his struggle against Britain, and they opposed the war by refusing to pay taxes, boycotting war loans, and refusing to furnish troops. In December 1814, delegates from New England gathered in Hartford, Connecticut, where they recommended a series of constitutional amendments to restrict the power of Congress to wage war, regulate commerce, and admit new states. The delegates also supported a

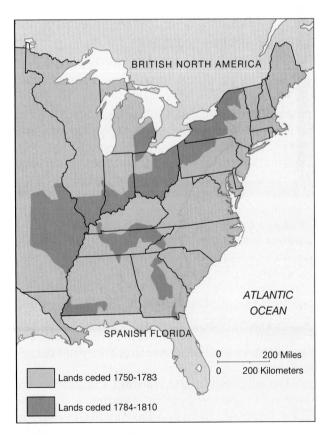

Indian Land Cessions

Before the War of 1812, Native Americans had already ceded much of their land to the federal government.

CHRONOLOGY OF KEY EVENTS

1801 John Marshall becomes chief justice; House of Representatives elects Thomas Jefferson as the third president; Jefferson sends eight ships to enforce a blockade of Tripoli

1802 Republican Congress repeals Judiciary Act of 1801

1803 *Marbury v. Madison* upholds the principle of judicial review; Jefferson purchases the Louisiana Territory from Napoleon for $15 million or 4 cents an acre; war resumes in Europe

1804 Lewis and Clark expedition sets out from St. Louis to explore Louisiana Territory; Vice President Aaron Burr kills Alexander Hamilton in a duel; impeachment of federal district Judge John Pickering and Supreme Court Justice Samuel Chase

1807 Aaron Burr is charged with treason; U.S. naval frigate *Chesapeake* is attacked by British man-of-war *Leopard;* Embargo Act

1809 Embargo Act is repealed; James Madison is sworn in as fourth president; Non-Intercourse Act prohibits trade with Britain and France

1810 Macon's Bill No. 2 reopens trade with Britain and France but says that if either country removes its trade restrictions, the United States will halt trade with the other nation; young Republicans who protest British interference with American shipping and favor expansion win congressional elections

1811 Madison, believing that France had repealed its restrictions on American shipping, stops trade with Britain; Battle of Tippecanoe in Indiana; Congress allows the charter of Bank of the United States to lapse

1812 Congress declares war against Britain; Americans surrender Detroit to British

1813 Captain Oliver Perry defeats British naval forces at the Battle of Lake Erie; General William Henry Harrison defeats British and northwestern Indians at Battle of the Thames

1814 General Andrew Jackson defeats Creek Indians at Battle of Horseshoe Bend; British burn Washington, D.C.; Commander Thomas Macdonough defeats British fleet on Lake Champlain; British invasion is turned back at Plattsburgh, New York; Hartford Convention meets; United States and Britain sign Treaty of Ghent, which ends the War of 1812

1815 Jackson defeats British at Battle of New Orleans

---

one-term president (to break the grip of Virginians on the presidency) and abolition of the three-fifths compromise (which increased the political clout of the South), and talked of seceding if they did not get their way.

The proposals of the **Hartford Convention** became public knowledge at the same time as the terms of the **Treaty of Ghent** and the American victory in the **Battle of New Orleans.** Euphoria over the war's end led many people to brand the Federalists as traitors. The party never recovered from this stigma and disappeared from national politics.

CONCLUSION

Early in the evening of February 11, 1815, the British sloop *Favourite,* flying a flag of truce, entered New York harbor bearing copies of the peace treaty ending the War of 1812. By 8:30 P.M. the news had spread throughout the city. Bells pealed and cannons boomed. Cheering crowds congregated in the streets, carrying candles. Despite bungling, incompetence, and threats of disunion, the new nation had fought Britain to a draw and affirmed its independence. *Niles' Register* summed up the prevailing mood: "Who would not be an American? Long live the Republic! All hail! Last asylum of oppressed humanity."

Between 1800 and 1815, the Jeffersonian Republicans had increased the nation's size, opened new lands to western settlement, and won international respect for American independence. In a climate of war and revolution, the new nation acquired Louisiana and the Southeast, defeated powerful Indian confederations in the Northwest and South, and evicted British troops from American soil. What emerged from this period was a strong, confident, and united nation.

CHAPTER SUMMARY AND KEY POINTS

In this chapter you read about the gestures of conciliation that Thomas Jefferson made to the Federalists after his election; the steps he took to reduce Federalist influence over the judiciary; how he reduced the military budget; and his purchase of Louisiana Territory. You also learned about British and French challenges to American neutrality and the actions that Presidents Jefferson and Madison took to maintain American neutrality. Finally, you learned about the causes and significance of the War of 1812.

- As president, Thomas Jefferson sought to implement his Republican principles, including a frugal, limited government, respect for states' rights, and encouragement for agriculture. He cut military expenditures, paid off the public debt, and repealed many taxes.

- His most important act was the purchase of the Louisiana Territory, which nearly doubled the size of the nation.

- The Jeffersonian era was marked by severe foreign policy challenges, including harassment of American shipping by North African pirates and by the British and French.

- In an attempt to stave off war with Britain and France, the United States attempted various forms of economic coercion.

- In a context of war and revolution, the United States succeeded in acquiring Louisiana and lands along the Gulf Coast and in Florida, defeated powerful Indian confederations in the Old Northwest and the South, and evicted British troops from American soil.

SUGGESTIONS FOR FURTHER READING

Stephen E. Ambrose, *Undaunted Courage: Meriwether Lewis, Thomas Jefferson and the Opening of the American West* (1997). An account of Lewis and Clark's two-and-a-half year expedition up the Missouri River, across the Rocky Mountains, down the Columbia, to the Pacific Ocean, and back.

R. David Edmunds, *Shawnee Prophet* (1983). A biography of Tenskwatawa, the religious leader who formed a pan-Indian coalition.

R. David Edmunds, *Tecumseh and the Quest for Indian Leadership* (1984). A biography of the leader of Indian resistance to American expansion in the Old Northwest.

Joseph J. Ellis, *American Sphinx: The Character of Thomas Jefferson* (1997). This National Book Award–winning study traces Jefferson's life and thought from the drafting of the Declaration of Independence through his retirement at Monticello.

Donald R. Hickey, *The War of 1812* (1989). The origins; military, diplomatic, and political history; and legacy of the War of 1812.

Drew McCoy, *The Elusive Republic: Political Economy in Jeffersonian America* (1980) and *The Last of the Fathers: James Madison and the Republican Legacy* (1989). Offer extensive information on Jeffersonian republicanism.

Merrill Peterson, *Thomas Jefferson and the New Nation* (1970). An especially valuable biography of Thomas Jefferson.

Novels

William Wells Brown, *Clotel; or the President's Daughter: A Narrative of Slave Life in the United States* (1853).

Barbara Chase Riboud, *Sally Hemings* (1979).

Gore Vidal, *Burr* (1973).

MEDIA RESOURCES

Web Sites

Getting the Word
http://www.monticello.org/gettingword/
Seven generations of oral histories of the descendants of Monticello's slaves.

Jefferson's Blood
http://www.pbs.org/wgbh/pages/frontline/shows/jefferson/
The companion site to the PBS Frontline program covering the controversy regarding Thomas Jefferson and his relationship with Sally Hemings, his slave, contains clips from the television show, as well as scientific and historical evidence surrounding the story.

Lewis and Clark
http://www.pbs.org/lewisandclark/
The companion site to the PBS series contains a time line, journals from the expedition, historians' reflections on the expedition, information on the Indian peoples that the expedition encountered, and lesson plans and activities.

Monticello
http://www.monticello.org/house/index.html
This site provides information about Jefferson's home and the people who worked on his plantation.

Thomas Jefferson
http://www.pbs.org/jefferson/
The companion site to the Ken Burns documentary contains documents and classroom activities.

Thomas Jefferson
http://www.pbs.org/jefferson/archives/interviews/frame.htm
Transcripts of interviews with leading authorities on Thomas Jefferson, including Joseph Ellis, John Hope Franklin, and Garry Wills.

Films and Videos

The Buccaneers (1938, 1958). A fanciful swashbuckling tale of pirate Jean Lafitte, who joins forces with General Andrew Jackson to defeat the British at the Battle of New Orleans during the War of 1812.

Jefferson in Paris (1995). Focusing on the mid-1780s, when widower and future president Jefferson replaced Benjamin Franklin as the U.S. representative in France, this film concentrates on his relationships with Maria Cosway and Sally Hemings.

John Paul Jones (1959). Hollywood biography of the American naval hero of the War of 1812.

Lewis and Clark: The Journey of the Corps of Discovery (1997). A historical documentary by Ken Burns.

Old Ironsides (1926). The story of the famous War of 1812 battleship.

Thomas Jefferson (1997). A historical documentary by Ken Burns.

KEY TERMS

Democratic-Republican Party   (p. 204)

Federalist Party   (p. 204)

Republican values   (p. 205)

Bank of the United States   (p. 207)

Judiciary Act of 1801   (p. 207)

Marbury v. Madison   (p. 208)

Judicial review   (p. 208)

Barbary pirates   (p. 208)

Louisiana Purchase   (p. 210)

Lewis and Clark Expedition   (p. 210)

Northern Confederacy   (p. 211)

Continental System   (p. 212)

Orders in Council   (p. 212)

Impressment   (p. 212)

Embargo of 1807   (p. 212)

Non-Intercourse Act   (p. 213)

Macon's Bill No. 2   (p. 213)

War Hawks   (p. 214)

Battle of Tippecanoe   (p. 214)

Battle of Horseshoe Bend   (p. 218)

War of 1812   (p. 218)

Hartford Convention   (p. 220)

Treaty of Ghent   (p. 220)

Battle of New Orleans   (p. 220)

PEOPLE YOU SHOULD KNOW

Alexander Hamilton   (p. 203)

Aaron Burr   (p. 203)

Thomas Jefferson   (p. 204)

John Marshall   (p. 207)

Samuel Chase   (p. 208)

Toussaint Louverture   (p. 210)

Napoleon Bonaparte   (p. 210)

James Madison   (p. 213)

Henry Clay   (p. 214)

John C. Calhoun   (p. 214)

William Henry Harrison   (p. 214)

Tenskwatawa   (p. 214)

Tecumseh   (p. 215)

Andrew Jackson   (p. 218)

REVIEW QUESTIONS

1. In what ways did Thomas Jefferson seek to conciliate the Federalists after he became president? In what ways did he implement his own principles?

2. What steps did President Jefferson take to reduce Federalist influence over the judiciary?

3. Why is *Marbury v. Madison* a landmark in American legal history?

4. How did Britain and France threaten American shipping? What steps did President Jefferson and President Madison take to pressure the French and British to recognize American neutrality?

5. Who favored war with Britain in 1812 and why? Who opposed the war and why?

6. Why did the United States fare poorly during the early stages of the War of 1812? Why was the United States ultimately able to fight Britain to a draw?

7. What was the significance of the War of 1812?

9 Nationalism, Economic Growth, and the Roots of Sectional Conflict, 1815–1824

FRANCIS LOWELL BUILDS A TEXTILE MILL IN MASSACHUSETTS

As the year 1810 began, **Francis Cabot Lowell,** a 36-year-old Boston importer, was bitterly discouraged. His health was failing and, as a result of war between Britain and France and the U.S. policy of discouraging trade by embargo and other legislation, his importing business was in ruins. Uncertain about which way to turn, he decided to travel abroad. While overseas, he discovered his life's calling. In Britain, he marveled at the textile factories at Manchester. Although it was illegal to export textile machinery or plans, Lowell carefully studied the power looms and secretly made sketches of the designs.

Upon his return to Boston in 1813, Lowell constructed textile machinery superior to any he had seen in England. The next year, in Waltham, Massachusetts, he and two associates spent a half million dollars to build the world's first factory able to convert raw cotton into cloth by power machinery under one roof.

To staff his new textile mill, Lowell chose a labor force different from that found in any previous factory. Determined to avoid the misery of England's textile mills, Lowell recruited his labor force not from the families of the poor or from young children but from among the virtuous daughters of New England farmers, who agreed to work in Lowell's mill for two or three years as a way of earning a dowry or an independent income. Because spinning and weaving had long been performed by women in the home, and because young women were willing to work for half or a third the wages of young men, they seemed to offer a perfect solution to the factory's labor needs.

To break down the prejudice against factory work as degrading and immoral, the company announced that it would employ only women of good moral character. It threatened to fire any employee guilty of smoking, drinking, lying, swearing, or any other immoral conduct. To keep a close watch over employees' moral character, the company required employees to attend church and provided boardinghouses where mill girls lived under the careful supervision of housekeepers of impeccable character. Within a few years, the new factory was overwhelmed with job applicants and was "more puzzled to get rid of hands than to employ them."

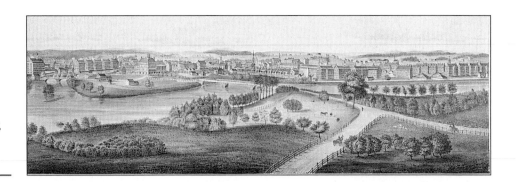

Lowell, Massachusetts, along the Merrimack River, was one of the first American mill towns.

The opening of the Boston Manufacturing Company's textile mill in 1814 marked a symbolic beginning to a new era in the nation's history. For Americans, the end of the War of 1812 unleashed a surge of nationalism, dramatic industrial growth, and rapid expansion to the West. In the years ahead, the United States would undergo an economic transformation, symbolized by improvements in transportation and agriculture, rapid urban growth, and many technological innovations.

In the aftermath of the war, patriotic fervor swept aside bitter political and sectional divisions. Intense nationalism was apparent in the adoption of programs to promote national economic growth, a series of Supreme Court decisions establishing the supremacy of the federal government and expanding the powers of Congress, and the proud assertion of American interest and power in foreign policy.

Paradoxically, it was during these years of nationalism and growth, known to contemporaries as the **Era of Good Feelings,** that sectional and political conflicts were exacerbated. Westward expansion, the rapid growth of industry in the North, and the strengthening of the federal government created problems that dominated American political life for the next 40 years.

THE GROWTH OF AMERICAN NATIONALISM

Early in the summer of 1817, as a conciliatory gesture toward the Federalists who had opposed the War of 1812, **James Monroe,** the nation's fifth president, embarked on a goodwill tour through the North. Everywhere Monroe went, citizens greeted him warmly, holding parades and banquets in his honor. In Federalist Boston, a crowd of 40,000 welcomed the Republican president. **John Quincy Adams,** Monroe's Secretary of State, expressed amazement at the acclaim with which the president was greeted: "Party spirit

has indeed subsided throughout the Union to a degree that I should have thought scarcely possible."

A Federalist newspaper, reflecting on the end of party warfare and the renewal of national unity, called the times the "Era of Good Feelings." The phrase accurately describes the early years of James Monroe's presidency, which were marked by a relative absence of political strife and opposition. With the collapse of the Federalist Party, the Jeffersonian Republicans dominated national politics. Reflecting a new spirit of political unity, the Republicans adopted many of the nationalistic policies of their former opponents, establishing a second national bank, a protective tariff, and improvements in transportation.

To the American people, James Monroe was the popular symbol of the Era of Good Feelings. A dignified and formal man, Monroe was the last president to don the fashions of the eighteenth century. He wore his hair in a powdered wig tied in a queue and dressed himself in a cocked hat, a black broadcloth tailcoat, knee breeches, long white stockings, and buckled shoes. His political values, too, were those of an earlier day. Like George Washington, Monroe worked to eliminate party and sectional rivalries by his attitudes and behavior. He hoped for a country without political parties, governed by leaders chosen on their merits. So great was his popularity that he won a second presidential term by an Electoral College vote of 231 to 1. A new era of national unity appeared to have dawned.

Neo-Hamiltonianism

Traditionally, the Republican Party stood for limited government, states' rights, and a strict interpretation of the Constitution. By 1815, however, the party had adopted former Federalist positions on a national bank, protective tariffs, a standing army, and national roads.

In a series of policy recommendations to Congress at the end of the War of 1812, President Madison revealed the extent to which Republicans had

THE PEOPLE SPEAK

Growing Up Female in the Early Republic

During the early nineteenth century, a new life stage emerged. Called "girlhood," it was a period of relative independence when a growing number of young women attended school or worked outside of a home. In her autobiography, the poet Lucy Larcom describes her girlhood and the growing expectation that young women had to prepare themselves for an independent life. After her father's death when she was 11, Lucy had to leave school and go to work in a Lowell, Massachusetts, textile mill. At first, she found mill work exciting, but she soon felt frustrated by the routine and the lack of education.

> It was not in my mother's nature closely to calculate costs, and in this way there came to be a continually increasing leak in the family purse. The older members of the family did everything they could, but it was not enough. I heard it said one day, in a distressed tone, "The children will have to leave school and go into the mill" . . .
>
> I thought it would be a pleasure to feel that I was not a trouble or a burden or expense to anybody. So I went to my first day's work in the mill with a light heart. The novelty of it made it seem easy, and it really was not hard, just to change the bobbins on the spinning-frames every three quarters of an hour or so, with half a dozen other little girls who were doing the same thing. . . .

> And for a little while it was only a new amusement; I liked it better than going to school and "making believe" I was learning when I was not. . . .
>
> I never cared much for the machinery. The buzzing and hissing and whizzing of pulleys and rollers and spindles and flyers around me often grew tiresome. . . .
>
> There were compensations for being shut in to daily toil so early. The mill itself had its lessons for us. But it was not, and could not be, the right sort of life for a child, and we were happy in the knowledge that, at the longest, our employment was only to be temporary. . . .
>
> But alas! I could not go [to high school]. The little money I could earn—one dollar a week, beside the price of my board—was needed in the family. . . .
>
> In the older times it was seldom said to little girls, as it always has been said to boys, that they ought to have some definite plan, while they were children, what to be and do when they were grown up. There was usually but one path open before them, to become good wives and housekeepers. . . . But girls, as well as boys, must often have been conscious of their own peculiar capabilities,—must have desired to make use of their individual powers. When I was growing up, they had already begun to be encouraged to do so.

Lucy Larcom, *A New England Girlhood* (Boston: Houghton Mifflin and Co., 1889), pp. 42–45, 120–121, 152–157.

---

adopted Federalist policies. He called for a program of national economic development directed by the central government, which included creation of a second Bank of the United States to provide for a stable currency, a protective tariff to encourage industry, a program of internal improvements to facilitate transportation, and a permanent 20,000-man army. In subsequent messages, he recommended an extensive system of roads and canals, new military academies, and establishment of a national university in Washington.

Old-style Republicans, who clung to the Jeffersonian ideal of limited government, dismissed Madison's proposals, but his nationalistic program found enthusiastic support among the new generation of political leaders. Convinced that inadequate roads, the lack of a national bank, and dependence on foreign imports had nearly resulted in a British victory in the war, these young Republicans were eager to use the federal government to promote national economic development.

Henry Clay, John C. Calhoun, and **Daniel Webster** were the principal leaders of the second generation of American political life—the period stretching from the War of 1812 to almost the eve of the Civil War. Each was destined to become the preeminent spokesperson of his region—Clay of the West, Calhoun of the South, Webster of the North. Each possessed extraordinary oratorical talent. Each served in the cabinet as secretary of state or secretary of war. They died within a few months of each other in the early 1850s.

The leader of this group was Henry Clay, a Republican from Kentucky. Clay was one of the so-called War Hawks who had urged President Madison to wage war against Britain. After the war, Clay became one of the strongest proponents of an active

Eager to use the federal government to promote economic development, young politicians Senator Henry Clay of Kentucky (left), Congressman John C. Calhoun of South Carolina (center), and Senator Daniel Webster of Massachusetts (right) supported a protective tariff to stimulate industry, a national bank to promote economic growth, and federally funded aid for transportation. Calhoun, elected to the Senate from South Carolina in 1832, became the nation's leading defender of states' rights, even defending his state's asserted right to "nullify" federal law within its territory.

federal role in national economic development. He used his position as Speaker of the House to advance an economic program that he later called the "**American System**." According to this plan, the federal government would erect a high protective tariff to keep out foreign goods, stimulate the growth of industry, and create a large urban market for western and southern farmers. Revenue from the tariff, in turn, would be used to finance internal improvements of roads and canals to stimulate the growth of the South and West.

Another leader of postwar nationalism was John C. Calhoun, a Republican from South Carolina. Calhoun, like Clay, entered Congress in 1811 and later served with distinction as secretary of war under Monroe and as vice president under both John Quincy Adams and Andrew Jackson. Later, Calhoun became the nation's leading exponent of states' rights, but at this point he seemed to John Quincy Adams, "above all sectional and factious prejudices more than any other statesman of this Union . . ."

The other dominant political figure of the era was Daniel Webster. Nicknamed "the Godlike Daniel" for his magnificent speaking style, Webster argued 168 cases before the Supreme Court. When he entered Congress as a Massachusetts Federalist, he opposed the War of 1812, the creation of a second na-

tional bank, and a protectionist tariff. But, later in his career, after industrial interests supplanted shipping and importing interests in the Northeast, Webster became a staunch defender of the national bank and a high tariff and perhaps was the nation's strongest exponent of nationalism and staunchest critic of states' rights. His argument that the United States was not only a union of states but also a union of people—would later be developed by Abraham Lincoln.

Strengthening American Finances

The severe financial problems created by the War of 1812 led to a wave of support for the creation of a second national bank. The demise of the first Bank of the United States just before the War of 1812 had left the nation ill-equipped to deal with the war's financial demands. To finance the war effort, the government borrowed from private banks at high interest rates. As demand for credit rose, the private banks issued bank notes greatly exceeding the amount of gold or silver that they held. One Rhode Island bank issued $580,000 in notes backed up by only $86.48 in gold and silver. The result was high inflation. Prices jumped 40 percent in just two years.

To make matters worse, the United States government was unable to redeem millions of dollars deposited in private banks. In 1814, after the British burned the nation's capital, many banks outside of New England stopped redeeming their notes in gold or silver. Soldiers, army contractors, and government securities holders went unpaid, and the Treasury temporarily went bankrupt. After the war was over, many banks still refused to resume payments in gold or silver.

In 1816, Congress voted by a narrow margin to charter a **second Bank of the United States** for 20 years and give it the privilege of holding government funds without paying interest for their use. Supporters of a second national bank argued that it would provide a safe place to deposit government funds and a convenient mechanism for transferring money between states. Supporters also claimed that a national bank would strengthen the banking system by refusing to accept the notes issued by over-speculative private banks and ensuring that bank notes were readily exchangeable for gold or silver. Opposition to a national bank came largely from private banking interests and traditional Jeffersonians, who considered a national bank to be unconstitutional and a threat to republican government.

Protecting American Industry

The War of 1812 provided tremendous stimulus to American manufacturing. It encouraged American manufacturers to produce goods previously imported from overseas. By 1816, 100,000 factory workers, two-thirds of them women and children, produced more than $40 million worth of manufactured goods a year. Capital investment in textile manufacturing, sugar refining, and other industries totaled $100 million.

Following the war, however, cheap British imports flooded the nation, threatening to undermine local industries. Congress responded to the flood of imports by continuing a tariff set during the War of 1812 to protect America's infant industries from low-cost competition. With import duties ranging from 15 to 30 percent on cotton, textiles, leather, paper, pig iron, wool, and other goods, the tariff promised to protect America's growing industries from foreign competition. Shipping and farming interests opposed the tariff on the grounds that it would make foreign goods more expensive to buy and would provoke foreign retaliation.

Conquering Space

Before 1812, westward expansion had proceeded slowly. Most Americans were nestled along the Atlantic coastline. More than two-thirds of the new nation's population still lived within 50 miles of the At-

The Conestoga wagon carried people and goods in the rush of westward expansion. Settlers moved west and north along the Ohio and Mississippi rivers before moving to open farmlands further inland.

lantic seaboard, and the center of population rested within 18 miles of Baltimore. Only two roads cut across the Allegheny Mountains, and no more than half a million pioneers had moved as far west as Kentucky, Tennessee, Ohio, or the western portion of Pennsylvania. Cincinnati was a town of 15,000 people; Buffalo and Rochester, New York, did not yet exist. Kickapoo, Miami, Wyandot, and other Native American peoples populated the areas that would become the states of Illinois, Indiana, Michigan, and Wisconsin, while Cherokee, Chickasaw, Choctaw, and Creek considered the future states of Alabama, Mississippi, and western Georgia their territory.

Between 1803, when Ohio was admitted to the Union, and the beginning of the War of 1812, not a single new state was carved out of the west. Thomas Jefferson estimated in 1803 that it would be a thousand years before settlers occupied the region between the Alleghenies and the Mississippi.

The end of the War of 1812 unleashed a rush of pioneers to Indiana, Illinois, Ohio, northern Georgia, western North Carolina, Alabama, Mississippi, Louisiana, and Tennessee. Congress quickly admitted five states to the Union: Louisiana in 1812, Indiana in 1816, Mississippi in 1817, Illinois in 1818, and Alabama in 1819. Pioneers demanded cheaper land and clamored for better transportation to move goods to eastern markets.

Farmers demanded that Congress revise legislation to make it easier to obtain land. Originally, Congress viewed federal lands as a source of revenue, and public land policies reflected that view. Under a policy adopted in 1785 and reaffirmed in 1796, the

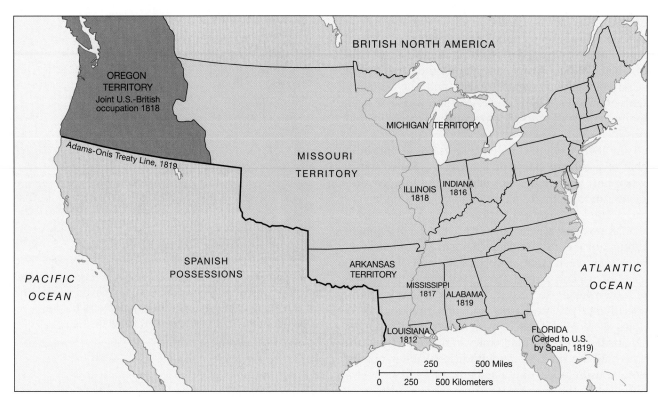

The United States in 1819

federal government only sold land in blocks of at least 640 acres. Although the minimum allotment was reduced to 320 acres in 1800, federal land policy continued to retard sales and concentrate ownership in the hands of a few large land companies and wealthy speculators.

In 1820 Congress sought to make it easier for farmers to purchase homesteads in the west by selling land in small lots suitable for operation by a family. Congress reduced the minimum allotment offered for sale from 320 to 80 acres. The minimum price per acre fell from $2 to $1.25. The second Bank of the United States encouraged land purchases by liberally extending credit. The result was a boom in land sales. For a decade, the government sold approximately a million acres of land annually.

Westward expansion also created a demand to expand and improve the nation's roads and canals. In 1808 Albert Gallatin, Thomas Jefferson's Treasury secretary, proposed a $20 million program of canal and road construction. As a result of state and sectional jealousies and charges that federal aid to transportation was unconstitutional, the federal government funded only a single turnpike, the National Road, at this time stretching from Cumberland, Maryland, to

Wheeling, Virginia (later West Virginia), but much later extending westward from Baltimore through Ohio and Indiana to Illinois.

In 1816 John C. Calhoun introduced a new proposal for federal aid for road and canal construction. Failure to link the nation together with an adequate system of transportation would, Calhoun warned, lead "to the greatest of calamities—disunion." "Let us," he exclaimed, "bind the republic together with a perfect system of roads and canals. Let us conquer space." Narrowly, Calhoun's proposal passed. But on the day before he left office, Madison vetoed the bill on constitutional grounds.

Despite this setback, Congress did adopt major parts of the nationalist neo-Hamiltonian economic program. It had established a second Bank of the United States to provide a stable means of issuing money and a safe depository for federal funds. It had enacted a tariff to raise duties on foreign imports and guard American industries from low-cost competition. It had also instituted a new public land policy to encourage western settlement. In short, Congress had translated the spirit of national pride and unity that the nation felt after the War of 1812 into a legislative program that placed the national interest above narrow sectional interests.

Judicial Nationalism

The decisions of the Supreme Court also reflected the nationalism of the postwar period. With **John Marshall** as chief justice, the Supreme Court greatly expanded its powers, prestige, and independence. When Marshall took office, in the last days of John Adams's administration in 1801, the Court met in the basement of the Capitol and was rarely in session for more than six weeks a year. Since its creation in 1789, the Court had only decided 100 cases.

In a series of critical decisions, the Supreme Court greatly expanded its authority. As previously noted (p. 208), *Marbury v. Madison* (1803) established the Supreme Court as the final arbiter of the Constitution and its power to declare acts of Congress unconstitutional. *Fletcher v. Peck* (1810) declared the Court's power to void state laws. *Martin v. Hunter's Lessee* (1816) gave the Court the power to review decisions by state courts.

After the War of 1812, Marshall wrote a series of decisions that further strengthened the powers of the national government. *McCulloch v. Maryland* (1819) established the constitutionality of the second Bank of the United States and denied to states the right to exert independent checks on federal authority. The case involved a direct attack on the second Bank of the United States by the state of Maryland, which had placed a tax on the bank notes of all banks not chartered by the state.

In his decision, Marshall dealt with two fundamental questions. The first was whether the federal government had the power to incorporate a bank. The answer to this question, the Court ruled, was yes because the Constitution granted Congress implied powers to do whatever was "necessary and proper" to carry out its constitutional powers—in this case, the power to manage a currency. In a classic statement of "broad" or "loose" construction of the Constitution, Marshall said, "Let the end be legitimate, let it be within the scope of the Constitution, and all means which are plainly adapted to that end, which are not prohibited, but consistent with the letter and spirit of the Constitution, are constitutional."

The second question raised was whether a state had the power to tax a branch of the Bank of the United States. The Court said no. The Constitution, the Court asserted, created a new government with sovereign power over the states. "The power to tax involves the power to destroy," the Court declared, and the states do not have the right to exert an independent check on the authority of the federal government.

During the postwar period, the Supreme Court also encouraged economic competition and development. In *Dartmouth v. Woodward* (1819) the Court promoted business growth by establishing the principle of sanctity of contracts. The case involved the efforts of the New Hampshire legislature to alter the charter of Dartmouth College, which had been granted by George III in 1769. The Court held that a charter was a valid contract protected by the Constitution and that states do not have the power to alter contracts unilaterally.

John Marshall established many basic principles of constitutional law in the 34 years he served as chief justice of the United States. Marshall and the six other members of the Supreme Court appear on the podium in this 1822 painting of the House of Representatives by Samuel F. B. Morse.

In *Gibbons v. Ogden* (1824), the Court broadened federal power over interstate commerce. The Court overturned a New York law that had awarded a monopoly over steamboat traffic on the Hudson River, ruling that the Constitution had specifically given Congress the power to regulate commerce.

Under John Marshall, the Supreme Court became the final arbiter of the constitutionality of federal and state laws. The Court's role in shifting sovereign power from the states to the federal government was an important development. It would become increasingly difficult in the future to argue that the union was a creation of the states, that states could exert an independent check on federal government authority, or that Congress's powers were limited to those specifically conferred by the Constitution.

Defending American Interests in Foreign Affairs

The War of 1812 stirred a new nationalistic spirit in foreign affairs. In 1815, this spirit resulted in a decision to end the raids by the **Barbary pirates** on American commercial shipping in the Mediterranean. For 17 years the United States had paid tribute to the ruler of Algiers. In March 1815, Captain **Stephen Decatur** and a fleet of 10 ships sailed into the Mediterranean, where they captured two Algerian gunboats, towed the ships into Algiers harbor, and threatened to bombard the city. As a result, all the North African states agreed to treaties releasing American prisoners without ransom, ending all demands for American tribute, and providing compensation for American vessels that had been seized.

After successfully defending American interests in North Africa, Monroe acted to settle old grievances with the British. Britain and the United States had left a host of issues unresolved in the peace treaty ending the War of 1812, including disputes over boundaries, trading and fishing rights, and rival claims to the Oregon region. The two governments moved quickly to settle these issues. The Rush-Bagot Agreement (1817) removed most military ships from the Great Lakes. In 1818, Britain granted American fishermen the right to fish in eastern Canadian waters, agreed to the 49th parallel as the boundary between the United States and Canada from Minnesota to the Rocky Mountains, and consented to joint occupation of the Oregon region.

The critical foreign policy issue facing the United States after the War of 1812 was the fate of Spain's crumbling New World empire. A source of particular concern was Florida, which was still under Spanish control. Pirates, fugitive slaves, and Native Americans used Florida as a sanctuary and as a jumping off point for raids on settlements in Georgia. In December 1817, to end these incursions, Monroe authorized General **Andrew Jackson** to lead a punitive expedition against the Seminole Indians in Florida. Jackson not only attacked the Seminoles and destroyed their villages but also overthrew the Spanish governor. He also court-martialed and executed two British citizens whom he accused of inciting the Seminoles to commit atrocities against Americans.

Jackson's actions provoked a furor in Washington. Spain protested Jackson's acts and demanded that he be punished. Secretary of War John C. Calhoun and other members of Monroe's cabinet urged the president to reprimand Jackson for acting without specific authorization. In Congress, Henry Clay called for Jackson's censure. Secretary of State Adams, however, saw in Jackson's actions an opportunity to wrest Florida from Spain.

Instead of apologizing for Jackson's conduct, Adams declared that the Florida raid was a legitimate act of self-defense. Adams informed the Spanish government that it would either have to police Florida effectively or cede it to the United States. Convinced that American annexation was inevitable, Spain ceded Florida to the United States in the Adams-Onis Treaty of 1819. In return, the United States agreed to honor $5 million in damage claims by Americans against Spain and renounced, at least temporarily, its claims to Texas.

At the same time, European intervention in the Pacific Northwest and Latin America became a new source of anxiety for American leaders. In 1821, Russia claimed control of the entire Pacific coast from Alaska to Oregon and closed the area to foreign shipping. This development coincided with rumors that Spain, with the help of its European allies, was planning to reconquer its former colonies in Latin America. European intervention threatened British as well as American interests. Not only did Britain have a flourishing trade with Latin America, which would decline if Spain regained its New World colonies, but it also occupied the Oregon region jointly with the United States. In 1823, British Foreign Minister George Canning proposed that the United States and Britain jointly announce their opposition to further European intervention in the Americas.

Monroe initially regarded the British proposal favorably. His secretary of state, John Quincy Adams, however, opposed a joint Anglo-American declaration. Secure in the knowledge that the British would use their fleet to support the American position, Adams convinced President Monroe to make an independent declaration of American policy. In his annual message to Congress in 1823, Monroe outlined the principles that have become known as the **Monroe Doctrine.** He announced that the Western Hemisphere was henceforth closed to any further European colonization, declaring that the United States would regard any attempt by European nations "to extend their system to any portion of this hemisphere as dangerous to our peace and safety." European countries with possessions in the hemisphere—Britain, France, the Netherlands, and Spain—were warned not to attempt expansion. Monroe also said that the United States would not interfere in internal European affairs.

For the American people, the Monroe Doctrine was the proud symbol of American hegemony in the Western Hemisphere. Unilaterally, the United States had defined its rights and interests in the New World. It is true that during the first half of the nineteenth century the United States lacked the military power to enforce the Monroe Doctrine and depended on the British navy to deter European intervention in the Americas, but the nation had clearly warned the European powers that any threat to American security would provoke American retaliation.

THE GROWTH OF THE AMERICAN ECONOMY

At the beginning of the nineteenth century, the United States was an overwhelmingly rural and agricultural nation. Most Americans lived on farms or in villages with fewer than 2500 inhabitants. The nation's population was small and scattered over a vast geographical area—just 5.3 million, compared to Britain's 15 million and France's 27 million.

Transportation and communications had changed little over the previous half-century. A coach ride between Boston and New York took three days. South of the Mason-Dixon line, except for a single stagecoach that traveled between Charleston and Savannah, no public transportation of any kind could be found.

American houses, clothing, and agricultural methods were surprisingly primitive. Fifty miles inland, half the houses were log cabins, lacking even glass windows. Farmers planted their crops in much the same way as had their parents and grandparents. Few farmers practiced crop rotation or used fertilizers or drained fields. They made plows out of wood, allowed their swine to run loose, and left their cattle outside except on the coldest nights.

Manufacturing was also quite backward. In rural areas, farm families grew their own food, produced their own soap and candles, wove their own blankets, and constructed their own furniture. The leading manufacturing industries, iron making, textiles, and clothes making, employed only about 15,000 people in mills or factories.

After the War of 1812, however, the American economy grew at an astonishing rate. The 25 years that followed Andrew Jackson's victory at New Orleans represented a critical period for the nation's economic growth, during which the United States overcame a series of serious obstacles that had stood in the way of sustained economic expansion. Improved transportation, rapid urbanization, increased farm productivity, and technological innovation transformed a rural, agricultural nation into one of the world's industrial leaders.

Accelerating Transportation

At the outset of the nineteenth century, the lack of reliable, low-cost transportation was a major barrier to American industrial development. The stagecoach, slow and cumbersome, was the main form of transportation. Twelve passengers, crowded along with their bags and parcels, traveled at just 4 miles an hour. In Connecticut and Massachusetts, Sunday travel was still forbidden by law.

Wretched roads plagued travelers. Larger towns had roads paved with cobblestones, but most roads were simply dirt paths left muddy and rutted by rain. The presence of tree stumps in the middle of many roads posed a serious obstacle to carriages.

The main form of public transportation in the early nineteenth century was the stagecoach. Unprotected from the weather, 12 passengers traveled with baggage between their knees at only 4 miles per hour.

In 1807, Robert Fulton demonstrated the feasibility of steam travel by launching his 160-ton side-wheeler, the *Clermont*, on the Hudson River.

Charles Dickens aptly described American roads as a "series of alternate swamps and gravel pits."

In 1791 builders first inaugurated a new era in transportation with the construction of a 66-mile-long turnpike between Philadelphia and Lancaster, Pennsylvania. This stimulated a craze for toll road construction. By 1811, 135 private companies in New York had invested $7.5 million in 1500 miles of road. By 1838, Pennsylvania had invested $37 million to build 2200 miles of turnpikes.

Despite the construction of turnpikes, the cost of transporting freight over land remained high. Because water transportation was cheaper, farmers often shipped their produce down the Mississippi, Potomac, or Hudson rivers by flatboat or raft. Un-

fortunately, water transportation was slow and few vessels were capable of going very far upstream. The trip downstream from Pittsburgh to New Orleans took a month; the trip upstream against the current took four months. Steam power offered the obvious solution, and inventors built at least 16 steamships before **Robert Fulton** successfully demonstrated the commercial practicality of steam navigation. In 1807 he sailed a 160-ton side-wheeler, the *Clermont*, 150 miles from New York City to Albany in only 32 hours. "Fulton's folly," as critics mocked it, opened a new era of faster and cheaper water transportation.

The building of canals further revolutionized water transportation. In 1825, the state of New York opened the **Erie Canal**, which connected the Great Lakes to the Atlantic Ocean. The canal was a stupendous engineering achievement. Three thousand workers, using hand labor, toiled for eight years to build the canal. They built 84 locks, each 15 feet wide and 90 feet long, to raise or lower barges 10 feet at a time.

Built almost entirely with state and local funding, "Clinton's Ditch"—nicknamed after the Erie Canal's chief backer, Governor DeWitt Clinton—sparked an economic revolution. Before the canal was built, it cost $100 and took 20 days to transport a ton of freight from Buffalo to New York City. After the canal was opened, the cost fell to $5 a ton and transit time was reduced to 6 days. By 1827, as a result of the canal, wheat from central New York State could be bought for less in Savannah, Georgia, than wheat grown in Georgia's interior.

The greatest engineering feat of the Erie Canal took place at the town of Lockport, where seven locks, each capable of raising or lowering a barge 10 feet, were constructed.

The success of the Erie Canal led other states to embark on expensive programs of canal building. Pennsylvanians spent $10 million to build a canal between Philadelphia and Pittsburgh. The states of Illinois, Indiana, and Ohio launched projects to connect the Ohio and Mississippi rivers to the Great Lakes. By 1840, 3326 miles of canals had been dug at a cost of $125 million.

Cities like Baltimore and Boston that were unable to reach the West with canals experimented with the railroad. Early railroads suffered from nagging engineering problems and vociferous opposition. Brakes were wholly inadequate, consisting of wooden blocks operated by a foot pedal. Boilers exploded so frequently that passengers had to be protected by bales of cotton. Engine sparks set fire to fields and burned unprotected passengers. One English traveler counted 13 holes burned in her dress after a short ride.

Vested interests, including turnpike and bridge companies, stagecoaches, ferries, and canals, sought laws to prohibit trains from carrying freight. A group of Boston doctors warned that bumps produced by trains traveling at 15 or 20 miles an hour would lead to many cases of "concussion of the brain." An Ohio school board declared that "such things as railroads . . . are impossibilities and rank infidelity."

Nonetheless, it quickly became clear after 1830 that railroads were destined to become the nation's chief means of moving freight. During the 1830s, construction companies laid down 3328 miles of track, roughly equal to all the miles of canals in the country. With an average speed of 10 miles an hour, railroads were faster than stagecoaches, canal boats, and steamboats, and, unlike water-going vessels, could travel in any season.

The transportation revolution sharply reduced the cost of shipping goods to market and stimulated agriculture and industry. New roads, canals, and railroads speeded the pace of commerce and strengthened ties between the East and West.

Speeding Communications

Poor communications had also impeded development. During the 1790s, it took 3 weeks for a letter to travel from New York to Cincinnati or Detroit and 4 weeks to arrive in New Orleans. In 1799 it took 1 week for news of George Washington's death to reach New York City from Virginia.

By the early 1830s, a decade before Samuel F. B. Morse invented the telegraph, the transmission of information had improved considerably as a result of improved roads and faster sailing ships. In 1831 it took just 15.5 hours for the text of Andrew Jackson's State of the Union address to travel from Washington to New York. By 1841 a letter traveled between New York and New Orleans in 9 days and between New York and Cincinnati in 5 days—three times faster than in 1815.

The volume of information transmitted also increased considerably. In 1790 the United States had just 92 newspapers, with a total annual circulation of less than 4 million. By 1820 the number of papers published had jumped to 512, with an annual circulation of 50 million. When Alexis de Tocqueville, a French observer, visited the United States in 1831, he was shocked at the amount of information available even in frontier regions: "I do not think that in the most enlightened rural districts of France there is an intellectual movement either so rapid or on such a scale as in this wilderness."

Transforming American Law

The growth of an industrial economy in the United States required a shift in American law. At the beginning of the nineteenth century, American law was rooted in concepts that reflected the values of a slowly changing, agricultural society. The law presumed that goods and services had a just price, independent of supply and demand. Courts forbade many forms of competition and innovation in the name of a stable society. Courts and judges legally protected monopolies and prevented lenders from charging high rates of interest. The law allowed property owners to sue for damages if a mill built upstream flooded their land or impeded their water supply. After 1815, however, the American legal system favored economic growth, profit, and entrepreneurial enterprise.

By the 1820s, courts, particularly in the Northeast, had begun to abandon many traditional legal doctrines that stood in the way of a competitive market economy. Courts dropped older doctrines that assumed that goods and services had an objective price, independent of supply and demand. Courts rejected many usury laws, which limited interest rates, and increasingly held that only the market could determine interest rates or prices or the equity of a contract.

To promote rapid economic growth, courts and state legislatures gave new powers and privileges to private firms. Companies building roads, bridges, canals, and other public works were given the power to appropriate land; private firms were allowed to avoid legal penalties for fires, floods, or noise they caused on the grounds that the companies served a public purpose. Courts also reduced the liability of companies for injuries to their own employees, ruling that an injured party had to prove negligence or carelessness on the part of an employer to collect damages. The legal barriers to economic expansion had been struck down.

Resistance to Technological Innovation

At the beginning of the nineteenth century, the United States lagged far behind Europe in the practical application of science and technology. There was probably just one steam engine in regular operation in the United States in 1800, one hundred years after simple engines had first been used in Europe. Inventors like Oliver Evans, who opened the first automated flour mill in 1785, and Samuel Fitch, who created the first American steamboat in 1786, failed because they were unable to finance their projects or persuade the public to use their inventions.

The inadequate state of higher education also slowed technological innovation. At the beginning of the nineteenth century, Harvard, the nation's most famous college, graduated just 39 men a year, no more than it had graduated in 1720. Harvard's entire undergraduate faculty consisted of the college president, a professor of theology, a professor of mathematics, a professor of Hebrew, and four tutors. All the nation's libraries put together contained barely 50,000 volumes.

By the 1820s, however, the United States had largely overcome resistance to technological innovation. When Friedrich List, a German traveler, visited the United States in the 1820s, he was astonished by the amount of public interest in technology. "Everything new is quickly introduced here," List wrote. "There is no clinging to old ways; the moment an American hears the word 'invention' he pricks up his ears."

How had Americans overcome resistance to technological innovation? The answer lies in the efforts of literally hundreds of inventors, tinkerers, and amateur scientists, who transformed European ideas into practical technologies. Their inventions inspired in Americans a boundless faith in technology.

Early American technology was pioneered largely by self-taught amateurs, whose zeal and self-assurance led them to create inventions that trained European scientists did not attempt. As early as the 1720s it was known that electricity could be conducted along a wire to convey messages, but it was not until 1844 that an American artist and inventor named **Samuel F. B. Morse** demonstrated the practicality of the telegraph and devised a workable code

for sending messages. A Frenchman built the first working steamship in 1783, but it was 24 years later that Robert Fulton, an American, produced the first commercially successful steamship. Eighteenth-century Europeans knew that ether would induce unconsciousness, but it was not until 1842 that a Georgia surgeon named Crawford Long used ether as an anesthetic.

Early Industrialization

In the 1820s and 1830s, America became the world's leader in adopting mechanization, standardization, and mass production. Manufacturers started to adopt labor-saving machinery that allowed workers to produce more goods at lower costs. So impressed were foreigners with these methods of manufacture that they called them the **American system of production.**

The single most important figure in the development of the American system of production was **Eli Whitney,** the inventor of the cotton gin. In 1798, Whitney persuaded the U.S. government to award him a contract for 10,000 muskets to be delivered within two years. Until then, rifles had been manufactured by skilled artisans, who made individual parts by hand and then carefully fitted the pieces together. When Whitney made his offer, the federal arsenal at Springfield, Massachusetts, was capable of producing only 245 muskets in two years. Whitney's idea was to develop precision machinery that would allow a worker with little manual skill to manufacture identical gun parts that would be interchangeable from one gun to another. The first year he produced 500 muskets.

Other industries soon adopted the American system of production. As early as 1800 manufacturers of wooden clocks began to use interchangeable parts. Makers of sewing machines used mass production techniques as early as 1846, and the next year, manufacturers mechanized the production of farm machinery.

Innovation was not confined to manufacturing. During the years following the War of 1812, American agriculture underwent a transformation nearly as profound and far-reaching as the revolution taking place in industry. No longer cut off from markets by the high cost of transportation, farmers began to grow larger crop surpluses and to specialize in cash crops. A growing demand for cotton for England's textile mills led to the introduction of long-staple cotton from the West Indies into the islands and lowlands of Georgia and South Carolina. Eli Whitney's invention of the cotton gin in 1793—which permitted an individual to clean 50 pounds of short-staple cotton in a single day, 50 times more than could be cleaned by hand—made it practical to produce the crop in the South. Other cash crops raised by southern farmers included rice, sugar, flax for linen, and hemp for rope fibers. In the Northeast, the growth of mill towns and urban centers created a growing demand for hogs, cattle, sheep, corn, wheat, wool, butter, milk, cheese, fruit, vegetables, and hay to feed horses.

As production for the market increased, farmers began to demand improved farm technology. In 1793 Charles Newbold, a New Jersey farmer, spent his entire fortune of $30,000 developing an efficient cast-iron plow. Farmers refused to use it, fearing that iron would poison the soil and cause weeds to grow. Twenty years later, a Scipio, New York, farmer named Jethro Wood patented an improved iron plow made out of interchangeable parts. Unlike wooden plows, which required two people and four oxen to plow an acre in a day, Wood's cast-iron plow allowed one person and one yoke of oxen to plow the same area. Demand was so great that manufacturers infringed on Wood's patents and produced thousands of copies of this new plow yearly.

A shortage of farm labor encouraged many farmers to adopt labor-saving machinery. Before the introduction in 1803 of the cradle scythe—a rake used to cut and gather up grain and deposit it in even piles—a farmer could not harvest more than half an acre a day. The horse rake—a device introduced in 1820 to mow hay—allowed a single farmer to perform the

This painting, dated 1832–1834, by Russell Smith depicts a saltworks, one of the leading industrial enterprises of the early nineteenth century.

work of 8 to 10 people. The invention in 1836 of a mechanical thresher, used to separate the wheat from the chaff, helped to halve the hours of labor required to produce an acre of wheat.

By 1830 the roots of America's future industrial growth had been firmly planted. Back in 1807, the nation had just 15 or 20 cotton mills, containing approximately 8000 spindles. By 1831 the number of spindles in use totaled nearly a million and a quarter. Factory production made household manufacture of shoes, clothing, textiles, and farm implements obsolete. The United States was well on its way to becoming one of the world's leading manufacturing nations.

The Growth of Cities

At the beginning of the nineteenth century, the United States was a nation of farms and rural villages. Only four cities had more than 10,000 inhabitants. Boston, which in 1800 contained just 25,000 inhabitants, looked much as it had before the Revolution. Its streets, still paved with cobblestones, were unlighted at night. New York City was so small that Wall Street (which is located near Manhattan Island's tip) was considered to be uptown and Broadway was a country drive. New York City's entire police force, which only patrolled at night, consisted of 2 captains, 2 deputies, and 72 assistants.

During the 1820s and 1830s, the nation's cities grew at an extraordinary rate. The urban population increased 60 percent a decade, five times as fast as that of the country as a whole. In 1810, New York City's population was less than 100,000. Two decades

With Eli Whitney's cotton gin, the amount of cotton fiber that a slave could separate from seed each day increased from 1 pound to 50 pounds.

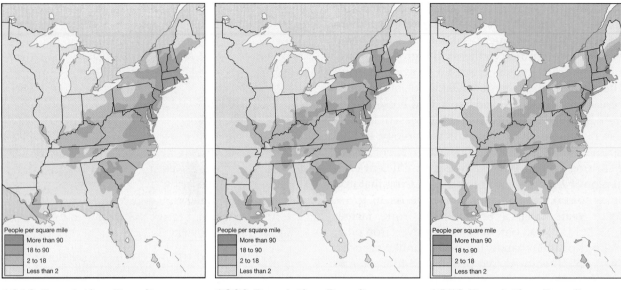

1810 Population Density   **1820 Population Density**   **1830 Population Density**

later it was more than 200,000. Western cities grew particularly fast.

The chief cause of the increase was the migration of sons and daughters away from farms and villages. The growth of commerce drew thousands of farm children to the cities to work as bookkeepers, clerks, and salespeople. The expansion of factories demanded thousands of laborers, mechanics, teamsters, and operatives. The need of those in rural areas to use services available only in urban centers also promoted the growth of cities, particularly in the West. Farmers needed their grain milled and their livestock butchered. In response, a grain processing and meat-packing industry sprouted up in "Porkopolis," Cincinnati. Manufacturers in Lexington produced hemp sacks and ropes for Kentucky farmers, and Louisville businesses cured and marketed tobacco.

Pittsburgh's growth illustrates these processes at work. Frontier farmers needed products made of iron, such as nails, horseshoes, and farm implements. Pittsburgh lay near western Pennsylvania's coalfields. Because it was cheaper to bring the iron ore to the coal supply for smelting than to transport the coal to the side of the iron mine, Pittsburgh became a major iron producer. Iron foundries and blacksmith shops proliferated. So did glass factories, which required large amounts of fuel to provide heat for glassblowing. As a result, Pittsburgh's population tripled between 1810 and 1830.

As urban areas grew many problems were exacerbated, including the absence of clean drinking water, the lack of cheap public transportation, and, most importantly, poor sanitation. Sanitation problems led to heavy urban mortality rates and frequent epidemics of typhoid, dysentery, typhus, cholera, and yellow fever.

Most city dwellers used outdoor privies, which emptied into vaults and cesspools that sometimes leaked into the soil and contaminated the water supply. Kitchen wastes were thrown into ditches; refuse was thrown into trash piles by the side of the streets. Every horse in a city deposited as much as 20 pounds of manure and urine on the streets each day. To help remove the garbage and refuse, many cities allowed packs of dogs, goats, and pigs to scavenge freely.

Although elite urbanites began to enjoy such amenities as indoor toilets, the cities' poorest inhabitants lived in slums. On New York's Lower East Side, many men, women, and children were crowded into damp, unlighted, ill-ventilated cellars with 6 to 20 persons living in a single room. Despite growing public awareness of the problems of slums and urban poverty, conditions remained unchanged for several generations.

THE GROWTH OF POLITICAL FACTIONALISM AND SECTIONALISM

The Era of Good Feelings began with a burst of nationalistic fervor. The economic program adopted by Congress, including a national bank and a protective tariff, reflected the growing feeling of national unity. The Supreme Court promoted the spirit of nationalism by establishing the principle of federal supremacy. Industrialization and improvements in transportation also added to the sense of national unity by contributing to the nation's economic strength and independence and by linking the West and the East together.

But this same period also witnessed the emergence of growing factional divisions in politics, including a deepening sectional split between the North and South. A severe economic depression between 1819 and 1822 provoked bitter division over questions of banking and tariffs. Geographic expansion exposed latent tensions over the morality of slavery and the balance of economic power. Political issues that arose during the Era of Good Feelings dominated American politics for the next 40 years.

The Panic of 1819

In 1819 a financial panic swept across the country. The growth in trade that followed the War of 1812 came to an abrupt halt. Unemployment mounted, banks failed, mortgages were foreclosed, and agricultural prices fell by half. Investment in western lands collapsed.

In Richmond, property values fell by half. In Philadelphia, 1808 individuals were committed to debtors' prison. In Boston, the figure was 3500.

For the first time in American history, the problem of urban poverty commanded public attention. In New York in 1819, the Society for the Prevention of Pauperism counted 8000 paupers out of a population of 120,000. The next year, the figure climbed to 13,000. Fifty thousand people were unemployed or irregularly employed in New York, Philadelphia, and Baltimore, and one foreign observer estimated that half a million people were jobless nationwide. To address the problem of destitution, newspapers appealed for old clothes and shoes for the poor, and churches and municipal governments distributed soup. Baltimore set up 12 soup kitchens in 1820 to give food to the poor.

The **Panic of 1819** had several causes, including a dramatic decline in cotton prices, a contraction of credit by the Bank of the United States designed to curb inflation, an 1817 congressional order requiring hard-currency payments for land purchases, and the closing of many factories due to foreign competition.

The panic unleashed a storm of popular protest. Many debtors agitated for "stay laws" to provide relief from debts as well as the abolition of debtors' prisons. Manufacturing interests called for increased protection from foreign imports, but a growing number of Southerners believed that high protective tariffs, which raised the cost of imported goods and reduced the flow of international trade, were the root of their troubles. Many people clamored for a reduction in the cost of government and pressed for sharp reductions in federal and state budgets. Others, particularly in the South and West, blamed the panic on the nation's banks and particularly the tight-money policies of the Bank of the United States.

By 1823 the panic was over. But it left a lasting imprint on American politics. The panic led to demands for the democratization of state constitutions, an end to restrictions on voting and officeholding, and heightened hostility toward banks and other "privileged" corporations and monopolies. The panic also exacerbated tensions within the Republican Party and aggravated sectional tensions as Northerners pressed for higher tariffs while Southerners abandoned their support of nationalistic economic programs.

The Missouri Crisis

In the midst of the panic, a crisis over slavery erupted with stunning suddenness. It was, Thomas Jefferson wrote, like "a firebell in the night." Missouri's application for statehood ignited the crisis, and the issue raised involved the status of slavery west of the Mississippi River.

East of the Mississippi, the Mason-Dixon line and the Ohio River formed a boundary between the North and South. States south of this line were slave states; states north of this line had either abolished slavery or adopted gradual emancipation policies. West of the Mississippi, however, no clear line demarcated the boundary between free and slave territory.

Representative James Tallmadge, a New York Republican, provoked the crisis in February 1819 by introducing an amendment to restrict slavery in Missouri as a condition of statehood. The amendment prohibited the further introduction of slaves into Missouri and provided for emancipation of all children of slaves at the age of 25. Voting along ominously sectional lines, the House approved the Tallmadge Amendment, but the amendment was defeated in the Senate.

Southern and northern politicians alike responded with fury. Southerners condemned the Tallmadge proposal as part of a northeastern plot to dominate the government. They declared the United States to be a union of equals, claiming that Congress had no power to place special restrictions upon a state.

Talk of disunion and civil war was rife. Senator Freeman Walker of Georgia envisioned "civil war . . . a brother's sword crimsoned with a brother's blood." Northern politicians responded with equal

Denmark Vesey and the Slave Conspiracy of 1822

"Do not open your lips! Die silent, as you shall see me do." Speaking from the gallows, Peter Poyas soon met his death with stoic dignity—as did five others on the second day of July in 1822. Among the five was Denmark Vesey, whose quiet composure at death reflected the steely courage with which he had led blacks in and around Charleston, South Carolina, in plotting insurrection. As their trials revealed, for over a year Vesey and his lieutenants had planned, recruited, and hoarded the provisions for the fight. Only betrayal by a few slaves had prevented what could well have become the bloodiest slave revolt in America's history.

Many whites were surprised at the revelation of Vesey's leadership. In their eyes he seemed to have few grievances. Born in the late 1760s in either Africa or the Caribbean, he served as a slave to Captain Joseph Vesey, a Bermuda slave trader who settled in Charleston in 1783 as a slave broker and ship merchandiser. In 1800 Denmark Vesey won $1500 in the East Bay Lottery. He then purchased his freedom for $600 and opened a carpentry shop; by 1817 he had amassed savings of several thousand dollars. He was literate and well traveled. He had once been offered the opportunity to return to Africa as a free man and rejected it. "What did he have to be upset about?" many whites must have asked. Well, for one thing, his wife and several of his children were still in bondage. He also deeply resented white interference in the lives of free blacks as well as slaves.

Vesey was a proud man and frequently rebuked friends who acquiesced to such traditional displays of deference as bowing to whites on the street. One remembered Vesey telling him "all men were born equal, and that he was surprised that anyone would degrade himself by such conduct; that he would never cringe to whites, nor ought any who had the feelings of a man."

As in cities throughout the nation, blacks in Charleston were meeting oppression by forging their own institutions and creating self-affirming communities. A key part of this process was religious independence. At the close of the War of 1812 black Methodists in Charleston outnumbered white ones 10 to 1. After an unsuccessful attempt by blacks to control their destinies within the white church, Morris Brown went to Philadelphia and was ordained by the African Methodist Episcopal church. In 1818, following a dispute over a burial ground, more than three-fourths of the 6000 black Methodists of Charleston withdrew from the white-led churches. Morris Brown was appointed bishop, and the African Church of Charleston was established.

White authorities regarded such independent churches as possible seedbeds of radicalism; therefore, they harassed church meetings and jailed church leaders. Beginning in 1820 legislation was passed to reduce the free black population of South Carolina. Finally, in 1821, the city of Charleston closed the Hampstead Church, which had been the leader of the independent church movement—and which included Denmark Vesey among its members. That closing became the spark that ignited Vesey to action. He began holding meetings, often in his own home, with other members of the congregation, including Rolla Bennett, "Gullah Jack" Pritchard, Monday Gell, and Ned and Peter Poyas. They became the nucleus of what came to be called the Vesey Conspiracy.

Later testimony indicates that Vesey was well aware of several recent events that convinced him that the tide of history was changing. Foremost was the successful slave rebellion in Haiti that began in 1791. Vesey "was in the habit of reading to me all the passages in the newspapers that related to St. Domingo, and apparently every pamphlet he could lay his hands on that had any connection with slavery," one rebel testified. Vesey was also knowledgeable about the debates over Missouri statehood; the same rebel reported, "He one day brought me a speech which he told me had been delivered in congress by a Mr. [Rufus] King on the subject of slavery; he told me this Mr. King was the black man's friend, that he, Mr. King, had declared . . . that slavery was a great disgrace to the country."

Vesey used religion as a potent force to spur blacks to join him in armed rebellion. At almost every meeting he "read to us from the Bible, how the children of Israel were delivered out of Egypt from bondage." He also frequently used the passage: "Behold the day of the Lord cometh, and thy spoil shall be divided in the midst of thee. For I shall gather all nations against Jerusalem to battle; and the city shall be taken." In addition, "Gullah Jack," born in Africa, was known as a powerful conjurer, and many were convinced his power could protect them from harm.

CLASS No. 1.

Comprises those prisoners who were found guilty and executed.

Prisoners Names.	Owners' Names.	Time of Commit.	How Disposed of.
Peter	James Poyas	June 18	
Ned	Gov. T. Bennett,	do.	Hanged on Tuesday
Rolla	do.	do.	the 2d July, 1822,
Batteau	do.	do.	on Blake's lands,
Denmark Vesey	A free black man	22	near Charleston.
Jessy	Thos. Blackwood	23	
John	Elias Horry	July 5	Do. on the Lines near
Gullah Jack	Paul Pritchard	do.	Ch.; Friday July 12.
Mingo	Wm. Harth	June 21	
Lot	Forrester	27	
Joe	P. L. Jore	July 6	
Julius	Thos. Forrest	8	
Tom	Mrs. Russell	10	
Smart	Robt. Anderson	do.	
John	John Robertson	11	
Robert	do.	do.	
Adam	do.	do.	
Polydore	Mrs. Faber	do.	Hanged on the Lines
Bacchus	Benj. Hammet	do.	near Charleston,
Dick	Wm. Sims	13	on Friday, 26th
Pharaoh	— Thompson	do.	July.
Jemmy	Mrs. Clement	18	
Mauidore	Mordecai Cohen	19	
Dean	— Mitchell	do.	
Jack	Mrs. Purcell	12	
Bellisle	Est. of Jos. Yates	18	
Naphur	do.	do.	
Adam	do.	do.	
Jacob	John S. Glen	16	
Charles	John Billings	18	
Jack	N. McNeill	22	
Cæsar	Miss Smith	do.	
Jacob Stagg	Jacob Lankester	23	Do. Tues. July 30.
Tom	Wm. M. Scott	24	
William	Mrs. Garner	Aug. 2	Do. Friday, Aug. 9.

There was a distinctly Pan-African cast to the conspiracy. A number of the leaders had lived in either Africa or the Caribbean. One of them, Monday Gell, had apparently corresponded with the president of Haiti. Charleston blacks were told that "Santo Domingo and Africa will assist us to get our liberty, if we will only make the motion first." The motion they planned was bold indeed. They were to attack the city at seven different points, capture weapons at the arsenal, set fire to the city, and kill all whites they encountered.

The plan was bold but not rashly undertaken. They prepared for a deadline in the second week of July 1822. Large numbers were needed and available. Blacks outnumbered whites 10 to 1 in the area surrounding Charleston, and recruiting extended to plantations as far away as 80 miles. The big problem was a shortage of arms until the arsenal was taken. So blacksmiths began making bayonets and spikes. Anything that could be used as a weapon was hoarded, along with gunpowder. Draymen, cartmen, and butchers were recruited to supply horses. Hundreds of blacks from all classes and occupations were contacted, but the nucleus remained skilled artisans, free and slave, from Charleston.

The dangers of advance planning and a widespread network were leaks and betrayal. For months luck held, but in late May 1822 a slave reported an attempt to recruit him to the insurrection. As authorities began to investigate, the betrayals escalated, and the authorities deployed military force to quash the rebellion before it had a chance to get started. Ten slaves were arrested on June 17 and 18, and the court began hearings. On June 22 Vesey was captured and stood trial the next day, while "Gullah Jack," the only major leader still free, tried to continue the revolt. Three days after the July 2 executions "Gullah Jack" was arrested. By August 9 more than 30 blacks had been hanged and many more deported.

White retaliation was swift and sure. So was white hysteria. The executions were public, and blacks were forbidden to dress in black or wear black crepe to mourn the dead. Examples were also made of the informers, who were freed and granted lifetime annuities. Finally, whites responded to Vesey's conspiracy with further antiblack legislation.

On the surface little good came from Denmark Vesey's bold plan. Its chances of success were meager at best. During Vesey's sentencing, the presiding magistrate told him, "It is difficult to imagine what *infatuation* could have prompted you to attempt an enterprise so wild and visionary. You were a free man; were comparatively wealthy; and enjoyed every comfort, compatible with your situation. You had therefore, much to risk and little to gain. From your age and experience you *ought* to have known, that success was impracticable." Nevertheless, Vesey took his indomitable stand. While recruiting for the Union army, the great black abolitionist Frederick Douglass called upon blacks "to remember Denmark Vesey."

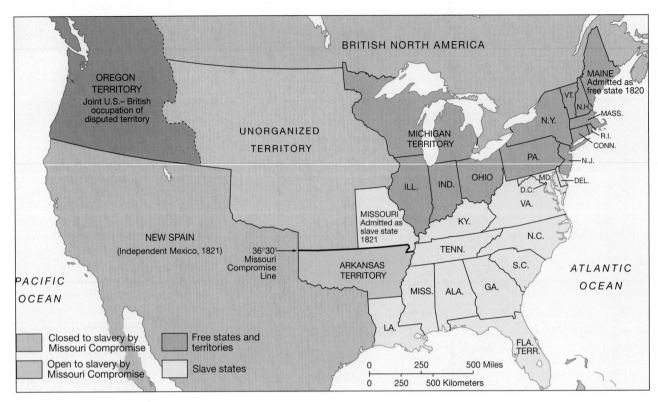

Missouri Compromise

The agreement reached in the Missouri Compromise temporarily settled the argument over slavery in the territories.

vehemence. Said Representative Tallmadge, "If blood is necessary to extinguish any fire which I have assisted to kindle, I can assure you gentlemen, while I regret the necessity, I shall not forbear to contribute my mite." Northern leaders argued that national policy, enshrined in the Northwest Ordinance, committed the government to halt the expansion of the institution of slavery. They warned that the extension of slavery into the West would inevitably increase the pressures to reopen the African slave trade.

Mass meetings convened in a number of cities in the Northeast. The vehemence of anti-Missouri feeling is apparent in an editorial that appeared in the New York *Advertiser:* "THIS QUESTION INVOLVES NOT ONLY THE FUTURE CHARACTER OF OUR NATION, BUT THE FUTURE WEIGHT AND INFLUENCE OF THE FREE STATES. IF NOW LOST— IT IS LOST FOREVER." Never before had passions over the issue of slavery been so heated or sectional antagonisms so overt.

Compromise ultimately resolved the crisis. In 1820, the Senate narrowly voted to admit Missouri as a slave state. To preserve the sectional balance, it also voted to admit Maine, which had previously been a

part of Massachusetts, as a free state, and to prohibit the formation of any further slave states from the territory of the Louisiana Purchase north of 36°30' north latitude. Henry Clay then skillfully steered the **Missouri Compromise** through the House, where a handful of antislavery representatives, fearful of the threat to the Union, threw their support behind the proposals.

Southerners won a victory in 1820, but they paid a high price. While many states would eventually be organized from the Louisiana Purchase area north of the compromise line, only two (Arkansas and part of Oklahoma) would be formed from the southern portion. If the South was to defend its political power against an antislavery majority, it had but two options in the future. It would either have to forge new political alliances with the North and West, or it would have to acquire new territory in the Southwest. The latter would inevitably reignite northern opposition to the further expansion of slavery.

The Era of Good Feelings ended on a note of foreboding. Although compromise had been achieved, it was clear that sectional conflict had not been resolved, only postponed. Sectional antagonism, Jeffer-

CHRONOLOGY OF KEY EVENTS

1785 Oliver Evans opens the first automated flour mill

1786 Samuel Fitch demonstrates his first steamboat

1793 Samuel Slater opens the first American textile mill at Pawtucket, Rhode Island; Eli Whitney invents the cotton gin

1807 Robert Fulton's *Clermont* demonstrates practicality of steam-powered navigation

1814 First factory to turn raw cotton into cotton cloth opens in Waltham, Massachusetts

1815 Congress declares war on Algiers

1816 Second Bank of the United States is chartered; Protective Tariff is passed; James Monroe is elected fifth president

1817– General Andrew Jackson invades Florida;
1818 Rush-Bagot convention between Britain and United States establishes American fishing rights and U.S.-Canadian boundary

1819 Panic of 1819; Spain cedes Florida to the United States and recognizes the western limits of the Louisiana Purchase in the Adams-Onis Treaty; *Dartmouth v. Woodward* upholds the sanctity of contracts; *McCulloch v. Maryland* upholds the constitutionality of the second Bank of the United States

1820 Missouri Compromise prohibits slavery in the northern half of the Louisiana Purchase; Missouri enters the union as a slave state and Maine as a free state

1822 Denmark Vesey's slave insurrection in South Carolina is exposed

1823 President James Monroe opposes any further European colonization or interference in the Americas, establishing the principle now known as the Monroe Doctrine

1824 *Gibbons v. Ogden* broadens federal power over interstate commerce

1825 Erie Canal opens

son wrote, "is hushed, indeed, for the moment. But this is a reprieve only, not a final sentence. A geographical line, coinciding with a marked principle, moral and political, once conceived and held up to the angry passions of men, will never be obliterated; and every new irritation will mark it deeper and deeper." John Quincy Adams agreed. The Missouri crisis, he wrote, is only the "title page to a great tragic volume."

CONCLUSION

The Era of Good Feelings came to a formal close on March 4, 1825, the day that John Quincy Adams was inaugurated as the nation's sixth president. Adams, who had served eight years as his predecessor's secretary of state, believed that James Monroe's terms in office would be regarded by future generations of Americans as a "golden age." In his inaugural address, he spoke with pride of the nation's achievements since the War of 1812. A strong spirit of nation-alism pervaded the nation and the country stood united under a single political party, the Republicans. The nation had settled its most serious disputes with England and Spain, extended its boundaries to the Pacific, asserted its diplomatic independence, encouraged the wars for national independence in Latin America, had developed a strong manufacturing system, and had begun to create a system of transportation adequate to a great nation.

The Era of Good Feelings marked a period of dramatic growth and intense nationalism, but it also witnessed the emergence of new political divisions as well as growing sectional animosities. The period following the War of 1812 brought rapid growth to cities, manufacturing, and the factory system in the North, while the South's economy remained centered on slavery and cotton. These two great sections were developing along diverging lines. Whether the spirit of nationalism or the spirit of sectionalism would triumph was the great question that would dominate American politics over the next four decades.

CHAPTER SUMMARY AND KEY POINTS

The War of 1812, climaxed by Andrew Jackson's smashing victory at the battle of New Orleans, stirred a new sense of nationalism and dynamism. In this chapter you learned about the forms the spirit of nationalism took in a series of Supreme Court decisions and in foreign policy. You also learned about industrial developments that increased productivity, promoted commercial development, and improved communication and transportation. Finally, you read about the Panic of 1819 and the Missouri Crisis, which led to the emergence of new political divisions and sectional animosities.

- The Era of Good Feelings was a period of dramatic growth and intense nationalism.

- The spirit of nationalism was apparent in Supreme Court decisions that established the supremacy of the federal government and expanded the powers of Congress. American interest and power in foreign policy was especially apparent in the Monroe Doctrine.

- Industrial development enhanced national self-sufficiency and united the nation with improved roads, canals, and river transportation.

- Forces for division were also at work. The financial Panic of 1819 led to the emergence of new political parties. The Missouri Crisis contributed to a growing sectional split between North and South.

SUGGESTIONS FOR FURTHER READING

Harry Ammon, *James Monroe: The Quest for National Identity* (1990). A biography of the last of the founders to serve as president.

Jeremy Atack and Peter Passell, *A New Economic View of American History,* 2nd ed. (1994) and Charles Sellers, *The Market Revolution, 1815–1846* (1991). Analyze thoroughly American economic development after 1815.

William Barney, *The Passage of the Republic* (1987). Offers a highly informative overview of the period.

Noble E. Cunningham, *The Presidency of James Monroe* (1996). Examines Monroe's responses to the wars for independence in Latin America, the decline of Spain's New World empire, the Panic of 1819, and the controversy over slavery in Missouri.

Ernest R. May, *The Making of the Monroe Doctrine* (1975). Examines American foreign policy during this period.

Novels

Richard Henry Dana, *Two Years Before the Mast* (1840).

Susan Warner, *The Wide, Wide World* (1850).

MEDIA RESOURCES

Web Sites

Prairietown, Indiana
http://www.indianapolis.in.us/cp/stories.html
Detailed information about America's movement westward and the everyday lives of Americans.

The Seminole Indians of Florida
http://www.seminoletribes.com/
The history of Florida's Seminoles.

Whole Cloth: Discovering Science and Technology Through American Textile History
http://www.si.edu/lemelson/centerpieces/whole_cloth/
The Jerome and Dorothy Lemelson Center for the Study of Invention and Innovation/Society for the History of Technology put together this site, which includes excellent activities and sources concerning early American manufacturing and industry.

The National Road
http://www.connerprairie.org/ntlroad.html
The National Road was a hot political topic in the early republic and was part of the beginning of the development of America's infrastructure.

Nineteenth Century Scientific American Online
http://www.history.rochester.edu/Scientific_American/
Magazines and journals are windows through which we can view society. This site provides online editions of one of the more interesting nineteenth-century journals.

Films and Videos

Africans in America (1998). The third part of this PBS documentary explores the status of African Americans, enslaved and free, between 1791 and 1831.

The Fighting Kentuckian (1949). In Alabama in 1818, a militiaman played by John Wayne falls in love with a French exile and discovers a plot to steal the land on which her fellow exiles plan to settle.

KEY TERMS

Era of Good Feelings (p. 226)

American System (p. 228)

Second Bank of the United States (p. 229)

Marbury v. Madison (p. 231)

McCulloch v. Maryland   (p. 231)

Dartmouth v. Woodward   (p. 231)

Barbary pirates   (p. 232)

Monroe Doctrine   (p. 233)

Erie Canal   (p. 234)

American system of production   (p. 236)

Panic of 1819   (p. 239)

Missouri Compromise   (p. 242)

PEOPLE YOU SHOULD KNOW

Francis Cabot Lowell   (p. 225)

James Monroe   (p. 226)

John Quincy Adams   (p. 226)

Henry Clay   (p. 227)

John C. Calhoun   (p. 227)

Daniel Webster   (p. 227)

John Marshall   (p. 231)

Stephen Decatur   (p. 232)

Andrew Jackson   (p. 232)

Robert Fulton   (p. 234)

Samuel F. B. Morse   (p. 236)

Eli Whitney   (p. 236)

REVIEW QUESTIONS

1. Why is the period following the War of 1812 called the "Era of Good Feelings"? What political, social, and economic developments contributed to a growing sense of nationalism after the conflict?

2. In what ways did the Supreme Court strengthen the authority of the national government?

3. What problems had to be overcome for the United States to develop a vigorous economy? How did the United States overcome the problems of scarce labor and poor transportation and communication?

4. Identify the main provisions of the Monroe Doctrine.

5. Explain how the Panic of 1819 and the Missouri Crisis ended the "Era of Good Feelings" and helped produce new sectional and party divisions.

10 Power and Politics in Jackson's America

THE ELECTION OF 1840: SYMBOL OVER SUBSTANCE

It was, without a doubt, one of the most exciting, colorful, and dirty presidential campaigns in American history. In 1840, **William Henry Harrison,** a military hero best known for fighting an alliance of Indians at the Battle of Tippecanoe in 1811, challenged the Democratic incumbent, **Martin Van Buren,** for the presidency.

Harrison's campaign began on Monday, May 4, 1840, when a huge procession made up of an estimated 75,000 people marched through the streets of Baltimore to celebrate Harrison's nomination by the Whig party convention. Although Harrison was college educated and brought up on a plantation with a workforce of some 200 slaves, his Democratic opponents had already dubbed him the "log cabin" candidate, who was happiest on his backwoods farm sipping hard cider. In response, Harrison's supporters enthusiastically seized on this image and promoted it in a number of colorful ways. They distributed barrels of hard cider, passed out campaign hats and placards, and mounted eight log cabins on floats.

Harrison's campaign brought many innovations to the art of electioneering. For the first time, a presidential candidate spoke out on his own behalf. Previous candidates had let others speak for them.

Harrison's backers also coined the first campaign slogans: "Tippecanoe and Tyler Too," "Van, Van is a used up man," and "Matty's policy, 12½ cents a day and french soup, Our policy, 2 Dollars a day and Roast Beef." They staged log-cabin raisings, including the erection of a 50-by-100-foot cabin on Broadway in New York City. They sponsored barbecues, including one in Wheeling, Virginia (now West Virginia), where a crowd devoured 360 hams, 26 sheep, 20 calves, 1500 pounds of beef, 8000 pounds of bread, 1000 pounds of cheese, and 4500 pies. Harrison's campaign managers even distributed whiskey bottles in the shape of log cabins, filled by the E. C. Booz Distillery of Philadelphia, thereby adding the word "booze" to the American vocabulary.

While defending their man as the "people's" candidate, Harrison's backers heaped an unprecedented avalanche of personal abuse on his Democratic opponent. The Whigs accused President Van Buren of eating off golden plates and lace tablecloths, drinking French wines, perfuming his whiskers, and wearing a corset. Whigs in Congress denied Van Buren an appropriation of $3665 to repair the White House

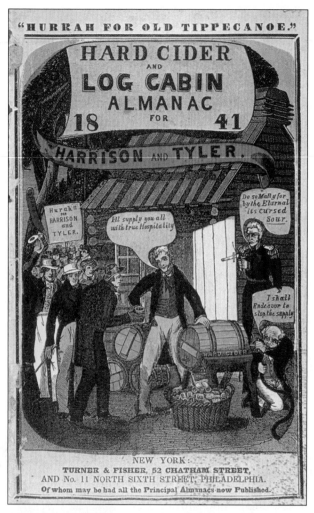

Campaign materials for the Hard Cider and Log Cabin campaign of Whig candidates William Henry Harrison and John Tyler in the election of 1840 included a variety of objects—ribbons, buttons, handkerchiefs, dishes, and printed materials such as *The Log Cabin*, the campaign newspaper, and the *Hard Cider and Log Cabin Almanac*. A 72-page copy of "Harrison Melodies" accompanied this almanac; more campaign songs were written for Harrison than for any other presidential candidate in any election before 1840—or since then.

lest he turn the executive mansion into a "palace as splendid as that of the Caesars." The object of this rough and colorful kind of campaigning was to show that the Democratic candidate harbored aristocratic leanings, while Harrison truly represented the people.

T he Harrison campaign provided a number of effective lessons for future politicians, most notably an emphasis on symbols and imagery over ideas and substance. Fearful of alienating voters and dividing the

Whig party, the political convention that nominated Harrison agreed to adopt no party platform. Harrison himself said not a single word during the campaign about his principles or proposals. He closely followed the suggestion of one of his advisers that he "rely entirely on the past" (that is, his reputation as a general and victor over the Indians) and offer no indication "about what he thinks now, or what he will do hereafter."

The new campaign techniques produced an overwhelming victory. In 1840, voter turnout was the highest it had ever been in a presidential election: nearly 80 percent of eligible voters cast ballots. The log cabin candidate for president won 53 percent of the popular vote and a landslide victory in the Electoral College.

POLITICAL DEMOCRATIZATION

When **James Monroe** began his second term as president in 1821, he rejoiced at the idea that the country was no longer divided by political parties, which he considered "the curse of the country," breeding disunity, demagoguery, and corruption. Yet even before Monroe's second term had ended, new political divisions had already begun to evolve, creating an increasingly democratic system of politics.

In 1821, American politics was still largely dominated by deference. Competing political parties were nonexistent and voters generally deferred to the leadership of local elites or leading families. Political campaigns tended to be relatively staid affairs. Direct appeals by candidates for support were considered in poor taste. Election procedures were, by later standards, quite undemocratic. Most states imposed property and taxpaying requirements on the white adult males who alone had the vote, and they conducted voting by voice. Presidential electors were generally chosen by state legislatures. Given the fact that citizens had only the most indirect say in the election of the president, it is not surprising that voting participation was generally extremely low, amounting to less than 30 percent of adult white males.

Between 1820 and 1840, a revolution took place in American politics. In most states, property qualifications for voting and officeholding were repealed; and voting by voice was largely eliminated. Direct methods of selecting presidential electors, county officials, state judges, and governors replaced indirect methods. Because of these and other political innovations, voter participation skyrocketed. By 1840 voting participation had reached unprecedented levels. Nearly 80 percent of adult white males went to the polls.

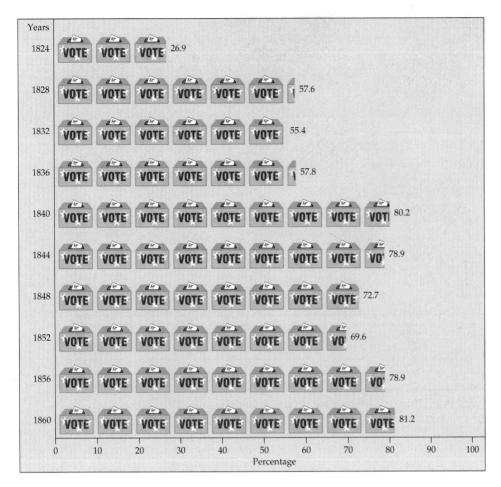

Years

1824 — 26.9
1828 — 57.6
1832 — 55.4
1836 — 57.8
1840 — 80.2
1844 — 78.9
1848 — 72.7
1852 — 69.6
1856 — 78.9
1860 — 81.2

Percentage
0 10 20 30 40 50 60 70 80 90 100

FIGURE 10.1
Voter Turnout,
1824–1860

A new two-party system, made possible by an expanded electorate, replaced the politics of deference to and leadership by elites. By the mid-1830s, two national political parties with marked philosophical differences, strong organizations, and wide popular appeal competed in virtually every state. Professional party managers used partisan newspapers, speeches, parades, rallies, and barbecues to mobilize popular support. Our modern political system had been born.

The Expansion of Voting Rights

The most significant political innovation of the early nineteenth century was the abolition of property qualifications for voting and officeholding. Hard times resulting from the panic of 1819 led many people to demand an end to property restrictions on voting and officeholding. In New York, for example, fewer than two adult males in five could legally vote for senator or governor. Under the new constitution adopted in 1821, all adult white males were allowed to vote, so long as they paid taxes or had served in the militia. Five years later, an amendment to the

state's constitution eliminated the taxpaying and militia qualifications, thereby establishing universal white manhood suffrage. By 1840, **universal white manhood suffrage** had largely become a reality. Only three states—Louisiana, Rhode Island, and Virginia—still restricted the suffrage to white male property owners and taxpayers.

To encourage popular participation in politics, most states also instituted statewide nominating conventions, opened polling places in more convenient locations, extended the hours that polls were open, and eliminated the earlier practice of voting by voice. This last reform did not truly institute the secret ballot, which was only adopted beginning in the 1880s, since voters during the mid-nineteenth century usually voted with straight-ticket paper ballots prepared by the political parties themselves. Each party had a different colored ballot, which voters deposited in a publicly viewed ballot box, so that those present knew who had voted for which party. By 1824 only 6 of the nation's 24 states still chose presidential electors in the state legislature, and eight years later the only state still to do so was South Carolina, which continued this practice until the Civil War.

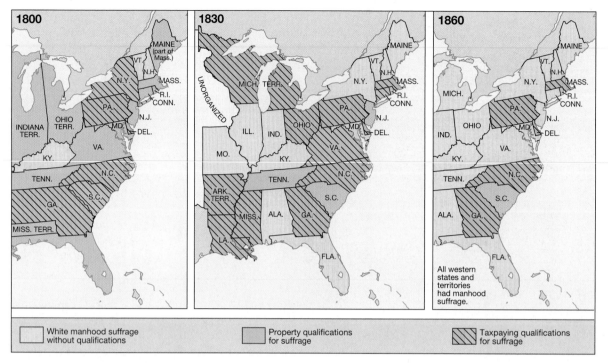

Extension of Male Suffrage

Some states and territories reserved the suffrage to white male property holders and taxpayers, while others permitted an alternative such as a period of residence.

In addition to removing property and tax qualifications for voting and officeholding, states also reduced residency requirements for voting. Immigrant males were permitted to vote in most states if they had declared their intention to become citizens. During the nineteenth century, 22 states and territories permitted immigrants who were not yet naturalized citizens to vote. States also allowed voters to choose presidential electors, governors, and county officials.

While universal white manhood suffrage was becoming a reality, restrictions on voting by African Americans and women remained in force. Only one state, New Jersey, had given unmarried women property holders the right to vote following the Revolution, but the state rescinded this right at the time it extended suffrage to all adult white men. Most states also explicitly denied the right to vote to free African Americans. By 1858 free blacks were eligible to vote in just four northern states: New Hampshire, Maine, Massachusetts, and Vermont.

Popular Attacks on Privilege

The democratic impulse that swept the country in the 1820s was also apparent in widespread attacks on special privilege and aristocratic pretension. Established churches, the bench, and the legal and medical professions all saw their elitist status diminished.

The judiciary became more responsive to public opinion through election, rather than appointment, of judges. To open up the legal profession, many states dropped formal training requirements to practice law. Some states also abolished training and licensing requirements for physicians, allowing unorthodox "herb and root" doctors, including many women, to compete freely with established physicians.

The surge of democratic sentiment had an important political consequence: the breakdown of the politics of deference and its terminology. The eighteenth-century language of politics—which included such terms as *faction, junto,* and *caucus*—was rooted in an elite-dominated political order. During the first quarter of the nineteenth century, a new democratic political vocabulary emerged that drew its words from everyday language. Instead of *standing* for public office, candidates *ran* for office. Politicians *logrolled* (made deals) or *straddled the fence* or promoted *pork barrel* legislation (programs that would benefit their constituents).

During the first quarter of the nineteenth century, local elites lost much of their influence. Professional politicians replaced them. In the 1820s, political inno-

ANTI MASONIC ALMANAC,
FOR THE YEAR
1831:
BY EDWARD GIDDINS.

By attacking special privilege and demanding equality of opportunity for all citizens, the Anti-Masonic party won broad support in New York and other Northern states.

vators such as Martin Van Buren, the son of a tavern keeper, and Thurlow Weed, a newspaper editor in Albany, New York, devised new campaign tools such as torchlight parades, subsidized partisan newspapers, and nominating conventions. These political bosses and manipulators soon discovered that the most successful technique for arousing popular interest in politics was to attack a privileged group or institution that had used political influence to attain power or profit.

The "**Anti-Masonic party**" was the first political movement to win widespread popular following using this technique. In the mid-1820s, a growing number of people in New York and surrounding states had come to believe that members of the fraternal order of Freemasons, who seemed to monopolize many of the region's most prestigious political offices and business positions, had used their connections to enrich themselves. They noted, for instance, that Masons held 22 of the nation's 24 governorships.

Then, in 1826, in the small town of Batavia, New York, William Morgan, a former Mason, disappeared.

Morgan had written an exposé of the organization in violation of the order's vow of silence, and rumor soon spread that he had been tied up with heavy cables and dumped into the Niagara River. When no indictments were brought against the alleged perpetrators of Morgan's kidnapping and presumed murder, many upstate New Yorkers accused local constables, justices of the peace, and judges, who were members of the Masons, of obstruction of justice.

By 1830 the Anti-Mason movement had succeeded in capturing half the vote in New York State and had gained substantial support throughout New England. In the mid-1830s, the Anti-Masons were absorbed into a new national political party, the Whigs.

THE REBIRTH OF PARTIES

The first years of the new republic had given rise to two competing political parties, the Federalists and the Democratic-Republicans. The first two parties, unlike present-day political parties, tended to have a strong sectional character, with the Federalists dominant in New England and the Republicans elsewhere.

After the War of 1812, the nation reverted to a period of one-party government in national politics. The decline of the Federalist Party created the illusion of national political unity, but appearances were deceptive. Without the discipline imposed by competition with a strong opposition party, the Republican Party began to fragment into cliques and factions.

During James Monroe's presidency, the Republican Party disintegrated as a stable national organization. Following his overwhelming victory in 1816, Monroe sought to promote the ideal expressed by George Washington in his Farewell Address: a nation free of partisan divisions. Like Washington, he appointed rival factional leaders, such as John Quincy Adams and John C. Calhoun, to his cabinet. He refused to use federal patronage to strengthen the Republican Party. He also took the position that Congress, not the president, was the best representative of the public will and, therefore, should define public policy.

The absence of a strong leader, however, led to the fragmentation of the Republican Party during Monroe's administration. Factional and sectional rivalries grew increasingly bitter and party machinery fell into disuse.

Birth of the Second Party System

Over time, local and personal factions began to coalesce into a new political party system. Three critical factors contributed to the creation of the

The Cholera Epidemic of 1832: Sinners and Saints

In the spring of 1832, Americans braced themselves for an attack by cholera—what one historian has called "the classic epidemic disease of the nineteenth century." They knew it was coming. Throughout the preceding year, newspapers had reported with alarm the disease's escape from its Asian homeland and its westward march across Europe. The press had turned shrill when cholera crossed the Atlantic Ocean—the last great barrier that shielded the Americas from this horrible plague—and struck Canada in June 1832. Despite the certainty that the disease would soon reach the United States, however, neither the federal, state, nor local governments did much to prevent or even prepare for an epidemic.

Nothing in their inventory of illnesses, not even the ravages of smallpox or malaria, had prepared Americans for the terror that seized them when cholera finally appeared. Their fear is easily understood: Cholera killed approximately half of those who contracted it, and it struck with unbelievable rapidity. A New Yorker who survived the 1832 epidemic testified that he was walking down the street when he suddenly fell forward on his face "as if knocked down with an axe."

Cholera's symptoms, which mimic those of severe arsenic poisoning, are indeed spectacular. Acute diarrhea, uncontrollable vomiting, and violent abdominal cramps mark the onset of the disease. Within hours, this sudden and massive loss of fluids causes de-hydration, and the victim's extremities feel cold, the face turns blue, and the feet and hands appear dark and swollen. Unless proper medical treatment is provided, death can follow within a few hours after the first symptoms appear, or, at most, within a few days. Even more than its devastating symptoms, it was the disease's ability to kill so swiftly that terrorized the public. "To see individuals well in the morning & buried before night, retiring apparently well & dead in the morning is something which is appalling to the boldest heart," exclaimed another survivor of America's first cholera epidemic.

The cause of cholera was not discovered until 1883 when Robert Koch, the famous scientist, led a commission to Egypt that isolated *Vibrio comma*, the guilty bacterium. These deadly germs settle in the intestines of their victims, after following a journey along any one of several pathways that lead to the human digestive tract. Although dirty hands or raw fruits and vegetables often transmit the disease, most cholera epidemics are spread by polluted drinking water from sewage-contaminated water systems.

Unfortunately, America's cities in 1832 harbored more than enough filth to nurture an epidemic. New York was especially dirty. Residents were required by law to pile their garbage in the gutter in front of their homes for removal by the city, but it seldom got collected. (With their characteristic sense of humor, New Yorkers dubbed these piles of stinking, decomposing garbage "corporation pie.") The only effective "sanitary engineers" in New York were the thousands of swine that roamed the streets gorging themselves on the refuse.

Thanks to this filth, cholera unleashed a great plague of death when it reached New York. Thousands died in the epidemic, producing so many bodies that the undertakers could not keep up with the volume and had to stack corpses in warehouses and public buildings to await burial. In short, cholera hit New York with the same force with which yellow fever had knocked Philadelphia to its knees in 1793 (see pp. 190–191).

In the midst of their suffering, New Yorkers could not help but wonder why some people contracted the disease while others escaped it. To answer this question, America's physicians espoused a doctrine of predisposing causes. People who kept God's laws, they explained, had nothing to fear, but the intemperate and the filthy stood at great risk. In fact, physicians elaborated their warnings about "predisposing" or "exciting" causes into a jeremiad against sin. Impiety, imprudence, idleness, drunkenness, gluttony, and sexual excess all left their devotees weakened and "artificially stimulated" their bodies to be vulnerable to cholera.

Because the disease was "decidedly vulgar," physicians predicted that it would confine itself largely to the lower classes—specifically, to blacks and to the Irish, who were thought by upper-class individuals to be the most intemperate and debauched members of society. Here, then, was a classic example of how the medical profession appropriated social attitudes regarding class and race to blame the victims of disease for their suffering.

The doctors appeared to be right, but for the wrong reasons. Cholera was indeed a "poor man's plague";

York's leading physicians (a practical thinker) even recommended plugging the patient's rectum with beeswax to halt the diarrhea.

Many Americans turned to quacks or treated themselves with home remedies. It made no difference. Those who survived the epidemic did so in spite of the medical care they received, not because of it.

Cholera receded from the land almost as quickly as it had come. By the fall of 1832 the epidemic had spent its fury, and by the winter it was gone. When it struck again in 1866, Americans had learned how to battle the disease. They no longer talked about cholera in moral terms as God's vengeance on the poor and the wicked. Instead, they approached it as a social problem amenable to human intervention. They imposed quarantines, opened emergency hospitals, increased the powers of health authorities, removed the trash and garbage from city streets, and cleaned up municipal water supplies. The contrast between 1832 and 1866 could not have been more complete.

Within the span of two generations, the public changed the way it viewed disease. American physicians became more scientific in handling and treating the sick—eloquent testimony to the medical advances in a modernizing society.

sin, however, was not the explanation. The upper classes suffered less because they fled the cities for country homes and lodges where pure water and low population density prevented infection. The poor, by contrast, could not afford to leave: they had to remain and take their chances.

Most of New York's lower classes lived in tiny, unvented apartments where entire families (and perhaps a boarder or two) occupied a single room; the most wretched subsisted in unfurnished cellars whose walls glistened with sewage and slime every time it rained. Instead of pure water imported in hogsheads from fresh water springs in the countryside (the

only water the wealthy would touch), the poor drew their drinking water from the river or from contaminated shallow wells. Though New Yorkers had long joked that their water was an excellent purgative, they might as well have called it "liquid death" when cholera swept the land.

Once cholera struck, physicians found that none of the traditional remedies of heroic medicine worked. In addition to bloodletting, they treated their patients with laudanum (the main ingredient of which was opium), tobacco smoke, enemas, and huge doses of calomel, a chalky mercury compound employed as a cathartic. In desperation, one of New

second party system. The first was the financial **panic of 1819** and the subsequent depression.

The panic resulted in significant political differences over such issues as debt relief, banking and monetary policy, and tariffs. Farmers, particularly in the South and West, demanded enactment of stay laws to postpone repayment of debts. Many artisans and farmers blamed banks for causing the panic by printing an excess of worthless paper money. They demanded that bank notes be replaced by hard money, gold and silver coinage. These groups often disagreed with pro-business interests, which called for the extension of credit, higher tariffs to protect infant industries, and government-financed transportation improvements to reduce the cost of trade.

A second source of political division was southern alarm over the slavery debates in Congress in 1819 and 1820. Many southern leaders feared that the **Missouri crisis** might spark a realignment in national politics along sectional lines. Such a development, John Quincy Adams wrote, was "terrible to the South—threatening in its progress the emancipation of all their slaves, threatening in its immediate effect that Southern domination which has swayed the Union for the last twenty years." Anxiety over the slavery debates in 1819 and 1820 induced many Southerners to seek political alliances with the North. As early as 1821, Old Republicans in the South—who opposed high tariffs, a national bank, and federally funded internal improvements—had begun to form a loose alliance with Senator Martin Van Buren of New York and the Republican party faction he commanded.

The third major source of political division was the selection of presidential candidates. The "Virginia dynasty" of presidents, a chain that had begun with George Washington and included Thomas Jefferson, James Madison, and James Monroe, was at its end by 1824. Traditionally, a caucus of the Republican Party's members of Congress selected the Republican Party's candidate. At the 1824 caucus, the members met in closed session and chose William Crawford, Monroe's secretary of the Treasury, as the party's candidate. Not all Republicans, however, supported this method of nominating candidates and, therefore, refused to participate.

When Crawford suffered a stroke and was left partially disabled, four other candidates emerged: Secretary of State **John Quincy Adams,** the son of the nation's second president and the only candidate from the North; **John C. Calhoun,** Monroe's secretary of war, who had little support outside of his native South Carolina; **Henry Clay,** the Speaker of the House; and General **Andrew Jackson,** the hero of the Battle of New Orleans and victor over the Creek and

Candidate	Party	Popular Vote	Electoral Vote
J. Q. Adams	No party designations	113,122	84
Jackson		151,271	99
Clay		47,531	37
Crawford		40,856	41

TABLE 10.1 Election of 1824

Seminole Indians. About the latter, Thomas Jefferson commented dryly, one might as well try "to make a soldier of a goose as a President of Andrew Jackson."

In the election of 1824, Jackson received the greatest number of votes both at the polls and in the Electoral College, followed (in electoral votes) by Adams, Crawford, and then Clay. But he failed to receive the constitutionally required majority of the electoral votes. As provided by the Twelfth Amendment of the Constitution, the election was, therefore, thrown into the House of Representatives, which was required to choose from among the top three vote getters in the Electoral College. There, Henry Clay persuaded his supporters to vote for Adams, commenting acidly that he did not believe "that killing two thousand five hundred Englishmen at New Orleans" was a proper qualification for the presidency. Adams was elected on the first ballot.

The Philadelphia *Observer* charged that Adams had made a secret deal to obtain Clay's support. Three days later, Adams's nomination of Clay as secretary of state seemed to confirm the charges of a "corrupt bargain." Jackson was outraged, since he could legitimately argue that he was the popular favorite. The general exclaimed, "The Judas of the West has closed the contract and will receive the thirty pieces of silver."

The Presidency of John Quincy Adams

John Quincy Adams was one of the most brilliant and well-qualified men ever to occupy the White House. A deeply religious, intensely scholarly man, he read Biblical passages at least three times a day—once in English, once in German, and once in French. He was fluent in seven foreign languages, including Greek and Latin. During his remarkable career as a diplomat and secretary of state, he negotiated the treaty that ended the War of 1812, acquired Florida, and conceived the Monroe Doctrine.

John Quincy Adams won the election of 1824 in the House of Representatives even though Andrew Jackson received the most popular votes.

But Adams lacked the political skills and personality necessary to create support for his program. Like his father, Adams lacked personal warmth. His adversaries mockingly described him as a "chip off the old iceberg."

Adams's problems as president did not arise exclusively from his temperament. His misfortune was to serve as president at a time of growing partisan divisions. The Republican Party had split into two distinct camps. Adams and his supporters, known as **National Republicans**, favored a vigorous role for the central government in promoting national economic growth, while the **Jacksonian Democrats** demanded a limited government and strict adherence to laissez-faire principles.

As the only president to lose both the popular vote and the electoral vote, Adams faced hostility from the start. Jackson and his supporters accused the new president of "corruptions and intrigues" to gain Henry Clay's support. Acutely aware of the fact that "two-thirds of the whole people [were] averse" to his election as president, Adams promised in his inaugural address to make up for this with "intentions upright and pure; a heart devoted to the welfare of our country." A staunch nationalist, Adams proposed an extraordinary program of federal support for scientific and economic development that included a national university, astronomical observatories ("lighthouses of the skies"), federal funding of roads and canals, and exploration of the country's territory—all to be financed by a high tariff.

Adams's advocacy of a strong federal government and a high tariff enraged defenders of slavery and states' rights advocates who clung to traditional Jeffersonian principles of limited government and strict construction of the Constitution. They feared that any expansion of federal authority might set a precedent for interference with slavery. Thomas Jefferson himself condemned Adams's proposals, declaring in a stinging statement that they would undermine the states and create a national elite—"an aristocracy . . . riding and ruling over the plundered ploughman and beggared yeomanry."

Adams met with further frustration because he was unwilling to adapt to the practical demands of politics. Adams made no effort to use his patronage powers to build support for his proposals and refused to fire federal officeholders who openly opposed his policies. During his entire term in office he removed just 12 incumbents, and these only for gross incompetence. He justified his actions by saying that he did not want to make "government a perpetual and unremitting scramble for office."

Adams's Indian policies also cost him supporters. Although he, like his predecessor Monroe, wanted to remove Native Americans in the South to an area west of the Mississippi River, he believed that the state and federal governments had a duty to abide by Indian treaties and to purchase, not merely annex, Indian lands. Adams's decision to repudiate and renegotiate a fraudulent treaty that stripped the Georgia Creek Indians of their land outraged land-hungry Southerners and Westerners.

Even in the realm of foreign policy, his strong suit prior to the presidency, Adams encountered difficulties. His attempts to acquire Texas from Mexico through peaceful means failed, as did his efforts to persuade Britain to permit more American trade with the British West Indies.

The "American System" and the "Tariff of Abominations"

President Adams was committed to using the federal government to promote national economic development. His program included a high protective tariff to promote industry, the sale of public lands at low prices to encourage western settlement, federally financed transportation improvements, expanded markets for western grain and southern cotton, and a strong national bank to regulate the economy.

Adams's secretary of state, Henry Clay, called this economic program the **American system** because it was supposed to promote growth in all parts of the country. But the program infuriated Southerners who believed that it favored northeastern industrial interests at their region's expense. Southerners particularly disliked a protective tariff, since it raised the cost of manufactured goods, which they did not produce.

Andrew Jackson's supporters in Congress sought to exploit the tariff question to embarrass Adams and help Jackson win the presidency in 1828. They framed a bill, which became known as the **Tariff of Abominations,** to win support for Jackson in Kentucky, Missouri, New York, Ohio, and Pennsylvania while weakening the Adams administration in New England. The bill raised duties on iron, hemp, and flax (which would benefit Westerners), while lowering the tariff on woolen goods (to the detriment of New England textile manufacturers). John Randolph of Virginia accurately described the object of the bill as an effort to encourage "manufactures of no sort or kind, except the manufacture of a President of the United States."

The Tariff of Abominations created a political uproar in the South, where it was denounced as unconstitutional and discriminatory. The tariff, Southerners insisted, was essentially a tax on their region to assist northern manufacturers. South Carolina expressed the loudest outcry against the tariff. At a public meeting in Charleston, protesters declared that a tariff was designed to benefit "one class of citizens [manufacturers] at the expense of every other class." Some South Carolinians called for revolutionary defiance of the national government.

Vice President John C. Calhoun, a skilled logician well versed in political theory, offered a theoretical framework for Southern discontent. Retreating from his early nationalistic position, the South Carolinian anonymously published the "South Carolina Exposition," an essay that advanced the principle of **nullification.** A single state, Calhoun maintained, might overrule or "nullify" a federal law within its own territory, until three-quarters of the states had upheld the law as constitutional. In 1828 the state of South Carolina decided not to implement this doctrine but rather to wait and see what attitude the next president would adopt toward the tariff.

The Election of 1828

"J. Q. Adams who can write" squared off against "Andy Jackson who can fight" in the election of 1828, one of the most bitter campaigns in American his-

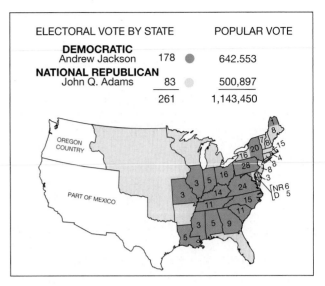

Election of 1828

tory. Jackson's followers repeated the charge that Adams was an "aristocrat" who had obtained office as a result of a "corrupt bargain." The Jackson forces also alleged that the president had used public funds to buy personal luxuries and had installed gaming tables in the White House. They even charged that Mrs. Adams had been born out of wedlock.

Adams's supporters countered by digging up an old story that Jackson had begun living with his wife before she was legally divorced from her first husband (which was technically true, although neither Jackson nor his wife Rachel knew her first husband was still living). They called the general a slave trader, a gambler, and a backwoods buffoon who could not spell more than one word out of four correctly. One Philadelphia editor published a handbill picturing the coffins of 12 men allegedly murdered by Jackson in numerous duels.

The Jackson campaign in 1828 was the first to appeal directly for voter support through a professional political organization. Skilled political organizers, like Martin Van Buren of New York, Amos Kendall of Kentucky, and Thomas Ritchie of Virginia, created an extensive network of campaign committees and subcommittees to organize mass rallies, parades, and barbecues, and to erect hickory poles, Jackson's symbol.

For the first time in American history, a presidential election was the focus of public attention, and voter participation increased dramatically. Twice as many voters cast ballots in the election of 1828 as in 1824, four times as many as in 1820. As in most previous elections, the vote divided along sectional lines. Jackson swept every state in the South and West and

Adams won the electoral votes of every state in the North except Pennsylvania and part of New York.

Contemporaries interpreted Jackson's resounding victory as a triumph for political democracy. Jackson's supporters called the vote a victory for the "farmers and mechanics of the country" over the "rich and well born." Even Jackson's opponents agreed that the election marked a watershed in the nation's political history, signaling the beginning of a new democratic age. One Adams supporter said bluntly, "a great revolution has taken place."

ANDREW JACKSON: THE POLITICS OF EGALITARIANISM

Supporters of Adams regarded Jackson's victory with deep pessimism. A justice of the Supreme Court declared, "The reign of King 'Mob' seems triumphant." Enthusiasts, however, greeted Jackson's victory as a great triumph for the people. At the inaugural, a cable stretched in front of the east portico of the Capitol to keep back the throngs snapped under the pressure of the surging crowd. As many as 20,000 well-wishers attended a White House reception to honor the new president, muddying rugs, breaking furniture, and damaging china and glassware. "It was a proud day for the people," commented one Kentucky newspaperman. "General Jackson is their own President."

In certain respects, Jackson was truly a self-made man. Born in 1767 in a frontier region along the North and South Carolina border, he was the first president to be born in a log cabin. His father, a poor farmer from northern Ireland, died two weeks before his birth, while his mother and two brothers died during the American Revolution. At the age of 13, Jackson volunteered to fight in the American Revolution. He was taken prisoner and a British officer severely slashed Jackson's hand and head when the boy refused to shine the officer's shoes.

Jackson soon rose from poverty to a career in law and politics, becoming Tennessee's first congressman, a senator, and judge on the state supreme court. Although he would later gain a reputation as the champion of the common people, in Tennessee he was allied by marriage, business, and political ties to the state's elite. As a land speculator, cotton planter, and attorney, he accumulated a large personal fortune and acquired more than 100 slaves. His candidacy for the presidency was initially promoted by speculators, creditors, and elite leaders in Tennessee who hoped to exploit Jackson's popularity to combat antibanking sentiment and fend off challenges to their dominance of state politics.

Expanding the Powers of the Presidency

In office, Jackson greatly enhanced the power and prestige of the presidency. While each member of Congress represented a specific regional constituency, only the president, Jackson declared, represented all the people of the United States.

Jackson convinced many Americans that their votes mattered. He espoused a political ideology of "democratic republicanism" that stressed the common peoples' virtue, intelligence, and capacity for self-government. He also expressed a deep disdain for the "better classes," which claimed a "more enlightened wisdom" than common men and women.

Endorsing the view that a fundamental conflict existed between working people and the "nonproducing" classes of society, Jackson and his supporters promised to remove any impediments to the ordinary citizen's opportunities for economic improvement. According to the Jacksonians, inequalities of wealth and power were the direct result of monopoly, favoritism, and special privileges, which made "the rich richer and the powerful more potent." Only free competition in an open marketplace would ensure that wealth would be distributed in accordance with each person's "industry, economy, enterprise, and prudence." The goal of the Jacksonians was to remove all obstacles that prevented farmers, artisans, and small shopkeepers from earning a greater share of the nation's wealth.

Nowhere was the Jacksonian ideal of openness made more concrete than in Jackson's theory of rotation in office, known as the **spoils system.** In his first annual message to Congress, Jackson defended the principle that public offices should be rotated among party supporters to help the nation achieve its republican ideals. Performance in public office, Jackson maintained, required no special intelligence or training, and rotation in office would ensure that the federal government did not develop a class of corrupt civil servants set apart from the people. His supporters advocated the spoils system on practical political grounds, viewing it as a way to reward party loyalists and build a stronger party organization. As Jacksonian Senator William Marcy of New York proclaimed, "To the victor belongs the spoils."

The spoils system opened government positions to many of Jackson's supporters, but the practice was neither as new nor as democratic as it appeared. During his first 18 months in office, Jackson replaced fewer than 1000 of the nation's 10,000 civil servants on political grounds, and fewer than 20 percent of federal officeholders were removed during his administration. Moreover, many of the men Jackson appointed to office had backgrounds of wealth and social eminence. Jackson did not originate the spoils system. By the time he took office, a number of states, including New York and Pennsylvania, practiced political patronage.

Clearing the Land of Indians

The first major political controversy of Jackson's presidency involved Indian policy. At the time Jackson took office, 125,000 Native Americans still lived east of the Mississippi River. Cherokee, Choctaw, Chickasaw, and Creek Indians—60,000 strong—held millions of acres in what would become the southern cotton kingdom stretching across Georgia, Alabama, and Mississippi. The key political issues were whether these Native American peoples would be permitted to block white expansion and whether the U.S. government and its citizens would abide by previously made treaties.

Since Jefferson's presidency, two conflicting policies, assimilation and removal, had governed the treatment of Native Americans. Assimilation encouraged Indians to adopt the customs and economic practices of white Americans. The government provided financial assistance to missionaries to Christianize and educate Native Americans and convince them to adopt single-family farms. Proponents defended assimilation as the only way Native Americans would be able to survive in a white-dominated society.

By the 1820s, the Cherokee had demonstrated the ability of Native Americans to adapt to changing conditions while maintaining their tribal heritage. **Sequoyah,** a leader of these people, had developed a written alphabet. Soon the Cherokee opened schools, established churches, built roads, operated printing presses, and even adopted a constitution.

The other policy—**Indian removal**—was first suggested by Thomas Jefferson as the only way to ensure the survival of Native American cultures. The goal of this policy was to encourage the voluntary migration of Indians westward to tracts of land where they could live free from white harassment. As early as 1817, James Monroe declared that the nation's security depended on rapid settlement along the southern coast and that it was in the best interests of Native Americans to move westward. In 1825 he set before Congress a plan to resettle all eastern Indians on tracts in the West where whites would not be allowed to live.

After initially supporting both policies, Jackson favored removal as the solution to the controversy. This shift in federal Indian policy came partly as a result of a controversy between the Cherokee nation and the state of Georgia. The Cherokee people had adopted a constitution asserting sovereignty over their land. The state responded by abolishing tribal rule and claiming that the Cherokee fell under its jurisdiction. The discovery of gold on Cherokee land triggered a land rush, and the Cherokee nation sued to keep white settlers from encroaching on their territory. In two important cases, *Cherokee Nation v. Georgia* in 1831 and *Worcester v. Georgia* in 1832, the Supreme Court ruled that states could not pass laws conflicting with federal Indian treaties and that the federal government had an obligation to exclude white intruders from Indian lands. Angered, Jackson is said to have exclaimed: "John Marshall has made his decision; now let him enforce it."

The primary thrust of Jackson's removal policy was to encourage Native Americans to sell their homelands in exchange for new lands in Oklahoma and Arkansas. Such a policy, the president maintained, would open new farmland to whites while offering Indians a haven where they would be free to develop at their own pace. "There," he wrote, "your

In 1809 a Cherokee named Sequoyah began to devise an alphabet consisting of letters based on English, Greek, and Hebrew. The Cherokee nation's weekly newspaper, the *Cherokee Phoenix*, was printed with this alphabet.

white brothers will not trouble you, they will have no claims to the land, and you can live upon it, you and all your children, as long as the grass grows or the water runs, in peace and plenty."

Pushmataha, a Choctaw chieftain, called on his people to reject Jackson's offer. Far from being a "country of tall trees, many water courses, rich lands and high grass abounding in games of all kinds," the promised preserve in the West was simply a barren desert. Jackson responded by warning that if the Choctaw refused to move west, he would destroy their nation.

During the winter of 1831, the Choctaw became the first tribe to walk the "**Trail of Tears**" westward. Promised government assistance failed to arrive, and malnutrition, exposure, and a cholera epidemic killed many members of the nation. Then, in 1836, the Creek suffered the hardships of removal. About 3500 of the tribe's 15,000 members died along the westward trek. Those who resisted removal were bound in chains and marched in double file.

Emboldened by the Supreme Court decisions declaring that Georgia law had no force on Indian territory, the Cherokees resisted removal. Fifteen thousand Cherokee joined in a protest against Jackson's policy: "Little did [we] anticipate that when taught to think and feel as the American citizen . . . [we] were to be despoiled by [our] guardian, to become strangers and wanderers in the land of [our] fathers, forced to return to the savage life, and to seek a new home in the wilds of the far west, and that without [our] consent." The federal government bribed a faction of the tribe to leave the land in exchange for transportation costs and $5 million, but most Cherokees held out until 1838, when the army evicted them from their land. All told, 4000 of the 15,000 Cherokee died along the trail to Indian Territory in what is now Oklahoma.

A number of other tribes also organized resistance against removal. In the Old Northwest, the Sauk and Fox Indians fought the **Black Hawk War** (1832) to recover ceded tribal lands in Illinois and Wisconsin. The

Trail of Tears (Indian Removal)

Andrew Jackson's Indian removal policy was known to many Native Americans as the Trail of Tears. Native Americans were herded westward off their lands to open the territory for expansion. The trek brought death to perhaps one-fourth of those who set out.

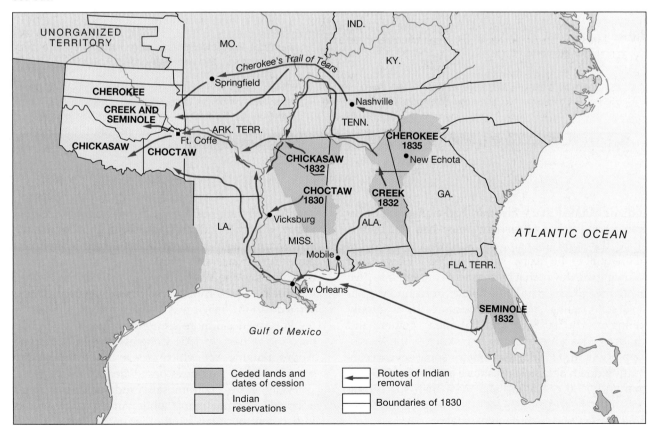

THE PEOPLE SPEAK

The Trail of Tears

In 1838 and 1839, the Cherokee nation was forced to give up its lands in western Georgia and migrate to present-day Oklahoma and Arkansas. Over 4000 of the 15,000 Cherokee who made the trek died along what became known as the Trail of Tears.

Eliza Whitmire was about five years old when she and her parents, who were enslaved to a Cherokee family, were forced to leave Georgia. She later described the process of removal:

> The weeks that followed General [Winfield] Scott's order to remove the Cherokees were filled with horror and suffering for the unfortunate Cherokees and their slaves. The women and children were driven from their homes, sometimes with blows and close on the heels of the retreating Indians came greedy whites to pillage the Indian's homes, drive off their cattle, horses, and pigs, and they even rifled the graves for any jewelry, or other ornaments that might have been buried with the dead. The Cherokees, after having been driven from their homes, were divided into detachments of nearly equal size and late in October, 1838, the first detachment started, the others following one by one. The aged, sick and young children rode in the wagons, which carried provisions and bedding, while others went on foot. The trip was made in the dead of winter and many died from exposure from sleet and snow, and all who lived to make this trip, or had parents who made it, will long remember it, as a bitter memory.

Source: Eliza Whitmire in George P. Rawick, ed. *The American Slave: A Composite Autobiography* (Westport CT.: Greenwood Press, 1972), 380–381.

Elizabeth Watts, a Cherokee woman whose mother was born along the Trail of Tears, described the trek westward.

> The soldiers gathered them up, all up, and put them in camps. They hunted them and ran them down until they got all of them. Even before they were loaded in wagons, many of them got sick and died. They were all grief-stricken; they lost all on earth they had. White men even robbed their dead's graves to get their jewelry and other little trinkets. They saw to stay was impossible and Cherokees told Gen. Scott they would go without further trouble and the long journey started. They did not all come at once. First one batch and then another. The sick, old, and babies rode on the grub and household wagons. The rest rode a horse, if they had one. Most of them walked. Many of them died along the way. They buried them where they died, in unmarked graves. It was a bitter dose and lingered in the mind of Mrs. Watts' Grandparents and parents until death took them. The road they traveled, history calls the "Trail of Tears." This trail was more than tears. It was death, sorrow, hunger, exposure, and humiliation to a civilized people as were the Cherokees.

Elizabeth Watts, *Indian Pioneer History Collection* [microform], Grant Foreman, ed. (Oklahoma City, Oklahoma: Indian Archives Division, Oklahoma Historical Society Microfilm Publications, 1978–1981).

General Winfield Scott ordered the Cherokee people not to resist the removal order:

> Chiefs, head-men and warriors! Will you then, by resistance, compel us to resort to arms? God forbid! Or will you, by flight, seek to hide yourselves in moun-

Indians claimed that when they had signed the treaty transferring title to their land, they had not understood the implications of the action. "I touched the goose quill to the treaty," said Chief Black Hawk, "not knowing, however, that by that act I consented to give away my village." The United States army and the Illinois state militia ended the resistance by wantonly killing nearly 500 Sauk and Fox men, women, and children who were trying to retreat across the Mississippi River. In Florida, the military spent seven years putting down Seminole resistance at a cost of $20 million and 1500 casualties, and even then succeeding only after the treacherous act of kidnapping the Seminole leader Osceola during peace talks.

By twentieth-century standards, Jackson's Indian policy was both callous and inhumane. Despite the semblance of legality—94 treaties were signed with Indians during Jackson's presidency—Native American migrations to the West almost always occurred under the threat of government coercion. Even before Jackson's death in 1845, it was obvious that tribal lands in the West were no more secure than Indian lands had been in the East. In 1851 Congress passed the Indian Appropriations Act, which sought to concentrate the western Native American population on reservations.

Why were such morally indefensible policies adopted? Because many white Americans regarded Indian control of land and other natural resources as

tains and forests, and thus oblige us to hunt you down? Remember that, in pursuit, it may be impossible to avoid conflicts. The blood of the white man or the blood of the red man may be spilt, and, if spilt, however accidentally, it may be impossible for the discreet and humane among you, or among us, to prevent a general war and carnage. Think of this, my Cherokee brethren! I am an old warrior, and have been present at many a scene of slaughter, but spare me, I beseech you, the horror of witnessing the destruction of the Cherokees.

Source: Edward J. Cashin (ed.), *A Wilderness Still The Cradle of Nature: Frontier Georgia* (Savannah: Beehive Press, 1994), pp. 137–138.

Lt. L. B. Webster, who accompanied the Cherokee along part of the Trail of Tears, reported a first-hand account of the journey:

We were eight days in making the journey (80 miles), and it was pitiful to behold the women & children who suffered exceedingly as they were all obliged to walk, with the exception of the sick. . . . I had three regular ministers of the gospel in my party, and . . . we have preaching or prayer meeting every night while on the march, and you may well imagine that under the peculiar circumstances of the case, among those sublime mountains and in the deep forest with the thunder often roaring in the distance, that nothing could be more solemn and impressive. And I always looked on with . . . awe, lest their prayers which I felt . . . ascending to Heaven and calling for justice to Him who alone can & will grant it . . . [might] fall upon my guilty head as one of the instruments of oppression.

Source: Trail of Tears Association,
http://www.arch.dcr.state.nc.us/tears/director.htm

Private John G. Burnett, who also accompanied the Cherokee westward, described what he saw:

Being acquainted with many of the Indians and able to fluently speak their language, I was sent as interpreter into the Smoky Mountain Country in May, 1838, and witnessed the execution and the most brutal order in the history of American warfare. I saw helpless Cherokees arrested and dragged from their homes, and driven at the bayonet point into the stockades. And in the chill of a drizzling rain on an October morning, I saw them loaded like cattle or sheep into six hundred and forty-five wagons and started toward the west.

One can never forget the sadness and solemnity of that morning. Chief John Ross led in prayer and when the bugle sounded and the wagons started rolling many of the children rose to their feet and waved their little hands good-by to their mountain homes, knowing they were leaving them forever. Many of these helpless people did not have blankets and many of them had been driven from home barefooted.

On the morning of November the 17th we encountered a terrific sleet and snow storm with freezing temperatures and from that day until we reached the end of the fateful journey on March the 26th, 1839, the sufferings of the Cherokees were awful. The trail of the exiles was a trail of death. They had to sleep in the wagons and on the ground without fire. And I have known as many as twenty-two of them to die in one night of pneumonia due to ill treatment, cold, and exposure.

Source: John G. Burnett, "The Cherokee Removal through the Eyes of a Private Soldier" in *Journal of Cherokee Studies* (Summer, 1978): 180–185.

---

a serious obstacle to their desire for expansion and as a potential threat to the nation's security. Even had the federal government wanted to, it probably lacked the resources and military means necessary to protect the eastern Indians from encroaching white farmers, squatters, traders, and speculators. By the 1830s, a growing number of missionaries and humanitarians agreed with Jackson that Indians needed to be resettled westward for their own protection. Removal failed in large part because of the nation's commitment to limited government and its lack of experience with social welfare programs. Contracts for food, clothing, and transportation were awarded to the lowest bidders, many of whom failed to fulfill their contractual responsibilities. Indians were resettled on semi-arid lands, unsuited for intensive farming. The tragic outcome was readily foreseeable.

The problem of preserving native cultures in the face of an expanding nation was not confined to the United States. Jackson's removal policy can only be properly understood when seen as part of a broader process: the political and economic conquest of frontier regions by expanding nation states. During the early decades of the nineteenth century, Western nations were penetrating into many frontier areas, including the steppes of Russia, the pampas of Argentina, the veldt of South Africa, the outback of Australia, and the American West. In each of these regions, national expansion was justified on the grounds of strategic interest (to preempt settlement by other powers) or in the name of opening valuable land to white settlement and development. And in each case, the removal or wholesale killing of native peoples accompanied expansion.

Sectional Disputes over Public Lands and Nullification

Bitter sectional disputes arose during Jackson's presidency over public lands and the tariff. After the Revolutionary War, the federal government owned one-quarter billion acres of public land; the Louisiana Purchase added another half-billion acres to the public domain. These public lands constituted the federal government's single greatest resource.

In 1820, to promote the establishment of farms, Congress encouraged the rapid sale of public land by reducing the minimum land purchase from 160 to just 80 acres at a price of $1.25 per acre. Still, a variety of groups favored even easier terms for land sales. Squatters, for example, who violated federal laws that forbade settlement before the completion of public surveys, pressured Congress to adopt preemption acts that would permit them to buy the land they occupied at the minimum price of $1.25 when it came up for sale. Urban workingmen—agitating under the slogan "Vote Yourself a Farm"—demanded free homesteads for any American who would settle the public domain. Transportation companies, which built roads, canals, and later railroads, called for grants of public land to help fund their projects.

In Congress, two proposals—"distribution" and "graduation"—competed for support. Under the distribution proposal, which was identified with Henry Clay, Congress would distribute the proceeds from the sale of public lands to the states, which would use it to finance transportation improvements. Senator Thomas Hart Benton of Missouri offered an alternative proposal, graduation. He proposed that Congress gradually reduce the price of unsold government land and finally give away unpurchased land.

At the end of 1829, a Connecticut senator proposed a cessation of public land sales. This transformed the debate over public lands into a sectional battle over the nature of the union. Senator Benton denounced the proposal as a brazen attempt by manufacturers to keep laborers from settling the West, fearing that westward migration would reduce the size of the urban workforce and, therefore, raise their wage costs.

Benton's speech prompted Robert Y. Hayne, a supporter of John C. Calhoun, to propose an alliance of southern and western interests based on a low tariff and cheap land. Affirming the principle of nullification, he called on the two sections to unite against attempts by the Northeast to strengthen the powers of the federal government.

Daniel Webster of Massachusetts answered Hayne in one of the most famous speeches in American history. The United States, Webster proclaimed, was not simply a compact of the states. It was a creation of the people, who had invested the Constitution and the national government with ultimate sovereignty. If a state disagreed with an action of the federal government, it had a right to sue in federal court or seek to amend the Constitution, but it had no right to nullify a federal law. That would inevitably lead to anarchy and civil war. It was delusion and

In his famous oration, Senator Daniel Webster answered Senator Robert Hayne's call for states' rights, proclaiming, "Liberty and Union, now and forever, one and inseparable."

folly to think that Americans could have "Liberty first and Union afterwards," Webster declared. "Liberty and Union, now and forever, one and inseparable."

Jackson revealed his position on the questions of states' rights and nullification at a Jefferson Day dinner on April 13, 1830. Fixing his eyes on Vice President John C. Calhoun, Jackson expressed his sentiments with the toast: "Our Union: It must be preserved." Calhoun responded to Jackson's challenge and offered the next toast: "The Union, next to our liberty, most dear. May we always remember that it can only be preserved by distributing equally the benefits and burdens of the Union."

Relations between Jackson and Calhoun had grown increasingly strained. Jackson had learned that when Calhoun was secretary of war under Monroe he had called for Jackson's court-martial for his conduct during the military occupation of Florida in 1818. Jackson was also angry because Mrs. Calhoun had snubbed the wife of Secretary of War John H. Eaton, because Mrs. Eaton was the twice-married daughter of a tavern keeper. Because Jackson's own late wife Rachel had been snubbed by society (partly because she smoked a pipe and partly because she had unknowingly married Jackson before a divorce from her first husband was final), the president had empathy for young Peggy Eaton. In 1831, Jackson reorganized his cabinet and forced Calhoun's supporters out. The next year, Calhoun became the first vice president to resign his office, when he became a senator from South Carolina.

In 1832, in an effort to conciliate the South, Jackson proposed a lower tariff. Revenue from the existing tariff (together with the sale of public lands) was so high that the federal debt was quickly being paid off; in fact on January 1, 1835, the United States Treasury had a balance of $440,000, not a penny of which was owed to anyone—the only time in U.S. history when the government was completely free of debt. The new tariff adopted in 1832 was somewhat lower than the Tariff of 1828 but still maintained the principle of protection. In protest, South Carolina's fiery "states' righters" declared both the Tariff of 1832 and the Tariff of 1828 null and void. To defend nullification, the state legislature voted to raise an army.

Jackson responded by declaring nullification illegal and then asked Congress to empower him to use force to execute federal law. Congress promptly enacted a Force Act. Privately, Jackson threatened to "hang every leader . . . of that infatuated people, sir, by martial law, irrespective of his name, or political or social position." He also dispatched a fleet of eight ships and a shipment of 5000 muskets to Fort Pinckney, a federal installation in Charleston harbor.

In Congress, Henry Clay, the "great compromiser" who had engineered the Missouri Compromise of 1820, worked feverishly to reduce South Carolina's sense of grievance. "He who loves the Union must desire to see this agitating question brought to a termination," he said. In less than a month, he persuaded Congress to enact a compromise tariff with lower levels of protection. South Carolinians backed down, rescinding the ordinance nullifying the federal tariff. As a final gesture of defiance, however, the state adopted an ordinance nullifying the Force Act.

In 1830 and 1831 South Carolina stood alone. No other southern state yet shared South Carolina's fear of federal power or its militant desire to assert the doctrine of **states' rights**. South Carolina's anxiety had many causes. By 1831 declining cotton prices and growing concern about the future of slavery had turned the state from a staunch supporter of economic nationalism into the nation's most aggressive advocate of states' rights. Increasingly, economic grievances fused with concerns over slavery. In 1832, the Palmetto State was one of just two states (the other was Mississippi) the majority of whose population was made up of slaves. By that year events throughout the hemisphere made South Carolinians desperately uneasy about the future of slavery. In 1831 and 1832 militant abolitionism had erupted in the North, slave insurrections had occurred in Southampton County, Virginia, and Jamaica, and Britain was moving to emancipate all slaves in the British Caribbean.

By using the federal tariff as the focus of their grievances, South Carolinians found an ideal way of debating the question of state sovereignty without debating the morality of slavery. Following the Missouri Compromise debates, a slave insurrection led by Denmark Vesey had been uncovered in Charleston in 1822. By 1832 South Carolinians did not want to stage debates in Congress that might bring the explosive slavery issue to the fore and possibly incite another slave revolt.

The Bank War

The major political issue of Jackson's presidency was his war against the second Bank of the United States. The banking system at the time Jackson assumed the presidency was completely different than it is today. At that time, the federal government coined only a limited supply of hard money and printed no paper money at all. The principal source of circulating currency—paper bank notes—was private commercial banks (of which there were 329 in 1829) chartered by the various states. These private, state-chartered banks supplied the credit necessary to finance land purchases, business operations, and economic growth. The notes they issued were promises to pay in gold or silver, but they were backed by a limited amount of precious metal and they fluctuated greatly in value.

In 1816, the federal government had chartered the **second Bank of the United States** partly in an effort to control the notes issued by state banks. By demanding payment in gold or silver, the national bank could discipline over-speculative private banks. The very idea of a national bank, however, was unpopular for various reasons. Many people blamed it for causing the Panic of 1819. Others resented its political influence. For example, Senator Daniel Webster was both the bank's chief lobbyist and a director of the bank's Boston branch. Wage earners and small-business owners blamed it for economic fluctuations and loan restrictions. Private banks resented its privileged position in the banking industry.

In 1832, Henry Clay, Daniel Webster, and other Jackson opponents in Congress, seeking an issue for that year's presidential election, passed a bill rechartering the second Bank of the United States. The bank's charter was not due to expire until 1836, but Clay and Webster wanted to force Jackson to take a clear probank or antibank position. Jackson had frequently attacked the bank as an agency through which speculators, monopolists, and other seekers after economic privilege cheated honest farmers and mechanics. Now, his adversaries wanted to force him either to sign the bill for recharter, alienating voters hostile to the bank, or veto it, antagonizing conservative voters who favored a sound banking system.

Jackson vetoed the bill in a forceful message that condemned the bank as a privileged "monopoly" created to make "rich men . . . richer by act of Congress." The bank, he declared, was "unauthorized by the Constitution, subversive of the rights of the States, and dangerous to the liberties of the people." In the presidential campaign of 1832, Henry Clay tried to make an issue of Jackson's bank veto, but Jackson swept to an easy second-term victory, defeating Clay by 219 electoral votes to 49.

Jackson interpreted his reelection as a mandate to undermine the bank still further. In September 1833, he ordered his Treasury secretary to divert federal revenues from the Bank of the United States to selected state banks, which came to be known as "pet" banks. The secretary of the Treasury and his assistant resigned rather than carry out the president's order. It was only after Jackson appointed a second new secretary that his order was implemented. Jackson's decision to divert federal deposits from the national bank prompted his adversaries in the Senate to formally censure the president's actions as arbitrary and unconstitutional. The bank's president, Nicholas Biddle, responded to Jackson's actions by reducing loans and calling in debts. "This worthy President," said Biddle, "thinks that because he has scalped Indi-

ans and imprisoned Judges he is to have his way with the Bank. He is mistaken." Jackson retorted: "The Bank . . . is trying to kill me, but I will kill it."

Jackson's decision to divert funds drew strong support from many conservative businesspeople who believed that the bank's destruction would increase the availability of credit and open up new business opportunities. Jackson, however, hated all banks and believed that the only sound currencies were gold and silver. Having crippled the Bank of the United States, he promptly launched a crusade to replace all bank notes with hard money. Denouncing "the power which the moneyed interest derives from a paper currency," the president prohibited banks that received federal deposits from issuing bills valued at less than $5. Then, in the Specie Circular of 1836, Jackson prohibited payment for public lands in anything but gold or silver. That same year, in another antibanking measure, Congress voted to deprive pet banks of federal deposits. Instead, nearly $35 million in surplus funds was distributed to the states to help finance internal improvements.

To Jackson's supporters, the presidential veto of the bank bill was a principled assault on a bastion of wealth and special privilege. His efforts to curtail the circulation of bank notes was an effort to rid the country of a tool used by commercial interests to exploit farmers and working men and women. To his critics, the veto was an act of economic ignorance that destroyed a valuable institution that promoted monetary stability, eased the long-distance transfer of funds, provided a reserve of capital on which other banks drew, and helped regulate the bank notes issued by private banks. Jackson's effort to limit the circulation of bank notes was a misguided act of a "backward-looking" president, who failed to understand the role of a banking system in a modern economy.

The effect of Jackson's banking policies remains a subject of debate. Initially, land sales, canal construction, cotton production, and manufacturing boomed following Jackson's decision to divert federal funds from the bank. At the same time, however, state debts rose sharply and inflation increased dramatically. Prices climbed 28 percent in just three years. Then in 1837, just after the election of Jackson's successor Democrat Martin Van Buren, a deep financial depression struck the nation. Cotton prices fell by half. In New York City, 50,000 people were thrown out of work and 200,000 lacked adequate means of support. Hungry mobs broke into the city's flour warehouse. From across the country came "rumor after rumor of riot, insurrection, and tumult." Not until the mid-1840s would the country fully pull out of the depression.

Who was to blame for the **Panic of 1837**? One school of thought holds Jackson responsible, arguing that his banking policies removed a vital check on

As this anti-Jackson cartoon illustrates, defenders of the second Bank of the United States regarded Jackson's banking policies as a threat to the nation's economic health.

the activities of state-chartered banks. Freed from the regulation of the second Bank of the United States, private banks rapidly expanded the volume of bank notes in circulation, contributing to the rapid increase in inflation. Jackson's Specie Circular of 1836, which sought to curb inflation by requiring that public land payments be made in hard currency, forced many Americans to exchange paper bills for gold and silver. Many private banks lacked sufficient reserves of hard currency and were forced to close their doors, triggering a financial crisis.

Another school of thought blames the panic on factors outside of Jackson's control. A surplus of cotton on the world market caused the price of cotton to drop sharply, throwing many southern and western cotton farmers into bankruptcy. Meanwhile, in 1836, Britain suddenly raised interest rates, which drastically reduced investment in the American economy and forced a number of states to default on loans from foreign investors.

If Jackson's policies did not necessarily cause the panic, they certainly made recovery more difficult. Jackson's handpicked successor, Martin Van Buren, responded to the economic depression in an extremely doctrinaire way. A firm believer in the Jeffersonian principle of limited government, Van Buren refused to provide government aid to business.

Fearful that the federal government might lose funds it had deposited in private banks, Van Buren convinced Congress in 1840 to adopt an independent treasury system. Under this proposal, federal funds were locked up in insulated subtreasuries, which were totally divorced from the banking system. As a result the banking system was deprived of funds that might have aided recovery.

The Jacksonian Court

Presidents' judicial appointments represent one of their most enduring legacies. In his two terms as president, Andrew Jackson appointed five of the seven justices on the Supreme Court. To replace Chief Justice John Marshall, who died in 1835, Jackson selected his Treasury secretary, **Roger B. Taney,** who would lead the court for nearly three decades. Under Taney, the first chief justice to wear trousers instead of knee breeches, the Court broke with tradition and sought to extend Jacksonian principles of promoting individual opportunity by removing traditional restraints on competition in the marketplace. The Taney Court upheld the doctrine of limited liability for corporations and provided legal sanction to state subsidies for canals, turnpikes, and railroads. Taken together, the decisions of the Taney Court played a vital role in the emergence of the American system of free enterprise.

One case in particular, that of *Charles River Bridge v. Warren Bridge*, raised an issue fundamental to the nation's future economic growth: whether state-granted monopolies would be allowed to block competition from new enterprises. In 1828, the state of Massachusetts chartered a company to build a bridge connecting Boston and neighboring Charlestown. The owners of an existing bridge sued, claiming that their 1785 charter included an implied right to a monopoly.

In its decision, the Court ensured that monopolistic privileges granted in the past would not be allowed to interfere with public welfare. The Court held that contracts conferred only explicitly stated rights. Any ambiguity in wording should be construed in the public interest. The decision epitomized the ideals of Jacksonian democracy: a commitment to removing artificial barriers to opportunity and an emphasis upon free competition in an open marketplace.

Jackson's Legacy

Andrew Jackson was one of the nation's most resourceful and effective presidents. In the face of hostile majorities in Congress, he carried out his most important policies, affecting banking, internal improvements, Native Americans, and tariffs. As president, Jackson used the veto power more often than had all earlier presidents together during the preceding 40 years, and used it in such a way that he succeeded in representing himself as the champion of the people against special interests in Congress. In addition, his skillful use of patronage and party organization and his successful manipulation of public symbols helped create the nation's first modern political party with truly national appeal.

And yet, despite his popular appeal, Jackson's legacy is a matter of great dispute among historians. His Indian policies continue to arouse passionate criticism, while his economic policies, contrary to his reputation as the president of the common man, did little to help small farmers, artisans, and working people. In fact, his policies actually weakened the ability of the federal government to regulate the nation's economy. Indeed, many historians now believe that slaveholders—not small farmers or working people—benefited most. His Indian policy helped to open new lands for slaveowners, and his view of limited government forestalled federal interference with slavery.

RISE OF A POLITICAL OPPOSITION

Although it took a number of years for Jackson's opponents to coalesce into an effective national political organization, by the mid-1830s the Whig party, as the opposition came to be known, was able to battle the Democratic Party on almost equal terms throughout the country.

A Party Formed by Coalition

A coalition of National Republicans, Anti-Masons, and disgruntled Democrats, who were united by their hatred of "King Andrew" Jackson and his "usurpations" of congressional and judicial author-

ity, came together in 1834 to form the **Whig party.** The party took its name from the seventeenth-century British Whig group that had defended English liberties against the usurpations of pro-Catholic Stuart Kings.

In 1836 the Whigs mounted their first presidential campaign, running three regional candidates against Martin Van Buren: Daniel Webster, the senator from Massachusetts who had substantial appeal in New England; Hugh Lawson White, who had appeal in the South; and William Henry Harrison, who fought an Indian alliance at the Battle of Tippecanoe and appealed to the West and to Anti-Masons in Pennsylvania and Vermont. The party strategy was to throw the election into the House of Representatives, where the Whigs would unite behind a single candidate. Van Buren easily defeated all his Whig opponents, winning 170 electoral votes to just 73 for his closest rival.

Following his strong showing in the election of 1836, William Henry Harrison received the united support of the Whig party in 1840. Benefiting from the Panic of 1837 and from a host of colorful campaign innovations as described at the beginning of this chapter, Harrison easily defeated Van Buren by a vote of 234 to 60 in the Electoral College.

Unfortunately, the 68-year-old Harrison caught cold while delivering a two-hour inaugural address in the freezing rain. Barely a month later he died of pneumonia, the first president to die in office. His successor, **John Tyler** of Virginia, was an ardent defender of slavery, a staunch advocate of states' rights, and a former Democrat, whom the Whigs had nominated to attract Democratic support to the Whig ticket.

A firm believer in the principle that the federal government should exercise no powers other than those expressly enumerated in the Constitution, Tyler rejected the entire Whig legislative program, which called for reestablishment of a national bank, an increased tariff, and federally funded internal improvements.

The Whig party was furious. An angry mob gathered at the White House, threw rocks through the windows, and burned the president in effigy. To protest Tyler's rejection of the Whig political agenda, all members of the cabinet but one resigned. Tyler became a president without a party. "His Accidency" vetoed nine bills during his four years in office, more than any previous one-term president, frustrating Whig plans to recharter the national bank and raise the tariff while simultaneously distributing proceeds of land sales to the states. In 1843 Whigs in the House of Representatives made Tyler the subject of the first serious impeachment attempt, but the resolutions failed by a vote of 127 to 83.

Curiously, it was during John Tyler's tumultuous presidency that the nation's new two-party system achieved full maturity. Before Tyler's ascension to office, the Whig party had been a loose conglomeration of diverse political factions unable to agree on a party platform. Tyler's presidency increased unity among Whigs who found common cause in their opposition to his policies. Never before had party identity been so high or partisan sentiment so strong.

Who Were the Whigs?

The Jacksonians made a great effort to persuade voters to identify their own cause with Thomas Jefferson and their Whig opponents with Alexander Hamilton. A radical Jacksonian Democrat made the point bluntly. "The aristocracy of our country . . . continually contrive to change their party name," wrote Frederick Robinson. "It was first Tory, then Federalist, then no party, then amalgamation, then National Republican, now Whig." In spite of Democratic charges to the contrary, however, the Whigs were not simply a continuation of the Federalist Party. Like the Democrats, the Whigs drew support from all parts of the nation. Indeed, the Whigs often formed the majority of the South's representatives in Congress. Like the Democrats, the Whigs were a coalition of sectional interests, class and economic interests, and ethnic and religious interests.

Democratic voters tended to be small farmers, residents of less-prosperous towns, and the Scots-Irish and Catholic Irish. Whigs tended to be educators and professionals; manufacturers; business-oriented farmers; British and German Protestant immigrants; upwardly aspiring manual laborers; free blacks; and active members of Presbyterian, Unitarian, and Congregational churches. The Whig coalition included supporters of Henry Clay's American System, states' righters, religious groups alienated by Jackson's Indian removal policies, and bankers and businesspeople frightened by the Democrats' anti-monopoly and antibank rhetoric.

Whereas the Democrats stressed class conflict, Whigs emphasized the harmony of interests between labor and capital, the need for humanitarian reform, and leadership by men of talent. The Whigs also idealized the "self-made man," who starts "from an humble origin, and from small beginnings rise[s] gradually in the world, as a result of merit and industry." Finally, the Whigs viewed technology and factory enterprise as forces for increasing national wealth and improving living conditions.

In 1848 and 1852 the Whigs tried to repeat their successful 1840 presidential campaign by nominating military heroes for the presidency. The party won the 1848 election with General Zachary Taylor, an Indian fighter and hero of the Mexican War, who had boasted that he had never cast a vote in a presidential election. Like Harrison, Taylor confined his campaign speeches to uncontroversial platitudes. "Old Rough and Ready," as he was known, died after just 1 year and 127 days in office. Then, in 1852, the Whigs nominated another Indian fighter and Mexican War hero, General Winfield Scott, who carried just four states for his dying party. "Old Fuss and Feathers," as he was called, was the last Whig nominee to play an important role in a presidential election.

CONCLUSION

A political revolution occurred in the United States between 1820 and 1840. Those two decades saw the abolition of property qualification for voting and office-holding, the elimination of voting by voice, an increase in voter participation, and the emergence of a new party system. Unlike America's first political parties, the Federalists and Republicans, the Jacksonian Democrats and the Whigs were parties with grassroots organization and support in all parts of the nation.

Andrew Jackson, the dominant political figure of the period, spelled out the new democratic approach to politics. In the name of eliminating special privilege and promoting equality of opportunity, he helped institute the national political nominating convention, defended the spoils system, destroyed the second Bank of the United States, and opened millions of acres of Indian lands to white settlement. A strong and determined leader, Jackson greatly expanded the power of the presidency. When South Carolina asserted the right of a state to nullify the federal tariff, Jackson made it clear that he would not tolerate defiance of federal authority. No matter how one evaluates his eight years in the White House, there can be no doubt that he left an indelible stamp on the nation's highest office; indeed, on a whole epoch in American history.

CHAPTER SUMMARY AND KEY POINTS

In this chapter you learned about the developments that transformed American politics between 1820 and 1840. You also learned about Andrew Jackson and the ways that he increased the power and prestige of the office of the president.

- The period from 1820 to 1840 was a time of important political developments.

- Property qualifications for voting and officeholding were repealed; voting by voice was eliminated.

- Direct methods of selecting presidential electors, county officials, state judges, and governors replaced indirect methods. Voter participation increased.

CHRONOLOGY OF KEY EVENTS

1820 Land Act reduces price of public land to $1.25 per acre

1821 New York State Constitutional Convention eliminates property qualification for voting

1824 House of Representatives elects John Quincy Adams as sixth president

1825 President Monroe calls for voluntary removal of Native Americans in the east to lands west of the Mississippi River

1826 Disappearance of William Morgan touches off Anti-Masonic movement in New York State

1828 John C. Calhoun's "South Carolina Exposition" spells out the doctrine of nullification; Congress passes Tariff of Abominations; Andrew Jackson is elected seventh president

1830 Indian Removal Act provides funds to purchase Indian homelands in exchange for land in present-day Oklahoma and Arkansas; Webster-Hayne debate on land policy and nature of the union; Anti-Masons hold the first national party convention

1832 Jackson vetoes the bill to recharter the second Bank of the United States; John C. Calhoun becomes the first vice president to resign; South Carolina nullifies the federal tariff; United States defeats the Sauk and Fox Indians in the Black Hawk War

1833 Congress adopts "Compromise Tariff," lowering tariff rates, but also passes "Force Bill," authorizing Jackson to enforce federal law in South Carolina

1835 Roger B. Taney succeeds John Marshall as chief justice

1836 Jackson issues the Specie Circular; Martin Van Buren is elected eighth president

1837 Panic of 1837; *Charles River Bridge v. Warren Bridge* decides against monopoly privilege, rejecting the notion of implied rights in contracts and ruling that ambiguities in charters should be resolved in the favor of public welfare

1840 Congress passes Van Buren's Independent Treasury Act; William Henry Harrison, a Whig, is elected ninth president

1841 Harrison's death makes John Tyler the tenth president; Dorr Rebellion against suffrage restrictions in Rhode Island is put down

---

• A new two-party system replaced the politics of deference to elites.

• The dominant political figure of this era was Andrew Jackson, who opened millions of acres of Indian lands to white settlement, destroyed the second Bank of the United States, and denied the right of a state to nullify the federal tariff.

SUGGESTIONS FOR FURTHER READING

Donald B. Cole, *The Presidency of Andrew Jackson* (1993), and Richard Latner, *The Presidency of Andrew Jackson* (1979). Valuable one-volume overviews of Jackson's presidency.

Daniel Feller, *The Jacksonian Promise* (1995). An up-to-date reinterpretation of the Jacksonian era.

Michael Holt, *Rise and Fall of the American Whig Party* (1999). A thorough reappraisal of Jackson's political opposition.

Daniel Walker Howe, *The Political Culture of the American Whigs* (1979). Examines the political ideologies of the Whig party.

Paul C. Nagel, *John Quincy Adams: A Public Life, a Private Life* (1999). The eventful life of the sixth president, who was also a Senator, a Harvard professor, Secretary of State, and, following his presidency, a member of the House of Representatives.

Edward Pessen, *Jacksonian America,* rev. ed. (1978), and Harry L. Watson, *Liberty and Power* (1990). Offer insightful surveys of the Jacksonian era.

Robert Remini, *Andrew Jackson and the Course of American Freedom* (1981), and *Andrew Jackson and the Course of American Democracy* (1984). Major biographies of Andrew Jackson.

Robert V. Remini, *Andrew Jackson and His Indian Wars* (2002). A history and interpretation of Andrew Jackson's Indian policies.

Robert V. Remini, *John Quincy Adams* (2002). A concise portrait of the life of the son of the second president who would become president himself.

Robert V. Remini, *Life of Andrew Jackson* (2001). A one-volume abridgement of the author's prize-winning three-volume biography.

Peter Temin, *The Jacksonian Economy* (1969). Reexamines Jackson's economic and banking policies.

Anthony F. C. Wallace, *The Long, Bitter Trail: Andrew Jackson and the Indians* (1993). Analyzes Jackson's Indian policies.

Novels

James Fenimore Cooper, *The Chainbearer* (1845).

James Fenimore Cooper, *The Ways of the Hour* (1850).

MEDIA RESOURCES

Web Sites

Alexis de Tocqueville

http://www.tocqueville.org/

This C-Span site contains extensive information about Tocqueville's visit to the United States and his observations about democracy.

Documents from the Gilder Lehrman Collection

http://www.gliah.uh.edu/modules/jacksonian/documents.cfm

Primary source documents relating to the major political controversies of the Jacksonian era.

Jacksonian Miscellanies

http://216.202.17.223/essays/Readings.htm

Primary sources on religion, transportation, communication, education, slavery and antislavery, manners, violence, and many other topics.

Medicine of the Jacksonian Era

http://www.connerprairie.org/historyonline/jmed.html

Information on the practice of medicine in Jacksonian America.

Films and Videos

Gangs of New York (2002). Martin Scorsese's epic portrait of conflict between Irish and native-born gangs in mid-nineteenth-century New York.

The President's Lady (1953). This film concentrates on Andrew Jackson's relationship with his wife Rachel, whose reputation causes scandal.

KEY TERMS

Universal white manhood suffrage   (p. 249)

Anti-Masonic party   (p. 251)

Second party system   (p. 254)

Panic of 1819   (p. 254)

Missouri crisis   (p. 254)

National Republicans   (p. 255)

Jacksonian Democrats   (p. 255)

American system   (p. 256)

Tariff of Abominations   (p. 256)

Nullification   (p. 256)

Spoils system   (p. 257)

Indian removal   (p. 258)

Trail of Tears   (p. 259)

Black Hawk War   (p. 259)

States' rights   (p. 263)

Second Bank of the United States   (p. 264)

Panic of 1837   (p. 264)

Charles River Bridge v. Warren Bridge   (p. 265)

Whig party   (p. 266)

PEOPLE YOU SHOULD KNOW

William Henry Harrison   (p. 247)

Martin Van Buren   (p. 247)

James Monroe   (p. 248)

John Quincy Adams   (p. 254)

John C. Calhoun   (p. 254)

Henry Clay   (p. 254)

Andrew Jackson   (p. 254)

Sequoyah   (p. 258)

Roger B. Taney   (p. 265)

John Tyler   (p. 266)

REVIEW QUESTIONS

1. What changes took place in voting, nominating procedures, party organization, and campaign strategies between 1820 and 1840?

2. What new political parties emerged in the 1820s and 1830s? How did these parties differ?

3. What groups were denied political participation under Jacksonian democracy?

4. Why did settlers want to move Native Americans west of the Mississippi River? How did Native Americans try to resist removal? Why is the removal of the Native Americans from their homelands in the Southeast known as the Trail of Tears?

5. Why did South Carolina try to nullify the federal tariff? What was President Jackson's reaction? How was the controversy resolved?

6. Why was President Jackson opposed to the Second Bank of the United States? What actions did he take to weaken the bank?

7. How did President Jackson strengthen the presidency?

11 America's First Age of Reform

CONNECTICUT SCHOOLMISTRESS PRUDENCE CRANDALL DEFIES THE LAW

In 1832, Sarah Harris, the 20-year-old daughter of a free black farmer, asked to be admitted to a female academy in Canterbury, Connecticut. She "wanted to get a little more learning," she told the academy's mistress, **Prudence Crandall.** At first, the 29-year-old teacher hesitated but finally agreed to let her enroll.

Almost immediately, white parents began to withdraw their daughters from the school. But Crandall, a Baptist who had been raised as a Quaker, refused to back down. She decided to convert her academy into a school for "the education of young ladies and little misses of color." She advertised for students and attracted more than 20 young black women from as far away as Boston, New York, and Philadelphia.

The Connecticut General Assembly responded by passing a law that prohibited the teaching of nonresident "colored" students without approval of local authorities. Twice, the young schoolteacher was arrested for defying the law. She was jailed temporarily when she refused to post bond. The first trial ended in a hung jury. The retrial led to a conviction.

While she appealed the verdict, Crandall and her students were subjected to insults and harassment. Local townspeople ostracized them. Local shopkeepers refused to sell them food. Local youths hurled rotten eggs and rocks at the schoolhouse. An arsonist tried to burn down the school. The students described the persecution they faced in song:

Sometimes when we have walked the streets
Saluted we have been
By guns and drums and cow bells, too
And horns of polished tin.
With warnings, threats, and words severe
They visit us at times
And gladly would they send us off
To Africa's burning climes.

Prudence Crandall, a Baptist schoolteacher, was jailed for teaching free African American children.

At a town meeting, Canterbury residents passed a resolution declaring that the school was part of a larger scheme by opponents of slavery "to promulgate their disgusting doctrines of [racial] amalgamation, and their pernicious sentiments of subverting the Union. Their pupils were to have been congregated here from all quarters under the false pretence of educating them, but really to TO SCATTER FIREBRANDS, arrows and death among the brethren of our own blood." Just two years earlier, a town meeting in New Haven, Connecticut, had rejected a proposal to construct a college for black men near Yale College by a vote of 702 to 4.

Late in July 1834, an appeals court dismissed the charges. A little more than a month later, on the evening of September 9, 1834, a group of townspeople attacked the school with crowbars. Crandall, her husband, and a number of students were inside. The mob broke the building's windows, overturned the furniture, and apparently attempted to set the build-

ing on fire. Fearful for students' safety, Crandall closed her school the next morning. Within a year, she and her husband had fled the state, first for New York, and later for Illinois and Kansas. In 1883, partly as a result of lobbying by the novelist Mark Twain, the Connecticut Assembly approved a pension for Crandall as reparations for the harassment she had undergone.

The decades before the Civil War saw the birth of the American reform tradition. Reformers—female and male, black and white—launched unprecedented campaigns to educate the deaf and the blind, rehabilitate criminals, extend equal rights to women, and abolish slavery. Our modern systems of free public schools, prisons, and hospitals for the infirm and the mentally ill are all legacies of this first generation of American reform.

SOURCES OF THE REFORM IMPULSE

What factors gave rise to the reform impulse and why was it unleashed with such vigor in pre–Civil War America? Reformers had many different reasons for wanting to change American society. Some hoped to remedy the distresses created by social disorder, violence, and widening class divisions. Others found motivation in a religious vision of a godly society on earth.

Social Problems on the Rise

During the early nineteenth century, poverty, lawlessness, violence, and vice appeared to be increasing at an alarming rate. In New York, the nation's largest city, crime rose far faster than the overall population. Between 1814 and 1834, the city's population doubled, but reports of crime quadrupled. Gangs, bearing such names as Plug Uglies and Bowery B'hoys, prowled the streets, stealing from warehouses and private residences. Public drunkenness was a common sight. By 1835, there were nearly 3000 drinking places in New York—one for every 50 persons over the age of 15. Prostitution also generated concern. By 1850, a reported 6000 "fallen women" strolled the city streets. Mob violence evoked particular fear. In a single decade, 1834–1844, 200 incidents of mob violence occurred in New York. Adding to the sense of alarm were scenes of heart-wrenching poverty, such as children standing barefoot outside hotels, selling matches.

Social problems were not confined to large cities like New York. During the decades before the Civil War, newspapers reported hundreds of incidences of

As early as the 1820s, urban slums like New York City's Five Points began to appear. These areas of poverty, crime, filth, and violence attracted beggars, pimps, prostitutes, and hoodlums.

duels, lynchings, and mob violence. In the slave states and southwestern territories men frequently resolved quarrels by dueling. In one 1818 duel between two cousins, the combatants faced off with shotguns at four paces! Lynchings too were widely reported. In 1835, the citizens of Vicksburg, Mississippi, attempted to rid the city of gambling and prostitution by raiding gaming houses and brothels and lynching five gamblers. In urban areas, mob violence increased in frequency and destructiveness. Between 1810 and 1819 there were 7 major riots; in the 1830s there were 115.

A nation in which the vice president had to carry a gun while presiding over the Senate—lest senators attack each other with knives or pistols—seemed to confirm criticism by Europeans that democracy inevitably led to anarchy. Incidents of crime and violence led many Americans to ask how a free society could maintain stability and moral order. Americans sought to answer this question through religion, education, and social reform.

A New Moral Sensibility

More than anxiety over lawlessness, violence, and vice sparked the reform impulse during the first decades of the nineteenth century. America's revolutionary heritage, the philosophy of the Enlightenment, and religious zeal all contributed to a sensitivity to human suffering and a boundless faith in humankind's capacity to improve social institutions.

Many pre–Civil War reformers saw their efforts as an attempt to realize the ideals enshrined in the Declaration of Independence. Invoking the principles of liberty and equality set forth in the Declaration, abolitionists such as William Lloyd Garrison attacked slavery and feminists such as Elizabeth Cady Stanton called for equal rights for women.

The philosophy of the **Enlightenment,** with its belief in the people's innate goodness and with its rejection of the inevitability of poverty and ignorance, was another important source of the reform impulse. Those who espoused the Enlightenment philosophy argued that the creation of a more favorable moral and physical environment could alleviate social problems.

Religion further strengthened the reform impulse. Almost all the leading reformers were devoutly religious men and women who wanted to deepen the nation's commitment to Christian principles. Two trends in religious thought—religious liberalism and evangelical revivalism—strengthened reformers' zeal. **Religious liberalism** was an emerging form of humanitarianism that rejected the harsh Calvinist doctrines of original sin and predestination. Its preachers stressed the basic goodness of human nature and each individual's capacity to follow the example of Christ.

William Ellery Channing (1780–1842) was America's leading exponent of religious liberalism, and his beliefs, proclaimed in a sermon he delivered in Baltimore in 1819, became the basis for American Unitarianism. The new religious denomination stressed individual freedom of belief, a united world under a single God, and the mortal nature of Jesus Christ, whom individuals should strive to emulate. Channing's beliefs stimulated many reformers to work toward improving the conditions of the physically handicapped, the criminal, the impoverished, and the enslaved.

The Second Great Awakening

Enthusiastic religious revivals swept the nation in the early nineteenth century, providing further religious motivation for the reform impulse. On August 6, 1801, some 25,000 men, women, and children gathered in the small frontier community of Cane Ridge, Kentucky, in search of religious salvation. Twenty-five thousand was a fantastically large number of people at a time when the population of the whole state of Kentucky was a quarter million, and the state's largest city, Lexington, had only 1795 residents. The Cane Ridge camp meeting went on for a week. Baptists, Methodists, and ministers of other denominations joined together to preach to the vast throng. Within three years, similar revivals occurred throughout Kentucky, Tennessee, and Ohio. This

Americans turned to revival meetings in times of social and economic upheaval. These meetings, which stressed new-birth conversions, could last for days.

great wave of religious fervor became known as the **Second Great Awakening.**

The revivals inspired a widespread sense that the nation was standing close to the **millennium,** a thousand years of peace and benevolence when sin, war, and tyranny would vanish from the earth. Evangelical leaders urged their followers to reject selfishness and materialism and repent their sins. To the revivalists, sin was no metaphysical abstraction. Luxury, high living, indifference to religion, preoccupation with worldly and commercial matters—all were denounced as sinful. If men and women did not seek God through Christ, the nation would face divine retribution. **Evangelical revivals** helped instill in Americans a belief that they had been chosen by God to lead the world toward "a millennium of republicanism."

Charles Grandison Finney (1792–1875), the "father of modern revivalism," led revivals throughout the Northeast. Finney became the North's leading revivalist. Despite his lack of formal theological training, he was remarkably successful in converting souls to Christ. Finney's message was that anyone could experience a redemptive change of heart and a resurgence of religious feeling. He prayed for sinners by name; he held meetings that lasted night after night for a week or more; he set up an "anxious bench" at the front of the meeting, where the almost-saved could receive special prayers. He also encouraged women to participate actively in revivals. If only enough people converted to Christ, Finney told his listeners, the millennium—Christ's reign on earth—would arrive within three years.

Revival meetings attracted both frontier settlers and city folk, slaves and masters, farmers and shopkeepers. The revivals had their greatest appeal among isolated farming families on the western and southern frontier and among upwardly mobile merchants, shopkeepers, artisans, skilled laborers in the expanding commercial and industrial towns of the North. They also drew support from social conservatives who feared that America would disintegrate into a state of anarchy without the influence of evangelical religion. Above all, revivals attracted large numbers of young women, who took an active role organizing meetings, establishing church societies, and editing religious publications.

Religious Diversity

The early nineteenth century was a period of extraordinary religious ferment. Church membership climbed steeply, until three-quarters of all Americans were affiliated with a church. The religious landscape grew increasingly diverse. A number of older denominations—notably the Baptists, Catholics, and Methodists—expanded rapidly while a host of new denominations and movements arose, including the African Methodist Episcopal church, the Disciples of Christ, the Mormons, and the Unitarian and Universalist churches.

During the late eighteenth century, church membership was low and falling. **Deism**—a movement that emphasized reason rather than revelation and denied that a divine creator interfered with the workings of the universe—and skepticism seemed to be spreading. A French immigrant claimed that "religious indifference is imperceptibly disseminated from one end of the continent to the other." Yet by 1830, foreign observers considered the United States the most religious country in the western world.

Religious revivals played a critical role in this outpouring of religion. In part, revivalism represented a response to the growing separation of church and state that followed the American Revolution. When states deprived established churches of state support (as did Virginia in 1785, Connecticut in 1818, and Massachusetts in 1833), Protestant ministers held revivals to ensure that America remained a God-fearing nation. The popularity of revivals also reflected the hunger of many Americans for an emotional religion that downplayed creeds and rituals and instead emphasized conversion.

No religious group grew more rapidly during the pre–Civil War era or faced more bitter hostility than the Roman Catholic Church. From just 25,000 members and 6 priests in 1776, the Catholic Church in America grew to 3 million members in 1860. With

English, French, German, Irish, and Mexican members, it was not only the nation's largest denomination, it was also America's first multicultural church. Concerned that many immigrants were only nominally Catholic, the Church established urban missions and launched religious revivals to strengthen Catholics' religious identity. Somewhat similar to the Protestant evangelical revivals, the Catholic revivals featured rousing sermons and encouraged piety, fervor, and devotion. By establishing its own schools and system of hospitals, orphanages, and benevolent societies, the Church sought to help Catholics preserve their faith in the face of Protestant proselytizing.

Prejudice and discrimination led African Americans to create their own churches. The first were established in Philadelphia, after the city's black Methodists were ordered to sit in a segregated gallery. Between 1804 and 1815, African Americans formed their own Baptist, Methodist, and Presbyterian churches in eastern cities. In 1816, the African Methodist Episcopal Church, the first autonomous black denomination, was founded.

Another religious group that grew sharply before the Civil War was American Jewry. At the beginning of the nineteenth century, there were only about 2000 Jews in the United States, six Jewish congregations, no Jewish newspapers, and not a single rabbi. By 1860, when the number of American Jews had climbed to 150,000, Jewish newspapers reached readers in 1250 communities, and Jews had served in the legislatures of Georgia, Indiana, New York, North Carolina, and South Carolina. Jews faced less discrimination and hostility than Catholics, in part because the Jewish community was scattered and in

part because most Jews shed the distinctive dress, long sideburns, and other customs that set European Jews apart. Yet, although they adapted to American life in many ways, Jews vigorously resisted threats to their identity, strongly opposing state laws that limited public office to Christians, bans against commerce on the Christian Sabbath, and the recitation of Christian prayers in schools.

MORAL REFORM

The earliest reformers wanted to persuade Americans to adopt more godly personal habits. They set up associations to battle profanity and Sabbath breaking, to place a Bible in every American home, and to curb the widespread heavy use of hard liquor. By discouraging drinking and gambling and encouraging observance of the Sabbath, reformers hoped to "restore the government of God" on earth.

One of the most dramatic attempts at moral reform involved Magdalene societies, which sought in the 1830s and 1840s to rehabilitate prostitutes and discourage male solicitation. The New York Moral Reform Society had 15,000 members in 1837 and branches in New England and upstate New York. Members walked into brothels and prayed for the prostitutes, publicized in the newspapers the names of men who patronized prostitutes, visited prostitutes in jails, and lobbied for state laws that would make male solicitation of prostitutes a crime.

The most extensive moral reform campaign was that against drinking, which was an integral part of American life. Many people believed that downing a

The temperance movement of the 1830s and 1840s used religious revivalist tactics to frighten drinkers into taking the "pledge" to abstain from drinking.

glass of whiskey before breakfast was conducive to good health. Instead of taking coffee breaks, people took a dram of liquor at 11 and again at 4 o'clock as well as drinks after meals "to aid digestion" and a nightcap before going to sleep. Campaigning politicians offered voters generous amounts of liquor during campaigns and as rewards for "right voting" on election day. On the frontier, one evangelist noted, "a house could not be raised, a field of wheat cut down, nor could there be a log rolling, a husking, a quilting, a wedding, or a funeral without the aid of alcohol."

Easily affordable to even the poorest Americans—a gallon of whiskey cost 25 cents in the 1820s—consumption had risen markedly since the beginning of the century. The supply of alcohol increased as farmers distilled growing amounts of corn into cheap whiskey, which could be transported more easily than bulk corn. By 1820 the typical adult American consumed more than 7 gallons of absolute alcohol a year (compared to 2.6 gallons today).

Reformers identified liquor as the cause of a wide range of social, family, and personal problems. Many middle-class women blamed alcohol for the abuse of wives and children and the squandering of family resources. Many businesspeople identified drinking with crime, poverty, and inefficient and unproductive employees.

The stage was set for the appearance of an organized movement against liquor. In 1826 the nation's first formal national **temperance** organization—the American Society for the Promotion of Temperance—was born. Led by socially prominent clergy and laypeople, the new organization called for total abstinence from distilled liquor. Within three years, 222 state and local antiliquor groups were laboring to spread this message.

By 1835 an estimated 2 million Americans had taken the "pledge" to abstain from hard liquor. Temperance reform drew support from many southerners and westerners who were otherwise indifferent or hostile to reform. Their efforts helped reduce annual per capita consumption of alcohol from 7 gallons in 1830 to 3 gallons a decade later, forcing 4000 distilleries to close.

The sudden arrival of hundreds of thousands of immigrants from "heavy drinking" cultures heightened the concerns of temperance reformers. Between 1830 and 1860, nearly 2 million Irish arrived in the United States along with an additional 893,000 Germans. In Ireland, land was in such short supply that many young men were unable to support a family by farming. The only solution was to delay marriage and socialize with other young men in "bachelor groups," a ritual that often involved drinking. These immigrants probably drank no more than most native-born Americans before the 1830s, but increasingly heavy drinking was regarded as a problem demanding government action.

Two new approaches to the temperance movement arose during the 1840s. The first was the Washingtonian movement in which reformed alcoholics sought to reform other drinkers. As many as 600,000 drinkers took the Washingtonian pledge of total abstinence. The second approach was a campaign to restrict the manufacture and sale of alcohol, culminating in adoption of the nation's first statewide prohibition law in Maine in 1851, which led to prohibition laws often being referred to as "Maine laws." Convinced that moral suasion was ineffective, a minister argued strongly in behalf of prohibition laws: "You might almost as well persuade the chained maniac to leave off howling, as to persuade him to leave off drinking."

SOCIAL REFORM

The nation's first reformers tried to improve the nation's moral and spiritual values by distributing Bibles and religious tracts, promoting observance of the Sabbath, and curbing drinking. Beginning in the 1820s a new phase of reform—social reform—spread across the country, directed at crime, illiteracy, poverty, and disease. Reformers sought to solve these social problems by creating new institutions to deal with them—including prisons, public schools, and asylums for the deaf, the blind, and the mentally ill.

The Problem of Crime in a Free Society

Before the American Revolution, punishment for crimes generally involved some form of corporal punishment, ranging from the death penalty for serious crimes to public whipping, confinement in stocks, and branding for lesser offenses. Jails were used as temporary confinement for criminal defendants awaiting trial or punishment. Conditions in these early jails were abominable. Cramped cells held large groups of offenders of both sexes and all ages; debtors were confined with hardened criminals. Prisoners customarily had to pay the expenses of food and lodging.

During the pre–Civil War decades reformers began to view crime as a social problem—a product of environment and parental neglect—rather than the result of original sin or innate human depravity. Reformers believed it was the duty of a humane society to remove the underlying causes of crime, to sympathize and show patience toward criminals and to try to reform them, instead of whipping or confining them in stocks.

Revulsion over the spectacle of public punishment led to the rapid construction of penal institutions in which the "disease" of crime could be quarantined and inmates could be gradually rehabilitated in a carefully controlled environment. Two rival prison systems competed for public support. After constructing Auburn Prison, New York state authorities adopted a system in which inmates worked in large workshops during the day and slept in separate cells at night. Convicts had to march in lockstep and refrain from speaking or even looking at each other. In Pennsylvania's Eastern State Penitentiary, constructed in 1829, authorities placed even greater stress on the physical isolation of prisoners. Every prison cell had its own exercise yard, work space, and toilet facilities. Under the Pennsylvania plan, prisoners lived and worked in complete isolation from each other. Called "penitentiaries" or "reformatories," these new prisons reflected the belief that hard physical labor and solitary confinement might encourage introspection and instill habits of discipline that would rehabilitate criminals.

The legal principle that a criminal act should be legally punished only if the offender was fully capable of distinguishing between right and wrong opened the way to one of the most controversial aspects of American jurisprudence—the **insanity defense.** The question arose dramatically in 1835 when a deranged Englishman named Richard Lawrence walked up to President Andrew Jackson and fired two pistols at him from a distance of six feet. Incredibly, both guns misfired, and Jackson was unhurt. Lawrence believed that Jackson's attack on the second Bank of the United States had prevented him from obtaining money that would have enabled him to claim the English throne. The court, ruling that Lawrence was clearly suffering from a mental delusion, found him insane and not subject to criminal prosecution; instead, he was confined to an asylum for treatment of his mental condition.

Another major effort in social reform was the drive to outlaw **capital punishment.** Before the 1830s, most states reduced the number of crimes punishable by death and began to perform executions out of public view, lest the public be stimulated to acts of violence by the spectacle of hangings. In 1847 Michigan became the first modern jurisdiction to outlaw the death penalty; Rhode Island and Wisconsin soon followed.

Imprisonment for debt also came under attack. As late as 1816, an average of 600 residents of New York City were in prison at any one time for failure to pay debts. More than half owed less than $50. New York's debtor prisons provided no food, furniture, or fuel for their inmates, who would have starved without the assistance of relatives or the charity of humane societies. In a Vermont case, state courts imprisoned a man for a debt of just 54 cents, and in Boston a woman was taken from her three children as a result of a $3 debt.

Increasingly, reformers regarded imprisonment for debt as irrational, since imprisoned debtors were unable to work and pay off their debts. Piecemeal reform led to the abolition of debtor prisons, as states eliminated the practice of jailing people for trifling debts and then forbade the jailing of women and veterans.

The Struggle for Public Schools

Of all the ideas advanced by antebellum reformers, none was more original than the principle that all American children should be educated to their full capacity at public expense. Reformers viewed education as the key to individual opportunity and the creation of an enlightened and responsible citizenry. Reformers also believed that public schooling could be an effective weapon in the fight against juvenile crime and an essential ingredient in the assimilation of immigrants.

From the early days of settlement, Americans attached special importance to education. During the seventeenth century, the New England Puritans required every town to establish a public school supported by fees from all but the very poorest families (a requirement later repealed). In the late eighteenth century, Thomas Jefferson popularized the idea that a democratic republic required an enlightened and educated citizenry. Early nineteenth-century educational reformers extended these ideas and struggled to make universal public education a reality. As a result of their efforts, the northern states were among the first jurisdictions in the world to establish tax-supported, tuition-free public schools.

At the beginning of the nineteenth century, the United States had the world's highest literacy rate—approximately 75 percent. Apprenticeship was a major form of education, supplemented by church schools, charity schools for the poor, and private academies for the affluent. Many youngsters learned to read in informal dame schools, in which a woman would take girls and boys into her own home. Formal schooling was largely limited to those who could afford to pay. Many schools admitted pupils regardless of age, mixing young children with young adults in their twenties. A single classroom could contain as many as 80 pupils.

The campaign for public schools began in earnest in the 1820s, when religiously motivated reformers advocated public education as an answer to poverty, crime, and deepening social divisions. At first, many reformers championed Sunday schools as a way "to reclaim the vicious, to instruct the ignorant, to secure the observance of the Sabbath . . . and to raise the standard of morals among the lower classes of society." But soon, reformers began to call for public schools.

Horace Mann (1796–1859) of Massachusetts, the nation's leading educational reformer, led the fight for government support for public schools. As a state legislator, in 1837 Mann took the lead in establishing a state board of education and his efforts resulted in a doubling of state expenditures on education. He also won state support for teacher training, an improved curriculum in schools, the grading of pupils by age and ability, and a lengthened school year. He was also partially successful in curtailing the use of corporal punishment. In 1852, three years after Mann left office to take a seat in the U.S. Congress, Massachusetts adopted the first compulsory school attendance law in American history.

Educational opportunities, however, were not available to all. Most northern cities specifically excluded African Americans from the public schools. It was not until 1855 that Massachusetts became the first state to admit students to public schools without regard to "race, color, or religious opinions."

Women and religious minorities also experienced discrimination. For women, education beyond the level of handicrafts and basic reading and writing was largely confined to separate female academies and seminaries for the affluent. Emma Hart Willard opened one of the first academies offering an advanced education to women in Philadelphia in 1814. Many public school teachers showed an anti-Catholic bias by using texts that portrayed the Catholic Church as a threat to republican values and reading passages from a Protestant version of the Bible. Beginning in New York City in 1840, Catholics decided to establish their own system of schools in which children would receive a religious education as well as training in the arts and sciences.

In higher education a few institutions opened their doors to African Americans and women. In 1833 Oberlin College, where Charles G. Finney taught, became the nation's first coeducational college. Four years later, Mary Lyon established the first women's college, Mount Holyoke, to train teachers and missionaries. A number of western state universities also admitted women. In addition, three colleges for African Americans were founded before the Civil War, and a few other colleges, including Ober-

lin, Harvard, Bowdoin, and Dartmouth, admitted small numbers of black students.

The reform impulse brought other changes in higher education. At the beginning of the nineteenth century, most colleges offered their students, who usually enrolled between the ages of 12 and 15, only a narrow training in the classics designed to prepare them for the ministry. During the 1820s and 1830s, in an effort to adjust to the "spirits and wants of the age," colleges broadened their curricula to include the study of history, literature, geography, modern languages, and the sciences. The entrance age was also raised and the requirements demanded of students were broadened.

The number of colleges also increased. Most of the new colleges, particularly in the South and West, were church-affiliated, but several states established public universities. Before the Civil War, 16 states provided some financial support to higher education, and by the 1850s, New York City offered tuition-free education from elementary school to college.

Asylums for Society's Outcasts

A number of reformers devoted their attention to the problems of the mentally ill, the deaf, and the blind. In 1841, **Dorothea Dix** (1802–1887), a 39-year-old former schoolteacher, volunteered to give religious instruction to women incarcerated in the East Cambridge, Massachusetts, House of Correction. Inside the House of Correction, she was horrified to find mentally ill inmates dressed in rags and confined to a single dreary, unheated room. Shocked by what she saw, she embarked on a lifelong crusade to reform the treatment of the mentally ill.

After a two-year secret investigation of every jail and almshouse in Massachusetts, Dix issued a report to the state legislature. The mentally ill, she found, were mixed indiscriminately with paupers and hardened criminals. Many were confined "in cages, closets, cellars, stalls, pens! Chained, naked, beaten with rods and lashed into obedience." Dix then carried her campaign for state-supported asylums nationwide, persuading more than a dozen state legislatures to improve institutional care for the insane.

Through the efforts of reformers such as Thomas Gallaudet and Samuel Gridley Howe, institutions to care for the deaf and blind began to appear. In 1817, **Thomas Hopkins Gallaudet** (1787–1851) established the nation's first school in Hartford, Connecticut, to teach deaf-mutes to read and write, read lips, and communicate through hand signals. **Samuel Gridley Howe** (1801–1876), the husband of Julia Ward Howe, composer of the "Battle Hymn of the Republic," accomplished for the blind what Gallaudet achieved for the deaf. He founded the country's first school for the blind in Boston and produced printed materials with raised type.

RADICAL REFORM

The initial thrust of reform—moral reform—was to rescue the nation from infidelity and intemperance. A second line of reform, social or humanitarian reform, attempted to alleviate such sources of human misery as crime, cruelty, disease, and ignorance. A third line of reform, radical reform, sought national regeneration by eliminating slavery and racial and sexual discrimination.

Early Antislavery Efforts

As late as the 1750s, no church had discouraged its members from owning or trading in slaves. Slaves could be found in each of the 13 American colonies, and before the American Revolution, only the colony of Georgia had temporarily sought to prohibit slavery (because its founders did not want a workforce that would compete with the convicts they planned to transport from England).

By the beginning of the nineteenth century, however, protests against slavery had become widespread. By 1804 nine states north of Maryland and Delaware had either emancipated their slaves or adopted gradual emancipation plans. Both the United States and Britain in 1808 outlawed the African slave trade.

The emancipation of slaves in the northern states and the prohibition against the African slave trade generated optimism that slavery was dying. Congress in 1787 had barred slavery from the Old Northwest, the region north of the Ohio River to the Mississippi River. The number of slaves freed by their masters had risen dramatically in the upper South during the 1780s and 1790s, and more antislavery societies had been formed in the South than in the North. At the present rate of progress, predicted one religious leader in 1791, within 50 years it will "be as shameful for a man to hold a Negro slave, as to be guilty of common robbery or theft."

By the early 1830s, however, the development of the Cotton Kingdom proved that slavery was not on the road to extinction. Despite the end of the African slave trade, the slave population continued to grow, climbing from 1.5 million in 1820 to over 2 million a decade later.

A widespread belief that blacks and whites could not coexist and that racial separation was necessary encouraged futile efforts at deportation and overseas colonization. In 1817 a group of prominent ministers and politicians formed the American Colonization Society to resettle free blacks in West Africa, encourage planters voluntarily to emancipate their slaves, and create a group of black missionaries who would spread Christianity in Africa. During the 1820s, Congress helped fund the cost of transporting free blacks to Africa.

A few blacks supported African colonization in the belief that it provided the only alternative to continued degradation and discrimination. **Paul Cuffe** (1759–1817), a Quaker sea captain who was the son of a former slave and an Indian woman, led the first experiment in colonization. In 1815 he transported 38 free blacks to the British colony of Sierra Leone, on the western coast of Africa, and devoted thousands of his own dollars to the cause of colonization. In 1822 the American Colonization Society established the colony of Liberia, in west Africa, for resettlement of free American blacks.

It soon became apparent that colonization was a wholly impractical solution to the nation's slavery problem. Each year the nation's slave population rose by roughly 50,000, but in 1830 the American Colonization Society succeeded in persuading only 259 free blacks to migrate to Liberia, bringing the total number of blacks colonized in Africa to a mere 1400.

The Rise of Abolitionist Sentiment in the North

Initially, free blacks led the movement condemning colonization and northern discrimination against African Americans. As early as 1817, more than 3000 members of Philadelphia's black community staged a protest against colonization, at which they denounced the policy as "little more merciful than death." In 1829 **David Walker** (1785–1830), the free black owner of a second-hand clothing store in Boston, issued the militant *Appeal to the Colored Citizens of the World*. The appeal threatened insurrection and violence if calls for the abolition of slavery and improved conditions for free blacks were ignored. The next year, some 40 black delegates from eight states held the first of a series of annual conventions denouncing slavery and calling for an end to discriminatory laws in the northern states.

The idea of abolition received impetus from **William Lloyd Garrison** (1805–1879). In 1829 the 25-year-old white Bostonian added his voice to the outcry against colonization, denouncing it as a cruel hoax designed to promote the racial purity of the northern population while doing nothing to end slavery in the South. Instead, he called for "**immediate emancipation.**" By immediate emancipation, he meant the immediate and unconditional release of slaves from bondage without compensation to slaveowners.

In 1831, Garrison founded *The Liberator,* a militant abolitionist newspaper that was the country's first publication to demand an immediate end to slavery. On the front page of the first issue, he defiantly declared: "I will not equivocate—I will not excuse—I will not retreat a single inch—AND I WILL BE HEARD." Incensed by Garrison's proclamation, the state of Georgia offered a $5000 reward to anyone who brought him to the state for trial.

Within four years, 200 antislavery societies had appeared in the North. In a massive propaganda campaign to proclaim the sinfulness of slavery, they distributed a million pieces of abolitionist literature and sent 20,000 tracts directly to the South.

Abolitionist Arguments and Public Reaction

Abolitionists attacked slavery on several grounds. Slavery was illegal because it violated the principles of natural rights to life and liberty embodied in the Declaration of Independence. Justice, said Garrison, required that the nation "secure to the colored population . . . all the rights and privileges that belong to them as men and as Americans." Slavery was sinful because slaveholders, in the words of abolitionist Theodore Weld, had usurped "the prerogative of God." Masters reduced a "God-like being" to a manipulable "THING." Slavery also encouraged sexual immorality and undermined the institutions of marriage and the family. Not only did slave masters sexually abuse and exploit slave women, abolitionists charged, but in some older southern states, such as Virginia and Maryland, they bred slaves for sale to the more recently settled parts of the Deep South.

Slavery was economically retrogressive, abolitionists argued, because slaves, motivated only by fear, did not exert themselves willingly. By depriving their labor force of any incentive for performing careful and diligent work, by barring slaves from acquiring and developing productive skills, planters hindered improvements in crop and soil management. Abolitionists also charged that slavery impeded the development of towns, canals, railroads, and schools.

Antislavery agitation provoked a harsh public reaction in both the North and the South. The U.S. postmaster general refused to deliver antislavery tracts to the South. In each session of Congress between 1836 and 1844 the House of Representatives adopted gag rules allowing that body automatically to table resolutions or petitions concerning the abolition of slavery.

Mobs led by "gentlemen of property and standing" attacked the homes and businesses of abolition-

This silk banner, bearing William Lloyd Garrison's bold and stirring words that appeared on the front page of the inaugural issue of *The Liberator,* was often on display at antislavery fairs during the nineteenth century.

ist merchants, destroyed abolitionist printing presses, disrupted antislavery meetings, and terrorized black neighborhoods. Crowds pelted abolitionist reformers with eggs and even stones. During antiabolitionist rioting in Philadelphia in October 1834, a white mob destroyed 45 homes in the city's black community. A year later, a Boston mob dragged Garrison through the streets and almost lynched him before authorities removed him to a city jail for his own safety.

In 1837, the abolitionist movement acquired its first martyr when an antiabolitionist mob in Alton, Illinois, murdered Reverend **Elijah Lovejoy,** editor of a militant abolitionist newspaper. Three times mobs destroyed Lovejoy's printing presses and attacked his house. When a fourth press arrived, Lovejoy armed himself and guarded the new press at the warehouse. The antiabolitionist mob set fire to the warehouse, shot Lovejoy as he fled the building, and dragged his mutilated body through the town.

Division Within the Antislavery Movement

Questions over strategy and tactics divided the antislavery movement. At the 1840 annual meeting of the American Anti-Slavery Society in New York, abolitionists split over such questions as women's right to participate in the administration of the organization and the advisability of nominating abolitionists as independent political candidates. Garrison won control of the organization, and his opponents promptly walked out. From this point on, no single organization could speak for abolitionism.

One group of abolitionists looked to politics as the answer to ending slavery and founded political parties for that purpose. The **Liberty party,** founded in 1839 under the leadership of Arthur and Lewis Tappan, wealthy New York City businessmen, and James G. Birney, a former slaveholder, called on Congress to abolish slavery in the District of Columbia, end the interstate slave trade, and cease admitting new slave states to the Union. The party also sought the repeal of local and state "black laws" in the North, which discriminated against free blacks, much as segregation laws would in the post-Reconstruction South. The Liberty party nominated Birney for president in 1840 and again in 1844. Although it gathered fewer than 7100 votes in its first campaign, it polled some 62,000 votes four years later and captured enough votes in Michigan and New York to deny Henry Clay the presidency.

In 1848 antislavery Democrats and Whigs merged with the Liberty party to form the Free Soil party. Unlike the Liberty party, which was dedicated to the abolition of slavery and equal rights for African Americans, the **Free Soil party** narrowed its demands to the abolition of slavery in the District of Columbia and the exclusion of slavery from the federal territories. The Free Soilers also wanted a homestead law to provide free land for western settlers, high tariffs to protect American industry, and federally sponsored internal improvements. Campaigning under the slogan "free soil, free speech, free labor, and free men," the new party polled 300,000 votes (or 10 percent) in the presidential election of 1848 and helped elect Whig candidate Zachary Taylor.

Other abolitionists, led by Garrison, took a more radical direction, advocating civil disobedience and linking abolitionism to other reforms such as women's rights, world government, and international peace. Garrison and his supporters established the New England Non-Resistance Society in 1838. Members refused to vote, to hold public office, or to bring suits in court. In 1854 Garrison attracted notoriety by publicly burning a copy of the Constitution, which he called "a covenant with death and an agreement with Hell" because it acknowledged the legality of slavery.

African Americans played a vital role in the abolitionist movement, staging protests against segregated churches, schools, and public transportation. In New York and Pennsylvania, free blacks launched petition drives for equal voting rights. Northern blacks also had a pivotal role in the "underground railroad," which provided escape routes for southern slaves through the northern states and into Canada. African American churches offered sanctuary to runaways, and black "vigilance" groups in cities such as New York and Detroit battled slave catchers who sought to recapture fugitive slaves.

Fugitive slaves, such as William Wells Brown, Henry Bibb, and **Harriet Tubman,** advanced abolitionism by publicizing the horrors of slavery. Their firsthand tales of whippings and separation from spouses and children combated the notion that slaves were contented under slavery and undermined belief in racial inferiority. Tubman risked her life by making 19 trips into slave territory to free as many as 300 slaves. Slaveholders posted a reward of $40,000 for the capture of the "Black Moses."

Frederick Douglass was the most famous fugitive slave and black abolitionist. The son of a Maryland slave woman and an unknown white father, Douglass was separated from his mother and sent to work on a plantation when he was six years old. At

Frederick Douglass, pictured here (seated to left of table) at a rally of the American Anti-Slavery Society in Syracuse, New York, became a lecturer for the society at the urging of William Lloyd Garrison. Douglass toured widely in the East and Midwest, condemning slavery and arguing for the Constitutional right of freedom for all Americans, regardless of color or gender.

Fugitive slave, abolitionist, and later spy for the Union during the Civil War, Harriet Tubman is pictured here at the extreme left with some of the slaves she helped escape. She led at least 19 raids into slave territory to escort more than 300 slaves to freedom in the northern states and Canada.

the age of 20, in 1838, he escaped to the North using the papers of a free black sailor. In the North, Douglass became the first runaway slave to speak out against slavery. When many Northerners refused to believe that this eloquent orator could possibly have been a slave, he responded by writing an autobiography that identified his previous owners by name. Although he initially allied himself with William Lloyd Garrison, Douglass later started his own newspaper, *The North Star,* and supported political action against slavery.

By the 1850s, many blacks had become pessimistic about defeating slavery. Some African Americans looked again to colonization as a solution. In the 15 months following passage of the federal Fugitive Slave Law in 1850, some 13,000 free blacks fled the North for Canada. In 1854, Martin Delany (1812–1885), a Pittsburgh doctor who had studied medicine at Harvard, organized the National Emigration Convention to investigate possible sites for black colonization in Haiti, Central America, and West Africa.

Other blacks argued in favor of violence. Black abolitionists in Ohio adopted resolutions encouraging slaves to escape and called on their fellow citizens to violate any law that "conflicts with reason, liberty and justice, North or South." A meeting of fugitive slaves in Cazenovia, New York, declared that "the State motto of Virginia, 'Death to Tyrants,' is as well the black man's as the white man's motto." By the late 1850s, a growing number of free blacks had concluded that it was just as legitimate to use vi-

olence to secure the freedom of the slaves as it had been to establish the independence of the American colonies.

Over the long run, the fragmentation of the antislavery movement worked to the advantage of the cause. Henceforth, Northerners could support whichever form of antislavery best reflected their views. Moderates could vote for political candidates with abolitionist sentiments without being accused of radical Garrisonian views or of advocating violence for redress of grievances.

The Birth of Feminism

The women's rights movement was a major legacy of radical reform. At the outset of the century, women could not vote or hold office in any state, they had no access to higher education, and they were excluded from professional occupations. American law accepted the principle that a wife had no legal identity apart from her husband. She could not be sued, nor could she bring a legal suit; she could not make a contract, nor could she own property. She was not permitted to control her own wages or gain custody of her children in case of separation or divorce.

Broad social and economic changes, such as the development of a market economy and a decline in the birthrate, opened employment opportunities for women. Instead of bearing children at two-year intervals after marriage, as was the general case throughout the colonial era, during the early nineteenth century women bore fewer children and ceased childbearing at younger ages. During these decades the first women's college was established, and some men's colleges first opened their doors to women students. More women were postponing marriage or not marrying at all; unmarried women gained new employment opportunities as "mill girls" and elementary school teachers; and a growing number of women achieved prominence as novelists, editors, teachers, and leaders of church and philanthropic societies.

Although there were many improvements in the status of women during the first half of the century, women still lacked political and economic status when compared with men. As the franchise was extended to larger and larger numbers of white males, including large groups of recent immigrants, the gap in political power between women and men widened. Even though women made up a core of supporters for many reform movements, men excluded them from positions of decision making and relegated them to separate female auxiliaries. Additionally, women lost economic status as production shifted away from the household to the factory and workshop. During the late eighteenth century, the need for a cash income led women and older children to engage in a variety of household industries, such as weaving and spinning. Increasingly, in the nineteenth century, these tasks were performed in factories and mills, where the workforce was largely male.

The fact that changes in the economy tended to confine women to a sphere separate from men had important implications for reform. Since women were believed to be uncontaminated by the competitive struggle for wealth and power, many argued that they had a duty—and the capacity—to exert an uplifting moral influence on American society.

Catharine Beecher (1800–1878) and Sarah J. Hale (1788–1879) helped lead the effort to expand women's roles through moral influence. Beecher, the eldest sister of Harriet Beecher Stowe, was one of the nation's most prominent educators before the Civil War. A woman of many talents and strong leadership, she wrote a highly regarded book on domestic science and spearheaded the campaign to convince school boards that women were suited to serve as schoolteachers. Hale edited the nation's most popular women's magazines, the *Ladies Magazine* and *Godey's Lady's Book*. She led the successful campaign to make Thanksgiving a national holiday (during Lincoln's administration), and she also composed the famous nursery rhyme "Mary Had a Little Lamb."

Both Beecher and Hale worked tirelessly for women's education (Hale helped found Vassar College). They gave voice to the grievances of women—the abysmally low wages paid to women in the needle trades (12.5 cents a day), the physical hardships endured by female operatives in the nation's shops and mills (where women worked 14 hours a day), and the minimizing of women's intellectual aspirations. Even though neither woman supported full equal rights for women, they were important transitional figures in the emergence of feminism. Each significantly broadened society's definition of "women's sphere" and assigned women vital social responsibilities: to shape their children's character, morally to uplift their husbands, and to promote causes of "practical benevolence."

Other women broke down old barriers and forged new opportunities in a more dramatic fashion. Frances Wright (1795–1852), a Scottish-born reformer and lecturer, received the nickname "The Great Red Harlot of Infidelity" because of her radical ideas about birth control, liberalized divorce laws, and legal rights for married women. In 1849 Elizabeth Blackwell (1821–1910) became the first American woman to receive a degree in medicine. A number of women became active as revivalists. Perhaps

Godey's Lady's Book offered its readers consumer information, household hints, fashion plates, dressmaking instructions, recipes, and sentimental songs as well as literary works by male and female authors. Sarah Hale, for forty years the editor of the magazine, supported women's education and economic independence but opposed women's participation in political activities, including voting.

the most notable was Phoebe Palmer (1807–1874), a Methodist preacher who ignited religious fervor among thousands of Americans and Canadians.

Catalyst for Women's Rights

A public debate over the proper role of women in the antislavery movement, especially their right to lecture to audiences composed of both sexes, led to the first organized movement for women's rights. By the mid-1830s more than a hundred female antislavery societies had been created, and women abolitionists were circulating petitions, editing abolitionist tracts, and organizing antislavery conventions. A key question was whether women abolitionists would be permitted to lecture to "mixed" audiences of men and women. In 1837 a national women's antislavery convention resolved that women should overcome this taboo: "The time has come for women to move in that sphere which providence has assigned her, and no longer remain satisfied with the circumscribed limits which corrupt custom and a perverted application of Scripture have encircled her."

Angelina Grimké (1805–1879) and her sister **Sarah** (1792–1873)—two sisters from a wealthy Charleston, South Carolina, slaveholding family— were the first women to break the restrictions and widen women's sphere through their writings and lectures before mixed audiences. In 1837 Angelina gained national notoriety by lecturing against slavery to audiences that included men as well as women. Shocked by this breach of the separate sexual spheres ordained by God, ministers in Massachusetts called on their fellow clergy to forbid women the right to speak from church pulpits. Sarah Grimké in 1840 responded with a pamphlet entitled *Letters on the Condition of Women and the Equality of the Sexes*, one of the first modern statements of feminist principles. She denounced the injustice of lower pay and denial of equal educational opportunities for women. Her pamphlet expressed outrage that women were "regarded by men, as pretty toys or as mere instruments of pleasure" and were taught to believe that marriage is "the *sine qua non* [indispensable element] of human happiness and human existence." Men and women, she concluded, should not be treated differently, since both were endowed with innate natural rights.

In 1840, after the American Anti-Slavery Society split over the issue of women's rights, the organization named three female delegates to a World Anti-Slavery Convention to be held in London later that year. There, these women were denied the right to participate in the convention on the grounds that their participation would offend British public opinion. The convention relegated them to seats in a balcony.

Eight years later, Lucretia Mott (1793–1880), who earlier had been denied the right to serve as a delegate to the World Anti-Slavery Convention, and **Elizabeth Cady Stanton** (1815–1902) organized the first women's rights convention in history. Held in July 1848 at Seneca Falls, New York, the convention drew up a Declaration of Sentiments, modeled on the Declaration of Independence, which opened with the phrase "All men and women are created equal." It named 15 specific inequities suffered by women, and after detailing "a history of repeated injuries and usurpations on the part of man toward woman," the document concluded that "he has endeavored, in every way that he could, to destroy her confidence in her own powers, to lessen her self-respect, and to make her willing to lead a dependent and abject life."

Among the resolutions adopted by the convention, only one was not ratified unanimously—that women be granted the right to vote. Of the 66 women and 34 men who signed the Declaration of Sentiments at the convention (including black abolitionist Frederick Douglass), only two lived to see the ratification of the women's suffrage amendment to the constitution 72 years later.

By mid-century women's rights conventions had been held in every northern state. Despite ridicule from the public press—the *Worcester* (Massachusetts) *Telegraph* denounced women's rights advocates as "Amazons"—female reformers contributed to important, if limited, advances against discrimination. They succeeded in gaining adoption of Married Women's Property Laws in a number of states, granting married women control over their own income and property. A New York law passed in 1860 gave women joint custody over children and the right to sue and be sued, and in several states women's rights reformers secured adoption of permissive divorce laws. A Connecticut law, for example, granted divorce for any "misconduct" that "permanently destroys the happiness of the petitioner and defeats the purposes of the marriage relationship."

Black women, too, were active in the campaign to extend equal rights to women. One of the most outspoken advocates for both women's rights and abolition was **Sojourner Truth,** born a slave known as Isabella in New York State's Hudson River Valley around 1797. She escaped from bondage in 1826, taking refuge with a farm family that later bought her freedom. She took the name Sojourner Truth in 1843, convinced that God had called on her to preach the truth throughout the country. Her fame as a preacher, singer, and orator for abolition and women's rights spread rapidly. At a women's rights convention in Akron, Ohio, in 1851, she is reported to have

THE PEOPLE SPEAK

The Struggle for Women's Rights

At the first convention in history dedicated to equal rights for women, held in Seneca Falls, New York, in 1848, the delegates adopted a "Declaration of Sentiments." Drafted by Elizabeth Cady Stanton and modeled on the Declaration of Independence, it listed a series of injuries that women had suffered at the hands of men and declared that women and men shared the same inalienable rights.

> We hold these truths to be self-evident: that all men and women are created equal. . . .
>
> The history of mankind is a history of repeated injuries and usurpations on the part of man toward woman, having in direct object the establishment of an absolute tyranny over her. To prove this, let facts be submitted to a candid world.
>
> He has never permitted her to exercise her inalienable right to the elective franchise.
>
> He has compelled her to submit to laws, in the formation of which she had no voice.
>
> He has withheld from her rights which are given to the most ignorant and degraded men—both natives and foreigners.
>
> Having deprived her of this first right of a citizen, the elective franchise, thereby leaving her without representation in the halls of legislation, he has opposed her on all sides.
>
> He has made her, if married, in the eye of the law, civilly dead.
>
> He has taken from her all rights in property, even to the wages she earns. . . .
>
> He has endeavored, in every way that he could, to destroy her confidence in her own powers, to lessen her self-respect, and to make her willing to lead a dependent and abject life.

Source: Seneca Falls Declaration and Resolutions, 1848, in Susan B. Anthony, Elizabeth Cady Stanton, and Matilda Joslyn Gage, eds., *History of Woman Suffrage* (Rochester, 1889), 1: 75–80.

Today Amelia Jenks Bloomer (1818–1894) is best known for the loose-fitting trousers that bear her name. But in the years before the Civil War, she was one of the country's leading advocates of women's rights and the founder of a magazine, *The Lily,* dedicated to "the Emancipation of Woman from Intemperance, Injustice, Prejudice and Bigotry." In 1855, the periodical published a letter denouncing marriage as "the *slavery of woman.*"

> Marriage is the *slavery of woman.* Marriage does not differ, in any of its essential features, from chattel slavery. The slave's earnings belong to the master, the earnings of the wife belong to the husband. The right of another to claim one's earnings, constitutes one a slave. In this respect, the essential feature of slavery, the wife and the chattel slave stand on a level. They may wear fine clothes, and "fare sumptuously every day," but in both cases the clothes they wear and the food they eat is the property of the master, and may be changed or withheld at his pleasure. If woman is endowed with one right more sacred than another, it is the right to her own children; but the wife nor the slave mother have no such right. In either case the legal owner of the child, as well as the mother, may separate them at will.

A leading lecturer on women's rights, Ernestine Potowsky Rose (1810-1892), migrated to New York from Poland in 1836 and led the fight for laws to grant women the right to own property in their own name. In 1860, she called on New York State to allow abused women to divorce their husbands.

> Divorce is now granted for some crimes; I ask it for others also. It is granted for a state's prison offense. I ask that personal cruelty to a wife, whom he swore to "love, cherish, and protect," may be made a heinous crime—a perjury and a state's prison offense, for which divorce shall be granted. Willful desertion for one year should be sufficient cause for divorce, for the willful deserter forfeits the sacred title of husband or wife. Habitual intemperance, or any other vice which makes the husband or wife intolerable or abhorrent to the other, ought to be sufficient cause for divorce. . . .
>
> But it is said that if divorce were easily granted, "men and women would marry to-day and unmarry to-morrow." Those who say that, only prove that they have no confidence in themselves, and therefore can have no confidence in others. . . . Remove the indissolubility [of marriage], and there would be less separation than now, for it would place the parties on their good behavior, the same as during courtship.

Source: Elizabeth Cady Stanton, *History of Woman Suffrage,* Vol. 1 (Rochester, N.Y.: Fowler and Wells, 1889), 729–31.

A legend in the abolitionist and women's rights movements, Sojourner Truth was born into slavery around 1797 and escaped from bondage in 1826.

demanded that Americans recognize the African American women's right to equality. "I could work as much and eat as much as a man—when I could get it—and bear de lash as well!" she told the crowd. "And a'n't I a woman?"

During the Civil War, Truth supported the Union, collecting food and supplies for black troops and struggling to make emancipation a war aim. When the war was over, she traveled across the North, collecting signatures on petitions calling on Congress to set aside western lands for former slaves. At her death in 1883, she could rightly be remembered as one of the nation's most eloquent opponents of discrimination in all forms.

Utopian Communities

Between the 1820s and 1840s, individuals who believed in the perfectibility of the social and political order founded hundreds of "**utopian communities.**" These experimental communal societies were called utopian communities because they provided blueprints for an ideal society.

The characteristics of these communities varied widely. One of the earliest perfectionist societies was popularly known as the **Shakers.** Founded in 1776

by "Mother" Ann Lee, an English immigrant, the Shakers believed that the millennium was at hand and that the time had come for people to renounce sin. Shaker communities regarded their male and female members as equals; thus, both sexes served as elders and deacons. Aspiring to live like the early Christians, the Shakers adopted communal ownership of property and a way of life emphasizing simplicity. Dress was kept simple and uniform. Shaker architecture and furniture are devoid of ornament—no curtains on windows, carpets on floors, or pictures on walls—but they are pure and elegant in form.

The two most striking characteristics of the Shaker communities were their dances and abstinence from sexual relations. The Shakers believed that religious fervor should be expressed through the head, heart, and mind, and their ritual religious practices included shaking, shouting, and dancing. Viewing sexual intercourse as the basic cause of human sin, the Shakers also adopted strict rules concerning celibacy. They attempted to replenish their membership by admitting volunteers and taking in orphans. Today, the Shakers have all but died out. Fewer than 20 members survived in the first decade of the twenty-first century.

Another utopian effort was Robert Owen's experimental community at New Harmony, Indiana, which reflected the influence of Enlightenment ideas. Owen, a paternalistic Scottish industrialist, was deeply troubled by the social consequences of the industrial revolution. Inspired by the idea that people are shaped by their environment, Owen purchased a site in Indiana where he sought to establish common ownership of property and abolish religion. At New Harmony the marriage ceremony was reduced to a

Officially named "The United Society of Believers in Christ's Second Appearing," the Shakers received their popular name from the movements they made during their religious dances.

single sentence and children were raised outside of their natural parents' home. The community lasted just three years, from 1825 to 1828.

Some 40 utopian communities based their organization on the ideas of the French theorist Charles Fourier, who hoped to eliminate poverty through the establishment of scientifically organized cooperative communities called "phalanxes." Each phalanx was to be set up as a "joint-stock company," in which profits were divided according to the amount of money members had invested, their skill, and their labor. In the phalanxes, women received equal job opportunities and equal pay, equal participation in decision making, and the right to speak in public assemblies. Although one Fourier community lasted for 18 years, most were unsuccessful.

The currents of radical antislavery thought inspired Frances Wright, a fervent Scottish abolitionist, to found Nashoba Colony in 1826, near Memphis, Tennessee, as an experiment in interracial living. She established a racially integrated cooperative community in which slaves were to receive an education and earn enough money to purchase their own freedom. Publicity about Fanny Wright's desire to abolish the nuclear family, religion, private property, and slavery created a furor, and the community dissolved after only four years.

Perhaps the most successful—and notorious—experimental colony was John Humphrey Noyes's Oneida Community. A lawyer who was converted in one of Charles G. Finney's revivals, Noyes believed that the millennium would occur only when people strove to become perfect through an "immediate and total cessation from sin."

In Putney, Vermont, in 1835 and in Oneida, New York, in 1848, Noyes established perfectionist communities that practiced communal ownership of property and "complex marriage." Complex marriage involved the marriage of each member of the community to every member of the opposite sex. Exclusive emotional or sexual attachments were forbidden, and sexual relations were arranged through an intermediary to protect a woman's individuality and give her a choice in the matter. Men were required to practice *coitus interruptus* (withdrawal) as a method of birth control, unless the group had approved of the couple's conceiving offspring. After the Civil War, the community conducted experiments in eugenics, the selective control of mating to improve the hereditary qualities of children. Other notable features of the community were mutual criticism sessions and communal child rearing. Noyes left the community in 1879 and fled to Canada to escape prosecution for adultery. As late as the early 1990s descendants of the original community could be found working at the Oneida silverworks, which became a corporation after Noyes's departure.

ARTISTIC AND CULTURAL FERMENT

In the late eighteenth century, many Americans wondered whether their country's infant democracy could produce great works of art. The revolutionary generation drew its models of art and architecture from the world of classical antiquity, especially the Roman republic. The new United States had few professional writers or artists. It lacked a large class of patrons to subsidize the arts. It published few magazines and housed only a single art museum. Above all, America seemed to lack the traditions out of which artists and writers could create great works.

Europeans treated American culture with contempt. They charged that America was too commercial and materialistic, too preoccupied with money and technology to produce great art and literature. "In the four quarters of the globe," asked one English critic, "who reads an American book? or goes to an American play? or looks at an American picture or statue?"

On August 31, 1837, a 34-year-old former Unitarian minister named Ralph Waldo Emerson (1803–1882) answered these critics. As he stood at the pulpit of the First Parish Church of Cambridge, Massachusetts—the very spot where Anne Hutchinson had been examined for heresy two centuries earlier—he delivered a talk, entitled "The American Scholar," that would be called America's "intellectual Declaration of Independence." In his address, Emerson urged Americans to cast off their "long apprenticeship to the learning of other lands" and abandon subservience to English models and create distinctly American forms of art rooted in the facts of American life.

Even before Emerson's call for a distinctly American culture, a number of authors had already begun to create literature emphasizing native scenes and characters. Washington Irving (1783–1859), who was probably the first American to support himself as a man of letters, demonstrated the possibility of creating art out of native elements in his classic tales "Rip Van Winkle" (1818) and "The Legend of Sleepy Hollow" (1820).

The poet Henry Wadsworth Longfellow was even more successful in transforming American legends into the stuff of art and reaching a broad popular audience. His narrative poems dramatizing scenes from America's past made such figures as Paul Revere, Miles Standish, John Alden, Priscilla Mullins, and Hiawatha household names. His simple evocative lines have been cherished by generations of American children:

> Under the spreading chestnut tree
> The village smithy stands
>
> I shot an arrow into the air,
> It fell to earth, I knew not where
>
> There was a little girl
> Who had a little curl
> Right in the middle of her forehead

Ironically, this popular poet was a "Boston Brahmin" (a member of one of Boston's leading families), an expert in linguistics, a professor of modern languages at Harvard, and a translator of the latest European poetry.

James Fenimore Cooper (1789–1851) was another successful mythmaker. His works gave us such staples of western fiction as the lone frontiersman, the faithful Indian companion, and the kidnap, chase, and rescue. He also made such words and phrases as "paleface," "on the warpath," and "war paint" part of the American vocabulary.

Born in Burlington, New Jersey, the son of a land speculator, Cooper grew up in the frontier community of Cooperstown in central New York. At 13, he enrolled at Yale but was expelled for blowing open a classmate's door with a charge of gunpowder and roping a donkey onto a professor's chair. He then went to sea as a common sailor. In 1819, following his return to Cooperstown, Cooper was reading a popular novel of the day aloud to his wife. He tossed the book aside and claimed that he could write a better one. His wife dared him to try, and during the remaining 32 years of his life he wrote 34 books.

In his second and third novels, *The Spy* (1821) and *The Pioneers* (1823), Cooper created one of the most enduring archetypes in American culture. His hero, the frontiersman Natty Bumppo (also known as Hawkeye, Leatherstocking, and Pathfinder) was an American knight at home in the wilderness. He became the prototype not only for future trappers and scouts but also for countless cowboys, detectives, and superheroes found in popular American fiction and film. Part of Natty Bumppo's appeal was that he gave expression to many of the misgivings early nineteenth-century Americans had about the cost of progress (his last words were "Let me sleep where I have lived—beyond the din of settlements"). An acute social critic, Cooper railed against the destruction of the natural environment, the violence directed at Native Americans, and the rapaciousness and materialism of an expansive American society.

Natty Bumppo, the legendary American frontiersman created by James Fenimore Cooper, from the frontispiece of Cooper's *Last of the Mohicans*. Bumppo, the hero of Cooper's Leatherstocking tales, has been called the most famous character in American fiction.

American Transcendentalism

On the afternoon of September 19, 1836, a number of Boston's leading young intellectuals met at the Boston home of the Reverend George Ripley. Ralph Waldo Emerson, who would shortly deliver his "American Scholar" address, was there, as was Bronson Alcott, a pioneering educational reformer and the father of novelist Louisa May Alcott. Orestes Brownson, a staunch advocate of the rights of workers, also attended. Their goal was "to see how far it would be possible for earnest minds to meet." Soon, other important thinkers joined the meetings, including novelist Nathaniel Hawthorne, feminist editor Margaret Fuller, educator Elizabeth Peabody, and pencil maker and poet Henry David Thoreau. So abstract and incomprehensible were their discussions to those outside their circle that unkind wits dubbed the group the "Transcendentalist Club." The nickname stuck, and these important thinkers, authors, and reformers came to be called **transcendentalists**.

The transcendentalists were a group of young New Englanders, mostly of Unitarian background, who found liberal religion too formal and rationalistic to meet their spiritual and emotional needs. Logic and reason, they believed, were incapable of explaining the fundamental mysteries of human existence. Where, then, could people find answers to life's fundamental problems? The deepest insights, the transcendentalists believed, were to be found within the human individual, through intuition.

The transcendentalists shared a common outlook: a belief that each person contains infinite and godlike potentialities; an emphasis on emotion and the senses over reason and intellect; and a glorification of nature as a creative, dynamic force in which people could discover their true selves and commune with the supernatural. Like the romantic artists and poets of Europe, they emphasized the individual, the subjective, the imaginative, the personal, the emotional, and the visionary.

The central figure in transcendentalism was **Ralph Waldo Emerson.** Trained, like his father, to be a liberal Unitarian minister, Emerson found his parents' faith unsatisfying. Unitarian theology and ritual, he wrote, was "corpse cold"; it was the "thin porridge or cold tea" of genteel Bostonians. Emerson's life was marked by personal tragedy and illness—his father died when he was a boy; his first wife died after less than two years of marriage; his firstborn son died at the age of five; a brother went insane. Consequently, Emerson could never believe that logic and reason offered answers to life's mysteries.

Appalled by the complacency, provinciality, and materialism of Boston's elite, the 29-year-old Emerson resigned as minister of the prestigious Second Church of Boston in 1832. Convinced that no external answers existed to the fundamental problems of life, he decided to look inward and "spin my thread from my own bowels." In his essays and public lectures, Emerson distilled the essence of the new philosophy: All people contain seeds of divinity, but society, traditionalism, and lifeless religious institutions thwart the fulfillment of these potentialities. In his essay "Nature" (1836), Emerson asserted that God's presence is inherent in both humanity and nature and can best be sensed through intuition rather than through reason. In his essay "Self-Reliance" (1841), he called on his readers to strive for true individuality in the face of intense social pressures for conformity: "Society everywhere is in conspiracy against the manhood of every one of its members. . . . The virtue in most request is conformity. . . . Whoso would be a man must be a nonconformist."

Although Emerson himself was not an active reformer (he once wrote that whenever he saw a reformer, he felt like asking, "What right, Sir, do you have to your one virtue?"), his philosophy inspired many reformers far more radical than he. His stress on the individual, his defense of nonconformity, and his vocal critique of the alienation and social fragmentation that had accompanied the growth of cities and industry led others to try to apply the principles of transcendentalism to their personal lives and to society at large.

Henry David Thoreau (1817–1862) was one of the transcendentalists who strove to realize Emersonian ideals in his personal life. A pencil maker, surveyor, and poet, Thoreau, like Emerson, was educated at Harvard. He felt nothing but contempt for

The title page from the first edition of Thoreau's *Walden*, published in 1854.

social conventions and wore a green coat to chapel because Harvard's rules required black. After college, he taught school and worked at his father's pencil factory, but these jobs brought him no fulfillment.

In March 1845, the 28-year-old Thoreau, convinced that his life was being frittered away by details, walked into the woods near Concord, Massachusetts, to live alone. He put up a cabin near Walden Pond as an experiment—to see if it was possible for a person to live truly free and uncommitted: "I went into the woods because I wished to live deliberately, to front only the essential facts of life, and see if I could not learn what it had to teach, and not, when I came to die, discover that I had not lived." The aim of his experiment was to break free from the distractions and artificialities of life, to shed himself of needless obligations and possessions, and to establish an original relationship with nature. His motto was "simplify, simplify."

During his 26 months at Walden Pond, he constructed his own cabin, raised his own food ("seven miles of beans"), observed nature, explored his inner self, and kept a 6000-page journal. He served as "self-appointed inspector of snow-storms and rain-storms," "surveyor of forest-paths," and protector of "wild-stock." He also spent a night in jail for refusing to pay taxes as a protest against the Mexican-American War. This incident led him to write the classic defense of nonviolent direct action, "Civil Disobedience."

Another figure who sought to realize transcendentalist ideals in her personal life was Margaret Fuller (1810–1850), editor of the transcendentalist journal *The Dial*. Often mocked as an egotist, she once said: "I know all the people worth knowing in America, and I find no intellect comparable to my own." She did indeed possess one of nineteenth-century America's towering minds. She was the first woman to use the Harvard College library and later became one of the nation's first woman journalists, writing for Horace Greeley's New York *Tribune*. A determined social reformer, she became a leading advocate of women's rights, publishing *Woman in the Nineteenth Century* in 1845. The book, in which she called for the complete equality of women and men, became a central work of the emerging women's rights movement. A partisan in Rome's revolution of 1849, she shocked Bostonians by taking an Italian revolutionary nobleman, 11 years her junior, as her lover, and bearing his child out of wedlock (they secretly married later). She died in a shipwreck off Long Island, at the age of 40, along with her husband and son. Edgar Allan Poe spoke for many Americans when he said of her: "Humanity is divided into men, women, and Margaret Fuller."

Another key figure in the transcendentalist circle was Bronson Alcott (1799–1888), a pioneer in the areas of child development and education. Often ridiculed—reviewers mockingly described one of his books as "clear as mud"—Alcott was far ahead of his time in his conception of education, which he viewed as a process of awakening and drawing out children's intellectual and moral capacities through dialogue, individualized instruction, nature study, and encouragement of creative expression through art and writing. Critics scoffed at his techniques, particularly his rejection of corporal punishment and his substitution of "vicarious atonement," a method of child discipline in which Alcott had naughty children spank him. When his own daughters misbehaved, Alcott went without dinner. Convinced that adults had a great deal to learn about children's physical, intellectual, and moral development, Alcott recorded 2500 pages of observations on the first years of his daughters' lives (who included Louisa May, later the author of *Little Women* and *Little Men*). He also published his dialogues with pupils on such controversial topics as the meaning of the Christian gospel and the processes of conception and birth.

Two dramatic attempts to apply the ideas of transcendentalism to everyday life were Brook Farm, a community located near Boston, and Fruitlands, a utopian community near Harvard, Massachusetts. In 1841, George Ripley, like Emerson a former Unitarian clergyman, established Brook Farm in an attempt to substitute transcendentalist ideals of "brotherly cooperation," harmony, and spiritual fulfillment for the "selfish competition," class division, and alienation that increasingly characterized the larger society. "Our ulterior aim is nothing less than Heaven on Earth," declared one community member. Brook Farm's residents, who never numbered more than 200, supported themselves by farming, teaching, and manufacturing clothing. The most famous member of the community was Nathaniel Hawthorne, who based his 1852 novel *The Blithedale Romance* on his experiences there. The community lasted in its original form just three years.

In 1843, Bronson Alcott and others attempted to form a "New Eden" at Fruitlands—a community where they could achieve human perfection through high thinking, manual labor, and dress and diet reform. Practices at Fruitlands included communal ownership of property, frequent cold-water baths, and a diet based entirely on native grains, fruits, herbs, and roots. Residents wore canvas shoes and linen tunics, so as not to have to kill animals for leather or use slave-grown cotton. Division of labor by gender, however, remained traditional. Responsibility for housekeeping and food preparation fell on

Alcott's wife Abba. Asked by a visitor if there were any beasts of burden at Fruitlands, Abba Alcott replied: "There is one woman."

A Literary Renaissance

Emerson's 1837 plea for Americans to cease imitating Europeans, speak with their own voices, and create art drawn from their own experiences coincided with an extraordinary burst of literary creativity. Nathaniel Hawthorne, Herman Melville, Edgar Allan Poe, Harriet Beecher Stowe, and Walt Whitman, like Emerson and Thoreau, produced literary works of the highest magnitude, yet in their own time many of their greatest works were greeted with derision, abuse, or indifference. It is a tragic fact that with the sole exception of Harriet Beecher Stowe, none of pre–Civil War America's greatest writers was able to earn more than a modest income from his or her books.

During his lifetime, Edgar Allan Poe (1809–1849) received far more notoriety from his legendary dissipation than from his poetry or short stories. The Boston-born son of two poor actors, Poe was raised by a Richmond, Virginia, merchant after his father abandoned the family and his mother died. For two years he went to the University of Virginia and briefly attended West Point, but drinking, gambling debts, and bitter fights with his guardian cut short his formal education. At the age of 24, he married a 13-year-old second cousin, who died a decade later of tuberculosis, brought on by cold and starvation. Found drunk and unconscious in Baltimore in 1849, Poe died at the age of 40.

Sorely underappreciated by contemporaries, Poe invented the detective novel; edited the *Southern Literary Messenger,* one of the country's leading literary journals; wrote incisive essays on literary criticism; and produced some of the most masterful poems and frightening tales of horror ever written. His literary techniques inspired a number of important French writers, including Charles Baudelaire, Stéphane Mallarmé, and Paul Valéry. Poe said that his writing style consisted of "the ludicrous heightened into the grotesque; the fearful coloured into the horrible; the witty exaggerated into the burlesque; the singular wrought into the strange and mystical."

Nathaniel Hawthorne (1804–1864), the author of *The Scarlet Letter* (1850), one of America's towering works of fiction, did not consider himself a novelist. He wrote "romances," he insisted—imaginative representations of moral problems, rather than novelistic depictions of social realities. A descendant of one of the Salem witch-trial judges, the Salem-born Hawthorne grew up in a somber and solitary atmosphere. His father, a sea captain, perished on a voyage when his son

In *The Scarlet Letter*, Nathaniel Hawthorne examined the theme of sin and its effects on the individual and on society. Hester Prynne is forced to wear a scarlet "A" on her dress as a symbol of her adultery, but by accepting her punishment and devoting herself to serving her community, she is reconciled to God. Her husband, Roger Chillingworth, is so consumed with revenge that he can neither forgive nor accept forgiveness. He must live in the private hell of alienation from God and society. Although the novel is set in seventeenth-century Puritan New England, the themes Hawthorne explores reflect the heritage of that Puritanism in his own age.

was just four years old, and Hawthorne's mother spent the remainder of her life in mourning. After attending Bowdoin College, where Henry Wadsworth Longfellow and future president Franklin Pierce were among his classmates, he began to write. It would not be until 1837, however, when he published *Twice-Told Tales*, that the 33-year-old Hawthorne first gained public recognition. He lived briefly at Brook Farm and participated in the transcendentalist circle but did not share their idealistic faith in humanity's innate goodness.

Hawthorne was a secretive, painfully shy man. But no pre–Civil War author wrote more perceptively about guilt—sexual, moral, and psychological. "In the depths of every human heart," he wrote in an

nb and a dungeon, though
revelry above may cause us
and the buried ones, or pris-
" In his fiction, Hawthorne,
ly nineteenth-century Ameri-
he larger society's faith in sci-
ess, and humanity's essential
greatest works project nineteenth-century concerns—about women's roles, sex-
uality, and religion—onto seventeenth-century Puritan settings. Some of his stories examine the hubris
of scientists and social reformers who dare tamper
with the natural environment and human nature.

Herman Melville (1819–1891), author of *Moby
Dick* (1851), possibly America's greatest romance,
had little formal education and claimed that his intellectual development did not begin until he was 25.
By then, he had already seen his father go bankrupt
and die insane, worked as a cabin boy on a merchant
ship, served as a common seaman on a whaling ship,
deserted in the Marquesas Islands, escaped on an
Australian whaler, and been imprisoned in Tahiti. He
drew on these experiences in his first two books,
Typee (1846) and *Omoo* (1847), which were popular
successes, but his third book *Mardi* (1849), a complex
blend of political and religious allegory, metaphysics,
and cosmic romance, failed miserably, foreshadow-
ing the reception of his later works.

Part of a New York literary circle called Young
America, Melville dreamed of creating a novel as
vast and energetic as the nation itself. In *Moby Dick,*
he produced such a masterwork. Based on the tale of
"Mocha-Dick," a gigantic white whale that sank a
whaling ship, *Moby Dick* combined whaling lore and
sea adventure into an epic drama of human arrogance, producing an allegory that explores what hap-
pens to a people who defy divine limits. Tragically,
neither *Moby Dick* nor Melville's later works found
an audience, and Melville spent his last years as a
deputy customs collector in New York. He died in utter obscurity, and his literary genius was rediscovered only in the 1920s.

In 1842, Ralph Waldo Emerson lectured in New
York and called for a truly original American poet
who could fashion verse out of "the factory, the railroad, and the wharf." Sitting in Emerson's audience
was a 22-year-old New York printer and journalist
named Walt Whitman (1819–1892). A carpenter's son
with only five years of schooling, Whitman soon became Emerson's ideal of the native American poet,
with the publication of *Leaves of Grass* in 1855. "A
mixture of Yankee transcendentalism and New York
rowdyism," *Leaves of Grass* was, wrote Emerson, "the
most extraordinary piece of wit & wisdom that

America has yet contributed." Most reviewers, however, reacted scornfully to the book, deeming it
"trashy, profane & obscene" for its sexual frankness.
A sprawling portrait of America, encompassing
every aspect of American life, from the steam-driven
Brooklyn ferry to the use of ether in surgery, the volume opens not with the author's name but simply
with his daguerreotype (a forerunner of the photograph). Unconventional in style—Whitman invented
"free verse" rather than use conventionally rhymed
or regularly metered verse—the volume stands out
as a landmark in the history of American literature
for its celebration of the diversity, the energy, and the
expansiveness of pre–Civil War America.

Ethnic Voices

During the years preceding the Civil War, America's
ethnic and racial minorities began to publish novels,
poems, histories, and autobiographies that explored
what it meant to be an outsider in a predominantly
white, Anglo-Saxon, Protestant society. The result
was a unique body of ethnic writing chronicling the
distinctive experience and changing self-image of
ethnic Americans.

One of the earliest forms of African-American literature was the slave narrative, graphic first-person
accounts of life in bondage, written by former slaves,
including William Wells Brown, Frederick Douglass,
and Josiah Henson (he was Harriet Beecher Stowe's
model for Uncle Tom). These volumes not only
awoke readers to the hardships and cruelties of life
under slavery, they also described the ingenious
strategies that fugitive slaves used to escape from
bondage. William and Ellen Craft, for example, disguised themselves as master and slave; Henry "Box"
Brown had himself crated in a box and shipped
north.

The 1850s saw the publication of the first four
novels by African Americans. William Wells Brown's
Clotel (1853), written by an abolitionist and escaped
slave, offers a fictional reworking of the story that
Thomas Jefferson fathered several children by a
slave mistress. In *The Garies and Their Friends* (1857),
Frank Webb, a Philadelphia free black, describes the
destructive effects of prejudice, discrimination, and
racial violence on two families, one lower class and
the other, wealthier, with a white husband and a mulatto wife. In *Blake* (1859), one of the most militant
novels produced during the nineteenth century,
Martin R. Delany, a physician and a reform activist,
tells the story of a black Cuban who repudiates organized religion and seeks to liberate blacks in Cuba
and the United States. Harriet Jacobs, a poverty-

stricken free black from Massachusetts, blends autobiography and fiction in *Incidents in the Life of a Slave Girl* (1859), which tells the story of an orphan who is indentured to an abusive white family, but who nevertheless achieves self-respect and self-reliance. Each of these novels draws on unique African American elements—including folklore and oral traditions—and gives expression to a distinctive "double consciousness," an awareness of being both African and American.

Native Americans, too, produced firsthand accounts of their lives. Among the most notable is the *Life of Ma-Ka-Tai-Me-she-kia-Kiak or Black Hawk* (1833), a classic spiritual and secular biography, in which the Sauk warrior explains why he resisted white efforts to seize Indian land in northwestern Illinois during the Black Hawk War (1832). William Apes, a Pequod, published one of the earliest histories from an Indian vantage point in 1836. John Rollin Ridge, a Cherokee journalist, published the first novel by an Indian in 1850, *The Life and Adventures of Joaquin Murieta*, which recounts the heroic adventures of a Robin Hood–like bandit in California who protects Mexican Americans from white exploitation. Much more than a simple adventure story, this novel is also a thinly veiled protest of the treatment of Native Americans by someone who had personally experienced the removal of the Cherokees from their tribal homelands in Georgia.

Mexican Americans responded to the arrival into the Southwest of white Americans through a variety of literary forms, including *corridos* (ballads), *chistes* (jokes), and autobiographies. The earliest autobiographical narrative was published by Padre Antonio José Martínez in 1838. Martínez resisted Father Jean-Baptiste Lamy's efforts to Americanize Catholic religious practices in New Mexico, a subject later treated in Willa Cather's 1927 novel *Death Comes to the Archbishop*. Other notable early autobiographies, written by José Antonio Mechaca and Juan Séguin, chronicle the decline of the landed Tejano elite following the Texas Revolution.

The famine years of the late 1840s—a period of massive Irish Catholic immigration and intense anti-Catholic prejudice—inspired a number of Irish American immigrants to reflect on their experience through fiction. Such authors as John Boyce, Hugh Quigley, and Mary Anne Sadlier used fiction to chronicle the sufferings of famine-stricken Ireland, the wrenching transatlantic passage, the disorientation of rural immigrants resettling in American cities, and the need for religious faith to help immigrants adjust to a challenging new environment. Sadlier, an orphan who migrated from Ireland in 1844, was the most prolific and influential nineteenth-century Irish-American novelist. Her 18 novels on Irish history and immigrant life offer a wealth of information about the famine generation and its religious beliefs and practices.

American Art

If Americans could produce literary masterpieces, were they also capable of creating visual art that would rival that of Europe? At the end of the eighteenth century, this seemed doubtful. Artistic implements, such as paints, brushes, and canvases, were difficult to obtain, and professional artists were few in number. Although a number of talented portrait painters—including John Singleton Copley, Charles Willson Peale, and Gilbert Stuart—appeared during the last half of the eighteenth century, most painters were simply skilled craftspeople, who devoted most of their time to painting houses, furniture, or signs.

Perhaps the biggest obstacle to the development of the visual arts was the fact that the revolutionary generation associated art with luxury, corruption, sensual appetite, and aristocracy. Commented one person: "When a people get a taste for the fine arts, they are ruined."

During the early nineteenth century, however, artists succeeded in overcoming public hostility toward the visual arts. One way artists gained a degree of respectability was through historical painting. The American public hungered for visual representations of the great events of the American Revolution, and works such as John Trumbull's Revolutionary War battle scenes and his painting of the Declaration of Independence (1818) fed the public's appetite. Romantic landscape paintings also attracted a large popular audience. Portrayals of the American landscape by artists of the Hudson River school, such as Thomas Cole, Albert Bierstadt, and Frederick Church, evoked a sense of the immensity, power, and grandeur of nature, which had not yet been tamed by an expansive American civilization.

A more favorable public attitude toward art was also evident in public campaigns to erect patriotic monuments, to landscape homes, and to beautify cities by restoring town greens and commons, constructing the first urban parks, and building the first modern "park" cemeteries. At the beginning of the nineteenth century, public monuments and statues were rarities; town commons were muddy, ill-kept areas, often containing buildings and packs of animals; houses lacked lawns; and cemeteries were unlandscaped collections of graves located near town centers.

Thomas Cole, *Schroon Mountain, The Adirondacks*, 1838. This painting captures the sense of awe at the grandeur and scenic beauty of the American landscape associated with artists of the Hudson River school.

Beginning in 1825, when an obelisk was erected at Bunker Hill to commemorate that Revolutionary War battle, Americans started to construct patriotic monuments. Around the same time, homeowners began to beautify their homes with lawns and landscaping, while cities established the nation's first urban parks. Construction of Mount Auburn cemetery in the 1830s in a pastoral setting outside Boston marked the beginning of the modern park cemetery, where the living could commune with the spirit of the dead (though the site was initially popular because it was a "green space" that could be used as a picnic ground). These beautification campaigns represented a response to the urban and industrial growth of cities that already threatened to destroy the physical beauty of city environments.

AMERICAN POPULAR CULTURE

Existing alongside the literary and artistic achievements of Emerson, Thoreau, and Melville was a vibrant popular culture. Consisting of penny newspapers, dime novels, minstrel shows, and other forms of popular amusement, this commercialized mass culture began to emerge at the dawn of the nineteenth century. By the eve of the Civil War, mass-circulation newspapers, inexpensive popular novels, and popular theater had become staples of American life.

One important aspect of popular culture was the penny press. Before the American Revolution, newspapers were few in number, expensive, short, small in circulation, infrequently printed, and aimed at a narrow audience. As late as 1765, there were only 23 weekly newspapers in the American colonies and no daily papers at all. At six cents a copy, these papers were out of reach of a popular audience; the contents of their four-page issues—announcements of ship arrivals, piracies, court actions, and maritime news—were of interest only to merchants. It was not until 1783 that the first daily newspaper, the *Pennsylvania Evening Post,* began to be published.

After the Revolution, political newspapers expressing the viewpoint of a particular political faction began to flourish. In the 1830s, when the development of the steam printing press dramatically cut printing costs and speeded production, the first mass-circulation newspapers began to appear. The first penny newspapers, Horatio David Sheppard's New York *Morning Post* and Benjamin H. Day's New York *Sun,* began publication in 1833.

The *Sun,* the first American paper to use newsboys to hawk papers on the street, soon discovered other ways of increasing its circulation. In the summer of 1835, the *Sun* announced that British astronomer Sir John Herschel had made "astronomical discoveries of the most wonderful description." With a new and powerful telescope, he had discovered "planets in other solar systems" and, most remarkably, the winged inhabitants of the moon. As a result of the "Great Moon Hoax," the *Sun's* circulation soared from 10,000 to 19,000. The *Sun's* success inspired other publishers to use hoaxes and stories of murders, railroad accidents, cannibalism, and freaks of nature—horror, gore, and perversity—to build circulation. English novelist Charles Dickens thought that appropriate names for newspapers would be the New York *Sewer* and the New York *Stabber.*

During the 1830s and 1840s, the modern mass-circulation newspaper emerged. Journalistic pioneers, such as James Gordon Bennett of the New York *Herald*, introduced features that we still associate with the daily newspaper, including crime stories, gossip columns, editorials, stock tables, and sports pages.

Along with the modern newspaper came magazines. From just five American magazines in 1794, the number rose to nearly 100 in 1825 and 600 in 1850. By 1850, there were magazines for almost every imaginable audience, with the proliferation of children's magazines, scientific journals, literary reviews, women's magazines, religious periodicals, and comics.

The Popular Novel

In 1860 an Oswego, New York, printer named Erastus Beadle issued his first dime novel, *Malaeska, The Indian Wife.* Critics attacked this book and others about heroes such as Daniel Boone as "devil-traps for the young," but within three years, Beadle had sold more than 2.5 million copies.

Well before Erastus Beadle introduced the dime novel (which usually sold for a nickel), opportunistic publishers had already produced murder trial transcripts, criminals' biographies, pirate tales, and westerns targeted at working-class and frontier readers. The respectable middle-class tended to read sentimental domestic tales, such as Susan Warner's *The Wide, Wide World,* one of the most popular mid-nineteenth-century novels; sentimental love poetry by authors such as Lydia Sigourney, "the sweet singer of Hartford"; or morally high-minded adventure tales, such as Richard Henry Dana, Jr.'s *Two Years Before the Mast* (1840) or historian Francis Parkman's *The Oregon Trail* (1847). Less educated Americans, however, favored adventure novels and urban crime novels.

Popular southern writers such as William Gilmore Simms and Robert Montgomery Bird produced tales of pirates and sea monsters for working-class and younger readers, and popular northern writers such as George Lippard, author of *New York: Its Upper Ten and Lower Million,* and Ned Buntline, author of *The Mysteries and Miseries of New York,* created tales of urban poverty and criminality. Although not great works of literature, the urban crime novels, in particular, offered valuable social commentary,

providing graphic details of aspects of pre–Civil War American life, such as teenage prostitution, urban poverty, class division, and social inequity, that were absent from the works of more respectable writers such as Washington Irving.

Much of the most popular American fiction produced before the Civil War was written by women. Although Nathaniel Hawthorne dismissed female novelists as "mere scribbling women," their works offered psychologically and sociologically insightful descriptions of drunken husbands brutalizing their wives, amoral men seducing and abandoning trusting young women, and callous employers exploiting ill-paid seamstresses and maids. The earliest woman-authored novel—Susanna Rowson's *Charlotte Temple* (1791), a story of a trusting heroine lured from her English home by a British officer and abandoned into poverty and premature death in New York—dealt with seduction and betrayal. At a time when the rate of illegitimate births was sharply rising (approaching 10 percent in New England), such stories offered a stark warning to young women.

By the 1820s, the form of women's literature most in demand was the "domestic novel," which typically described the "trials and triumphs" of a young woman who encounters hardships in a hostile society and discovers the resources within herself to surmount these difficulties. Authors such as Maria Cummins, Catharine Sedgwick, and Susan Warner gave expression to an early feminist vision. Their books upheld "feminine" values—of duty, tenderness, and self-sacrifice—as an alternative to the acquisitive, pecuniary values of the dominant society and called on women to attain a sense of self-respect and self-worth.

Forms of Popular Entertainment

A freewheeling, irreverent spirit pervaded American popular culture before the Civil War—a spirit typified by P. T. Barnum, nineteenth-century America's most famous purveyor of popular entertainment. A Connecticut Yankee born in Bridgeport in 1810, Barnum is reputed to have said that "there is a sucker born every minute." A staunch advocate of temperance, antislavery, and women's rights, Barnum made a fortune through pioneering campaigns of advertising and self-promotion. A critic said that an appropriate motto for Barnum would be: "Lie and swindle as much as you please . . . but be sure you read your Bible and drink no brandy!"

Throughout his life, the "prince of humbugs" never stopped believing that the public enjoyed hav-

Gouging Fights and Backcountry Honor

Nobody ever called them pretty. Eastern and European travelers to the American southern back-country employed many descriptive and emotive adjectives—disgusting, brutal, savage, uncivilized, disgraceful, barbaric, unsightly—but never once pretty. And, indeed, backcountry fights, whether called "gouging" matches, "rough-and-tumble" contests, or "no holds barred" battles, were not attractive affairs. Men fought all out, using fists, hands, feet, elbows, knees, teeth, and whatever other part of their anatomy promised to do bodily damage to their opponents. Capturing the temper of these battles, Anglican minister Charles Woodmason counseled, "I would advise you when You do fight Not to act like Tygers and Bears as these Virginians do—Biting one anothers Lips and Noses off, and *gouging* one another—that is, thrusting out one anothers Eyes, and kicking one another on the Cods, to the Great damage of many a Poor Woman."

The goal of a gouging match was the disfigurement of one's opponent. This could be accomplished in any number of ways, but the most popular was eye gouging. Fighters manicured their fingernails hard and sharp so that they could use them as a fulcrum to pry out their adversary's eye. On seeing a renowned fighter badly mauled, a passerby remarked, "'You have come off badly this time; I doubt?' 'Have I,' says he triumphantly, showing from his pocket at the same time an eye; which he had extracted during the combat, and preserved as a trophy."

Reading descriptions of these sanguinary contests provokes a series of questions. Who would engage in such activities? And why? Were the contests considered sports or manifestations of blood feuds? And what of the spectators and the law—did they enjoy and allow and condone such barbarities? Finally, what do the contests tell us about the society in which they flourished?

Gouging centered in the region of rivers and largely untamed backcountry south of the Ohio River. It was a land of dangers and violence and early deaths. Organized groups of Native Americans threatened settlers. Wild animals roamed the heavily wooded forests. Outlaws practiced their professions almost unchecked by the law. High infant mortality rates, short life expectancies, dangerous occupations, and random violence stood as grim reminders that life in this region of nature was, as philosopher Thomas Hobbes once noted, "solitary, poor, nasty, brutish, and short."

The men who disfigured each other in gouging matches had been hardened by their environment and their occupations. Many worked on the rivers as roustabouts, rivermen, or gamblers. Others were hunters, herders, or subsistence farmers. No plantations dotted their world; no landed aristocrats dominated them. As a leading historian of the subject commented, "the upland folk lived in an intensely local, kin-based society. Rural hamlets, impassable roads, and provincial isolation—not growing towns, internal improvements, or in-ternational commerce—characterized the backcountry."

The work these men performed was physically demanding and dangerous. Working on a Mississippi barge or trapping game in the backcountry exposed men to all the forces of nature and did not foster a gentle view of life. Death and pain were everywhere to be seen. Mark Twain remembered such men from his boyhood experiences in a raw river town: "Rude, uneducated, brave, suffering terrific hardships with sailorlike stoicism; heavy drinkers, coarse frolickers . . . , heavy fighters, reckless fellows, every one, elephantinely jolly, foul witted, profane, prodigal of their money, bankrupt at the end of the trip, fond of barbaric finery, prodigious braggarts." They were not Jacksonian men on the make or respectable churchgoers. Rather they were men who worked hard, played hard, and drank hard.

Since they spent most of their lives in the company of other men, much of their sense of self-worth came from how their companions viewed them. They did not use money or piety as yardsticks for measuring the worth of a man. Bravery, strength, conviviality, and a jealous sense of personal honor determined the cut of a man. The ability to drink, boast, and fight with equal ability marked a backcountry Renaissance man.

Question a man's honor and you questioned in the most profound sense his manhood. If aristocratic Southerners dueled over such slights, backcountry laborers gouged over them. Northerners found this touchy sense of honor perplexing. Philip Vickers Fithian, a New Jerseyite who traveled to the South in the 1770s,

commented about the reason for one fight, "I suppose either that they are lovers, and one has in Jest or reality some way supplanted the other; or has in a merry hour called him a *Lubber* or a *Thick-Skull,* or a *Buckskin,* or a *Scotsman,* or perhaps one has mislaid the other's hat, or knocked a peach out of his Hand, or offered him a dram without wiping the mouth of the Bottle." Any excuse, thought Fithian, could lead to mortal combat. But he misread the situation. In truth, any insult, no matter how slight, could be judged serious enough to provoke violence.

Once men exchanged angry words and angrier challenges, their combat provided entertainment for their companions. At the fights, drinking and boasting continued, and the line between participant and spectator was hazy. One fight often led to another

and general melees were not uncommon. Were such contests sports? Probably not, but it was not a question that anyone would have posed. Just as there was little distinction between participant and spectator, there was little difference between sport and battery.

Gouging matches were certainly not civilized affairs, and as civilized behavior and culture penetrated the backcountry, men ceased to settle their differences in such brutal contests. This is not to say that they stopped fighting. Rather they "defended their honor" in more "civilized" ways. Bowie knives, swords, and pistols replaced honed thumbnails and filed teeth as the weapons of choice. And these "affairs of honor" were held before a few solemn witnesses rather than a host of cheering friends.

But if gouging became a relic of another age, it remained a particularly telling relic. It provides an important clue to the values of the southern backcountry. How men fought—just as how they worked or played—indicates much about their lives. The men who gouged led strenuous, often violent lives. They were not the sort of men to turn pale at the sight of blood or even at the sight of an eyeless eye socket. They admired toughness, fearlessness, and even meanness—not piety, gentleness, and sensitivity.

During an earlier time, it was considered an unmanly sign of fear for a person to carry a weapon. But more refined sensibilities reversed this notion. By the mid-nineteenth century weapon carrying had become an indication of manliness.

State legislator and Congressman David Crockett gained popularity as frontiersman folk hero Davy Crockett with the 1834 publication of *A Narrative of the Life of David Crockett of the State of Tennessee.* Over the next two decades a series of popular pamphlets known as Davy Crockett almanacs recounted the exploits and adventures of the backwoodsman, who boasted that he could "walk like an ox, run like a fox, swim like an eel, and spout like an earthquake."

ing its wits tested. He got his start exhibiting a slave woman named Joice Heth, whom he claimed was 161 years old and had served as George Washington's nursemaid (an autopsy later revealed that she was 80 at her death). Barnum achieved fame and fortune from his 25-cent American Museum in New York, which contained the "Feejee mermaid," which had the head of a monkey and the body of a fish; a working model of Niagara Falls; the 25-inch-tall General Tom Thumb; and Jumbo, an immense white elephant. After the Civil War, Barnum closed his museum and opened "the greatest show on earth," a spectacular three-ring circus. With his hoaxes, humbugs, and shameless self-promotion, Barnum epitomized the buoyant, irreverence of antebellum popu-

lar culture—which taught Americans to pay gladly for entertainment.

A rowdy, boisterous spirit was particularly evident in popular humor. The word *grotesque* sums up a defining characteristic of American humor before the Civil War. Employing crude language, wild exaggeration, pungent images, and incongruity, the writings of such early American humorists as James Kirke Paulding and George Washington Harris paved the way for the later success of Artemus Ward, Bret Harte, and Mark Twain.

No form of humor was more popular than the tall tale, an incredibly exaggerated account of improbable events. The most famous comic hero was Davy Crockett, loosely based on the life of the frontier hero and Whig politician who died at the Alamo. More than 50 wildly popular Crockett almanacs and humor pamphlets described him as a high-spirited, resourceful braggart, "half-man, half-alligator." He is depicted as an ardent opponent of corruption in business and politics, who spends his leisure time riding on streaks of lightning and lighting his pipe with the sun.

American popular culture found one of its most well-received forms of expression on the stage. A typical night at the theater included not only a play but also various musical interludes and a comic opera, as well as demonstrations of magic tricks, tightrope walking, fireworks, acrobatics, or pantomime. Melodramas were an especially popular form of theatrical entertainment, often describing a villain's efforts to strip a young maiden of her virtue and fortune. Emphasizing action over characterization, melodramas were filled with thrilling fights, daring escapes, and breathtaking rescues, and featured elaborate scenery, including working waterfalls and volcanoes.

Critics condemned the theater as a "Synagogue of Satan" that attracted "the most depraved and yet the most enticing companions the community affords." Antebellum theaters were rowdy places where liquor dealers and prostitutes plied their wares, and audiences interacted directly with actors and musicians. Theatergoers were not passive spectators. They ate during performances and expressed their praise with boisterous clapping. When they were displeased, they yelled and hissed and pelted actors with rotten eggs, stones, and even chairs. Some performances actually ignited riots—usually when an English actor was accused of insulting the United States. The most famous, the Astor Place Riot of 1849, resulted in dozens of injuries.

Oratory was a particularly popular form of entertainment. Americans attended sermons, political speeches, poetry readings, and public lectures with

Although Stephen Foster actually knew little about the South, his songs, such as "Old Folks at Home" and "My Old Kentucky Home," gave expression to a sentimental picture of the antebellum South. Foster also wrote songs for blackface minstrel shows, like Christy's Minstrels, a popular form of entertainment in the 1830s and 1840s.

an enthusiasm unmatched in American history. The lyceum movement, founded by Josiah Holbrook, a Connecticut farmer, in 1826, sponsored traveling lectures on the arts, literature, philosophy, religion, and science, including such prominent figures as Ralph Waldo Emerson and the Whig politician Daniel Webster.

Perhaps the most distinctive feature of pre–Civil War popular culture was the minstrel show. The first uniquely American entertainment form, the minstrel show provided comedy, music, dance, and novelty acts to audiences hungry for entertainment. Offering humor that ranged from comedy skits to slapstick and one-liners—often mocking pompous politicians and pretentious professionals—the minstrel shows also introduced many of America's most enduring popular songs, including "Turkey in the Straw" and "Dixie."

Minstrel shows popularized the songs of Stephen Foster (1826–1864), the most acclaimed American composer of the mid-nineteenth century. Foster wrote more than 200 songs during his lifetime, mainly senti-

mental ballads and love songs (such as "Old Folks at Home," "My Old Kentucky Home," and "Beautiful Dreamer") and up tempo, rhythmic comic songs (such as "Camptown Races" and "Oh! Susanna"). At a time when the country was undergoing rapid urbanization and industrialization, Foster's music responded to a deep nostalgia for a simpler era. Although Foster died in utter poverty—at the age of 37 in the paupers' wing of New York's Bellevue Hospital, with just 37 cents in his pocket—he, more than any other composer, stimulated popular enthusiasm for American music.

The minstrel shows are difficult to interpret, in part because they relied on blackface humor that we find particularly abhorrent. Reflecting the racism of the broader society, minstrel shows presented a denigrating portrayal of African Americans. Racial stereotypes were the minstrel shows' stock in trade. Actors wore grotesque makeup, spoke in ludicrous dialects, and presented plantation life in a highly romanticized manner. Yet if the minstrel shows expressed the virulent racism of many white Americans, the blackface minstrel had another side. His humor frequently mocked whites and challenged traditional values. Moreover, the shows often incorporated elements of African-American folklore and showed black men and women outwitting white masters.

Pseudoscience also captured the popular fancy during the decades before the Civil War. During the early nineteenth century, science was advancing so rapidly that it was difficult to distinguish authentic scientific discoveries from hoaxes. Before the Civil War, Americans were fascinated by a variety of pseudosciences. Phrenology linked human character to the shape of and bumps on a person's skull. Animal magnetism was the belief in a universal electrical fluid influencing physics and even human psychology. Audiences flocked to see demonstrations of mesmerism (the control of a hypnotized person by a medium) and spiritualism (the direct communication with spirits of the deceased through trance visions or séances).

Phrenology had particular appeal to pre–Civil War Americans. Discovered by a physician from Vienna named Franz Gall and imported into the United States in 1832, phrenology exerted an extraordinary impact on popular culture. One American phrenology journal claimed a circulation of 50,000, and many employers required prospective employees to have their heads read. One of the earliest examples of a "science" of human behavior, phrenology held that distinct portions of the brain were devoted to distinct impulses—such as combativeness, amativeness (sexual love), and adhesiveness (comradely affection)—and that peoples' mental attributes could be read through their facial features. Phrenology claimed to offer young men and women a way to evaluate potential spouses and employers a tool for judging potential employees.

lightenment faith in reason, and liberal and evangelical religious principles, educational reformers created a system of free public education; prison reformers constructed specialized institutions to reform criminals; temperance reformers sought to end the drinking of liquor; and utopian socialists established ideal communities to serve as models for a better world.

America's first age of reform was also an era of extraordinary intellectual and artistic ferment. The decades preceding the Civil War witnessed the growth of a mass audience for art, literature, and drama; the rise of a vibrant commercial mass culture; and the popularization of some of the most distinctive products of American culture, including the penny press, the minstrel show, and the western adventure novel. Authors such as James Fenimore Cooper and Henry Wadsworth Longfellow created a distinctly American literature employing native scenes and characters. The Transcendentalists developed a philosophy that rejected external authority and tradition and instead emphasized each person's infinite potentialities and glorified nature as a creative force. And especially during the 1850s, a host of writers—including Nathaniel Hawthorne, Harriet Jacobs, and Herman Melville—produced works of literature that rank among the greatest ever produced in this country.

The Civil War brought this period of ferment and experimentation to a close. The war's grim brutality undercut the spirit of hope and boundless possibilities that had pervaded pre–Civil War America. Nevertheless, the reformers, writers, and artists of the early nineteenth century would stand as an example and an inspiration to future generations of Americans.

Conclusion

The pre–Civil War reform era came to a symbolic end in 1865 when William Lloyd Garrison, the abolitionist, closed down his militant abolitionist newspaper *The Liberator* and called on the American Anti-Slavery Society to disband. Its mission, he announced, had been accomplished.

The first half of the nineteenth century witnessed the rise of the first secular movements in history to educate the deaf and the blind, care for the mentally ill, extend equal rights to women, and abolish slavery. Inspired by the revolutionary ideals of the Declaration of Independence and the Bill of Rights, the En-

Chapter Summary and Key Points

In this chapter you learned about the religious, cultural, and social factors that gave rise to efforts to suppress the drinking of hard liquor; to rehabilitate criminals; establish public schools; care for the mentally ill, the deaf, and the blind; abolish slavery; and extend women's rights. In addition you read about the efforts of authors and artists to create distinctly American forms of literature and art.

- During the first half of the nineteenth century, the Declaration of Independence, the Enlightenment faith in reason, and liberal and evangelical religion inspired efforts at reform.

CHRONOLOGY OF KEY EVENTS

1776 Mother Ann Lee founds the first Shaker community in America near Albany, New York

1801 Cane Ridge, Kentucky, revival meeting

1807 Congress outlaws the African slave trade

1816 American Colonization Society is founded

1819 Washington Irving publishes "Rip Van Winkle"

1825 Charles Finney leads his first religious revivals in New York State; Robert Owen founds New Harmony community in Indiana

1826 American Society for the Promotion of Temperance is founded

1829 David Walker issues his *Appeal to the Colored Citizens of the World*

1831 William Lloyd Garrison begins publishing the militant abolitionist newspaper *The Liberator*

1833 First penny newspapers—New York *Sun* and New York *Morning Post*—are published; first coeducational college in the United States—Oberlin—is founded

1834 Antiabolitionist rioting takes place in Philadelphia

1837 Emerson presents his address on the "American Scholar"; Angelina Grimké lectures to mixed audiences of men and women; Massachusetts creates first state board of education and appoints Horace Mann secretary; abolitionist Elijah P. Lovejoy is killed by a proslavery mob in Alton, Illinois

1838 Frederick Douglass escapes from slavery

1840 Washington temperance movement begins; Liberty party is founded; and James G. Birney runs for president as Liberty party candidate; Sarah Grimké publishes *Letters on the Condition of Women and the Equality of the Sexes,* one of the earliest public defenses of sexual equality

1841 Dorothea Dix begins crusade on behalf of the mentally ill; Brook Farm is founded

1843 "Isabella" takes name Sojourner Truth and begins to speak out on behalf of women's rights and against slavery

1845 Henry David Thoreau begins living at Walden Pond

1848 First women's rights convention is held in Seneca Falls, New York; Free Soil party receives 10 percent of presidential vote

1849 Astor Place riot in New York City

1850 Nathaniel Hawthorne publishes *The Scarlet Letter*

1851 Herman Melville publishes *Moby Dick*

1852 Massachusetts adopts the first compulsory education law; Harriet Beecher Stowe's *Uncle Tom's Cabin* sells a million copies in its first year and a half

1854 Henry David Thoreau publishes *Walden*

1855 Walt Whitman publishes *Leaves of Grass*

- Educational reformers created the nation's first system of free public schools; prison reformers created institutions to rehabilitate criminals; temperance reformers sought to end the drinking of liquor; abolitionists sought to overthrow slavery; women's rights advocates fought for the vote, expanded educational opportunities, and married women's property rights; and utopian socialists established ideal communities to serve as blueprints for a better world.

- This period also saw the rise of vibrant commercial mass culture and the emergence of such distinctive aspects of American culture as the penny press, the minstrel show, and the western adventure novel.

- James Fenimore Cooper and Henry Wadsworth Longfellow created literature that employed native scenes and characters.

- Transcendentalists popularized a philosophy that rejected authority and tradition and emphasized each person's infinite potentialities and glorified nature as a creative force.

Suggestions for Further Reading

Robert Abzug, *Cosmos Crumbling: American Reform and the Religious Imagination* (1994) shows how religious ideals and motives influenced the major reforms of the pre–Civil War era, including abolition, temperance, and woman's rights.

Steven Mintz, *Moralists and Modernizers: America's Pre–Civil War Reformers* (1995) offers an overview and interpretation of America's first age of reform, combining portraits of leading reformers with discussions of religion and specific reform movements.

David Reynolds, *Beneath the American Renaissance: The Subversive Imagination in the Age of Emerson and Melville* (1989). An exploration of the popular culture and popular writers of the pre–Civil War decades.

Ronald G. Walters, *American Reformers, 1815–1860* (1997) examines the beliefs, rhetoric, and tactics of leading reformers.

Novels

Nathaniel Hawthorne, *The Blithedale Romance* (1852).
Herman Melville, *Moby Dick* (1851).

Media Resources
Web Sites
Abolition
http://lcweb.loc.gov/exhibits/african/afam005.html
This Library of Congress exhibit includes antislavery petitions, songs, children's magazines, and other original sources documenting the struggle to abolish slavery.

Divining America
http://www.nhc.rtp.nc.us:8080/tserve/siteguide.htm
This site includes essays by leading religious historians on American Jewish experience in the nineteenth century; Mormonism; Evangelicalism and the Second Great Awakening; Evangelicalism as a social movement; African-American religion; and Roman Catholics and immigration.

Documents from the Gilder Lehrman Collection
http://www.gliah.uh.edu/modules/precivilwar/documents.cfm
Primary sources that document the reform movements of the pre–Civil War era.

History of Women's Suffrage
http://www.rochester.edu/SBA/historysba.htm
This site provides information about the first women's Rights Convention in Seneca Falls, New York in 1848, as well as women's struggle for the vote.

Worcester Women's History
http://www.assumption.edu/HTML/academic/history/WWHP/hr.html
Speeches, letters, and other primary source documents relating to the first national women's rights convention in Worcester, Mass., in 1850.

Films and Videos

Not for Ourselves Alone: The Story of Elizabeth Cady Stanton and Susan B. Anthony (2001). A historical documentary by Ken Burns.

Key Terms

Enlightenment   (p. 273)
Religious liberalism   (p. 273)
Second Great Awakening   (p. 274)
Millennium   (p. 274)
Evangelical revivals   (p. 274)
Deism   (p. 274)
Temperance   (p. 276)
Insanity defense   (p. 277)
Capital punishment   (p. 277)
Imprisonment for debt   (p. 277)
Colonization   (p. 279)
Immediate emancipation   (p. 279)
Liberty party   (p. 281)
Free Soil party   (p. 281)
Utopian communities   (p. 286)
Shakers   (p. 286)
Transcendentalists   (p. 288)

People You Should Know

Prudence Crandall   (p. 271)
William Ellery Channing   (p. 273)
Charles Grandison Finney   (p. 274)
Horace Mann   (p. 278)
Dorothea Dix   (p. 278)
Thomas Hopkins Gallaudet   (p. 278)
Samuel Gridley Howe   (p. 278)
Paul Cuffe   (p. 279)

David Walker   (p. 279)

William Lloyd Garrison   (p. 279)

Elijah Lovejoy   (p. 280)

Harriet Tubman   (p. 281)

Frederick Douglass   (p. 281)

Angelina and Sarah Grimké   (p. 284)

Elizabeth Cady Stanton   (p. 284)

Sojourner Truth   (p. 284)

Ralph Waldo Emerson   (p. 289)

Henry David Thoreau   (p. 289)

REVIEW QUESTIONS

1. Describe the social and religious roots of the reform movements of the early nineteenth century.

2. In what ways did moral reformers try to change the behavior of early nineteenth-century Americans? How successful were they?

3. Describe the efforts of pre–Civil War reformers in each of the following areas: (a) educational reform; (b) the treatment of criminals; and (c) the treatment of the mentally ill.

4. Why did the abolition movement arouse resentment among many Northerners as well as many Southerners?

5. Why did a movement for women's rights emerge in the mid-nineteenth century? Identify the movement's achievements.

6. In what ways did American literature and art give expression to a distinctive national identity in the years before the Civil War?

12 The Divided North, The Divided South

ELI WHITNEY'S COTTON GIN REVITALIZES SLAVERY

In the early 1790s, slavery appeared to be a dying institution. Slave imports into the New World were declining and slave prices were falling because the crops grown by slaves—tobacco, rice, and indigo—did not generate enough income to pay for their upkeep. In Maryland and Virginia, planters were replacing tobacco, a labor-intensive crop that needed a slave labor force, with wheat and corn, which did not. At the same time, leading Southerners, including Thomas Jefferson, denounced slavery as a source of debt, economic stagnation, and moral dissipation. A French traveler reported that people throughout the South "are constantly talking of abolishing slavery, of contriving some other means of cultivating their estates."

Then **Eli Whitney** of Massachusetts gave slavery a new lease on life. Even as a teenager, Whitney was considered a mechanical genius. At the age of 12, he produced a violin that "made tolerable good musick." At 15 he took over his father's workshop in Westborough, Massachusetts, and began manufacturing nails. By the time he was 18, he had begun to produce hatpins for women's bonnets and men's walking sticks. But young Whitney hoped to become something more than a clever mechanic, and at the age of 23 he abandoned his father's workshop and entered college.

In 1792, just after graduating from Yale, Whitney traveled south in search of employment as a tutor. His journey was filled with disasters. During the boat trip, he became seasick. Before he could recover, his boat ran aground on rocks near New York City. Then he contracted smallpox. The only good thing to happen during his journey was that he was befriended by a charming southern widow named Catharine Greene, whose late husband, General Nathanael Greene, had been a leading general during the American Revolution. When he arrived in the South, Whitney discovered that his promised salary as a tutor had been cut in half. So he quit the job and accepted Greene's invitation to visit her plantation near Savannah, Georgia.

During his visit, Whitney became intrigued with the problem encountered by southern planters in producing short-staple cotton. The booming textile industry had created a high demand for the crop, but it could not be marketed until the

While seeking employment in the South, Yankee schoolteacher Eli Whitney developed a simple machine for separating cotton from its seeds. The "cotton gin" met the increasing demand for cotton and breathed new life into the institution of slavery.

seeds had been extracted from the cotton boll, a laborious and time-consuming process.

From a slave known only by the name Sam, Whitney learned that a comb could be used to remove seeds from cotton. In just 10 days, Whitney devised a way of mechanizing the comb. Within a month, Whitney's cotton engine (gin for short) could separate fiber from seeds faster than 50 people working by hand.

Whitney's invention revitalized slavery in the South by stimulating demand for slaves to raise short-staple cotton. Between 1792, when Whitney arrived on the Greene plantation, and 1794, the price of slaves doubled. By 1825 field hands, who brought $500 apiece in 1794, were worth $1500. As the price of slaves rose, so too did the number of slaves. During the first decade of the nineteenth century, the number of slaves in the United States increased by 33 percent; during the following decade (after the African slave trade became illegal), the slave population grew another 29 percent.

As the institution of slavery expanded in the South, it declined in the North. In 1777, Vermont's constitution outlawed slavery, making it the first area in the New World to prohibit slavery. Judicial decisions freed slaves in Massachusetts and New Hampshire, and other northern states adopted gradual emancipation acts. By the beginning of the nineteenth century, the new republic was fatefully divided into a slave section and a free section.

A Divided Culture

By 1860 most Americans believed that the Mason-Dixon line divided the nation into two distinctive cultures: a commercial North and an agrarian South. This belief—that the cultures of the North and South were fundamentally different—was not a new idea on the eve of the Civil War. During the bitter political battles of the 1790s, New England Federalists pictured the South as a backward, economically stagnant society in which manual labor was degraded and wealth was dissipated in personal luxury. Many southern Republicans countered by denouncing the corrupt, grasping, materialistic society of the North.

Many factors contributed to this sense of sectional difference. Diction, work habits, diet, and labor systems distinguished the two sections. One section depended on slave-based agriculture; the other emphasized commercial agriculture based on family farms and a developing industrial sector resting on wage labor.

The North was over 50 percent more populous than the South. Urban centers grew as European immigrants arrived in greater and greater numbers. Commerce, financial institutions, manufacturing, and transportation were developing rapidly. In contrast, the South had primitive transportation facilities, and it had smaller and fewer cities. Most important of all, a third of the South's population lived in slavery.

Despite these differences, the pre–Civil War North and South shared many important characteristics. Both regions were predominantly rural, both had booming economies, and both were engaged in speculation and trade. They shared western expansion, the enactment of democratic political reforms, and the same national political parties. Nevertheless, most Americans thought of their nation as divided into two halves, a commercial civilization and an agrarian civilization, each operating according to entirely different sets of values.

THE EMERGENCE OF A NEW INDUSTRIAL ORDER IN THE NORTH

To all outward appearances, life in the North in 1790 was not much different than in 1740. The vast majority of the people—more than 90 percent—still lived and worked on farms or in small rural villages. Less than 1 Northerner in 13 worked in trade or manufacturing.

Conditions of life remained primitive. The typical house—a single-story one- or two-room log or wood frame structure—was small, sparsely furnished, and afforded little personal privacy. Sleeping, eating, and work spaces were not sharply differentiated, and mirrors, curtains, upholstered chairs, carpets, desks, and bookcases were luxuries enjoyed only by wealthy families.

Even prosperous farming or merchant families lived simply. Many families ate meals out of a common pot or bowl, just as their ancestors had in the seventeenth century. Standards of cleanliness remained exceedingly low. Bedbugs were constant sleeping companions, and people seldom bathed or even washed their clothes or dishes.

Daily life was physically demanding. Most families made their own cloth, clothing, and soap. Because they lacked matches, they lit fires by striking a flint again and again with a steel striker until a spark ignited some tinder. Because there was no indoor plumbing, chamber pots had to be used and emptied. Homes were usually heated by a single open fireplace and illuminated by candles. Housewives hand-carried water from a pump, well, or stream and threw the dirty water or slops out the window. Family members hauled grain to a local grist mill or else milled it by hand. They cut, split, and gathered wood and fed it into a fireplace.

By 1860, however, profound and far-reaching changes had taken place. Commercial agriculture had replaced subsistence agriculture. Household production had been supplanted by centralized manufacturing outside the home. And nonagricultural employment had begun to overtake agricultural employment: Nearly half of the North's population made a living outside the agricultural sector.

These economic transformations were all results of the industrial revolution, which affected every aspect of life. It raised living standards, transformed the work process, and relocated hundreds of thousands of people across oceans and from rural farms and villages into fast-growing industrial cities.

The most obvious consequence of this revolution was an impressive increase in wealth, per capita income, and commercial, middle-class job opportunities. Between 1800 and 1860, output increased 12-fold, and purchasing power doubled. New middle-class jobs proliferated. Increasing numbers of men found work as agents, bankers, brokers, clerks, merchants, professionals, and traders.

Living standards rose sharply, at least for the rapidly expanding middle class. Instead of making cloth and clothing at home, families began to buy them. Instead of hand milling grains, an increasing number of families began to buy processed grains. Kerosene lamps replaced candles as a source of light; coal replaced wood as fuel; friction matches replaced crude flints. Even poorer families began to cook their food on cast-iron cook stoves and to heat their rooms with individual-room heaters. The advent of railroads and the first canned foods brought year-round variety to the northern diet.

Physical comfort increased markedly. Padded seats, spring mattresses, and pillows became more common. By 1860 many urban middle-class families had central heating, indoor plumbing, and wall-to-wall carpeting.

Houses became larger and more affordable. The invention in the 1830s of the balloon frame—a light-weight house frame made up of boards nailed together—as well as prefabricated doors, window frames, shutters, and sashes resulted in larger and more reasonably priced houses. The cost of building a house fell by 40 percent, and two-story houses, with four or five rooms, became increasingly common.

A revolution in values and sensibility accompanied these changes in the standard of living. Standards of cleanliness and personal hygiene rose sharply. People bathed more frequently, washed their clothes more often, and dusted, swept, and scrubbed their houses more regularly. Standards of propriety also rose. The respectable classes began to blow their noses into handkerchiefs, instead of wiping them with their sleeves, and to dispose of their spittle in spittoons.

Northerners regarded all of these changes as signs of progress. A host of northern political leaders, mainly Whigs and later Republicans, celebrated the North as a region of bustling cities, factories, railroads, and prosperous farms and independent craftsmen—a stark contrast to an impoverished, backward, slave-owning South, suffering from soil exhaustion and economic and social decline.

Although the industrial revolution brought many material benefits, critics decried its negative consequences. Labor leaders deplored the bitter suffering of factory and sweatshop workers, the breakdown of craft skills, the vulnerability of urban workers to layoffs and economic crises, and the maldistribution of wealth and property. Conservatives lamented the disintegration of an older household-centered economy in which husbands, wives, and children had labored together. Southern writers, such as George Fitzhugh, argued that the North's growing class of free laborers were slaves of the marketplace, suffering even more insecurity than the South's chattel slaves, who were provided for in sickness and old age.

During the early nineteenth century, the industrial revolution transformed northern society, altering the way people worked and lived and contributing to growing sectional differences between the North and South. How and why did the industrial revolution occur when it did? What were its consequences? How did it fuel sectional antagonisms?

The Transformation of the Rural Countryside

In 1790 most farm families in the rural North produced most of what they needed to live. Instead of using money to purchase necessities, families entered into complex exchange relationships with relatives and neighbors and bartered to acquire the goods they needed. To supplement their meager incomes, farm families often did piecework for shopkeepers and craftsmen. In the late eighteenth century these "household industries" provided work for thousands of men, women, and children in rural areas. Shopkeepers or master craftsmen supplied farm families with raw materials and paid them piece rates to produce such items as linens and farm utensils.

Between 1790 and the 1820s, a new pattern emerged. Subsistence farming gave way to commercial agriculture as farmers increasingly began to grow cash crops for sale and used the proceeds to buy goods produced by others. In New Hampshire farmers raised sheep for wool; in western Massachusetts they began to fatten cattle and pigs for sale to Boston; in eastern Pennsylvania they specialized in dairy products.

After 1820, the household industries that had employed thousands of women and children began to decline. They were replaced by manufacturing in city shops and factories. New England farm families began to buy their shoes, furniture, cloth, and sometimes even their clothes ready-made. Small rural factories closed their doors, and village artisans who produced for local markets found themselves unable to compete against cheaper city-made goods. As local opportunities declined, many long-settled farm

Agriculture and Industry, 1850

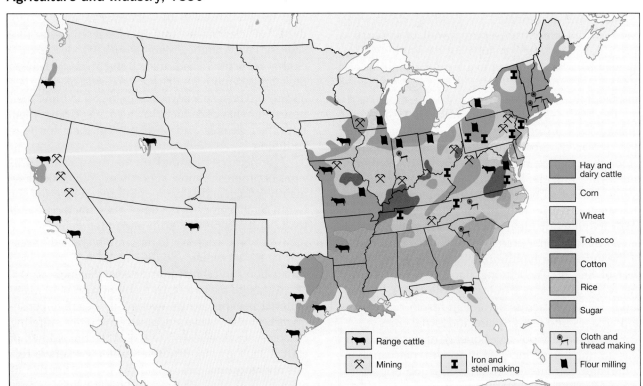

areas suffered sharp population losses. Convinced that "agriculture is not the road to wealth, nor honor, nor to happiness," thousands of young people left the fields for cities.

The Disruption of the Artisan System of Labor

In the late eighteenth century, the North's few industries were small. Skilled craftspeople, known as *artisans* or *mechanics,* performed most manufacturing in small towns and larger cities. These craftspeople manufactured goods in traditional ways—by hand in their own homes or in small shops located nearby—and marketed the goods they produced. Matthew Carey, a Philadelphia newspaperman, personified the early nineteenth-century artisan-craftsman. He not only wrote articles and editorials that appeared in his newspaper, he also set the paper's type, operated the printing press, and hawked the newspaper.

The artisan class was divided into three subgroups. At the highest level were self-employed master craftspeople. They were assisted by skilled journeymen, who owned their own tools but lacked the capital to set up their own shops, and by apprentices, teenage boys who typically worked for three years in exchange for training in a craft.

Urban artisans did not draw a sharp separation between home and work. A master shoemaker might make shoes in a 10-foot square shed located immediately in back of his house. A printer would bind books or print newspapers in a room below his family's living quarters. Typically, a master craftsperson lived in the same house with his assistants. The household of Everard Peck, a Rochester, New York, publisher, was not unusual. It included his wife, his children, his brother, his business partner, a day laborer, and four journeyman printers and bookbinders.

Nor did urban artisans draw a sharp division between work and leisure. Work patterns tended to be irregular and were frequently interrupted by leisure breaks during which masters and journeymen would drink whiskey or other alcoholic beverages. During slow periods or periodic layoffs, workers enjoyed fishing trips and sleigh rides or cockfights, as well as drinking and gambling at local taverns. Artisans often took unscheduled time off to attend boxing matches, horse races, and exhibitions by traveling musicians and acrobats.

The first half of the nineteenth century witnessed the decline of the **artisan system of labor.** Skilled tasks, previously performed by artisans, were divided and subcontracted to less expensive unskilled laborers. Small shops were replaced by large "machineless" factories, which made the relationship between employer and employee increasingly impersonal. Many master craftspeople abandoned their supervisory role to foremen and contractors and substituted unskilled teenage boys for journeymen. Words like *employer, employee, boss,* and *foreman*—descriptive of the new relationships—began to be widely used.

Between 1790 and 1850 the work process—especially in the building trades, printing, and such rapidly expanding consumer-oriented manufacturing industries as tailoring and shoemaking—was radically reorganized. The changes in the shoemaking industry in Rochester, New York, during the 1820s and 1830s illustrate this process. Instead of producing an entire shoe, a master would fit a customer, rough-cut the leather uppers, and then send the uppers and soles to a boardinghouse, where a journeyman would shape the leather. Then, the journeyman would send the pieces to a binder, a woman who worked in her home, who would sew the shoes together. Finally, the binder would send the shoe back to the master for sale to the customer. Tremendous gains in productivity sprang from the division and specialization of labor.

By 1850, the older household-based economy, in which assistants lived in the homes of their employers, had disappeared. Young men moved out of rooms in their master's home and into hotels or boardinghouses in distinct working-class neighborhoods. The older view that workers should be attached to a particular master, who would supervise their behavior and assume responsibility for their welfare, declined. This paternalistic view was replaced by a new conception of labor as a commodity, like cotton, that could be acquired or disposed of according to the laws of supply and demand.

In the factory system of production, machines lowered the costs of producing goods, but workers faced increasing demands to tend more machines and put out greater numbers of items.

The Introduction of the Factory System

In 1789 the Pennsylvania legislature placed an advertisement in British newspapers offering a cash bounty to any English textile worker who would migrate to the state. **Samuel Slater**, who was just finishing an apprenticeship in a Derbyshire textile mill, read the ad. He went to London, booked passage to America, and landed in Philadelphia. There he learned that Moses Brown, a Quaker merchant, had just completed a mill in Pawtucket, Rhode Island, and needed a manager. Slater applied for the job and received it, along with a promise that if he made the factory a success he would receive all the business's profits, less the cost and interest on the machinery.

On December 21, 1790, the mill opened. Seven boys and two girls, all between the ages of 7 and 12, operated the little factory's 72 spindles. Slater soon discovered that these children, "constantly employed under the immediate inspection of a [supervisor]," could produce three times as much as whole families working in their homes. To keep the children awake and alert, Slater whipped them with a leather strap

Young women made up the bulk of the workforce in the early textile mills.

or sprinkled them with water. On Sundays the children attended a special school Slater founded for their education.

The opening of Slater's mill marked the beginning of the **factory system**, a widespread movement to consolidate manufacturing operations under a single roof. During the last years of the eighteenth century, merchants and master craftspeople who were discontented with the inefficiencies of their workforce created the nation's first modern factories. Within these centralized workshops, employers closely supervised employees, synchronized work to the clock, and punished infractions of rules with heavy fines or dismissal. In 1820, only 350,000 Americans worked in factories or mills. Four decades later, on the eve of the Civil War, the number had soared to two million.

For an inexpensive and reliable labor force, many factory owners turned to child labor. During the early phases of industrialization, textile mills and agricultural tool, metal goods, nail, and rubber factories had a ravenous appetite for cheap teenage laborers. In many mechanized industries, from a quarter to over half of the workforce was made up of young men or women under the age of 20.

During the first half of the nineteenth century, unmarried women made up a majority of the workforce in cotton textile mills and a substantial minority of workers in factories manufacturing ready-made clothing, hats, and shoes. Women were also employed in significant numbers in the manufacture of buttons, furniture, gloves, gunpowder, shovels, and tobacco.

Unlike farm work or domestic service, employment in a mill offered female companionship and an independent income. Wages were twice what a woman could make as a seamstress, tailor, or school-

Cotton Textile Industry

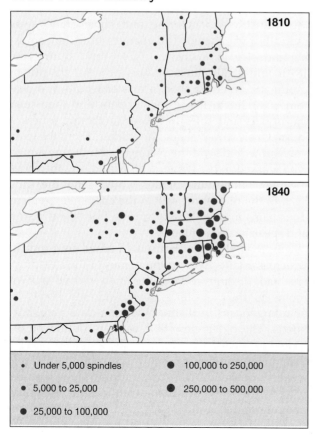

1810

1840

- Under 5,000 spindles
- 5,000 to 25,000
- 25,000 to 100,000
- 100,000 to 250,000
- 250,000 to 500,000

teacher. Furthermore, most mill girls viewed the work as only temporary before marriage. Most worked in the mills fewer than four years, and frequently interrupted their stints in the mill for several months at a time with trips back home.

By the 1830s, increasing competition among textile manufacturers caused deteriorating working conditions that drove native-born women out of the mills. Employers cut wages, lengthened the workday, and required mill workers to tend four looms instead of just two. Hannah Borden, a Fall River, Massachusetts, textile worker, was required to have her loom running at 5 A.M. She was given an hour for breakfast and half an hour for lunch. Her workday ended at 7:30 P.M., $14\frac{1}{2}$ hours after it had begun. For a six-day workweek, she received between $2.50 and $3.50.

The mill girls militantly protested the wage cuts. In 1834 and again in 1836, the mill girls went out on strike. An open letter spelled out the workers' complaints: "sixteen females [crowded] into the same hot, ill-ventilated attic"; a workday "two or three hours longer . . . than is done in Europe"; and workers compelled to "stand so long at the machinery . . . that varicose veins, dropsical swelling of the feet and limbs, and prolapsus uter[us], diseases that end only with life, are not rare but common occurrences."

During the 1840s, fewer and fewer native-born women were willing to work in the mills. "Slavers," which were long, black wagons that criss-crossed the Vermont and New Hampshire countryside in search of mill hands, arrived empty in Rhode Island and Massachusetts mill towns. Increasingly, employers replaced the native-born mill girls with a new class of permanent factory operatives: immigrant women from Ireland.

Labor Protests

In 1806 journeyman shoemakers in New York City organized one of the nation's first labor strikes. The workers' chief demands were not higher wages and shorter hours. Instead, they protested the changing conditions of work. They staged a "turn-out" or "stand-out," as a strike was then called, to protest the use of cheap unskilled and apprentice labor and the subdivision and subcontracting of work. The strike ended when a court ruled that a labor union was guilty of criminal conspiracy if workers struck to obtain wages higher than those set by custom. The court found the journeyman shoemakers guilty and fined them $1 plus court costs.

By the 1820s, a growing number of journeymen were organizing to protest employer practices that were undermining the independence of workers, re-ducing them to the status of "a humiliating servile dependency, incompatible with the inherent natural equality of men." Unlike their counterparts in Britain, American journeymen did not protest against the introduction of machinery into the workplace. Instead, they vehemently protested wage reductions, declining standards of workmanship, and the increased use of unskilled and semiskilled workers. Journeymen charged that manufacturers had reduced "them to degradation and the loss of that self-respect which had made the mechanics and laborers the pride of the world." They insisted that they were the true producers of wealth and that manufacturers, who did not engage in manual labor, were unjust expropriators of wealth. In 1834 journeymen established the National Trades' Union, the first national organization of American wage earners. By 1836 union membership had climbed to 300,000.

Despite bitter employer opposition, some gains were made. In 1842, in the landmark case *Commonwealth v. Hunt,* the Massachusetts Supreme Court established a new precedent by recognizing the right of unions to exist. In addition to establishing the nation's first labor unions, journeymen also formed political organizations, known as Working Men's parties, as well as mutual benefit societies, libraries, educational institutions, and producers' and consumers' cooperatives. Working men and women published at least 68 labor papers, and they agitated for free public education, reduction of the workday, and abolition of

During the 1830s, rapid inflation and mounting competition for jobs encouraged the growth of unions. By 1836, an estimated 300,000 American workers were union members.

capital punishment, state militias, and imprisonment for debt. Following the Panic of 1837, land reform was one of labor's chief demands. One hundred sixty acres of free public land for those who would actually settle the land was the demand, and "Vote Yourself a Farm" became the popular slogan.

The Movement for a 10-Hour Day

Labor's greatest success was a campaign to establish a 10-hour workday in most major northeastern cities. In 1835 carpenters, masons, and stonecutters in Boston staged a seven-month strike in favor of a 10-hour day. The strikers demanded that employers reduce excessively long hours worked in the summer and spread them throughout the year. Quickly, the movement for a 10-hour workday spread to Philadelphia, where carpenters, bricklayers, plasterers, masons, leather dressers, and blacksmiths went on strike. Textile workers in Paterson, New Jersey, were the first factory operatives to strike for a reduction in work hours. Soon, women textile operatives in Lowell, Massachusetts, added their voices to the call for a 10-hour day, contending that such a law would "lengthen the lives of those employed, by giving them a greater opportunity to breathe the pure air of heaven" as well as provide "more time for mental and moral cultivation."

In 1840 the federal government introduced a 10-hour workday on public works projects. In 1847 New Hampshire became the first state to adopt a 10-hour day law. It was followed by Pennsylvania in 1848. Both states' laws, however, included a clause that allowed workers to voluntarily agree to work more than a 10-hour day. Despite the limitations of these state laws, agitation for a 10-hour day did result in a reduction in the average number of hours worked, to approximately 11½ by 1850.

The Laboring Poor

In January 1850, police arrested John McFeaing in Newburyport, Massachusetts, for stealing wood from the wharves. McFeaing pleaded necessity and a public investigation was conducted. Investigators found McFeaing's wife and four children living "in the extremity of misery. The children were all scantily supplied with clothing and not one had a shoe to his feet. There was not a stick of firewood or scarcely a morsel of food in the house, and everything betokened the most abject want and misery." McFeaing's predicament was not uncommon at that time.

The quickening pace of trade and finance during the early nineteenth century not only increased the demand for middle-class clerks and shopkeepers, it also dramatically increased demand for unskilled workers, who earned extremely low incomes and led difficult lives.

In 1851 Horace Greeley, editor of the New York *Tribune*, estimated the minimum weekly budget needed to support a family of five. Essential expenditures for rent, food, fuel, and clothing amounted to $10.37 a week. In that year, a shoemaker or a printer earned just $4 to $6 a week, a male textile operative $6.50 a week, and an unskilled laborer just $1 a week. The only manual laborers able to earn Greeley's minimum were blacksmiths and machinists.

Frequent unemployment compounded the problems of the unskilled. In Massachusetts upward of 40 percent of all workers were out of a job for part of a year, usually for four months or more. Fluctuations in demand, inclement weather, interruptions in transportation, technological displacement, fire, injury, and illness all could leave workers jobless.

Typically, a male laborer earned just two-thirds of his family's income. Wives and children earned the other third. Many married women performed work in the home, such as embroidery and making artificial flowers, tailoring garments, or doing laundry. The wages of children were critical for a family's standard of living. Children under the age of 15 contributed 20 percent of the income of many working-class families. These children worked not because their parents were heartless, but because children's earnings were absolutely essential to the family's survival.

To provide protection against temporary unemployment, many working-class families scrimped and saved to buy a house or maintain a garden. In Newburyport, Massachusetts, many workers bought farm property on the edge of town. On New York City's East Side, many families kept goats and pigs. Ownership of a house was a particularly valuable source of security, since a family could always obtain extra income by taking in boarders and lodgers.

Immigration Begins

During the summer of 1845, a "blight of unusual character" devastated Ireland's potato crop, the basic staple in the Irish diet. A few days after potatoes were dug from the ground, they began to turn into a slimy, decaying, blackish "mass of rottenness." Expert panels, convened to investigate the blight's cause, suggested that it was a result of "static electricity" or the smoke that billowed from railroad locomotives or "mortiferous vapours" rising from underground volcanoes. In fact, the cause was a fungus that had traveled from America to Ireland.

"Famine fever"—dysentery, typhus, and infestations of lice—soon spread through the Irish countryside. Observers reported seeing children crying with

THE PEOPLE SPEAK

The Irish Potato Famine

Between 1845 and 1850, at least 750,000 Irish people died of starvation or disease as a result of the blight that destroyed the island's potato crop. Another two million people migrated from their homeland. Newspaper accounts of the devastation included these excerpts from *The Cork Examiner*.

> Melancholy indeed are the latest accounts from all parts of this extensive county. . . .
>
> In the parish of Kilmore 14 died on Sunday; 3 of these were buried in coffins, 11 were buried without other covering than the rags they wore when alive.
>
> Stretched on a bed of straw lies a dying husband and father; and grouped around that couch are a wretched wife and children, who devour wild weeds themselves, that they might leave the only remaining morsel of food to the dying man!
>
> "Is this tide of horror to roll on unchecked? Will the Imperial rulers of this slavish province wait until one-half of the 'Irish savages' be swept away? For to this it will soon come."

Source: The Cork Examiner. "Scenes of Misery," January 11, 1847.

Very few first-hand accounts of migration from Ireland survive. Here, a passenger aboard one of the famine ships provides a detailed account of an eight-week voyage from Liverpool to New York in the winter of 1847–1848.

> The day advertised for sailing was the 12th of [November 1847], but in consequence of not having got in the cargo, which consisted of pig iron and earthen-ware, we were detained ten days . . . and one day to stop a leak. . . . The immigrants . . . having left Ireland a week, some a fortnight, before the day fixed for sailing, this detention of eleven days was severely felt by those poor creatures, many of them having consumed half of their provisions, without the means of obtaining more. . . . On Friday, November 26, 1847, we set sail. . . .
>
> [A] storm commenced[;] it rained so heavily the whole day we could not make a fire on deck to cook our victuals with. . . .

> About midnight, a number of boxes and barrels broke loose . . . breaking the water cans and destroying everything capable of being destroyed by them. . . . In a few minutes the boxes and barrels broke to atoms, scattering the contents in all directions—tea, coffee, sugar, potatoes, pork, shorts, trowsers, vests, coasts, handkerchiefs &c., &c. were mingled in one confused mass. The cries of the women and children was heart-rending; some praying, others weeping bitterly, as they saw their provisions and clothes (the only property they possessed) destroyed. The passengers being sea sick, were vomiting in all parts of the vessel. . . .
>
> We had been at sea four weeks. . . . I felt sure . . . that however good the motives were which induced the captain to take a southerly passage, that the dreadful scourge, the ship fever, (which was already on board our ship) would be increased by it; an opinion . . . verified by the number of cases and deaths increasing. . . .
>
> Most of those who died of ship-fever were delirious, some a day, others only a few hours previous to death. . . .
>
> When we had been at sea a month, the steward discovered the four hogsheads [for water], by oversight or neglect, had not been [filled]. On the following morning . . . our water was reduced from two quarts to one quart per day for an adult and one pint for a child. . . . My provisions were consumed, and I had nothing but ship allowance to subsist upon, which was scarcely sufficient to keep us from perishing, being only a pound of seabiscuit (full of maggots) and a pint of water. . . . I was seized with the ship-fever; at first I was so dizzy that I could not walk without danger of falling; I was suffering from a violent pain in my head, my brains felt as if they were on fire, my tongue clove to the roof of my mouth and my lips were parched with excessive thirst. . . .
>
> This disastrous voyage . . . [came] to an end, after an absence of exactly eight weeks from the shores of my native land, (the day we arrived at Staten Island being Friday, the 21st of January, 1848). My whole lifetime did not seem so long as the last two months appeared to me. . . .

Source: William Smith, An Emigrant's Narrative, or a Voice from the Steerage (New York, 1850).

pain and looking "like skeletons, their features sharpened with hunger and their limbs wasted, so that there was little left but bones, their hands and arms." Masses of bodies were buried without coffins, a few inches below the soil.

Over the next 10 years, 750,000 Irish died and another 2 million left their homeland for Great Britain, Canada, and the United States. Freighters that carried American and Canadian timber to Europe offered fares as low as $17 to $20 between Liverpool

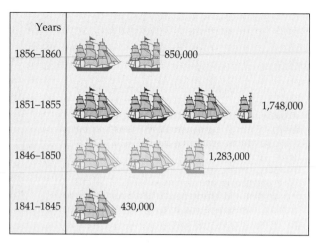

FIGURE 12.1
Total Immigration, 1841–1860

and Boston—fares subsidized by English landlords eager to be rid of the starving peasants. As many as 10 percent of the emigrants perished while still at sea. In 1847, 40,000 (or 20 percent) of those who set out from Ireland died along the way. "If crosses and tombs could be erected on water," wrote the U.S. commissioner for emigration, "the whole route of the emigrant vessels from Europe to America would long since have assumed the appearance of a crowded cemetery."

At the beginning of the nineteenth century, only about 5000 immigrants arrived in the United States each year. During the 1830s, however, **immigration** climbed sharply as 600,000 immigrants poured into the country. This figure jumped to 1.7 million in the 1840s, when harvests all across Europe failed, and reached 2.6 million in the 1850s. Most of these immigrants came from Germany, Ireland, and Scandinavia, pushed from their homelands by famine, eviction from farmlands by landlords, political unrest, and the destruction of traditional handicrafts by factory enterprises. Attracted to the United States by the prospects of economic opportunity and political and religious freedom, many dispossessed Europeans braved the voyage across the Atlantic.

Each immigrant group migrated for its own distinct reasons and adapted to American society in its own unique ways. Poverty forced most Irish immigrants to settle in their port of origin. By the 1850s, the Irish comprised half the population of New York and Boston. Young, unmarried, Catholic, and largely of peasant background, the immigrants faced the difficult task of adapting to an urban and a predominantly Protestant environment. Confronting intense discrimination in employment, most Irish men

found work as manual laborers, while Irish women took jobs mainly in domestic service. Discrimination had an important consequence: It encouraged Irish immigrants to become actively involved in politics. With a strong sense of ethnic identity, high rates of literacy, and impressive organizational talents, Irish politicians played an important role in the development of modern American urban politics.

Unlike Irish immigrants, who settled primarily in northeastern cities and engaged in politics, German immigrants tended to move to farms or frontier towns in the Midwest and were less active politically. While some Germans fled to the United States to escape political persecution following the revolutions of 1830 and 1848, most migrated for quite a different reason: to sustain traditional ways of life. The industrial revolution severely disrupted traditional patterns of life for German farmers, shopkeepers, and practitioners of traditional crafts (like baking, brewing, and carpentering). In the Midwest's farmland and frontier cities, including Cincinnati and St. Louis, they sought to reestablish old German lifeways, setting up German fraternal lodges, coffee circles, and educational and musical societies. German immigrants carried important aspects of German culture with them, which quickly became integral parts of American culture, including the Christmas tree and the practice of Christmas gift giving, the kindergarten, and the gymnasium. Given Germany's strong educational and craft traditions, it is not surprising that German immigrants would be particularly prominent in the fields of engineering, optics, drug manufacture, and metal and tool making, as well as in the labor movement.

The Divided North

During the decades preceding the Civil War, an article of faith among Northerners was that their society offered unprecedented economic equality and opportunity and was free of rigid class divisions and glaring extremes of wealth and poverty. The North was a land where even a "humble mechanic" had "every means of winning independence which are extended only to rich monopolists in England." How accurate is this picture of the pre–Civil War North as a land of opportunity, where material success was available to all?

In fact, the percentage of wealth held by those at the top of the economic hierarchy appears to have increased substantially before the Civil War. While the proportion of wealth controlled by the richest 10 percent rose from 50 percent in the 1770s to 70 percent in 1860, the real wages of unskilled northern workers stagnated or, at best, rose modestly. By 1860 half of

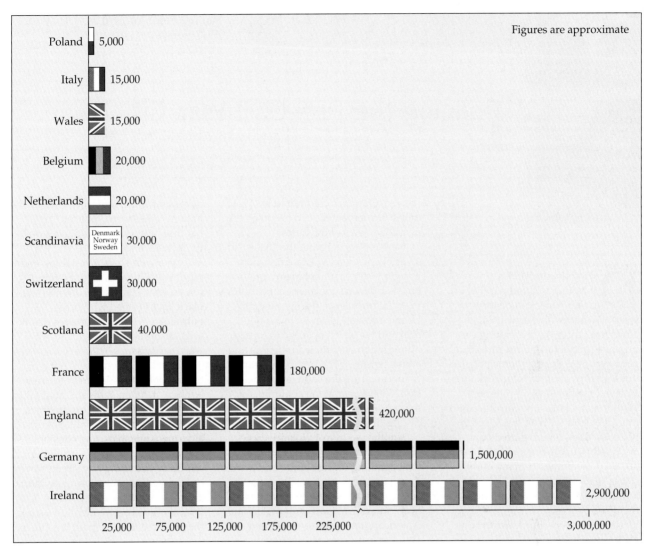

FIGURE 12.2
Immigration by Country of Origin, 1840–1860

all free whites held fewer than 1 percent of the North's real and personal property, while the richest 1 percent owned 27 percent of the region's wealth—a level of inequality comparable to that found in early nineteenth-century Europe and greater than that found in the United States today. In towns as different as Stonington, Connecticut, and Chicago, Illinois, between two-thirds and three-quarters of all households owned no property.

The first stages of industrialization and urbanization in the North, far from diminishing social inequality, actually widened class distinctions and intensified social stratification. At the top of the social and economic hierarchy was an elite class of families, linked together by intermarriage, membership in ex-

clusive social clubs, and residence in exclusive neighborhoods, as rich as the wealthiest families of Europe. At the bottom were the working poor—immigrants, casual laborers, African Americans, widows, and orphans—who might be thrown out of work or their home at any time. Poor, propertyless unskilled laborers composed a vast floating population, which trekked from city to city in search of work. They congregated in urban slums like Boston's Ann Street and New York's Five Points, where starving children begged for pennies and haggard prostitutes plied their trade.

Between these two extremes were family farmers and a rapidly expanding urban middle class of shopkeepers, merchants, bankers, agents, and brokers.

Policing the Pre–Civil War City

During the mid-1830s, a wave of rioting without parallel in earlier American history swept the nation. In April 1834, in New York, three days of rioting pitting pro-Democrat against pro-Whig gangs erupted during municipal elections. In July, another New York mob stormed the house of a prominent abolitionist, carried the furniture into the street, and set it on fire. Over the next two days, a mob gutted New York's Episcopal African Church and attacked the homes of many of the city's African Americans. The state militia had to be called out to quell the disturbances.

Rioting was not confined to New York City. On August 11, 1834, a mob composed of lower-class men and boys sacked and burned a convent in Charlestown, Massachusetts, near the site of Bunker Hill, following a series of impassioned anti-Catholic sermons by the Reverend Lyman Beecher, the father of novelist Harriet Beecher Stowe. Two months later, a proslavery riot swept through Philadelphia, destroying 45 homes in the city's African American community.

Altogether there were at least 115 incidents of mob violence during the 1830s, compared to just 7 incidents in the 1810s and 21 incidents in the 1820s. *Niles' Register,* a respected newspaper of the time, reported that a "spirit of riot or a disposition to 'take the law into their own hands' prevails in every quarter." Abraham Lincoln, then a young Springfield, Illinois, attorney, echoed these sentiments. "Outrages committed by mobs," he lamented, had become "the everyday news of the times."

Mob violence during the 1830s had a variety of sources. A rate of urban growth faster than that in any previous decade was one major contributor to social turbulence during the 1830s. Urban populations grew by 60 percent and the sharp upsurge in foreign immigration heightened religious and ethnic tensions. The number of immigrants entering the country jumped from 5000 a year at the beginning of the century to over 50,000 annually during the 1830s.

Another source of violence came with abolitionism, which emerged at the beginning of the decade and produced a violent reaction. The belief that abolitionists favored miscegenation—interracial marriages of African Americans and whites—enflamed anti–African American sentiment. The mobs that attacked African American homes and churches, burned white abolitionists' homes and businesses, and disrupted antislavery meetings were often led by "gentlemen of property and standing." These old-stock merchants and bankers feared that abolitionist appeals to the middle class and especially to women and children threatened their patriarchal position in local communities and even in their own families.

The birth of a new two-party political system also contributed to a growing climate of violence. Mob violence frequently broke out on election days as rival Democratic and Whig gangs tried to steal ballot boxes and keep the opposition's voters from reaching local polling places.

Traditional methods of preserving public order proved totally inade-quate by the 1830s. Earlier in time, the nation's cities were "policed" by a handful of unpaid, untrained, ununiformed, and unarmed sheriffs, aldermen, marshals, constables, and night watchmen. In New England towns, tithingmen armed with long black sticks tipped with brass patrolled streets searching for drunkards, disorderly children, and wayward servants.

These law officers were not a particularly effective deterrent to crime. Night watchmen generally held other jobs during the day and sometimes slept at their posts at night. Sheriffs, aldermen, marshals, and constables made a living not by investigating crimes or patrolling city streets but by collecting debts, foreclosing on mortgages, and serving court orders. Victims of crime had to offer a reward if they wanted these unpaid law officers to investigate a case.

This early system of maintaining public order worked in previous decades when the rates of serious crime were extremely low and citizens had informal mechanisms that helped maintain order. Most cities were small and compact and lacked any distinct working-class ghettoes. Shopkeepers usually lived at or near their place of business, and apprentices, journeymen, and laborers tended to live in or near the house of their master. Under these circumstances, the poor and the working class were subject to close supervision by their social superiors. By the mid-1830s, however, this older pattern of social organization had clearly broken down. Class-segregated neighborhoods grew increasingly common. Youth gangs, organized along ethnic and neighborhood lines, proliferated.

Older mechanisms of social control weakened.

After 1830, drunken brawls, robberies, beatings, and murders all increased in number. Fear of crime led city leaders to look for new ways of preserving public order. Many municipal leaders regarded the new professional police force established in London in 1829 by the British Parliament as a model. London's police, nicknamed "bobbies" after Prime Minister Robert Peel, were trained, full-time professionals. They wore distinctive uniforms to make them visible to the public, patrolled regular beats, and lived in the neighborhoods they patrolled.

Initially, resistance to the establishment of professional police forces in American cities was intense. Taxpayers feared the cost of a police force. Local political machines feared the loss of the night watch as a source of political patronage. During the late 1830s and 1840s, rising crime rates overcame opposition to the establishment of a professional police force.

Boston appointed the nation's first police officers in 1838.

In New York City, the turning point came in 1841 following the unsolved murder of Mary Rogers, who worked in a tobacco shop. On July 25, 1841, she disappeared. Three days later, the body of the "beautiful cigar girl" was found in a river. The coroner said she had died not from drowning but from being abused and murdered by a gang of ruffians. The case aroused intense passion in New York City, prompting vocal demands for an end to waterfront gangs. The city's constables, however, said that they would only investigate the murder if they were promised a substantial reward. The public was outraged. In 1844, the New York state legislature authorized the establishment of a professional police force to investigate crimes and patrol streets in New York City.

The life of a mid-nineteenth-century police officer was exceptionally hard. In many cities, members of gangs, like New York's Bowery B'hoys, Baltimore's Rip Raps, and Philadelphia's Schuylkill Rangers, actually outnumbered police officers. Young toughs regularly harassed police officers. Many officers resisted wearing uniforms on the grounds that any distinctive dress made them readily identifiable targets for street gangs. In New York City, four officers were killed in the line of duty in a single year.

After 1850, in large part as a result of more efficient policing, the number of street disorders in American cities began to drop. Despite the introduction of the Colt revolver and other easily concealed and relatively inexpensive handguns during the middle years of the century, homicide rates, too, began to decline. By the eve of the Civil War, the nation's cities had become far less violent and far more orderly places than they had been two decades before.

This was a highly mixed group that ranged from prosperous entrepreneurs and professionals to hard-pressed journeymen, who found their skills increasingly obsolete.

Does this mean that the pre–Civil War North was not the fluid, "egalitarian" society that many Northerners claimed? The answer is a qualified "no." In the first place, the North's richest individuals, unlike Europe's aristocracy, were a working class, engaged in commerce, insurance, finance, shipbuilding, manufacturing, landholding, real estate, and the professions. More important, wealthy Northerners publicly rejected the older Hamiltonian notion that the rich and wellborn were superior to the masses of people. During the early decades of the nineteenth century, wealthy Northerners shed the wigs, knee breeches, ruffled shirts, and white-topped boots that had symbolized high social status in colonial America and began to dress like other men, signaling their acceptance of an ideal of social equality. One wealthy Northerner succinctly summarized the new ideal: "These phrases, the higher orders, and lower orders, are of European origin, and have no place in our Yankee dialect."

Above all, it was the North's relatively high rates of economic and social mobility that gave substance to a widespread belief in equality of opportunity. Although few rich men were truly "self-made" men who had climbed from "rags to riches," there were many dramatic examples of upward mobility and countless instances of more modest climbs up the ladder of success. Industrialization rapidly increased the number of nonmanual jobs in commerce, industry, and the professions. There were new opportunities for lawyers, bookkeepers, business managers, brokers, and clerks. Giving additional reinforcement to the belief in opportunity was a remarkable rate of physical mobility. Each decade, fully half the residents of northern communities moved to a new town.

Even at the bottom of the economic hierarchy, prospects for advancement increased markedly after 1850. During the 1830s and 1840s, less than 1 unskilled worker in 10 managed in the course of a decade to advance to a white-collar job. After 1850, the percentage doubled. The sons of unskilled laborers were even more likely to advance to skilled or white-collar employment. Even the poorest unskilled laborers often were able to acquire a house and a savings account as they grew older, and their children did better yet. It was the reality of physical and economic mobility that convinced the overwhelming majority of Northerners that they lived in a uniquely open society, in which differences in wealth or status were the result of hard work and ambition.

SOUTHERN DISTINCTIVENESS

In 1785 Thomas Jefferson jotted down a brief list of differences between North and South.

In the North they are:

cool
sober
laborious
independent
jealous of their own liberties and just to those of
    others
interested
chicaning
superstitious and hypocritical in their religion.

In the South they are:

fiery
voluptuary
indolent
unsteady
zealous for their own liberties, but trampling on
    those of others
generous
candid
without attachment or pretensions to any religion but that of the heart.

Pre–Civil War Americans regarded Southerners as a distinct people, who possessed their own values and ways of life. It was widely though mistakenly believed that the North and South had originally been settled by two distinct groups of immigrants, each with its own ethos. Northerners were said to be the descendants of seventeenth-century English Puritans, while Southerners were the descendants of England's country gentry. In the eyes of many pre–Civil War Americans this contributed to the evolution of two distinct kinds of Americans: the aggressive, individualistic, money-grubbing Yankee and the southern cavalier. According to the popular stereotype, the cavalier, unlike the Yankee, was violently sensitive to insult, indifferent to money, and preoccupied with honor.

The Plantation Legend

During the three decades before the Civil War, popular writers created a stereotype, now known as the **plantation legend,** which described the South as a land of aristocratic planters, beautiful southern belles, poor white trash, faithful household slaves, and superstitious field hands.

This image of the South as "a land of cotton" where "old times" are "not forgotten" received its most popular expression in 1859 in a song called

"Dixie," written by a Northerner named Dan D. Emmett to enliven shows given by a troupe of black-faced minstrels on the New York stage. In the eyes of many Northerners, uneasy with their increasingly urban, individualistic, commercial society, the culture of the South seemed to have many things absent from the North—a leisurely pace of life, a clear social hierarchy, and an indifference to money.

The Old South: Images and Realities

Despite the strength of the plantation stereotype, the South was, in reality, a diverse and complex region. Though Americans today often associate the old South with cotton plantations, large parts of the South were unsuitable for plantation life. In the mountainous regions of eastern Tennessee and western Virginia, few plantations or slaves were to be found. Nor did southern farms and plantations devote their efforts exclusively to growing cotton or other cash crops, such as rice and tobacco. Unlike the slave societies of the Caribbean, which produced crops exclusively for export, the South devoted much of its energy to raising food and livestock.

The pre–Civil War South encompassed a wide variety of regions that differed geographically, economically, and politically. Such regions included the Piedmont, Tidewater, coastal plain, piney woods, Delta, Appalachian mountains, upcountry, and a fertile "black belt"—regions that clashed repeatedly over such political questions as debt relief, taxes, apportionment of representation, and internal improvements.

The white South's social structure was much more complex than the popular stereotype of proud aristocrats disdainful of honest work and ignorant, vicious, exploited poor whites. The old South's intricate social structure included many small slaveowners and relatively few large ones. Large slaveholders were extremely rare. In 1860 only 11,000 Southerners—three-quarters of one percent of the white population—owned more than 50 slaves; a mere 2358 owned as many as 100 slaves. However, although large slaveholders were few in number, they owned most of the South's slaves. Over half of all slaves lived on plantations with 20 or more slaves and a quarter lived on plantations with more than 50 slaves.

Slave ownership was relatively widespread. In the first half of the nineteenth century, one-third of all southern white families owned slaves, and a majority of white southern families either owned slaves, had owned them, or expected to own them. These slaveowners were a diverse lot. A few were African American, mulatto, or Native American; one-tenth were women; and more than 1 in 10 worked as artisans, businesspeople, or merchants rather than as farmers or planters. Few led lives of leisure or refinement. The average slaveowner lived in a log cabin rather than a mansion and was a farmer rather than a planter. The average holding varied between four

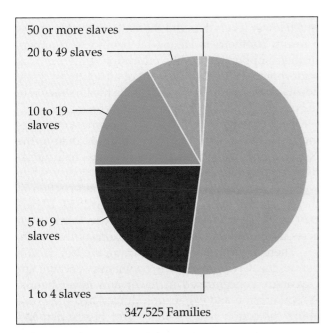

FIGURE 12.3
Slaveowning Population, 1850

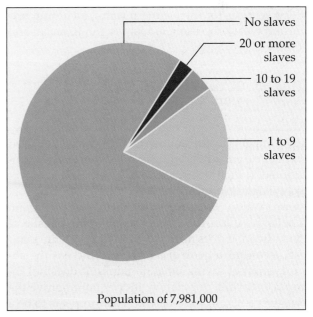

FIGURE 12.4
Southern White Population, 1860

and six slaves, and most slaveholders possessed no more than five.

White women in the South, despite the image of the hoop-skirted southern belle, suffered under heavier burdens than their northern counterparts. They married earlier, bore more children, and were more likely to die young. They lived in greater isolation, had less access to the company of other women, and lacked the satisfactions of voluntary associations and reform movements. Their education was briefer and much less likely to result in opportunities for independent careers.

The plantation legend was misleading in still other respects. Slavery was neither dying nor unprofitable. In 1860 the South was richer than any country in Europe except England, and it had achieved a level of wealth unmatched by Italy or Spain until the eve of World War II.

The southern economy generated enormous wealth and was critical to the economic growth of the entire United States. Well over half of the richest 1 percent of Americans in 1860 lived in the South. Even more important, southern agriculture helped finance early nineteenth-century American economic growth. Before the Civil War, the South grew 60 percent of the world's cotton, provided over half of all U.S. export earnings, and furnished 70 percent of the cotton consumed by the British textile industry. Cotton exports paid for a substantial share of the capital and technology that laid the basis for America's industrial revolution. In addition, precisely because the South specialized in agricultural production, the North developed a variety of businesses that provided services for the southern states, including textile and meat processing industries and financial and commercial facilities.

Impact of Slavery on the Southern Economy

Although slavery was highly profitable, it had a negative impact on the southern economy. It impeded the development of industry and cities and contributed to high debts, soil exhaustion, and a lack of technological innovation. The philosopher and poet Ralph Waldo Emerson said that "slavery is no scholar, no improver; it does not love the whistle of the railroad; it does not love the newspaper, the mailbag, a college, a book or a preacher who has the absurd whim of saying what he thinks; it does not increase the white population; it does not improve the soil; everything goes to decay." There appears to be a large element of truth in Emerson's observation.

The South, like other slave societies, did not develop urban centers for commerce, finance, and industry on a scale equal to those found in the North. Vir-

ginia's largest city, Richmond, had a population of just 15,274 in 1850. That same year, Wilmington, North Carolina's largest city, had only 7264 inhabitants, while Natchez and Vicksburg, the two largest cities in Mississippi, had fewer than 3000 white inhabitants.

Southern cities were small because they failed to develop diversified economies. Unlike the cities of the North, southern cities rarely became processing or finishing centers and southern ports rarely engaged in international trade. Their primary functions were to market and transport cotton or other agricultural crops, supply local planters and farmers with such necessities as agricultural implements, and produce the small number of manufactured goods, such as cotton gins, needed by farmers.

An overemphasis on slave-based agriculture led Southerners to neglect industry and transportation improvements. As a result, manufacturing and transportation lagged far behind that of the North. In 1860 the North had approximately 1.3 million industrial workers, whereas the South had 110,000, and northern factories manufactured nine-tenths of the industrial goods produced in the United States.

The South's transportation network was primitive by northern standards. Traveling the 1460 overland miles from Baltimore to New Orleans in 1850 meant riding five different railroads, two stagecoaches, and two steamboats. Most southern railroads served primarily to transport cotton to southern ports, where the crop could be shipped on northern vessels to northern or British factories for processing.

Because of high rates of personal debt, southern states kept taxation and government spending at much lower levels than did the states in the North. As a result, Southerners lagged far behind Northerners in their support for public education. Illiteracy was widespread. In 1850, 20 percent of all southern white adults could not read or write, while the illiteracy rate in New England was less than half of 1 percent.

Because large slaveholders owned most of the region's slaves, wealth was more stratified than in the North. In the Deep South, the middle class held a relatively small proportion of the region's property, while wealthy planters owned a very significant portion of the productive lands and slave labor. In 1850, 17 percent of the farming population held two-thirds of all acres in the rich cotton-growing regions of the South.

There are indications that during the last decade before the Civil War slave ownership became increasingly concentrated in fewer and fewer hands. As soil erosion and exhaustion diminished the availability of cotton land, scarcity and heavy demand forced the price of land and slaves to rise beyond the reach of most, and in newer cotton-growing regions, yeomen farmers were pushed off the land as planters expanded their holdings. In Louisiana, for example,

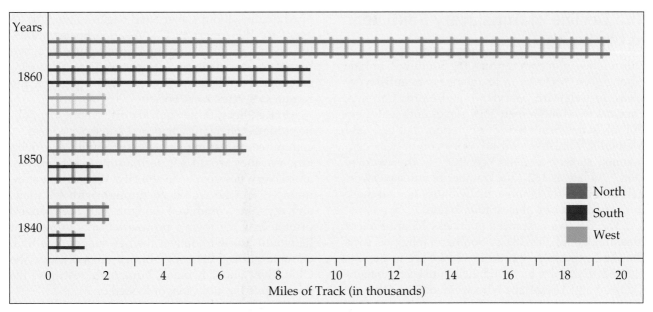

FIGURE 12.5
Railroad Growth, 1840–1860

An overemphasis on slave-based agriculture led Southerners to neglect transportation improvements.

nearly half of all rural white families owned no land. During the 1850s, the percentage of the total white population owning slaves declined significantly. By 1860, the proportion of whites holding slaves had fallen from about one-third to one-fourth. As slave and land ownership grew more concentrated, a growing number of whites were forced by economic pressure to leave the land and move to urban centers.

Growth of a Distinctive Southern Identity

Beginning in the 1830s, the South developed a new and aggressive sense of "nationalism" that was rooted in its sense of distinctiveness and its perception that it was ringed by enemies. The South began to conceive of itself more and more as the true custodian of America's revolutionary heritage. Southern travelers who ventured into the North regarded it as a "strange and distant land" and expressed disgust about its vice-ridden cities and its grasping materialism.

At the same time, southern intellectuals began to defend slavery as a positive factor. After 1830, white Southerners stopped referring to slavery as a necessary evil. Instead, they argued that it was a beneficial institution that created a hierarchical society superior to the leveling democracy of the North. By the late 1840s, a new and more explicitly racist rationale for slavery had emerged.

With the emergence of militant abolitionism in the North, sharpened by slave uprisings in Jamaica and Southampton County, Virginia, the South began to see itself as surrounded by enemies. Southern leaders responded aggressively. On the Senate floor in 1837, **John C. Calhoun** pronounced slavery "a good—a positive good" and set the tone for future southern proslavery arguments. Before the 1830s, southern statements on slavery had been defensive; afterward, they were defiant.

In the 1840s, a growing number of southern ministers, journalists, and politicians began to denounce the North's form of capitalism as "wage slavery." The condition of free labor, they argued, was actually "worse than slavery," because slaveholders, unlike greedy northern employers, provide for their employees "when most needed, when sickness or old age has overtaken [them]." Northern workers, they declared, were simply "slaves without masters."

During the 1840s, more and more Southerners defended slavery on explicitly racial grounds. In doing so, they drew on new pseudoscientific theories of racial inferiority. Some of these theories came from Europe, which was seeking justification of imperial expansion over nonwhite peoples in Africa and Asia. Other racist ideas were drawn from northern scientists, who employed an elaborate theory of "polygenesis," which claimed that Africans and whites were separate species.

The Decline of Antislavery Sentiment in the South

During the eighteenth century, the South was unique among slave societies in its openness to antislavery ideas. In Delaware, Maryland, and North Carolina, Quakers freed more than 1500 slaves and sent them out of state. Scattered Presbyterian, Baptist, and Methodist ministers and advisory committees condemned slavery as a sin "contrary to the word of God." As late as 1827, the number of antislavery organizations in the South actually outnumbered those in the free states by at least four to one.

The South's historical openness to antislavery ideas ended in the 1830s. Southern religious sects that had expressed opposition to slavery in the late eighteenth century modified their antislavery beliefs. Quakers and Unitarians who were strongly antagonistic to slavery emigrated. By the second decade of the century, antislavery sentiment was confined to Kentucky, the Piedmont counties of North Carolina, and the mountains in eastern Tennessee.

State law and public opinion stifled debate and forced conformity to proslavery arguments. Southern state legislatures adopted a series of laws suppressing criticism of the institution. In 1830 Louisiana made it a crime to make any statement that might produce discontent or insubordination among slaves. Six years later, Virginia made it a felony for any member of an abolition society to come into the state and for any citizen to deny the legality of slavery.

The silent pressure of public opinion also limited public discussion of the slavery question. College presidents or professors suspected of sympathizing with abolitionists lost their jobs. Mobs attacked editors who dared to print articles critical of slavery. One Richmond, Virginia, editor fought eight duels in two years to defend his views on slavery. In Parkville, Missouri, and Lexington, Kentucky, crowds dismantled printing presses of antislavery newspapers. An "iron curtain" was erected against the invasion of antislavery propaganda.

Only once, in the wake of Nat Turner's famous slave insurrection in 1831, did a southern state openly debate the possibility of ending slavery. These debates in the Virginia legislature in January and February 1832 ended with the defeat of proposals to abolish slavery.

James G. Birney was one of many Southerners to discover that it was hopeless to work for slave emancipation in the South. Birney was born into a wealthy Kentucky slaveholding family, and, like many members of the South's slaveowning elite, was educated at Princeton. After graduation, he moved to Huntsville, Alabama, where he practiced law and operated a cotton plantation. In Huntsville, he developed qualms about slavery and began to work as an agent for the American Colonization Society. Soon, his doubts about slavery had grown into an active hatred for the institution. He returned to Kentucky, emancipated his slaves and in 1835 organized the Kentucky Anti-Slavery Society.

In Kentucky, Birney quickly discovered that public opinion vehemently opposed antislavery ideas. A committee of leading citizens in Danville informed him that they would not permit him to establish an antislavery newspaper in the city. When Birney announced that he would go through with his plans anyway, the committee bought out the paper's printer, and the town's postmaster announced that he would refuse to deliver the newspaper. In a final effort to publish his paper, Birney moved across the Ohio River into Cincinnati, but a mob destroyed his press while the city's mayor looked on.

The defense of slavery after 1830 also led to hostility toward all social reforms. One southern newspaper editor declared that the South "has uniformly rejected the isms which infest Europe and the Eastern and Western states of this country." Many Southerners spoke proudly of rejecting the reforms that flourished in the North. The South, said one South Carolina scientist, was "the breakwater which is to stay that furious tide of social and political heresies now setting toward us from the shores of the old world." Only the temperance movement made headway in the South.

"Reforming" Slavery from Within

Many white Southerners felt genuine moral doubts about slavery. For the most part, however, these doubts were directed into efforts to reform the institution by converting slaves to Christianity, revising slave codes to make them less harsh, and making slavery conform to the ideal depicted in the Old Testament.

During the early eighteenth century, ministers from such denominations as the Quakers, Moravians, and Anglicans launched the first concerted campaigns to convert slaves in the American colonies to Christianity. Missionaries established schools and taught several thousand slaves to read and recite Scripture. They stressed that Christian slaves would make more loyal and productive workers, less likely to stage insurrections. The Great Awakening of the 1730s and 1740s stimulated renewed efforts to promote Christianization, but not until the early nineteenth century did most slaveowners express concern for converting their slaves to Christianity.

There were also early nineteenth-century efforts to ameliorate the harshness of the early slave codes. The eighteenth-century codes permitted owners to punish slaves by castration and cutting off limbs. Slaveholders had no specific obligations for housing, feeding, or clothing slaves, and many observers reported seeing slaves half-clothed or naked. Few eighteenth-century masters showed any concern for slave marriages, families, or religion.

During the early nineteenth century, the southern states enacted new codes regulating the punishment of slaves and setting minimum standards for maintenance. State legislatures defined killing a slave with malice as murder and made dismemberment and some other cruel punishments illegal. Three states forbade the sale of young slave children from their parents, and four states permitted slaves to be taught to read and write.

Many of the new laws went unenforced, but they suggest that a new code of values and behavior was emerging. **Paternalism** was the defining characteristic of this new code. According to this new ideal, slaveholding was "a duty and a burden" carrying strict moral obligations. A humane master of a plantation was supposed to show concern for the spiritual and physical well-being of his slaves.

These minimal efforts to reform slavery were, however, accompanied by tighter restrictions on other aspects of slave life. Private manumissions

---

Iron collars, iron masks, leg shackles, and spurs were just a few of the devices that slaveowners might use to punish their slaves for such offenses as attempting to run away, damaging property, disobeying an order, or failing to work as long and as hard as the owner desired.

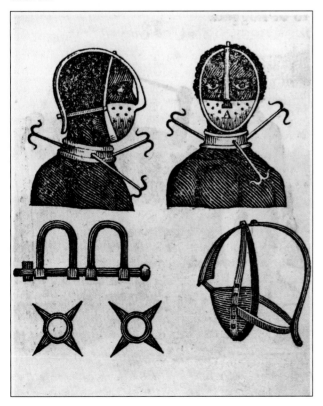

were made illegal. Southern states instituted the death penalty for any slaves involved in plotting a rebellion. Most states prohibited slaves from owning firearms, horses, or drums, which might be used during an insurrection; these states also placed tight restrictions on slave funerals and barred African American preachers from conducting religious services unless a white person was present. To restrict contact between free African Americans and slaves, a number of southern states required manumitted slaves to leave the state. Other restrictive laws quarantined vessels containing black sailors and imprisoned those who stepped on shore.

Southern Nationalism

Seeking to free their region from cultural, economic, and religious dependence on the North, southern "nationalists" sought to promote southern economic self-sufficiency, to create southern-oriented educational and religious institutions, and to develop a distinctive southern literature. Beginning in 1837, southern leaders held the first of a series of commercial conventions in an attempt to diversify the southern economy and to rescue the South from northern "pecuniary and commercial supremacy."

Efforts to develop the southern economy were surprisingly successful. Southern railroad mileage quadrupled between 1850 and 1860—although southern track mileage still trailed that of the free states by 14,000. By 1860 Richmond manufactured more tobacco than any other America city and exported more goods to South America than any other American port, including New York.

Other southern nationalists strove to create southern-oriented educational institutions to protect the young from, in Jefferson's words, "imbibing opinions and principles in discord" with those of the South. Schoolbooks, declared one southern magazine, "have slurs and innuendoes at slavery; the geographies are more particular in stating the resources of the Northern States; the histories almost ignore the South; the arithmetics contain in their examples reflections upon the Southern states."

The struggle for independent southern colleges achieved considerable success. By 1860 Virginia had 23 colleges and Georgia had 32, while New York had 17 colleges and Massachusetts just 8. In 1856 the University of Virginia had 558 students, compared to only 361 at Harvard.

Regional independence was also called for in religion. Due in large part to fear of antislavery agitation, southern Baptists, Methodists, and Presbyterians sought to sever their denominational affiliations with northern churches. In the early 2000s, only the Baptists remain divided.

Southerners also called for a distinctive and peculiarly southern literature. More than 30 periodicals were founded with the word "Southern" in their title, all intended to "breathe a Southern spirit, and sustain a strictly Southern character." Authors such as Nathaniel Beverly Tucker and William Gilmore Simms called on the South to write on southern themes and to overcome the taunts of "Englishmen and Northernmen" that they were intellectually inferior.

Southern Radicalism

By the early 1850s, a growing number of aggressive Southerners had moved beyond earlier calls for separate southern factories, colleges, and churches. Militant nationalists called for the reopening of the slave trade and aggressive annexations of new slave territory in Latin America and the Caribbean.

In a bid to acquire new lands for slavery a filibustering expedition was launched from New Orleans in 1851 to secure Cuba for the South. After this failed, extreme southern nationalists supported the efforts of William Walker, "the gray-eyed man of destiny," to extend slave labor into Latin America. In 1853, with considerable southern support, Walker raised a private army and unsuccessfully invaded Mexico. Two years later, he launched the first of three invasions of Nicaragua. On his final foray in 1860, he was taken prisoner by a British officer, handed over to Honduran authorities, and, at the age of 36, executed by a firing squad. In the late 1850s, another group of ardent southern expansionists, the Knights of the Golden Circle, developed plans to create an independent slave empire stretching from Maryland and Texas to northern South America and the West Indies. The only practical effect of these schemes was to arouse northern opinion against an aggressive southern slavocracy.

SLAVERY

The primary distinguishing characteristic of the South was its dependence on slave labor. During the decades before the Civil War, 4 million African Americans, one-third of the South's population, labored as slaves.

Two unrelated incidents suggest the complexity of the institution of slavery. The first took place in 1811. Lilburne and Isham Lewis, two nephews of Thomas Jefferson, ordered Lilburne's slaves to strap a slave named George to the kitchen floor of their southwest Kentucky farm. The 17-year-old slave had run away, returned, and then broken a treasured pitcher. Enraged and probably drunk, Lilburne seized an ax and nearly decapitated the young slave.

Then the brothers had their terrorized slaves dismember the victim and throw the pieces on the fire.

The second picture of slavery is from 1825. In that year, Joseph Davis, a Mississippi planter, met Robert Owen, the Scottish industrialist and utopian reformer. Inspired by Owen's vision of society operating according to the principles of voluntary cooperation, Davis attempted to reorganize his plantation at Davis Bend, 30 miles south of Vicksburg. Davis provided enslaved families with two-room cabins and supplied food freely. His most famous innovation was a form of self-government for the slave community. No slave of the more than 300 on his plantation could be punished without being tried and convicted by a jury of his peers. Later, Joseph's younger brother, Jefferson Davis, the future president of the Confederacy, put a similar system into practice on his plantation.

The overwhelming majority of enslaved African Americans were overworked, poorly clad, and inadequately housed and received the minimum of medical care. Debt, the death of a master, or merely the prospect of economic gain frequently tore slave husbands from wives and slave parents from children. And yet, as brutal and destructive as the institution of slavery was, enslaved African Americans were able to sustain ties to their African past and to maintain a cultural life. Through religion, folklore, music, and family life as well as more direct forms of resistance, the enslaved were able to sustain a vital culture supportive of human dignity.

The Legal Status of Slaves

Every southern state enacted a **slave code** that defined the slaveowners' power and the slaves' status as property. The codes stated that a slave, like a domestic animal, could be bought, sold, and leased. A master also had the right to compel a slave to work. The codes prohibited slaves from owning property, testifying against whites in court, or from making contracts. Slave marriages were not recognized by law. Under the slave codes, slavery was lifelong and hereditary, and any child born to a slave woman was the property of her master.

The slave codes gave slaves limited legal rights. To refute abolitionist contentions that slavery was unjust and inhumane, southern legislators adopted statutes regulating slaves' hours of labor and establishing certain minimal standards for slave upkeep. Most states also defined the wanton killing of a slave as murder, prohibited cruel and unusual punishments, and extended to slaves accused of capital offenses the right to trial by jury and legal counsel. Whipping, however, was not regarded by southern legislatures as a cruel punishment, and slaves were

In a particularly cruel twist, an African slave is forced to whip a fellow slave as the white slave owner watches. Punishments and tortures that slaves might be forced to endure included, in addition to whipping, chaining, confinement, and branding.

prohibited from bringing suit to seek legal redress for violations of their rights.

The main goal of the slave codes was to regulate slaves' lives. Slaves were forbidden to strike whites or use insulting language toward white people, hold a meeting without a white person present, visit whites or freed slaves, or leave plantations without permission. The laws prohibited whites and free blacks from teaching slaves to read and write, gambling with slaves, or supplying them with liquor, guns, or poisonous drugs. Most of the time, authorities loosely enforced these legal restrictions, but whenever fears of slave uprisings spread, enforcement tightened.

Slave Labor

Simon Gray was a slave. He was also the captain of a Mississippi River flatboat and the builder and operator of a number of sawmills. Emanuel Quivers, too, was a slave. He worked at the Tredegar Iron Works of Richmond, Virginia. Andrew Dirt was also a slave. He was an overseer.

Slaves performed all kinds of work. During the 1850s, half a million slaves lived in southern towns and cities, where they were hired out by their owners to work in ironworks, textile mills, tobacco factories, laundries, shipyards, and mechanics' homes. Other slaves labored as lumberjacks, as deckhands and fire tenders on riverboats, and in sawmills, gristmills, and quarries. Many other slaves were engaged in construction of roads and railroads. Most slaves, to be sure, were field hands, raising cotton, hemp, rice, tobacco, and sugar cane. Even on plantations, however, not all slaves were menial laborers. Some worked as skilled artisans such as blacksmiths, shoemakers, or carpenters; others held domestic posts, such as coachmen or house servants; and still others held managerial posts. At least two-thirds of the slaves worked under the supervision of black foremen of gangs, called drivers. Not infrequently they managed the whole plantation in the absence of their masters.

For most slaves, slavery meant backbreaking fieldwork on small farms or larger plantations. On the typical plantation, slaves worked "from day clean to first dark." Solomon Northrup, a free black who was kidnapped and enslaved for 12 years on a Louisiana cotton plantation, wrote a graphic description of the work regimen imposed on slaves: "The hands are required to be in the cotton field as soon as it is light in the morning, and, with the exception of ten or fifteen minutes, which is given them at noon to swallow their allowance of cold bacon, they are not permitted to be a moment idle until it is too dark to see, and when the moon is full, they often times labor till the middle of the night." Even then, the slaves' work was not over; it was still necessary to feed swine and mules, cut wood, and pack the cotton. At planting time or harvest time, work was even more exacting as planters required slaves to stay in the fields 15 or 16 hours a day.

To maximize productivity, slaveowners assigned each hand a specific set of tasks throughout the year. During the winter, field slaves ginned and pressed cotton, cut wood, repaired buildings and fences, and cleared fields. In the spring and summer, field hands plowed and hoed fields, killed weeds, and planted and cultivated crops. In the fall, slaves picked, ginned, and packed cotton, shucked corn, and gathered peas. Elderly slaves cared for children, made clothes, and prepared food.

Labor on large plantations was as rigidly organized as in a factory. Under the **gang system,** which was widely used on cotton plantations, field hands were divided into plow gangs and hoe gangs, each commanded by a driver. Under the **task system,** mainly used on rice plantations, each hand was given a specific daily work assignment.

Because slaves had little direct incentive to work hard, slaveowners combined a variety of harsh penalties with positive incentives. Some masters denied disobedient slaves passes to leave the plantation or forced them to work on Sundays or holidays. Other planters confined disobedient hands to private or public jails, and one Maryland planter required a slave to eat the worms he had failed to pick off tobacco plants. Chains and shackles were widely used

Hardworking slaves on a plantation pick and carry cotton while white overseers look on.

to control runaways. Whipping was a key part of the system of discipline and motivation. On one Louisiana plantation, at least one slave was lashed every four and one-half days. In his diary, Bennet H. Barrow, a Louisiana planter, recorded flogging "every hand in the field," breaking his sword on the head of one slave, shooting another slave in the thigh, and cutting another with a club "in 3 places very bad."

Physical pain alone, however, was not enough to elicit hard work. To stimulate productivity, some masters gave slaves small garden plots and permitted them to sell their produce. Others distributed gifts of food or money at the end of the year. Still other planters awarded prizes, holidays, and year-end bonuses to particularly productive slaves. One Alabama master permitted his slaves to share in the profits of the cotton, peanut, and pea crops.

Material Conditions of Slave Life

Deprivation and physical hardship were the hallmarks of life under slavery. It now seems clear that the material conditions of slave life may have been even worse than those of the poorest, most downtrodden free laborers in the North and Europe. Although the material conditions for slaves improved greatly in the nineteenth century, slaves remained much more likely than southern or northern whites to die prematurely, suffer malnutrition or dietary deficiencies, or lose a child in infancy.

Plantation records reveal that over half of all slave babies died during their first year of life—a rate twice that of white babies. Although slave children's death rate declined after the first year of life, it remained twice the white rate. The average slave's small size indicates a deficient diet. At birth, over half of all slave children weighed less than five pounds—or what is today considered underweight. Throughout their childhoods, slaves were smaller than white children of the same age. The average slave children

did not reach three feet in height until their fourth birthdays. At that age they were five inches shorter than a typical child today and about the same height as a child in present-day Bangladesh. At 17, slave men were shorter than 96 percent of present-day American men, and slave women were smaller than 80 percent of American women.

The slaves' diet was monotonous and unvaried, consisting largely of cornmeal, salt pork, and bacon. Only rarely did slaves drink milk or eat fresh meat or vegetables. This diet provided enough bulk calories to ensure that slaves had sufficient strength and energy to work as productive field hands, but it did not provide adequate nutrition. As a result, slaves were small for their ages, suffered from vitamin and protein deficiencies, and were victims of such ailments as beriberi, kwashiorkor, and pellagra. Poor nutrition and high rates of infant and child mortality contributed to a short average life expectancy—just 21 or 22 years compared to 40 to 43 years for whites.

The physical conditions in which slaves lived were appalling. Lacking privies, slaves had to urinate and defecate in the cover of nearby bushes. Lacking any sanitary disposal of garbage, they were surrounded by decaying food. Chickens, dogs, and pigs lived next to the slave quarters, and in consequence, animal feces contaminated the area. Such squalor contributed to high rates of dysentery, typhus, diarrhea, hepatitis, typhoid fever, and intestinal worms.

Slave quarters were cramped and crowded. The typical cabin—a single, windowless room, with a chimney constructed of clay and twigs and a floor made up of dirt or planks resting on the ground—ranged in size from 10 feet by 10 feet to 21 feet by 21 feet. These small cabins often contained five, six, or more occupants. On some plantations, slaves lived in single-family cabins; on others, two or more shared the same room. On the largest plantations, unmarried men and women were sometimes lodged together in barracklike structures. Josiah Henson, the

The dirt-floored, poorly ventilated, roughly built log one-room huts in which slaves lived were breeding grounds for disease. When slave owners realized they were losing the productive labor of their frequently ill slaves, they provided them with sturdier, better constructed cabins—still made of logs, but with wooden floors and glazed windows.

Kentucky slave who served as the model for Harriet Beecher Stowe's Uncle Tom, described his plantation's cabins this way:

> We lodged in log huts. . . . Wooden floors were an unknown luxury. In a single room were huddled, like cattle, ten or a dozen persons, men, women, and children. . . . There were neither bedsteads nor furniture. . . . Our beds were collections of straw and old rags. . . . The wind whistled and the rain and snow blew in through the cracks, and the damp earth soaked in the moisture till the floor was muddy as a pig sty.

Slave Family Life

In 1858, after being sold away from his family, a Georgia slave named Abream Scriven wrote the following words to his wife: "Give my love to my dear father and mother and tell them good bye for me. . . . My dear wife for you and all my children my pen cannot express the grief I feel to be parted from you. I remain your true husband until death."

Slavery severely strained family life. Slave sales frequently broke up slave families. During the Civil War, nearly 20 percent of former slaves reported that an earlier marriage had been terminated by "force." The sale of children from parents was even more common. Over the course of a lifetime, the average slave had a fifty-fifty chance of being sold at least once and was likely to witness the sale of several members of his or her immediate family.

Even in instances in which marriages were not broken by sale, slave husbands and wives often resided on separate farms and plantations and were owned by different individuals. On large plantations, one slave father in three had a different owner than his wife and could visit his family only at his master's discretion. On smaller holdings divided ownership occurred even more frequently. The typical farm and plantation were so small that it was difficult for many slaves to find a spouse at all. As a former slave put it, men "had a hell of a time getting a wife during slavery."

Other obstacles stood in the way of an independent family life. Living accommodations undermined privacy. Many slaves had to share their single-room cabins with relatives and other slaves who were not related to them. On larger plantations, food was cooked in a common kitchen and young children were cared for in a communal nursery while their parents worked in the fields. Even on model plantations, children between the ages of 7 and 10 were taken from their parents and sent to live in separate cabins.

Slavery imposed rigid limits on the authority of slave parents. Nearly every slave child went through an experience similar to one recalled by a young South Carolina slave named Jacob Stroyer. Stroyer was being trained as a jockey. His trainer beat him regularly, for no apparent reason. Stroyer appealed to his father for help, but his father simply said to work harder, "for I cannot do anything for you." When Stroyer's mother argued with the trainer, she was whipped for her efforts. From this episode, he learned a critical lesson: The ability of slave parents to protect their own children was sharply limited.

Of all the evils associated with slavery, abolitionists most bitterly denounced the sexual abuse suffered by slave women. Abolitionists claimed that slaveholders adopted deliberate policies to breed slaves for sale in the lower South—"like oxen for the shambles"—and kept "black harems" and sexually exploited slave women. Some masters did indeed take slave mistresses and concubines. One slave, Henry Bibb, said that a slave trader forced Bibb's wife to become a prostitute.

Planters also sought to increase slave birthrates through a variety of economic incentives. Many slaveholders gave bounties in the form of cash or household goods to mothers who bore healthy children and increased rations and lightened the workload of pregnant and nursing women.

And yet, despite the constant threat of sale and family breakup, African Americans managed to forge strong family ties and personal relationships; despite the fact that southern law provided no legal sanction for slave marriages, most slaves established *de facto* arrangements that were often stable over long periods of time; despite frequent family disruption, a majority of slaves grew up in families headed by a father and a mother. Nuclear family ties stretched outward to an involved network of extended kin. Through the strength and flexibility of their kin ties, African Americans fought the psychologically debilitating effects of slavery.

Contrary to what early nineteenth-century abolitionists charged, the sexual life of slaves was not casual or promiscuous nor did slave women become mothers at a particularly early age. Some slave women, like some white women, engaged in intercourse and bore children before settling into a permanent union. Most slave women settled into long-lasting monogamous relationships in their early 20s, which lasted, unless broken by sale, until she or her husband died.

Slave Cultural Expression

Notwithstanding the harshness and misery of life under slavery, slaves developed a distinctive life and culture. Through their families, their religion, and their cultural traditions, slaves were able to nurture an autonomous culture and community, beyond the direct control of their masters.

During the late eighteenth and early nineteenth centuries, slaves embraced Christianity, but they molded and transformed it to meet their own needs. Slave religious beliefs were a mixture of African traditions and Christianity. From their African heritage, slaves brought a hopeful and optimistic view of life, which contrasted sharply with evangelical Protestantism's emphasis on human sinfulness. In Protestant Christianity the slaves found an emphasis on love and the spiritual equality of all people that strengthened their ties to others. Many slaves fused the figures of Moses, who led his people to freedom, and Jesus, who suffered on behalf of all humankind, into a promise of deliverance in this world.

A major form of African American religious expression was the **spiritual.** Slave spirituals, such as "Go Down Moses" with its refrain "let my people go," indicated that slaves identified with the history of the Hebrew people, who had been oppressed and enslaved, but who achieved eventual deliverance.

In addition to the spiritual, storytelling was another important form of slave cultural expression. Slave folktales were much more than amusing stories; slaves used them to comment on the people around them and to convey lessons for everyday living. Among the most popular slave folktales were animal trickster stories, like the Brer Rabbit tales, derived from similar African stories, which told of powerless creatures who achieve their will through wit and guile rather than power and authority. These tales taught slave children how to function in a white-dominated world and held out the promise that the powerless would eventually triumph over the strong.

Slave Resistance

It was a basic tenet of the proslavery argument that slaves were docile, contented, faithful, and loyal. "Our slave population is not only a happy one," said a Virginia legislator, "but it is a contented, peaceful, and harmless one."

In fact, there is no evidence that the majority of slaves were contented. One scholar has identified more than 200 instances of attempted insurrection or rumors of slave resistance between the seventeenth century and the Civil War. And many slaves who did not directly rebel made their masters' lives miserable through a variety of indirect protests against slavery, including sabotage, stealing, malingering, murder, arson, and infanticide.

Four times during the first 31 years of the nineteenth century, slaves attempted major insurrections. In 1800, a 24-year-old Virginia slave named **Gabriel,** who was a blacksmith, led a march of perhaps 50 armed slaves on Richmond. The plot failed when a storm washed out the road to Richmond, giving the Virginia militia time to arrest the rebels. White authorities executed Gabriel and 25 other conspirators.

In 1811 in southern Louisiana, between 180 and 500 slaves, led by Charles Deslondes, a free mulatto from Haiti, marched on New Orleans, armed with axes and other weapons. Slaveowners retaliated by killing 82 blacks and placing the heads of 16 leaders on pikes.

In 1822 **Denmark Vesey,** a former West Indian slave who had been born in Africa, bought his freedom, and moved to Charleston, South Carolina. There he apparently devised a conspiracy to take over the city on a summer Sunday when many

Slave religious expression, like that depicted in this 1860 painting *Plantation Burial*, by John Antrobus, often combined the beliefs and practices of white Christian slave owners with rituals imported from Africa.

whites would be vacationing outside the city. Using his connections as a leader in the African Church of Charleston, Vesey drew support from skilled African American artisans, carpenters, harness makers, mechanics, and blacksmiths as well as from field slaves. Before the revolt could take place, however, a domestic slave of a prominent Charlestonian informed his master. The authorities proceeded to arrest 131 African Americans and hang 37.

The best-known slave revolt took place nine years later in Southampton County in southern Virginia. On August 22, 1831, **Nat Turner,** a trusted Baptist preacher, led a small group of fellow slaves into the home of his master Joseph Travis and killed the entire Travis household. By August 23, Turner's force had increased to between 60 and 80 slaves and had killed more than 50 whites. The local militia counterattacked and killed about 100 African Americans. Twenty more slaves, including Turner, were later executed. Turner's revolt sparked a panic that spread as far south as Alabama and Louisiana. One Virginian worried that "a Nat Turner might be in any family."

Slave uprisings were much less frequent and less extensive in the American South than in the West Indies or Brazil. Outright revolts did not occur more often because the chances of success were minimal and the consequences of defeat catastrophic. As one Missouri slave put it, "I've seen Marse Newton and Marse John Ramsey shoot too often to believe they can't kill" a slave.

The conditions that favored revolts elsewhere were absent in the South. In Jamaica, slaves outnumbered whites 10 to 1, whereas in the South whites were a majority in every state except Mississippi and South Carolina. In addition, slaveholding units in the South were much smaller than in other slave societies in the Western Hemisphere. Half of all U.S. slaves worked on units of 20 or less; in contrast, many sugar plantations in Jamaica had more than 500 slaves.

The unity of the white population in defense of slavery made the prospects for a successful rebellion bleak. In Virginia in 1830, 100,000 of the state's 700,000 whites were members of the state militia. Finally, southern slaves had few havens to which to escape. The major exception was the swamp country in Florida, where former slave **maroons** joined with Seminole Indians in resisting the U.S. army.

Recognizing that open resistance would be futile or even counterproductive, most plantation slaves expressed their opposition to slavery in a variety of subtle ways. Most day-to-day resistance took the form of breaking tools, feigning illness, doing shoddy work, stealing, and running away. These acts of resistance most commonly occurred when a master or overseer overstepped customary bounds. Through these acts, slaves tried to establish a right to proper treatment.

Free African Americans

In 1860, 488,000 African Americans were not slaves. After the American Revolution, slaveowners freed thousands of slaves, and countless others emancipated themselves by running away. In Louisiana, a large free Creole population had emerged under Spanish and French rule, and in South Carolina a Creole population had arrived from Barbados. The number of free blacks in the Deep South increased rapidly with the arrival of thousands of light-colored refugees from the slave revolt in Haiti.

Free African Americans varied greatly in status. Most lived in poverty, but in a few cities, such as New Orleans, Baltimore, and Charleston, they worked as skilled carpenters, shoemakers, tailors, and millwrights. In the lower South, a few achieved high occupational status and actually bought slaves of their own. One of the wealthiest former slaves was William Ellison, the son of a slave mother and a white planter. As a slave apprenticed to a skilled artisan, Ellison had learned how to make cotton gins, and at the age of 26 bought his freedom with his overtime earnings. At his death in 1861, he had acquired the home of a former South Carolina governor, a shop, lands, and 63 slaves worth more than $100,000.

Free people of color occupied an uneasy middle ground between the dominant whites and the masses of slaves. Legally, courts denied them the right to serve on juries or to testify against whites. Some, like William Ellison, distanced themselves from those black people who remained in slavery and even bought and sold slaves. Others identified with slaves and poor free slaves and took the lead in establishing separate African American churches.

In addition to the more than 250,000 free African Americans who lived in the South, another 200,000 lived in the North. Although they made up no more than 3.8 percent of the population of any northern state, free African Americans faced intense legal, economic, and social discrimination, which kept them desperately poor. They were prohibited from marrying whites and were forced into the lowest paying jobs. Whites denied them equal access to education, relegated them to segregated jails, cemeteries, asylums, and schools, forbade them from testifying against whites in court, and, in all but four states—New Hampshire, Maine, Massachusetts, and Vermont—denied them the right to vote.

In the North as well as the South, most free African Americans faced economic hardship and substandard living conditions. Northern African Americans typically lived in tenements, sheds, and stables. An 1847 visitor described the typical black dwelling in Philadelphia as "a desolate pen," 6 feet square, without windows, beds, or furniture, possessing a leaky roof and a floor so low in the ground "that more or less water comes in on them from the yard in rainy weather." According to the *New York Express,* the principal residence of a free black in that city was a house with eight or ten rooms, "and in these are crowded not infrequently two or three hundred souls."

During the 1830s or even earlier, African Americans in both the North and South began to suffer from heightened discrimination and competition from white immigrants in both the skilled trades and such

Although many free African Americans lived in poverty, some worked as skilled carpenters, tailors, millwrights, or sawyers.

traditional occupations as domestic service. In the late 1850s, the plight of free African Americans worsened. In states such as South Carolina and Maryland, they faced a new crisis. White mechanics and artisans, bitter over the competition they faced from free people of color, demanded that the states legislate the reenslavement of African Americans. During the winter of 1859, politicians in the South Carolina legislature introduced 20 bills restricting the freedom of African Americans. None passed. The next summer, Charleston officials went house to house, demanding that free people of color provide documentary proof of their freedom and threatening to reenslave those who lacked evidence. A panic followed, and hundreds of free blacks emigrated to the North. Some 780 emigrated from South Carolina before secession; 2000 more left during the first month and a half of 1861.

CONCLUSION

In 1857 **Hinton Rowan Helper,** the son of a western North Carolina farmer, published one of the most politically influential books ever written by an Ameri-

CHRONOLOGY OF KEY EVENTS

1790 Samuel Slater opens the nation's first textile mill in Pawtucket, Rhode Island

1793 Eli Whitney obtains a patent for the cotton gin

1800 Gabriel slave insurrection is uncovered in Richmond, Virginia

1806 Journeyman shoemakers in New York stage one of the nation's first labor strikes

1811 Charles Deslondes's slave insurrection in southern Louisiana is suppressed

1822 Denmark Vesey's slave rebellion is uncovered in South Carolina

1831 Nat Turner's slave insurrection in Southampton County, Virginia

1832 Virginia legislature defeats proposal to abolish slavery

1834 National Trades' Union is organized; Massachusetts mill girls stage their first strike

1837 Panic of 1837 begins

1838 Boston establishes the nation's first modern police force

1840 Ten-hour day is established for federal employees

1842 Massachusetts Supreme Court, in *Commonwealth v. Hunt*, recognizes unions' right to exist

1844 Methodist church divides over slavery issue

1845 Potato blight strikes Ireland; Baptists split over the slavery issue

1848 Revolutions in Europe; Free Soil party is organized to oppose expansion of slavery into new territories

1857 Hinton Helper publishes *The Impending Crisis of the South*

can. Entitled *The Impending Crisis of the South*, the book argued that slavery was incompatible with economic progress. Using statistics drawn from the 1850 census, Helper maintained that by every possible measure the North was growing far faster than the South and that slavery was the cause of the South's economic backwardness.

Helper's thesis was that southern slavery was inefficient and wasteful, inferior in all respects to the North's free labor system. Helper argued that slavery was incompatible with economic progress; it impoverished the South, degraded labor, inhibited urbanization, thwarted industrialization, and stifled innovation. A rabid racist, Helper accompanied a call for the abolition of slavery with a demand for black colonization overseas. He concluded his book with a call for the South's nonslaveholders to overthrow the region's planter elite.

Helper's book created a nationwide furor. A leading antislavery newspaper distributed 500 copies a day, viewing the book as the most effective propaganda against slavery ever written. Many Southerners burned it, fearful that it would divide the white population and undermine the institution of slavery.

By 1857, when Helper's book appeared, the North and South had become in the eyes of many

Americans two distinct civilizations, with their own distinctive sets of values and ideals: one increasingly urban and industrial, the other committed to slave labor. Although the two sections shared many of the same ideals, ambitions, and prejudices, they had developed along diverging lines. In increasing numbers, Northerners identified their society with progress and believed that slavery was an intolerable obstacle to innovation, self-improvement, and commercial and economic growth. A growing number of Southerners, in turn, regarded their rural and agricultural society as the true embodiment of republican values. The great question before the nation was whether it could continue to exist half slave, half free.

CHAPTER SUMMARY AND KEY POINTS

In the decades before the Civil War, diverging economic developments contributed to growing sectional differences between the North and South. In this chapter you learned about the breakdown of the artisan system of labor and the rise of the factory system in the North as well as the growth of labor protests and increases in immigration. You also read about the impact of slavery on the southern economy, the legal status of slaves, the material conditions of slave life, slave family life and cultural expression, and forms of slave resistance.

- Far-reaching changes took place in the northern economy between 1790 and 1860. Commercial agriculture replaced subsistence agriculture. Household production was replaced by factory production.

- Massive foreign immigration greatly increased the size of cities.

- In the South, slavery impeded the development of industry and cities and discouraged technological innovation.

- About one-third of the South's population labored as slaves. Slaves performed all kinds of work, but slavery mainly meant backbreaking fieldwork.

- Deprivation and physical hardship were the hallmark of life under slavery. Slave sales frequently broke up slave families.

- Nevertheless, slaves were able—through their families, religion, and cultural traditions—to sustain an autonomous culture and community beyond the direct control of their masters. In addition, slaves resisted slavery through insurrection and a variety of indirect protests against slavery.

Suggestions for Further Reading

William J. Cooper, Jr., *The South and the Politics of Slavery* (1978) and Cooper and Thomas E. Terrill, *The American South* (1990) are valuable studies of the pre–Civil War South.

Peter Kolchin, *American Slavery, 1619–1877* (1993) offers an insightful overview of slavery.

Stephanie, McCurry, *Masters of Small Worlds: Yeoman Households, Gender Relations, and the Political Culture of the Antebellum South Carolina Low Country* (1995). Explores the place of small landholders in plantation society.

Christine Stansell, *City of Women: Sex and Class in New York, 1789–1860* (2nd edition, 1987). Reconstructs the experiences of working-class women in America's largest city.

Sean Wilentz, *Chants Democratic: New York City and the Rise of the American Working Class, 1788–1850.* (1984) provides extensive information on the antebellum northern working class.

Novels

Maria S. Cummins, *The Lamplighter* (1854).

Richard Henry Dana, *Two Years Before the Mast* (1840).

Harriet Jacobs, *Incidents in the Life of a Slave Girl* (1861).

Toni Morrison, *Beloved* (1987).

Susan Warner, *The Wide, Wide World* (1850).

Media Resources

Web Sites

African American Religion
http://www.nhc.rtp.nc.us:8080/tserve/nineteen/nkeyinfo/nafrican.htm
Laurie Maffly-Kipp, an authority on religious history, examines the fusion of African and Christian religious beliefs and practices.

African American Spirituals
http://www.authentichistory.com/audio/antebellum/AAspirituals.html
Early recordings of African American spirituals.

"Been Here So Long": Selections from the WPA American Slave Narratives
http://newdeal.feri.org/asn/index.htm
Slave narratives are some of the more interesting primary sources about slavery.

Africans in America: America's Journey Through Slavery
http://www.pbs.org/wgbh/aia/home.html
This PBS site contains images and documents recounting slavery in America.

Amistad Trials (1839–1840)
http://www.law.umkc.edu/faculty/projects/ftrials/amistad/AMISTD.HTM
Images, chronology, court and official documents constitute this site by Dr. Doug Linder at University of Missouri–Kansas City Law School.

The Atlantic Slave Trade and Slave Life in the Americas
http://gropius.lib.virginia.edu/Slavery/index.html
Images of slavery and the slave trade.

Everyday Life in New England
http://www.osv.org/education/resources.htm
This site provides information about everyday life in New England during the early nineteenth century.

Exploring Amistad
http://amistad.mysticseaport.org/main/welcome.html
Mystic Seaport runs this site, which includes extensive collections of historical resources relating to the revolt and subsequent trial of enslaved Africans.

Interpreting the Irish Famine
http://www.people.virginia.edu/~eas5e/Irish/Famine.html
This site includes photographs and reporting and commentaries by Irish, English, and American observers.

Life in Pre–Civil War America
http://www.connerprairie.org/histon.html
Documents and articles on diverse life in Indiana and the United States before the Civil War, including women's lives, clothing, medicine and disease, food, transportation, and religion.

North American Slave Narratives

http://metalab.unc.edu/docsouth/neh/neh.html
This site includes all the narratives of fugitive and former slaves published in broadsides, pamphlets, or book form in English up to 1920 and many of the biographies of fugitive and former slaves published in English before 1920.

The Settlement of African Americans in Liberia

http://www.loc.gov/exhibits/african/perstor.html
This site contains images and text relating to the colonization movement to return African Americans to Africa.

Underground Railroad

http://www.cr.nps.gov/delta/under.htm
National Park Service site about the Underground Railroad, with special reference to the lower Mississippi Valley.

Views of the Famine

http://vassun.vassar.edu/~sttaylor/FAMINE/
This site contains contemporary newspaper illustrations and articles about the Irish famine of 1845–1851 and includes 100 early engravings from the *Illustrated London News,* the *Pictorial Times,* and *Punch.*

Films and Videos

Africans in America (1998). A PBS documentary history of slavery.

Amistad (1997). Steven Spielberg's recreation of the 1839 incident in which kidnapped Africans overcame their captors and were subsequently put on trial in the United States for piracy.

Beloved (1998). The screen adaptation of Toni Morrison's novel about the psychic legacies of slavery, based on the story of Margaret Garner, a fugitive slave who killed her own child rather than have her offspring grow up in slavery.

Gangs of New York (2002). Martin Scorsese's epic portrait of conflict between Irish and native-born gangs in mid-nineteenth century New York.

NightJohn (1996). This made-for-television drama tells the story of a slave who risks his life to teach other slaves to read.

Roots (1977). Based on Alex Haley's best-selling novel, the first episode of this television mini-series focuses on the enslavement and resistance of the African warrior Kunta Kinte.

Sankofa (1993). Named after an Akan word that means one must return to the past to move forward, the movie tells the story of a fashion model who is possessed by spirits lingering in Cape Coast Castle in Ghana and travels back to the slave past.

KEY TERMS

Artisan system of labor   (p. 309)

Factory system   (p. 310)

Immigration   (p. 314)

Plantation legend   (p. 318)

Paternalism   (p. 323)

Slave code   (p. 324)

Gang system   (p. 325)

Task system   (p. 325)

Spiritual   (p. 328)

Maroons   (p. 329)

PEOPLE YOU SHOULD KNOW

Eli Whitney   (p. 305)

Samuel Slater   (p. 310)

John C. Calhoun   (p. 321)

James G. Birney   (p. 322)

Gabriel   (p. 328)

Denmark Vesey   (p. 328)

Nat Turner   (p. 329)

Hinton Rowan Helper   (p. 330)

REVIEW QUESTIONS

1. In what ways were Northerners and Southerners similar? In what ways were they different?

2. How was industrialization both a force for unity and a force for division in the pre–Civil War United States?

3. How did the northern economy change during the early nineteenth century?

4. Why did an increasing number of immigrants come to the United States during the 1840s and 1850s? Why did some Americans resent the immigrants?

5. How did the invention of the cotton gin affect southern society?

6. Why did some Southerners try to promote industry and a distinctive southern culture during the 1840s and 1850s?

7. Explain how the size of a plantation and the crop grown affected the conditions under which slaves worked and lived.

8. How were enslaved African Americans able to sustain a sense of dignity and independence under slavery? In what ways did they resist slavery?

13 Cultures Collide in the Far West

SOCIAL BANDITS: ROBIN HOODS OF THE SOUTHWEST

In 1920 an enormously popular figure burst onto the Hollywood screen. Zorro, a California version of Robin Hood, was Hollywood's first swashbuckling hero. Played by some of Hollywood's biggest stars—including Douglas Fairbanks, Sr., and Tyrone Power—Zorro was a gifted horseman and master of disguise. He wore a mask, wielded a cape and a sword with panache, and announced his presence by slashing the letter Z on a wall. Like the legendary English outlaw, he robbed from the rich and gave to the poor—but he had a crucial difference: he was Hispanic. In more than a dozen feature films and a long-running Walt Disney television series, Don Diego Vegas, the son of a prominent wealthy California *alcalde* (administrator and judge), deeply resents the exploitation of California's peasants. He adopts the secret identity of Zorro, robs tax collectors, and returns the money to the poor.

Zorro was the fictional creation of a popular novelist named Johnston Culley. But the figure he portrayed—the **social bandit** protecting the interests of ordinary Mexicans (and later Mexican Americans) in the Southwest—was based on reality. Especially after Americans moved into the Southwest, many Mexicans struggled to preserve their culture, economy, and traditional rights. Some Mexicans in Texas and California—such as the legendary Joaquín Murieta—turned to banditry as a way to resist exploitation and avenge injustice. Though called *bandidos*, these figures did not rob banks or stagecoaches; instead, they sought to protect the rights and interests of poorer Mexicans and Mexican Americans.

One of the most famous social bandits was **Juan Nepomuceno Cortina** of Texas. Born in 1824 to a wealthy, established family, Cortina fought for Mexico in its war with the United States between 1846 and 1848. After the war, he saw many Mexicans reduced to second-class citizenship, mistreated by local police officers and Texas Rangers, and cheated out of their cattle and land. "Flocks of vampires, in the guise of men," he wrote, robbed Mexicans "of their property, incarcerated, chased, murdered, and hunted [them] like wild beasts." In July 1859, he saw a marshal in Brownsville beating a Mexican farmhand. Cortina ordered the marshal to stop, and when he refused, shot him in the shoulder. Then, in September, Cortina and other Mexicans raided Brownsville, proclaimed a Republic of the Rio Grande, and raised the Mexican flag. A force consisting of Texas Rangers and the United

The popularity of Zorro, the fictional recreation of the social bandits who sought to protect the rights of Mexicans and Mexican Americans in the nineteenth century, continues to the present day. A recent incarnation of the folk hero was the character played by Antonio Banderas in the movie *The Mask of Zorro*, released in 1998.

States Army eventually forced Cortina and his supporters to retreat into Mexico. Cortina would later serve as governor of the Mexican state of Tamaulipas.

U ntil recently, American popular culture presented the story of America's westward expansion largely from the perspective of white Americans. Countless western novels and films depicted the westward movement primarily through the eyes of explorers, missionaries, soldiers, trappers, traders, and pioneers. Theodore Roosevelt captured their perspective in a book entitled *The Winning of the West*, an epic tale of white civilization conquering the western wilderness. But there are other sides to the story. To properly understand America's surge to the Pacific, one must understand it from multiple perspectives, including the viewpoint of the people who already inhabited the region: Mexicans and Native Americans.

THE HISPANIC AND NATIVE AMERICAN WEST

When Americans ventured westward, they did not enter uninhabited land. Large parts of the Far West were inhabited by Native Americans and Mexicans, who had lived on those lands for hundreds of years and established their own distinctive ways of life.

Spanish America

Until 1821, Spain ruled the area that now includes the states of Arizona, California, Colorado, Nevada, New Mexico, Texas, and Utah. Spanish explorers, priests, and soldiers first entered the area in the early sixteenth century, half a century before the first English colonists arrived at Jamestown. Between 1528 and 1800 Spain established imperial claims and isolated outposts in an area extending from Mexico to Montana and from California to the Mississippi River. Spain established permanent settlements in the region partly as a way to keep out other European powers. In the late sixteenth century, Spain planted a colony in New Mexico and a century later built the first settlements in what is now Arizona and Texas. In the late eighteenth century, fears of British and Russian occupation of the Pacific Coast led Spain also to establish outposts in California.

Unlike England or France, Spain did not actively encourage settlement or economic development in its northern empire. Instead, Spain concentrated much of its energies in Mexico. Spain restricted manufacturing and trade and discouraged migration to regions north of Mexico. In 1821, the year Mexico gained its independence, Spanish settlement was concentrated in just four areas: in southern Arizona, along California's coast, in New Mexico, and in Texas. Santa Fe, Spain's largest settlement, had only 6000 Spanish inhabitants, and San Antonio a mere 1500.

Despite these small numbers, Spain would leave a lasting cultural imprint on the entire region. Such institutions as the rodeo and the cowboy (the *vaquero*) had their roots in Spanish culture. Place names, too, bear witness to the Spanish heritage: Los Angeles, San Diego, and San Francisco were founded by Spanish explorers and priests. To this day, Spanish architecture—adobe walls, tile roofs, wooden beams, and intricate mosaics—continues to characterize the Southwest. By introducing horses and livestock, Spanish colonists and missionaries transformed the southwestern economy and that area's physical appearance. As livestock devoured the region's tall, native grasses, a new and distinctively southwestern environment arose, one of cactus, sagebrush, and mesquite.

The first American cowboys borrowed the clothing and customs of Mexican cowhands known as *vaqueros*.

The Mission System

The Spanish clergy, particularly Jesuits and Franciscans, played a critical role in settling the Southwest using the **mission system.** Their missions were designed to spread Christianity among, and establish

California Missions

Mission life reached its peak of development in California.

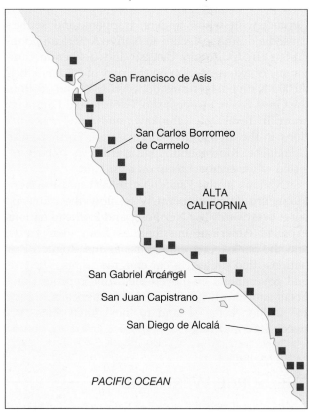

San Francisco de Asís

San Carlos Borromeo de Carmelo

ALTA CALIFORNIA

San Gabriel Arcángel

San Juan Capistrano

San Diego de Alcalá

PACIFIC OCEAN

control over, native populations. In some areas, they forced Indians to live in mission communities, where the priests taught them weaving, blacksmithing, candle-making, and leather-working, and forced them to work in orchards, workshops, and fields for long hours. The missions were most successful in New Mexico (despite an Indian revolt in 1680) and California and far less successful in Arizona and Texas.

Mission life reached its peak in California, an area Spain did not begin to colonize until 1769. Spain built 21 missions between 1769 and 1823, extending from San Diego northward to Sonoma. By 1830, 30,000 of California's 300,000 Native Americans worked on missions, where they harvested grain and herded 400,000 cattle, horses, goats, hogs, and sheep.

Impact of Mexican Independence

By the early nineteenth century, resistance to Spanish colonial rule was growing. In 1810, Miguel Hidalgo y Costilla, a Mexican priest, led a revolt against Spain, which, although short-lived, represented the beginning of the **Mexican struggle for independence.** Mexico finally achieved independence in 1821.

The War of Independence marked the beginning of a period of far-reaching change in the Southwest. Among the most important consequences of the collapse of Spanish rule was the opening of the region to American economic penetration. Mexican authorities in New Mexico and Arizona allowed American traders to bring American goods into the area and trappers to hunt for beaver. Texas and California were also opened to American commerce and settlement. By 1848, Americans made up about half of California's non-Indian population.

Mexican independence also led to the demise of the mission system. After the revolution the missions were "secularized"—broken up and their property sold or given away to private citizens. In 1833–1834 the Mexican government confiscated California mission properties and exiled the Franciscan friars. As a result, mission properties fell into private hands. By 1846, mission land and cattle had passed into the hands of 800 private landowners called *rancheros*, who controlled 8 million acres of land in units called *ranchos*, which ranged in size from 4500 to 50,000 acres. These ranchos were run like feudal estates. They were worked by Native Americans, who were treated like slaves. Indeed, the death rate of Native Americans who worked on ranchos was twice that among southern slaves.

Native Americans

In 1840, before large numbers of pioneers and farmers crossed the Mississippi, at least 300,000 people lived in the Southwest, on the Great Plains, in California, and on the northwest Pacific Coast. This population was divided into more than 200 nations whose lifestyles ranged from sedentary farming to nomadic hunting and gathering. Their social organization was equally diverse, each nation having its own language, religious beliefs, kinship patterns, and system of government.

The best known of the western Indians are the 23 Indian tribes—including the Cheyenne and Sioux—who lived on the Great Plains and hunted buffalo, antelope, deer, and elk for subsistence. For many present-day Americans, the Plains Indians, riding on horseback, wearing warbonnets, and living in tepees, are regarded as the typical American Indians. In fact, however, the Plains Indians first acquired the horse from the Spanish in the sixteenth century. Not until the middle of the eighteenth century did these tribes have a large supply of horses and not until the early to mid-nineteenth century did most Plains Indians have firearms.

South and west of the Plains, in the huge, arid region that is now Arizona and New Mexico, sophisticated farmers, like the Hopi, Zuni, and other Pueblo groups, coexisted alongside migratory hunters, like the Apaches and Navajos. In the Great Basin, the harsh barren region between the Sierra Nevada and the Rocky Mountains, nations like the Paiute and the Gosiute lived on berries, nuts, roots, insects, and reptiles.

More than 100,000 Native Americans lived in California when the area was acquired by the United States in 1848. Most lived in small villages in the winter but moved during the rest of the year gathering wild plants and seeds, hunting small game, and fishing in the ocean and rivers.

Comanche Chasing Buffalo with Bows and Lances, by George Catlin. Catlin lived in many different nations of the Plains and produced an important record of Native American life, both in his book *Letters and Notes on the Manners, Customs and Condition of the North American Indians*, published in 1841, and in hundreds of sketches, engravings, and paintings.

The large number of tribes living along the northwest Pacific Coast developed an elaborate social hierarchy based on wealth and descent. These people found an abundant food supply in the sea, coastal rivers, and forests. They took salmon, seal, whale, and otter from the coastal waters and hunted deer, moose, and elk in the forests.

Impact of Contact

Contact with white traders, trappers, and settlers caused a dramatic decline in Native American populations. In California, disease and deliberate campaigns of extermination on the part of settlers killed 70,000 Native Americans between 1849 and 1859. In the Great Basin, trappers shot Gosiute and Paiute for sport. In Texas, the Karankawa and many other nations in the area largely disappeared. Further west, Comanche, Kiowa, and Apache warriors bitterly resisted white encroachment on their land.

Nations in the Pacific Northwest and northern Plains struggled desperately to slow the pioneers' surge westward. The Nez Perce and Flathead nations expelled American missionaries from their lands, and the Snake, Cheyenne, Shasta, and Rogue River nations tried futilely to cut emigrant roots. The federal government employed the army to protect pioneers and forced western Native Americans to cede 147 million acres of land to the United States between 1853 and 1857.

THE SURGE WESTWARD

Early in April 1846, 87 pioneers led by George Donner, a well-to-do 62-year-old farmer, set out from Illinois for California. As this group of pioneers headed westward, they never imagined the hardship that awaited them. Like many emigrants, they were ill prepared for the dangerous trek. The pioneers' 27 wagons were loaded not only with necessities but also with fancy foods, liquor, and such luxuries as built-in beds and stoves.

In Wyoming, the party decided to take a short-cut, having read in a guidebook that pioneers could save 400 miles by cutting south of the Great Salt Lake. At first the trail was "all that could be desired," but soon huge boulders and dangerous mountain passes slowed the expedition to a crawl. During one stretch, the party traveled only 36 miles in 21 days. In late October, the **Donner party** reached the eastern Sierra Nevada and prepared to cross the Truckee Pass, the last remaining barrier before they arrived in California's Sacramento Valley. They climbed the high Sierra ridges in an attempt to cross the pass, but early snows blocked their path.

Trapped, the party built crude tents covered with clothing, blankets, and animal hides, which were soon buried under 14 feet of snow. The pioneers intended to slaughter their livestock for food, but many of the animals perished in 40-foot snowdrifts. To survive, the Donner party was forced to eat mice, their rugs, and even their shoes. In the end, surviving members of the party escaped starvation only by eating the flesh of those who died.

Finally, in mid-December, 17 men and women made a last-ditch effort to cross the pass to find help. They took only a six-day supply of rations, consisting of finger-sized pieces of dried beef—two pieces per person per day. During a severe storm two of the group died. The surviving members of the party "stripped the flesh from their bones, roasted and ate it, averting their eyes from each other, and weeping." More than a month passed before seven frostbitten survivors reached an American settlement. By then, the rest had died and two Native American guides had been shot and eaten.

Relief teams immediately sought to rescue the pioneers still trapped near Truckee Pass. The situation that the rescuers found was unspeakably gruesome. Surviving members of the Donner party were delirious from hunger and exposure. One survivor was found in a small cabin next to the cannibalized body of a young boy. Of the original 87 members of the party, only 47 survived.

It took white Americans a century and a half to expand as far west as the Appalachian Mountains, a few hundred miles from the Atlantic coast. It took another 50 years to push the frontier to the Mississippi river. By 1830, fewer than 100,000 pioneers had crossed the Mississippi.

During the 1840s, however, tens of thousands of Americans ventured beyond the Mississippi River. Inspired by the new vision of the West as a paradise

Margaret Reed was one of only 47 survivors of the original party of 87 pioneers to reach California.

of plenty, filled with fertile valleys and rich land, thousands of families chalked GTT ("Gone to Texas") on their gates or painted "California or Bust" on their wagons and joined the trek westward. By 1850 pioneers had pushed the edge of American settlement all the way to Texas, the Rocky Mountains, and the Pacific Ocean.

Opening the West

Before the nineteenth century, mystery shrouded the Far West. Mapmakers knew very little about the shape, size, or topography of the land west of the Mississippi River. French, British, and Spanish trappers, traders, and missionaries had traveled the Upper and Lower Missouri River, and the British and Spanish had explored the Pacific Coast, but most of western North America was unknown to white Americans or Europeans.

The popular conception of the West was largely a mixture of legend and guesswork. Even educated people like Thomas Jefferson believed that the West was populated by primeval beasts, that a "Northwest Passage" connected the Missouri River and the Pacific Ocean, and that only a single ridge of mountains, known as the "Stony Mountains," needed to be crossed before one could see the Pacific Ocean.

Pathfinders

In 1803 President Thomas Jefferson appointed his personal secretary, **Meriwether Lewis,** and **William Clark,** a former U.S. military officer, to explore the Missouri and Columbia rivers as far as the Pacific Ocean. As a politician interested in the rapid settlement and commercial development of the West, Jefferson wanted Lewis and Clark to establish American claims to the region west of the Rocky Mountains, gather information about furs and minerals in the region, and identify sites

Guided by the Native American woman Sacajewa, Meriwether Lewis and army captain William Clark led a party of 34 soldiers and 10 civilians up the Missouri River, across the northern Rocky Mountains, and along the tributaries of the Columbia River to the Pacific Ocean. Sergeant Patrick Glass, a member of the expedition, kept a journal recording the events and adventures of the two-year journey. This drawing shows Clark and his men building a line of huts.

for trading posts and settlements. The president also instructed the expedition to collect information covering the diversity of life in the West, ranging from climate, geology, and plant growth to fossils of extinct animals and Indian religions, laws, and customs.

In 1806, the year that Lewis and Clark returned from their 8000-mile expedition, a young army lieutenant named Zebulon Pike left St. Louis to explore the southern border of the Louisiana Territory, just as Lewis and Clark had explored the territory's northern portion. Traveling along the Arkansas River, Pike saw the towering peak that bears his name. He and his party then traveled into Spanish territory along the Rio Grande and Red River. Pike's description of the wealth of Spanish towns in the Southwest attracted American traders to the region.

Pike's report of his expedition, published in 1810, helped to create one of the most influential myths about the Great Plains: that this region was nothing more than a "**Great American Desert**," a treeless and waterless land of dust storms and starvation. "Here," wrote Pike, is "barren soil, parched and dried up for eight months of the year . . . [without] a speck of vegetation." This image of the West as a region of wild beasts and deserts received added support from another government-sponsored expedition, one led by Major Stephen H. Long in 1820 in search of the source of the Red River. Long's report described the West as "wholly unfit for cultivation, and . . . uninhabitable by a people depending upon agriculture for their subsistence." This report helped implant the image of the "Great American Desert" even more deeply in the American mind, retarding western settlement for a generation.

The view of the West as a dry, barren wasteland was not fully offset until the 1840s when another government-sponsored explorer, John C. Frémont, mapped much of the territory between the Mississippi Valley and the Pacific Ocean. His glowing descriptions of the West as a paradise of plenty captivated the imagination of many midwestern families who, by the 1840s, were eager for new lands to settle.

Mountain Men

Traders and trappers were more important than government explorers in opening the West to white settlement. **Mountain men** trapped beaver and bartered with Native Americans for pelts. They blazed the great western trails through the Rockies and Sierra Nevada and stirred the popular imagination with stories of redwood forests, geysers, and fertile valleys in California and Oregon. These men also undermined the ability of western Native Americans to resist white incursions by making them dependent on manufactured goods and pitting tribes against one another. They killed off animals that provided a major part of the Great Plains hunting economy, distributed alcohol, and spread disease.

When Lewis and Clark completed their expedition, they brought back reports of rivers and streams teeming with beaver and otter in the northern Rockies. Starting in 1807, keelboats ferried fur trappers up the Missouri River. By the mid-1830s these mountain men had marked out the overland trails that would lead pioneers to Oregon and California.

The Rocky Mountain Fur Company played a central role in opening the western fur trade. Instead of buying skins from the Native Americans, the company ran ads in St. Louis newspapers asking for white trappers willing to go to the wilderness. In 1822, it sent a hundred trappers along the upper Missouri River. Three years later the company introduced the **"rendezvous" system**, under which trappers met once a year at an agreed-on meeting place to barter pelts for supplies. "The rendezvous," wrote one participant, "is one continued scene of drunkenness, gambling, and brawling and fighting, as long as the money and the credit of the trappers last."

At the same time that mountain men searched for beaver in the Rockies and along the Columbia River, other groups trapped furs in the Southwest, at that time part of Mexico. In 1827, Jedediah Smith and a party of 15 trappers, after nearly dying of thirst, discovered a westward route to California. Jim Beckwourth, a mountain man who was the son of a Virginia slave, later discovered a pass through the Sierra Nevada that became part of the overland trail to California.

In 1827 Jedediah Smith led a party of trappers through Utah, across the Colorado River, then across the Mojave Desert and the San Bernardino Mountains to the Pacific.

The western fur trade lasted only until 1840, when the last annual rendezvous was held. Beaver hats for gentlemen went out of style in favor of silk hats; thus, the era of the mountain man, dressed in a fringed buckskin suit, came to an end. Fur-bearing animals had been trapped out, and profits from trading, which amounted to as much as 2000 percent during the early years, fell steeply. Instead of hunting furs,

some trappers became scouts for the U.S. Army or pilots for the wagon trains that were beginning to carry pioneers to California and Oregon.

Trailblazing

The Santa Fe and Oregon trails were the two principal routes to the Far West. William Becknell, an American trader, opened the **Santa Fe Trail** in 1821. His 800-mile journey from Missouri to Santa Fe took two months. When he could find no water, Becknell drank blood from a mule's ear and the contents of a buffalo's stomach. Ultimately, the trail tied the New Mexican Southwest economically to the United States and hastened American penetration of the region.

The Santa Fe Trail served primarily commercial functions. From the early 1820s until the 1840s, an average of 80 wagons and 150 traders used the trail each year. Mexican settlers in Santa Fe purchased cloth, hardware, glass, and books. On their return east, American traders carried Mexican blankets, beaver pelts, wool, mules, and silver. By the 1830s, traders had extended the trail into California with branches reaching Los Angeles and San Diego. By the 1850s and 1860s more than 5000 wagons a year took the trail across long stretches of desert, dangerous water crossings, and treacherous mountain passes. The Santa Fe Trail made the New Mexican Southwest economically dependent on the United

Western Trails

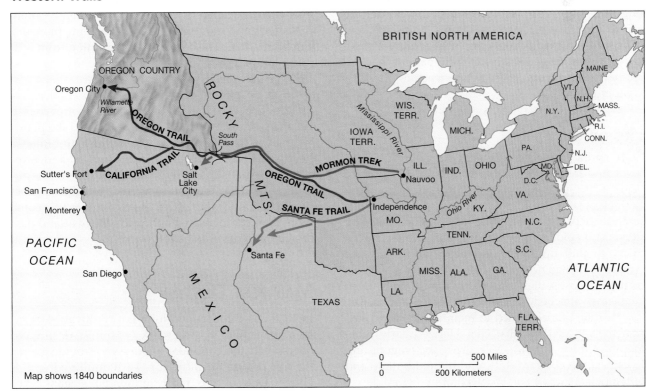

Map shows 1840 boundaries

States and brought Americans into the areas that became Arizona, California, and New Mexico.

In 1811 and 1812 fur trappers marked out the **Oregon Trail**, the longest and most famous pioneer route in American history. This trail crossed about 2000 miles from Independence, Missouri, to the Columbia River country of Oregon. During the 1840s, 12,000 pioneers traveled the trail's entire length to Oregon.

Travel on the Oregon Trail was a tremendous test of human endurance. The journey by wagon train took six months. Settlers encountered prairie fires, sudden blizzards, and impassable mountains. Cholera and other diseases were common; food, water, and wood were scarce. Only the stalwart dared brave the physical hardship of the westward trek.

Settling the Far West

During the 1840s thousands of pioneers headed westward toward California and Oregon. In 1841, the first party of 69 pioneers left Missouri for California, led by an Ohio schoolteacher named John Bidwell. The members of the party knew little about western travel: "We only knew that California lay to the west." The hardships the party endured were nearly unbearable. They were forced to abandon their wagons and eat their pack animals, "half roasted, dripping with blood." But American pioneering of the Far West had begun. Over the next 25 years, 350,000 more made the trek along the overland trails.

The rugged pioneer life was not a new experience for most of the early western settlers. Most pioneers migrated to the Far West from states that border the Mississippi River—Arkansas, Illinois, Louisiana, and Missouri—which had only recently acquired statehood. Either these settlers or their parents had already moved several times before reaching the Mississippi Valley.

Life on the Trail

Each spring, pioneers gathered at Council Bluffs, Iowa, and Independence and St. Joseph, Missouri, to begin a 2000-mile journey westward. For many families, the great spur for emigration was economic. The financial depression of the late 1830s, accompanied by floods and epidemics in the Mississippi Valley, forced many to pull up stakes and head west. Said one woman: "We had nothing to lose, and we might gain a fortune." Most settlers traveled in family units. Even single men attached themselves to family groups.

At first, pioneers tried to maintain the rigid sexual division of labor that characterized early nineteenth-century America. Men drove the wagons and livestock, stood guard duty, and hunted buffalo and antelope for extra meat. Women got up before dawn,

Life along the westward trails was a tremendous test of human endurance. Pioneers encountered arid desert, difficult mountain passes, dangerous rivers, and quicksand.

collected wood and "buffalo chips" (animal dung used for fuel), hauled water, kindled campfires, kneaded dough, and milked cows. The demands of the journey forced a blurring of gender-role distinctions for women who, in addition to domestic chores, performed many duties previously reserved for men. They drove wagons, yoked cattle, and loaded wagons. Some men did such things as cooking, previously regarded as women's work.

Accidents, disease, and sudden disaster were ever-present dangers. Diseases such as typhoid, dysentery, and mountain fever killed many pioneers. Emigrant parties also suffered devastation from buffalo stampedes, prairie fires, and floods. At least 20,000 emigrants died along the Oregon Trail.

Still, despite the hardships of the experience, few emigrants ever regretted their decision to move west. As one pioneer put it: "Those who crossed the plains . . . never forgot the ungratified thirst, the intense heat and bitter cold, the craving hunger and utter physical exhaustion of the trail. . . . But there was another side. True they had suffered, but the satisfaction of deeds accomplished and difficulties overcome more than compensated and made the overland passage a thing never to be forgotten."

MANIFEST DESTINY

In 1845 an editor named John L. O'Sullivan referred in a magazine to America's "manifest destiny to overspread the continent allotted by Providence for the free development of our yearly multiplying millions." One of the most influential slogans ever coined, the term **manifest destiny** expressed the romantic emotion that led Americans to risk their lives to settle the Far West.

The idea that America had a special destiny to stretch across the continent motivated many people to migrate west. Manifest destiny inspired a 29-year-old named Stephen F. Austin to talk of grandly colonizing the Mexican province of Texas with "North American population, enterprise and intelligence." It led expansionists—united behind the slogan "54°40' or fight!"—to demand that the United States should own the entire Pacific Northwest all the way to Alaska. Aggressive nationalists invoked the idea to justify the displacement of Native Americans from their land, war with Mexico, and American expansion into Cuba and Central America. More positively, the idea of manifest destiny also inspired missionaries, farmers, and pioneers, who dreamed only of transforming plains and fertile valleys into farms and small towns.

Gone to Texas

In 1822, when the first caravan of American traders traversed the Santa Fe Trail and the first hundred fur trappers searched the Rocky Mountains for beaver, a small number of Americans followed trails to another frontier—Texas.

American settlement in Texas began with the encouragement of first the Spanish and then the Mexican governments. In the summer of 1820, Moses Austin, a bankrupt 59-year-old Missourian, asked Spanish authorities for a large Texas land tract that he would promote and sell to American pioneers. The following year the Spanish government gave him permission to settle 300 families in Texas. Spain welcomed the Americans for two reasons—to provide a buffer against illegal U.S. settlers, who were creating problems in east Texas even before the grant was made to Austin, and to help develop the land, since only 3500 native Mexicans had settled in Texas (which was then part of the Mexican state of Coahuila y Tejas).

Moses Austin soon died, but his son Stephen carried out his dream to colonize Texas. By 1824, he had attracted 272 colonists to Texas and persuaded the new government of Mexico that encouragement of American immigration was the best way to develop the area. To promote colonization, Mexico in 1825 gave land agents 67,000 acres of land for every 200 families that they brought to Texas. Mexico imposed two conditions on land ownership: settlers had to become Mexican citizens and convert to Roman Catholicism. By 1830 there were 16,000 Americans in Texas.

As the Anglo population swelled, Mexican authorities grew increasingly suspicious of the growing American presence in Texas, and in 1827 the govern-

ment sent General Manuel de Mier y Terán to investigate the situation. In his report Terán warned that unless the Mexican government took timely measures, American settlers in Texas were certain to rebel. Differences in language and culture, Terán believed, had produced bitter enmity between the colonists and native Mexicans. The colonists, he noted, refused to learn the Spanish language, maintained their own separate schools, and conducted most of their trade with the United States. They complained bitterly that they had to travel more than 500 miles to reach a Mexican court and resented the efforts of Mexican authorities to deprive them of the right to vote.

To reassert its authority over Texas, the Mexican government reaffirmed its constitutional prohibition against slavery throughout Mexico, established a chain of military posts occupied by convict soldiers, levied customs duties, restricted trade with the United States, and decreed an end to further American immigration. These actions might have provoked Texans to revolution. But in 1832 **General Antonio López de Santa Anna** became Mexico's president. Colonists hoped that he would make Texas a self-governing state within the Mexican republic, separate from the much more populous Coahuila, thereby eliminating any reason for rebellion. Once in power, however, Santa Anna proved to be far less liberal than many Americans had believed. In 1834 he overthrew Mexico's constitutional government, abolished state governments, and made himself dictator. When Stephen Austin went to Mexico City to try to settle the Texans' grievances, Santa Anna imprisoned him in a Mexican jail for a year.

On November 3, 1835, American colonists adopted a constitution and organized a temporary government but voted overwhelmingly against declaring independence. A majority of settlers hoped to attract the support of Mexican liberals in a joint effort to depose Santa Anna and restore power to the state governments, hopefully including a separate state of Texas.

While holding out the possibility of compromise, the Texans prepared for war. The provisional government elected Sam Houston, a former Tennessee governor and close friend of Andrew Jackson, to lead whatever military forces he could muster. In the middle of 1835 scattered local outbursts erupted against Mexican rule. Then, in 1836 a band of 300 to 500 Texans captured Mexico's military headquarters in San Antonio. The Texas Revolution was under way.

Soon the ominous news reached Texas that Santa Anna himself was marching north with 7000 soldiers to crush the revolt. In actuality, Santa Anna's army was not particularly impressive; it was filled with raw recruits and included many Mayan troops who spoke and understood little Spanish. When Houston learned

One of the most colorful leaders of the struggle for Texas independence, Sam Houston lived for a time with the Cherokee, was a popular hero of the Creek War, and later served as a congressman and governor of Texas.

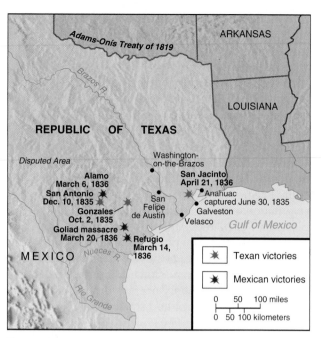

Texas Revolution

The revolution left Texas a lone republic, unrecognized by Mexico and unwanted by the United States.

that Santa Anna's initial goal was to recapture San Antonio, he ordered the city abandoned. But Texas rebels decided to defend the town and made their stand at an abandoned Spanish mission, the **Alamo.** The Texans were led by William Travis and Jim Bowie and included the frontier hero David Crockett.

For 12 days Mexican forces laid siege to the Alamo. At 5 A.M., March 6, 1836, Mexican troops scaled the mission's walls. By 8 A.M., the fighting was over. One hundred eighty-three defenders lay dead, including several Mexicans who had fought for Texas independence.

Two weeks after the defeat at the Alamo, James Fannin and his men surrendered to Mexican forces near Goliad with the understanding that they would be treated as prisoners of war. Instead, Santa Anna ordered more than 350 Texans shot.

These defeats, however, had an unexpected side effect. They gave Sam Houston time to raise and train an army. Volunteers from the American South flocked to his banner. On April 21 his army of less than 800 men surprised and utterly defeated Santa Anna's army as it camped out on the San Jacinto River, east of present-day Houston. The next day Houston's army

captured Santa Anna himself and forced him to sign a treaty granting Texas its independence, a treaty that was never ratified by the Mexican government because it was acquired under duress.

For most Mexican settlers in Texas, defeat meant that they would be relegated to second-class social, political, and economic positions. The new Texas constitution denied citizenship and property rights to those who failed to support the revolution. All persons of Hispanic ancestry were considered in the "denial" category unless they could prove otherwise. Consequently, many Mexican landowners fled the region.

Texas grew rapidly following independence. In 1836, 5000 immigrants arrived in Texas, boosting its population to 30,000. By 1847 its population had reached 140,000. The region also grew economically. Although cotton farming dominated the Texas economy, cattle were becoming an increasingly important industry. Many Mexican landowners abandoned cattle after the Texas Revolution, and by the 1840s large numbers of wild cattle roamed the range. By 1850 the first American cowboys were driving 60,000 cattle a year to New Orleans and California.

The Texas Question

Texas had barely won its independence when it decided to become a part of the United States. A referendum held soon after the Battle of San Jacinto showed Texans favoring annexation by a vote of 3277 to 93.

The **Texas annexation** question became one of the most controversial issues in American politics in the late 1830s and early 1840s. The issue was not Texas but slavery. The admission of Texas to the Union would upset the sectional balance of power in the U.S. Senate, just as the admission of Missouri had threatened 15 years earlier. President Andrew Jackson, acutely conscious of the opposition to admitting Texas as a slave state, agreed only to recognize Texan independence. In 1838, John Quincy Adams, then a member of the House of Representatives, staged a 22-day filibuster that successfully blocked annexation. It appeared that Congress had settled the Texas question. For the time being, Texas would remain an independent republic.

At this point, proslavery Southerners began to popularize a conspiracy theory that would eventually bring Texas into the Union as a slave state. In 1841 John Tyler, an ardent defender of slavery, succeeded to the presidency on the death of William Henry Harrison. Tyler and his secretary of state, John C. Calhoun, argued that Britain was scheming to annex Texas and transform it into a haven for runaway slaves. According to this theory, British slave emancipation in the West Indies had been a total economic disaster, and the British now hoped to undermine slavery in the American South by turning Texas into a British satellite state. In fact, British abolitionists, but not the British government, were working to convince Texas to outlaw slavery in exchange for British foreign aid. Sam Houston did his part to excite American fears by conducting highly visible negotiations with the British government. If the United States would not annex Texas, Houston warned, Texas would seek the support of "some other friend." In the spring of 1844 Calhoun hammered out an annexation treaty with Texas diplomats, but the agreement failed to gain the required two-thirds majority for Senate ratification.

The Texas question became the major political issue in the presidential campaign of 1844. **James K. Polk,** the Democratic candidate, was a strong supporter of annexation, and his victory encouraged Tyler to attempt to annex Texas again in the waning months of his administration. This time Tyler submitted the measure in the form of a resolution, which required only a simple majority of both houses. Congress narrowly approved the resolution in 1845, making Texas the twenty-eighth state.

Webster-Ashburton Treaty

Today the 4000-mile United States-Canadian border is one of the world's most peaceful international boundaries. During the decades before the Civil War, by contrast, the border between the United States and British America was the scene of constant tensions. In 1837 many Americans viewed an insurrection in eastern Canada as an opportunity to annex the country. Americans who lived near the Canadian border aided the rebels, and in one incident several hundred western New Yorkers crossed into Canada and staged an abortive attack on a band of British soldiers. After British forces suppressed the uprising, New Yorkers provided safe haven for the insurrection's leaders. When the rebels began to launch raids into Canada from western New York State, Canadian officials crossed the U.S. border, killed a Canadian rebel, and burned an American ship, the *Caroline*, which had supplied the rebels. When Americans demanded an apology and reparations, Canadian officials refused. Almost immediately, another dispute erupted over the Maine boundary as American and Canadian lumberjacks and farmers battled for possession of northern Maine and western New Brunswick.

The **Webster-Ashburton Treaty of 1842** settled these controversies. The treaty awarded the United States most of the disputed territory in Maine and New Brunswick and guaranteed free navigation on many rivers and lakes along the Canadian border. The Webster-Ashburton Treaty left one major border controversy unresolved: the Canadian-American boundary in the Pacific Northwest.

Oregon

Disputes between the United States and Britain over the **Oregon country** emerged early in the nineteenth century. In 1810 John Jacob Astor, an American who had made a fortune in the Great Lakes fur trade, decided to open a trading post, named Astoria, at the mouth of the Columbia River. He hoped the post would secure a monopoly over the western fur trade for shipping the furs to eager customers in China. The venture failed, however, and for nearly two decades the fur trade was dominated by the British Hudson's Bay Company.

As British fur traders expanded their activities in the Pacific Northwest, American politicians grew alarmed that Britain would gain sovereignty over the region. American diplomats moved quickly to solidify American claims to Oregon. Spain, Russia, Britain, and the United States all claimed rights to the Pacific Northwest. In 1818 Britain and the United States agreed that nationals of both countries could trade in the region; this agreement was renewed in 1827. In 1819 American negotiators persuaded Spain to cede its claims to Oregon to the United States, and two years later Secretary of State John Quincy Adams warned Russia that the United States would oppose any Russian attempts to occupy the territory.

Tejanos at the Alamo

General Antonio López de Santa Anna, backed by some 2400 Mexican troops, put the Alamo under siege on February 23, 1836. On that day Santa Anna ordered the hoisting of a red flag, meaning "no quarter," or no mercy toward potential prisoners of war. This only hardened the resolve of the Alamo's small contingent of defenders, including the legendary Jim Bowie, Davy Crockett, and William Barret Travis. Also inside the Alamo were men like Juan Seguin and Gregorio Esparza. They represented a handful of Tejano defenders. As native residents of Texas (named the province of Tejas in 1691 by the conquering Spanish), they despised Santa Anna for having so recently overthrown the Mexican Constitution of 1824 in favor of dictatorship.

San Antonio was a center of the Tejano population of Texas. Juan Seguin's father, Don Erasmo, was a wealthy local rancher who in earlier years had encouraged the opening of the Mexican province of Coahuila y Tejas to nonnatives from the United States. Most of the Americans settled far to the east of San Antonio, but those who traveled to the Tejano settlements knew Don Erasmo as a generous host who entertained lavishly at his *hacienda*, "Casa Blanca." His son Juan was also locally prominent and had helped immeasurably in driving Mexican troops under General Martin Perfecto de Cós, Santa Anna's brother-in-law, out of San Antonio late in 1835. His reward was

a commission as a captain of Texas cavalry.

Much less is known about Gregorio Esparza. He lived with his wife and four children in San Antonio when Juan Seguin recruited him for his cavalry company. When Santa Anna's advance troops appeared on February 23, Esparza quickly gathered up his family and rushed for protection behind the thick walls of the old Spanish mission known locally as the Alamo.

The Alamo defenders were in an all but impossible position, especially with Santa Anna tightening his siege lines every day. Inside the Alamo, the defenders looked to Jim Bowie for leadership, but he was seriously ill with pneumonia. So they accepted orders from William Barret Travis. With 1000 troops, Travis had argued, the Alamo would never fall. His numbers, however, were hardly more than 150. As a result, Travis regularly sent out couriers with urgent messages for relief. His words were direct. He would never "surrender or retreat." He would "die like a soldier who never forgets what is due to his own honor and that of his country." For those at the Alamo, the alternatives were now "Victory or death."

Late in February Travis, who would gain only 32 troops as reinforcements, prepared yet another appeal, this time addressed to Sam Houston, commander-in-chief of the Texas army. Time was running out, Travis wrote. "If they overpower us," he explained, "we hope posterity and our country will do our memory justice. Give me help, oh my country!" Travis handed the message to Juan Seguin, who borrowed Jim Bowie's horse and rode off with his aide, Antonio Cruz, under the

cover of a driving rainstorm. They eventually found Houston, far to the east, but there was nothing anyone could do now to save those defenders still with Travis.

Early on the morning of March 6, 1836, the Alamo fell to 1800 attacking Mexican soldiers. The fighting was so brutal that 600 of Santa Anna's troops lay dead or wounded before the last of the 183 defenders faced mutilation from countless musket balls, bayonet thrusts, or summary executions after the battle. Gregorio Esparza was torn to shreds as the Mexicans reached the church inside the courtyard. Only women, children, Colonel Travis's slave Joe, and one Tejano, who claimed that he was a prisoner, survived. Later that day Mrs. Esparza got permission to bury her husband with Christian rites. Santa Anna issued orders to have the bodies of all other defenders heaped into piles and set on fire.

During the next several weeks Santa Anna's troops pushed steadily eastward with the goal of destroying another Texas army being hastily assembled by Sam Houston. The Seguins, father and son, played key parts in providing resistance. Don Erasmo worked furiously to collect needed food supplies, and Juan led troops in harassing and delaying the Mexican column, all of which aided in the staging of Houston's stunning victory over Santa Anna at the Battle of San Jacinto on April 21, 1836—the day the Republic of Texas secured its independence.

As the Texas Revolution gained momentum in late 1835 and early 1836, Tejanos had to choose which side to support. Some hoped that uniting with the Americans would

Worse yet, according to the Americans, they behaved at times like depraved, violent, less-than-human creatures as personified by Santa Anna at the Alamo and by Mexican troops later at Goliad, where nearly 400 captured rebels were systematically shot to death. Wrote one American veteran of the Texas Revolution late in life: "I thought that I could kill Mexicans as easily as I could deer and turkeys." He apparently did so while shouting: "Remember the Alamo! Remember Goliad!"

This veteran, like so many others looking back at the days of the Texas Revolution, only recalled selected portions of the Alamo story. They talked of the bravery of Bowie, Crockett, and Travis but ignored the courage of Tejanos like Don Erasmo and Juan Seguin and Gregorio Esparza. Nor did they remember that Juan Seguin received an honorable military discharge before serving as mayor of San Antonio until 1842, when Anglo rumormongers accused him of supporting an attempted military invasion from Mexico. To save himself, Seguin had to flee across the border. Eventually he returned to his native Texas and quietly lived out his days far removed from the public limelight. No doubt Seguin wondered whether he had made the right decision in not joining the side of Santa Anna, especially as he experienced the racial and cultural malice directed at Mexican Americans as the United States surged forward toward the Pacific. Although his thoughts are not known, it is fortunate that his story and those of other Tejano resisters have not been forgotten. Surely they too deserve remembrance as heroes of the Alamo and the Texas Revolution.

force Santa Anna to renounce his dictatorship in favor of the liberal 1824 constitution. Few Tejanos actually favored independence because they knew that Americans held them in contempt. This caused men like Gregorio Esparza's brother to join Santa Anna's army and fight against the Alamo defenders. He suspected that heavy-handed rule under the Mexican dictator could not be worse and might well be better than living under culturally and racially intolerant Americans.

From the very outset, Americans entering Texas spoke of Tejanos and Mexicans as debased human beings, comparable in many ways to Native American "savages" blocking the westward movement of white European civilization. In 1831 colonizer Stephen F. Austin wrote: "My object, the sole and only desire of my ambitions since I first saw Texas, was to . . . settle it with an intelligent, honorable, and enterprising people." Four years later Austin still wanted to see Texas "Americanized, that is, settled by a population that will harmonize with their neighbors on the East, in language, political principles, common origin, sympathy, and even interest." The success of the Texas Revolution, from Austin's point of view, would ensure that Americans pouring into the region would not be ruled by what they considered an inferior native populace.

Increasingly, before and after 1836, American migrants employed terms of racial and cultural derision to describe the native Tejanos. They were the most "lazy, indolent, poor, starved set of people as ever the sun shined upon"; they were "slaves of popish superstitions and despotism"; and they would "spend days in gambling to gain a few bits" rather than "make a living by honest industry." With their mixture of blood from Spanish, Native American, and African parents, the native populace represented a "mongrel" race, a "swarthy looking people much resembling . . . mulattoes."

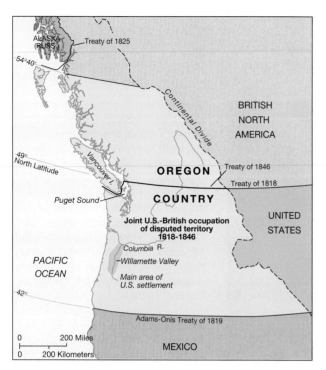

Oregon Country, Pacific Northwest Boundary Dispute

The United States and Great Britain nearly came to blows over the disputed boundary in Oregon.

But U.S. politicians, merchants, and fur traders were unsuccessful in promoting American settlement of Oregon. In the end, it was neither commerce nor politics, but religion that led to American settlement of the region.

The first missionaries arrived in Oregon in 1834. The most famous were Marcus Whitman, a young doctor, and his wife Narcissa Prentiss Whitman, who were sent west in 1836 by the Methodists. The couple founded a mission near present-day Walla Walla, Washington, and persisted in their efforts to convert Native Americans to Christianity until 1847, when a severe epidemic of measles broke out in the area. Many Native Americans blamed the epidemic on white missionaries, and the Whitmans and 12 others were murdered.

Before his death, Marcus Whitman made an epic 3000-mile journey to Boston, during which he publicized the attractions of the Pacific Northwest and the need to offset British influence in the region. On his return trip to Oregon in 1843, Whitman guided nearly 900 immigrants along the Oregon Trail. By the mid-1840s, 6000 Americans had moved to Oregon.

The rapid influx of land-hungry Americans into Oregon in the mid-1840s forced Britain and the United States to decide the status of Oregon. In the presidential election of 1844, the Democratic party demanded the "re-occupation" of Oregon and the annexation of the entire Pacific Northwest coast up to the edge of Russian-held Alaska, which was fixed at 54°40'. This demand helped James K. Polk win the presidency in 1844.

In truth, Polk had little desire to go to war with Britain. As an ardent proslavery Southerner, he did not want to add new free states to the Union. Furthermore, he believed that the northernmost portions of the Oregon country were unsuitable for agriculture. Therefore, in 1846—despite the expansionist slogan "54°40' or fight!"—he readily accepted a British compromise to extend the existing United States–Canadian boundary along the 49th parallel from the Rocky Mountains to the Pacific Ocean.

The Mormon Frontier

Pioneers migrated to the West for a variety of reasons. Some moved west in the hope of economic and social betterment, others out of a restless curiosity and an urge for adventure. The Mormons migrated for an entirely different reason—to escape religious persecution.

The **Mormon church** had its beginnings in upstate New York, which was a hotbed of religious fervor. Methodist, Baptist, Presbyterian, and Universalist preachers all eagerly sought converts. Fourteen-year-old **Joseph Smith, Jr.,** the son of a farmer, listened closely to these preachers but was uncertain which way to turn.

In the spring of 1820, Smith went into the woods near Palmyra, New York, to seek divine guidance. According to his account, a brilliant light revealed "two personages," who announced that they were God the Father and Christ the Savior. They told him that all existing churches were false and that the true church of God was about to be reestablished on earth.

In 1823, Smith had another revelation that told him of the existence of buried golden plates that contained a lost section from the Bible describing a tribe of Israelites that had lived in America. Smith wrote that he unearthed the golden plates and four years later translated them into English. The messages on the plates were later published as the *Book of Mormon*.

By the 1830s Smith attracted several thousand followers from rural areas of the North and the frontier Midwest. The converts were usually small farmers, mechanics, and traders who had been displaced by the growing commercial economy and who were repelled by the rising tide of liberal religion and individualism in early nineteenth-century America.

Because Smith said that he conversed with angels and received direct revelations from God, local authorities threatened to indict him for blasphemy. He and his followers responded by moving to Ohio,

Saints [Mormons] *Driven from Jackson County, Missouri,* by C. C. A. Christensen. Mormon settlements in Missouri were repeatedly attacked and destroyed by mobs between 1832 and 1839, when the Mormons moved to Illinois.

where they built their first temple and experimented with an economy planned and controlled by the church. From Ohio, the Mormons moved to Missouri. There, proslavery mobs attacked the Mormons, accusing them of inciting slave insurrections. Fifteen thousand Mormons fled Missouri after the governor proclaimed them enemies who "had to be exterminated, or driven from the state."

In 1839, the Mormons resettled along the east bank of the Mississippi River in Nauvoo, Illinois, which soon grew into the second largest city in the state. Both Illinois Whigs and Democrats eagerly sought support among the Mormons, who usually voted as a bloc. In exchange for their votes, the state legislature awarded Nauvoo a special charter that made the town an autonomous city-state, complete with its own 2000-man militia.

But trouble arose again. A dissident group within the church published a newspaper denouncing the practice of polygamy and attacking Joseph Smith for trying to become "king or lawgiver to the church." On Smith's orders, city officials destroyed the dissidents' printing press. Under the protection of the Illinois governor, Smith and his brother were then confined to a jail cell in Carthage, Illinois. Late in the afternoon of June 27, 1844, a mob broke into Smith's cell, shot him and his brother, and threw their bodies out of a second-story window.

Why did the Mormons seem so menacing? Anti-Mormonism was rooted in a struggle for economic and political power. Individualistic frontier settlers felt threatened by Mormon communalism. By voting as their elders told them to and controlling land as a bloc, Mormons seemed to have an unfair advantage in the struggle for wealth and power.

Mormonism was also denounced as a threat to fundamental social values. Protestant ministers railed against it as a threat to Christianity because Mormons rejected the legitimacy of the established churches and insisted that the *Book of Mormon* was sacred Scripture, equal in importance to the Bible. The Mormons were also accused of corrupt moral values. Before the church changed its rules in 1890, some Mormons practiced polygyny, which they saw as an effort to reestablish the patriarchal Old Testament family. Polygyny also served an important social function by absorbing single or widowed women into Mormon communities. Contrary to popular belief, it was not widely practiced. Altogether, only 10 to 20 percent of Mormon families were polygamous and nearly two-thirds involved a man and two wives.

After Joseph Smith's murder, the Mormons decided to migrate across a thousand miles of unsettled prairie and desert in search of a new refuge outside the boundaries of the United States. In 1846 a new leader, **Brigham Young,** led the Mormons to the Great Salt Lake. As governor of the Mormon state of Deseret and later as governor of Utah, Young oversaw the building of Salt Lake City and 186 other Mormon communities, developed church-owned businesses, and established cooperative irrigation projects.

Early nineteenth-century American society attached enormous importance to individualism, secularism, monogamous marriage, and private property, and the Mormons were believed to threaten each of these values. But in a larger sense the Mormons' aspirations were truly American. They sought nothing less than the establishment of the Kingdom of God on earth—a dream that was, of course, not new in this country. In seeking to build God's kingdom the

Mormons were carrying on a quest that had been begun by their Puritan ancestors two centuries before.

WAR WITH MEXICO

When Brigham Young led the Mormons west, he was seeking a homeland outside the boundaries of the United States. But even before he arrived at the Great Salt Lake during the summer of 1847, Utah, as well as California, Nevada, and parts of Arizona, Colorado, New Mexico, and Wyoming, became part of the United States as a result of a war with Mexico.

Why War?

Fifteen years before the United States plunged into civil war, it fought a war against Mexico that added a half million square miles of territory to the United States. Not only was it the first American war fought almost entirely outside the United States, it was also the first American war to be reported by daily newspapers as it was occurring. It was also a controversial war that bitterly divided American public opinion. Finally, it was the war that gave young military officers such as Ulysses S. Grant, Robert E. Lee, Thomas ("Stonewall") Jackson, William Tecumseh Sherman, and George McClellan their first experience in a major conflict.

The Mexican-American War was the nation's first war to be reported in newspapers as it was happening.

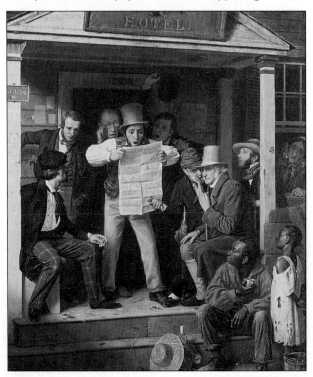

The underlying cause of the **Mexican-American War** was the inexorable movement of American pioneers into the Far West. As Americans marched westward, they moved into land claimed by Mexico, and inevitably Mexican and American interests clashed.

The immediate reason for the conflict was the annexation of Texas in 1845. Despite its defeat at San Jacinto in 1836, Mexico refused to recognize Texan independence and warned the United States that annexation would be tantamount to a declaration of war. In early 1845, when Congress voted to annex Texas, Mexico cut diplomatic relations, but took no further action.

Polk told his commanders to prepare for the possibility of war. He ordered American naval vessels in the Gulf of Mexico to position themselves outside Mexican ports. Secretly, he warned the Pacific fleet to prepare to seize ports along the California coast in the event of war. Anticipating a possible Mexican invasion of Texas, he dispatched American forces in Louisiana to Corpus Christi.

Peaceful settlement of the two countries' differences still seemed possible. In the fall of 1845, the president sent an envoy, John Slidell, to Mexico with a proposal to settle the disputes peacefully. The most significant controversies concerned Texas's boundary and the Mexican government's failure to compensate American citizens for losses during Mexico's years of political turmoil. Slidell was authorized to cancel the damage claims and pay $5 million in reparations if the Mexicans agreed to recognize the Rio Grande as the southwestern boundary of Texas (earlier the Spanish government had defined the Texas boundary as the Nueces River, 130 miles to the north of the Rio Grande). No Americans lived between the Nueces and the Rio Grande, although many Mexicans lived in the region.

Polk not only wanted to settle the boundary and claims disputes, he also wanted to acquire Mexico's two northwestern provinces, California and New Mexico. He directed Slidell to offer up to $5 million for the province of New Mexico—which included Nevada and Utah and parts of four other states—and up to $25 million for California.

Polk was anxious to acquire California because in mid-October 1845 he had been led to believe that Britain was on the verge of making California a protectorate. It was widely believed that Mexico had agreed to cede California to Britain as payment for outstanding debts. Immediate preventive action seemed necessary. Polk, therefore, instructed his consul in Monterey to encourage Californians to agitate for annexation by the United States. He also dispatched a young Marine Corps lieutenant, Archibald H. Gillespie, to California, apparently to foment revolt against Mexican authority.

TABLE 13.1	
Road to War: Mexican-American War	
1821	Spain allows Moses Austin to settle 300 American families in Texas; Mexico gains its independence from Spain.
1827	Mexico establishes a chain of military posts in Texas and decrees an end to further American immigration.
1834	General Santa Anna declares Mexico a dictatorship.
1836	American settlers are defeated in the siege of the Alamo; Americans win the battle of San Jacinto; Texas gains independence.
1845	Congress annexes Texas; Mexico cuts diplomatic ties with the United States.
1846	Mexican cavalry crosses the Rio Grande; United States declares war.

The Mexican government, already incensed over the annexation of Texas, refused to negotiate. The Mexican president, José Herrera, refused to receive Slidell and ordered his leading commander, General Mariano Paredes y Arrillaga, to assemble an army and reconquer Texas. Paredes proceeded to topple Herrera's government and declared himself president, but he also refused to receive Slidell.

The failure of Slidell's mission led Polk to order Brigadier General Zachary Taylor to march 3000 troops from Corpus Christi, Texas, to "defend the Rio Grande." Late in March 1846 Taylor and his men set up camp along the Rio Grande, directly across from the Mexican city of Matamoros, on a stretch of land claimed by both Mexico and the United States.

On April 25, a Mexican cavalry force crossed the Rio Grande and clashed with a small American squadron, forcing the Americans to surrender after the loss of several lives. Polk used this episode as an excuse to declare war.

Hours before he received word of the skirmish on May 9, Polk and his cabinet had already decided to press for war with Mexico. On May 11, Polk asked Congress to acknowledge that a state of war already existed. "Mexico," the president announced, "has passed the boundary of the United States, has invaded our territory, and shed American blood upon the American soil." Congress responded with a declaration of war.

The Mexican-American War was extremely controversial. Its supporters blamed Mexico for the hostilities because it had severed relations with the United States, threatened war, refused to receive an American emissary, and refused to pay the damage claims of American citizens. Opposition leaders denounced the war as an immoral land grab by an expansionist power against a weak neighbor that had been independent barely two decades. The war's critics claimed that Polk deliberately provoked Mexico into war by ordering American troops into disputed territory. A Delaware senator declared that ordering Taylor to the Rio Grande was "as much an act of aggression on our part as is a man's pointing a pistol at another's breast."

Critics argued that the war was an expansionist power play dictated by an aggressive southern slavocracy intent on acquiring more land for cotton cultivation and more slave states to better balance the northern free states in the U.S. Senate. "Bigger pens to cram with slaves" was the way poet James Russell Lowell put it. Others blamed the war on expansion-minded Westerners who were hungry for land, and on eastern trading interests, which dreamed of establishing "an American Boston or New York" in San Francisco to increase trade with Asia. Mexicans denounced the war as a brazen attempt by the United States to seize Mexican territory.

The War

American strategy was based on a three-pronged attack. Colonel Stephen Kearny had the task of securing New Mexico, naval forces under Commodore John D. Sloat blockaded the California coast, and General Zachary Taylor invaded Mexico.

Kearny easily accomplished his mission. In less than two months he marched his 1700-man army more than a thousand miles. On August 16, 1846, he occupied Santa Fe and declared New Mexico's inhabitants American citizens. In California, American settlers in the Sacramento Valley, fearful that Mexican authorities were about to expel them, revolted even before reliable reports of the outbreak of war reached the area. The so-called Bear Flag Revolt soon came to an end, and by January 1847 U.S. naval forces under Commodore Robert F. Stockton and an expeditionary force under Captain John C. Frémont had brought the region under American control. Meanwhile, the main U.S. army under Taylor's command had taken Matamoros, and by late September captured Monterrey, Mexico's largest northern city.

Following hard-fought battles at Chapultepec Castle and other locations in the Valley of Mexico, General Winfield Scott's forces occupied Mexico City. U. S. infantry and calvary units stood at attention as their commander entered the historic plaza at the center of the city, the *Zocalo*.

Although the American invasion of Mexico's northernmost provinces was completely successful, the Mexican government did not surrender. In June 1846 Colonel A. W. Doniphan led 856 Missouri cavalry volunteers 3000 miles across mountains and desert into the northern Mexican province of Chihuahua. He occupied El Paso and then captured the capital city of Chihuahua. Further south, 6000 volunteers under the command of Zachary Taylor held their ground against a Mexican force of 15,000 at the battle of Buena Vista on February 22 and 23, 1847.

Despite an impressive string of American victories, Mexico still refused to negotiate. Switching strategy, Polk ordered General Winfield Scott to invade central Mexico from the sea, march inland, and capture Mexico City. On March 9, 1847, the Mexicans allowed an American force of 10,000 men to land unopposed at Veracruz on the Gulf of Mexico. Scott's army then began to march on the Mexican capital. On April 18, at a mountain pass near Jalapa, a 9000-man American force met 13,000 Mexican troops and in bitter hand-to-hand fighting forced the Mexicans to flee. As Scott's army pushed on toward Mexico City, it stormed a Mexican fortress at Contreras and then routed a large Mexican force at Churubusco on August 19 and 20.

For two weeks, Scott observed an armistice to allow the Mexicans to consider peace proposals. When the negotiations failed, Scott's 6000 remaining men attacked El Molino del Rey and stormed Chapultepec, a fortified castle guarding Mexico City's gates.

Despite the capture of their capital, the Mexicans refused to surrender. Hostile crowds staged demonstrations in the streets, and snipers fired shots and hurled stones and broken bottles from the tops of flat-roofed Mexican houses. To quell the protests, General Scott ordered the streets "swept with grape and canister" and artillery "turned upon the houses whence the fire proceeded." Outside the capital, belligerent civilians attacked army supply wagons and guerrilla fighters harassed American troops.

War Fever and Antiwar Protests

During the first few weeks following the declaration of war, a frenzy of prowar hysteria swept the country. Two hundred thousand men responded to a call for 50,000 volunteers. Novelist Herman Melville observed, "a military ardor pervades all ranks. . . . Nothing is talked about but the halls of the Montezumas." In New York, placards bore the slogan "Mexico or Death." Many newspapers, especially in the North declared that the war would benefit the Mexican people by bringing them the blessings of democracy and liberty. The *Boston Times* said that an American victory "must necessarily be a great blessing" because it would introduce "the reign of law where license has existed for a generation."

In Philadelphia, 20,000 turned out for a prowar rally, and in Cincinnati, 12,000 celebrated Zachary Taylor's victories with cannon salutes, parades, and speeches. In Tennessee, 30,000 men volunteered for 3000 positions as soldiers, prompting one applicant to complain that it was "difficult even to purchase a place in the ranks." The war was particularly popular in the West. Of the 69,540 men who were accepted for service, more than 40,000 were from the western states.

From the war's very beginning, however, a small but highly visible group of intellectuals, clergy, pacifists, abolitionists, and some Whig and Democratic politicians denounced the war as brutal aggression against a "poor, feeble, distracted country." Abolitionist William Lloyd Garrison's militant newspaper, the *Liberator*, expressed open support for the Mexican people: "Every lover of Freedom and humanity throughout the world must wish them the most triumphant success."

Most Whigs supported the war—in part because two of the leading American generals, Zachary Taylor and Winfield Scott, were Whigs, and in part because they remembered that opposition to the War of 1812 had destroyed the Federalist Party. Many prominent

Whigs, from the South as well as the North, however, openly expressed opposition. Thomas Corwin of Ohio denounced the war as merely the latest example of American injustice to Mexico. Daniel Webster, a frequent Whig presidential candidate, mockingly described the conflict as a "war of pretexts"—the pretext that Mexico had refused to receive an American emissary, had refused to pay American financial claims, and had invaded American territory.

A freshman Whig congressman from Illinois named Abraham Lincoln lashed out against the war, calling it immoral, proslavery, and a threat to the nation's republican values. One of Lincoln's constituents branded him "the Benedict Arnold of our district," and his own party denied him renomination.

As newspapers informed their readers about the hardships and savagery of life on the front, public enthusiasm for the war began to wane. The war did not turn out to be the romantic exploit that Americans envisioned. Troops complained that their food was "green with slime"; their meat, they said, would stick "if thrown against a smooth plank." Diarrhea, amoebic dysentery, measles, and yellow fever ravaged American soldiers. Seven times as many Americans died of disease and exposure as died of battlefield injuries. Of the 90,000 Americans who served in the war, only 1721 died in action. Another 11,155 died from diseases and exposure to the elements.

Public support for the war was further eroded by reports of brutality against Mexican civilians. After one of their members was murdered, the Arkansas volunteer cavalry surrounded a group of Mexican peasants and began an "indiscriminate and bloody massacre of the poor creatures." A young lieutenant named George G. Meade reported that volunteers in Matamoros robbed the citizens, stole their cattle, and killed innocent civilians "for no other object than their own amusement." If only a tenth of the horror stories were true, General Winfield Scott wrote, it was enough "to make Heaven weep, & every American of Christian morals blush for his country."

During wartime the party in power has often lost support. The Mexican-American War was no exception. In the congressional election of 1846, which took place half a year after the outbreak of war, the Democrats lost control of the House of Representatives to the Whigs.

Peace

Difficult negotiations followed the war. After American troops entered Mexico City, Mexican president Santa Anna resigned and the Mexican Congress retreated to a provincial capital to try to reorganize. More than two months passed before a new civilian government was able to gain control over the country and name a peace negotiator.

As Americans waited impatiently for a final peace settlement, they grew increasingly divided over their war aims. Ultraexpansionists, who drew support from such cities as Baltimore, New York, and Philadelphia as well as from the West, wanted the United States to annex all of Mexico. Many Southerners, led by John C. Calhoun, called for withdrawal to the Rio Grande. They opposed annexation of any territory below the Rio Grande because they did not want to extend American citizenship to Mexicans. Most Democratic Party leaders wanted to annex at least the one-third of Mexico south and west of the Rio Grande.

Then suddenly on February 22, 1848, word reached Washington that a peace treaty had been signed. On February 2, 1848, Nicholas Trist, a Spanish-speaking State Department official, signed the **Treaty of Guadalupe Hidalgo,** ending the Mexican-American War. Trist had actually been ordered home two months earlier by Polk, but he had continued negotiating anyway, fearing that his recall would be "deadly to the cause of peace."

According to the treaty, Mexico ceded to the United States only those areas that Polk had originally sought to purchase. Mexico ceded California, Nevada, New Mexico, Utah, and parts of Arizona, Colorado, Kansas, and Wyoming to the United States for $15 million and the assumption of $3.25 million in debts owed to Americans by Mexico. The treaty also settled the Texas border dispute in favor of the United States, placing the Texas-Mexico boundary at the Rio Grande.

Ultraexpansionists called on Polk to throw out the treaty, but a war-weary public wanted peace. Polk quickly submitted the treaty to the Senate, which ratified it overwhelmingly. The war was over.

The Fate of Mexican Americans

The 80,000 Mexicans who lived in the Southwest did not respond to the Mexican-American War with a single voice. Some welcomed the Americans; many others, recognizing the futility of resistance, responded to the American conquest with ambivalence. A number openly resisted the American military advance. For example, in 1847, disaffected Mexicans and Pueblo Indians in Taos, New Mexico, staged an unsuccessful revolt, in which they killed the American-imposed governor. One observer described the dominant view: "The native sons have hope that the Americans will tire of a long and stubborn war and that in some time they will be left to live in their land in peace and tranquility."

Although American officials promised to protect Mexican property and religious rights and the Treaty of Guadalupe Hidalgo explicitly guaranteed Mexi-

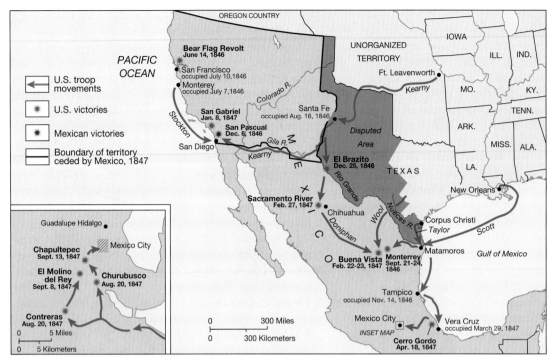

Mexican-American War

The terms of the Treaty of Guadalupe Hidalgo, which ended the Mexican-American War, increased the size of the United States by one-third.

cans "all the rights of citizens," they quickly found themselves reduced to second-class citizenship.

In Texas—where memories of the Alamo fueled anti-Mexican sentiment—Mexicans found themselves increasingly outnumbered and outvoted. By 1850 Anglos outnumbered Mexican Americans in Texas 20 to 1. While delegates to Texas's constitutional convention rejected a motion to restrict voting to "white persons," violent intimidation kept Mexican Americans from the polls. In south Texas, large landowners and political bosses used their economic power to manipulate the votes of Mexican American cowboys and laborers.

In California, too, Mexican Americans were outnumbered and vulnerable to discrimination. During the early years of the Gold Rush, Mexican Americans were robbed, beaten, and lynched with impunity. The 1850 Foreign Miners' Tax imposed a $20 a month tax on Mexican American miners, even though the Treaty of Guadalupe Hidalgo had granted them citizenship. In 1855 the state legislature outlawed bullfights, refused to provide for translation of laws into Spanish (as required by the state constitution), and adopted an antivagrancy act aimed at Mexican American laborers.

Only in New Mexico—where Mexican Americans made up a majority of the population—did Mexican Americans play an important political role. With sizable representation in territorial and local government, Spanish-speaking New Mexicans were able to prevent discriminatory legislation. The New

Mexico Constitution, for example, prohibited school segregation, reaffirmed the rights conferred in the Treaty of Guadalupe Hidalgo, and made Spanish and English equal languages of government. At that time, New Mexico included much of Arizona and Colorado. Anglo New Mexicans convinced Congress to create a separate Colorado Territory in 1861 and a separate Arizona Territory in 1862 partly to gain political control of those areas.

Across the Southwest, Mexican Americans lost land, despite provisions in the Treaty of Guadalupe Hidalgo that guaranteed Spanish and Mexican land grants and Mexican American property rights. In California, many Mexicans were forced to sell land to pay onerous taxes that fell heaviest on the Spanish speakers. In Texas, speculators purchased many Mexican land grants, and squatters simply seized abandoned land. In Arizona and New Mexico, where it took years of expensive litigation to confirm land titles, many Mexicans sold land to pay legal bills. In New Mexico, litigation over land claims was still dragging on in the 1970s.

Loss of land had important implications for the future. Increasingly, Mexican American men were forced to support themselves as migratory unskilled laborers in mines, on farms, and on railroads, and women found employment as domestic servants and farm laborers. Displaced from their land, Mexican Americans were forced to live in segregated neighborhoods and communities, known as *barrios* and *colonias*.

The War's Significance

The story of America's conflict with Mexico tends to be overshadowed by the story of the Civil War, which began only a decade and a half later. In fact, the conflict had far-reaching consequences. It increased the nation's size by a third, but it also created deep political divisions that threatened the nation's future.

The most significant result of the Mexican-American War was to reignite the question of slavery in the western territories—the very issue that had divided the country in 1819. Even before the war began, philosopher Ralph Waldo Emerson predicted that the United States would "conquer Mexico, but it will be as the man who swallows the arsenic which will bring him down in turn. Mexico will poison us." The war convinced a growing number of Northerners that southern slaveowners had precipitated the conflict to open new lands to slavery and acquire new slave states. And most significant of all, the war weakened the party system and made it increasingly difficult for congressional leaders to prevent the issue of slavery from dominating congressional activity.

Political Crisis of the 1840s

Before the Mexican-American War, the major political issues that divided Americans were questions of tariffs, banking, internal improvements, and land. Political positions on these issues largely divided along party lines. After the outbreak of war with Mexico a new issue began to dominate American politics—the extension of slavery in the western territories. Public opinion began to polarize and party cohesion began to break down as party factional and sectional divisions grew more important than traditional party coalitions.

The question of slavery burst into the public spotlight one summer evening in 1846. Congressman David Wilmot, a Pennsylvania Democrat, introduced an amendment, known as the **Wilmot Proviso,** to a war appropriations bill. The proviso forbade slavery in any territory acquired from Mexico. Throughout the North, thousands of working men and women and farmers feared that free workers would be unable to compete successfully against slave labor. "If slavery is not excluded by law," said one northern congressman, "the presence of the slave will exclude the laboring white man."

Southerners denounced the Wilmot Proviso as "treason to the Constitution." Polk tried to quiet the debate between "southern agitators and northern fanatics" by assuring moderate Northerners that slavery could never take root in the arid Southwest, but his efforts were to no avail. With the strong support of Westerners, the amendment passed the House twice, but was defeated in the Senate. Although the Wilmot Proviso did not become law, the issue it raised—the

Territorial Growth to 1853

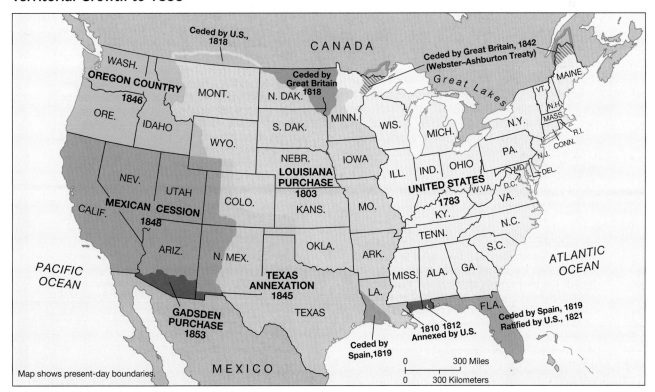

extension of slavery into the western territories—contributed to the growth of political factionalism.

Growing sectional tensions were also evident in the founding of the Free Soil party in 1848. This sectional party opposed the westward expansion of slavery and favored free land for western homesteaders. Under the slogan "free soil, free speech, free labor, and free men," the party nominated Martin Van Buren as its presidential nominee in 1848 and polled 291,000 votes. This was enough to split the Democratic vote and throw the election to Whig candidate Zachary Taylor.

Up until the last month of 1848, the debate over slavery in the Mexican cession seemed academic. Most Americans thought of the newly acquired territory as a wasteland filled with "broken mountains and dreary desert." Then, in a farewell address, Polk electrified Congress with news that gold had been discovered in California—and suddenly the question of slavery was of inescapable importance.

The Gold Rush

On January 24, 1848, less than 10 days after the signing of the peace treaty ending the Mexican-American War, James W. Marshall, a 36-year-old carpenter and handyman, noticed several bright bits of yellow mineral. Marshall was building a sawmill in California's Sacramento Valley for John A. Sutter, a Swiss-born rancher. To test if the bits were fool's gold, which shatters when struck by a hammer, or real gold, which is malleable, Marshall "tried it between two rocks, and found that it could be beaten into a different shape but not broken. He told the men working with him: "Boys, by God, I believe I have found a gold mine."

On March 15, 1849, a San Francisco newspaper, the *Californian*, printed the first account of Marshall's discovery. Within two weeks the paper had lost its staff and was forced to shut down its printing press. In its last edition, it told its readers: "The whole

THE PEOPLE SPEAK

A San Francisco Merchant Protests Discrimination Against the Chinese

The Gold Rush brought tens of thousands of people from around the world, including China, to California. In 1849, there were only 54 Chinese immigrants in California, but by 1876, the number had increased to 116,000. Although emigrants from China made up only a small proportion of California's immigrants, they faced intense prejudice and discrimination. In 1852, California Governor John Bigler proposed restricting immigration from China. In the following public letter, Norman Assing, a prominent San Francisco merchant, restaurant owner, and community leader, denounces the governor's proposal.

To His Excellence Gov. Bigler

Sir:—I am a Chinaman, a republican, and a lover of free institutions; am much attached to the principles of the Government and the United States; and therefore take the liberty of addressing you as the chief of the government of the state. Your official position gives you a great opportunity of good or evil. . . . The effect of your late message has been . . . to prejudice the public mind against my people, to enable those with the opportunity to hunt them down, and rob them of the rewards of their toil. . . .

You are deeply convinced you say "that to enhance the prosperity and to preserve the tranquility of this state, Asiatic immigration must be checked". . . . You argue that this is a republic of a particular race—that the constitution of the United States admits of no asylum to any other than the pale face. This proposition is false in the extreme; and you know it. The declaration of your independence, and all the acts of your government, your people, and your history, are against you. . . .

We would beg to remind you that when your nation was a wilderness, and the nation from who you sprung *barbarous*, we exercised most of the arts and virtues of civilized life; that we are possessed of a language and literature, and that men skilled in science and the arts are numerous amongst us; that the producers of our manufactories, our sail and work-shops, form no small share of the commerce of the world; and that for centuries colleges, schools, charitable institutions, asylums and hospitals, have been as common as in your own land. . . . We came amongst you as mechanics or traders, and following every honorable business of life. You do not find us as pursuing occupations of a degrading character, except you consider labor degrading, which I am sure you do not. . . . As far as the aristocracy of *skin* is concerned, ours might compare with many of the European races; nor do we . . . believe that the framers of your declaration of rights ever suggested the propriety of establishing an aristocracy of *skin*.

Source: Daily Alta California (May 5, 1852).

country, from San Francisco to Los Angeles . . . resounds with the sordid cry of Gold! Gold! Gold! while the field is left half-planted, the house half-built, and everything neglected but the manufacture of picks and shovels."

In 1849, 80,000 men arrived in California—half by land and half by ship, around the tip of South America or across the Isthmus of Panama. Only half were Americans; the rest came from Europe, Latin America, and China. Soldiers deserted; sailors jumped ship; husbands abandoned wives; apprentices ran away from their masters; farmers and businesspeople deserted their livelihoods. Within a year, California's population had swollen from 14,000 to 100,000.

The **gold rush** transformed California from a quiet society into one that was wild, unruly, ethnically diverse, and violent. In San Francisco alone there were more than 500 bars and 1000 gambling dens. There were a thousand murders in San Francisco during the early 1850s, but only one conviction. "Forty-niners" slaughtered Native Americans for sport, drove Mexicans from the mines on penalty of death, and sought to restrict the immigration of foreigners, especially the Chinese. Since the military government was incapable of keeping order, leading merchants formed vigilance committees, which attempted to rule by lynch law and the establishment of "popular" courts.

California's gold rush era lasted less than a decade. By the mid-1850s, the lone miner who prospected for gold with a pick, a shovel, and a washpan was already an anachronism. Mining companies using heavy machinery replaced the individual miner.

CHRONOLOGY OF KEY EVENTS

1803 Louisiana Purchase

1804 Lewis and Clark Expedition sets out from St. Louis to explore the northern region of Louisiana Purchase territory

1810 Mexican War for Independence against Spanish rule begins; John Jacob Astor attempts to plant a trading post in Oregon

1811–1812 Fur trappers mark out the Oregon Trail

1818 United States and Britain agree to joint occupation of Oregon

1819 Spain cedes its claims to Oregon to the United States

1821 Mexico gains independence from Spain; first American traders traverse the Santa Fe Trail; Stephen Austin founds American colony in Texas

1822 The Rocky Mountain Fur Company begins to send trappers into the frontier

1830 Joseph Smith, Jr., founds Church of Christ, later renamed Church of Jesus Christ of Latter-Day Saints

1833–1834 Mexican government confiscates California missions

1834 Santa Anna overthrows Mexico's constitutional government and makes himself dictator; first American missionaries arrive in Oregon

1835 Scattered local outbursts erupt in Texas against Mexican rule

1836 Texas Revolution

1838 John Quincy Adams's filibuster defeats move to annex Texas

1841 First party of pioneers leaves Missouri for California; Congress recognizes squatters' rights in the Preemption Bill

1844 Joseph Smith, Jr., assassinated at Carthage, Illinois

1845 Texas is admitted as twenty-eighth state; Mexican government breaks off diplomatic relations with the United States

1846 The United States declares war on Mexico; Britain and the United States divide Oregon along 49th parallel; Donner party becomes trapped in Sierra Nevada; Brigham Young leads the Mormons to the Great Salt Lake Valley; Wilmot Proviso, barring slavery from any territory acquired from Mexico, is proposed.

1848 Gold is discovered at Sutter's Mill in California; Treaty of Guadalupe Hidalgo ends the Mexican War

1849 Gold rush brings 80,000 gold prospectors to California

Systems of dams exposed whole river bottoms. Drilling machines drove shafts 700 feet into the earth. Hydraulic mining machines blasted streams of water against mountainsides. The mythical era of California gold mining had already come to a close.

CONCLUSION

By 1860 the gold rush was over. Prospectors had found more than $350 million worth of gold. Certainly, some fortunes were made, but few struck it rich. Even James W. Marshall, who discovered the first gold bits, and John A. Sutter, on whose ranch the gold was first found, died penniless.

By 1850 the American flag flew over an area that stretched from sea to sea. In the span of just five years the United States had increased its size by a third and acquired an area that now includes the states of Arizona, California, Colorado, Idaho, Nevada, New Mexico, Oregon, Texas, Utah, Washington, and Wyoming.

The exploration and settlement of the Far West is one of the great epics of nineteenth-century history. But America's dramatic territorial expansion also created severe problems. In addition to providing the United States with its richest mines, greatest forests, and most fertile farmland, the Far West intensified the sectional conflict between the North and South and raised the fateful and ultimately divisive question of whether slavery should be permitted in the western territories. Could democratic political institutions resolve the question of slavery in the western territories? That question would dominate American politics in the 1850s.

CHAPTER SUMMARY AND KEY POINTS

By 1850, the United States had acquired vast new territory in the West. In this chapter you read about the Native Americans and Mexicans who lived in the trans-Mississippi West. You learned about the exploration of the Far West and the forces that drove traders, missionaries, and pioneers westward. Finally, you read about the way that United States acquired Texas, the Great Southwest, and the Pacific Northwest by annexation, negotiation, and war.

- Until 1821, Spain ruled the area that now includes Arizona, California, Colorado, Nevada, New Mexico, Texas, and Utah. The Mexican war for independence opened the region to American economic penetration.

- Government explorers, traders, and trappers helped to open the West to white settlement. In

the 1820s thousands of Americans moved into Texas, and during the 1840s thousands of pioneers headed westward toward Oregon and California, seeking land and inspired by manifest destiny, the idea that America had a special destiny to stretch across the continent.

- Between 1844 and 1848 the United States expanded its boundaries into Texas, the Southwest, and the Pacific Northwest.

- It acquired Texas by annexation; Oregon and Washington by negotiation with Britain; and Arizona, California, Colorado, Idaho, Nevada, New Mexico, Oregon, Utah, and Wyoming as a result of war with Mexico.

SUGGESTIONS FOR FURTHER READING

H. W. Brands, *The Age of Gold: The California Gold Rush and the New American Dream* (2002). A history of the men and women who went west to seek their fortune.

John Mack Faragher, *Women and Men on the Overland Trail* (2nd edition, 2001). Examines the dynamics of the westward movement, dispelling many myths about female and male roles.

Patricia Nelson Limerick, *The Legacy of Conquest: The Unbroken Past of the American West* (1987). Reinterprets the history of the West as a region where diverse peoples struggled for control of land, resources, and cultural dominance.

Patricia Nelson Limerick, *Something in the Soil: Legacies and Reckonings in the New West* (2000). An examination of the history and environments of the American West.

Clyde Milner, II, Anne M. Butler, and David R. Lewis, *Major Problems in the History of the American West* (2nd edition, 1997). Primary and secondary sources documenting the history of the American West.

Richard White, *"It's Your Misfortune and None of My Own": A New History of the American West* (1991). Offers a comprehensive history of the American West incorporating the most recent historical scholarship.

Novels

Willa Cather, *Death Comes for the Archbishop* (1927).

A.B. Guthrie, *The Big Sky* (1947).

Laura Ingalls Wilder, *Little House on the Prairie* Series (1932–1943).

MEDIA RESOURCES

Web Sites

Documents from the Gilder Lehrman Collection
http://www.gliah.uh.edu/modules/westward/documents.cfm

Primary sources that document America's westward expansion.

History of the West
http://memory.loc.gov/ammem/award97/codhtml/hawphome.html
Over 30,000 photographs, drawn from the holdings of the Western History and Genealogy Department at Denver Public Library, illuminate many aspects of the history of the American West. Most of the photographs were taken between 1860 and 1920.

Lewis and Clark
http://www.pbs.org/lewisandclark/
The companion site to the PBS series contains a time line, journals from the expedition, historians' reflections on the expedition, information on the Indian peoples that the expedition encountered, and lesson plans and activities.

New Perspectives on the West
http://www3.pbs.org/weta/thewest/
Companion site to the public television documentary, *The West*. This site includes an interactive time line tracing events from pre-Columbian times to the early twentieth century; an interactive map covering the territory and the times; an interactive biographical dictionary of historical figures; and documentary materials including memoirs, journals, letters, photos, and transcripts.

Pioneering the Upper Midwest: Books from Michigan, Minnesota, and Wisconsin, ca. 1820–1910
http://memory.loc.gov/ammem/umhtml/umhome.html
This Library of Congress site looks at first-person accounts, biographies, promotional literature, local histories, ethnographic and antiquarian texts, colonial archival documents, and other works from the seventeenth to the early twentieth century. It covers many topics and issues that affected Americans in the settlement and development of the upper Midwest.

Films and Videos

The Alamo (1960). John Wayne plays David Crockett in this highly romanticized recreation of the battle of the Alamo.

Jeremiah Johnson (1972). Set around 1850, this film depicts an ex-soldier who would rather live alone as a mountain man in Colorado than deal with society's constraints.

Last Command (1955). This version of the battle of the Alamo focuses on the life of Jim Bowie.

Oregon Trail (1939). A collection of 15 serials detailing the tribulations of a wagon train headed for Oregon.

The West (1996). An eight-part documentary history by Ken Burns and Stephen Ives.

KEY TERMS

Social bandit (p. 335)
Mission system (p. 337)
Mexican struggle for independence (p. 337)
Donner party (p. 339)
Great American Desert (p. 340)
Mountain men (p. 340)
Rendezvous system (p. 340)
Santa Fe Trail (p. 341)
Oregon Trail (p. 342)
Manifest destiny (p. 343)
Alamo (p. 344)
Texas annexation (p. 345)
Webster-Ashburton Treaty of 1842 (p. 345)
Oregon country (p. 345)
Mormon church (p. 348)
Mexican-American War (p. 350)
Treaty of Guadalupe Hidalgo (p. 353)
Wilmot Proviso (p. 355)
Gold rush (p. 357)

PEOPLE YOU SHOULD KNOW

Juan Nepomuceno Cortina (p. 335)
Meriwether Lewis (p. 339)
William Clark (p. 339)
General Antonio López de Santa Anna (p. 343)
James K. Polk (p. 345)
Joseph Smith, Jr. (p. 348)
Brigham Young (p. 349)

REVIEW QUESTIONS

1. Describe the role of each of the following in the settlement of the Far West: (a) trappers and traders; (b) government explorers; and (c) missionaries.

2. Why did Anglo-American settlers in Texas rebel against the Mexican government?

3. What is the meaning of the phrase "manifest destiny"? Explain why Americans expanded west of the Mississippi River during the 1840s.

4. Why did the United States and Mexico go to war in 1846? Why did the war arouse bitter controversy?

14 The House Divided

JOHN SMITH DYE AND THE SLAVE POWER CONSPIRACY

Early in 1864, a New York writer named John Smith Dye published a book entitled *The Adder's Den or Secrets of the Great Conspiracy to Overthrow Liberty in America*. In his volume, Dye set out to prove that for more than 30 years a ruthless southern "slave power" had engaged in a deliberate, systematic plan to subvert civil liberties, pervert the Constitution, and extend slavery into the western territories.

In Dye's eyes, the entire history of the United States was the record of the South's repeated plots to expand slavery. An arrogant and aggressive "slave power," he maintained, had entrenched slavery in the Constitution, caused financial panics to sabotage the North's economy, dispossessed Indians from their native lands, and fomented revolution in Texas and war with Mexico to expand the South's slave empire. Most important of all, he insisted, the southern slavocracy had secretly assassinated two presidents by poison and unsuccessfully attempted to murder three others.

According to Dye, this campaign of political assassination began in 1835 when John C. Calhoun, outraged by Andrew Jackson's opposition to states' rights and nullification, encouraged a deranged man named Richard Lawrence to kill Jackson. This plot failed when Lawrence's pistols misfired. Six years later, in 1841, Dye alleged, a successful attempt was made on William Henry Harrison's life. After he refused to cooperate in a southern scheme to annex Texas, Harrison died of symptoms resembling arsenic poisoning. This left John Tyler, a strong defender of slavery, in the White House.

The next president to die at the hands of the slave power, according to Dye, was Zachary Taylor. A Louisiana slave owner who had commanded American troops in the Mexican War, Taylor had shocked Southerners by opposing the extension of slavery into California. Just 16 months after taking office, Taylor died suddenly of acute gastroenteritis, caused, claimed Dye, by arsenic poisoning. (A 1991 postmortem examination of Taylor's remains disproved this theory.) He was succeeded by Vice President Millard Fillmore, who was more sympathetic to the southern cause. Just three years later, Dye maintained, an attempt was made on the life of Millard Fillmore's successor, Franklin Pierce, a New Hampshire Democrat whom the slave power considered unreliable. On the way to his inauguration,

In 1864, New York economist John Smith Dye argued that the slave power had secretly poisoned two presidents—William Henry Harrison and Zachary Taylor—and had conspired to murder three others.

Pierce's railroad car derailed and rolled down an embankment. The president and his wife escaped injury, but their 12-year-old son was killed. From that point on, Pierce toed the southern line.

According to Dye, the next attempt came on February 23, 1857. President-elect James Buchanan,

a Pennsylvania Democrat, was dining at Washington's National Hotel. Buchanan had won the Democratic presidential nomination in the face of fierce southern opposition, and, in Dye's view, the slavocracy wanted to remind Buchanan who was in charge. Southern agents sprinkled arsenic on the lump sugar used by Northerners to sweeten their tea. Because Southerners drank coffee and used granulated sugar, no Southerners were injured. According to Dye, 60 Northerners, including the President, were poisoned and 38 died. Frightened by this brush with death, Buchanan became a reliable tool of the slave power.

In fact, no credible evidence supports any of John Smith Dye's sensational allegations. Historians neither have uncovered any connection between John C. Calhoun and the assassination attempt on Andrew Jackson, nor have they found any proof that Harrison's and Taylor's deaths resulted from poisoning or that southern agents derailed Pierce's train, nor have they located any evidence at all that 60 Northerners were poisoned at the dinner for President-elect Buchanan. Yet even if his charges were without foundation, Dye was not alone in interpreting events in conspiratorial terms. His book *The Adder's Den* was only one of the most extreme examples of conspiratorial charges that had been made by abolitionists since the late 1830s.

By the 1850s a growing number of Northerners had come to believe that an aggressive southern slave power had seized control of the federal government and threatened to subvert republican ideals of liberty, equality, and self-rule. At the same time, an increasing number of Southerners had begun to believe that antislavery radicals dominated northern politics and would "rejoice" in the ultimate consequences of abolition—race war and racial amalgamation that would surely follow emancipation. Sectional animosities were becoming increasingly ideological and inflamed, moving the torn nation closer to secession and civil war.

During the 1850s, the American political system was incapable of containing the sectional disputes between the North and South that had smoldered for more than half a century. One major political party—the Whigs—collapsed. Another—the Democrats—split into northern and southern factions. With the breakdown of the party system, the issues raised by slavery exploded. The bonds that had bound the country for more than seven decades began to unravel.

THE CRISIS OF 1850

In 1849 an expedition of Texas slaveowners and their slaves arrived in the California gold fields. As curious prospectors looked on, the Texans staked out claims and put their slaves to work panning for gold. White miners considered it unfair that they should have to compete with slave labor. They held a mass meeting and resolved "that no slave or Negro should own claims or even work in the mines." They ordered the Texans out of the gold fields within 24 hours.

Three days later, the white miners elected a delegate to a convention that had been called to frame a state constitution for California and to apply for admission to the Union. At the convention, the miners' delegate proposed that "neither slavery nor involuntary servitude" should ever "be tolerated" in California. The convention adopted his proposal unanimously.

California's application for admission to the Union as a free state in September 1849 raised the question that would dominate American politics during the 1850s: Would slavery be allowed to expand into the West or would the West remain free soil? It was the issue of slave expansion—and not the morality of slavery—that would make antislavery a respectable political position in the North, polarize public opinion, and initiate the chain of events that would lead the United States to civil war.

California's application for statehood made slavery's expansion an unavoidable political issue. Southerners feared that California's admission as a free state would upset the sectional balance of power. The free states already held a commanding majority in the House of Representatives because they had a much greater population than did the slave states. Therefore, the political power of proslavery Southerners depended on maintaining a balance of power in the Senate. Since the Missouri Compromise, Congress had paired the admission of a free state and a slave state. In 1836 and 1837, Congress had admitted Arkansas as a slave state and Michigan as a free state. In 1845 Florida and Texas had joined the Union as slave states, but Congress restored the sectional balance by admitting Iowa as a free state in 1846 and Wisconsin in 1848. If California were admitted as a free state, there would be 16 free states and only 15 slave states. The sectional balance of power in the Senate would be disrupted, and the South feared that it would lose its ability to influence political events.

The instability of the Democratic and Whig parties, and the growing political power of northern opponents of slave expansion, further dimmed chances of a peaceful compromise. When the Thirty-first Congress convened in December 1849, neither the Democrats nor the Whigs had a stable majority. Southern Whigs were deserting their party in droves, and northern and southern Democrats were badly split. The parties were so divided that it took 3 weeks and 63 ballots simply to elect the Speaker of the House.

In the North, opponents of the westward expansion of slavery made striking gains, particularly within the Democratic Party. Coalitions of Democrats and Free Soilers in Connecticut, Illinois, Indiana, Massachusetts, New York, Ohio, Vermont, and Wisconsin elected congressmen determined to prevent southern expansion. Every northern state legislature, except Iowa's, asserted that Congress had the power and duty to exclude slavery from the territories.

Southern hotspurs talked openly of secession. Robert Toombs of Georgia declared that if the North deprived the South of the right to take slaves into California and New Mexico, "I am for disunion." Such bold talk inched the South closer to secession.

The South's Dilemma

Why were the South's political leaders so worried about whether slavery would be permitted in the West when geography and climate made it unlikely that slavery would ever prosper in the area? The answer lies in the South's growing awareness of its minority

In California white miners refused "to swing a pick side by side with the Negro." Their delegate to the California constitutional convention of 1849 proposed that "neither slavery nor industry servitude . . . shall ever be tolerated in this state."

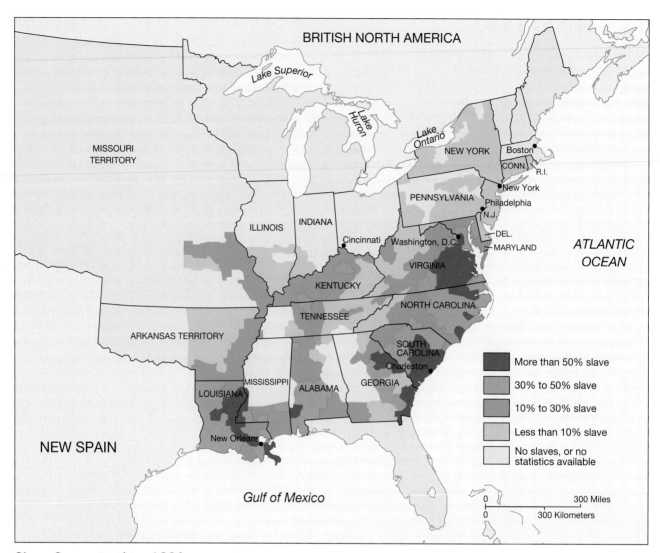

Slave Concentration, 1820

status in the Union, of the elimination of slavery in many other areas of the Western Hemisphere, and of the decline of slavery in the upper South. For more and more Southerners, the region's future depended on whether the West was opened or closed to slavery.

By 1850, New World slavery was confined to Brazil, Cuba, Puerto Rico, a small number of Dutch colonies, and the American South. British slave emancipation in the Caribbean had been followed by an intensified campaign to eradicate the international slave trade. In areas such as Brazil and Cuba, slavery could not long survive once the slave trade was cut off, because the slave populations of these countries had a skewed sex ratio and were unable to naturally reproduce their numbers. Only in the American South could slavery survive without the Atlantic slave trade.

Exacerbating southern fears about slavery's future was a sharp decline in slavery in the upper South. Between 1830 and 1860, the proportion of slaves in Missouri's population fell from 18 to 10 percent; in Kentucky from 24 to 19 percent; in Maryland from 23 to 13 percent. The South's leaders feared that in the future the upper South would soon become a region of free labor.

By mid-century, the South's slaveowners faced a further dilemma. Within the region itself, slave ownership was increasingly concentrated in fewer and fewer hands. Abolitionists were stigmatizing the South as out of step with the times. Many of the South's leading politicians feared that these criticisms of slavery would weaken lower-class white support for slavery.

The desire to ensure the support for slavery among poorer whites led some Southerners to agitate for reopening the African slave trade, believing that nonslaveholding Southerners would only support the institution if they had a chance to own slaves themselves. Most Southern leaders, however, believed the best way to perpetuate slavery was through westward expansion, and they wanted con-

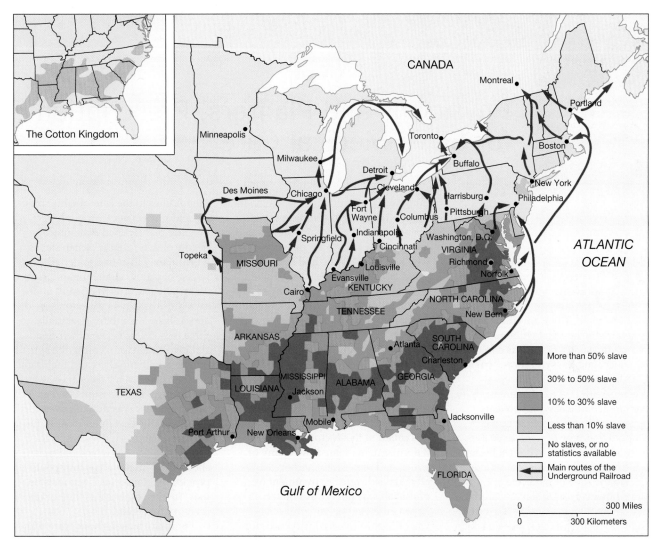

The Cotton Kingdom

Minneapolis
Des Moines
Topeka
MISSOURI
Cairo
Springfield
ARKANSAS
TEXAS
LOUISIANA
Port Arthur
New Orleans
Mobile
MISSISSIPPI
Jackson
ALABAMA
TENNESSEE
KENTUCKY
Louisville
Evansville
Cincinnati
Indianapolis
Fort Wayne
Chicago
Milwaukee
Detroit
Cleveland
Columbus
Pittsburgh
Harrisburg
Buffalo
Toronto
Montreal
Portland
Boston
New York
Philadelphia
Washington, D.C.
VIRGINIA
Richmond
Norfolk
NORTH CAROLINA
New Bern
SOUTH CAROLINA
Charleston
Atlanta
GEORGIA
Jacksonville
FLORIDA
CANADA
ATLANTIC OCEAN
Gulf of Mexico

More than 50% slave
30% to 50% slave
10% to 30% slave
Less than 10% slave
No slaves, or no statistics available
Main routes of the Underground Railroad

0   300 Miles
0   300 Kilometers

Slave Concentration, 1860/The Cotton Kingdom

crete assurance that Congress would not infringe on the right to take slaves into the western territories. Without such a guarantee, declared an Alabama politician, "This union cannot stand."

The Compromise of 1850: The Illusion of Sectional Peace

Ever since **David Wilmot** had proposed in 1846 that slavery be prohibited from any territory acquired from Mexico, opponents of slavery had argued that Congress possessed the power to regulate slavery in all of the territories. Ardent proslavery Southerners vigorously disagreed.

Politicians had repeatedly but unsuccessfully tried to work out a compromise. One simple proposal had been to extend the **Missouri Compromise** line to the Pacific Ocean. Slavery, thus, would have been forbidden north of 36°30' north latitude but permitted

south of that line. This proposal attracted the support of moderate Southerners but generated little support outside the region. Another proposal, supported by two key Democratic senators, Lewis Cass of Michigan and **Stephen Douglas** of Illinois, was known as squatter sovereignty or **popular sovereignty**. It declared that the people actually living in a territory should decide whether or not to allow slavery.

Henry Clay, the aging statesman known as the "Great Compromiser" for his efforts on behalf of the Missouri Compromise and the Compromise Tariff of 1832 (which resolved the nullification crisis), once again appealed to Northerners and Southerners to place national patriotism ahead of sectional loyalties. He believed that compromise could be effective only if it addressed all the issues dividing the two regions. He proposed that California be admitted as a free state; that territorial governments be established in New Mexico and Utah without any restrictions on

Physicians and Planters, Prescription for Slave Medical Care

"So perverse and stubbornly foolish are these people," one slaveholder wrote of his bondsmen, "they are either running into the hospital without cause or braving such a disease as cholera, by concealing the symptoms." Maintenance of slaves' health presented masters with diverse dilemmas. In the continual battle of wills between slaves and their owners over the amount and type of work to be performed, pretending to be sick became a form of "striking" for some slaves. Due to the state of medicine at the time, however, other slaves feared the cure more than the disease. Determining who really was sick was a tricky but crucial matter. Complicating the task were issues of profits, humanitarianism, and racism. Sick slaves could produce few profits; dead slaves none. At the same time, to provide healthy living conditions and constant medical care cost money, which cut into profits. Most masters liked to see themselves as paternalists who took good care of their "slave children." Planters and physicians consequently spent much time trying to determine appropriate responses to slave illnesses.

Feigning illness was an art that some slaves learned through trial and error. Some complaints worked better than others, as the Virginia slave James L. Smith discovered. He detested shooing crows from the cornfield but knew that if he acted sick "they will give me something that will physic me to death." That some-thing was frequently ipecac, which induced vomiting. In response to an earlier stomach complaint Smith's mistress had "made me drunk with whiskey"—a state he had not enjoyed. So he finally decided to claim to have injured his leg and stayed in his room, eating less, to give his claim credibility. Two weeks later, after the crows had deserted the cornfield for the cherry orchard, Smith "began to grow better very fast."

For the same reason that Smith concocted certain imaginary complaints, a number of slaves concealed symptoms of real diseases. Most masters called in the doctor only after the failure of home remedies—many of which had unpleasant and occasionally fatal side effects. Treatment by a physician was not always better. Nineteenth-century medical science was still primitive and had cures for only a handful of conditions. Otherwise doctors resorted to the use of excessive drugs and diuretics, leeching and bloodletting, purging and sweating, all of which caused discomfort and often weakened the body's ability to fight the disease. Many slaves, therefore, preferred to treat themselves with herbal cures that had been quietly passed down through the generations. Some home remedies in the slaves' quarters were superior to those of whites and were occasionally reported in medical journals. Others, however, were based on superstition, and conjurers sometimes caused treatable diseases to progress to irreversible states. For some slaves the decision to conceal an illness was an act of independence. Even though an unannounced illness meant they had to continue to work while sick, some slaves preferred that to surrendering their bodies to the care of white owners and physicians.

Once planters had overcome the hurdle of determining which slaves were ill, they then had to decide on a course of action. Here humanitarian and profit concerns frequently intersected. Slaveowners were concerned about slaves' health for essentially three reasons: protecting their financial investment, preventing the spread of illness to themselves and their families, and concern for the slaves as human beings. The decision of when to call in a doctor was difficult even for those with the best intentions. To his overseer, Thomas Jefferson specified certain illnesses for which physicians should be summoned as they could provide "certain relief," but insisted that "in most other cases they oftener do harm than good."

For many reasons home care was the first resort of most planters in all cases except those in which the value of professional care was obvious. Treatments for some illnesses were fairly standardized, well known, and easily performed by laymen. Many planters questioned the need to pay a doctor to treat such maladies. Through various suppliers, they obtained such commonly used drugs as calomel, castor oil, ipecac, laudanum, opium, camphor, and quinine. They consulted various household medical guides about proper dosages. Frequently the home cures worked as well as or better than professional services. Often, however, planters misdiagnosed. Even if the improper treatment made the condition no worse, it prolonged the course of the illness until too late for effective treatment.

Some slaveholders consciously waited until everything else had

failed before they called in a doctor. Planter Robert Garter of Virginia sent a dying patient to a physician with a note: "I do not wish to continue practice any longer on Peter—and now I deliver him to you." Such actions infuriated doctors, who were then blamed for their low cure rates. On some plantations where the doctor was not summoned until death was at hand, slaves superstitiously began to link the doctor's arrival with life's departure, giving them another reason to conceal their symptoms.

There were limits to paternalism. The growing knowledge of the impact of environment on health did not induce many planters to improve the living quarters or diets of their bondsmen. That cut into profits too drastically for the perceived benefits. Hence inadequate diets, clothing, and shelter dramatically decreased slaves' health. Economic and humane considerations were offset by a racism that placed less value on slave life. Landon Carter administered rattlesnake powder to his slaves during an attack of "bilious fever." It seemed to help but produced unpleasant side effects. "I wish my own fears did not prevent my giving it to my Children," Carter wrote in his diary—displaying a willingness to "experiment" on slaves that was not uncommon for physicians or planters. Slaves had no authority to refuse any kind of treatment.

African Americans were sometimes treated differently from whites because of perceived physiological differences. A number of the perceptions were accurate assessments distilled from experience. Physicians could not help but note variations in the susceptibility to specific diseases or in the response to treatment between the two groups. Modern researchers have found physiological bases for some of their observations, such as the effect of the sickle-cell trait—more common in African Americans than in the rest of the population—on some malarial viruses. At the time, however, those differences were often used and exaggerated as justification for both slavery and inadequate health care. Some asserted that African American bodies were uniquely suited for hard labor as well as slavery—a proposal not supported by mortality statistics.

Samuel W. Cartwright of Louisiana was a leading medical apologist for slavery. He argued that African Americans were intellectually inferior because dark pigmentation was more than skin deep. "Even the negro's brain and nerves," he wrote, "are tinctured with a shade of pervading darkness." To support his claims of African American bodies and minds being built for slavery, Cartwright explained all "unslavelike" behavior as diseases peculiar to African Americans. Careless habits were a symptom of what he called *Dysaetesia Aethipica.* Slaves who ran away were affected with *Drapetomania.* He could not accept that either could be rational forms of resistance to slavery. The health care of slaves illustrates the interplay of medicine and public values. Physicians became apologists for slavery and built lucrative careers on treating "Negro illnesses." Although slaves often sought to control their medical destinies through secret self-treatment, ultimate authority over their bodies rested in the property rights of their owners. Those owners most frequently acted on the basis of self-interest, which sometimes, but not always, coincided with benevolence. Few valued African American life as highly as white. Medical care, like most other life-and-death matters, was controlled by the white establishment.

Seventy-three-year-old Henry Clay pleads his case for sectional compromise. The Senate chamber was so crowded when he made his speech that the temperature reached 100 degrees.

slavery; that Texas relinquish its claims to land in New Mexico in exchange for federal assumption of Texas's unpaid debts; that Congress enact a stringent and enforceable fugitive slave law; and that the slave trade—but not slavery—be abolished in the District of Columbia.

Clay's proposal ignited an eight-month debate in Congress and led **John C. Calhoun** to threaten Southern secession. On March 4, 1850, Calhoun, the "Sentinel of the South," offered his response to Clay's compromise proposal. Calhoun was dying of tuberculosis and was too ill to speak publicly, so a colleague read his speech. He warned the North that the only way to save the Union was to "cease the agitation of the slave question," concede "to the South an equal right" to the western territories, return runaway slaves, and accept a constitutional amendment that would protect the South against northern violations of its rights. In the absence of such concessions, Calhoun argued, the South's only option was to secede.

Three days later, **Daniel Webster**, the North's most spellbinding orator, abandoned his previous opposition to the expansion of slavery into the western territories and threw his support behind Clay's compromise. "Mr. President," he began, "I wish to speak today not as a Massachusetts man, nor as Northern man, but as an American. . . . I speak today for the preservation of the Union. Hear me for my cause." The 68-year-old Massachusetts Whig called on both sides to resolve their differences in the name of patriotism. The North, he insisted, could afford to be gener-

ous because climate and geography ensured that slavery would never be profitable in the western territories. He concluded by warning his listeners that "there can be no such thing as a peaceable secession."

Webster's speech provoked a storm of outrage from northern opponents of compromise. Senator **William H. Seward** of New York called Webster a "traitor to the cause of freedom." But Webster's speech did have one important effect. It reassured moderate Southerners that powerful interests in the North were committed to compromise.

Still, opposition to compromise was fierce. Whig President **Zachary Taylor** argued that California, New Mexico, Oregon, Utah, and Minnesota should all be admitted to statehood before the question of slavery was addressed—a proposal that would have given the North a 10-vote majority in the Senate. William H. Seward, speaking for abolitionists and other opponents of slave expansion, denounced the compromise as conceding too much to the South and proclaimed that there was a "higher law" than the Constitution, a law that demanded an end to slavery. At the same time, many Southern extremists bridled at the idea of admitting California as a free state. In July, northern and southern senators opposed to the very idea of compromise joined ranks to defeat a bill that would have admitted California to the Union and organized New Mexico and Utah without reference to slavery.

Compromise appeared to be dead. A bitterly disappointed and exhausted Henry Clay dejectedly left the Capitol, his efforts apparently for naught. Then with unexpected suddenness the outlook changed. On the evening of July 9, 1850, President Taylor died of gastroenteritis, five days after taking part in a Fourth of July celebration dedicated to the building of the Washington Monument. Taylor's successor was **Millard Fillmore**, a 50-year-old New Yorker who was an ardent supporter of compromise.

In Congress, leadership in the fight for a compromise passed to Stephen Douglas, a Democratic senator from Illinois. An arrogant and dynamic leader, 5 feet 4 inches in height, with stubby legs, a massive head, bushy eyebrows, and a booming voice, Douglas was known as the "Little Giant." Douglas abandoned Clay's strategy of gathering all issues dividing the sections into a single "omnibus" bill. Instead, he introduced Clay's proposals one at a time. In this way, he was able to gather support from varying coalitions of Whigs, Democrats, Northerners, and Southerners on each issue. At the same time, banking and business interests as well as speculators in Texas bonds lobbied and even bribed members of Congress to support compromise. Despite these manipulations, the compromise proposals never succeeded in gathering solid congressional support. In the end, only 4

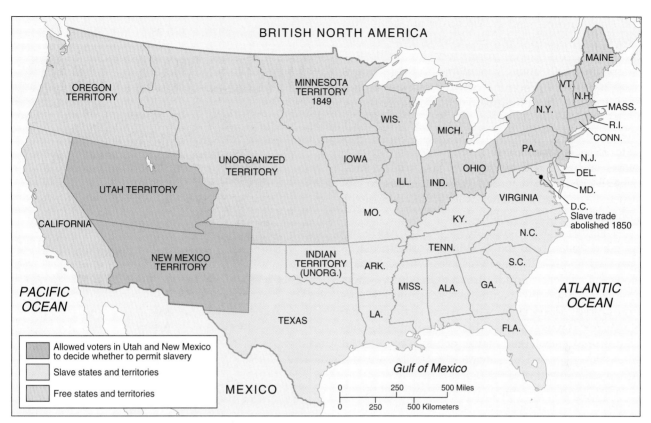

BRITISH NORTH AMERICA

Compromise of 1850

▓	Allowed voters in Utah and New Mexico to decide whether to permit slavery
░	Slave states and territories
░	Free states and territories

senators and 28 representatives voted for every one of the measures. Nevertheless, they all passed.

As finally approved, the **Compromise of 1850** admitted California as a free state, allowed the territorial legislatures of New Mexico and Utah to settle the question of slavery in those areas, set up a stringent federal law for the return of runaway slaves, abolished the slave trade in the District of Columbia, and gave Texas $10 million to abandon its claims to territory in New Mexico east of the Rio Grande.

The compromise created the illusion that the territorial issue had been resolved once and for all. "There is rejoicing over the land," wrote one Northerner, "the bone of contention is removed; disunion, fanaticism, violence, insurrection are defeated." Sectional hostility had been defused; calm had returned. But, as one southern editor correctly noted, it was "the calm of preparation, and not of peace."

The Fugitive Slave Law

The most divisive element in the Compromise of 1850 was the **Fugitive Slave Law,** which permitted any African American to be sent South solely on the affidavit of anyone claiming to be his or her owner. As a result, free African Americans were in danger of being

placed in slavery. The law also stripped runaway slaves of such basic legal rights as the right to a jury trial and the right to testify in one's own defense. The law further stipulated that accused runaways stand trial in front of special commissioners, not a judge or a jury, and that the commissioners be paid $10 if a fugitive was returned to slavery but only $5 if the fugitive was freed—a provision that many Northerners regarded as a bribe to ensure that any African American accused of being a runaway would be found guilty. Finally, the law required all U.S. citizens to assist in the capture of escapees. Anyone who refused to aid in the capture of a fugitive, interfered with the arrest of a slave, or tried to free a slave already in custody was subject to a heavy fine and imprisonment.

The Fugitive Slave Law kindled widespread outrage in the North and converted thousands of Northerners to the free soil doctrine that slavery should be barred from the western territories. "We went to bed one night old-fashioned, conservative, compromise, Union Whigs," wrote a Massachusetts factory owner, "and waked up stark mad Abolitionists."

Efforts to enforce the new law provoked wholesale opposition. Riots directed against the law broke out in many cities. In Christiana, Pennsylvania, in 1851, a gun battle broke out between abolitionists and slave catchers, and in Wisconsin, an abolitionist editor named Sherman M. Booth freed Joshua Glover, a fugitive slave, from a local jail. In Boston, federal marshals and 22 companies of state troops were needed to prevent a crowd from storming a courthouse to free a fugitive named Anthony Burns.

Eight northern states attempted to invalidate the law by enacting "personal liberty" laws that forbade state officials from assisting in the return of runaways and extended the right of jury trial to fugitives. Southerners regarded these attempts to obstruct the return of runaways as a violation of the Constitution and federal law.

The free black communities of the North responded defiantly to the 1850 law. Northern blacks provided about 1500 fugitive slaves with sanctuary along the **Underground Railroad** to freedom. Others established vigilance committees to protect blacks from hired kidnappers who were searching the North for runaways. And 15,000 free blacks, convinced that they could never achieve equality in America, emigrated to Canada, the Caribbean, and Africa after adoption of the federal law.

One northern moderate who was repelled by the Fugitive Slave Law was a 41-year-old Maine mother of six named **Harriet Beecher Stowe.** In 1852 she published *Uncle Tom's Cabin,* the single most widely read attack on slavery ever written. Stowe had learned about slavery while living in Cincinnati, Ohio, across from slaveholding Kentucky. Her book awakened millions of Northerners to the moral evil of slavery. Southerners denounced Stowe as a

> ### 135,000 SETS, 270,000 VOLUMES SOLD.
> # UNCLE TOM'S CABIN
> # FOR SALE HERE.
> AN EDITION FOR THE MILLION, COMPLETE IN 1 Vol., PRICE 37 1-2 CENTS.
> " " IN GERMAN, IN 1 Vol., PRICE 50 CENTS.
> " " IN 2 Vols., CLOTH, 6 PLATES, PRICE $1.50.
> SUPERB ILLUSTRATED EDITION, IN 1 Vol., WITH 153 ENGRAVINGS,
> PRICES FROM $2.50 TO $5.00.
> ## The Greatest Book of the Age.

Apologists for slavery denounced *Uncle Tom's Cabin* as inaccurate. Harriet Beecher Stowe responded by writing *The Key to Uncle Tom's Cabin,* which provided documentary proof of the abuses she described in her novel.

Harriet Beecher Stowe.

"wretch in petticoats," but in the North the book sold a million copies in sixteen months. No novel has ever exerted a stronger influence on American public opinion. Legend has it that when President Lincoln met Mrs. Stowe during the Civil War, he said, "So this is the little woman who made this big war."

DISINTEGRATION OF THE PARTY SYSTEM

As late as 1850, the two-party system was, to all outward appearances, still healthy. Every state, except for South Carolina, had two effective political parties. Voter participation was extremely high, and in presidential elections neither the Whigs nor the Democrats were able to gain more than 53 percent of the popular vote. Then, in the space of just five years, the two-party system began to disintegrate in response to two issues: massive foreign immigration and the reemergence of the issue of the expansion of slavery.

The Know Nothings

The most momentous shift in party sentiment in American history took place in the early 1850s following the rise of a party vigorously opposed to immigrants and Catholics. This party, which was known as the American party or **Know Nothing Party,** crippled the Whig party, weakened the Democratic Party, and made the political system incapable of resolving the growing crisis over slavery.

Hostility toward immigrants and Catholics had deep roots in American culture. The Protestant religious revivals of the 1820s and 1830s stimulated a "No Popery" movement. Prominent northern clerics, mostly Whig in politics, accused the Catholic Church of conspiring to overthrow democracy and subject the United States to Catholic despotism. Popular fiction offered graphic descriptions of priests seducing women during confession and nuns cutting unborn infants from their mothers' wombs and throwing them to dogs. A popular children's game was called "break the Pope's neck." Anti-Catholic sentiment culminated in mob rioting and in the burning of churches and convents. In 1834, for example, a Philadelphia mob rampaged through Irish neighborhoods, burning churches and houses.

A massive wave of immigration from Ireland and Germany after 1845 led to a renewed outburst of antiforeign and anti-Catholic sentiment. Between 1846 and 1855, more than three million foreigners arrived in America. In cities such as Chicago, Milwaukee, New York, and St. Louis, immigrants actually outnumbered native-born citizens. **Nativists**—ardent opponents of immigration—capitalized on deep-seated Protestant antagonism toward Catholics, working-class fear of economic competition from cheaper immigrant labor, and resentment among native-born Americans of the growing political power of foreigners. Nativists charged that Catholics were responsible for a sharp increase in poverty, crime, and drunkenness and were subservient to a foreign leader, the Pope.

To native-born Protestant workers, the new immigrants posed a tangible economic threat. Economic slumps in 1851 and 1854 resulted in severe unemployment and wage cuts. Native workers blamed Irish and German immigrants for their plight. The immigrants also posed a political threat. Concentrated in the large cities of the eastern seaboard, Irish immigrants voted as blocs and quickly built up strong political organizations.

One example of anti-Catholic hostility was the formation of a secret fraternal society made up of native-born Protestant working men. This secret society, "The Order of the Star Spangled Banner," soon formed the nucleus of a new political party known as the Know Nothing or the American party. The party received its name because when members were asked about the workings of the party, they were supposed to reply, "I know nothing."

The sudden growth of the Know Nothing party is one of the most extraordinary stories in American political history. In the North, the Know Nothings drew support from many native-born Protestants hostile toward Catholics and immigrants. In the South and in the border states, the party attracted voters disturbed by the mounting sectional disputes over slavery. Throughout the country, the Know Nothings capitalized on a popular longing for new political leaders.

By 1855 the Know Nothings had captured control of the legislatures in New England, except in Vermont and Maine, and were the dominant opposition party to the Democrats in New York, Pennsylvania, Maryland, Virginia, Tennessee, Georgia, Alabama, Mississippi, and Louisiana. In the presidential election of 1856, the party supported Millard Fillmore and won more than 21 percent of the popular vote and 8 electoral votes. In Congress, the party had 5 senators and 43 representatives. Between 1853 and 1855, the Know Nothings replaced the Whigs as the nation's second largest party.

Respectable public opinion spoke out vehemently against the dangers posed by the party. In 1855 an Illinois Whig politician named **Abraham Lincoln** denounced the Know Nothings in eloquent terms:

> I am not a Know-Nothing. How could I be? How can any one who abhors the oppression of Negroes be in favor of degrading classes of white people? Our progress in degeneracy appears to me pretty rapid, as a nation we began by declaring "all men are created equal." We now practically read it, "all men are created equal, except Negroes." When the Know-Nothings get control, it will read "all men are created equal, except Negroes, and foreigners, and Catholics." When it comes to this I should prefer emigrating to some country where they make no pretense of loving liberty—to Russia, for example, where despotism can be taken pure and without the base alloy of hypocrisy.

By 1856, however, the Know Nothing party was already in decline. Many Know Nothing officeholders were relatively unknown men with little political experience. In the states where they gained control, the Know Nothings proved unable to enact their legislative program, which included a 21-year residency period before immigrants could become citizens and vote, a limitation on political officeholding to native-born Americans, and restrictions on the sale of liquor.

After 1855 a new and explosive sectional party, the Republicans, supplanted the Know Nothing party in the North. By 1856 northern workers felt more threatened by the southern slave power than by the Pope and Catholic immigrants. At the same time, fewer and fewer Southerners were willing to support a party that ignored the question of the expansion of slavery. As a result, the Know Nothing party rapidly dissolved.

Nevertheless, the Know Nothings left an indelible mark on American politics. The Know Nothing movement eroded loyalty to the national political parties, helped destroy the Whig party, and undermined the capacity of the political system to contain the divisive issue of slavery.

Young America

For nearly four years following the Compromise of 1850, agitation over the question of the expansion of slavery abated. Most Americans were weary of the continuing controversy and turned their attention away from politics to focus instead on railroads, cotton, and trade. The early 1850s were dominated by dreams of greater American influence abroad—in areas such as Asia, the Caribbean, and Central America. Majestic clipper ships raced from New York to China in as few as 104 days. Steamship and railroad promoters launched ambitious schemes to build transit routes across Central America to link California and the Atlantic Coast.

In 1853 Commodore Matthew Perry sailed into Tokyo Bay with two steam frigates and two sailing ships, ending Japan's era of isolation from the western world. The whole world appeared to be opening up to American influence.

Franklin Pierce, a New Hampshire Democrat elected as the nation's fourteenth president in 1852, tried to unite the country with an aggressive program of foreign expansion called "Young America." He sought to annex Hawaii, expand American influence in Honduras and Nicaragua, and acquire new territory from Mexico and Spain. He announced that his administration would not be deterred "by any timid forebodings of evil" raised by the slavery question. Each effort to expand the country's boundaries, however, only provoked new sectional disputes because any acquisition would have posed the question of its status with regard to slavery.

Pierce was the first **"doughface"** president. He was, in the popular phrase, "a Northern man with Southern principles." Many Northerners suspected that Pierce's real goal was the acquisition of new territory for slavery. This suspicion was first raised in 1853, when the president instructed James Gadsden, his minister to Mexico, to purchase as much Mexican territory as possible, to provide a route for a southern railroad from New Orleans to California. The **Gadsden Purchase** of 1854 added 29,640 square miles to the United States in what is now Arizona and New Mexico.

Commodore Matthew Perry's display of armor and technology led Japan to accept the Treaty of Kanagawa, opening Japanese ports to American trade. These drawings were done by artists dispatched by Japanese officials to keep a visual record of Perry's activities.

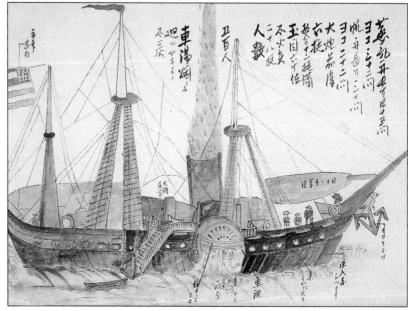

Cuba was the next object of Pierce's ambitions. Southern slaveholders coveted Cuba's 300,000 slaves. Other Americans wanted to free Cuba's white population from Spanish rule. In 1854 Pierce instructed his ambassador to Spain to offer $130 million for Cuba, but Spain refused the offer. That same year, at a meeting in Ostend, Belgium, three of Pierce's diplomatic ministers (including a future Democratic president, James Buchanan) sent a dispatch, later titled the **Ostend Manifesto**, to the secretary of state. It urged the military seizure of Cuba if Spain continued to refuse to sell the island. The Ostend Manifesto outraged Northerners, who regarded it as a brazen attempt to expand U.S. slavery in defiance of Spain's sovereign rights.

The Kansas-Nebraska Act

In 1854, less than four years after the Compromise of 1850, a piece of legislation was introduced in Congress that revived the issue of the expansion of slavery, shattered all illusions of sectional peace, and reordered the political landscape by destroying the Whig party, dividing the Democratic party, and creating the Republican party. Ironically, the author of

this legislation was Senator Stephen A. Douglas, the very man who had pushed the earlier compromise through Congress—and a man who had sworn after the passage of the Compromise of 1850 that he would never make a speech on the slavery question again.

As chairman of the Senate Committee on Territories, Douglas proposed that the area west of Iowa and Missouri—which had been set aside as a permanent Indian reservation—be organized as the Nebraska territory and opened to white settlement. Douglas had sought to achieve this objective since 1844, but southern congressmen had objected because Nebraska was located in the northern half of the Louisiana Purchase where the Missouri Compromise prohibited slavery. To forestall southern opposition, Douglas's original bill ignored both the Missouri Compromise and the status of slavery in the Nebraska territory. It simply provided that Nebraska, when admitted as a state, could enter the Union "with or without slavery," as its "constitution may prescribe."

Southern senators, however, demanded that Douglas add a clause specifically repealing the Missouri Compromise and stating that the question of

Kansas-Nebraska Act of 1854

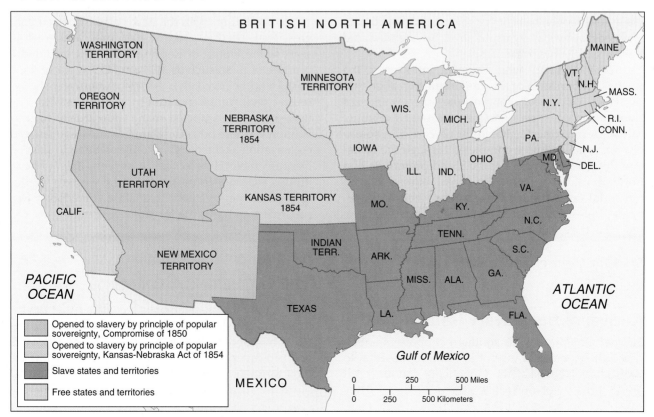

slavery would be determined on the basis of popular sovereignty. Douglas relented to southern pressure. In its final form, Douglas's bill created two territories, Kansas and Nebraska, and declared that the Missouri Compromise was "inoperative and void." With solid support from southern Whigs and southern Democrats and the votes of half of the northern Democratic congressmen, the measure passed. On May 30, 1854, President Pierce signed the measure into law.

Why did Douglas risk reviving the slavery question? His critics accused him of yielding to the southern pressure because of his presidential ambitions and a desire to enhance the value of his holdings in Chicago real estate and western lands. They charged that the Illinois senator's chief interest in opening up Kansas and Nebraska was to secure a right-of-way for a transcontinental railroad that would make Chicago the transportation center of mid-America.

Douglas's supporters, on the other hand, pictured him as a statesman laboring for western development and a sincere believer in popular sovereignty as a solution to the problem of slavery in the western territories. Douglas had long insisted that the democratic solution to the slavery issue was to allow the people who actually settled a territory to decide whether slavery would be permitted or forbidden. Popular sovereignty, he believed, would allow the nation to "avoid the slavery agitation for all time to come." Moreover, he believed that because of climate and geography slavery could never be extended into Kansas and Nebraska anyway.

To understand why Douglas introduced the **Kansas-Nebraska Act,** it is important to realize that by 1854 political and economic pressure to organize Kansas and Nebraska had become overwhelming. Midwestern farmers agitated for new land. A southern rail route had been completed through the Gadsden Purchase in December 1853, and promoters of a northern route for a transcontinental railroad viewed territorial organization as essential. Missouri slaveholders, already bordered on two sides by free states, believed that slavery in their state was doomed if they were surrounded by a free territory. All wanted to see the region opened to settlement.

Revival of the Slavery Issue

Neither Douglas nor his southern supporters anticipated the extent and fury of northern opposition to the Kansas-Nebraska Act. Opponents denounced it as "a gross violation of a sacred pledge." They burned so many figures of Douglas from trees, the Illinois senator joked, "I could travel from Boston to Chicago by the light of my own effigy."

Douglas predicted that the "storm will soon spend its fury," but it did not subside. Northern Free Soilers regarded the Missouri Compromise line as a "sacred compact" that had forever excluded slavery from the northern half of the Louisiana Purchase. Now, they feared that under the guise of popular sovereignty, the southern slave power threatened to spread slavery across the entire western frontier.

No single piece of legislation ever passed by Congress had more far-reaching political consequences. The Kansas-Nebraska Act brought about nothing less than a dramatic realignment of the two-party system. Conservative Whigs abandoned their party and joined the Democrats, while northern Democrats with free soil sentiments repudiated their own elected representatives. In the elections of 1854, 44 of the 51 northern Democratic representatives who voted for the act were defeated.

The chief beneficiary of these defections was a new political organization, the **Republican Party.** A combination of diverse elements, it stood for the belief that slavery must be barred from the western territories. It contained antislavery radicals, moderate and conservative Free Soilers, old-line Whigs, former Jacksonian Democrats, nativists, and antislavery immigrants.

In the fall of 1854, the new party contested congressional elections for the first time and won 46 seats in the House of Representatives. It included a number of men, such as William H. Seward of New York, who believed that African Americans should receive civil rights, including the right to vote. The new party also attracted many individuals, such as Salmon P. Chase and Abraham Lincoln, who favored colonization as the only workable solution to slavery. Despite their differences, however, all of these groups shared a conviction that the western territories should be saved for free labor. "Free labor, free soil, free men," was the Republican slogan.

THE GATHERING STORM

Because the Kansas-Nebraska Act stated that the future status of slavery in the territories was to be decided by popular vote, both antislavery Northerners and proslavery Southerners competed to win the region for their section. Because Nebraska was too far north to attract slave owners, Kansas became the

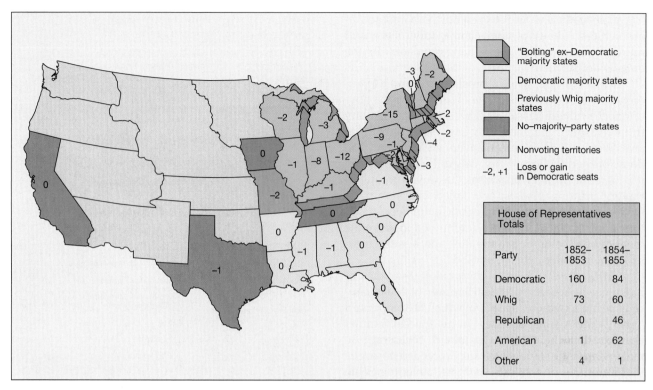

Gains and Losses in the Congressional Election of 1854

The sectional rift grew even sharper after the Kansas-Nebraska Act.

Party	1852–1853	1854–1855
Democratic	160	84
Whig	73	60
Republican	0	46
American	1	62
Other	4	1

House of Representatives Totals

Legend:
- "Bolting" ex–Democratic majority states
- Democratic majority states
- Previously Whig majority states
- No–majority–party states
- Nonvoting territories
- −2, +1 Loss or gain in Democratic seats

arena of sectional conflict. For six years, proslavery and antislavery factions fought in Kansas as popular sovereignty degenerated into violence.

"Bleeding Kansas" and "Bleeding Sumner"

Across the drought-stricken Ohio and Mississippi valleys, thousands of land-hungry farmers hoped to stake a claim to part of Kansas's 126,000 square miles of territory. Along with these pioneers came a small contingent of settlers whose express purpose was to keep Kansas free soil. Even before the 1854 act had been passed, the New England Emigrant Aid Company was promoting the emigration of antislavery New Englanders to Kansas to "vote to make it free." By the summer of 1855, more than 9000 pioneers— mainly midwestern Free Soilers—had settled in Kansas.

Slaveholders from Missouri expressed alarm at the activities of the Emigrant Aid Society. In response, they formed organizations to "repel the wave of fanaticism which threatens to break upon

our border." One Missouri lawyer told a cheering crowd that he would hang any "free soil" emigrant who came into Kansas.

Competition between proslavery and antislavery factions reached a climax on May 30, 1855, when Kansas held territorial elections. Although only 1500 men were registered to vote, 6000 ballots were cast, many of them by proslavery "border ruffians" from Missouri. As a result, a proslavery legislature was elected, which passed laws stipulating that only proslavery men could hold office or serve on juries.

Free Soilers called the election a fraud and held their own "Free State" convention in Topeka in the fall of 1855. At this convention, delegates drew up a constitution that not only prohibited slavery in Kansas but also barred free African Americans from the territory. Like the Free Soilers who settled California and Oregon, most Northerners in Kansas wanted the territory to be free and white.

When Congress convened in January 1856, it was confronted by two rival governments in Kansas. President Franklin Pierce threw his support behind the proslavery legislature and asked Congress to admit Kansas to the Union as a slave state.

Violence broke out between northern and southern settlers over rival land claims, town sites, and railroad routes—and, most dangerous of all, the question of slavery.

In one episode, when a proslavery grand jury indicted several members of the Free Soil Topeka government for high treason, 800 proslavery men, many from Missouri, marched into Lawrence, Kansas, to arrest the leaders of the antislavery government. The posse burned the local hotel, called the Free Soil Hotel, looted a number of houses, destroyed two antislavery printing presses, and killed one man. One member of the posse declared: "Gentlemen, this is the happiest day of my life. I determined to make the fanatics bow before me in the dust and kiss the territorial laws. I have done it, by God."

On May 19, 1856—two days before the "sack of Lawrence"—Senator **Charles Sumner** of Massachusetts began a two-day speech in which he denounced "The Crime Against Kansas." In his speech, Sumner charged that there was a southern conspiracy to make Kansas a slave state. He proceeded to argue that a number of southern senators, including Senator Andrew Butler of South Carolina, stood behind this conspiracy. Launching into a bitter personal diatribe, Sumner accused Senator Butler of taking "the harlot, Slavery," for his "mistress" and proceeded to make fun of a medical disorder from which Senator Butler suffered. At the rear of the Senate chamber, Stephen Douglas muttered: "That damn fool will get himself killed by some other damned fool."

Two days later, Senator Butler's nephew, Congressman Preston Brooks of South Carolina, entered a nearly empty Senate chamber. Brooks was convinced that he had a duty to "avenge the insult to my State." Sighting Sumner at his desk, Brooks charged at him and began striking the Massachusetts senator over the head with a cane. He swung so hard that the cane broke into pieces. Brooks caned Sumner, rather than challenging him to a duel, because he regarded the Senator as his social inferior. Thus, he wanted to use the same method slaveholders used to chastise slaves. Although it took Sumner three years to recover from his injuries and return to his Senate seat, he promptly became a martyr to the cause of freedom in the North, where a million copies of his "Crime Against Kansas" speech were distributed. In the South, Brooks was hailed as a hero. Merchants in Charleston bought the congressman a new cane, inscribed "Hit him again." A vote to expel Brooks from Congress failed because every Southern representative but one voted against the measure. Instead, Brooks was censured. He promptly resigned his seat and was immediately reelected.

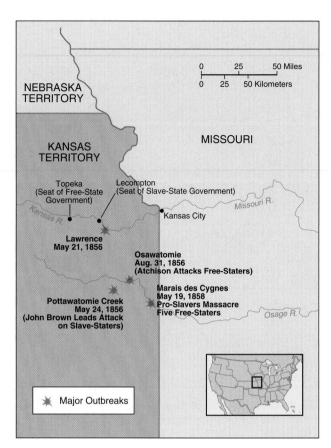

Bleeding Kansas

When the territory of Kansas was established under the principle of popular sovereignty, violence erupted between proslavery and antislavery forces. A preview of the Civil War occurred when a proslavery mob from Missouri ransacked antislavery Lawrence, Kansas. The term "Bleeding Kansas" became a battle cry for antislavery advocates.

The caning of Sumner had repercussions in strife-torn Kansas. **John Brown**, a devoted Bible-quoting Calvinist who believed he had a personal responsibility to overthrow slavery, announced that the time had come "to fight fire with fire" and "strike terror in the hearts of proslavery men." The next day, in reprisal for the "sack of Lawrence" and the assault on Sumner, Brown and six companions dragged five proslavery men and boys from their beds at Pottawatomie Creek, split open their skulls with a sword, cut off their hands, and laid out their entrails.

A war of revenge erupted in Kansas. Columns of proslavery Southerners ransacked free farms, while they searched for Brown and the other "Pottawatomie killers." Armed bands looted enemy stores and farms. At Osawatomie, proslavery forces attacked John Brown's headquarters, leaving a dozen men dead.

Clutching a pen in one hand and a copy of his "Crime Against Kansas" speech in the other, Senator Charles Sumner attempts to defend himself against an attack by South Carolina Congressman Preston Brooks.

John Brown's men killed four Missourians, and proslavery forces retaliated by blockading the free towns of Topeka and Lawrence. Before it was over, guerrilla warfare in eastern Kansas left 200 dead.

The Election of 1856

The presidential election of 1856 took place in the midst of Kansas's civil war. President Pierce hoped for renomination to a second term in office, but northern indignation over the Kansas-Nebraska Act led the Democrats to seek out a less controversial candidate. On the seventeenth ballot, northern and western Democrats succeeded in winning the nomination for **James Buchanan,** a 65-year-old Pennsylvania bachelor, who had been minister to Great Britain during the struggle over the Kansas-Nebraska bill. The dying Whig party and the southern wing of the Know Nothing party nominated former President Millard Fillmore.

The Republican Party held its first national convention in Philadelphia and adopted a platform denying the authority of Congress and of territorial legislatures "to give legal existence to slavery" in the territories. The convention nominated the dashing young explorer and soldier **John C. Frémont** for president as young Republicans chanted, "Free Speech, Free Soil and Frémont." Frémont was a romantic figure who had led more than a dozen major explorations of the Rocky Mountains and Far West. After accepting the Republican nomination, he declared that Kansas should be admitted to the Union as a free state. This was his only public utterance during the entire 1856 campaign. A few weeks later, the northern wing of the Know Nothing party threw its support behind Frémont.

The election was one of the most bitter in American history and the first in which voting divided along rigid sectional lines. The Democratic strategy was to picture the Republican Party as a hotbed of radicalism. Democrats called the Republicans the party of disunion and described Frémont as a "black abolitionist" who would destroy the union. Republicans responded by accusing the Democrats of being accomplices in a conspiracy to extend slavery.

Although Buchanan garnered only 45 percent of the popular vote because of the presence of Fillmore, he narrowly carried five northern states, giving him a comfortable margin in the Electoral College. Buchanan won 174 Electoral College votes to 114 for Frémont and 8 for Fillmore.

The election results showed how polarized the nation had become. The South, except for Maryland, voted solidly Democratic. Frémont did not receive a single vote south of the Mason-Dixon line. At the same time, the northernmost states were solidly Republican.

In their first presidential campaign, the Republicans had made an extraordinarily impressive showing. Eleven free states voted for Frémont. If only two more states had voted in his favor, the Republicans would have won the election.

The Supreme Court Speaks

In his inaugural address, Buchanan declared that "the great object of my administration will be to arrest . . . the agitation of the slavery question in the North." He then predicted that a forthcoming Supreme Court decision would once and for all settle the controversy over slavery in the western territories. Two days after Buchanan's inauguration, the high court handed down its decision.

On March 6, 1857, the Supreme Court finally decided a question that Congress had evaded for decades: whether Congress had the power to prohibit slavery in the territories. Repeatedly, Congress had declared that this was a constitutional question that the Supreme Court should settle. Now, for the first time, the Supreme Court offered its answer.

The case originated in 1846, when a Missouri slave, **Dred Scott,** sued to gain his freedom. Scott argued that while he had been the slave of an army surgeon, he had lived for four years in Illinois, a free state, and Wisconsin, a free territory, and that his residence on free soil had erased his slave status. By a 7–2 margin, the Court ruled that Dred Scott had no right to sue in federal court, that the Missouri Compromise was unconstitutional, and that Congress had no right to exclude slavery from the territories.

All nine justices rendered separate opinions, but Chief Justice **Roger Taney** delivered the opinion that expressed the position of the Court's majority. His opinion represented a judicial defense of the most extreme proslavery position.

The chief justice made two sweeping rulings. The first was that Dred Scott had no right to sue in federal court because neither slaves nor free blacks were citizens of the United States. At the time the Constitution was adopted, the chief justice wrote, blacks had been "regarded as beings of an inferior order" with "no rights which the white man was bound to respect."

Second, Taney declared that Congress had no right to exclude slavery from the federal territories since any law excluding slave property from the territories was a violation of the Fifth Amendment prohibition against the seizure of property without due process of law. For the first time since *Marbury v. Madison* in 1803, the Court declared an act of Congress unconstitutional. The Missouri Compromise was unconstitutional, the Court declared, because it prohibited slavery north of 36°30′. Newspaper headlines summarized the Court's rulings: "SLAVERY ALONE NATIONAL—THE MISSOURI COMPROMISE UNCONSTITUTIONAL—NEGROES CANNOT BE CITIZENS—THE TRIUMPH OF SLAVERY COMPLETE."

In a single decision, the Court sought to resolve all the major constitutional questions raised by slavery. It declared that the Declaration of Independence and the Bill of Rights were not intended to apply to African Americans. It stated that the Republican Party platform—barring slavery from the western territories—was unconstitutional. And it ruled that Stephen Douglas's doctrine of "popular sovereignty"—which stated that territorial governments had the power to prohibit slavery—was also unconstitutional.

Republicans reacted with scorn. The decision, said the *New York Tribune*, carried as much moral weight as "the judgment of a majority of those congregated in any Washington barroom." Radical abolitionists called for secession. Many Republicans—including an Illinois politician named Abraham Lincoln—regarded the decision as part of a slave power conspiracy to legalize slavery throughout the United States.

The Dred Scott decision was a major political miscalculation. In its ruling, the Supreme Court sought to solve the slavery controversy once and for all. Instead the Court intensified sectional strife, undercut possible compromise solutions to the divisive issue of the expansion of slavery, and weakened the moral authority of the judiciary.

In the sweeping Dred Scott decision, Chief Justice Roger Taney sought to resolve the constitutional questions raised by slavery. The decision, which remained a major source of controversy until the eruption of the Civil War, intensified divisions between proslavery and antislavery factions.

The Lecompton Constitution: "A Swindle and a Fraud"

Late in 1857, President Buchanan faced a major test of his ability to suppress the slavery controversy. In September, proslavery forces in Kansas met in Lecompton, the territorial capital, to draft a constitution that would bring Kansas into the Union as a slave state. Recognizing that a proslavery constitution would be defeated in a free and fair election, proslavery delegates withheld the new state charter from the territory's voters. Instead, they offered voters a referendum on whether they preferred "the constitution with slavery" or "the constitution without slavery." In either case, however, the new constitution guaranteed slave ownership as a sacred right. Free Soilers boycotted the election and, as a result, "the constitution with slavery" was approved by a 6000-vote margin.

President Buchanan—afraid that the South would secede if Kansas were not admitted to the

Union as a slave state—accepted the proslavery **Lecompton Constitution** as a satisfactory application of the principle of popular sovereignty. He then demanded that Congress admit Kansas as the sixteenth slave state.

Stephen Douglas was aghast. "A small minority" of proslavery men in Kansas, he said, had "attempted to cheat and defraud the majority by trickery and juggling." Appalled by this travesty of the principle of popular sovereignty, Douglas broke with the Buchanan administration.

After a rancorous debate, the Senate passed a bill that admitted Kansas as a slave state under the Lecompton Constitution. But the House of Representatives rejected this measure and instead substituted a compromise, known as the English bill, which allowed Kansans to vote on the proslavery constitution. As a thinly veiled bribe to encourage Kansans to ratify the document, the English bill offered Kansas a huge grant of public land if it approved the Lecompton Constitution. In 1858, while federal troops guarded the polls, Kansas voters overwhelmingly rejected the proslavery constitution.

The bloody battle for Kansas had come to an end. Free Soilers took control of the territorial legislature and repealed the Kansas territorial slave code. Stripped of any legal safeguards for their slave property, most Kansas slaveowners quickly left the territory. When the federal census was taken in 1860, just two slaves remained in Kansas.

But the nation would never be the same. To antislavery Northerners, the Lecompton controversy showed that the slave power was willing to subvert democratic processes in an attempt to force slavery on a free people. In Kansas, they charged, proslavery forces had used violence, fraud, and intimidation to expand the territory open to slavery. To the more extreme opponents of slavery in the North, the lesson was clear. The only way to preserve freedom and democratic procedures was to destroy slavery and the slave power through force of arms.

CRISIS OF THE UNION

In 1858, Senator William H. Seward of New York examined the sources of the conflicts between the North and the South. Some people, said Seward, thought the sectional conflict was "accidental, unnecessary, the work of interested or fanatical agitators, and therefore ephemeral." But Seward believed that these people were wrong. The roots of the conflict went far deeper. "It is an irrepressible conflict," Seward said, "between opposing and enduring forces."

By 1858, a growing number of Northerners were convinced that two fundamentally antagonistic societies had evolved in the nation, one dedicated to freedom, the other opposed. They had come to believe that their society was locked in a life-and-death struggle with a southern society dominated by an aggressive slave power, which had seized control of the federal government and imperiled the liberties of free people. Declared the *New York Tribune:* "We are not one people. We are two peoples. We are a people for Freedom and a people for Slavery. Between the two, conflict is inevitable."

At the same time, an increasing number of Southerners expressed alarm at the growth of antislavery and anti-South sentiment in the North. They were convinced that Republicans would not only insist on halting slavery's expansion but would also seek to undermine the institution where it already existed. As the decade closed, the dominant question of American political life was whether the nation's leaders could find a peaceful way to resolve the differences separating the North and South.

The Lincoln-Douglas Debates

The critical issues dividing the nation—slavery versus free labor, popular sovereignty, and the legal and political status of African Americans—were brought into sharp focus in a series of dramatic forensic duels during the 1858 election campaign for U.S. senator from Illinois. The campaign pitted a little-known lawyer from Springfield named Abraham Lincoln against Senator Stephen A. Douglas, the front-runner for the Democratic presidential nomination in 1860. (Senators, at the time, were elected by state legislators, and Douglas and Lincoln were actually campaigning for candidates from their party for the state legislature.)

The contest received intense national publicity. One reason for the public attention was that the political future of Stephen Douglas was at stake. Douglas had openly broken with the Buchanan administration over the proslavery Lecompton Constitution and had joined with Republicans to defeat the admission of Kansas to the Union as a slave state. Now, many wondered, would Douglas assume the leadership of the free soil movement?

The public knew little about the man the Republicans selected to run against Douglas. Lincoln had been born on February 12, 1809, in a log cabin and grew up on the wild Kentucky and Indiana frontier. At the age of 21, he moved to Illinois, where he worked as a clerk in a country store, became a local postmaster and a lawyer, and served four terms in the lower house of the Illinois General Assembly. A Whig in politics, Lincoln was elected in 1846 to the U.S. House of Representatives, but his stand against the Mexican War had made him too unpopular to win reelection. After the passage of the Kansas-Nebraska Act in 1854, Lincoln reentered politics, and in 1858 the Republican Party nominated him to run against Douglas for the Senate.

Lincoln accepted the nomination with the famous words: "'A house divided against itself cannot stand.' I believe this Government cannot endure permanently half-slave and half-free." He did not believe the Union would fall, but he did predict that it would cease to be divided. Lincoln proceeded to argue that Stephen Douglas's Kansas-Nebraska Act and the Supreme Court's Dred Scott decision were part of a conspiracy to make slavery lawful "in all the States, old as well as new—North as well as South."

For four months Lincoln and Douglas crisscrossed Illinois, traveling nearly 10,000 miles and participating in seven face-to-face debates before crowds of up to 15,000.

During the course of the **Lincoln-Douglas debates,** the two candidates presented two sharply contrasting views of the problem of slavery. Douglas argued that slavery was a dying institution that had reached its natural limits and could not thrive where climate and soil were inhospitable. He asserted that the problem of slavery could best be resolved if it were treated as essentially a local problem. Lincoln, on the other hand, regarded slavery as a dynamic, expansionistic institution, hungry for new territory. He argued that if Northerners allowed slavery to spread unchecked, slaveowners would make slavery a national institution and would reduce all laborers, white as well as black, to a state of virtual slavery.

The sharpest difference between the two candidates involved the issue of African Americans' legal rights. Douglas was unable to conceive of African Americans as anything but inferior to whites, and he was unalterably opposed to their citizenship. "I want citizenship for whites only," he declared. Lincoln said that he, too, was opposed to granting free blacks full legal rights. But he insisted that African Americans were equal to Douglas and "every living man" in their right to life, liberty, and the fruits of their own labor.

The debates reached a climax on a damp, chilly August 27. At Freeport, Illinois, Lincoln asked Douglas to reconcile the Supreme Court's Dred Scott decision, which denied Congress the power to exclude slavery from a territory, with popular sovereignty. Could the residents of a territory "in any lawful way" exclude slavery prior to statehood? Douglas replied that the residents of a territory could exclude slavery by refusing to pass laws protecting slaveholders' property rights. "Slavery cannot exist a day or an hour anywhere," he declared, "unless it is supported by local police regulations."

Any way he answered, Douglas was certain to alienate northern Free Soilers or proslavery Southerners. The Dred Scott decision had given slave owners the right to take their slavery into any western territories. Now Douglas said that territorial settlers could exclude slavery, despite what the Court had ruled. Douglas won reelection, but his cautious statements antagonized Southerners and northern Free Soilers alike.

In the final balloting, the Republicans outpolled the Democrats. The Democrats, however, had gerrymandered the voting districts so skillfully that they kept control of the state legislature.

The question of the legal status of slavery in the territories was the major issue Illinois senatorial candidates Stephen A. Douglas and Abraham Lincoln discussed in their series of seven debates in 1858. Lincoln lost the Senate race to Douglas, nicknamed the "Little Giant" in reference to his short stature but outstanding oratorical skills. The debates, however, helped bring Lincoln to national prominence, and two years later he defeated Douglas for the presidency.

Although Lincoln failed to win a Senate seat, his battle with Stephen Douglas had catapulted him into the national spotlight and made him a serious presidential possibility in 1860. As Lincoln himself noted, his defeat was "a slip and not a fall."

Harpers Ferry

On August 19, 1859, John Brown, the Kansas abolitionist, and Frederick Douglass, the celebrated African American abolitionist and former slave, met in an abandoned stone quarry near Chambersburg, Pennsylvania. For three days, the two men discussed whether violence could be legitimately used to free the nation's slaves. The Kansas guerrilla leader asked Douglass if he would join a band of raiders who would seize a federal arsenal and spark a mass uprising of slaves. "When I strike," Brown said, "the bees will begin to swarm, and I shall need you to help hive them."

"No," Douglass replied. Brown's plan, he knew, was suicidal. Brown had earlier proposed a somewhat more realistic plan. According to that scheme, Brown would have launched guerrilla activity in the Virginia mountains, providing a haven for slaves and an escape route into the North. That scheme had a chance of working, but Brown's new plan was hopeless.

Up until the Kansas-Nebraska Act, abolitionists were averse to the use of violence. Opponents of slavery hoped to use moral suasion and other peaceful means to eliminate slavery. By the mid-1850s, however, the abolitionists' aversion to violence had begun to fade. In 1858 William Lloyd Garrison complained that his followers were "growing more and more warlike." On the night of October 16, 1859, violence came, and John Brown was its instrument.

Brown's plan was to capture the federal arsenal at Harpers Ferry, Virginia (now West Virginia), and arm slaves from the surrounding countryside. His long-range goal was to drive southward into Tennessee and Alabama, raiding federal arsenals and inciting slave insurrections. Failing that, he hoped to ignite a sectional crisis that would destroy slavery.

At eight o'clock Sunday evening, October 16, John Brown led a raiding party of approximately 21 men toward **Harpers Ferry,** where they captured the lone night watchman and cut the town's telegraph lines. Encountering no resistance, Brown's raiders seized the federal arsenal, an armory, and a rifle works along with several million dollars worth of arms and munitions. Brown then sent out several detachments to round up hostages and liberate slaves.

But Brown's plans soon went awry. As news of the raid spread, many townspeople and local militia companies cut off Brown's escape routes and trapped his men in the armory. Twice, Brown sent men carrying flags of truce to negotiate. On both occasions, drunken mobs, yelling "Kill them, kill them," gunned the men down.

Two days later U.S. Marines, commanded by Colonel Robert E. Lee and Lieutenant J. E. B. Stuart, arrived in Harpers Ferry. Brown and his men took refuge in a fire engine house and battered holes through the building's brick wall to shoot through. A hostage later described the climactic scene: "With one son dead by his side and another shot through, he felt the pulse of his dying son with one hand and held his rifle with the other and commanded his men . . . encouraging them to fire and sell their lives as dearly as they could."

Later that morning, Colonel Lee's marines stormed the engine house and rammed down its doors. Brown and his men continued firing until the leader of the storming party cornered Brown and knocked him unconscious with a sword. Five of Brown's party escaped, 10 were killed, and seven, including Brown himself, were taken prisoner.

A week later, John Brown was put on trial in a Virginia court, even though his attack had occurred on federal property. During the six-day proceedings, Brown refused to plead insanity as a defense. He was found guilty of treason, conspiracy, and murder, and was sentenced to die on the gallows.

The trial's high point came at the very end when Brown was allowed to make a five-minute speech. His words helped convince thousands of Northerners that this grizzled man of 59, with his "piercing eyes" and "resolute countenance," was a martyr to the cause of freedom. Brown denied that he had come to Virginia to commit violence. His only goal, he said, was to liberate the slaves. "If it is deemed necessary," he told the Virginia court, "that I should forfeit my life for the furtherance of the ends of justice and mingle my blood . . . with the blood of millions in this slave country whose rights are disregarded by wicked, cruel, and unjust enactments, I say let it be done."

Brown's execution was set for December 2. Before he went to the gallows, Brown wrote one last message: "I . . . am now quite certain that the crimes of this guilty land will never be purged away but with blood." At 11 A.M., he was led to the execution site, a halter was placed around his neck, and a sheriff led him over a trapdoor. The sheriff cut the rope and the trapdoor opened. As the old man's body convulsed on the gallows, a Virginia officer cried out: "So perish all enemies of Virginia!"

Across the North, church bells tolled, flags flew at half-mast, and buildings were draped in black

John Brown, convicted of treason against Virginia, conspiring to promote a slave insurrection, and murder, mounts the scaffold on which he is to be hanged. While he was mourned by many in the North as a martyr for the antislavery cause, Southerners and moderate Northerners regarded the radical abolitionist as a violent, fanatical madman.

THE PEOPLE SPEAK

John Brown Defends His Raid on Harpers Ferry (1859)

At the very end of his trial in a Virginia court for treason, conspiracy, and murder, John Brown delivered a five-minute speech in which he defended his raid on Harpers Ferry.

I have, may it please the Court, a few words to say.

In the first place, I deny everything but what I have all along admitted: of a design on my part to free slaves. I intended certainly to have made a clean thing of that matter, as I did last winter, when I went into Missouri and there took slaves without the snapping of a gun on either side, moving them through the country, and finally leaving them in Canada. I designed to have done the same thing again on a larger scale. That was all I intended. I never did intend murder, or treason, or the destruction of property, or to exercise or incite slaves to rebellion, or to make insurrection.

I have another objection, and that is that it is unjust that I should suffer such a penalty. . . . Had I so interfered in behalf of the rich, the powerful, the intelligent, the so-called great . . . it would have been all right. Every man in this Court would have deemed it an act worthy of reward rather than punishment.

This Court acknowledges . . . the validity of the law of God. I see a book kissed, which I suppose to be the Bible, or at least the New Testament, which teaches me that all things whatsoever I would that men should do to me, I should do even so to them. It teaches me, further, to remember them that are in bonds as bound with them. I endeavored to act up to that instruction. I say I am yet too young to understand that God is any respecter of persons. I believe that to have interfered as I have done . . . in behalf of His despised poor, I did no wrong, but right. Now, if it is deemed necessary that I should forfeit my life for the furtherance of the ends of justice, and mingle my blood further with the blood of my children and with the blood of millions in this slave country whose rights are disregarded by wicked, cruel, and unjust enactments, I say let it be done.

Source: John Brown, "Last Statement to the Court," in *The Life and Execution of Captain John Brown, Known as "Old Brown of Ossawatomie"* (New York, 1859).

CHRONOLOGY OF KEY EVENTS

1846 Wilmot Proviso, banning slavery from any territory acquired from Mexico, is proposed

1850 Compromise of 1850

1852 Harriet Beecher Stowe publishes *Uncle Tom's Cabin*

1853 Gadsden Purchase from Mexico

1854 Ostend Manifesto calls on the United States to acquire Cuba from Spain; Commodore Matthew Perry negotiates a treaty opening Japan to American trade; Kansas-Nebraska Act reignites sectional controversy over slavery; "Bleeding Kansas" begins; conventions of Free Soilers form the Republican party

1856 "Sack of Lawrence"—proslavery Missourians loot and burn several buildings in Lawrence, Kansas; "Bleeding Sumner"—Congressman Preston Brooks of South Carolina beats Senator Charles Sumner of Massachusetts with a cane; John Brown's raid on Pottawatomie Creek, Kansas

1857 Dred Scott decision

1858 Kansas voters reject the Lecompton constitution; Lincoln-Douglas debates

1859 John Brown's raid at Harpers Ferry

bunting. Ralph Waldo Emerson compared Brown to Jesus Christ and declared that his death had made "the gallows as glorious as the cross." William Lloyd Garrison, previously the strongest exponent of nonviolent opposition to slavery, announced that Brown's death had convinced him of "the need for violence" to destroy slavery. He told a Boston meeting that "every slave holder has forfeited his right to live" if he opposed immediate emancipation.

Prominent northern Democrats and Republicans, including Stephen Douglas and Abraham Lincoln, spoke out forcefully against Brown's raid and his tactics. Lincoln expressed the views of the Republican leadership when he denounced Brown's raid as an act of "violence, bloodshed, and treason" that deserved to be punished by death. But southern whites refused to believe that politicians like Lincoln and Douglas represented the true opinion of most Northerners. These men condemned Brown's "invasion," observed a Virginia senator, "only because it failed."

CONCLUSION

For 40 years the debate over the extension of slavery had divided North and South. National leaders had tried on several occasions to reach a permanent, workable solution to the problem, without success. With the collapse of the Whigs and the rise of the Republicans, the American political process could no longer contain the fierce antagonisms and mutual distrust that separated the two regions.

In 1859, John Brown's raid convinced many white Southerners that a majority of Northerners wished to free the slaves and incite a race war. Southern extremists, known as "fire-eaters," told large crowds that John Brown's attack on Harpers Ferry was "the first act in the grand tragedy of emancipation, and the subjugation of the South in bloody treason." After Harpers Ferry, Southerners increasingly believed that secession and creation of a slaveholding confederacy were now the South's only options. A Virginia newspaper noted that there were "thousands of men in our midst who, a month ago, scoffed at the idea of a dissolution of the Union as a madman's dream, but who now hold the opinion that its days are numbered." The final bonds that had held the Union together had come unraveled.

CHAPTER SUMMARY AND KEY POINTS

During the 1850s the nation's political system became incapable of resolving sectional disputes between North and South. In this chapter you read about the Compromise of 1850, including the Fugitive Slave Law; the demise of the Whig party and the emergence of the Republican party; the Kansas-Nebraska Act; violence in Kansas; the controversial Supreme Court decision in the case of Dred Scott; and John Brown's raid on Harpers Ferry.

- For 40 years, attempts were made to resolve conflicts between North and South. The Missouri Compromise prohibited slavery in the northern half of the Louisiana Purchase.

- The acquisition of vast new territories during the 1840s reignited the question of slavery in the western territories. The Compromise of 1850 was an attempt to solve this problem by admitting California as a free state but allowing slavery in the rest of the Southwest. But the compromise included a fugitive slave law opposed by many Northerners.

- The Kansas-Nebraska Act proposed to solve the problem of status there by popular sovereignty. But this led to violent conflict in Kansas and the rise of the Republican Party.

- The Dred Scott decision eliminated possible compromise solutions to the sectional conflict and John Brown's raid on Harpers Ferry convinced many Southerners that a majority of Northerners wanted to free the slaves and incite race war.

Suggestions for Further Reading

Tyler Anbinder, *Nativism and Slavery: The Northern Know Nothings and the Politics of the 1850s* (1992) and William E. Gienapp, *Origins of the Republican Party* (1987). Analyze shifts in voting patterns in the 1850s.

Borritt, Gabor, ed., *Why the Civil War Came* (1995). A collection of essays by leading scholars that explores the causes of the conflict.

William J. Cooper, Jr., *Liberty and Slavery* (1983). Examines white southern attitudes on the eve of the Civil War.

Eric Foner, *Free Soil, Free Labor, Free Men* (1970). Explores northern attitudes.

Don E. Fehrenbacher, *The Dred Scott Case* (1978). Thoroughly examines this landmark Supreme Court decision.

William W. Freehling, *The Road to Disunion* (1990); Bruce Levine, *Half Slave and Half Free: The Roots of the Civil War* (1992); David M. Potter, *The Impending Crisis* (1976); and Kenneth M. Stampp, *America in 1857* (1990). Explore the causes of the Civil War.

Novels

Harriet Jacobs, *Incidents in the Life of a Slave Girl* (1861).

Harriet Beecher Stowe, *Uncle Tom's Cabin* (1852).

Media Resources
Web Sites

19th-Century Documents
http://www.yale.edu/lawweb/avalon/19th.htm
The full text of the Fugitive Slave Act, the Kansas-Nebraska Act, and other important antebellum political documents.

Bleeding Kansas
http://www.ukans.edu/carrie/kancoll/galbks.htm
Books, diaries, autobiographies, and letters documenting the struggle over slavery in territorial Kansas.

Documents from the Gilder Lehrman Collection
http://www.gliah.uh.edu/modules/coming_civilwar/documents.cfm
Primary sources documenting the decade preceding the Civil War.

John Brown's Holy War
http://www.pbs.org/wgbh/amex/brown/
The companion site to the PBS documentary contains a time line, maps, glossary, and historical overviews on a variety of topics related to John Brown's raid on Harpers Ferry.

***Uncle Tom's Cabin* and American Culture**
http://jefferson.village.virginia.edu/utc/
Texts, images, songs, objects, and film clips relating to Harriet Beecher Stowe's *Uncle Tom's Cabin*.

Films and Videos

Abe Lincoln in Illinois (1940). This screen biography retells Lincoln's life from his log-cabin birth to his departure for the White House.

John Brown's Holy War (1999). This PBS documentary chronicles the life and times of the man whose armed crusade against slavery ended in his execution at Harpers Ferry.

Santa Fe Trail (1941). A fanciful recreation of the fight for Kansas during the 1850s with Ronald Reagan, Errol Flynn, and Olivia De Haviland.

Young Mr. Lincoln (1940). Biography of Abraham Lincoln from his log-cabin upbringing to Springfield attorney.

Key Terms

Missouri Compromise   (p. 365)

Popular sovereignty   (p. 365)

Compromise of 1850   (p. 369)

Fugitive Slave Law   (p. 369)

Underground Railroad   (p. 370)

Know Nothing Party   (p. 371)

Nativists   (p. 371)

Doughface   (p. 372)

Gadsden Purchase   (p. 372)

Ostend Manifesto   (p. 373)

Kansas-Nebraska Act   (p. 374)

Republican Party   (p. 374)

Lecompton Constitution   (p. 379)

Lincoln-Douglas debates   (p. 380)

Harpers Ferry   (p. 381)

PEOPLE YOU SHOULD KNOW

David Wilmot   (p. 365)

Stephen Douglas   (p. 365)

Henry Clay   (p. 365)

John C. Calhoun   (p. 368)

Daniel Webster   (p. 368)

William H. Seward   (p. 368)

Zachary Taylor   (p. 368)

Millard Fillmore   (p. 368)

Harriet Beecher Stowe   (p. 370)

Abraham Lincoln   (p. 371)

Franklin Pierce   (p. 372)

Charles Sumner   (p. 376)

John Brown   (p. 376)

James Buchanan   (p. 377)

John C. Frémont   (p. 377)

Dred Scott   (p. 377)

Roger Taney   (p. 378)

REVIEW QUESTIONS

1. Why did California's application for statehood cause heated debate in Congress?

2. In what ways did Southerners benefit from the Compromise of 1850? In what ways did Northerners benefit?

3. Why did the Fugitive Slave Law anger many Northerners?

4. What issue led to the formation of the Republican Party?

5. How was the issue of slavery to be decided in Kansas and Nebraska? Why did the status of slavery in Kansas become a divisive issue during the 1850s?

6. What did the Supreme Court rule in the Dred Scott decision? What was the ruling's significance?

7. What were the major differences in the attitudes of Abraham Lincoln and Stephen Douglas toward slavery?

8. Why did John Brown's raid convince many Southerners that their states should secede from the Union?

15 A Nation Shattered by Civil War, 1860–1865

Thomas Rushin and Alvin Flint, Jr.: "Johnny Reb" and "Billy Yank" at Antietam

Looking eastward from Sharpsburg into the mountains of western Maryland, General Robert E. Lee uttered the fateful words: "We will make our stand." Behind him was the Potomac River and to his front was Antietam Creek. Having invaded Union territory in early September 1862, Lee dispersed his Army of Northern Virginia, some 50,000 strong, across the countryside to capture strategic points such as Harpers Ferry and to rally the citizens of this border slaveholding state behind the Confederate cause. Now he issued orders for his troops to reassemble with all haste at Sharpsburg. A major battle was in the making. General George B. McClellan's Army of the Potomac, numbering nearly 100,000 soldiers, was rapidly descending upon Lee's position.

Early on the morning of September 17, the great battle began. As the day progressed, Union forces attacked in five uncoordinated waves, which allowed Lee to maneuver his heavily outnumbered troops from point to point, warding off federal assaults. As usual, Lee calculated his opponent's temperament correctly. McClellan was too timid to throw everything into the battle at once. As darkness fell, the Confederates still held their lines. Lee knew, however, that if McClellan attacked again the next morning, the southern army might well be annihilated.

Among those rebel troops who had marched into Maryland was 25-year-old **Thomas Jefferson Rushin.** He had grown up secure in his social station as the second son of Joel Rushin, a prospering west Georgia cotton planter who owned 21 slaves. Thomas was anxious to show those far-off "Black Republican" Yankees that Southern gentlemen would never shrink from battle in defense of their way of life. He enlisted in Company K of the Twelfth Georgia Volunteers in June 1861. At 5:30 A.M. on September 17, 1862, Sergeant Rushin waited restlessly north of Sharpsburg—where the first Union assault occurred.

As dawn beckoned, Rushin and his comrades first heard skirmish fire, then the booming of cannons. Out in an open field they soon engaged Yankee troops appearing at the edge of a nearby woods. The Twelfth Georgia Volunteers stood their ground until they pulled back at 6:45 A.M. By the time that order came, 62 of the Georgians lay dead or wounded, among them the lifeless remains of Thomas Jefferson Rushin.

The human toll of the Civil War was overwhelming for contemporaries and remains so for later generations. Thomas Jefferson Rushin (left) and Alvin Flint, Jr. (right), were young casualties of the Battle of Antietam.

To the south of Sharpsburg, the battle would soon heat up. At 9:00 A.M. General Ambrose E. Burnside's Union soldiers prepared to cross a stone bridge over Antietam Creek. On the other side was sharply rising ground, on top of which troops in gray waited, ready to shoot at any person bold enough to venture onto what became known as Burnside Bridge.

The Eleventh Connecticut Volunteers were among those poised for the advance. Included in their number was 18-year-old Private **Alvin Flint, Jr.,** who had enlisted a few months before in Company D. He was from Hartford, where his father, Alvin, Sr., worked in a papermaking factory. Flint's departure from home was sorrowful because his mother had just died of consumption. A few weeks later he received word that his younger sister had succumbed to the same disease.

Flint's own sense of foreboding must have been overwhelming as he charged toward the bridge. In an instant, he became part of the human carnage, as minié balls poured down from across the bridge. Bleeding profusely from a mortal wound, he died before stretcher-bearers from the Ambulance Corps could reach him.

Flint had not known that his father and younger brother had recently joined another Connecticut regiment, affording Alvin, Sr., the chance to visit the battlefield a month later in search of his son's remains. Deeply distressed, his father wrote the *Hartford Courant* and decried the loss of "my boy" who "was brutally murdered" because of this "hellish, wicked rebellion." "Oh how dreadful was that place to me," he wrote in agony, where his son "had been buried like a beast of the field!"

Fifty-three-year-old Alvin Flint, Sr., gave up, returned to his regiment, and marched toward Fredericksburg, Virginia, where another major battle took place in December 1862. A month later the two remaining Flints died of typhoid fever, a disease then raging through the Army of the Potomac.

As the human toll mounted higher and higher, Civil War battlefields became hallowed ground. Southerners named these sites after towns while Northerners named them for nearby landmarks like rivers and streams. In the South the Battle of Sharpsburg symbolized a valiant stand against overwhelming odds. In the North the Battle of Antietam represented a turning point in the war because Union troops, at last, controlled the field of combat after Lee, astonished that McClellan did not continue the fight, ordered a retreat back into Virginia on the evening of September 18.

Different names for the same battle could not change the results. With 23,000 dead and wounded soldiers, Antietam turned out to be the bloodiest one-day action of the Civil War. Before the slaughter ended in 1865, total casualties reached 1.2 million people, including 620,000 dead—more than the total number of United States troops who lost their lives in World Wars I and II combined. Back in April 1861, when the Confederates fired on Fort Sumter, no one foresaw such carnage. No one imagined bodies as "thick as human leaves" decaying in fields around Sharpsburg, or how "horrible" looking would be "the faces of the dead."

The coming of the Civil War could be compared to a time bomb ready to explode. The fundamental issue was slavery, or more specifically whether the "peculiar institution" would be allowed to spread across the American landscape. Southerners feared that northern leaders would use federal authority to declare slavery null and void throughout the land. The South made its stand on the principle of states' rights and voted to secede. The North, in response, went to war to save the Union, but always lurking in the background was the issue of permitting the continued existence of slavery. The carnage of the war settled the matter. A few days after Antietam, President Abraham Lincoln announced the Emancipation Proclamation, which transformed the Civil War into a struggle to end slavery—and the way of life it supported—as a means of destroying Confederate resistance and preserving the federal Union.

FROM SECESSION TO FULL-SCALE WAR

On April 23, 1860, the Democratic party gathered in Charleston, South Carolina, to select a presidential candidate. No nominating convention faced a more difficult task. The delegates argued bitterly among themselves, and many southern delegates walked out of the convention. The breaking up of the Democratic party cleared the way for Lincoln's election, which in turn provoked the secession of seven southern states by February 1861. As the Union fell apart, all Americans watched closely to see how "Honest Abe," the "Railsplitter" from Illinois, would handle the secession crisis.

Electing a New President

Even before the Democratic convention met, evidence was abundant that the party was crumbling. Early in 1860 **Jefferson Davis** of Mississippi introduced a series of resolutions in the U.S. Senate calling for federal protection of slavery in all western territories. More extreme **fire-eaters,** such as William L. Yancey of Alabama, not only embraced Davis's proposal but announced that he and others would leave the convention if the party did not defend their inalienable right to hold slaves and nominate a Southerner for president. After the convention rejected an extreme proslavery platform, delegates from eight southern states walked out.

Those who remained tried to nominate a candidate, but after dozens of ballots no one received a two-thirds majority. So the delegates gave up and agreed to reconvene in Baltimore in another six weeks. That convention also failed to produce a consensus. Finally, in two separate meetings, northern delegates named Stephen A. Douglas as their candidate, and southern delegates chose John C. Breckinridge of Kentucky.

To confuse matters further, a short-lived party, the Constitutional Unionists, emerged. This coalition of former Whigs, Know Nothings, and Unionist Democrats adopted a platform advocating "no political principle other than the Constitution of the country, the union of the states, and the enforcement of the laws." The Constitutional Unionists nominated John Bell of Tennessee, who enjoyed some support in the border states and drew votes away from both Douglas and Breckinridge, thereby making it easier for the sectional Republican party to carry the election.

When the Republicans gathered in Chicago during mid-May, they were very optimistic, especially with the Democrats hopelessly divided. Delegates constructed a platform with many promises, including high tariffs in an appeal to gain the support of northern manufacturers and a homestead law in a bid to win the backing of citizens wanting free farmland. On the slave expansion issue there was no hint of compromise. "The normal condition of all the territory of the United States is that of freedom," the platform read, and no federal, state, or local legislative body could ever "give legal existence to slavery in any territory." The platform, however, did not call for an end to slavery in states where that institution already existed.

To ensure victory, Republican party regulars sought a candidate, as one of them stated, "of popular origin, . . . who had no record to defend and no radicalism of an offensive character." This left out

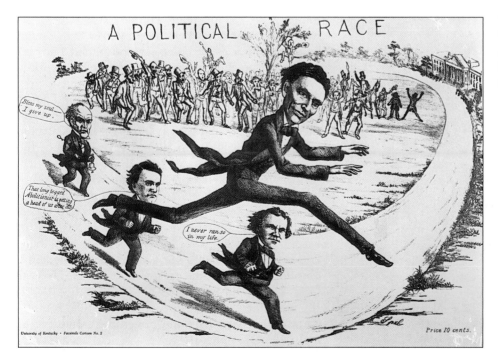

This 1860 cartoon shows Abraham Lincoln, "the fittest of all candidates," outdistancing his opponents.

Senator **William H. Seward,** the front-runner, who was widely known as a strong antislavery advocate. Seward fell short of a majority on the first ballot. Then the skilled floor managers of **Abraham Lincoln,** the local favorite from Illinois—the Republican party had failed to carry this state in 1856—started what became a landslide for their candidate.

The 1860 presidential campaign took place in a lightning-charged atmosphere of threats and fears bordering on hysteria. Rumors of slave revolts, town burnings, and the murder of women and children swept the South. Newspapers reported the imminence of John Brown–style invasions and of slaves stockpiling strychnine to poison water supplies. In one Alabama town, a mob hanged a stranger, thinking him to be an abolitionist. Across the South militia companies armed themselves and started to drill just in case that "black-hearted abolitionist fanatic" Lincoln won the election.

According to custom, Lincoln stayed home during the campaign and let others speak for him. His supporters inflamed sectional tensions by bragging that slavery would never survive their candidate's presidency. Stephen Douglas, desperately trying "to save the Union," announced, "I will go South." He embarked on the first nationwide speaking tour of a presidential nominee. Once under way, southern Democrats asked Douglas to withdraw from the election in favor of Breckinridge, whom they thought had a better chance to beat Lincoln. Douglas refused, asserting that only he could defeat the Republican candidate.

On election day, November 6, 1860, Lincoln won only 39.9 percent of the popular vote, but he received 180 electoral college votes, 57 more than the combined total of his opponents. The vote was purely sectional; Lincoln's name did not appear on the ballots of 10 southern states. Even when totaling all the popular votes against him, Lincoln still would have won in the electoral college by 17 votes because he carried the most populous states—all in the North. His election dramatically demonstrated to Southerners their minority status.

Secession Rends the Union

Lincoln said to a friend during the campaign that Southerners "have too much good sense, and good temper, to attempt the ruin of the government." He told others he would support a constitutional amendment protecting slavery where it already existed, but Southerners believed otherwise. The choice for the South, as the Mississippi secession convention framed the alternatives, was either to "submit to degradation, and to the loss of [slave] property worth four billions," or to leave the Union. No matter what, "the South will never submit" was the common refrain. Secession, then, meant liberation from the oppression of Black Republicans.

South Carolina led the way when its legislature, in the wake of Lincoln's victory, unanimously called for a secession convention. On December 20, 1860, the delegates voted 169 to 0 to leave the Union. The rationale had long since been developed by John C. Calhoun. State authority was superior to that of the nation, and as sovereign entities, states could as freely leave as they had freely joined the Union. South Carolina, as the delegates proclaimed, had "resumed her position among the nations of the world."

By early February 1861 the states of Georgia, Florida, Alabama, Mississippi, Louisiana, and Texas had also voted for secession. Representatives from the seven states first met in Montgomery, Alabama, on February 8 and proclaimed a new nation, the Confederate States of America. They elected Jefferson Davis provisional president and wrote a plan of government, which they modeled on the federal Constitution except for their emphasis on states' rights. The southern government would consist of an executive branch headed by a president, a two-house Congress, and a Supreme Court. The Confederate constitution limited the president to a single six-year term, required a two-thirds vote of Congress to admit new states or enact appropriations bills, and forbade protective tariffs and government funding of internal improvements.

Election of 1860

ELECTORAL VOTE BY STATE		POPULAR VOTE
REPUBLICAN Abraham Lincoln	180	1,865,593
DEMOCRATIC, SOUTHERN John C. Breckenridge	72	848,356
DEMOCRATIC, NORTHERN Stephen A. Douglas	12	1,382,713
CONSTITUTIONAL UNION John Bell	39	592,906
	303	4,689,568

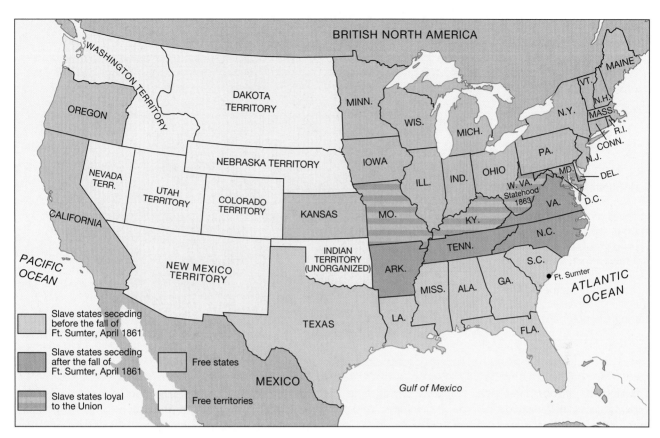

Secession

For some Northerners, such as newspaper editor Horace Greeley of the *New York Tribune*, the intelligent course was to let the "wayward sisters" of the South "depart in peace." A more conciliatory approach, as suggested in December 1860 by Senator John J. Crittenden of Kentucky, was to enshrine the old Missouri Compromise line of 36°30' in a constitutional amendment that would also promise no future restrictions on slavery where it existed. Neither alternative appealed to Lincoln. Secession was unconstitutional, he maintained, and appeasement, especially any plan endorsing the spread of slavery, was unacceptable. "On the territorial question," he stated, "I am inflexible." These words killed the Crittenden Compromise.

President-elect Lincoln, pressured from all sides to do something, decided instead to do nothing until after his inauguration. He had continued to hope that pro-Unionist sentiment in the South would win out over secessionist feelings. Also, eight slave states remained in the Union and controversial statements might have pushed some or all of them into the Confederate camp. Lincoln would make his moves prudently, indeed so carefully that some leading Republicans misread him as a bumbling, inept fool. William Seward, his future secretary of state, even politely offered to run the presidency on Lincoln's behalf.

Lincoln Takes Command

On February 11, 1861, Lincoln left his beloved home of Springfield, Illinois, for the last time. All the way to the nation's capital, as his special train stopped in town after town, the president-elect spoke in vague, conciliatory terms. Between stops, he worked on his inaugural address, which embodied his plan.

On March 4, Lincoln raised his hand and swore to uphold the Constitution as the nation's sixteenth president. Then he read his inaugural address, with its powerful but simple message. The Union was "perpetual," and secession was illegal. To resist federal authority was both "insurrectionary" and "revolutionary." As president, he would support the Union by maintaining possession of federal properties in the South. Then Lincoln appealed to the southern people: "We are not enemies, but friends." And he warned: "In your hands, my dissatisfied countrymen, and not in mine, is the momentous issue of civil war. . . . You can have no conflict without yourselves being the aggressors."

Even as he spoke, Lincoln knew the seceding states had taken possession of all federal military installations within their borders—with the principal exceptions of Fort Sumter, guarding the entrance to

Fort Sumter, at the entrance to Charleston Harbor, was the site of the first shots fired in the Civil War. Although the intense shelling continued for 34 hours and destroyed much of the fort, not a single member of the garrison's force was killed during the bombardment.

Charleston harbor, and Fort Pickens along the Florida coast at Pensacola. The next day Lincoln received an ominous report. Major Robert Anderson, in command of Fort Sumter, was running out of provisions and would have to abandon his position within six weeks unless resupplied.

Lincoln had a month to back off or decide on a showdown. He consulted his cabinet, only to get sharply conflicting advice. Finally, he sent an emissary to South Carolina to gather intelligence. At the end of March he received a distressing report. South Carolinians, the agent informed him, had "no attachment to the Union" and were anxious for war. Now Lincoln realized how grossly he had overestimated the extent of pro-Union feeling in the South. The president resolved to stand firm.

Knowing full well the implications of his actions, Lincoln ordered the navy to take provisions to Fort Sumter. Just before the expedition left, he sent a message to South Carolina's governor, notifying him that "if such attempt be not resisted, no effort to throw in men, arms, or ammunition, will be made." The rebels, from the president's point of view, would have to decide whether they wanted war.

Before the supply expedition arrived, Confederate General P. G. T. Beauregard presented Major Anderson with a demand that he and his troops withdraw from Fort Sumter. Anderson replied that he would do so if not resupplied. Knowing that help was on the way, Confederate officials ordered the cannonading of Fort Sumter. The firing commenced at 4:30 A.M. on April 12, 1861. Thirty-four hours later, Major Anderson surrendered. On April 15, Lincoln announced that an "insurrection" existed and called for 75,000 volunteers to put down the South's rebellion. The Civil War had begun.

An Accounting of Resources

The firing on Fort Sumter caused both jubilation and consternation. Most citizens thought a battle or two would quickly end the conflict, so they rushed to enlist, not wanting to miss the action. The emotional outburst was particularly strong in the South where up to 200,000 enthusiasts tried to join the fledgling Confederate military machine. Several thousand had to be sent home, since it was impossible to muster them into the service in so short a time with even the bare essentials of war—uniforms, weapons, camp equipment, and food rations.

Professional military men like Lieutenant Colonel **Robert E. Lee,** who had experienced combat in the Mexican War, were less enthusiastic. "I see only that a fearful calamity is upon us," he wrote. Lee was anxious "for the preservation of the Union," but he felt compelled to defend the "honor" of Virginia, should state leaders vote for secession. If that happened, he would resign his military commission and "go back in sorrow to my people and share the misery of my native state."

On April 17, Virginians seceded in direct response to Lincoln's declaration of an insurrection. By late May, North Carolina, Tennessee, and Arkansas had also voted to leave the Union, meaning that 11 states containing a population of nearly 9 million people, including 3.5 million slaves, ultimately pro-

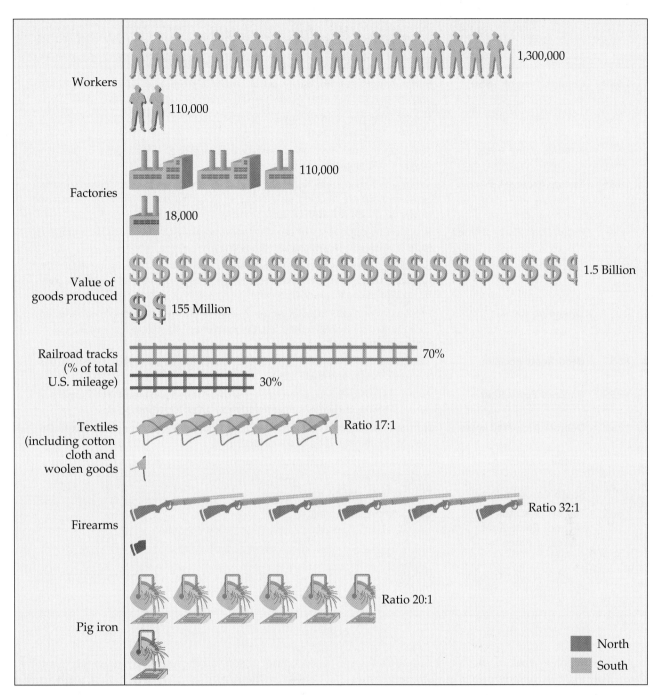

FIGURE 15.1
Resources, North and South

claimed their independence. On the other hand, four slaveholding states bordering the North—Delaware, Maryland, Kentucky, and Missouri—equivocated about secession. Lincoln understood that sustaining the loyalty of the border states was critical. Besides making it more difficult for the Confederates to carry the war into the North, their presence gave the Union, with 23 million people, a decisive population edge, a major asset should a prolonged military struggle ensue.

Set in this frame, Robert E. Lee's gloom reflected more than a personal dilemma about conflicting loyalties; it also related to a realistic appraisal of what were overwhelming northern advantages going into the war. The value of northern property was twice that of the South; the banking capital advantage was 10 to 1, and it was 8 to 1 in investment capital. The North could easily underwrite the production of war goods, whereas the South would have to struggle, given its scarce capital resources and an industrial

TABLE 15.1

Road to War: Civil War

1850	**Compromise of 1850**	Series of acts that appear to settle sectional strife over slavery; most controversial feature was a strict law for the return of fugitive slaves.
1852	**Uncle Tom's Cabin**	Harriet Beecher Stowe's novel, which sells a million copies in 18 months, arouses antislavery sentiment in the North.
	Know Nothing Party	Anti-Catholic, anti-immigrant party grows largely at the expense of the Whig party, weakening the party system.
1854	**Kansas-Nebraska Act**	Organizes Kansas and Nebraska territories and provides that slavery in those territories will be decided on the basis of popular sovereignty; reopens issue of slavery in the territories.
	Republican Party formed	Founded by opponents of the Kansas-Nebraska Act, the party is committed to halting slavery's westward expansion.
1856	**"Bleeding Sumner"**	Senator Charles Sumner of Massachusetts denounces "The Crime Against Kansas"; three days later, Representative Preston Brooks of South Carolina beats him unconscious with a cane.
	"Bleeding Kansas"	Proslavery Kansans attack Lawrence, center of free soil settlers; a band led by John Brown avenges the "Sack of Lawrence" by killing five people at Pottawatomie Creek.
1857	**Dred Scott decision**	Declares the Missouri Compromise unconstitutional and holds that Negroes are not citizens of the United States.
1859	**Harpers Ferry Raid**	An armed group led by John Brown seizes the federal arsenal at Harpers Ferry, Virginia; Brown is subsequently executed for treason.
1860	**Democratic party splits**	Northern Democrats nominate Stephen Douglas for president; Southern Democrats nominate John Breckinridge.
	Lincoln's election	Republican candidate Abraham Lincoln, committed to halting the westward spread of slavery, wins election.
	South Carolina secedes	The Union begins to disintegrate.
1861	**Ten other states secede; Confederate States of America forms**	Compromise efforts fail.
	South Carolina troops fire on Fort Sumter	President Lincoln responds by declaring a state of insurrection and calls for 75,000 volunteers to put down the rebellion.

capacity far below that of the North. In 1861 there were just 18,000 Confederate manufacturing establishments employing 110,000 workers. By comparison, the North had 110,000 establishments utilizing the labor of 1.3 million workers.

By other crucial resource measures, such as railroad mileage, representing the capacity to move armies and supplies easily, the Union was far ahead of the Confederacy. The North had 22,000 miles of track, as compared to 9000 for the South. In 1860 U.S. manufacturers produced 470 locomotives, only 17 of which were built in the South. That same year the North produced 20 times as much pig iron, 17 times the clothing, and 32 times as many firearms. Indeed, Northern factories manufactured nearly 97 percent of all firearms, a major reason that the Confederacy

could not absorb all those enthusiasts who wanted to enlist in the spring of 1861. The South went to war with a serious weapons shortage.

What is remarkable is that the South, despite this imbalance, performed so well in the early going and that the North fared so poorly. Among the South's assets, at least in 1861, was sheer geographic size. As long as the Confederacy maintained a defensive military posture, the North would have to demonstrate an ability to win more than an occasional battle. It would have to conquer a massive region. This factor alone emboldened Southern leaders. In analogies alluding to the American Revolution, they discussed how the British, with superior resources, had failed to reconquer the colonies. If Southerners maintained their resolve, something more likely to happen when soldiers were defending homes and families, nothing, it appeared, could extinguish their desire for national independence.

In addition, the South held an initial advantage in generalship. When secession occurred, regular army officers, some of them trained at West Point, had to decide which side to serve. Most, like Robert E. Lee, stood with their states. There were about 300 available West Pointers, and some 120 joined the Confederate army. Of those senior in age, the South gained more initial talent with Lee (54), Joseph E. Johnston (54), and Albert Sidney Johnston (58), when compared to the North's draw of Henry W. Halleck (46), Joseph Hooker (47), and George G. Meade (46).

As mature senior commanders, men like the two Johnstons and Lee quickly gravitated to the top of the new Confederate command structure. The Union structure, however, was already in place, with the aging hero of the Mexican War, "Old Fuss and Feathers" **Winfield Scott** (74) serving as general in chief in April 1861. Younger West Pointers, such as **Ulysses S. Grant** (39), **William Tecumseh Sherman** (41), and **George B. McClellan** (34), were not even in the service. Grant had developed a drinking problem after the Mexican War and was running a general store in Illinois; Sherman had fared poorly as a banker in San Francisco and was heading a military academy in Louisiana; and McClellan was in the railroad business. So even with their West Point credentials, Grant and Sherman had to work through the pack of lackluster military professionals in line ahead of them.

Then there was the matter of civilian leadership. At the outset the South appeared to have the advantage. Jefferson Davis, the Confederacy's new president, possessed superb qualifications. Besides being a wealthy slaveholder, he had a West Point education, had fought in the Mexican War, had served in Congress, and had been Franklin Pierce's secretary of war (1853–1857). Further, he looked like a president. "He bears the marks of greatness," wrote an admirer in 1862, because "above all, the gentleman is apparent, the thorough, high-bred, polished gentleman."

Appearances, however, were deceptive. Davis was a hard-working but often ineffective administrator. He would not delegate authority and became tangled up in details; he surrounded himself with weak assistants; he held strong opinions on all subjects; and he was invariably rude with those who disagreed with him. Perhaps worst of all, he was not an inspirational leader, something the South desperately needed after war weariness set in. A close associate aptly described Davis in 1865: "Few men could be more chillingly, freezingly cold."

Abraham Lincoln, by comparison, lacked the outward demeanor of a cultured gentleman. Republican campaign literature of 1860 stated: "We know Old Abe does not look very handsome, but if all the ugly men in the U.S. vote for him, he will surely be elected." Worse yet, Lincoln's credentials were unimpressive. He had little formal schooling; he spent an impoverished childhood in Kentucky and Indiana before moving to Illinois and succeeding as a country lawyer; he had served only one term in Congress; and he had virtually no military experience, except for a brief stint as a militia captain during the Black Hawk War (1832). As Lincoln liked to joke, he "fought, bled, and came away" barely alive—not because of contact with "fighting Indians" but because of "many bloody struggles with the mosquitoes."

Many Northerners shook their heads as Lincoln entered the White House. With his tall, thin frame and long legs, he seemed to stumble as he walked, half hunched over in baggy clothes. When he listened, he appeared to be daydreaming; yet he did listen, and when he spoke in return, stated one newspaper reporter, "the dull, listless features dropped like a mask." Citizens soon found that Lincoln viewed himself as a man of the people, eager to do anything necessary to save the Union. They saw him bear up under unbelievable levels of criticism. Even those who disagreed with him came to admire his ability to reflect and think through the implications of proposed actions—and then to move forward decisively. As "Old Abe" or "Father Abraham," he emerged as an inspirational leader in the North's drive for victory.

"FORWARD TO RICHMOND!" AND "ON TO WASHINGTON!"

War hysteria was pervasive after Fort Sumter, and Southerners exuded confidence. As a Virginian wrote, "all of us are . . . ripe and ready. . . . I go for taking Boston and Cincinnati. I go for wiping them out." Another, having sent forth five sons, offered his daughter who "desires me to say . . . that if you will furnish her with suitable arms she will undertake deeds of daring that will astonish many of the sterner sex." Northerners were equally delirious with war fever. In New York a woman reported on "the terrible excitement" of a city full of "excited crowds" reveling in "the incessant movement and music of marching regiments."

The populace clearly wanted a fight. Throughout the North the war cry was "Forward to Richmond!" referring to the Virginia city 100 miles south of Washington that had been selected as the permanent capital of the Confederacy. Throughout the South anyone shouting "On to Washington!" could expect to hear cheering voices in return. The land between the two capitals soon became a major combat zone. President

The departure of the Seventh Regiment from New York conveys the sense of enthusiasm everyone had early in the war.

Lincoln, bowing in mid-July to pressure for a demonstration of Union superiority in arms, ordered General Irvin McDowell and 30,000 half-trained **Billy Yanks** to engage General P. G. T. Beauregard and his **Johnny Rebs,** who were gathering at sleepy Manassas Junction, lying near a creek called Bull Run, 25 miles southwest of the federal capital.

The Battle of Bull Run (First Manassas) occurred on Sunday, July 21. Citizens of Washington packed picnic lunches and went out to observe the engagement. Because the battlefield soon became shrouded in smoke, they saw little except Union soldiers finally breaking off and fleeing past them in absolute panic for their lives. Bull Run had its glorious moments, such as when Virginians under **Thomas J. Jackson** held onto a key hill despite a crushing federal assault. This stand earned Jackson his nickname, "Stonewall," and he became the South's first authentic war hero. The North had no heroes. As Union troops straggled back into Washington, they "looked pretty well whipped." Bull Run, with 2700 Union and 2000 Confederate casualties, proved to Lincoln that the warring sections were in for a long-term struggle.

Planning the Union Offensive

Bull Run showed the deficiencies of both sides. Union troops had not been trained well enough to stand the heat of battle. The Confederates were so disorganized after sweeping their adversaries from the field that they could not take advantage of the rout and strike a mortal blow at Washington. Lincoln now realized, too, that he had to develop a comprehensive strategy—a detailed war plan—to break the South's will of resistance. Also, he needed to find young, energetic generals who could organize Union

forces and guide them to victory. Devising a war strategy proved to be much easier than locating military leaders with the capacity to execute those plans.

Well before Bull Run, Lincoln had turned to Winfield Scott for an overall strategic design, and the general in chief came up with the **Anaconda Plan**—which, like the snake, was capable of squeezing the resolve out of the Confederacy. The three essential coils included a full naval blockade of the South's coastline to cut off shipments of war goods and other supplies from Europe; a campaign to gain control of the Mississippi River, thereby splitting the Confederacy into two parts; and a placement of armies at key points to ensure that Southerners could not wiggle free of the squeeze. Once accomplished, Scott predicted, pro-Unionists would rise up, discredit secessionist hotheads, and lead the South back into the Union, all in a year's time.

Lincoln liked certain features. He ordered the blockade, a seemingly impossible assignment, given a southern coastline stretching for 3550 miles and containing 189 harbors and navigable rivers. In early 1861 the United States Navy had only 7600 seamen and 90 warships, 21 of which were unusable. But with a burst of energy under Secretary Gideon Welles, the navy expanded to 20,000 sailors and 264 ships by late 1861 and continued building to 650 vessels and 100,000 sailors thereafter. The blockade became more effective with each passing month, and it also was a political success. Neutral powers generally respected

FIGURE 15.2
Comparative Troop Strength, North and South

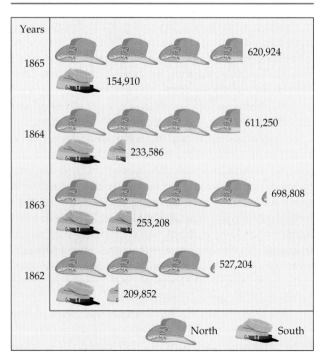

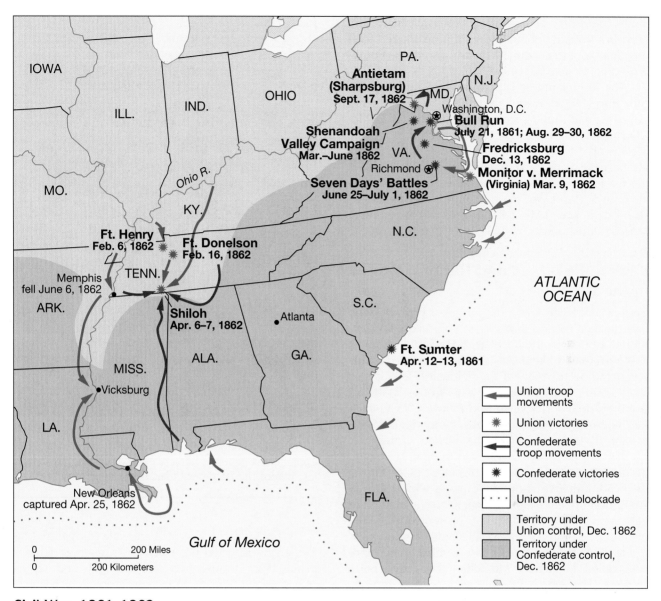

Civil War, 1861–1862

the blockade, which seriously hampered southern efforts to gain essential war matériel from abroad.

Lincoln also agreed with Scott that splitting the Confederacy was critical. He ordered Generals Henry W. Halleck, headquartered in St. Louis, and Don Carlos Buell, based in Louisville, to build great armies for the western theater. The president likewise worked with the Navy Department to devise the means to gain control of the Mississippi River. The latter effort resulted in the risky campaign of Captain David G. Farragut, whose fleet of 24 wooden ships and 19 mortar vessels captured New Orleans on April 25, 1862. Farragut's triumph was a major first step in cutting the South apart and crippling dreams of independence.

The third aspect of the Anaconda Plan, Lincoln thought, was naive. Fort Sumter had convinced him that the slaveholding elite had too powerful a grip on

the southern populace to expect any significant rallying of pro-Unionists. Nor should armies sit on the sidelines or train endlessly and wait for a decisive battle. After all, Bull Run had accomplished little except to embarrass Lincoln. By July 1861 the president was talking about truly muscular federal armies, mightier than anything the South, with its limited resources, could ever muster. After Bull Run he got Congress to authorize the enlistment of 500,000 additional volunteer troops, far beyond the number recommended by Scott.

For a man with no formal training in military strategy, Lincoln was way ahead of the generals immediately surrounding him. As he explained to one of them, "we have the greater numbers," and if "superior forces" could strike "at different points at the same time," breakthroughs would occur, and the

South could then be disemboweled from the inside. Lincoln's thinking pointed toward unrestrained total war, implying the complete destruction of the South, if need be, to save the Union.

The former militia captain needed ranking officers who viewed overall strategy as he did. Lincoln hoped he had found such a person in George B. McClellan, whom he brought to Washington to replace McDowell. McClellan happened to be in the public eye because he had just directed a small force in saving the territory of western Virginia from Confederate raiders. (West Virginia joined the Union as a separate state in 1863.) McClellan turned out to be one of Lincoln's mistakes.

Yankee Reverses and Rebel Victories in the East

George McClellan was a man of great bravado who had finished second in his West Point class and authored a book on the art of war. He could organize and train troops like no one else, as evidenced by his command of the Army of the Potomac. He was also an inspiring leader, adored by his troops. With his usual brashness McClellan told Lincoln: "I can do it all." Unfortunately, the cocksure commander was incapable of using effectively what he had wrought.

Lincoln gave McClellan everything necessary to do the job. Not only did the president place him at the head of the Army of the Potomac, which at peak strength numbered 150,000 troops, but he made him general in chief after Winfield Scott retired in the fall of 1861. The problem was McClellan's unwillingness to move his showcase force into combat. When Lincoln called for action, McClellan demanded more soldiers. The rebels, he claimed from spy reports, had 220,000 troops at Manassas Junction—the actual number was closer to 36,000. To counter this mythical force, McClellan wanted at least 273,000 men before entering the field.

To give McClellan his due, his approach to the war was different from Lincoln's. He intended to maneuver his army but avoid large battles. He wanted to save soldiers' lives, not expend them. He thought he could threaten Southerners into submission by getting them to realize the futility of standing up to so superior a force—and so brilliant a general in command.

For Lincoln, now convinced that only crushing victories orchestrated along several fronts could break the Confederate will, McClellan had contracted a bad case of "the slows." In January 1862 the angry president laughed and told a friend, "I am thinking of taking the field myself." By March he no longer covered his feelings. So that McClellan would concentrate on actual fighting, Lincoln removed him as general in chief and ordered him to use the Army of the Potomac.

Everett B. D. Julio, *Last Meeting of Lee and Jackson*, 1869. This romanticized portrayal of the two Confederate generals depicts them discussing strategy just before the Battle of Chancellorsville in May 1863.

What followed was the Peninsula campaign. McClellan transported his army down through Chesapeake Bay, landing between the York and James rivers, about 75 miles to the southeast of Richmond. In May his army moved forward at a snail's pace, which allowed the Confederates time to mass 70,000 troops. By the end of the month McClellan's advance units were approaching the outskirts of Richmond. Rebel forces under Joseph E. Johnston struck the main Union army near the Chickahominy River on May 31 and June 1. The Battle of Seven Pines cost a total of 10,000 casualties, among them a seriously wounded General Johnston.

Johnston's misfortune opened the way for Robert E. Lee, then advising President Davis on military matters, to assume command of the Army of Northern Virginia. Evaluating his opponent, Lee called in "Stonewall" Jackson's corps from the Shenandoah Valley and aggressively went after the Union army. McClellan all but panicked. Insisting that his army now faced 200,000 rebels (the number was 90,000), he retreated after two inconclusive fights north of the Chickahominy. What ensued was the Battle of the Seven Days (June 25–July 1) in which combined casualties reached 30,000, two-thirds sustained by the Confederates. Still, Lee's offensive punches prevailed—and saved Richmond. McClellan soon boarded his troops on waiting transport ships and returned to Washington.

The aggressive Lee, meanwhile, sensed other opportunities. In defending Richmond the rebels had abandoned their advanced post at Manassas Junction. A Union force numbering 45,000 under General John Pope moved into position there. Having just come in from the western theater, Pope was as blind to danger as McClellan was cautious. He thought the enemy a trifle and kept exhorting his officers to "study the probable lines of retreat of our opponents." What Pope did not factor in was the audacity of Lee, who, once sure of McClellan's decision to retreat, wheeled about and rushed northward straight toward Pope.

Lee broke all the rules by dividing his force and sending Jackson's corps in a wide, looping arc around Pope. On August 29, Jackson began a battle known as Second Bull Run (Second Manassas). When Pope turned to face Jackson, Lee hit him from the other side. The battle raged for another day and ended with Union troops again fleeing for Washington. Combined casualties were 19,000 (10,000 for the North).

Even with another monstrous body count, the Army of the Potomac had gained nothing in over a year's campaigning. A tired, frustrated Lincoln said: "We might as well stop fighting." The president knew he had to get the war off dead center, and he was already devising plans to do so, which included an emancipation proclamation. Lee gave Lincoln the opportunity to announce that document when he led his victorious army into Maryland in early September, moving toward Antietam and yet another rendezvous with McClellan.

Federal Breakthrough in the West

The two Union western commanders, Henry W. Halleck and Don Carlos Buell, also suffered from "the slows." Neither responded to Lincoln's pleas for action. Halleck, however, was not afraid to let his subordinates take chances. Brigadier General Ulysses S. Grant had a good idea about how to break through 50,000 Confederate troops—under the overall command of General Albert Sidney Johnston—spread thinly along a 150-mile line running westward from Bowling Green, Kentucky, to the Mississippi River. The weak points were the two rebel forts, Henry and Donelson, guarding the Tennessee and Cumberland rivers in far northern Tennessee.

Grant sensed that a combined land and river offensive might reduce these forts, thereby cutting through the rebel defensive line and opening states such as Tennessee to full-scale invasion. Working

Union commander Ulysses S. Grant discusses war strategies with his men near Spotsylvania, Virginia, in 1864. After Grant led Union forces to victory at Fort Henry, Fort Donelson, Shiloh, Vicksburg, Chattanooga, Lookout Mountain, and Missionary Ridge, President Lincoln appointed him commander of all Union forces.

with Flag Officer Andrew H. Foote, who commanded the Union gunboats, the Federals captured both forts in February 1862. Grant even earned the nickname "Unconditional Surrender" when he told the Fort Donelson commander to choose between capitulation or annihilation, which netted the Union side 15,000 rebel prisoners.

After puncturing the Confederate line, Grant's army of 40,000 poured into Tennessee, following after Johnston, who retreated all the way to Corinth in northern Mississippi. Cautioned by Halleck "to strike no blow until we are strong enough to admit no doubt of the result," Grant settled his army in at Pittsburgh Landing, 25 miles north of Corinth along the Tennessee River—with advanced lines around a humble log church bearing the name Shiloh. There he waited for reinforcements marching south under Buell. Flushed with confidence, Grant did not bother to order a careful posting of picket guards.

When Johnston received additional troops under Beauregard, he decided to attack. At dawn on April 6, 40,000 rebels overran Grant's outer lines, and for two days the battle raged before the Federals drove off the Confederates. The Battle of Shiloh (Pittsburgh Landing) resulted in 20,000 combined casualties. General Johnston died the first day from a severe leg wound, which cost the South a valued commander. Grant, so recently hailed as a war hero, now faced severe criticism for not having secured his lines. Some even claimed that he was dead drunk when the rebels first struck, undercutting—at least for the moment—thoughts of elevating him to higher command.

With other Union victories along the Mississippi corridor, and with Farragut's capture of New Orleans, the Union western offensive was making headway. The only portion of the Mississippi River yet to be conquered was a 110-mile stretch running north from Port Hudson, Louisiana, to Vicksburg, Mississippi. Since the rebels had powerful artillery batteries trained on the river, Union gunboats could not pass through this strategic zone and complete the dissection of the Confederacy. General Grant would redeem his reputation in 1863 by conquering Vicksburg after a prolonged siege.

TO AND FROM EMANCIPATION: THE WAR ON THE HOME FRONT

Rarely a man of humor, Jefferson Davis laughed when he read a letter from a young woman demanding that her soldiering boyfriend be sent home to wed her. Even though "I is willin" to marry him, she wrote, the problem was "Jeem's capt'in," who "ain't willin" to let him leave the front. She begged Davis to intervene, promising that "I'll make him go straight back when he's done got married and fight just as hard as ever." Thinking it good for morale, Davis ordered the leave. True to his bride's word, "Jeem," once married, did return to his unit in one of thousands of incidents involving ordinary citizens who were trying to maintain the normal rhythms of life in the midst of a terrible war.

Keeping up morale—and the will to endure at all costs—was a major challenge for both sides, once citizens at home accepted the reality of a long and bloody conflict. How civilian leaders in the North and the South handled these problems had a direct bearing on the outcome of the conflict. Northern leaders, drawing on greater resources, proved more adept at finding solutions designed to keep up morale while breaking the southern will to continue the war.

An Abundance of Confederate Shortages

With their society lacking an industrial base, southern leaders realized the great need to secure material aid from Europe, just as the American colonists had received vital foreign support to sustain their rebellion against Britain. Overconfident secession enthusiasts expected Europe's dependence on cotton to assure them unofficial assistance, if not diplomatic recognition as an independent nation. "Cotton," predicted the *Charleston Mercury*, "would bring England to her knees." It did not. A glut then existed in the European marketplace, and British textile manufacturers after 1861 turned to Egypt, India, and Brazil as sources for new supplies of cotton.

ANTIETAM

"We Will Make Our Stand"

As George B. McClellan moved his Army of the Potomac into Maryland during September 1862, in pursuit of Robert E. Lee's Army of Northern Virginia, a Union soldier stumbled upon cigars lying in a field wrapped in a piece of paper. The paper was a copy of Lee's orders regarding his invasion of Maryland. The Confederate general had divided his force to strike at such vulnerable federal posts as Harpers Ferry.

McClellan now had the opportunity to destroy separate components of Lee's army. The methodical Union general did speed up his advance but not at a fast enough pace to take advantage of circumstances.

Learning of McClellan's discovery, Lee issued urgent orders for his units to reassemble at Sharpsburg. Most critical were "Stonewall" Jackson's soldiers, who had easily captured Harpers Ferry and a Union garrison of 12,000 on September 15. Had McClellan attacked Lee on the 16th before Jackson's troops covered the 15 miles from Harpers Ferry to Sharpsburg, he might have crushed his opponent. As usual, McClellan acted slowly, preferring to refine his battle plan for the 17th.

There was nothing wrong with the plan. The idea was to throw the weight of Union troops against Lee's left flank, north of Sharpsburg. Meanwhile, General Ambrose E. Burnside was to create a diversion by crossing the stone bridge over Antietam Creek southeast of town, thereby pinning down rebels that could be shifted to support Lee's left flank.

The Union army, however, never got its punches coordinated. Three assaults on Lee's left, from dawn until late morning, proved futile. Then the battle shifted toward the center, where soldiers fought along a sunken farm road, since known as Bloody Lane. In the early afternoon, Burnside finally got his troops across the bridge. They threatened to crush Lee's right flank before a column of Confederates rushing north from Harpers Ferry cut off their thrust.

Antietam was the bloodiest day of the war. Once again, President Lincoln was furious with McClellan's unaggressive generalship, and he eventually removed him from command. More important, the appearance of a Union victory, based on Lee's retreat back into Virginia, gave Lincoln what he needed, the opportunity to announce his Emancipation Proclamation.

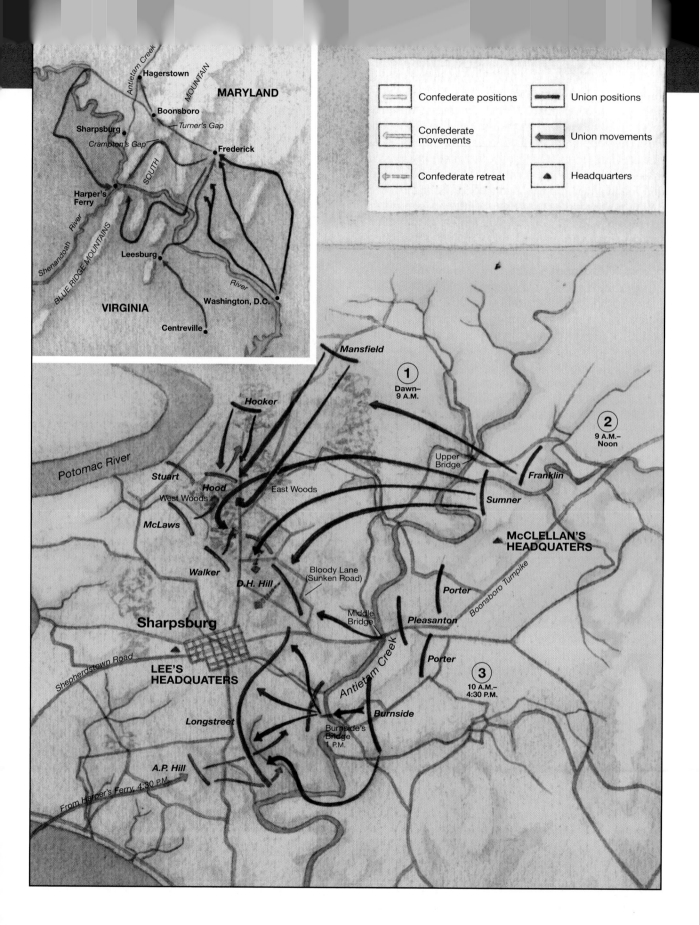

MARYLAND

Hagerstown

Antietam Creek

Boonsboro

Turner's Gap

Sharpsburg

Crampton's Gap

SOUTH MOUNTAIN

Frederick

Harper's Ferry

Shenandoah River

BLUE RIDGE MOUNTAINS

Leesburg

River

Washington, D.C.

VIRGINIA

Centreville

	Confederate positions		Union positions
	Confederate movements		Union movements
	Confederate retreat	▲	Headquarters

Mansfield

1 Dawn– 9 A.M.

2 9 A.M.– Noon

Hooker

Upper Bridge

Franklin

Potomac River

Stuart

Hood

West Woods

East Woods

Sumner

McLaws

McCLELLAN'S HEADQUATERS

Walker

D.H. Hill

Bloody Lane (Sunken Road)

Porter

Boonsboro Turnpike

Sharpsburg

Middle Bridge

Pleasanton

Antietam Creek

Porter

3 10 A.M.– 4:30 P.M.

LEE'S HEADQUATERS

Shepherdstown Road

Longstreet

Burnside

Burnside's Bridge 1 P.M.

A.P. Hill

From Harper's Ferry 4:30 P.M.

Some British leaders saw advantages to a prolonged war in which the Union and Confederacy ripped each other apart. Wrote Lincoln's minister to Russia, "I saw at a glance where the feeling of England was. They hoped for our ruin! They are jealous of our power. They care neither for the South nor the North." In addition, Britain had long since abandoned slavery, and leaders had moral qualms about publicly recognizing a slave power. Having so little to gain except the possible destruction of the rising—and still much-hated—American nation, the English government chose to remain on the sidelines. Queen Victoria announced her country's neutrality in May 1861.

Despite concerted southern diplomatic efforts, other European nations followed Britain's lead and officially ignored the Confederacy. Some of these countries depended heavily on northern grain crops to help feed their populace. Grain rather than "king cotton" was most vital to their national well-being.

The Confederacy, however, received small amounts of clandestine aid from Europe. In 1862 English shipyards constructed two commerce raiders, the *Florida* and the *Alabama*, before protests from the Lincoln administration ended such activity. By 1865 blockade runners had transported an estimated 600,000 European-produced weapons into southern ports. The Richmond government also obtained about $710 million in foreign loans, secured by promises to deliver cotton; but the tightening Union naval blockade made the exportation of cotton difficult, discouraging further European loans because of the mounting risk of never being paid back.

From the very outset, Union naval superiority was a critical factor in isolating the South. There was a moment of hope in March 1862, when a scuttled U.S. naval vessel, the *Merrimack,* now covered with iron plates, given a huge ram, and renamed the CSS *Virginia,* steamed out into Norfolk Bay and battered a fleet of wooden Union blockade vessels. Losing engine power, the *Virginia* retreated, then returned the next day to discover a new adversary, the USS *Monitor,* also clad in iron and ready to fight. The *Virginia* held its own in the ensuing battle but finally backed away, as if admitting that whatever the South tried, the North could counter it effectively. The Confederacy simply lacked the funds to build a naval fleet of any consequence, a disadvantage that allowed the Union navy to dominate the sea lanes.

The effects of cutting the South off from external support were profound. By the spring of 1862 citizens at home were experiencing many shortages—and getting mad about it. Such common items as salt, sugar, and coffee had all but disappeared, and shoes and clothing were at a premium. In 1863 bread riots broke out in several southern cities, including Richmond, where citizens demanded basic food amid

Although neither the *Monitor* (foreground) nor the *Merrimack* (*CSS Virginia*) won a decisive victory when they met, they helped introduce a new era in naval warfare by demonstrating the superior capacity of ironclads over wooden vessels.

shouts of, "we are starving." Shortages abetted rapid inflation, as did the overprinting of Confederate dollars. The central government put a total of $1.5 billion into circulation to help pay for the war. Between 1861 and 1865 prices spiraled upward on the average of 7000 percent.

Once it was obvious that cotton would not bring significant foreign support, Jefferson Davis tried to turn adversity to advantage by urging citizens to raise less cotton and grow more food. Farm women, thrown into new roles as heads of households with husbands and older sons off at war, did so, but then Richmond-based tax collectors appeared and started seizing portions of these crops—wheat, corn, and peas—to feed the armies. For struggling wives, this was too much. Many wrote their husbands and begged them to come home. Some did, thus aggravating an increasing desertion problem.

Most Southerners, in trying to comprehend so many difficulties, blamed their central government. When the Confederate Congress, for example, enacted a conscription act in April 1862—the first draft law in U.S. history—because of rapidly declining enlistments, a North Carolina soldier wrote: "I would like to know what has been done to the main principle for which we are now fighting—*States' Rights!*— Where is it? . . . When we hear men comparing the despotism of the *Confederacy* with that of the Lincoln government—*something must be wrong.*" The fault lay with power-hungry leaders like Davis, many argued, not with a political philosophy inherently at odds with the need for effective, centralized military planning to defeat the North's war machine.

In the months that followed, accusations of political high-handedness in Richmond could be heard everywhere. The draft law, for example, allowed individuals to purchase substitutes, and with rapid inflation, avoiding service became solely a wealthy man's prerogative. When the central government in October 1862 exempted from the draft all those managing 20 or more slaves, ordinary citizens were furious with their planter leaders. Some started referring to the contest as "a rich man's war and a poor man's fight."

These were very serious problems. In defending the institution of slavery, wealthy planters had touted states' rights to rally their more humble neighbors on behalf of independence. With all the shortages and sacrifices, however, disaffection with these same planters was on the rise because they were violating the tenets of states' rights and adopting laws favoring their class. In combination with a dawning realization that the North had overpowering resources and numbers, some Southerners were concluding, even before the end of 1862: "The enemy is superior to us in everything but courage." Courage, especially when leaders in Richmond appeared to be so self-serving, could not be sustained in perpetuity.

Directing the Northern War Effort

Although Abraham Lincoln focused most of his energies on military matters, he did not neglect other vital areas, including diplomatic relations with foreign powers and domestic legislation. His diplomatic objective was to keep European nations from supporting the Confederacy, and his domestic goal was to maintain high levels of popular support for the war effort. Lincoln was successful on both counts, but he took many risks, the most dramatic being his announcement of an emancipation proclamation.

Unlike Jefferson Davis, Lincoln delegated authority whenever he could. In foreign affairs he relied heavily on Secretary of State William Seward, whom European leaders came to regard as hotheaded but effective. Early in the war, for example, Lord John Russell, Britain's foreign secretary, met briefly—and unofficially—with fire-eating William L. Yancey, who was in London to seek diplomatic recognition for the Confederacy. When informed of the meeting, Seward drafted a strong letter, which Lincoln toned down, all but threatening the British with war. Russell never saw the text, but he learned about it and decided not to meet again with commissioners of the Confederacy. "For God's sakes," Russell stated, "let us if possible, keep out of it." Certainly Britain had nothing to gain by provoking the Union too much, especially over so remote a possibility as according the Confederacy diplomatic recognition.

There were some intense diplomatic moments, such as in November 1861, when the U.S. warship *San Jacinto* intercepted a British packet vessel, the *Trent*, and seized two Confederate envoys, James M.

Mason and John Slidell, who were on their way to the courts of Europe. England vehemently protested such an overt violation of maritime law—stopping and searching neutral vessels on the high seas. The often-bellicose Seward took these complaints seriously, and he and Lincoln, with the skillful help of the U.S. Ambassador to England, **Charles Francis Adams,** the son and grandson of two former presidents, smoothed matters over by apologizing for the *Trent* affair and releasing the envoys from jail.

Then, a few months later, Seward received reports that English shipyards were completing two ironclad ram vessels, similar to the CSS *Virginia*. This time the United States threatened serious repercussions. In response, British officials confiscated the ironclads, thus averting another crisis. All in all, Seward and Lincoln helped convince the major European powers that they could "commit no graver error than to mix . . . in our affairs." With Europe maintaining a posture of neutrality, the North could fully concentrate on defeating the South.

Also helping the Yankee cause was wartime prosperity, which Lincoln and a Republican-dominated Congress tried to sustain. In 1862 Congress passed the Homestead Act, which granted 160 acres free to individuals who agreed to farm that land for at least five years; the Morrill Land Grant Act, which offered immense parcels of public land to states that established agricultural colleges; and the Pacific Railway Act, which laid the basis for constructing a transcontinental railroad after the war. Under the leadership of Lincoln's treasury secretary, Salmon P. Chase, Congress approved National Banking acts in 1863 and 1864, which clamped down on irresponsible financial practices and provided for a uniform national currency. Also, the Republican Congress, to protect the North's manufacturing interests from foreign competition, approved tariff acts that raised import duties nearly 50 percent.

Under the watchful eye of Secretary Chase, the government likewise resorted to various expedients to finance the war effort. In 1861 Congress approved a modest income tax with rates that fell only on the wealthy. The government also taxed the states, borrowed heavily (around $2.2 billion), and issued **greenbacks,** a fiat currency that, like Confederate dollars, had no backing in gold or silver but held its value better because of slowly growing confidence in the Union war effort. At no time did the Lincoln administration need to confiscate farm goods, a morale booster in and of itself.

Historians have debated whether the economic boom in the North generated by the Civil War sped up the process of industrialization in the United States. By some measures, such as the annual rate of economic growth during the 1860s, the war injured

TABLE 15.2

Previous Occupations of Sampled White Union and Confederate Soldiers*

Civil War soldiers came rather evenly from all occupational categories, an indication that fighting the war did not fall disproportionately on any one economic group. Confederate claims to the contrary, Union armies were not made up heavily of the foreign-born. Although 31 percent of all white northern males of military age were foreign-born, only 26 percent of white Union soldiers were nonnatives. By comparison, some 10 percent of all southern troops were foreign-born, even though only 7.5 percent of Confederate males of military age were nonnatives. The South, then, drew more heavily on its supply of foreign-born residents than did the North, just as the Confederacy called upon a far greater proportion of its eligible population (90 percent as compared to 40 percent for the Union) to fight the war. Running out of troops by late 1864, the only source left for the South was the slave population.

Occupational Categories	Union Troops	Total Male Population North (1860 census)	Confederate Troops	Total Male Population South (1860 census)
Farmers and farm laborers (includes southern planters)	47.5	42.9	61.5	57.5
Skilled laborers	25.1	24.9	14.1	15.7
Unskilled laborers	15.9	16.7	8.5	12.7
White collar and commercial	5.1	10.0	7.0	8.3
Professional	3.2	3.5	5.2	5.0
Miscellaneous and unknown	3.2	2.0	3.7	0.8

Source: Ordeal by Fire: The Civil War and Reconstruction by James M. McPherson. Copyright © 1982 by Alfred A. Knopf, Inc. Reprinted by permission.

*All numbers are in percentages.

the economy. No decade in American history before the Great Depression years of the 1930s saw less economic growth, but most of this seeming downturn had to do with the destruction of the southern economy. By war's end in 1865, two-fifths of all southern livestock had been killed; more than half of the Confederacy's farm machinery had been destroyed; and countless plantations and family farms had been ruined. In the North, by comparison, per capita commodity output rose by 56 percent during the decade of the 1860s, and the amount of working capital to underwrite business activity expanded by 50 percent. Entrepreneurs, John D. Rockefeller and Andrew Carnegie among them, made huge profits from war contracts. Their new-found capital base and ideas about the advantages of large-scale business organization certainly foreshadowed the rapid postwar transition to a full-scale industrial economy.

The intense level of governmental activity resulted in charges that Lincoln's real purpose was to become a dictator. These accusations started soon after Fort Sumter, when the new president, acting by himself since Congress was not then in session, declared an insurrection and began a military buildup. Shortly thereafter, secession-minded Marylanders attacked Yankee troops moving through Baltimore to the federal capital. To quell such turbulence, Lincoln suspended the writ of habeas corpus in Maryland and ordered the arrest and jailing of leading advocates of secession, including Baltimore's mayor and several state legislators.

The question of whether the president had the power to curtail constitutionally guaranteed rights, even when facing wartime emergencies, quickly produced a response from Supreme Court Chief Justice Roger B. Taney, a Marylander himself. In a federal circuit court case, *Ex Parte Merryman* (1861), Taney proclaimed Lincoln's action illegal by arguing that only Congress had the authority to suspend writs of habeas corpus in times of rebellion. Lincoln ignored Taney's ruling, and John Merryman, one of those arrested, languished in a military prison with no set trial date on vague charges of having incited Marylanders to secede from the Union.

During the war Lincoln authorized the arrest of some 14,000 dissidents and had them jailed without any prospect for trials. He was careful, however, not to suppress his political opponents, particularly leading members of the Democratic party. The president worked to have open and fair elections, operating on a distinction between legitimate dissent in support of the nation and willful attempts to subvert the Union. Most agree that Lincoln, given the tense wartime climate, showed sensitivity toward basic rights. At the same time he clearly tested the limits of presidential powers.

Some of his political opponents, mostly Peace Democrats who favored negotiating an end to the war and letting the South leave the Union, regularly described Lincoln as a doer of all evil. These **Copperheads,** as their detractors called them, had some support in the Midwest. They rallied around individuals such as Congressman Clement L. Vallandigham of Ohio. In 1863 Union military officials arrested him on nonspecific charges, but Lincoln ordered him set free and banished to the South. Vallandigham then moved to Canada where he conducted a vigorous election campaign to become governor of Ohio, which he decisively lost. Lincoln wisely ignored the matter, hoping that Vallandigham and other Peace Democrats, who most of all liked to bewail the **Emancipation Proclamation,** could not muster enough popular support to undermine the Union cause.

Issuing the Emancipation Proclamation

Abraham Lincoln believed fervently in the ideals of the Declaration of Independence, which gave Americans "the right to rise" out of poverty, as he described his own experience, and "get through the world respectably." He also admired the Declaration's emphasis on human liberty, which made chattel slavery inconsistent with the ideals of the Revolution. Slavery, he wrote as early as 1837, was "founded both on injustice and bad policy."

After becoming president, Lincoln promised not to interfere with slavery in established southern states. When warfare began, he seemed to move with indecisive steps toward emancipation. His only war aim, he claimed well into the spring of 1862, was to save the Union. When in August 1861 General John C. Frémont, then heading federal military operations in Missouri, declared an end to slavery in that state, the president not only rescinded the proclamation but severely rebuked Frémont by removing him from command in Missouri.

For a person who despised slavery, Lincoln held back in resolving the emancipation question for many reasons. First, he did not want to drive slaveholding border states such as Missouri into the Confederacy. Second, he worried about pervasive racism;

white Northerners had willingly taken up arms to save the Union, but he wondered whether they would keep fighting to liberate the slave population. Third, if he moved too fast, he reasoned, he might lose everything, including the Union itself, should northern peace advocates seize upon popular fears of emancipation and create an overwhelming demand to stop the fighting in favor of southern independence. Fourth, he had personal doubts as to whether black Americans and white Americans could ever live together in freedom.

For all these reasons Lincoln moved cautiously, allowing people and events to decide the issue. He did not seek close identity with radical Republicans in Congress, led by Charles Sumner and Benjamin Wade in the Senate and Thaddeus Stevens in the House, men who built a strong coalition in favor of ending slavery. When these same radicals scoffed at his proposals for compensated emancipation at $500 a head, or for colonization in Central America or Liberia, he stated, "I can only go just as fast as I can see how to go." Lincoln did support a series of radical-sponsored bills adopted by Congress in the spring and early summer of 1862. One act abolished slaveholding in the nation's capital and western territories; and a second bill, the Confiscation Act, freed all slaves belonging to rebel masters fighting against the Union.

By the summer of 1862, Lincoln had finally made up his mind. The war's death toll, he now reasoned, had become too great; all the maiming and killing had to have some larger purpose, transcending the primary objective of preserving the Union. For Lincoln, the military contest had become a test to see whether the republic, at long last, had the capacity to live up to the ideals of the American Revolution. This could be determined only by announcing the Emancipation Proclamation.

Lincoln knew he was gambling with northern morale at a time when Union victories were all but nonexistent, when enlistments were in decline, and when war weariness had set in. He was aware that racists, such as the person who wrote and called him a "god-damned black nigger," would spread their poison far and wide. So the president waited for the right moment, such as after an important battlefield triumph, to quiet his critics, who would surely say that emancipation was a desperate measure designed to cover up presidential mismanagement of the war.

As a shrewd politician, Lincoln began to prepare Northerners for what was coming. He explained to readers of Horace Greeley's *New York Tribune* in late August: "If I could save the Union without freeing *any* slave, I would do it; and if I could save it by freeing *all* the slaves, I would do it; and if I could save it by freeing some and leaving others alone, I would

Allegory of Freedom with Martin Delaney, c. 1863, artist unknown. On the same day that he issued the Emancipation Proclamation, President Lincoln announced a new program to enlist black troops for the Union Army. Martin R. Delaney, physician, abolitionist, writer, and lecturer, persuaded Lincoln to allow him to recruit an all-black unit. Early in 1865, Delaney was commissioned major of infantry of the 104th Colored Troops, becoming the first black line field officer in the U.S. Army.

also do that." Sidestepping any pronouncement of high ideals in public, the president would treat his assault on slavery as a war measure designed to ensure total military victory.

On September 22, 1862, five days after the Battle of Antietam, Lincoln announced his preliminary Emancipation Proclamation, which called on Southerners to lay down their arms and return to the Union by year's end or to accept the abolition of slavery. Getting no formal response, on January 1, 1863, he declared all slaves in the Confederacy "forever free." The final document called emancipation "an act of justice, warranted by the Constitution upon military necessity." Out of necessity, too, slavery could continue to exist in the four Union border states—to ensure a united front against the rebels.

In private, Lincoln referred to the horrible carnage at Antietam as "an indication of Divine will" that had forever "decided the question" of emancipation "in favor of the slaves." He did not see how slavery, even in the loyal border states, could long outlast the war, and he happily envisioned a republic now moving forward toward the realization of its ideals.

Lincoln did something else in the wake of Antietam. He fired George McClellan for not using his superior troop strength to destroy Lee's army when the opportunity had so clearly presented itself. In trying to save soldiers' lives, Lincoln reasoned, McClellan's timidity would actually cost thousands more in the days ahead. So the president kept searching for a commander with the capacity to bring down the Confederacy in a war now dedicated to abolishing slavery as a means to preserve the Union.

Emancipation Tests Northern Resolve

Reaction to the preliminary proclamation varied widely. With Democrats in Congress calling for Lincoln's impeachment, some cabinet members urged the president to reconsider. They also feared repercussions in the upcoming November elections. The Republicans did lose seats, but they still controlled Congress, despite the efforts of many Democrats to smear "Black Republican" candidates. Certainly, too, frustration with so many battlefield reverses, as much as news of the proclamation, hurt the Republicans at the polls.

Others, however, criticized Lincoln for not going far enough. Abolitionists chided him for offering only half a loaf, and female activists like **Susan B. Anthony** and Elizabeth Cady Stanton formed the Woman's Loyal National League, dedicated to the eradication of slavery in all the states. Foreign opinion generally applauded Lincoln, although a few commentators made caustic remarks about a curious new "principle" that no American would henceforth be allowed to own slaves "unless he is loyal to the United States."

In the Confederacy, the planter elite played on traditional racist attitudes and used the proclamation to rally white citizens wavering in their resolve. Here was proof, shouted planter leaders, that every indignity the South had suffered was part of a never-

Despite an excellent record in combat, black soldiers often found themselves the victims of discrimination. Black regiments were kept separate from white units and were commanded by white officers.

ending abolitionist plot to stir up slave rebellions and "convert the quiet, ignorant black son of toil into a savage incendiary and brutal murderer."

Back in the North, African Americans were jubilant. Wrote **Frederick Douglass,** "We shout for joy that we live to record this righteous decree." Standing outside the White House on New Year's Day, 1863, a group of African Americans sang praises to the president, shouting that "they would hug him to death" if he would "come out of that palace" and greet them. For African Americans the Civil War meant liberation at last.

Up until this point, black Americans had found the war frustrating. Federal officials had blocked their attempts to enlist. Not wanting to stir up racial violence, Lincoln had danced around the issue. Most early African American enlistments were in the navy. Finally, in 1862, Secretary of War Edwin M. Stanton, with the president's backing, called for the enlistment of African Americans—North and South—in land forces. In a model program, Colonel Thomas Wentworth Higginson, one of the financial sponsors of radical abolitionist John Brown, worked with former slaves in the Sea Island region of South Carolina, an area under Union control, to mold them into a well-trained regiment (the 1st South Carolina Volunteers). They fought effectively in the coastal region running south to Florida.

The success of Higginson's troops broke down some racial stereotypes by demonstrating that African Americans could master the art of war. No regiment proved that more dramatically than the 54th Massachusetts Infantry. Like all other black regiments, the 54th trained separately from white units and received its commands from white officers. This regiment prepared itself for combat during the spring of 1863 under 26-year-old **Robert Gould Shaw,** the scion of a wealthy Boston antislavery family. Then the unit shipped out to the front lines in coastal South Carolina.

On July 18, 1863, the 54th Massachusetts Infantry led an early evening assault against an army more than twice its numbers that was defending Fort Wagner, a major bastion protecting Charleston harbor for the Confederacy. Eventually repulsed after fierce fighting, the 54th experienced more than a 40 percent casualty rate that evening. Shaw, who had complete confidence in his troops, was shot dead in the charge. After the battle the rebel defenders tried to mock Shaw, even in death as a Confederate stated, by burying him in a common grave "with his niggers!" Their attempted insult failed. Shaw became a martyred war hero in the North, and his surviving troops, wrote one of them, swore "Revenge for our galant Curnel." The 54th still expected "to Plant the Stars and Stripes on the Sity of Charleston" or die in the effort, this soldier declared with conviction.

Before the war ended, 179,000 African Americans had served in the Union army (10 percent of total land forces), and another 29,000 in the navy (25 percent of total naval forces). About 135,000 were former slaves, delighted to be free at last of their masters. Some 44,000 died fighting to save the Union and to defend the prize of freedom for black Americans. Twenty-four received the Congressional Medal of Honor for extraordinary bravery in battle. Among them was Sergeant William H. Carney of the 54th Massachusetts, whose citation praised him for grabbing the regimental flag after its bearer was shot down and leading the troops forward into the outer works of Fort Wagner. Carney, a runaway slave from Virginia, then planted the flag and engaged in hand-to-hand combat. Severely wounded, he reluctantly retreated with flag in hand, not suspecting that he would become the first African American Medal of Honor recipient in the Civil War—and in American history.

Because of the Emancipation Proclamation, African Americans could "march through . . . fine thoroughfares," explained one black observer, as "Negro soldiers!—with banners flying." Still, as they marched, they received lower pay until protests ended such discrimination in 1864; and they quite often drew menial work assignments, such as digging

THE PEOPLE SPEAK

A Request for Equal Pay for Equal Work

Young James Henry Gooding, a free northern African American, settled in the port town of New Bedford, Massachusetts, in 1856, where he found employment with the whaling fleet. Early in 1863 he enlisted in the 54th Massachusetts Infantry. Gooding was anxious to demonstrate that African Americans were just as capable as whites of fighting effectively in battle. The stereotype at that time was that blacks were better suited for more menial assignments, ranging from digging trenches and latrines to guarding campsites well behind battle lines. Such thinking served as an excuse for the federal government to establish lower wages for black soldiers—$10 per month minus $3 for clothing—than for whites—$10 per month plus an additional sum for clothing. Once given the opportunity, Gooding and the rest of his 54th Massachusetts comrades showed how courageously they could fight, as in the case of the assault on Fort Wagner in July 1863. A few months later after further combat, Gooding sent a letter to President Lincoln in which he called for equal pay for all soldiers, regardless of race. His well-articulated plea was representative of those that finally caused the federal government to mandate in the summer of 1864 equal pay for all soldiers. In Gooding's case, equal wages came too late. Wounded, then captured in combat early in 1864, he was thrown into the horrid Confederate prison camp at Andersonville, Georgia, where he died in July 1864. His words, as contained in his letter to Lincoln that follows, remain a timeless statement on behalf of fair and equitable treatment.

Camp of the 54th Mass. Colored Regt. Morris Island.

Dept of the South. Sept. 28th, 1863.

Your Excellency, Abraham Lincoln:

Your Excellency will pardon the presumption of an humble individual like myself, in addressing you, but the earnest Solicitation of my Comrades in Arms beside the genuine interest felt by myself in the matter is my excuse, for placing before the Executive head of the Nation our Common Grievance. . . .

Now the main question is, Are we <u>Soldiers</u>, or are we <u>Labourers</u>? We are fully armed, and equipped, have done all the various Duties pertaining to a Soldier's life, have conducted ourselves to the complete satisfaction of General Officers, who . . . now accord us all the encouragement and honour due us; have shared the perils and Labour of Reducing the first stronghold that flaunted a Traitor Flag; and more, Mr. President. Today the Anglo-Saxon Mother, Wife, or Sister are not alone in tears for departed Sons, Husbands and Brothers. The patient, trusting Descendants of Afric's Clime have dyed the ground with blood, in defense of the Union, and Democracy. Men, too, your Excellency, who know in a measure the cruelties of the Iron heel of oppression, which in years gone by, the very Power their blood is now being spilled to maintain, ever ground them to the dust.

But When the war trumpet sounded o'er the land, when men knew not the Friend from the Traitor, the Black man laid his life at the Altar of the Nation,—and he was refused. When the arms of the Union were beaten, in the first year of the War, . . . again the black man begged the privilege of aiding his Country in her need, to be again refused.

And now he is in the War, and how has he conducted himself? Let their dusky forms rise up . . . and give the answer. Let the rich mould around Wagner's parapets be upturned, and there will be found an Eloquent answer. Obedient and patient and Solid as a wall are they. All we lack is a paler hue and a better acquaintance with the Alphabet.

Now your Excellency, we have done a Soldier's Duty. Why Can't we have a Soldier's pay? You caution the Rebel Chieftain, that the United States knows no distinction in her Soldiers. She insists on having all her Soldiers of whatever creed or Color, to be treated according to the usages of War. Now if the United States exacts uniformity of treatment of her Soldiers from the Insurgents, would it not be well and consistent to set the example herself by paying all her <u>Soldiers</u> alike? . . .

We appeal to you, Sir, as the Executive of the Nation, to have us justly Dealt with. The Regt. do pray that they be assured their service will be fairly appreciated by paying them as American <u>Soldiers</u>, not as menial hirelings. Black men, you may well know, are poor; three dollars per month for a year will supply their needy Wives and little ones with fuel. If you, as Chief Magistrate of the Nation, will assure us of our whole pay, we are content. Our Patriotism, our enthusiasm will have a new impetus, to exert our energy more and more to aid our Country. Not that our hearts ever flagged in Devotion, . . . now that we are sworn to serve her. Please give this a moment's attention.

James Henry Gooding.

Source: Virginia M. Adams, ed., *On the Altar of Freedom: A Black Soldier's Civil War Letters from the Front* (University of Massachusetts Press, 1991).

Although outnumbered nearly two to one, the Confederates soundly defeated the northern army under the command of General Joseph Hooker at the Battle of Chancellorsville in May, 1863. The four days of fighting cost each side thousands of casualties. A major loss for the Southerners was General Thomas A. "Stonewall" Jackson, who was accidentally wounded by his own troops and died of pneumonia a few days later.

latrines and burying the dead after battle. Emancipation, African Americans soon realized, was just the beginning of a monumental struggle that lay ahead—beyond the Civil War—to overcome the prejudice and hatred that had locked them in slavery for over two centuries.

BREAKING CONFEDERATE RESISTANCE, 1863–1865

During the spring of 1863, Union war sentiment sagged to a low point. Generals kept demanding more troops; yet with the exception of African American enlistees, few stepped forth as new volunteers. Congress faced this reality in March and passed a Conscription Act, which provided for the drafting of males between the ages of 20 and 45. Draftees could buy exemptions for $300.00—an average wage for half a year—or hire substitutes. All told, federal conscription produced 166,000 soldiers, roughly three-fourths of whom were substitutes.

Conscription infuriated many Northerners, particularly day laborers who lacked the income to buy their way out of the service. Riots took place in several cities. The worst were in New York where Irish workers, sensing a plot to force them into the Union army so that newly freed slaves would get their jobs, vented their rage in mid-July 1863. The rampaging started when workers assaulted a building in which a draft lottery was taking place. For a week the streets were not safe, particularly for African Americans, who in a few cases were beaten to death or

hanged by roaming mobs. Only the intervention of federal troops ended the New York draft riots, but not before at least 100 people had died.

Moderate Republicans wondered whether the northern war effort could outlast such serious turmoil on the home front, but Lincoln would not back down on emancipation. As a Senate leader said of him, "he is stubborn as a mule when he gets his back up." The president kept approaching the war effort with the same grim determination, even as he continued his search for a commanding general with the talent and tenacity to achieve total military victory.

The Tide Turns: Gettysburg and Vicksburg

Before relieving McClellan of command, Lincoln had named a new general in chief, Henry W. Halleck. "Old Brains," as the soldiers called him because of his West Point education and voluminous writings on military strategy, moved to Washington from the western theater in the summer of 1862. Life in the field was one thing; life in the nation's capital was another. The pressures of office caused Halleck to have a nervous breakdown.

Lincoln did not replace Halleck but functioned as his own general in chief until the spring of 1864. His greatest frustration was with commanders of the Army of the Potomac, which the masterful Robert E. Lee kept subjecting to embarrassing defeats. After dismissing McClellan, Lincoln named General Ambrose E. Burnside, famous for his huge sideburns, to head the eastern army. Burnside did not have "the

Pickett's Charge at Gettysburg

For two days the death toll mounted, but nothing conclusive had yet happened in the Battle of Gettysburg. Late on the evening of July 2, 1863, General Robert E. Lee made the momentous decision. The next afternoon, on the third day of fighting, 13,000 troops under the command of Major General George E. Pickett would attack the center of the Union line, which stretched for 3 miles south of Gettysburg along Cemetery Ridge, a mile to the east of Lee's 5-mile line along Seminary Ridge. His soldiers, Lee believed with pride, could do anything. The question was whether, in the face of concentrated enemy fire, they could drive off their adversaries and achieve a victory so crushing that it would result in independence for the South.

Late on the morning of July 3, Pickett's officers and men started to assemble under the cover of woods along Seminary Ridge. The fear of death lurked among them, but they spoke of courage and the need "to force manhood to the front." In numerous engagements they had seen their comrades die in ghastly ways from metal hurled by Yankee weapons. They suppressed thoughts of death as best they could and prayed for God's help in girding themselves up for battle.

Like their commanders, these "Johnny Rebs" were battle-hardened veterans who knew what to expect as they marched across the open fields toward Cemetery Ridge. At first, solid shot from enemy artillery, fired mostly from cannons called Napoleons, would fly at them from up to a mile away. As they moved closer, within 400 yards or so, enemy cannons would unleash canisters, or large tin cans filled with lethal cast-iron pellets. Once in flight, the cans fell away, and the pellets ripped human beings to shreds. Within 200 yards, if not before, "Billy Yanks" would start firing their rifled muskets, the basic infantry weapon of the Civil War. With grooves inside the barrel, the rifled musket shot the minié ball, really an elongated bullet, up to 400 yards or more with accuracy. For Civil War soldiers, all of these weapons made the offensive charge a deadly proposition.

To reduce enemy firepower, Lee ordered a heavy cannonade to weaken the Union center. He hoped to knock out enemy artillery units and cause mayhem among the massed infantry on Cemetery Ridge. The bombardment began at 1:00 P.M. and lasted for over one and a half hours. Federal cannons quickly responded in what proved to be the greatest artillery barrage of the Civil War. One officer compared the noise to "that from the falls of Niagara." Another stated "that the earth shook as if in fright." When Southern officers spotted Union cannoneers pulling their artillery pieces back to greater cover, they concluded that much damage had been done. They were wrong. Sensing that so great a cannonade would be followed by an infantry attack, Brigadier General Henry J. Hunt, artillery chief for the Army of the Potomac, had ordered his units to regroup and reload with canister shot.

As the battlefield fell silent, another drama played itself out. Lieutenant General James Longstreet, Lee's valuable deputy, was adamantly opposed to the assault, believing it would only produce a senseless slaughter. Still, as Pickett's corps commander, his responsibility was to order the charge. A little after 2:30 P.M., Pickett rode up to Longstreet and said: "General, shall we advance?" Longstreet looked away and made no reply. The handsomely dressed Pickett, described by one officer as a "desperate-looking character" with long, flowing locks of hair, saluted and stated grandly: "I am going to lead my division forward, sir."

Soon Pickett was riding among the assembled regiments and shouting: "Up men and to your posts! Don't forget today that you are from old Virginia." The afternoon was excruciatingly hot, and the soldiers had been lying down to protect themselves from the Union cannonade. Now with officers urging them into line, the men were soon ready to leave the woods and press forward with red battle flags unfurled before them. Even before the advance, a few soldiers fell to the ground, suffering from "seeming sunstroke," but more likely from fear. As for the rest, wrote a rebel lieutenant, they formed a "beautiful line of battle."

From the Union vantage point on Cemetery Ridge, officers and soldiers whispered back and forth that "the enemy is advancing." The waiting Yankees "grew pale" as they crouched behind stone fences and hastily constructed earthworks. Pickett's front stretched for half a mile, and the rebels moved forward in three battle lines, "man touching man, rank pressing rank, and line supporting line." At first, Union artillery fire was sporadic, cutting only

occasional holes in Pickett's proud lines. When soldiers fell, torn to bits by cannon balls, those beside them closed ranks, as if nothing had happened.

While the Confederates advanced, Union infantry troops held their fire, reported Major General Winfield S. Hancock, whose corps took the brunt of Pickett's Charge. Then when Pickett's front line closed to about 300 yards, Union officers gave the command to fire. Hunt's artillery belched forth with canister shot, and a hailstorm of minié balls flew through the air. Rebel officers suddenly realized how little damage Lee's cannon barrage had done. They had been deceived by Hunt's decision to pull back his cannons. There was no serious weakness in the Union line.

Still the Confederates came on, now at double-quick step, determined to break through or to die honorably in the attempt. Rebel soldiers leveled their muskets, yet few got off shots before being struck down. Only 5000 men reached the stone wall, where they temporarily breached the Union line. Those who made it were shot, stabbed by bayonets, captured, or driven back in hand-to-hand combat. In little more than 20 minutes Pickett's Charge was all over. Wrote General Hancock afterward, the Confederates "were repulsed . . . and sought safety in flight or by throwing themselves on the ground to escape our fire. Their battle flags were ours and the victory was won."

Retreating as best they could, fewer than half of the rebels got back to Seminary Ridge. Pickett, a survivor among the officers, rode up to Lee in tears and shouted that his division had been massacred. Lee replied softly: "Never mind, general; all this has been *my* fault. It is *I* who have lost this fight, and you must help me out of it in the best way you can." Then Lee rode among the broken soldiers, soothing them by saying over and over again: "All this will come right in the end. . . . All good men must rally."

Gettysburg was the high mark of human carnage during the Civil War. Combined Union and Confederate losses of 50,000 or more after three days of battle were greater than total British and American casualties in eight years of fighting during the War for American Independence. The huge increase in human carnage reflected many changes in the conduct of war over the previous 80 years. Armies had grown dramatically in size, and significant technological improvements in weaponry, as represented in the expanded range and ac- curacy of the rifled musket over its smoothbore predecessor, turned Civil War battlefields into deadly killing zones.

Soldiers of Robert E. Lee's generation had been trained in the advantages of offensive tactical maneuvers. The massed charge of infantry troops during the Mexican War of 1846–1848, in which Lee and many other high-ranking Civil War officers fought, had worked in storming positions without great loss of life. This was before the United States had fully adopted the rifled musket, which occurred during the 1850s.

After Gettysburg, Lee never attempted another massed charge of soldiers. His army fought primarily on the defensive until its surrender in April 1865. And as Union troops buried slain rebels after Lee's retreat on July 4, they spoke of how the Confederates had "advanced magnificently, unshaken by shot and shell" into the jaws of death. Certainly, too, more than one Yankee reflected on the irony of the words painted on a sign hanging from a tree on Cemetery Hill: "All persons found using firearms in these grounds will be prosecuted with the utmost rigor of the law."

slows." He rushed his troops south and, on December 13, 1862, foolishly engaged Lee in a frontal assault at Fredericksburg, Virginia. His force outnumbered Lee's by a ratio of three to two; but Burnside's casualties that day were nearly 11,000, as compared to under 5000 for the Army of Northern Virginia.

Shattered by the defeat, Burnside offered strong hints to Lincoln about finding a replacement. Lincoln accommodated him and elevated "Fighting Joe" Hooker, whose ambitions to command the Army of the Potomac were well-known. Hooker did raise sagging troop morale, even if his headquarters, according to one critic, represented "a combination of barroom and brothel." With self-assurance, Hooker promised Lincoln that he could capture Richmond. The president only wanted to know when, reminding Hooker that the hen was the wisest of all animals "because she never cackles until the egg is laid."

Moving south in late April 1863, Hooker got 75,000 troops across the Rappahannock River and quickly squared off with Lee's Confederates in what became a bloody brawl known as the Battle of Chancellorsville (May 1–4). The intense action resulted in a combined casualty count of 21,000 before Hooker pulled back across the river on the evening of May 5. "Stonewall" Jackson, shot accidentally by his own pickets, died a few days later, costing the South an authentic military genius. As for Hooker, the embar-

rassment of Chancellorsville soon brought to an end his command of the Army of the Potomac.

At this juncture, with the war taking such a toll on the Virginia countryside, Lee asked Jefferson Davis for permission to lead his troops northward into Pennsylvania. There they could disrupt rail traffic, live off the land, intimidate civilians, and, most important, try to win a battle so overwhelming that Lincoln would be forced to accept peace terms favorable to the Confederacy. During June, Lee executed his plan, and the Army of the Potomac tagged along far to the east, keeping an eye fixed on the Confederate offensive challenge. Late in the month, Lincoln asked George G. Meade, a lackluster but competent general, to assume command. On July 1, 1863, the two armies squared off against one another just west of a small Pennsylvania town called Gettysburg.

The Battle of Gettysburg, lasting three days, was the bloodiest engagement of the war, with combined casualties of over 50,000. On the third day, hoping that he could split and rout his adversary, Lee massed soldiers under General George E. Pickett for an assault on the center of the Union line. Pickett's Charge, sometimes called "the high tide of the Confederacy," saw some 13,000 rebels hurtling across a mile of open, gradually rising fields. For the Union soldiers it was a turkey shoot, costing Lee at least 7000 casualties. Late the next day, Lee retreated, his army battered but not

Civil War, 1863–1865

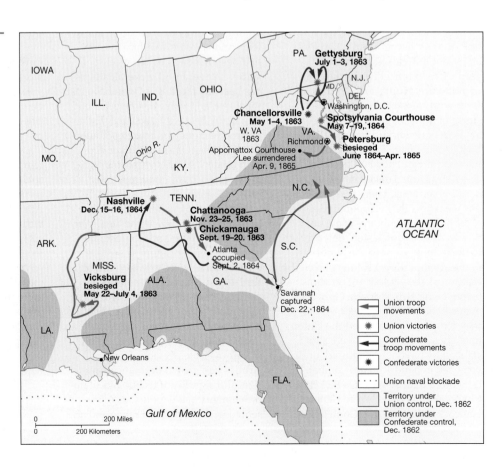

yet broken. Rather than boldly pursuing, the Union force followed along at a safe distance, causing Lincoln to accuse Meade of acting like "an old woman trying to shoo her geese across the creek."

Still, Gettysburg was a decisive battle. Never again would Lee have the troop strength to carry the war into enemy territory. Further, the timing of the engagement was important, because the federal siege of Vicksburg on the Mississippi River was just ending successfully.

Early in 1863 General Grant had secured permission to attempt the reduction of that city. Through a series of intricate maneuvers, he moved 75,000 troops south through eastern Arkansas into Louisiana, then swept east across the Mississippi River and slowly turned west in a wide arc, securing his lines against rebel marauders along the way. By late May, Grant had Vicksburg under siege, and his artillery bombarded that city and its defenders for six weeks. Reduced to living in caves and eating rats, troops under General John C. Pemberton and local citizens held out valiantly until they could take no more. On July 4, 1863, the day after Pickett's Charge, Grant accepted Vicksburg's surrender. A few days later rebel defenders capitulated at Port Hudson, Louisiana. Union forces had finally severed the Confederacy.

With these triumphs the war had turned against the South. The combat was far from over, Lincoln fully appreciated, as he rode a train to Gettysburg to dedicate a national memorial cemetery before a large crowd in November 1863. At Gettysburg he urged all citizens to "resolve that these dead shall not have died in vain; . . . and that government of the people, by the people, for the people, shall not perish from the earth."

Crushing Blows from Grant and Sherman

Vicksburg revived Grant's tarnished reputation, and after Union forces suffered an embarrassing defeat at the Battle of Chickamauga in northwestern Georgia on September 19–20, 1863, Lincoln named him overall commander of western forces. Once in the vicinity, Grant quickly restored federal fortunes in the campaign to capture Chattanooga, Tennessee (November 1863). Now the opportunity was at hand to plunge an army into Georgia to cut away at the heart of the Confederacy.

Early in 1864, Lincoln decided to name Grant general in chief, despite critics who described the western commander as a dirty, uncouth little man who drank too much whiskey—to which Lincoln reputedly said that if he could get the brand name he would send abundant supplies to his other generals. Grant arrived in Washington during March and soon unveiled his war plan. Promising to limit "the carnage . . . to a single year," Grant wanted Union armies to advance on "a common center" inside the Confederacy. They were to pursue the enemy relentlessly. Further, in a virtual declaration of **total war,** he wanted to destroy all property that could be used to support the rebel armies.

To ensure no faint-hearted maneuvers, Grant decided to travel with General Meade, who was still in command of the Army of the Potomac. The target was not Richmond but Lee's army, which Grant intended to grind into dust. The general in chief called on his old ally, General William Tecumseh Sherman, then commanding western forces, to march to Atlanta and destroy key southern railheads there. As Sherman proceeded, he was to challenge the Confederate Army of Tennessee under General Joseph E. Johnston, who had recovered from wounds suffered while defending Richmond back in the spring of 1862.

Grant and Sherman began operations in May 1864, and the spectacle made for blood-soaked newspaper headlines. Grant moved across the Rappahannock River and engaged Lee in the Battle of the Wilderness (May 5–6). Union forces took a drubbing, but something was different. They did not retreat but rolled southeastward in what became the month-long campaign for Virginia. Again and again, Johnny Rebs and Billy Yanks clashed at such places as Spotsylvania Courthouse (May 7–19) and Cold Harbor (June 1–3), within a few miles of Richmond. Finally, the two exhausted armies settled along siege lines at Petersburg, 20 miles southeast of the Confederate capital, with Grant waiting for Lee's army to disintegrate.

There had been nothing quite like the Virginia campaign before. Grant started with 120,000 soldiers, and half of them were casualties by early June. To preserve his army, Lee lived up to one of his nicknames, "King of Spades," by repeatedly ordering his troops to dig up earth, indeed anything, to provide cover from the relentless fury of federal minié balls flying at them. By the time Lee reached the Petersburg trenches in mid-June, his army had been reduced by more than a third, to 40,000.

In the North, Peace Democrats called Grant a "butcher," but the general in chief, with Lincoln's backing, held tight to the war plan. Winning was now only a matter of time since the president, as the manager of the Union's superior resources, could supply more troops and keep waging a war of attrition. The South, however, had little manpower left to draw on. Of an estimated 1.2 million white males between the ages of 16 and 50, some 90 percent had already seen Confederate military service; the comparable figure for the North was 40 percent.

In late 1864 Jefferson Davis admitted the South's need for new troop strength when he called for the conscription of slaves. Furious planters, apparently blinded by self-interest, screamed about protecting states' rights and once again denounced President Davis as a tyrant. One leader proclaimed: "The day that the Army of [Northern] Virginia allows a Negro regiment to enter their lines as soldiers they will be degraded, ruined, and disgraced." Finally, the Richmond government in March 1865 called for the enlistment of 300,000 slaves, but too late "to gain our independence," as a Georgian noted with irony, "by the valor of our slaves." The war was over before southern African American regiments could be organized.

If the Confederacy had any hope for survival in the fall of 1864, it centered on the upcoming presidential election. The Republicans, calling themselves the National Union party, renominated Lincoln in June. His new vice presidential running mate was Andrew Johnson, a Democrat who had served as Tennessee's Union war governor after Grant's invasion of that state in early 1862. The Democrats nominated General George B. McClellan. The party's platform promised a negotiated end to the war, even should that mean independence for the Confederacy—a position McClellan himself thought too extreme to support. A despairing Lincoln, looking at the horrible casualty figures in Virginia, feared repudiation at the polls by a populace too sickened by the carnage to let him finish the fight.

Lincoln's pessimism proved groundless. He had not counted on General Sherman's army, moving

Sally L. Tompkins opened a private hospital in Richmond to care for wounded Confederate soldiers after the first Battle of Bull Run.

slowly toward Atlanta in the face of stout rebel resistance. In early September, Sherman wired the president: "Atlanta is ours, and fairly won." News of the capture of this major Confederate railroad and manufacturing center thrilled Northerners. The Confederacy was obviously in serious trouble. Voters gave Lincoln a resounding victory. On November 8, 1864, he received 55 percent of the popular vote and 212 electoral college votes, as compared to just 21 for McClellan. Lincoln's reelection especially pleased Union soldiers in the field, such as one of Sherman's corporals, who wrote excitedly that his comrades now marched forward "with our Hartes contented nowing that we have a president that will not declare peace on no other terms then an Uncondishnell Surrender."

Total War Forces Surrender

In the eighteenth century, warfare rarely affected the whole populace. Armies were small, and combat could be conducted in war zones away from population centers. By comparison, the Civil War touched nearly every American life. Families gave fathers and sons to the armed services; and women assumed the

TABLE 15.3		
Incidence of Disease Among Union Soldiers		

Sickness was a chronic problem in both the Union and Confederate armies. White federal troops were ill on the average of 2.50 times a year, and black soldiers were ill on the average of 3.33 times a year. Black soldiers also died at a more rapid rate from their illnesses. There is no satisfactory explanation for these higher rates.

	Whites	Blacks
Average annual number of sick cases per 1000 troops	2435	3299
Average annual number of deaths from sickness per 1000 troops	53.4	143.4

Source: From *The Life of Billy Yank: The Common Soldier of the Union* by Bell Irvin Wiley. Copyright 1952 © by Bell I. Wiley. Reprinted by permission of Louisiana State University Press.

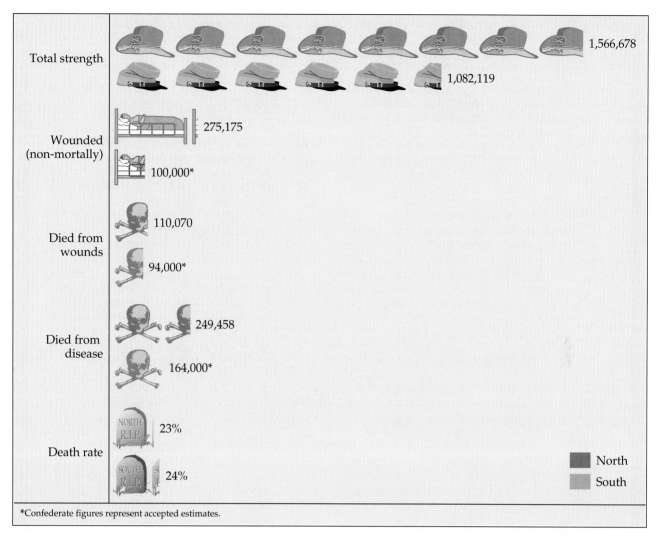

Total strength	1,566,678
	1,082,119
Wounded (non-mortally)	275,175
	100,000*
Died from wounds	110,070
	94,000*
Died from disease	249,458
	164,000*
Death rate	NORTH R.I.P. 23%
	SOUTH R.I.P. 24%

■ North
□ South

*Confederate figures represent accepted estimates.

FIGURE 15.3
The Human Cost of War

Many soldiers died as a result of inadequate care of wounds and diseases.

management of farms or moved to the cities and took jobs to keep factories humming in the production of war goods. Hundreds of women, more rigidly segregated from combat than had been the case at the time of the American Revolution, became nurses who fought to save thousands of lives.

Serving the fallen was grim work. Too often hospitals were centers of filth, horrible agony, and death. Such women as Dorothea Dix, superintendent of Union army nurses, and **Clara Barton,** who later founded the American Red Cross (1881), endured incredible personal privation to comfort those in pain. Still, they could hardly relieve the suffering. Medicine was too primitive to cope with such killer diseases as typhoid fever and malaria that swept through army camps and cut down Alvin Flint, Sr., and thousands of other soldiers.

Since physicians lacked a sense of the importance of sterilization, germs spread rapidly as surgeons cut off arms and legs to save wounded soldiers from gangrene poisoning. Troops on both sides would have agreed with the Alabama private who wrote in 1862: "I beleave the doctors kills more than they cure." Of those who survived the crude surgery of the times, only a small portion recovered in the type of clean, well-managed hospital run by **Sally L. Tompkins** in Richmond. Indeed, Confederate leaders did not officially permit the use of female nurses until the autumn of 1862. Once they did, they found that death rates were lower than in hospitals employing only male nurses.

To force an end to all the suffering and killing, General Sherman, after taking Atlanta, proposed to march his troops first eastward to Savannah, Georgia,

CHRONOLOGY OF KEY EVENTS

1860 Democratic party links along sectional lines; Republican nominee Abraham Lincoln is elected the sixteenth president (November); Senator John J. Crittenden offers a series of compromise proposals to end the sectional crisis (December); South Carolina votes to secede from the Union (December)

1861 Six Deep South States—Georgia, Florida, Alabama, Mississippi, Louisiana, and Texas—secede (January–February); Confederate States of America is formed by the seceding states (February); Fort Sumter falls to Confederate artillery (April); Lincoln declares an "insurrection," calls for volunteer troops, and announces a naval blockade (April); western section of Virginia breaks away to form West Virginia and later joins the Union in 1863 (June); South wins at Bull Run, or First Manassas (July)

1862 Union forces penetrate the South's western defenses, seizing Forts Henry and Donelson in Tennessee and capturing Memphis, Tennessee; Corinth, Mississippi; and New Orleans, Louisiana (February–June). Confederacy adopts a draft law (April); Homestead Act offers 160 acres of western acreage to citizens who will occupy and improve the land for five years (May); in the Battle of the Seven Days, the Second Battle of Bull Run (Second Manassas), and the Battle of Fredericksburg, Confederates prevent Union forces from breaking through to Richmond (June–December); Morrill Act gives states land grants to endow agricultural colleges (July); at Antietam (Sharpsburg), McClellan's army halts a Confederate offensive into Maryland and forces Lee to retreat to Virginia (September); Lincoln issues prelimi-

nary Emancipation Proclamation—all slaves in states still in rebellion on January 1, 1863, would be freed (September)

1863 National Bank Act creates nation's first centralized banking system (February); the Union passes a draft law (March); Congress affirms Lincoln's suspension of habeas corpus to persons who resist the draft, discourage enlistments, or aid the rebel cause (March); Lee leads army into Pennsylvania (June); Confederates are defeated at Gettysburg and forced to withdraw to Virginia (July); capture of Vicksburg and Port Hudson place Mississippi River under Union control (July); New York City faces violence in draft riots (July); African American soldiers in 54th Massachusetts regiment lead assault on Fort Wagner in Charleston harbor (July); Union army secures strategic railroad center at Chattanooga, Tennessee (November)

1864 General Ulysses S. Grant pursues Lee's army through Virginia to Confederate entrenchments at Petersburg (May–June); William T. Sherman's army marches from Chattanooga and takes Atlanta, then marches through Georgia (May–December); Union General Philip H. Sheridan's army takes control of the Shenandoah Valley (September–October); Four Southern state governors recommend using slaves as Confederate soldiers (October)

1865 Lee retreats from his Richmond-Petersburg defenses and surrenders at Appomattox (April); John Wilkes Booth assassinates Lincoln at Ford's Theater in Washington, D.C., and Andrew Johnson becomes the seventeenth president (April)

then north toward Grant's army in Virginia. He intended to "demonstrate the vulnerability of the South," he wrote, "and make its inhabitants feel that war and individual ruin are synonymous terms." Before year's end Sherman's soldiers cut a 60-mile-wide swath through Georgia. Then, in January 1865, they entered South Carolina, which they thought of as "the birth place of Dark Treason" against the Union. "South Carolina cried out the first for war," penned

an Iowa soldier, "and she shall have it to her hearts content." In systematic fashion Sherman's army broke the southern will to keep fighting by burning and leveling everything in sight.

As word of Sherman's devastating march reached Lee's troops in the Petersburg trenches, they deserted in droves, wanting to return home to help protect their loved ones. By late March, Lee's Army of Northern Virginia had fewer than 35,000 troops, compared to

Grant's total of 115,000. The situation was all but hopeless, so the Confederate commander ordered a retreat to the west, and Richmond fell on April 3. Grant's soldiers moved quickly to encircle the disintegrating rebel army. They soon had their prey entrapped.

On April 9, 1865, Lee met with Grant and surrendered at Appomattox. The two generals reminisced for a few moments about their previous service in the Mexican War. They said goodbye, but not before Grant graciously allowed the Confederates to keep their horses—they had to give up their arms—so that they could more easily plow their fields and plant crops after returning home. Lee's surrender served as a signal to other Confederate forces to lay down their arms and accept military defeat. The Civil War, at long last, had ended.

CONCLUSION

At noon on Good Friday, April 14, 1865, a crowd gathered to watch Major General Robert Anderson raise over Fort Sumter the very same U.S. flag that he had surrendered four years earlier. A genuinely moved Anderson said: "I thank God that I have lived to see this day." Then he hoisted up the "weather-beaten, frayed, and shell-torn old flag" as Union naval vessels out in Charleston harbor fired their cannons in salute. Citizens at the fort wept and cheered, realizing that the national tragedy was finally over, a tragedy that had forever sealed the fate of secession. The states, while far from reunited, would continue together as a nation.

Just a few hours later another shot rang out, this time in the nation's capital. John Wilkes Booth, a Confederate sympathizer and racist fanatic who hated Abraham Lincoln for emancipating African Americans, gained access to the presidential box at Ford's Theater and assassinated the president at point blank range. At 7:22 A.M. the next morning, four years to the day after he had declared an insurrection and called up federal troops, Lincoln died quietly at the age of 56.

In his last days Lincoln felt the elation of knowing that a war begun to preserve the Union had achieved its objective. Further, in recognition of the horrible price in lives maimed and destroyed, he took pride in the elimination of slavery from the American landscape, which he called the "act" that would put "my name . . . into history." Lincoln had also started to speak openly of citizenship for African Americans as part of his reconstruction plans. Even as the American people mourned his passing, they too turned to the difficult task of how best to bring

the South—defeated, destroyed, but still with a dogged streak of defiance—back into the United States.

CHAPTER SUMMARY AND KEY POINTS

Abraham Lincoln's election to the presidency in the autumn of 1860 set off a chain of events that sent the nation spiraling into civil war. Southern states reacted to Lincoln's victory by seceding from the Union. The relative strengths and weaknesses of the North and South, the military history of the war, and the dramatic political, economic, and social changes growing out of the conflict are keys to understanding how the Civil War both preserved the Union and helped bring an end to chattel slavery in the United States.

- President Lincoln's opposition to the expansion of slavery into the western territories led seven states in the lower South to secede from the Union and to establish the Confederate States of America.

- After Lincoln notified South Carolina's governor that he intended to resupply Fort Sumter in Charleston harbor, the Confederacy fired on the installation, leading the president to declare that an insurrection existed in the South.

- Early in the war, the Union succeeded in blockading Confederate harbors, and by mid-July 1862 it had cut the Confederacy in two by regaining control of Kentucky, Missouri, and much of Tennessee, as well as most of the Mississippi River.

- In the Eastern Theater in 1861 and 1862, Southern forces repulsed Union attempts to capture its capital in Richmond, Virginia. In September 1862 (at Antietam in Maryland) and July 1863 (at Gettysburg in Pennsylvania), General Robert E. Lee tried and failed to win a major victory on Northern soil to help provoke intervention in the war by European powers on behalf of the Confederacy.

- In the autumn of 1862 President Lincoln concluded that emancipation was a military and political necessity. The Emancipation Proclamation broadened the war from a contest to save the Union to a conflict to abolish slavery.

- During the war, Congress enacted the Homestead Act, offering free public land to western settlers. Land grants would be given to support the construction of a transcontinental railroad.

The federal government also raised the tariff, enacted the first income tax, and established a system of federally chartered banks.

SUGGESTIONS FOR FURTHER READING

Catherine Clinton and Nina Silber, eds., *Divided Houses: Gender and the Civil War* (1992). Challenging essays focusing on gender-related issues, including prescribed identities for men and women during the Civil War era.

William C. Davis, *Look Away!: A History of the Confederate States of America* (2002). Engaging survey of the military, legal, political, and economic structures of the Confederate states as well as the problems caused by trying to sustain independence during the Civil War.

David Herbert Donald, *Lincoln* (1995). Highly readable, perceptive one-volume biography of the nation's sixteenth president.

Joseph T. Glatthaar, *Forged in Battle: The Civil War Alliance of Black Soldiers and White Officers* (1990). Valuable analysis of racial attitudes as reflected in the wartime service experiences of African Americans.

Howard Jones, *Union in Peril: The Crisis over British Intervention in the Civil War* (1992). Important revisionist analysis of the reasons the Confederacy failed to gain powerful foreign allies, a serious impediment to securing independence.

James McPherson, *Crossroads of Freedom: Antietam* (2002). Gripping re-examination of the bloodiest battle of the Civil War, which proved to be a critical victory for the Union.

————, *Battle Cry of Freedom: The Civil War Era* (1988). Winner of a Pulitzer Prize, the best detailed introduction to the war period in its broad-ranging complexities.

Emory M. Thomas, *General Robert E. Lee: A Biography* (1995). Balanced one-volume study of the talented—and charismatic—Confederate general and folk hero.

Ronald C. White, Jr., *Lincoln's Greatest Speech: The Second Inaugural* (2002). Incisive reading of a key Civil War document calling for a generous reconciliation with the South only a few weeks before the end of the war and Lincoln's assassination.

Novels

Stephen Crane, *The Red Badge of Courage* (1895).

Charles Frazier, *Cold Mountain: A Novel* (1997).

Paulette Jiles, *Enemy Women: A Novel* (2002).

MacKinlay Kantor, *Andersonville* (1955).

Jeffrey M. Shaara, *Gods and Generals* (1996).

————, *The Last Full Measure* (1998).

Michael Shaara, *The Killer Angels* (1974).

MEDIA RESOURCES

Web Sites

The American Civil War Homepage
http://funnelweb.utcc.utk.edu/~hoemann/cwarhp.html
This site has a good collection of hypertext links to the most useful identified electronic files about the American Civil War.

The Valley of the Shadow: Living the Civil War in Pennsylvania and Virginia
http://jefferson.village.virginia.edu/vshadow/vshadow.html
This project tells the histories of two communities on either side of the Mason-Dixon line during the Civil War. It includes a narrative and an electronic archive of sources.

Civil War @ Charleston
http://www.awod.com/gallery/probono/cwchas/cwlayout.html
This site covers the history of the Civil War in and around Charleston, South Carolina.

Abraham Lincoln Association
http://www.alincolnassoc.com/
This site allows you to search digital versions of Lincoln's papers.

The Papers of Jefferson Davis
http://jeffersondavis.rice.edu
This site tells about the collection of Jefferson Davis Papers and includes a chronology of his life, a family genealogy, some key Davis documents on-line, and a collection of related links.

Crisis at Fort Sumter
http://www.tulane.edu/~latner/CrisisMain.html
This well-crafted use of hypermedia with assignments or problems explains and explores the events in and around the start of the Civil War.

U.S. Civil War Center
http://www.cwc.lsu.edu/
This is a site whose mission is to "locate, index, and/or make available all appropriate private and public data regarding the Civil War and to promote the study of the Civil War from the perspectives of all professions, occupations, and academic disciplines."

American Civil War (1861–1865) Archive
http://users.iamdigex.nef/bdboyle/cw.html
This excellent site marshals diverse information about the Civil War.

Civil War Women
http://scriptorium.lib.duke.edu/collections/civil-war-women.html
This site includes original documents, links, and biographical information about several women and their lives during the Civil War.

History of African Americans in the Civil War—United States Colored Troops
http://www.itd.nps.gov/cwss/africanh.html
This National Park Service site explores the history of the USCT (United States Colored Troops).

Assassination of President Abraham Lincoln
http://memory.loc.gov/ammem/alhtml/alrintr.html
Part of the American Memory series with an introduction, time line, and gallery.

Selected Civil War Photographs
http://memory.loc.gov/ammem/cwphtml/cwphome.html
Library of Congress site with more than 1000 photographs, many from Matthew Brady.

A Time Line of the Civil War
http://www.historyplace.com/civilwar/index.html
A complete time line of the Civil War, well illustrated with photographs.

KEY TERMS

Fire-eaters   (p. 389)
Billy Yank   (p. 396)
Johnny Reb   (p. 396)
Anaconda Plan   (p. 396)
Greenbacks   (p. 403)
Copperheads   (p. 405)
Emancipation Proclamation   (p. 405)
Total war   (p. 413)

PEOPLE YOU SHOULD KNOW

Thomas Jefferson Rushin   (p. 387)
Alvin Flint, Jr.   (p. 388)
Jefferson Davis   (p. 389)
William H. Seward   (p. 390)
Abraham Lincoln   (p. 390)

Robert E. Lee   (p. 392)
Winfield Scott   (p. 395)
Ulysses S. Grant   (p. 395)
William Tecumseh Sherman   (p. 395)
George B. McClellan   (p. 395)
Thomas J. ("Stonewall") Jackson   (p. 396)
Charles Francis Adams   (p. 403)
Susan B. Anthony   (p. 406)
Frederick Douglass   (p. 407)
Robert Gould Shaw   (p. 407)
Clara Barton   (p. 415)
Sally L. Tompkins   (p. 415)

REVIEW QUESTIONS

1. Examine the numerous problems that contributed to the dissolution of the Democratic Party and the consequences this breakup had for the coming of the Civil War. Why did Abraham Lincoln's election prompt secession?

2. Evaluate the reasons for the Civil War by considering the following: On what principles did the South secede from the Union? On what principles did the North go to war? How did these principles change during the course of the war?

3. Compare and contrast the strengths and weaknesses of the North and the South as the Civil War started. Be sure to include a survey of available resources as well as an assessment of the political leadership of the two regions.

4. Compare and contrast the military leaders, strategies, and tactics of the North and the South. How effective were the various generals in the battlefield?

5. Discuss the role of slavery as an issue during the Civil War. What were the experiences of African Americans? Why did Lincoln issue the Emancipation Proclamation? How did Northerners and Southerners react to the proclamation?

6. Assess the ways in which the Civil War became a "total war." What did the war accomplish?

16 The Nation Reconstructed: North, South, and the West, 1865–1877

THOMAS PINCKNEY CONFRONTS HIS FORMER SLAVES

As Thomas Pinckney approached El Dorado, his plantation on the Santee River in South Carolina, he felt a quiver of apprehension. Pinckney, a captain in the defeated Confederate army, had stayed the night with neighbors before going to reclaim his land. "Your negroes sacked your house," they reported, "stripped it of furniture, bric-a-brac, heirlooms, and divided these among themselves. They got it in their heads that the property of whites belongs to them." Pinckney remembered the days when his return home had been greeted with slaves' chants of "Howdy do, Master! Howdy do, Boss!" Now he was welcomed with an eerie silence. He did not even see any of his former slaves until he went into the house. There, a single servant seemed genuinely glad to see him, but she pleaded ignorance as to the whereabouts of any others. He lingered about the house until after the dinner hour. Still no one appeared, so he informed the servant that he would return in the morning and expected to see all his former slaves.

On his ride back the next day, Pinckney nostalgically recalled his days as a small boy when the slaves had seemed happy to see him as he accompanied his mother on her Saturday afternoon rounds. He could not believe he had any reason to fear his "own people" whom he "could only remember as respectful, happy and affectionate." He probably mistook their previous displays of submissiveness as expressions of a genuine affection that would not be altered by freedom. Yet he was armed this time, and after summoning his former slaves, he quickly noticed that they too were armed. Their sullen faces reflected their defiant spirits.

Pinckney told them, "Men, I know you are free. I do not wish to interfere with your freedom. But I want my old hands to work my lands for me. I will pay wages." They remained silent as he gave further reassurances. Finally one responded, "O yes, we gwi wuk! We gwi wuk fuh ourse'ves. We ain' gwi wuk fuh no white man." Pinckney was confused and asked how they expected to support themselves and where they would go. They quickly informed him that they intended to stay and work "right here on de lan' whar we wuz bo'n an' whar belongs tuh us." One former slave, dressed in a Union army uniform, stood beside his cabin, brought his rifle down with a crash, and declared, "I'd like tuh see any man put me outer dis house."

This 1865 illustration by Thomas Nast illustrates the optimism that came with emancipation and contrasts the opportunities of freedom with the horrors of slavery.

Pinckney had no intention of allowing the former slaves to work the land for themselves. He joined with his neighbors in an appeal to the Union commander at Charleston, who sent a company of troops and addressed the blacks himself. They still refused to work under his terms, so Pinckney decided to "starve" them into submission. He denied them access to food and supplies. Soon his head plowman begged food for his hungry family, claiming he wanted to work, "But de other niggers dee won' let me wuk." Pinckney held firm, and the man returned several days later saying, "Cap'n, I come tuh ax you tuh lemme wuk fuh you, suh." Pinckney pointed him to the plow and let him draw his rations. Slowly, his other former slaves drifted back to work. "They had suffered," he later recalled, "and their ex-master had suffered with them."

All over the South this scenario was acted out with variations, as former masters and former slaves sought to define their new relationships. Whites tried to keep the blacks a dependent labor source; African Americans struggled to win as much independence as possible. Frequently Union officials were called upon to arbitrate; the North had a stake in the final outcome. At the same time the other sections of the nation faced similar problems of determining the status of heterogeneous populations whose interests were sometimes in conflict with the majority. The war had reaped a costly harvest of death and hostility, but at the same time it accelerated the modernization of the economy and society. Western expansion forced Americans to deal with the often hostile presence of the Plains Indians; the resumption of large-scale immigration raised issues of how to adapt to an increasingly pluralistic society made up of many different ethnic and religious groups. More and more the resolution of conflicting interests became necessary: farmer versus industrialist, whites versus blacks, Republicans versus Democrats, Indians versus settlers, North versus South, management versus labor, immigrant versus native born, men versus women, one branch of government versus another. Complicating these issues were unresolved questions about federal authority, widespread racial prejudice in both North and South, and strongly held beliefs in the sanctity of property rights.

Reconstruction offered an opportunity to balance conflicting interests with justice and fairness. In the end, however, the government was unwilling to establish ongoing programs and permanent mechanisms to protect the rights of minorities. As on Pinckney's plantation, economic power usually became the determining factor in establishing relationships. Northerners were distracted by issues related to industrialization and Westerners by conflicts with the Plains Indians. Authorities sacrificed the interests of both African Americans and the Indians of the West to the goals of national unity and economic growth. Yet in the ashes of failure were left two cornerstones on which the future could be built—the Fourteenth and Fifteenth amendments to the Constitution.

POSTWAR CONDITIONS AND ISSUES

General William T. Sherman proclaimed, "War is all hell." Undoubtedly it was for most soldiers and civilians caught up in the actual throes of battle and for the families of the 360,000 Union and 258,000 Confederate soldiers who would never return home. The costs of war, however, were not borne equally. Many segments of the North's economy were stimulated by wartime demands, and with the once powerful southern planters no longer there, Congress enacted programs to aid industrial growth. Virtually exempt from the devastation of the battlefield, the North built railroads and industries and increased agricultural production at the same time that torn-up southern rails were twisted around trees, southern factories were put to the torch, and southern farmland lay choked with weeds.

In 1865 Southerners were still reeling from the bitter legacy of total war. General Philip Sheridan announced that after his troops had finished in the Shenandoah Valley even a crow would have to carry rations to fly over the area. One year after the war, Carl Schurz noted that along the path of Sherman's march the countryside still "looked for many miles like a broad black streak of ruin and desolation." Much of what was not destroyed was confiscated, and emancipation divested Southerners of another $2 billion to $4 billion in assets. The decline of southern wealth has been estimated at more than 40 percent during the four years of war.

The War's Impact on Individuals

Returning soldiers and their wives had to reconstruct relationships disrupted by separation—and the assumption of control by the women on farms and plantations. War widows envied them that adjustment. While the homeless wandered, one plantation mistress moaned, "I have not one human being in the wide world to whom I can say 'do this for me.'" Another noted, "I have never even so much as washed out a pocket handkerchief with my own hands, and now I have to do all my work." Southerners worried about how to meet their obligations; Confederate currency and bonds were worthless except as collectors' items—and even as collectors' items, they were too plentiful to have much value. One planter remarked dryly that his new son "promises to suit the times, having remarkably large hands as if he might one day be able to hold plough handles." Many white Southerners, rich and poor, suffered a self-

induced paranoia. They imagined the end of slavery would bring a nightmare of black revenge, rape, and pillage unless whites retained social control.

For four million former slaves, emancipation had come piecemeal, following the course of the northern armies. It was not finalized until the ratification of the Thirteenth Amendment in December 1865. Most slaves waited patiently for the day of freedom, continuing to work the plantations but speaking up more boldly. Sometimes the Yankees came, proclaimed them free, and then left them to the mercy of their masters. Most, therefore, reacted cautiously to test the limits of their new freedom.

Many African Americans had to leave their plantations, at least for a short time, to feel liberated. A few were confused as to the meaning of freedom and thought they would never have to work again. Soon, most learned they had gained everything—and nothing. As **Frederick Douglass,** the famous black abolitionist, noted, the freedman "was free from the individual master but a slave of society. He had neither money, property, nor friends."

The wartime plight of homeless and hungry blacks as well as whites impelled Congress to take unprecedented action, establishing on March 3, 1865, the Bureau of Refugees, Freedmen, and Abandoned Lands (**Freedmen's Bureau**), within the War Department. The bureau was to provide "such issues of provisions, clothing, and fuel" as were needed to relieve "destitute and suffering refugees and their wives and children." It was a massive task. The bureau issued 22 million in rations between 1865 and 1870. Never before had the national government assumed responsibility for relief. Feeding and clothing the population had not been deemed its proper function. Considered drastic action, warranted only by civil war, the bureau was supposed to operate for just a year, but was extended for five years.

Under Commissioner **Oliver O. Howard,** the bureau had its own courts to deal with land and labor disputes. Agents in every state provided rations and medical supplies and helped to negotiate labor contracts between former slaves and landowners. The quality of the service rendered to the former slaves depended on the ability and motivation of the individual agents. One of the most lasting benefits of the bureau was the schools it established. During and after the war, African Americans of all ages flocked to schools to taste the previously forbidden fruit of education. The former slaves shrewdly recognized the keys to the planters' power—land, literacy, and the vote. The white South had legally denied all three to African Americans in slavery, and now many former slaves were determined to have them all.

Some former bondsmen had a firmer grasp of reality than their "liberators." Southern whites had

Day of Jubilo: Slaves Confront Emancipation

Rooted in Africa, the oral tradition became one of the tools slaves used to maintain a sense of self-worth. Each generation heard the same stories, and storytelling did not die with slavery. The day that slaves first learned of their emancipation remained vivid in their own minds and later in those of their descendants. The great-grandchildren of a strong-willed woman named Caddy relished the family account of her first taste of freedom:

> Caddy threw down that hoe,
> she marched herself up to the
> big house, then she looked
> around and found the mistress.
> She went over to the mistress,
> she flipped up her dress and
> told the white woman to do
> some thing. She said it mean
> and ugly. This is what she said:
> *Kiss my ass!*

Caddy's reaction was not typical. There was no typical response. Reminiscences of what was called the "Day of Jubilo" formed a tapestry as varied as the range of personality. Some, however, seem to have occurred more frequently than others. Many former slaves echoed one man's description of his and his mother's action when their master announced their emancipation: "Jes like tarpins or turtles after 'mancipation. Jes stick our heads out to see how the land lays."

Caution was a shrewd and realistic response. One of the survival lessons in slavery had been not to trust whites too much. This had been reinforced during the war when Union troops moved through regions proclaiming emancipation only to depart, leaving blacks at the mercy of local whites. One elderly slave described the aftermath to a Union correspondent. "Why, the day after you left, they jist had us all out in a row and told us they was going to shoot us, and they did hang two of us; and Mr. Pierce, the overseer, knocked one with a fence rail and he died the next day. Oh, Master! we seen stars in de day time."

Environment played a role in slaves' reactions to the Day of Jubilo. Urban slaves frequently enjoyed more freedom than plantation slaves. Even before emancipation such black social institutions as schools and churches emerged in many cities. When those cities were liberated, organized celebrations occurred quickly. In Charleston 4000 black men and women paraded before some 10,000 spectators. Two black women sat in one mule-drawn cart while a mock auctioneer shouted, "How much am I offered?" In the next cart a black-draped coffin was inscribed with the words "Slavery Is Dead." Four days after the fall of Richmond blacks there held a mass rally of some 1500 people in the First African Church.

Knowledge of their freedom came in many forms to the slaves. Rural slaves were less likely to enjoy the benefits of freedom as early as urban slaves. Many heard of the Emancipation Proclamation through the slave grapevine or from Union soldiers long before its words became reality for them. Masters sometimes took advantage of the isolation of their plantations to keep their slaves in ignorance or to make freedom seem vague and frightening. Their ploys usually failed, but learned patterns of deference made some former slaves unwilling to challenge their former masters. Months after emancipation one North Carolina slave continued to work without compensation, explaining to a northern correspondent, "No, sir; my mistress never said anything to me that I was to have wages, nor yet that I was free; nor I never said anything to her. Ye see I left it to her honor to talk to me about it, because I was afraid she'd say I was insultin' to her and presumin', so I wouldn't speak first. She ha'n't spoke yet." There were, however, limits to his patience; he intended to ask her for wages at Christmas.

Numerous blacks described the exuberance they felt. One elderly Virginia man went to the barn, jumped from one stack of straw to another, and "screamed and screamed!" A Texan remembered, "We all felt like horses" and "everybody went wild." Other blacks recalled how slave songs and spirituals were updated, and "purty soon ev'ybody fo' miles around was singin' freedom songs."

Quite a few slaves learned of freedom when a Union officer or Freedmen's Bureau agent read them the Emancipation Proclamation—often over the objections of the master. "Dat one time," Sarah Ford declared, "Massa Charley can't open he mouth, 'cause de captain tell him to shut up, dat he'd do the talkin'." Some masters, however, still sought to have the

called for him." Education was the key for others. "If I nebber does do nothing more while I live," a Mississippi freedman vowed, "I shall give my children a chance to go to school, for I considers education next best ting to liberty."

Most came to a good understanding of the benefits and limits of their new status. One explained, "Why, sar, all I made before was Miss Pinckney's, but all I make now is my own." Another noted, "You could change places and work for different men." One newly freed slave wrote his brother, "I's mighty well pleased tu git my eatin' by de 'sweat o' my face, an all I ax o' ole masser's tu jes' keep he hands off o' de Lawd Almighty's property, fur *dat's me*." A new sense of dignity was cherished by many. An elderly South Carolina freedman rejoiced, "Don't hab me feelins hurt now. Used to hab me feelins hurt all de times. But don't hab em hurt now, no more." Charlie Barbour exulted over one thing: "I won't wake up some mornin' fer fin' dat my mammy or some ob de rest of my family am done sold." Most agreed with Margrett Millin's answer when she was asked decades later whether she had liked slavery or freedom better. "Well, it's dis way. In slavery I owns nothin'. In freedom I's own de home and raise de family. All dat cause me worryment and in slavery I has no worryment, but I takes de freedom."

last word. A Louisiana planter's wife announced immediately after the Union officer departed, "Ten years from today I'll have you all back 'gain."

Fear did not leave all slaves as soon as their bondage was lifted. Jenny Proctor of Alabama recalled that her fellow slaves were stunned by the news. "We didn' hardly know what he means. We jes' sort of huddle 'round together like scared rabbits, but after we knowed what he mean, didn' many of us go, 'cause we didn' know where to of went." James Lucas, a former slave of Jefferson Davis, explained, "folks dat ain' never been free don' rightly know de *feel* of bein' free. Dey don' know de meanin' of it."

Former slaves quickly learned that one could not eat or wear freedom.

"Dis livin' on liberty," one declared, "is lak young folks livin' on love after they gits married. It just don't work." They searched for the real meaning of liberty in numerous ways. Some followed the advice of a black Florida preacher, "You ain't none 'o you, gwinter feel rale free till you shakes de dus ob de Ole Plantashun offen you feet," and moved. Others declared their independence by legalizing their marriages and taking new names or publicly using surnames they had secretly adopted while in slavery. "We had a real sho' nuff weddin' wid a preacher," one recalled. "Dat cost a dollar." When encouraged to take his old master's surname, a black man declared, "Him's nothing to me now. I don't belong to he no longer, an' I don't see no use in being

long claimed to "know our Negroes" better than outsiders could. Ironically, this was proven false, but the reverse *was* true. Ex-slaves knew their ex-masters very well. One freedman pleaded, "Gib us our own land and we can take care ourselves; but widout land, de ole massas can hire us or starve us, as dey please." The events on Pinckney's plantation proved the wisdom of that statement.

Later generations have laughed at the widespread rumor among former slaves that they were to receive "forty acres and a mule" from the government, but the rumor did have some basis. During the war, General Sherman was plagued with swarms of former slaves following his army, and in January 1865 he issued **Special Field Order 15** setting aside a strip of abandoned coastal lands from Charleston, South Carolina, to Jacksonville, Florida, for the exclusive use of former slaves. African Americans were to be given "possessory titles" to 40-acre lots. Three months later, the bill establishing the Freedmen's Bureau gave the agency control of thousands of acres of abandoned and confiscated lands to be rented to "loyal refugees and freedmen" in 40-acre plots for three-year periods with an option to buy at a later date. By June 1865, 40,000 African Americans were cultivating land. In the Sea Islands and elsewhere, they proved they could be successful independent farmers. Yet land reform was not a popular cause among whites. Although a few congressmen continued to advocate land confiscation and redistribution, the dream of "forty acres and a mule" was a casualty of the battle for control of Reconstruction when Andrew Johnson's pardons returned most confiscated lands. Indeed, the issue of economic security for the former slaves was obscured by other questions that seemed more important to whites.

Unresolved Issues

At war's end some issues had been settled, but at a terrible cost. As historian David Potter noted, "slavery was dead, secession was dead, and six hundred thousand men were dead." A host of new problems had arisen from the nature of civil war and the results of that war as well as the usual postwar dislocations. Many questions remained that shaped Reconstruction.

The first of these concerned the status of the former slaves. They were indeed free, but were they citizens? The **Dred Scott decision** (1857) had denied citizenship to all African Americans. Even if it were decided that they were citizens, what rights were conferred by that citizenship? Would they be segregated as free blacks in the antebellum North had often been? Also, citizenship did not automatically confer suffrage; women were proof of that. Were the freedmen to be given the ballot? These weighty matters were complicated by racial prejudice as well as constitutional and partisan questions.

The Constitution had been severely tested by civil war, and many felt it had been twisted by the desire to save the Union. Once the emergency was over, how were constitutional balance and limits to be restored? Except during the terms of a few strong presidents, Congress had been the most powerful branch of government during the nation's first 70 years. Lincoln had assumed unprecedented powers, and Congress was determined to regain its ascendancy. The ensuing battle directly influenced Reconstruction policies and their implementation.

Secession was dead, but what about states' rights? Almost everyone agreed that a division of power between the national and state governments was crucial to the maintenance of freedom. The fear of centralized tyranny remained strong. There was reluctance to enlarge federal power into areas traditionally controlled by the states, even though action in some of those areas was essential to craft the kind of peace many desired. Hesitation to reduce states' rights produced timid and compromised solutions to such issues as suffrage.

Another constitutional question concerned the status of the former Confederate states and how they were to be readmitted to the Union. There was no constitutional provision for failed secession, and many people debated whether the South had actually left the Union or not. The query reflected self-interest rather than an intellectual inquiry. Ironically, Southerners and their Democratic sympathizers now argued that the states had never legally separated from the rest of the nation, thus denying validity to the Confederacy in order to quickly regain their place in the Union. Extremists on the other side—**Radical Republicans**—insisted that the South had reverted to the status of conquered territory, forfeiting all rights as states. Under territorial governments, Representative Thaddeus Stevens declared, Southerners could "learn the principles of freedom and eat the fruit of foul rebellion." Others, including Lincoln, believed that the Confederate states had remained in the Union but had forfeited their rights. This constitutional hair-splitting grew out of the power struggle between the executive and legislative branches to determine which had the power to readmit the states and on what terms.

Influencing all these issues were partisan politics. Although not provided for in the Constitution, political parties had played a major role in the evolving American government. The road to war had disrupted the existing party structure—killing the Whig party, dividing the Democratic party, and creating the Republican party. The first truly sectional party, the Republican party had very few adherents in the

South. Its continued existence was dubious in the face of the probable reunion of the northern and southern wings of the Democratic party. Paradoxically, the political power of the South, and in turn the Democratic party, was increased by the abolition of slavery. As slaves, only three-fifths of African Americans had been counted for representation; with the end of slavery, all African Americans would be counted. Thus the Republican party's perceived need to make itself a national party also colored the course of Reconstruction.

PRESIDENTIAL RECONSTRUCTION

Early in the conflict, questions regarding the reconstruction of the nation were secondary to winning the war—without victory there would be no nation to reconstruct. Nonetheless, Lincoln had to take some action as Union forces pushed into the South. Authority had to be imposed in the reclaimed territory, so the president named military governors for Tennessee, Arkansas, and Louisiana in 1862 after federal armies occupied most of those states. He also began formulating plans for civilian government for those states and future Confederate areas as they came under the control of Union forces. The result was a Proclamation of Amnesty and Reconstruction issued in December 1863 on the constitutional basis of the president's power to pardon.

Lincoln's Plan

Called the **10 percent plan,** Lincoln's provisions were incredibly lenient. Rebels could receive presidential pardon by merely swearing their future allegiance to the Union and their acceptance of the end of slavery. In other words, former Confederates were not required to say they were sorry—only to promise they would be good in the future. A few people were excluded from pardons, such as Confederate military and civilian officers. After only 10 percent of the number who had voted in 1860 had taken the oath, a state could form a civilian government. When such states produced a constitution outlawing slavery, Lincoln promised to recognize them as reconstructed. He did not demand any provisions for protecting black rights or allowing black suffrage.

Tennessee, Arkansas, and Louisiana met Lincoln's requirements and soon learned they had only cleared the first barrier in what became a long obstacle course. Radical Republicans, such as Representative **Thaddeus Stevens** of Pennsylvania and Senator **Charles Sumner** of Massachusetts, were outraged by the president's generosity. They thought the provi-

sions did not adequately punish Confederate treason, restructure southern society, protect the rights of African Americans, or aid the Republican party. The Radicals were in a minority, but many moderate Republicans were also dismayed by Lincoln's leniency, and shared the Radical view that Reconstruction was a congressional, not a presidential, function. As a result Congress recognized neither the three states' elected congressmen nor their electoral votes in the 1864 election.

After denying the president's right to reconstruct the nation, Congress drew up a plan for reconstruction: the **Wade-Davis Bill.** Its terms were much more stringent. A majority, rather than 10 percent, of each states' voters had to declare their allegiance in order to form a government. Only those taking "ironclad" oaths of their past Union loyalty were allowed to participate in the making of new state constitutions. Barely a handful of high-ranking Confederates, however, were to be permanently barred from political participation. The only additional requirement imposed by Congress was the repudiation of the Confederate debt; Northerners did not want Confederate bondholders to benefit from their "investment in treason" at a cost to loyal taxpayers. Congress would determine when a state had met these requirements.

Constitutional collision was postponed by Lincoln's pocket veto of the bill and his assassination on April 14, 1865. While most of the nation mourned, some Radicals rejoiced at the results of John Wilkes Booth's action. Lincoln had been a formidable opponent and had articulated his position on the South in his second inaugural address. Calling for "malice toward none" and "charity for all," he proposed to "bind the nation's wounds" and achieve "a just and lasting peace." His successor, **Andrew Johnson,** on the other hand, had announced, "Treason is a crime, and crime must be punished." Johnson was a Tennessee Democrat and Unionist; he had been the only Southerner to remain in the Senate after his state seceded. Placed on the 1864 Republican "Union" ticket as a gesture of unity, Johnson's political affiliation was less than clear, but some considered him a weaker opponent than Lincoln. Radical Senator Benjamin Wade proclaimed, "By the gods there will be no trouble now in running this government."

Radicals found comfort in, but miscalculated, Johnson's hatred of the planters. He hated them for their aristocratic domination of the South, not for their slaveholding. Born of humble origins in Raleigh, North Carolina, and illiterate until adulthood, Johnson entered politics in Tennessee as a successful tailor. A champion of the people, he called the planters a "cheap purse-proud set . . . not half as good as the man who earns his bread by the sweat of his brow." Favoring free public education and a

North Carolina–born Andrew Johnson, a former governor of Tennessee and a U.S. senator from that state, was the only senator from a seceding state to remain loyal to the Union. In 1862 Lincoln appointed him military governor of Tennessee, and in 1864 Johnson was selected as Lincoln's running mate.

homestead act, Johnson was elected mayor, congressman, governor, and senator, before being appointed military governor of Tennessee and then becoming vice president. Although he shared the Radicals' hatred and distrust of the planters, he was a firm believer in black inferiority and did not support the Radical aim of black legal equality. He also advocated strict adherence to the Constitution and strongly supported states' rights.

Johnson's Plan

In the end Johnson did not reverse Lincoln's lenient policy. Congress was not in session when Johnson became president so he had about eight months to pursue policies without congressional interference. He issued his own proclamation of amnesty in May 1865 that excluded everyone with taxable property worth more than $20,000. Closing one door, he opened another by providing for personal presiden-

tial pardons for excluded individuals. By year's end he had issued about 13,000 pardons in response to 15,000 requests. The most important aspect of the pardons was Johnson's claim that they restored all rights, including property rights. Thus many former slaves with crops in the ground suddenly found their masters back in charge—a disillusioning first taste of freedom that foreclosed further attempts at widespread land redistribution.

Johnson's amnesty proclamation did not immediately end the Radicals' honeymoon period with him, but his other proclamation issued on the same day caused deep concern. In it, he announced plans for the reconstruction of North Carolina—a plan that would set the pattern for all southern states. A native Unionist was named provisional governor with the power to call a constitutional convention elected by loyal voters. Omitting Lincoln's 10 percent provision, Johnson did eventually require ratification of the Thirteenth Amendment, repudiation of Confederate debts, and state constitutional provisions abolishing slavery and renouncing secession. He also recommended limited black suffrage, primarily to stave off congressional attempts to give the vote to all black males.

Although more stringent than Lincoln's plan, Johnson's plan fell short of the Radicals' hopes. Many moderates might have accepted it if the South had complied with the letter and the spirit of Johnson's proposals. Instead, Southerners seemed determined to ignore their defeat, even to make light of it. The state governments, for the most part, met the minimum requirements (Mississippi and South Carolina refused to repudiate the debt and Mississippi declined to ratify the Thirteenth Amendment). Their apparent acceptance, however, grew out of a belief that very little had actually changed, and Southerners proceeded to show almost total disregard for northern sensibilities. Presenting themselves, like prodigal sons, for admission to Congress were four Confederate generals and six Confederate cabinet officials. As the crowning indignity, Confederate Vice President Alexander H. Stephens was also elected. Most Northerners were not exceedingly vindictive. Still the North did expect some sign of change and hoped for some indication of repentance by the former rebels.

Black Codes in the South

At the very least, Northerners expected adherence to the abolition of slavery, and the South was blatantly forging new forms of bondage. African Americans were to be technically free, but Southern whites expected them to work and live as they had before emancipation. To accomplish this, the new state governments enacted a series of laws known as the **Black Codes.** This legislation granted certain rights denied to slaves. Freedmen had the right to marry, own property, sue and be sued, and testify in court. Complex legalisms, however, often took away what was apparently given. Black Codes in all states prohibited racial intermarriage. Some forbade freedmen to own certain types of property, such as alcoholic beverages and firearms. Most so tightly restricted black legal rights that they were practically nonexistent. Black Codes imposed curfews on African Americans, segregated them, and outlawed their right to congregate in large groups.

The Black Codes did more than merely provide means of racial control; they also sought to fashion a labor system as close to slavery as possible. Some required that African Americans obtain special licenses for any job except agricultural labor or domestic service. Most mandated the signing of yearly labor contracts, which sometimes required African Americans to call the landowner "master" and allowed withholding wages for minor infractions. To accomplish the same objective, Mississippi prohibited black ownership or even rental of land. Mandatory apprenticeship programs took children away from their parents, and vagrancy laws allowed authorities to arrest blacks "wandering or strolling about in idleness" and use them on chain gangs or rent them out to planters for as long as a year.

When laws failed, some southern whites resorted to violence. In Memphis, whites resented the presence of black troops at nearby Fort Pickering. A local paper asserted "the negro can do the country more good in the cotton field than in the camp" and chastised "the dirty, fanatical, nigger-loving Radicals of this city." In May 1866 a street brawl erupted between white policemen and recently discharged black soldiers. That night, after the soldiers had returned to the fort, white mobs attacked the black section of the city, with the encouragement of the police and local officials, one of whom urged the mob to "go ahead and kill the last damned one of the nigger race." The reign of terror lasted over 40 hours and left 46 blacks and 2 whites dead. This and other outbreaks of violence disgusted northern voters.

Most Northerners would not have insisted on black equality or suffrage, but the South had regressed too far. Some Black Codes were even identical to the old slave codes, with the word negro substituted for slave. At the same time, reports of white violence against blacks filtered back to Washington. It is no wonder that upon finally reconvening in December 1865, Congress refused to seat the representatives and senators from the former Confederate states and instead proceeded to investigate conditions in the South.

CONGRESSIONAL RECONSTRUCTION

To discover what was really happening in the South, Congress established the **Joint Committee on Reconstruction,** which conducted inquiries and interviews that provided graphic and chilling examples of white repression and brutality toward African Americans. Prior to the committee's final report, even moderates were convinced that action was necessary. In early 1866 Congress passed a bill to extend the life of the Freedmen's Bureau. The bill also granted the agency new powers to establish special courts for disputes concerning former slaves and to promote black education. Johnson vetoed it, claiming that the bureau was constitutional only in wartime conditions. Now,

Southern whites frequently vented their frustration on blacks. Following a Radical Republican meeting in New Orleans on July 30, 1866, rioting erupted; 37 blacks and 3 white sympathizers were killed in the fighting. This cartoon shows Andrew Johnson looking with apparent approval at the violence. The crown illustrates disapproval of Johnson's "tyrannical" actions.

he claimed, the country had returned "to a state of peace and industry."

At first Johnson prevailed; his veto was not overridden. Then he made a mistake. In an impromptu speech on Washington's birthday, Johnson launched into a bitter attack on the Joint Committee on Reconstruction. Even moderates were offended. In mid-March 1866 Congress passed the Civil Rights Act. It declared that "all persons born in the United States and not subject to any foreign power, excluding Indians not taxed," were citizens and entitled to "full and equal benefit of all laws." Congress was responding to the Black Codes, but Johnson deemed the bill both unconstitutional and unwise. He vetoed it. This time, however, Congress overrode the veto. It then passed a slightly revised Freedmen's Bureau bill in July and enacted it over Johnson's veto. Even though the South had ignored much of Johnson's advice, such as granting limited suffrage to blacks, he stubbornly held to his conviction that reconstruction was complete and labeled his congressional opponents as "traitors."

His language did not create a climate of cooperation. Congress was concerned about the constitutional questions he raised and his challenge to congressional authority. To protect its handiwork and establish an alternate program of reconstruction, it drafted the **Fourteenth Amendment.** Undoubtedly the most significant legacy of Reconstruction, the first article of the amendment defined citizenship and its basic rights. Every person born in the United States and subject to its jurisdiction is declared a citizen. It also forbids any state from abridging "the privileges and immunities" of citizenship, from depriving any person of "due process of law," and from denying citizens the "equal protection of the laws." Although 100 years passed before its provisions were enforced as intended, the amendment has been interpreted to mean that states as well as the federal government are bound by the Bill of Rights—an important constitutional change that paved the way for the civil rights decisions and laws of the twentieth century.

The remaining sections of the amendment spelled out Congress's minimum demands for postwar change and was the South's last chance for a lenient peace. A creation of the congressional moderates, the amendment did not require black suffrage but reduced the "basis of representation" proportionately for those states not allowing it. Former Confederate leaders were also barred from holding office unless pardoned by Congress—not the president. Thus Congress repudiated Johnson's power to control Reconstruction. Finally, neither Confederate war debts nor compensation to former slaveholders were ever to be paid. The amendment, which passed Congress in June 1866, was then sent to the states for ratification.

TABLE 16.1

Reconstruction Amendments, 1865–1870

Amendment	Main Provisions	Congressional Passage (2/3 majority in each house required)	Ratification Process (3/4 of all states including ex-Confederate states required)
Thirteenth	Slavery prohibited in United States	January 1865	December 1865 (27 states, including 8 southern states)
Fourteenth	1. National citizenship 2. State representation in Congress reduced proportionally to number of voters disfranchised 3. Former Confederate leaders denied right to hold office 4. Only Congress could pardon former Confederates	June 1866	Rejected by 12 southern and border states, February 1867 Radicals make readmission of southern states hinge on ratification Ratified July 1868
Fifteenth	Denial of franchise because of race, color, or past servitude explicitly prohibited	February 1869	Ratification required for readmission of Virginia, Texas, Mississippi, Georgia Ratified March 1870

"Radical" Reconstruction

Everyone assumed that the 1866 congressional elections would be a referendum on the Fourteenth Amendment and that their position would prevail. At President Johnson's urging, all former Confederate states but Tennessee refused to ratify it. In the end the Republicans won overwhelming victories, which they interpreted as a mandate for congressional reconstruction. The election results along with the South's intransigence finally gave the Radicals an upper hand. In 1867 Congress passed the **Military Reconstruction Act** that raised the price of readmission. The act declared all existing "Johnson governments," except Tennessee's, void and divided the South into five military districts headed by military governors granted broad powers to govern. Delegates to new constitutional conventions were to be elected by all qualified voters—a group that by congressional stipulation included black males and excluded former Confederate leaders. Following the ratification of a new state constitution providing for black suffrage, elections were to be held and the state would be required to ratify the Fourteenth Amendment. When that amendment became part of the Constitution and Congress approved the new state constitutions, the states would be granted representation in Congress once again.

Obviously, Johnson was not pleased with the congressional plan; he vetoed it, only to see his veto overridden. Nevertheless, as commander in chief he reluctantly appointed military governors, and by the end of 1867 elections had been held in every state except Texas. Because many white Southerners boycotted the elections, the South came under the control of Republicans supported by Union forces. To many in the North, however, Southerners had brought more radical measures upon themselves by their inflexibility. As the *Nation* declared in 1867,

> Six years ago, the North would have rejoiced to accept any mild restrictions upon the spread of slavery as a final settlement. Four years ago, it would have accepted peace on the basis of gradual emancipation. Two years ago, it would have been content with emancipation and equal civil rights for the colored people without the extension of suffrage. One year ago, a slight extension of the suffrage would have satisfied it.

Congress realized the plan it had enacted was unprecedented and subject to challenge by the other two branches of government. To check Johnson's power to disrupt, Congress took two other actions on the same day it passed the Military Reconstruction Act. The Command of the Army Act limited presidential military power. The **Tenure of Office Act**

Reconstruction and Redemption

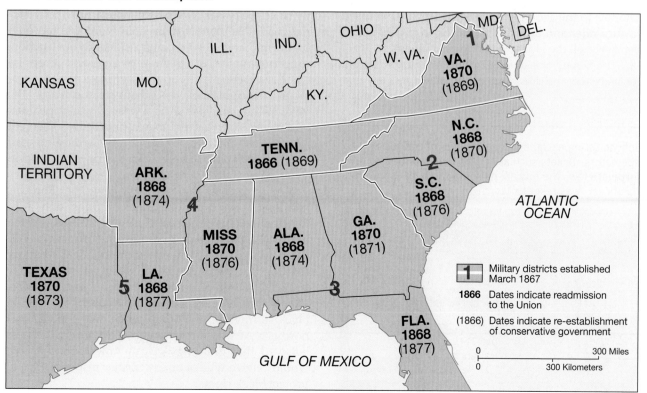

required Senate consent for the removal of any official whose appointment had required the Senate's confirmation. It was meant in part to protect Secretary of War **Edwin M. Stanton,** who supported the Radicals. Both acts represented the Radicals' anger toward Johnson.

The Supreme Court had also shown its willingness to challenge Reconstruction actions in two important cases of 1866. In *Ex parte Milligan* the justices struck down the conviction of a civilian by a military tribunal in an area where civil courts were operating. Another decision ruled as void a state law barring former Confederates from certain professions on the basis that the act was *ex post facto*. Nevertheless, other decisions reflected a hesitation to tackle some of the thornier issues of Reconstruction. Important cases were pending, and Congress acted in March 1868 to limit the court's power to review cases. Because the congressional action was clearly constitutional, the Supreme Court acquiesced and in *Texas v. White* (1869) even acknowledged congressional power to reframe state governments.

President Johnson was not so accommodating. He sought to sabotage military reconstruction by continuing to pardon former Confederates, removing military commanders who were Radical sympathizers, and naming former Confederates to federal positions. Congress was angry but could not find adequate grounds for impeachment. Johnson did not attempt to mend fences. After an unsuccessful attempt to replace Secretary of War Stanton with Ulysses S. Grant, on February 21 he named Lorenzo Thomas to the cabinet position. Stanton also refused to surrender and barricaded himself in his office. On February 24, the House voted impeachment.

The Senate was given 11 articles of impeachment for its trial of the president. Eight related to the viola-

tion of the Tenure of Office Act and another to a violation of the Command of the Army Act. These articles were merely the pretext for impeachment. Only the last two reflected the real reasons for congressional action. Those articles accused Johnson of "inflammatory and scandalous harangues" against Congress and of "unlawfully devising and contriving" to obstruct congressional will. The heated and bitter trial lasted from March 5 to May 26. Johnson did not attend, but his lawyers made a good legal case that he had not technically violated the Tenure of Office Act since Stanton had been appointed by Lincoln. They tried to keep the trial focused on indictable offenses. Radical prosecutors continued to argue that Johnson had committed "high crimes and misdemeanors," but they also asserted that a president could be removed for political reasons, even without being found legally guilty of crimes. Thus Congress asserted the power to remove a president for disagreeing with it.

The vote for conviction fell one short of the required two-thirds majority, when seven Republicans broke ranks and voted against conviction. This set the precedent that a president must be guilty of serious misdeeds to be removed from office. The outcome was a political blow to the Radicals, costing them some support. The action, however, did make Johnson more cooperative for the last months of his presidency.

Black Suffrage

In the 1868 presidential election, the Republicans won with **Ulysses S. Grant,** whose Civil War victories made his name a household word. He ran on a platform that endorsed congressional reconstruction, urged repayment of the national debt, and defended black suffrage in the South as necessary but supported the right of each northern state to restrict the vote. His slogan, "Let us have peace," was appealing, but his election was less than a ringing endorsement for Radical policies. The military hero who had seemed invincible barely won the popular vote in several key states.

While Charles Sumner and a few other Radicals had long favored national black suffrage, only after the Republicans' electoral close call in 1868 did the bulk of the party begin to consider a suffrage amendment. Many were swayed by the political certainty that the black vote would be theirs and might give them the margin of victory in future close elections. Others were embarrassed by the hypocrisy of forcing black suffrage on the South while only 7 percent of northern African Americans could vote. Still others believed that granting African Americans the vote would relieve whites of any further responsibility to protect black rights.

Johnson's impeachment drew crowds of curious spectators. Tickets such as this one were issued to a fortunate few. The original date of March 13, shown on this ticket, was reset to March 23.

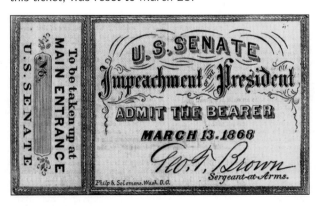

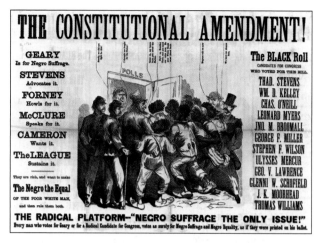

Many Northerners were opposed to the Fifteenth Amendment. Highly racist posters, such as this one from Pennsylvania, were used against politicians who supported the amendment.

Suffrage supporters faced many objections to such an amendment. One was based on the lack of popular support. At that time only seven northern states granted blacks the right to vote, and since 1865, referendum proposals for black suffrage in eight states had been voted down. In fact, only in Iowa and Minnesota (both containing minuscule black populations) had voters supported the extension of the vote. The amendment was so unpopular that, ironically, it could never have won adoption without its ratification by the southern states, where black suffrage already existed.

A more serious challenge was the question of whether Congress could legislate suffrage at all. Before Reconstruction the national government had never taken any action regarding the right to vote; suffrage had been considered not a right but a privilege which only the states could confer. The Radical answer was that the Constitution expressly declared that "the United States shall guarantee to every State in this Union a republican form of government." Charles Sumner further asserted that "anything for human rights is constitutional" and that black rights could only be protected by black votes.

Senator George Vickers sarcastically asked: "Does not the doctrine of human rights asserted by the senator apply as well to females as to males?" Although he was "no advocate for woman suffrage," he noted that "if the Congress of the United States had been composed exclusively of women we should have had no civil war. We might have had a war of words, but that would have been all." When one senator did propose female suffrage, a colleague informed him that "to extend the right of suffrage to

negroes in this country I think is necessary for their protection; but to extend the right of suffrage to women is not necessary."

Some women, such as Elizabeth Cady Stanton and **Susan B. Anthony,** did not want to rely upon their fathers, brothers, or husbands to protect their rights. As leaders of the Women's Loyal League, both had worked hard for the adoption of the Thirteenth Amendment, only to be rewarded by inclusion of the word *male* in the Fourteenth Amendment of the Constitution—the first time that word appears. Some women, such as Lucy Stone of the American Woman Suffrage Association, accepted the plea of long-time woman suffrage supporter Frederick Douglass that it was the "Negro's hour," and worked for ratification. Anthony, however, vowed "[I will] cut off this right arm of mine before I will ever work for or demand the ballot for the Negro and not the woman." Such differences played a role in splitting the women's movement in 1869 between those working for a national suffrage amendment and those who concentrated their efforts on the state level. Anthony and Stanton founded the National Woman Suffrage Association to battle for a constitutional amendment and other feminist reforms. Others became disillusioned with that approach and established the American Woman Suffrage Association, which focused on obtaining suffrage on a state-by-state basis.

Actually, women did not lose much by not being included in the **Fifteenth Amendment.** To meet the various objections, compromise was necessary. The resulting amendment did not grant the vote to anyone. It merely stated that the vote could not be denied "on account of race, color, or previous condition of servitude." Suffrage was still essentially to be controlled by the states, and other bases of exclusion were not deemed unconstitutional. These loopholes would eventually allow white Southerners to make a mockery of the amendment.

Although congressional reconstruction was labeled "Radical," compromise had instead produced another essentially moderate plan. What Congress did *not* do is as important as what it did. It did not even guarantee the right to vote. There was only one execution for war crimes and only Jefferson Davis was imprisoned for more than a few months. For all but a handful, former Confederates were not permanently barred from voting or holding office. By 1872 only about 200 were still denied the right to hold office. Most local southern governments were undisturbed. Land as well as rights were restored to former rebels, eliminating the possibility of extensive land redistribution. Most areas that had traditionally been the states' domain remained so, free from federal meddling. For example, no requirements were placed on the states to provide any education to former slaves. The only attempt by the national government to meet the basic needs of its citizens was the temporary Freedmen's Bureau—justified only as an emergency measure. The limited nature of Reconstruction doomed it as an opportunity to provide means for the protection of minority rights.

Such congressional moderation reflected the spirit of the age. Enduring beliefs in the need for strict construction of the Constitution and in states' rights presented formidable barriers to truly radical changes. Property rights were considered sacrosanct—even for "traitors." Cherished ideals of self-reliance and the conviction that a person determined his or her own destiny led many to support **Horace Greeley**'s call to "break up our Freedmen's Bureaus and all manner of coddling devices and let the negroes take care of themselves." Few agreed with Charles Sterns who argued that even a hog could not root without a snout—that there could be no equality of opportunity where one group had long been allowed an unfair advantage. Many instead sided with an editorialist for the *New York Herald* who wrote of the bill to extend the life of the Freedmen's Bureau: "The bill ought to be called an act to support the negroes in idleness by the honest labor of white people, or an act to establish a gigantic and corrupt political machine for the benefit of the radical faction and a swarm of officeholders." Clearly the idea of affirmative action or even equal opportunity had less support then than it did 100 years later.

Tainting every action was the widespread conviction that African Americans were not equal to whites. Many Northerners were more concerned with keeping blacks in the South than with abstract black rights. In 1866, for example, New York Senator Roscoe Conkling catered to the northern fear of black immigration while calling for support of the Fourteenth Amendment:

> Four years ago mobs were raised, passions were aroused, votes were given, upon the idea that emancipated negroes were to burst in hordes upon the North. We then said, give them liberty and rights in the South, and they will stay there and never come into a cold climate. We say so still, and we want them let alone, and that is one thing that this part of the amendment is for.

Even Radical Representative George Julian admitted to his Indiana constituents, "the real trouble is that we hate the negro. It is not his ignorance that offends us, but his color."

The plan for Reconstruction evolved fitfully, buffeted first one way and then another by the forces of the many issues unresolved at war's end. If permanent changes were very limited, nonetheless precedents had been set for later action, and for a brief time congressional reconstruction brought about the most democratic governments the South had ever seen—or would see for another hundred years.

RECONSTRUCTION IN THE SOUTH

Any dictated peace would probably have been unpalatable to Southern whites. They were especially leery of any action that seemed to threaten white supremacy—whether or not that was the intended result. Even before the war, suspicion greeted every Northern move. Southerners continued to see a radical abolitionist behind every bush.

Most Southerners criticized and condemned the Freedmen's Bureau from its first day to its last. Many believed its agents were partial to African Americans. As one Mississippi planter declared, "The negro is a sacred animal. The Yankees are about negroes like the Egyptians were about cats." Actually there was a great diversity in the background and goals of bureau agents. Some were idealistic young New Englanders who, like the Yankee schoolmarms, came south to aid in the transition to freedom. Others were army officers whose first priority was to maintain order—often by siding with the landowners. All were overworked, underpaid, and under pressure.

The results of bureau actions were mixed in regard to conditions for African Americans. The agents helped to negotiate labor contracts that African Americans were forced to sign to obtain rations. Frequently the wages were well below the rate at which slaves had been hired out by their owners before the war. While it should be remembered that money was

Freed persons realized that education was a key to real freedom and flocked to schools opened by the Freedmen's Bureau, the American Missionary Association, and other groups.

scarce at the time, these contracts helped to keep African Americans on the farm—someone else's farm. On the other hand, between 1865 and 1869 the bureau issued over 21 million rations, of which about 5 million went to whites. Thus it showed that the government could establish and administer a massive relief program, as it would again do during the depression of the 1930s. The bureau also operated more than 40 hospitals, opened hundreds of schools, and accomplished the Herculean task of resettling some 30,000 people displaced by the war.

Carpetbaggers, Scalawags, and Black Republicans

Until Congressional Reconstruction, Southern governments were largely unchanged. Afterwards, however, Republican officeholders joined bureau agents in directing the course of Reconstruction. Despised by many whites, these men, depending on their origins, were derisively labeled "carpetbaggers," "scalawags," and "nigrahs." Opponents considered all three groups despicable creatures whose "black and tan" governments were tyrannizing native whites, while engaged in an orgy of corruption. Myths created about Southern Republicans lingered long after the restoration of Democratic party rule.

Northerners who came to the South during or after the war and became engaged in politics were called **carpetbaggers.** According to their critics, they arrived with a few meager belongings in their carpetbags, which would expand to hold ill-gotten gains from looting an already devastated South. Probably what most infuriated whites was the carpetbaggers' willingness to cooperate with African Americans. Calling them "a kind of political dry-nurse for the negro population," native whites accused the carpetbaggers of cynically exploiting former slaves for their own gain. Many agreed with the charge that the carpetbaggers were standing "right in the public eye, stealing and plundering, many of them with both arms around negroes, and their hands in their rear pockets, seeing if they cannot pick a paltry dollar out of them."

White Southerners who voted for Republicans were labeled **scalawags.** The term, said to be derived from Scalloway, "a district in the Shetland Islands where small, runty cattle and horses were bred," had been used previously as a "synonym for scamp, loafer, or rascal." Thus southern white Republicans were depicted as people "paying no taxes, riding poor horses, wearing dirty shirts, and having no use for soap." Such men were said to have "sold themselves for office" and become a "subservient tool and accomplice" of the carpetbaggers.

Most detested by white Southerners were the black Republicans. Having long characterized African Americans as inferior creatures dependent on white management for survival, Southerners loathed the prospect of blacks in authority. They feared that the former slaves would exact payment for their years of bondage. Democrats also knew that racism was their best rallying cry to regain power. Thus Reconstruction governments were denounced for "Ethiopian minstrelsy, Ham radicalism in all its glory." Whites claimed ignorant freedmen, incapable of managing their own affairs, were allowed to run the affairs of state with disastrous results.

Such legends persisted for a long time, despite contrary facts. Southern whites had determined even before Reconstruction began that it would be "the most galling tyranny and most stupendous system of organized robbery that is to be met with in history." The truth was, as W. E. B. Du Bois later wrote, "There is one thing that the white South feared more than negro dishonesty, ignorance, and incompetency, and that was negro honesty, knowledge, and efficiency." To a surprising degree they got what they most feared.

Black voters were generally as fit to vote as the millions of illiterate whites enfranchised by Jacksonian democracy. Black officials as a group were as qualified as their white counterparts. In South Carolina two-thirds of them were literate, and in all states most of the acknowledged leaders were well educated and articulate. They usually had been members of the northern or southern free black elite or part of the slave aristocracy of skilled artisans and household slaves. Hiram Revels, a U.S. senator from Mississippi, was the son of free blacks who had sent him to college in the North. James Walker Hood, the presiding officer of the North Carolina constitutional convention of 1867, was a black carpetbagger from Pennsylvania who came to the state as an African Methodist Episcopal Zion missionary. Some, such as Francis Cardoza of South Carolina, were the privileged mulatto sons of white planters. Cardoza had been educated in Scottish and English universities. During Reconstruction 14 such men served in the U.S. House of Representatives and 2 in the Senate. By 1901, 6 others were elected to the House, before southern black political power was effectively demolished.

Even if black Republicans had been incompetent, they could hardly be held responsible for the perceived abuses of so-called black reconstruction. Only in South Carolina did African Americans have a majority of the delegates to the constitutional convention provided for by the Reconstruction Acts. Neither did they dominate the new governments; only for a two-year period in South Carolina did blacks control both houses of the legislature. None were elected governor, although P. B. S. Pinchback, the lieutenant governor of Louisiana, did serve as acting governor for a short time. When the vote was restored to ex-

African Americans participated in politics at all levels. This poster shows Senators Blanche K. Bruce and Hiram Revels flanking Frederick Douglass, who was appointed to several important positions, including Minister Resident and Counsel General to Haiti, Recorder of Deeds, and U.S. Marshall.

Confederates, African Americans comprised only one-third of the voters of the South, and only in two states did they have a majority.

Actually, carpetbaggers dominated most Republican governments to an extent not warranted by their numbers. They accounted for less than 1 percent of the party's voters but held a third of the offices. Their power was especially obvious in the higher offices. Over half of the South's Republican governors and almost half of the Republican congressmen and senators were former Northerners. Although some carpetbaggers did resemble their stereotypes, most did not. Many had come south before black enfranchisement and could not have predicted political futures based on black votes. Most were Union veterans whose wartime exposure to the region convinced them that they could make a good living there without having to shovel snow. Some brought with them much needed capital for investment in their new home. A few came with a sense of mission to educate blacks and reform southern society.

Obviously, if African Americans constituted only a third of the population and carpetbaggers less than 1 percent, those two groups had to depend on the votes of a sizable number of native white Southerners to obtain office in some regions of the South. Those men came from diverse backgrounds. Some scalawags were members of the old elite of bankers, merchants, industrialists, and even some planters who, as former Whigs, favored the "Whiggish" economic policies of the Republican party and hoped to control and use the black vote for their own pur-poses. On discovering their inability to dominate the Republican governments, most of these soon drifted into alliance with the Democrats. The majority of southern white Republican voters were yeomen farmers and poor whites from areas where slavery had been unimportant. They had long resented planter domination and had opposed secession.

To win their vote the Republicans appealed to class interests. In Georgia they proclaimed, "Poor White men of Georgia: Be a Man! Let the Slave-holding aristocracy no longer rule you. Vote for a constitution which educates your children free of charge; relieves the poor debtor from his rich creditor; allows a liberal homestead for your families; and more than all, places you on a level with those who used to boast that for every slave they were entitled to three-fifths of a vote in congressional representation." Many accepted such arguments and joined African Americans to put Republicans into office. The coalition, however, was always shaky, given the racism of poor whites. The scalawags actually represented a swing vote that finally swung toward the Democratic party of white supremacy later in the 1870s.

Character of Republican Rule

While the coalition lasted, the Republican governments became the most democratic that the South had ever had. More people could vote for more offices, all remaining property requirements for voting and office holding were dropped, representation was made fairer through reapportionment, and more offices became elective rather than appointive. Salaries for public officials made it possible to serve without being wealthy. Most important, universal male suffrage was enacted with the support of black legislators. Ironically, by refusing to deny southern whites what had been denied to them—the vote—African Americans sowed the seeds of their own destruction.

The Republican state constitutions, which brought the South firmly into the mainstream of national reform, often remained in effect years after the end of Reconstruction. Legislatures abolished automatic imprisonment for debt and reduced the use of the death penalty. More institutions for the care of the indigent, orphans, mentally ill, deaf, and blind were established. Tax structures were overhauled, reducing head taxes and increasing property taxes to relieve somewhat poorer taxpayers. At the same time, southern railroads, harbors, and bridges were rebuilt.

Reforms also affected the status of women, increasing their rights in the possession of property and divorce. Although giving women legal control of their property was mainly intended to protect the families of their debt-ridden husbands, African Americans in particular pushed for more radical changes. When William Whipper's motion to give South Carolina women the vote did not receive a second, he declared:

> However frivolous you may think it, I know the time will come when every man and woman in this country will have the right to vote. I acknowledge the superiority of woman. There are large numbers of the sex

who have an intelligence more than equal to our own. Is it right or just to deprive these intelligent beings of the privileges which we enjoy? The time will come when you will have to meet this question. It will continue to be agitated until it must ultimately triumph.

The area in which black legislators had the most success was laying the foundations for public education. Antebellum provisions for public schools below the Mason-Dixon line were meager to nonexistent. In every state African Americans were among the main proponents of state-supported schools, but most accepted segregated facilities as necessary compromises. Some black parents did not even desire integration; they believed their children could not flourish in environments tainted by white supremacy. By 1877 some 600,000 blacks were in schools, but only the University of South Carolina and the public schools of New Orleans were integrated.

As desirable as many of the new social services were, they required money and money was scarce. Railroads and bridges also needed to be rebuilt. The necessary tax increases were bound to be unpopular, as were soaring state debts. Both were blamed on corruption, with some justification. Louisiana governor Henry C. Warmouth netted some $100,000 in a year in which his salary was only $8000. A drunken South Carolina governor signed an issue of state bonds for a woman in a burlesque show. One black man was paid $9000 to repair a bridge with an original cost of only $500. Contracts for rebuilding and expanding railroads, subsidies to industries, and bureaucracies for administering social services offered generous opportunities for graft and bribery. When these occurred, southern whites loudly proclaimed that they knew it would happen if shifty former slaves were given the keys to the till.

Actually, although African Americans received a large share of the blame, they received little of the profit. A smaller percentage of blacks than whites were involved in the scandals. Also the corruption that the Democrats denounced at every turn was rather meager compared with the shenanigans of such contemporary northern Democratic regimes as the Boss Tweed Ring of New York. There seemed to be an orgy of national corruption that infected both parties. Indeed, in the South a Democratic state treasurer who came to office after Reconstruction deserves the dubious distinction of being the largest embezzler of the era.

The "tyranny" that so distressed southern whites did not include wholesale disfranchisement or confiscation of their lands. In fact, the demands of most African Americans were quite reasonable and moderate. Their goals were expressed by the declarations of the many postwar black conventions, such as a

African Americans eagerly participated in politics when allowed. As depicted in this sketch of the 1867 election in the nation's capital, they served as polling place judges and lined up as early as 2 A.M. to vote.

Virginia one in 1865 that declared, "All we ask is an *equal chance* with the white *traitors* varnished and japanned with the oath of amnesty."

Black and White Economic and Social Adaptation

Just as the former slaves on Thomas Pinckney's plantation had learned, blacks everywhere soon realized that the economic power of whites had diminished little. If anything, land became more concentrated in the hands of a few. In one Alabama county, the richest 10 percent of landowners increased their share of landed wealth from 55 to 63 percent between 1860 and 1870. Some African Americans, usually through hard work and incredible sacrifice, were able to obtain land. The percentage of blacks owning property increased from less than 1 to 20 percent. Indeed, African Americans seemed to fare better than poor whites. One observer noted, "The negro, bad as his condition is, seems to me, on the whole, to accommodate himself more easily than the white to the change of situation." The truth of his assertion is reflected in the fact that the percentage of whites owning land dropped from 80 to 67 percent. Increasingly, poor blacks and whites became agricultural laborers on someone else's land.

The black landless farmers, like the slaves before them, were not mere pawns. If they could not control their destinies, at least they could shape them. As one northern observer wrote, "They have a mine of strategy to which the planter sooner or later yields." Through strikes and work slowdowns, African Americans resisted contract and wage labor because working in gangs under white supervision smacked too much of slavery. When they could not own land, they preferred to rent it, but the few who had the cash to do so found few southern whites would risk the wrath of their neighbors by breaking the taboo against renting to blacks.

Sharecropping emerged both as a result of blacks' desire for autonomy and whites' lack of cash. Landowners gave blacks as well as poor whites a plot of land to work in return for a share of the crops. Freedom from white supervision was so desirable to former slaves that they sometimes hitched mule teams to their old slave cabins and carried them off to their assigned acres. To put distance between themselves and slavery, many black men would not allow their wives and children to work in the fields.

Sharecropping at first seemed to be a good bargain for African Americans because they frequently negotiated their way to a half-share of the crops. Their portion of the profits from southern agriculture, including all provisions, rose from 22 percent under slavery to 56 percent by the end of Reconstruction. Moreover, they were making more for working less. Fewer family members worked and black men labored shorter hours; as a group African Americans worked one-third fewer hours than under slavery. Per capita black income increased quickly after the war to about one-half that of whites, but then it stagnated.

Sharecropping later proved to be disastrous for most blacks and poor whites. They needed more than land to farm; they also required seeds, fertilizers, and provisions to live on until they harvested their crops. To obtain these they often borrowed against their share of the crops. Falling crop prices, high credit rates, and sometimes cheating by creditors left many to harvest a growing burden of debt with each crop. In many states, when the Democrats regained power, laws favoring creditors were passed. These led to debt peonage for many sharecroppers.

If most former slaves did not win economic freedom, they benefited from freedom in other ways. It was no longer illegal to learn to read and write, and African Americans pursued education with much zeal. Many even paid as much as 10 percent of their limited incomes for tuition. They began to learn the fundamentals, and a growing number also sought higher education. Between 1860 and 1880 over 1000 African Americans earned college degrees. Some went north to college, but most went to 1 of the 13 southern colleges established by the American Missionary Association or by black and white churches with the assistance of the Freedmen's Bureau. Such schools as Howard and Fisk were a permanent legacy of Reconstruction.

African Americans were also able to enjoy and expand their rich cultural heritage. Religion was a central focus for most, just as it had been in slavery. Withdrawing from white congregations with segregated pews and self-serving sermons on the duty of servants to their masters, blacks everywhere established separate black churches. The membership in such antebellum denominations as the African Methodist Episcopal soared. In essence, black Christians declared their religious independence, and their churches became centers of political and social activities as well as religious ones. As one carpetbagger noted, "The colored preachers are *the great power* in controlling and uniting the colored vote." The churches also functioned as vehicles for self-help and sources of entertainment.

Most African Americans desired racial intermingling no more than whites. Many could not feel free until they had removed themselves and their children as far as possible from white arrogance. They created separate congregations and acquiesced to segregated schooling. Nevertheless, they did not want to be publicly humiliated by such measures as separate railroad cars. They frequently used their limited political power to protect civil rights through clauses in state constitutions and legislation, as well as by appeals for the enforcement of national laws. Consequently, black Southerners did enjoy the use of public facilities to a greater degree than they would during the 75 years following Reconstruction.

The very changes that gave African Americans hope during Reconstruction distressed poor whites. Black political equality rankled them, but much more serious was their own declining economic status. As their landownership declined, more whites became dependent on sharecropping and low-wage jobs, primarily in the textile industry. Even these meager opportunities were eagerly greeted; as one North Carolina preacher proclaimed, "Next to God, what this town needs is a cotton mill." Economic competition between poor whites and blacks was keen, but their common plight also favored cooperation based on class interest. The economic pressures applied by the white elite frequently hurt both groups as well as middle-class yeomen farmers, and for brief periods during Reconstruction they warily united in politics. Invariably, however, these attempts were shattered by upper-class appeals to white supremacy and racial unity.

Ironically, although poor whites were perceived by nearly everyone as the group most hostile to blacks, the two shared many aspects of a rich southern cultural heritage. Both groups developed colorful dialects. For each, aesthetic expression was based on utility—reflecting their need to use wisely what little they had. Their quilts were not merely functional but often quite beautiful. In religion and recreation, their experiences were similar. At camp meetings and revivals, poor whites practiced a highly emotional religion, just as many black Southerners did. Both groups spun yarns and sang songs that reflected the perils of their existence and provided folk heroes. They also shared many superstitions as well as useful folk remedies. Race, however, was a potent wedge between them that upper-class whites frequently exploited for their own political and economic goals.

Planters no longer dominated the white elite; sharecropping turned them and others into absentee landlords. The sons of the old privileged families joined the growing ranks of lawyers, railroad entrepreneurs, bankers, industrialists, and merchants. In some ways, the upper and middle classes began to merge, but in many places the old elite and their sons still enjoyed a degree of deference and political leadership. Their hostility toward African Americans was not as intense, largely because they possessed means of control. When their control slipped, however, they also became ranting racists.

So strongly were all southern whites imbued with a belief in white superiority that most could not imagine total black equality. A Freedmen's Bureau agent reported in 1866 that "a very respectable old citizen . . . swore that, if he could not thrash a negro who insulted him, he would leave the country." White attitudes toward blacks were as irrational as they were generalized. Most whites exempted the blacks they knew from such generalizations. As an Alabama planter declared in 1865, "If all were like some of mine I wouldn't say anything. They're as intelligent and well behaved as anybody. But I can't stand free niggers anyhow!"

Violent White Resistance

Large numbers of whites engaged in massive resistance to Reconstruction. Unlike the resistance of southern blacks 100 years later, however, this brand of resistance was not passive but very aggressive. In 1866, some bored young men in Pulaski, Tennessee, organized a social club with all the trappings of fraternal orders—secret rituals, costumes, and practical jokes. They soon learned that their antics intimidated African Americans; thenceforth the **Ku Klux Klan** grew into a terrorist organization, copied all over the South under various names. A historian of the Klan asserts that it "whipped, shot, hanged, robbed, raped, and otherwise outraged Negroes and Republicans

This 1874 cartoon by Thomas Nast illustrates northern concern about southern violence and disillusionment about Reconstruction. It contrasts sharply with Nast's highly optimistic 1865 illustration of emancipation on page 422.

THE PEOPLE SPEAK

Testimony Against the Klan

The terrorism committed by the Ku Klux Klan is documented in the published proceedings of the Joint Committee on Reconstruction. Here Daniel H. Smith of Mississippi tells of his narrow escape from a lynching in his testimony before the committee.

Question. Have you ever been attacked by disguised men?

Answer. Yes, sir.

Question. You may state the particulars to the committee.

Answer. After I came here in 1866, and was near Brooksville, a gentleman up there named Elm tried to hire my wife, and told me he would give me a school on the place, if I would let my wife go and wait on him. When I mentioned it to her she was not willing to go there. I would not try to force her there, and he fell out with me about it. After he fell out with me about it, he met me, and asked me what sort of way I had done, and cursed me. I told him I thought I done my duty; that my wife was not willing to go. He told me he generally made negroes like me do as he wanted them to do; he didn't ask no negro what they did; he generally made them do it; and a good many words passed between us. I told him I thought I had done my duty. He threatened to kill me a time or two up there if I did not do it. When I was coming from Brooksville one night, I saw two men up here in the road before me, with white sheets around them. They lit off of horses and told me to stop. They knowed I was going to Brooksville; they always knew it; for I was teaching a colored school near Brooksville, and always went to Brooksville Saturday evening, and sometimes it was after night before I returned home. In returning back I saw two people with sheets around them, and when they ordered me to stop I did so, and they got down and asked if that was Daniel Smith. I told them it was not, it was Alleck Billips. He was a man that resembles me very much, and was about my height, and, it being dark, they could not tell whether it was me or not, and I don't think they had taken very particular notice of my features and face. They drew a rope out, and said if it had been Daniel H. Smith they aimed to hang him with that rope that night. Then they went on and asked me if I had been a good negro to my master Charley; that was Charley Sherrod. I told them I had been very good and obedient to him, and got away from them that night by telling them that falsehood. The year after

that, or a shorter time than a year, I moved away from there down here to where I am now. . .

Question. What is the feeling among the whites, so far as you have conversed with them or heard an expression of opinion in relation to colored suffrage or negroes voting?

Answer. Well, sir, they do not believe in it. . . . Out in the part of the county where I live I have known a great many of them to tell the colored people, so as to disappoint them, that there was no election—that it had all been given over. A great many ignorant people would think the employer knew, and that he told them the truth. They would deprive them in that way of their votes. And, again, they would tell them to take their wagons, and go to such a place, and haul so and so away from there. They would manage in all such ways to keep the black people away. Since I have been in the State they came to me and asked me when the election was, and I would tell them. I do not believe, sir, that the generality, the majority of the white people that were around in the neighborhood, generally appreciated me very much on account of my being a negro. I have heard them speak so very bitterly, though I have always behaved myself to them and been very obedient, and never put myself in the way to create any disturbance in any way. . . .

Question. Do the white people here favor the colored people buying lands and having homes?

Answer. No, sir. . . . [T]hey say that if you suffer the colored people here to own land they cannot get any laborers then, for where a colored man owns a piece of land, as many as can do so will go to their own land, and that will defeat them from getting labor.

Question. So that the white owners of the soil you think are generally opposed to your people becoming owners of land?

Answer. Yes, sir; or stocks [livestock] in any way; they don't believe in that. I have known a great many people that have lost their stock. Sometimes the employers would go out and shoot the stock down, if they found them in the wrong place. They did not tell them who killed them.

Testimony of Daniel H. Smith, Macon, Mississippi, November 7, 1871, in U.S. Congress. *Testimony Taken by the Joint Select Committee to Inquire into the Condition of Affairs in the Late Insurrectionary States.* Government Printing Office, Washington, D.C., Vol. II, pp. 570–573, 574, 1872.

across the South in the name of preserving white civilization." Led by former confederate officer Nathan Bedford Forrest, a major goal of the Klan was to intimidate Republican voters and restore Democrats to office. In South Carolina, when blacks working for a scalawag began to vote, Klansmen visited the plantation and "whipped every nigger man they could lay their hands on." The group's increasing lawlessness alarmed many people and led to congressional action. The Klan was broken up by three Enforcement Acts (1870–1871) that gave the president the right to suspend habeas corpus against "armed combinations" interfering with any citizen's right to vote. In 1871 Grant did so in nine South Carolina counties. Disbanding the Klan, however, did little to decrease southern violence or the activities of similar terrorist groups.

Some black Southerners were probably never allowed to vote freely. At the peak of Reconstruction, fewer than 30,000 federal troops were stationed in the entire South—hardly enough to protect the rights of 4.5 million African Americans. As troops were being withdrawn, Democrats sought to regain control of their states. They made appeals to white supremacy and charged the Republicans with corruption. Without secret ballots, landowners could threaten sharecroppers with eviction for "improper" voting. In addition to economic intimidation, violence against African Americans escalated in most states as the Democrats increased their political power. When victory seemed close, Democrats justified any means to the desired end that they called "redemption." A South Carolina Democratic campaign plan in 1876 urged, "Never threaten a man individually. If he deserves to be threatened, the necessities of the times require that he should die. A dead Radical is very harmless." One Democratic candidate for governor in Louisiana proclaimed, "We shall carry the next election if we have to ride saddle-deep in blood to do it." In six heavily black counties in Mississippi such tactics proved highly successful—reducing Republican votes from more than 14,000 in 1873 to only 723 in 1876. Beginning with Virginia and Tennessee in 1869, by 1876 all but three states—Louisiana, Florida, and South Carolina—had Democratic **Redeemer governments.** The final collapse of Reconstruction became official the following year with the withdrawal of federal troops from the three unredeemed states.

RECONSTRUCTION IN THE NORTH AND WEST

In the end, the South could be said to have lost the war but won the peace. After 1877 Southern whites found little resistance to their efforts to forge new institutions to replace both the economic benefits and racial control of slavery. By 1910 they had devised a system of legalized repression that gave whites many of the benefits of slavery without all the responsibilities. Surely this was not what the North had envisioned after Appomattox. How did it happen? Much of the answer is found in events occurring in the North and West.

Northern Shifts in Attitudes

The basic cause for the decline of Reconstruction can be seen in an 1874 conversation between two northern Republicans during which one declared that the people were "tired out with this wornout cry of 'Southern Outrages!!!' Hard times and heavy taxes make them wish the . . . 'everlasting nigger' were in [hell] or Africa. . . . It is amazing the change that has taken place in the last two years in the public sentiment." A shifting political climate, economic hard times, increasing preoccupation with other issues, and continued racism combined to make most Northerners wash their hands of the responsibility for the protection of black rights.

Although his slogan "Let us have peace" was appealing, Ulysses S. Grant proved to be a poor choice for the presidency. Not only was he politically inexperienced, but he also lacked a taste for politics. Haunted by a fear of failure and socially insecure, Grant was too easily influenced by men of wealth and prestige. He made some dismal appointments and remained loyal to individuals who did not merit his trust. The result was a series of scandals. Grant was not personally involved, but his close association with the perpetrators blemished both his and his party's image. The first major scandal surfaced in 1872; it involved **Credit Mobilier,** a dummy construction company used to milk money from railroad investors in order to line the pockets of a few insiders, including Vice President Schuyler Colfax and a number of other prominent Republicans. Later, bribes and kickback schemes surfaced that involved Indian trading posts, post office contracts, and commissions for tax collection. Such revelations as well as the corruption in some southern Republican governments did little to enhance the public image of the party, and Democrats were quick to make corruption a major issue in both the North and the South.

Although by the 1872 presidential election, there had only been a hint of scandal, some Republicans were disenchanted. In that election the Republican party was split; a number, calling themselves Liberal Republicans, formed a separate party. They supported their own candidate, *New York Tribune* editor Horace Greeley, rather than Grant. Among Greeley's campaign pledges was a more moderate southern policy. Even with the Democrats also nominating Greeley, Grant easily won reelection, but the fear of disgruntled Republicans merging with Democrats remained. By 1874 Republicans were becoming aware that the black vote would not save them. That year Democrats captured the House and gained in the Senate, following further revelations of Republican corruption.

At least as detrimental to Republican political fortunes was a depression that followed the **Panic of 1873,** which was caused by overinvestment in railroads and risky financial deals. Lasting six years, it was the most serious economic downturn the nation had yet experienced. Whatever their cause, depressions usually result in "voting the rascals out." Democratic fortunes were bound to rise as the people's fell. Yet economic distress had an even wider impact on Reconstruction. People's attention became focused on their pocketbooks rather than on abstract ideals of equality and justice.

Actually, the Panic of 1873 merely brought into clearer focus the vast changes occurring in the North during Reconstruction. The South had never had the undivided attention of the rest of the nation. Such events as the completion of the first transcontinental railroad in 1869 often overshadowed reports of "Southern outrages." The United States was experiencing the growing pains of economic modernization and western expansion. The Republican platform of 1860 had called for legislation favoring both of these as well as stopping the expansion of slavery. Comprised of diverse interest groups, the party went through a battle for its soul during Reconstruction. For a while the small abolitionist faction had gained some ascendancy due to postwar developments. By

the late 1870s, however, the Republican party had forsaken its reformist past to become a protector of privilege rather than a guarantor of basic rights. In effect, Republicans and Democrats joined hands in conservative support of railroad and industrial interests.

Western Expansion, Racism, and Native Americans

The major reason for the decline of Reconstruction was the pervasive belief in white supremacy. There could be little determination to secure equal rights for those who were considered unequal in all other respects. Reconstruction became a failed opportunity to resolve justly the status of one minority, and the climate of racism almost ensured failure for others as well. Western expansion not only diverted attention from Reconstruction but also raised the question of what was to be done about the Plains Indians. They, too, were considered inferior to whites. William H. Seward, who later became secretary of state, spoke for most white Americans when in 1860 he described blacks as "a foreign and feeble element like the Indians, incapable of assimilation." Indeed, while Reconstruction at first offered hope to African Americans, for Native Americans hope was fading.

In the end, African Americans were oppressed; Native Americans were exterminated or separated into shrinking reservations. From the white viewpoint the reason was obvious. As a so-called scientific treatise of the 1850s explained, "The *Barbarous* races of America . . . although nearly as low in intellect as the Negro races, are essentially untameable. Not merely have all attempts to civilize them failed, but also every endeavor to enslave them." Because most Africans,

Black troops, known as "buffalo soldiers," fought in the western campaigns to subdue the Plains Indians. African Americans often sought unsuccessfully to prove their loyalty and win respect and rights through military service.

like Europeans, depended on agriculture rather than hunting, they adapted more easily to agricultural slavery. Black labor was valuable, if controlled; Native Americans were merely barriers to expansion.

Cultural Differences

When settlers first began moving onto the Great Plains, they encountered about 250,000 Plains Indians and 13 million buffalo. Some groups, including the Zuni, Hopi, Navaho, and Pawnee, were fairly settled and depended on gardening and farming. Others, such as the Sioux, Apache, and Cheyenne, however, were nomadic hunters who followed the buffalo herds over vast tracts of land. These herds played a crucial role in most Plains Indians' culture—providing almost all the basic necessities. Indians ate the buffalo meat, made clothing and teepees out of the hides, used the fats for cosmetics, fashioned the bones into tools, made thread from the sinews, and even burned dried buffalo droppings as fuel. To settlers, however, the buffalo were barriers to western expansion. The herds interfered with construction, knocked over telegraph poles and fences, and could derail trains during stampedes.

Other cultural differences caused misunderstandings between settlers and Native Americans. Among Anglo-Americans, capitalism fostered competition and frontier living promoted individualism. On the other hand, Plains Indians lived in tribes based on kinship ties. As members of an extended family that included distant cousins, Indians were taught to place the welfare of the group over the interests of the individual. The emphasis within a tribe was on cooperation rather than competition. Some tribes might be richer than other tribes, but there was seldom a large gap between the rich and the poor within a tribe.

Power as well as wealth was usually shared. Tribes were loosely structured rather than tightly organized. Chiefs seldom had much individual power. The Cheyenne, for example, had a council of 44 to advise the chief. Instead of having a lot of political power, chiefs were generally religious and ceremonial leaders. Anglo-Americans did not always understand their limited power. Whites incorrectly believed that an individual Indian could make decisions and sign agreements that would be considered legal by their fellow Indians.

Another major cultural difference between the newly arriving settlers and the Plains Indians was their attitudes toward the land. Most Native Americans had no concept of private property. Chief Joseph of the Nez Percé eloquently expressed the view: "The earth was created by the assistance of the sun, and it should be left as it was. . . . The country was made without lines of demarcation, and it is no man's business to divide it."

Native Americans refused to draw property lines and borders because of how they viewed the place of people in the world. Whites tended to see land, plants, and animals as resources to be exploited. Native Americans, on the other hand, stressed the unity of all life—and its holiness.

Most of the Plains Indians believed that land could be utilized but never owned. The idea of owning land was as absurd as owning the air people breathed. To some, the sacredness of the land made farming against their religion. Chief Somohalla of the Wanapaun explained why his people refused to farm. "You ask me to plow the ground! Shall I take a knife and tear my mother's bosom? . . . You ask me to cut grass and make hay and sell it, and be rich like white men! But how dare I cut off my mother's hair?"

Indians had great reverence for all land. In addition, some particular pieces of land were considered especially sacred or holy. Certain bodies of water were seen as sources of healing and sites for worship. Some areas were burial grounds, where the spirits of ancestors were believed to reside. White settlers had little understanding of or respect for such Indian sentiments. The results could be tragic where interests collided.

From the white viewpoint, the most significant characteristic of many of the Plains Indian tribes, such as the Cheyenne, Sioux, and Arapaho, was their ability as mounted warriors. Using horses introduced by the Spanish, they had resisted white encroachment for two centuries. Most had no desire for assimilation; they merely wanted to be left alone. "If the Indians had tried to make the whites live like them," one Sioux declared, "the whites would have resisted, and it was the same way with the Indians."

Although some tribes could coexist peacefully with settlers, the nomadic tribes had a way of life that was incompatible with miners, railroad developers, cattle ranchers, and farmers. To Anglo-Americans the Indians were barriers to expansion. They agreed with Theodore Roosevelt that the West was not meant to be "kept as nothing but a game reserve for squalid savages." Thus U.S. Indian policy focused on getting more territory for white settlement. Prior to Reconstruction this was done by signing treaties that divided land between Native Americans and settlers and restricted the movement of each on the lands of the other. Frequently Indian consent was fraudulently obtained, and white respect for Indian land depended on how desirable it was for settlement. As the removal of the Southern Cherokees to Oklahoma had shown in the 1830s, compatibility of cultures did not protect Native Americans from the greed of whites.

During the Civil War, Sioux, Cheyenne, and Arapaho braves rejected the land cessions made by their chiefs. Violence against settlers erupted as frontier troop strength was reduced to fight the Confederacy. The war also provided an excuse to nullify previous

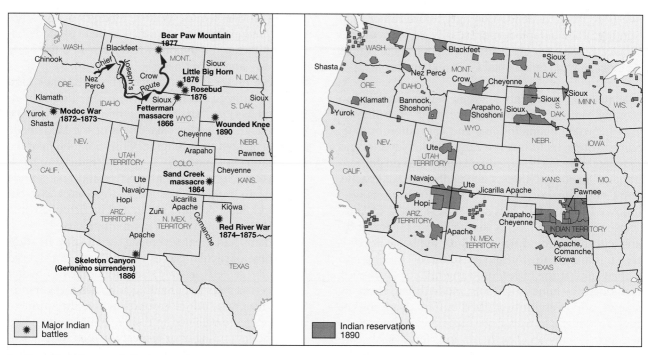

Indian Battles and Reservations

treaties and pledges with the Native Americans resettled in Oklahoma under Andrew Jackson's Indian removal policy. Some did support the Confederacy, but all suffered the consequences of Confederate defeat. Settlers moved into the most desirable land, pushing the Indians farther south and west. Some Native Americans began to resist.

Confrontation and Annihilation By the close of the Civil War, Indian hostility had escalated, especially after an 1864 massacre. The territorial governor of Colorado persuaded most of the warring Cheyennes and Arapahos to come to Fort Lyon on Sand Creek, promising them protection. Colonel J. M. Chivington's militia, however, attacked an Indian camp flying a white flag and the American flag and killed hundreds of Native American men, women, and children. The following year Congress established a committee to investigate the causes of conflict. Its final report in 1867 led to the creation of an **Indian Peace Commission** charged with negotiating settlements. At two conferences in 1867 and 1868, Indian chiefs were asked to restrict their tribes to reservations in the undesirable lands of Oklahoma and the Black Hills of the Dakotas in return for supplies and assistance from the government.

Most Indians did not consider the offer very generous. Some acquiesced and others resisted, but in the end federal authorities subdued or killed them all. Several factors made their resistance unsuccessful. Railroads had penetrated the West, bringing in

both settlers and federal troops more rapidly. Most important, however, was the destruction of the buffalo herds. Just as modern Americans would be helpless without oil or electricity, the Plains Indians' culture could not survive the near extinction of the buffalo by professional and sport hunters. In 1872 the Indian commissioner accurately forecasted that in a few years the "most powerful and hostile bands of today" would be "reduced to the condition of suppliants for charity."

In 1876, the final year of Reconstruction, Lieutenant Colonel George A. Custer's defeat at Little Bighorn called attention to the "Indian problem." The stage was set for this confrontation with Chief Sitting Bull's Sioux warriors and their Cheyenne allies two years earlier when gold was discovered in the Black Hills. The territory suddenly became tempting, and miners began pouring into the lands guaranteed to the Indians only five years before. "The white man is in the Black Hills just like maggots," one Indian lamented.

Despite Sitting Bull's victory, the die had been cast during Reconstruction. All that remained were "mopping up" exercises. Federal authorities solved the Indian problem by reducing the number of Native Americans to a level that posed no threat. Still, white Americans would not leave the Indians alone to practice their religion and culture. The last major bloody confrontation occurred during the cold December of 1890 on the Pine Ridge Reservation (Sioux) in South Dakota. Poorly fed and supplied on the reservation, dissatisfied with their present, and longing for the

A Native American watercolor rendering of the Battle of Little Bighorn depicts its aftermath. As Sitting Bull and others stand watching, Sioux and Cheyenne warriors ride horseback over the corpses of Custer (*left center*) and his troops.

glories of their past, members of the Teton Sioux took up the **Ghost Dance,** a ritual that promised the faithful the mystical disappearance of the whites and the return of their lands. An inept government agent overreacted, calling in troops to suppress the Ghost Dance and arrest the Sioux leader Sitting Bull, whom the government considered the focal point of Indian resistance. When Indian police killed Sitting Bull, some Sioux took up arms and left the reservation. Near Wounded Knee Creek, U.S. soldiers, armed with rapid-fire Hotchkiss guns, attempted to disarm the Indians. When one Indian resisted, soldiers opened fire, killing more than 300 men, women, and children. The **Battle of Wounded Knee,** which resembled more a slaughter than a battle, ended the violent era of Indian and white relations.

Ethnocide and Assimilation By the time of Wounded Knee, the U.S. government had adopted a policy that emphasized ethnocide rather than genocide. An assault on tribalism, ethnocide—the calculated destruction of a culture—was an attempt by white Americans to force Native Americans to assimilate into their culture. Although not as bloody as the Indian wars, ethnocide was even more destructive to Native American societies.

At the heart of this new policy was the destruction of the reservation system. Reservations encouraged tribal unity, and, as such, distinctiveness from white American society. Congress believed that the solution was to treat Indians less like members of individual tribes and more like autonomous individuals. As a first step, in 1871 Congress had ruled that no Indian tribe "shall be acknowledged or recognized as an independent nation, tribe or power, with whom

This photograph, showing the mass burial of the victims after the massacre at Wounded Knee, illustrates the callous disregard of the value of Native American lives.

the United States may contract by treaty." Then in an attempt to destroy Indian culture, in 1887 Congress passed the **Dawes Severalty Act,** which authorized the president to divide tribal lands and redistribute the lands among tribal members, giving 160 acres to each head of a family and lesser amounts to bachelors, women, and children. Although the plots would be held in trust for 25 years to prevent Indians from immediately selling the land, the object of the legislation was to make Indians individual landowners. In addition, all Native Americans receiving land grants were also made citizens of the United States.

Henry Lauren Dawes, a senator from Massachusetts, was motivated by what he believed were the best interests of the Native Americans. Like other reformers, he believed that the most effective solution to the Indian problem was to assimilate Indians into mainstream white American culture. To this end, other reformers opened Indian schools to teach Indian children to be mechanics and farmers and to train them for citizenship. Richard Pratt, an army officer who founded the Carlisle Indian Industrial School in Pennsylvania in 1879, maintained that the fastest and surest way to assimilate Indians was to remove Indian children from reservations and send them to boarding schools in the East. By 1905 there were 25 boarding schools patterned after Carlisle. The schools emphasized ruthless assimilation. The "Rules for Indian Schools" called for compulsory observation of the Christian Sabbath, all formal and casual conversation in English, and instruction in "the sports and games enjoyed by white youth, such as baseball, hopscotch, croquet, marbles, bean bags, dominoes, checkers." Even more boarding schools were established on reservations to serve the same ends. What surprised reformers the most, however, was the failure of these schools to break tribal loyalties or destroy Indian culture.

While the reformers opened schools, Congress continued its efforts to break up the reservations. The Curtis Act of 1898 ended tribal sovereignty in Indian Territory, voiding tribal control of mineral rights, abolishing tribal laws and courts, and imposing the laws and courts of the United States on the Indians. The Dead Indian Act (1902) permitted Indians to sell allotted lands they had inherited, thereby circumventing the 25-year trust period imposed by the Dawes Act. Four years later, Congress continued its assault on the trust period with the Burke Act, which eliminated the trust period altogether and allowed the secretary of the interior to decide when Indians were competent to manage their own affairs. Finally, in 1924 Congress enacted the Snyder Act, which granted all Indians born in the United States full citizenship. As far as Congress was concerned, the United States had now assimilated its true natives.

TABLE 16.2	
Native Americans and the Federal Government Following the Civil War	
1864	Sand Creek Massacre
1867	Creation of the Indian Peace Commission
1876	Battle of Little Big Horn
1887	Dawes Severalty Act
1890	Ghost Dance and Wounded Knee
1898	Curtis Act
1902	Dead Indian Act
1906	Burke Act
1924	Snyder Act

Reformers believed that these acts would end the tribal system and lead to assimilation. The legislation, however, served only the land interests of white Americans. By 1932 the allotment program had taken 90 million acres of land away from tribal control. Far from being assimilated, Indians saw their own culture attacked and partially destroyed, while at the same time they were never fully accepted into the dominant American culture.

Final Retreat from Reconstruction

The exact nature of the Native Americans' status, like that of African Americans, was determined after Reconstruction was over. The treatment of both, as well as of immigrants, would be justified by the increasingly virulent racism of whites, which was given "scientific" support by the scholars of the late nineteenth century. The patriotism engendered by the 1876 centennial of the Declaration of Independence also fostered a desire for unity among white Americans at the expense of nonwhites.

By 1876, fewer Americans championed black rights than had at the close of the war. Neither could Northerners who believed that the only good Indian was a dead Indian condemn southern whites for their treatment of African Americans. Some of the old abolitionist Radicals had grown tired of what had become a protracted and complex problem. They therefore justified their withdrawal from the fight by the failures of some southern Reconstruction governments. Those least likely to do so, such as Thaddeus Stevens and Charles Sumner, were dead. Until his death in 1874, Sumner had struggled to get Congress to pass a civil rights act that would spell out more specifically the guarantees of the Fourteenth Amendment. He proposed that segregation of all public facilities, including schools, be declared illegal and the right of African Americans to serve on juries specified. After his death, in part as a tribute to him but mostly as one provision of a larger political bargain, Congress en-

This 1877 cartoon shows President Hayes as a railroad conductor ushering two Louisiana carpetbaggers out of the state.

acted the **Civil Rights Act of 1875.** The act did not include Sumner's clause on schools and did not provide any means of enforcement. For African Americans it was a paper victory that marked an end of national action on their behalf. Never effectively enforced, the act was rendered totally impotent by Supreme Court decisions of the late nineteenth century.

By 1876 all the elements were present for a national retreat on Reconstruction: the distraction of economic distress, a deep desire for unity among whites, the respectability of racism, a frustrated weariness with black problems by former allies, a growing conservatism on economic and social issues, a changing political climate featuring a resurgence of the Democratic party, and finally a general public disgust with the failure of Reconstruction. The presidential election of that year sealed the fate of Reconstruction and brought about an official end to it.

Corruption was a major issue in the 1876 election and the Democrats chose **Samuel J. Tilden,** a New Yorker whose claim to fame was breaking up the notorious Boss Tweed Ring. The Republicans nominated **Rutherford B. Hayes,** a man who had offended few—largely by doing little. Although Hayes had been elected governor of Ohio three times, to one observer he was "a third rate nonentity, whose only recommendation is that he is obnoxious to no one." As would become typical of most elections during the decades following Reconstruction, the campaign did not focus on any burning issues. The Democrats

ran against Republican corruption. The Republicans ran against Democratic violence in the South. "Our strong ground," Hayes wrote, "is the dread of a solid South, *rebel rule,* etc., etc. . . . It leads people away from 'hard times'; which is our deadliest foe."

The election itself was so riddled with corruption and violence that no one can ever know what would have happened in a fair election. One thing is certain. The Democrats gained strength. Tilden won the popular vote and led Hayes in undisputed electoral votes 184 to 165. However, 185 votes were needed for election, and 20 votes were disputed—19 of them from Louisiana, Florida, and South Carolina. They were the only southern states still under Republican rule with the backing of federal troops. In each, rival election boards sent in different returns.

With no constitutional provision for such an occurrence, the Republican Senate and Democratic House established a special commission to decide which returns were valid. The 15-member Electoral Commission had 5 members each from the House, the Senate, and the Supreme Court. At first it was evenly divided with 7 Republicans and 7 Democrats; politically independent Supreme Court Justice David Davis was the swing vote. Illinois Democrats then made a mistake and selected Davis as their senator. Thus, a Republican justice was appointed to replace him on the Electoral Commission, which proceeded to vote along party lines, 8 to 7, to give all the

Election of 1876

UNCONTESTED ELECTORAL VOTE	ELECTORAL TOTAL	POPULAR VOTE
REPUBLICAN Rutherford B. Hayes 165	185 ●	4,034,311
DEMOCRATIC Samuel J. Tilden 184	184 ●	4,288,546
GREENBACK Peter Cooper —	—	75,983
349		8,398,830

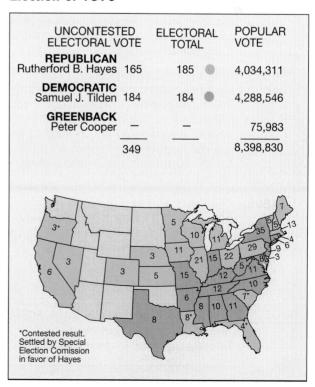

*Contested result. Settled by Special Election Comission in favor of Hayes

disputed votes to Hayes. Democrats were outraged, and a constitutional crisis seemed in the making if a united Democratic front in the House voted to reject the commission's findings.

A series of agreements between Hayes's advisors and southern Democratic congressmen averted the crisis. In what came to be called the **Compromise of 1877,** Hayes agreed to support federal aid for southern internal improvements, especially a transcontinental railroad. He also promised to appoint a southern Democrat to his cabinet and to allow southern Democrats a say in the allocation of federal offices in their region. Most important, however, was his pledge to remove the remaining federal troops from the South. In return southern Democrats promised to protect black rights and to support the findings of the Electoral Commission. On March 2, the House voted to accept the report and declare Hayes the presidential winner by an electoral vote of 185 to 184. After taking office, Hayes removed the troops, and the remaining Republican governments in the South soon collapsed.

Scholars once considered the Compromise of 1877 an important factor in the end of Reconstruction. Actually, its role was more symbolic than real; it merely buried the corpse. The battle for the Republican party's soul had been lost by its abolitionist faction well before the election of 1876. The Democratic party had never sought to extend or protect blacks' rights. The Supreme Court began to interpret the Fourteenth and Fifteenth amendments very narrowly, stripping them of their strength. Thus African Americans were left with a small number of allies, and one by one many of their rights were lost during the next four decades.

CONCLUSION

As the Civil War ended, many unresolved issues remained. The most crucial involved the status of the former slaves and of the former Confederate states.

CHRONOLOGY OF KEY EVENTS

1863 Lincoln proclaims 10 percent plan for Reconstruction, which requires states to abolish slavery and have 10 percent of the citizens who had voted in the 1860 election subscribe to an oath to support the Constitution and the Union

1864 Lincoln vetoes Wade-Davis Bill on grounds that it imposes too severe conditions on the readmission of the seceded states; Sand Creek Massacre of Indians in Colorado

1865 Congress establishes Freedmen's Bureau to aid former slaves and refugees; Confederate army surrenders at Appomattox; John Wilkes Booth assassinates Lincoln at Ford's Theater in Washington, D.C.; Andrew Johnson becomes seventeenth president; Thirteenth Amendment is ratified, abolishing slavery

1866 Civil Rights Act provides that all persons born in the United States are citizens and possess equal legal and property rights; Fourteenth Amendment is proposed

1867 Reconstruction Act, passed over Johnson's veto, divides the South into five military districts, each governed by an army general. It requires each state to adopt a constitution disqualifying former Confederate officials from holding office, to grant black citizens the right to vote, and to ratify the Fourteenth Amendment

1868 House of Representatives impeaches President Johnson; he escapes conviction in the Senate by one vote; Fourteenth Amendment is ratified, guaranteeing citizenship to black Americans; Indian peace conference leads to establishment of reservations in Oklahoma and the Black Hills of the Dakotas; Ulysses S. Grant is elected eighteenth president

1870 Fifteenth Amendment is ratified, outlawing exclusion from the vote on the basis of race

1870–1871 Ku Klux Klan Acts are passed, which outlaw use of force to prevent people from voting and authorize use of federal troops to enforce the laws; Tweed Ring in New York City is exposed

1872 Credit Mobilier scandal is exposed

1876 Custer is defeated at Little Bighorn; disputed presidential election between Tilden and Hayes

1877 Electoral Commission awards disputed ballots to Republican Rutherford B. Hayes, who becomes nineteenth president

The destinies of both were inextricably intertwined. Anything affecting the status of either influenced the fate of the other. Quick readmission of the states with little change would doom black rights. Enforced equality of African Americans under the law would create turbulence and drastic change in the South. This difficult problem was further complicated by constitutional, economic, and political considerations, ensuring that the course of Reconstruction would be chaotic and contradictory.

Presidential Reconstruction under both Lincoln and Johnson favored rapid reunification and white unity more than changes in the racial structure of the South. The South, however, refused to accept a meaningful end of slavery, as was blatantly demonstrated by the Black Codes. Congressional desire to reestablish legislative supremacy and the Republican need to build a national party combined with this southern intransigence to unite Radical and moderate Republicans on the need to protect black rights and to restructure the South. What emerged from congressional reconstruction were Republican governments that expanded democracy and enacted needed reforms but were deeply resented by many southern whites. At the core of that resentment was not disgust over incompetence or corruption but hostility to black political power in any form.

Given the pervasiveness of racial prejudice, what is remarkable is not that the Freedmen's Bureau, the constitutional amendments, and the civil rights legislation did not produce permanent change but that these actions were taken at all. Cherished ideas of property rights, limited government, and self-reliance, as well as an almost universal belief in black inferiority, almost guaranteed that the experiment would fail. The first national attempt to resolve fairly and justly the question of minority rights in a pluralistic society was abandoned in less than a decade. After Native American populations had been decimated, the government sought to eradicate all elements of their culture that differed from that of the dominant society. Indians, blacks, and women saw the truth of the Alabama planter's words of 1865: "Poor elk—poor buffaloe—poor Indian—poor Nigger—this is indeed a white man country." However, less than a century later seeds planted by the amendments would finally germinate, flower, and be harvested.

CHAPTER SUMMARY AND KEY POINTS

The 12 years following the Civil War carried vast consequences for the nation's future. They helped set the pattern for future race relations and defined the federal government's role in promoting racial equality.

- Immediately following the war, all-white southern legislatures passed Black Codes, which denied blacks the right to purchase or rent land.

- These efforts to force former slaves to work on plantations led congressional Republicans to seize control of Reconstruction from President Andrew Johnson, deny representatives from the former Confederate states their congressional seats, and pass the Civil Rights Act of 1866 and draft the Fourteenth Amendment, extending citizenship rights to African Americans and guaranteeing equal protection of the laws.

- In 1870, the Fifteenth Amendment gave voting rights to black men.

- The freedmen, in alliance with carpetbaggers and southern white Republicans known as scalawags, temporarily gained power in every former Confederate state except Virginia. The Reconstruction governments drew up democratic state constitutions, expanded women's rights, provided debt relief, and established the South's first state-funded schools.

- Internal divisions within the southern Republican party, white terrorism, and northern apathy allowed white southern Democrats known as Redeemers to return to power.

- During Reconstruction former slaves and many small white farmers became trapped in a new system of economic exploitation known as sharecropping.

- Native Americans unsuccessfully resisted efforts to restrict them to reservations.

SUGGESTIONS FOR FURTHER READING

Eugene H. Berwanger, *The West and Reconstruction* (1981). Focuses on the events happening in the West during the Reconstruction era.

Richard Nelson Current, *Those Terrible Carpetbaggers* (1988). Refutes the long-standing myth that Northerners in the South after the Civil War were ill-educated people whose only goal was private gain.

William A. Dunning, *Reconstruction, Political and Economic* (1907). One of the first history books written about Reconstruction, it greatly influenced those that followed by presenting the era as a period of tyrannical and corrupt rule of the South.

Eric Foner, *Nothing But Freedom: Emancipation and Its Legacy* (1983). Compares and contrasts the postemancipation experience of African Americans with that of former slaves in the Caribbean.

————, *Reconstruction: America's Unfinished Revolution, 1863–1877* (1988). Comprehensive history of the period, which emphasizes African Americans' central role in defining the period's political and social agenda.

Leon Litwack, *Been in the Storm So Long: The Aftermath of Slavery* (1979). Examines the varied responses of African Americans in the South to emancipation.

James McPherson, *Ordeal by Fire: The Civil War and Reconstruction,* 3rd ed. (2000). A readable and balanced survey of the era.

James Roark, *Masters Without Slaves* (1977). Describes the experience of the former slave owners after emancipation.

Mark W. Summers, *The Era of Good Stealings* (1993). Investigates political corruption during the Reconstruction period.

Joel Williamson, *The Crucible of Race* (1984). Explores the evolution of southern race relations after Reconstruction.

Novels

Howard Bahr, *The Year of Jubilo* (2000).

Howard Fast, *Freedom Road* (1944).

Albion Tourgee, *A Fool's Errand* (1879).

Margaret Walker, *Jubilee* (1966).

MEDIA RESOURCES

Web Sites

Ulysses S. Grant (American Experience) Web site

http://www.pbs.org/wgbh/amex/grant/
A companion to the PBS program with documents, timeline, definitions of people and events, and three broadband interactive sites.

Not For Ourselves Alone: The Story of Elizabeth Cady Stanton and Susan B. Anthony

http://www.pbs.org/stantonanthony/index.html
Web site companion to the PBS series that includes essays, documents, and other resources relating to women's rights.

Jump Jim Crow, Or What Difference Did Emancipation Make?

http://www.lib.Berkeley.edu/~ljones/Jimcrow/index.html
A collection of images, songs, and stories relating to the rise of segregation; also includes texts of segregation laws and a glossary.

Finding Precedence: The Impeachment of Andrew Johnson

http://www.impeach-andrewjohnson.com/
Based upon *Harper's Weekly* articles, includes pictures, cartoon, articles, and explanations of the key issues.

Finding Precedence: Hayes vs. Tilden

http://elections.harpweek.com/controversy.htm

Provides a day-by-day account with cartoons, illustrations, and biographies.

Freedmen and Southern Society

http://www.inform.umd.edu/ARHU/Depts/History/Freedman/home.html
Contains a chronology and sample documents from several print collections or primary sources about emancipation and freedom in the 1860s.

Black History at Harpweek

http://blackhistory.harpweek.com/
Drawn from the pages of *Harper's Weekly,* includes pictures, articles, cartoons, and other resources.

Native American Documents Project

http://www.csusm.edu/nadp/nadp.htm
California State University at San Marcos provides digital documents relating to Native Americans.

Diary and Letters of Rutherford B. Hayes

http://www.ohiohistory.org/onlinedoc/hayes/index.cfm
The Rutherford B. Hayes Presidential Center in Fremont, Ohio, maintains this searchable database of Hayes's writings.

Indian Affairs: Laws and Treaties

http://www.library.okstate.edu/kappler/
Digitized text at Oklahoma State that includes preremoval treaties with the Five Civilized Tribes and other tribes.

Geronimo

http://odur.let.rug.nl/~usa/B/geronimo/geronixx.htm
Contains biographical and autobiographical information about this famous Native American who resisted European domination.

Images of African Americans from the Nineteenth Century

http://digital.nypl.org/schomburg/images_aa19/
Schomburg Center for Research in Black Culture at New York Public Library provides numerous photographs and other visuals.

The Valley of the Shadow

http://jefferson.village.virginia.edu/vshadow2/
Focuses on a northern and a southern town during the Civil War and its aftermath.

Films and Videos

Ulysses S. Grant. A documentary produced by PBS about the life and career of Grant.

Fight No More Forever. Episode 6 of the PBS series *New Perspectives on the West* which covers the battle over the Plains between Native Americans and the federal government.

One Sky Above Us. Episode 8 of *New Perspectives on the West* which discusses the West in the 1890s and the Ghost Dance.

Last Stand at Little Big Horn. One of the most frequently depicted and least understood moments in American history is covered in this *American Experience* tape from PBS.

Geronimo and the Apache Resistance. An account of the battles of Geronimo and the Apaches from PBS.

Birth of a Nation. 1915 movie classic that gives a one-sided, southern view of Reconstruction and illustrates the popular myths about that era.

Dances with Wolves. 1990 movie with Kevin Costner that chronicles the interactions between Civil War hero Lt. John Dunbar and the peaceful Lakota Sioux.

KEY TERMS

Freedmen's Bureau   (p. 423)

Special Field Order 15   (p. 426)

Dred Scott decision   (p. 426)

Radical Republicans   (p. 426)

Ten percent plan   (p. 427)

Wade-Davis Bill   (p. 427)

Black Codes   (p. 428)

Joint Committee on Reconstruction   (p. 429)

Fourteenth Amendment   (p. 430)

Military Reconstruction Act   (p. 431)

Tenure of Office Act   (p. 431)

Fifteenth Amendment   (p. 433)

Carpetbaggers   (p. 435)

Scalawags   (p. 435)

Sharecropping   (p. 438)

Ku Klux Klan   (p. 439)

Redeemer governments   (p. 441)

Credit Mobilier   (p. 441)

Panic of 1873   (p. 442)

Indian Peace Commission   (p. 444)

Ghost Dance   (p. 445)

Battle of Wounded Knee   (p. 445)

Dawes Severalty Act   (p. 446)

Civil Rights Act of 1875   (p. 447)

Compromise of 1877   (p. 448)

PEOPLE YOU SHOULD KNOW

Frederick Douglass   (p. 423)

Oliver O. Howard   (p. 423)

Thaddeus Stevens   (p. 427)

Charles Sumner   (p. 427)

Andrew Johnson   (p. 427)

Edwin M. Stanton   (p. 432)

Ulysses S. Grant   (p. 432)

Susan B. Anthony   (p. 433)

Horace Greeley   (p. 434)

Samuel J. Tilden   (p. 447)

Rutherford B. Hayes   (p. 447)

REVIEW QUESTIONS

1. How were the Civil War and Reconstruction's impacts on black and white Southerners interrelated, and how did the impacts affect the actions of each group?

2. To what extent were white Southerners responsible for what they considered to be the harsh conditions of congressional Reconstruction?

3. Just how radical was Radical Reconstruction?

4. What factors led to the decline of Reconstruction?

5. How were white Americans' treatments of African Americans and Native Americans similar, and how did the treatment of each group differ?

APPENDIX

The Declaration of Independence

The Constitution of the United States of America

Amendments to the Constitution

Presidential Elections

Present Day United States

Present Day World

For additional reference material, go to www.ablongman.com/martin5e/appendix
The online appendix includes the following:

The Declaration of Independence

In Congress, July 4, 1776

The Unanimous Declaration of the Thirteen United States of America

When, in the course of human events, it becomes necessary for one people to dissolve the political bonds which have connected them with another, and to assume, among the powers of the earth, the separate and equal station to which the laws of nature and of nature's God entitle them, a decent respect to the opinions of mankind requires that they should declare the causes which impel them to the separation.

We hold these truths to be self-evident: That all men are created equal; that they are endowed by their Creator with certain unalienable rights; that among these are life, liberty, and the pursuit of happiness; that, to secure these rights, governments are instituted among men, deriving their just powers from the consent of the governed; that whenever any form of government becomes destructive of these ends, it is the right of the people to alter or to abolish it, and to institute new government, laying its foundation on such principles, and organizing its powers in such form, as to them shall seem most likely to effect their safety and happiness. Prudence, indeed, will dictate that governments long established should not be changed for light and transient causes; and accordingly all experience hath shown that mankind are more disposed to suffer, while evils are sufferable, than to right themselves by abolishing the forms to which they are accustomed. But when a long train of abuses and usurpations, pursuing invariably the same object, evinces a design to reduce them under absolute despotism, it is their right, it is their duty, to throw off such government, and to provide new guards for their future security. Such has been the patient sufferance of these colonies; and such is now the necessity which constrains them to alter their former systems of government. The history of the present King of Great Britain is a history of repeated injuries and usurpations, all having in direct object the establishment of an absolute tyranny over these states. To prove this, let facts be submitted to a candid world.

He has refused his assent to laws, the most wholesome and necessary for the public good.

He has forbidden his governors to pass laws of immediate and pressing importance, unless suspended in their operation till his assent should be obtained; and, when so suspended, he has utterly neglected to attend to them.

He has refused to pass other laws for the accommodation of large districts of people, unless those people would relinquish the right of representation in the legislature, a right inestimable to them, and formidable to tyrants only.

He has called together legislative bodies at places unusual, uncomfortable, and distant from the depository of their public records, for the sole purpose of fatiguing them into compliance with his measures.

He has dissolved representative houses repeatedly, for opposing, with manly firmness, his invasions on the rights of the people.

He has refused for a long time, after such dissolutions, to cause others to be elected; whereby the legislative powers, incapable of annihilation, have returned to the people at large for their exercise; the state remaining, in the mean time, exposed to all the dangers of invasions from without and convulsions within.

He has endeavored to prevent the population of these states; for that purpose obstructing the laws for naturalization of foreigners; refusing to pass others to encourage their migration hither, and raising the conditions of new appropriations of lands.

He has obstructed the administration of justice, by refusing his assent to laws for establishing judiciary powers.

He has made judges dependent on his will alone, for the tenure of their offices, and the amount and payment of their salaries.

He has erected a multitude of new offices, and sent hither swarms of officers to harass our people and eat out their substance.

He has kept among us, in times of peace, standing armies, without the consent of our legislatures.

He has affected to render the military independent of, and superior to, the civil power.

He has combined with others to subject us to a jurisdiction foreign to our constitution, and unacknowledged by our laws, giving his assent to their acts of pretended legislation:

For quartering large bodies of armed troops among us;

For protecting them, by a mock trial, from punishment for any murder which they should commit on the inhabitants of these states;

For cutting off our trade with all parts of the world;

For imposing taxes on us without our consent;

For depriving us, in many cases, of the benefits of trial by jury;

For transporting us beyond seas, to be tried for pretended offenses;

For abolishing the free system of English laws in a neighboring province, establishing therein an arbitrary government, and enlarging its boundaries, so as to render it at once an example and fit instrument for introducing the same absolute rule into these colonies;

For taking away our charters abolishing our most valuable laws, and altering fundamentally the forms of our governments;

For suspending our own legislatures, and declaring themselves invested with power to legislate for us in all cases whatsoever.

He has abdicated government here, by declaring us out of his protection and waging war against us.

He has plundered our seas, ravaged our coasts, burned our towns, and destroyed the lives of our people.

He is at this time transporting large armies of foreign mercenaries to complete the works of death, desolation, and tyranny already begun with circumstances of cruelty and perfidy scarcely paralleled in the most barbarous ages, and totally unworthy the head of a civilized nation.

He has constrained our fellow-citizens, taken captive on the high seas, to bear arms against their country, to become the executioners of their friends and brethren, or to fall themselves by their hands.

He has excited domestic insurrection among us, and has endeavored to bring on the inhabitants of our frontiers the merciless Indian savages, whose known rule of warfare is an undistinguished destruction of all ages, sexes, and conditions.

In every stage of these oppressions we have petitioned for redress in the most humble terms; our repeated petitions have been answered only by repeated injury. A prince, whose character is thus marked by every act which may define a tyrant, is unfit to be the ruler of a free people.

Nor have we been wanting in our attentions to our British brethren. We have warned them, from time to time, of attempts by their legislature to extend an unwarrantable jurisdiction over us. We have reminded them of the circumstances of our emigration and settlement here. We have appealed to their native justice and magnanimity; and we have conjured them, by the ties of our common kindred, to disavow these usurpations, which would inevitably interrupt our connections and correspondence. They, too, have been deaf to the voice of justice and of consanguinity. We must, therefore, acquiesce in the necessity which denounces our separation, and hold them, as we hold the rest of mankind, enemies in war, in peace friends.

We, therefore, the representatives of the United States of America, in General Congress assembled, appealing to the Supreme Judge of the world for the rectitude of our intentions, do, in the name and by the authority of the good people of these colonies, solemnly publish and declare, that these United Colonies are, and of right ought to be, FREE AND INDEPENDENT STATES; that they are absolved from all allegiance to the British crown, and that all political connection between them and the state of Great Britain is, and ought to be, totally dissolved; and that, as free and independent states, they have full power to levy war, conclude peace, contract alliances, establish commerce, and do all other acts and things which independent states may of right do. And for the support of this declaration, with a firm reliance on the protection of Divine Providence, we mutually pledge to each other our lives, our fortunes, and our sacred honor.

JOHN HANCOCK

BUTTON GWENNETT	THS. NELSON, JR.	RICHD. STOCKTON
LYMAN HALL	FRANCIS LIGHTFOOT LEE	JNO. WITHERSPOON
GEO. WALTON	CARTER BRAXTON	FRAS. HOPKINSON
WM. HOOPER	ROBT. MORRIS	JOHN HART
JOSEPH HEWES	BENJAMIN RUSH	ABRA. CLARK
JOHN PENN	BENJA. FRANKLIN	JOSIAH BARTLETT
EDWARD RUTLEDGE	JOHN MORTON	WM. WHIPPLE
THOS. HEYWARD, JUNR.	GEO. CLYMER	SAML. ADAMS
THOMAS LYNCH, JUNR.	JAS. SMITH	JOHN ADAMS
ARTHUR MIDDLETON	GEO. TAYLOR	ROBT. TREAT PAINE
SAMUEL CHASE	JAMES WILSON	ELBRIDGE GERRY
WM. PACA	GEO. ROSS	STEP. HOPKINS
THOS. STONE	CAESAR RODNEY	WILLIAM ELLERY
CHARLES CARROLL OF CARROLLTON	GEO. READ	ROGER SHERMAN
GEORGE WYTHE	THO. M'KEAN	SAM'EL. HUNTINGTON
RICHARD HENRY LEE	WM. FLOYD	WM. WILLIAMS
TH. JEFFERSON	PHIL. LIVINGSTON	OLIVER WOLCOTT
BENJA. HARRISON	FRANS. LEWIS	MATTHEW THORNTON
	LEWIS MORRIS	

The Constitution of the United States of America

PREAMBLE

We the People of the United States, in Order to form a more perfect Union, establish Justice, insure domestic Tranquility, provide for the common defence, promote the general Welfare, and secure the Blessings of Liberty to ourselves and our Posterity, do ordain and establish this Constitution for the United States of America.

ARTICLE I.

Section 1   All legislative Powers herein granted shall be vested in a Congress of the United States, which shall consist of a Senate and House of Representatives.

Section 2   The House of Representatives shall be composed of Members chosen every second Year by the People of the several States, and the Electors in each State shall have the Qualifications requisite for Electors of the most numerous Branch of the State Legislature.

No Person shall be a Representative who shall not have attained to the Age of twenty five Years, and been seven Years a Citizen of the United States, and who shall not, when elected, be an inhabitant of that State in which he shall be chosen.

Representatives and direct Taxes shall be apportioned among the several States which may be included within this Union, according to their respective Numbers, *which shall be determined by adding to the whole Number of free Persons, including those bound to Service for a Term of Years, and excluding Indians not taxed, three fifths of all other Persons.*[*] The actual Enumeration shall be made within three Years after the first Meeting of the Congress of the United States, and within every subsequent Term of ten Years, in such Manner as they shall by Law direct. The Number of Representatives shall not exceed one for every thirty Thousand, but each State shall have at Least one Representative; *and until such enumeration shall be made, the State of New Hampshire shall be entitled to chuse three, Massachusetts eight, Rhode-Island and Providence Plantations one, Connecticut five, New York six, New Jersey four, Pennsylvania eight, Delaware one, Maryland six, Virginia ten, North Carolina five, South Carolina five, and Georgia three.*

When vacancies happen in the Representation from any State, the Executive Authority thereof shall issue Writs of Election to fill such Vacancies.

[*]*Passages no longer in effect are printed in italic type.*

The House of Representatives shall choose their Speaker and other Officers; and shall have the sole Power of Impeachment.

Section 3   The Senate of the United States shall be composed of two Senators from each State, *chosen by the Legislature thereof,* for six Years; and each Senator shall have one Vote.

Immediately after they shall be assembled in Consequence of the first Election, they shall be divided as equally as may be into three Classes. The Seats of the Senators of the first Class shall be vacated at the Expiration of the second Year, of the second Class at the Expiration of the fourth Year, and of the third Class at the Expiration of the sixth Year so that one third may be chosen every second Year; *and if Vacancies happen by Resignation, or otherwise, during the Recess of the Legislature of any state, the Executive thereof may make temporary Appointments until the next Meeting of the Legislature, which shall then fill such Vacancies.*

No Person shall be a Senator who shall not have attained to the Age of thirty Years, and been nine Years a Citizen of the United States, and who shall not, when elected, be an Inhabitant of that State for which he shall be chosen.

The Vice President of the United States shall be President of the Senate, but shall have no Vote, unless they be equally divided.

The Senate shall choose their other Officers, and also a President *pro tempore,* in the Absence of the Vice President, or when he shall exercise the Office of President of the United States.

The Senate shall have the sole Power to try all Impeachments. When sitting for that Purpose, they shall be on Oath or Affirmation. When the President of the United States is tried the Chief Justice shall preside: And no Person shall be convicted without the Concurrence of two thirds of the Members present.

Judgment in Cases of Impeachment shall not extend further than to removal from Office, and disqualification to hold and enjoy any Office of honor, Trust or Profit under the United States: but the Party convicted shall nevertheless be liable and subject to Indictment, Trial, Judgment and Punishment, according to Law.

Section 4   The Times, Places and Manner of holding Elections for Senators and Representatives, shall be prescribed in each State by the Legislature thereof; but the Congress may at any time by Law make or alter such Regulations, except as to the Places of choosing Senators.

The Congress shall assemble at least once in every Year, and such Meeting shall be on the first Monday in December, unless they shall by Law appoint a different Day.

Section 5   Each House shall be the Judge of the Elections, Returns and Qualifications of its own Members, and a Majority of each shall constitute a Quorum to do Business; but a smaller Number may adjourn from day to day, and may be authorized to compel the Attendance of absent Members, in such Manner, and under such Penalties as each House may provide.

Each House may determine the Rules of its Proceedings, punish its Members for disorderly Behaviour, and, with the Concurrence of two thirds, expel a Member.

Each House shall keep a Journal of its Proceedings, and from time to time publish the same, excepting such Parts as may in their Judgment require Secrecy; and the Yeas and Nays of the Members of either House on any question shall, at the Desire of one fifth of those Present, be entered on the Journal.

Neither House, during the Session of Congress, shall, without the Consent of the other, adjourn for more than three days, nor to any other Place than that in which the two Houses shall be sitting.

Section 6   The Senators and Representatives shall receive a Compensation for their Services, to be ascertained by Law, and paid out of the Treasury of the United States. They shall in all Cases, except Treason, Felony and Breach of the Peace, be privileged from Arrest during their Attendance at the Session of their respective Houses, and in going to and returning from the same; and for any Speech or Debate in either House, they shall not be questioned in any other Place.

No Senator or Representative shall, during the Time for which he was elected, be appointed to any civil Office under the Authority of the United States, which shall have been created, or the Emoluments whereof shall have been encreased during such time, and no Person holding any Office under the United States, shall be a Member of either House during his Continuance in Office.

Section 7   All Bills for raising Revenue shall originate in the House of Representatives; but the Senate may propose or concur with Amendments as on other Bills.

Every Bill which shall have passed the House of Representatives and the Senate, shall, before it become a Law, be presented to the President of the United States; If he approve he shall sign it, but if not he shall return it, with his Objections to the House in which it shall have originated, who shall enter the Objections at large on their Journal, and proceed to reconsider it. If after such Reconsideration two thirds of that House shall agree to pass the Bill, it shall be sent, together with the Objections, to the other House, by which it shall likewise be reconsidered, and if approved by two thirds of that House, it shall become a Law. But in all such Cases the Votes of both Houses shall be determined by Yeas and Nays, and the Names of the Persons voting for and against the Bill shall be entered on the Journal of each House respectively. If any Bill shall not be returned by the President within ten Days (Sundays excepted) after it shall have been presented to him, the Same shall be a Law, in like Manner as if he had signed it, unless the Congress by their Adjournment prevent its Return, in which Case it shall not be a Law.

Every Order, Resolution, or Vote to which the Concurrence of the Senate and House of Representatives may be necessary (except on a question of Adjournment) shall be presented to the President of the United States; and before the Same shall take Effect, shall be approved by him, or being disapproved by him, shall be repassed by two thirds of the Senate and House of Representatives, according to the Rules and Limitations prescribed in the Case of a Bill.

Section 8   The Congress shall have Power To lay and collect Taxes, Duties, Imposts and Excises, to pay the Debts and provide for the common Defence and general Welfare of the United States; but all Duties, Imposts and Excises shall be uniform throughout the United States;

To borrow Money on the credit of the United States;

To regulate Commerce with foreign Nations, and among the several States, and with the Indian Tribes;

To establish an uniform Rule of Naturalization, and uniform Laws on the subject of Bankruptcies throughout the United States;

To coin Money, regulate the Value thereof, and of foreign Coin, and fix the Standard of Weights and Measures;

To provide for the Punishment of counterfeiting the Securities and current Coin of the United States;

To establish Post Offices and post Roads;

To promote the Progress of Science and useful Arts, by securing for limited Times to Authors and Inventors the exclusive Right to their respective Writings and Discoveries;

To constitute Tribunals inferior to the supreme Court;

To define and punish Piracies and Felonies committed on the high Seas, and Offences against the Law of Nations;

To declare War, grant Letters of Marque and Reprisal, and make Rules concerning Captures on Land and Water;

To raise and support Armies, but no Appropriation of Money to that Use shall be for a longer Term than two Years;

To provide and maintain a Navy;

To make Rules for the Government and Regulation of the land and naval Forces;

To provide for calling forth the Militia to execute the Laws of the Union, suppress Insurrections and repel Invasions;

To provide for organizing, arming, and disciplining the Militia, and for governing such Part of them as may be employed in the Service of the United States, reserving to the States respectively, the Appointment of the Officers, and the Authority of training the Militia according to the discipline prescribed by Congress;

To exercise exclusive Legislation in all Cases whatsoever, over such District (not exceeding ten Miles square) as may, by Cession of particular States, and the Acceptance of Congress, become the Seat of the Government of the United States, and to exercise like Authority over all Places purchased by the Consent of the Legislature of the State in which the Same shall be, for the Erection of Forts,

Magazines, Arsenals, dock-Yards, and other needful Buildings;—And

To make all Laws which shall be necessary and proper for carrying into Execution the foregoing Powers, and all other Powers vested by this Constitution in the Government of the United States, or in any Department of Officer thereof.

Section 9 The Migration or Importation of such Persons as any of the States now existing shall think proper to admit, shall not be prohibited by the Congress prior to the Year one thousand eight hundred and eight, but a Tax or duty may be imposed on such Importation, not exceeding ten dollars for each Person.

The Privilege of the Writ of Habeas Corpus shall not be suspended, unless when in Cases of Rebellion or Invasion the public Safety may require it.

No Bill of Attainder or ex post facto Law shall be passed.

No Capitation, or other direct, Tax shall be laid, unless in Proportion to the Census or Enumeration herein before directed to be taken.

No Tax or Duty shall be laid on Articles exported from any State.

No Preference shall be given by any Regulation of Commerce or Revenue to the Ports of one State over those of another: nor shall Vessels bound to, or from, one State, be obliged to enter, clear, or pay Duties in another.

No Money shall be drawn from the Treasury, but in Consequence of Appropriations made by Law; and a regular Statement and Account of the Receipts and Expenditures of all public Money shall be published from time to time.

No Title of Nobility shall be granted by the United States: And no Person holding any Office of Profit or Trust under them, shall, without the Consent of the Congress, accept of any present, Emolument, Office, or Title, of any kind whatever, from any King, Prince, or foreign State.

Section 10 No State shall enter into any Treaty, Alliance, or Confederation; grant Letters of Marque and Reprisal; coin Money; emit Bills of Credit; make any Thing but gold and silver Coin a Tender in Payment of Debts; pass any Bill of Attainder, ex post facto Law, or Law impairing the obligation of Contracts, or grant any Title of Nobility.

No State shall, without the Consent of the Congress, lay any Imposts or Duties on Imports or Exports, except what may be absolutely necessary for executing its inspection Laws: and the net Produce of all Duties and Imposts, laid by any State on Imports or Exports, shall be for the Use of the Treasury of the United States; and all such Laws shall be subject to the Revision and Control of the Congress.

No State shall, without the Consent of Congress, lay any Duty of Tonnage, keep Troops, or Ships of War in time of Peace, enter into any Agreement or Compact with another State, or with a foreign Power, or engage in War, unless actually invaded, or in such imminent Danger as will not admit of delay.

Article II.

Section 1 The executive Power shall be vested in a President of the United States of America. He shall hold his Office during the Term of four Years, and, together with the Vice President, chosen for the same Term, be elected, as follows:

Each State shall appoint, in such Manner as the Legislature thereof may direct, a Number of Electors, equal to the whole Number of Senators and Representatives to which the State may be entitled in the Congress: but no Senator or Representative, or Person holding an Office of Trust or Profit under the United States, shall be appointed an Elector.

The Electors shall meet in their respective States, and vote by Ballot for two Persons, of whom one at least shall not be an Inhabitant of the same State with themselves. And they shall make a List of all the Persons voted for, and of the Number of Votes for each; which List they shall sign and certify, and transmit sealed to the Seat of the Government of the United States, directed to the President of the Senate. The President of the Senate shall, in the Presence of the Senate and House of Representatives, open all the Certificates, and the Votes shall then be counted. The Person having the greatest Number of Votes shall be the President, if such Number be a Majority of the whole number of Electors appointed; and if there be more than one who have such Majority, and have an equal Number of Votes, then the House of Representative shall immediately choose by Ballot one of them for President; and if no Person have a Majority, then from the five highest on the List the said House shall in like Manner choose the President. But in choosing the President, the Votes shall be taken by States, the Representation from each State having one Vote; A quorum for this Purpose shall consist of a Member or Members from two thirds of the States, and a Majority of all the States shall be necessary to a Choice. In every Case, after the Choice of the President, the Person having the greatest Number of Votes of the Electors shall be the Vice President. But if there should remain two or more who have equal Votes, the Senate shall choose from them by Ballot the Vice President.

The Congress may determine the time of choosing the Electors, and the Day on which they shall give their Votes; which Day shall be the same throughout the United States.

No person except a natural born Citizen, *or a Citizen of the United States, at the time of the Adoption of this Constitution,* shall be eligible to the Office of President; neither shall any Person be eligible to that Office who shall not have attained to the Age of thirty five Years, and been fourteen Years a Resident within the United States.

In Case of the Removal of the President from Office, or of his Death, Resignation, or Inability to discharge the Powers and Duties of the said Office, the Same shall devolve on the Vice President, and the Congress may by Law provide for the Case of Removal, Death, Resignation or Inability, both of the President and Vice President, declaring what Officer shall then act as President, and such Officer shall act accordingly, until the Disability be removed, or a President shall be elected.

The President shall, at stated Times, receive for his Services, a Compensation, which shall neither be increased nor diminished during the Period for which he shall have been elected, and he shall not receive within that period any other Emolument from the United States, or any of them.

Before he enter on the Execution of his Office, he shall take the following Oath or Affirmation:—"I do solemnly swear (or affirm) that I will faithfully execute the Office of President of the United States, and will to the best of my Ability, preserve, protect and defend the Constitution of the United States."

Section 2 The President shall be Commander in Chief of the Army and Navy of the United States, and of the Militia of the several States, when called into the actual Service of the United States; he may require the Opinion, in writing, of the principal Officer in each of the executive Departments, upon any Subject relating to the Duties of their respective Offices, and he shall have Power to grant Reprieves and Pardons for Offences against the United States, except in Cases of Impeachment.

He shall have Power, by and with the Advice and Consent of the Senate, to make Treaties, provided two thirds of the Senators present concur; and he shall nominate, and by and with the Advice and Consent of the Senate, shall appoint Ambassadors, other public Ministers and Consuls, Judges of the supreme Court, and all other Officers of the United States, whose Appointments are not herein otherwise provided for, and which shall be established by Law: but the Congress may by Law vest the Appointment of such inferior Officers, as they think proper in the President alone, in the Courts of Law, or in the Heads of Departments.

The President shall have Power to fill up all Vacancies that may happen during the Recess of the Senate, by granting Commissions which shall expire at the End of their next Session.

Section 3 He shall from time to time give to the Congress Information of the State of the Union, and recommend to their Consideration such Measures as he shall judge necessary and expedient; he may, on extraordinary Occasions, convene both Houses, or either of them, and in Case of disagreement between them, with Respect to the Time of Adjournment, he may adjourn them to such Time as he shall think proper; he shall receive Ambassadors and other public Ministers; he shall take Care that the Laws be faithfully executed, and shall Commission all the officers of the United States.

Section 4 The President, Vice President and all civil Officers of the United States, shall be removed from Office on Impeachment for, and Conviction of, Treason, Bribery or other high Crimes and Misdemeanors.

ARTICLE III.

Section 1 The judicial Power of the United States, shall be vested in one supreme Court, and in such inferior Courts as the Congress may from time to time ordain and establish. The Judges, both of the supreme and inferior Courts, shall hold their offices during good Behaviour, and shall, at stated Times, receive for their Services, a Compensation, which shall not be diminished during their Continuance in Office.

Section 2 The judicial Power shall extend to all Cases, in Law and Equity, arising under this Constitution, the Laws of the United States, and Treaties made, or which shall be made, under their Authority;—to all Cases affecting Ambassadors, other public Ministers and Consuls;—to all Cases of admiralty and maritime Jurisdiction;—to Controversies to which the United States shall be a Party;—to Controversies between two or more States;—between a State and Citizens of another State;—between Citizens of different States,—between Citizens of the same State claiming Lands under Grants of different States, and between a State, or the Citizens thereof, and foreign States, Citizens or Subjects.

In all Cases affecting Ambassadors, other public Ministers and Consuls, and those in which a State shall be Party, the supreme Court shall have original Jurisdiction. In all the other Cases before mentioned, the supreme Court shall have appellate Jurisdiction, both as to Law and Fact, with such Exceptions, and under such Regulations as the Congress shall make.

The Trial of all Crimes, except in Cases of Impeachment, shall be by Jury; and such Trial shall be held in the State where the said Crimes shall have been committed, but when not committed within any State, the Trial shall be at such Place or Places as the Congress may by Law have directed.

Section 3 Treason against the United States, shall consist only in levying War against them, or in adhering to their Enemies, giving them Aid and Comfort. No person shall be convicted of Treason unless on the Testimony of two Witnesses to the same overt Act, or on Confession in open Court.

The Congress shall have Power to declare the Punishment of Treason, but no Attainder of Treason shall work Corruption of Blood, or Forfeiture except during the Life of the Person attainted.

ARTICLE IV.

Section 1 Full Faith and Credit shall be given in each State to the public Acts, Records, and judicial Proceedings of every other State. And the Congress may be general Laws prescribe the Manner in which such Acts, Records and Proceedings shall be proved, and the Effect thereof.

Section 2 The Citizens of each State shall be entitled to all Privileges and Immunities of Citizens in the several States.

A Person charged in any State with Treason, Felony, or other Crime, who shall flee from Justice, and be found in another State, shall on Demand of the executive Authority of the State from which he fled, be delivered up, to be removed to the State having Jurisdiction of the Crime.

No Person held to Service or Labour in one State, under the Laws thereof, escaping into another, shall, in Consequence of any Law or Regulation therein, be discharged from such Service or Labour, but shall be delivered up on Claim of the Party to whom such Service or Labour may be due.

Section 3 New States may be admitted by the Congress into this Union; but no new State shall be formed or erected within the Jurisdiction of any other State; nor any

State be formed by the Junction of two or more States, or Parts of States, without the Consent of the Legislatures of the States concerned as well as of the Congress.

The Congress shall have Power to dispose of and make all needful Rules and Regulations respecting the Territory or other Property belonging to the United States; and nothing in this Constitution shall be so construed as to Prejudice any Claims of the United States, or of any particular States.

Section 4 The United States shall guarantee to every State in this Union a Republican Form of Government, and shall protect each of them against Invasion; and on Application of the Legislature, or of the Executive (when the Legislature cannot be convened) against domestic violence.

ARTICLE V.

The Congress, whenever two thirds of both Houses shall deem it necessary, shall propose Amendments to this Constitution, or, on the Application of the Legislatures of two thirds of the several States, shall call a Convention for proposing Amendments, which, in either Case, shall be valid to all Intents and Purposes, as Part of this Constitution, when ratified by the Legislatures of three fourths of the several States, or by Conventions in three fourths thereof, as the one or the other Mode of Ratification may be proposed by the Congress; Provided *that no Amendment which may be made prior to the Year One thousand eight hundred and eight shall in any Manner affect the first and fourth Clauses in the Ninth Section of the first Article;* and that no State without its Consent, shall be deprived of its equal Suffrage in the Senate.

ARTICLE VI.

All Debts contracted and Engagements entered into, before the Adoption of this Constitution, shall be as valid against the United States under this Constitution, as under the Confederation.

This Constitution, and Laws of the United States which shall be made in Pursuance thereof; and all Treaties made, or which shall be made, under the Authority of the United States, shall be the supreme Law of the Land; and the Judges in every State shall be bound thereby, any Thing in the Constitution or Laws of any State to the Contrary notwithstanding.

The Senators and Representatives before mentioned, and the Members of the several State Legislatures, and all executive and Judicial Officers, both of the United States and of the several States, shall be bound by Oath or Affirmation, to support this Constitution; but no religious Test shall ever be required as a Qualification to any Office of public Trust under the United States.

ARTICLE VII.

The Ratification of the Conventions of nine States, shall be sufficient for the Establishment of this Constitution—between the States so ratifying the Same.

Done in Convention by the Unanimous Consent of the States present the Seventeenth Day of September in the Year of our Lord one thousand seven hundred and Eighty seven and of the Independence of the United States of America the Twelfth IN WITNESS whereof We have hereunto subscribed our Names,

GEORGE WASHINGTON,
President and Deputy from Virginia

New Hampshire
JOHN LANGDON
NICHOLAS GILMAN

Massachusetts
NATHANIEL GORHAM
RUFUS KING

Connecticut
WILLIAM S. JOHNSON
ROGER SHERMAN

New York
ALEXANDER HAMILTON

New Jersey
WILLIAM LIVINGSTON
DAVID BREARLEY
WILLIAM PATERSON
JONATHAN DAYTON

Pennsylvania
BENJAMIN FRANKLIN
THOMAS MIFFLIN
ROBERT MORRIS
GEORGE CLYMER
THOMAS FITZSIMONS
JARED INGERSOLL
JAMES WILSON
GOUVERNEUR MORRIS

Delaware
GEORGE READ
GUNNING BEDFORD, JR.
JOHN DICKINSON
RICHARD BASSETT
JACOB BROOM

Maryland
JAMES MCHENRY
DANIEL OF ST. THOMAS JENIFER
DANIEL CARROLL

Virginia
JOHN BLAIR
JAMES MADISON, JR.

North Carolina
WILLIAM BLOUNT
RICHARD DOBBS SPRAIGHT
HU WILLIAMSON

South Carolina
J. RUTLEDGE
CHARLES C. PINCKNEY
PIERCE BUTLER

Georgia
WILLIAM FEW
ABRAHAM BALDWIN

Amendments to the Constitution

The first ten amendments (the Bill of Rights) were adopted in 1791.

AMENDMENT I

Congress shall make no law respecting an establishment of religion, or prohibiting the free exercise thereof; or abridging the freedom of speech, or of the press; or the right of the people peaceably to assemble, and to petition the Government for a redress of grievances.

AMENDMENT II

A well regulated Militia being necessary to the security of a free State, the right of the people to keep and bear Arms, shall not be infringed.

AMENDMENT III

No Soldier shall, in time of peace be quartered in any house, without the consent of the Owner, nor in time of war, but in a manner to be prescribed by law.

AMENDMENT IV

The right of the people to be secure in their persons, houses, papers, and effects, against unreasonable searches and seizures, shall not be violated, and no Warrants shall issue, but upon probable cause, supported by Oath or affirmation, and particularly describing the place to be searched, and the persons or things to be seized.

AMENDMENT V

No person shall be held to answer for a capital, or otherwise infamous crime, unless on a presentment or indictment of a Grand Jury, except in cases arising in the land or naval forces, or in the Militia, when in actual service in time of War or public danger; nor shall any person be subject for the same offense to be twice put in jeopardy of life or limb; nor shall be compelled in any criminal case to be a witness against himself, nor be deprived of life, liberty, or property, without due process of law; nor shall private property be taken for public use, without just compensation.

AMENDMENT VI

In all criminal prosecutions, the accused shall enjoy the right to a speedy and public trial, by an impartial jury of the State and district wherein the crime shall have been committed, which district shall have been previously ascertained by law, and to be informed of the nature and cause of the accusation; to be confronted with the witnesses against him; to have compulsory process for obtaining witnesses in his favor, and to have the Assistance of Counsel for his defence.

AMENDMENT VII

In Suits at common law, where the value in controversy shall exceed twenty dollars, the right of trial by jury shall be preserved, and no fact trial by a jury, shall be otherwise re-examined in any Court of the United States, than according to the rules of the common law.

AMENDMENT VIII

Excessive bail shall not be required, nor excessive fines imposed, nor cruel and unusual punishments inflicted.

AMENDMENT IX

The enumeration in the Constitution, of certain rights, shall not be construed to deny or disparage others retained by the people.

AMENDMENT X

The powers not delegated to the United States by the Constitution, nor prohibited by it to the States, are reserved to the States respectively, or to the people.

AMENDMENT XI

[Adopted 1798]

The Judicial power of the United States shall not be construed to extend to any suit in law or equity, commenced or prosecuted against one of the United States by Citizens of another State, or by Citizens or Subjects of any Foreign State.

AMENDMENT XII

[Adopted 1804]

The Electors shall meet in their respective states, and vote by ballot for President and Vice-President, one of whom, at least, shall not be an inhabitant of the same state with themselves; they shall name in their ballots the person voted for as President, and in distinct ballots the person voted for as Vice-President, and they shall make distinct lists of all persons voted for as President, and of all persons voted for as Vice-President, and of the number of votes for each, which lists they shall sign and certify, and transmit sealed to the seat of the government of the United States, directed to the President of the Senate;—The President of the Senate shall, in the presence of the Senate and House of Representatives, open all the certificates and the votes shall then be counted;—The person having the greatest number of votes for President, shall be the President, if such number be a majority of the whole number of Electors appointed; and if no person have such majority, then from the persons having the highest numbers not exceeding three on the list of those voted for as President, the House of Representatives shall choose immediately, by ballot, the President. But in choosing the President, the votes shall be taken by states, the representation from each state having one vote; a quorum for this purpose shall consist of a member or members from two-thirds of the states, and a majority of all the states shall be necessary to a choice. And if the House of Representatives shall not choose a President whenever the right of choice shall devolve upon them, before *the fourth day of March* next following, then the Vice-President shall act as President, as in the case of the death or other constitutional disability of the President.—The person having the greatest number of votes as Vice-President, shall be the Vice-President, if such number be a majority of the whole number of Electors appointed, and if no person have a majority, then from the two highest numbers on the list, the Senate shall choose the Vice-President; a quorum for the purpose shall consist of two-thirds of the whole number of Senators, and a majority of the whole number shall be necessary to a choice. But no person constitutionally ineligible to the office of President shall be eligible to that of Vice President of the United States.

AMENDMENT XIII

[Adopted 1865]

Section 1 Neither slavery nor involuntary servitude, except as a punishment for crime whereof the party shall have been duly convicted, shall exist within the United States, or any place subject to their jurisdiction.

Section 2 Congress shall have power to enforce this article by appropriate legislation.

AMENDMENT XIV

[Adopted 1868]

Section 1 All persons born or naturalized in the United States, and subject to the jurisdiction thereof, are citizens of the United States and of the State wherein they reside. No State shall make or enforce any law which shall abridge the privileges or immunities of citizens of the United States; nor shall any State deprive any person of life, liberty, or property, without due process of law; nor deny to any person within its jurisdiction the equal protection of the laws.

Section 2 Representatives shall be apportioned among the several States according to their respective numbers, counting the whole number of persons in each State, excluding Indians not taxed. But when the right to vote at any election for the choice of electors for President and Vice-President of the United States, Representatives in Congress, the Executive and Judicial officers of a State, or the members of the Legislature thereof, is denied to any of the male inhabitants of such State, being twenty-one years of age, and citizens of the United States, or in any way abridged, except for participation in rebellion, or other crime, the basis of representation therein shall be reduced in the proportion which the number of such male citizens shall bear to the whole number of male citizens twenty-one years of age in such State.

Section 3 No person shall be a Senator or Representative in Congress, or elector of President and Vice-President, or hold any office, civil or military, under the United States, or under any State, who, having previously taken an oath, as a member of Congress, or as an officer of the United States, or as a member of any State legislature, or as an executive or judicial officer of any State, to support the Constitution of the United States, shall have engaged in insurrection or rebellion against the same, or given aid or comfort to the enemies thereof. But Congress may by a vote of two-thirds of each House, remove such disability.

Section 4 The validity of the public debt of the United States, authorized by law, including debts incurred for payment of pensions and bounties for services in suppressing insurrection or rebellion, shall not be questioned. But neither the United States nor any State shall assume or pay any debt or obligation incurred in aid of insurrection or rebellion against the United States, or any claim for the loss or emancipation of any slave; but all such debts, obligations and claims shall be held illegal and void.

Section 5 The Congress shall have power to enforce, by appropriate legislation, the provisions of this article.

AMENDMENT XV

[Adopted 1870]

Section 1 The right of citizens of the United States to vote shall not be denied or abridged by the United States or by any State on account of race, color, or previous condition of servitude.

Section 2 The Congress shall have power to enforce this article by appropriate legislation.

AMENDMENT XVI

[Adopted 1913]

The Congress shall have power to lay and collect taxes on incomes, from whatever source derived, without apportionment among the several States, and without regard to any census or enumeration.

AMENDMENT XVII

[Adopted 1913]

The Senate of the United States shall be composed of two Senators from each State, elected by the people thereof, for six years; and each Senator shall have one vote. The electors in each State shall have the qualifications requisite for electors of the most numerous branch of the State legislatures.

When vacancies happen in the representation of any State in the Senate, the executive authority of such State shall issue writs of election to fill such vacancies: *Provided*, That the legislature of any State may empower the executive thereof to make temporary appointments until the people fill the vacancies by election as the legislature may direct.

This amendment shall not be so construed as to affect the election or term of any Senator chosen before it becomes valid as part of the Constitution.

AMENDMENT XVIII

[Adopted 1919, Repealed 1933]

Section 1 After one year from the ratification of this article the manufacture, sale, or transportation of intoxicating liquors within, the importation thereof into, or the exportation thereof from the United States and all territory subject to the jurisdiction thereof for beverage purposes is hereby prohibited.

Section 2 The Congress and the several States shall have concurrent power to enforce this article by appropriate legislation.

Section 3 This article shall be inoperative unless it shall have been ratified as an amendment to the Constitution by the legislatures of the several States, as provided in the Constitution, within seven years from the date of the submission hereof to the States by the Congress.

AMENDMENT XIX

[Adopted 1920]

Section 1 The right of citizens of the United States to vote shall not be denied or abridged by the United States or by any State on account of sex.

Section 2 Congress shall have power to enforce this article by appropriate legislation.

AMENDMENT XX

[Adopted 1933]

Section 1 The terms of the President and Vice-President shall end at noon on the 20th day of January, and the terms of Senators and Representatives at noon on the 3d day of January, of the years in which such terms would have ended if this article had not been ratified and the terms of their successors shall then begin.

Section 2 The Congress shall assemble at least once in every year, and such meeting shall begin at noon on the 3d day of January, unless they shall by law appoint a different day.

Section 3 If, at the time fixed for the beginning of the term of the President, the President elect shall have died, the Vice-President elect shall become President. If a President shall not have been chosen before the time fixed for the beginning of his term, or if the President elect shall have failed to qualify, then the Vice-President elect shall act as President until a President shall have qualified; and the Congress may by law provide for the case wherein neither a President elect nor a Vice-President elect shall have qualified, declaring who shall then act as President, or the manner in which one who is to act shall be selected, and such person shall act accordingly until a President or Vice-President shall have qualified.

Section 4 The Congress may by law provide for the case of the death of any of the persons from whom the House of Representatives may choose a President whenever the right of choice shall have devolved upon them, and for the case of the death of any of the persons from whom the Senate may choose a Vice-President whenever the right of choice shall have devolved upon them.

Section 5 Sections 1 and 2 shall take effect on the 15th day of October following the ratification of this article.

Section 6 This article shall be inoperative unless it shall have been ratified as an amendment to the Constitution by the legislatures of three fourths of the several States within seven years from the date of its submission.

AMENDMENT XXI

[Adopted 1933]

Section 1 The eighteenth article of amendment to the Constitution of the United States is hereby repealed.

Section 2 The transportation or importation into any State, Territory, or possession of the United States for delivery or use therein of intoxicating liquors in violation of the laws thereof, is hereby prohibited.

Section 3   This article shall be inoperative unless it shall have been ratified as an amendment to the Constitution by conventions in the several States, as provided in the Constitution, within seven years from the date of the submission hereof to the States by the Congress.

AMENDMENT XXII

[Adopted 1951]

Section 1   No person shall be elected to the office of the President more than twice, and no person who has held the office of President, or acted as President, for more than two years of a term to which some other person was elected President shall be elected to the office of the President more than once. But this Article shall not apply to any person holding the office of President when this Article was proposed by the Congress, and shall not prevent any person who may be holding the office of President, or acting as President, during the term within which this Article becomes operative from holding the office of President or acting as President during the remainder of such term.

Section 2   This article shall be inoperative unless it shall have been ratified as an amendment to the Constitution by the legislatures of three-fourths of the several States within several years from the date of its submission to the States within seven years from the date of its submission to the States by the Congress.

AMENDMENT XXIII

[Adopted 1961]

Section 1   The District constituting the seat of Government of the United States shall appoint in such manner as the Congress shall direct:

A number of electors of President and Vice-President equal to the whole number of Senators and Representatives in Congress to which the District would be entitled if it were a State, but in no event more than the least populous State; they shall be in addition to those appointed by the States, but they shall be considered, for the purposes of the election of President and Vice-President, to be electors appointed by a State; and they shall meet in the District and perform such duties as provided by the twelfth article of amendment.

Section 2   The Congress shall have power to enforce this article by appropriate legislation.

AMENDMENT XXIV

[Adopted 1964]

Section 1   The right of citizens of the United States to vote in any primary or other election for President or Vice-President, for electors for President or Vice-President, or for Senator or Representative in Congress, shall not be denied or abridged by the United States or any state by reason of failure to pay any poll tax or other tax.

Section 2   The Congress shall have the power to enforce this article by appropriate legislation.

AMENDMENT XXV

[Adopted 1967]

Section 1   In case of the removal of the President from office or his death or resignation, the Vice-President shall become President.

Section 2   Whenever there is a vacancy in the office of the Vice-President, the President shall nominate a Vice-President who shall take the office upon confirmation by a majority vote of both houses of Congress.

Section 3   Whenever the President transmits to the President pro tempore of the Senate and the Speaker of the House of Representatives his written declaration that he is unable to discharge the powers and duties of his office, and until he transmits to them a written declaration to the contrary, such powers and duties shall be discharged by the Vice-President as Acting President.

Section 4   Whenever the Vice-President and a majority of either the principal officers of the executive departments or of such other body as Congress may by law provide, transmit to the President pro tempore of the Senate and the Speaker of the House of Representatives their written declaration that the President is unable to discharge the powers and duties of his office, the Vice-President shall immediately assume the powers and duties of the office as Acting President.

Thereafter, when the President transmits to the President pro tempore of the Senate and the Speaker of the House of Representatives his written declaration that no inability exists, he shall resume the powers and duties of his office unless the Vice-President and a majority of either the principal officers of the executive department or of such other body as Congress may by law provide, transmit within four days to the President pro tempore of the Senate and the Speaker of the House of Representatives their written declaration that the President is unable to discharge the powers and duties of his office. Thereupon Congress shall decide the issue, assembling within 48 hours for that purpose if not in session. If the Congress, within 21 days after receipt of the latter written declaration, or, if Congress is not in session, within 21 days after Congress is required to assemble, determines by two-thirds vote of both houses that the President is unable to discharge the powers and duties of his office, the Vice-President shall continue to discharge the same as Acting President; otherwise, the President shall resume the powers and duties of his office.

AMENDMENT XXVI

[Adopted 1971]

Section 1   The right of citizens of the United States, who are 18 years of age or older, to vote shall not be denied or abridged by the United States or any state on account of age.

Section 2   The Congress shall have the power to enforce this article by appropriate legislation.

AMENDMENT XXVII

[Adopted 1992]

No law varying the compensation for the services of the Senators and Representatives shall take effect, until an election of Representatives shall have intervened.

Presidential Elections

Year	Candidates	Parties	Popular Vote	Electoral Vote	Voter Participation
1789	GEORGE WASHINGTON		*	69	
	John Adams			34	
	Others			35	
1792	GEORGE WASHINGTON		*	132	
	John Adams			77	
	George Clinton			50	
	Others			5	
1796	JOHN ADAMS	Federalist	*	71	
	Thomas Jefferson	Democratic-Republican		68	
	Thomas Pinckney	Federalist		59	
	Aaron Burr	Dem.-Rep.		30	
	Others			48	
1800	THOMAS JEFFERSON	Dem.-Rep.	*	73	
	Aaron Burr	Dem.-Rep.		73	
	John Adams	Federalist		65	
	C. C. Pinckney	Federalist		64	
	John Jay	Federalist		1	
1804	THOMAS JEFFERSON	Dem.-Rep.	*	162	
	C. C. Pinckney	Federalist		14	
1808	JAMES MADISON	Dem.-Rep.	*	122	
	C. C. Pinckney	Federalist		47	
	George Clinton	Dem.-Rep.		6	
1812	JAMES MADISON	Dem.-Rep.	*	128	
	De Witt Clinton	Federalist		89	
1816	JAMES MONROE	Dem.-Rep.	*	183	
	Rufus King	Federalist		34	
1820	JAMES MONROE	Dem.-Rep.	*	231	
	John Quincy Adams	Dem.-Rep.		1	
1824	JOHN Q. ADAMS	Dem.-Rep.	108,740 (30.5%)	84	26.9%
	Andrew Jackson	Dem.-Rep.	153,544 (43.1%)	99	
	William H. Crawford	Dem.-Rep.	46,618 (13.1%)	41	
	Henry Clay	Dem.-Rep.	47,136 (13.2%)	37	
1828	ANDREW JACKSON	Democratic	647,286 (56.0%)	178	57.6%
	John Quincy Adams	National Republican	508,064 (44.0%)	83	
1832	ANDREW JACKSON	Democratic	687,502 (55.0%)	219	55.4%
	Henry Clay	National Republican	530,189 (42.4%)	49	
	John Floyd	Independent		11	
	William Wirt	Anti-Mason	33,108 (2.6%)	7	
1836	MARTIN VAN BUREN	Democratic	765,483 (50.9%)	170	57.8%
	W. H. Harrison	Whig		73	
	Hugh L. White	Whig	739,795 (49.1%)	26	
	Daniel Webster	Whig		14	
	W. P. Magnum	Independent		11	
1840	WILLIAM H. HARRISON	Whig	1,274,624 (53.1%)	234	80.2%
	Martin Van Buren	Democratic	1,127,781 (46.9%)	60	
	J. G. Birney	Liberty	7069	—	

*Electors selected by state legislatures

Year	Candidates	Parties	Popular Vote	Electoral Vote	Voter Participation
1844	**JAMES K. POLK**	Democratic	1,338,464 (49.6%)	170	78.9%
	Henry Clay	Whig	1,300,097 (48.1%)	105	
	J. G. Birney	Liberty	62,300 (2.3%)	—	
1848	**ZACHARY TAYLOR**	Whig	1,360,967 (47.4%)	163	72.7%
	Lewis Cass	Democratic	1,222,342 (42.5%)	127	
	Martin Van Buren	Free-Soil	291,263 (10.1%)	—	
1852	**FRANKLIN PIERCE**	Democratic	1,601,117 (50.9%)	254	69.6%
	Winfield Scott	Whig	1,385,453 (44.1%)	42	
	John P. Hale	Free-Soil	155,825 (5.0%)	—	
1856	**JAMES BUCHANAN**	Democratic	1,832,955 (45.3%)	174	78.9%
	John C. Frémont	Republican	1,339,932 (33.1%)	114	
	Millard Fillmore	American	871,731 (21.6%)	8	
1860	**ABRAHAM LINCOLN**	Republican	1,865,593 (39.8%)	180	81.2%
	Stephen A. Douglas	Democratic	1,382,713 (29.5%)	12	
	John C. Breckinridge	Democratic	848,356 (18.1%)	72	
	John Bell	Union	592,906 (12.6%)	39	
1864	**ABRAHAM LINCOLN**	Republican	2,213,655 (55.0%)	212	73.8%
	George B. McClellan	Democratic	1,805,237 (45.0%)	21	
1868	**ULYSSES S. GRANT**	Republican	3,012,833 (52.7%)	214	78.1%
	Horatio Seymour	Democratic	2,703,249 (47.3%)	80	
1872	**ULYSSES S. GRANT**	Republican	3,597,132 (55.6%)	286	71.3%
	Horace Greeley	Democratic	2,834,125 (43.9%)	66	
1876	**RUTHERFORD B. HAYES**	Republican	4,034,311 (48.0%)	185	81.8%
	Samuel J. Tilden	Democratic	4,288,546 (51.0%)	184	
1880	**JAMES A. GARFIELD**	Republican	4,454,416 (48.5%)	214	79.4%
	Winfield S. Hancock	Democratic	4,444,952 (48.1%)	155	
1884	**GROVER CLEVELAND**	Democratic	4,874,986 (48.5%)	219	77.5%
	James G. Blaine	Republican	4,851,981 (48.2%)	182	
1888	**BENJAMIN HARRISON**	Republican	5,439,853 (47.9%)	233	79.3%
	Grover Cleveland	Democratic	5,540,309 (48.6%)	168	
1892	**GROVER CLEVELAND**	Democratic	5,556,918 (46.1%)	277	74.7%
	Benjamin Harrison	Republican	5,176,108 (43.0%)	145	
	James B. Weaver	People's	1,041,028 (8.5%)	22	
1896	**WILLIAM McKINLEY**	Republican	7,104,779 (51.1%)	271	79.3%
	William J. Bryan	Democratic People's	6,502,925 (47.7%)	176	
1900	**WILLIAM McKINLEY**	Republican	7,207,923 (51.7%)	292	73.2%
	William J. Bryan	Dem.-Populist	6,358,133 (45.5%)	155	
1904	**THEODORE ROOSEVELT**	Republican	7,623,486 (57.9%)	336	65.2%
	Alton B. Parker	Democratic	5,077,911 (37.6%)	140	
	Eugene V. Debs	Socialist	402,283 (3.0%)	—	
1908	**WILLIAM H. TAFT**	Republican	7,678,908 (51.6%)	321	65.4%
	William J. Bryan	Democratic	6,409,104 (43.1%)	162	
	Eugene V. Debs	Socialist	420,793 (2.8%)	—	
1912	**WOODROW WILSON**	Democratic	6,293,454 (41.9%)	435	58.8%
	Theodore Roosevelt	Progressive	4,119,538 (27.4%)	88	
	William H. Taft	Republican	3,484,980 (23.2%)	8	
	Eugene V. Debs	Socialist	900,672 (6.0%)	—	
1916	**WOODROW WILSON**	Democratic	9,129,606 (49.4%)	277	61.6%
	Charles E. Hughes	Republican	8,538,221 (46.2%)	254	
	A. L. Benson	Socialist	585,113 (3.2%)	—	
1920	**WARREN G. HARDING**	Republican	16,152,200 (60.4%)	404	49.2%
	James M. Cox	Democratic	9,147,353 (34.2%)	127	
	Eugene V. Debs	Socialist	919,799 (3.4%)	—	
1924	**CALVIN COOLIDGE**	Republican	15,725,016 (54.0%)	382	48.9%
	John W. Davis	Democratic	8,386,503 (28.8%)	136	
	Robert M. La Follette	Progressive	4,822,856 (16.6%)	13	

Year	Candidates	Parties	Popular Vote	Electoral Vote	Voter Participation
1928	**HERBERT HOOVER**	Republican	21,391,381 (58.2%)	444	56.9%
	Alfred E. Smith	Democratic	15,016,443 (40.9%)	87	
	Norman Thomas	Socialist	267,835 (0.7%)	—	
1932	**FRANKLIN D. ROOSEVELT**	Democratic	22,821,857 (57.4%)	472	56.9%
	Herbert Hoover	Republican	15,761,841 (39.7%)	59	
	Norman Thomas	Socialist	881,951 (2.2%)	—	
1936	**FRANKLIN D. ROOSEVELT**	Democratic	27,751,597 (60.8%)	523	61.0%
	Alfred M. Landon	Republican	16,679,583 (36.5%)	8	
	William Lemke	Union	882,479 (1.9%)	—	
1940	**FRANKLIN D. ROOSEVELT**	Democratic	27,244,160 (54.8%)	449	62.5%
	Wendell L. Willkie	Republican	22,305,198 (44.8%)	82	
1944	**FRANKLIN D. ROOSEVELT**	Democratic	25,602,504 (53.5%)	432	55.9%
	Thomas E. Dewey	Republican	22,006,285 (46.0%)	99	
1948	**HARRY S TRUMAN**	Democratic	24,105,695 (49.5%)	304	53.0%
	Thomas E. Dewey	Republican	21,969,170 (45.1%)	189	
	J. Strom Thurmond	State-Rights Democratic	1,169,021 (2.4%)	38	
	Henry A. Wallace	Progressive	1,156,103 (2.4%)	—	
1952	**DWIGHT D. EISENHOWER**	Republican	33,936,252 (55.1%)	442	63.3%
	Adlai E. Stevenson	Democratic	27,314,992 (44.4%)	89	
1956	**DWIGHT D. EISENHOWER**	Republican	35,575,420 (57.6%)	457	60.6%
	Adlai E. Stevenson	Democratic	26,033,066 (42.1%)	73	
	Other	—	—	1	
1960	**JOHN F. KENNEDY**	Democratic	34,227,096 (49.9%)	303	62.8%
	Richard M. Nixon	Republican	34,108,546 (49.6%)	219	
	Other	—	—	15	
1964	**LYNDON B. JOHNSON**	Democratic	43,126,506 (61.1%)	486	61.7%
	Barry M. Goldwater	Republican	27,176,799 (38.5%)	52	
1968	**RICHARD M. NIXON**	Republican	31,770,237 (43.4%)	301	60.6%
	Hubert H. Humphrey	Democratic	31,270,533 (42.7%)	191	
	George Wallace	American Indep.	9,906,141 (13.5%)	46	
1972	**RICHARD M. NIXON**	Republican	47,169,911 (60.7%)	520	55.2%
	George S. McGovern	Democratic	29,170,383 (37.5%)	17	
	Other	—	—	1	
1976	**JIMMY CARTER**	Democratic	40,828,587 (50.0%)	297	53.5%
	Gerald R. Ford	Republican	39,147,613 (47.9%)	241	
	Other	—	1,575,459 (2.1%)	—	
1980	**RONALD REAGAN**	Republican	43,901,812 (50.7%)	489	52.6%
	Jimmy Carter	Democratic	35,483,820 (41.0%)	49	
	John B. Anderson	Independent	5,719,722 (6.6%)	—	
	Ed Clark	Libertarian	921,188 (1.1%)	—	
1984	**RONALD REAGAN**	Republican	54,455,075 (59.0%)	525	53.3%
	Walter Mondale	Democratic	37,577,185 (41.0%)	13	
1988	**GEORGE H. W. BUSH**	Republican	48,886,000 (53.4%)	426	57.4%
	Michael S. Dukakis	Democratic	41,809,000 (45.6%)	111	
1992	**BILL CLINTON**	Democratic	43,728,375 (43%)	370	55.0%
	George H. W. Bush	Republican	38,167,416 (38%)	168	
	H. Ross Perot	Independent	19,237,247 (19%)	—	
1996	**BILL CLINTON**	Democratic	47,402,357 (49%)	379	49.0%
	Robert Dole	Republican	39,198,755 (41%)	159	
	H. Ross Perot	Reform	8,085,402 (8%)	—	
2000	**GEORGE W. BUSH**	Republican	50,456,167 (47.88%)	271	51.2%
	Al Gore	Democratic	50,996,064 (48.39%)	266*	
	Ralph Nader	Green	2,864,810 (2.72%)	—	
	Other	—	834,774 (< 1%)	—	

*One District of Columbia Gore elector abstained.

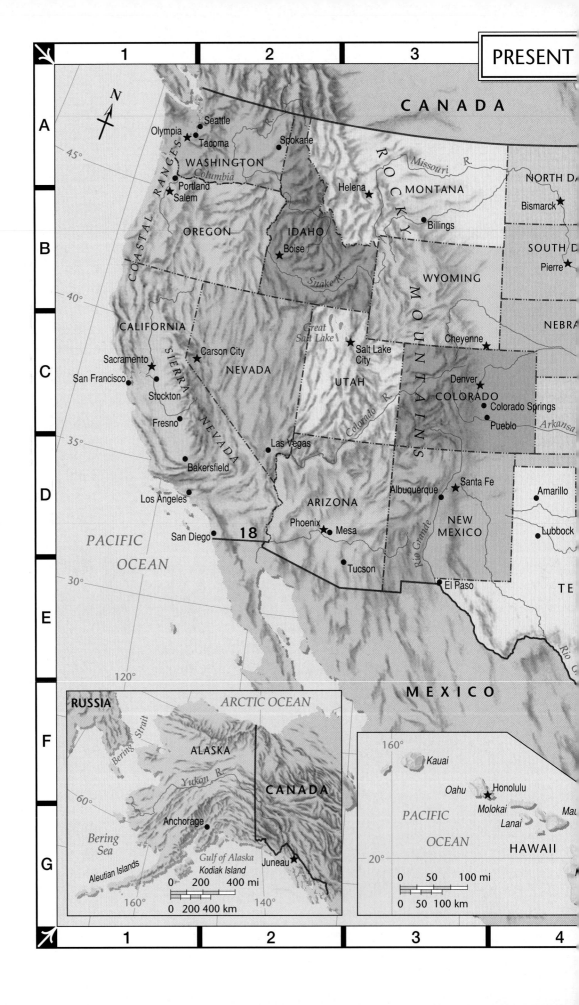

CANADA

A

1   2   3

N

45°

Olympia
Seattle
Tacoma
Spokane

WASHINGTON
Columbia

Portland
Salem

OREGON

Helena
MONTANA

Billings

NORTH D

Bismarck

B

40°

Boise
IDAHO

Snake R.

WYOMING

SOUTH D

Pierre

NEBRA

CALIFORNIA

Great
Salt Lake

Salt Lake
City

Cheyenne

Sacramento
Carson City

San Francisco
NEVADA

Stockton

UTAH

Denver
COLORADO

Colorado Springs

C

Fresno

Colorado R.

Pueblo

Arkansa

35°

Las Vegas

Bakersfield

Los Angeles

ARIZONA

San Diego   18

Phoenix
Mesa

Albuquerque
Santa Fe

NEW
MEXICO

Amarillo

Lubbock

D

30°

Tucson

Rio Grande

El Paso

TE

PACIFIC

OCEAN

120°

MEXICO

E

RUSSIA
ARCTIC OCEAN

160°

Bering Strait

ALASKA

Yukon R.

CANADA

Kauai

Oahu   Honolulu

Molokai
Lanai

Mau

PACIFIC
OCEAN

HAWAII

F

60°

Anchorage

Bering
Sea

Gulf of Alaska
Kodiak Island
Juneau

Aleutian Islands

0   200   400 mi

0   200 400 km

0   50   100 mi

0   50 100 km

20°

G

160°   140°

1   2   3   4

COASTAL RANGES

SIERRA NEVADA

ROCKY MOUNTAINS

Missouri R.

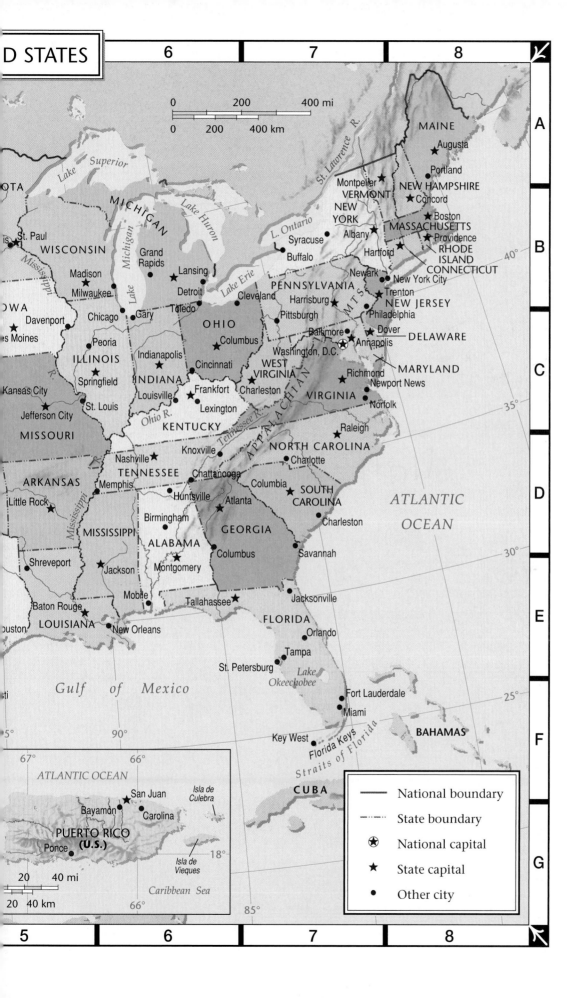

6   7   8

A
B
C
D
E
F
G

0   200   400 mi
0   200   400 km

MAINE
★ Augusta
• Portland
Montpelier ★   NEW HAMPSHIRE
VERMONT   ★ Concord
NEW   ★ Boston
YORK   MASSACHUSETTS
Syracuse •   • Albany   ★ Providence
L. Ontario   Hartford   RHODE
Buffalo •   ISLAND
  CONNECTICUT
St. Lawrence R.

Lake Superior

MICHIGAN

Lake Huron

MINNESOTA
St. Paul •
WISCONSIN
Grand
Rapids •   Lansing ★
Madison ★
Milwaukee •
Lake Michigan
Detroit •
IOWA   Lake Erie
Davenport •   Chicago •   Gary •   Toledo •
Des Moines •   OHIO
Peoria •   Cleveland •
ILLINOIS   Columbus ★
Indianapolis ★   PENNSYLVANIA
Springfield •   INDIANA   Cincinnati •   Pittsburgh •
Kansas City •   Louisville •   Frankfort ★
St. Louis •   Lexington •
Jefferson City ★   Ohio R.   KENTUCKY
MISSOURI

Mississippi R.

Newark •
New York City •
Harrisburg ★   Trenton ★
  NEW JERSEY
Philadelphia •
Baltimore •   Dover •
Washington, D.C. ✪   Annapolis ★   DELAWARE
  MARYLAND
WEST   Richmond ★
VIRGINIA   Newport News •
Charleston ★   VIRGINIA
  Norfolk •

APPALACHIAN MTS.

40°
35°

Raleigh ★
Knoxville •   NORTH CAROLINA
Nashville ★   Charlotte •
TENNESSEE   Chattanooga •
ARKANSAS   Memphis •   Columbia ★   SOUTH
  Huntsville •   CAROLINA
Little Rock ★   Atlanta ★
  Birmingham •   Charleston •
MISSISSIPPI   ALABAMA   GEORGIA
  Jackson ★   Columbus •   Savannah •
Shreveport •   Montgomery ★
  Mobile •   Tallahassee ★

Tennessee R.

ATLANTIC
OCEAN

30°

Baton Rouge ★
LOUISIANA   Jacksonville •
Houston •   New Orleans •
  FLORIDA
  Orlando •
  Tampa •
Gulf of Mexico   St. Petersburg •   Lake
  Okeechobee
  Fort Lauderdale •
  Miami •
  BAHAMAS
Key West •   Florida Keys
  Straits of Florida
  CUBA

85°   90°   25°

Mississippi R.

67°   66°
ATLANTIC OCEAN
Isla de
Culebra
San Juan ★
Bayamón •   • Carolina
PUERTO RICO
(U.S.)
Ponce •
  Isla de
  Vieques
20   40 mi
20   40 km   66°
18°
85°   Caribbean Sea

—— National boundary
–··–··– State boundary
✪ National capital
★ State capital
• Other city

5   6   7   8

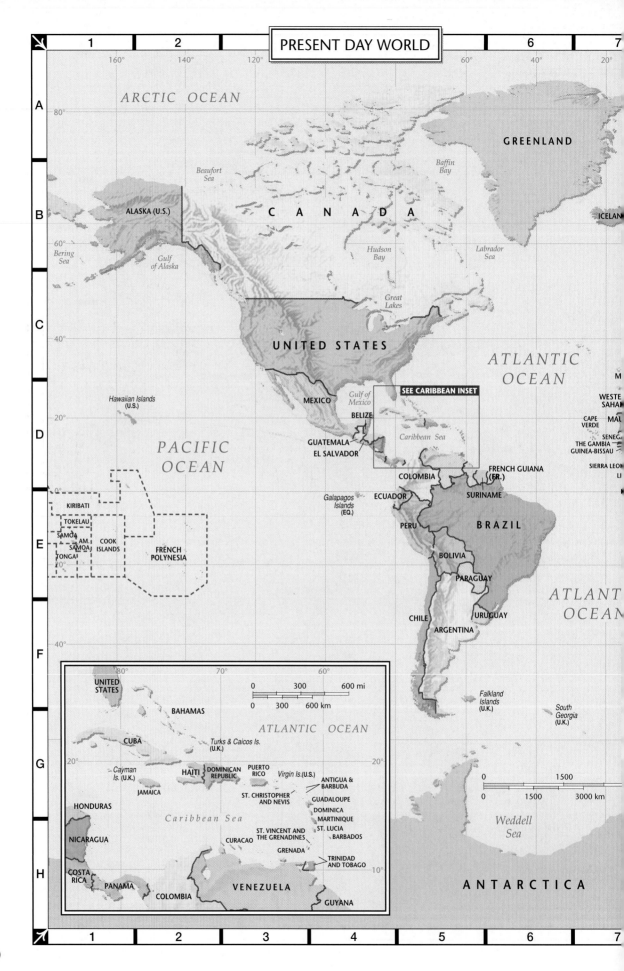

PRESENT DAY WORLD

ARCTIC OCEAN

GREENLAND

Baffin Bay

ALASKA (U.S.)

C A N A D A

ICELA

Beaufort Sea

Bering Sea

Gulf of Alaska

Hudson Bay

Labrador Sea

Great Lakes

UNITED STATES

ATLANTIC OCEAN

Hawaiian Islands (U.S.)

MEXICO

Gulf of Mexico

SEE CARIBBEAN INSET

WESTE SAHA

CAPE VERDE

MAL

BELIZE

Caribbean Sea

SENEG THE GAMBIA GUINEA-BISSAU

PACIFIC OCEAN

GUATEMALA EL SALVADOR

SIERRA LEO

LI

COLOMBIA

FRENCH GUIANA (FR.)

KIRIBATI

Galapagos Islands (EQ.)

ECUADOR

SURINAME

TOKELAU

PERU

B R A Z I L

SAMOA

AM. SAMOA

COOK ISLANDS

FRENCH POLYNESIA

BOLIVIA

ATLANT

TONGA

PARAGUAY

OCEAN

CHILE

URUGUAY

ARGENTINA

Falkland Islands (U.K.)

South Georgia (U.K.)

UNITED STATES

0   300   600 mi

0   300   600 km

BAHAMAS

ATLANTIC OCEAN

CUBA

Turks & Caicos Is. (U.K.)

Cayman Is. (U.K.)

HAITI

DOMINICAN REPUBLIC

PUERTO RICO

Virgin Is.(U.S.)

ANTIGUA & BARBUDA

JAMAICA

ST. CHRISTOPHER AND NEVIS

GUADALOUPE

DOMINICA

HONDURAS

Caribbean Sea

MARTINIQUE

ST. LUCIA

0   1500

NICARAGUA

CURACAO

ST. VINCENT AND THE GRENADINES

BARBADOS

0   1500   3000 km

GRENADA

Weddell Sea

COSTA RICA

TRINIDAD AND TOBAGO

PANAMA

COLOMBIA

VENEZUELA

A N T A R C T I C A

GUYANA

A-20

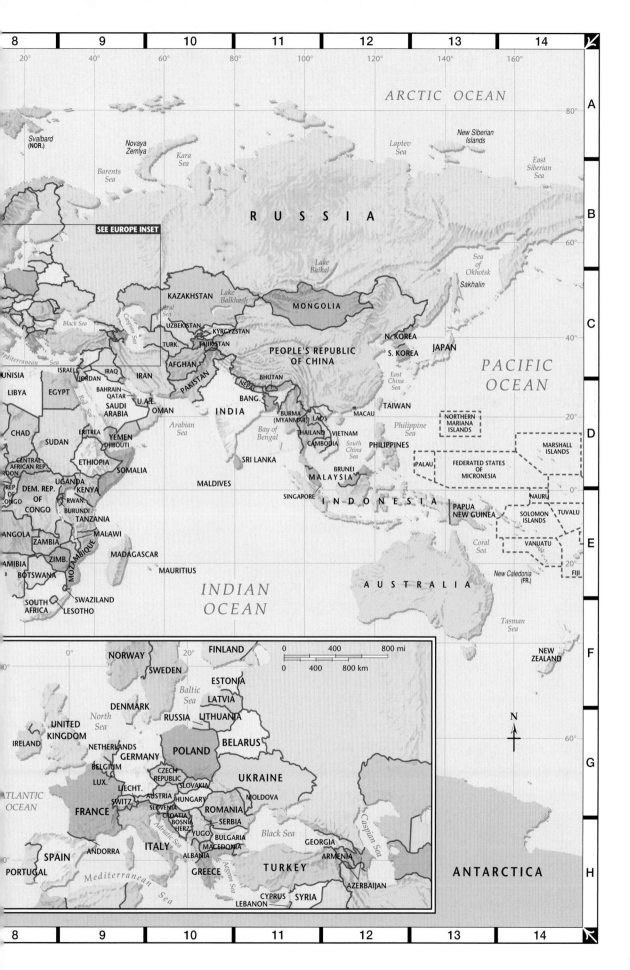

Agricultural Adjustment Act (AAA) (p. 680) New Deal program of 1933 led by Secretary of Agriculture Henry Wallace; it was an effort to develop a partnership between the government and major agricultural producers that would raise prices by reducing the supply of farm goods. Large producers in farm cooperatives would agree upon a "domestic allotment" plan that would assign acreage quotas to each producer, and those who cut production to comply with the quotas would be paid for land left fallow.

Alamo (p. 344) A former Spanish mission in San Antonio, Texas, where, in 1836, a Texan force of about 180 was besieged by the Mexican army during Texas's war for independence.

Alien and Sedition acts (p. 195) Four acts passed in 1798 designed to curb criticism of the federal government. Adopted during a time of conflict with France, the acts lengthened the period before an immigrant could obtain citizenship, gave the president power to deport dangerous aliens, and provided for the prosecution of those who wrote "false, scandalous, and malicious" writings against the U.S. government.

Alliance movement (p. 535) Started in 1877 as a farmers' club in Texas, the group expanded into a network of organizations devoted to improving the plight of farmers, eventually through political action

Allies (p. 617) In World War I, the United States, Great Britain, France, and Russia, the alliance that opposed and defeated the Central Powers of Germany and Austria-Hungary and their allies; in World War II, primarily the United States, Great Britain, (free) France, and the Soviet Union that opposed and defeated the Axis powers of Germany, Italy, and Japan.

Al-Qaeda (p. 894) An international terrorist network led by Osama bin Laden that staged the plane hijackings and attacks on the Pentagon and New York's World Trade Center of September 11, 2001.

Amateurism (p. 512) A belief that nonprofessional athletes are the pure embodiment of sports. The concept is noble in its outlook that "the game" should be played for the joy of participation and competition. It was somewhat marred in that elitist elements could manipulate the playing field to exclude people without access to expensive equipment or facilities.

American exceptionalism (p. 554) Notion that the United States houses biologically superior people and can spread democracy to the rest of the world. An intellectual foundation of expansion and racism in the late nineteenth and early twentieth centuries.

American Federation of Labor (p. 482) A confederation of labor unions founded in 1886, it was composed mainly of skilled craft unions and was the first na-tional labor organization to survive and experience a degree of success, largely because of its conservative leadership that accepted industrial capitalism.

American Indian Movement (AIM) (p. 840) An activist organization founded in 1968 to protect the civil rights of Native Americans and to pressure state and federal governments to strictly observe treaty obligations. To dramatize its demands, AIM occupied the Bureau of Indian Affairs Building in Washington, D.C., in 1972 and Wounded Knee, South Dakota, in 1973.

American System (of Henry Clay) (pp. 228, 256) Henry Clay's program for the national economy, which included a protective tariff to stimulate industry, a national bank to provide credit, and federally funded internal improvements to expand the market for farm products.

American system of production (p. 236) The high cost of labor led to the establishment of a system of mass production through the manufacture of interchangeable parts and the standardization of the tasks performed by workers.

Amos 'n Andy (p. 649) Popular radio show first aired in 1926 from Chicago station WMAQ; it spread vicious racial stereotypes about African Americans.

Anaconda Plan (p. 396) General Winfield Scott designed this strategic plan in the early days of the Civil War to give direction to the Union war effort against the South. The plan advocated a full naval blockade of the South's coastline, a military campaign to gain control of the Mississippi River, and the placement of armies at key points in the South to squeeze—like the anaconda snake—the life out of the Confederacy. In various ways, this plan helped inform overall Union strategy in militarily defeating the South.

Antifederalists (p. 174) These were opponents of the Constitution of 1787 who sought to continue the confederation of sovereign states and to keep power as close as possible to the people. In actuality, the Antifederalists were true federalists in seeking to balance powers among the states and the national government. Their confused identity may have cost them support in attempting to prevent ratification of the Constitution. See *Federalists*.

Anti-Masonic party (p. 251) A political organization that emerged following the alleged kidnapping and murder in 1826 of William Morgan, who had threatened to expose the secrets of the Masonic order. In 1831, the Anti-Masons held the first political nominating convention and issued the first written party platform. In 1834, Anti-Masons helped form the Whig party.

Antinomian (p. 45) Literally meaning against the laws of human governance. Antinomians believed that once they had earned saving grace, God would offer them direct revelation by which to order the steps of their lives. As such, human institutions, such as churches and government, were no longer necessary. Mainline Puritans believed Antinomianism would produce only social chaos and destroy the Bay Colony's mission, so they repudiated and even exiled prominent persons like Anne Hutchinson, who advocated such doctrines.

Artisan system of labor (p. 309)   A system of manufacturing that preceded the rise of the factory system, under which apprentices and skilled journeymen worked for self-employed master craftsmen in the master's home or a small shop nearby.

Ashcan School (p. 506)   Originating in the first decade of the twentieth century, a school of art centered on the experiences of urban life. An impressionistic offshoot, it is characterized by use of unmixed primary colors and quick brushstrokes while being concerned with content over technique.

Asiento (p. 84)   A trade agreement growing out of the War of the Spanish Succession (1702–1713) that allowed the English to sell 4800 slaves annually in New Spain. The English regularly cheated and traded much more extensively in the Spanish empire than provided for in the *Asiento*, which resulted in further warfare between Britain and Spain, beginning in 1739 with the start of the War of Jenkins's Ear.

Associationism (p. 660)   Concept proposed by Herbert Hoover as Secretary of Commerce under President Warren G. Harding, that called for voluntary trade associations to foster cooperation in industry and agriculture through commissions, trade practice controls, and ethical standards.

Atlanta Compromise (p. 473)   A term used to describe an 1895 speech by Booker T. Washington, who called upon African Americans to defer agitation in return for white Southerners' support for black educational and economic advancement.

Axis Powers (p. 715)   In World War II, the alliance of German and Italy, and later Japan.

Baltimore (p. 559)   U.S. warship that, on October 16, 1891, arrived at Valparaiso, Chile. A liberty party from the ship was involved in a riot and 2 sailors were killed and 16 injured. Aggressive and jingoistic parties used the incident to call for war against Chile.

Bank of the United States (pp. 186, 207)   A central bank, chartered by the federal government in 1791. Proposed by Alexander Hamilton, the bank collected taxes, held government funds, and regulated state banks. The bank's charter expired in 1811. A second Bank of the United States was created in 1816. See *Second Bank of the United States*.

Barbary pirates (pp. 208, 232)   During the late eighteenth and early nineteenth centuries, pirates from the North African states of Tripoli, Tunis, Morocco, and Algiers captured merchant ships and held their crews for ransom.

Bare-knuckle boxing (p. 518)   Precursor to more legitimate forms of professional boxing, bare-knuckles competitors did not use gloves and would fight until one man could not continue. The brutality of the matches brought about demands for rules and a general cleanup of the sport.

Battle of the Bulge (p. 718)   Last major Axis counteroffensive of World War II, December 16–26, 1944, when German armored divisions, driving toward Antwerp, slashed 60 miles to the Franco-Belgium border before being delayed and finally defeated by Allied forces at Bastogne.

Bay of Pigs fiasco (p. 788)   A plan to assassinate Cuban leader Fidel Castro and liberate Cuba with a trained military force of political exiles. The limited 1961 invasion was an unmitigated military failure and actually strengthened Castro's position in Cuba.

Beat generation (p. 778)   A cultural style and artistic movement of the 1950s that rejected traditional American family life and material values and celebrated African American culture. The Beats tapped an underground dissatisfaction with mainstream American culture.

Berlin airlift (p. 739)   During 1948 and 1949 the Soviet Union cut off all ground communication between the western sectors of Berlin (occupied by Britain, France, and the United States) and West Germany. The apparent purpose was to starve the three countries out of Berlin and allow the Soviets to have complete control of the city. In response to this challenge a massive airlift was conducted, supplying the city's basic needs by air for over a year. When the Soviets saw that there was no sign of capitulation and that the airlift was making great political capital for their opponents, the land blockade was abruptly and quietly lifted.

Big Stick Diplomacy (p. 599)   The proclaimed foreign policy of Theodore Roosevelt, it was based on the proverb, "Speak softly and carry a big stick," and advocated the threat of force to achieve the United States' goals, especially in the Western Hemisphere.

Bill of Rights (p. 184)   The first 10 amendments to the U.S. Constitution, which protect the rights of individuals from the powers of the national government. Congress and the states ratified the 10 amendments in 1791.

Billy Yank (p. 396)   This term referred to common soldiers serving in Union armies during the Civil War. See *Johnny Reb*.

Birds of passage (p. 491)   Immigrants who never intended to make the United States their home. Unable to make a living in their native countries, they came to America, worked and saved, and returned home. About 20 to 30 percent of immigrants returned home.

Black Codes (p. 428)   Laws passed by southern state legislatures during Reconstruction, while Congress was out of session. These laws limited the rights of former slaves and led Congress to ratify the Fourteenth Amendment.

Black Hawk War (p. 259)   In 1832, the Sauk and Fox Indians, who had lost their land in northern Illinois as a result of a disputed treaty, attempted to reclaim their lands but were defeated by state militia and army regulars.

Black Like Me (p. 768)   Novel by John Howard Griffin recounting his experiences as a white man disguised as an African American. His book told of the dreadful conditions that were permitted under the Jim Crow laws in the American South. This book was a first look into the situation for many white Americans.

Black Muslims (p. 822)   Founded in 1930, a group led by Elijah Muhammad that emphasized racial separation and worked to improve African American living conditions and root out activities that were exploited by racists.

Black Panther party (p. 824)   A militant black nationalist organization formed in 1966 in Oakland, California, by Huey Newton and Bobby Seale. The group advocated racial separation and black power.

Black power (p. 824)   A rallying cry for more militant blacks advocated by younger leaders like Stokely Carmichael and H. Rap Brown, beginning in the mid-1960s. It called for African Americans to form their own economic, political, and cultural institutions.

Black Sox scandal (p. 651)   Scandal in which eight Chicago White Sox baseball players threw the 1919 World Series and were ultimately banned from the sport.

Black Tuesday (p. 663)   October 29, 1929, the day of the stock market crash that helped to initiate the Great Depression.

Bombingham (p. 819)   Name given to Birmingham, Alabama, due to the number of bombs that were used against civil rights activists during the 1960s. In one explosion four young girls preparing for choir practice were killed in the basement of the Sixteenth Street Baptist Church.

Bonus Army (p. 676)   Group of unemployed World War I veterans who marched on Washington, D.C., in June 1932 to ask for immediate payment of their war pensions.

Bosnia-Herzegovina (p. 903)   A former Yugoslav republic that was the site of ethnic conflict between Serbs, Croats, and Muslims during the 1990s.

Brain trust (p. 678)   Close advisers to President Franklin Delano Roosevelt during the early days of his first term whose policy suggestions influenced much New Deal legislation.

Brown v. Board of Education of Topeka (p. 772)   Supreme Court decision of 1954 that overturned the "separate but equal doctrine" that justified Jim Crow laws. Chief Justice Earl Warren argued that "separate educational facilities are inherently unequal."

Cabinet (p. 184)   This term refers to the heads of the executive departments in the federal government.

Calvinism (p. 20)   Broadly influential Protestant theology emanating from the French theologian John Calvin, who fled to Switzerland, where he reordered life in the community of Geneva according to his conception of the Bible. Calvinism emphasized the power and omnipotence of God and the importance of seeking to earn saving grace and salvation, even though God had already determined (the concept of predestination) who would be eternally saved or damned.

Camp David Accords (p. 882)   Historic 1979 peace agreement negotiated between Egypt and Israel at the U.S. presidential retreat at Camp David, Maryland, with the help of U.S. President Jimmy Carter. Under the pact, Israel agreed to return captured territory to Egypt and to negotiate Palestinian autonomy in the West Bank and Gaza Strip. The pact normalized relations between the two nations and provided a framework for peace in the Middle East.

Capital punishment (p. 277)   During the early nineteenth century, a reform movement arose to end the death penalty.

Carpetbaggers (p. 435)   People who moved to the South during or following the Civil War and became active in politics, they helped to bring Republican control of southern state governments during Reconstruction and were bitterly resented by most white Southerners.

Cautious revolutionaries (p. 154)   Sometimes called reluctant revolutionaries, these leaders lacked a strong trust in the people to rise above their own self-interest and provide for enlightened legislative policies (see *Public virtue*). At the time of the American Revolution, they argued in favor of forms of government that could easily check the popular will. To assure political stability, they believed that political decision making should be in the hands of society's proven social and economic elite. John Dickinson, John Adams (very much an eager revolutionary), and Robert Morris might be described as cautious revolutionaries. See *Radical revolutionaries*.

Central Powers (p. 618)   In World War I, Germany and Austria-Hungary and their allies.

Charles River Bridge v. Warren Bridge (p. 265)   Landmark 1837 Supreme Court case which held that any ambiguities in contracts should be interpreted in the public interest.

China Lobby (p. 740)   An informal group of media leaders and political pundits who criticized the communist takeover of China, claiming the United States could have prevented it.

Chinese Exclusion Act (p. 496)   The success of the immigrants from China during the third quarter of the nineteenth century caused concern among "native-born" Americans in the West as the century closed. In order to prevent a greater influx of competitors, the Chinese Exclusion Act was passed in 1882 to suspend immigration from China for ten years. In 1892 a ten-year extension was passed and in 1902 the act was extended indefinitely.

Cincinnati Red Stockings (p. 509)   An early baseball team that helped to establish the requirements for "steady, temperate habits, and constant training" in professional sports.

Citizen Genêt Affair (p. 188)   When French envoy Charles Genêt attempted in 1794 to encourage Americans to launch naval attacks against the British, the U.S. government demanded his recall. This incident aggravated tensions between the United States and France.

City upon a Hill (p. 41)   Phrase from John Winthrop's sermon, "A Model of Christian Charity," in which he challenged his fellow Puritans to build a model, ideal community in America that would serve as an example of how the rest of the world should order its existence. Here was the beginning of the idea of America as a special, indeed exceptional society, therefore worthy of emulation by others. The concept of American exceptionalism has helped to define American history and culture down to the present.

Civil Rights Act of 1875 (p. 447)   An act that spelled out more specifically the rights guaranteed by the Fourteenth Amendment. It was meant to prohibit segregation of public accommodations but was greatly undermined by Supreme Court decisions.

Civil Rights Act of 1964 (p. 822)   Landmark legislation that prohibited discrimination on the basis of race, sex, religion, or national origin in employment and public facilities such as hotels, restaurants, and playgrounds. It established the Equal Employment Opportunity Commission.

Civil Service Commission (p. 530)   Established by the Pendleton Act in 1883, this body oversees the granting of federal jobs and administers tests given to applicants.

Coercive Acts (p. 114)   Also known as the Intolerable Acts, they consisted of four pieces of punitive legislation from King and Parliament in the spring of 1774 to punish colonists in Massachusetts who had dumped £10,000 worth of tea into Boston harbor in December 1773.

Coinage Act of 1873 (p. 529)   Called the "Crime of 73" by farmers and others who wanted to inflate the currency, this act halted the minting of silver dollars.

Cold War (p. 734)   The period between the end of World War II (1945) and the final dissolution of the Soviet Union (1991) in which the Western powers, led by the United States and comprised mainly of the NATO countries (with Japan), and the Soviet bloc (including the USSR and the Warsaw Pact nations of Eastern Europe) maintained a "short-of-war" condition. Any confrontation directly between the USSR and the United States could get out of hand and result in nuclear war. Thus the two superpowers found it useful to compete via third parties, such as Israel and the Arab nations or North and South Korea. The period could be characterized by "limited war fought for limited goals."

Colonization (p. 279)   The effort to encourage masters to emancipate their slaves voluntarily and to resettle free blacks in Africa.

Columbian Exchange (p. 27)   The process of transferring plants, animals, foods, diseases, wealth, and culture between Europe and the Americas, beginning at the time of Christopher Columbus and continuing throughout the era of exploration and expansion. The exchange often resulted in the devastation of Native American peoples and cultures, so much so that the process is sometimes referred to as the "Columbian collision."

Committee on Public Information (p. 627)   U.S. propaganda agency during World War I.

Committees of correspondence (p. 112)   As American leaders became increasingly anxious about a perceived British imperial conspiracy to deprive them of their liberties, they set up networks of communication among the colonies. Beginning in 1773 colonial assemblies began to appoint committees of correspondence to warn each other about possible abuses. In some colonies, such as Massachusetts, local communities also organized such committees, all with the intention of being vigilant against arbitrary acts from British officials.

Common Sense (p. 131)   This best-selling pamphlet by Thomas Paine, first published in January 1776, denounced the British monarchy, called for American independence, and encouraged the adoption of republican forms of government. Paine's bold words helped crack the power of reconciliationist leaders in the Second Continental Congress who did not believe the colonies could stand up to British arms and survive as an independent nation.

Compromise of 1850 (p. 369)   A series of measures passed by Congress to resolve sectional tensions. Congress admitted California to the Union as a free state; organized the territories of New Mexico, Nevada, Arizona, and Utah without mention of slavery; paid Texas $10 million to relinquish land claims in New Mexico; abolished the slave trade in the District of Columbia (but not slavery); and enacted a law requiring the return of fugitive slaves.

Compromise of 1877 (p. 448)   A bargain made between southern Democrats and Republican candidate Rutherford B. Hayes after the disputed presidential election of 1876. The southern Democrats pledged to let Hayes take office in return for his promise to withdraw the remaining federal troops from the southern states. The removal of the last troops in 1877 marked the end of Reconstruction.

Coney Island (p. 514)   Popular site of New York amusement parks opening in 1890s, attracting working-class Americans with rides and games celebrating abandon and instant gratification.

Congress of Industrial Organization (CIO) (p. 684)   Group formed in 1935 by union leaders of unskilled workers in mass-production industries, including auto, glass, radio, rubber, and steelworkers.

Congress of Racial Equality (CORE) (p. 818)   Formed in 1942, this group was instrumental in organizing the sit-ins of the 1960s. CORE promoted nonviolent protest as a means to social change. In July 1966 CORE shifted to an endorsement of black power and repudiated the nonviolent aspect of their protests.

Conscription (p. 631)   Compulsory draft of enrollees to serve in the military; put into effect in World War I by the Selective Service Act in May 1917.

Containment (p. 738)   George Kennan's paper, "The Sources of Soviet Conduct," suggested that the Soviets would expand only when the United States allowed them to do so. By containing them within their current borders and not allowing any other nations to convert to communism, the Soviets could be controlled and would decay from within. The policy of containment was to be enforced by economic, political, and military means. This defensive policy may have prolonged the Cold War.

Continental System (p. 212)   As part of France's conflict with Britain, Napoleon in 1806 and 1807 issued decrees that sought to prevent neutral nations, including the United States, from trading with Britain.

Contract With America (p. 900)   A 1994 campaign document in which Republican congressional candidates committed themselves to a constitutional amendment requiring a balanced federal budget, stiff work requirements for welfare recipients, and term limits for elected officials.

Copperheads (p. 405)   Not every person living in the North during the Civil War favored making war against the Confederacy. Such persons came to be identified as Copperheads. Often affiliated with the Democratic party and residing in the Midwest, Copperheads favored a negotiated peace settlement that would allow the South to leave the Union. Some of them were arbitrarily thrown into jail without proper *habeas corpus* proceedings after publicly advocating their views.

Court packing (p. 688) President Franklin Roosevelt's controversial plan to make the Supreme Court more sympathetic to his views and less likely to reject his legislative proposals as unconstitutional. FDR proposed to reorganize the Supreme Court by appointing up to six new members, one new justice for each sitting member over the age of 70 who did not retire, thus increasing the size of the Court from 9 to 16 members, and offering generous pension benefits for justices who did retire. FDR's plan was denounced on all sides as an attempt to circumvent the constitutional systems of checks and balances and the separation of powers.

Coverture (p. 48) The concept which contends that the legal identity of women is subordinated first to their fathers and then to their husbands, as the sanctioned heads of households. See *Patriarchal.*

Coxey's Army (p. 542) A movement founded by Jacob S. Coxey to help the unemployed during the depression of the 1890s, it brought out-of-work people to Washington, D.C., to demand that the federal government provide jobs and inflate the currency.

Credit Mobilier (p. 441) A financial scandal during Ulysses S. Grant's administration in 1872 involving his vice president, which tarnished the Republican party's image.

Cuban missile crisis (p. 788) The conflict in 1962 prompted by Soviet installation of missiles on Cuba. After days of genuine fear on both sides, the two sides negotiated an agreement whereby the Soviet Union removed the missiles and the United States pledged not to invade Cuba.

Cuban Revolution (of 1895) (p. 575) A revolt by local Cubans against the Spanish rulers of the island, starting in 1895. The ruthless suppression of this revolt by the Spanish would provide fuel for the coming Spanish-American War.

Cuban Revolution (of 1959) (p. 767) A revolt against the corrupt regime of Fulgencio Batista led by Fidel Castro. Castro, a medical doctor by training, called for local ownership of national industries and resources. As most of these were owned by American interests, the U.S. government did not support the revolution. When Castro declared himself a communist after the revolution was successful, U.S.-Cuba relations became even more strained.

Cult of domesticity (p. 513) Adherents held that women should be mothers, wives, and caregivers. Not only did this limit them in the world at large, it also prevented women from participating in most competitive sports.

Dartmouth v. Woodward (p. 231) A landmark 1819 Supreme Court decision protecting contracts. In the case, Chief Justice John Marshall ruled that the charters of business corporations are contracts and thus protected under the U.S. Constitution.

Dawes Severalty Act (p. 446) Legislation passed in 1887 to authorize the president to divide tribal land and distribute it to individual Native Americans; it gave 160 acres to each head of the household in an attempt to assimilate Indians into citizenship.

D-Day (p. 717) June 6, 1944, the day Allied forces landed on the beaches of Normandy, in France, leading to the defeat of Germany in World War II.

Declension (p. 52) A term associated with the Massachusetts Bay Colony, referring to the declining zeal of later generations or movement away from the utopian ideals of those Puritan leaders, such as John Winthrop, who founded the colony. As an example of declension, see *Half-way covenant.*

Deism (p. 274) A form of Christianity that rejects miracles, revelation, and the literal truth of the Bible.

Democratic-Republican Party (pp. 187, 204) One of the United States's first two political parties, it was founded by Thomas Jefferson and James Madison in opposition to the economic and foreign policies of Alexander Hamilton.

Department of Homeland Security (p. 907) A cabinet department set up in 2002 to prevent, protect against, and respond to acts of terrorism. Its responsibilities include controlling the nation's borders, analyzing intelligence, and coordinating emergency responses to terrorist attacks.

Deregulation (p. 880) An economic policy, begun during the administration of Jimmy Carter, which freed air and surface transportation, the savings and loan industry, natural gas, and other industries from many government economic controls.

Détente (p. 881) A relaxation of tensions between the United States and the Soviet Union that was begun by President Richard M. Nixon.

Dien Bien Phu (p. 789) Vietminh siege of 13,000 French soldiers in 1954 at a remote military outpost. The French surrender led to the 1956 elections designed to reunify Vietnam.

Direct taxes (p. 98) Also called "internal" taxes, such as visibly placed taxes on newspapers, pamphlets, and a host of other items such as those listed in the Stamp Act of 1765. Direct taxes are those that people know they are paying, such as state sales taxes or federal income taxes today. See *Indirect taxes.*

Divine Right (p. 37) Long-held belief that monarchs were God's political stewards on earth. Because their authority to rule supposedly came directly from God, the decision making of monarchs was held to be infallible and thus could not be questioned. Some of England's Stuart kings in the seventeenth century viewed themselves as ruling by divine right, a position that numerous subjects rejected, even to the point of a civil war in the 1640s and the beheading of Charles I in 1649.

Dollar diplomacy (p. 601) The diplomatic policy of President William Howard Taft; it called for increasing American influence in the world through economic investment rather than military force.

Dominican Republic (p. 551) Country which forms the eastern two-thirds of the island of Santo Domingo (the balance is the country of Haiti). President Ulysses S. Grant wanted the Dominican Republic not only as an asset to the U.S. economy but also as a haven for African Americans suffering from the depredations of the Ku Klux Klan.

Domino theory (p. 791) The U.S. belief that if one country in a region were to fall under communist control then other countries, like a row of dominoes, would fall one after the other. The U.S. resolve was that the communists would not gain a "toehold" in any of the areas friendly to the United States.

Donner party (p. 339)   A party of pioneers who were stranded on their way to California in late 1846. Of the original 87 emigrants, 39 died.

Double V campaign (p. 712)   African American term for their dual struggle to combat fascism abroad and discrimination at home during and after World War II.

Doughface (p. 372)   A Northerner with sympathies toward the slave-holding South.

Dred Scott decision (p. 426)   Supreme Court ruling in the 1857 case of *Dred Scott v. Sanford* that slaves were not citizens of the United States and thus were not eligible to bring suit in a federal court, and that Congress had no power to exclude slavery from any part of U.S. territory.

Dumbbell tenements (p. 501)   Apartment buildings built to minimal codes and designed to cram the largest number of people into the smallest amount of space. The dumbbell indentation in the middle of the building, although unsightly, conformed to the Tenement Reform Law of 1879, which required all rooms to have access to light and air.

Dunmore's Ethiopian regiment (p. 130)   In November 1775 John Murray, Lord Dunmore (Virginia's last royal governor), issued an emancipation proclamation that freed all slaves and indentured servants living in Virginia who were willing to bear arms against their rebellious masters. As many as 2000 slaves fled to the British banner, and some became members of Dunmore's Ethiopian regiment. With little training in arms, this regiment fared poorly in a battle with Virginia militia in December 1775. An outbreak of smallpox later killed many of the exslaves who responded to Dunmore's proclamation.

Dust Bowl (p. 679)   Area from northern Texas to the Dakotas that suffered from severe drought and dust storms during the 1930s, with the damage compounded by previous overgrazing and overfarming.

Eighteenth Amendment (p. 629)   Amendment that established prohibition by banning the manufacture, sale, or transportation of alcohol in the United States and its territories, ratified in 1919.

Electric trolley (p. 498)   Public transportation for urban neighborhoods, using electric current from overhead wires. Between 1888 and 1902, 97 percent of urban transit mileage was electrified.

Emancipation Proclamation (p. 405)   President Abraham Lincoln issued a preliminary proclamation in September 1862 that all slaves would be declared free in those states that were still in rebellion against the Union at the beginning of 1863. Receiving no official response from the Confederacy, Lincoln announced the Emancipation Proclamation on January 1, 1863. All slaves in the rebellious Confederate states were to be forever free. However, slavery could continue to exist in border states that were not at war against the Union. Lincoln's Emancipation Proclamation represented the beginning of the end of chattel slavery in the United States.

Embargo of 1807 (p. 212)   An attempt to stop British and French interference with American shipping by prohibiting foreign trade.

Emergency Banking Relief Act (p. 678)   First New Deal program, March 9, 1933, which allowed solvent banks to stay open under government supervision and permitted the Reconstruction Finance Corporation to buy the stock of troubled banks and keep them open for reorganization.

Emergency Quota Act (p. 497)   Prelude to the National Origins Act, this 1921 law limited to 3 percent annually the number of new immigrants of any nationality, based on the number of the group counted in the 1910 census.

Enclosure Movement (p. 22)   As the demand for wool heightened in England during the sixteenth century because of the emerging textile industry, Parliament passed laws that allowed profit-seeking landowners to fence in their open fields to raise more sheep. Thousands of peasants who, as renters, had been farming these lands for generations were evicted and thrown into poverty. Many moved to the cities, where as "sturdy beggars" they too often found little work. In time, some migrated to English colonies in America, where work opportunities were far more abundant.

Encomienda **System** (p. 17)   The government in Spain gave away large tracts of conquered land in Spanish America, including whole villages of indigenous peoples, to court favorites, including many *conquistadores.* These new landlords, or *encomenderos,* were supposed to educate the natives and teach them the Roman Catholic faith. The system, however, was rife with abuse. Landlords rarely offered much education, preferring instead to exploit the labor of the local inhabitants, whom they treated like slaves.

Enlightenment (pp. 78, 273)   A broadly influential philosophical and intellectual movement that began in Europe during the eighteenth century. The Enlightenment unleashed a tidal wave of new learning, especially in the sciences and mathematics, that helped promote the notion that human beings, through the use of their reason, could solve society's problems. The Enlightenment era, as such, has also been called the Age of Reason. Benjamin Franklin and Thomas Jefferson were leading proponents of Enlightenment thinking in America.

Enola Gay (p. 724)   B-29 Superfortress plane that dropped the atomic bomb, "Little Boy," on Hiroshima, Japan, August 6, 1945. The *Bock's Car* dropped the second bomb on Nagasaki on August 9.

Enumerated goods (p. 63)   Products grown or extracted from England's North American colonies that could be shipped only to England or other colonies within the empire. Goods on the first enumeration list included tobacco, indigo, and sugar. Later on furs, molasses, and rice would be added to a growing list of products that the English colonies could not sell directly to foreign nations.

Equal Employment Opportunity Commission (EEOC) (p. 832)   A commission set up to investigate complaints of employment discrimination by Title VII of the 1964 Civil Rights Act.

Equal Rights Amendment (p. 833)   Proposed constitutional amendment that would prohibit discrimination on the basis of gender.

Era of Good Feelings (pp. 226, 653)   Phrase used to describe the years following the War of 1812, when one party, the Jeffersonian Republicans, dominated politics, and a spirit of nationalism characterized public policy.

Erie Canal (p. 234) Built between 1817 and 1825, the Erie Canal linked the Hudson River with the Great Lakes, cutting travel time from Buffalo to New York from 20 to 6 days and freight charges from $100 to $5 a ton.

Espionage Act (p. 627) Law passed in June 1917 to combat spying, sabotage, or obstruction of the war effort by giving postal officials authority to ban newspapers and magazines from the mails and threatening individuals convicted of obstructing the draft with $10,000 fines and 20 years in jail.

Europeanizing (p. 76) As the British North American colonies matured during the eighteenth century, many prospering colonists sought to ape the latest fashions and lifestyles of wealthy persons in England and on the European continent. This imitative trend has been described as the "Europeanizing" of American society in the years before the American Revolution.

Evangelical Revivalism (Revivals) (p. 274) A current of Protestant Christianity emphasizing personal conversion, repentance of sin, and the authority of Scripture.

Executive Order 9835 (p. 747) This order established the Federal Loyalty Program, which authorized the FBI to investigate all government employees in an attempt to root out communists. Thousands of federal workers lost their jobs but not one charge was ever filed under this order.

Executive Privilege (p. 192) The doctrine, first asserted by President George Washington, that the constitutional principle of separation of powers allows the Executive Branch the right to withhold certain requests for information from Congress and the Judiciary.

Existentialism (p. 652) Philosophy which maintains that life has no transcendent purpose and that each individual must salvage personal meaning from the void. Novelists of the 1920s such as F. Scott Fitzgerald and Ernest Hemingway foreshadowed this philosophy in their works.

Factory system (p. 310) During the industrial revolution of the nineteenth century, large numbers of workers were concentrated under one roof, where they were subjected to strict supervision and close discipline.

Fair Deal (p. 746) Failed 1948 legislative package proposed by President Truman; it included an expansion of Social Security, federal aid to education, a higher minimum wage, a national plan for medical insurance, and civil rights legislation for minorities.

Fallen Timbers, Battle of (p. 189) General Anthony Wayne's victory over an Indian confederation near present-day Toledo, Ohio, in 1794, opened the Ohio country to white settlement.

Farewell Address (p. 193) In this 1796 statement, in which he expressed his intention not to run for a third term as president, George Washington warned of the dangers of party divisions, sectionalism, and permanent alliances with foreign nations.

Fascism (p. 700) Political philosophy that emerged just prior to World War II; it espoused one-party government, strict government control of business and labor, and severe restrictions on personal liberty.

Federal Emergency Relief Act (p. 678) New Deal program enacted May 12, 1933, which gave $500 million to state-run welfare agencies.

Federal Reserve System (p. 598) The central banking system of the United States, established with passage of the Federal Reserve Act of 1913, charged with the responsibility of managing the country's money supply through such means as lowering or raising interest rates. A board of seven members (the Federal Reserve Board), appointed by the U.S. president, oversees the 12 regional banks of the Federal Reserve System.

Federalist Papers (p. 174) These 85 newspaper essays, written in support of ratification of the Constitution of 1787 in New York by James Madison, Alexander Hamilton, and John Jay, described the proposed plan of national government as a sure foundation for long-term political stability and enlightened legislation. Although having little effect on the ratification debate in New York, the papers soon became classics of political philosophy about the Constitution as the framework of federal government for the American republic.

Federalist Party (pp. 187, 204) One of the United States's first two political parties, it was founded by Alexander Hamilton to promote his policies, which included a national bank and friendly relations with Britain. It advocated a strong central government.

Federalists (p. 174) In the campaign to ratify the Constitution of 1787, nationalists started referring to themselves as federalists, which conveyed the meaning that they were in favor of splitting authority between their proposed strong national government and the states. The confusion in terminology may have helped win some support among citizens worried about a powerful—and potentially tyrannical—national government. Some leading nationalists of the 1780s became Federalists in the 1790s. See *Antifederalists.* The term also refers to a political party founded by Alexander Hamilton in the 1790s to support his economic program.

Femes sole (p. 49) A legal concept that allowed single, adult women to own and manage their own property and households, as distinct from legal subordination to fathers or husbands. See *Coverture* and *Patriarchal.*

Feminist theory (p. 833) Theory that analyzes the economic, psychological, and social roots of female subordination and argues that gender distinctions structure virtually every aspect of individual lives.

Fifteenth Amendment (p. 433) Passed by Congress in February 1869 and ratified by the required three-quarters of the states in March 1870, this amendment prohibited the denial of the right to vote on the basis of race, color, or past servitude. It did not specifically grant the vote to anyone and was successfully circumvented by southern states following Reconstruction.

Fire-eaters (p. 389) Radical leaders in the South during the years leading up to the Civil War, the fire-eaters were persons who took an extreme proslavery position. They repeatedly expressed their desire to see slavery spread throughout the United States, and they used states' rights arguments to support their uncompromising position.

Fireside chats (p. 678) Weekly radio addresses by President Franklin Roosevelt in which he explained his actions directly to the American people.

First Continental Congress (p. 115) This body was the most important expression of intercolonial protest activity up to 1774. Called in response to Parliament's Coercive Acts, the delegates met in Philadelphia for nearly two months. More radical delegates dominated the deliberations. Before dissolving itself, the Congress called for ongoing resistance, even military preparations to defend American communities, and a second congress, should King and Parliament not redress American grievances.

First Hundred Days (p. 678)   President Franklin Roosevelt's first 100 days in office, when he proposed and Congress passed 15 major bills that reshaped the U.S. economy.

Flapper (p. 652)   Term for a liberated woman who flaunted conventional ideas of propriety in dress and manners during the 1920s.

Flexible response (p. 790)   Approach to foreign policy of the Kennedy administration based on developing and maintaining conventional, counterinsurgency (antiguerrilla), and nuclear forces so that the United States would be able to choose from among these options in response to a communist threat anywhere in the world.

Fourteen Points (p. 634)   President Woodrow Wilson's formula for peace after World War I.

Fourteenth Amendment (p. 430)   Ratified in June 1868, this amendment defined citizenship and the rights of citizenship and specified changes required of the former Confederate states.

Free silver (p. 521)   A slogan of the 1890s, its advocates called for the inflation of the currency by minting more silver.

Free Soil party (p. 281)   An antislavery political party founded in 1848.

Freedmen's Bureau (Bureau of Refugees, Freedmen, and Abandoned Lands) (p. 423)   An organization established by Congress on March 3, 1865, to deal with the dislocations of the Civil War. It provided relief, helped settle disputes, and founded schools and hospitals.

Freedom of Information Act (p. 877)   This law allows the public and press to request declassification of government documents.

Freedom riders (p. 818)   Civil rights activists who in 1961 demonstrated that despite a federal ban on segregated travel on interstate buses, segregation prevailed in parts of the South.

French Revolution (p. 187)   A social and political revolution that took place in France between 1789 and 1799 and resulted in the overthrow of the French monarchy and the social system over which it ruled.

Fugitive Slave Law (p. 369)   The most controversial element of the Compromise of 1850, the Fugitive Slave Law provided for the return of runaway slaves to their masters.

Gadsden Purchase (p. 372)   The purchase of 30,000 square miles of land from Mexico in 1854 for a southern railroad fixed the southern boundary of the continental United States.

Gang system (p. 325)   A system of plantation labor under which field hands were divided into plow gangs and hoe gangs under the command of a driver. See *Task system*.

Gay and lesbian liberation (p. 841)   A movement among homosexuals to free themselves from the social stigma long associated with same-sex relations.

Ghost Dance (p. 445)   A movement among the Sioux in the 1890s that promised the disappearance of the white man and the return of their lands.

Gilded Age (p. 523)   A term used to describe the late nineteenth century, it highlighted the superficiality of the culture, wealth, and politics of the era.

Glass-Steagall Act (p. 678)   New Deal program that provided a federal guarantee on all bank deposits under $5000 (with creation of the Federal Deposit Insurance Corporation), separated commercial and investment banking, and strengthened the Federal Reserve's ability to stabilize the economy.

Globalization (p. 896)   Emerging patterns of trade, finance, manufacturing, and entertainment that cross international boundaries.

Gold Rush (p. 357)   Some 80,000 gold seekers moved to California in 1849 after the announcement that gold had been discovered in the Sacramento Valley.

Golden door (p. 496)   Nineteenth-century Chinese term for the United States, perhaps derived from the "Golden Gate" through which many arrived in this country from China.

Good Neighbor policy (p. 698)   During the administration of President Franklin D. Roosevelt, the U.S. policy of not interfering in the internal affairs of hemispheric neighbors.

Gospel of wealth (p. 458)   The belief that God ordains certain people to amass money and use it to further God's purposes; it justified the concentration of wealth as long as the rich used their money responsibly.

Grand Alliance (p. 715)   In World War II, the alliance between the United States, Great Britain, and France.

Great American Desert (p. 340)   A term applied to the arid, treeless land west of the Missouri River and east of the Rocky Mountains, which helped impede settlement of the Great Plains until after the Civil War.

Great Awakening (p. 79)   Spilling over into the colonies from a wave of revivals in Europe, the Awakening placed renewed emphasis on vital religious faith, partially in reaction to more secular, rationalist thinking characterizing the Enlightenment. Beginning as scattered revivals in the 1720s, the Awakening grew into a fully developed outpouring of rejuvenated faith by the 1740s. Key figures included Jonathan Edwards and George Whitefield. The Awakening's legacy included more emphasis on personal choice, as opposed to state mandates about worship, in matters of religious faith.

Great Migration (p. 630)   The mass movement of African Americans from the South to the North during World War I.

Great Society (pp. 826, 863)   The liberal reform program of President Lyndon Johnson. The program included civil rights legislation, increased public spending to help the poor, Medicare and Medicaid programs, educational legislation, and liberalized immigration policies.

Great Strike of 1877 (p. 480)   A spontaneous strike of the railroads that paralyzed two thirds of the nation's tracks for two weeks, it eventually failed after President Rutherford Hayes sent federal troops to restore control.

Greenback party (p. 529)   A political party founded in 1874 to promote the issuance of legal tender paper currency not backed by precious metals in order to inflate the money supply and relieve the suffering of people hurt by the era's deflation; most of its members merged with the Populist party.

Greenbacks (p. 403)   To help fund the military forces used against the Confederacy during the Civil War, the federal Congress issued a paper currency known as greenbacks. Even though greenbacks had no backing in specie (hard currency), this currency held its value fairly well because of mounting confidence the Union would prevail in the war. See also *Specie*.

Gulf of Tonkin Resolution (p. 792)   Following two reported attacks on the *U.S.S. Maddox* in 1964, American president Lyndon B. Johnson asked for and received this authorization from Congress to "take all necessary measures" to repel attacks, prevent aggression, and protect American security. It allowed Johnson to act without Congressional authorization on military matters in Vietnam.

Haciendas (p. 17)   Vast landed estates awarded to full-blooded Spaniards. The native populace on these estates existed in a state of peonage and had to share their crops and labor with the *hacienda* owners. The *hacienda* system replaced the somewhat harsher *encomienda* system. See *Encomienda* System.

Half-Way Covenant (p. 52)   Realizing that many children of the Massachusetts Bay Colony's first generation were not actively seeking God's saving grace and full church membership, the question was how to keep the next generation of children active in church affairs. The solution, agreed to in 1662, was to permit the baptism of children and grandchildren of professing saints, thereby according them half-way membership. Full church membership still would come only after individuals testified to a conversion experience. This compromise on standards of membership was seen as a sign of declension. See *Declension*.

Harlem Renaissance (p. 659)   Self-conscious African American cultural, literary, and artistic movement centered in Harlem in New York City during the 1920s.

Harpers Ferry, Virginia (p. 381)   The site of abolitionist John Brown's raid on the federal arsenal in 1859, which heightened sectional tensions and brought the nation closer to Civil War.

Hartford Convention (p. 220)   Convention held in late 1814 and early 1815 by New Englanders opposed to the War of 1812, which recommended constitutional amendments to weaken the power of the South and to restrict Congress's power to impose embargoes or declare war.

Hatch Act of 1887 (p. 472)   Aimed at increasing agricultural production, it provided federal support to the states for agricultural research.

Hay-Bunau-Varilla Treaty (p. 600)   The treaty with the new nation of Panama in 1903 that granted the United States the right to use the Panama Canal for payment of $10 million and an annual rental fee of $250,000.

Haymarket Square riot (p. 481)   A violent encounter between police and protestors in 1886 in Chicago, which led to the execution of four protest leaders, it scared the public with the specter of labor violence and demonstrated government's support of industrialists over workers.

Headright (p. 36)   As an economic incentive to encourage English settlement in Virginia and other English colonies during the seventeenth century, sponsoring parties would offer 50 acres of land per person to those who migrated or who paid for the passage of others willing to migrate to America. Because of Virginia's high death rate and difficult living conditions, headrights functioned as an inducement to help bolster the colony's low settlement rate.

Hessians (p. 133)   Six German principalities provided 30,000 soldiers to Great Britain to fight against the American rebels during the War for Independence. More than half of these troops-for-hire came from Hesse-Cassel. Hessian thus would serve as the generic term for all German mercenaries fighting in the war, whether or not they came from Hesse-Cassel.

Hiss-Chambers affair (p. 733)   An early event in the anti-communist Red Scare. Whittaker Chambers accused Alger Hiss of being a communist and passing national security secrets to the Soviets. Hiss denied Chambers's allegations. This was an important milestone in Richard Nixon's political career.

Holy experiment (p. 66)   Tolerance of religious diversity was at the core of William Penn's vision for a colony in America. As such, the colony of Pennsylvania represented a "holy experiment" for Penn. He encouraged people of all faiths to live together in harmony and to maintain peaceful relations with Native Americans in the region. The residents of early Pennsylvania never fully embraced Penn's vision, but the colony was open to religious dissenters and became a model for the diversity that later characterized America.

Homestead strike (p. 540)   An unsuccessful strike at Carnegie Steel's Homestead plant in 1892, that led to violence, including the stabbing of plant manager Henry Frick by anarchist Alexander Berkman.

Hooverizing (p. 652)   Herbert Hoover's program as director of the Food Administration to conserve food during World War I.

Hoovervilles (p. 671)   Shantytowns of the Great Depression, named after President Herbert Hoover.

Horseshoe Bend, Battle of (p. 218)   This 1814 battle in which an American army of 2600 under Andrew Jackson, combined with 600 Indians, defeated a Creek army of 1000, was the decisive battle of the Creek War (1813–1814).

House Un-American Activities Committee (HUAC) (p. 749)   Committee that investigated subversive right- and left-wing movements. During the Cold War, it was best known for its two investigations of the American film industry.

Hudson Highlands strategy (p. 140)   The British tried to execute this strategy early in the War for American Independence but never successfully implemented it. The idea was to gain control of the Hudson River–Lake Champlain corridor running north from New York City and south from Montreal, Canada. Had the British done so, the effect would have been to cut off New England, the initial center of rebellion, from the rest of the colonies. New England could then have been reconquered in detail. The failure to coordinate the movements of British forces in 1776 and 1777 resulted in the capture of John Burgoyne's army at Saratoga, New York, in October 1777, which ended any attempt to snuff out the rebellion by retaking New England.

Hungarian revolution (p. 764)   Revolt against Soviet domination of the Hungarian government in 1956. The Soviet army was at first expelled from the country, but Khrushchev soon crushed the popular uprising with overwhelming military force.

Hydraulic society (p. 857)   Defined by historian Donald Worster as "a social order based on the intensive manipulation of water and its products in an arid setting," it characterized the irrigated societies of the modern West, allowing for agricultural productivity and a massive demographic shift westward.

Immediate emancipation (p. 279)   The doctrine advanced by the abolitionist William Lloyd Garrison that slaves should be immediately freed without compensation to their masters.

Immigration (p. 314)   The movement of people from one country to another.

Implied powers (p. 185)   The view that the national government's powers are not limited to those stated explicitly in the U.S. Constitution.

Impressment (p. 212)   The British practice of seizing seamen from American merchant ships and forcing them to serve in the British navy. Impressment was one of the causes of the War of 1812.

Imprisonment for debt (p. 277)   During the early nineteenth century, reformers succeeded in restricting imprisonment of debtors.

Indentured servitude (p. 35)   In an effort to entice English subjects to the colonies, parties would offer legal bonded contracts that would exchange the cost of passage across the Atlantic for up to seven years of labor in America. Indenture contracts also required masters to provide food, clothing, farm tools, and sometimes land when the term of bonded service had expired, thus allowing former servants the opportunity to gain full economic independence in America.

Indian New Deal (p. 687)   New Deal programs aimed specifically at Native Americans. The Indian Emergency Conservation Program provided work relief on Indian reservations; the Indian Reorganization Act of 1934 terminated the allotment program of the Dawes Severalty Act of 1887, provided funds for Native American groups to purchase new land, offered government recognition of Native American constitutions, and repealed prohibitions on Native American languages and customs.

Indian Peace Commission (p. 444)   Established by Congress in 1867, the commission sought to negotiate settlements with the Plains Indians, asking them to restrict their tribes to reservations in order to promote western settlement.

Indian removal (p. 258)   President Andrew Jackson's Indian policies resulted in the removal of some 46,000 Indians east of the Mississippi to Oklahoma and Arkansas, opening 25 million acres of land to white settlement.

Indirect taxes (p. 98)   Also called "external" taxes, such as hidden trade duties placed on goods like those embodied in the Townshend Duties of 1767. Indirect taxes are those that people may not realize they are paying when they make purchases, such as the Townshend trade duty on tea or excise taxes placed on items like alcohol and smoking products today. See *Direct taxes.*

Indulgences (p. 19)   Redemption certificates pardoning persons from punishment in the afterlife that were being sold by the Roman Catholic church. Martin Luther particularly condemned this practice in his Ninety-five Theses, bringing on the Protestant Reformation.

Industrial Workers of the World (p. 626)   Organized in 1905, the IWW, or "Wobblies," were a militant socialist labor union that advocated one union for all workers and frequently employed the language of class warfare to dramatize demands.

Influence of Sea Power upon History (p. 558)   An 1890 book by Alfred Thayer Mahan that argued nations expand their world power through foreign commerce and a strong navy. Strongly influenced American politicians who advocated expansion.

Initiative and Referendum (p. 537)   Procedures that allow citizens to propose legislation through petitions, adopted by numerous states at the turn of the century but rarely used until the 1970s.

Insanity defense (p. 277)   The legal principle that a criminal act should only be punished if the offender was fully capable of distinguishing right from wrong.

Institutional economists (p. 581)   Progressive-era economists who rejected static economic theories and conducted field research to determine how the economy actually worked.

Interstate Commerce Commission (p. 531)   The first federal regulatory agency, established by passage of the Interstate Commerce Act in 1887 to regulate the railroads. The ICC's powers were expanded to oversee other forms of transportation and communication.

Iran-Contra Affair (p. 888)   A political scandal of the mid-1980s in which the Reagan administration attempted to secure release of U.S. hostages held in Lebanon by authorizing the sale of arms to Iran. Some of the proceeds were then channeled to opponents of the government of Nicaragua.

Iranian Hostage Crisis (p. 883)   In November 1979 Iranian students seized the U.S. embassy compound in Tehran and held 52 Americans inside hostage for 444 days.

Iron Curtain (p. 736)   A term coined by Winston Churchill to describe the psychological and political boundary between Western and Eastern Europe. The image was amplified when the Soviets started fortifying and sealing the western frontiers of Warsaw Pact states that bordered Western European nations. The Iron Curtain was meant as much to keep the current resident in as it was to keep Western nations out.

Jacksonian Democrats (p. 255)   Made up of opponents of the administration of John Quincy Adams, Jacksonian Democrats favored strong presidential power, states' rights, Indian removal, the sale of federal land in the West at low prices, and territorial expansion. They opposed government assistance for banks and other "privileged" corporations, subsidies for internal improvements, and protective tariffs.

Jawboning (p. 673)   President Herbert Hoover's initial response to the Great Depression, persuading business leaders to maintain prices and wages and labor spokesmen not to strike or demand higher wages.

Jay's Treaty (p. 192)   This controversial 1794 treaty averted war between the United States and Britain by removing British forts on American soil, providing compensation for seizures from American ships, and permitting limited U.S. trade with the British West Indies.

Jazz (p. 507) Musical style based on improvisation within a band format, combining African traditions of repetition, call and response, and strong beat with European structure.

Jazz Age (p. 649) Catch phrase coined by author F. Scott Fitzgerald to denote the 1920s, which gave rise to popular jazz artists such as Duke Ellington, Louis Armstrong, Fletcher Henderson, and Benny Goodman as Americans' attention shifted from politics and world events to popular culture.

Jim Crow laws (p. 768) Laws enacted by states to promote the theory of "separate but equal" facilities for whites and nonwhites. The actual purpose of these laws was to segregate the population and, implicitly, demonstrate that whites were superior.

Johnny Reb (p. 396) This term referred to common soldiers serving in Confederate armies during the Civil War. See *Billy Yank*.

Joint Committee on Reconstruction (p. 429) A congressional committee made up of both senators and representatives established in 1866 to investigate conditions in the southern states that were readmitted to the Union by President Andrew Johnson.

Joint Stock Trading Companies (p. 24) These companies were given the right to develop trade between England and certain geographic regions, such as Russia or India. Investors would pool their capital, in return for shares of stock, to underwrite trading ventures. One such company, the Virginia Company, failed to secure profits for its investors but laid the basis for the first major English colony in the Americas.

Judicial review (p. 208) The power of the courts to determine the constitutionality of acts of other branches of government and to declare unconstitutional acts null and void.

Judiciary Act of 1789 (p. 184) The first Congress established a federal court system, including federal district and appeals courts.

Judiciary Act of 1801 (p. 207) Passed by the Federalists after they had lost control of Congress in the election of 1800, the act reduced the size of the Supreme Court, created a new set of circuit courts, and increased the number of district court judges. The Jeffersonian Republicans repealed the act in 1801.

Kansas-Nebraska Act of 1854 (p. 374) Controversial legislation that opened Kansas and Nebraska to white settlement, repealed the Compromise of 1820, and led opponents to form the Republican party.

Kefauver Crime Committee (p. 750) Communists were not the only group targeted by congressional investigative committees in the 1950. Senator Estes Kefauver chaired a probe into organized crime in the United States during this time. The committee was a hit on television and helped popularize the U.S. interest in eavesdropping on governmental procedures.

Kellogg-Briand Pact (p. 697) Pact signed by 62 nations in 1928 that renounced war and allowed countries to defend themselves with force only if attacked. The pact lacked enforcement measures and so was unsuccessful in preventing war.

Kentucky and Virginia resolutions (p. 196) Resolutions passed by the legislatures of Kentucky and Virginia in opposition to the Alien and Sedition Acts of 1789; they represented the first statement of states' rights principles and provided a basis for the doctrine of nullification and secession.

Knights of Labor (p. 482) A labor organization founded in 1869, that called for the unity of all workers, rejected industrial capitalism, and favored cooperatively owned businesses but was discredited by such labor violence as the Haymarket Square riot and did not survive the depression of the 1890s.

Know-Nothing Party (p. 371) A nativist, antiforeign, anti-Catholic political party that arose in the early and mid-1850s following massive Irish and Catholic immigration during the late 1840s. Know-Nothings drew support from native-born workingmen who felt threatened by immigration and from white Southerners in the border states troubled by agitation over the slavery issue. Between 1853 and 1856, the Know-Nothing party replaced the Whigs as the second largest party in New England and some other states.

Korean War (p. 744) Perceiving that the draw-down of U.S. forces after World War II had weakened American military power to a tremendous extent, the government of North Korea launched an invasion aimed at overthrowing the South Korean government and unifying the country. The United States managed to hold onto the southwestern corner of South Korea long enough to move forces into the country and counterattack into North Korea. The approach of U.S. forces to the Yalu River brought the Chinese communists into the war and the United States was thrown back to near the original dividing line between the two countries. At that point a stalemate developed which continues into the twenty-first century.

Kosovo (p. 903) A predominantly Albanian part of Yugoslavia that was the site of a NATO air campaign in 1999, which reversed Serbian efforts to expel Albanian Kosovars from their homes.

Ku Klux Klan (pp. 439, 657) A secret organization founded in the southern states during Reconstruction to terrorize and intimidate former slaves and prevent them from voting or holding public office. Officially disbanded in 1869, a second antiblack, anti-Catholic, and anti-Semitic Klan emerged in 1915 that aimed to preserve "Americanism."

Laissez-faire (p. 460) An economic theory based on the ideas of Adam Smith; it contended that in a free economy self-interest would lead individuals to act in ways that benefited society as a whole and therefore government should not intervene.

Landed states (p. 156) In its final form the Articles of Confederation did not provide for a national domain but allowed so-called landed states, or those states that had title claim to western lands based on English colonial charters, to maintain control of these areas. The landed states included New Hampshire, Massachusetts, Connecticut, New York, Virginia, North Carolina, South Carolina, and Georgia. The landless states objected to their exclusion from western territory, so much so that the landed states, with Virginia in the lead, began in 1781 to release their claims to the national government, thereby establishing a national domain for future development. See also *Landless states* and *National domain*.

Landless states (p. 156) Five states, including Rhode Island, New Jersey, Pennsylvania, Delaware, and Maryland, had no claim to western lands based on colonial charters. At the time of the ratification of the Articles of Confederation, Maryland demanded full access to western lands as its price for approval of the Articles. Virginia, a landed state, agreed to turn over its claim under specified conditions, which not only helped bring about ratification but also facilitated the formation of a national domain of western lands that would be developed on behalf of the whole republic. See also *Landed states* and *National domain*.

Large policy (p. 558) Bold foreign policy put forth by Henry Cabot Lodge and others, advocating a canal through the Central American isthmus and a strong American naval presence in the Caribbean and Pacific.

League of Nations (p. 634) Point Fourteen of Wilson's Fourteen Points, the proposal to establish an international organization to guarantee the territorial integrity of independent nations.

Lecompton Constitution (p. 379) In an election in 1857 in which Free Soil voters abstained, Kansas adopted a proslavery constitution. When President Buchanan urged Congress to admit Kansas as a slave state under the Lecompton Constitution, Stephen Douglas broke with the administration. In 1858, Kansas voters decisively defeated the Lecompton Constitution.

Lend-Lease Act (p. 704) The program by which the United States provided arms and supplies to the Allies in World War II before joining the fighting.

Lewis and Clark Expedition (p. 210) The first overland expedition to the Pacific coast and back, led by Meriwether Lewis and William Clark and initiated by President Thomas Jefferson, took place between 1804 and 1806.

Liberty party (p. 281) An antislavery political party founded in 1839.

Lincoln-Douglas debates (p. 380) A series of seven debates between Republican Abraham Lincoln and Democratic senator Stephen Douglas in the 1858 Illinois Senate campaign that dramatized the issues of slavery in the western territory and popular sovereignty.

Literacy testing (p. 496) Politicians' idea to restrict immigration from southern and eastern Europe and China in the 1890s. Such bills were killed by presidential veto. Superseded by the quota system of restricting undesirable immigration.

Little Rock crisis (p. 773) Conflict in 1957 in which Arkansas Governor Orval Faubus sent the Arkansas National Guard to prevent the racial integration of Little Rock's Central High School. After a crucial delay, President Eisenhower federalized the National Guard troops and sent in 1000 paratroopers to foster the school's integration.

Loose interpretation (p. 186) The view that the national government has the power to create agencies or enact statutes to fulfill the powers granted by the U.S. Constitution.

Louisiana Purchase (p. 210) Territory purchased from France in 1803 for $15 million that extended from the Mississippi River to the Rocky Mountains and that doubled the size of the country.

Loyal Nine (p. 100) This informal group of pro-colonial rights leaders in Boston helped organize resistance against unwanted British policies, such as the Stamp Act. Working with more visible popular leaders like Samuel Adams and street leaders like Ebenezer Mackintosh, the Loyal Nine both planned and gave overall direction to controlled violent protests in defying the imperial will and protecting the community's interests in Boston during the 1760s.

LSD (Lysergic Acid Diethylamide) (p. 830) A psychoactive drug developed originally to help in research on mental illness. The strong hallucinogenic character of the drug made it a favorite of the counterculture in the 1960s.

Lusitania (p. 619) British ship carrying American passengers sunk by a German submarine on May 15, 1915.

Lyndon's war (p. 792) Another name for the war in Vietnam, used by antiwar activists to indicate who they felt was responsible for continuing U.S. involvement in Vietnam.

Macon's Bill No. 2 (p. 213) An attempt to stop British and French interference with American trade.

Manhattan Project (p. 724) The secret government program to develop an atomic bomb during World War II.

Manifest destiny (p. 343) A concept that justified American expansion westward and southward across North America.

Manila Bay, Battle of (p. 565) A decisive victory against the Spanish navy in the Philippine Islands. Commodore Dewey's Asiatic Fleet sailed from China and destroyed the Spanish on May 1, 1898. This was the first fleet action between "modern" warships.

Manitou (p. 12) Native Americans considered everything on the planet—trees, plants, and animals—to be spiritually alive or filled with spirits. Manitou is the term for spirits.

Manumission (p. 167) The freeing or emancipation of chattel slaves by their owners, which became more common in the upper South in the wake of so much talk during the American Revolution about human liberty. George Washington was among those planters who provided for the manumission of his slaves after the death of his wife Martha.

Marbury v. Madison (pp. 208, 231) This landmark 1803 Supreme Court decision, which established the principle of judicial review, marked the first time that the Court declared an act of Congress unconstitutional.

Maroons (p. 329) Escaped slaves who formed communities of runaways.

Marquis of Queensberry Rules (p. 509) Standardized boxing rules of the late nineteenth century, creating structured three-minute rounds with one-minute rest periods, outlawing wrestling throws and holds, and specifying the number of rounds.

Marshall Plan (p. 737) A massive foreign aid program to Western Europe of $17 billion over four years, beginning in 1948. Named after Secretary of State George Marshall, the program restored economic prosperity to the region and stabilized its system of democracy and capitalism.

Matrilineal (p. 8) Unlike European nations that were male based, or patrilineal, in organization, many Native American societies structured tribal and family power and authority through women. Quite often, use rights to land and personal property passed from mother to daughter, and the eldest women chose male chiefs. Matrilineal societies thus placed great importance on the capacities of women to provide for the long-term welfare of their tribes.

McCullouch v. Maryland (p. 231)   A landmark 1819 Supreme Court decision establishing Congress's power to charter a national bank and declaring unconstitutional a tax imposed by Maryland on the bank's Baltimore branch.

McKinley Tariff Act (p. 560)   An act passed to remove all tariffs on foreign sugar and placing a two-cent per pound bounty on American-produced sugar. The negative effect on Hawaiian sugar production helped Queen Liliuokalani in her drive to purge American influences in Hawaii.

Mercantilism (p. 63)   An economic system built on the assumption that the world's supply of wealth is fixed and that nations must export more goods than they import to assure a steady supply of gold and silver into national coffers. Mercantile thinkers saw the inflow of such wealth as the key to maintaining and enhancing national power and self-sufficiency. Within this context, the accumulation and development of colonies was of great importance, since colonies could supply scarce raw materials to parent nations and serve as markets for finished goods.

Mexican struggle for independence (p. 337)   Mexico's struggle against Spanish rule began in 1810 and independence was achieved in 1821.

Mexican-American War (p. 350)   A war between the United States and Mexico that took place between 1846 and 1848.

Military Reconstruction Act (p. 431)   A law passed after the South's refusal to accept the Fourteenth Amendment in 1867, it nullified existing state governments and divided the South into five military districts headed by military governors.

Mill towns (p. 474)   Established by factory owners to supply necessary goods and services for their workers, these towns often caused employees to become very dependent on the mills.

Millennium (p. 274)   In the biblical Book of Revelation, the millennium is a period of a thousand years during which Christ is to rule on Earth.

Mission system (p. 337)   A system used by the Spanish for colonial settlement, the mission system sought to convert the native population to Christianity and use its labor in farming, ranching, and handicrafts.

Missionary diplomacy (p. 601)   Name given to the diplomatic policy of Woodrow Wilson; it called for the United States to use its influence to promote democracy around the world.

Mississippi Plan (p. 542)   Provisions in the 1890 Mississippi constitution designed to disfranchise African Americans through poll taxes, literacy tests, and residency requirements. These provisions were widely copied by other southern states.

Missouri Compromise (pp. 242, 365)   An act passed by Congress in 1820 that admitted Missouri to the Union as a slave state and Maine as a free state, and prohibited slavery in the portion of the Louisiana Purchase north of Missouri's border.

Missouri crisis (p. 254)   The political debate that followed the 1819 proposal of Representative James Tallmadge of New York that Missouri be admitted to the Union only if it prohibited further slaves from entering the state and freed its slaves when they reached the age of 25.

Modern Republicanism (p. 760)   Also called *dynamic conservatism*, President Eisenhower's domestic agenda advocated conservative spending approaches without drastically cutting back New Deal social programs.

Molly Maguires (p. 479)   Leaders of a secret fraternal society of Irish immigrants, they waged guerilla warfare in the coalfields during 1877, disrupting the operation of several mines and attacking a few mining officials.

Monroe Doctrine (p. 233)   In this 1823 statement of American foreign policy, President James Monroe declared that the United States would not allow European powers to establish new colonies in the Western Hemisphere or to expand the boundaries of existing colonies.

Mormon church (p. 348)   The Church of Jesus Christ of Latter-Day Saints is a religious group organized by Joseph Smith, Jr., in 1830.

Mosinee's Red May Day (p. 744)   Mosinee, Wisconsin, became a communist puppet state for a day in 1950. The local American Legionnaires dressed up as Soviets and took over the town to try to illustrate what (according to them) life would be like in the United States under a Soviet-style government. This was one symptom of the Red Scare that would soon make communist-hunting also a sport in the United States.

Motion pictures (p. 514)   A revolutionary form of entertainment that came into being at the close of the nineteenth century. Using a series of still pictures projected fast enough onto a screen to produce the illusion of continuous action, they brought scenes and events that previously had been experienced only through still photography to life.

Mountain men (p. 340)   The name given to the buckskin-clad trappers, explorers, and traders who engaged in the fur trade in the early nineteenth century.

Muckrakers (p. 583)   Investigative journalists during the Progressive era, they wrote sensational exposés of social and political problems that helped spark the reform movements of their day.

Mugwumps (p. 525)   A reform faction of the Republican party in the 1870s and 1880s that crusaded for honest and effective government and sometimes supported Democratic reform candidates.

Muller v. Oregon (p. 582)   Case through which the Supreme Court in 1908, using social science research, upheld governments' rights to set limits to the working hours of women.

My Lai (p. 806)   A village in South Vietnam, scene of a massacre of unarmed civilians on February 25, 1968. The only person convicted of this crime was Lt. William Calley.

Nation of Islam (p. 822)   Founded by Wallace D. Fard during the Great Depression of the 1930s, the Nation of Islam emphasized black economic self-sufficiency and black nationalism under the leadership of Elijah Muhammad.

National American Woman Suffrage Association (p. 527) An organization formed in 1890 from two factions of the suffrage movement, NAWSA sought a constitutional amendment to grant women the right to vote throughout the nation, eventually leading to the Nineteenth Amendment.

National Anti-Cigarette League (p. 656) Organization formed in 1903, the embodiment of the movement to end cigarette smoking in the United States, closely allied with Prohibition. The group won success in many states but never nationally, and the movement dissipated by the end of the 1920s.

National Association for the Advancement of Colored People (NAACP) (pp. 590, 658) Organization established in 1909 to fight for African American civil rights through legal action.

National Child Labor Committee (p. 592) Founded in 1904 by Edgar Gardner Murphy and Florence Kelley, this organization fought to bring an end to child labor.

National Defense Education Act (p. 767) A reaction to the apparent lead in education held by the Soviets in light of their *Sputnik* space program. The aim of the act was to improve science and mathematical skills in the American school system.

National domain (p. 156) All territory west of the original thirteen states that was to be developed on behalf of the new American republic and, ultimately, made into new states. The national domain came into existence in the 1780s when the so-called landed states started to cede their sea-to-sea charter claims to the national government. See also *Landed states* and *Landless states*.

National Labor Union (p. 482) Founded in 1866, it was the first union to attempt to organize all workers, supported a variety of reform causes, but failed during the depression of the mid-1870s.

National Organization for Women (NOW) (p. 833) A feminist advocacy group, founded in 1966, that promotes equity for women in the workplace and reproductive rights, and opposes sexual harassment and violence against women.

National Origins Act of 1924 (pp. 497, 657) Law that restricted immigration to 2 percent for any given nationality, based on the total amounts from the 1890 census. Use of the 1890 census effectively restricted immigrants from eastern and southern Europe. Combined with the Emergency Quota Act, this law effectively stifled immigration from southern and eastern Europe and stopped Asian immigration completely.

National Recovery Administration (NRA) (p. 680) The federal government's plan to revive industry during the Great Depression through rational planning.

National Republicans (p. 255) The name that supporters of John Quincy Adams took following his defeat in the presidential election of 1828. National Republicans were committed to using the federal government to promote economic and social development.

National Security Council Paper Number 68 (NSC-68) (p. 741) Influential National Security Council document arguing communism was a monolithic world movement directed from the Kremlin and advocating a massive military buildup to counteract the encroachment of communism.

National System of Interstate and Defense Highways Act (p. 761) Legislation adapted in 1956 that created the national highway system of 41,000 miles, costing $26 billion and taking 13 years to construct. It solidified the central role of the automobile in American culture.

National Urban League (p. 658) Organization founded in 1911 by social workers, white philanthropists, and conservative African Americans on the basis of Booker T. Washington's conciliatory approach to race relations; that league concentrated on finding jobs for urban African Americans.

Nationalists (p. 156) Revolutionary leaders who favored a stronger national government than the one provided for in the Articles of Confederation. They believed that only a powerful national government, rather than self-serving states, could deal effectively with the many vexing problems besetting the new nation. George Washington, Alexander Hamilton, and James Madison were prominent nationalists.

Nativism (p. 494) A backlash against immigration by white native-born Protestants. Nativism could be based on racial prejudice (professors and scientists sometimes classified eastern Europeans as innately inferior), religion (Protestants distrusted Catholics and Jews), politics (immigrants were often associated with radical political philosophies), and economics (labor leaders resented competition).

Nativists (p. 371) People who are strongly hostile toward immigrants.

Naturalism (p. 505) Literary style of the late nineteenth and early twentieth century in which the individual was seen as a helpless victim in a world in which biological, social, and psychological forces determined his or her fate.

Navigation System (p. 63) To effect mercantilist goals, King and Parliament legislated a series of Navigation Acts (1651, 1660, 1663, 1673, 1696) that established England as the central hub of trade in its emerging empire. Various rules of trade, as embodied in the Navigation Acts, made it clear that England's colonies in the Americas existed first and foremost to serve the parent nation's economic interests, regardless of what might be best for the colonists.

Neutrality (p. 618) U.S. policy of impartiality during World Wars I and II.

New Deal (p. 676) President Franklin Delano Roosevelt's program designed to bring about economic recovery and reform during the Great Depression.

New Freedom (p. 597) A phrase used in the 1912 presidential election campaign to describe Woodrow Wilson's plan for restoring economic freedom by busting the trusts.

New Humanists (p. 689) Depression-era intellectuals who extolled classical civilization as a bulwark against modern values, exemplified by Lewis Mumford's 1934 work, *Technics and Civilization*.

New Left (p. 828) Collective term for the various political action youth groups that developed during the 1960s. Most of these groups were interested in ending the war in Vietnam and bringing about political change in the United States.

New Lights (p. 82) As the Great Awakening spread during the 1730s and 1740s, various religious groups fractured into two camps, sometimes known as the New Lights and Old Lights. The New Lights placed emphasis on a "new birth" conversion experience—gaining God's saving grace. They also demanded ministers who had clearly experienced conversions themselves. See *Old Lights*.

New Look (p. 763)   President Eisenhower's adjustment to the doctrine of containment. He advocated saving money by emphasizing nuclear over conventional weapons, on the premise that the next major world conflict would be nuclear.

New Nationalism (p. 597)   Slogan used by Theodore Roosevelt in the 1912 presidential election campaign to describe his plan for combating the power of big corporations through government regulation rather than trust busting.

New Navy (p. 557)   After the Civil War the United States Navy dwindled from first to near last among the industrialized nations. In the 1880s and 1890s a movement was undertaken to build new warships to be used to extend U.S. influence around the world. The debate over the building of these ships echoed the debate over U.S. involvement in the world at large.

New Orleans, Battle of (p. 220)   In January 1815, a ragtag army consisting of frontier fighters, pirates, and freed slaves under the command of Andrew Jackson decisively defeated a British force trying to capture New Orleans. The battle took place after the signing of the Treaty of Ghent, which ended the War of 1812.

New South (p. 473)   The ideology following Reconstruction that the South could be restored to its previous glory through a diversified economy; it was used to rally Southerners and convince outside investors to underwrite regional industrialization by extolling the resources, labor supply, and racial harmony of the South.

Niagara movement (p. 589)   Begun in 1905 by W. E. B. Du Bois and William Monroe Trotter, this group sought to counteract the accommodationist program of Booker T. Washington, helping to set the stage for the organization of the National Association for the Advancement of Colored People (NAACP).

1963 March on Washington (p. 821)   In 1963, some 250,000 demonstrators marched on Washington to demand passage of meaningful civil rights legislation, an end to school segregation and police brutality, a federal law ending discrimination in the workplace, self-government for the District of Columbia, and an increase in the minimum wage and public works programs for the unemployed. This landmark civil rights protest ended with hundreds of thousands of people congregated on Capitol Mall in Washington, D.C., to hear, among others, Dr. Martin Luther King, Jr., deliver his "I have a dream" speech.

Nineteenth Amendment (p. 653)   Passed in 1920, the Constitutional guarantee of women's right to vote.

Nixon Doctrine (p. 800)   President Richard Nixon's argument in favor of "Vietnamization," the notion that the South Vietnamese would carry more of the war's combat burden. This plan never reached full realization because of the South Vietnamese inability to carry on the war effort without American troops.

Non-Intercourse Act (p. 213)   An 1809 statute that replaced the Embargo of 1807. It forbade trade with Britain, France, and their possessions, but reopened trade with other countries.

Nonseparatists (p. 39)   Religious dissenters from England who wanted to purify, rather than separate from, what they viewed as the corrupted, state-supported Anglican church, or Church of England. By and large, the Puritans were nonseparatists, and some of them banded together to form a utopian community of believers in America. The Massachusetts Bay Colony was to be a model society that would show how godly societies and churches were to be properly organized. See *Separatists*.

North American Free Trade Agreement (NAFTA) (p. 900)   A 1994 agreement that reduced trade barriers between the United States, Canada, and Mexico.

North Atlantic Treaty Organization (NATO) (p. 739)   An organization founded in 1949 whose members signed a mutual defense pact to protect those countries bordering the North Atlantic, or having need to traverse it frequently. As these countries were the United States and its allies and the main threat to those countries was the Soviet Union, the purpose of NATO, defense against a Soviet attack on Western Europe, was clear. In response to the creation of NATO, the Soviet Union invited its communist allies in Europe to join the Warsaw Pact.

Northern Confederacy (p. 211)   Fearful that the Louisiana Purchase of 1803 would reduce their region's political influence, a number of Federalists plotted to establish an independent confederacy that would include New Jersey, New York, and New England. The scheme was repudiated by Alexander Hamilton.

Northwest Passage (p. 19)   During the Age of Exploration, adventurers from England, France, and the Netherlands sought an all-water route across North America. The goal was to gain access to Oriental material goods and riches while avoiding contact with the developing Spanish empire farther to the south in Central and South America.

Nullification (p. 256)   The doctrine, devised by John C. Calhoun, that a state has the power to "nullify" federal legislation within its borders.

Office of Price Administration (OPA) (p. 708)   Office formed in 1942 that had the authority to freeze prices and wages, control rents, and institute rationing of scarce items during World War II.

Ohio Gang (p. 660)   Friends and cronies of President Warren G. Harding who received governmental jobs during his term and subsequently plunged his administration into disgrace.

Oil crisis (p. 879)   Oil supply disruptions and soaring oil prices that the United States experienced in 1973 and 1979. In 1973, Middle Eastern nations imposed an embargo on oil shipments to punish the West for supporting Israel in that year's Arab-Israeli war. A second oil shock occurred when the Iranian Revolution disrupted oil shipments to the western nations.

Old Lights (p. 82)   As the Great Awakening spread during the 1730s and 1740s, various religious groups fractured into two camps, sometimes known as the Old Lights and the New Lights. The Old Lights were not very enthusiastic about the Awakening, particularly in terms of what they viewed as popular excesses in seeking after God's grace. Old Light ministers emphasized formal schooling in theology as a source of their religious authority, and they emphasized good order in their churches. See *New Lights.*

Open Door note (p. 572)   Policy set forth in 1899 by Secretary of State John Hay preventing further partitioning of China by European powers, and protecting the principle of free trade.

Operation Just Cause (p. 902)   Name given to an American military intervention in Panama in December 1989, which was launched after Panama's leader, Manuel Noriega, who was indicted on drug-related charges, invalidated civilian elections and declared a state of war with the United States.

Opium and cocaine (p. 515)   Two drugs that were beginning to have an impact on the social structure of the United States as early as the 1890s. The unrestricted and uncontrolled sale of these drugs caused concern that they were linked to crime and racial unrest.

Orders in Council (p. 212)   British government policies that imposed an economic blockade on European ports during the Napoleonic wars.

Oregon country (p. 345)   The United States and Britain both claimed territory in the Pacific Northwest. In 1846 they agreed to divide the territory along the 49th parallel.

Oregon Trail (p. 342)   Westward pioneer route stretching 2,000 miles from Missouri to the mouth of the Columbia River on the Pacific Coast.

Ostend Manifesto (p. 373)   A plan devised in 1854 by three U.S. diplomats, including future president James Buchanan, to purchase or seize Cuba and its 300,000 slaves.

Pale of Settlement (p. 493)   Area of settlement for Polish Jews after Russia conquered Poland in the eighteenth century. This area was a ghetto for over 90 percent of Russian Jews and was the only area where they were allowed to live without special permit. Increasing repression of their religion in Russia caused large numbers of Russian Jews to emigrate to the United States and other countries "beyond the Pale."

Paleo-Indians (p. 5)   Those nomadic people who first came to the Americas via the land bridge from Asia and traveled in small bands while constantly searching for food.

Panama Canal Treaty (p. 882)   A 1977 treaty providing for transfer of control of the Panama Canal to Panamanians by 2000.

Panic of 1819 (pp. 239, 254)   A financial panic that brought the economic expansion that followed the War of 1812 to a close and resulted in bank failures, mortgage foreclosures, and widespread unemployment.

Panic of 1837 (p. 264)   A financial depression that lasted until the early 1840s.

Panic of 1873 (p. 442)   A financial collapse caused by overinvestment in railroads that ushered in a six-year economic depression.

Panic of 1893 (p. 538)   Caused primarily by a European depression, coupled with overexpansion of the American economy, this stock market crash ushered in one of the nation's worse depressions.

Paternalism (p. 323)   The belief held by many slaveowners in the pre–Civil War South that slaveholding was a duty and a burden and that they had to care for and discipline slaves as parents do children.

Patriarchal (p. 48)   Patriarchal social and political systems are denoted by power and authority residing in males, such as the father of the family. Such authority then passes from father to son through the generations, and males, in general, control decision making. See *coverture.*

Patrons of Husbandry (p. 535)   An organization founded in 1867 to aid farmers through its local granges; it was responsible for state laws regulating railroads, established cooperatives to help with marketing problems, and provided a social outlet for rural areas. Officially entitled the National Grange of the Patrons of Husbandry, the organization was also known as the *Granger movement,* and its local branches were called *granges.*

Peace without victory (p. 623)   President Woodrow Wilson's plan for a peaceful postwar world order, to be maintained by a League of Nations.

Peaceful coexistence (p. 764)   An attempt to warm the Cold War, in which Eisenhower and Khrushchev sought to improve relations between their countries. Incidents such as the U-2 shoot-down over the USSR and the Cuban missile crisis strained this policy.

Pearl Harbor (p. 706)   The main base of the U.S. Pacific fleet, which Japan attacked on December 7, 1941. Following that attack, the United States entered World War II.

Pendleton Act (p. 530)   A law passed in 1883 to eliminate political corruption in the federal government, it outlawed political contributions by appointed officeholders and established the Civil Service Commission to administer competitive examinations for coveted government jobs.

Permanent immigrants (p. 493)   Immigrants coming to America to settle permanently, often due to ethnic and religious persecution at home.

Perpetual servitude (p. 53)   Indentured servitude represented temporary service for a specified period, usually from four to seven years, to a legally designated owner. Perpetual servitude meant being owned by some other person for life—and ultimately, even through the generations. In the early days of Virginia, both English subjects and African Americans were indentured servants, but over time blacks would be subjected to perpetual servitude as chattel, defined as the movable property of their all-powerful masters and without legal rights of any kind.

Philippine Islands (p. 565)   A group of over 4,000 islands in the western Pacific, owned by Spain prior to the Spanish-American War. The Filipino struggle for independence from Spain shifted to resistance against U.S. occupation of the islands after the war.

Ping-pong diplomacy (p. 803)   Communist China's chairman Mao Tse-tung sent a table tennis team to the world championships in Nagoya, Japan, and then invited an American team to compete in Japan in 1971. This small gesture paved the way for President Nixon's visit to China in February 1972.

Planned urban growth (p. 503)   Ultimately this was a proposal that the city should serve the public (the public city), differing from earlier views that the city should cater to the wealthy and ambitious (the private city). City planners looked at the city as a place where ordinary people, with families and lives to live, resided. Such a place would have to include plans for a healthy environment for those people. Inclusion of parks, schools, and public services were part of the public city ideal, but much work would be needed to recover from the private city concept.

Plantation legend (p. 318)   A stereotype, created by popular pre–Civil War writers, that depicted the South as a region of aristocratic planters, beautiful Southern belles, poor white trash, and faithful household slaves.

Platt Amendment (p. 567)   An amendment to the Army Appropriation Bill in 1901, limiting Cuban independence by giving the United States two naval bases on Cuba and the right to intervene in Cuban affairs if the American government felt Cuban independence was threatened.

Plessy v. Ferguson (pp. 475, 593)   A Supreme Court decision in 1896 that ruled "separate but equal" facilities for African Americans were constitutional under the Fourteenth Amendment; it had the effect of legalizing segregation and led to the passage of much discriminatory legislation known as Jim Crow laws.

Political slavery (p. 111)   During the 1760s and 1770s many colonial leaders believed that if they did not keep resisting unwanted British policies, they would fall into a state of political slavery in which they had no liberties. As such, they would be akin to chattel slaves in their midst. Comprehending how potentially tyrannical chattel slavery was spurred on many colonists to defend American liberties, even to the point of open rebellion.

Ponzi scheme (p. 662)   Scheme in which Charles Ponzi promised to return $15 to anyone who lent him $10 for 90 days in order to buy foreign currencies at low prices and sell them for higher prices. Ponzi received $15 million in eight months and returned less than $200,000 to investors.

Pools (p. 462)   Agreements among railroad administrators to divide the total volume of freight among their lines, usually to be able to raise prices.

Popular sovereignty (p. 365)   The principle, incorporated into the Compromise of 1850 and the Kansas-Nebraska Act of 1854, that the people living in the western territories should decide whether or not to permit slavery.

Populist (People's) party (p. 537)   A political party established in 1892 primarily by remnants of the Farmers' Alliance and Greenback party, it sought to inflate the currency with silver dollars and to establish an income tax; some of its platform was adopted by the Democrats in 1896, and it died out after the defeat of joint candidate William Jennings Bryan.

Port Huron Statement (p. 828)   The founding document of the Students for a Democratic Society (SDS), adopted in June 1962, it attacked racial discrimination, alienating work, and uncontrolled exploitation of natural resources. The statement also called for participatory democracy and the active involvement of citizens in decisions that might affect their lives.

Potsdam Conference (p. 721)   Suburb of Berlin where Allied leaders convened in July 1945 for their last wartime meeting of World War II, the first test for President Truman. The Potsdam Declaration de-

manded that Japan immediately surrender and that any other action would lead to "prompt and utter destruction."

Pragmatism (p. 582)   A distinctly American philosophy proposed by William James, it contends that any concept should be tested and its validity determined by its outcome and that the truth of an idea is found in the conduct it dictates or inspires.

Price Revolution (p. 22)   The large influx of gold and silver into Europe from Spanish America during the sixteenth century, along with increased demand for limited supplies of goods, set off a threefold rise in prices (the "great inflation") that caused profound economic turmoil, social disruption, and political instability among European peoples and nations.

Progressive (Bull Moose) party (p. 597)   A political party established in 1912 by supporters of Theodore Roosevelt after William H. Taft won the Republican presidential nomination. The party proposed a broad program of reform but Bull Moose candidate Roosevelt and Republican nominee Taft lost to the Democratic candidate, Woodrow Wilson.

Prohibition (p. 656)   The ban of the production, sale, and consumption of alcoholic beverages. The Eighteenth Amendment to the U.S. Constitution, adopted in 1919, established prohibition. The amendment was repealed in 1933, with adoption of the Twenty-first Amendment.

Protestant Reformation (p. 19)   A religious reform movement formally begun in 1517 when the German friar Martin Luther openly attacked abuses of Roman Catholic doctrine. Luther contended that the people could read scripture for themselves in seeking God's grace and that the Bible, not church doctrine, was the ultimate authority in human relationships. Luther's complaints helped foster a variety of dissenting religious groups, some of which would settle in America to get away from various forms of oppression in Europe.

Public virtue (p. 133)   A cornerstone of good citizenship in republican states, public virtue involved the subordination of individual self-interest to serving the greater good of the whole community. Revolutionary leaders believed that public virtue was essential for a republic to survive and thrive. If absent, governments would be torn apart by competing private interests and succumb to anarchy, at which point tyrants would emerge to offer political stability but with the loss of dearly won political liberties.

Public Works Administration (PWA) (p. 681)   One of many works programs under the Federal Emergency Relief Act of the New Deal, which hired unemployed workers for various public projects, thus providing people with money to spend on industrial products.

Pullman strike (p. 541)   Called by the American Railway Union in 1894, this strike at the Pullman plant at Chicago was defeated by the use of federal troops.

Purity crusaders (p. 586)   Beginning in the 1890s, these people sought the prohibition of alcohol and prostitution and supported censorship and the regulation of narcotics.

Quasi War with France (p. 195)   An undeclared naval war fought entirely at sea by the United States and France between 1798 and 1801.

Radical Republicans (p. 426)   A faction of the Republican Party during Reconstruction, the Radicals favored forcing the former Confederate states to make fundamental changes before they could be readmitted to the Union. Eventually the Radicals won control of the Republican party because of Southerners' refusal to accept more lenient plans for Reconstruction.

Radical revolutionaries (p. 154)   At the time of the American Revolution, this group argued in favor of establishing more democratic forms of government. Radical revolutionaries had a strong trust in the people, viewed them as inherently virtuous (see *Public virtue*), and believed that citizens could govern themselves. Samuel Adams, Thomas Jefferson, and Thomas Paine might be described as radical revolutionaries. See *Cautious revolutionaries.*

Rage militaire (p. 122)   A term meaning a passion for arms, the rage militaire characterized the attitudes of American colonists as the war with Great Britain began in 1775. When the ravages and deprivations of warfare became more self-evident, however, this early enthusiasm gave out. In 1776 Thomas Paine criticized the "summer soldiers and sunshine patriots" among the colonists who seemed so eager to fight at the beginning of the War for Independence but who so quickly dropped out as the dangers of engaging in warfare increased.

Rationalism (p. 78)   A main tenet of the Enlightenment era, meaning a firm trust in the ability of the human mind to solve earthly problems, thereby lessening the role of—and reliance on—God as an active force in the ordering of human affairs.

Reagan Doctrine (p. 885)   President Ronald Reagan's 1985 pledge of American aid to insurgent movements attempting to overthrow Soviet-backed regimes in the Third World.

Rebates (p. 462)   Discounts from the normal shipping rate, they were given by the railroads to attract business in the middle of the 19th century.

Reconstruction Finance Corporation (RFC) (p. 673)   Corporation created by Congress in 1932 and authorized to loan $2 billion to banks, savings and loan associations, railroads, and life insurance companies in the hopes of spurring production and hiring in the private sector.

Red Scare (p. 633)   Fear of radicalism and Communism following World War I, triggered by labor strikes and bombings which resulted in widespread vigilantism as well as extreme measures by government.

Redeemer governments (p. 441)   A popular name for the Democratic state governments in the South that replaced the Republican-dominated ones established during Reconstruction.

Redemptioners (p. 74)   The redemptioner labor system was similar to that of indentured servitude in providing a way for persons without financial means to get to America. Normally, the family had to locate someone to pay for its passage in return for a set number of years of labor. If no buyer could be found, then ships captains could sell the family's labor, most likely on less desirable terms for the family, to recoup the costs of passage. Thousands of Germans migrated to America as redemptioners in the eighteenth century.

Referendum   See *Initiative and Referendum.*

Reform Darwinists (p. 581)   Sociologists who rejected the determinism of the Social Darwinists, they accepted evolutionary theory but held that people could shape their environment rather than only be shaped by it and accepted human intervention in society.

Religious liberalism (p. 273)   A religious viewpoint that rejected the Calvinist doctrines of original sin and predestination and stressed the basic goodness of human nature.

Remember the *Maine*! (p. 564)   A national catch phrase following the mysterious 1898 explosion of the U.S. battleship *Maine* in Havana harbor that inflamed public opinion, leading to the Spanish-American War.

Removal (Indian Removal Policy) (p. 258)   A policy of resettling eastern Indian tribes on lands west of the Mississippi River.

Renaissance (p. 10)   Beginning in the 1400s, the European Renaissance represented an intellectual and cultural flowering in the arts, literature, philosophy, and the sciences. One of the most important tenets of the Renaissance was the belief in human progress, or the betterment of society.

Rendezvous system (p. 340)   Between 1825 and 1840, fur companies held gatherings where fur trappers could trade their skins for supplies.

Republican motherhood (p. 165)   This definition of motherhood, emanating from the American Revolution, assigned mothers the task of raising dutiful children, especially sons, who would be prepared to serve the nation in disinterested fashion (see *Public virtue).* Mothers thus acquired the special charge of assuring that future generations could uphold the tenets of republicanism. This expanded role for mothers meant that women, not men, would be responsible for the domestic sphere of life.

Republican party (p. 374)   A political party established following enactment of the Kansas-Nebraska Act of 1854 that was opposed to the extension of slavery into the western territories.

Republican values (p. 205)   A set of values widely held during the Revolutionary and post-Revolutionary eras that the new nation's survival depended upon nurturing virtue and goodness of character among its citizens.

Republicanism (p. 153)   At the time of the American Revolution, republicanism referred to the concept that sovereignty, or ultimate political authority, is vested in the people—the citizens of the nation. As such, republican governments not only derive their authority from the consent of the governed but also predicate themselves on the principles of rule by law and legislation by elected representatives.

Restrictive covenant (p. 646)   A formal deed restriction that bound white property owners in a given neighborhood to sell only to whites.

Resumption Act of 1875 (p. 529)   This act required that all paper money of the United States be backed by either gold or silver.

Revenue Act of 1942 (p. 708)   World War II measure that raised corporate taxes, increased the excess profits tax, and levied a 5 percent withholding tax on anyone earning over $642 a year; it attempted to slow inflation by reducing consumer purchasing power.

Rock and roll (p. 777)   Musical style new to the 1950s, combining black rhythm and blues with white country music. Listened to mostly by young Americans and embodied by Elvis Presley, the music challenged notions of sexual propriety and racial division.

Roderigue Hortalez & Cie. (p. 139)   Prior to its formal involvement in the War for Independence, the French government supplied the American rebels with critically needed war goods through a bogus private trading firm known as Roderigue Hortalez & Cie. French officials did so because they hoped to see the power of Great Britain reduced but without becoming directly engaged in the war itself. Once the Franco-American alliance came into being in 1778, the French could abandon such ruses in favor of open support of their rebel allies.

Roe v. Wade (p. 834)   A case from Texas that was heard before the Supreme Court in 1973 and considered whether a woman had the right to an abortion. The Court decision was that the decision to have an abortion was a private matter of concern only to the woman and her physician, and that only in the last three months of pregnancy could the government limit the right to abortion.

Roosevelt recession (p. 689)   Economic relapse following the 1936 elections when industrial production fell by 40 percent and unemployment rose by 4 million.

Rough Riders (p. 568)   A group of volunteer cavalry led by Theodore Roosevelt during the Cuban campaign of the Spanish-American War.

Rwanda (p. 903)   A central African nation that was the site of the killing of approximately 800,000 Tutsis and moderate Hutus in 1994.

Sacco and Vanzetti case (p. 657)   Italian immigrants, anarchists Nicola Sacco and Bartolomeo Vanzetti were arrested and tried for the robbery and murders of two men in Braintree, Massachusetts. The state did not prove its case but won by exploiting the men's radical views. They were put to death on July 14, 1921.

Sagebrush rebellion (p. 868)   Failed movement led by conservative western politicians to cede federal control of western land to individual states, promoting private ownership and commercial development.

Salutary neglect (p. 73)   This term signifies England's relatively benign neglect of its American colonies from about 1690 to 1760. During these years King and Parliament rarely legislated constraints of any kind and allowed the colonists much autonomy in provincial and local matters. In turn, the colonists supported the parent nation's economic and political objectives. This harmonious period came to an end after the Seven Year's War when King and Parliament began asserting more control over the American colonists through taxes and trade regulations.

Samoa (p. 559)   Pacific island where the United States and Germany gathered warships in 1889. Both sides wanted control of the island as a coaling station, but a typhoon blew both fleets about badly and the Germans withdrew.

Santa Fe Trail (p. 341)   Westward trading route stretching southward from Missouri to Santa Fe, New Mexico, which William Becknell started in 1821.

Scalawags (p. 435)   Southern white Republicans during Reconstruction, they came from every class and had a variety of motives but were pictured by their opponents as ignorant and degraded.

Scopes "Monkey Trial" (p. 656)   Trial against John Scopes in 1925 for teaching Charles Darwin's theory of evolution in a Tennessee public school.

Second Bank of the United States (pp. 229, 264)   A national bank chartered in 1816 to hold government funds, ease the transfer of money across state lines, and regulate private banks. Its federal charter expired in 1836.

Second Continental Congress (p. 125)   This body gathered in Philadelphia during May 1775 after the shooting war with Great Britain had started. The second Congress functioned as a coordinating government for the colonies and states in providing overall direction to the patriot war effort. It continued as a central legislative body under the Articles of Confederation until 1789 when a new national legislature, the federal Congress as established under the Constitution of 1787, first convened.

Second Great Awakening (p. 274)   A wave of religious fervor and revivalism that swept the United States from the early nineteenth century through the Civil War.

Second New Deal (p. 685)   The second stage of President Franklin Delano Roosevelt's economic recovery and reform program, launched January 4, 1935.

Second party system (p. 254)   A new two-party system, pitting the Democrats against the Whigs, had appeared by 1834. The two parties began to split over the issue of slavery during the 1840s and the second party system came to an end in the early 1850s.

Sedition Act (p. 627)   Law passed in 1918 which expanded the Espionage Act of 1917 and made a federal offense of using "disloyal, profane, scurrilous, or abusive language" about the Constitution, the government, the American uniform, or the flag.

Separatists (p. 39)   Religious dissenters from England who believed that the state-supported Anglican church, or Church of England, was too corrupt to be reformed. Thus, like the Pilgrims, they often migrated elsewhere to form their own religious communities. See *Nonseparatists.*

Settlement house movement (p. 587)   A reform movement growing out of Jane Addams's Hull House in the late nineteenth century, it led to the formation of community centers in which mainly middle-class women sought to meet the needs of recent immigrants to urban centers.

Shakers (p. 286)   A religious group that called itself the United Society of Believers and originated in England in the mid-eighteenth century, the Shakers emphasized celibacy, sexual equality, and communal living.

Shamans (p. 8)   Shamans were medicine men in Native American cultures. Sometimes called "powwows," shamans kept the lore of taboos to help guard against the overexploitation of nature, and they prescribed various rituals and medicines to help preserve and restore good health.

Sharecropping (pp. 438, 472)   A system of labor to replace slavery that allowed landless farmers to work the land of others for a share of the crops they produced. It was favored by freedpeople over gang labor but sometimes led to virtual peonage.

Shaysites (p. 161)   Beset by a hard-hitting economic depression after the War for American Independence, these farmers from western Massachusetts finally rose up in rebellion against their state government in 1786 because they had failed to obtain tax relief. One leader of the uprising was Daniel Shays, from whom the Shaysites derived their name.

Sherman Antitrust Act (p. 532)   A law passed in 1890 to break up trusts and monopolies, it was rarely enforced except against labor unions and most of its power was stripped away by the Supreme Court, but it began federal attempts to prevent unfair, anticompetitive business practices.

Sherman Silver Purchase Act (p. 532)   Passed in 1890 in response to popular pressure, this act required the government to purchase 4.5 million ounces of silver each month at the ratio of 16 to 1.

Sit-in (p. 816)   A tactic of nonviolent direct action originally used by labor unions during the Great Depression; civil rights activists adopted this method of resistance to protest segregation in whites-only facilities.

Sixteen to one (16 to 1) (p. 529)   Referring to the mint ratio between silver and gold, this became a rallying cry for those who favored the expansion of the currency.

Skyscraper (p. 499)   Buildings with steel frameworks that exceeded the previous limitations of brick buildings. The lighter and stronger steel skeletons allowed structures to climb above the seven-story maximum. Architect William LeBaron Jenny's first skyscraper was ten stories tall. Cities could now build up instead of out, concentrating people and business in small areas.

Slave codes (p. 324)   Legal codes that defined the slaveholders' power and the slaves' status as property.

Smog (p. 860)   The chemical-laden fog caused by automobile engines, a serious problem in southern California. Like nuclear waste and the shrinking water supply, it reflects the problems associated with the rapid population shift to the West in modern times.

Social bandit (p. 335)   A Robin Hood–like figure who defends poor people against exploitation.

Social Darwinism (pp. 458, 554)   The application of Charles Darwin's evolutionary theories of natural selection and "survival of the fittest" to racial and social groups; it justified the concentration of wealth and lack of governmental protection of the weak. In the late 19th and early 20th centuries Social Darwinism was used to justify racism.

Social Gospel (p. 582)   A movement among Christian theologians, it applied Christian doctrines to social problems and advocated creating living conditions conducive to saving souls by tackling the problems of the poor.

Social Security Act (p. 684)   New Deal legislation enacted in 1935 to provide monthly stipends for workers aged 65 or older and to provide assistance to the indigent elderly, blind and handicapped persons, and dependent children who did not have a wage-earning parent. The act also established the nation's first federally funded system of unemployment insurance.

Southern Agrarians (p. 689)   Eleven white southern intellectuals who issued "I'll Take My Stand," a manifesto that urged a return to the agrarian way of life in light of the Great Depression.

Southern strategy (p. 142)   Once France formally entered the War for Independence in 1778 on the American side, the British had to concern themselves with protecting such vital holdings as their sugar islands in the Caribbean region. Needing to disperse their troop strength, the idea of the Southern strategy was to tap into a perceived reservoir of loyalist numbers in the southern colonies. Reduced British forces could employ these loyalists as troops in subduing the rebels and as civil officials in reestablishing royal governments. The plan failed for many reasons, including a shortfall of loyalist support and an inability to hold ground once conquered in places like South Carolina.

Spanish-American War (p. 565)   The 1898 war between Spain and the United States regarding the fate of Cuba. As a result of the war, Cuba gained independence and America acquired the Philippines and Puerto Rico.

Special Field Order 15 (p. 426)   An 1865 order issued by Union General William T. Sherman that set aside a strip of abandoned lands from Charleston, South Carolina, to Jacksonville, Florida, to be divided up into 40-acre lots for the use of the exslaves.

Specie (p. 93)   A term for hard coin, such as gold or silver, that can also back and give a fixed point of valuation to paper currencies.

Spirituals (p. 328)   Religious songs composed by enslaved African Americans.

Spoils system (pp. 257, 530)   The policy of awarding political or financial help with a government job. Abuses of the spoils system led to the passage in 1883 of the Pendleton Act, which created the Civil Service Commission to award government jobs on the basis of merit.

Sputnik (p. 766)   Russian satellite that successfully orbited the earth in 1957, prompting Americans to question their own values and educational system. The hysteria over Soviet technological superiority led to the 1958 National Defense Education Act.

Stagflation (p. 880)   The economic conditions of slow economic growth, rising inflation, and flagging productivity that characterized the American economy during the 1970s.

Stalwarts and Half-breeds (p. 525)   Two factions of the Republican party in the late nineteenth century, they were primarily focused on which group would get government jobs.

Stamp Act Congress (p. 102)   This intercolonial body of political leaders from nine colonies met for a few days in October 1765 to consider ways to protest the Stamp Act. The delegates drafted a petition declaring that Parliament should not tax Americans, since they were not represented in that legislative body. The Congress showed that the colonies, when aggrieved, could act in unity, an important precedent for further intercolonial resistance efforts in years to come.

States' rights (p. 263)   The doctrine that the states possess certain rights and powers that supersede those of the federal government.

Storyville (p. 507)   The red-light district of New Orleans, Louisiana, a major area of development for jazz music.

Strategic Arms Limitation Treaty of 1972 (SALT I) (p. 803)   Arms control treaty signed by President Richard

Nixon and Soviet premier Leonid Brezhnev. Although it froze the deployment only of relatively inconsequential intercontinental ballistic missiles, this first treaty would lead to more comprehensive arms reduction treaties in the future.

Streetcar suburbs (p. 499)   Residential areas outside the urban center that were made accessible by mass transit. In the last part of the nineteenth century the people who could afford suburban real estate, the upper and middle classes, fled the ever more crowded cities and left the poorer classes behind. This economic division exacerbated the social and political divisions developing at the time.

Strict construction (p. 185)   The view that the powers of the national government are limited to those described in the U.S. Constitution.

Student Nonviolent Coordinating Committee (SNCC) (p. 817)   A civil rights organization formed in 1960 to coordinate nonviolent direct-action, such as sit-ins and voter-registration and desegregation campaigns in the South.

Students for a Democratic Society (SDS) (pp. 796, 828)   Founded in Port Huron, Michigan, in 1962, this radical organization aimed to rid American society of poverty, racism, and violence through an individually oriented approach called participatory democracy. By 1968, the organization had over 100,000 followers and was responsible for demonstrations at nearly 1000 colleges.

Submarine warfare (p. 619)   War waged by submarines, silent underground vessels that Germany introduced during World War I. Submarine tactics violated international law since they attacked from under water and depended on the element of surprise.

Suburban threat (p. 776)   A growing fear in the 1950s that the sameness of the suburban landscape would cause the residents to become homogeneous to the point of losing their individuality. Critics pointed out that people in the cities had very similar problems and that the phenomenon was overstated.

Suez Canal Crisis (p. 765)   Egyptian President Gamal Abdel Nasser nationalized the Suez Canal in 1956 after the United States withdrew a promised loan when Nasser appeared to be making friends with the Soviets. England and France responded by occupying the canal, and Israel invaded Egypt. The United States refused to support the Europeans and the invading parties withdrew.

***Sussex* pledge** (p. 622)   Agreement between Germany and the United States during World War I in which Germany promised not to launch surprise submarine attacks on passenger and merchant ships. The pledge was the result of the U.S. threat to sever diplomatic ties with Germany following the March 24, 1916, attack on the *Sussex*, an unarmed French passenger ship that was carrying several Americans.

Taft-Hartley Act (p. 745)   Legislation in 1947 that reflected the conservative postwar mood. It outlawed the closed shop, gave presidential power to delay strikes with a "cooling-off" period, and curtailed the political and economic power of organized labor.

Taliban (p. 906)   An Islamic fundamentalist political and military movement, intensely hostile to both Communism and Western (including U.S.) interests, that

seized control of Afghanistan during the 1990's. Following the terrorist attacks of September 11, 2001, U. S. armed forces entered Afghanistan and overthrew the Taliban in retaliation for their having allowed the terrorist network al-Qaeda to use Afghan territory for military purposes.

Tariff of Abominations (p. 256)   An 1828 protective tariff opposed by many Southerners.

Task system (p. 325)   A system of plantation labor found mainly on rice plantations in which each field hand was given a specific daily work assignment. See *Gang system.*

Teapot Dome scandal (p. 660)   Scandal in which President Warren G. Harding's Secretary of the Interior Albert B. Fall was convicted of accepting large bribes in exchange for leasing drilling rights on federal naval oil reserves. This was the first conviction of a cabinet member for crimes in office.

Temperance (p. 276)   The pre-Civil War reform movement that sought to curb the drinking of hard liquor.

Ten percent plan (p. 427)   Lincoln's plan for Reconstruction in December 1863 that provided for the readmission to the Union of the former Confederate states. It stated that when 10 percent of a state's 1860 voters took an oath of loyalty, a civilian government could be formed.

Tennessee Valley Authority (TVA) (p. 679)   Organization established by Congress in May 1933 to build 21 dams to generate electricity for tens of thousands of farm families and to develop the region in other ways. In 1935 President Franklin D. Roosevelt signed an executive order to create the Rural Electrification Administration to bring the electricity generated by government dams to America's hinterland.

Tenure of Office Act (p. 431)   Enacted in 1867, the law required the president to get the consent of the Senate before removing certain appointed officers. The goal was to prevent President Andrew Johnson from removing Secretary of War Edwin Stanton and became a basis for Johnson's impeachment by the House of Representatives.

Tet offensive (p. 794)   As American military and political leaders suggested victory in Vietnam was in sight, North Vietnam launched an offensive in January 1968 against major South Vietnamese targets. Although the United States repelled the Tet offensive, it prompted waves of criticism from those who felt the government had been misleading the American people.

Texas annexation (p. 345)   Following the Texas Revolution, a treaty that would have annexed Texas to the United States failed to pass. Texas remained an independent republic until 1845, when a convention voted to accept a joint congressional resolution admitting Texas to the Union.

Tippecanoe, Battle of (p. 214)   An 1811 battle in which an American force under William Henry Harrison defeated an Indian confederacy led by the Shawnee Prophet Tenskwatawa.

Tory (p. 131)   In England during the eighteenth century the Tory party was closely identified with the king's interests and monarchism, or in the minds of many American patriots, with tyrannical government. As the Revolution dawned, tory became a term of derision applied to those colonists who sought to maintain their allegiance to the British crown. They preferred to think of themselves as loyalists, since they were not rebelling against but were still supporting British imperial authority in America.

Total War (p. 403)   As opposed to limited war, total war usually denotes a military conflict in which warfare ultimately affects the entire population, civilian as well as military. The American Civil War, at least in its latter stages, might serve as an example of total war because of the destruction of both military and civilian resources in the South by Union armies operating under General Grant and especially General Sherman during 1864 and 1865.

Trail of Tears (p. 259)   The forced migration of the Cherokee Indians in 1838 and 1839 from western Georgia to Oklahoma resulted in the deaths of some 4,000 people.

Transcendentalists (p. 288)   A group of New England intellectuals who glorified nature and believed that each person contains godlike potentialities.

Treaty of Ghent (p. 220)   This 1814 treaty ended the War of 1812.

Treaty of Guadalupe Hidalgo (p. 353)   The peace agreement that ended the Mexican-American War, under which Mexico recognized the Rio Grande as the boundary with Texas and ceded to the United States California, Nevada, New Mexico, Utah, and parts of Arizona, Colorado, Kansas, and Wyoming in exchange for $15 million and the assumption of $3.25 million in debts owed to Americans by Mexico.

Treaty of Versailles (p. 637)   The treaty that ended World War I.

Triangle Shirtwaist Company (p. 592)   A fire at this company on March 25, 1911, which killed 147 workers—most of them women—opened the eyes of many Americans to workplace dangers, leading to pressure for reform.

Truman Doctrine (p. 737)   President Truman made a speech in March 1947 and set the course of U.S. foreign policy for the next generation, painting international affairs as a struggle between free democratic governments and tyrannical communist governments, and advocating American intervention to protect democratic governments.

Trust (p. 463)   A form of business organization that allowed a single board of trustees to oversee competing firms; the term came to apply when any single entity had the power to control competition within a given industry, such as oil production.

Twenty-Fourth Amendment (p. 822)   This amendment, adopted in 1964, barred a poll tax in federal elections.

U-2 spy planes (p. 781)   Ultra-high flying surveillance aircraft used by the United States to take reconnaissance photos. The U.S. government denied that the planes were flying over Russia until one was shot down and the pilot captured. The incident caused a downturn in U.S.-Soviet relations.

UN police action (p. 742)   President Truman's term for the war in Korea. As the Soviet member of the UN Security Council was absent when the vote was taken to send troops to aid South Korea, the United Nations was officially against the North Korean aggression. Many UN members sent at least token forces to assist

in the war, and the UN resolution gave legitimacy to the U.S.-led resistance to the spread of communism in this theater.

Underground Railroad (p. 370)   The routes used by enslaved African Americans to escape from slavery. Some escapes were made by individuals or small groups who fled on their own; other escapes were highly organized.

United Farm Workers (p. 835)   This union of agricultural workers came into being in 1966 as a result of a merger between the Agricultural Workers Organizing Committee, established in 1959 by the AFL-CIO, and the National Farm Workers Association, started by César Chávez and Dolores Huerta in 1962. It established credit unions, health plans, and community centers for farm laborers.

Universal white manhood suffrage (p. 249)   The elimination of property, tax-paying, and religious qualification for voting in the early nineteenth century extended the vote to all native-born white men.

Utopian communities (p. 286)   Hundreds of experimental communities were established in America during the eighteenth and nineteenth centuries inspired by religious and secular ideals. Despite their differences, all shared a vision of extending the intimacy of the family to a broader range of social relationships.

V-E Day (p. 720)   May 8, 1945, Victory in Europe Day, the day Germany surrendered to the Allies in World War II.

Vertical integration (p. 464)   The practice of controlling every phase of production by owning the sources of raw materials and often the transportation facilities needed to distribute the product; it was a means of gaining a competitive edge over rival companies.

Vice-admiralty courts (p. 97)   The English government established these courts in its North American colonies to deal with issues of maritime law, including smuggling. If judges condemned vessels for smuggling, they would share in profits from the sale of such craft and their cargoes. Judges made all rulings without juries and thus could clearly benefit from their own decisions, which caused many colonists to view these courts as centers of despotic imperial power. The Stamp Act of 1765 stated that colonists who did not pay stamp duties could be tried in vice-admiralty courts, which became another colonial grievance—in this case the prospect of being convicted and sent to jail without a jury trial, a violation of fundamental English liberties.

Vietcong (p. 789)   An offshoot of the Vietminh in South Vietnam. Their political goal was the reunification of the two Vietnams under the rule of the communist North.

Vietminh (p. 789)   Communist guerrilla force ("Viet" for Vietnam and "Minh" for their leader, Ho Chi Minh) who fought the French colonial forces after World War II.

Vietnam (p. 783)   Country in Southeast Asia, part of French Indochina until after World War II. Ho Chi Minh led guerrilla fighters (the Vietminh) in a war for independence when the French refused to grant independence despite promises made during the war. This refusal initiated a conflict of long duration that eventually involved the U.S. military in a war to prevent the divided North and South Vietnams from being reunified under Ho's communist government. When the United States withdrew, North Vietnam overran South Vietnam and united the country.

Virtual representation (p. 98)   King George III's chief minister, George Grenville, employed this concept in 1765 in relation to the Stamp Act. He insisted that all colonists were represented in Parliament by virtue of being English subjects, regardless of where they lived. Grenville was attempting to counter the colonists' position that King and Parliament had no authority to tax them, since the Americans had no elected representatives serving in Parliament.

Voting Rights Act of 1965 (p. 822)   This law prohibited literacy tests and sent federal examiners to the South to register voters.

Wade-Davis Bill (p. 427)   Congress's answer to Lincoln's plan for Reconstruction that required a majority of a state's voters to express their loyalty to the Union. It also limited participation in the forming of a new government to those who took an "iron clad" oath of past loyalty to the Union. It was pocket-vetoed by Lincoln.

Wagner Act (National Labor Relations Act) (p. 684)   New Deal legislation enacted in 1935 guaranteeing the right of workers to form unions and bargain collectively. The act established the National Labor Relations Board (NLRB) to settle union-management disputes over unfair labor practices.

War cabinet (p. 624)   Six boards established by President Woodrow Wilson to unify the nation's efforts toward World War I that conferred broad powers on the federal government. Included in the effort were the War Industries Board, the Fuel Administration, the War Trade Board, the Shipping Administration, and the U.S. Railroad Administration. The War Industries Board was the central unit, designed to coordinate government purchases of military supplies.

War Hawks (p. 214)   Nickname applied to young Republicans in Congress who pushed for war against Britain in 1812.

War Labor Board (WLB) (p. 708)   Board established in 1942 that had power to set wages, hours, and working conditions for the duration of World War II.

War of 1812 (p. 218)   War between Britain and the United States. Causes included British interference with American shipping, impressment of seamen, a desire to end British aid to Indians, and an American desire for expansion.

War Powers Act (p. 876)   This 1973 law required presidents to win specific authorization from Congress to engage U.S. forces in foreign combat for more than 90 days.

War Production Board (WPB) (p. 707)   The board was established in January 1942 to help mobilize the U.S. economy for war production.

War Refugee Board (p. 714)   World War II authority that set up refugee camps in Italy, North Africa, and the United States to help save Jewish refugees.

War Relocation Authority (p. 714)   Program of forcible relocation of Japanese Americans to internment camps during World War II. In December 1944, the Supreme Court ruled that as a civilian authority the War Relocation Authority had no right to incarcerate law-abiding citizens, and the camps closed.

Watergate break-in (p. 873)   During the 1972 presidential campaign, burglars, tied to the Nixon White House, were caught installing eavesdropping devices in Democratic party headquarters in the Watergate Complex in Washington, D.C. Revelations of White House efforts to obstruct the investigation of the break-in, of financial irregularities, and the use of government agencies for partisan purposes led President Nixon to resign in 1974.

Watts Riot of 1965 (p. 824)   A riot in Los Angeles's South Central neighborhood in 1965 left 34 people dead and marked the beginning of four "long, hot" summers of riots.

Webster-Ashburton Treaty (p. 345)   An 1842 treaty that fixed the present-day border between Maine and Canada.

Whig party (Whigs) (pp. 111, 266)   During the eighteenth century in England the Whig party was a loosely organized coalition of political leaders opposed to any hint of arbitrary authority that might emanate from the monarchy and royally appointed officials in government. Like the radical whig pamphleteers, they also viewed themselves as defenders of liberty, which is one reason why many American leaders, even though not organized as a political party, called themselves whigs. During the 1830s and 1840s in the United States, there was a Whig party that opposed the policies of Andrew Jackson, Martin Van Buren, and other members of the Democratic party.

Whiskey Rebellion (p. 188)   Popular protests against a federal tax on liquor in western Pennsylvania in 1794 were quickly dissolved when President Washington sent 15,000 troops to the area to demonstrate the central government's willingness to enforce federal law.

White man's burden (p. 555)   The belief that the white race was naturally superior and should take on the task of "civilizing" the rest of the races. This required them to spread their cultures and religions around the world.

Wilmot Proviso (p. 355)   An amendment attached to an appropriations bill during the Mexican-American War that would have forbade slavery in any territory acquired from Mexico. The amendment passed the House in 1846 and 1847 but was defeated in the Senate.

Woman's Christian Temperance Union (WCTU) (p. 586)   An organization led by Frances Willard to stop the abuse of alcohol; it joined forces with other groups in the movement for the prohibition of alcohol to reduce such problems as wife abuse. Founded in 1874, the WCTU proved instrumental in the passage of the Eighteenth Amendment to the Constitution.

Women's Army Corps (WAC) (p. 711)   The auxiliary women's unit to the U.S. army.

Workmen's compensation laws (p. 592)   Legislation establishing mandatory insurance to be carried by employers to cover on-the-job injuries to their workers; it was a reform that provided protection to workers while also lowering the financial risk to employers.

Works Progress Administration (WPA) (p. 682)   Works program of the Second New Deal that established a much larger system of work relief for the unemployed than earlier efforts.

Wounded Knee, Battle of (p. 445)   The massacre of more than 300 Native Americans in 1890 by federal troops. It became a symbol of white oppression of Indians.

Writs of assistance (p. 100)   Blanket search warrants used by English customs collectors in the colonies to try to catch suspected smugglers. These writs did not require any form of prior evidence to justify searches, which the colonies viewed as yet another imperial violation of fundamental English liberties.

XYZ Affair (p. 195)   A diplomatic incident in 1797 and 1798 that occurred when three agents of French foreign minister Charles Talleyrand demanded a $250,000 bribe and a $10 million loan as a precondition for negotiations.

Yalta Conference (p. 729)   The meeting between President Franklin Roosevelt, British prime minister Winston Churchill, and Soviet premier Joseph Stalin at Yalta in the Russian Crimea in February 1945 to determine the post–World War II world order.

Yellow journalism (p. 563)   Sensationalistic press accounts of the volatile Cuban situation in the 1890s, printed by William Randolph Hearst's *New York Journal* and Joseph Pulitzer's *New York World*. These stories helped mobilize prointerventionist public opinion prior to the Spanish-American war.

Zimmermann telegram (p. 623)   Telegram from German Foreign Minister Arnold Zimmermann to the German ambassador to Mexico pledging a Mexican-German alliance against the United States, which helped bring the United States into World War I.

CREDITS

Page abbreviations are as follows: (T)top, (C)center, (B)bottom, (L)left, (R)right.

Title page and chapter openers: *First row:* Picture Collection, The Branch Libraries, New York Public Library, Astor, Lenox, and Tilden Foundations. *Second row:* Robert Lindneux, *Trail of Tears,* Woolaroc Museum, Bartlesville, Oklahoma; Library of Congress; and Library of Congress. *Third row: John Adams* by John Trumbull, White House Historical Association (White House Collection); Library of Congress; Library of Congress; Library of Congress and Library of Congress. *Fourth row:* Robert Lindneux, *Trail of Tears,* Woolaroc Museum, Bartlesville, Oklahoma; Library of Congress; ©PhotoDisc; and Library of Congress.

CHAPTER 1

4 The Granger Collection, New York 6 Peabody Museum of Archaeology and Ethnology, Harvard University 7 Tony Linck 10 © Bettmann/CORBIS 11 The Art Archive/Marine Museum Lisbon/Dagli Orti 13 Hulton|Archive/Getty Images 14 Rare Book Division, New York Public Library, Astor, Lenox and Tilden Foundations 17 The Granger Collection, New York 19 © Scala/Art Resource 21 The Art Archive/University Library Geneva/Dagli Orti 23 The Granger Collection, New York 25 Hulton|Archive/Getty Images

CHAPTER 2

34 North Wind Picture Archives 35 The Granger Collection, New York 37 Reproduced courtesy of the Trustees of the British Museum, London 39 Bishop Roberts, "Charleston Harbor," Colonial Williamsburg Foundation 41 © National Portrait Gallery, Smithsonian Institution/Art Resource, NY 43 Courtesy of the Pilgrim Society, Plymouth, Massachusetts 44 The Granger Collection, New York 45 Brown County Library 46(L) Rare Book Division, New York Public Library, Astor, Lenox and Tilden Foundations 46(R) Courtesy of the Huntington Library, Art Collections, and Botanical Gardens, San Marino, California 48 John Greenwood, "Abigail Gerrish with her Grandmother, Abigail (Flint) Holloway Gerrish," 1750. Photograph courtesy Peabody Essex Museum 51 Library of Congress 53 © Lee Snider/CORBIS 54 The Granger Collection, New York 56 Abby Aldrich Rockefeller Folk Art Museum, Williamsburg, VA

CHAPTER 3

62 Bernard Gallagher 64 Library of Congress 67 Benjamin West, "Penn's Treaty with the Indians," 1771–72. Courtesy of the Pennsylvania Academy of the Fine Arts, Philadelphia, Gift of Mrs. Sarah Harrison (The Joseph Harrison, Jr. Collection), 1878.1.10 71 Elias C. Larrabee, "Accusation of a Witch." Photograph courtesy Peabody Essex Museum 79 Benjamin West, "Benjamin Franklin Drawing Electricity from the Sky." Philadelphia Museum of Art, Mr. and Mrs. Wharton Sinkler Collection 81 The Granger Collection, New York 82 John Wollaston, "Portrait of George Whitfield," c. 1742. The National Portrait Gallery, London 83 Brown University Library 84 George Catlin, "La Salle Erecting a Cross and Taking Possession of the Land. March 25, 1682," c 1847–1848. National Gallery of Art, Paul Mellon Collection, (1965.16.335). Photo © 2003 Board of Trustees, National Gallery of Art, Washington 87 Library of Congress 88 The Granger Collection, New York

CHAPTER 4

94 Hulton|Archive/Getty Images 95 Sir Joshua Reynolds, "King George III". Royal Academy of Arts, London 99 Library of Congress 101 Library of Congress 103 Library of Congress 106 Rare Book Division, New York Public Library, Astor, Lenox and Tilden Foundations 107 Index of American Design, National Gallery of Art, Washington, DC. © 2003 Board of Trustees, National Gallery of Art, Washington 109 Library of Congress 110 Courtesy of the Massachusetts Historical Society, (MHS Image #67) 112 Charles DeWolf Brownell, "The Burning of the Gaspee," 1892. The Rhode Island Historical Society, (Rhi X4 1) 113 Private Collection/Bridgeman Art Library 115 North Wind Picture Archives

CHAPTER 5

122 Courtesy of The Valley Forge Historical Society 125 Courtesy Concord Free Public Library 129 The Granger Collection, New York 131(L) Independence National Historical Park 131(R) Library of Congress 132 US Capitol Historical Society 134 Library of Congress 136 The Granger Collection, New York 137 The Granger Collection, New York 140 © Giraudon/Bridgeman Art Library 142 Hulton|Archive/Getty Images 145 South Carolina Historical Society 146 Library of Congress

CHAPTER 6

152(L) Courtesy of the Atwater Kent Museum, PA 152(R) Library of Congress 155 The Granger Collection, New York 159 Courtesy of the Pennsylvania Academy of Fine Arts, Philadelphia, Bequest of Richard Ashhurst 161 © CORBIS 164 Courtesy of the Massachusetts Historical Society 166 Museum of Art, Rhode Island School of Design. Museum Appropriation, (17.361) 169 "The Cheney Family," c. 1795. National Gallery of Art, Gift of Edgar William and Bernice Chrysler Garbisch, (1958.9.9). Photo © 2003 Board of Trustees, National Gallery of Art, Washington, DC 170(T, L) The Granger Collection, New York 170(T, R) Schomburg Center for Research in Black Culture, Art and Artifacts Division, The New York Public Library, Astor, Lenox and Tilden Foundations 170(B) Library of Congress 171 Junius Brutus Stearns, "Washington as Statesman at the Constitutional Convention," 1856. Virginia Museum of Fine Arts, Richmond, Gift of Edgar William and Bernice Chrysler Garbisch. Photo Ron Jennings/©Virginia Museum of Fine Arts 172 Library of Congress

CHAPTER 7

182(L) Rare Book Division, New York Public Library, Astor, Lenox and Tilden Foundations 182(R) White House Photo Office 183 Library of Congress 184 North Wind Picture Archives 186 Library of Congress 188 Frederick Kemmelmeyer, "Washington Reviewing the Western Army at Fort Cumberland, Maryland." The Metropolitan Museum of Art, Gift of Edgar William and Bernice Chrysler Garbisch, 1963 (63.201.2). Photograph © 1983 The Metropolitan Museum of Art 191 © CORBIS 192 Library of Congress 193 John Singleton Copley, "John Adams," Courtesy of the Harvard University Portrait Collection, Harvard University Art Museums. Bequest of Ward Nicholas Boylston, 1828 to Harvard College 194 White House Historical Association, White House Collection, (127) 195 Library of Congress 197 CORBIS

CHAPTER 8

204(T) © Hulton|Archive/Getty Images 204(B) National Museum of American History, Smithsonian Institution, Washington, DC 205 © Robert Llewellyn 209 The Mariners' Museum, Newport News, VA 210(L) Bror Thure de Thulstrap, "Raising of the American Flag Louisiana Transfer Ceremonies," 1903. Louisiana State Museum, Loan of the Louisiana Historical Society **210(R)** North Wind Picture Archives **214** Library of Congress **217(L)** Library of Congress **217(R)** The Field Museum, Chicago (#A93851) **219** Anne S. K. Brown Military Collection, Brown University Library

CHAPTER 9

226 Rare Book Division, New York Public Library, Astor, Lenox and Tilden Foundations **228(C)** © National Portrait Gallery, Smithsonian Institution/Art Resource, NY **228(L)** Library of Congress **228(R)** The Granger Collection, New York **229** © Shelburne Museum, Shelburne, Vermont **231** Samuel F.B. Morse, "The Old House of Representatives," 1822. In the Collection of The Corcoran Gallery of Art, Washington, DC **233** Pavel Petrovich Svinin, "Travel by Stagecoach near Trenton, New Jersey". The Metropolitan Museum of Art, Rogers Fund, 1942 (42.95.11). Photograph © 1984 The Metropolitan Museum of Art **234(B)** Mary Keys, "Lockport on the Erie Canal", 1832. Munson-Williams-Proctor Arts Institute, Museum of Art, Utica, New York **234(T)** Rare Book Division, New York Public Library, Astor, Lenox and Tilden Foundations **237(L)** National Museum of American History, Smithsonian Institution, Washington, DC **237(R)** Russell Smith, "Saltworks," 1832–34. Courtesy of the Atwater Kent Museum, PA **241** The Granger Collection, New York

CHAPTER 10

248 The Granger Collection, New York **251** Rare Book Division, New York Public Library, Astor, Lenox and Tilden Foundations **253** Library of Congress **255** The Metropolitan Museum of Art, Gift of I.N. Phelps Stokes, Edward S. Hawes, Alice Mary Hawes, Marion Augusta Hawes, 1937. (37.14.34) **258** The Newberry Library, Chicago **262** Library of Congress **265** The Granger Collection, New York

CHAPTER 11

272 Carl A. Kroch Library, Cornell University **273** Brown Brothers **274** Courtesy of New Bedford Whaling Museum **275** Library of Congress **280** Courtesy of the Massachusetts Historical Society **282** © Bettmann/CORBIS **283(T)** © Madison County Historical Society, Oneida, NY **283(B)** Culver Pictures, Inc. **286(L)** Library of Congress **286(R)** Mary Evans Picture Library **288** Library of Congress **289** Courtesy Concord Free Public Library **291** The Granger Collection, New York **294** Thomas Cole, "View of Schroon Mountain, Essex County, New York, After a Storm," 1838. The Cleveland Museum of Art, Hinman B. Hurlburt Collection, (1335.1917). Photo © The Cleveland Museum of Art, 2003 **297** Courtesy, American Antiquarian Society **298** Rare Book Division, New York Public Library, Astor, Lenox and Tilden Foundations **299** The Granger Collection, New York

CHAPTER 12

306 SuperStock, Inc. **309** North Wind Picture Archives **310** Library of Congress **311** Library of Congress **317** The Granger Collection, New York **323** Library of Congress **325** North Wind Picture Archives **326** Library of Congress **327** North Wind Picture Archives **329** Historic New Orleans Collection, (1960.046) **330** The

Collection of Jay P. Altmayer

CHAPTER 13

336 The Kobal Collection/Tristar/Amblin/Ricco Torres **337** Thomas Gilcrease Institute of American History and Art, Tulsa **338** George Catlin, "Comanche Chasing Buffalo with Bows and Lances," 1832–33. Courtesy the Library, American Museum of Natural History, New York **339** Bancroft Library, University of California, Berkeley **340** The Granger Collection, New York **341** Library of Congress **342** National Archives **344** Stephen Seymour Thomas, "The Equestrian Portrait of Sam Houston," San Jacinto Museum of History, Houston **347** Friends of the Governor's Mansion, TX **349** C.C.A Christensen, "Saints Driven from Jackson County, Missouri," Courtesy of Brigham Young University Museum of Art. All Rights Reserved. **350** Richard Caton Woodville, Sr., "War News from Mexico," 1846. National Gallery of Art. Photo © 2003 Board of Trustees, National Gallery of Art, Washington **352** North Wind Picture Archives

CHAPTER 14

362 Indiana Historical Society **363** Courtesy of the California History Room, California State Library, Sacramento, CA **367** © Smithsonian American Art Museum, Washington, DC/Art Resource, NY **368** Library of Congress **370(T)** © Collection of The New-York Historical Society, (Acc. No. 38219) **370(B)** The Metropolitan Museum of Art, Gift of I.N. Phelps Stokes, Edward S. Hawes, Alice Mary Hawes, and Marion Augusta Hawes, 1937. (37.14.40) **372(L)** Library of Congress **372(R)** Library of Congress **377** Library of Congress **378** Missouri Historical Society, St. Louis **380** AP/Wide World Photos **382** The New York Public Library, Astor, Lenox and Tilden Foundations

CHAPTER 15

388(L) Georgia Department of Archives and History **388(R)** Library of Congress **389** Library of Congress **392** Library of Congress **396** George Hayward, "Departure of the Seventh Regiment, N.Y.S.M., April 19, 1861," Courtesy, Museum of Fine Arts, Boston. Reproduced with permission. Photo © 2003 Museum of Fine Arts, Boston. All Rights Reserved **398** Anne S.K. Brown Military Collection, Brown University Library **399** Library of Congress **402** Chicago Historical Society **406** The Granger Collection, New York **407** Chicago Historical Society **409** The Granger Collection, New York **411** The State Museum of Pennsylvania, Pennsylvania Historical Museum Commission **414** Valentine Richmond History Center

CHAPTER 16

422 Library of Congress **425** The Granger Collection, New York **428** Library of Congress **429** Library of Congress **432** Library of Congress **433** Library of Congress **434** Valentine Richmond History Center **436** Library of Congress **437** Culver Pictures, Inc. **439** Library of Congress **442** Library of Congress **445(T)** Courtesy of the Southwest Museum, Los Angeles **445(B)** Nebraska State Historical Society, Photographic Collections **447** Culver Pictures, Inc.

INDEX

Page abbreviations are as follows: (t)tables, (f)figures, (m)maps, (i)illustrations.

CHAPTER 1 • THE PEOPLING AND UNPEOPLING OF AMERICA

SUMMARY

In this chapter you read about the original inhabitants of the Americas and the diverse cultures that existed in North and South America in 1492. You also read about the developments in Europe that led Europeans to explore and colonize new lands, and about the far-reaching consequences of the encounter between the Old and New Worlds.

KEY POINTS

- The European voyages of discovery brought two worlds together, producing what scholars call the Columbian Exchange.

- The Indians taught Europeans about tobacco, corn, potatoes, and varieties of beans, peanuts, tomatoes, and other crops unknown in Europe.

- In return, Europeans introduced the Indians to wheat, oats, barley, and rice, as well as to grapes for wine and various melons. Europeans also brought with them domesticated animals including horses, pigs, sheep, goats, and cattle.

- The exchange was not evenly balanced. Killer diseases killed millions of Indians. The survivors were drawn into European trading networks that disrupted earlier patterns of life.

CHAPTER SYNOPSIS

Approximately 30,000 years ago, the Paleo-Indians, the ancestors of Native Americans, followed herds of animals from Siberia across Beringia, a land bridge connecting Asia and North America, into Alaska. By 8,000 B.C.E., these peoples had spread across North and South America.

Complex, agriculturally-based cultures developed in several regions, including the Mayas and Aztecs in Mesoamerica, the Incas in Peru, and the Moundbuilders and Mississippians in the Ohio and Mississippi River Valleys. An estimated 500,000 to 800,000 Indians lived in eastern North America. Along the Atlantic coast, small agriculturally oriented groups predominated.

Although the Vikings reached eastern Canada around 1000 c.e., their settlements left no lasting impact on the Americas. Sustained European expansion was the result of several factors. The Crusades opened up new horizons in commerce and knowledge. Advances in geographical knowledge and naval science made sea travel less hazardous. Other stimuli included the printing press and the publication of Marco Polo's adventures, which captured the imaginations of many Europeans. The rise of competing nation-states headed by monarchs created a favorable environment for exploration.

Prince Henry of Portugal sponsored voyages that increased knowledge of the sea while opening new trade routes to Africa and India. The Portuguese success led Spain to sponsor the voyage by Christopher Columbus that resulted in the European discovery of the Americas.

Between 1492 and 1620, Spain, England, and France established permanent settlements in the New World. Europe's New World empires took three distinct forms. There were empires of conquest, commerce, and settlement.

In Mexico and Central and South America, the Spanish, unlike the English or the French, viewed Indians as a usable labor force—to be put to work to raising crops, tending animals, and extracting valuable minerals from mines. In the early 1500s Spanish policy forced many Indians to work on Spanish estates. Under the encomienda system, colonists were granted the right to demand tribute from Indians living on a given piece of land. Often the colonists forced the Indians to farm or work in mines as payment. Gradually, the Indians became bound to the land because they had no other way to pay tribute.

The Spanish crown exercised central authority over Spain's New World empire. Trade was restricted to merchants licensed by the Council of the Indies. Unlike the later British colonies, Spanish colonists were not allowed to established representative assemblies.

The Conquest had negative consequences for the Spanish economy. The inflow of bullion created runaway inflation. Manufactured imports overwhelmed Spanish industry. It also led the Spanish crown to seek to dominate Europe, leading to a series of foreign wars that ended in defeat and made it impossible to enforce its exclusive claims to the Western Hemisphere.

For more than a century, Spain and Portugal were the only European powers with New World colonies. After 1600, however, other European countries began to emulate their example. France's New World empire was based largely on trade. In 1504, French fishermen sailed into the Gulf of St. Lawrence, looking for cod. Gradually, the French realized that they could increase their profits by trading with the Indians for furs. In exchange for pelts, the French coureurs de bois (traders) supplied Indians with textiles, muskets, and other European goods. By the end of the sixteenth century, a thousand ships a year were engaged in the fur trade along the St. Lawrence River and the interior, where the French constructed forts, missions, and trading posts.

Relations between the French and Indians were less violent than in Spanish or English colonies. In part, this reflected the small size of France's New World population. The French government had little interest in encouraging immigration and the number of settlers in New France remained small, totaling just 3,000 in 1663. Virtually all these settlers were men—mostly traders or Jesuit priests—and many took Indian wives or concubines, helping to promote relations of mutual dependency. Common trading interests also encouraged accommodation between the French and the Indians. Missionary activities, too, proved somewhat less divisive in New France than in New Mexico or New England, since France's Jesuit priests did not require them to immediately abandon their tribal ties or their traditional way of life.

At first, the English Crown delegated authority to form overseas settlements to private profit-making corporations known as joint-stock companies. In planning its American colonies, the English drew upon their experience colonizing Ireland. In the 1580s, England's first attempt to settle in North America ended in disaster as the Roanoke colony along the North Carolina coast mysteriously disappeared without a trace. England's first permanent colony was established in Jamestown by the Virginia Company in 1607.

The European voyages of discovery brought two worlds together. The Indians taught Europeans about tobacco, corn, potatoes, and varieties of beans, peanuts, tomatoes, and other crops unknown in Europe. In return, Europeans introduced the Indians to wheat, oats, barley, and rice, as well as to grapes for wine and various melons. Europeans also brought with them domesticated animals including horses, pigs, sheep, goats, and cattle. The Columbian Exchange, however, was not evenly balanced. Killer diseases killed millions of Indians. The survivors were drawn into European trading networks that disrupted earlier patterns of life.

OBJECTIVES

After reading this chapter, you should be able to:

1. Trace the settlement of the Americas by Paleo-Indians; the impact of the agricultural revolution on Native American life; the diversity and size of Native American cultures; and the defining characteristics of the Indian cultures of the Eastern Woodlands on the eve of European contact.

2. Identify the factors—including rapid population growth, commerce, new learning, and the rise of competing nation-states—that encouraged Europeans to explore and colonize new lands, and explain why Portugal and Spain were the first to become involved in overseas exploration.

3. Trace the development of Spain's New World empire and explain why the Spanish Conquistadors were able to conquer large portions of the Americas.

4. Explain why England and France were slow to challenge Spain's supremacy in the Americas.

5. Trace the relationship between the European Renaissance and the Protestant Reformation and subsequent exploration and settlement of the New World.

6. Explain how Ireland served as a model for later English colonization; why the colony at Roanoke Island failed; and why the colony of Virginia was able to survive.

7. Describe the similarities and differences between Spanish, English, Dutch, and French colonization.

KEY TERMS

Beringia
Aztecs, Mayas, and Incas
Mississippian culture
Matrilineal
Black Death
Renaissance
Conquistadors
Encomienda System
Haciendas

Mestizos
Las Casas and the Black Legend
Northwest Passage
Protestant Reformation
Indulgences
Enclosure Movement
Price Revolution
Joint-Stock Trading Companies
Columbian Exchange

KEY FIGURES

Squanto	Christopher Columbus
Columbus	Hernan Cortes
Las Casas	Martin Luther
Marco Polo	Richard Hakluyt
Johann Gutenberg	Sir Humphrey Gilbert
Prince Henry the Navigator	Captain John Smith
Ferdinand and Isabella	

PRACTICE TEST

CHAPTER 1 • THE PEOPLING AND UNPEOPLING OF AMERICA

_____ 1. The Patuxet Indian, Squanto
   a. was raised by English Pilgrims
   b. taught the Pilgrims how to grow Indian corn
   c. after being captured and taken to England, preferred to remain there

_____ 2. Where did the Paleo-Indians, who first migrated to the Americas, come from?
   a. Northeastern Asia
   b. Scandinavia
   c. The South Pacific

_____ 3. At the time of Columbus's arrival in the New World in 1492, the New World
   a. was largely unpopulated
   b. had no more than a million inhabitants
   c. was the home of millions of people

_____ 4. Before the arrival of the Europeans, Native Americans had developed all of the following EXCEPT
   a. the planting and harvesting of food crops
   b. living in villages and intertribal trade networks
   c. hunting from horseback

_____ 5. Which of the following statements about the Native American peoples north of Mexico around 1500 is TRUE?
   a. These peoples had developed no large towns or monumental structures
   b. These peoples developed essentially similar economies and ways of life
   c. These peoples were linguistically and culturally diverse

_____ 6. In the century after Europeans arrived, the Indian population in the Americas
   a. doubled
   b. remained at the same level
   c. fell by 50 to 90 percent

_____ 7. Prior to contact with Europeans, Indian peoples had adapted to their environment in all but one of the following ways. Select the EXCEPTION.
   a. In the Pacific Northwest, tribes such as the Chinooks fished for salmon
   b. In the Southwest, the Hopi and Zuni relied on agriculture and practiced irrigation
   c. On the Plains, Indian peoples hunted from horseback

_____ 8. Unlike the Europeans, the eastern Indians
   a. did not recognize individual ownership of land
   b. did not organize themselves into separate nations
   c. did not practice religion

_____ 9. Europeans made their first contact with the Americas
   a. around 5,000 B.C.
   b. around 1,000 A.D.
   c. in 1492

_____ 10. The main stimulus for European expansion during the 15th century was a growing interest in
   a. converting non-European peoples to Christianity
   b. increasing trade with the Far East
   c. proving that the world was round

_____ 11. The European nation that took the lead in exploring the west coast of Africa was
   a. France
   b. Portugal
   c. Spain

_____ 12. Christopher Columbus
   a. was the first European to reach the Americas
   b. understood that he had reached a new world
   c. thought Asia was only 4,500 miles from Spain, when it was actually 12,000 miles away

_____ 13. The major factor that contributed to Cortez's defeat of the Aztecs was
     a. the superior numbers of the Spanish Conquistadors
     b. the superiority of Spanish weapons
     c. European diseases, such as smallpox, typhoid, and diphtheria, which took a heavy toll on the native population

_____ 14. The encomienda system
     a. gave Spanish landlords control of the labor of whole villages of Indians
     b. was a system of trade between Mexico and Spain
     c. represented an attempt by the Catholic Church to protect the Indians from brutal treatment in gold and silver mines

_____ 15. All but one of the following factors delayed England and France from exploring and settling the New World. Select the EXCEPTION.
     a. Ignorance about the amount of wealth that Spain extracted from the New World
     b. Political and religious turmoil that diverted the royal government from supporting trading stations and permanent settlements
     c. Spain's success in defeating outsiders who tried to colonize on Spanish territory.

_____ 16. Which of the following did NOT encourage many people in England to consider migrating to the New World during the early seventeenth century?
     a. The enclosure of traditional common lands
     b. Rapid population growth
     c. Government subsidies to people who were willing to migrate to the New World

_____ 17. Jamestown, England's first permanent North American settlement,
     a. was financed using royal funds
     b. was an immediate financial success
     c. found wealth in the production of tobacco

_____ 18. Which of the following statements about the "Columbian exchange" is FALSE?
     a. Indians taught Europeans about maize, potatoes, squashes, pumpkins, tobacco, and tomatoes
     b. Europeans brought wheat, oats, barley, race, grapes, horses, pigs, sheep, goats, and cattle to the New World
     c. Indians introduced Europeans to smallpox and measles

Chapter 2 • Plantations and Cities Upon a Hill, 1620–1700

SUMMARY

In this chapter you read about the beginnings of English settlement in North America in the 1600s. You read about the diverse reasons why European settlers came to America and the difficulties they encountered as a result of varied climates, topographies, and Indian populations. In addition, you learned about the differences between life in the Chesapeake colonies and in New England, and about how chattel slavery took root in the southernmost colonies.

KEY POINTS

- Permanent, hereditary slavery took root slowly in the American colonies.
- Initially, settlers in the Chesapeake relied on white indentured servants as their labor force, and at least some of the blacks who arrived in the region were able to acquire property.
- Between 1640 and 1670, a sharp distinction emerged between short-term servitude for whites and permanent slavery for blacks.
- A crucial difference arose between the southern-most colonies, whose economy was devoted to production of staple crops, and the more diverse economies of the northern colonies.

CHAPTER SYNOPSIS

The southern colonies of Maryland, Virginia, and the Carolinas developed around an economic system based upon cash crops raised by indentured servants and then increasingly by slaves imported from Africa. The northern colonies, in contrast, developed a more diverse economy based on family farms, crafts, and trade.

Tobacco made land in the Chesapeake region of Maryland and Virginia valuable and ignited a violent conflict with Indians over land. Tobacco also encouraged a dispersed settlement pattern with an absence of towns and an urban merchant class. To attract settlers, Virginia created a representative assembly and granted headrights, private land ownership. After Virginia became a royal colony, dissent forced the crown to establish the House of Burgesses to provide local representation in government.

Maryland was founded as a proprietary colony awarded to the Calvert family and as a haven for Catholics. Like Virginia, its economy was based upon tobacco.

Religious strife in England led to the execution of King Charles I, parliamentary rule by the Puritans, and then the restoration of the monarchy. To repay some supporters, the new king, Charles II, granted them Carolinas, which was partly settled by farmers from Barbados, who transplanted the Caribbean plantation system of cash crops cultivated by African slaves.

Settlement of New England was part of the religious upheaval known as the Reformation. Protestant religious reformers denied the authority of the Pope and challenged fundamental Catholic doctrines. Puritans believed that the Church of England needed to be purged of Catholic customs that had no Biblical sanction. The English Crown regarded religious unity as necessary to maintain royal authority, and those who threatened church unity were persecuted.

The first group of Puritans to move to New England were the Pilgrims. In 1620, they settled Plymouth colony. More influential were the Puritans, who emigrated in the twelve years after 1630. They were committed to creating a godly community that would serve as a city upon a hill, a model of how England could be transformed and purified. The vast majority were sober married couples. Family life in New England was much more stable and long-lived than farther south.

In Puritan New England, everyone was legally required to attend church services. Church membership was confined to visible saints, those who could demonstrate their godliness, and participation in politics was confined to adult male church members. Puritan Massachusetts was not a theocracy, a state ruled by religious authorities. The Puritans held to the modern conception that church and civil government were distinct, and did not elect ministers to public office. A number of dissenting Puritans, including Roger Williams, defended religious liberty as a natural right.

During the 17th century, a rapidly growing population and an increase in trade contributed to the spread of commercial values in New England. Many ministers regarded the growing dominance of commercial values as a sign of decline or declension.

OBJECTIVES

After reading this chapter, you should be able to:

1. Describe the major difficulties that early settlers in Virginia encountered and how these difficulties were overcome.

2. Describe the similarities and differences in the relations between Indians and English colonists in the Chesapeake and New England colonies.

3. Describe the beliefs of the Puritans and how their beliefs influenced life in New England.

4. Compare and contrast the characteristics of life in New England the Chesapeake colonies during the seventeenth century.

5. Describe the differences between indentured servitude and chattel slavery and the factors that led to the shift from indentured servitude to enslavement in the southern colonies.

KEY TERMS

Indentured Servitude
Headrights
Divine Right
Separatists and Non Separatists
Puritans
Antinomian
Patriarchal
Coverture
Declension
Jeremiads
Half-Way Covenant
Perpetual Servitude

KEY FIGURES

John Punch
Sir Edwin Sandys
Powhatan
John Rolfe
Opechancanough
Sir George Calvert and Cecilius Calvert, Lords Baltimore
John Winthrop
Roger Williams
Anne Hutchinson
Metacomet or King Philip

PRACTICE TEST

CHAPTER 2 • PLANTATIONS AND CITIES UPON A HILL, 1620–1700

SUMMARY

_____ 1. A distinction between short-term servitude for whites and life-long, inheritable slavery for blacks became firmly fixed in Virginia
   a. before 1620
   b. between 1640 and 1670
   c. only after 1700

_____ 2. The English who signed a contract temporarily exchanging their labor for payment of their passage to America were called
   a. burgesses
   b. headrights
   c. indentured servants

_____ 3. Problems faced by Jamestown included all of the following EXCEPT
   a. inadequate food and agricultural methods
   b. disease
   c. conflicting religious beliefs

_____ 4. The Virginia colony was finally able to achieve lasting economic success by
   a. growing and exporting tobacco
   b. exporting cedar and sassafras
   c. mining silver and gold

_____ 5. To raise tobacco, Virginia planters initially relied primarily upon
   a. slaves imported from Africa
   b. foreign immigrants
   c. white indentured servants

_____ 6. To attract a supply of laborers from England, the Virginians introduced all but one of the following reforms in 1618. Select the EXCEPTION
   a. Virginia ended martial law
   b. Virginia abolished indentured servitude
   c. Virginia promised to establish a local representative assembly

_____ 7. Settlers to Virginia in the 17th century
   a. usually migrated in family groups
   b. usually came as indentured servants
   c. were about equally divided between males and females

_____ 8. England's Stuart kings viewed overseas colonization in all but one of the following ways. Select the EXCEPTION.
   a. As a way to enhance England's stature among the nations of Europe
   b. As a dumping ground for troublesome groups in England
   c. As an expensive luxury that England could not afford

_____ 9. Which of the following statements about Maryland is TRUE?
   a. Maryland was founded by the Dutch
   b. Maryland was originally settled by Puritans
   c. To protect Catholics, the colony's 1649 Act of Religious Toleration guaranteed voting rights to adult males who believed in the doctrine of the Trinity

_____ 10. Which of the following was NOT true about Massachusetts Bay Colony?
   a. Voting privileges were granted only to church members
   b. Church leaders held significant political authority
   c. The colony's government was obligated to enforce moral commandments

_____ 11. Roger Williams was banished from Massachusetts Bay Colony because he
   a. insisted that the colony had to purchase land from Indians in fair agreements
   b. challenged the colony's leaders because they refused to require all settlers to attend church on the Sabbath
   c. argued that all settlers had to belong to the Church of England

_____ 12. Anne Hutchinson earned the disfavor of Massachusetts by
   a. declaring that God could offer direct revelations to individuals
   b. defending those accused of witchcraft
   c. demanding freedom of religion for Catholics

_____ 13. Religious freedom was expressly granted in the colony of
   a. Massachusetts Bay
   b. Connecticut
   c. Rhode Island

_____ 14. King Philip's War in 1675 and 1676 pitted
   a. the French against the English
   b. the Spanish against the Virginians
   c. the followers of a Wampanoag chieftain against New Englanders

_____ 15. A difference between northern and southern English colonies that was to have major future implications was the
   a. different religions of the two sections
   b. single-crop economy of the southern colonies versus the more diverse economies of the northern colonies
   c. different types of local government

_____ 16. Compared to the southern colonies,
   a. New England was healthier and New Englanders bore more children
   b. fewer New Englanders married and had a shorter life expectancy
   c. New Englanders were less likely to cross the Atlantic in family units

_____ 17. All but one of the following factors contributed to the shift toward slave labor in the southern colonies in the late 17th century. Select the EXCEPTION.
   a. Legislation decreed that slavery was inheritable and was passed through the mother
   b. A decline in the number of white indentured servants as economic conditions improved in England
   c. The fact that slaves cost less than indentured servants

_____ 18. What percentage of African slaves forcibly imported to the New World were brought to British North America?
   a. 5 percent
   b. 30 percent
   c. 50 percent

_____ 19. Which of the following statements about colonial slavery is FALSE?
   a. Enslaved Africans, who were expert at raising and herding animals, developed a thriving trade in cattle in the colonies
   b. Enslaved Africans who came from rice growing areas in Africa fostered rice production in the colonies
   c. In the New World, enslaved Africans were unable to maintain distinctive cultural traditions

CHAPTER 3 • PROVINCIAL AMERICA IN UPHEAVAL, 1660–1760

SUMMARY

In this chapter, you read about England's efforts to create an empire based on mercantilist principles. You learned about how England acquired additional North American colonies, about British efforts to assert new authority over the thirteen American colonies, and the conflicts that these efforts to assert control produced. You also learned about the forces that transformed colonial life, including an expanding population, economic stratification, the Enlightenment, and the Great Awakening. Finally, you read about the European wars for empire that were partly fought in North America.

KEY POINTS

- Between 1660 and 1760, England laid the foundations for a great empire. It began to create a formal system of empire and imposed a series of imperial laws upon its American colonies.

- From time to time, when the imperial laws became too restrictive, the colonists resisted these impositions, and Britain responded with a system of accommodation known as "salutary neglect."

- The colonists also became embroiled in a series of contests for empire between Britain, France and Spain.

- By the 1760s—after Britain had decisively defeated the French—the colonists were in a position to challenge their subordinate position within the British empire.

CHAPTER SYNOPSIS

After 1650, the English Crown and Parliament attempted to increase their control over American commerce. Underlying these restrictive trade policies was an economic theory known as mercantilism. Mercantilist theory asserted that colonies exist to benefit the parent nation by supplying staple crops and raw materials. This assumption led to the passage of the Navigation Acts, which banned foreign merchants and vessels from participating in colonial trade; declared that certain enumerated goods could be shipped only to England or other colonies; and specified that European goods destined for the colonies had to pass through England.

By the late 1690s, the English had displaced the Dutch as Europe's leading commercial power. In 1664, Charles II gave his brother, James, the Duke of York, title to all Dutch lands in North America, on the condition that they be conquered. New York and New Jersey were formed out of the lands that the Dutch surrendered.

Pennsylvania was founded partially as payment for a debt owed the Penn family by King Charles II. Having adopted the Quaker faith, William Penn wanted to found a colony in which all faiths would live in harmony. He also wanted peaceful relations with the Indians, buying their lands and treating them fairly.

Violent uprising took place in many colonies. Virginians blamed the Navigation Acts for a glutted tobacco market that threatened their economy; they also bridled under the rule of royal governor Sir William Berkeley. Nathaniel Bacon raised a force that attacked neighboring Indians and staged an uprising against Berkeley. The uprising petered out after Bacon's death from dysentery. But when the Crown starting sending royal governors to Virginia with detailed instructions about managing the colony, Virginia's leading planters began to work together to protect the colony's interests.

The Crown also tried to assert authority over the colonies by sending customs officials to America and by seeking to set up a large administrative unit, the Dominion of New England, stretching from Nova Scotia to the Delaware River. After King James II flaunted his Roman Catholic beliefs, English leaders drove him from England; gave the throne to James's Protestant daughter Mary and her husband, William of Orange, a Dutch prince; and adopted the Declaration of Right (1689), which guaranteed Parliament's voice in political affairs. The "Glorious Revolution" sparked rebellions in New England, New York, and Maryland. Under William and Mary there was a movement toward Crown appointed governors existing alongside legislative assemblies that expressed and defended local concerns. Until the 1760s, a balance was maintained between imperial authority and local autonomy.

By the early 1760s, the colonists were in a position to challenge their subordinate status within the British empire. Between 1700 and 1760, the colonial population grew from 250,000 to 1.6 million people. This was due to natural reproduction, the importation of enslaved Africans, and the migration of non-English peoples, especially Germans and Scot-Irish, into New York and Pennsylvania. Meanwhile, a prospering economy contributed to the emergence of wealthy elite families that dominated the colonial assemblies and defended local autonomy.

The Great Awakening, a succession of religious revivals, contributed to a growing acceptance of religious pluralism and a questioning of established authority.

Between 1689 and 1763, England, France and Spain fought four imperial wars. The defeat of the French in the Seven Years' War set the stage of renewed conflict between Britain's North American colonies and the British Crown and Parliament.

OBJECTIVES

After reading this chapter, you should be able to:

1. Define mercantilism and describe the obligations of colonies under England's mercantilist policies.

2. Describe the similarities and differences between the Middle Colonies and the New England and southern colonies.

3. Explain the political and social turmoil that occurred in Massachusetts, New York, and Virginia in the 1670s and 1680s and describe its impact on the long-term development of the colonies.

4. Identify the Enlightenment and the Great Awakening and describe their impact on colonial society, culture, and politics.

5. Describe the military conflicts among the British, French, and Spanish in the Americas from the 1690s through the 1750s and explain why Britain ultimately emerged triumphant in 1763.

KEY TERMS
Mercantilism
Enumerated Goods
Navigation System
Holy Experiment
Bacon's Rebellion
Dominion of New England
Glorious Revolution
Salutary Neglect
Redemptioners
Enlightenment
Rationalism
Great Awakening
New Lights
Old Lights
Seven Years' War

KEY FIGURES
Hannah Dustan
Eliza Lucas
William Penn
Nathaniel Bacon
Benjamin Franklin
Jonathan Edwards
George Whitefield

CHAPTER 3 • PROVINCIAL AMERICA IN UPHEAVAL, 1660–1760

_____ 1. Eliza Lucas
  a. was a New Englander who was captured in an Indian raiding party, but succeeded in killing her captors
  b. demonstrated that indigo, a source of a blue dye, could be grown profitably in South Carolina
  c. was the first slave woman to publish poetry in the American colonies

_____ 2. Mercantilists believed that colonies could contribute to England's wealth in all of the following ways EXCEPT by
  a. supplying valuable raw materials
  b. purchasing English manufactured goods
  c. becoming economically self-sufficient

_____ 3. New Netherland had all but one of the following EXCEPT
  a. an ethnically diverse population
  b. a weak and unstable government
  c. a locally elected representative assembly

_____ 4. Quakers believed
  a. that all persons had an "inner light" that allowed them to speak with God
  b. that all human beings were equal in the sight of God
  c. both of the above

_____ 5. William Penn, the Quaker founder of Pennsylvania,
  a. sought to create a colony that would exclusively be settled by Quakers
  b. promised that he would not take land from Indians unless the transfer was sanctioned by tribal chieftains
  c. only allowed English colonists to settle in his colony

_____ 6. Bacon's Rebellion in Virginia was a result of all of the following EXCEPT
  a. the frustration caused by rising taxes and falling tobacco prices
  b. a growing desire for independence from England
  c. resentment against the royal governor's Indian policies

_____ 7. What was the result of Bacon's Rebellion?
  a. Nathaniel Bacon became Virginia's royal governor
  b. Virginia's planter elite settled their differences and began to work together to protect the colony's interests
  c. The Church of England was disestablished in Virginia

_____ 8. What was the Dominion of New England intended to provide?
  a. Greater self-government for the New England colonies
  b. Greater royal control over the New England colonies
  c. More economic self-sufficiency for New England

_____ 9. Which of the following statements about the Glorious Revolution is FALSE?
  a. It allowed New Englanders to overthrow the Dominion of New England
  b. It increased the power of the English Crown
  c. It enabled Parliament to place strict limitations on royal power

_____ 10. News that James II had been driven from the English throne in 1688 sparked rebellions in:
  a. Ohio
  b. Massachusetts, New York, and Maryland
  c. Kentucky

_____ 11. Which of the following statements about the Salem witchcraft hysteria is FALSE?
  a. Twenty men and women were executed after refusing to admit they practiced witchcraft
  b. Most of the original accusers of witches were young, unmarried women
  c. The event strengthened belief in the Puritan religion throughout New England

_____ 12. Because it was deemed a violation of mercantilist principles, Parliament forbade the colonists from exporting
   a. woolen products, beaver or felt hats, and iron or steel products
   b. tobacco, rice and indigo
   c. salted fish and animal furs

_____ 13. What does the phrase "era of salutary neglect" refer to?
   a. The frightful months of the Salem witchcraft trials in the 1690s
   b. The early 18th century, when Parliament voluntarily restrained its administration of colonial affairs
   c. The late 17th century, when the colonists switched from indentured servitude to slave labor

_____ 14. Colonial America in the first half of the 18th century was characterized by all the following EXCEPT
   a. rapid population growth
   b. widespread ownership of farm property
   c. ethnic homogeneity

_____ 15. Which of the following statements is FALSE? Between 1700 and 1775,
   a. the colonial population grew 10-fold, from 250,000 to 2.5 million and the black population rose from 28,000 to 500,000
   b. over 100,000 Scots-Irish and over 100,000 Germans migrated to the colonies
   c. over half of the colonies' population migrated west of the Appalachian mountains

_____ 16. Compared to the 17th century,
   a. wealth was becoming more equally distributed in the colonies during the 18th century
   b. colonial society in the 18th century was becoming more economically stratified, with extremes of wealth and poverty becoming more visible
   c. life expectancy in the 18th century was sharply declining and the death rate was rapidly rising

_____ 17. Enlightenment thinkers assumed all but one of the following. Select the EXCEPTION.
   a. That human beings are rational creatures capable of solving social and political problems
   b. That there were natural laws that governed the universe
   c. That God plays an active role in the affairs of ordinary people

_____ 18. "Whig" pamphleteers in England, who were widely read by colonial gentlemen,
   a. warned that government ministers would try to grab authority and power for themselves
   b. argued that government should be run by men of noble birth and wealth
   c. contended that the mass of the population was unfit to exercise political power

_____ 19. What was the effect of the Great Awakening?
   a. a heightened respect for an educated clergy
   b. declining respect for established authority
   c. an increase in unity among the colonial churches

_____ 20. How many wars did France and Britain fight in North America between 1689 and 1763?
   a. none
   b. one
   c. four

_____ 21. The only colony to attempt to ban slavery before the Revolution was
   a. Massachusetts
   b. New York
   c. Georgia

_____ 22. Which of the following statements about the Seven Years' War is FALSE?
   a. The conflict began as a result of conflicts between American traders and land speculators and the French over control of the Ohio Valley
   b. The war ended in a stalemate
   c. The conflict resulted in the fall of the French empire in North America

CHAPTER 4 • BREAKING THE BONDS OF EMPIRE, 1760–1775

SUMMARY

This chapter traces the road to revolution. You read about the problems created by the Seven Years' War, and British efforts to suppress American smuggling, to prevent warfare with Indians, and to pay the cost of stationing troops in the colonies. You also read about the emerging patterns of resistance in the colonies, including petitions, pamphlets, intimidation, boycotts, and intercolonial meetings. Finally, you learned about the series of events, including the Boston Massacre, the Boston Tea Party, and the Coercive Acts, that ruptured relations between Britain and its American colonies.

KEY POINTS

- The roots of the American Revolution can be traced to the year 1763 when British leaders began to tighten imperial reins. Once harmonious relations between Britain and the colonies became increasingly conflict-driven.
- Britain's land policy prohibiting settlement in the West irritated colonists as did the arrival of British troops. The most serious problem was the need for money to support the empire.
- Attempts through the Sugar Act, the Stamp Act, and the Townshend Acts to raise money rather than control trade met with growing resistance in the colonies.
- Tensions increased further after Parliament passed the Coercive Acts and the First Continental Congress took the first steps toward independence from Britain.

CHAPTER SYNOPSIS

The Seven Years' War removed France from North America, but it came at a high cost. Britain's national debt doubled during the conflict and British leaders were eager to end American smuggling operations with France and Spain, which had prolonged hostilities. A pressing concern was establishing friendly relations with the Indians who allied themselves with France.

George Grenville vowed to end the previous period of salutary neglect. To halt illegal trading, he stationed British naval ships in American waters, where juryless vice-admiralty courts ruled on smuggling charges. He issued the Proclamation of 1763 that made settlement beyond the Allegheny and Appalachian Mountains illegal. A component of the Proclamation was stationing 10,000 British troops in North America, with the colonists paying the annual costs of 250,000 pounds sterling.

Grenville wanted to establish Parliament's right to levy direct taxes on the colonists, instead of indirect levies, like customs duties. He instituted the Sugar Act, which placed duties on foreign items, and the Currency Act that voided colonial paper currency. The Stamp Act was Parliament's first attempt to directly tax the colonists and precipitated widespread protests that united the colonies in a common cause.

In 1763, the colonists were proud members of the British empire, but wanted greater local autonomy. Mild protests against the Sugar Act were followed by strident protests against the Stamp Act that included hangings in effigy and attacks against the homes of colonial administrators.

OBJECTIVES

After reading this chapter, you should be able to:

1. Explain why Britain's success in the Seven Years' War produced an imperial crisis with the American colonies after 1763.
2. Explain why the Stamp Act produced fury among the colonists and identify the tactics that the colonists used to resist British policies.
3. Explain why George Grenville, Charles Townshend, and Lord Frederick North wanted to tax the colonists.
4. Discuss the significance of the Boston Massacre and the Boston Tea Party and explain why the Coercive Acts and the Quebec Act proved to be major blunders for Lord North's administration.

KEY TERMS
Specie
Vice Admiralty Courts
Virtual Representation
Writs of Assistance
Loyal Nine
Stamp Act Congress
Townshend Duties
Whigs
Political Slavery
Committees of Correspondence
First Continental Congress

KEY FIGURES
Samuel Adams
Thomas Hutchinson
George Grenville
Patrick Henry
Charles Townshend
Lord Frederick North

CHAPTER 4 • BREAKING THE BONDS OF EMPIRE, 1760–1775

_____ 1. Samuel Adams
   a. was a wealthy Boston merchant who served as Massachusetts Bay Colony's lieutenant governor and held a number of other prominent government offices
   b. used his position as a local tax collector to line his own pockets
   c. led opposition in Boston to the British practice of placing power in the hands of individuals who held many government offices

_____ 2. Following the Seven Years' War, the British government
   a. continued a policy of salutary neglect toward the North American colonies
   b. took the position that the colonists should help pay for their defense and for debts incurred on their behalf
   c. provided large loans and grants to help the colonies rebuild after the conflict

_____ 3. In the treaty ending the Seven Years' War, Britain gained control of
   a. the territory between the Mississippi River and the Rocky Mountains
   b. all of French Canada and most territory east of the Mississippi River
   c. France's possessions in the West Indies

_____ 4. Immediately following the Seven Years' War, Britain tightened control over the colonies in all but one of the following ways. Select the EXCEPTION.
   a. It stationed British naval vessels in American waters to seize colonial ships engaged in illegal trade
   b. It prohibited colonial settlement west of the Appalachian Mountains
   c. It revoked the colonies' charters

_____ 5. Which of the following was NOT a major problem facing Britain at the end of the Seven Years' War?
   a. A large national debt
   b. Indian uprisings on the western frontier
   c. The threat of rebellion from French settlers in Canada and Spanish settlers in Florida

_____ 6. The primary purpose of the Proclamation of 1763 was to
   a. to punish the colonists for failing to support British soldiers during the Seven Years' War
   b. prevent costly Indian wars
   c. encourage rapid development of the West

_____ 7. The Stamp Act was the first _____ the British Parliament imposed on the North American colonies.
   a. customs duty
   b. direct tax
   c. export tax

_____ 8. The colonists protested the Stamp Act with the slogan
   a. "moderation in the defense of liberty is no virtue"
   b. "liberty, equality, fraternity"
   c. "no taxation without representation"

_____ 9. To protest the Stamp Tax, Boston's Sons of Liberty used all the following tactics EXCEPT
   a. personal threats and intimidation
   b. property destruction
   c. the assassination of tax collectors

_____ 10. Parliament repealed the Stamp Act because
   a. of violent intimidation of British officials
   b. of the effectiveness of the colonists' boycott of English trade
   c. it feared that the colonists would otherwise demand independence

_____ 11. The Declaratory Act
   a. repealed the Stamp Act
   b. declared that the Sons of Liberty were traitors
   c. asserted Parliament's absolute authority over the colonies

_____ 12. The Townshend Duties imposed a tax on
   a. printed documents
   b. imported goods
   c. real estate and personal income

_____ 13. The colonists resisted British policies from 1763 to 1775 in all but one of the following ways. Select the EXCEPTION.
   a. by petitioning the king and Parliament for redress of grievances
   b. through economic boycotts and intimidation of British officials by colonial crowds
   c. by murdering British customs agents

_____ 14. Boston was the focal point of colonial protest against British policies for all but one of the following reasons. Select the EXCEPTION.
   a. Because Boston was a major port whose citizens' livelihood was affected by the Sugar Act, the Townshend Duties, and the Tea Act
   b. Because Boston was the colonies' only large city
   c. Because Boston had effective leaders, like Samuel Adams, and propagandists, like Paul Revere

_____ 15. In 1770, in the Boston Massacre, British solders sent to maintain order quelled a crowd of rioting colonists and killed:
   a. 5
   b. 50
   c. 55

_____ 16. Crispus Attucks was
   a. highly regarded in colonial times as an archer
   b. a Shakespearean actor remembered for his Othello
   c. among those killed in the Boston Massacre

_____ 17. The Boston Tea Party of 1773 was
   a. a colonial fund-raiser organized by Boston society ladies and gentlemen
   b. a publicity stunt set up by coffee importers
   c. a protest against the British policies regarding tea

_____ 18. In response to the Boston Tea Party, Parliament did all of the following EXCEPT
   a. It closed the port of Boston
   b. It restricted the political rights of the citizens of Massachusetts
   c. It limited the authority of the Massachusetts governor

_____ 19. The Coercive Acts
   a. Suspended Massachusetts's charter; replaced elective offices with royal appointments; restricted town meetings; and allowed British troops to be quartered in unoccupied homes
   b. were supported by most colonists outside of Massachusetts as proper punishment for the Boston Tea Party
   c. were effective in calming resistance to British rule in Massachusetts

_____ 20. Why were colonists alarmed by the Quebec Act?
   a. Because it extended the boundaries of Quebec to the Ohio River and provided for no popularly elected assembly in Quebec
   b. Because it placed the Roman Catholic Church on an equal footing with the Protestant churches in the thirteen colonies
   c. Because it made French the official language in northern New England

_____ 21. Which of the following statements about the First Continental Congress in 1774 is FALSE?
   a. Radicals wanted military preparations, intercolonial cooperation, and a well-policed economic boycott
   b. Conservatives wanted reconciliation with Britain and a plan of union that would give the colonies a measure of self-government
   c. When it ended its deliberations, the First Continental Congress declared the independence of the colonies

_____ 22. By 1774, a growing number of colonists believed that
   a. the British Parliament was in the hands of power-hungry ministers who were plotting to deprive them of their rights and liberties
   b. resistance to British authority in the thirteen colonies was declining
   c. most members of Parliament were sympathetic to the colonists' concerns

CHAPTER 5 • THE TIMES THAT TRIED MANY SOULS, 1775–1783

SUMMARY

Before the colonies gained independence, they had to fight a long and bitter war. In this chapter you learned why the colonists hesitated before declaring independence. You also learned why moderates hoping for reconciliation were overwhelmed by proponents of independence.

KEY POINTS

- Fighting between Britain and the colonists broke out in Massachusetts in April 1775.
- The British had many advantages in the war, including a large, well-trained army and navy and many Loyalists who supported the British empire.
- But many colonists were alienated by Lord Dunmore's promise of freedom to slaves who joined the royal army, and were inspired by Thomas Paine's *Common Sense*.
- Excellent leadership by George Washington; the aid of such European nations as France; and tactical errors by British commanders contributed to the American victory.

CHAPTER SYNOPSIS

Convinced that the time had come to crush resistance to British authority once and for all, the British government opened what they thought would be a brief military lesson in obedience. The first skirmishes at Lexington and Concord demonstrated American resolve and fighting ability. Despite attempts to reconcile differences with the British in the face of the first battles, the Second Continental Congress authorized the creation of an army under the leadership of George Washington. Eventually, two blocs emerged in Congress. Those seeking independence were centered in New England, and those opposing such action came primarily from the middle colonies. The failed American attack on Quebec and the bloody loss to the British at Bunker Hill removed the early euphoria from the rebellion.

Before the end of 1775, fighting had also shifted to the South. In Virginia, Lord Dunmore, the last royal governor, sought to break the rebellion of the planters by offering slaves freedom in exchange for military service. An African-American regiment was formed, suffering a bad defeat at the hand of better-trained Virginia militiamen. As a result, royal authority in Virginia ended, and Lord Dunmore fled the colony in the midst of a devastating smallpox epidemic. Royal governments in most colonies collapsed and were replaced by provincial legislatures. Massachusetts and other colonies then sought permission from the Continental Congress to form governments based on written constitutions.

Moderates attempted to stem the growing tide toward independence. Their efforts failed as military battles, and the popularity of Thomas Paine's *Common Sense* turned the mood of the patriots to independence. Thomas Jefferson's Declaration of Independence expressed both the philosophy of rebellion leading to independence and the promise of the new country.

Having initially underestimated the ability of the colonists, the British government prepared to fight a sustained war, made much more difficult by geography and the lack of any political center whose capture would hasten the end of hostilities. The British strategy involved concentrating troops in New York City, where large numbers of loyalists lived, and using land and naval forces, including German mercenaries, to crush the rebel army. The British mounted a huge offensive in New York, hoping to end the conflict within a single campaign season. However, the British failed to trap Washington's force in Brooklyn, saving the rebellion from possible early defeat.

Washington's army retreated first into New Jersey and then into Pennsylvania. Washington attacked the British at Trenton and then Princeton, New Jersey, saving the Continental army from extinction. Meanwhile, the British failed to defend many loyalists or to make effective use of those who joined nearly 70 regiments to help the British army regain control in America.

Washington realized he needed a professional and dedicated army if the new nation was to win its independence. With promises of regular pay, food, clothing, and possibly cash bonuses and land, the Continental army was formed by enlisting the economically deprived and the unfree. Most were young, unskilled, and landless men who had grown up in poverty. Supplementing these troops were indentured servants and African-Americans—slave and free. Women were recruited as auxiliaries to cook and care for the wounded and sick, among other things. Some even saw combat.

Aid for the rebel cause came from Europe, as many nations hoped to benefit from the British loss. France provided covert war supplies through a trading company set up just for that purpose, including loans and cash subsidies. British military failures in 1777—notably an abortive effort to cut off New England from the rest of the colonies by sending an army under General Burgoyne south from Canada—triggered formal French intervention on the part of the colonists.

The French alliance revived rebel hopes and victory against Britain became a real possibility. Meanwhile, British leaders devised a new strategy to cope with what had become less a rebellion than a transatlantic war, particularly after Spain joined the conflict as a French ally. The so-called southern strategy changed the theater of operations to the southern colonies where it was mistakenly believed more loyalists lived. General Sir Henry Clinton replaced William Howe and evacuated Philadelphia, narrowly escaping a devastating defeat by Washington's troops at Monmouth. In the southern colonies, operations revolved around using loyalist troops supported by a British army to secure areas and set up royal governments. Georgia was the first target, and it was quickly taken. In addition, the British sought alliances with the Cherokee, Chickasaw, Creeks, and Choctaw, but a Cherokee defeat led to the withdrawal of these nations from the war.

Following the conquest of Georgia, Clinton captured Charleston, South Carolina. Leaving Lord Cornwallis in command, Clinton returned to New York. Cornwallis defeated rebel troops at Camden, South Carolina. The shifting fortunes of war reached a low point for the rebels in 1780 as mutinies, defeats, the betrayal of Benedict Arnold, and falling troop strength beset the patriot effort. But Cornwallis had overextended his forces in the South, making them vulnerable. A major portion of his loyalist troops were defeated at King's Mountain, North Carolina. Guerrilla raids led by Frances Marion and others in South Carolina harassed British troops and supporters in South Carolina.

The changing fortunes of war continued to favor the rebels. General Nathanael Greene was appointed commander of the southern rebel forces. He split his forces in three, letting two groups act as bait for British troops. When the British army wore itself out chasing the two columns, then the third would attack. After a defeat at Hannah's Cowpens in South Carolina, Cornwallis fought Greene's forces at Guilford Courthouse, North Carolina. Though the Americans withdrew, the British suffered twice as many casualties. Cornwallis eventually retreated to Yorktown near Chesapeake Bay. While a French naval force sealed off any retreat by sea, Washington surrounded Cornwallis's army and forced it to surrender.

Facing French and Spanish attacks on British vessels in the English channel and French and Spanish threats to Gibraltar and the British West Indies, as well as attacks on Pensacola, Florida, and in India, the British opened negotiations with the Americans in 1782. A final agreement, signed in 1783, established American independence but also laid the groundwork for future conflicts between Britain and the United States.

OBJECTIVES

After reading this chapter, you should be able to:

1. Explain the factors that contributed to the desire of the colonists to challenge Britain militarily by the Spring of 1775.

2. Discuss why many leaders of the Second Continental Congress were hesitant to move toward formal independence.

3. Discuss the text of the Declaration of Independence, including the way it summarized colonial grievances and provided a vision of a future independent American republic.

4. Discuss the composition of the British and American military forces.

5. Assess the role of the French, Spanish, Dutch, and Native Americans in the colonists' struggle for independence

6. Explain why the Americans emerged victorious in the Revolution.

KEY TERMS
Rage Militaire
Second Continental Congress
Dunmore's Ethiopian Regiment
Common Sense
Tory
Hessians
Roderigue Hortalez & Cie.
Hudson Highlands Strategy
Southern Strategy

KEY FIGURES
Joseph Plumb Martin
George Washington
Thomas Gage
"Gentleman Johnny" Burgoyne
Sir Henry Clinton
William Howe
Lord Dunmore
Thomas Paine
Charles Cornwallis

CHAPTER 5 • THE TIMES THAT TRIED MANY SOULS, 1775–1783

_____ 1. In 1774 and 1775, British ministers believed that they were embarking on
   a. a brief but decisive action against a handful of colonial traitors
   b. a protracted war of revolution in North America
   c. the beginnings of a conflict that would involve the armies of the major powers of Europe

_____ 2. The opening battle of the War for Independence was fought at
   a. Lexington Green
   b. Yorktown
   c. Bunker Hill

_____ 3. Lord Dunmore, the royal governor of Virginia, outraged many colonists when he
   a. offered to free any slaves who took up arms for the British
   b. threatened to confiscate slaves and sell them to West Indian sugar planters
   c. cut off the African slave trade

_____ 4. What did Thomas Paine's popular pamphlet _Common Sense_ advocate?
   a. independence for the colonies
   b. a negotiated reconciliation with Britain
   c. submission to Parliamentary authority

_____ 5. The British king against whom the 13 Colonies rebelled was:
   a. George II
   b. George III
   c. George IV

_____ 6. The Fourth of July commemorates the
   a. start of the American Revolution
   b. adoption of the Declaration of Independence.
   c. end of the American Revolution

_____ 7. The Declaration of Independence was largely the work of
   a. Benjamin Franklin
   b. Alexander Hamilton
   c. Thomas Jefferson

_____ 8. According to the Declaration of Independence, "all men ... are endowed by their Creator with certain unalienable Rights . . ." Among the rights specified in the Declaration are:
   a. The right to trial by jury
   b. The right to bear arms
   c. The pursuit of happiness

_____ 9. As adopted by the Second Continental Congress, the Declaration of Independence did all but one of the following. Select the EXCEPTION.
   a. It argued that Britain had robbed Americans of their natural rights and liberties
   b. It accused the British of beginning an unjustified war against the colonists
   c. It accused Britain of imposing the slave trade upon the colonies

_____ 10. During the Revolutionary War, the Continental army consisted primarily of
   a. poor recruits
   b. foreign mercenaries
   c. land-holding farmers

_____ 11. The people who opposed the Revolution were called:
   a. Loyalists
   b. Whigs
   c. Republicans

_____ 12. For most of the war, Washington's chief accomplishment was:
   a. Keeping the army together
   b. Winning many battles, major and minor
   c. Killing large numbers of British soldiers

_____ 13. The British occupied all of the following cities at some point during the Revolution EXCEPT:
   a. Boston
   b. New York
   c. New Orleans

_____ 14. What was the primary significance of the battle of Saratoga?
   a. It led England to initiate talks to end the war
   b. It led to a successful colonial invasion of Canada
   c. It encouraged the French to publicly commit to an alliance with the colonists

_____ 15. From December 1777 to June 1778, the Continental Army underwent severe hardships when it was camped at:
   a. Yorktown in Virginia
   b. Saratoga in northern New York
   c. Valley Forge southeast Pennsylvania

_____ 16. The second half of the war was fought almost entirely in:
   a. The South
   b. The mid-Atlantic
   c. New England

_____ 17. To win the Revolution, America needed the help of:
   a. The Hessians
   b. The Indians
   c. The French

_____ 18. The general who commanded the British army at Yorktown was:
   a. Gen. Burgoyne
   b. Gen. Cornbury
   c. Gen. Cornwallis

_____ 19. Why was the British General forced to surrender his army at Yorktown?
   a. Because the French fleet controlled the entry into Chesapeake Bay
   b. Because his troops had staged a mutiny and were unwilling to fight
   c. Because he had run out of ammunition

_____ 20. The Revolutionary War lasted from:
   a. 1775–1777
   b. 1775–1783
   c. 1776–1779

_____ 21. England failed to win the Revolution primarily because
   a. of inadequate troop strength
   b. of a lack of financial support from Parliament
   c. it was afraid of losing other parts of its empire

CHAPTER 6 • SECURING THE REPUBLIC AND ITS IDEALS, 1776–1789

SUMMARY

In this chapter you learned about the creation of new state governments based on the principles of popular sovereignty, rule of law, and legislation by elected representatives. You also learned about the internal difficulties besetting the new republic, such as financing the war, the threat of a military coup, a hard-hitting economic depression, and popular demands for tax relief. In addition, you read about efforts to extend the boundaries of freedom, including the efforts to expand freedom of religion, to make land more readily available, to increase women's educational opportunities, and to address the problem of slavery. Finally, you learned about the drafting of the U.S. Constitution, a plan for a more powerful central government.

KEY POINTS

- Between 1776 and 1789 a variety of efforts were made to realize the nation's republican ideals.
- New state governments were established in most states, expanding voting and officeholding rights.
- Lawmakers let citizens decide which churches to support with their tax monies.
- Several states adopted bills of rights guaranteeing freedom of speech, assembly, and the press, as well as trial by jury.
- Western lands were opened to settlement.
- Educational opportunities for women increased
- Most northern states either abolished slavery or adopted a gradual emancipation plan, while some southern states made it easier for slaveowners to manumit individual slaves.
- Concern for the new nation's political stability led leading revolutionary leaders to draft a new Constitution in 1787, which worked out compromises between large and small states and between northern and southern states.
- The federal system balanced power between the national government and the state governments; within the national government, power was divided among three separate branches in a system of checks and balances.

CHAPTER SYNOPSIS

Having won the Revolutionary War and having negotiated a favorable peace settlement, the Americans still had to establish stable governments. Although American leaders agreed that government had to be based upon republican principles—defined in terms of popular sovereignty, rule of law, and legislation enacted by elected representatives—they disagreed on whether the people would act democratically or tyrannically. This debate influenced the character of revolutionary governments established by the states and the national government.

Following the collapse of royal colonial rule, ten new state constitutions were produced by 1777, and a design for a new national government was developed. These constitutions had three common traits: popular sovereignty; expanded suffrage and office-holding rights for free, white, adult males; and limited power for the national government. Pennsylvania had the most liberal constitution, opening suffrage to all white, male citizens. At the other extreme, Maryland largely retained its colonial constitution and imposed property requirements for voting, holding office, and becoming governor. New Jersey did not include gender restrictions in its constitution, meaning women voted until they were disenfranchised in 1807.

The task of planning the national government fell to John Dickinson, who at first had opposed declaring independence. Dickinson's draft called for a strong central government, but the war postponed debate and revision until late 1777. The revised version was almost the opposite of that proposed by Dickinson. Fearing tyranny, the members of the Congress had placed sovereignty and power in the states, not even providing the national government with the power of taxation. The Articles of Confederation had not so much created a nation as a loose union of states with very little center, pleasing radicals such as Samuel Adams and Thomas Jefferson, but worrying others.

The new nation faced many internal difficulties that threatened the union but which created a strong bloc of nationalists who sought a new, stronger national government. The first issue involved ratifying the Articles, which required a unanimous vote, but was stalled by questions over the distribution of lands west of the Appalachians. The Articles left the question of future settlement to those states enjoying sea-to-sea colonial charters. Maryland had no such claims and objected to this clause, refusing to sign the Articles until the so-called landed states relinquished their charter titles to Congress. They did, and on March 1, 1781, the United States had its first constitution.

An equally pressing issue involved paying the costs of the war at a time when both the states and national government were hard pressed for funds. Soldiers experienced shortages of supplies and pay. With taxation blocked, the national government issued paper money and certificates of indebtedness, but since neither had solid backing, they proved worthless. Led by Robert Morris, a group of congressional delegates proposed an impost of 5 percent on foreign trade goods to raise revenue for the national government, which required amending the Articles. Rhode Island blocked such a move, precipitating plans for a military coup by troops stationed at Newburgh, New York, in 1782, which was stopped by a dramatic appearance by George Washington. Other attempts to raise funds failed, showing the weakness of the national government.

Following the signing of the peace treaty, economic conditions worsened as a depression hit the new nation in late 1783. Trade with Britain suffered from the Orders in Council while negotiations with Spain threatened southern and western interests leading to talk of dissolving the union. These events and the rebellion led by Daniel Shays against land confiscation for payment of back taxes in western Massachusetts made nationalists even more committed to constitutional change.

During this period of war and upheaval, a movement arose to secure human rights. Virginia led the way by appending a Declaration of Rights to its state constitution that guaranteed freedom of speech, assembly, and the press, along with trial by jury. Their example was soon followed by several other states. A major issue throughout the colonies was the disestablishment of state-supported churches, where again Virginia was the pioneer, and other states quickly followed.

Another question was organization of the land west of the Appalachian Mountains, particularly in the Ohio region. The national government effectively resolved this problem through the Ordinances of 1785 and 1787. Though there had been hope such lands would be made available to landless poor and to Continental soldiers, the need for revenue caused the government to sell off much of the territory to speculators.

Women also had their hopes of securing more rights and status shattered. However, charged with the task of raising their children as good citizens, women found the concept of "republican motherhood" brought them more authority in their households, and greater educational opportunities.

The contradictions between the concepts of liberty and equality and their practice were most evident in the issue of slavery. Northern states either abolished slavery or adopted gradual emancipation acts. In the South, some planters, such as George Washington, liberated their slaves in their wills. Most, even if they opposed slavery, failed to free their slaves. Freed African-Americans found that abolishing slavery did not remove discrimination or alter Euro-American attitudes regarding racial inferiority. African-American communities did arise in northern cities, but African-Americans were considered second-class citizens. Nonetheless, some African-Americans, including Benjamin Banneker who helped design the nation's capitol, overcame racial hostility to lead noteworthy lives.

Beginning in 1786 with a meeting in Albany, nationalists waged a strong campaign for a new constitution that eventually resulted in the U. S. Constitution. The Constitutional Convention that met in Philadelphia in 1787 was attended by successful, wealthy, and powerful men who had in common the goal of a strong central government. Success depended upon compromising on a number of vexing issues.

James Madison took the leading role, having worked out a plan of national government that served as the basis of debate. But since his Virginia Plan favored large states in terms of legislative representation, the small states offered their own New Jersey Plan. The resulting "Great Compromise" created the bicameral legislature of the House of Representatives based on popular sovereignty and the Senate, apportioned equally by states. The issue of slavery threatened to divide the Convention, but again compromise was achieved. The final stumbling block was the president and executive power. A system of checks and balances combined with a electoral process that insulated the president from potential manipulation by public opinion was quickly accepted.

Drafting the Constitution was only half of the process of changing the government. The other half was getting it ratified by a divided nation. The nationalists favoring ratification became known as the Federalists. Their opponents were the Antifederalists. In a series of newspaper articles, Federalist leaders James Madison, Alexander Hamilton, and John Jay effectively presented the argument for ratification. The Antifederalist proponents proved less successful in arguing their points and could not block ratification. But their efforts did result in amending the Constitution so it included a Bill of Rights.

OBJECTIVES

After reading this chapter, you should be able to:

1. Discuss some of the internal problems that plagued the early republic and how these problems were aggravated by the weak government established by the Articles of Confederation.

2. Identify and state the significance of the Newburgh Conspiracy of 1783 and Shays's Rebellion of 1786–1787.

3. Examine the contradictions between the Revolution's rhetoric of liberty and the actual conditions faced by African Americans, women, and the propertiless poor.

4. Explain why the Constitution of 1787 might be described as a bundle of compromises.

KEY TERMS
Republicanism
Public Virtue
Radical Revolutionaries
Cautious Revolutionaries
Nationalists
Shaysites
Republican Motherhood
Manumission
Federalists
Antifederalists
The Federalist Papers

KEY FIGURES
Nancy Shippen
Phillis Wheatley
John Dickinson
Robert Morris
John Jay
Daniel Shays
Benjamin Banneker
James Madison
Alexander Hamilton

CHAPTER 6 • SECURING THE REPUBLIC AND ITS IDEALS, 1776–1789

_____ 1. Phillis Wheatley
   a. was the daughter of a wealthy Philadelphia physician
   b. fought in the Revolution disguised as a man
   c. had been captured by slave catchers on Africa's West Coast and later became a published poet

_____ 2. Which of the following statements about the new state constitutions drafted after the Revolution is FALSE?
   a. The 13 states drafted their first state constitutions between 1775 and 1780
   b. The new state constitutions stressed representative government, rule of law, and popular sovereignty
   c. The state constitutions emphasized executive power and expanded the authority of state governors

_____ 3. A unique feature of New Jersey's state constitution was that it
   a. created a one-chamber legislature
   b. allowed some women to vote
   c. did not provide for a governor

_____ 4. Because of the new state constitutions, more _____ began to hold high political office than before the Revolution.
   a. free blacks
   b. wealthy elitists
   c. common white males

_____ 5. The Articles of Confederation represented a victory for those who wanted
   a. a strong central government
   b. strong executive authority
   c. state sovereignty

_____ 6. Disgruntled military officers at Newburgh
   a. feared that Congress was going to abolish the army
   b. feared they would not be paid their back pay or their pensions
   c. overthrew George Washington as head of the Continental army

_____ 7. After the Revolution, New England farmers, merchants, and shipbuilders were hard hit by being excluded from trade with
   a. the southern states
   b. France
   c. the British West Indies

_____ 8. What was the cause of Shays's Rebellion?
   a. economic depression
   b. religious intolerance
   c. racial conflict

_____ 9. The significance of Shays's Rebellion was that it seemed to demonstrate
   a. the success of the original state constitutions
   b. the need for a stronger national government
   c. the depth of the conflict between white Americans and neighboring Indian tribes

_____ 10. The American Revolution led to all but one of the following. Select the EXCEPTION.
   a. It led to the abolition of slavery or the adoption of gradual emancipation laws in the northern states
   b. It led to the disestablishment of the established churches in many states
   c. It resulted in significant gains in the political rights of women and a more equal distribution of wealth in America

_____ 11. The Northwest Ordinance of 1787
    a. granted free homesteads to families of modest means
    b. banned slavery in territories north of the Ohio River
    c. allowed territories to print currency and mint coins

_____ 12. Increasing educational opportunities for women in the Revolutionary era were meant to
    a. secure political rights for women
    b. encourage women to achieve individual development and self-fulfillment
    c. make women better mothers

_____ 13. Following the Revolution, some southern states
    a. enacted legislation making it illegal to discriminate against blacks
    b. made it easier for planters to free individual slaves
    c. provided financial compensation to owners who freed their slaves

_____ 14. In 1787, the Framers of the Constitution opened a convention in Philadelphia to write a constitution for the following purpose:
    a. To declare independence from England
    b. To create a federal government and define its powers
    c. To establish the 13 original states

_____ 15. The outcome of the debates over slavery at the Constitutional Convention suggests that the top priority of the delegates was to:
    a. abolish slavery
    b. perpetuate slavery
    c. create a strong union with a powerful central government

_____ 16. Delegates to the Constitutional Convention agreed that
    a. a state's slave populations should not count in determining that state's representation in Congress
    b. Congress could not abolish the international slave trade unless southern slave states agreed
    c. Each slave would count for three-fifths of a white person in apportioning representation in the House of Representatives

_____ 17. Delegates at the Constitutional Convention decided that the President could NOT
    a. be elected by direct vote of the people
    b. serve as commander in chief of the armed forces
    c. negotiate treaties with foreign nations

_____ 18. _The Federalist Papers_ expressed the views of
    a. supporters of the Constitution
    b. Antifederalists
    c. state legislatures

_____ 19. The Constitution, when finished, reflected the delegates' faith in all of the following EXCEPT
    a. checks and balances
    b. popular sovereignty and federalism
    c. direct democracy

_____ 20. One objection of the Antifederalists to the new constitution was that it did NOT contain a
    a. procedure for ratifying or amending the Constitution
    b. specific list of the powers granted to the national government
    c. list of the individual rights of the people

CHAPTER 7 • THE FORMATIVE DECADE, 1790–1800

SUMMARY

In this chapter you learned how the United States adopted a bill of rights protecting the rights of the individual against the power of the central government; enacted a financial program that secured the government's credit and stimulated the economy; created the first political parties to involve the voting population in national politics; and built a new national capital in Washington, D.C.

KEY POINTS

- During the first 12 years under the new Constitution, the Federalists established a strong and vigorous national government.

- Alexander Hamilton's economic program attracted foreign investment and stimulated economic growth.

- The creation of political parties was an unexpected development that involved the voting population in politics.

- Presidents George Washington and John Adams succeeded in keeping the nation free from foreign entanglements during the nation's first crucial years.

- Despite bitter party battles, threats of secession, and foreign interference with American shipping and commerce, the new nation had overcome every obstacle it had faced.

CHAPTER SYNOPSIS

The United States in 1790 had an overwhelmingly rural population. Yet while most people lived on the Atlantic coast, the West was the most rapidly growing area. In the following ten years, tremendous economic advances occurred. The number of state chartered corporations increased tenfold. Export quadrupled and mechanized mills were built. Education, too, experienced substantial growth, especially in the number of colleges and female academies.

Creating the machinery of government was among the many pressing tasks facing the United States in 1790. Congress passed bills to impose taxes, duties, and tariffs to raise money. It also created the structure of the executive branch by establishing the departments of States, Treasury, and War. The Judiciary Act of 1789 had organized the federal court system. Passage of the Bill of Rights eased fears of government tyranny.

George Washington defined the powers of the nation's chief executive. Though Washington consulted with cabinet officials, he made the final decisions on various issues. He also established the precedent that the president could dismiss presidential appointees without Senate approval, and negotiate treaties.

The nation's most pressing problems were economic, particularly the $54 million debt owed by the national government and the $25 million owed by the states. Supported by wealthy, influential citizens, Alexander Hamilton advocated a strong federal government. He developed a multifaceted financial program that placed the nation on a sound economic footing. Through a compromise that located the future national capitol on the Virginia-Maryland border, Hamilton secured congressional passage of a plan for the federal government to assume the state and federal debts and pay them off through loans secured at a lower interest rate. He also established a Bank of the United States, despite bitter protests over its constitutionality. His proposal to aid industrial development was rejected. Raising fundamental disagreements between Hamiltonians and Jeffersonians over the future development of the nation.

Though initially opposed by Washington and others, by 1796, two political parties had emerged. Federalists supported the ideas of Alexander Hamilton and enjoyed political patronage in the Washington administration. In response, James Madison and Thomas Jefferson founded the Republican party. In addition to domestic policy differences, attitudes toward the French Revolution and the subsequent war between Britain and France divided the parties. Washington's policy of neutrality prevailed.

Crises in 1793 and 1794 tested the Washington administration and fueled political divisions. The Genet affair of 1793 led Federalists to claim the Republicans were undermining the Washington administration. In 1794, Washington's strong military response to the Whisky Rebellion prompted criticisms by Jefferson that the government had stifled legal protest.

In the 1790s, the government opened western lands for white settlement through treaties, acquisitions, and wars with Native Americans. Native American responded to the deteriorating situation with religious revitalization movements and by forming loose confederacies.

The refusal of the British to evacuate forts in western U. S. territory combined with the seizure of cargoes and American sailors by British ships stimulated widespread protest in America. The potential crisis was defused by a treaty with Britain negotiated by John Jay. Jeffersonian Republicans denounced the treaty as submission to Britain. They thought it provided unfair advantages to shipping and commercial interests. As a result Washington's popularity declined, but it revived when a subsequent treaty with Spain opened the Mississippi River to American trade. The Spanish also recognized the western and southern borders of the United States.

Washington's retirement in 1796 led to the election of John Adams as president. Adams was the first president to live in Washington, D.C. and the White House. One of Adams's first challenges was resolving an undeclared naval war with France. When negotiations stalled and French officials demanded bribes, the "XYZ affair" led many Americans to demand war. Adams eventually negotiated a peaceful settlement. The Convention of 1800 dissolved the U.S.-France alliance, but also involved the Americans forgiving $20 million in damages incurred because of French seizure of American ships may have cost. In preserving peace, Adams probably cost himself a second term as president.

In 1798, during the quasi-war with France, Congress passed the Alien and Sedition Acts to block political opposition and reduce sympathy for France. These repressive acts prompted many foreigners to leave the United States. In addition Federalist prosecutors and judges used the Sedition Act to attack Republican papers and to suppress dissent. In response, the Virginia and Kentucky legislatures passed resolutions that raised issues of states rights and nullification.

In a close, bitterly contested election, the victory of Thomas Jefferson over John Adams showed that national leadership could pass peacefully from one political party to another.

OBJECTIVES

After reading this chapter, you should be able to:

1. Describe the most serious problems facing the new nation when George Washington became president.

2. Identify the political precedents set by President Washington.

3. Discuss the measures that Alexander Hamilton proposed to create a strong central government and a prospering economy and explain why his opponents opposed these measures.

4. Distinguish between the philosophies of the Federalists and the Republicans and explain the factors that led to the rise of political parties in the United States.

5. Discuss the successes and failures of President John Adams.

6. Explain why Congress enacted the Alien and Sedition Acts and why the Jeffersonians opposed these measures.

KEY TERMS
Bill of Rights
Cabinet
Alexander Hamilton
Strict Construction
Implied Powers
Loose Interpretation
Bank of the United States
Federalists
Republicans
Farewell Address
Alien and Sedition Acts

KEY FIGURES
James Thomson Callender
George Washington
Alexander Hamilton
Thomas Jefferson
James Madison
Edmond Charles Genet
John Jay
John Adams
Aaron Burr

CHAPTER 7 • THE FORMATIVE DECADE, 1790–1800

_____ 1. The United States was the first modern nation to
   a. enact laws through a national legislature
   b. create a national bank
   c. achieve independence through a successful revolution against colonial rule

_____ 2. All of the following occurred in the United States between 1789 and 1800 EXCEPT
   a. rapid demographic and economic growth
   b. the emergence of political parties
   c. the growth of large industrial centers

_____ 3. To put the new national government into operation, Congress did all but one of the following. Select the EXCEPTION.
   a. It imposed a tax on imports
   b. It organized the federal judiciary
   c. It defined the powers of the president

_____ 4. The U.S. Constitution specified that
   a. there should be federal district and appeals courts and that the courts have the power to declare federal laws unconstitutional
   b. the president should personally run the executive branch
   c. the federal government should be divided into executive, legislative, and judicial branches of government

_____ 5. The Bill of Rights is
   a. contained in the preamble to the Constitution
   b. Article I of the original Constitution
   c. the first 10 amendments to the Constitution

_____ 6. The Bill of Rights
   a. guaranteed the right of the judiciary to overrule federal and state laws
   b. guaranteed that the federal government could not infringe upon the rights of the people
   c. established the supremacy of the federal government over the states

_____ 7. The Bill of Rights guaranteed citizens all of the following EXCEPT
   a. a free press, free speech, and free exercise of religion
   b. the right to a trial by jury
   c. the right to vote

_____ 8. The most pressing problem facing the new government in 1790 was
   a. the threat of foreign invasion
   b. the existence of a sizeable national debt
   c. bitter conflict between competing political parties

_____ 9. Which of the following proposals by Alexander Hamilton was NOT approved by Congress?
   a. That the federal government assume the indebtedness of the states
   b. That the new nation create a Bank of the United States modeled on the Bank of England
   c. That the United States aid its infant industries by imposing a high tariff on imported goods and fund internal improvements in transportation

_____ 10. The United States established its national capital in Washington, D.C. because
   a. Washington was located halfway between New England and Georgia
   b. George Washington provided the land for the capital near his home at Mount Vernon
   c. of a compromise between Hamilton and Thomas Jefferson and James Madison that gained Southern support for Hamilton's plan to pay off Revolutionary war debts

_____ 11. Thomas Jefferson argued that a national bank was a violation of the
   a. strict construction of the Constitution
   b. the principle of executive privilege
   c. Bill of Rights

_____ 12. All of the following precedents were established during Washington's presidency EXCEPT
     a. a presidential cabinet
     b. executive privilege
     c. judicial review

_____ 13. Competing political parties began to emerge as a result of
     a. Hamilton's financial program
     b. the Whiskey Rebellion
     c. Washington's Proclamation of Neutrality

_____ 14. Generally, the _____ viewed the French Revolution negatively as an assault on private property and Christianity.
     a. Federalists
     b. Jeffersonian Republicans
     c. Antifederalists

_____ 15. America's relations with Britain were troubled by all of the following EXCEPT
     a. Britain's refusal to remove its troops from forts in the Old Northwest
     b. British seizure of Americans ships and sailors and its encouragement of Indian attacks on American settlers
     c. Britain's refusal to recognize American boundaries in the Southwest

_____ 16. In the Jay Treaty, Britain agreed to all of the following EXCEPT
     a. evacuating forts in the Old Northwest
     b. permitting American merchants some trade with the British West Indies
     c. repaying slaveowners for slaves who had fled to the British army during the Revolution

_____ 17. In his Farewell Address, George Washington warned Americans against the dangers of foreign alliances and
     a. political parties
     b. the Three-Fifths Compromise
     c. allowing presidents to serve more than two successive terms in office

_____ 18. The Election of 1796 was the first presidential election to have all the following EXCEPT
     a. competing political parties
     b. nominations of vice presidents
     c. the outcome decided in the House of Representatives

_____ 19. What event led to an undeclared naval war between the United States and France?
     a. Genet Affair
     b. XYZ Affair
     c. Fries Rebellion

_____ 20. The Alien and Sedition Acts did NOT
     a. lengthen the period required of immigrants to become citizens of the United States and allow the president to deport aliens in time of war
     b. bar immigrants from the United States
     c. make it a crime to attack the government with malicious statements

_____ 21. The Jeffersonian Republicans considered the Alien and Sedition Acts a clear violation of the
     a. Bill of Rights
     b. Three-Fifths Compromise
     c. doctrine of judicial review

_____ 22. The Kentucky and Virginia Resolutions asserted that _____ had the right to declare an act of Congress unconstitutional and null and void.
     a. the Supreme Court
     b. the states
     c. the president

_____ 23. An immediate result of the Election of 1800 was a change in the constitution regarding the
     a. qualifications for citizens voting in presidential elections
     b. power of the House of Representatives
     c. voting procedures in the Electoral College

CHAPTER 8 • THE JEFFERSONIANS IN POWER, 1800–1815

SUMMARY

In this chapter you read about the gestures of conciliation that Thomas Jefferson made to the Federalists after his election; the steps he took to reduce Federalist influence over the judiciary; how he reduced the military budget; and his purchase of Louisiana Territory. You also learned about British and French challenges to American neutrality and the actions that Presidents Jefferson and Madison took to maintain American neutrality. Finally, you learned about the causes and significance of the War of 1812.

KEY POINTS

- As president, Thomas Jefferson sought to implement his Republican principles, including a frugal, limited government; respect for states' rights, and encouragement for agriculture. He cut military expenditures, paid off the public debt, and repealed many taxes.

- His most important act was the purchase of Louisiana Territory, which nearly doubled the size of the nation.

- The Jeffersonian era was marked by severe foreign policy challenges, including harassment of American shipping by North African pirates and by the British and French.

- In a attempt to stave off war with Britain and France, the United States attempted various forms of economic coercion.

- In a context of war and revolution, the United States succeeded in acquiring Louisiana and lands along the Gulf Coast and in Florida, defeated powerful Indian confederations in the Old Northwest and the South, and evicted British troops from American soil.

CHAPTER SYNOPSIS

As president, Thomas Jefferson believed that his mission was to restore the nation to Republican principles, from which Federalists had strayed. He believed that the yeoman farmer was the backbone of democracy, and that only an educated citizenship could create a republic where talent and ability would determine success. Jefferson was a contradictory figure who opposed slavery and tyranny, yet owned slaves and relegated women to an inferior status.

Jefferson repudiated many of the "monarchical practices" of Washington and Adams, striving for simplicity and informality. Politically, he believed that the president should not dictate to Congress, refusing to initiate legislation publicly or to veto laws solely on policy grounds. He also established the tradition of sending written messages to Congress rather than appearing personally, a standard practice until Woodrow Wilson's presidency. To achieve economy in government, Jefferson cut military spending, trimmed the budget, eliminated many taxes, and fired all federal tax collectors. During his eight years in office, the federal debt was cut by a third. He also reduced the residency requirement for citizenship from 14 to 5 years. He also let the Sedition Act lapse and freed all those imprisoned under its provisions.

Because he was committed to the principle that merit should be the criterion for filling government offices, Jefferson refused to fire Federalist employees, except for the "midnight" appointments made by John Adams in his last weeks in office. He did move, however, to weaken Federalist control of the courts. Republicans repealed the Judiciary Act of 1801. The Republicans also attempted to use impeachment to reshape the courts, but the tactic failed, helping to establish the principle of judicial independence. A controversy over the appointment of William Marbury as a judge helped establish the principle of judicial review. In his opinion in Marbury v. Madison, Supreme Court Chief Justice John Marshall held that the section of the act under which Marbury sued was unconstitutional.

Foreign policy dominated Jefferson's second term. One crisis involved the Barbary pirates who preyed on American vessels in the Mediterranean. Jefferson refused to pay tribute and sent a naval force to blockade Tripoli. Although the United States forced Tripoli to back down, it was forced to pay tribute to other North African states until 1816.

Another crisis occurred after Spain secretly ceded Louisiana territory to France in 1800. The French closed the port of New Orleans to American farmers, evoking talk of war and raising the threat of a new French colonial empire in North America. An American delegation was sent to France to purchase New Orleans and the Gulf Coast. France's failure to suppress a slave revolt in Haiti convinced Napoleon to sell Louisiana territory for $15 million. The Louisiana Purchase doubled the size of the country.

Two conspiracies threatened to break up the Union. Recognizing that the admission of western states would weaken their political influence, some Federalists hoped to form a new confederacy including New England, New Jersey, New York, and Canada. This attempt failed. It was followed by a bizarre plan, whose details remained unknown, devised by Aaron Burr and James Wilkinson, the military governor of Louisiana. Wilkinson betrayed Burr, who was then arrested and tried for treason, winning an acquittal.

The United States became embroiled in a military conflict between France and Britain, that lasted, with brief interruptions, for 25 years. France instituted the Continental System, closing European ports to British shipping and authorizing the seizure of neutral vessels that stopped in British ports. Britain responded with Orders in Council that required neutral ships to obtain a trading license and pay a tariff at a British port.

The most overt violation of America's neutral rights was the British practice of impressments, which, by 1811, forced almost 11,000 American sailors into the British Navy. A crisis erupted when three American sailors were killed by broadsides fired by the British man-of-war Leopard on the American frigate Chesapeake. With war threatening, Jefferson persuaded Congress in 1807 to institute an embargo on foreign shipping and exports. This action was both unpopular and costly and was lifted in 1809.

Under President James Madison, Congress replaced the embargo with the Non-Intercourse Act, which reopened trade with all countries except Britain and France. In 1810, Macon's Bill #2 replaced the Non-Intercourse Act, restoring trade with France and Britain. When France repealed its restrictions on American trade, the United States closed trade with Britain. In 1812, the United States declared war on England, a decision opposed by most Federalists. Sentiment for war was fanned by a desire to acquire territory in Canada and in Florida as well as a desire to attack Indians. The discovery of British guns at the battle of Tippecanoe convinced Americans that Britain was involved in Indian attacks.

The United States was unprepared for war, but succeeded in stopping a British invasion at Niagara. It also stopped a British attempt to take Baltimore, after a British force captured and burned Washington, D.C. In the Southeast, a force led by Andrew Jackson defeated the Creek Indians at the Battle of Horseshoe Bend and decimated a British force at the Battle of New Orleans. Ironically, the victory took place two weeks after a peace treaty had been signed.

Though considered a footnote to the Napoleonic wars, the War of 1812 was of crucial significance to the United States. It destroyed the ability of Indians east of the Mississippi River to resist American expansion. The victory also strengthened the U.S. position over Spain in the South, leading to the cession of Florida and recognition of a boundary line that ran to the Pacific Ocean. Finally, the opposition of the Federalists to the war led to their party's demise.

OBJECTIVES

After reading this chapter, you should be able to:

1. Discuss the ways that Thomas Jefferson sought to conciliate the Federalists after he became president and how he implemented his own principles.

2. Describe the steps Jefferson took to reduce Federalist influence over the judiciary.

3. Explain why *Marbury v. Madison* is a landmark in American legal history.

4. Explain how Britain and France threatened American shipping and the steps that Presidents Jefferson and Madison took to pressure the French and British to respect American rights.

5. Identify who favored and who opposed war with Britain in 1812; explain why the United States was able to fight Britain to a draw; and describe the significance of the conflict.

KEY TERMS
Judiciary Act of 1801
Marbury v. Madison
Judicial Review
Impressment
Embargo of 1807
Non-Intercourse Act
Macon's Bill No. 2
Hartford Convention

KEY FIGURES
Aaron Burr
John Marshall
Toussaint Louverture
James Madison
Andrew Jackson

CHAPTER 8 • THE JEFFERSONIANS IN POWER, 1800–1815

_____ 1. In 1804, while he was still Vice President, Aaron Burr was indicted for
   a. bribery
   b. murder
   c. shoplifting

_____ 2. Upon becoming President, Thomas Jefferson pledged his administration to all the following EXCEPT
   a. limited government
   b. states rights
   c. a stronger military and a more aggressive foreign policy

_____ 3. Thomas Jefferson viewed _____ as God's chosen people.
   a. merchants
   b. planters
   c. yeoman farmers

_____ 4. Jefferson supported all of the following EXCEPT
   a. religious freedom
   b. an educated citizenry
   c. a loose interpretation of the Constitution

_____ 5. To implement President Jefferson's principles, the Republican-dominated Congress
   a. revoked the charter of the Bank of the United States
   b. lowered the price of public lands
   c. formed a military and economic alliance with France

_____ 6. As President, Jefferson
   a. refused to initiate legislation or to veto congressional bills
   b. regularly appeared before Congress to lobby for his agenda
   c. gave frequent public speeches across the country in order to involve the public in government

_____ 7. Which of the following statements about Jefferson's presidency is FALSE?
   a. He fired all federal tax collectors
   b. He eliminated taxes on whiskey, houses, and slaves and cut the federal debt by a third
   c. He increased the size of the army and navy

_____ 8. Which of the following statements about the Louisiana Purchase is FALSE?
   a. It doubled the country's size
   b. It gave the United States control of the Mississippi River and the port of New Orleans
   c. It required the adoption of a Constitutional Amendment to permit government purchases of land

_____ 9. The Supreme Court case of _Marbury v. Madison_
   a. permitted the court to overturn state laws
   b. established the authority of the Supreme Court to invalidate federal laws it thought to be unconstitutional
   c. upheld the constitutionality of the Bank of the United States

_____ 10. John Marshall's decision in _Marbury v. Madison_ established the precedent for
   a. implied powers
   b. executive privilege
   c. judicial review

_____ 11. The Jeffersonian Republicans
   a. controlled the judiciary
   b. strongly defended the principle of an independent judiciary
   c. impeached and removed one federal judge and brought proceedings against a Supreme Court Justice

_____ 12. Why was Aaron Burr tried for treason?
   a. For murdering Alexander Hamilton in a duel
   b. For conspiring to create a Northern Confederacy consisting of New Jersey, New York, New England, and Canada
   c. For plotting to set up an independent nation in the Mississippi Valley

_____ 13. Impressment involved the
   a. seizure of American ships
   b. forcible conscription of American seamen into the British navy
   c. violation of another country's neutral rights

_____ 14. The Embargo of 1807
   a. led Britain to end its practice of impressments
   b. stimulated smuggling and evasion of the law by Americans
   c. strengthened the Jeffersonian Republican party

_____ 15. President James Madison initially dealt with foreign interference in American shipping by
   a. greatly increasing the size of the army and navy
   b. having U.S. naval vessels accompany American merchant ships
   c. attempting to use economic pressures to persuade Britain and France to alter their policies

_____ 16. Supporters of the War of 1812 viewed war with Britain as an opportunity to do all but one of the following. Select the EXCEPTION.
   a. To defend the nation's honor and expand the nation's territory
   b. To conquer the islands of the British West Indies
   c. To remove western Indians from the path of white settlement

_____ 17. Which of the following proposals was NOT adopted by the Hartford Convention?
   a. Restrictions on the powers of Congress and abolition of the Three-Fifths Compromise
   b. Limiting the president to a single term in office
   c. Immediate secession of New England from the Union

_____ 18. Which of the following was NOT a consequence of the War of 1812?
   a. It effectively destroyed the Indians' ability to resist future American expansion
   b. It led to the demise of the Federalist party
   c. It led Spain to surrender Texas to the United States

_____ 19. The Battle of New Orleans
   a. was the major British victory of the War of 1812
   b. occurred after the War of 1812 was over
   c. was the only battle of the war fought in the South

CHAPTER 9 • NATIONALISM, ECONOMIC GROWTH, AND THE ROOTS OF SECTIONAL CONFLICT, 1815–1824

SUMMARY

The War of 1812, climaxed by Andrew Jackson's smashing victory at the battle of New Orleans, stirred a new sense of nationalism and dynamism. In this chapter you learned about the forms the spirit of nationalism took in a series of Supreme Court decisions and in foreign policy. You also learned about industrial developments that increased productivity, promoted commercial development, and improved communication and transportation. Finally, you read about the Panic of 1819 and the Missouri Crisis, which led to the emergence of new political divisions and sectional animosities.

KEY POINTS

- The Era of Good Feelings was a period of dramatic growth and intense nationalism.

- The spirit of nationalism was apparent in Supreme Court decisions that established the supremacy of the federal government and expanded the powers of Congress. American interest and power in foreign policy was especially apparent in the Monroe Doctrine.

- Industrial development enhanced national self-sufficiency and united the nation with improved roads, canals, and river transportation.

- Forces for division were also at work. The financial Panic of 1819 led to the emergence of new political parties. The Missouri Crisis contributed to a growing sectional split between North and South.

CHAPTER SYNOPSIS

The presidency of James Monroe became known as the "Era of Good Feelings" because of the relative absence of political strife. Monroe's policies followed the nonpartisan tradition of Washington. The Federalist party had collapsed, and the Republican party had adopted many of Federalist policies.

The willingness of Republicans to accept Federalist programs was apparent in proposals made by James Madison at the end of the War of 1812. A national bank, protective tariffs, a standing army, and internal improvements were warmly welcomed by the new generation of Republican leaders, including Henry Clay, John C. Calhoun, and Daniel Webster, who represented western, southern, and eastern interests, respectively.

Clay devised the "American System" that called for protective tariffs to keep out foreign goods and stimulate industrial growth while creating a large urban market for agricultural products. The tariff revenues would then be used to build roads and canals to stimulate western and southern growth. The need to protect the nascent American industrial base became apparent when cheap British goods flooded American markets after 1815. As a result, Congress continued the protective duties established during the War of 1812, providing protection to America's emerging industries.

The movement for a second national bank was a response to the financial problems created by the War of 1812. The first bank had expired in 1811, leaving the United States ill-prepared to cope with the war's financial demands. In 1816, Congress chartered a second national bank for 20 years.

The return of peace unleashed a large migration into western lands leading to the rapid admission of four states: Indiana (1816), Mississippi (1817), Illinois (1818), and Alabama (1819). Settlers demanded cheaper land and improved transportation to move goods to markets. In 1820, Congress reduced the minimum purchase to 80 acres and the minimum price to $1.25 per acre, stimulating a land boom that resulted in sales of almost one million acres annually. Settlement spurred calls for improved transportation but a variety of factors stymied all federal government efforts before 1815, except for the National Road.

The spirit of nationalism was reflected in Supreme Court decisions. In a series of rulings after 1815, the Court became the final arbiter of the constitutionality of state and federal laws.

The victory in the War of 1812 had a significant impact on foreign policy, too. The United States decided to end the raids on American shipping by the Barbary pirates and stop tribute payments. A fleet of ships was sent to the Mediterranean where the threat of military action produced an agreement by all North African states to free American prisoners without ransom, end tribute payments, guarantee noninterference with American commerce, and pay compensation for vessels seized. The next step was settling old grievances with the British. The Rush-Bagot Treaty (1817) removed most military ships from the Great Lakes. The following year, American fishing interests gained access to eastern Canadian waters and the 49th parallel was agreed upon as the northern boundary between the United States and Canada from Minnesota to the Rockies. The British also consented to joint occupancy of the Oregon region.

The most pressing issue was the collapse of Spain's New World empire. The deposing of the Spanish king by Napoleon in 1808 led Spain's American colonies to declare their independence, arousing sympathy in the United States. But there was concern over possible European intervention to restore monarchical order. An invasion into Florida by Andrew Jackson to halt raids by Indians, fugitive slaves, and pirates led to the acquisition of that territory under the Adams-Onis Treaty (1819). The Monroe Doctrine, issued in 1823, declared the Americas closed to further colonization in return for noninterference by the United States in European affairs.

After the War of 1812, the American economy grew at an astounding rate. A major obstacle to economic development before 1815 was poor transportation. Overland costs were prohibitively high. Shipping by water was cheaper but slow and posed great problems when going upstream. The development of the steamboat by Robert Fulton revolutionized water travel, as did the building of canals. The construction of the Erie Canal stimulated an economic revolution that bound the farms of the Midwest to eastern markets. It also unleashed a spurt of canal building. Eastern cities experimented with railroads which quickly became the chief method of moving freight. The emerging transportation revolution greatly reduced the cost of bringing goods to market, stimulating both agriculture and industry. The new roads, canals, and railroads helped bind the East and West together. The telegraph also stimulated development by improving communication.

The emerging industrial economy produced a corresponding shift in the law. Previously, courts had made decisions on the basis of fair price regardless of supply and demand. The rise of the market economy required different assumptions. In conjunction with state legislatures, the courts provided private firms with new powers, including the power allowed to appropriate land. Company liability for injuries to employees were reduced, too.

Initially, economic progress. was slowed by a lack of skilled mechanics, an inadequate system of collegiate education, and resistance to the changes technological innovation brought. By the 1820s, attitudes had changed regarding progress, thanks in large part to the numerous inventors who basically transformed European theories into practical inventions. Another factor was the emergence of the United States as a leader in industrial production techniques. Eli Whitney pioneered the method of production using interchangeable parts that became the foundation of the American System of manufacture. Transportation improvements combined with market demands stimulated cash crop cultivation. Agricultural production was also transformed by the iron plow and later the mechanical thresher.

Economic development contributed to the rapid growth of cities. Between 1820 and 1840, the urban population of the nation increased by 60 percent each decade. The migration of people from farm areas to the cities provided the major impetus for growth. The influx of people, however, intensified existing urban problems, such as access to clean drinking water, improved public transportation, and, most importantly sanitation that resulted in high mortality rates from disease. While conditions for the wealthy improved, many poor people lived in slum areas.

The image of the "Era of Good Feelings" masked emerging tensions that arose as a result of an economic depression and a controversy over slavery. In 1819, a financial panic swept the country. The resulting depression. produced mounting unemployment, bank failures, foreclosures, plummeting crop prices, and the collapse of western land investments. The panic was caused by a sharp drop in cotton prices, contraction of credit by the Bank of the United States to stem inflation, a congressional order requiring cash payments for land purchases, and the closing of factories in the face of foreign competition. A wave of protest arose that led to demands for greater democratization. In addition, the economic collapse intensified bad feelings toward banks and monopolies. In seeking solutions, the divergent needs of the North and South became evident, renewing sectional feelings.

Sectionalism became even more overt in the Missouri Crisis. The question of admitting Missouri as a slave state threatened the delicate balance of slave and free states in Congress. The Tallmadge amendment sought to restrict slavery in Missouri as a condition for statehood. A series of compromises resolved this inflammatory issue as Maine was admitted as a free state and Missouri as a slave state. In addition, it was agreed that north of 36° 30' latitude no slave state would be formed in the Louisiana Purchase territory. The controversy and the compromise showed that the nation still harbored deep sectional distinctions that threatened the security of the Union.

OBJECTIVES

After reading this chapter, you should be able to:

1. Explain why the period following the War of 1812 is called the "Era of Good Feelings" and describe the political, social, and economic developments that contributed to a growing sense of nationalism.

2. Describe the ways that the Supreme Court strengthened the authority of the national government.

3. Identify the problems that had to be overcome for the United States to develop a vigorous economy.

4. Explain how the Panic of 1819 and the Missouri Crisis produced new sectional and party divisions.

KEY TERMS
Era of Good Feelings
McCullough v. Maryland
Dartmouth v. Woodward
Monroe Doctrine
American System of Production

KEY FIGURES
Francis Cabot Lowell
James Monroe
Henry Clay
John C. Calhoun
Daniel Webster
Eli Whitney
Denmark Vesey

CHAPTER 9 • NATIONALISM, ECONOMIC GROWTH, AND THE ROOTS OF SECTIONAL CONFLICT, 1815–1824

_____ 1. What did Francis Cabot Lowell invest in when his importing business was ruined by the Embargo Act and War of 1812?
   a. Textile manufacturing
   b. Railroads
   c. Western lands

_____ 2. In the immediate aftermath of the War of 1812, the United States experienced a strong surge of
   a. sectional animosity
   b. party strife
   c. nationalism

_____ 3. The Era of Good Feelings was the period under
   a. James Madison when good relations with Britain were developed
   b. James Monroe when political factionalism was at a low point
   c. James Monroe just before the 1824 presidential election

_____ 4. The War of 1812 convinced many younger Republican members of Congress that the United States needed all the following EXCEPT
   a. a national bank
   b. a protective tariff and federally funded internal improvements
   c. federal government support for education

_____ 5. The rise of industry between 1815 and 1825 can be attributed to all of the following EXCEPT
   a. improved transportation
   b. advances in technology
   c. government support for education and research

_____ 6. The Supreme Court decision in _McCulloch v. Maryland_ involved
   a. the sanctity of contracts
   b. the constitutionality of the Second Bank of the United States
   c. the federal government's power over the interstate slave trade

_____ 7. The Monroe Doctrine did all but one of the following. Select the EXCEPTION.
   a. It warned Europeans not to interfere in the internal affairs of Western hemispheric nations
   b. It pledged that the United States would not interfere in internal European affairs
   c. It promised that the United States would not interfere in the affairs of other Western hemispheric nations

_____ 8. The American system of manufacturing depended on the use of all of the following EXCEPT
   a. mass production
   b. skilled craftsmanship
   c. mechanization and interchangeable parts

_____ 9. After the War of 1812, American farming became less
   a. mechanized
   b. commercialized
   c. self-sufficient

_____ 10. Debtors blamed the Panic of 1819 on all the following EXCEPT
   a. high protective tariffs and the high cost of government
   b. the policies of the Second Bank of the United States
   c. the Federalist party

_____ 11. Which of the following statements about the Panic of 1819 is FALSE?
   a. It led many states to end restrictions on voting by white men
   b. It led many debtors to demand "stay laws" and many manufacturers to call for high protective tariffs
   c. It led Congress to fund public works projects including an extensive system of national roads

_____ 12. The Missouri Crisis was generated by the need to decide the status of slavery
   a. west of the Mississippi River
   b. north of the Ohio River
   c. in the Southwest

_____ 13. Which of the following provisions was NOT included in the Missouri Compromise?
   a. no future slave states were to be admitted to the Union
   b. Missouri was to be admitted to the Union as a slave state
   c. Maine was to be admitted to the Union as a free state

_____ 14. As a result of the Missouri Compromise,
   a. there were temporarily more slave states than free states
   b. slavery was banned in the northern half of Louisiana Territory
   c. free blacks were barred from Louisiana Territory

CHAPTER 10 • POWER AND POLITICS IN JACKSON'S AMERICA

SUMMARY

In this chapter you learned about the political revolution that transformed American politics between 1820 and 1840. You also learned about Andrew Jackson and the ways that he increased the power and prestige of the office of the president.

KEY POINTS

- The period from 1820 to 1840 was a time of important political developments.
- Property qualifications for voting and officeholding were repealed; voting by voice was eliminated.
- Direct methods of selecting presidential electors, county officials, state judges, and governors replaced indirect methods. Voter participation increased.
- A new two-party system replaced by the politics of deference to elites.
- The dominant political figure of this era was Andrew Jackson, who opened millions of acres of Indian lands to white settlement, destroyed the Second Bank of the United States, and denied the right of a state to nullify the federal tariff.

CHAPTER SYNOPSIS

In 1820, American politics was dominated by deference. Competing parties were non-existent and voters deferred to the leadership of local elites. Political campaigns were staid affairs and most states imposed property and tax-paying requirements on the adult white males who alone had the vote. Voting was conducted by voice.

Between 1820 and 1840, however, a democratic revolution occurred in American politics. Property qualifications for voting and officeholding were repealed. Voters began to directly elect presidential electors, governors, and county officials. To provide for greater participation, states instituted nominating conventions, opened polling places in convenient locations, and eliminated voting by voice. A new two-party system emerged.

During James Monroe's presidency, the Republican party split into factions. Over time, these factions coalesced into two competing parties. Three factors contributed to the rise of the second party system. First were strong disagreements over debt relief, banking, monetary, and tariffs following the financial Panic of 1819. Second, the slavery issue came to a head over the admission of Missouri as a slave state. The third cause was disagreement over presidential candidates since the Virginia dynasty had ended with Monroe. The election of 1824 saw the emergence of four candidates, each of whom had a distinct constituency. Though Andrew Jackson won the most popular and electoral votes, he failed to receive the constitutionally mandated majority of electoral votes. This threw the election to the House of Representatives, where Henry Clay's support of John Quincy Adams led to his election.

Though one of the most well-qualified men to serve as president, John Quincy Adams' presidency was largely a failure. This was partly due to his cold personality and his lack of an electoral mandate. But he also suffered from intensifying partisanship and sectional tension. Adams headed the National Republicans, who favored a strong, national government that provided federal aid to internal improvements and scientific advancement. Andrew Jackson led the opposition. Many slaveowners opposed Adams because they believed that expansion of federal authority had the potential of interfering with slavery.

Adams's political philosophy also worked against him. He refused to use his powers of patronage to gain support for his program. His Indian policies also created opposition. He supported removal across the Mississippi River, but felt that the government had to abide by signed treaties and had to purchase, not simply annex, Indian lands. In foreign policy, Adams failed to acquire Texas, nor could he persuade Britain to open the British West Indies to greater American trade.

Andrew Jackson's supporters in Congress used the tariff to try and embarrass Adams while promoting their candidate for president. In 1828, they framed the "Tariff of Abominations" which created an uproar in the South, leading John C. Calhoun to introduce his theory of nullification, under which a single state might nullify a federal law within its territory.

After a bitter campaign that featured personal attacks on both candidates, Andrew Jackson won a crushing victory. He was aided by the first direct appeal to voters by a professional political organization that had created a vast network of partisan newspapers and campaign committees. The number of people casting ballots rose dramatically.

Andrew Jackson greatly increased the power and prestige of the presidency. He was the first to declare that the president and not Congress represented the people. He believed that a conflict existed between working people and "non-producing" classes, and vowed to remove any obstacles to economic opportunity. Thus, he attacked monopolies and special privileges, seeking to instill free competition in an open marketplace. He also advocated the "spoils system."

The first major controversy of his presidency involved Indian policy. At the time he took office, 125,000 Indians lived east of the Mississippi River. The thrust of Jackson's policies was to encourage Indians to sell their lands in exchange for new lands in Oklahoma and Arkansas. The end result was that the Southeastern Indians were forced to walk the "Trail of Tears" westward, along which many died. The Sauk, Fox, and Seminoles unsuccessfully organized physical resistance against removal.

The sale of public land and the tariff on imported goods produced major controversies. Many farm families wanted cheap or free public lands, while many white Southerners wanted a low tariff. To pacify the South, in 1832, Jackson proposed a reduced tariff, but one that maintained the principle of protection. States' rights advocates in South Carolina declared the tariffs of 1828 and 1832 null and void. As military action threatened, Henry Clay achieved a compromise.

The major political issue of Jackson's presidency was his war against the Second Bank of the United States. He considered the bank unconstitutional and a privileged monopoly. The issue came to a head in 1832 when Congressional opponents of Jackson passed a bill to recharter the Second Bank, even though its current charter did not expire until 1836. Jackson vetoed the bill, and though this veto became an issue in the presidential campaign of 1832, the President easily defeated Henry Clay. Considering his victory as a mandate to attack the bank, he ordered federal revenues diverted from the bank to selected state banks. Jackson then launched a drive to remove all paper currency from circulation and replace it with hard coinage. A short-lived economic boom followed Jackson's decision to divert funds from the second Bank of the United States, but just after the election of Democratic President Martin Van Buren, the nation fell into a deep depression.

Formed in 1834, the Whig Party competed with the Democrats on almost equal terms throughout the nation. The Whigs lost the election of 1836, but won in 1840. Plagued by the continuing depression, Democratic President Martin Van Buren lost the 1840 election to William Henry Harrison who died just 30 days after taking office. Harrison's successor was John Tyler, a strict constructionist, who rejected the entire Whig program and served only one term.

Both the Whigs and the Democrats were true national parties showing strength in all sections. But the parties drew upon very different bases and had profound differences in philosophy and policy.

OBJECTIVES

After reading this chapter, you should be able to:

1. Describe the changes that took place in voting, nominating procedures, party organization, and campaign strategies between 1820 and 1840.

2. Explain why new political parties emerged in the United States in the 1820s and 1830s and how these parties differed in their principles and their bases of support.

3. Identify the groups that were denied political participation under Jacksonian democracy.

4. Explain why settlers wanted to move Native Americans west of the Mississippi River and why the removal of Indians from their homelands is known as the Trail of Tears.

5. Explain why South Carolina tried to nullify the federal tariff and how the controversy was resolved.

6. Describe how Andrew Jackson strengthened the office of the presidency.

KEY TERMS
Anti-Masons
American System
Tariff of Abominations
Nullification
Spoils System
Removal
Second Bank of the United States
Panic of 1837
Charles River Bridge case
Whig Party

KEY FIGURES
James Monroe
John Quincy Adams
Andrew Jackson
John C. Calhoun
Daniel Webster
Henry Clay

PRACTICE TEST

CHAPTER 10 • POWER AND POLITICS IN JACKSON'S AMERICA

_____ 1. The Whig Party campaign for the presidency in 1840
   a. was the first in which a party adopted a written platform
   b. emphasized principles and specific programs
   c. was the first with slogans and the first in which a presidential candidate spoke out on his own behalf

_____ 2. The dominant symbol of the Whig campaign in 1840 was
   a. the railroad
   b. the log cabin
   c. the hickory tree

_____ 3. In 1820,
   a. There were two competing parties in national politics
   b. There was one-party government in national politics
   c. There was a party concentrated in New England, a party in the South, and another party in the West

_____ 4. Between 1820 and 1840, democracy came to imply that the right to vote should be extended to
   a. all taxpayers
   b. those who had a stake in society
   c. all adult white men

_____ 5. Increasing democracy in politics during the Jacksonian era included all but one of the following. Select the EXCEPTION.
   a. establishment of national presidential nominating conventions
   b. establishment of a civil service based on merit
   c. direct election of presidential electors

_____ 6. During the Jacksonian era,
   a. women gained the right to vote in three states
   b. free blacks received the right to vote in most northern states
   c. property qualifications for voting and officeholding were abolished in most states

_____ 7. The Anti-Masons
   a. were a political party that attacked special privilege
   b. later merged with the Jacksonian Democrats
   c. were wealthy men who used political influence to attain power and profit

_____ 8. Which of the following factors did NOT contribute to the rise of the Second Party System?
   a. the financial Panic of 1819
   b. selection of a presidential candidate in 1824
   c. disagreements over foreign policy

_____ 9. John Quincy Adams
   a. favored federal support for science and economic development
   b. received the largest number of popular and electoral votes in the election of 1824
   c. opposed protective tariffs

_____ 10. John Quincy Adams's policies can best be described as
   a. nationalist
   b. strict constructionist
   c. socialist

_____ 11. Andrew Jackson's supporters accused John Quincy Adams of
   a. introducing the spoils system into national politics
   b. having struck a corrupt bargain with Henry Clay to win the presidency
   c. ruthlessly removing Indians from their homelands

_____ 12. In the presidential election of 1828, Andrew Jackson's support came mainly from
    a. the South and West
    b. New England
    c. supporters of Henry Clay's American System

_____ 13. Jackson defended the spoils system by claiming that
    a. the system insured that the best qualified people were placed in important government positions
    b. the duties of public office were simple enough for any person of intelligence to perform
    c. governmental functions would be performed with greater continuity and consistency

_____ 14. Jackson's policy toward Indians emphasized
    a. removal of Indians to lands west of the Mississippi
    b. the purchase of Indian lands
    c. government protection of Indian rights on the lands that they inhabited

_____ 15. In the case of *Worcester v. Georgia,* the Supreme Court
    a. ruled that the Second Bank of the United States was unconstitutional
    b. denied the right of a state to extend its jurisdiction over Indian tribal lands
    c. held that property qualifications for voting and officeholding violated the Constitution

_____ 16. The Trail of Tears was the consequence of Andrew Jackson's Indian policy of
    a. assimilation
    b. removal
    c. graduation

_____ 17. All of the following factors contributed to the tariff crisis of 1832 EXCEPT
    a. Southern fears that federal power would soon extend to the emancipation of slaves
    b. the attempt by Northern politicians to forge an alliance with Westerners against slavery
    c. economic troubles in South Carolina and a belief that protective tariffs discriminated against the southern states

_____ 18. The Nullification Doctrine
    a. stated that the federal government might overrule a state law
    b. proposed that a single state might block enforcement of federal laws it considered unconstitutional
    c. stated that states had a right to secede from the Union

_____ 19. Andrew Jackson responded to the nullification doctrine with
    a. sympathy
    b. neutrality
    c. open opposition

_____ 20. Andrew Jackson opposed the Bank of the United States because
    a. it possessed great power and influence without being under democratic control
    b. the bank's president illegally bribed members of Congress
    c. he felt that the bank was an impediment to interstate commerce and increased inflation and rising prices

_____ 21. As President, Andrew Jackson
    a. was unwavering in his devotion to states' rights
    b. promoted high tariffs, internal improvements, a national bank, and an active government role in the economy
    c. strengthened the office of the presidency

_____ 22. The political party that formed in opposition to Jackson's policies was
    a. the Whigs
    b. the Republicans
    c. the Federalists

_____ 23. The various factions in the Whig Party coalition were united in their common opposition to
    a. slavery
    b. humanitarian reform
    c. Andrew Jackson

CHAPTER 11 • AMERICA'S FIRST AGE OF REFORM

SUMMARY

In this chapter you learned about the religious, cultural, and social factors that gave rise to efforts to suppress the drinking of hard liquor; to rehabilitate criminals; establish public schools; care for the mentally ill, the deaf, and the blind; abolish slavery; and extend women's rights. In addition you read about the efforts of authors and artists to create distinctly American forms of literature and art.

KEY POINTS

- During the first half of the 19th century, the Declaration of Independence, the Enlightenment faith in reason, and liberal and evangelical religion inspired efforts at reform.

- Educational reformers created the nation's first system of free public schools; prison reformers created institutions to rehabilitate criminals; temperance reformers sought to end the drinking of liquor; abolitionists sought to overthrow slavery; women's rights advocates fought for the vote, expanded educational opportunities, and married women's property rights; and utopian socialists established ideal communities to serve as blueprints for a better world.

- This period also saw the rise of vibrant commercial mass culture; and the emergence of such distinctive aspects of American culture as the penny press, the minstrel show, and the western adventure novel.

- James Fenimore Cooper and Henry Wadsworth Longfellow created literature that employed native scenes and characters.

- Transcendentalists popularized a philosophy that rejected authority and tradition and emphasized each person's infinite potentialities and glorified nature as a creative force.

CHAPTER SYNOPSIS

During the first half of the nineteenth century, reformers launched unprecedented campaigns to reduce drinking, establish prisons, create public schools, educate the deaf and the blind, abolish slavery, and extend equal rights to women. America's first age of reform was accompanied by a cultural flowering of equal magnitude and impact.

Increasing poverty, lawlessness, violence, and vice encouraged efforts to reform American society. So, too, did the ideals enshrined in the Declaration of Independence, the philosophy of the Enlightenment, and liberal and evangelical religion. A wave of religious revivalism known as the Second Great Awakening convinced many Americans that the Millennium was at hand, and that America had been chosen by God to lead the world into the thousand years of peace through adherence to Republican ideas. The revivals were often led by itinerant preachers like Charles Grandison Finney and had their greatest appeal among isolated frontier farm families and upwardly mobile, lower-middle-class and working-class people in northern cities. Young women proved particularly drawn to the revivalist creed.

The earliest reformers sought to persuade Americans to lead more godly daily lives. They battled profanity and Sabbath breaking, attacked prostitution, distributed religious tracts and sought to place a Bible in every American home, and attempted to curb the use of hard liquor.

Beginning in the 1820s, social reformers sought to solve the problems of crime and illiteracy by creating prisons, public schools, and asylums for the deaf, the blind, and the mentally ill. Viewing crime as a product of environment and parental neglect, rather than the result of original sin, reformers rejected corporal punishment and instead emphasized the construction of prisons, where inmates could be rehabilitated. Other reformers campaigned for public schools as a solution to juvenile crime and the assimilation of immigrants and a way to promote individual opportunity and an informed, responsible citizenry. Meanwhile, Dorothea Dix led the crusade for better treatment of the mentally ill, while reformers Gallaudet and Samuel Howe championed efforts on behalf of the deaf and the blind.

Other reformers sought to abolish slavery and eliminate racial and gender discrimination. The emancipation of slaves in the north states following the Revolution and the prohibition against the African slave trade in 1807 created optimism that slavery was a dying institution. But the rapid growth of the slave population and the expansion of slavery into the Cotton Kingdom proved that slavery was not disappearing. At first, some opponents of slavery favored colonization of freed slaves in Liberia. But by 1830 it was clear that colonization was an impractical solution to slavery. In 1829, David Walker threatened insurrection if slavery was not abolished. In 1831, William Lloyd Garrison called for immediate emancipation without compensation to slave owners.

Abolitionists attacked slavery as sinful, illegal and economically inefficient. Antislavery agitation provoked an often violent public response in the North and South. Mobs attacked the homes of abolitionist leaders, destroyed abolitionist presses, broke up antislavery meetings, and rampaged through black neighborhoods. The Postmaster General refused to deliver antislavery tracts to the South. Between 1836 and 1844, the House of Representatives automatically tabled petitions concerning the abolition of slavery.

Some abolitionists believed that politics offered the best hope of abolishing slavery, and founded the Liberty, Free-Soil, and the Republican parties for that purpose. Other abolitionists favored a more radical approach, stressing civil disobedience and linked abolition to other reform goals such as women's rights and peace. African-Americans were at the forefront of the antislavery movement. Many risked their lives to transport runaway slaves on the underground railroad.

The women's rights movement was another major legacy of the pre-Civil War decades. Contributing to the rise of this movement were a reduction of the birth rate, new employment opportunities, and the establishment of the first coeducational and women's colleges. Other factors included a widening gap in political power, as the vote was extended to all white men, including many immigrants; the decline of household industries; and the discrimination women faced in many reform movements. The movement's achievements included the first convention dedicated to women's rights; enactment of the first laws granting married women control over their own income and property; and easier access to divorce and custody rights for mothers after divorce.

Before the Civil War, hundreds of utopian communities were founded to serve as models for an ideal society. Some, like the Shakers, were inspired by religion. Others, like New Harmony, were secular in origin. Many advocated communal upbringing of children and collective ownership of property. Among the most radical utopian experiments were Nashoba, an interracial community in Tennessee, and Oneida, a "free love" community in western New York.

At the end of the 18th century, the United States had few professional writers or artists and lacked a class of patrons to subsidize the arts. The art and literature that existed was derivative of foreign models, and Europeans treated American culture with contempt. But during the decades before the Civil War, distinctively American art and literature emerged. Early in the 19th century, Washington Irving, Henry Wadsworth Longfellow, and James Fenimore Cooper began to create literature emphasizing native scenes and characters. American Transcendentalism, a branch of the Romantic movement in Europe, contributed to the growth of a distinctive American literature. It glorified nature and expressed the idea that each individual possessed infinite, godlike potential, and stressed emotion over reason and intellect. Central figures in American Transcendentalism included Ralph Waldo Emerson, Henry David Thoreau, Margaret Fuller, a woman rights advocate, and Bronson Alcott, a pioneer in child development and education. There were two attempts to form utopian communities applying the philosophy of Transcendentalism to everyday life.

One result of the cultural ferment was the emergence of a true American literary tradition that rivaled that of Europe. Works by Edgar Allen Poe, Nathaniel Hawthorne, Herman Melville, and Walt Whitman signaled the coming of age of American literature. Minorities participated in the literary explosion. African-American writers such as Frederick Douglass and William Wells Brown helped establish the slave narrative as a literary form. In the 1850s, novels appeared by African-American and Native American writers. Mexican-Americans and Irish immigrants also contributed works on their experiences.

Beginning with historical paintings of the American Revolution, artists attracted a large audience. Landscape painting also proved popular. Parks and monuments also appeared as part of the artistic flowering. An indigenous popular culture also emerged between 1800 and 1860, consisting of penny newspapers, dime novels, and minstrel shows. Popular novels offered a wide variety of styles and content at a low cost. Much popular fiction was produced by women novelists.

The most famous purveyor of popular culture was P. T. Barnum. He pandered to the public's thirst for the bizarre in his exhibitions and American Museum in New York. Pseudoscience also captured public attention, while popular humor revolved around the tall tale. In addition, variety and minstrel shows provided inexpensive entertainment, largely to northern working-class audiences.

OBJECTIVES

After reading this chapter, you should be able to:

1. Describe the social and religious roots of the reform movements of the early 19th century.

2. Identify the ways that moral reformers tried to change the behavior of early 19th century Americans.

3. Describe the efforts of reformers in the areas of education, the treatment of criminals, and the treatment of the mentally ill.

4. Explain the emergence of the abolitionist and women's rights movements.

5. Describe how American literature and art gave expression to a distinctive national identity in the years before the Civil War.

KEY TERMS

Enlightenment
Religious Liberalism
Evangelical Revivalism
Temperance
Insanity Defense
Capital Punishment
Imprisonment for Debt
Colonization
Abolition
Women's Rights
Transcendentalists

KEY FIGURES

Sojourner Truth
William Ellery Channing
Charles Grandison Finney
Horace Mann
Prudence Crandall
Dorothea Dix
Thomas Hopkins Gallaudet
Samuel Gridley Howe
Paul Cuffe
David Walker
William Lloyd Garrison
Frederick Douglass
Angelina and Sarah Grimke
Elizabeth Cady Stanton
Ralph Waldo Emerson
Henry David Thoreau
Stephen Foster

CHAPTER 11 • AMERICA'S FIRST AGE OF REFORM

_____ 1. Prudence Crandall
  a. was jailed for teaching free African American students
  b. was a leading advocate for women's rights
  c. played an active role on the Underground Railroad

_____ 2. The reform impulse of the early 19th century was sparked by all of the following EXCEPT
  a. the ideals enshrined in the Declaration of Independence
  b. the ideas espoused by the Enlightenment
  c. a faith in the ability of government to solve all social problems

_____ 3. Early 19th century religious liberals stressed
  a. the doctrine of original sin
  b. predestination
  c. the essential goodness of human nature

_____ 4. Early nineteenth century evangelical Protestants believed in all of the following EXCEPT
  a. That national redemption depended on each person accepting Jesus Christ as a personal savior
  b. That sin was not a metaphysical abstraction but took concrete forms, such as drunkenness and dueling
  c. That religious people should not involve themselves in reform movements

_____ 5. The religious revivals that spread across the nation before the Civil War inspired a widespread sense that:
  a. the world was facing imminent destruction
  b. the nation had to overcome sin or face divine retribution
  c. human progress was inevitable

_____ 6. The leading evangelist of the Second Great Awakening was
  a. William Ellery Channing
  b. Charles Grandison Finney
  c. John Humphrey Noyes

_____ 7. At first, early 19th century moral reformers believed that they could attain their goals through _____, later they came to believe that reform depended on _____.
  a. moral suasion; government action
  b. legislation; moral appeals
  c. public education; individual conversion

_____ 8. Temperance reformers wanted to eliminate
  a. prostitution
  b. Sabbath-breaking
  c. the drinking of hard liquor

_____ 9. In 1820,
  a. Americans drank more than twice as much alcohol as they do today
  b. Americans drank the same amount of alcohol they do today
  c. Americans drank less alcohol than they do today

_____ 10. The first state to adopt a law to prohibit the sale and manufacture of alcohol was
  a. Maine in 1851
  b. South Carolina in 1860
  c. Ohio in 1875

_____ 11. Pre-Civil War reformers believed that crime was rooted in
  a. humanity's sinful nature
  b. heredity
  c. social conditions and faulty childrearing

_____ 12. Early 19th century reformers believed that criminals could be rehabilitated by
   a. removing criminals from society and encouraging them to develop habits of self-discipline
   b. inflicting harsh physical punishment on criminals
   c. subjecting criminals to public scorn and ridicule

_____ 13. Early 19th century reformers succeeded in getting a number of states to abolish
   a. the insanity defense
   b. solitary confinement
   c. the death penalty

_____ 14. Horace Mann did NOT view public education as a way to
   a. provide individual opportunity
   b. provide formal religious instruction
   c. fight juvenile delinquency and assimilate immigrants

_____ 15. The leading proponent of asylums for the mentally ill was
   a. Dorothea Dix
   b. Prudence Crandall
   c. Sojourner Truth

_____ 16. Before 1820, there was reason to believe that slavery was a dying institution because of all of the following EXCEPT
   a. Congress had outlawed the African slave trade
   b. the northern states had abolished slavery or instituted gradual emancipation schemes
   c. the slave population had begun to decline

_____ 17. Colonizationists believed that
   a. racial discrimination meant that freed slaves would have to be resettled overseas
   b. slaves should be freed at once
   c. the United States had a divine mission to spread across the North American continent

_____ 18. William Lloyd Garrison advocated
   a. transporting freed blacks to Africa
   b. immediate abolition of slavery in the South without compensation to slaveowners
   c. voting for politicians who opposed slavery

_____ 19. At first, abolitionists tried to achieve their goals by
   a. electing antislavery candidates to Congress
   b. appealing to the moral conscience of southern slaveholders
   c. offering to compensate slaveholders who voluntarily freed their own slaves

_____ 20. In the North, the appearance of abolition in the 1830s was greeted with
   a. strong support
   b. apathy
   c. hostile violence

_____ 21. In 1840, the antislavery movement divided over the issue of
   a. temperance
   b. women's rights
   c. the use of violence to end slavery

_____ 22. The first African American fugitive slave to publicly speak against slavery was
   a. William Lloyd Garrison
   b. John Brown
   c. Frederick Douglass

_____ 23. The first women's rights convention in history was held in 1848 in
   a. Philadelphia
   b. Boston
   c. Seneca Falls, New York

_____ 24. The first women's rights convention
   a. accused men of establishing a tyranny over women
   b. declared that women should have greater rights, but not the right to vote
   c. said that men and women should occupy separate but equal spheres of life

_____ 25. The mid-19th century women's rights movement succeeded in all of the following EXCEPT
   a. gaining married women greater legal control over their income and property
   b. liberalizing divorce and child custody laws
   c. gaining women the right to vote

_____ 26. Brook Farm in Massachusetts and New Harmony in Indiana were
   a. refuges for runaway slaves
   b. experiments to promote states' rights
   c. model communities designed to achieve a better social order

_____ 27. Almost all of the utopian communities in early 19th century America abolished
   a. religion
   b. private property
   c. the family

_____ 28. Ralph Waldo Emerson urged American writers and artists to
   a. challenge Americans' faith in progress
   b. create distinctly American forms of art rooted in the facts of American life
   c. investigate the bleaker aspects of American life, including poverty and racism

_____ 29. The Transcendentalists believed that the answers to the mysteries of human existence were to be found through
   a. intuition
   b. the application of reason
   c. the study of the Bible

_____ 30. Which of the following statements about Henry David Thoreau is FALSE?
   a. He wrote a classic defense of non-violent civil disobedience
   b. He lived for over two years in a cabin at Walden Pond in Massachusetts
   c. He was best known as an active campaigner for prison reform

_____ 31. Unlike most early 19th-century writers, _____ questioned society's faith in progress and humanity's basic goodness.
   a. Hawthorne and Melville
   b. Emerson and Thoreau
   c. Longfellow and Whitman

CHAPTER 12 • THE DIVIDED NORTH, THE DIVIDED SOUTH

SUMMARY

In the decades before the Civil War, diverging economic developments contributed to growing sectional differences between the North and South. In this chapter you learned about the breakdown of the artisan system of labor and the rise of the factory system in the North; the growth of labor protests and increases in immigration. You also read about the impact of slavery on the southern economy, the legal status of slaves, the material conditions of slave life, slave family life and cultural expression, and forms of slave resistance.

KEY POINTS

- Far-reaching changes took place in the northern economy between 1790 and 1860. Commercial agriculture replaced subsistence agriculture. Household production was replaced by factory production.
- Massive foreign immigration greatly increased the size of cities.
- In the South, slavery impeded the development of industry and cities and discouraged technological innovation.
- About one-third of the South's population labored as slaves. Slaves performed all kinds of work, but slavery mainly meant backbreaking field work.
- Deprivation and physical hardship were the hallmark of life under slavery. Slave sales frequently broke up slave families.
- Nevertheless, slaves were able—through their families, religion, and cultural traditions—to sustain an autonomous culture and community beyond the direct control of their masters. In addition, slaves resisted slavery through insurrection and a variety of indirect protests against slavery.

CHAPTER SYNOPSIS

In the decades before the Civil War, northern and southern development followed increasingly different paths. By 1860, the North contained 50 percent more people than the South. It was more urbanized and attracted many more European immigrants. The northern economy was more diversified into agricultural, commercial, manufacturing, financial, and transportation sectors. In contrast, the South had smaller and fewer cities and a third of its population lived in slavery.

The period between 1790 and 1860 witnessed a transformation of northern society, fueled largely by the Industrial Revolution that raised standards of living, transformed the work process, and instigated a massive migration from northern rural areas and Europe into burgeoning industrial cities. The changes in the North were heralded as offering dramatic contrast to the backward, poverty-stricken, declining South. Yet critics of industrialism also emerged, including southern apologists who claimed that the slaves were better off than the free working classes of the North.

In 1790, most farm families were largely self-sufficient. Beginning in the late eighteenth century, many families supplemented or earned their income by manufacturing products at home. By 1820, self-sufficient agriculture had given way to commercial agriculture that produced crops for sale, and a cash economy. After 1820, the emergence of factories led to the decline of household industries, causing distress in many rural regions and forcing a large number of young people to migrate to cities in search of work. By 1860, the artisan system of production declined as factories emerged. The work process became characterized by a division and specialization of labor that increased productivity. Labor became a commodity.

The economic changes resulted from the emergence of the factory system were transplanted from England to America by Samuel Slater in 1790. The idea of having a centralized workplace that consolidated all manufacturing systems appealed to many merchants and craftspeople. It allowed for close supervision of employees and regulated the workday. To acquire cheap labor and reduce costs, many factories hired children and unmarried women. By the 1830s, increasing competition among textile manufacturers led to deteriorating working conditions. As a result, many native-born women quit their jobs. They were replaced by immigrant women from Ireland.

Workers strongly protested against changes that adversely affected them. The first labor strike took place in 1806. Eventually, unions were organized. The greatest labor success was in partially establishing the ten-hour day. By 1850, the average workday had been reduced to 11.5 hours.

The changes in the economy led to a substantial increase in the demand for unskilled workers who earned very low income and lived precarious lives, in part due to frequent unemployment. After 1830, America experienced a surge of immigration from Germany, Scandinavia, and later Ireland. By the 1850s, one-half of the populations of New York and Boston were Irish. German immigrants largely moved to the Midwest.

The North was considered as a place where opportunities for mobility existed, but, in reality, society was becoming increasingly stratified between the wealthy and the poor. Industrialization and urbanization made class distinctions wider and stratification more acute. This process was intensified by the influx of immigrants, many of whom were relegated to the lowest classes. The upper classes were linked by status, intermarriage, and social relationships. In between were the urban middle classes and family farmers. Still the North was imbued with democratic principles. The wealthy comprised a working class that rejected notions of superiority and wore the same styles of dress as the middle class. Enough examples existed of people rising from poverty to wealth to support beliefs in social mobility and opportunity. Frequent internal migration fueled this feeling of mobility. After 1850, workers near the bottom of the economic ladder had expanded job opportunities.

The perception that the North and South were distinct was partially fueled by a belief that different peoples had settled these regions. Northerners were considered descendants of Puritans and Southerners were thought of as descendants of England's country gentry. In part, this misperception was propagated by popular writers who created the "Plantation Legend" stereotype. In reality, the South was both diverse and complex. Neither plantation life nor its slave system of labor was ubiquitous throughout the region. Staple crops were not the only products of southern agriculture. Geographic, economic, political, and cultural diversity characterized the South.

The popular image of southern society divided between proud aristocrats and venal poor whites was a stereotype. Large slaveholders were scarce, though they owned most of the slaves. The average owner lived in a log cabin and possessed fewer than five slaves. In spite of the prevailing image of the southern belle, white women were less fortunate than their northern counterparts. They married young, lived in relative isolation, and were less educated.

The notion that the South was poor and that slavery was dying was also a false image. The region was wealthy and the economy was growing. In addition, the southern economy largely financed the Industrial Revolution in the United States, and stimulated the development of industries in the North to service southern agriculture. However, although slavery had proven highly profitable, its overall impact on the southern economy was negative. It inhibited industrialization and urbanization, while contributing to large debts, soil exhaustion, and the retarded state of technology. In addition, class stratification was intensified because wealth and land tended to be concentrated in the hands of the large slaveowners.

The regional identification of the South intensified during the decades before the Civil War, partly in response to antislavery agitation in the North. Slaveowners no longer called slavery a necessary evil. Instead, they said it was a beneficial institution that helped create a society superior to that of the North. This argument was supported by new pseudoscientific theories that backed claims of racial inferiority. Concurrently, any antislavery sentiment in the South was rooted out by state law and public opinion.

As the South sought greater independence from the North, campaigns were launched in support of economic diversification, education, religious independence, and the creation of a uniquely southern literature. The drive toward self-sufficiency resulted in substantial increases in southern railroads, a growth in the number of southern colleges, and the creation of southern churches. By the 1850s, southern nationalism had become more aggressive and extreme. Unsuccessful attempts were even launched to extend slavery into Latin America.

Slave labor distinguished the South from the rest of the nation. One-third of the region's population worked as slaves in the decades prior to the Civil War. Overworked, poorly clad, inadequately housed, largely removed from medical care, and subject to sudden dislocation from family and friends, the destructiveness of slavery did not emasculate the slaves nor leave them defenseless. Legally, state codes defined slave status and offered regulations regarding living conditions, punishment, slave rights, and behavior toward whites. Enforcement of the codes was often loose though tightened in times of slave revolts.

The work performed by slaves was extremely diverse and not confined to agriculture, though that was where most slave labor was concentrated. The majority of slaves faced backbreaking tasks on farms or plantations, working from sun up to sunset. On large plantations, gangs commanded by black drivers predominated. To ensure hard work by unwilling laborers, slaveowners used a combination of rewards and punishments.

The material conditions of slave life were very poor, though they improved somewhat during the nineteenth century. Mortality rates were high, particularly among infants. The diet of slaves was largely corn meal, salt pork, and bacon that provided sufficient calories but inadequate nutrition. Deleterious living conditions contributed to high rates of disease. The small, crowded living quarters typically consisted of a small, windowless room where as many as six or more people lived.

Even though slavery exacted a heavy toll on family life, strong family and kinship ties existed. Slave marriages were stable and long-lasting. Family life was structured around a two-parent household but expanded into a large network of extended kin. The prospect and reality of being sold strained these relationships, as did the limits slavery placed on parental authority and the sexual abuse suffered by slave women.

Supported by family life, religion, and African traditions, slaves created a vibrant and distinctive culture. Many converted to Christianity, but molded the religion to meet their own needs, often mixing it with African retentions. Folktales commented on slave life, while providing lessons for children on how to function in the white-dominated world.

Slaves actively resisted the institution of slavery. The most overt form was armed rebellion; more prevalent were the breaking of tools, faking illness, shoddy work, stealing, and running away. These acts often occurred when slaves felt the slaveowner and overseer had overstepped traditional bounds.

The situation of the free African-Americans varied greatly, though most lived in poverty. Their legal status was on shifting middle ground between the white society and the slaves. Over half the free blacks in 1860 lived in the South. In both North and South, they faced severe restrictions and discrimination.

OBJECTIVES

After reading this chapter, you should be able to:

1. Describe the similarities and differences between the North and the South.

2. Explain how industrialization was both a force for unity and division in the pre-Civil War United States.

3. Explain why an increasing number of immigrants came to the United States during the 1840s and 1850s.

4. Describe how the institution of slavery affected southern society.

5. Explain how some Southerners tried to promote industry and a distinctive southern culture during the 1840s and 1850s.

6. Explain how the size of a plantation and the crop grown affected the conditions under which slaves and lived and how enslaved African Americans were able to sustain a sense of dignity and independence under slavery, as well as the ways that they resisted bondage.

KEY TERMS
Cotton Gin
Plantation Legend
Slave Codes
Spirituals
Maroons

KEY FIGURES
Eli Whitney
Gabriel
Denmark Vesey
Nat Turner
Hinton Rowan Helper

CHAPTER 12 • THE DIVIDED NORTH, THE DIVIDED SOUTH

_____ 1. Eli Whitney invented the _____ which revitalized _____.
   a. steamboat; western trade
   b. cotton gin; slavery
   c. spinning ginny; the textile industry

_____ 2. The pre-Civil War North differed from the South in that the North
   a. was overwhelmingly urban
   b. had a booming economy
   c. had a rapidly growing European immigrant population

_____ 3. Which was the most distinctive feature of the pre-Civil War South?
   a. Most Southerners worked in agriculture
   b. Slavery was legal and widely used
   c. The South's population was larger than the North's

_____ 4. Compared to 1790, in 1860 fewer people were engaged in
   a. commercial agriculture
   b. factory labor
   c. household crafts

_____ 5. For middle-class Northerners in the early 19th century, the industrial revolution increased all the following EXCEPT
   a. living standards
   b. job opportunities
   c. housing costs

_____ 6. Early 19th century artisans
   a. were divided into three ranks, masters, journeymen, and apprentices
   b. drew a sharp distinction between the home and the workplace
   c. rigidly divided up their life between work time and leisure time

_____ 7. By the Civil War
   a. relations between employers and employees had grown more impersonal
   b. skilled craftsmanship was increasing in importance
   c. middle-class mothers were working for wages in sharply increasing numbers

_____ 8. Who organized the first labor unions in America?
   a. unskilled laborers
   b. skilled journeymen
   c. working women

_____ 9. The greatest success for workers generated by the early 19th century labor protest was
   a. enactment of a minimum wage
   b. establishment of a ten-hour work day
   c. passage of workmen's compensation laws

_____ 10. Among the early 19th century laboring poor
   a. wages were low but unemployment was infrequent
   b. wives typically earned two-thirds of the family's income
   c. children's wages were critical to the family's standard of living

_____ 11. Where did most immigrants who entered the United States in the 1840s and '50s come from?
   a. Scandinavia
   b. Ireland and Germany
   c. England and Scotland

_____ 12. The Irish immigrated to America after 1845
   a. to avoid serving in the British Army
   b. because the potato blight wiped out their food supply
   c. because the British Army forced them to

_____ 13. The widespread belief in equality of opportunity in early 19th century America was true to the extent that there was
    a. a high rate of physical mobility
    b. an even distribution of wealth and an absence of genuine poverty
    c. an absence of class divisions

_____ 14. In the northern stereotype, the pre-Civil War South was all of the following EXCEPT
    a. a classless society
    b. a land of cotton plantations
    c. a leisurely society indifferent to money

_____ 15. In the pre-Civil War South
    a. most slaves worked on small farms
    b. most whites owned slaves
    c. most slaveholders owned five or fewer slaves

_____ 16. In the pre-Civil War South, slavery
    a. impeded urbanization
    b. was unprofitable
    c. promoted industrialization

_____ 17. In the pre-Civil War South, _____ was much higher than in the North.
    a. the literacy rate
    b. the concentration of wealth
    c. government spending

_____ 18. Between 1820 and 1860, the South's defense of slavery became more
    a. apologetic
    b. explicitly racist
    c. infrequently expressed

_____ 19. Pre-Civil War white Southerners defended slavery by arguing that it helped the South achieve _____ than the North.
    a. more commerce and industry
    b. a more stable social order
    c. greater social equality

_____ 20. Slave law
    a. treated slaves as property that could be bought, sold, and leased
    b. required slaves and whites to attend separate schools
    c. recognized the institution of marriage

_____ 21. All of the following organized slave insurrections in the early 19th century EXCEPT
    a. Denmark Vesey
    b. Nat Turner
    c. William Walker

_____ 22. Slave rebellions in the pre-Civil War South were relatively infrequent because of all but one of the following reasons. Select the EXCEPTION.
    a. Slaves were outnumbered by whites
    b. Whites were firmly united against slaves
    c. Because slaves were content under slavery

CHAPTER 13 • CULTURES COLLIDE IN THE FAR WEST

SUMMARY

By 1850, the United States had acquired vast new territory in the West. In this chapter you read about the Native Americans and Mexicans who lived in the trans-Mississippi West. You learned about the exploration of the Far West and the forces that drove traders, missionaries, and pioneers westward. Finally, you read about the way that United States acquired Texas, the Great Southwest, and the Pacific Northwest by annexation, negotiation, and war.

KEY POINTS

- Until 1821, Spain ruled the area that now includes Arizona, California, Colorado, Nevada, New Mexico, Texas, and Utah. The Mexican war for independence opened the region to American economic penetration.

- Government explorers, traders, and trappers helped to open the West to white settlement. In the 1820s, thousands of Americans moved into Texas, and during the 1840s, thousands of pioneers headed westward toward Oregon and California, seeking land and inspired by *manifest destiny*, the idea that America had a special destiny to stretch across the continent.

- Between 1844 and 1848 the United States expanded its boundaries into Texas, the Southwest, and the Pacific Northwest.

- It acquired Texas by annexation; Oregon and Washington by negotiation with Britain; and Arizona, California, Colorado, Idaho, Nevada, New Mexico, Oregon, Utah, and Wyoming as a result of war with Mexico.

CHAPTER SYNOPSIS

The West was not virgin land when Americans entered it. Most of the West was already occupied by Indians and Mexicans. In 1840, at least 300,000 Indians lived in the West and comprised more than 200 different ethnic and political groupings with diverse life styles, ranging from nomadic hunting and gathering to sedentary agriculture and fishing. Some 80,000 Mexicans also lived in the Far West.

The Mexican war for independence from Spain profoundly influenced the development of the Southwest. It encouraged American settlement in Texas and California and helped undermine the mission system by which Spanish priests had tried to convert the indigenous population to Christianity. The Revolution began in 1810, but independence was not achieved until 1821. A consequence of the removal of Spanish authority was the entry of American settlements and traders in California and Texas. The mission system, meanwhile, collapsed as the Mexican government confiscated mission property and the land was divided up into huge private ranchos worked by native Americans who were treated like slaves.

Before the nineteenth century, mystery shrouded the West because much of western North America had not been explored by Europeans. Beginning with the Louisiana Purchase, a large body of knowledge about the region was collected by American explorers, hunters, soldiers, naturalists, traders, and trappers. The beginning was the 8,000-mile, two-year expedition led by Meriwether Lewis and William Clark to explore the Missouri and Columbia rivers to the Pacific. In 1806, Lieutenant Zebulon Pike explored the southern portion of the Louisiana Territory, proclaiming the territory a vast desert. This perception continued until the 1840s when John C. Fremont provided a contrasting vision of the West as a land of plenty.

More significant to the opening of the West than the government explorers were the traders and trappers who became the first to economically exploit western resources. These mountain men blazed trails and provided much information to spur the imagination of Americans. They also undermined traditional Indian life by making them dependent upon trade goods, despoiling hunting grounds, distributing alcohol, and spreading disease. The beaver trade lasted until about 1840 after which many trappers served as army scouts or pilots for wagon trains.

One of the first western territories to experience rapid, widespread settlement was Iowa. Opened to white settlers in 1832, eight years later Iowa's population was 40,000.

Two major passages west were the Santa Fe and Oregon trails. The former tied the New Mexican economy to the United States and hastened American encroachment into the region. Originally stretching from Missouri to Santa Fe, it was extended to California in the 1830s. The Oregon Trail was mapped out in 1811 and 1812 by fur trappers. It became the longest and most famous pioneer route, stretching 2,000 miles from Independence, Missouri, to Oregon.

Between 1841 and 1865, over 350,000 pioneers made the overland trip from Iowa or Missouri to California and Oregon. The rigors of the trip blurred the traditional sexual divisions of labor. Accidents, disease, and other disasters claimed at least 20,000 lives, but the survivors never forgot the suffering or satisfaction of completing the overland passage.

In 1845, John L. O' Sullivan coined the phrase "manifest destiny," which summed up the feelings of many Americans regarding the nation's mission to extend from coast to coast. This belief in the God-given right to settle the continent and spread democracy animated and justified westward expansion.

Stephen Austin founded the first American settlement in Texas in 1822. By 1830, 16,000 Americans lived in Texas, far outnumbering the Mexican population. The Mexican government feared a takeover by the Americans and sought to reassert its control. In 1835, the Americans revolted and won their independence the following year, setting up the Republic of Texas. Though many Texans wanted to join the United States, the slave question delayed admission until 1845.

The westward expansion also raised issues regarding the boundaries of the United States, particularly the border with Canada Controversies in the East were resolved by the Webster-Ashburton Treaty of 1842, but the question of the Pacific Northwest remained unresolved.

The United States, Britain, Russia, and Spain all had claims to Oregon. The British had dominated the region primarily to support the fur trade, but an 1818 agreement with the United States opened the region to trade for both nations. By 1821, only the United States and Great Britain maintained claims on Oregon territory. American settlement was sparse until a missionary effort was undertaken in the 1830s. Spurred by rosy accounts of the land, "Oregon fever" prompted over 6,000 Americans to migrate to the territory in the 1840s. The influx of settlers forced Britain and the United States to address the issue of Oregon. Though expansionists clamored for war and annexation to the Alaska border, President James K. Polk agreed to a compromise agreement that extended the existing boundary at the 49th parallel from the Rocky Mountains to the Pacific.

Religion led to the settlement of Utah by the Mormons. Originating in upstate New York, the Mormon Church faced persecution there, moving first to Kirtland, Ohio, and eventually to Nauvoo, Illinois. The murder of Joseph Smith led Brigham Young to lead the church to the Great Salt Lake in present-day Utah in 1846, where the Mormons created a church-centered society.

In 1846, the United States went to war against Mexico and added half a million square miles of territory to the United States. American settlement of the Far West was the basic cause of war with Mexico, while the annexation of Texas provided the immediate cause. While prepared to go to war to settle boundary and claims disputes and to acquire New Mexico and California, President Polk first tried a diplomatic solution. When negotiations collapsed, the president ordered the army into disputed territory along the Riot Grande river, provoking an attack that he used as an excuse to declare war. The Mexican War was a very controversial, with its supporters arguing that it was the nation's destiny to expand, while detractors denounced the war as a land grab benefiting only Southern slaveowners.

The initial American campaign entailed a three-pronged attack on northern Mexico. Although completely successful, the loss of New Mexico and California did not force the Mexican government to surrender. Polk ordered the army to invade central Mexico. The capture of Mexico City in late 1847 failed, however, to force the Mexicans into negotiations. In 1848, an American envoy negotiated a treaty that gave the United States only the parts of Mexico Polk had initially tried to purchase. Although unpopular among ultra-expansionists, a war-weary public's desire for peace prompted Congress to ratify the treaty.

Although it increased the nation's size by a third, the Mexican war also created deep political divisions by reintroducing the issue of slavery in the West. The Wilmot Proviso, which would have barred slavery from any territory acquired from Mexico, polarized public opinion and undermined party cohesion. Initially, the debate seemed academic, but when Polk announced the discovery of gold, the slavery issue became inescapable, as tens of thousands of Americans and foreigners flocked to California, making the territory eligible for statehood.

OBJECTIVES

After reading this chapter, you should be able to:

1. Describe the role of trappers and traders, government explorers, and missionaries in the settlement of the Far West.

2. Explain why Anglo-American settlers in Texas rebelled against the Mexican government.

3. Explain the meaning of the phrase "manifest destiny" and why Americans expanded west of the Mississippi River during the 1840s.

4. Explain why the United States and Mexico went to war in 1846 and the war's significance.

KEY TERMS
Manifest Destiny
Treaty of Guadalupe Hildago
Wilmot Proviso
Gold Rush

KEY FIGURES
Stephen Austin
Sam Houston
General Antonio Lopez de Santa Anna
Joseph Smith, Jr.
Brigham Young

PRACTICE TEST

CHAPTER 13 • CULTURES COLLIDE IN THE FAR WEST

_____1. The Donner Party
   a. found a shortcut that trimmed months off the overland journey to California
   b. was the first group of pioneers to travel the overland trails to California
   c. got caught by early snows in the Sierra Nevada Mountains and suffered horribly

_____ 2. Which was NOT a purpose of the Lewis and Clark expedition?
   a. To determine whether the region was suitable for slavery
   b. To establish American claims to the region west of the Rocky Mountains
   c. To collect scientific information on the trans-Mississippi West

_____ 3. Settlement of the Great Plains was mainly delayed by
   a. opposition from Spain
   b. the absence of adequate transportation
   c. the myth that the area was the Great American Desert

_____ 4. The major force that encouraged Americans to move to Texas and the Pacific Northwest was
   a. government encouragement
   b. gold
   c. land hunger

_____ 5. The primary motive behind Spain's establishment of settlements in Texas, New Mexico, and California
   a. was the abundance of gold and silver mined in the region
   b. to defend the area from intrusion by other European powers
   c. to rid the area of its Indian inhabitants

_____ 6. Where was the Spanish mission system most successfully employed?
   a. in Arizona
   b. in Colorado
   c. in California

_____ 7. The Mexican Revolution against Spanish authority quickly led to all the following EXCEPT
   a. migration of American traders into the Southwest
   b. the demise of the rancheros
   c. the demise of the mission system

_____ 8. Where was the home of the Indians who most effectively utilized the horse in America?
   a. the Great Basin
   b. the Great Plains
   c. the Pacific Northwest

_____ 9. Contact with white traders, trappers and settlers caused
   a. the Plains Indians to move to the Southwest
   b. a dramatic decline in the Native American population
   c. the retreat of Native Americans into Spanish missions for protection

_____ 10. Most of the pioneers who migrated to the Far West came from ____ and usually _____ migrated before.
   a. the Old South; had not
   b. New England; had
   c. the Mississippi Valley; had

_____ 11. Overland pioneers usually did all the following EXCEPT
   a. travel in family units
   b. suffer severe physical hardships and abandon a rigid sexual division of labor on the trail
   c. regret their decision to migrate

_____ 12. The idea that the United States was divinely ordained to spread across the North American continent was called
   a. the mission system
   b. noblesse oblige
   c. manifest destiny

_____ 13. When American moved to Texas in the early and mid-1820s, the Mexican government required them to:
   a. learn Spanish and convert to Catholicism
   b. cease trading with the United States
   c. immediately free their slaves

_____ 14. The primary issue in the controversy over U.S. annexation of Texas was
   a. Texas's status as an independent republic
   b. the legality of slavery in Texas
   c. popular opposition to annexation among Texans

_____ 15. James K. Polk's election to the presidency in 1844 was considered a popular mandate for
   a. declaring war on Texas
   b. banning slavery from the western territories
   c. annexing Texas

_____ 16. The United States acquired the Pacific Northwest as a result of
   a. war with Russia
   b. purchase from Russia
   c. negotiations with Britain

_____ 17. Early 19th century converts to the Mormon faith were often seeking
   a. a freer expression of individualism
   b. the establishment of the Kingdom of God on earth through communal and cooperative effort
   c. the spirit of adventure in westward migration

_____ 18. The person who led the Mormons to the Great Salt Lake was
   a. Joseph Smith
   b. Brigham Young
   c. Marcus Whitman

_____ 19. The Mormons were persecuted because they seemed to threaten all but one of the following values. Select the EXCEPTION.
   a. Private property and monogamous marriage
   b. Separation of church and state
   c. Religious piety

_____ 20. President Polk based his war message to Congress on the claim that
   a. Mexico had refused to repay its debts to the United States
   b. Mexicans had killed American soldiers on American soil
   c. Mexico and Britain were plotting to halt American expansion into the Southwest

_____ 21. The Mexican War was least popular among
   a. white Southerners
   b. Westerners
   c. abolitionists

_____ 22. The Mexican War
   a. received virtually unanimous support from the American people
   b. was fought entirely outside the United States
   c. ended in a stalemate

_____ 23. The Treaty of Guadalupe Hidalgo that ended the war included
   a. the banning of slavery in all Mexican territories ceded to the United States
   b. denial of citizenship rights to Mexicans living in areas acquired by the United States
   c. the acquisition of the northern third of Mexico by the United States

_____ 24. The Wilmot Proviso was an attempt to
   a. keep Mexican territory from being annexed by the United States
   b. ban slavery from any Mexican territory ceded to the United States
   c. annex all of Mexico to the United States

CHAPTER 14 • THE HOUSE DIVIDED

SUMMARY

During the 1850s the nation's political system became incapable of resolving sectional disputes between North and South. In this chapter you read about the Compromise of 1850, including the Fugitive Slave Law; the demise of the Whig party and the emergence of the Republican party; the Kansas-Nebraska Act; violence in Kansas; the controversial Supreme Court decision in the case of Dred Scott; and John Brown's raid on Harpers Ferry.

KEY POINTS

- For forty years, attempts were made to resolve conflicts between North and South. The Missouri Compromise prohibited slavery in the northern half of the Louisiana Purchase.

- The acquisition of vast new territories during the 1840s reignited the question of slavery in the western territories. The Compromise of 1850 was an attempt to solve this problem by admitting California as a free state but allowing slavery in the rest of the Southwest. But the compromise included a fugitive slave law opposed by many Northerners.

- The Kansas-Nebraska Act proposed to solve the problem of status there by popular sovereignty. But this led to violent conflict in Kansas and the rise of the Republican party.

- The Dred Scott decision eliminated possible compromise solutions to the sectional conflict and John Brown's raid on Harpers Ferry convinced many Southerners that a majority of Northerners wanted to free the slaves and incite race war.

CHAPTER SYNOPSIS

California's 1849 request for admission to the Union as a free state raised the question that would dominate American politics over the next decade: would slavery be allowed to expand into the West or not? California's request threatened to upset the sectional balance of power in the Senate which Southerners believed was essential because the larger population in the North gave that section a majority in the House. Since the Missouri Compromise, admission to the Union had been paired between free and slave states, but there was no state to pair with California. Party instability and growing antislavery sentiment dimmed chances of a peaceful settlement.

The South faced a dilemma because of its growing minority status in the Union, the hemispheric trend toward abolition, and the decline of slavery in the Upper South. In addition, slave ownership within the region was becomingly increasingly concentrated into fewer hands, potentially weakening lower-class white support. Westward expansion provided the best option for proving slavery's viability. Southerners wanted the government to guarantee that slaves could be taken into western territories.

To provide for California's admission and resolve other issues dividing the Union, Henry Clay proposed a compromise. Admit California as a free state. Establish territorial governments in New Mexico and Utah without antislavery clauses. Have the government assume Texas' unpaid debt in exchange for the state relinquishing its claims to land in New Mexico. Have Congress enact and enforce a strict Fugitive Slave Law. Continue slavery in the nation's capital but end the slave trade. His proposal stimulated much debate in Congress and was opposed by President Zachary Taylor. It seemed dead, but after Taylor's sudden demise, President Millard Fillmore revived the idea. Illinois Senator Stephen Douglas devised a plan where Clay's single bill was divided into separate proposals that allowed changing alignments and secured passage. Many thought the compromise settled the issue of slave expansion, but this proved illusory.

The Fugitive Slave Law proved the most controversial element of the Compromise of 1850 as it permitted the transport of any black south on presentation of an affidavit by anyone claiming ownership. This potentially stripped free blacks of their rights and accorded runaway slaves no basic legal rights. The law stimulated outrage throughout the North changing thousands of people into free-soil advocates. Wide opposition also was evident in attempts to enforce the law. Harriet Beecher Stowe wrote *Uncle Tom's Cabin* as a response to the law, thereby alerting millions in the North to the evils of slavery.

As late as 1850, the two-party system appeared healthy. But it began to disintegrate as the issues of foreign immigration and expansion of slavery arose. The Know Nothing party, an anti-immigrant, anti-Catholic third party emerged in the North in response to the large immigration from Germany and Ireland that began in the mid-1840s. Urban, native-born workers saw the Irish and German immigrants as the source of their troubles. By 1855, the party had gained control of all the legislatures in New England except Vermont and Maine. The Know Nothings comprised the dominant opposition party to the Democrats in nine other states in the North and South. However this success proved temporary as political inexperience and failure to enact their program led to the party's decline by 1856. The Know Nothings influenced political developments by eroding party loyalty and helping speed the demise of the Whigs.

In 1854, the Kansas-Nebraska Act again threatened the unity of the country as the issue of slavery's expansion turned violent. Senator Stephen A. Douglas of Illinois asked that Kansas and Nebraska be opened to white settlement. To forestall southern opposition he proposed that popular sovereignty determine the status of slavery when statehood arose, and included a clause voiding the Missouri Compromise. The bill passed.

Northern opposition to the Kansas-Nebraska Act was both widespread and intense. The political fallout included increasing desertion of conservative Whigs to the Democrats and the repudiation of elected representatives by free-soil northern Democrats. In addition, anti-Nebraska groups emerged, out of which developed the Republican party, whose party slogan was "free labor, free soil, and free men."

Kansas became the pivot point for the contest between pro and anti-slavery forces. From the drought-stricken Ohio and Mississippi valleys, farmers and some free-soil advocates flooded into Kansas. Slaveholders in neighboring Missouri tried to stem the movement through fear and at the ballot box. In 1855, a proslavery legislature was elected, but free-soilers declared the election a fraud and held their own convention in Topeka, drawing up an antislavery constitution that was approved by the voters. Kansas requested admission as a free state. President Pierce recommended Kansas's admission to the Union as a slave state. Meanwhile, the territory suffered a reign of terror launched by both sides that culminated with proslavery forces sacking the free-soil town of Lawrence.

In Congress, Senator Charles Summer charged that a southern conspiracy was at work in Kansas, accusing Senator Butler of South Carolina of being part of it. Butler's nephew, Congressman Preston Brooks, retaliated by beating Summer on the head with a cane. Brooks became a hero in the South, while Summer acquired martyr status in the North. The assault on Summer led John Brown to seek revenge by murdering five proslavery advocates in Kansas. This precipitated a war of revenge that resulted in hundreds of deaths.

In the midst of the controversy and violence, Democratic candidate James Buchanan faced the Republican nominee John C. Fremont and former President Millard Fillmore in the presidential election of 1856. The bitter campaign ended with Buchanan the victor, but the results showed the increasing polarization of the nation. Except for Maryland, the South voted Democratic. The North went overwhelmingly, but not totally, Republican.

The Supreme Court added fuel to the growing fire with its decision in the Dred Scott case. The ruling basically said that Scott had no right to sue for freedom because blacks—free or slave—were not citizens, and that Congress could not exclude slavery from the territories. In seeking to resolve the slavery controversy, the court eliminated any hope for compromise, weakened its moral authority, and fanned sectional flames.

In Kansas, the proslavery forces met in Lecompton and drafted their own constitution. Afraid of southern secession, Buchanan demanded Congress admit Kansas as a slave state. The Senate agreed but the House rejected the measure and offered a compromise. The voters, however, overwhelmingly voted against the Lecompton Constitution. Free-soilers gained control of the legislature and repealed the slave code, driving most slaveowners out of the state. The lesson Northerners believed they had learned was that the slave power would stop at nothing to ensure the expansion of slavery.

By 1858, many Northerners were convinced that the nation contained two basically antagonistic societies, one dedicated to freedom and one opposed. They believed their society was locked in a life and death struggle with a southern slaveocracy that had seized the federal government and threatened fundamental liberties. At the same time, many white Southerners became convinced that the total elimination of slavery was the northern goal.

Many of the issues dividing the nation were brought into focus in the Lincoln-Douglas debates that took place during the 1858 Illinois senatorial election. Although Abraham Lincoln was little known, incumbent Stephen Douglas was the leading candidate for the Democratic presidential nomination, and so the election drew national attention. Their speeches illuminated two sharply contrasting views of slavery. Douglas won reelection, but his statements had dimmed his presidential hopes. Lincoln was thrust into the national spotlight as a Republican leader.

In 1859, John Brown attempted to instigate a slave insurrection by seizing the federal arsenal at Harper's Ferry. After the army surrounded the facility, Marines led by Colonel Robert E. Lee stormed the arsenal and captured Brown, who was tried and executed for treason. His death made him a martyr in the North, though many lashed out strongly against his tactics and the raid.

Southerners viewed the northern reaction to Brown's raid as proof that the North wanted to end slavery and begin a race war. Extremists called "fire-eaters" came to the forefront inciting public passions. Secession seemed the only alternative. The issue that had divided the nation for over 40 years, and that all the compromises could not resolve, was coming to a head.

OBJECTIVES

After reading this chapter, you should be able to:

1. Explain why California's application for statehood provoked a major sectional controversy between the North and South.

2. Identify and state the significance of the Compromise of 1850, the Fugitive Slave Law, the Kansas-Nebraska Act, and the Dred Scott Decision

3. Describe the major differences in the attitudes of Abraham Lincoln and Stephen Douglas toward slavery.

4. Explain why John Brown's raid convinced many Southerners that their states should secede from the Union.

KEY TERMS
Popular Sovereignty
Compromise of 1850
Fugitive Slave Law
Kansas Nebraska Act
Dred Scott Decision
Harpers Ferry

KEY FIGURES
Henry Clay
Daniel Webster
John C. Calhoun
Stephen Douglass
Charles Sumner
Abraham Lincoln
Frederick Douglass
John Brown

CHAPTER 14 • THE HOUSE DIVIDED

_____ 1. According to 19th century economist John Smith Dye, the entire history of the United States was a record of
   a. abolitionist attempts to instigate slave rebellion in the South
   b. Southern plots to expand slavery
   c. efforts by the federal government to destroy states' rights

_____ 2. What was the central issue that dominated American politics during the 1850s?
   a. Whether slavery would be permitted in the western territories
   b. Conflicts between the United States and Britain over the Canadian border
   c. Banking and tariff policy

_____ 3. In 1850, Southerners feared that the sectional balance of power would be upset by
   a. the demise of the Whig party
   b. California's admission as a free state
   c. the repeal of the Missouri Compromise

_____ 4. By 1850, white Southerners feared for the future of slavery for all but one of the following reasons. Select the EXCEPTION.
   a. Because Britain and France had abolished slavery in their Caribbean possessions
   b. Because slave ownership was increasingly concentrated in few hands in the South and slavery was declining in the Upper South
   c. Because Congress had banned slavery from territories ceded by Mexico in the Treaty of Guadalupe Hidalgo

_____ 5. In the Congressional debate in 1850, John C. Calhoun
   a. said there must be a constitutional amendment to protect southern rights
   b. a higher law than the Constitution necessitated the abolition of slavery
   c. an unfavorable environment would keep slavery out of the western territories

_____ 6. The most divisive element in the Compromise of 1850 was the proposal regarding the
   a. return of runaway slaves
   b. slave trade in the District of Columbia
   c. admission of California to the Union

_____ 7. The Fugitive Slave Law
   a. generally went unenforced
   b. required ordinary citizens to assist in the capture of runaway slaves
   c. protected the basic civil liberties of free blacks

_____ 8. The two-party system disintegrated in the 1850s in response to two issues: slavery expansion and
   a. foreign policy
   b. foreign immigration
   c. protective tariffs

_____ 9. Between 1853 and 1855, the _____ replaced the Whigs as the nation's second largest party.
   a. Democrats
   b. Know Nothings
   c. Republicans

_____ 10. During the 1850s, prejudice surfaced with particular vehemence against
   a. Germans
   b. Masons
   c. Catholics

_____ 11. In the politics of the 1850s, "a Northern man with Southern principles" was called a
   a. nativist
   b. doughface
   c. Know Nothing

_____ 12. American acquisition of Cuba was the goal of the
    a. Gadsden Purchase
    b. Ostend Manifesto
    c. American Party

_____ 13. The Kansas-Nebraska Act provided that slavery in these two territories be decided by
    a. Congress
    b. popular sovereignty
    c. the Supreme Court

_____ 14. Opponents of the Kansas-Nebraska Act were primarily upset because it
    a. repealed the Missouri Compromise
    b. guaranteed that slavery would expand into Kansas
    c. was incompatible with the Compromise of 1850

_____ 15. What was the consequence of the Kansas Nebraska Act?
    a. It led to the revival of the Whig Party
    b. It led to the collapse of the Democratic party
    c. It led to the formation of the Republican party

_____ 16. The diverse elements that made up the Republican party shared a belief that
    a. African Americans should have the same civil rights as white Americans
    b. residents of a territory should determine the fate of slavery there by popular vote
    c. all western territories should be closed to slavery

_____ 17. Who was the abolitionist senator who was severely beaten when he condemned the South for the "Crime Against Kansas"?
    a. Preston Brooks
    b. Charles Sumner
    c. Andrew Butler

_____ 18. The Dred Scott decision ruled that the _____ was unconstitutional.
    a. Kansas-Nebraska Act
    b. Compromise of 1850
    c. Missouri Compromise

_____ 19. In the Dred Scott decision, the Supreme Court declared that
    a. a slave taken into a free state automatically became free
    b. free blacks, but not slaves, had a right to sue in federal court
    c. Congress had no power to exclude slavery from the federal territories

_____ 20. In his "House Divided" speech in 1858, Abraham Lincoln predicted that
    a. the controversy over slavery would destroy the Union
    b. Republicans would win the presidency in 1860
    c. slavery would either be abolished or legalized throughout the Union

_____ 21. In the Lincoln-Douglas debates in 1858, Lincoln stated that he
    a. favored the full social and political equality of whites and blacks
    b. regarded slavery as a dynamic and expansionistic institution
    c. believed that the problem of slavery in the territories could best be resolved at the local level

_____ 22. During the Lincoln-Douglas debate at Freeport, Ill., Douglas upset Southerners by arguing that
    a. the Dred Scott decision was unconstitutional
    b. blacks had an equal rights to life, liberty, and the fruit of their own labor
    c. regardless of the Dred Scott decision, local laws could still exclude slavery from a territory

_____ 23. With his raid on Harpers Ferry, John Brown hoped to
    a. force the North and South to compromise on the slavery question
    b. incite a slave insurrection
    c. make Kansas a free territory

CHAPTER 15 • A NATION SHATTERED BY CIVIL WAR, 1860–1865

SUMMARY

In this chapter you learned about the coming of the Civil War; the relative strengths and weakness of the North and South; the military history of the war; as well as the dramatic political, economic, and social changes that the war produced.

KEY POINTS

- The election of a Republican president opposed to the expansion of slavery into the western territories led seven states in the lower South to secede from the Union and to establish the Confederate States of America.

- After Lincoln notified South Carolina's governor that he intended to resupply Fort Sumter in Charleston harbor, the Confederacy fired on the installation, leading the President to declare that an insurrection existed in the South.

- Early in the war, the Union succeeded in blockading Confederate harbors, and by mid-July 1862 it had divided the Confederacy in two by wresting control of Kentucky, Missouri, and much of Tennessee, as well as Mississippi River.

- In the Eastern Theater in 1861 and 1862, the Confederacy stopped Union attempts to capture its capital in Richmond, Virginia. In September 1862 (at Antietam in Maryland) and July 1863 (at Gettysburg in Pennsylvania), Robert E. Lee tried and failed to provoke European intervention in the war by winning a victory on Northern soil.

- After futile pleas to the border states to free slaves voluntarily, Lincoln in the summer of 1862 decided that emancipation was a military and political necessity. The Emancipation Proclamation transformed the war from a conflict to save the Union to a war to abolish slavery. It also authorized the enlistment of African Americans.

- During the war Congress enacted the Homestead Act offered free public land to western settlers; and land grants supported construction of a transcontinental railroad. The government also raised the tariff, enacted the first income tax, and established a system of federally-chartered banks.

CHAPTER SYNOPSIS

At the Democratic convention of 1860, southern delegates bolted the convention, splitting their party, and paving the way for the Republican victory. Northern delegates chose Stephen A. Douglas as their candidate. John C. Breckinridge was selected by southern delegates, while the short-lived Constitutional Unionists named John C. Bell. Abraham Lincoln emerged as the Republican standard bearer. In an atmosphere of fear and growing hysteria, punctuated by violence, the campaign progressed. On November 6, 1860, Lincoln won the election with a minority of the popular vote but an overwhelming edge in the electoral college. He carried every Northern state, which Southerners took as proof of their minority status in the Union.

Though Lincoln tried to reassure the South that he would not push for abolition, opinion in that section saw only two options: submission to the North or secession. South Carolina was the first state to secede and was followed by six others who met in Montgomery, Alabama to frame the new Confederate States of America. Public opinion was divided on how to respond, but Lincoln's stance was unequivocal. The Union was perpetual and secession illegal. When the Confederates opened fire on Fort Sumter, the bloodiest war in American history began.

The Confederacy contained 11 states with a population of almost 9 million, including 3.5 million slaves. But neither Delaware, Maryland, Missouri, or Kentucky joined their fellow slaveholding states in secession. With these border states the Union contained 23 million people. Apart from a larger population, the North had other advantages, including greater capital resources, more manufacturing, much more railroad mileage, and almost a monopoly on firearms production. As long as the South waged a defensive war, it had its size as an advantage and a seemingly better qualified leadership. Over the course of the conflict, however, Lincoln emerged as the stronger leader.

The first battle went to the Confederates who routed Union soldiers at Bull Run. The loss convinced Lincoln of the need for a detailed and comprehensive war plan. He also recognized that younger, more energetic generals were needed to organize and lead the army. Prior to Bull Run, Lincoln had asked General-in-Chief Winfield

Scott to design a strategy for prosecuting the war. Scott produced the "Anaconda Plan," which combined a naval blockade, a military thrust to control the Mississippi River and split the Confederacy in two, plus the stationing of armies at key points to contain southern troops. The goal was to squeeze the fighting resolve out of the South, which Scott estimated would take a year. Lincoln ordered the blockade to be implemented, which required large-scale shipbuilding and an equally large expansion of the navy. Lincoln also thought that splitting the South was a good idea. He ordered a combined navy and army effort to gain control of the Mississippi. A major step was the capture of New Orleans in 1862. But Lincoln differed with Scott over the third component. He pushed for a massive build-up of the army and a much more aggressive military posture. He placed George McClellan in charge of the army.

McClellan had amply demonstrated that his strengths lay in organizing and training his troops and in serving as an inspirational leader who was well-liked by his soldiers. But, he proved unwilling to engage the enemy in combat, in part because his military strategy conflicted with that of Lincoln, who grew frustrated and ordered him into battle. The ensuing peninsula campaign was marked by two very costly battles that led to the promotion of Robert E. Lee to the head of the Confederate forces and the retreat of McClellan to Washington. Lee achieved another victory at the Second Battle of Bull Run.

The western campaign also initially suffered from inaction. But Ulysses S. Grant's troops cut through a 150-mile rebel line from Bowling Green, Kentucky, to the Mississippi River, capturing Fort Donelson and advancing into Tennessee. A rebel counterattack led to the Battle of Shiloh that the Union won at a high cost.

Maintaining high morale among the troops and the civilian population was a major challenge facing both governments. Northern leaders proved more successful at morale building. The South believed their situation paralleled that of the colonies during the Revolutionary War. Success depended upon establishing relations with European nations to receive much needed material aid. They mistakenly thought that Europe's dependence upon southern cotton would aid in this quest. It did not. The British declared neutrality and stayed out of the conflict, as did other European nations. The need for western grain to feed their populations and moral qualms over slavery influenced these decisions. Still, the Confederacy did receive small amounts of aid from Europe, primarily through blockade runners and foreign loans.

The South faced severe problems. The blockade caused severe shortages of such everyday items as salt, sugar, and even shoes. Bread riots erupted in several cities in 1863. Compounding matters was rising inflation. When Jefferson Davis urged that southern farmers grow more food and less cotton, government confiscation of the crops led many women to plead with their soldier husbands to come home. These appeals exacerbated the desertion problem. The actions of the government eroded public confidence and led to continuing attacks on government policy. Another problem was the ability of wealthy planters to buy their way out of military service by securing substitutes, aggravating class tensions. The prevailing belief that the South's greatest weapon was its courage was increasingly undermined by the seemingly self-serving actions of the planter aristocracy in collusion with the government.

In the North, Lincoln sought to maintain public morale and to keep European nations from supporting the Confederacy. Secretary of State William Seward effectively defended Union interests and convinced European nations to remain neutral. Domestically, the Union experienced prosperity that Lincoln and the Congress helped sustain by passing a variety of legislation. A major morale booster was the refusal of the government to confiscate farm goods. The prosecution of the war led Lincoln to vastly expand the powers of the presidency, leading to charges of virtual dictatorship. Yet, he avoided prosecuting any political opponents and ensured that elections were open and fair. When the "Copperhead" movement for a negotiated peace arose, Lincoln ignored the matter.

For fear of alienating the border states, Lincoln initially moved cautiously regarding the emancipation of slaves. But by Summer 1862, the mounting death toll led him to change his mind. He announced a preliminary Emancipation Proclamation in September 1862, followed by the formal Proclamation on January 1, 1863. The public response was varied, but enthusiastically welcomed by blacks, who now sought enlistment in the war. Of the 179,000 African-Americans who served in the Union forces, 135,000 were former slaves.

The low point in the northern war effort occurred in the Spring and Summer of 1863 when morale sagged and conscription efforts led to riots among the Irish immigrants in New York City. During this period, Lincoln relieved McClellan of command, naming Ambrose Burnside in his place. Burnside rushed south and engaged Lee at Fredericksburg, experiencing a numbing defeat. Burnside was then replaced by Joseph Hooker who was defeated by Lee at Chancellorsville, though the rebel victory was marred by the death of "Stonewall" Jackson. Lee then moved north into Pennsylvania where he met a federal force under George Meade at Gettysburg. The three-day battle ended with a Union victory as Lee withdrew. In the West, Grant won another victory by taking

Vicksburg, thus giving the Union control of the Mississippi River and cutting the Confederacy in two. After the Union forces suffered another embarrassing defeat at Chickamauga, Lincoln named Grant commander of the western army. Grant captured Chattanooga, opening Georgia to invasion.

Early in 1864, Lincoln promoted Grant to general-in-chief. The new commander shifted strategy in the North away from capturing Richmond to destroying Lee's army. Although Grant was defeated in the Battle of the Wilderness, he did not withdraw but rolled southeastward, seeking more engagements. Despite heavy casualties, Grant pursued Lee's greatly reduced army to Petersburg. The only hope for the Confederacy was the election of a peace candidate in the 1864 Union presidential election. The Democrats nominated McClellan and the Republicans named Lincoln. The capture of Atlanta by William Tecumseh Sherman's army led northern voters to reelect Lincoln by an overwhelming margin.

The war had affected the lives of almost every American. Women in increasing numbers were employed as nurses in the medical facilities where prevailing practices combined with epidemic disease probably killed more people than were saved.

To speed the end of the war, Sherman requested that he march his troops to Savannah and then turn north to meet Grant, leaving a swath of devastation and destruction in his wake to sap southern morale and their ability to fight. Knowledge of Sherman's march led to increased desertion among Lee's forces. On April 9, 1865, Lee and Grant met at Appomattox where the rebel leader surrendered.

OBJECTIVES

After reading this chapter, you should be able to:

1. Describe the problems that contributed to the breakup of the Democratic party in 1860.

2. Explain why Abraham Lincoln's election as president prompted secession.

3. Compare and contrast the strengths and weaknesses of the North and South as the Civil War started.

4. Compare and contrast the military leaders and strategies of the North and the Confederacy.

5. Describe the circumstances that led President Lincoln to issue the Emancipation Proclamation.

6. Identify the social changes that the war precipitated, particularly with regard to the role of blacks.

KEY TERMS
Fire-eaters
Billy Yank
Johnny Reb
Anaconda Plan
Greebacks
Copperheads
Emancipation Proclamation
Total War

KEY FIGURES
Abraham Lincoln
Jefferson Davis
Robert E. Lee
Ulysses Grant
William Tecumseh Sherman

CHAPTER 15 • A NATION SHATTERED BY CIVIL WAR, 1860–1865

_____ 1. What was the bloodiest one-day battle of the Civil War?
   a. First Battle of Bull Run
   b. Antietam
   c. Vicksburg

_____ 2. In the election of 1860, Abraham Lincoln
   a. won a majority of the popular vote
   b. was nominated because he was a radical abolitionist
   c. did not win a single electoral vote in the South

_____ 3. During the secession crisis, Abraham Lincoln overestimated
   a. the South's commitment to slavery
   b. Northerners' devotion to the Union
   c. the extent of pro-Union sentiment in the South

_____ 4. Confederate artillery fired on Fort Sumter when news was received that Lincoln had
   a. decided to launch a preemptive attack to force the Confederate states back into the Union
   b. decided to resupply the fort
   c. proclaimed that the South was in a state of insurrection against the federal government

_____ 5. As the Civil War began, the South had an initial superiority of
   a. industrial capacity
   b. railroad mileage
   c. military leadership

_____ 6. As president of the Confederacy, Jefferson Davis was
   a. an inspirational leader
   b. an ineffective administrator
   c. easy to work with

_____ 7. During the Civil War, the Republican dominated Congress passed legislation to do all the following EXCEPT
   a. make free homesteads available to individual settlers
   b. establish agricultural colleges
   c. lower tariff rates

_____ 8. In _Ex Parte Merryman_, the Supreme Court declared that President Lincoln acted unconstitutionally when he
   a. declared the South in a state of insurrection
   b. suspended writs of habeas corpus in order to jail secessionists in Maryland
   c. issued the Emancipation Proclamation to free the slaves

_____ 9. President Lincoln's cautious approach to making the abolition of slavery a war goal
   a. reflected his own personal ambiguity about the morality of slavery
   b. disappointed most Northerners
   c. resulted from his concern about losing slaveholding border states to the Confederacy

_____ 10. The Emancipation Proclamation freed slaves in
   a. the slave states that remained in the Union
   b. the Confederate states
   c. the border states

_____ 11. In public, President Lincoln justified the Emancipation Proclamation on the grounds
   a. that slavery was immoral
   b. that it was a way to quiet the Peace Democrats
   c. that it would contribute to a military victory for the Union

_____ 12. Twice Robert E. Lee commanded a Confederate Army in major battles on Union soil. These were the battles of
   a. First and Second Bull Run
   b. Antietam and Gettysburg
   c. Fredericksburg and Shiloh

_____ 13. Abraham Lincoln's reelection chances in 1864 received a tremendous boost from
   a. the inability of the Democrats to agree on a candidate to oppose him
   b. popular enthusiasm for the Emancipation Proclamation
   c. General William Tecumseh Sherman's capture of Atlanta

_____ 14. Sherman's march to the sea was designed to
   a. offer his troops an opportunity to loot and plunder the South
   b. destroy the South's capacity to continue fighting
   c. draw Lee's attention away from northern Virginia

CHAPTER 16 • THE NATION RECONSTRUCTED: NORTH, SOUTH, AND THE WEST, 1865–1877

SUMMARY

The twelve years following the Civil War carried vast consequences for the nation's future. They helped set the pattern for future race relations and defined the federal government's role in promoting racial equality.

KEY POINTS

- Immediately following the war, all-white Southern legislatures passed black codes which denied blacks the right to purchase or rent land.

- These efforts to force former slaves to work on plantations led Congressional Republicans to seize control of Reconstruction from President Andrew Johnson, deny representatives from the former Confederate states their Congressional seats, and pass the Civil Rights Act of 1866 and draft the 14th Amendment, extending citizenship rights to African Americans and guaranteeing equal protection of the laws.

- In 1870, the 15th Amendment gave voting rights to black men

- The freedmen, in alliance with carpetbaggers and southern white Republicans known as scalawags, temporarily gained power in every former Confederate state except Virginia. The Reconstruction governments drew up democratic state constitutions, expanded women's rights, provided debt relief, and established the South's first state-funded schools.

- Internal divisions within the southern Republican party, white terror, and northern apathy allowed white southern Democrats known as Redeemers to return to power.

- During Reconstruction former slaves and many small white farmers became trapped in a new system of economic exploitation known as sharecropping.

CHAPTER SYNOPSIS

The Civil War left the former Confederacy's economy in shambles. The large number of homeless and hungry led the government to establish the Bureau of Refugees, Freedmen and Abandoned Lands to provide relief and to settle land and labor disputes. The Freedmen's Bureau also founded schools to which African Americans, young and old, flocked. It also forced former slaves to sign labor contracts that tied them to the land and paid substandard wages. Former slaves viewed literacy, land, and the vote as the keys to securing freedom, but planters largely retained their land holdings.

Lincoln's plan for Reconstruction—the 10 percent plan, devised during the war—granted rebels a presidential pardon after they swore allegiance to the Union and accepted the end of slavery. Certain Confederate officials were excluded, particularly former U. S. officials who had resigned to serve the Confederacy, and rebels accused of mistreating captured black Union soldiers. When 10 percent of those who voted in 1860 took the oath, the state could form a civilian government to draft a constitution that outlawed slavery. Once reconstructed, Lincoln promised to recognize the states. Lincoln's plan did not address the status of the ex-slaves. Although Tennessee, Arkansas, and Louisiana met these requirements, many Republicans considered Lincoln's plan too lenient. They also believed Reconstruction was a congressional matter, and so refused to recognize these states.

Congress presented its own plan in the Wade-Davis Bill. It required an oath from a majority of the states' voters to form a government and permanently barred a small number of high Confederate officials from participating in politics. It mandated a repudiation of the Confederate debt to forestall profiteering from treason. Congress would decide when these requirements were met by each state. Lincoln threatened to veto the bill, but his assassination ended this threat.

Andrew Johnson was considered a less formidable opponent to Congressional plans, but he pursued a plan similar to Lincoln's. He issued an amnesty proclamation that applied to all rebels except those owning more than $20,000 worth of property, who had to apply for a presidential pardon that was readily given. Johnson restored all property rights to southern whites. His reconstruction plan allowed a native Unionist to call for a constitutional convention without Lincoln's 10 percent requirement. Readmission, however, required ratifying the Thirteenth Amendment, repudiating the Confederate debt, abolishing slavery, renouncing secession, and providing limited black suffrage.

Southerners, however, angered many Northerners with their actions. New state governments enacted black codes that greatly circumscribed black freedom and rights, attempting to force the ex-slaves into a labor system similar to slavery. There was also violence perpetrated against African-Americans. Congress refused to seat the new Southern representatives and conducted an inquiry into prevailing conditions in the South.

The investigation by the congressional Joint Committee on Reconstruction documented the brutality of whites against blacks. When Congress extended the life of the Freedmen's Bureau and expanded its power, Johnson vetoed the bill. His attack on the committee angered Congress, which passed the Civil Rights Act and then overrode Johnson's veto. It then passed a revised Freedmen's Bureau Bill over Johnson's veto. Next, Congress drafted the Fourteenth Amendment that reversed the Dred Scott decision and extended citizenship rights and guaranteed due process and equal protection under the laws. The overwhelming victory by the Republicans in the 1866 elections, in the face of Johnson's campaign to oust the Radicals, was seen as a mandate for congressional reconstruction.

Congress passed the Military Reconstruction Act that divided the South into five military districts and provided for new constitutional conventions that included black participation and excluded former rebel leaders. Each state had to provide for black suffrage and ratify the Fourteenth Amendment. Only after the amendment was ratified were states granted representation in Congress. Johnson's veto was overridden. Congress also passed bills that limited presidential military power and required Senate consent for the removal of any official confirmed by that body. Any opposition from the Supreme Court was eliminated by bills that limited the court's power to review cases. Johnson's attempt to block Reconstruction and remove Secretary of War Stanton led the House to impeach him. After the Senate failed by one vote to convict the president, Johnson's opposition to Congressional Reconstruction ended.

The election of Grant in 1868 led Congress to debate the issue of black suffrage, raising the question of the vote for women. The controversy over the Fifteenth Amendment split the women's movement. The Fifteenth Amendment declared that the right to vote shall not be abridged on account of race, color, or previous condition of servitude.

Congressional reconstruction did not harshly punish most Confederates; nor did it lead to major reforms in land ownership. But it did allow coalitions of blacks, northern white migrants, and some southern whites, to head state government that implemented many reforms. Meanwhile, many southern whites, committed to white supremacy, opposed these governments.

Many officeholders were northern carpetbaggers, typically veterans who saw opportunity in the South. Scalawags (white southern Republicans) included former Whigs and yeoman farmers and poor whites. Many of the latter two groups had resented planter domination and had opposed secession. The Republicans appealed to these classes by voicing opposition to the slave aristocracy, but most southern whites returned to Democratic ranks in the late 1870s.

The Republican reconstruction governments were the most democratic the South had ever experienced. Any remaining property requirements for voting or running for office were removed. Reapportionment was largely fair, and salaries for public officials increased so that the non-wealthy could serve, too. Women enjoyed expanded rights and taxation was made more equitable. The greatest success was establishing public education. The devastated state of the South and the scarcity of money hindered progress. Recovery created a large tax burden and a rising debt that was partially due to corruption.

Landholdings became even more concentrated into fewer hands. Although some blacks succeeded in acquiring land, most blacks and an increasing number of whites worked as paid laborers. Sharecropping arose from the desire for black autonomy and the lack of cash among white landowners. The system seemed to offer opportunity, but tenants were often reduced to debt peonage.

Racial violence was directed against blacks by organizations such as the Ku Klux Klan. The federal government suppressed the Klan, but violence against blacks persisted, "Redeemer" governments to emerge.

Events transpiring in the North and West contributed to Reconstruction's failure. By the mid-1870s, Northerners had grown weary of Reconstruction. Scandals haunted the Grant administration, splitting the Republican party in 1872. Though Grant won reelection, by 1874, the Democrats signaled their return to power by capturing the House of Representatives and increasing their numbers in the Senate. Growing public disenchantment was fueled by the Panic of 1873, caused by overspeculation, which thrust the nation into its most serious economic depression up until that time.

The panic highlighted the tremendous changes occurring in the North during this period. The completion of the transcontinental railroad eclipsed reports of violations of African Americans' civil rights. The Republicans were committed to economic modernization and western expansion of the United States. In the process, the Republicans abandoned reform and became the party of conservatism that protected vested interests.

The major reason for Reconstruction's decline was white supremacy, which was also evident in western expansion and the treatment of the Plains Indians. A major obstacle to white settlement was the massive herds of buffalo that provided many Native Americans with food, clothing, and other necessities of life. In addition, cultural differences created problems between white settlers and the Native Americans, particularly the divergent concepts of land use and land ownership. Indian resistance led to outbreaks of violence, but proved futile. The rise of the Ghost Dance in the late 1880s fueled white fears of Native American uprisings that ended with the Wounded Knee massacre in 1890. Wounded Knee closed the era of violence between whites and Indians, but solutions to Native American problems remained illusive.

The government and reformers launched several efforts to assimilate Native Americans into American society by destroying their traditional culture. The Dawes Severalty Act of 1887 distributed tribal lands to individual Native American families. Subsequent acts also sought to weaken tribal culture. In addition, boarding schools arose to educate Native American children in the ways of mainstream American

The disputed presidential election of 1876 ended with a compromise that allowed the victory of Republican Rutherford B. Hayes. The removal of troops from the South and the demise of the few remaining Republican governments symbolically ended the Reconstruction era, though the battle for African American rights had been lost years earlier.

OBJECTIVES

After reading this chapter, you should be able to:

1. Describe Presidents Lincoln's and Johnson's plans to readmit the Confederate states to the Union as well as the more stringent Congressional plan.

2. Trace the contributions made to civil rights during Reconstruction.

3. Describe the power struggle between President Andrew Johnson and Congress, including the vote over the president's impeachment.

4. Identify the groups that ruled the southern state governments from 1866 to 1877.

5. Explain why Reconstruction ended in 1877.

KEY TERMS
Freedmen's Bureau
Radical Republicans
Black Codes
Military Reconstruction Act
Carpetbaggers
Scalawags
Sharecropping
Ku Klux Klan
Wounded Knee
Dawes Severalty Act
Compromise of 1877

KEY FIGURES
Andrew Johnson
Thaddeus Stevens
Edwin M. Stanton
Charles Sumner
Colonel J.M. Chivington
George A. Custer
Rutherford Hayes

CHAPTER 16 • THE NATION RECONSTRUCTED: NORTH, SOUTH, AND THE WEST, 1865–1877

_____ 1. Slavery was abolished in the United States by
    a. the Emancipation Proclamation
    b. the 13th Amendment
    c. the surrender of Robert E. Lee's army at Appomattox

_____ 2. Originally, the Freedmen's Bureau main function was to provide _____ for the freedmen.
    a. protection from the violence perpetrated by former Confederates
    b. food and clothing
    c. transportation to the North and West

_____ 3. The Freedmen's Bureau was most successful in providing freedmen with
    a. land
    b. schools
    c. economic independence

_____ 4. After the Civil War, most southern freedmen wanted to
    a. own their own land
    b. work for wages
    c. move to the North

_____ 5. The Black Codes
    a. sought to fashion a labor system as close to slavery as possible
    b. guaranteed the civil rights of African Americans
    c. were abolished by the 13th Amendment

_____ 6. As Reconstruction began, the _____ clause of the Constitution seemed to work to an unfair advantage for the South and the Democratic party.
    a. necessary and proper
    b. Three-Fifths
    c. due process

_____ 7. President Johnson's plan for Reconstruction required all of the following EXCEPT
    a. That the former Confederate states abolish slavery
    b. That Confederate officials apply to the President for a pardon
    c. That the former Confederate states give freedmen the vote

_____ 8. The main purpose of the Black Codes was to
    a. open economic opportunities to blacks
    b. put blacks in an economically dependent position
    c. build up the Republican party in the South

_____ 9. The 14th Amendment guaranteed _____ to freedmen.
    a. land ownership
    b. the right to vote
    c. citizenship

_____ 10. The governments of the South during the Reconstruction era are best characterized as
    a. corrupt and inefficient
    b. progressive and beneficial to the South, though run by people who had generally not held power in the South prior to the war
    c. worse than the governments that ruled the South prior to Reconstruction, and run by Northerners who had no real interest in the region

_____ 11. The Reconstruction governments in the South
    a. stripped plantation owners of their land
    b. implemented needed reforms in education and tax structure
    c. were directed, in every southern state, by African American legislators

_____ 12. President Johnson's impeachment was provoked by his
   a. dismissal of Secretary of War Edwin Stanton
   b. hostility toward black freedmen
   c. pardoning of ex-Confederate planter aristocrats

_____ 13. During Reconstruction, Congress
   a. redistributed Confederate lands to the freedmen
   b. imprisoned the civilian and military leaders of the Confederacy
   c. insisted that former slaves become full citizens of the United States

_____ 14. The Ku Klux Klan and _____ shared the goal of restoring white Democrats to political office in the South.
   a. redeemers
   b. carpetbaggers
   c. scalawags

_____ 15. The decline of Congressional Reconstruction resulted from all the following EXCEPT
   a. intimidation and violence by the Ku Klux Klan
   b. the waning of reforming idealism in the North and corruption in the Grant administration
   c. the return of economic prosperity in the 1870s

_____ 16. The Credit Mobilier scandal involved
   a. illegal post office contracts
   b. fraudulent railroad investments
   c. exploitation of Indians

_____ 17. Resistance by the Plains Indians was unsuccessful for all of the following reasons EXCEPT
   a. a viral infection killed most of the Indians' horses
   b. the buffalo was hunted to near extinction
   c. railroads allowed U.S. troops to be deployed rapidly and brought large numbers of settlers to the Plains

_____ 18. The Dawes Act of 1887 undermined Indian cultures by
   a. breaking up reservations into individual landholdings
   b. forbidding Indian religious practices
   c. ordering the education of Indian children in white-run boarding schools

_____ 19. The candidate who received the largest popular vote in the election of 1876 was
   a. Ulysses S. Grant
   b. Rutherford Hayes
   c. Samuel J. Tilden

_____ 20. The dispute over contested electoral votes in the 1876 election was decided by
   a. the House of Representatives
   b. the Supreme Court
   c. an electoral commission

_____ 21. In the Compromise of 1877, Republican candidate Rutherford B. Hayes promised the South all but one of the following. Select the EXCEPTION.
   a. federal aid for southern railroads
   b. to revoke the Civil Rights Act of 1875
   c. appointment of a Southern Democrat to his cabinet